T0135189

Lecture Notes in Computer Science　13682

More information about this series at https://link.springer.com/bookseries/558

Shai Avidan · Gabriel Brostow ·
Moustapha Cissé · Giovanni Maria Farinella ·
Tal Hassner (Eds.)

Computer Vision – ECCV 2022

17th European Conference
Tel Aviv, Israel, October 23–27, 2022
Proceedings, Part XXII

 Springer

Editors
Shai Avidan
Tel Aviv University
Tel Aviv, Israel

Gabriel Brostow ⓘ
University College London
London, UK

Moustapha Cissé
Google AI
Accra, Ghana

Giovanni Maria Farinella ⓘ
University of Catania
Catania, Italy

Tal Hassner ⓘ
Facebook (United States)
Menlo Park, CA, USA

ISSN 0302-9743 ISSN 1611-3349 (electronic)
Lecture Notes in Computer Science
ISBN 978-3-031-20046-5 ISBN 978-3-031-20047-2 (eBook)
https://doi.org/10.1007/978-3-031-20047-2

This Springer imprint is published by the registered company Springer Nature Switzerland AG
The registered company address is: Gewerbestrasse 11, 6330 Cham, Switzerland

Foreword

Organizing the European Conference on Computer Vision (ECCV 2022) in Tel-Aviv during a global pandemic was no easy feat. The uncertainty level was extremely high, and decisions had to be postponed to the last minute. Still, we managed to plan things just in time for ECCV 2022 to be held in person. Participation in physical events is crucial to stimulating collaborations and nurturing the culture of the Computer Vision community.

There were many people who worked hard to ensure attendees enjoyed the best science at the 16th edition of ECCV. We are grateful to the Program Chairs Gabriel Brostow and Tal Hassner, who went above and beyond to ensure the ECCV reviewing process ran smoothly. The scientific program includes dozens of workshops and tutorials in addition to the main conference and we would like to thank Leonid Karlinsky and Tomer Michaeli for their hard work. Finally, special thanks to the web chairs Lorenzo Baraldi and Kosta Derpanis, who put in extra hours to transfer information fast and efficiently to the ECCV community.

We would like to express gratitude to our generous sponsors and the Industry Chairs, Dimosthenis Karatzas and Chen Sagiv, who oversaw industry relations and proposed new ways for academia-industry collaboration and technology transfer. It's great to see so much industrial interest in what we're doing!

Authors' draft versions of the papers appeared online with open access on both the Computer Vision Foundation (CVF) and the European Computer Vision Association (ECVA) websites as with previous ECCVs. Springer, the publisher of the proceedings, has arranged for archival publication. The final version of the papers is hosted by SpringerLink, with active references and supplementary materials. It benefits all potential readers that we offer both a free and citeable version for all researchers, as well as an authoritative, citeable version for SpringerLink readers. Our thanks go to Ronan Nugent from Springer, who helped us negotiate this agreement. Last but not least, we wish to thank Eric Mortensen, our publication chair, whose expertise made the process smooth.

October 2022

Rita Cucchiara
Jiří Matas
Amnon Shashua
Lihi Zelnik-Manor

Preface

Welcome to the proceedings of the European Conference on Computer Vision (ECCV 2022). This was a hybrid edition of ECCV as we made our way out of the COVID-19 pandemic. The conference received 5804 valid paper submissions, compared to 5150 submissions to ECCV 2020 (a 12.7% increase) and 2439 in ECCV 2018. 1645 submissions were accepted for publication (28%) and, of those, 157 (2.7% overall) as orals.

846 of the submissions were desk-rejected for various reasons. Many of them because they revealed author identity, thus violating the double-blind policy. This violation came in many forms: some had author names with the title, others added acknowledgments to specific grants, yet others had links to their github account where their name was visible. Tampering with the LaTeX template was another reason for automatic desk rejection.

ECCV 2022 used the traditional CMT system to manage the entire double-blind reviewing process. Authors did not know the names of the reviewers and vice versa. Each paper received at least 3 reviews (except 6 papers that received only 2 reviews), totalling more than 15,000 reviews.

Handling the review process at this scale was a significant challenge. To ensure that each submission received as fair and high-quality reviews as possible, we recruited more than 4719 reviewers (in the end, 4719 reviewers did at least one review). Similarly we recruited more than 276 area chairs (eventually, only 276 area chairs handled a batch of papers). The area chairs were selected based on their technical expertise and reputation, largely among people who served as area chairs in previous top computer vision and machine learning conferences (ECCV, ICCV, CVPR, NeurIPS, etc.).

Reviewers were similarly invited from previous conferences, and also from the pool of authors. We also encouraged experienced area chairs to suggest additional chairs and reviewers in the initial phase of recruiting. The median reviewer load was five papers per reviewer, while the average load was about four papers, because of the emergency reviewers. The area chair load was 35 papers, on average.

Conflicts of interest between authors, area chairs, and reviewers were handled largely automatically by the CMT platform, with some manual help from the Program Chairs. Reviewers were allowed to describe themselves as senior reviewer (load of 8 papers to review) or junior reviewers (load of 4 papers). Papers were matched to area chairs based on a subject-area affinity score computed in CMT and an affinity score computed by the Toronto Paper Matching System (TPMS). TPMS is based on the paper's full text. An area chair handling each submission would bid for preferred expert reviewers, and we balanced load and prevented conflicts.

The assignment of submissions to area chairs was relatively smooth, as was the assignment of submissions to reviewers. A small percentage of reviewers were not happy with their assignments in terms of subjects and self-reported expertise. This is an area for improvement, although it's interesting that many of these cases were reviewers hand-picked by AC's. We made a later round of reviewer recruiting, targeted at the list of authors of papers submitted to the conference, and had an excellent response which helped provide enough emergency reviewers. In the end, all but six papers received at least 3 reviews.

The challenges of the reviewing process are in line with past experiences at ECCV 2020. As the community grows, and the number of submissions increases, it becomes ever more challenging to recruit enough reviewers and ensure a high enough quality of reviews. Enlisting authors by default as reviewers might be one step to address this challenge.

Authors were given a week to rebut the initial reviews, and address reviewers' concerns. Each rebuttal was limited to a single pdf page with a fixed template.

The Area Chairs then led discussions with the reviewers on the merits of each submission. The goal was to reach consensus, but, ultimately, it was up to the Area Chair to make a decision. The decision was then discussed with a buddy Area Chair to make sure decisions were fair and informative. The entire process was conducted virtually with no in-person meetings taking place.

The Program Chairs were informed in cases where the Area Chairs overturned a decisive consensus reached by the reviewers, and pushed for the meta-reviews to contain details that explained the reasoning for such decisions. Obviously these were the most contentious cases, where reviewer inexperience was the most common reported factor.

Once the list of accepted papers was finalized and released, we went through the laborious process of plagiarism (including self-plagiarism) detection. A total of 4 accepted papers were rejected because of that.

Finally, we would like to thank our Technical Program Chair, Pavel Lifshits, who did tremendous work behind the scenes, and we thank the tireless CMT team.

October 2022

Gabriel Brostow
Giovanni Maria Farinella
Moustapha Cissé
Shai Avidan
Tal Hassner

Organization

General Chairs

Rita Cucchiara   University of Modena and Reggio Emilia, Italy
Jiří Matas   Czech Technical University in Prague, Czech
Republic
Amnon Shashua   Hebrew University of Jerusalem, Israel
Lihi Zelnik-Manor   Technion – Israel Institute of Technology, Israel

Program Chairs

Shai Avidan   Tel-Aviv University, Israel
Gabriel Brostow   University College London, UK
Moustapha Cissé   Google AI, Ghana
Giovanni Maria Farinella   University of Catania, Italy
Tal Hassner   Facebook AI, USA

Program Technical Chair

Pavel Lifshits   Technion – Israel Institute of Technology, Israel

Workshops Chairs

Leonid Karlinsky   IBM Research, Israel
Tomer Michaeli   Technion – Israel Institute of Technology, Israel
Ko Nishino   Kyoto University, Japan

Tutorial Chairs

Thomas Pock   Graz University of Technology, Austria
Natalia Neverova   Facebook AI Research, UK

Demo Chair

Bohyung Han   Seoul National University, Korea

Social and Student Activities Chairs

Tatiana Tommasi   Italian Institute of Technology, Italy
Sagie Benaim   University of Copenhagen, Denmark

Diversity and Inclusion Chairs

Xi Yin   Facebook AI Research, USA
Bryan Russell   Adobe, USA

Communications Chairs

Lorenzo Baraldi   University of Modena and Reggio Emilia, Italy
Kosta Derpanis   York University & Samsung AI Centre Toronto,
                  Canada

Industrial Liaison Chairs

Dimosthenis Karatzas   Universitat Autònoma de Barcelona, Spain
Chen Sagiv   SagivTech, Israel

Finance Chair

Gerard Medioni   University of Southern California & Amazon,
                  USA

Publication Chair

Eric Mortensen   MiCROTEC, USA

Area Chairs

Lourdes Agapito   University College London, UK
Zeynep Akata   University of Tübingen, Germany
Naveed Akhtar   University of Western Australia, Australia
Karteek Alahari   Inria Grenoble Rhône-Alpes, France
Alexandre Alahi   École polytechnique fédérale de Lausanne,
                  Switzerland
Pablo Arbelaez   Universidad de Los Andes, Columbia
Antonis A. Argyros   University of Crete & Foundation for Research
                  and Technology-Hellas, Crete
Yuki M. Asano   University of Amsterdam, The Netherlands
Kalle Åström   Lund University, Sweden
Hadar Averbuch-Elor   Cornell University, USA

Hossein Azizpour	KTH Royal Institute of Technology, Sweden
Vineeth N. Balasubramanian	Indian Institute of Technology, Hyderabad, India
Lamberto Ballan	University of Padova, Italy
Adrien Bartoli	Université Clermont Auvergne, France
Horst Bischof	Graz University of Technology, Austria
Matthew B. Blaschko	KU Leuven, Belgium
Federica Bogo	Meta Reality Labs Research, Switzerland
Katherine Bouman	California Institute of Technology, USA
Edmond Boyer	Inria Grenoble Rhône-Alpes, France
Michael S. Brown	York University, Canada
Vittorio Caggiano	Meta AI Research, USA
Neill Campbell	University of Bath, UK
Octavia Camps	Northeastern University, USA
Duygu Ceylan	Adobe Research, USA
Ayan Chakrabarti	Google Research, USA
Tat-Jen Cham	Nanyang Technological University, Singapore
Antoni Chan	City University of Hong Kong, Hong Kong, China
Manmohan Chandraker	NEC Labs America, USA
Xinlei Chen	Facebook AI Research, USA
Xilin Chen	Institute of Computing Technology, Chinese Academy of Sciences, China
Dongdong Chen	Microsoft Cloud AI, USA
Chen Chen	University of Central Florida, USA
Ondrej Chum	Vision Recognition Group, Czech Technical University in Prague, Czech Republic
John Collomosse	Adobe Research & University of Surrey, UK
Camille Couprie	Facebook, France
David Crandall	Indiana University, USA
Daniel Cremers	Technical University of Munich, Germany
Marco Cristani	University of Verona, Italy
Canton Cristian	Facebook AI Research, USA
Dengxin Dai	ETH Zurich, Switzerland
Dima Damen	University of Bristol, UK
Kostas Daniilidis	University of Pennsylvania, USA
Trevor Darrell	University of California, Berkeley, USA
Andrew Davison	Imperial College London, UK
Tali Dekel	Weizmann Institute of Science, Israel
Alessio Del Bue	Istituto Italiano di Tecnologia, Italy
Weihong Deng	Beijing University of Posts and Telecommunications, China
Konstantinos Derpanis	Ryerson University, Canada
Carl Doersch	DeepMind, UK

Matthijs Douze   Facebook AI Research, USA
Mohamed Elhoseiny   King Abdullah University of Science and
                                Technology, Saudi Arabia
Sergio Escalera   University of Barcelona, Spain
Yi Fang   New York University, USA
Ryan Farrell   Brigham Young University, USA
Alireza Fathi   Google, USA
Christoph Feichtenhofer   Facebook AI Research, USA
Basura Fernando   Agency for Science, Technology and Research
                                (A*STAR), Singapore
Vittorio Ferrari   Google Research, Switzerland
Andrew W. Fitzgibbon   Graphcore, UK
David J. Fleet   University of Toronto, Canada
David Forsyth   University of Illinois at Urbana-Champaign, USA
David Fouhey   University of Michigan, USA
Katerina Fragkiadaki   Carnegie Mellon University, USA
Friedrich Fraundorfer   Graz University of Technology, Austria
Oren Freifeld   Ben-Gurion University, Israel
Thomas Funkhouser   Google Research & Princeton University, USA
Yasutaka Furukawa   Simon Fraser University, Canada
Fabio Galasso   Sapienza University of Rome, Italy
Jürgen Gall   University of Bonn, Germany
Chuang Gan   Massachusetts Institute of Technology, USA
Zhe Gan   Microsoft, USA
Animesh Garg   University of Toronto, Vector Institute, Nvidia,
                                Canada
Efstratios Gavves   University of Amsterdam, The Netherlands
Peter Gehler   Amazon, Germany
Theo Gevers   University of Amsterdam, The Netherlands
Bernard Ghanem   King Abdullah University of Science and
                                Technology, Saudi Arabia
Ross B. Girshick   Facebook AI Research, USA
Georgia Gkioxari   Facebook AI Research, USA
Albert Gordo   Facebook, USA
Stephen Gould   Australian National University, Australia
Venu Madhav Govindu   Indian Institute of Science, India
Kristen Grauman   Facebook AI Research & UT Austin, USA
Abhinav Gupta   Carnegie Mellon University & Facebook AI
                                Research, USA
Mohit Gupta   University of Wisconsin-Madison, USA
Hu Han   Institute of Computing Technology, Chinese
                                Academy of Sciences, China

Bohyung Han	Seoul National University, Korea
Tian Han	Stevens Institute of Technology, USA
Emily Hand	University of Nevada, Reno, USA
Bharath Hariharan	Cornell University, USA
Ran He	Institute of Automation, Chinese Academy of Sciences, China
Otmar Hilliges	ETH Zurich, Switzerland
Adrian Hilton	University of Surrey, UK
Minh Hoai	Stony Brook University, USA
Yedid Hoshen	Hebrew University of Jerusalem, Israel
Timothy Hospedales	University of Edinburgh, UK
Gang Hua	Wormpex AI Research, USA
Di Huang	Beihang University, China
Jing Huang	Facebook, USA
Jia-Bin Huang	Facebook, USA
Nathan Jacobs	Washington University in St. Louis, USA
C.V. Jawahar	International Institute of Information Technology, Hyderabad, India
Herve Jegou	Facebook AI Research, France
Neel Joshi	Microsoft Research, USA
Armand Joulin	Facebook AI Research, France
Frederic Jurie	University of Caen Normandie, France
Fredrik Kahl	Chalmers University of Technology, Sweden
Yannis Kalantidis	NAVER LABS Europe, France
Evangelos Kalogerakis	University of Massachusetts, Amherst, USA
Sing Bing Kang	Zillow Group, USA
Yosi Keller	Bar Ilan University, Israel
Margret Keuper	University of Mannheim, Germany
Tae-Kyun Kim	Imperial College London, UK
Benjamin Kimia	Brown University, USA
Alexander Kirillov	Facebook AI Research, USA
Kris Kitani	Carnegie Mellon University, USA
Iasonas Kokkinos	Snap Inc. & University College London, UK
Vladlen Koltun	Apple, USA
Nikos Komodakis	University of Crete, Crete
Piotr Koniusz	Australian National University, Australia
Philipp Kraehenbuehl	University of Texas at Austin, USA
Dilip Krishnan	Google, USA
Ajay Kumar	Hong Kong Polytechnic University, Hong Kong, China
Junseok Kwon	Chung-Ang University, Korea
Jean-Francois Lalonde	Université Laval, Canada

Ivan Laptev	Inria Paris, France
Laura Leal-Taixé	Technical University of Munich, Germany
Erik Learned-Miller	University of Massachusetts, Amherst, USA
Gim Hee Lee	National University of Singapore, Singapore
Seungyong Lee	Pohang University of Science and Technology, Korea
Zhen Lei	Institute of Automation, Chinese Academy of Sciences, China
Bastian Leibe	RWTH Aachen University, Germany
Hongdong Li	Australian National University, Australia
Fuxin Li	Oregon State University, USA
Bo Li	University of Illinois at Urbana-Champaign, USA
Yin Li	University of Wisconsin-Madison, USA
Ser-Nam Lim	Meta AI Research, USA
Joseph Lim	University of Southern California, USA
Stephen Lin	Microsoft Research Asia, China
Dahua Lin	The Chinese University of Hong Kong, Hong Kong, China
Si Liu	Beihang University, China
Xiaoming Liu	Michigan State University, USA
Ce Liu	Microsoft, USA
Zicheng Liu	Microsoft, USA
Yanxi Liu	Pennsylvania State University, USA
Feng Liu	Portland State University, USA
Yebin Liu	Tsinghua University, China
Chen Change Loy	Nanyang Technological University, Singapore
Huchuan Lu	Dalian University of Technology, China
Cewu Lu	Shanghai Jiao Tong University, China
Oisin Mac Aodha	University of Edinburgh, UK
Dhruv Mahajan	Facebook, USA
Subhransu Maji	University of Massachusetts, Amherst, USA
Atsuto Maki	KTH Royal Institute of Technology, Sweden
Arun Mallya	NVIDIA, USA
R. Manmatha	Amazon, USA
Iacopo Masi	Sapienza University of Rome, Italy
Dimitris N. Metaxas	Rutgers University, USA
Ajmal Mian	University of Western Australia, Australia
Christian Micheloni	University of Udine, Italy
Krystian Mikolajczyk	Imperial College London, UK
Anurag Mittal	Indian Institute of Technology, Madras, India
Philippos Mordohai	Stevens Institute of Technology, USA
Greg Mori	Simon Fraser University & Borealis AI, Canada

Vittorio Murino	Istituto Italiano di Tecnologia, Italy
P. J. Narayanan	International Institute of Information Technology, Hyderabad, India
Ram Nevatia	University of Southern California, USA
Natalia Neverova	Facebook AI Research, UK
Richard Newcombe	Facebook, USA
Cuong V. Nguyen	Florida International University, USA
Bingbing Ni	Shanghai Jiao Tong University, China
Juan Carlos Niebles	Salesforce & Stanford University, USA
Ko Nishino	Kyoto University, Japan
Jean-Marc Odobez	Idiap Research Institute, École polytechnique fédérale de Lausanne, Switzerland
Francesca Odone	University of Genova, Italy
Takayuki Okatani	Tohoku University & RIKEN Center for Advanced Intelligence Project, Japan
Manohar Paluri	Facebook, USA
Guan Pang	Facebook, USA
Maja Pantic	Imperial College London, UK
Sylvain Paris	Adobe Research, USA
Jaesik Park	Pohang University of Science and Technology, Korea
Hyun Soo Park	The University of Minnesota, USA
Omkar M. Parkhi	Facebook, USA
Deepak Pathak	Carnegie Mellon University, USA
Georgios Pavlakos	University of California, Berkeley, USA
Marcello Pelillo	University of Venice, Italy
Marc Pollefeys	ETH Zurich & Microsoft, Switzerland
Jean Ponce	Inria, France
Gerard Pons-Moll	University of Tübingen, Germany
Fatih Porikli	Qualcomm, USA
Victor Adrian Prisacariu	University of Oxford, UK
Petia Radeva	University of Barcelona, Spain
Ravi Ramamoorthi	University of California, San Diego, USA
Deva Ramanan	Carnegie Mellon University, USA
Vignesh Ramanathan	Facebook, USA
Nalini Ratha	State University of New York at Buffalo, USA
Tammy Riklin Raviv	Ben-Gurion University, Israel
Tobias Ritschel	University College London, UK
Emanuele Rodola	Sapienza University of Rome, Italy
Amit K. Roy-Chowdhury	University of California, Riverside, USA
Michael Rubinstein	Google, USA
Olga Russakovsky	Princeton University, USA

Mathieu Salzmann   École polytechnique fédérale de Lausanne, Switzerland
Dimitris Samaras   Stony Brook University, USA
Aswin Sankaranarayanan   Carnegie Mellon University, USA
Imari Sato   National Institute of Informatics, Japan
Yoichi Sato   University of Tokyo, Japan
Shin'ichi Satoh   National Institute of Informatics, Japan
Walter Scheirer   University of Notre Dame, USA
Bernt Schiele   Max Planck Institute for Informatics, Germany
Konrad Schindler   ETH Zurich, Switzerland
Cordelia Schmid   Inria & Google, France
Alexander Schwing   University of Illinois at Urbana-Champaign, USA
Nicu Sebe   University of Trento, Italy
Greg Shakhnarovich   Toyota Technological Institute at Chicago, USA
Eli Shechtman   Adobe Research, USA
Humphrey Shi   University of Oregon & University of Illinois at Urbana-Champaign & Picsart AI Research, USA
Jianbo Shi   University of Pennsylvania, USA
Roy Shilkrot   Massachusetts Institute of Technology, USA
Mike Zheng Shou   National University of Singapore, Singapore
Kaleem Siddiqi   McGill University, Canada
Richa Singh   Indian Institute of Technology Jodhpur, India
Greg Slabaugh   Queen Mary University of London, UK
Cees Snoek   University of Amsterdam, The Netherlands
Yale Song   Facebook AI Research, USA
Yi-Zhe Song   University of Surrey, UK
Bjorn Stenger   Rakuten Institute of Technology
Abby Stylianou   Saint Louis University, USA
Akihiro Sugimoto   National Institute of Informatics, Japan
Chen Sun   Brown University, USA
Deqing Sun   Google, USA
Kalyan Sunkavalli   Adobe Research, USA
Ying Tai   Tencent YouTu Lab, China
Ayellet Tal   Technion – Israel Institute of Technology, Israel
Ping Tan   Simon Fraser University, Canada
Siyu Tang   ETH Zurich, Switzerland
Chi-Keung Tang   Hong Kong University of Science and Technology, Hong Kong, China
Radu Timofte   University of Würzburg, Germany & ETH Zurich, Switzerland
Federico Tombari   Google, Switzerland & Technical University of Munich, Germany

Todd Zickler   Harvard University, USA
Wangmeng Zuo   Harbin Institute of Technology, China

Technical Program Committee

Davide Abati
Soroush Abbasi
    Koohpayegani
Amos L. Abbott
Rameen Abdal
Rabab Abdelfattah
Sahar Abdelnabi
Hassan Abu Alhaija
Abulikemu Abuduweili
Ron Abutbul
Hanno Ackermann
Aikaterini Adam
Kamil Adamczewski
Ehsan Adeli
Vida Adeli
Donald Adjeroh
Arman Afrasiyabi
Akshay Agarwal
Sameer Agarwal
Abhinav Agarwalla
Vaibhav Aggarwal
Sara Aghajanzadeh
Susmit Agrawal
Antonio Agudo
Touqeer Ahmad
Sk Miraj Ahmed
Chaitanya Ahuja
Nilesh A. Ahuja
Abhishek Aich
Shubhra Aich
Noam Aigerman
Arash Akbarinia
Peri Akiva
Derya Akkaynak
Emre Aksan
Arjun R. Akula
Yuval Alaluf
Stephan Alaniz
Paul Albert
Cenek Albl

Filippo Aleotti
Konstantinos P.
    Alexandridis
Motasem Alfarra
Mohsen Ali
Thiemo Alldieck
Hadi Alzayer
Liang An
Shan An
Yi An
Zhulin An
Dongsheng An
Jie An
Xiang An
Saket Anand
Cosmin Ancuti
Juan Andrade-Cetto
Alexander Andreopoulos
Bjoern Andres
Jerone T. A. Andrews
Shivangi Aneja
Anelia Angelova
Dragomir Anguelov
Rushil Anirudh
Oron Anschel
Rao Muhammad Anwer
Djamila Aouada
Evlampios Apostolidis
Srikar Appalaraju
Nikita Araslanov
Andre Araujo
Eric Arazo
Dawit Mureja Argaw
Anurag Arnab
Aditya Arora
Chetan Arora
Sunpreet S. Arora
Alexey Artemov
Muhammad Asad
Kumar Ashutosh

Sinem Aslan
Vishal Asnani
Mahmoud Assran
Amir Atapour-Abarghouei
Nikos Athanasiou
Ali Athar
ShahRukh Athar
Sara Atito
Souhaib Attaiki
Matan Atzmon
Mathieu Aubry
Nicolas Audebert
Tristan T.
    Aumentado-Armstrong
Melinos Averkiou
Yannis Avrithis
Stephane Ayache
Mehmet Aygün
Seyed Mehdi
    Ayyoubzadeh
Hossein Azizpour
George Azzopardi
Mallikarjun B. R.
Yunhao Ba
Abhishek Badki
Seung-Hwan Bae
Seung-Hwan Baek
Seungryul Baek
Piyush Nitin Bagad
Shai Bagon
Gaetan Bahl
Shikhar Bahl
Sherwin Bahmani
Haoran Bai
Lei Bai
Jiawang Bai
Haoyue Bai
Jinbin Bai
Xiang Bai
Xuyang Bai

Yang Bai
Yuanchao Bai
Ziqian Bai
Sungyong Baik
Kevin Bailly
Max Bain
Federico Baldassarre
Wele Gedara Chaminda
   Bandara
Biplab Banerjee
Pratyay Banerjee
Sandipan Banerjee
Jihwan Bang
Antyanta Bangunharcana
Aayush Bansal
Ankan Bansal
Siddhant Bansal
Wentao Bao
Zhipeng Bao
Amir Bar
Manel Baradad Jurjo
Lorenzo Baraldi
Danny Barash
Daniel Barath
Connelly Barnes
Ioan Andrei Bârsan
Steven Basart
Dina Bashkirova
Chaim Baskin
Peyman Bateni
Anil Batra
Sebastiano Battiato
Ardhendu Behera
Harkirat Behl
Jens Behley
Vasileios Belagiannis
Boulbaba Ben Amor
Emanuel Ben Baruch
Abdessamad Ben Hamza
Gil Ben-Artzi
Assia Benbihi
Fabian Benitez-Quiroz
Guy Ben-Yosef
Philipp Benz
Alexander W. Bergman

Urs Bergmann
Jesus Bermudez-Cameo
Stefano Berretti
Gedas Bertasius
Zachary Bessinger
Petra Bevandić
Matthew Beveridge
Lucas Beyer
Yash Bhalgat
Suvaansh Bhambri
Samarth Bharadwaj
Gaurav Bharaj
Aparna Bharati
Bharat Lal Bhatnagar
Uttaran Bhattacharya
Apratim Bhattacharyya
Brojeshwar Bhowmick
Ankan Kumar Bhunia
Ayan Kumar Bhunia
Qi Bi
Sai Bi
Michael Bi Mi
Gui-Bin Bian
Jia-Wang Bian
Shaojun Bian
Pia Bideau
Mario Bijelic
Hakan Bilen
Guillaume-Alexandre
   Bilodeau
Alexander Binder
Tolga Birdal
Vighnesh N. Birodkar
Sandika Biswas
Andreas Blattmann
Janusz Bobulski
Giuseppe Boccignone
Vishnu Boddeti
Navaneeth Bodla
Moritz Böhle
Aleksei Bokhovkin
Sam Bond-Taylor
Vivek Boominathan
Shubhankar Borse
Mark Boss

Andrea Bottino
Adnane Boukhayma
Fadi Boutros
Nicolas C. Boutry
Richard S. Bowen
Ivaylo Boyadzhiev
Aidan Boyd
Yuri Boykov
Aljaz Bozic
Behzad Bozorgtabar
Eric Brachmann
Samarth Brahmbhatt
Gustav Bredell
Francois Bremond
Joel Brogan
Andrew Brown
Thomas Brox
Marcus A. Brubaker
Robert-Jan Bruintjes
Yuqi Bu
Anders G. Buch
Himanshu Buckchash
Mateusz Buda
Ignas Budvytis
José M. Buenaposada
Marcel C. Bühler
Tu Bui
Adrian Bulat
Hannah Bull
Evgeny Burnaev
Andrei Bursuc
Benjamin Busam
Sergey N. Buzykanov
Wonmin Byeon
Fabian Caba
Martin Cadik
Guanyu Cai
Minjie Cai
Qing Cai
Zhongang Cai
Qi Cai
Yancheng Cai
Shen Cai
Han Cai
Jiarui Cai

Bowen Cai
Mu Cai
Qin Cai
Ruojin Cai
Weidong Cai
Weiwei Cai
Yi Cai
Yujun Cai
Zhiping Cai
Akin Caliskan
Lilian Calvet
Baris Can Cam
Necati Cihan Camgoz
Tommaso Campari
Dylan Campbell
Ziang Cao
Ang Cao
Xu Cao
Zhiwen Cao
Shengcao Cao
Song Cao
Weipeng Cao
Xiangyong Cao
Xiaochun Cao
Yue Cao
Yunhao Cao
Zhangjie Cao
Jiale Cao
Yang Cao
Jiajiong Cao
Jie Cao
Jinkun Cao
Lele Cao
Yulong Cao
Zhiguo Cao
Chen Cao
Razvan Caramalau
Marlène Careil
Gustavo Carneiro
Joao Carreira
Dan Casas
Paola Cascante-Bonilla
Angela Castillo
Francisco M. Castro
Pedro Castro

Luca Cavalli
George J. Cazenavette
Oya Celiktutan
Hakan Cevikalp
Sri Harsha C. H.
Sungmin Cha
Geonho Cha
Menglei Chai
Lucy Chai
Yuning Chai
Zenghao Chai
Anirban Chakraborty
Deep Chakraborty
Rudrasis Chakraborty
Souradeep Chakraborty
Kelvin C. K. Chan
Chee Seng Chan
Paramanand Chandramouli
Arjun Chandrasekaran
Kenneth Chaney
Dongliang Chang
Huiwen Chang
Peng Chang
Xiaojun Chang
Jia-Ren Chang
Hyung Jin Chang
Hyun Sung Chang
Ju Yong Chang
Li-Jen Chang
Qi Chang
Wei-Yi Chang
Yi Chang
Nadine Chang
Hanqing Chao
Pradyumna Chari
Dibyadip Chatterjee
Chiranjoy Chattopadhyay
Siddhartha Chaudhuri
Zhengping Che
Gal Chechik
Lianggangxu Chen
Qi Alfred Chen
Brian Chen
Bor-Chun Chen
Bo-Hao Chen

Bohong Chen
Bin Chen
Ziliang Chen
Cheng Chen
Chen Chen
Chaofeng Chen
Xi Chen
Haoyu Chen
Xuanhong Chen
Wei Chen
Qiang Chen
Shi Chen
Xianyu Chen
Chang Chen
Changhuai Chen
Hao Chen
Jie Chen
Jianbo Chen
Jingjing Chen
Jun Chen
Kejiang Chen
Mingcai Chen
Nenglun Chen
Qifeng Chen
Ruoyu Chen
Shu-Yu Chen
Weidong Chen
Weijie Chen
Weikai Chen
Xiang Chen
Xiuyi Chen
Xingyu Chen
Yaofo Chen
Yueting Chen
Yu Chen
Yunjin Chen
Yuntao Chen
Yun Chen
Zhenfang Chen
Zhuangzhuang Chen
Chu-Song Chen
Xiangyu Chen
Zhuo Chen
Chaoqi Chen
Shizhe Chen

Xiaotong Chen

Xiaozhi Chen

Dian Chen

Defang Chen

Dingfan Chen

Ding-Jie Chen

Ee Heng Chen

Tao Chen

Yixin Chen

Wei-Ting Chen

Lin Chen

Guang Chen

Guangyi Chen

Guanying Chen

Guangyao Chen

Hwann-Tzong Chen

Junwen Chen

Jiacheng Chen

Jianxu Chen

Hui Chen

Kai Chen

Kan Chen

Kevin Chen

Kuan-Wen Chen

Weihua Chen

Zhang Chen

Liang-Chieh Chen

Lele Chen

Liang Chen

Fanglin Chen

Zehui Chen

Minghui Chen

Minghao Chen

Xiaokang Chen

Qian Chen

Jun-Cheng Chen

Qi Chen

Qingcai Chen

Richard J. Chen

Runnan Chen

Rui Chen

Shuo Chen

Sentao Chen

Shaoyu Chen

Shixing Chen

Shuai Chen

Shuya Chen

Sizhe Chen

Simin Chen

Shaoxiang Chen

Zitian Chen

Tianlong Chen

Tianshui Chen

Min-Hung Chen

Xiangning Chen

Xin Chen

Xinghao Chen

Xuejin Chen

Xu Chen

Xuxi Chen

Yunlu Chen

Yanbei Chen

Yuxiao Chen

Yun-Chun Chen

Yi-Ting Chen

Yi-Wen Chen

Yinbo Chen

Yiran Chen

Yuanhong Chen

Yubei Chen

Yuefeng Chen

Yuhua Chen

Yukang Chen

Zerui Chen

Zhaoyu Chen

Zhen Chen

Zhenyu Chen

Zhi Chen

Zhiwei Chen

Zhixiang Chen

Long Chen

Bowen Cheng

Jun Cheng

Yi Cheng

Jingchun Cheng

Lechao Cheng

Xi Cheng

Yuan Cheng

Ho Kei Cheng

Kevin Ho Man Cheng

Jiacheng Cheng

Kelvin B. Cheng

Li Cheng

Mengjun Cheng

Zhen Cheng

Qingrong Cheng

Tianheng Cheng

Harry Cheng

Yihua Cheng

Yu Cheng

Ziheng Cheng

Soon Yau Cheong

Anoop Cherian

Manuela Chessa

Zhixiang Chi

Naoki Chiba

Julian Chibane

Kashyap Chitta

Tai-Yin Chiu

Hsu-kuang Chiu

Wei-Chen Chiu

Sungmin Cho

Donghyeon Cho

Hyeon Cho

Yooshin Cho

Gyusang Cho

Jang Hyun Cho

Seungju Cho

Nam Ik Cho

Sunghyun Cho

Hanbyel Cho

Jaesung Choe

Jooyoung Choi

Chiho Choi

Changwoon Choi

Jongwon Choi

Myungsub Choi

Dooseop Choi

Jonghyun Choi

Jinwoo Choi

Jun Won Choi

Min-Kook Choi

Hongsuk Choi

Janghoon Choi

Yoon-Ho Choi

Yukyung Choi
Jaegul Choo
Ayush Chopra
Siddharth Choudhary
Subhabrata Choudhury
Vasileios Choutas
Ka-Ho Chow
Pinaki Nath Chowdhury
Sammy Christen
Anders Christensen
Grigorios Chrysos
Hang Chu
Wen-Hsuan Chu
Peng Chu
Qi Chu
Ruihang Chu
Wei-Ta Chu
Yung-Yu Chuang
Sanghyuk Chun
Se Young Chun
Antonio Cinà
Ramazan Gokberk Cinbis
Javier Civera
Albert Clapés
Ronald Clark
Brian S. Clipp
Felipe Codevilla
Daniel Coelho de Castro
Niv Cohen
Forrester Cole
Maxwell D. Collins
Robert T. Collins
Marc Comino Trinidad
Runmin Cong
Wenyan Cong
Maxime Cordy
Marcella Cornia
Enric Corona
Huseyin Coskun
Luca Cosmo
Dragos Costea
Davide Cozzolino
Arun C. S. Kumar
Aiyu Cui
Qiongjie Cui

Quan Cui
Shuhao Cui
Yiming Cui
Ying Cui
Zijun Cui
Jiali Cui
Jiequan Cui
Yawen Cui
Zhen Cui
Zhaopeng Cui
Jack Culpepper
Xiaodong Cun
Ross Cutler
Adam Czajka
Ali Dabouei
Konstantinos M. Dafnis
Manuel Dahnert
Tao Dai
Yuchao Dai
Bo Dai
Mengyu Dai
Hang Dai
Haixing Dai
Peng Dai
Pingyang Dai
Qi Dai
Qiyu Dai
Yutong Dai
Naser Damer
Zhiyuan Dang
Mohamed Daoudi
Ayan Das
Abir Das
Debasmit Das
Deepayan Das
Partha Das
Sagnik Das
Soumi Das
Srijan Das
Swagatam Das
Avijit Dasgupta
Jim Davis
Adrian K. Davison
Homa Davoudi
Laura Daza

Matthias De Lange
Shalini De Mello
Marco De Nadai
Christophe De
  Vleeschouwer
Alp Dener
Boyang Deng
Congyue Deng
Bailin Deng
Yong Deng
Ye Deng
Zhuo Deng
Zhijie Deng
Xiaoming Deng
Jiankang Deng
Jinhong Deng
Jingjing Deng
Liang-Jian Deng
Siqi Deng
Xiang Deng
Xueqing Deng
Zhongying Deng
Karan Desai
Jean-Emmanuel Deschaud
Aniket Anand Deshmukh
Neel Dey
Helisa Dhamo
Prithviraj Dhar
Amaya Dharmasiri
Yan Di
Xing Di
Ousmane A. Dia
Haiwen Diao
Xiaolei Diao
Gonçalo José Dias Pais
Abdallah Dib
Anastasios Dimou
Changxing Ding
Henghui Ding
Guodong Ding
Yaqing Ding
Shuangrui Ding
Yuhang Ding
Yikang Ding
Shouhong Ding

Haisong Ding	Samuel Dooley	Max Ehrlich
Hui Ding	Gianfranco Doretto	Mahsa Ehsanpour
Jiahao Ding	Michael Dorkenwald	Iván Eichhardt
Jian Ding	Keval Doshi	Farshad Einabadi
Jian-Jiun Ding	Zhaopeng Dou	Marvin Eisenberger
Shuxiao Ding	Xiaotian Dou	Hazim Kemal Ekenel
Tianyu Ding	Hazel Doughty	Mohamed El Banani
Wenhao Ding	Ahmad Droby	Ismail Elezi
Yuqi Ding	Iddo Drori	Moshe Eliasof
Yi Ding	Jie Du	Alaa El-Nouby
Yuzhen Ding	Yong Du	Ian Endres
Zhengming Ding	Dawei Du	Francis Engelmann
Tan Minh Dinh	Dong Du	Deniz Engin
Vu Dinh	Ruoyi Du	Chanho Eom
Christos Diou	Yuntao Du	Dave Epstein
Mandar Dixit	Xuefeng Du	Maria C. Escobar
Bao Gia Doan	Yilun Du	Victor A. Escorcia
Khoa D. Doan	Yuming Du	Carlos Esteves
Dzung Anh Doan	Radhika Dua	Sungmin Eum
Debi Prosad Dogra	Haodong Duan	Bernard J. E. Evans
Nehal Doiphode	Jiafei Duan	Ivan Evtimov
Chengdong Dong	Kaiwen Duan	Fevziye Irem Eyiokur
Bowen Dong	Peiqi Duan	Yaman
Zhenxing Dong	Ye Duan	Matteo Fabbri
Hang Dong	Haoran Duan	Sébastien Fabbro
Xiaoyi Dong	Jiali Duan	Gabriele Facciolo
Haoye Dong	Amanda Duarte	Masud Fahim
Jiangxin Dong	Abhimanyu Dubey	Bin Fan
Shichao Dong	Shiv Ram Dubey	Hehe Fan
Xuan Dong	Florian Dubost	Deng-Ping Fan
Zhen Dong	Lukasz Dudziak	Aoxiang Fan
Shuting Dong	Shivam Duggal	Chen-Chen Fan
Jing Dong	Justin M. Dulay	Qi Fan
Li Dong	Matteo Dunnhofer	Zhaoxin Fan
Ming Dong	Chi Nhan Duong	Haoqi Fan
Nanqing Dong	Thibaut Durand	Heng Fan
Qiulei Dong	Mihai Dusmanu	Hongyi Fan
Runpei Dong	Ujjal Kr Dutta	Linxi Fan
Siyan Dong	Debidatta Dwibedi	Baojie Fan
Tian Dong	Isht Dwivedi	Jiayuan Fan
Wei Dong	Sai Kumar Dwivedi	Lei Fan
Xiaomeng Dong	Takeharu Eda	Quanfu Fan
Xin Dong	Mark Edmonds	Yonghui Fan
Xingbo Dong	Alexei A. Efros	Yingruo Fan
Yuan Dong	Thibaud Ehret	Zhiwen Fan

Zicong Fan
Sean Fanello
Jiansheng Fang
Chaowei Fang
Yuming Fang
Jianwu Fang
Jin Fang
Qi Fang
Shancheng Fang
Tian Fang
Xianyong Fang
Gongfan Fang
Zhen Fang
Hui Fang
Jiemin Fang
Le Fang
Pengfei Fang
Xiaolin Fang
Yuxin Fang
Zhaoyuan Fang
Ammarah Farooq
Azade Farshad
Zhengcong Fei
Michael Felsberg
Wei Feng
Chen Feng
Fan Feng
Andrew Feng
Xin Feng
Zheyun Feng
Ruicheng Feng
Mingtao Feng
Qianyu Feng
Shangbin Feng
Chun-Mei Feng
Zunlei Feng
Zhiyong Feng
Martin Fergie
Mustansar Fiaz
Marco Fiorucci
Michael Firman
Hamed Firooz
Volker Fischer
Corneliu O. Florea
Georgios Floros

Wolfgang Foerstner
Gianni Franchi
Jean-Sebastien Franco
Simone Frintrop
Anna Fruehstueck
Changhong Fu
Chaoyou Fu
Cheng-Yang Fu
Chi-Wing Fu
Deqing Fu
Huan Fu
Jun Fu
Kexue Fu
Ying Fu
Jianlong Fu
Jingjing Fu
Qichen Fu
Tsu-Jui Fu
Xueyang Fu
Yang Fu
Yanwei Fu
Yonggan Fu
Wolfgang Fuhl
Yasuhisa Fujii
Kent Fujiwara
Marco Fumero
Takuya Funatomi
Isabel Funke
Dario Fuoli
Antonino Furnari
Matheus A. Gadelha
Akshay Gadi Patil
Adrian Galdran
Guillermo Gallego
Silvano Galliani
Orazio Gallo
Leonardo Galteri
Matteo Gamba
Yiming Gan
Sujoy Ganguly
Harald Ganster
Boyan Gao
Changxin Gao
Daiheng Gao
Difei Gao

Chen Gao
Fei Gao
Lin Gao
Wei Gao
Yiming Gao
Junyu Gao
Guangyu Ryan Gao
Haichang Gao
Hongchang Gao
Jialin Gao
Jin Gao
Jun Gao
Katelyn Gao
Mingchen Gao
Mingfei Gao
Pan Gao
Shangqian Gao
Shanghua Gao
Xitong Gao
Yunhe Gao
Zhanning Gao
Elena Garces
Nuno Cruz Garcia
Noa Garcia
Guillermo
    Garcia-Hernando
Isha Garg
Rahul Garg
Sourav Garg
Quentin Garrido
Stefano Gasperini
Kent Gauen
Chandan Gautam
Shivam Gautam
Paul Gay
Chunjiang Ge
Shiming Ge
Wenhang Ge
Yanhao Ge
Zheng Ge
Songwei Ge
Weifeng Ge
Yixiao Ge
Yuying Ge
Shijie Geng

Zhengyang Geng
Kyle A. Genova
Georgios Georgakis
Markos Georgopoulos
Marcel Geppert
Shabnam Ghadar
Mina Ghadimi Atigh
Deepti Ghadiyaram
Maani Ghaffari Jadidi
Sedigh Ghamari
Zahra Gharaee
Michaël Gharbi
Golnaz Ghiasi
Reza Ghoddoosian
Soumya Suvra Ghosal
Adhiraj Ghosh
Arthita Ghosh
Pallabi Ghosh
Soumyadeep Ghosh
Andrew Gilbert
Igor Gilitschenski
Jhony H. Giraldo
Andreu Girbau Xalabarder
Rohit Girdhar
Sharath Girish
Xavier Giro-i-Nieto
Raja Giryes
Thomas Gittings
Nikolaos Gkanatsios
Ioannis Gkioulekas
Abhiram
    Gnanasambandam
Aurele T. Gnanha
Clement L. J. C. Godard
Arushi Goel
Vidit Goel
Shubham Goel
Zan Gojcic
Aaron K. Gokaslan
Tejas Gokhale
S. Alireza Golestaneh
Thiago L. Gomes
Nuno Goncalves
Boqing Gong
Chen Gong

Yuanhao Gong
Guoqiang Gong
Jingyu Gong
Rui Gong
Yu Gong
Mingming Gong
Neil Zhenqiang Gong
Xun Gong
Yunye Gong
Yihong Gong
Cristina I. González
Nithin Gopalakrishnan
    Nair
Gaurav Goswami
Jianping Gou
Shreyank N. Gowda
Ankit Goyal
Helmut Grabner
Patrick L. Grady
Ben Graham
Eric Granger
Douglas R. Gray
Matej Grcić
David Griffiths
Jinjin Gu
Yun Gu
Shuyang Gu
Jianyang Gu
Fuqiang Gu
Jiatao Gu
Jindong Gu
Jiaqi Gu
Jinwei Gu
Jiaxin Gu
Geonmo Gu
Xiao Gu
Xinqian Gu
Xiuye Gu
Yuming Gu
Zhangxuan Gu
Dayan Guan
Junfeng Guan
Qingji Guan
Tianrui Guan
Shanyan Guan

Denis A. Gudovskiy
Ricardo Guerrero
Pierre-Louis Guhur
Jie Gui
Liangyan Gui
Liangke Gui
Benoit Guillard
Erhan Gundogdu
Manuel Günther
Jingcai Guo
Yuanfang Guo
Junfeng Guo
Chenqi Guo
Dan Guo
Hongji Guo
Jia Guo
Jie Guo
Minghao Guo
Shi Guo
Yanhui Guo
Yangyang Guo
Yuan-Chen Guo
Yilu Guo
Yiluan Guo
Yong Guo
Guangyu Guo
Haiyun Guo
Jinyang Guo
Jianyuan Guo
Pengsheng Guo
Pengfei Guo
Shuxuan Guo
Song Guo
Tianyu Guo
Qing Guo
Qiushan Guo
Wen Guo
Xiefan Guo
Xiaohu Guo
Xiaoqing Guo
Yufei Guo
Yuhui Guo
Yuliang Guo
Yunhui Guo
Yanwen Guo

Akshita Gupta
Ankush Gupta
Kamal Gupta
Kartik Gupta
Ritwik Gupta
Rohit Gupta
Siddharth Gururani
Fredrik K. Gustafsson
Abner Guzman Rivera
Vladimir Guzov
Matthew A. Gwilliam
Jung-Woo Ha
Marc Habermann
Isma Hadji
Christian Haene
Martin Hahner
Levente Hajder
Alexandros Haliassos
Emanuela Haller
Bumsub Ham
Abdullah J. Hamdi
Shreyas Hampali
Dongyoon Han
Chunrui Han
Dong-Jun Han
Dong-Sig Han
Guangxing Han
Zhizhong Han
Ruize Han
Jiaming Han
Jin Han
Ligong Han
Xian-Hua Han
Xiaoguang Han
Yizeng Han
Zhi Han
Zhenjun Han
Zhongyi Han
Jungong Han
Junlin Han
Kai Han
Kun Han
Sungwon Han
Songfang Han
Wei Han

Xiao Han
Xintong Han
Xinzhe Han
Yahong Han
Yan Han
Zongbo Han
Nicolai Hani
Rana Hanocka
Niklas Hanselmann
Nicklas A. Hansen
Hong Hanyu
Fusheng Hao
Yanbin Hao
Shijie Hao
Udith Haputhanthri
Mehrtash Harandi
Josh Harguess
Adam Harley
David M. Hart
Atsushi Hashimoto
Ali Hassani
Mohammed Hassanin
Yana Hasson
Joakim Bruslund Haurum
Bo He
Kun He
Chen He
Xin He
Fazhi He
Gaoqi He
Hao He
Haoyu He
Jiangpeng He
Hongliang He
Qian He
Xiangteng He
Xuming He
Yannan He
Yuhang He
Yang He
Xiangyu He
Nanjun He
Pan He
Sen He
Shengfeng He

Songtao He
Tao He
Tong He
Wei He
Xuehai He
Xiaoxiao He
Ying He
Yisheng He
Ziwen He
Peter Hedman
Felix Heide
Yacov Hel-Or
Paul Henderson
Philipp Henzler
Byeongho Heo
Jae-Pil Heo
Miran Heo
Sachini A. Herath
Stephane Herbin
Pedro Hermosilla Casajus
Monica Hernandez
Charles Herrmann
Roei Herzig
Mauricio Hess-Flores
Carlos Hinojosa
Tobias Hinz
Tsubasa Hirakawa
Chih-Hui Ho
Lam Si Tung Ho
Jennifer Hobbs
Derek Hoiem
Yannick Hold-Geoffroy
Aleksander Holynski
Cheeun Hong
Fa-Ting Hong
Hanbin Hong
Guan Zhe Hong
Danfeng Hong
Lanqing Hong
Xiaopeng Hong
Xin Hong
Jie Hong
Seungbum Hong
Cheng-Yao Hong
Seunghoon Hong

Yi Hong
Yuan Hong
Yuchen Hong
Anthony Hoogs
Maxwell C. Horton
Kazuhiro Hotta
Qibin Hou
Tingbo Hou
Junhui Hou
Ji Hou
Qiqi Hou
Rui Hou
Ruibing Hou
Zhi Hou
Henry Howard-Jenkins
Lukas Hoyer
Wei-Lin Hsiao
Chiou-Ting Hsu
Anthony Hu
Brian Hu
Yusong Hu
Hexiang Hu
Haoji Hu
Di Hu
Hengtong Hu
Haigen Hu
Lianyu Hu
Hanzhe Hu
Jie Hu
Junlin Hu
Shizhe Hu
Jian Hu
Zhiming Hu
Juhua Hu
Peng Hu
Ping Hu
Ronghang Hu
MengShun Hu
Tao Hu
Vincent Tao Hu
Xiaoling Hu
Xinting Hu
Xiaolin Hu
Xuefeng Hu
Xiaowei Hu

Yang Hu
Yueyu Hu
Zeyu Hu
Zhongyun Hu
Binh-Son Hua
Guoliang Hua
Yi Hua
Linzhi Huang
Qiusheng Huang
Bo Huang
Chen Huang
Hsin-Ping Huang
Ye Huang
Shuangping Huang
Zeng Huang
Buzhen Huang
Cong Huang
Heng Huang
Hao Huang
Qidong Huang
Huaibo Huang
Chaoqin Huang
Feihu Huang
Jiahui Huang
Jingjia Huang
Kun Huang
Lei Huang
Sheng Huang
Shuaiyi Huang
Siyu Huang
Xiaoshui Huang
Xiaoyang Huang
Yan Huang
Yihao Huang
Ying Huang
Ziling Huang
Xiaoke Huang
Yifei Huang
Haiyang Huang
Zhewei Huang
Jin Huang
Haibin Huang
Jiaxing Huang
Junjie Huang
Keli Huang

Lang Huang
Lin Huang
Luojie Huang
Mingzhen Huang
Shijia Huang
Shengyu Huang
Siyuan Huang
He Huang
Xiuyu Huang
Lianghua Huang
Yue Huang
Yaping Huang
Yuge Huang
Zehao Huang
Zeyi Huang
Zhiqi Huang
Zhongzhan Huang
Zilong Huang
Ziyuan Huang
Tianrui Hui
Zhuo Hui
Le Hui
Jing Huo
Junhwa Hur
Shehzeen S. Hussain
Chuong Minh Huynh
Seunghyun Hwang
Jaehui Hwang
Jyh-Jing Hwang
Sukjun Hwang
Soonmin Hwang
Wonjun Hwang
Rakib Hyder
Sangeek Hyun
Sarah Ibrahimi
Tomoki Ichikawa
Yerlan Idelbayev
A. S. M. Iftekhar
Masaaki Iiyama
Satoshi Ikehata
Sunghoon Im
Atul N. Ingle
Eldar Insafutdinov
Yani A. Ioannou
Radu Tudor Ionescu

Umar Iqbal
Go Irie
Muhammad Zubair Irshad
Ahmet Iscen
Berivan Isik
Ashraful Islam
Md Amirul Islam
Syed Islam
Mariko Isogawa
Vamsi Krishna K. Ithapu
Boris Ivanovic
Darshan Iyer
Sarah Jabbour
Ayush Jain
Nishant Jain
Samyak Jain
Vidit Jain
Vineet Jain
Priyank Jaini
Tomas Jakab
Mohammad A. A. K.
    Jalwana
Muhammad Abdullah
    Jamal
Hadi Jamali-Rad
Stuart James
Varun Jampani
Young Kyun Jang
YeongJun Jang
Yunseok Jang
Ronnachai Jaroensri
Bhavan Jasani
Krishna Murthy
    Jatavallabhula
Mojan Javaheripi
Syed A. Javed
Guillaume Jeanneret
Pranav Jeevan
Herve Jegou
Rohit Jena
Tomas Jenicek
Porter Jenkins
Simon Jenni
Hae-Gon Jeon
Sangryul Jeon

Boseung Jeong
Yoonwoo Jeong
Seong-Gyun Jeong
Jisoo Jeong
Allan D. Jepson
Ankit Jha
Sumit K. Jha
I-Hong Jhuo
Ge-Peng Ji
Chaonan Ji
Deyi Ji
Jingwei Ji
Wei Ji
Zhong Ji
Jiayi Ji
Pengliang Ji
Hui Ji
Mingi Ji
Xiaopeng Ji
Yuzhu Ji
Baoxiong Jia
Songhao Jia
Dan Jia
Shan Jia
Xiaojun Jia
Xiuyi Jia
Xu Jia
Menglin Jia
Wenqi Jia
Boyuan Jiang
Wenhao Jiang
Huaizu Jiang
Hanwen Jiang
Haiyong Jiang
Hao Jiang
Huajie Jiang
Huiqin Jiang
Haojun Jiang
Haobo Jiang
Junjun Jiang
Xingyu Jiang
Yangbangyan Jiang
Yu Jiang
Jianmin Jiang
Jiaxi Jiang

Jing Jiang
Kui Jiang
Li Jiang
Liming Jiang
Chiyu Jiang
Meirui Jiang
Chen Jiang
Peng Jiang
Tai-Xiang Jiang
Wen Jiang
Xinyang Jiang
Yifan Jiang
Yuming Jiang
Yingying Jiang
Zeren Jiang
ZhengKai Jiang
Zhenyu Jiang
Shuming Jiao
Jianbo Jiao
Licheng Jiao
Dongkwon Jin
Yeying Jin
Cheng Jin
Linyi Jin
Qing Jin
Taisong Jin
Xiao Jin
Xin Jin
Sheng Jin
Kyong Hwan Jin
Ruibing Jin
SouYoung Jin
Yueming Jin
Chenchen Jing
Longlong Jing
Taotao Jing
Yongcheng Jing
Younghyun Jo
Joakim Johnander
Jeff Johnson
Michael J. Jones
R. Kenny Jones
Rico Jonschkowski
Ameya Joshi
Sunghun Joung

Felix Juefei-Xu
Claudio R. Jung
Steffen Jung
Hari Chandana K.
Rahul Vigneswaran K.
Prajwal K. R.
Abhishek Kadian
Jhony Kaesemodel Pontes
Kumara Kahatapitiya
Anmol Kalia
Sinan Kalkan
Tarun Kalluri
Jaewon Kam
Sandesh Kamath
Melna Kan
Menelaos Kanakis
Takuhiro Kaneko
Di Kang
Guoliang Kang
Hao Kang
Jaeyeon Kang
Kyoungkook Kang
Li-Wei Kang
MinGuk Kang
Suk-Ju Kang
Zhao Kang
Yash Mukund Kant
Yueying Kao
Aupendu Kar
Konstantinos Karantzalos
Sezer Karaoglu
Navid Kardan
Sanjay Kariyappa
Leonid Karlinsky
Animesh Karnewar
Shyamgopal Karthik
Hirak J. Kashyap
Marc A. Kastner
Hirokatsu Kataoka
Angelos Katharopoulos
Hiroharu Kato
Kai Katsumata
Manuel Kaufmann
Chaitanya Kaul
Prakhar Kaushik

Yuki Kawana
Lei Ke
Lipeng Ke
Tsung-Wei Ke
Wei Ke
Petr Kellnhofer
Aniruddha Kembhavi
John Kender
Corentin Kervadec
Leonid Keselman
Daniel Keysers
Nima Khademi Kalantari
Taras Khakhulin
Samir Khaki
Muhammad Haris Khan
Qadeer Khan
Salman Khan
Subash Khanal
Vaishnavi M. Khindkar
Rawal Khirodkar
Saeed Khorram
Pirazh Khorramshahi
Kourosh Khoshelham
Ansh Khurana
Benjamin Kiefer
Jae Myung Kim
Junho Kim
Boah Kim
Hyeonseong Kim
Dong-Jin Kim
Dongwan Kim
Donghyun Kim
Doyeon Kim
Yonghyun Kim
Hyung-Il Kim
Hyunwoo Kim
Hyeongwoo Kim
Hyo Jin Kim
Hyunwoo J. Kim
Taehoon Kim
Jaeha Kim
Jiwon Kim
Jung Uk Kim
Kangyeol Kim
Eunji Kim

Daeha Kim
Dongwon Kim
Kunhee Kim
Kyungmin Kim
Junsik Kim
Min H. Kim
Namil Kim
Kookhoi Kim
Sanghyun Kim
Seongyeop Kim
Seungryong Kim
Saehoon Kim
Euyoung Kim
Guisik Kim
Sungyeon Kim
Sunnie S. Y. Kim
Taehun Kim
Tae Oh Kim
Won Hwa Kim
Seungwook Kim
YoungBin Kim
Youngeun Kim
Akisato Kimura
Furkan Osman Kınlı
Zsolt Kira
Hedvig Kjellström
Florian Kleber
Jan P. Klopp
Florian Kluger
Laurent Kneip
Byungsoo Ko
Muhammed Kocabas
A. Sophia Koepke
Kevin Koeser
Nick Kolkin
Nikos Kolotouros
Wai-Kin Adams Kong
Deying Kong
Caihua Kong
Youyong Kong
Shuyu Kong
Shu Kong
Tao Kong
Yajing Kong
Yu Kong

Zishang Kong
Theodora Kontogianni
Anton S. Konushin
Julian F. P. Kooij
Bruno Korbar
Giorgos Kordopatis-Zilos
Jari Korhonen
Adam Kortylewski
Denis Korzhenkov
Divya Kothandaraman
Suraj Kothawade
Iuliia Kotseruba
Satwik Kottur
Shashank Kotyan
Alexandros Kouris
Petros Koutras
Anna Kreshuk
Ranjay Krishna
Dilip Krishnan
Andrey Kuehlkamp
Hilde Kuehne
Jason Kuen
David Kügler
Arjan Kuijper
Anna Kukleva
Sumith Kulal
Viveka Kulharia
Akshay R. Kulkarni
Nilesh Kulkarni
Dominik Kulon
Abhinav Kumar
Akash Kumar
Suryansh Kumar
B. V. K. Vijaya Kumar
Pulkit Kumar
Ratnesh Kumar
Sateesh Kumar
Satish Kumar
Vijay Kumar B. G.
Nupur Kumari
Sudhakar Kumawat
Jogendra Nath Kundu
Hsien-Kai Kuo
Meng-Yu Jennifer Kuo
Vinod Kumar Kurmi

Yusuke Kurose
Keerthy Kusumam
Alina Kuznetsova
Henry Kvinge
Ho Man Kwan
Hyeokjun Kweon
Heeseung Kwon
Gihyun Kwon
Myung-Joon Kwon
Taesung Kwon
YoungJoong Kwon
Christos Kyrkou
Jorma Laaksonen
Yann Labbe
Zorah Laehner
Florent Lafarge
Hamid Laga
Manuel Lagunas
Shenqi Lai
Jian-Huang Lai
Zihang Lai
Mohamed I. Lakhal
Mohit Lamba
Meng Lan
Loic Landrieu
Zhiqiang Lang
Natalie Lang
Dong Lao
Yizhen Lao
Yingjie Lao
Issam Hadj Laradji
Gustav Larsson
Viktor Larsson
Zakaria Laskar
Stéphane Lathuilière
Chun Pong Lau
Rynson W. H. Lau
Hei Law
Justin Lazarow
Verica Lazova
Eric-Tuan Le
Hieu Le
Trung-Nghia Le
Mathias Lechner
Byeong-Uk Lee

Chen-Yu Lee
Che-Rung Lee
Chul Lee
Hong Joo Lee
Dongsoo Lee
Jiyoung Lee
Eugene Eu Tzuan Lee
Daeun Lee
Saehyung Lee
Jewook Lee
Hyungtae Lee
Hyunmin Lee
Jungbeom Lee
Joon-Young Lee
Jong-Seok Lee
Joonseok Lee
Junha Lee
Kibok Lee
Byung-Kwan Lee
Jangwon Lee
Jinho Lee
Jongmin Lee
Seunghyun Lee
Sohyun Lee
Minsik Lee
Dogyoon Lee
Seungmin Lee
Min Jun Lee
Sangho Lee
Sangmin Lee
Seungeun Lee
Seon-Ho Lee
Sungmin Lee
Sungho Lee
Sangyoun Lee
Vincent C. S. S. Lee
Jaeseong Lee
Yong Jae Lee
Chenyang Lei
Chenyi Lei
Jiahui Lei
Xinyu Lei
Yinjie Lei
Jiaxu Leng
Luziwei Leng

Jan E. Lenssen	Kailin Li	Xu Li
Vincent Lepetit	Kenneth Li	Ya-Li Li
Thomas Leung	Kun Li	Yao Li
María Leyva-Vallina	Kunpeng Li	Yongjie Li
Xin Li	Aoxue Li	Yijun Li
Yikang Li	Chenglong Li	Yiming Li
Baoxin Li	Chenglin Li	Yuezun Li
Bin Li	Changsheng Li	Yu Li
Bing Li	Zhichao Li	Yunheng Li
Bowen Li	Qiang Li	Yuqi Li
Changlin Li	Yanyu Li	Zhe Li
Chao Li	Zuoyue Li	Zeming Li
Chongyi Li	Xiang Li	Zhen Li
Guanyue Li	Xuelong Li	Zhengqin Li
Shuai Li	Fangda Li	Zhimin Li
Jin Li	Ailin Li	Jiefeng Li
Dingquan Li	Liang Li	Jinpeng Li
Dongxu Li	Chun-Guang Li	Chengze Li
Yiting Li	Daiqing Li	Jianwu Li
Gang Li	Dong Li	Lerenhan Li
Dian Li	Guanbin Li	Shan Li
Guohao Li	Guorong Li	Suichan Li
Haoang Li	Haifeng Li	Xiangtai Li
Haoliang Li	Jianan Li	Yanjie Li
Haoran Li	Jianing Li	Yandong Li
Hengduo Li	Jiaxin Li	Zhuoling Li
Huafeng Li	Ke Li	Zhenqiang Li
Xiaoming Li	Lei Li	Manyi Li
Hanao Li	Lincheng Li	Maosen Li
Hongwei Li	Liulei Li	Ji Li
Ziqiang Li	Lujun Li	Minjun Li
Jisheng Li	Linjie Li	Mingrui Li
Jiacheng Li	Lin Li	Mengtian Li
Jia Li	Pengyu Li	Junyi Li
Jiachen Li	Ping Li	Nianyi Li
Jiahao Li	Qiufu Li	Bo Li
Jianwei Li	Qingyong Li	Xiao Li
Jiazhi Li	Rui Li	Peihua Li
Jie Li	Siyuan Li	Peike Li
Jing Li	Wei Li	Peizhao Li
Jingjing Li	Wenbin Li	Peiliang Li
Jingtao Li	Xiangyang Li	Qi Li
Jun Li	Xinyu Li	Ren Li
Junxuan Li	Xiujun Li	Runze Li
Kai Li	Xiu Li	Shile Li

Sheng Li
Shigang Li
Shiyu Li
Shuang Li
Shasha Li
Shichao Li
Tianye Li
Yuexiang Li
Wei-Hong Li
Wanhua Li
Weihao Li
Weiming Li
Weixin Li
Wenbo Li
Wenshuo Li
Weijian Li
Yunan Li
Xirong Li
Xianhang Li
Xiaoyu Li
Xueqian Li
Xuanlin Li
Xianzhi Li
Yunqiang Li
Yanjing Li
Yansheng Li
Yawei Li
Yi Li
Yong Li
Yong-Lu Li
Yuhang Li
Yu-Jhe Li
Yuxi Li
Yunsheng Li
Yanwei Li
Zechao Li
Zejian Li
Zeju Li
Zekun Li
Zhaowen Li
Zheng Li
Zhenyu Li
Zhiheng Li
Zhi Li
Zhong Li

Zhuowei Li
Zhuowan Li
Zhuohang Li
Zizhang Li
Chen Li
Yuan-Fang Li
Dongze Lian
Xiaochen Lian
Zhouhui Lian
Long Lian
Qing Lian
Jin Lianbao
Jinxiu S. Liang
Dingkang Liang
Jiahao Liang
Jianming Liang
Jingyun Liang
Kevin J. Liang
Kaizhao Liang
Chen Liang
Jie Liang
Senwei Liang
Ding Liang
Jiajun Liang
Jian Liang
Kongming Liang
Siyuan Liang
Yuanzhi Liang
Zhengfa Liang
Mingfu Liang
Xiaodan Liang
Xuefeng Liang
Yuxuan Liang
Kang Liao
Liang Liao
Hong-Yuan Mark Liao
Wentong Liao
Haofu Liao
Yue Liao
Minghui Liao
Shengcai Liao
Ting-Hsuan Liao
Xin Liao
Yinghong Liao
Teck Yian Lim

Che-Tsung Lin
Chung-Ching Lin
Chen-Hsuan Lin
Cheng Lin
Chuming Lin
Chunyu Lin
Dahua Lin
Wei Lin
Zheng Lin
Huaijia Lin
Jason Lin
Jierui Lin
Jiaying Lin
Jie Lin
Kai-En Lin
Kevin Lin
Guangfeng Lin
Jiehong Lin
Feng Lin
Hang Lin
Kwan-Yee Lin
Ke Lin
Luojun Lin
Qinghong Lin
Xiangbo Lin
Yi Lin
Zudi Lin
Shijie Lin
Yiqun Lin
Tzu-Heng Lin
Ming Lin
Shaohui Lin
SongNan Lin
Ji Lin
Tsung-Yu Lin
Xudong Lin
Yancong Lin
Yen-Chen Lin
Yiming Lin
Yuewei Lin
Zhiqiu Lin
Zinan Lin
Zhe Lin
David B. Lindell
Zhixin Ling

Zhan Ling
Alexander Liniger
Venice Erin B. Liong
Joey Litalien
Or Litany
Roee Litman
Ron Litman
Jim Little
Dor Litvak
Shaoteng Liu
Shuaicheng Liu
Andrew Liu
Xian Liu
Shaohui Liu
Bei Liu
Bo Liu
Yong Liu
Ming Liu
Yanbin Liu
Chenxi Liu
Daqi Liu
Di Liu
Difan Liu
Dong Liu
Dongfang Liu
Daizong Liu
Xiao Liu
Fangyi Liu
Fengbei Liu
Fenglin Liu
Bin Liu
Yuang Liu
Ao Liu
Hong Liu
Hongfu Liu
Huidong Liu
Ziyi Liu
Feng Liu
Hao Liu
Jie Liu
Jialun Liu
Jiang Liu
Jing Liu
Jingya Liu
Jiaming Liu

Jun Liu
Juncheng Liu
Jiawei Liu
Hongyu Liu
Chuanbin Liu
Haotian Liu
Lingqiao Liu
Chang Liu
Han Liu
Liu Liu
Min Liu
Yingqi Liu
Aishan Liu
Bingyu Liu
Benlin Liu
Boxiao Liu
Chenchen Liu
Chuanjian Liu
Daqing Liu
Huan Liu
Haozhe Liu
Jiaheng Liu
Wei Liu
Jingzhou Liu
Jiyuan Liu
Lingbo Liu
Nian Liu
Peiye Liu
Qiankun Liu
Shenglan Liu
Shilong Liu
Wen Liu
Wenyu Liu
Weifeng Liu
Wu Liu
Xiaolong Liu
Yang Liu
Yanwei Liu
Yingcheng Liu
Yongfei Liu
Yihao Liu
Yu Liu
Yunze Liu
Ze Liu
Zhenhua Liu

Zhenguang Liu
Lin Liu
Lihao Liu
Pengju Liu
Xinhai Liu
Yunfei Liu
Meng Liu
Minghua Liu
Mingyuan Liu
Miao Liu
Peirong Liu
Ping Liu
Qingjie Liu
Ruoshi Liu
Risheng Liu
Songtao Liu
Xing Liu
Shikun Liu
Shuming Liu
Sheng Liu
Songhua Liu
Tongliang Liu
Weibo Liu
Weide Liu
Weizhe Liu
Wenxi Liu
Weiyang Liu
Xin Liu
Xiaobin Liu
Xudong Liu
Xiaoyi Liu
Xihui Liu
Xinchen Liu
Xingtong Liu
Xinpeng Liu
Xinyu Liu
Xianpeng Liu
Xu Liu
Xingyu Liu
Yongtuo Liu
Yahui Liu
Yangxin Liu
Yaoyao Liu
Yaojie Liu
Yuliang Liu

Yongcheng Liu
Yuan Liu
Yufan Liu
Yu-Lun Liu
Yun Liu
Yunfan Liu
Yuanzhong Liu
Zhuoran Liu
Zhen Liu
Zheng Liu
Zhijian Liu
Zhisong Liu
Ziquan Liu
Ziyu Liu
Zhihua Liu
Zechun Liu
Zhaoyang Liu
Zhengzhe Liu
Stephan Liwicki
Shao-Yuan Lo
Sylvain Lobry
Suhas Lohit
Vishnu Suresh Lokhande
Vincenzo Lomonaco
Chengjiang Long
Guodong Long
Fuchen Long
Shangbang Long
Yang Long
Zijun Long
Vasco Lopes
Antonio M. Lopez
Roberto Javier
    Lopez-Sastre
Tobias Lorenz
Javier Lorenzo-Navarro
Yujing Lou
Qian Lou
Xiankai Lu
Changsheng Lu
Huimin Lu
Yongxi Lu
Hao Lu
Hong Lu
Jiasen Lu

Juwei Lu
Fan Lu
Guangming Lu
Jiwen Lu
Shun Lu
Tao Lu
Xiaonan Lu
Yang Lu
Yao Lu
Yongchun Lu
Zhiwu Lu
Cheng Lu
Liying Lu
Guo Lu
Xuequan Lu
Yanye Lu
Yantao Lu
Yuhang Lu
Fujun Luan
Jonathon Luiten
Jovita Lukasik
Alan Lukezic
Jonathan Samuel Lumentut
Mayank Lunayach
Ao Luo
Canjie Luo
Chong Luo
Xu Luo
Grace Luo
Jun Luo
Katie Z. Luo
Tao Luo
Cheng Luo
Fangzhou Luo
Gen Luo
Lei Luo
Sihui Luo
Weixin Luo
Yan Luo
Xiaoyan Luo
Yong Luo
Yadan Luo
Hao Luo
Ruotian Luo
Mi Luo

Tiange Luo
Wenjie Luo
Wenhan Luo
Xiao Luo
Zhiming Luo
Zhipeng Luo
Zhengyi Luo
Diogo C. Luvizon
Zhaoyang Lv
Gengyu Lyu
Lingjuan Lyu
Jun Lyu
Yuanyuan Lyu
Youwei Lyu
Yueming Lyu
Bingpeng Ma
Chao Ma
Chongyang Ma
Congbo Ma
Chih-Yao Ma
Fan Ma
Lin Ma
Haoyu Ma
Hengbo Ma
Jianqi Ma
Jiawei Ma
Jiayi Ma
Kede Ma
Kai Ma
Lingni Ma
Lei Ma
Xu Ma
Ning Ma
Benteng Ma
Cheng Ma
Andy J. Ma
Long Ma
Zhanyu Ma
Zhiheng Ma
Qianli Ma
Shiqiang Ma
Sizhuo Ma
Shiqing Ma
Xiaolong Ma
Xinzhu Ma

Gautam B. Machiraju
Spandan Madan
Mathew Magimai-Doss
Luca Magri
Behrooz Mahasseni
Upal Mahbub
Siddharth Mahendran
Paridhi Maheshwari
Rishabh Maheshwary
Mohammed Mahmoud
Shishira R. R. Maiya
Sylwia Majchrowska
Arjun Majumdar
Puspita Majumdar
Orchid Majumder
Sagnik Majumder
Ilya Makarov
Farkhod F.
    Makhmudkhujaev
Yasushi Makihara
Ankur Mali
Mateusz Malinowski
Utkarsh Mall
Srikanth Malla
Clement Mallet
Dimitrios Mallis
Yunze Man
Dipu Manandhar
Massimiliano Mancini
Murari Mandal
Raunak Manekar
Karttikeya Mangalam
Puneet Mangla
Fabian Manhardt
Sivabalan Manivasagam
Fahim Mannan
Chengzhi Mao
Hanzi Mao
Jiayuan Mao
Junhua Mao
Zhiyuan Mao
Jiageng Mao
Yunyao Mao
Zhendong Mao
Alberto Marchisio

Diego Marcos
Riccardo Marin
Aram Markosyan
Renaud Marlet
Ricardo Marques
Miquel Martí i Rabadán
Diego Martin Arroyo
Niki Martinel
Brais Martinez
Julieta Martinez
Marc Masana
Tomohiro Mashita
Timothée Masquelier
Minesh Mathew
Tetsu Matsukawa
Marwan Mattar
Bruce A. Maxwell
Christoph Mayer
Mantas Mazeika
Pratik Mazumder
Scott McCloskey
Steven McDonagh
Ishit Mehta
Jie Mei
Kangfu Mei
Jieru Mei
Xiaoguang Mei
Givi Meishvili
Luke Melas-Kyriazi
Iaroslav Melekhov
Andres Mendez-Vazquez
Heydi Mendez-Vazquez
Matias Mendieta
Ricardo A. Mendoza-León
Chenlin Meng
Depu Meng
Rang Meng
Zibo Meng
Qingjie Meng
Qier Meng
Yanda Meng
Zihang Meng
Thomas Mensink
Fabian Mentzer
Christopher Metzler

Gregory P. Meyer
Vasileios Mezaris
Liang Mi
Lu Mi
Bo Miao
Changtao Miao
Zichen Miao
Qiguang Miao
Xin Miao
Zhongqi Miao
Frank Michel
Simone Milani
Ben Mildenhall
Roy V. Miles
Juhong Min
Kyle Min
Hyun-Seok Min
Weiqing Min
Yuecong Min
Zhixiang Min
Qi Ming
David Minnen
Aymen Mir
Deepak Mishra
Anand Mishra
Shlok K. Mishra
Niluthpol Mithun
Gaurav Mittal
Trisha Mittal
Daisuke Miyazaki
Kaichun Mo
Hong Mo
Zhipeng Mo
Davide Modolo
Abduallah A. Mohamed
Mohamed Afham
    Mohamed Aflal
Ron Mokady
Pavlo Molchanov
Davide Moltisanti
Liliane Momeni
Gianluca Monaci
Pascal Monasse
Ajoy Mondal
Tom Monnier

Aron Monszpart
Gyeongsik Moon
Suhong Moon
Taesup Moon
Sean Moran
Daniel Moreira
Pietro Morerio
Alexandre Morgand
Lia Morra
Ali Mosleh
Inbar Mosseri
Sayed Mohammad
    Mostafavi Isfahani
Saman Motamed
Ramy A. Mounir
Fangzhou Mu
Jiteng Mu
Norman Mu
Yasuhiro Mukaigawa
Ryan Mukherjee
Tanmoy Mukherjee
Yusuke Mukuta
Ravi Teja Mullapudi
Lea Müller
Matthias Müller
Martin Mundt
Nils Murrugarra-Llerena
Damien Muselet
Armin Mustafa
Muhammad Ferjad Naeem
Sauradip Nag
Hajime Nagahara
Pravin Nagar
Rajendra Nagar
Naveen Shankar Nagaraja
Varun Nagaraja
Tushar Nagarajan
Seungjun Nah
Gaku Nakano
Yuta Nakashima
Giljoo Nam
Seonghyeon Nam
Liangliang Nan
Yuesong Nan
Yeshwanth Napolean

Dinesh Reddy
    Narapureddy
Medhini Narasimhan
Supreeth
    Narasimhaswamy
Sriram Narayanan
Erickson R. Nascimento
Varun Nasery
K. L. Navaneet
Pablo Navarrete Michelini
Shant Navasardyan
Shah Nawaz
Nihal Nayak
Farhood Negin
Lukáš Neumann
Alejandro Newell
Evonne Ng
Kam Woh Ng
Tony Ng
Anh Nguyen
Tuan Anh Nguyen
Cuong Cao Nguyen
Ngoc Cuong Nguyen
Thanh Nguyen
Khoi Nguyen
Phi Le Nguyen
Phong Ha Nguyen
Tam Nguyen
Truong Nguyen
Anh Tuan Nguyen
Rang Nguyen
Thao Thi Phuong Nguyen
Van Nguyen Nguyen
Zhen-Liang Ni
Yao Ni
Shijie Nie
Xuecheng Nie
Yongwei Nie
Weizhi Nie
Ying Nie
Yinyu Nie
Kshitij N. Nikhal
Simon Niklaus
Xuefei Ning
Jifeng Ning

Yotam Nitzan
Di Niu
Shuaicheng Niu
Li Niu
Wei Niu
Yulei Niu
Zhenxing Niu
Albert No
Shohei Nobuhara
Nicoletta Noceti
Junhyug Noh
Sotiris Nousias
Slawomir Nowaczyk
Ewa M. Nowara
Valsamis Ntouskos
Gilberto Ochoa-Ruiz
Ferda Ofli
Jihyong Oh
Sangyun Oh
Youngtaek Oh
Hiroki Ohashi
Takahiro Okabe
Kemal Oksuz
Fumio Okura
Daniel Olmeda Reino
Matthew Olson
Carl Olsson
Roy Or-El
Alessandro Ortis
Guillermo Ortiz-Jimenez
Magnus Oskarsson
Ahmed A. A. Osman
Martin R. Oswald
Mayu Otani
Naima Otberdout
Cheng Ouyang
Jiahong Ouyang
Wanli Ouyang
Andrew Owens
Poojan B. Oza
Mete Ozay
A. Cengiz Oztireli
Gautam Pai
Tomas Pajdla
Umapada Pal

Simone Palazzo
Luca Palmieri
Bowen Pan
Hao Pan
Lili Pan
Tai-Yu Pan
Liang Pan
Chengwei Pan
Yingwei Pan
Xuran Pan
Jinshan Pan
Xinyu Pan
Liyuan Pan
Xingang Pan
Xingjia Pan
Zhihong Pan
Zizheng Pan
Priyadarshini Panda
Rameswar Panda
Rohit Pandey
Kaiyue Pang
Bo Pang
Guansong Pang
Jiangmiao Pang
Meng Pang
Tianyu Pang
Ziqi Pang
Omiros Pantazis
Andreas Panteli
Maja Pantic
Marina Paolanti
Joao P. Papa
Samuele Papa
Mike Papadakis
Dim P. Papadopoulos
George Papandreou
Constantin Pape
Toufiq Parag
Chethan Parameshwara
Shaifali Parashar
Alejandro Pardo
Rishubh Parihar
Sarah Parisot
JaeYoo Park
Gyeong-Moon Park

Hyojin Park
Hyoungseob Park
Jongchan Park
Jae Sung Park
Kiru Park
Chunghyun Park
Kwanyong Park
Sunghyun Park
Sungrae Park
Seongsik Park
Sanghyun Park
Sungjune Park
Taesung Park
Gaurav Parmar
Paritosh Parmar
Alvaro Parra
Despoina Paschalidou
Or Patashnik
Shivansh Patel
Pushpak Pati
Prashant W. Patil
Vaishakh Patil
Suvam Patra
Jay Patravali
Badri Narayana Patro
Angshuman Paul
Sudipta Paul
Rémi Pautrat
Nick E. Pears
Adithya Pediredla
Wenjie Pei
Shmuel Peleg
Latha Pemula
Bo Peng
Houwen Peng
Yue Peng
Liangzu Peng
Baoyun Peng
Jun Peng
Pai Peng
Sida Peng
Xi Peng
Yuxin Peng
Songyou Peng
Wei Peng

Weiqi Peng
Wen-Hsiao Peng
Pramuditha Perera
Juan C. Perez
Eduardo Pérez Pellitero
Juan-Manuel Perez-Rua
Federico Pernici
Marco Pesavento
Stavros Petridis
Ilya A. Petrov
Vladan Petrovic
Mathis Petrovich
Suzanne Petryk
Hieu Pham
Quang Pham
Khoi Pham
Tung Pham
Huy Phan
Stephen Phillips
Cheng Perng Phoo
David Picard
Marco Piccirilli
Georg Pichler
A. J. Piergiovanni
Vipin Pillai
Silvia L. Pintea
Giovanni Pintore
Robinson Piramuthu
Fiora Pirri
Theodoros Pissas
Fabio Pizzati
Benjamin Planche
Bryan Plummer
Matteo Poggi
Ashwini Pokle
Georgy E. Ponimatkin
Adrian Popescu
Stefan Popov
Nikola Popović
Ronald Poppe
Angelo Porrello
Michael Potter
Charalambos Poullis
Hadi Pouransari
Omid Poursaeed

Shraman Pramanick
Mantini Pranav
Dilip K. Prasad
Meghshyam Prasad
B. H. Pawan Prasad
Shitala Prasad
Prateek Prasanna
Ekta Prashnani
Derek S. Prijatelj
Luke Y. Prince
Véronique Prinet
Victor Adrian Prisacariu
James Pritts
Thomas Probst
Sergey Prokudin
Rita Pucci
Chi-Man Pun
Matthew Purri
Haozhi Qi
Lu Qi
Lei Qi
Xianbiao Qi
Yonggang Qi
Yuankai Qi
Siyuan Qi
Guocheng Qian
Hangwei Qian
Qi Qian
Deheng Qian
Shengsheng Qian
Wen Qian
Rui Qian
Yiming Qian
Shengju Qian
Shengyi Qian
Xuelin Qian
Zhenxing Qian
Nan Qiao
Xiaotian Qiao
Jing Qin
Can Qin
Siyang Qin
Hongwei Qin
Jie Qin
Minghai Qin

Yipeng Qin
Yongqiang Qin
Wenda Qin
Xuebin Qin
Yuzhe Qin
Yao Qin
Zhenyue Qin
Zhiwu Qing
Heqian Qiu
Jiayan Qiu
Jielin Qiu
Yue Qiu
Jiaxiong Qiu
Zhongxi Qiu
Shi Qiu
Zhaofan Qiu
Zhongnan Qu
Yanyun Qu
Kha Gia Quach
Yuhui Quan
Ruijie Quan
Mike Rabbat
Rahul Shekhar Rade
Filip Radenovic
Gorjan Radevski
Bogdan Raducanu
Francesco Ragusa
Shafin Rahman
Md Mahfuzur Rahman
    Siddiquee
Hossein Rahmani
Kiran Raja
Sivaramakrishnan
    Rajaraman
Jathushan Rajasegaran
Adnan Siraj Rakin
Michaël Ramamonjisoa
Chirag A. Raman
Shanmuganathan Raman
Vignesh Ramanathan
Vasili Ramanishka
Vikram V. Ramaswamy
Merey Ramazanova
Jason Rambach
Sai Saketh Rambhatla

Clément Rambour
Ashwin Ramesh Babu
Adín Ramírez Rivera
Arianna Rampini
Haoxi Ran
Aakanksha Rana
Aayush Jung Bahadur
    Rana
Kanchana N. Ranasinghe
Aneesh Rangnekar
Samrudhdhi B. Rangrej
Harsh Rangwani
Viresh Ranjan
Anyi Rao
Yongming Rao
Carolina Raposo
Michalis Raptis
Amir Rasouli
Vivek Rathod
Adepu Ravi Sankar
Avinash Ravichandran
Bharadwaj Ravichandran
Dripta S. Raychaudhuri
Adria Recasens
Simon Reiß
Davis Rempe
Daxuan Ren
Jiawei Ren
Jimmy Ren
Sucheng Ren
Dayong Ren
Zhile Ren
Dongwei Ren
Qibing Ren
Pengfei Ren
Zhenwen Ren
Xuqian Ren
Yixuan Ren
Zhongzheng Ren
Ambareesh Revanur
Hamed Rezazadegan
    Tavakoli
Rafael S. Rezende
Wonjong Rhee
Alexander Richard

Christian Richardt
Stephan R. Richter
Benjamin Riggan
Dominik Rivoir
Mamshad Nayeem Rizve
Joshua D. Robinson
Joseph Robinson
Chris Rockwell
Ranga Rodrigo
Andres C. Rodriguez
Carlos Rodriguez-Pardo
Marcus Rohrbach
Gemma Roig
Yu Rong
David A. Ross
Mohammad Rostami
Edward Rosten
Karsten Roth
Anirban Roy
Debaditya Roy
Shuvendu Roy
Ahana Roy Choudhury
Aruni Roy Chowdhury
Denys Rozumnyi
Shulan Ruan
Wenjie Ruan
Patrick Ruhkamp
Danila Rukhovich
Anian Ruoss
Chris Russell
Dan Ruta
Dawid Damian Rymarczyk
DongHun Ryu
Hyeonggon Ryu
Kwonyoung Ryu
Balasubramanian S.
Alexandre Sablayrolles
Mohammad Sabokrou
Arka Sadhu
Aniruddha Saha
Oindrila Saha
Pritish Sahu
Aneeshan Sain
Nirat Saini
Saurabh Saini

Takeshi Saitoh
Christos Sakaridis
Fumihiko Sakaue
Dimitrios Sakkos
Ken Sakurada
Parikshit V. Sakurikar
Rohit Saluja
Nermin Samet
Leo Sampaio Ferraz
    Ribeiro
Jorge Sanchez
Enrique Sanchez
Shengtian Sang
Anush Sankaran
Soubhik Sanyal
Nikolaos Sarafianos
Vishwanath Saragadam
István Sárándi
Saquib Sarfraz
Mert Bulent Sariyildiz
Anindya Sarkar
Pritam Sarkar
Paul-Edouard Sarlin
Hiroshi Sasaki
Takami Sato
Torsten Sattler
Ravi Kumar Satzoda
Axel Sauer
Stefano Savian
Artem Savkin
Manolis Savva
Gerald Schaefer
Simone Schaub-Meyer
Yoni Schirris
Samuel Schulter
Katja Schwarz
Jesse Scott
Sinisa Segvic
Constantin Marc Seibold
Lorenzo Seidenari
Matan Sela
Fadime Sener
Paul Hongsuck Seo
Kwanggyoon Seo
Hongje Seong

Dario Serez
Francesco Setti
Bryan Seybold
Mohamad Shahbazi
Shima Shahfar
Xinxin Shan
Caifeng Shan
Dandan Shan
Shawn Shan
Wei Shang
Jinghuan Shang
Jiaxiang Shang
Lei Shang
Sukrit Shankar
Ken Shao
Rui Shao
Jie Shao
Mingwen Shao
Aashish Sharma
Gaurav Sharma
Vivek Sharma
Abhishek Sharma
Yoli Shavit
Shashank Shekhar
Sumit Shekhar
Zhijie Shen
Fengyi Shen
Furao Shen
Jialie Shen
Jingjing Shen
Ziyi Shen
Linlin Shen
Guangyu Shen
Biluo Shen
Falong Shen
Jiajun Shen
Qiu Shen
Qiuhong Shen
Shuai Shen
Wang Shen
Yiqing Shen
Yunhang Shen
Siqi Shen
Bin Shen
Tianwei Shen

Xi Shen
Yilin Shen
Yuming Shen
Yucong Shen
Zhiqiang Shen
Lu Sheng
Yichen Sheng
Shivanand Venkanna
  Sheshappanavar
Shelly Sheynin
Baifeng Shi
Ruoxi Shi
Botian Shi
Hailin Shi
Jia Shi
Jing Shi
Shaoshuai Shi
Baoguang Shi
Boxin Shi
Hengcan Shi
Tianyang Shi
Xiaodan Shi
Yongjie Shi
Zhensheng Shi
Yinghuan Shi
Weiqi Shi
Wu Shi
Xuepeng Shi
Xiaoshuang Shi
Yujiao Shi
Zenglin Shi
Zhenmei Shi
Takashi Shibata
Meng-Li Shih
Yichang Shih
Hyunjung Shim
Dongseok Shim
Soshi Shimada
Inkyu Shin
Jinwoo Shin
Seungjoo Shin
Seungjae Shin
Koichi Shinoda
Suprosanna Shit

Palaiahnakote
  Shivakumara
Eli Shlizerman
Gaurav Shrivastava
Xiao Shu
Xiangbo Shu
Xiujun Shu
Yang Shu
Tianmin Shu
Jun Shu
Zhixin Shu
Bing Shuai
Maria Shugrina
Ivan Shugurov
Satya Narayan Shukla
Pranjay Shyam
Jianlou Si
Yawar Siddiqui
Alberto Signoroni
Pedro Silva
Jae-Young Sim
Oriane Siméoni
Martin Simon
Andrea Simonelli
Abhishek Singh
Ashish Singh
Dinesh Singh
Gurkirt Singh
Krishna Kumar Singh
Mannat Singh
Pravendra Singh
Rajat Vikram Singh
Utkarsh Singhal
Dipika Singhania
Vasu Singla
Harsh Sinha
Sudipta Sinha
Josef Sivic
Elena Sizikova
Geri Skenderi
Ivan Skorokhodov
Dmitriy Smirnov
Cameron Y. Smith
James S. Smith
Patrick Snape

Mattia Soldan
Hyeongseok Son
Sanghyun Son
Chuanbiao Song
Chen Song
Chunfeng Song
Dan Song
Dongjin Song
Hwanjun Song
Guoxian Song
Jiaming Song
Jie Song
Liangchen Song
Ran Song
Luchuan Song
Xibin Song
Li Song
Fenglong Song
Guoli Song
Guanglu Song
Zhenbo Song
Lin Song
Xinhang Song
Yang Song
Yibing Song
Rajiv Soundararajan
Hossein Souri
Cristovao Sousa
Riccardo Spezialetti
Leonidas Spinoulas
Michael W. Spratling
Deepak Sridhar
Srinath Sridhar
Gaurang Sriramanan
Vinkle Kumar Srivastav
Themos Stafylakis
Serban Stan
Anastasis Stathopoulos
Markus Steinberger
Jan Steinbrener
Sinisa Stekovic
Alexandros Stergiou
Gleb Sterkin
Rainer Stiefelhagen
Pierre Stock

Ombretta Strafforello
Julian Straub
Yannick Strümpler
Joerg Stueckler
Hang Su
Weijie Su
Jong-Chyi Su
Bing Su
Haisheng Su
Jinming Su
Yiyang Su
Yukun Su
Yuxin Su
Zhuo Su
Zhaoqi Su
Xiu Su
Yu-Chuan Su
Zhixun Su
Arulkumar Subramaniam
Akshayvarun Subramanya
A. Subramanyam
Swathikiran Sudhakaran
Yusuke Sugano
Masanori Suganuma
Yumin Suh
Yang Sui
Baochen Sun
Cheng Sun
Long Sun
Guolei Sun
Haoliang Sun
Haomiao Sun
He Sun
Hanqing Sun
Hao Sun
Lichao Sun
Jiachen Sun
Jiaming Sun
Jian Sun
Jin Sun
Jennifer J. Sun
Tiancheng Sun
Libo Sun
Peize Sun
Qianru Sun

Shanlin Sun
Yu Sun
Zhun Sun
Che Sun
Lin Sun
Tao Sun
Yiyou Sun
Chunyi Sun
Chong Sun
Weiwei Sun
Weixuan Sun
Xiuyu Sun
Yanan Sun
Zeren Sun
Zhaodong Sun
Zhiqing Sun
Minhyuk Sung
Jinli Suo
Simon Suo
Abhijit Suprem
Anshuman Suri
Saksham Suri
Joshua M. Susskind
Roman Suvorov
Gurumurthy Swaminathan
Robin Swanson
Paul Swoboda
Tabish A. Syed
Richard Szeliski
Fariborz Taherkhani
Yu-Wing Tai
Keita Takahashi
Walter Talbott
Gary Tam
Masato Tamura
Feitong Tan
Fuwen Tan
Shuhan Tan
Andong Tan
Bin Tan
Cheng Tan
Jianchao Tan
Lei Tan
Mingxing Tan
Xin Tan

Zichang Tan
Zhentao Tan
Kenichiro Tanaka
Masayuki Tanaka
Yushun Tang
Hao Tang
Jingqun Tang
Jinhui Tang
Kaihua Tang
Luming Tang
Lv Tang
Sheyang Tang
Shitao Tang
Siliang Tang
Shixiang Tang
Yansong Tang
Keke Tang
Chang Tang
Chenwei Tang
Jie Tang
Junshu Tang
Ming Tang
Peng Tang
Xu Tang
Yao Tang
Chen Tang
Fan Tang
Haoran Tang
Shengeng Tang
Yehui Tang
Zhipeng Tang
Ugo Tanielian
Chaofan Tao
Jiale Tao
Junli Tao
Renshuai Tao
An Tao
Guanhong Tao
Zhiqiang Tao
Makarand Tapaswi
Jean-Philippe G. Tarel
Juan J. Tarrio
Enzo Tartaglione
Keisuke Tateno
Zachary Teed

Ajinkya B. Tejankar
Bugra Tekin
Purva Tendulkar
Damien Teney
Minggui Teng
Chris Tensmeyer
Andrew Beng Jin Teoh
Philipp Terhörst
Kartik Thakral
Nupur Thakur
Kevin Thandiackal
Spyridon Thermos
Diego Thomas
William Thong
Yuesong Tian
Guanzhong Tian
Lin Tian
Shiqi Tian
Kai Tian
Meng Tian
Tai-Peng Tian
Zhuotao Tian
Shangxuan Tian
Tian Tian
Yapeng Tian
Yu Tian
Yuxin Tian
Leslie Ching Ow Tiong
Praveen Tirupattur
Garvita Tiwari
George Toderici
Antoine Toisoul
Aysim Toker
Tatiana Tommasi
Zhan Tong
Alessio Tonioni
Alessandro Torcinovich
Fabio Tosi
Matteo Toso
Hugo Touvron
Quan Hung Tran
Son Tran
Hung Tran
Ngoc-Trung Tran
Vinh Tran

Phong Tran
Giovanni Trappolini
Edith Tretschk
Subarna Tripathi
Shubhendu Trivedi
Eduard Trulls
Prune Truong
Thanh-Dat Truong
Tomasz Trzcinski
Sam Tsai
Yi-Hsuan Tsai
Ethan Tseng
Yu-Chee Tseng
Shahar Tsiper
Stavros Tsogkas
Shikui Tu
Zhigang Tu
Zhengzhong Tu
Richard Tucker
Sergey Tulyakov
Cigdem Turan
Daniyar Turmukhambetov
Victor G. Turrisi da Costa
Bartlomiej Twardowski
Christopher D. Twigg
Radim Tylecek
Mostofa Rafid Uddin
Md. Zasim Uddin
Kohei Uehara
Nicolas Ugrinovic
Youngjung Uh
Norimichi Ukita
Anwaar Ulhaq
Devesh Upadhyay
Paul Upchurch
Yoshitaka Ushiku
Yuzuko Utsumi
Mikaela Angelina Uy
Mohit Vaishnav
Pratik Vaishnavi
Jeya Maria Jose Valanarasu
Matias A. Valdenegro Toro
Diego Valsesia
Wouter Van Gansbeke
Nanne van Noord

Simon Vandenhende
Farshid Varno
Cristina Vasconcelos
Francisco Vasconcelos
Alex Vasilescu
Subeesh Vasu
Arun Balajee Vasudevan
Kanav Vats
Vaibhav S. Vavilala
Sagar Vaze
Javier Vazquez-Corral
Andrea Vedaldi
Olga Veksler
Andreas Velten
Sai H. Vemprala
Raviteja Vemulapalli
Shashanka
    Venkataramanan
Dor Verbin
Luisa Verdoliva
Manisha Verma
Yashaswi Verma
Constantin Vertan
Eli Verwimp
Deepak Vijaykeerthy
Pablo Villanueva
Ruben Villegas
Markus Vincze
Vibhav Vineet
Minh P. Vo
Huy V. Vo
Duc Minh Vo
Tomas Vojir
Igor Vozniak
Nicholas Vretos
Vibashan VS
Tuan-Anh Vu
Thang Vu
Mårten Wadenbäck
Neal Wadhwa
Aaron T. Walsman
Steven Walton
Jin Wan
Alvin Wan
Jia Wan

Jun Wan
Xiaoyue Wan
Fang Wan
Guowei Wan
Renjie Wan
Zhiqiang Wan
Ziyu Wan
Bastian Wandt
Dongdong Wang
Limin Wang
Haiyang Wang
Xiaobing Wang
Angtian Wang
Angelina Wang
Bing Wang
Bo Wang
Boyu Wang
Binghui Wang
Chen Wang
Chien-Yi Wang
Congli Wang
Qi Wang
Chengrui Wang
Rui Wang
Yiqun Wang
Cong Wang
Wenjing Wang
Dongkai Wang
Di Wang
Xiaogang Wang
Kai Wang
Zhizhong Wang
Fangjinhua Wang
Feng Wang
Hang Wang
Gaoang Wang
Guoqing Wang
Guangcong Wang
Guangzhi Wang
Hanqing Wang
Hao Wang
Haohan Wang
Haoran Wang
Hong Wang
Haotao Wang

Hu Wang
Huan Wang
Hua Wang
Hui-Po Wang
Hengli Wang
Hanyu Wang
Hongxing Wang
Jingwen Wang
Jialiang Wang
Jian Wang
Jianyi Wang
Jiashun Wang
Jiahao Wang
Tsun-Hsuan Wang
Xiaoqian Wang
Jinqiao Wang
Jun Wang
Jianzong Wang
Kaihong Wang
Ke Wang
Lei Wang
Lingjing Wang
Linnan Wang
Lin Wang
Liansheng Wang
Mengjiao Wang
Manning Wang
Nannan Wang
Peihao Wang
Jiayun Wang
Pu Wang
Qiang Wang
Qiufeng Wang
Qilong Wang
Qiangchang Wang
Qin Wang
Qing Wang
Ruocheng Wang
Ruibin Wang
Ruisheng Wang
Ruizhe Wang
Runqi Wang
Runzhong Wang
Wenxuan Wang
Sen Wang

Shangfei Wang
Shaofei Wang
Shijie Wang
Shiqi Wang
Zhibo Wang
Song Wang
Xinjiang Wang
Tai Wang
Tao Wang
Teng Wang
Xiang Wang
Tianren Wang
Tiantian Wang
Tianyi Wang
Fengjiao Wang
Wei Wang
Miaohui Wang
Suchen Wang
Siyue Wang
Yaoming Wang
Xiao Wang
Ze Wang
Biao Wang
Chaofei Wang
Dong Wang
Gu Wang
Guangrun Wang
Guangming Wang
Guo-Hua Wang
Haoqing Wang
Hesheng Wang
Huafeng Wang
Jinghua Wang
Jingdong Wang
Jingjing Wang
Jingya Wang
Jingkang Wang
Jiakai Wang
Junke Wang
Kuo Wang
Lichen Wang
Lizhi Wang
Longguang Wang
Mang Wang
Mei Wang

Min Wang
Peng-Shuai Wang
Run Wang
Shaoru Wang
Shuhui Wang
Tan Wang
Tiancai Wang
Tianqi Wang
Wenhai Wang
Wenzhe Wang
Xiaobo Wang
Xiudong Wang
Xu Wang
Yajie Wang
Yan Wang
Yuan-Gen Wang
Yingqian Wang
Yizhi Wang
Yulin Wang
Yu Wang
Yujie Wang
Yunhe Wang
Yuxi Wang
Yaowei Wang
Yiwei Wang
Zezheng Wang
Hongzhi Wang
Zhiqiang Wang
Ziteng Wang
Ziwei Wang
Zheng Wang
Zhenyu Wang
Binglu Wang
Zhongdao Wang
Ce Wang
Weining Wang
Weiyao Wang
Wenbin Wang
Wenguan Wang
Guangting Wang
Haolin Wang
Haiyan Wang
Huiyu Wang
Naiyan Wang
Jingbo Wang

Jinpeng Wang
Jiaqi Wang
Liyuan Wang
Lizhen Wang
Ning Wang
Wenqian Wang
Sheng-Yu Wang
Weimin Wang
Xiaohan Wang
Yifan Wang
Yi Wang
Yongtao Wang
Yizhou Wang
Zhuo Wang
Zhe Wang
Xudong Wang
Xiaofang Wang
Xinggang Wang
Xiaosen Wang
Xiaosong Wang
Xiaoyang Wang
Lijun Wang
Xinlong Wang
Xuan Wang
Xue Wang
Yangang Wang
Yaohui Wang
Yu-Chiang Frank Wang
Yida Wang
Yilin Wang
Yi Ru Wang
Yali Wang
Yinglong Wang
Yufu Wang
Yujiang Wang
Yuwang Wang
Yuting Wang
Yang Wang
Yu-Xiong Wang
Yixu Wang
Ziqi Wang
Zhicheng Wang
Zeyu Wang
Zhaowen Wang
Zhenyi Wang

Zhenzhi Wang
Zhijie Wang
Zhiyong Wang
Zhongling Wang
Zhuowei Wang
Zian Wang
Zifu Wang
Zihao Wang
Zirui Wang
Ziyan Wang
Wenxiao Wang
Zhen Wang
Zhepeng Wang
Zi Wang
Zihao W. Wang
Steven L. Waslander
Olivia Watkins
Daniel Watson
Silvan Weder
Dongyoon Wee
Dongming Wei
Tianyi Wei
Jia Wei
Dong Wei
Fangyun Wei
Longhui Wei
Mingqiang Wei
Xinyue Wei
Chen Wei
Donglai Wei
Pengxu Wei
Xing Wei
Xiu-Shen Wei
Wenqi Wei
Guoqiang Wei
Wei Wei
XingKui Wei
Xian Wei
Xingxing Wei
Yake Wei
Yuxiang Wei
Yi Wei
Luca Weihs
Michael Weinmann
Martin Weinmann

Congcong Wen
Chuan Wen
Jie Wen
Sijia Wen
Song Wen
Chao Wen
Xiang Wen
Zeyi Wen
Xin Wen
Yilin Wen
Yijia Weng
Shuchen Weng
Junwu Weng
Wenming Weng
Renliang Weng
Zhenyu Weng
Xinshuo Weng
Nicholas J. Westlake
Gordon Wetzstein
Lena M. Widin Klasén
Rick Wildes
Bryan M. Williams
Williem Williem
Ole Winther
Scott Wisdom
Alex Wong
Chau-Wai Wong
Kwan-Yee K. Wong
Yongkang Wong
Scott Workman
Marcel Worring
Michael Wray
Safwan Wshah
Xiang Wu
Aming Wu
Chongruo Wu
Cho-Ying Wu
Chunpeng Wu
Chenyan Wu
Ziyi Wu
Fuxiang Wu
Gang Wu
Haiping Wu
Huisi Wu
Jane Wu

Jialian Wu
Jing Wu
Jinjian Wu
Jianlong Wu
Xian Wu
Lifang Wu
Lifan Wu
Minye Wu
Qianyi Wu
Rongliang Wu
Rui Wu
Shiqian Wu
Shuzhe Wu
Shangzhe Wu
Tsung-Han Wu
Tz-Ying Wu
Ting-Wei Wu
Jiannan Wu
Zhiliang Wu
Yu Wu
Chenyun Wu
Dayan Wu
Dongxian Wu
Fei Wu
Hefeng Wu
Jianxin Wu
Weibin Wu
Wenxuan Wu
Wenhao Wu
Xiao Wu
Yicheng Wu
Yuanwei Wu
Yu-Huan Wu
Zhenxin Wu
Zhenyu Wu
Wei Wu
Peng Wu
Xiaohe Wu
Xindi Wu
Xinxing Wu
Xinyi Wu
Xingjiao Wu
Xiongwei Wu
Yangzheng Wu
Yanzhao Wu

Yawen Wu
Yong Wu
Yi Wu
Ying Nian Wu
Zhenyao Wu
Zhonghua Wu
Zongze Wu
Zuxuan Wu
Stefanie Wuhrer
Teng Xi
Jianing Xi
Fei Xia
Haifeng Xia
Menghan Xia
Yuanqing Xia
Zhihua Xia
Xiaobo Xia
Weihao Xia
Shihong Xia
Yan Xia
Yong Xia
Zhaoyang Xia
Zhihao Xia
Chuhua Xian
Yongqin Xian
Wangmeng Xiang
Fanbo Xiang
Tiange Xiang
Tao Xiang
Liuyu Xiang
Xiaoyu Xiang
Zhiyu Xiang
Aoran Xiao
Chunxia Xiao
Fanyi Xiao
Jimin Xiao
Jun Xiao
Taihong Xiao
Anqi Xiao
Junfei Xiao
Jing Xiao
Liang Xiao
Yang Xiao
Yuting Xiao
Yijun Xiao

Yao Xiao

Zeyu Xiao

Zhisheng Xiao

Zihao Xiao

Binhui Xie

Christopher Xie

Haozhe Xie

Jin Xie

Guo-Sen Xie

Hongtao Xie

Ming-Kun Xie

Tingting Xie

Chaohao Xie

Weicheng Xie

Xudong Xie

Jiyang Xie

Xiaohua Xie

Yuan Xie

Zhenyu Xie

Ning Xie

Xianghui Xie

Xiufeng Xie

You Xie

Yutong Xie

Fuyong Xing

Yifan Xing

Zhen Xing

Yuanjun Xiong

Jinhui Xiong

Weihua Xiong

Hongkai Xiong

Zhitong Xiong

Yuanhao Xiong

Yunyang Xiong

Yuwen Xiong

Zhiwei Xiong

Yuliang Xiu

An Xu

Chang Xu

Chenliang Xu

Chengming Xu

Chenshu Xu

Xiang Xu

Huijuan Xu

Zhe Xu

Jie Xu

Jingyi Xu

Jiarui Xu

Yinghao Xu

Kele Xu

Ke Xu

Li Xu

Linchuan Xu

Linning Xu

Mengde Xu

Mengmeng Frost Xu

Min Xu

Mingye Xu

Jun Xu

Ning Xu

Peng Xu

Runsheng Xu

Sheng Xu

Wenqiang Xu

Xiaogang Xu

Renzhe Xu

Kaidi Xu

Yi Xu

Chi Xu

Qiuling Xu

Baobei Xu

Feng Xu

Haohang Xu

Haofei Xu

Lan Xu

Mingze Xu

Songcen Xu

Weipeng Xu

Wenjia Xu

Wenju Xu

Xiangyu Xu

Xin Xu

Yinshuang Xu

Yixing Xu

Yuting Xu

Yanyu Xu

Zhenbo Xu

Zhiliang Xu

Zhiyuan Xu

Xiaohao Xu

Yanwu Xu

Yan Xu

Yiran Xu

Yifan Xu

Yufei Xu

Yong Xu

Zichuan Xu

Zenglin Xu

Zexiang Xu

Zhan Xu

Zheng Xu

Zhiwei Xu

Ziyue Xu

Shiyu Xuan

Hanyu Xuan

Fei Xue

Jianru Xue

Mingfu Xue

Qinghan Xue

Tianfan Xue

Chao Xue

Chuhui Xue

Nan Xue

Zhou Xue

Xiangyang Xue

Yuan Xue

Abhay Yadav

Ravindra Yadav

Kota Yamaguchi

Toshihiko Yamasaki

Kohei Yamashita

Chaochao Yan

Feng Yan

Kun Yan

Qingsen Yan

Qixin Yan

Rui Yan

Siming Yan

Xinchen Yan

Yaping Yan

Bin Yan

Qingan Yan

Shen Yan

Shipeng Yan

Xu Yan

Yan Yan
Yichao Yan
Zhaoyi Yan
Zike Yan
Zhiqiang Yan
Hongliang Yan
Zizheng Yan
Jiewen Yang
Anqi Joyce Yang
Shan Yang
Anqi Yang
Antoine Yang
Bo Yang
Baoyao Yang
Chenhongyi Yang
Dingkang Yang
De-Nian Yang
Dong Yang
David Yang
Fan Yang
Fengyu Yang
Fengting Yang
Fei Yang
Gengshan Yang
Heng Yang
Han Yang
Huan Yang
Yibo Yang
Jiancheng Yang
Jihan Yang
Jiawei Yang
Jiayu Yang
Jie Yang
Jinfa Yang
Jingkang Yang
Jinyu Yang
Cheng-Fu Yang
Ji Yang
Jianyu Yang
Kailun Yang
Tian Yang
Luyu Yang
Liang Yang
Li Yang
Michael Ying Yang

Yang Yang
Muli Yang
Le Yang
Qiushi Yang
Ren Yang
Ruihan Yang
Shuang Yang
Siyuan Yang
Su Yang
Shiqi Yang
Taojiannan Yang
Tianyu Yang
Lei Yang
Wanzhao Yang
Shuai Yang
William Yang
Wei Yang
Xiaofeng Yang
Xiaoshan Yang
Xin Yang
Xuan Yang
Xu Yang
Xingyi Yang
Xitong Yang
Jing Yang
Yanchao Yang
Wenming Yang
Yujiu Yang
Herb Yang
Jianfei Yang
Jinhui Yang
Chuanguang Yang
Guanglei Yang
Haitao Yang
Kewei Yang
Linlin Yang
Lijin Yang
Longrong Yang
Meng Yang
MingKun Yang
Sibei Yang
Shicai Yang
Tong Yang
Wen Yang
Xi Yang

Xiaolong Yang
Xue Yang
Yubin Yang
Ze Yang
Ziyi Yang
Yi Yang
Linjie Yang
Yuzhe Yang
Yiding Yang
Zhenpei Yang
Zhaohui Yang
Zhengyuan Yang
Zhibo Yang
Zongxin Yang
Hantao Yao
Mingde Yao
Rui Yao
Taiping Yao
Ting Yao
Cong Yao
Qingsong Yao
Quanming Yao
Xu Yao
Yuan Yao
Yao Yao
Yazhou Yao
Jiawen Yao
Shunyu Yao
Pew-Thian Yap
Sudhir Yarram
Rajeev Yasarla
Peng Ye
Botao Ye
Mao Ye
Fei Ye
Hanrong Ye
Jingwen Ye
Jinwei Ye
Jiarong Ye
Mang Ye
Meng Ye
Qi Ye
Qian Ye
Qixiang Ye
Junjie Ye

Sheng Ye
Nanyang Ye
Yufei Ye
Xiaoqing Ye
Ruolin Ye
Yousef Yeganeh
Chun-Hsiao Yeh
Raymond A. Yeh
Yu-Ying Yeh
Kai Yi
Chang Yi
Renjiao Yi
Xinping Yi
Peng Yi
Alper Yilmaz
Junho Yim
Hui Yin
Bangjie Yin
Jia-Li Yin
Miao Yin
Wenzhe Yin
Xuwang Yin
Ming Yin
Yu Yin
Aoxiong Yin
Kangxue Yin
Tianwei Yin
Wei Yin
Xianghua Ying
Rio Yokota
Tatsuya Yokota
Naoto Yokoya
Ryo Yonetani
Ki Yoon Yoo
Jinsu Yoo
Sunjae Yoon
Jae Shin Yoon
Jihun Yoon
Sung-Hoon Yoon
Ryota Yoshihashi
Yusuke Yoshiyasu
Chenyu You
Haoran You
Haoxuan You
Yang You

Quanzeng You
Tackgeun You
Kaichao You
Shan You
Xinge You
Yurong You
Baosheng Yu
Bei Yu
Haichao Yu
Hao Yu
Chaohui Yu
Fisher Yu
Jin-Gang Yu
Jiyang Yu
Jason J. Yu
Jiashuo Yu
Hong-Xing Yu
Lei Yu
Mulin Yu
Ning Yu
Peilin Yu
Qi Yu
Qian Yu
Rui Yu
Shuzhi Yu
Gang Yu
Tan Yu
Weijiang Yu
Xin Yu
Bingyao Yu
Ye Yu
Hanchao Yu
Yingchen Yu
Tao Yu
Xiaotian Yu
Qing Yu
Houjian Yu
Changqian Yu
Jing Yu
Jun Yu
Shujian Yu
Xiang Yu
Zhaofei Yu
Zhenbo Yu
Yinfeng Yu

Zhuoran Yu
Zitong Yu
Bo Yuan
Jiangbo Yuan
Liangzhe Yuan
Weihao Yuan
Jianbo Yuan
Xiaoyun Yuan
Ye Yuan
Li Yuan
Geng Yuan
Jialin Yuan
Maoxun Yuan
Peng Yuan
Xin Yuan
Yuan Yuan
Yuhui Yuan
Yixuan Yuan
Zheng Yuan
Mehmet Kerim Yücel
Kaiyu Yue
Haixiao Yue
Heeseung Yun
Sangdoo Yun
Tian Yun
Mahmut Yurt
Ekim Yurtsever
Ahmet Yüzügüler
Edouard Yvinec
Eloi Zablocki
Christopher Zach
Muhammad Zaigham
    Zaheer
Pierluigi Zama Ramirez
Yuhang Zang
Pietro Zanuttigh
Alexey Zaytsev
Bernhard Zeisl
Haitian Zeng
Pengpeng Zeng
Jiabei Zeng
Runhao Zeng
Wei Zeng
Yawen Zeng
Yi Zeng

Yiming Zeng
Tieyong Zeng
Huanqiang Zeng
Dan Zeng
Yu Zeng
Wei Zhai
Yuanhao Zhai
Fangneng Zhan
Kun Zhan
Xiong Zhang
Jingdong Zhang
Jiangning Zhang
Zhilu Zhang
Gengwei Zhang
Dongsu Zhang
Hui Zhang
Binjie Zhang
Bo Zhang
Tianhao Zhang
Cecilia Zhang
Jing Zhang
Chaoning Zhang
Chenxu Zhang
Chi Zhang
Chris Zhang
Yabin Zhang
Zhao Zhang
Rufeng Zhang
Chaoyi Zhang
Zheng Zhang
Da Zhang
Yi Zhang
Edward Zhang
Xin Zhang
Feifei Zhang
Feilong Zhang
Yuqi Zhang
GuiXuan Zhang
Hanlin Zhang
Hanwang Zhang
Hanzhen Zhang
Haotian Zhang
He Zhang
Haokui Zhang
Hongyuan Zhang

Hengrui Zhang
Hongming Zhang
Mingfang Zhang
Jianpeng Zhang
Jiaming Zhang
Jichao Zhang
Jie Zhang
Jingfeng Zhang
Jingyi Zhang
Jinnian Zhang
David Junhao Zhang
Junjie Zhang
Junzhe Zhang
Jiawan Zhang
Jingyang Zhang
Kai Zhang
Lei Zhang
Lihua Zhang
Lu Zhang
Miao Zhang
Minjia Zhang
Mingjin Zhang
Qi Zhang
Qian Zhang
Qilong Zhang
Qiming Zhang
Qiang Zhang
Richard Zhang
Ruimao Zhang
Ruisi Zhang
Ruixin Zhang
Runze Zhang
Qilin Zhang
Shan Zhang
Shanshan Zhang
Xi Sheryl Zhang
Song-Hai Zhang
Chongyang Zhang
Kaihao Zhang
Songyang Zhang
Shu Zhang
Siwei Zhang
Shujian Zhang
Tianyun Zhang
Tong Zhang

Tao Zhang
Wenwei Zhang
Wenqiang Zhang
Wen Zhang
Xiaolin Zhang
Xingchen Zhang
Xingxuan Zhang
Xiuming Zhang
Xiaoshuai Zhang
Xuanmeng Zhang
Xuanyang Zhang
Xucong Zhang
Xingxing Zhang
Xikun Zhang
Xiaohan Zhang
Yahui Zhang
Yunhua Zhang
Yan Zhang
Yanghao Zhang
Yifei Zhang
Yifan Zhang
Yi-Fan Zhang
Yihao Zhang
Yingliang Zhang
Youshan Zhang
Yulun Zhang
Yushu Zhang
Yixiao Zhang
Yide Zhang
Zhongwen Zhang
Bowen Zhang
Chen-Lin Zhang
Zehua Zhang
Zekun Zhang
Zeyu Zhang
Xiaowei Zhang
Yifeng Zhang
Cheng Zhang
Hongguang Zhang
Yuexi Zhang
Fa Zhang
Guofeng Zhang
Hao Zhang
Haofeng Zhang
Hongwen Zhang

Hua Zhang
Jiaxin Zhang
Zhenyu Zhang
Jian Zhang
Jianfeng Zhang
Jiao Zhang
Jiakai Zhang
Lefei Zhang
Le Zhang
Mi Zhang
Min Zhang
Ning Zhang
Pan Zhang
Pu Zhang
Qing Zhang
Renrui Zhang
Shifeng Zhang
Shuo Zhang
Shaoxiong Zhang
Weizhong Zhang
Xi Zhang
Xiaomei Zhang
Xinyu Zhang
Yin Zhang
Zicheng Zhang
Zihao Zhang
Ziqi Zhang
Zhaoxiang Zhang
Zhen Zhang
Zhipeng Zhang
Zhixing Zhang
Zhizheng Zhang
Jiawei Zhang
Zhong Zhang
Pingping Zhang
Yixin Zhang
Kui Zhang
Lingzhi Zhang
Huaiwen Zhang
Quanshi Zhang
Zhoutong Zhang
Yuhang Zhang
Yuting Zhang
Zhang Zhang
Ziming Zhang

Zhizhong Zhang
Qilong Zhangli
Bingyin Zhao
Bin Zhao
Chenglong Zhao
Lei Zhao
Feng Zhao
Gangming Zhao
Haiyan Zhao
Hao Zhao
Handong Zhao
Hengshuang Zhao
Yinan Zhao
Jiaojiao Zhao
Jiaqi Zhao
Jing Zhao
Kaili Zhao
Haojie Zhao
Yucheng Zhao
Longjiao Zhao
Long Zhao
Qingsong Zhao
Qingyu Zhao
Rui Zhao
Rui-Wei Zhao
Sicheng Zhao
Shuang Zhao
Siyan Zhao
Zelin Zhao
Shiyu Zhao
Wang Zhao
Tiesong Zhao
Qian Zhao
Wangbo Zhao
Xi-Le Zhao
Xu Zhao
Yajie Zhao
Yang Zhao
Ying Zhao
Yin Zhao
Yizhou Zhao
Yunhan Zhao
Yuyang Zhao
Yue Zhao
Yuzhi Zhao

Bowen Zhao
Pu Zhao
Bingchen Zhao
Borui Zhao
Fuqiang Zhao
Hanbin Zhao
Jian Zhao
Mingyang Zhao
Na Zhao
Rongchang Zhao
Ruiqi Zhao
Shuai Zhao
Wenda Zhao
Wenliang Zhao
Xiangyun Zhao
Yifan Zhao
Yaping Zhao
Zhou Zhao
He Zhao
Jie Zhao
Xibin Zhao
Xiaoqi Zhao
Zhengyu Zhao
Jin Zhe
Chuanxia Zheng
Huan Zheng
Hao Zheng
Jia Zheng
Jian-Qing Zheng
Shuai Zheng
Meng Zheng
Mingkai Zheng
Qian Zheng
Qi Zheng
Wu Zheng
Yinqiang Zheng
Yufeng Zheng
Yutong Zheng
Yalin Zheng
Yu Zheng
Feng Zheng
Zhaoheng Zheng
Haitian Zheng
Kang Zheng
Bolun Zheng

Haiyong Zheng
Mingwu Zheng
Sipeng Zheng
Tu Zheng
Wenzhao Zheng
Xiawu Zheng
Yinglin Zheng
Zhuo Zheng
Zilong Zheng
Kecheng Zheng
Zerong Zheng
Shuaifeng Zhi
Tiancheng Zhi
Jia-Xing Zhong
Yiwu Zhong
Fangwei Zhong
Zhihang Zhong
Yaoyao Zhong
Yiran Zhong
Zhun Zhong
Zichun Zhong
Bo Zhou
Boyao Zhou
Brady Zhou
Mo Zhou
Chunluan Zhou
Dingfu Zhou
Fan Zhou
Jingkai Zhou
Honglu Zhou
Jiaming Zhou
Jiahuan Zhou
Jun Zhou
Kaiyang Zhou
Keyang Zhou
Kuangqi Zhou
Lei Zhou
Lihua Zhou
Man Zhou
Mingyi Zhou
Mingyuan Zhou
Ning Zhou
Peng Zhou
Penghao Zhou
Qianyi Zhou

Shuigeng Zhou
Shangchen Zhou
Huayi Zhou
Zhize Zhou
Sanping Zhou
Qin Zhou
Tao Zhou
Wenbo Zhou
Xiangdong Zhou
Xiao-Yun Zhou
Xiao Zhou
Yang Zhou
Yipin Zhou
Zhenyu Zhou
Hao Zhou
Chu Zhou
Daquan Zhou
Da-Wei Zhou
Hang Zhou
Kang Zhou
Qianyu Zhou
Sheng Zhou
Wenhui Zhou
Xingyi Zhou
Yan-Jie Zhou
Yiyi Zhou
Yu Zhou
Yuan Zhou
Yuqian Zhou
Yuxuan Zhou
Zixiang Zhou
Wengang Zhou
Shuchang Zhou
Tianfei Zhou
Yichao Zhou
Alex Zhu
Chenchen Zhu
Deyao Zhu
Xiatian Zhu
Guibo Zhu
Haidong Zhu
Hao Zhu
Hongzi Zhu
Rui Zhu
Jing Zhu

Jianke Zhu
Junchen Zhu
Lei Zhu
Lingyu Zhu
Luyang Zhu
Menglong Zhu
Peihao Zhu
Hui Zhu
Xiaofeng Zhu
Tyler (Lixuan) Zhu
Wentao Zhu
Xiangyu Zhu
Xinqi Zhu
Xinxin Zhu
Xinliang Zhu
Tangguang Zhu
Yichen Zhu
Yixin Zhu
Yanjun Zhu
Yousong Zhu
Yuhao Zhu
Ye Zhu
Feng Zhu
Zhen Zhu
Fangrui Zhu
Jinjing Zhu
Linchao Zhu
Pengfei Zhu
Sijie Zhu
Xiaobin Zhu
Xiaoguang Zhu
Zezhou Zhu
Zhenyao Zhu
Kai Zhu
Pengkai Zhu
Bingbing Zhuang
Chengyuan Zhuang
Liansheng Zhuang
Peiye Zhuang
Yixin Zhuang
Yihong Zhuang
Junbao Zhuo
Andrea Ziani
Bartosz Zieliński
Primo Zingaretti

Nikolaos Zioulis
Andrew Zisserman
Yael Ziv
Liu Ziyin
Xingxing Zou
Danping Zou
Qi Zou

Shihao Zou
Xueyan Zou
Yang Zou
Yuliang Zou
Zihang Zou
Chuhang Zou
Dongqing Zou

Xu Zou
Zhiming Zou
Maria A. Zuluaga
Xinxin Zuo
Zhiwen Zuo
Reyer Zwiggelaar

Contents – Part XXII

ByteTrack: Multi-object Tracking by Associating Every Detection Box

Yifu Zhang[1], Peize Sun[2], Yi Jiang[3], Dongdong Yu[3], Fucheng Weng[1],
Zehuan Yuan[3], Ping Luo[2], Wenyu Liu[1], and Xinggang Wang[1]([✉])

[1] Huazhong University of Science and Technology, Wuhan, China
xgwang@hust.edu.cn
[2] The University of Hong Kong, Hong Kong, China
[3] ByteDance Inc., Beijing, China

Abstract. Multi-object tracking (MOT) aims at estimating bounding boxes and identities of objects in videos. Most methods obtain identities by associating detection boxes whose scores are higher than a threshold. The objects with low detection scores, *e.g.* occluded objects, are simply thrown away, which brings non-negligible true object missing and fragmented trajectories. To solve this problem, we present a simple, effective and generic association method, tracking by associating almost every detection box instead of only the high score ones. For the low score detection boxes, we utilize their similarities with tracklets to recover true objects and filter out the background detections. When applied to 9 different state-of-the-art trackers, our method achieves consistent improvement on IDF1 score ranging from 1 to 10 points. To put forwards the state-of-the-art performance of MOT, we design a simple and strong tracker, named ByteTrack. For the first time, we achieve 80.3 MOTA, 77.3 IDF1 and 63.1 HOTA on the test set of MOT17 with 30 FPS running speed on a single V100 GPU. ByteTrack also achieves state-of-the-art performance on MOT20, HiEve and BDD100K tracking benchmarks. The source code, pre-trained models with deploy versions and tutorials of applying to other trackers are released at https://github.com/ifzhang/ByteTrack.

Keywords: Multi-object tracking · Data association · Detection boxes

1 Introduction

Was vernünftig ist, das ist wirklich; und was wirklich ist, das ist vernünftig.
— *G. W. F. Hegel*

Tracking-by-detection is the most effective paradigm for multi-object tracking (MOT) in current. Due to the complex scenarios in videos, detectors are prone

Supplementary Information The online version contains supplementary material available at https://doi.org/10.1007/978-3-031-20047-2_1.

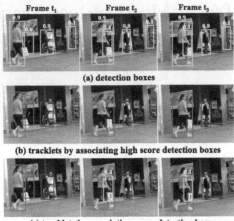

Fig. 1. Examples of our method which associates almost every detection box. (a) shows all the detection boxes with their scores. (b) shows the tracklets obtained by previous methods which associates detection boxes whose scores are higher than a threshold, *i.e.* 0.5. The same box color represents the same identity. (c) shows the tracklets obtained by our method. The dashed boxes represent the predicted box of the previous tracklets using Kalman filter. The two low score detection boxes are correctly matched to the previous tracklets based on the large IoU.

to make imperfect predictions. State-of-the-art MOT methods [1–3, 6, 13, 18, 46, 58, 69, 71, 84] need to deal with true positive / false positive trade-off in detection boxes to eliminate low confidence detection boxes [4, 41]. However, is it the right way to eliminate all low confidence detection boxes? Our answer is NO: as Hegel said "What is reasonable is real; that which is real is reasonable." Low confidence detection boxes sometimes indicate the existence of objects, *e.g.* the occluded objects. Filtering out these objects causes irreversible errors for MOT and brings non-negligible missing detection and fragmented trajectories.

Figure 1 (a) and (b) show this problem. In frame t_1, we initialize three different tracklets as their scores are all higher than 0.5. However, in frame t_2 and frame t_3 when occlusion happens, red tracklet's corresponding detection score becomes lower *i.e.* 0.8 to 0.4 and then 0.4 to 0.1. These detection boxes are eliminated by the thresholding mechanism and the red tracklet disappears accordingly. Nevertheless, if we take every detection box into consideration, more false positives will be introduced immediately, *e.g.* , the most right box in frame t_3 of Fig. 1 (a). To the best of our knowledge, very few methods [31, 61] in MOT are able to handle this detection dilemma.

In this paper, we identify that the similarity with tracklets provides a strong cue to distinguish the objects and background in low score detection boxes. As shown in Fig. 1 (c), two low score detection boxes are matched to the tracklets by the motion model's predicted boxes, and thus the objects are correctly recovered. At the same time, the background box is removed since it has no matched tracklet.

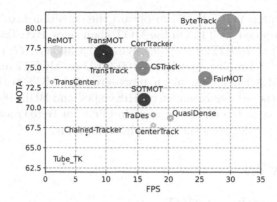

Fig. 2. MOTA-IDF1-FPS comparisons of different trackers on the test set of MOT17. The horizontal axis is FPS (running speed), the vertical axis is MOTA, and the radius of circle is IDF1. Our ByteTrack achieves 80.3 MOTA, 77.3 IDF1 on MOT17 test set with 30 FPS running speed, outperforming all previous trackers. Details are given in Table 4.

For making full use of detection boxes from high scores to low ones in the matching process, we present a simple and effective association method BYTE, named for each detection box is a basic unit of the tracklet, as byte in computer program, and our tracking method values every detailed detection box. We first match the high score detection boxes to the tracklets based on motion similarity or appearance similarity. Similar to [6], we adopt Kalman filter [30] to predict the location of the tracklets in the new frame. The similarity can be computed by the IoU or Re-ID feature distance of the predicted box and the detection box. Figure 1 (b) is exactly the results after the first matching. Then, we perform the second matching between the unmatched tracklets, *i.e.* the tracklet in red box, and the low score detection boxes using the same motion similarity. Figure 1 (c) shows the results after the second matching. The occluded person with low detection scores is matched correctly to the previous tracklet and the background (in the right part of the image) is removed.

As the integrating topic of object detection and association, a desirable solution to MOT is never a detector and the following association; besides, well-designed of their junction area is also important. The innovation of BYTE lies in the junction area of detection and association, where low score detection boxes are bridges to boost both of them. Benefiting from this integration innovation, when BYTE is applied to 9 different state-of-the-art trackers, including the Re-ID-based ones [34,48,68,84], motion-based ones [70,87], chain-based one [49] and attention-based ones [58,79], notable improvements are achieved on almost all the metrics including MOTA, IDF1 score and ID switches. For example, we increase the MOTA of CenterTrack [87] from 66.1 to 67.4, IDF1 from 64.2 to 74.0 and decrease the IDs from 528 to 144 on the half validation set of MOT17 (Fig. 2).

Towards pushing forwards the state-of-the-art performance of MOT, we propose a simple and strong tracker, named ByteTrack. We adopt a recent high-performance detector YOLOX [25] to obtain the detection boxes and associate them with our proposed BYTE. On the MOT challenges, ByteTrack ranks 1st on both MOT17 [45] and MOT20 [17], achieving 80.3 MOTA, 77.3 IDF1 and 63.1 HOTA with 30 FPS running speed on V100 GPU on MOT17 and 77.8 MOTA, 75.2 IDF1 and 61.3 HOTA on much more crowded MOT20. ByteTrack also achieves state-of-the-art performance on HiEve [38] and BDD100K [78] tracking benchmarks. We hope the efficiency and simplicity of ByteTrack could make it attractive in real applications such as social computing.

2   Related Work

2.1   Object Detection in MOT

Object detection is one of the most active topics in computer vision and it is the basis of multi-object tracking. The MOT17 dataset [45] provides detection results obtained by popular detectors such as DPM [23], Faster R-CNN [51] and SDP [76]. A large number of methods [3,9,13,15,29,72,90] focus on improving the tracking performance based on these given detection results.

Tracking by Detection. With the rapid development of object detection [11, 21,22,24,27,36,50,51,57,59,63], more and more methods begin to utilize more powerful detectors to obtain higher tracking performance. The one-stage object detector RetinaNet [36] begin to be adopted by several methods such as [40,49]. CenterNet [88] is the most popular detector adopted by most methods [61,64,66, 70,84,86,87] for its simplicity and efficiency. The YOLO series detectors [8,50,63] are also adopted by a large number of methods [16,34,35,68,74] for its excellent balance of accuracy and speed. Most of these methods directly use the detection boxes on a single image for tracking.

However, the number of missing detections and very low scoring detections begin to increase when occlusion or motion blur happens in the video sequence, as is pointed out by video object detection methods [42,60]. Therefore, the information of the previous frames are usually leveraged to enhance the video detection performance.

Detection by Tracking. Tracking can also adopted to help obtain more accurate detection boxes. Some methods [13–16,53,90] utilize single object tracking (SOT) [5] or Kalman filter [30] to predict the location of the tracklets in the following frame and fuse the predicted boxes with the detection boxes to enhance the detection results. Other methods [35,85] leverage tracked boxes in the previous frames to enhance feature representation of the following frame. Recently, Transformer-based [19,39,62,65] detectors [12,91] are adopted by several methods [10,43,58,79] for its strong ability to propagate boxes between frames. Our method also utilize the similarity with tracklets to strength the reliability of detection boxes.

After obtaining the detection boxes by various detectors, most MOT methods [34,40,48,58,68,70,84] only keep the high score detection boxes by a threshold, *i.e.* 0.5, and use those boxes as the input of data association. This is because the low score detection boxes contain many backgrounds which harm the tracking performance. However, we observe that many occluded objects can be correctly detected but have low scores. To reduce missing detections and keep the persistence of trajectories, we keep all the detection boxes and associate across every of them.

2.2   Data Association

Data association is the core of multi-object tracking, which first computes the similarity between tracklets and detection boxes and leverage different strategies to match them according to the similarity.

Similarity Metrics. Location, motion and appearance are useful cues for association. SORT [6] combines location and motion cues in a very simple way. It first adopts Kalman filter [30] to predict the location of the tracklets in the new frame and then computes the IoU between the detection boxes and the predicted boxes as the similarity. Some recent methods [56, 58, 70, 87] design networks to learn object motions and achieve more robust results in cases of large camera motion or low frame rate. Location and motion similarity are accurate in the short-range matching. Appearance similarity are helpful in the long-range matching. An object can be re-identified using appearance similarity after being occluded for a long period of time. Appearance similarity can be measured by the cosine similarity of the Re-ID features. DeepSORT [69] adopts a stand-alone Re-ID model to extract appearance features from the detection boxes. Recently, joint detection and Re-ID models [34, 40, 48, 68, 83, 84, 89] becomes more and more popular because of their simplicity and efficiency.

Matching Strategy. After similarity computation, matching strategy assigns identities to the objects. This can be done by Hungarian Algorithm [32] or greedy assignment [87]. SORT [6] matches the detection boxes to the tracklets by once matching. DeepSORT [69] proposes a cascaded matching strategy which first matches the detection boxes to the most recent tracklets and then to the lost ones. MOTDT [13] first utilizes appearance similarity to match and then utilize the IoU similarity to match the unmatched tracklets. QDTrack [48] turns the appearance similarity into probability by a bi-directional softmax operation and adopts a nearest neighbor search to accomplish matching. Attention mechanism [62] can directly propagate boxes between frames and perform association implicitly. Recent methods such as [43, 79] propose track queries to find the location of the tracked objects in the following frames. The matching is implicitly performed in the attention interaction process without using Hungarian Algorithm.

All these methods focus on how to design better association methods. However, we argue that the way detection boxes are utilized determines the upper bound of data association and we focus on how to make full use of detection boxes from high scores to low ones in the matching process.

3   BYTE

We propose a simple, effective and generic data association method, BYTE. Different from previous methods [34,48,68,84] which only keep the high score detection boxes, we keep almost every detection box and separate them into high score ones and low score ones. We first associate the high score detection boxes to the tracklets. Some tracklets get unmatched because they do not match to an appropriate high score detection box, which usually happens when occlusion, motion blur or size changing occurs. We then associate the low score detection boxes and these unmatched tracklets to recover the objects in low score detection boxes and filter out background, simultaneously. The pseudo-code of BYTE is shown in Algorithm 1.

The input of BYTE is a video sequence V, along with an object detector Det. We also set a detection score threshold τ. The output of BYTE is the tracks $\mathcal{T}$ of the video and each track contains the bounding box and identity of the object in each frame.

For each frame in the video, we predict the detection boxes and scores using the detector Det. We separate all the detection boxes into two parts $\mathcal{D}_{high}$ and $\mathcal{D}_{low}$ according to the detection score threshold τ. For the detection boxes whose scores are higher than τ, we put them into the high score detection boxes $\mathcal{D}_{high}$. For the detection boxes whose scores are lower than τ, we put them into the low score detection boxes $\mathcal{D}_{low}$ (line 3 to 13 in Algorithm 1).

After separating the low score detection boxes and the high score detection boxes, we adopt Kalman filter to predict the new locations in the current frame of each track in $\mathcal{T}$ (line 14 to 16 in Algorithm 1).

The first association is performed between the high score detection boxes $\mathcal{D}_{high}$ and all the tracks $\mathcal{T}$ (including the lost tracks $\mathcal{T}_{lost}$). Similarity#1 can be computed by either by the IoU or the Re-ID feature distances between the detection boxes $\mathcal{D}_{high}$ and the predicted box of tracks $\mathcal{T}$. Then, we adopt Hungarian Algorithm [32] to finish the matching based on the similarity. We keep the unmatched detections in $\mathcal{D}_{remain}$ and the unmatched tracks in $\mathcal{T}_{remain}$ (line 17 to 19 in Algorithm 1).

BYTE is highly flexible and can be compatible to other different association methods. For example, when BYTE is combined with FairMOT [84], Re-ID feature is added into * first association * in Algorithm 1, others are the same. In the experiments, we apply BYTE to 9 different state-of-the-art trackers and achieve notable improvements on almost all the metrics.

The second association is performed between the low score detection boxes $\mathcal{D}_{low}$ and the remaining tracks $\mathcal{T}_{remain}$ after the first association. We keep the unmatched tracks in $\mathcal{T}_{re-remain}$ and just delete all the unmatched low score detection boxes, since we view them as background. (line 20 to 21 in Algorithm 1). We find it important to use IoU alone as the Similarity#2 in the second association because the low score detection boxes usually contains severe occlusion or motion blur and appearance features are not reliable. Thus, when apply BYTE to other Re-ID based trackers [48,68,84], we do not adopt appearance similarity in the second association.

Algorithm 1: Pseudo-code of BYTE.

Input: A video sequence V; object detector Det; detection score threshold τ
Output: Tracks $\mathcal{T}$ of the video

1 Initialization: $\mathcal{T} \leftarrow \emptyset$
2 **for** *frame f_k in V* **do**
     /* Figure 2(a) */
     /* predict detection boxes & scores */
3      $\mathcal{D}_k \leftarrow \text{Det}(f_k)$
4      $\mathcal{D}_{high} \leftarrow \emptyset$
5      $\mathcal{D}_{low} \leftarrow \emptyset$
6   **for** *d in $\mathcal{D}_k$* **do**
7   **if** *d.score > τ* **then**
8 | $\mathcal{D}_{high} \leftarrow \mathcal{D}_{high} \cup \{d\}$
9   **end**
10   **else**
11 | $\mathcal{D}_{low} \leftarrow \mathcal{D}_{low} \cup \{d\}$
12   **end**
13   **end**

     /* predict new locations of tracks */
14   **for** *t in $\mathcal{T}$* **do**
15 | $t \leftarrow \text{KalmanFilter}(t)$
16   **end**

     /* Figure 2(b) */
     /* first association */
17   Associate $\mathcal{T}$ and $\mathcal{D}_{high}$ using **Similarity#1**
18     $\mathcal{D}_{remain} \leftarrow$ remaining object boxes from $\mathcal{D}_{high}$
19     $\mathcal{T}_{remain} \leftarrow$ remaining tracks from $\mathcal{T}$

     /* Figure 2(c) */
     /* second association */
20   Associate $\mathcal{T}_{remain}$ and $\mathcal{D}_{low}$ using similarity#2
21     $\mathcal{T}_{re-remain} \leftarrow$ remaining tracks from $\mathcal{T}_{remain}$

     /* delete unmatched tracks */
22     $\mathcal{T} \leftarrow \mathcal{T} \setminus \mathcal{T}_{re-remain}$

     /* initialize new tracks */
23   **for** *d in $\mathcal{D}_{remain}$* **do**
24 | $\mathcal{T} \leftarrow \mathcal{T} \cup \{d\}$
25   **end**
26 **end**
27 Return: $\mathcal{T}$

Track rebirth [69,87] is not shown in the algorithm for simplicity. In green is the key of our method.

After the association, the unmatched tracks will be deleted from the tracklets. We do not list the procedure of track rebirth [13,69,87] in Algorithm 1 for simplicity. Actually, it is necessary for the long-range association to preserve the identity of the tracks. For the unmatched tracks $\mathcal{T}_{re-remain}$ after the second association, we put them into $\mathcal{T}_{lost}$. For each track in $\mathcal{T}_{lost}$, only when it exists for more than a certain number of frames, $i.e.$ 30, we delete it from the tracks $\mathcal{T}$. Otherwise, we remain the lost tracks $\mathcal{T}_{lost}$ in $\mathcal{T}$ (line 22 in Algorithm 1). Finally, we initialize new tracks from the unmatched high score detection boxes $\mathcal{D}_{remain}$ after the first association. (line 23 to 27 in Algorithm 1). The output of each individual frame is the bounding boxes and identities of the tracks $\mathcal{T}$ in the current frame. Note that we do not output the boxes and identities of $\mathcal{T}_{lost}$.

To put forwards the state-of-the-art performance of MOT, we design a simple and strong tracker, named ByteTrack, by equipping the high-performance detector YOLOX [25] with our association method BYTE.

4   Experiments

4.1   Setting

Datasets. We evaluate BYTE and ByteTrack on MOT17 [45] and MOT20 [17] datasets under the "private detection" protocol. Both datasets contain training sets and test sets, without validation sets. For ablation studies, we use the first half of each video in the training set of MOT17 for training and the last half for validation following [87]. We train on the combination of CrowdHuman dataset [55] and MOT17 half training set following [58,70,79,87]. We add Cityperson [81] and ETHZ [20] for training following [34,68,84] when testing on the test set of MOT17. We also test ByteTrack on HiEve [38] and BDD100K [78] datasets. HiEve is a large scale human-centric dataset focusing on crowded and complex events. BDD100K is the largest driving video dataset and the dataset splits of the MOT task are 1400 videos for training, 200 videos for validation and 400 videos for testing. It needs to track objects of 8 classes and contains cases of large camera motion.

Metrics. We use the CLEAR metrics [4], including MOTA, FP, FN, IDs, $etc.$, IDF1 [52] and HOTA [41] to evaluate different aspects of the tracking performance. MOTA is computed based on FP, FN and IDs. Considering the amount of FP and FN are larger than IDs, MOTA focuses more on the detection performance. IDF1 evaluates the identity preservation ability and focus more on the association performance. HOTA is a very recently proposed metric which explicitly balances the effect of performing accurate detection, association and localization. For BDD100K dataset, there are some multi-class metrics such as mMOTA and mIDF1. mMOTA/mIDF1 is computed by averaging the MOTA/IDF1 of all the classes.

Implementation Details. For BYTE, the default detection score threshold τ is 0.6, unless otherwise specified. For the benchmark evaluation of MOT17, MOT20 and HiEve, we only use IoU as the similarity metrics. In the linear assignment step, if the IoU between the detection box and the tracklet box is smaller than 0.2, the matching will be rejected. For the lost tracklets, we keep it for 30 frames in case it appears again. For BDD100K, we use UniTrack [67] as the Re-ID model. In ablation study, we use FastReID [28] to extract Re-ID features for MOT17.

For ByteTrack, the detector is YOLOX [25] with YOLOX-X as the backbone and COCO-pretrained model [37] as the initialized weights. For MOT17, the training schedule is 80 epochs on the combination of MOT17, CrowdHuman, Cityperson and ETHZ. For MOT20 and HiEve, we only add CrowdHuman as additional training data. For BDD100K, we do not use additional training data and only train 50 epochs. The input image size is 1440 ×800 and the shortest side ranges from 576 to 1024 during multi-scale training. The data augmentation includes Mosaic [8] and Mixup [80]. The model is trained on 8 NVIDIA Tesla V100 GPU with batch size of 48. The optimizer is SGD with weight decay of 5×10^{-4} and momentum of 0.9. The initial learning rate is 10^{-3} with 1 epoch warm-up and cosine annealing schedule. The total training time is about 12 h. Following [25], FPS is measured with FP16-precision [44] and batch size of 1 on a single GPU.

4.2   Ablation Studies on BYTE

Similarity Analysis. We choose different types of similarity for the first association and the second association of BYTE. The results are shown in Table 1. We can see that either IoU or Re-ID can be a good choice for `Similarity#1` on MOT17. IoU achieves better MOTA and IDs while Re-ID achieves higher IDF1. On BDD100K, Re-ID achieves much better results than IoU in the first association. This is because BDD100K contains large camera motion and the annotations are in low frame rate, which causes failure of motion cues. It is important to utilize IoU as `Similarity#2` in the second association on both datasets because the low score detection boxes usually contains severe occlusion or motion blur and thus Re-ID features are not reliable. From Table 1 we can find that using IoU as `Similarity#2` increases about 1.0 MOTA compared to Re-ID, which indicates that Re-ID features of the low score detection boxes are not reliable.

Comparisons with Other Association Methods. We compare BYTE with other popular association methods including SORT [6], DeepSORT [69] and MOTDT [13] on the validation set of MOT17 and BDD100K. The results are shown in Table 2.

SORT can be seen as our baseline method because both methods only adopt Kalman filter to predict the object motion. We can find that BYTE improves the MOTA metric of SORT from 74.6 to 76.6, IDF1 from 76.9 to 79.3 and decreases IDs from 291 to 159. This highlights the importance of the low score detection boxes and proves the ability of BYTE to recover object boxes from low score one.

DeepSORT utilizes additional Re-ID models to enhance the long-range association. We surprisingly find BYTE also has additional gains compared with

Table 1. Comparison of different type of similarity metrics used in the first association and the second association of BYTE on the MOT17 and BDD100K validation set.

Similarity#1	Similarity#2	MOT17			BDD100K		
		MOTA↑	IDF1↑	IDs↓	mMOTA↑	mIDF1↑	IDs↓
IoU	Re-ID	75.8	77.5	231	39.2	48.3	29172
IoU	IoU	**76.6**	79.3	**159**	39.4	48.9	27902
Re-ID	Re-ID	75.2	78.7	276	45.0	53.4	10425
Re-ID	IoU	76.3	**80.5**	216	**45.5**	**54.8**	**9140**

Table 2. Comparison of different data association methods on the MOT17 and BDD100K validation set. The best results are shown in **bold**.

Method		MOT17			BDD100K			
	w/ Re-ID	MOTA↑	IDF1↑	IDs↓	mMOTA↑	mIDF1↑	IDs↓	FPS
SORT		74.6	76.9	291	30.9	41.3	10067	**30.1**
DeepSORT	✓	75.4	77.2	239	24.5	38.2	10720	13.5
MOTDT	✓	75.8	77.6	273	26.7	39.8	14520	11.1
BYTE (ours)		**76.6**	79.3	**159**	39.4	48.9	27902	29.6
BYTE (ours)	✓	76.3	**80.5**	216	**45.5**	**54.8**	**9140**	11.8

DeepSORT. This suggests a simple Kalman filter can perform long-range association and achieve better IDF1 and IDs when the detection boxes are accurate enough. We note that in severe occlusion cases, Re-ID features are vulnerable and may lead to identity switches, instead, motion model behaves more reliably.

MOTDT integrates motion-guided box propagation results along with detection results to associate unreliable detection results with tracklets. Although sharing the similar motivation, MOTDT is behind BYTE by a large margin. We explain that MOTDT uses propagated boxes as tracklet boxes, which may lead to locating drifts in tracking. Instead, BYTE uses low-score detection boxes to re-associate those unmatched tracklets, therefore, tracklet boxes are more accurate.

Table 2 also shows the results on BDD100K dataset. BYTE also outperforms other association methods by a large margin. Kalman filter fails in autonomous driving scenes and it is the main reason for the low performance of SORT, DeepSORT and MOTDT. Thus, we do not use Kalman filter on BDD100K. Additional off-the-shelf Re-ID models greatly improve the performance of BYTE on BDD100K.

Robustness to Detection Score Threshold. The detection score threshold τ_{high} is a sensitive hyper-parameter and needs to be carefully tuned in the task of multi-object tracking. We change it from 0.2 to 0.8 and compare the MOTA and IDF1 score of BYTE and SORT. The results are shown in Fig. 3. From the results we can see that BYTE is more robust to the detection score threshold

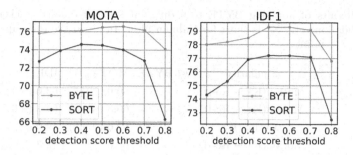

Fig. 3. Comparison of the performances of BYTE and SORT under different detection score thresholds. The results are from the validation set of MOT17.

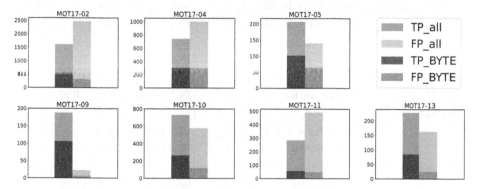

Fig. 4. Comparison of the number of TPs and FPs in all low score detection boxes and the low score tracked boxes obtained by BYTE. The results are from the validation set of MOT17.

than SORT. This is because the second association in BYTE recovers the objects whose scores are lower than τ_{high}, and thus considers almost every detection box regardless of the change of τ_{high}.

Analysis on Low Score Detection Boxes. To prove the effectiveness of BYTE, we collect the number of TPs and FPs in the low score boxes obtained by BYTE. We use the half training set of MOT17 and CrowdHuman for training and evaluate on the half validation set of MOT17. First, we keep all the low score detection boxes whose scores range from τ_{low} to τ_{high} and classify the TPs and FPs using ground truth annotations. Then, we select the tracking results obtained by BYTE from low score detection boxes. The results of each sequence are shown in Fig. 4. We can see that BYTE obtains notably more TPs than FPs from the low score detection boxes even though some sequences (*i.e.* MOT17-02) have much more FPs in all the detection boxes. The obtained TPs notably increases MOTA from 74.6 to 76.6 as is shown in Table 2.

Applications on Other Trackers. We apply BYTE on 9 different state-of-the-arts trackers, including JDE [68], CSTrack [34], FairMOT [84], TraDes

Table 3. Results of applying BYTE to 9 different state-of-the-art trackers on the MOT17 validation set. "K" is short for Kalman filter. In green are the improvements of at least +1.0 point.

Method	Similarity	w/ BYTE	MOTA↑	IDF1↑	IDs↓
JDE [68]	Motion(K) + Re-ID		60.0	63.6	473
	Motion(K) + Re-ID	✓	60.3 (+0.3)	64.1 (+0.5)	418
	Motion(K)	✓	60.6 (+0.6)	66.0 (+2.4)	360
CSTrack [34]	Motion(K) + Re-ID		68.0	72.3	325
	Motion(K) + Re-ID	✓	69.2 (+1.2)	73.9 (+1.6)	285
	Motion(K)	✓	69.3 (+1.3)	71.7 (-0.6)	279
FairMOT [84]	Motion(K) + Re-ID		69.1	72.8	299
	Motion(K) + Re-ID	✓	70.4 (+1.3)	74.2 (+1.4)	232
	Motion(K)	✓	70.3 (+1.2)	73.2 (+0.4)	236
TraDes [70]	Motion + Re-ID		68.2	71.7	285
	Motion + Re-ID	✓	68.6 (+0.4)	71.1 (-0.6)	259
	Motion(K)	✓	67.9 (-0.3)	72.0 (+0.3)	178
QDTrack [48]	Re-ID		67.3	67.8	377
	Motion(K) + Re-ID	✓	67.7 (+0.4)	72.0 (+4.2)	281
	Motion(K)	✓	67.9 (+0.6)	70.9 (+3.1)	258
CenterTrack [87]	Motion		66.1	64.2	528
	Motion	✓	66.3 (+0.2)	64.8 (+0.6)	334
	Motion(K)	✓	67.4 (+1.3)	74.0 (+9.8)	144
CTracker [49]	Chain		63.1	60.9	755
	Motion(K)	✓	65.0 (+1.9)	66.7 (+5.8)	346
TransTrack [58]	Attention		67.1	68.3	254
	Attention	✓	68.6 (+1.5)	69.0 (+0.7)	232
	Motion(K)	✓	68.3 (+1.2)	72.4 (+4.1)	181
MOTR [79]	Attention		64.7	67.2	346
	Attention	✓	64.3 (-0.4)	69.3 (+2.1)	263
	Motion(K)	✓	65.7 (+1.0)	68.4 (+1.2)	260

[70], QDTrack [48], CenterTrack [87], Chained-Tracker [49], TransTrack [58] and MOTR [79]. Among these trackers, JDE, CSTrack, FairMOT, TraDes adopt a combination of motion and Re-ID similarity. QDTrack adopts Re-ID similarity alone. CenterTrack and TraDes predict the motion similarity by the learned networks. Chained-Tracker adopts the chain structure and outputs the results of two consecutive frames simultaneously and associate in the same frame by IoU. TransTrack and MOTR adopt the attention mechanism to propagate boxes among frames. Their results are shown in the first line of each tracker in Table 3. To evaluate the effectiveness of BYTE, we design two different modes to apply BYTE to these trackers.

Table 4. Comparison of the state-of-the-art methods under the "private detector" protocol on MOT17 test set. The best results are shown in **bold**. MOT17 contains rich scenes and half of the sequences are captured with camera motion. **ByteTrack** ranks 1st among all the trackers on the leaderboard of MOT17 and outperforms the second one ReMOT by a large margin on almost all the metrics. It also has the highest running speed among all trackers.

Tracker	MOTA↑	IDF1↑	HOTA↑	FP↓	FN↓	IDs↓	FPS↑
Tube_TK [47]	63.0	58.6	48.0	27060	177483	4137	3.0
MOTR [79]	65.1	66.4	–	45486	149307	2049	–
CTracker [49]	66.6	57.4	49.0	22284	160491	5529	6.8
CenterTrack [87]	67.8	64.7	52.2	**18498**	160332	3039	17.5
QuasiDense [48]	68.7	66.3	53.9	26589	146643	3378	20.3
TraDes [70]	69.1	63.9	52.7	20892	150060	3555	17.5
MAT [26]	69.5	63.1	53.8	30660	138741	2844	9.0
SOTMOT [86]	71.0	71.9	–	39537	118983	5184	16.0
TransCenter [73]	73.2	62.2	54.5	23112	123738	4614	1.0
GSDT [66]	73.2	66.5	55.2	26397	120666	3891	4.9
Semi-TCL [33]	73.3	73.2	59.8	22944	124980	2790	–
FairMOT [84]	73.7	72.3	59.3	27507	117477	3303	25.9
RelationTrack [77]	73.8	74.7	61.0	27999	118623	**1374**	8.5
PermaTrackPr [61]	73.8	68.9	55.5	28998	115104	3699	11.9
CSTrack [34]	74.9	72.6	59.3	23847	114303	3567	15.8
TransTrack [58]	75.2	63.5	54.1	50157	86442	3603	10.0
FUFET [54]	76.2	68.0	57.9	32796	98475	3237	6.8
SiamMOT [35]	76.3	72.3	–	–	–	–	12.8
CorrTracker [64]	76.5	73.6	60.7	29808	99510	3369	15.6
TransMOT [16]	76.7	75.1	61.7	36231	93150	2346	9.6
ReMOT [75]	77.0	72.0	59.7	33204	93612	2853	1.8
ByteTrack (ours)	**80.3**	**77.3**	**63.1**	25491	**83721**	2196	**29.6**

– The first mode is to insert BYTE into the original association methods of different trackers, as is shown in the second line of the results of each tracker in Table 3. Take FairMOT [84] for example, after the original association is done, we select all the unmatched tracklets and associate them with the low score detection boxes following the * second association * in Algorithm 1. Note that for the low score objects, the Re-ID features are not reliable so we only adopt the IoU between the detection boxes and the tracklet boxes after motion prediction as the similarity. We do not apply the first mode of BYTE to Chained-Tracker because we find it is difficult to implement in the chain structure.

Table 5. Comparison of the state-of-the-art methods under the "private detector" protocol on MOT20 test set. The best results are shown in **bold**. The scenes in MOT20 are much more crowded than those in MOT17. **ByteTrack** ranks 1st among all the trackers on the leaderboard of MOT20 and outperforms the second one SOTMOT by a large margin on all the metrics. It also has the highest running speed among all trackers.

Tracker	MOTA↑	IDF1↑	HOTA↑	FP↓	FN↓	IDs↓	FPS↑
MLT [82]	48.9	54.6	43.2	45660	216803	2187	3.7
FairMOT [84]	61.8	67.3	54.6	103440	88901	5243	13.2
TransCenter [73]	61.9	50.4	–	45895	146347	4653	1.0
TransTrack [58]	65.0	59.4	48.5	27197	150197	3608	7.2
CorrTracker [64]	65.2	69.1	–	79429	95855	5183	8.5
Semi-TCL [33]	65.2	70.1	55.3	61209	114709	4139	–
CSTrack [34]	66.6	68.6	54.0	**25404**	144358	3196	4.5
GSDT [66]	67.1	67.5	53.6	31913	135409	3131	0.9
SiamMOT [35]	67.1	69.1	–	–	–	–	4.3
RelationTrack [77]	67.2	70.5	56.5	61134	104597	4243	2.7
SOTMOT [86]	68.6	71.4	–	57064	101154	4209	8.5
ByteTrack (ours)	**77.8**	**75.2**	**61.3**	26249	**87594**	**1223**	**17.5**

Table 6. Comparison of the state-of-the-art methods under the "private detector" protocol on HiEve test set. The best results are shown in **bold**. HiEve has more complex events than MOT17 and MOT20. **ByteTrack** ranks 1st among all the trackers on the leaderboard of HiEve and outperforms the second one CenterTrack by a large margin on all the metrics.

Tracker	MOTA↑	IDF1↑	MT↑	ML↓	FP↓	FN↓	IDs↓
DeepSORT [69]	27.1	28.6	8.5%	41.5%	5894	42668	2220
MOTDT [13]	26.1	32.9	8.7%	54.6%	6318	43577	1599
IOUtracker [7]	38.6	38.6	28.3%	27.6%	9640	28993	4153
JDE [68]	33.1	36.0	15.1%	24.1%	9526	33327	3747
FairMOT [84]	35.0	46.7	16.3%	44.2%	6523	37750	**995**
CenterTrack [87]	40.9	45.1	10.8%	32.2%	3208	36414	1568
ByteTrack (Ours)	**61.7**	**63.1**	**38.3%**	**21.6%**	**2822**	**22852**	1031

- The second mode is to directly use the detection boxes of these trackers and associate using the whole procedure in Algorithm 1, as is shown in the third line of the results of each tracker in Table 3.

We can see that in both modes, BYTE can bring stable improvements over almost all the metrics including MOTA, IDF1 and IDs. For example, BYTE increases CenterTrack by 1.3 MOTA and 9.8 IDF1, Chained-Tracker by 1.9 MOTA and 5.8 IDF1, TransTrack by 1.2 MOTA and 4.1 IDF1. The results in

Table 3 indicate that BYTE has strong generalization ability and can be easily applied to existing trackers.

4.3   Benchmark Evaluation

We compare ByteTrack with the state-of-the-art trackers on the test set of MOT17, MOT20 and HiEve under the private detection protocol in Table 4, Table 5 and Table 6, respectively. All the results are directly obtained from the official MOT Challenge evaluation server[1] and the Human in Events server[2].

MOT17. ByteTrack ranks 1st among all the trackers on the leaderboard of MOT17. Not only does it achieve the best accuracy (*i.e.* 80.3 MOTA, 77.3 IDF1 and 63.1 HOTA), but also runs with highest running speed (30 FPS). It outperforms the second-performance tracker [75] by a large margin (*i.e.* +3.3 MOTA, +5.3 IDF1 and +3.4 HOTA). Also, we use less training data than many high performance methods such as [34,35,54,64,84] (29K images vs. 73K images). It is worth noting that we only leverage the simplest similarity computation method Kalman filter in the association step compared to other methods [34,48,58,66,79,84] which additionally adopt Re-ID similarity or attention mechanisms. All these indicate that ByteTrack is a simple and strong tracker.

MOT20. Compared with MOT17, MOT20 has much more crowded scenarios and occlusion cases. The average number of pedestrians in an image is 170 in the test set of MOT20. ByteTrack also ranks 1st among all the trackers on the leaderboard of MOT20 and outperforms other trackers by a large margin on almost all the metrics. For example, it increases MOTA from 68.6 to 77.8, IDF1 from 71.4 to 75.2 and decreases IDs by 71% from 4209 to 1223. It is worth noting that ByteTrack achieves extremely low identity switches, which further indicates that associating every detection boxes is very effective under occlusion cases.

Human in Events. Compared with MOT17 and MOT20, HiEve contains more complex events and more diverse camera views. We train ByteTrack on Crowd-Human dataset and the training set of HiEve. ByteTrack also ranks 1st among all the trackers on the leaderboard of HiEve and outperforms other state-of-the-art trackers by a large margin. For example, it increases MOTA from 40.9 to 61.3 and IDF1 from 45.1 to 62.9. The superior results indicate that ByteTrack is robust to complex scenes (Table 7).

BDD100K. BDD100K is multiple categories tracking dataset in autonomous driving scenes. The challenges include low frame rate and large camera motion. We utilize a simple ResNet-50 ImageNet classification model from UniTrack [67] to compute appearance similarity. ByteTrack ranks first on the leaderboard of BDD100K. It increases mMOTA from 36.6 to 45.5 on the validation set and 35.5 to 40.1 on the test set, which indicates that ByteTrack can also handle the challenges in autonomous driving scenes.

---

[1] https://motchallenge.net.
[2] http://humaninevents.org.

Table 7. Comparison of the state-of-the-art methods on BDD100K test set. The best results are shown in **bold**. **ByteTrack** ranks 1st among all the trackers on the leaderboard of BDD100K and outperforms the second one QDTrack by a large margin on most metrics. The methods denoted by * are the ones reported on the leaderboard of BDD100K.

Tracker	Split	mMOTA↑	mIDF1↑	MOTA↑	IDF1↑	FN↓	FP↓	IDs↓	MT↑	ML↓
Yu *et al.* [78]	Val	25.9	44.5	56.9	66.8	122406	52372	8315	8396	3795
QDTrack [48]	Val	36.6	50.8	63.5	**71.5**	108614	46621	**6262**	9481	3034
ByteTrack(Ours)	Val	**45.5**	**54.8**	**69.1**	70.4	**92805**	**34998**	9140	**9626**	**3005**
Yu *et al.* [78]	Test	26.3	44.7	58.3	68.2	213220	100230	14674	16299	6017
DeepBlueAI*	Test	31.6	38.7	56.9	56.0	292063	**35401**	25186	10296	12266
Madamada*	Test	33.6	43.0	59.8	55.7	209339	76612	42901	16774	**5004**
QDTrack [48]	Test	35.5	52.3	64.3	**72.3**	201041	80054	**10790**	17353	5167
ByteTrack(Ours)	Test	**40.1**	**55.8**	**69.6**	71.3	**169073**	63869	15466	**18057**	5107

5   Conclusion

We present a simple yet effective data association method BYTE for multi-object tracking. BYTE can be easily applied to existing trackers and achieve consistent improvements. We also propose a strong tracker ByteTrack, which achieves 80.3 MOTA, 77.3 IDF1 and 63.1 HOTA on MOT17 test set with 30 FPS. ByteTrack is very robust to occlusion for its accurate detection performance and the help of associating low score detection boxes. It also sheds light on how to make the best use of detection results to enhance multi-object tracking. We hope the high accuracy, fast speed and simplicity of ByteTrack can make it attractive in real applications.

Acknowledgement. This work was in part supported by NSFC (No. 61733007 and No. 61876212). Ping Luo is supported by the General Research Fund of HK No.27208720, No. 17212120, and No. 17200622.

References

1. Bae, S.H., Yoon, K.J.: Robust online multi-object tracking based on tracklet confidence and online discriminative appearance learning. In: Proceedings of the IEEE Conference on Computer Vision and Pattern Recognition, pp. 1218–1225 (2014)
2. Berclaz, J., Fleuret, F., Turetken, E., Fua, P.: Multiple object tracking using k-shortest paths optimization. IEEE Trans. Pattern Anal. Mach. Intell. **33**(9), 1806–1819 (2011)
3. Bergmann, P., Meinhardt, T., Leal-Taixe, L.: Tracking without bells and whistles. In: ICCV, pp. 941–951 (2019)
4. Bernardin, K., Stiefelhagen, R.: Evaluating multiple object tracking performance: the clear mot metrics. EURASIP J. Image Video Process. **2008**, 1–10 (2008)
5. Bertinetto, L., Valmadre, J., Henriques, J.F., Vedaldi, A., Torr, P.H.S.: Fully-convolutional Siamese networks for object tracking. In: Hua, G., Jégou, H. (eds.) ECCV 2016. LNCS, vol. 9914, pp. 850–865. Springer, Cham (2016). https://doi.org/10.1007/978-3-319-48881-3_56

6. Bewley, A., Ge, Z., Ott, L., Ramos, F., Upcroft, B.: Simple online and realtime tracking. In: ICIP, pp. 3464–3468. IEEE (2016)

7. Bochinski, E., Eiselein, V., Sikora, T.: High-speed tracking-by-detection without using image information. In: 2017 14th IEEE International Conference on Advanced Video and Signal Based Surveillance (AVSS), pp. 1–6. IEEE (2017)

8. Bochkovskiy, A., Wang, C.Y., Liao, H.Y.M.: YOLOv4: optimal speed and accuracy of object detection. arXiv preprint arXiv:2004.10934 (2020)

9. Brasó, G., Leal-Taixé, L.: Learning a neural solver for multiple object tracking. In: Proceedings of the IEEE/CVF Conference on Computer Vision and Pattern Recognition, pp. 6247–6257 (2020)

10. Cai, J., Xu, M., Li, W., Xiong, Y., Xia, W., Tu, Z., Soatto, S.: MeMOT: multi-object tracking with memory. In: Proceedings of the IEEE/CVF Conference on Computer Vision and Pattern Recognition, pp. 8090–8100 (2022)

11. Cai, Z., Vasconcelos, N.: Cascade R-CNN: delving into high quality object detection. In: CVPR, pp. 6154–6162 (2018)

12. Carion, N., Massa, F., Synnaeve, G., Usunier, N., Kirillov, A., Zagoruyko, S.: End-to-end object detection with transformers. In: Vedaldi, A., Bischof, H., Brox, T., Frahm, J.-M. (eds.) ECCV 2020. LNCS, vol. 12346, pp. 213–229. Springer, Cham (2020). https://doi.org/10.1007/978-3-030-58452-8_13

13. Chen, L., Ai, H., Zhuang, Z., Shang, C.: Real-time multiple people tracking with deeply learned candidate selection and person re-identification. In: 2018 IEEE International Conference on Multimedia and Expo (ICME), pp. 1–6. IEEE (2018)

14. Chu, P., Fan, H., Tan, C.C., Ling, H.: Online multi-object tracking with instance-aware tracker and dynamic model refreshment. In: 2019 IEEE Winter Conference on Applications of Computer Vision (WACV), pp. 161–170. IEEE (2019)

15. Chu, P., Ling, H.: FAMNet: joint learning of feature, affinity and multi-dimensional assignment for online multiple object tracking. In: ICCV, pp. 6172–6181 (2019)

16. Chu, P., Wang, J., You, Q., Ling, H., Liu, Z.: TransMOT: spatial-temporal graph transformer for multiple object tracking. arXiv preprint arXiv:2104.00194 (2021)

17. Dendorfer, P., et al.: MOT20: a benchmark for multi object tracking in crowded scenes. arXiv preprint arXiv:2003.09003 (2020)

18. Dicle, C., Camps, O.I., Sznaier, M.: The way they move: tracking multiple targets with similar appearance. In: Proceedings of the IEEE International Conference on Computer Vision, pp. 2304–2311 (2013)

19. Dosovitskiy, A., et al.: An image is worth 16x16 words: transformers for image recognition at scale. arXiv preprint arXiv:2010.11929 (2020)

20. Ess, A., Leibe, B., Schindler, K., Van Gool, L.: A mobile vision system for robust multi-person tracking. In: CVPR, pp. 1–8. IEEE (2008)

21. Fang, Y., et al.: You only look at one sequence: rethinking transformer in vision through object detection. Adv. Neural. Inf. Process. Syst. **34**, 26183–26197 (2021)

22. Fang, Y., Yang, S., Wang, S., Ge, Y., Shan, Y., Wang, X.: Unleashing vanilla vision transformer with masked image modeling for object detection. arXiv preprint arXiv:2204.02964 (2022)

23. Felzenszwalb, P., McAllester, D., Ramanan, D.: A discriminatively trained, multi-scale, deformable part model. In: CVPR, pp. 1–8. IEEE (2008)

24. Fu, J., Zong, L., Li, Y., Li, K., Yang, B., Liu, X.: Model adaption object detection system for robot. In: 2020 39th Chinese Control Conference (CCC), pp. 3659–3664. IEEE (2020)

25. Ge, Z., Liu, S., Wang, F., Li, Z., Sun, J.: YOLOX: exceeding YOLO series in 2021. arXiv preprint arXiv:2107.08430 (2021)

26. Han, S., et al.: MAT: motion-aware multi-object tracking. arXiv preprint arXiv:2009.04794 (2020)
27. He, K., Gkioxari, G., Dollár, P., Girshick, R.: Mask R-CNN. In: ICCV, pp. 2961–2969 (2017)
28. He, L., Liao, X., Liu, W., Liu, X., Cheng, P., Mei, T.: FastReID: a PyTorch toolbox for general instance re-identification. arXiv preprint arXiv:2006.02631 (2020)
29. Hornakova, A., Henschel, R., Rosenhahn, B., Swoboda, P.: Lifted disjoint paths with application in multiple object tracking. In: International Conference on Machine Learning, pp. 4364–4375. PMLR (2020)
30. Kalman, R.E.: A new approach to linear filtering and prediction problems. J. Fluids Eng. **82**(1), 35–45 (1960)
31. Khurana, T., Dave, A., Ramanan, D.: Detecting invisible people. arXiv preprint arXiv:2012.08419 (2020)
32. Kuhn, H.W.: The Hungarian method for the assignment problem. Naval Res. Logistics Q. **2**(1–2), 83–97 (1955)
33. Li, W., Xiong, Y., Yang, S., Xu, M., Wang, Y., Xia, W.: Semi-TCL: semi-supervised track contrastive representation learning. arXiv preprint arXiv:2107.02396 (2021)
34. Liang, C., et al.: Rethinking the competition between detection and ReID in multi-object tracking. arXiv preprint arXiv:2010.12138 (2020)
35. Liang, C., Zhang, Z., Zhou, X., Li, B., Lu, Y., Hu, W.: One more check: making "fake background" be tracked again. arXiv preprint arXiv:2104.09441 (2021)
36. Lin, T.Y., Goyal, P., Girshick, R., He, K., Dollár, P.: Focal loss for dense object detection. In: ICCV, pp. 2980–2988 (2017)
37. Lin, T.-Y., et al.: Microsoft COCO: common objects in context. In: Fleet, D., Pajdla, T., Schiele, B., Tuytelaars, T. (eds.) ECCV 2014. LNCS, vol. 8693, pp. 740–755. Springer, Cham (2014). https://doi.org/10.1007/978-3-319-10602-1_48
38. Lin, W., et al.: Human in events: a large-scale benchmark for human-centric video analysis in complex events. arXiv preprint arXiv:2005.04490 (2020)
39. Liu, Z., et al.: Swin transformer: hierarchical vision transformer using shifted windows. arXiv preprint arXiv:2103.14030 (2021)
40. Lu, Z., Rathod, V., Votel, R., Huang, J.: RetinaTrack: online single stage joint detection and tracking. In: Proceedings of the IEEE/CVF Conference on Computer Vision and Pattern Recognition, pp. 14668–14678 (2020)
41. Luiten, J., et al.: HOTA: a higher order metric for evaluating multi-object tracking. Int. J. Comput. Vision **129**(2), 548–578 (2021)
42. Luo, H., Xie, W., Wang, X., Zeng, W.: Detect or track: towards cost-effective video object detection/tracking. In: Proceedings of the AAAI Conference on Artificial Intelligence, vol. 33, pp. 8803–8810 (2019)
43. Meinhardt, T., Kirillov, A., Leal-Taixe, L., Feichtenhofer, C.: TrackFormer: multi-object tracking with transformers. arXiv preprint arXiv:2101.02702 (2021)
44. Micikevicius, P., et al.: Mixed precision training. arXiv preprint arXiv:1710.03740 (2017)
45. Milan, A., Leal-Taixé, L., Reid, I., Roth, S., Schindler, K.: MOT16: a benchmark for multi-object tracking. arXiv preprint arXiv:1603.00831 (2016)
46. Milan, A., Roth, S., Schindler, K.: Continuous energy minimization for multitarget tracking. IEEE Trans. Pattern Anal. Mach. Intell. **36**(1), 58–72 (2013)
47. Pang, B., Li, Y., Zhang, Y., Li, M., Lu, C.: TubeTK: adopting tubes to track multi-object in a one-step training model. In: Proceedings of the IEEE/CVF Conference on Computer Vision and Pattern Recognition, pp. 6308–6318 (2020)

48. Pang, J., et al.: Quasi-dense similarity learning for multiple object tracking. In: Proceedings of the IEEE/CVF Conference on Computer Vision and Pattern Recognition, pp. 164–173 (2021)
49. Peng, J., et al.: Chained-tracker: chaining paired attentive regression results for end-to-end joint multiple-object detection and tracking. In: Vedaldi, A., Bischof, H., Brox, T., Frahm, J.-M. (eds.) ECCV 2020. LNCS, vol. 12349, pp. 145–161. Springer, Cham (2020). https://doi.org/10.1007/978-3-030-58548-8_9
50. Redmon, J., Farhadi, A.: YOLOv3: an incremental improvement. arXiv preprint arXiv:1804.02767 (2018)
51. Ren, S., He, K., Girshick, R., Sun, J.: Faster R-CNN: towards real-time object detection with region proposal networks. In: Advances in Neural Information Processing Systems, pp. 91–99 (2015)
52. Ristani, E., Solera, F., Zou, R., Cucchiara, R., Tomasi, C.: Performance measures and a data set for multi-target, multi-camera tracking. In: Hua, G., Jégou, H. (eds.) ECCV 2016. LNCS, vol. 9914, pp. 17–35. Springer, Cham (2016). https://doi.org/10.1007/978-3-319-48881-3_2
53. Sanchez-Matilla, R., Poiesi, F., Cavallaro, A.: Online multi-target tracking with strong and weak detections. In: Hua, G., Jégou, H. (eds.) ECCV 2016. LNCS, vol. 9914, pp. 84–99. Springer, Cham (2016). https://doi.org/10.1007/978-3-319-48881-3_7
54. Shan, C., et al.: Tracklets predicting based adaptive graph tracking. arXiv preprint arXiv:2010.09015 (2020)
55. Shao, S., et al.: CrowdHuman: a benchmark for detecting human in a crowd. arXiv preprint arXiv:1805.00123 (2018)
56. Shuai, B., Berneshawi, A., Li, X., Modolo, D., Tighe, J.: SiamMOT: Siamese multi-object tracking. In: Proceedings of the IEEE/CVF Conference on Computer Vision and Pattern Recognition, pp. 12372–12382 (2021)
57. Sun, P., et al.: What makes for end-to-end object detection? In: Proceedings of the 38th International Conference on Machine Learning. Proceedings of Machine Learning Research, vol. 139, pp. 9934–9944. PMLR (2021)
58. Sun, P., et al.: TransTrack: multiple-object tracking with transformer. arXiv preprint arXiv:2012.15460 (2020)
59. Sun, P., et al.: Sparse R-CNN: end-to-end object detection with learnable proposals. In: Proceedings of the IEEE/CVF Conference on Computer Vision and Pattern Recognition, pp. 14454–14463 (2021)
60. Tang, P., Wang, C., Wang, X., Liu, W., Zeng, W., Wang, J.: Object detection in videos by high quality object linking. IEEE Trans. Pattern Anal. Mach. Intell. **42**(5), 1272–1278 (2019)
61. Tokmakov, P., Li, J., Burgard, W., Gaidon, A.: Learning to track with object permanence. arXiv preprint arXiv:2103.14258 (2021)
62. Vaswani, A., et al.: Attention is all you need. In: Advances in Neural Information Processing Systems, pp. 5998–6008 (2017)
63. Wang, C.Y., Bochkovskiy, A., Liao, H.Y.M.: YOLOv7: trainable bag-of-freebies sets new state-of-the-art for real-time object detectors. arXiv preprint arXiv:2207.02696 (2022)
64. Wang, Q., Zheng, Y., Pan, P., Xu, Y.: Multiple object tracking with correlation learning. In: Proceedings of the IEEE/CVF Conference on Computer Vision and Pattern Recognition, pp. 3876–3886 (2021)
65. Wang, W., et al.: Pyramid vision transformer: a versatile backbone for dense prediction without convolutions. arXiv preprint arXiv:2102.12122 (2021)

66. Wang, Y., Kitani, K., Weng, X.: Joint object detection and multi-object tracking with graph neural networks. arXiv preprint arXiv:2006.13164 (2020)
67. Wang, Z., Zhao, H., Li, Y.L., Wang, S., Torr, P.H., Bertinetto, L.: Do different tracking tasks require different appearance models? arXiv preprint arXiv:2107.02156 (2021)
68. Wang, Z., Zheng, L., Liu, Y., Li, Y., Wang, S.: Towards real-time multi-object tracking. In: Vedaldi, A., Bischof, H., Brox, T., Frahm, J.-M. (eds.) ECCV 2020. LNCS, vol. 12356, pp. 107–122. Springer, Cham (2020). https://doi.org/10.1007/978-3-030-58621-8_7
69. Wojke, N., Bewley, A., Paulus, D.: Simple online and realtime tracking with a deep association metric. In: 2017 IEEE International Conference on Image Processing (ICIP), pp. 3645–3649. IEEE (2017)
70. Wu, J., Cao, J., Song, L., Wang, Y., Yang, M., Yuan, J.: Track to detect and segment: an online multi-object tracker. In: Proceedings of the IEEE/CVF Conference on Computer Vision and Pattern Recognition, pp. 12352–12361 (2021)
71. Xiang, Y., Alahi, A., Savarese, S.: Learning to track: online multi-object tracking by decision making. In: ICCV, pp. 4705–4713 (2015)
72. Xu, J., Cao, Y., Zhang, Z., Hu, H.: Spatial-temporal relation networks for multi-object tracking. In: Proceedings of the IEEE/CVF International Conference on Computer Vision, pp. 3988–3998 (2019)
73. Xu, Y., Ban, Y., Delorme, G., Gan, C., Rus, D., Alameda-Pineda, X.: TransCenter: transformers with dense queries for multiple-object tracking. arXiv preprint arXiv:2103.15145 (2021)
74. Yan, B., et al.: Towards grand unification of object tracking. arXiv preprint arXiv:2207.07078 (2022)
75. Yang, F., Chang, X., Sakti, S., Wu, Y., Nakamura, S.: ReMOT: a model-agnostic refinement for multiple object tracking. Image Vis. Comput. **106**, 104091 (2021)
76. Yang, F., Choi, W., Lin, Y.: Exploit all the layers: fast and accurate CNN object detector with scale dependent pooling and cascaded rejection classifiers. In: Proceedings of the IEEE Conference on Computer Vision and Pattern Recognition, pp. 2129–2137 (2016)
77. Yu, E., Li, Z., Han, S., Wang, H.: RelationTrack: relation-aware multiple object tracking with decoupled representation. arXiv preprint arXiv:2105.04322 (2021)
78. Yu, F., et al.: BDD100K: a diverse driving dataset for heterogeneous multitask learning. In: Proceedings of the IEEE/CVF Conference on Computer Vision and Pattern Recognition, pp. 2636–2645 (2020)
79. Zeng, F., Dong, B., Wang, T., Chen, C., Zhang, X., Wei, Y.: MOTR: end-to-end multiple-object tracking with transformer. arXiv preprint arXiv:2105.03247 (2021)
80. Zhang, H., Cisse, M., Dauphin, Y.N., Lopez-Paz, D.: mixup: beyond empirical risk minimization. arXiv preprint arXiv:1710.09412 (2017)
81. Zhang, S., Benenson, R., Schiele, B.: CityPersons: a diverse dataset for pedestrian detection. In: CVPR, pp. 3213–3221 (2017)
82. Zhang, Y., Sheng, H., Wu, Y., Wang, S., Ke, W., Xiong, Z.: Multiplex labeling graph for near-online tracking in crowded scenes. IEEE Internet Things J. **7**(9), 7892–7902 (2020)
83. Zhang, Y., Wang, C., Wang, X., Liu, W., Zeng, W.: VoxelTrack: multi-person 3D human pose estimation and tracking in the wild. IEEE Trans. Pattern Anal. Mach. Intell. (2022)
84. Zhang, Y., Wang, C., Wang, X., Zeng, W., Liu, W.: FairMOT: on the fairness of detection and re-identification in multiple object tracking. Int. J. Comput. Vision **129**(11), 3069–3087 (2021)

85. Zhang, Z., Cheng, D., Zhu, X., Lin, S., Dai, J.: Integrated object detection and tracking with tracklet-conditioned detection. arXiv preprint arXiv:1811.11167 (2018)
86. Zheng, L., Tang, M., Chen, Y., Zhu, G., Wang, J., Lu, H.: Improving multiple object tracking with single object tracking. In: Proceedings of the IEEE/CVF Conference on Computer Vision and Pattern Recognition, pp. 2453–2462 (2021)
87. Zhou, X., Koltun, V., Krähenbühl, P.: Tracking objects as points. In: Vedaldi, A., Bischof, H., Brox, T., Frahm, J.-M. (eds.) ECCV 2020. LNCS, vol. 12349, pp. 474–490. Springer, Cham (2020). https://doi.org/10.1007/978-3-030-58548-8_28
88. Zhou, X., Wang, D., Krähenbühl, P.: Objects as points. arXiv preprint arXiv:1904.07850 (2019)
89. Zhou, X., Yin, T., Koltun, V., Krähenbühl, P.: Global tracking transformers. In: Proceedings of the IEEE/CVF Conference on Computer Vision and Pattern Recognition, pp. 8771–8780 (2022)
90. Zhu, J., Yang, H., Liu, N., Kim, M., Zhang, W., Yang, M.-H.: Online multi-object tracking with dual matching attention networks. In: Ferrari, V., Hebert, M., Sminchisescu, C., Weiss, Y. (eds.) ECCV 2018. LNCS, vol. 11209, pp. 379–396. Springer, Cham (2018). https://doi.org/10.1007/978-3-030-01228-1_23
91. Zhu, X., Su, W., Lu, L., Li, B., Wang, X., Dai, J.: Deformable DETR: deformable transformers for end-to-end object detection. arXiv preprint arXiv:2010.04159 (2020)

Robust Multi-object Tracking
by Marginal Inference

Yifu Zhang[1], Chunyu Wang[2], Xinggang Wang[1], Wenjun Zeng[3],
and Wenyu Liu[1(✉)]

[1] Huazhong University of Science and Technology, Wuhan, China
`liuwy@hust.edu.cn`
[2] Microsoft Research Asia, Beijing, China
[3] Eastern Institute for Advanced Study, Ningbo, China

Abstract. Multi-object tracking in videos requires to solve a fundamental problem of one-to-one assignment between objects in adjacent frames. Most methods address the problem by first discarding impossible pairs whose feature distances are larger than a threshold, followed by linking objects using Hungarian algorithm to minimize the overall distance. However, we find that the distribution of the distances computed from Re-ID features may vary significantly for different videos. So there isn't a single optimal threshold which allows us to safely discard impossible pairs. To address the problem, we present an efficient approach to compute a marginal probability for each pair of objects in real time. The marginal probability can be regarded as a normalized distance which is significantly more stable than the original feature distance. As a result, we can use a single threshold for all videos. The approach is general and can be applied to the existing trackers to obtain about one point improvement in terms of IDF1 metric. It achieves competitive results on MOT17 and MOT20 benchmarks. In addition, the computed probability is more interpretable which facilitates subsequent post-processing operations.

Keywords: Multi-object tracking · Data association · Marginal probability

1 Introduction

Multi-object tracking (MOT) is one of the most active topics in computer vision. The state-of-the-art methods [25,31,37,40,45,48,58,60] usually address the problem by first detecting objects in each frame, and then linking them to trajectories based on Re-ID features. Specifically, it computes distances between objects in adjacent frames, discards impossible pairs with large distances, and determines the matched pairs by minimizing the overall distance by applying the Hungarian algorithm [20].

This work was done when Yifu Zhang was an intern of Microsoft Research Asia.

Supplementary Information The online version contains supplementary material available at https://doi.org/10.1007/978-3-031-20047-2_2.

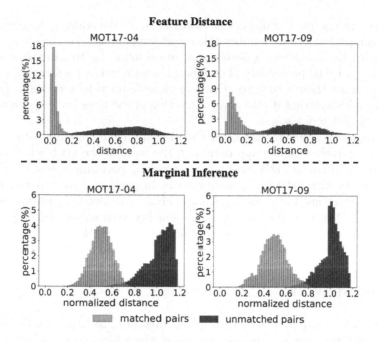

Fig. 1. Distance distribution of the matched pairs and unmatched pairs, respectively, on two videos. The top shows the distances directly computed from Re-ID features the bottom shows our normalized distances (marginal probability).

The core of the linking step is to find a threshold where the distances between the matched objects are smaller than it, while those of the unmatched ones are larger than it. The threshold setting is done by experience and has not received sufficient attention. However, our experiment shows that even the best Re-ID model cannot discard all impossible pairs without introducing false negatives using a single threshold because the distances may vary significantly on different frames as shown in Fig. 1 (top). We can see that the optimal threshold to discriminate matched and unmatched pairs is 0.2 for video "MOT17-04" and 0.4 for "MOT17-09" which are very different.

We argue in this work that we should put a particular value of distance into context when we determine whether it is sufficiently small to be a matched pair. For example, in Fig. 1 (top), 0.2 is a large distance for video "MOT17-04" but it is a small one for "MOT17-09" considering their particular distance distributions. To achieve this goal, we propose to compute a marginal probability for each pair of objects being matched by considering the whole data association space which consists of all possible one-to-one assignment structures. The marginal probability is robust to distance distribution shift and significantly improves the linking accuracy in our experiment. For example, in the "Public Detection" track of the MOT17 challenge, the IDF1 score improves from 59.6% to 65.0%.

We consider a possible matching between all the detections and trajectories as one structure. However, naively enumerating all structures is intractable especially when the number of objects in videos is large. We address the complexity issue by computing a small number of low-cost supporting structures which often overlap with the maximum a posterior solution found by Hungarian algorithm [4,48]. The marginal probability of each pair is computed by performing marginal inference among these structures. Our experiments on videos with a large number of objects show that it takes only a fraction of the time to compute without affecting the inference speed.

The approach is general and applies to almost all existing multi-object trackers. We extensively evaluate approach with the state-of-the-art trackers on multiple datasets. It consistently improves the tracking performances of all methods on all datasets with little extra computation. In particular, we empirically find that it is more robust to occlusion. When occlusion occurs, the distance between two (occluded) instances of the same person becomes larger and the conventional methods may treat them as two different persons. However, the marginal probability is less affected and the two instances can be correctly linked.

2   Related Work

Most *state-of-the-art* multi-object tracking methods [25,31,37,45,48,51,56,58, 60] follow the *tracking-by-detection* paradigm which form trajectories by associating detections in time. They first adopt detectors such as [12,22,33,34,61] to get the location of the objects and then link the detections to the existing trajectories according to similarity. Similarity computation and matching strategy are two key components of data association in the *tracking-by-detection* paradigm. We review different methods from the two aspects and compare them to our approach.

2.1   Similarity Computation

Location, motion, and appearance are three important cues to compute similarity between detections and tracks. IOU-Tracker [6] computes the spatial overlap of detections in neighboring frames as similarity. SORT [4] adopts Kalman Filter [47] as a motion model to predict the future locations of objects. The similarity is computed by the IoU of predicted locations and detected locations. The two trackers are widely used in practice due to their speed and simplicity. However, both the two trackers will cause a large number of identity switches when encountering camera motion and crowded scenes. To decrease the identity switches, DeepSORT [48] adopts a deep neural network to extract appearance features as appearance cues can refind lost objects. The final similarity is a weighted sum of motion similarity computed by Kalman Filter and cosine similarity of the appearance features. Bae *et al.* [1] also proposes an online discriminative appearance learning method to handle similar appearances of different objects. Many *state-of-the-art* methods [9,25,31,42,45,57,58] follow [48] to compute the similarity using location, motion and appearance cues. Some methods

[37,49] utilize networks to encode appearance and location cues into similarity score. Recently, some methods [25,31,45,58] combine the detection task and re-identification task in a single neural network to reduce computation cost. JDE [45] first proposes a joint detection and embedding model to first achieve a (near) real-time MOT system. FairMOT [58] deeply studies the reasons for the unfairness between detection and re-identification task in anchor-based models and proposes a high-resolution anchor-free model to extract more discriminative appearance features. QDTrack [31] densely samples hundreds of region proposals on a pair of images for contrastive learning of appearance features to make use of the majority of the informative regions on the images. It gets very high-quality appearance features and can achieve *state-of-the-art* results only using appearance cues.

Our method also uses the location, motion, and appearance cues to compute similarity. However, we find that the appearance feature distance distribution may vary significantly for different videos. We achieve a more stable distribution by computing the marginal probability based on appearance features.

2.2 Matching Strategy

After computing similarity, most methods [1,4,9,37,42,45,48,49,58] use Hungarian Algorithm [20] to complete matching. Bae *et al.* [1] matches tracklets in different ways according to their confidence values. Confident tracklets are locally matched with online-provided detections and fragmented tracklets are globally matched with confident tracklets or unmatched detections. The advantage of confidence-based tracklets matching is that it can handle track fragments due to occlusion or unreliable detections. DeepSORT [48] proposes a cascade matching strategy, which first matches the most recent tracklets to the detections and then matches the lost tracklets. This is because recent tracklets are more reliable than lost tracklets. MOTDT [9] proposes a hierarchical matching strategy. It first associates using the appearance and motion cues. For the unmatched tracklets and detections (usually under severe occlusion), it matches again by IoU. JDE [45] and FairMOT [58] also follow the hierarchical matching strategy proposed by MOTDT. QDTrack [31] applies a bi-directional softmax to the appearance feature similarity and associates objects with a simple nearest neighbor search. All these methods need to set a threshold to decide whether the detections match the tracklets. If the distance is larger than the threshold, the matching is rejected. It is very challenging to set an optimal threshold for all videos because the distance distribution may vary significantly as the appearance model is data-driven. The work most related to our approach is Rezatofighi *et al.* [35] which also uses probability for matching. However, their motivation and the solution to compute probability are different from ours.

We follow the matching strategy of [9,45,58] which hierarchically uses appearance, motion, and location cues. The main difference is that we turn the appearance similarity into marginal probability (normalized distance) to achieve a more stable distance distribution. The motion model and location cues are more generalized, so we do not turn them into probability. The matching is also completed by the Hungarian Algorithm. Our marginal probability is also more robust to occlusion as it decreases the probability of false matching. We can thus set a looser (higher) matching threshold to refind some lost/occluded objects.

3   Method

3.1   Problem Formulation

Suppose we have M detections and N history tracks at frame t, our goal is to assign each detection to one of the tracks which has the same identity. Let $\mathbf{d}_t^1, ..., \mathbf{d}_t^M$ and $\mathbf{h}_t^1, ..., \mathbf{h}_t^N$ be the Re-ID features of all M detections and N tracks at frame t, respectively. We compute a cosine similarity matrix $\mathbf{S}_t \in [0, 1]^{M \times N}$ between all the detections and tracks as follows:

$$\mathbf{S}_t(i, j) = \frac{\mathbf{d}_t^i \cdot \mathbf{h}_t^j}{||\mathbf{d}_t^i|| \cdot ||\mathbf{h}_t^j||}, \tag{1}$$

where $i \in \{1, ..., M\}$ and $j \in \{1, ..., N\}$. For simplicity, we replace $\{1, ..., M\}$ by $\mathbb{M}$ and $\{1, ..., N\}$ by $\mathbb{N}$ in the following myparagraphs.

Based on the similarity $\mathbf{S}_t$, we compute a marginal probability matrix $\mathbf{P}_t \in [0, 1]^{M \times N}$ for all pairs of detections and tracks. $\mathbf{P}_t(i, j)$ represents the marginal probability that the i_{th} detection is matched to the j_{th} track. We compute $\mathbf{P}_t(i, j)$ considering all possible matchings. Let $\mathbb{A}$ denote the space which consists of all possible associations (or matchings). Under the setting of multi-object tracking, each detection matches at most one track and each track matches at most one detection. We define the space $\mathbb{A}$ as follow:

$$\mathbb{A} = \left\{ A = \left(m_{ij} \right)_{i \in \mathbb{M}, j \in \mathbb{N}} \middle| m_{ij} \in \{0, 1\} \right. \tag{2}$$

$$\wedge \sum_{i=0}^{M} m_{ij} \leqslant 1, \forall j \in \mathbb{N} \tag{3}$$

$$\left. \wedge \sum_{j=0}^{N} m_{ij} \leqslant 1, \forall i \in \mathbb{M} \right\}, \tag{4}$$

where A is one possible matching. We define $\mathbb{A}_{ij}$ as a subset of $\mathbb{A}$, which contains all the matchings where the i_{th} detection is matched to the j_{th} track:

$$\mathbb{A}_{ij} = \{A \in \mathbb{A} \mid m_{ij} = 1\} \tag{5}$$

The marginal probability $\mathbf{P}_t(i, j)$ can be computed by marginalizing $\mathbb{A}_{ij}$ as follows:

$$\mathbf{P}_t(i, j) = \sum_{A \in \mathbb{A}_{ij}} p(A), \tag{6}$$

where $p(A)$ is a joint probability representing the probability of one possible matching A and can be computed as follows:

$$p(A) = \prod_{\forall q \in M, \forall r \in N} \left(\frac{\exp\left(\mathbf{S}_t(q,r)\right)}{\sum_{r=1}^{N} \exp\left(\mathbf{S}_t(q,r)\right)} \right) \tag{7}$$

The most difficult part to obtain $\mathbf{P}_t(i,j)$ is to computing all possible matchings in $\mathbb{A}_{ij}$ because the total number of matchings is n-permutation.

3.2 Our Solution

We consider the structured problems. We view each possible matching between all the detections and tracks as a structure $\mathbf{k} \in \{0,1\}^{MN}$, which can be seen as a flattening of the matching matrix. We define all the structures in the space $\mathbb{A}$ as $\mathbf{K} \in \{0,1\}^{MN \times D}$, where D is the number of all possible matchings and $MN \ll D$.

We often use the structured log-potentials to parametrize the structured problems. The scores of the structures can be computed as $\boldsymbol{\theta} := \mathbf{K}^\top \boldsymbol{S}$, where $\boldsymbol{S} \in \mathbb{R}^{MN}$ is a flattening of the similarity matrix $\mathbf{S}_t$. Suppose we have variables V and factors F in a factor graph [19], $\boldsymbol{\theta}$ can be computed as:

$$\theta_o := \sum_{v \in V} S_{V,v}(o_v) + \sum_{f \in F} S_{F,f}(o_f), \tag{8}$$

where o_v and o_f are local structures at variable and factor nodes. $\boldsymbol{S}_V$ and $\boldsymbol{S}_F$ represent the log-potentials. In our linear assignment setting, we only have variables and thus $\boldsymbol{\theta}$ can be written in matrix notation as $\boldsymbol{\theta} = \mathbf{K}^\top \boldsymbol{S}_V$.

The optimal matching between detections and tracks can be viewed as the MAP inference problem, which seeks the highest-scoring structure. It can be rewritten using the structured log-potentials as follows:

$$\mathrm{MAP}_{\mathbf{K}}(\boldsymbol{S}) := \underset{\mathbf{v}:=\mathbf{Ky}, \mathbf{y} \in \triangle^D}{\arg\max} \; \boldsymbol{\theta}^\top \mathbf{y} \tag{9}$$

$$= \underset{\mathbf{v}:=\mathbf{Ky}, \mathbf{y} \in \triangle^D}{\arg\max} \; \boldsymbol{S}_V{}^\top \mathbf{v}, \tag{10}$$

where $\mathbf{v} \in \{0,1\}^{MN}$ is the highest-scoring structure and $\{\mathbf{v} = \mathbf{Ky}, \mathbf{y} \in \triangle^D\}$ is the Birkhoff polytope [5]. In linear assignment, the structure $\mathbf{v}$ can be obtained by Hungarian algorithm [20].

The main challenge of computing the marginal probability as in Eq. 6 is that the total number of structures D is very large and usually not tractable. To address the problem, we propose to compute a small number of low-cost and often-overlapping structures instead of enumerating all of them. In [29], Niculae et al. show that this can be achieved by regularizing the MAP inference problem with a squared l_2 penalty on the returned posteriors which was inspired by [27]. Computing multiple structures which approximate the MAP inference problem can be written as follows:

$$\mathrm{L2MAP}_{\mathbf{K}}(\boldsymbol{S}) := \underset{\mathbf{v}:=\mathbf{Ky}, \mathbf{y} \in \triangle^D}{\arg\max} \; \boldsymbol{\theta}^\top \mathbf{y} - \frac{1}{2}\|\mathbf{Ky}\|_2^2 \tag{11}$$

$$= \underset{\mathbf{v}:=\mathbf{Ky}, \mathbf{y} \in \triangle^D}{\arg\max} \; \boldsymbol{S}_V{}^\top \mathbf{v} - \frac{1}{2}\|\mathbf{v}\|_2^2, \tag{12}$$

The result is a quadratic optimization problem and it can be solved by the conditional gradient (CG) algorithm [21]. The Eq. 11 can be written by function f as follows:

$$f(\mathbf{v}) := \boldsymbol{S_V}^\top \mathbf{v} - \frac{1}{2}||\mathbf{v}||_2^2, \tag{13}$$

A linear approximation to f around a point $\mathbf{v}'$ is:

$$\hat{f}(\mathbf{v}) := (\nabla_\mathbf{v} f)^\top \mathbf{v} = (\boldsymbol{S_V} - \mathbf{v}')^\top \mathbf{v}, \tag{14}$$

We can turn the optimization problem of $\hat{f}$ into an MAP inference problem. The variable scores of the MAP inference problem at each step is $\boldsymbol{S_V} - \mathbf{v}'$. At each step, we use Hungarian algorithm to solve the MAP inference problem and get a high-scoring structure $\mathbf{z} \in \{0, 1\}^{MN}$. Then we use $\mathbf{z}$ to substitute $\mathbf{v}'$ for another step. After a small number of steps, we obtain a set of high-scoring and often-overlapping structures $\mathbb{Z} = \{\mathbf{z}_1, ..., \mathbf{z}_n\}$, where n is the number of steps. We compute the marginal probability $\mathbf{P}_t$ by marginalizing $\mathbb{Z}$ following Eq. 6:

$$\mathbf{P}_t(i, j) = \sum_{\mathbf{z} \in \mathbb{Z}_{ij}} \left(\frac{\exp(-\mathbf{C}_t^\top \mathbf{z})}{\sum_{v=1}^n \exp(-\mathbf{C}_t^\top \mathbf{z}_v)} \right) \tag{15}$$

where $\mathbb{Z}_{ij}$ contains all structures that the i_{th} detection is matched to the j_{th} track and $\mathbf{C}_t \in [0, 1]^{MN}$ is a flattened feature distance matrix $\boldsymbol{S_V}$.

3.3   Tracking Algorithm

Our tracking algorithm jointly considers appearance, motion, and location cues. In each frame, we adopt Hungarian algorithm [20] to perform matching two times hierarchically: 1) marginal probability matching, 2) IoU matching.

We first define some thresholds in our tracking algorithm. Thresholds C_t and C_d are the confidence thresholds for the detections. Thresholds T_p and T_{IoU} are for the marginal probability matching and IoU matching, respectively.

In the first frame, we initialize all detections with scores larger than C_d as new tracks. In the following frame t, we first match between all N tracks and all M medium detections using marginal probability $\mathbf{P}_t \in [0, 1]^{M \times N}$ calculated by Eq. 15 and the Mahalanobis distance $\mathbf{M}_t \in \mathbb{R}^{M \times N}$ computed by Kalman Filter proposed in [48]. The cost matrix is computed as follows:

$$\mathbf{D}_p = \omega(1 - \mathbf{P}_t) + (1 - \omega)\mathbf{M}_t, \tag{16}$$

where ω is a weight that balances the appearance cue and the motion cue. We set ω to be 0.98 in our experiments. We adopt Hungarian algorithm to perform the first matching and we reject the matching whose distance is larger than T_p. It is worth noting that T_p may vary significantly for different frames or videos if we directly utilize the appearance feature similarity for matching. The marginal probability matching has a significantly more stable T_p.

For the unmatched detections and tracks, we perform the second matching using IoU distance with the threshold T_{IoU}. This works when appearance features are not reliable (*e.g.* occlusion).

Finally, we mark lost for the unmatched tracks and save it for 30 frames. For the unmatched detections, if the score is larger than C_t, we initialize a new track. We also update the appearance features following [58].

4 Experiments

4.1 MOT Benchmarks and Metrics

Datasets. We evaluate our approach on MOT17 [28] and MOT20 [11] benchmarks. The two datasets both provide a training set and a test set, respectively. The MOT17 dataset has videos captured by both moving and stationary cameras from various viewpoints at different frame rates. The videos in the MOT20 dataset are captured in very crowded scenes so there is a lot occlusion happening. There are two evaluation protocols which either use the provided public detections or private detections generated by any detectors. In particular, the MOT17 dataset provides three sets of public detections generated DPM [13], Faster R-CNN [34] and SDP [52], respectively and we evaluate our approach on all of them. The MOT20 dataset provides one set of public detections generated by Faster R-CNN.

Metrics. We use the CLEAR metric [3] and IDF1 [36] to evaluate different aspects of multi-object tracking. Multi-Object Tracking Accuracy (MOTA) and Identity F1 Score (IDF1) are two main metrics. MOTA focuses more on the detection performance. IDF1 focuses on identity preservation and depends more on the tracking performance.

4.2 Implementation Details

We evaluate our approach with two existing feature extractors. The first is the state-of-the-art one-stage method FairMOT [58] which jointly detects objects and estimates Re-ID features in a single network. The second is the state-of-the-art two-stage method following the framework of DeepSORT [48] which adopts Scaled-YOLOv4 [43] as the detection model and BoT [26] as the Re-ID model. The input image is resized to 1088×608. In the linking step, we set $C_d = 0.4$, $C_t = 0.5$, $T_p = 0.8$, $T_{IoU} = 0.5$. We set the number of steps n to be 100 when computing the marginal probability. The inference speed of the models is listed as follows: 40 FPS for Scaled-YOLOv4, 26 FPS for FairMOT and 17 FPS for BoT.

Public Detection. In this setting, we adopt FairMOT [58] and our marginal inference data association method. Following the previous works of Tracktor [2] and CenterTrack [60], we only initialize a new trajectory if it is near a public detection (*e.g.* IoU is larger than a threshold). In particular, we set a strict

IoU threshold 0.75 to make our trajectories as close to the public detections as possible. The FairMOT model is pre-trained on the COCO dataset [23] and finetuned on the training set of MOT17 and MOT20, respectively.

Private Detection. We adopt the detection model Scaled-YOLOv4 [43] and Re-ID model BoT [26] implemented by FastReID [14] in the private detection setting. We train Scaled-YOLOv4 using the YOLOv4-P5 [43] model on the same combination of different datasets as in FairMOT [58]. We train BoT on Market1501 [59], DukeMTMC [36] and MSMT17 [46]. All the training process is the same as the references except the training data. For the Re-ID part, we multiply the cosine distance by 500 to make it evenly distributed between 0 and 1.

Ablation Study. For ablation study, we evaluate on the training set of MOT17 and MOT20. To make it more similar to real-world applications, our training data and evaluation data have different data distribution. We also use different detection models and Re-ID models to evaluate the generalization ability of our method. We select three models, FairMOT, Scaled-YOLOv4, and BoT. We adopt FairMOT either as a joint detection and Re-ID model or a separate Re-ID model. We adopt Scaled-YOLOv4 as a detection model and BoT as a Re-ID model. We train Scaled-YOLOv4 on the CrowdHuman [38] dataset. We train FairMOT on the HiEve [24] dataset. We train BoT on the Market1501, DukeMTMC, and MSMT17 datasets. The matching threshold is 0.4 for the distance-based method and 0.8 for the probability-based method.

4.3   Evaluation of the Marginal Probability

More Stable Distribution. In this part, we try to prove that marginal probability is more stable than feature distance. We compare the IDF1 score of the two different methods and also plot the distance distribution between detections and tracks of each method. We adopt different detection models and Re-ID models and evaluate on different datasets. The results are shown in Table 1. We can see that the marginal probability matching method has about 1 point IDF1 score higher than the distance-based matching method in most settings. The optimal threshold for each video is different. However, it is not realistic to set different thresholds for different videos in some testing scenarios or real-world applications. So we set one threshold for all videos in a dataset. One reason for the performance gain is that the optimal threshold for each video is similar in the probability-based method, which means a single threshold is suitable for most videos.

To obtain the distance distribution, we adopt Scaled-YOLOv4 [43] as the detector and FairMOT [58] as the Re-ID model to perform tracking on the training set of MOT17. We find the optimal threshold for each video by grid search and plot the distance distribution between detections and tracks in each video. The saved distance is the input of the first matching in our tracking algorithm. As is shown in Fig. 1, the marginal probability distribution of each video is similar and is more stable than feature distance distribution. Also, the optimal threshold for each video is similar in the probability-based matching method and varies significantly in the distance-based matching method.

Table 1. Comparison of probability-based method and distance-based method. "P" is short for probability and "D" is short for distance. "Det" is short for detection model and "Re-ID" is short for Re-ID model.

Dataset	Det	ReID	Match	MOTA↑	IDF1↑
MOT17	FairMOT	FairMOT	D	47.6	58.0
MOT17	FairMOT	FairMOT	P	47.6	**58.2 (+0.2)**
MOT17	Scaled-YOLOv4	FairMOT	D	71.5	72.5
MOT17	Scaled-YOLOv4	FairMOT	P	71.4	**73.6 (+1.1)**
MOT17	Scaled-YOLOv4	BoT	D	71.5	74.8
MOT17	Scaled-YOLOv4	BoT	P	71.6	**75.7 (+0.9)**
MOT20	FairMOT	FairMOT	D	43.2	45.9
MOT20	FairMOT	FairMOT	P	43.1	**46.7 (+0.8)**
MOT20	Scaled-YOLOv4	FairMOT	D	73.9	69.3
MOT20	Scaled-YOLOv4	FairMOT	P	74.1	**70.1 (+0.8)**
MOT20	Scaled-YOLOv4	BoT	D	74.0	69.5
MOT20	Scaled-YOLOv4	BoT	P	74.2	**70.2 (+0.7)**

More Robust to Occlusion. There are many occlusion cases in multi-object tracking datasets [11,28]. Even state-of-the-art detectors cannot detect objects under severe occlusions. Therefore, in many cases, an object will reappear after being occluded for a few frames. The key to getting a high IDF1 score is to preserve the identities of these reappeared objects, which is also a main challenge in multi-object tracking. Using appearance features is an effective way to preserve the identities of the occluded objects. However, we find in our experiments that the appearance feature distances of the same object increases linearly with the increase of the number of interval frames and the distance becomes even larger in the case of occlusion, as is shown in Fig. 2. The feature distance becomes very large after 20 frames. Thus, it is difficult to retrieve the lost object because it needs a high matching threshold, which may lead to other wrong matchings.

Another reason for the IDF1 performance gain of our method is that marginal probability is more robust to occlusion. We show some detailed visualization results of how our approach deals with occlusion and retrieve the lost object. As is shown in the second line of Fig. 3, our approach can keep the identity unchanged in the case of severe occlusion. We adopt Kalman Filter to filter some impossible matchings (distance is infinity). The distance matrix in Fig. 3 is the input of the Hungarian Algorithm in the first matching. The distance of the occluded person is 0.753 in the distance-based method and the distance is 0.725 in the probability-based method. From the distance distribution figure, we can see that the optimal matching threshold is 0.6 for the distanced-based method and 0.8 for the probability-based method. Only the probability-based method can preserve the identity of the occluded person as 0.725 is smaller than 0.8. Because we consider all possible matchings to compute the marginal probability, the probability of many impossible pairs can be very low (*e.g.* 0) and the distance is very large (*e.g.* 1) after using 1 to minus the probability. After adding the motion distance, the final distance is compressed between 0.8 to 1.2 and thus we can set a relatively high matching threshold (*e.g.* 0.8) and successfully retrieve the lost object with a large distance (*e.g.* 0.7). Also, by comparing 0.725 to 0.753, we can see that the marginal probability can make the distance of correct-matched occluded pairs lower.

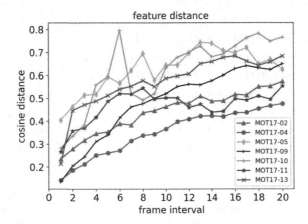

Fig. 2. Visualization of cosine distances of the appearance features at different frame intervals. The appearance features are extracted by the BoT Re-ID model. We show the results of all the sequences from the MOT17 training set.

4.4   Ablation Studies

In this section, we compare different methods to compute marginal probability and evaluate different components of our matching strategy. We also evaluate the time-consuming of our method. We adopt Scaled-YOLOv4 [43] as the detector, BoT [26] as the Re-ID model and evaluate on MOT17 training sets. We utilize powerful deep learning models and domain-different training data and evaluation data to make our setting as close to real-world applications as possible, which can better reflect the real performance of our method.

Probability Computation. We compare different methods to compute the marginal probability, including softmax, bi-directional softmax, and our marginal inference method. The softmax method is to compute softmax probability between each track and all the detections. Bi-directional softmax is to

Fig. 3. Visualization of how our approach preserves object identity in the case of occlusion. The first line is the distanced-based method and the second line is the probability-base method. We show tracking visualizations, distance values, and distance distribution for both methods. The tracking results are from frame 686 and frame 700 of the MOT17-11 sequence. The occluded person is highlighted by the red dotted ellipse. The distance value is computed by the track and detection of the occluded person in frame 700. The occluded person is not detected from frame 687 to frame 699 and it is set as a lost track. (Color figure online)

compute probability between each track and all the detections along with each detection and all the tracks. We average the two probabilities to get the final probability.

The results are shown in Table 2. We can see that the bi-directional softmax method has the highest MOTA and lowest ID switches while our method has the highest IDF1 score. The softmax-based methods only consider one-to-n matchings and lack global consideration. Our method can approximate all possible matchings and thus has global consideration. Our method has sightly more ID switches than bi-softmax because sometimes the ID will switch 2 times and then turn to be correct in some cases of severe occlusion. In such cases, the IDF1 score is still high and we argue that IDF1 score is more important.

Matching Strategy. We evaluate the effect of different components in the matching strategy, including appearance features, sparse probability, Kalman Filter and IoU. As is shown in Table 3, appearance and motion cues are complementary. IoU matching often works when appearance features are unreliable (*e.g.* occlusion). Finally, the marginal probability matching further increase the IDF1 score by about 1 point.

Table 2. Comparison of different methods to compute probability. "Bi-softmax" is short for bi-directional softmax. "Marginal" is short for marginal inference.

Method	MOTA↑	IDF1↑	IDs↓
Distance	71.5	74.8	499
Softmax	71.6	73.7	477
Bi-softmax	71.6	74.7	**405**
Marginal (Ours)	**71.6**	**75.7**	449

Table 3. Ablation study of different components in the matching strategy. "A" is short for appearance features, "P" is short for probability, "K" is short for Kalman Filter.

A	K	IoU	P	MOTA↑	IDF1↑	IDs↓
✓				68.8	71.9	792
✓	✓			70.1	73.6	777
✓	✓	✓		71.5	74.8	499
✓	✓	✓	✓	**71.6**	**75.7**	**449**

Time-Consuming. We compute the time-consuming of the linking step using videos with different density (average number of pedestrians per frame). We compare the distance-based matching method to the probability-based matching method. We choose videos with different density from the MOT17 training set. As is shown in Fig. 4, it takes only a fraction of time (less than 10 ms) to compute the marginal probability.

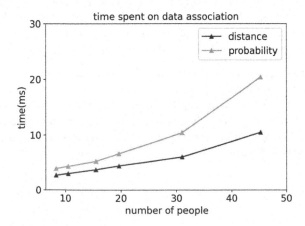

Fig. 4. Visualization of the time-consuming of data association. We evaluate two different methods on the training set of MOT17.

Table 4. Comparison of the state-of-the-art methods on MOT17 test sets. We report results under both public detection and private detection protocols.

Public detection								
Mode	Method	MOTA↑	IDF1↑	MT↑	ML↓	FP↓	FN↓	IDs↓
Off	MHT_DAM [18]	50.7	47.2	491	869	22875	252889	2314
Off	jCC [17]	51.2	54.5	493	872	25937	247822	1802
Off	FWT [15]	51.3	47.6	505	830	24101	247921	2648
Off	eHAF [39]	51.8	54.7	551	893	33212	236772	1834
Off	TT [55]	54.9	63.1	575	897	20236	233295	1088
Off	MPNTrack [8]	58.8	61.7	**679**	**788**	17413	213594	**1185**
Off	Lif_T [16]	**60.5**	**65.6**	637	791	**14966**	**206619**	1189
On	MOTDT [9]	50.9	52.7	413	841	24069	250768	2474
On	FAMNet [10]	52.0	48.7	450	787	14138	253616	3072
On	DeepMOT [50]	53.7	53.8	458	861	11731	247447	1947
On	Tracktor++v2 [2]	56.3	55.1	498	831	**8866**	235449	1987
On	CenterTrack [60]	61.5	59.6	621	752	14076	200672	2583
On	MTracker (Ours)	**62.1**	**65.0**	**657**	**730**	24052	**188264**	**1768**
Private detection								
Mode	Method	MOTA↑	IDF1↑	MT↑	ML↓	FP↓	FN↓	IDs↓
On	TubeTK [30]	63.0	58.6	735	468	27060	177483	4137
On	CTracker [32]	66.6	57.4	759	570	22284	160491	5529
On	CenterTrack [60]	67.8	64.7	816	579	**18489**	160332	**3039**
On	FairMOT [58]	73.7	72.3	1017	408	27507	117477	3303
On	PermaTrackPr [41]	73.8	68.9	1032	405	28998	115104	3699
On	TransTrack [40]	75.2	63.5	1302	**240**	50157	86442	3603
On	CorrTracker [44]	76.5	73.6	1122	300	29808	99510	3369
On	MTracker (Ours)	**77.3**	**75.9**	**1314**	276	45030	**79716**	3255

4.5   Benchmark Evaluation

We compare our Marginal Inference Tracker (MTracker) with the state-of-the-art methods on the test sets of MOT17 and MOT20 under both public detection and private detection protocols. We list the results of both online methods and offline methods for completeness. We only compare directly to the online methods for fairness. For public detection results, we adopt the one-shot tracker FairMOT [58] to jointly perform detection and Re-ID and follow CenterTrack [60] to use public detections to filter the tracklets with a more strict IoU distance. For private detection results, we adopt a more powerful detector Scaled-Yolov4 [43] and Re-ID model BoT [26].

Table 4 and Table 5 show our results on the test sets of MOT17 and MOT20. For public detection results, MTracker achieves high IDF1 score and low ID

Table 5. Comparison of the state-of-the-art methods on MOT20 test sets. We report results under both public detection and private detection protocols. The methods denoted by * are the ones reported on CVPR2019 Challenge in which the videos and ground-truth are almost the same as MOT20.

Public detection								
Mode	Method	MOTA↑	IDF1↑	MT↑	ML↓	FP↓	FN↓	IDs↓
Off	IOU19 [6]*	35.8	25.7	126	389	24427	319696	15676
Off	V-IOU [7]*	46.7	46.0	288	306	33776	261964	2589
Off	MPNTrack [8]	**57.6**	**59.1**	**474**	**279**	**16953**	**201384**	**1210**
On	SORT20 [4]	42.7	45.1	208	326	27521	264694	4470
On	TAMA [53]*	47.6	48.7	342	**297**	38194	252934	2437
On	Tracktor++ [2]*	51.3	47.6	313	326	16263	253680	2584
On	Tracktor++v2 [2]	52.6	52.7	365	331	**6930**	236680	1648
On	MTracker (Ours)	**55.6**	**65.0**	**444**	388	12297	**216986**	**480**
Private detection								
Mode	Method	MOTA↑	IDF1↑	MT↑	ML↓	FP↓	FN↓	IDs↓
On	MLT [54]	48.9	54.6	384	274	45660	216803	**2187**
On	FairMOT [58]	61.8	67.3	**855**	**94**	103440	**88901**	5243
On	TransTrack [40]	65.0	59.4	622	167	27197	150197	3608
On	CorrTracker [44]	65.2	69.1	-	-	79429	95855	5183
On	MTracker (Ours)	**66.3**	**67.7**	707	146	**41538**	130072	2715

switches and outperforms the state-of-the-art methods by a large margin. On MOT17 test sets, the IDF1 score of MTracker is 5.4 points higher than CenterTrack and the ID switches are reduced by 30%. On MOT20 test sets, the IDF1 score of MTracker is 12.3 points higher than Tractor++v2 [2] and the ID switches are reduced by 70%. The high IDF1 score and low ID switches indicate that our method has strong identity preservation ability, which reveals the advantages of the marginal probability. For the private detection results, we use the same training data as FairMOT and substantially outperforms it on both MOTA and IDF1 score.

5   Conclusion

We present an efficient and robust data association method for multi-object tracking by marginal inference. The obtained marginal probability can be regarded as "normalized distance" and is significantly more stable than the distances based on Re-ID features. Our probability-based data association method has several advantages over the classic distance-based one. First, we can use a single threshold for all videos thanks to the stable probability distribution. Second, we empirically find that marginal probability is more robust to occlusion.

Third, our approach is general and can be applied to the existing state-of-the-art trackers [48,58] easily. We hope our work can benefit real applications where data distribution always varies significantly.

Acknowledgement. This work was in part supported by NSFC (No. 61733007 and No. 61876212) and MSRA Collaborative Research Fund.

References

1. Bae, S.H., Yoon, K.J.: Robust online multi-object tracking based on tracklet confidence and online discriminative appearance learning. In: Proceedings of the IEEE Conference on Computer Vision and Pattern Recognition, pp. 1218–1225 (2014)
2. Bergmann, P., Meinhardt, T., Leal-Taixe, L.: Tracking without bells and whistles. In: ICCV, pp. 941–951 (2019)
3. Bernardin, K., Stiefelhagen, R.: Evaluating multiple object tracking performance: the clear mot metrics. EURASIP J. Image Video Process. **2008**, 1–10 (2008)
4. Bewley, A., Ge, Z., Ott, L., Ramos, F., Upcroft, B.: Simple online and realtime tracking. In: ICIP, pp. 3464–3468. IEEE (2016)
5. Birkhoff, G.: Tres observaciones sobre el algebra lineal. Univ. Nac. Tucuman, Ser. A **5**, 147–154 (1946)
6. Bochinski, E., Eiselein, V., Sikora, T.: High-speed tracking-by-detection without using image information. In: 2017 14th IEEE International Conference on Advanced Video and Signal Based Surveillance (AVSS), pp. 1–6. IEEE (2017)
7. Bochinski, E., Senst, T., Sikora, T.: Extending IOU based multi-object tracking by visual information. In: 2018 15th IEEE International Conference on Advanced Video and Signal Based Surveillance (AVSS), pp. 1–6. IEEE (2018)
8. Brasó, G., Leal-Taixé, L.: Learning a neural solver for multiple object tracking. In: Proceedings of the IEEE/CVF Conference on Computer Vision and Pattern Recognition, pp. 6247–6257 (2020)
9. Chen, L., Ai, H., Zhuang, Z., Shang, C.: Real-time multiple people tracking with deeply learned candidate selection and person re-identification. In: 2018 IEEE International Conference on Multimedia and Expo (ICME), pp. 1–6. IEEE (2018)
10. Chu, P., Ling, H.: FamNet: joint learning of feature, affinity and multi-dimensional assignment for online multiple object tracking. In: ICCV, pp. 6172–6181 (2019)
11. Dendorfer, P., et al.: MOT20: a benchmark for multi object tracking in crowded scenes. arXiv:2003.09003 [cs], March 2020. arxiv.org/abs/1906.04567. arXiv: 2003.09003
12. Fang, Y., Yang, S., Wang, S., Ge, Y., Shan, Y., Wang, X.: Unleashing vanilla vision transformer with masked image modeling for object detection. arXiv preprint arXiv:2204.02964 (2022)
13. Felzenszwalb, P.F., Girshick, R.B., McAllester, D., Ramanan, D.: Object detection with discriminatively trained part-based models. IEEE Trans. Pattern Anal. Mach. Intell. **32**(9), 1627–1645 (2009)
14. He, L., Liao, X., Liu, W., Liu, X., Cheng, P., Mei, T.: FastReID: a PyTorch toolbox for real-world person re-identification. arXiv preprint arXiv:2006.02631 (2020)
15. Henschel, R., Leal-Taixé, L., Cremers, D., Rosenhahn, B.: Fusion of head and full-body detectors for multi-object tracking. In: Proceedings of the IEEE Conference on Computer Vision and Pattern Recognition Workshops, pp. 1428–1437 (2018)

16. Hornakova, A., Henschel, R., Rosenhahn, B., Swoboda, P.: Lifted disjoint paths with application in multiple object tracking. In: International Conference on Machine Learning, pp. 4364–4375. PMLR (2020)
17. Keuper, M., Tang, S., Andres, B., Brox, T., Schiele, B.: Motion segmentation & multiple object tracking by correlation co-clustering. IEEE Trans. Pattern Anal. Mach. Intell. **42**(1), 140–153 (2018)
18. Kim, C., Li, F., Ciptadi, A., Rehg, J.M.: Multiple hypothesis tracking revisited. In: Proceedings of the IEEE International Conference on Computer Vision, pp. 4696–4704 (2015)
19. Kschischang, F.R., Frey, B.J., Loeliger, H.A.: Factor graphs and the sum-product algorithm. IEEE Trans. Inf. Theory **47**(2), 498–519 (2001)
20. Kuhn, H.W.: The Hungarian method for the assignment problem. Naval Res. Logistics Q. **2**(1–2), 83–97 (1955)
21. Lacoste-Julien, S., Jaggi, M.: On the global linear convergence of Frank-Wolfe optimization variants. arXiv preprint arXiv:1511.05932 (2015)
22. Lin, T.Y., Goyal, P., Girshick, R., He, K., Dollár, P.: Focal loss for dense object detection. In: ICCV, pp. 2980–2988 (2017)
23. Lin, T.-Y., et al.: Microsoft COCO: common objects in context. In: Fleet, D., Pajdla, T., Schiele, B., Tuytelaars, T. (eds.) ECCV 2014. LNCS, vol. 8693, pp. 740–755. Springer, Cham (2014). https://doi.org/10.1007/978-3-319-10602-1_48
24. Lin, W., et al.: Human in events: a large-scale benchmark for human-centric video analysis in complex events. arXiv preprint arXiv:2005.04490 (2020)
25. Lu, Z., Rathod, V., Votel, R., Huang, J.: RetinaTrack: online single stage joint detection and tracking. In: Proceedings of the IEEE/CVF Conference on Computer Vision and Pattern Recognition, pp. 14668–14678 (2020)
26. Luo, H., Gu, Y., Liao, X., Lai, S., Jiang, W.: Bag of tricks and a strong baseline for deep person re-identification. In: Proceedings of the IEEE/CVF Conference on Computer Vision and Pattern Recognition Workshops (2019)
27. Martins, A., Astudillo, R.: From softmax to sparsemax: A sparse model of attention and multi-label classification. In: ICML, pp. 1614–1623. PMLR (2016)
28. Milan, A., Leal-Taixé, L., Reid, I., Roth, S., Schindler, K.: MOT16: a benchmark for multi-object tracking. arXiv preprint arXiv:1603.00831 (2016)
29. Niculae, V., Martins, A., Blondel, M., Cardie, C.: SparseMAP: differentiable sparse structured inference. In: ICML, pp. 3799–3808. PMLR (2018)
30. Pang, B., Li, Y., Zhang, Y., Li, M., Lu, C.: TubeTK: adopting tubes to track multi-object in a one-step training model. In: Proceedings of the IEEE/CVF Conference on Computer Vision and Pattern Recognition, pp. 6308–6318 (2020)
31. Pang, J., Qiu, L., Chen, H., Li, Q., Darrell, T., Yu, F.: Quasi-dense instance similarity learning. arXiv preprint arXiv:2006.06664 (2020)
32. Peng, J., et al.: Chained-tracker: chaining paired attentive regression results for end-to-end joint multiple-object detection and tracking. arXiv preprint arXiv:2007.14557 (2020)
33. Redmon, J., Farhadi, A.: YOLOv3: an incremental improvement. arXiv preprint arXiv:1804.02767 (2018)
34. Ren, S., He, K., Girshick, R., Sun, J.: Faster R-CNN: towards real-time object detection with region proposal networks. In: Advances in Neural Information Processing Systems, pp. 91–99 (2015)
35. Rezatofighi, S.H., Milan, A., Zhang, Z., Shi, Q., Dick, A., Reid, I.: Joint probabilistic data association revisited. In: Proceedings of the IEEE International Conference on Computer Vision, pp. 3047–3055 (2015)

36. Ristani, E., Solera, F., Zou, R., Cucchiara, R., Tomasi, C.: Performance measures and a data set for multi-target, multi-camera tracking. In: Hua, G., Jégou, H. (eds.) ECCV 2016. LNCS, vol. 9914, pp. 17–35. Springer, Cham (2016). https://doi.org/10.1007/978-3-319-48881-3_2
37. Shan, C., et al.: FGAGT: flow-guided adaptive graph tracking. arXiv preprint arXiv:2010.09015 (2020)
38. Shao, S., et al.: CrowdHuman: a benchmark for detecting human in a crowd. arXiv preprint arXiv:1805.00123 (2018)
39. Sheng, H., Zhang, Y., Chen, J., Xiong, Z., Zhang, J.: Heterogeneous association graph fusion for target association in multiple object tracking. IEEE Trans. Circuits Syst. Video Technol. **29**(11), 3269–3280 (2018)
40. Sun, P., et al.: TransTrack: multiple-object tracking with transformer. arXiv preprint arXiv:2012.15460 (2020)
41. Tokmakov, P., Li, J., Burgard, W., Gaidon, A.: Learning to track with object permanence. arXiv preprint arXiv:2103.14258 (2021)
42. Voigtlaender, P., et al.: MOTS: multi object tracking and segmentation. In: CVPR, pp. 7942–7951 (2019)
43. Wang, C.Y., Bochkovskiy, A., Liao, H.Y.M.: Scaled-YOLOv4: scaling cross stage partial network. arXiv preprint arXiv:2011.08036 (2020)
44. Wang, Q., Zheng, Y., Pan, P., Xu, Y.: Multiple object tracking with correlation learning. In: Proceedings of the IEEE/CVF Conference on Computer Vision and Pattern Recognition, pp. 3876–3886 (2021)
45. Wang, Z., Zheng, L., Liu, Y., Wang, S.: Towards real-time multi-object tracking. arXiv preprint arXiv:1909.12605 (2019)
46. Wei, L., Zhang, S., Gao, W., Tian, Q.: Person transfer GAN to bridge domain gap for person re-identification. In: Proceedings of the IEEE Conference on Computer Vision and Pattern Recognition, pp. 79–88 (2018)
47. Welch, G., Bishop, G., et al.: An introduction to the Kalman filter (1995)
48. Wojke, N., Bewley, A., Paulus, D.: Simple online and realtime tracking with a deep association metric. In: 2017 IEEE International Conference on Image Processing (ICIP), pp. 3645–3649. IEEE (2017)
49. Xu, J., Cao, Y., Zhang, Z., Hu, H.: Spatial-temporal relation networks for multi-object tracking. In: Proceedings of the IEEE/CVF International Conference on Computer Vision, pp. 3988–3998 (2019)
50. Xu, Y., Osep, A., Ban, Y., Horaud, R., Leal-Taixé, L., Alameda-Pineda, X.: How to train your deep multi-object tracker. In: Proceedings of the IEEE/CVF Conference on Computer Vision and Pattern Recognition, pp. 6787–6796 (2020)
51. Yan, B., et al.: Towards grand unification of object tracking. In: ECCV (2022)
52. Yang, F., Choi, W., Lin, Y.: Exploit all the layers: fast and accurate CNN object detector with scale dependent pooling and cascaded rejection classifiers. In: Proceedings of the IEEE Conference on Computer Vision and Pattern Recognition, pp. 2129–2137 (2016)
53. Yoon, Y.C., Kim, D.Y., Song, Y.M., Yoon, K., Jeon, M.: Online multiple pedestrians tracking using deep temporal appearance matching association. Inf. Sci. **561**, 326–351 (2020)
54. Zhang, Y., Sheng, H., Wu, Y., Wang, S., Ke, W., Xiong, Z.: Multiplex labeling graph for near-online tracking in crowded scenes. IEEE Internet Things J. **7**(9), 7892–7902 (2020)
55. Zhang, Y., et al.: Long-term tracking with deep tracklet association. IEEE Trans. Image Process. **29**, 6694–6706 (2020)

56. Zhang, Y., et al.: ByteTrack: multi-object tracking by associating every detection box. arXiv preprint arXiv:2110.06864 (2021)
57. Zhang, Y., Wang, C., Wang, X., Liu, W., Zeng, W.: VoxelTrack: multi-person 3D human pose estimation and tracking in the wild. IEEE Trans. Pattern Anal. Mach. Intell. (2022)
58. Zhang, Y., Wang, C., Wang, X., Zeng, W., Liu, W.: FairMOT: on the fairness of detection and re-identification in multiple object tracking. Int. J. Comput. Vision **129**(11), 3069–3087 (2021)
59. Zheng, L., Shen, L., Tian, L., Wang, S., Wang, J., Tian, Q.: Scalable person re-identification: a benchmark. In: Proceedings of the IEEE International Conference on Computer Vision, pp. 1116–1124 (2015)
60. Zhou, X., Koltun, V., Krähenbühl, P.: Tracking objects as points. In: Vedaldi, A., Bischof, H., Brox, T., Frahm, J.-M. (eds.) ECCV 2020. LNCS, vol. 12349, pp. 474–490. Springer, Cham (2020). https://doi.org/10.1007/978-3-030-58548-8_28
61. Zhou, X., Wang, D., Krähenbühl, P.: Objects as points. arXiv preprint arXiv:1904.07850 (2019)

PolarMOT: How Far Can Geometric Relations Take us in 3D Multi-object Tracking?

Aleksandr Kim$^{(\boxtimes)}$, Guillem Brasó, Aljoša Ošep, and Laura Leal-Taixé

Technical University of Munich, Munich, Germany
{aleksandr.kim,guillem.braso,aljosa.osep,leal.taixe}@tum.de

Abstract. Most (3D) multi-object tracking methods rely on appearance-based cues for data association. By contrast, we investigate *how far we can get* by only encoding geometric relationships between objects in 3D space as cues for data-driven data association. We encode 3D detections as nodes in a graph, where spatial and temporal pairwise relations among objects are encoded via *localized polar* coordinates on graph edges. This representation makes our geometric relations invariant to global transformations and smooth trajectory changes, especially under non-holonomic motion. This allows our graph neural network to learn to effectively encode *temporal and spatial* interactions and fully leverage contextual and motion cues to obtain final scene interpretation by posing data association as edge classification. We establish a new state-of-the-art on nuScenes dataset and, more importantly, show that our method, *PolarMOT*, generalizes remarkably well across different locations (Boston, Singapore, Karlsruhe) and datasets (nuScenes and KITTI).

Keywords: 3D multi-object tracking · Graph neural networks · Lidar scene understanding

1 Introduction

Intelligent agents such as autonomous vehicles need to understand dynamic objects in their surroundings to safely navigate the world. 3D multi-object tracking (MOT) is, therefore, an essential component of autonomous intelligent systems (Fig. 1).

State-of-the-art methods leverage the representational power of neural networks to learn appearance models [56,63] or regress velocity vectors [61] as cues for data association. While powerful, such methods need to be trained for the specific environments in which they are deployed. Methods such as [9,55] rely

Supplementary Information The online version contains supplementary material available at https://doi.org/10.1007/978-3-031-20047-2_3.

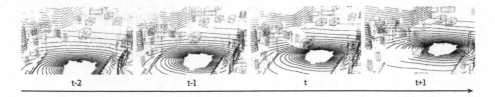

Fig. 1. PolarMOT tracks objects in 3D (offline and online) using a graph neural network that learns to associate 3D bounding boxes over time solely based on their relative geometric features and spatio-temporal interactions.

on motion as the key cue for association and can thus generalize across different environments. However, performance-wise they lag behind data-driven methods as they treat individual objects in isolation and do not consider their interactions.

In this work, we investigate *how far we can get* by learning to track objects given *only geometric cues* in the form relative pose differences between 3D bounding boxes *without* relying on any appearance information. This approach is not coupled to any specific object detector, sensor modality, or region-specific appearance models. Consequentially, it generalizes well across different environments and geographic locations, as we experimentally demonstrate. By contrast to prior work [55] that rely on individual object motion as the main association cue, our method can learn how objects move as a group, taking into account their interactions to better adapt to dynamic environments and crowded scenarios.

As graphs are a natural representation for such long-term agent interactions, we represent our scene as a *sparse, multiplex* graph, which is then processed by a graph neural network (Fig. 2). We encode 3D detection as nodes, while edges represent their *spatial* and *temporal* relations and denote possible associations and influences. After several message passing steps in this graph, our neural network outputs binary classifications for all *temporal* edges. All nodes connected with a positive edge form a track and thus get assigned a consistent track ID [5].

One of our main insights is that encoding pairwise geometric relations, *i.e.*, edge features, in *localized polar* instead of Cartesian space is the key to good generalization and robustness and enables our model to effectively learn to track by *solely* relying on geometric cues. The pair-specific nature of the features makes them invariant to global transforms. Thus, features encoding relations between different detections of an object that moves consistently will be *stable*, regardless of the route geometry or point of reference. Such polar representation also naturally encodes non-holonomic motion prior, *i.e.*, a motion that is constrained by heading direction and is well parametrized by heading angle and velocity.

We evaluate our method on KITTI [13] and nuScenes dataset [8]. Our ablations reveal that our proposed graph structure and edge feature parametrization are pivotal for our final model to achieve 66.4 average AMOTA, setting a new state-of-the-art on nuScenes MOT dataset among lidar-based methods. More importantly, we show that our learning-based framework that relies only on geometry leads to strong generalization across different geographic regions (Boston, Singapore, Karlsruhe) and datasets (nuScenes, KITTI), without fine-tuning. We are not suggesting to *not use* appearance cues, but rather point out we can get very far with a minimalistic, graph-based tracking, solely relying on geometric cues and inferring object properties implicitly from their interactions.

To **summarize**, (i) we propose a minimalistic, graph-based 3D tracker that relies only on geometric cues and, without any bells and whistles or image/lidar input, establish new state-of-the-art on the nuScenes dataset; (ii) we suggest a graph-based representation of the scene that encodes temporal and spatial relations via a localized polar representation. This is not only to achieve state-of-the-art performance on benchmarks but, more importantly, is the key to strong generalization; (iii) as efficiency and online operation are crucial for robotic/AV scenarios, we construct a sparse graph and only establish links that are feasible based on maximal possible velocity and show how such sparse graphs can be constructed in an online fashion. We hope our code and models, available at polarmot.github.io, will run on friendly future robots!

2   Related Work

This section reviews relevant related work in 2D and 3D multi-object tracking (MOT) based on the well-established *tracking-by-detection* paradigm.

2D MOT. Early methods for vision-based MOT rely on hand-crafted appearance models [10,32] and motion cues [23,32], in conjunction with optimization frameworks for data association that go beyond simple bi-partite matching [20]. These include quadratic pseudo-boolean optimization [25], graph-based methods [6,7,40,45,64], conditional random fields [10,32] and lifted multi-cuts [50]. Orthogonally, the community has also been investigating lifting data association from image projective space to 3D using via (*e.g.*, stereo) depth maps [24,25,30,37,38,46].

In the era of deep learning, the community has been focusing on learning strong appearance models [22,49,54], future target locations [2,59] or predicting offset vectors as cues for association [65]. Recently, we have witnessed a resurgence in graph-based approaches for tracking. MPNTrack [5] encodes 2D object detections as nodes while edges represent possible associations among them. Then, a message passing [14] graph neural network (GNN) [15] is used to update node/edge representation with temporal context, as needed for reliable binary edge classification to obtain final tracks. Just as [5], we (i) encode detections as nodes, while edges represent hypothetical associations, and we (ii) learn to classify edges to obtain the final set of tracks. Different to [5], we tackle 3D MOT using *only* geometric cues. Our model encodes both, temporal and spatial relations and, importantly, encodes them via *localized polar coordinates*, that encode non-holonomic motion prior. Moreover, beyond *offline* use-case, we show how to construct *sparse* graphs in *online* fashion, as needed in mobile robotics.

3D MOT. Early methods for 3D detection and tracking [11,39] model vehicles as cuboids or rely on bottom-up point cloud segmentation [16,33,51] and track

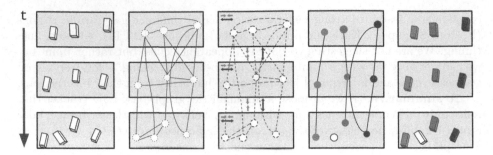

Fig. 2. Given a set of 3D bounding boxes in a sequence, *PolarMOT* constructs a graph encoding detections as nodes, and their geometric relations as *spatial* and *temporal* edges. After refining edge features via message passing with wider spatial and temporal context, we classify edges to obtain object track predictions. (Color figure online)

objects using (extended) Kalman filter. Thanks to developments in deep point-based representation learning [42,43,52,66], we nowadays have strong backbones, as needed for 3D object detection [21,41,47,60,61,66], tracking [9,12,55] and segmentation [1]. AB3DMOT [55] shows that well-localized lidar-based 3D object detections work very well in conjunction with a simple Kalman filter based tracking framework [4]. Association can be performed based on 3D bounding box overlap or centroid-based Mahalanobis distance [9] to increase robustness to lower frame rates. State-of-the-art CenterPoint [61] learns to detect objects as points and regresses velocity vectors needed for the association. Similar to ours, OGR3MOT [62] also tackles 3D MOT using message passing networks based framework, proposed by [5]. However, it represents detections *and* tracks as two distinct types of nodes, thus effectively maintaining two subgraphs. *Different* to that, *our PolarMOT* implicitly derives node embeddings from relational (edge) features parametrized via proposed local polar coordinates. A recent body of work proposes to fuse image and lidar data [17,56,63]. GNN3DMOT [56] utilizes GNNs to learn appearance and motion features for data association jointly. This approach relies on Hungarian algorithm to perform data association based on the learned features. *Different* to that, we *only* use 3D geometric cues and perform association directly via edge classification in end-to-end manner.

3   Message Passing Networks for Multi-object Tracking

Our work is inspired by MPNTrack [5], an image-based MOT method that we summarize for completeness. MPNTrack models detections as graph nodes and represents possible associations via edges. After propagating features via neural message passing [14], edges are classified as active/inactive.

MPNTrack processes a clip of frames with detected objects, and outputs classifications of links between them. For each clip, input is a set of object detections $\mathcal{O} = \{o_i\}_{i=1}^{n}$, represented via an (appearance) embedding vector, 2D position and timestamp. Then, a graph $G = (V, E)$ where $V = \mathcal{O}$ and $E \subset \mathcal{O} \times \mathcal{O}$. MPNTrack

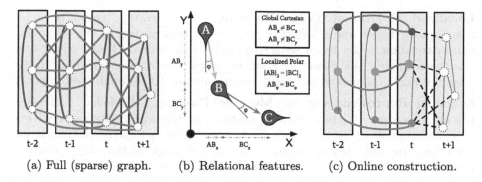

(a) Full (sparse) graph.   (b) Relational features.   (c) Online construction.

Fig. 3. The key contributions of our work: multiplex input graph with *inter-frame (temporal)* and *intra-frame (spatial)* edges, relative geometric features in localized polar coordinates and continuously evolving online graph construction.

encodes only inter-frame edges and heuristically prunes them for sparsity. Each node $o_i \in V$ and edge $e_{ij} \in E$ (connecting o_i, o_j) have corresponding initial embeddings $h_i^{(0)}$ and $h_{(i,j)}^{(0)}$ obtained from appearance and position cues. These embeddings are propagated across the graph via neural message passing for a fixed number of iterations L to obtain updated edge features $h_{(i,j)}^{(1,...,L)}$.

More specifically, edge embeddings are updated at each message passing step based on embeddings from the previous step of the edge itself and its neighboring nodes. Nodes are then updated based on previous embeddings of the node and neighboring edges, which are aggregated separately for forward and backward directions in time. After L message passing updates, edges are classified based on their embeddings from all steps, $h_{(i,j)}^{(1,...,L)}$, where positive classification implies that two connected detections are part of the same track (identity).

4 PolarMOT

In this section, we provide a high-level overview of our *PolarMOT*, followed by a detailed discussion of our key ideas and components.

4.1 Method Overview

PolarMOT encodes the overall geometric configuration of detected objects and the relative pose changes between them as primary cues for tracking.

Sparse Graph-Based Scene Representation. We use a graph to represent object detections as nodes, and their geometric relations as edges. We encode both *temporal* and *spatial* relations among objects in two levels of our *sparse multiplex* graph (Fig. 3a). The *temporal* level connects nodes across different frames with inter-frame edges, while the *spatial* level connects nodes of the same frame with intra-frame edges. For sparsity, we *only* link nodes that are mutually reachable based on the maximal velocity of their semantic class.

Localized Relational Polar Encoding. We encode geometric relations among nodes via a localized polar-based representation (Fig. 3b). Our parametrization is not based on a shared global coordinate frame but is specific to each pair's local frame. This makes our parametrization *invariant* to the reference world frame, and induces a *non-holonomic* (directional) motion prior.

Learning Representation via Message Passing. We follow a message passing procedure [14] to iteratively update our features through alternating edge/node updates (Fig. 2, *center*). Node features are not extracted from input detections. Instead, they are learned *implicitly* through mutual object interactions.

Edge Classification. To obtain object tracks, we classify our *temporal* edges using a multi-layer perceptron based on final edge representations (Fig. 2, *right*).

Online Graph Construction. For *online* tracking, we continuously evolve our input graph after each frame, while maintaining both sparsity and high connectivity (Fig. 3c). For online processing, we connect past track predictions directly to the most recent detections, thus allowing our network to infer historical context effectively via message passing on the graph topology.

4.2 Message Passing on a Sparse Multiplex Graph

Representation. Following [5], we represent each individual object detection as a *node* of the graph with *edges* encoding relations between objects. More precisely, we model *temporal* and *spatial* relations between objects (graph nodes) by encoding our 3D detections via a *sparse*, undirected *multiplex* graph with two distinct levels/edge types (Fig. 3a). In the *first level* we model temporal connections via undirected *inter-frame* edges between nodes across frames [5], which describe potential motion of objects. Each edge connects two distinct detections across frames. The edge features denote the likelihood of an object moving from pose/node A to pose/node B in the elapsed time. In the *second level*, we introduce undirected *intra-frame* edges (*i.e.*, links between nearby detections from the same frame) to model spatial context. These edges act as pathways to exchange frame-specific context and are meant to express the mutual influence of moving targets' motion patterns. This should intuitively help with difficult and ambiguous cases that arise in crowded scenarios. Both inter- and intra-frame edges connect the same set of nodes, but convey semantically different information, effectively turning our graph into a multiplex network with two distinct levels. *Intra-frame* edges are excluded from edge classification.

Sparse Graph Construction. To handle occlusions, we connect nodes across any number of frames. Doing this naively would potentially result in a prohibitively dense graph. To ensure graph sparsity, we take full advantage of the 3D domain, and rely on physical constraints to establish only *relevant*, physically-plausible spatial or temporal relations. For *inter-frame edges*, if the physical distance between two detections is greater than the maximal velocity of the detected class, we consider it impossible for them to belong to the same object and do not form an edge. For *intra-frame edges*, we allow distance up to twice the maximal velocity to connect objects that could collide in the next frame if moving towards each other and, therefore, influence each other's movement.

Message Passing. Following the general message passing framework, our model performs a fixed number of alternating *edge* and *node* updates to obtain enhanced node/edge representation, as needed for edge classification.

Edge Update: At every message passing iteration $l = 1, \ldots, L$, we first update edge embeddings by learning to fuse the edge and connected node embeddings from the previous message passing iteration. More precisely, we update edge embedding $h_{(i,j)}$ between nodes o_i and o_j as follows:

$$h_{(i,j)}^{(l)} = \text{MLP}_{\text{edge}} \left(\left[h_i^{(l-1)}, h_{(i,j)}^{(l-1)}, h_j^{(l-1)} \right] \right). \tag{1}$$

During each update, the edge embedding from the previous message passing iteration $l - 1$, i.e., $h_{(i,j)}^{(l-1)}$, is concatenated with embeddings $(h_i^{(l-1)}, h_j^{(l-1)})$ of the connected nodes. The result is then fused by MLP_{edge}, a Multi-Layer Perceptron (MLP), which produces the fused edge features $h_{(i,j)}^{(l)}$ (Eq. 1). This edge embedding update is identical for all edge types and directions.

Node Update: To update nodes, first, we construct messages for each edge $h_{(i,j)}^{(l)}$ via learned fusion of *its updated edge* and *neighboring nodes'* features:

$$m_{(i,j)}^{(l)} = \begin{cases} \text{MLP}_{\text{past}} \left([h_i^{(l-1)}, h_{(i,j)}^{(l)}, h_j^{(l-1)}] \right) \text{ if } t_j < t_i, \\ \text{MLP}_{\text{pres}} \left([h_i^{(l-1)}, h_{(i,j)}^{(l)}, h_{(j)}^{(l-1)}] \right) \text{ if } t_i = t_j, \\ \text{MLP}_{\text{fut}} \left([h_i^{(l-1)}, h_{(i,j)}^{(l)}, h_j^{(l-1)}] \right) \text{ if } t_j > t_i. \end{cases} \tag{2}$$

Via *inter-frame edges* we produce two messages for each temporal direction: we produce *past* features via MLP_{past} and *future* features via MLP_{fut} (only in offline tracking settings). At the same time, we produce *present* features via MLP_{pres} for each *intra-frame*, spatial, edge. Using separate MLPs allows our model to learn different embeddings for each type of relationship.

Node Aggregation: Then, each node $h_i^{(l)}$ *aggregates* incoming messages using an element-wise max operator, separately for past, present and future edges to maintain contextual awareness. The resulting aggregated vectors are concatenated and fused via MLP_{node}:

$$h_i^{(l)} = \text{MLP}_{\text{node}}([\max_{t_j < t_i} m_{(i,j)}^{(l)}, \max_{t_i = t_j} m_{(i,j)}^{(l)}, \max_{t_j > t_i} m_{(i,j)}^{(l)}]). \tag{3}$$

As we do not use any object-specific information (*e.g.*, appearance), we rely on the model to implicitly learn node features from their interactions.

Initialization: We *initialize* edge embeddings with relational features (as detailed in Sect. 4.3) processed by $\text{MLP}_{\text{edge\_init}}$ (Eq. 4). These are then directly aggregated to produce *initial node embeddings* via $\text{MLP}_{\text{node\_init}}$ (Eq. 5):

$$\text{(initial edge)} \quad h_{(i,j)}^{(1)} = \text{MLP}_{\text{edge\_init}}(h_{(i,j)}^{(0)}), \tag{4}$$

$$\text{(initial node)} \quad h_i^{(1)} = \text{MLP}_{\text{node\_init}}([\max_{t_j < t_i} h_{(i,j)}^{(1)}, \max_{t_i = t_j} h_{(i,j)}^{(1)}, \max_{t_j > t_i} h_{(i,j)}^{(1)}]). \tag{5}$$

Tracking via Edge Classification.   After graph construction and message passing, we classify *inter-frame* edges, which encode *temporal* relations. Positive classification implies the same object identity for both detections (*i.e.*, a consistent track ID). Any edge connecting nodes of the same track should be labeled as positive, regardless of the time difference between the connected nodes.

4.3   Localized Relational Polar Encoding

Depth sensors do not provide comparatively rich appearance information as images; however, they do provide accurate distance measurements to objects. Therefore, we fully focus on efficiently representing relative poses via edge features and learn node features implicitly. This leads to the question of how to represent geometric relations between objects efficiently? We start by representing each 3D detection as an oriented point with two planar coordinates x, y and orientation ϕ around vertical axis z, as differences in elevation, tilt, and spatial dimensions are insignificant between objects of the same class.

Global Cartesian Coordinates.   Traditionally, spatial geometric relations between objects are parametrized in Cartesian coordinates relative to some reference frame, encoding an edge $h_{i,j}^{(0)}$ connecting nodes o_i and o_j as:

$$h_{i,j}^{(0)} = \Delta(o_i, o_j) = \begin{bmatrix} \Delta x \\ \Delta y \\ \dots \end{bmatrix} = \begin{bmatrix} o_i^x - o_j^x \\ o_i^y - o_j^y \\ \dots \end{bmatrix}. \tag{6}$$

As shown in Fig. 3b, for *identical* pose changes $\overrightarrow{AB}$ and $\overrightarrow{BC}$, global Cartesian features are *not identical*, as they depend on the orientation of the reference frame. *Identical motion non-intuitively leads to different relational features.*

Localized Polar Coordinates.   We propose a different representation, which depends (i) only on the relevant pair of objects, o_i and o_j, and (ii) is more suitable for encoding directional non-holonomic motion. Our parametrization (Fig. 3b) expresses differences in poses A and B through a velocity vector, expressed in *polar coordinates*, where the center of the first detection A is the *pole* (*i.e.*, the origin of the polar coordinate frame), and its heading direction (downward) is the *polar axis*. This vector includes two components: *velocity* $|AB|$ (*i.e.*, distance between objects by detection time difference), and *polar angle* φ, *i.e.*, the angle between $\overrightarrow{AB}$ and the polar axis of A (downward vector). We also include differences in object orientation (o^ϕ) and detection time difference (o^t):

$$h_{i,j}^{(0)} = \Delta(o_i, o_j) = \begin{bmatrix} v \\ \varphi_{i,j} \\ \Delta\phi \\ \Delta t \end{bmatrix} = \begin{bmatrix} \frac{\|o_i - o_j\|_2}{\Delta t} \\ \angle\left(o_i^{head}, o_j - o_i \right) \\ o_i^\phi - o_j^\phi \\ o_i^t - o_j^t \end{bmatrix}. \tag{7}$$

We remove the dependency on an arbitrary reference frame by computing each feature relative to individual localized frames. *Now, identical motion between $\overrightarrow{AB}$ and $\overrightarrow{BC}$ leads to identical feature representation.*

Polar coordinates explicitly encode the change in heading angle (φ). This intuitively encodes a *smooth, non-holonomic* motion prior. For example, polar features for trajectory $\overrightarrow{KL}$ and an (improbable) trajectory $\overrightarrow{MN}$ significantly differ, while their Cartesian coordinates do not. These key characteristics allow *PolarMOT* to generalize well even when trained with a small number of labeled samples (Sect. 5.4), especially important for rarely observed object classes.

4.4   Online Graph Construction

In this section, we propose an online graph construction approach that makes our method applicable to *online* applications. We maintain a *single* input graph for the whole sequence, which we continuously evolve with each incoming frame. This construction is identical to the *offline* setting, as discussed in Sect. 4.2. In each frame, edges are classified based on past-frame information *only*. There are multiple ways of maintaining a single input graph over a sequence of frames.

MPNTrack++: Dense.   First approach is a simple extension of prior offline GNN methods [5,26], where previous track associations do not influence the graph structure. At each frame, new nodes and edges are added to a continuously growing *dense* graph. *Such model is unaware of past track estimates.*

Prune Inactive: Consecutive.   Past track estimates are a valuable cue that could be leveraged to resolve ambiguous associations. To this end, [62] propose to simply prune all past (negative) edges. This option encodes track history and maintains sparsity and due to frame-by-frame processing, preserved track edges always connect temporally *consecutive* nodes in each track. However, over time, the temporal distance from the current frame to early track nodes is increasing, making them unreachable within a limited number of message passing iterations. *This approach thus has a limited temporal receptive field.*

Ours: Prune + Skip.   We propose a simple solution, that retains graph sparsity and provides global temporal receptive field from each newly-added node. After each frame, we remove all *past negative* edges *and* ensure we have, for each track, an edge between *each* most-recent track node and *all* past nodes from its track, see Fig. 3c. Moreover, new nodes (detections) at each frame are *only* connected to the most-recent track node for each existing track. By continuously evolving the graph in this manner we maintain sparsity, provide previous tracking decisions to the model through the input graph topology (this makes our model autoregressive) and keep all nodes reachable during message passing: any two connected nodes have at most two edges between them. *This allows our model to learn historical context directly via message passing to make well-informed edge classification, as needed for long-term tracking.*

4.5   Implementation Details

Network Structure.   In *PolarMOT*, we use only fully connected (FC) layers with the leaky ReLU [35] nonlinearity, and the dimensionality of the edge and

Table 1. Results of state-of-the-art methods for 3D multi-object tracking on the NuScenes test set. Legend: L – lidar, B – 3D bounding boxes

Method name	Input modality	IDs ↓ total	Recall ↑ average	AMOTA ↑ average	Class-specific AMOTA ↑						
					Car	Ped	Bicycle	Bus	Motor	Trailer	Truck
Ours	3D (B)	**242**	**70.2**	**66.4**	**85.3**	**80.6**	34.9	70.8	**65.6**	**67.3**	60.2
OGR3MOT [62]	3D (B)	288	69.2	65.6	81.6	78.7	**38.0**	**71.1**	64.0	67.1	59.0
CenterPoint [61]	3D (L)	684	68.0	65.0	81.8	78.0	33.1	71.5	58.7	69.3	**62.5**
IPRL-TRI [9]	3D (B)	950	60.0	55.0	71.9	74.5	25.5	64.1	48.1	49.5	51.3
AlphaTrack [63]	3D + 2D	718	72.3	69.3	84.2	74.3	47.1	72.0	72.8	72.0	62.6
EagerMOT [17]	3D + 2D	1156	72.7	67.7	81.0	74.4	58.3	74.0	62.5	63.6	59.7

node features is 16 and 32 respectively. Our MLP_{node} and MLP_{node_init} consist of 3 FC layers. Remaining MLPs consist of 2 layers with 70k parameters in total.

Training and Augmentation. We train *PolarMOT* only on keyframes from the nuScenes [8] dataset, which we augment with noise dropout to mimic real detection performance. To mimic occlusions and false negatives, we randomly drop full frames, individual bounding boxes, and edges. To mimic false positives, we randomly add bounding boxes. We also perturb boxes by adding Gaussian noise to 3D positions and orientation. We train *PolarMOT* with focal loss [27], which is well suited for our imbalanced binary classification case. We use Radam optimizer [19,28] using cosine annealing with warm restarts [29] for 180 epochs with batch size of 64. For more details, we refer to the supplementary.

5   Experimental Evaluation

This section outlines our evaluation setting: datasets, metrics and 3D object detections used as input during evaluations (Sect. 5.1). Next, in Sect. 5.2, we discuss our *offline* tracking results on the nuScenes test set and *online* and *offline* performance on the validation set compared to the current state-of-the-art. Then, we justify our design decisions and discuss the benefits of our contributions via thorough ablation studies (Sect. 5.3). Finally, we demonstrate the generalization capabilities of *PolarMOT* by showing that it can be applied to different datasets and locations without fine-tuning (Sect. 5.4).

5.1   Evaluation Setting

Datasets. We evaluate our method on nuScenes [8] and KITTI [13] tracking datasets. NuScenes was recorded in four locations across two cities: Boston, USA, and Singapore. It contains 150 scenes, recorded with a 32-beam lidar sensor, and provides two scans per second (2 Hz). KITTI tracking dataset was recorded in Karlsruhe, Germany, using a 64-beam lidar sensor at 10 Hz frame rate. Unless otherwise specified, we follow the official train/validation/test splits.

Evaluation Metric. On the nuScenes dataset, we follow the official evaluation protocol that reports per-class and average AMOTA [55], which averages the

Table 2. Online vs. offline tracking on the nuScenes validation set [8]

Method name	Input modality	IDs ↓ total	Recall ↑ average	AMOTA ↑ average	Class-specific AMOTA ↑						
					Car	Ped	Bicycle	Bus	Motor	Trailer	Truck
Ours *offl.*	3D	**213**	75.14	**71.14**	**85.83**	**81.70**	54.10	**87.36**	72.32	48.67	**68.03**
Ours *onl.*	3D	439	72.46	67.27	81.26	78.79	49.38	82.76	67.19	45.80	65.70
CenterPoint *onl.*	3D	562	70.62	65.91	84.23	77.29	43.70	80.16	59.16	**51.47**	65.39

Table 3. Ablation on parametrization of geometric relations among objects on nuScenes validation set. Trained on the **official mini** training set

Localized polar	Normalized by time	IDs ↓ total	Recall ↑ average	AMOTA ↑ average	Class-specific AMOTA ↑						
					Car	Ped	Bicycle	Bus	Motor	Trailer	Truck
✓	✓	430	**62.12**	**57.96**	**85.16**	**80.80**	**44.02**	**80.68**	45.83	**5.41**	**63.83**
✓	✗	652	55.07	52.17	81.51	80.14	06.66	79.53	53.82	0	63.51
✗	✓	1321	41.06	40.41	78.77	78.80	0	67.62	0	0	57.66

CLEAR-MOT [3] MOTA metric across different recall thresholds. On KITTI, we also report sAMOTA [55] and HOTA [31] metrics, which allows us to analyze detection and association errors separately. We also report the number of identity switches (IDs) at the best performing recall. In the supplementary, we provide extended tables and evaluations that we omitted for brevity.

Object Detections. On nuScenes, for a fair comparison with CenterPoint [61], we use their provided 3D detections (without the estimated velocity vectors). On KITTI, we use PointGNN [48] detections provided by EagerMOT [17].

5.2   Benchmark Results

We compare our method to state-of-the-art 3D MOT on the official nuScenes benchmark. In Table 1 (*top*) we compare methods that rely *only* on the 3D input. As can be seen, our model ranks highest overall (66.4 avg. AMOTA compared to 2nd best 65.6). Our method only lags behind methods that additionally rely on rich visual signal (AlphaTrack and EagerMOT). While our focus was on effectively leveraging geometric relations, this hints that our approach could potentially further benefit from sensor fusion, which we leave for future work.

Online Tracking. To confirm that our approach successfully handles online scenarios, we evaluate it on the nuScenes validation set with streaming inputs. In Table 2 we compare our *offline* and *online* versions, and compare both to *online* state-of-the-art CenterPoint [61] using the same 3D detections for all.

Not surprisingly, our *offline* model achieves the top performance at 71.14 avg. AMOTA. When switching to *online* inference, we achieve 67.27 avg. AMOTA (-3.87), outperforming CenterPoint by $+1.36$ avg AMOTA (from 65.91). As expected, there is a noticeable difference between our *offline* and *online* variants, as the online version is effectively exposed to only half of the context available to its offline counterpart, which observes both past and future detections.

Table 4. Ablation for intra-frame edges on the nuScenes validation set

Intra-frame connections	IDs ↓ total	Recall ↑ average	AMOTA ↑ average	Class-specific AMOTA ↑						
				Car	Ped	Bicycle	Bus	Motorcycle	Trailer	Truck
✓	213	**75.14**	**71.14**	**85.83**	**81.70**	**54.10**	**87.36**	**72.32**	**48.67**	68.03
✗	198	72.74	70.09	85.44	80.51	52.88	86.78	69.87	46.61	**68.54**

Table 5. Sparse graph construction: the impact of reducing/increasing the maximal velocity threshold on online tracking (nuScenes validation set)

Max edge distance	IDs ↓ total	Recall ↑ average	AMOTP ↓ average	AMOTA ↑ Car	Class-specific AMOTA ↑					
					Ped	Bicycle	Bus	Motorcycle	Trailer	Truck
0.5x	1123	65.14	0.718	58.61	76.90	46.66	46.89	77.35	62.73	40.09	59.63
1.0x	**439**	**72.46**	**0.595**	**67.27**	81.26	**78.79**	49.38	82.76	**67.19**	**45.80**	65.70
2.0x	467	69.74	0.642	65.42	**81.28**	72.15	46.84	**83.45**	63.57	44.94	**65.70**

5.3   Model Ablation

Edge Parametrization. To measure the impact of our proposed representation of geometric relations, we train three models with different relative feature parametrizations. The main advantage of our *proposed polar* representation is in the inductive bias that helps the model better understand long trajectories and non-holonomic motion. We conduct this experiment in the low data regime using the official nuScenes mini-split (1% of training data) and evaluate them on the (non-overlapping) validation set (150 seq.) and report results in Table 3.

First row reports results obtained with our proposed model (time-normalized localized polar parametrization, together with orientation and time difference, as explained in Sect. 4.3). This approach yields 57.96 avg. AMOTA. Next is the model without time normalization, where the features include distance between nodes instead of velocity. Despite the time difference still being available in this configuration, we see that performing explicit time normalization yields an improvement of +**5.79** avg. AMOTA, confirming our intuition that encoding relative velocity instead of distance improves tracking by making features invariant to trajectory length. Lastly, we evaluate a model with the commonly-used global Cartesian representation and see that simply switching to our proposed localized polar parametrization gives a significant improvement of +17.55 avg. AMOTA. This validates our intuition that incorporating a domain-appropriate inductive bias improves generalization from scarce data. For completeness, we provide evaluations of all three configurations trained on the full training set in the supplementary.

Intra-frame Connections. *Does spatial context matter?* Table 4 shows that adding spatial *intra-frame* edges improves avg. AMOTA by +1.05 and significantly improves recall (+2.4%) at a marginal increase in IDs (+15). For better contextual awareness, we aggregate messages from temporal and spatial edges separately. An ablation study of this technique is in the supplementary material.

Table 6. Online graph construction analysis (nuScenes validation set)

Track connectivity	IDs ↓ total	Recall ↑ average	AMOTA ↑ average	Class-specific AMOTA ↑						
				Car	Pedestrian	Bicycle	Bus	Motorcycle	Trailer	Truck
Ours	**439**	**72.46**	**67.27**	**81.26**	**78.79**	49.38	**82.76**	**67.19**	**45.80**	**65.70**
Consecutive	485	69.90	66.03	81.04	77.37	48.84	82.45	66.58	40.66	65.23
Dense	1024	68.58	61.39	71.08	75.20	**49.70**	79.78	52.03	41.15	60.79

Table 7. CenterPoint (CP) [61] and our method when trained on training data from one city, and evaluated on the validation data from another

Train city → eval city	Tracking model	IDs ↓ total	Recall ↑ average	AMOTA ↑ average	Class-specific AMOTA ↑						
					Car	Ped	Bicycle	Bus	Motor	Trailer	Truck
Boston	Ours	**145**	**64.48**	**63.12**	**82.26**	**72.81**	**31.49**	77.70	**43.17**	0	**71.28**
→ Singapore	CP	306	61.02	59.71	79.26	67.47	20.52	**78.86**	41.13	0	71.04
Singapore	Ours	**104**	52.30	**50.28**	**78.60**	**82.59**	**36.70**	**71.22**	**28.71**	11.31	42.83
→ Boston	CP	314	**53.32**	47.06	77.01	76.18	34.86	71.07	13.54	**13.18**	**43.55**

Sparse Graph Construction. *What is the impact of our sparse graph construction on tracking performance?* In Table 5 we compare results obtained by models using half (0.5x) and double (2.0x) of the measured maximal velocity values to constrain edges with the ones from our default model (1x). Reducing maximum allowed velocity (0.5x) removes valuable edges that hypothesize valid associations, while permitting higher values (2x) introduces irrelevant edges. In both cases, we observe a significant performance drop across all metrics (recall, precision, AMOTA), due to message passing becoming less complete and noisier and edge classification more challenging. This confirms that our data-driven physics-based sparse graph construction is the optimal approach.

Evolving Online Graph Connectivity. To validate our proposed approach to online graph connectivity, we present ablation experiments that confirm the advantage of our technique over alternatives discussed in Sect. 4.4. As shown in Table 6, our experimental results align with our expectations based on the theoretical properties of each option. *Dense* (MPNTrack++) linking (61.39 avg. AMOTA) completely ignores past trajectories and produces the lowest results. Next, *consecutive* (prune inactive) chaining introduces a significant improvement with 66.03 avg. AMOTA. Finally, our proposed *prune + skip* connectivity leads to a significant improvement over both alternatives with 67.27 avg. AMOTA.

5.4   Generalization Study

In this section, we show how *PolarMOT* generalizes across geographic locations and datasets. To this end, we (i) use the nuScenes dataset, recorded in Singapore and Boston, to train the model on one city and evaluate on the other and (ii) evaluate our model, trained on nuScenes, on KITTI data without any fine-tuning.

Cross-City Generalization: Boston ↔ Singapore. In this cross-city evaluation we compare our method to CenterPoint (we use detections from the corresponding re-trained CenterPoint model). As shown in Table 7, our method generalizes significantly better: +3.41 avg. AMOTA on Boston (trained) → Singapore (evaluated) and +3.33 avg. AMOTA on Singapore → Boston. In both cases we also observe a significant improvement in both recall and number of ID-switches. This confirms that our method generalizes very well across regions, which we believe is largely due to our feature parametrization (Sect. 4.3).

Cross-Dataset Generalization: nuScenes → KITTI. We report our results on the unofficial KITTI 3D MOT benchmark [55] in Table 8, and on the official KITTI 2D MOT benchmark in Table 9. We *only* evaluate our nuScenes-trained model on KITTI dataset, which we consider an ultimate generalization experiment, as KITTI dataset was recorded using a different sensor under a different frame rate in a different geographical location (Karlsruhe, Germany). For 2D MOT evaluation we simply project our estimated 3D tracks to the image plane. We note that entries are not directly comparable, as different methods use different input detections. However, we observe our method is on-par with Eager-MOT [18], which uses lidar and cameras, and the same set of 3D detections.

Table 8. Unofficial KITTI 3D MOT validation set benchmark [55]. Our model was trained **only** on nuScenes dataset

Method name	3D input	2D input	IDs ↓ Car	Ped	sAMOTA ↑ Car	Ped	MOTA ↑ Car	Ped	Recall ↑ Car	Ped
Ours *online*	✓	✗	31	9	94.32	**94.08**	93.93	**93.48**	94.54	**93.66**
PC-TCNN [58]	✓	✗	**1**	–	**95.44**	–	unpub	–	unpub	–
EagerMOT [17]	✓	✓	2	36	94.94	92.95	**96.61**	93.14	**96.92**	93.61
GNN3DMOT [56]	✓	✓	10	–	93.68	–	84.70	–	unpub	–
AB3DMOT [55]	✓	✗	0	1	91.78	73.18	83.35	66.98	92.17	72.82

Table 9. KITTI 2D MOT test set benchmark. Our model was trained **only** on nuScenes dataset

Method name	3D input	2D input	IDs ↓ Car	Ped	HOTA ↑ Car	Ped	AssA ↑ Car	Ped	AssRe ↑ Car	Ped	MOTA ↑ Car	Ped
Ours *online*	✓	✗	462	270	75.16	43.59	76.95	48.12	80.00	51.95	85.08	46.98
PC-TCNN [58]	✓	✗	**37**	–	**80.90**	–	**84.13**	–	**87.46**	–	**91.70**	–
PermaTrack [53]	✗	✓	258	403	78.03	48.63	78.41	45.61	81.14	49.63	91.33	65.98
PC3T [57]	✓	✗	225	–	77.80	–	81.59	–	84.77	– 5	88.81	–
Mono_3D_KF [44]	✗	✓	162	267	75.47	42.87	77.63	46.31	80.23	52.86	88.48	45.44
EagerMOT [17]	✓	✓	239	496	74.39	39.38	74.16	38.72	76.24	40.98	87.82	49.82
SRK_ODESA [34]	✗	✓	380	511	68.51	**50.87**	63.08	48.78	65.89	53.45	87.79	**68.04**
3D-TLSR [36]	✗	✓	–	175	–	46.34	–	**51.32**	–	**54.45**	–	53.58
MPNTrack [5]	✗	✓	–	397	–	45.26	–	47.28	–	52.18	–	46.23

PolarMOT is top-performer on the 3D benchmark and among top-4 on the 2D benchmark, performing consistently well on *car* and *pedestrian* classes.

6 Conclusion

We presented *PolarMOT* for 3D multi-object tracking that solely relies on 3D bounding boxes as input without appearance/shape information. Our key contribution is a GNN that encodes spatial and temporal geometric relations via localized polar coordinates. This parametrization enables us to effectively learn to understand long-range temporal and spatial context via message passing and, solely from object interactions, learn a scene representation suitable for tracking via edge classification. We also propose an online graph construction technique to apply *PolarMOT* to streaming data. Our method establishes a new state-of-the-art on the nuScenes dataset among methods that do not rely on image data and, more importantly, generalizes well across geographic regions and datasets.

Acknowledgement. This research was partially funded by the Humboldt Foundation through the Sofja Kovalevskaja Award.

References

1. Aygün, M., et al.: 4D panoptic lidar segmentation. In: CVPR (2021)
2. Bergmann, P., Meinhardt, T., Leal-Taixé, L.: Tracking without bells and whistles. In: ICCV (2019)
3. Bernardin, K., Stiefelhagen, R.: Evaluating multiple object tracking performance: the clear mot metrics. JIVP **2008**, 1–10 (2008)
4. Bewley, A., Ge, Z., Ott, L., Ramos, F., Upcroft, B.: Simple online and realtime tracking. In: ICIP (2016)
5. Braso, G., Leal-Taixé, L.: Learning a neural solver for multiple object tracking. In: CVPR (2020)
6. Brendel, W., Amer, M.R., Todorovic, S.: Multi object tracking as maximum weight independent set. In: CVPR (2011)
7. Butt, A.A., Collins, R.T.: Multi-target tracking by Lagrangian relaxation to min-cost network flow. In: CVPR, June 2013
8. Caesar, H., et al.: nuScenes: a multimodal dataset for autonomous driving. In: CVPR (2020)
9. Chiu, H.K., Prioletti, A., Li, J., Bohg, J.: Probabilistic 3D multi-object tracking for autonomous driving. In: ICRA (2021)
10. Choi, W.: Near-online multi-target tracking with aggregated local flow descriptor. In: ICCV (2015)
11. Dellaert, F., Thorpe, C.: Robust car tracking using Kalman filtering and Bayesian templates. In: Conference on Intelligent Transportation Systems (1997)
12. Frossard, D., Urtasun, R.: End-to-end learning of multi-sensor 3D tracking by detection. ICRA (2018)
13. Geiger, A., Lenz, P., Urtasun, R.: Are we ready for autonomous driving? The KITTI vision benchmark suite. In: CVPR (2012)

14. Gilmer, J., Schoenholz, S.S., Riley, P.F., Vinyals, O., Dahl, G.E.: Neural message passing for quantum chemistry. In: International Conference on Machine Learning, pp. 1263–1272. PMLR (2017)
15. Gori, M., Monfardini, G., Scarselli, F.: A new model for learning in graph domains. In: IJCNN (2005)
16. Held, D., Levinson, J., Thrun, S., Savarese, S.: Combining 3D shape, color, and motion for robust anytime tracking. In: RSS (2014)
17. Kim, A., Ošep, A., Leal-Taixé, L.: EagerMOT: 3D multi-object tracking via sensor fusion. In: ICRA (2021)
18. Kim, D., Woo, S., Lee, J.Y., Kweon, I.S.: Video panoptic segmentation. In: CVPR (2020)
19. Kingma, D.P., Ba, J.: Adam: a method for stochastic optimization. In: ICLR (2015)
20. Kuhn, H.W., Yaw, B.: The Hungarian method for the assignment problem. Naval Res. Logist. Q., 83–97 (1955)
21. Lang, A.H., Vora, S., Caesar, H., Zhou, L., Yang, J., Beijbom, O.: PointPillars: fast encoders for object detection from point clouds. In: CVPR (2019)
22. Leal-Taixé, L., Canton-Ferrer, C., Schindler, K.: Learning by tracking: Siamese CNN for robust target association. In: CVPR Workshops (2016)
23. Leal-Taixé, L., Fenzi, M., Kuznetsova, A., Rosenhahn, B., Savarese, S.: Learning an image-based motion context for multiple people tracking. In: CVPR (2014)
24. Leibe, B., Leonardis, A., Schiele, B.: Robust object detection with interleaved categorization and segmentation. IJCV **77**(1–3), 259–289 (2008)
25. Leibe, B., Schindler, K., Cornelis, N., Gool, L.V.: Coupled object detection and tracking from static cameras and moving vehicles. PAMI **30**(10), 1683–1698 (2008)
26. Li, J., Gao, X., Jiang, T.: Graph networks for multiple object tracking. In: WACV (2020)
27. Lin, T.Y., Goyal, P., Girshick, R., He, K., Dollár, P.: Focal loss for dense object detection. In: ICCV (2017)
28. Liu, L., et al.: On the variance of the adaptive learning rate and beyond. In: ICLR, April 2020
29. Loshchilov, I., Hutter, F.: SGDR: stochastic gradient descent with warm restarts. In: ICLR (2017)
30. Luiten, J., Fischer, T., Leibe, B.: Track to reconstruct and reconstruct to track. RAL **5**(2), 1803–1810 (2020)
31. Luiten, J., et al.: HOTA: a higher order metric for evaluating multi-object tracking. IJCV **129**, 548–578 (2020)
32. Milan, A., Roth, S., Schindler, K.: Continuous energy minimization for multitarget tracking. PAMI **36**(1), 58–72 (2014)
33. Moosmann, F., Stiller, C.: Joint self-localization and tracking of generic objects in 3D range data. In: ICRA (2013)
34. Mykheievskyi, D., Borysenko, D., Porokhonskyy, V.: Learning local feature descriptors for multiple object tracking. In: ACCV (2020)
35. Nair, V., Hinton, G.E.: Rectified linear units improve restricted Boltzmann machines. In: ICML (2010)
36. Nguyen, U., Heipke, C.: 3d pedestrian tracking using local structure constraints. ISPRS J. Photogrammetry Remote Sens. **166**, 347–358 (2020)
37. Ošep, A., Mehner, W., Mathias, M., Leibe, B.: Combined image- and world-space tracking in traffic scenes. In: ICRA (2017)
38. Ošep, A., Mehner, W., Voigtlaender, P., Leibe, B.: Track, then decide: category-agnostic vision-based multi-object tracking. In: ICRA (2018)

39. Petrovskaya, A., Thrun, S.: Model based vehicle detection and tracking for autonomous urban driving. AR **26**, 123–139 (2009)
40. Pirsiavash, H., Ramanan, D., Fowlkes, C.C.: Globally-optimal greedy algorithms for tracking a variable number of objects. In: CVPR (2011)
41. Qi, C.R., Liu, W., Wu, C., Su, H., Guibas, L.J.: Frustum PointNets for 3D object detection from RGB-D data. In: CVPR (2017)
42. Qi, C.R., Su, H., Mo, K., Guibas, L.J.: PointNet: deep learning on point sets for 3D classification and segmentation. In: CVPR (2017)
43. Qi, C.R., Yi, L., Su, H., Guibas, L.J.: PointNet++: deep hierarchical feature learning on point sets in a metric space. In: NeurIPS (2017)
44. Reich, A., Wuensche, H.J.: Monocular 3D multi-object tracking with an EKF approach for long-term stable tracks. In: FUSION (2021)
45. Schulter, S., Vernaza, P., Choi, W., Chandraker, M.K.: Deep network flow for multi-object tracking. In: CVPR (2017)
46. Sharma, S., Ansari, J.A., Krishna Murthy, J., Madhava Krishna, K.: Beyond pixels. leveraging geometry and shape cues for online multi-object tracking. In: ICRA (2018)
47. Shi, S., Wang, X., Li, H.: PointRCNN: 3D object proposal generation and detection from point cloud. In: CVPR (2019)
48. Shi, W., Rajkumar, R.: Point-GNN: graph neural network for 3d object detection in a point cloud. In: CVPR (2020)
49. Son, J., Baek, M., Cho, M., Han, B.: Multi-object tracking with quadruplet convolutional neural networks. In: CVPR (2017)
50. Tang, S., Andres, B., Andriluka, M., Schiele, B.: Subgraph decomposition for multi-target tracking. In: CVPR (2015)
51. Teichman, A., Levinson, J., Thrun, S.: Towards 3D object recognition via classification of arbitrary object tracks. In: ICRA (2011)
52. Thomas, H., Qi, C.R., Deschaud, J.E., Marcotegui, B., Goulette, F., Guibas, L.J.: KPConv: flexible and deformable convolution for point clouds. In: ICCV (2019)
53. Tokmakov, P., Li, J., Burgard, W., Gaidon, A.: Learning to track with object permanence. In: ICCV (2021)
54. Voigtlaender, P., et al.: MOTS: multi-object tracking and segmentation. In: CVPR (2019)
55. Weng, X., Wang, J., Held, D., Kitani, K.: 3D multi-object tracking: a baseline and new evaluation metrics. In: IROS (2020)
56. Weng, X., Wang, Y., Man, Y., Kitani, K.: GNN3DMOT: graph neural network for 3D multi-object tracking with multi-feature learning. In: CVPR (2020)
57. Wu, H., Han, W., Wen, C., Li, X., Wang, C.: 3D multi-object tracking in point clouds based on prediction confidence-guided data association. IEEE TITS **23**, 5668–5677 (2021)
58. Wu, H., Li, Q., Wen, C., Li, X., Fan, X., Wang, C.: Tracklet proposal network for multi-object tracking on point clouds. In: IJCAI (2021)
59. Xu, Y., Ošep, A., Ban, Y., Horaud, R., Leal-Taixé, L., Alameda-Pineda, X.: How to train your deep multi-object tracker. In: CVPR (2020)
60. Yan, Y., Mao, Y., Li, B.: Second: sparsely embedded convolutional detection. Sensors **18**(10), 3337 (2018)
61. Yin, T., Zhou, X., Krähenbühl, P.: Center-based 3D object detection and tracking. In: CVPR (2021)
62. Zaech, J.N., Liniger, A., Dai, D., Danelljan, M., Van Gool, L.: Learnable online graph representations for 3D multi-object tracking. IEEE R-AL , 5103–5110 (2022)

63. Zeng, Y., Ma, C., Zhu, M., Fan, Z., Yang, X.: Cross-modal 3D object detection and tracking for auto-driving. In: IROS (2021)
64. Zhang, L., Yuan, L., Nevatia, R.: Global data association for multi-object tracking using network flows. In: CVPR (2008)
65. Zhou, X., Koltun, V., Krähenbühl, P.: Tracking objects as points. In: Vedaldi, A., Bischof, H., Brox, T., Frahm, J.-M. (eds.) ECCV 2020. LNCS, vol. 12349, pp. 474–490. Springer, Cham (2020). https://doi.org/10.1007/978-3-030-58548-8_28
66. Zhou, Y., Tuzel, O.: VoxelNet: end-to-end learning for point cloud based 3D object detection. In: CVPR (2018)

Particle Video Revisited: Tracking Through Occlusions Using Point Trajectories

Adam W. Harley$^{(\boxtimes)}$, Zhaoyuan Fang, and Katerina Fragkiadaki

Carnegie Mellon University, Pittsburgh, USA
{aharley,zhaoyuaf,katef}@cs.cmu.edu

Abstract. Tracking pixels in videos is typically studied as an optical flow estimation problem, where every pixel is described with a displacement vector that locates it in the next frame. Even though wider temporal context is freely available, prior efforts to take this into account have yielded only small gains over 2-frame methods. In this paper, we revisit Sand and Teller's "particle video" approach, and study pixel tracking as a long-range motion estimation problem, where every pixel is described with a trajectory that locates it in multiple future frames. We re-build this classic approach using components that drive the current state-of-the-art in flow and object tracking, such as dense cost maps, iterative optimization, and learned appearance updates. We train our models using long-range amodal point trajectories mined from existing optical flow data that we synthetically augment with multi-frame occlusions. We test our approach in trajectory estimation benchmarks and in keypoint label propagation tasks, and compare favorably against state-of-the-art optical flow and feature tracking methods.

1 Introduction

In 2006, Sand and Teller [25] wrote that there are two dominant approaches to motion estimation in video: feature matching and optical flow. This is still true today. In their paper, they proposed a new motion representation called a "particle video", which they presented as a middle-ground between feature tracking and optical flow. The main idea is to represent a video with a set of particles that move across multiple frames, and leverage long-range temporal priors while tracking the particles.

Methods for feature tracking and optical flow estimation have greatly advanced since that time, but there has been relatively little work on estimating long-range trajectories at the pixel level. Feature correspondence methods [4,39] currently work by matching the features of each new frame to the features of

Project page: https://particle-video-revisited.github.io.

© The Author(s), under exclusive license to Springer Nature Switzerland AG 2022
S. Avidan et al. (Eds.): ECCV 2022, LNCS 13682, pp. 59–75, 2022.
https://doi.org/10.1007/978-3-031-20047-2_4

Fig. 1. Persistent Independent Particles. Our method takes an RGB video as input, and estimates trajectories for any number of target pixels. Left: targets and their trajectories, shown separately. Right: trajectories overlaid on the pixels.

one or more source frames [17], without taking into account temporal context. Optical flow methods today produce such exceedingly-accurate estimates within pairs of frames [32] that the motion vectors can often be chained across time without much accumulation of error, but as soon as the target is occluded, it is no longer represented in the flow field, and tracking fails.

Particle videos have the potential to capture two key elements missing from feature-matching and optical flow: (1) persistence through occlusions, and (2) multi-frame temporal context. If we attend to a pixel that corresponds to a point on the world surface, we should expect that point to exist across time, even if appearance and position and visibility all vary somewhat unpredictably. Temporal context is of course widely known to be relevant for flow-based methods, but prior efforts to take multi-frame context into account have yielded only small gains. Flow-based methods mainly use consecutive pairs of frames, and occasionally leverage time with a simple constant-velocity prior, which weakly conditions the current flow estimate on previous frames' flow [23,32].

We propose Persistent Independent Particles (PIPs), a new particle video method, which takes a T-frame RGB video as input, along with the (x, y) coordinate of a target to track, and produces a $T \times 2$ matrix as output, representing the positions of the target across the given frames. The model can be queried for any number of particles, at any positions within the first frame's pixel grid. A defining feature of our approach, which differentiates it from both the original particle video algorithm and modern flow algorithms, is that it makes an extreme trade-off between spatial awareness and temporal awareness. *Our model estimates the trajectory of every target independently.* Computation is shared between particles within a video, which makes inference fast, but each particle produces its own trajectory, without inspecting the trajectories of its neighbors. This extreme choice allows us to devote the majority of parameters into a module that simultaneously learns (1) temporal priors, and (2) an iterative inference mechanism that searches for the target pixel's location in all input frames. The value of the temporal prior is that it allows the model to *fail* its correspondence task at multiple intermediate frames. As long as the pixel is "found" at some sparse timesteps within the considered temporal span, the model can use its prior to estimate plausible positions for the remaining timesteps. This is helpful because appearance-based correspondence is impossible in some frames, due to occlusions, moving out-of-bounds, or difficult lighting.

We train our model entirely in synthetic data, which we call FlyingThings++, based on the FlyingThings [20] optical flow dataset. Our dataset includes multi-frame amodal trajectories, with challenging synthetic occlusions caused by moving objects. In our experiments on both synthetic and real video data, we demonstrate that our particle trajectories are more robust to occlusions than flow trajectories—they can pick up an entity upon re-appearance—and also provide smoother and finer-grained correspondences than current feature-matching methods, thanks to its temporal prior. We also propose a method to link the model's moderate-length trajectories into arbitrarily-long trajectories, relying on a simultaneously-estimated visibility cue. Figure 1 displays sample outputs of our model on RGB videos from the DAVIS benchmark [22]. Our code and data are publicly available at https://particle-video-revisited.github.io.

2   Related Work

2.1   Optical Flow

Many classic methods track points independently [18,35], and such point tracks see wide use in structure-from-motion [2,15,21] and simultaneous localization and mapping systems [31]. While earlier optical flow methods use optimization techniques to estimate motion fields between two consecutive frames [3,29], recent methods learn such displacement fields supervised from synthetic datasets [6,10]. Many recent works use iterative refinements for flow estimation by leveraging coarse-to-fine pyramids [28]. Instead of coarse-to-fine refinements, RAFT [32] mimics an iterative optimization algorithm, and estimates flow through iterative updates of a high resolution flow field based on 4D correlation volumes constructed for all pairs of pixels from per-pixel features. Inspired by RAFT, we also perform iterative updates of the position estimations using correlations as an input, but unlike RAFT we additionally update features.

Ren et al. [23] propose a fusion approach for multi-frame optical flow estimation. The optical flow estimates of previous frames are used to obtain multiple candidate flow estimations for the current timestep, which are then fused into a final prediction by a learnable module. In contrast, our method explicitly reasons about multiframe context, and iteratively updates its estimates across all frames considered. Note that without using multiple frames, it is impossible to recover an entity after occlusion. Janai et al. [12] is closer to our method, since it uses 3 frames as multiframe context, and explicitly reasons about occlusions. That work uses a constant velocity prior [24] to estimate motion during occlusion. In contrast, we devote a large part of the model capacity to learning an accurate temporal prior, and iteratively updates its estimates across all frames considered, in search of the object's re-emergence from occlusion. Note that without using multiple frames, it is impossible to recover an entity after occlusion. Additionally, our model is the only work that aims to recover *amodal* trajectories that do not terminate at occlusions but rather can recover and re-connect with a visual entity upon its re-appearance.

2.2 Feature Matching

Wang and Jabri ct al. [11,39] leverage cycle consistency of time for feature matching. This allows unsupervised learning of features by optimizing a cycle consistency loss on the feature space across multiple time steps in unlabelled videos. Lai et al. [16,17] and Yang et al. [43] learn feature correspondence through optimizing a proxy reconstruction objective, where the goal is to reconstruct a target frame (color or flow) by linearly combining pixels from one or more reference frames. Instead of using proxy tasks, supervised approaches [8,13,38,40] directly train models using ground truth correspondences across images. Features are usually extracted per-image and a transformer-based processor locates correspondences between images. In our work, we reason about point correspondences over a long temporal horizon, incorporating motion context, instead of using pairs of frames like these works.

2.3 Tracking with Temporal Priors

Our work argues for using wide temporal context to track points, but this is not new for visual tracking in general. For decades, research on object-centric trackers has dealt with occlusions [46] and appearance changes [19], and non-linear pixel-space temporal priors [26], similar to our work. Here, we merely aim to bring the power of these object-tracking techniques down to the point level.

3   Persistent Independent Particles (PIPs)

3.1   Setup and Overview

Our work revisits the classic Particle Video [25] problem with a new algorithm, which we call Persistent Independent Particles (PIPs).[1] We take as input an RGB video with T frames, and the (x_1, y_1) coordinate of a pixel on the first frame, indicating the target to track. As output, we produce per-timestep coordinates (x_t, y_t) tracking the target across time, and per-timestep visibility/occlusion estimates $v_t \in [0, 1]$. The model can be queried for N target points in parallel, and some computation will be shared between them, but the model does not share information between the targets' trajectories.

At training time, we query the model with points for which we have ground-truth trajectories and visibility labels. We supervise the model's (x_t, y_t) outputs with a regression objective, and supervise v_t with a classification objective. At test time, the model can be queried for the trajectories of any number of points.

---

[1] The countable dots on playing cards, dice, or dominoes are also called "pips".

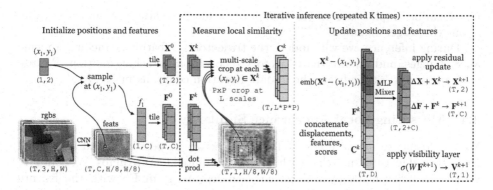

Fig. 2. Persistent Independent Particles (PIPs) architecture. Given an RGB video as input, along with a location in the first frame indicating what to track, our model initializes a multi-frame trajectory, then computes features and correlation maps, and iteratively updates the trajectory and its corresponding sequence of features, with a deep MLP-Mixer model. From the computed features, the model also estimates a visibility score for each timestep of the trajectory.

We use the words "point" and "particle" interchangeably to mean the things we are tracking, and use the word "pixel" more broadly to indicate any discrete cell on the image grid. Note that although the tracking targets are specified with single pixel coordinates, tracking successfully requires (at least) taking into account the local spatial context around the specified pixel.

Our overall approach has four stages, somewhat similar to the RAFT optical flow method [32]: extracting visual features (Sect. 3.2), initializing a list of positions and features for each target (Sect. 3.3), locally measuring appearance similarity (Sect. 3.4), and repeatedly updating the positions and features for each target (Sect. 3.5). Figure 2 shows an overview of the method.

3.2 Extracting Features

We begin by extracting features from every frame of the input video. In this step, each frame is processed independently with a 2D convolutional network (i.e., no temporal convolutions). The network produces features at 1/8 resolution.

3.3 Initializing Each Target

After computing feature maps for the video frames, we compute a feature vector for the target, by bilinearly sampling inside the first feature map at the first (given) coordinate, obtaining a feature vector f_1, with C channels. We use this sampled feature to initialize a trajectory of features, by simply tiling the feature across time, yielding a matrix $\mathbf{F}^0$ sized $T \times C$. This initialization implies an appearance constancy prior.

We initialize the target's trajectory of positions in a similar way. We simply copy the initial position across time, yielding a matrix $\mathbf{X}^0$, shaped $T \times 2$. This initialization implies a zero-velocity prior, which essentially assumes nothing about the target's motion.

During inference, we will update the trajectory of features, tracking appearance changes, and update the trajectory of positions, tracking motion. We use the superscript k to indicate the update iteration count, as in $\mathbf{X}^k, \mathbf{F}^k$.

3.4   Measuring Local Appearance Similarity

We would like to measure how well our trajectory of positions, and associated trajectory of features, matches with the pre-computed feature maps. We compute visual similarity maps by correlating each feature f_t in $\mathbf{F}^k$ with the feature map of the corresponding timestep, and then obtain "local" scores by bilinearly sampling a crop centered at the corresponding position (x_t, y_t). This step returns patches of un-normalized similarity scores, where large positive values indicate high similarity between the target's feature and the convolutional features at this location. The sequence of score patches is shaped $T \times P \cdot P$, where P is the size of the patch extracted from each correlation map. Similar to RAFT [32], we find it is beneficial to create a spatial pyramid of these score patches, to obtain similarity measurements at multiple scales. We denote our set of multi-scale score crops $\mathbf{C}^k$, shaped $T \times P \cdot P \cdot L$, where L is the number of levels in the pyramid.

3.5   Iterative Updates

The main inference step for our model involves updating the sequence of positions, and updating the sequence of features. To perform this update, we take into account all of the information we have computed thus far: the feature matrix $\mathbf{F}^k$, the correlation matrix $\mathbf{C}^k$, and displacements computed from the position matrix $\mathbf{X}^k$. To compute displacements from $\mathbf{X}^k$, we subtract the given position (x_1, y_1) from each element of the matrix. Using displacements instead of absolute positions makes all input trajectories appear to start at $(0, 0)$, which makes our model translation-invariant. To make the displacements easier to process by the model, we employ sinusoidal position encodings [37], motivated by the success of these encodings in vision transformers [5].

We concatenate this broad set of inputs on the channel dimension, yielding a new matrix shaped $T \times D$, and process them with a 12-block MLP-Mixer [34], which is a parameter-efficient all-MLP architecture with design similarities to a transformer. As output, this module produces updates for the sequence of positions and sequence of features, $\Delta \mathbf{X}$ and $\Delta \mathbf{F}$, which we apply with addition: $\mathbf{F}^{k+1} = \mathbf{F}^k + \Delta \mathbf{F}$, and $\mathbf{X}^{k+1} = \mathbf{X}^k + \Delta \mathbf{X}$. After each update, we compute new correlation pyramids at the updated coordinates, using the updated features.

The update module is iterated K times. After the last update, the positions $\mathbf{X}^K$ are treated as the final trajectory, and the features $\mathbf{F}^K$ are sent to a linear layer and sigmoid, to estimate per-timestep visibility scores $\mathbf{V}^K$.

3.6   Supervision

We supervise the model using the L_1 distance between the ground-truth trajectory and the estimated trajectory (across iterative updates), with exponentially increasing weights, similar to RAFT [32]:

$$\mathcal{L}_{\text{main}} = \sum_{k}^{K} \gamma^{K-k} ||\mathbf{X}^k - \mathbf{X}^*||_1, \tag{1}$$

where K is the number of iterative updates, and we set $\gamma = 0.8$. Note that this loss is applied even when the target is occluded, or out-of-bounds, which is possible since we are using synthetically-generated ground truth. This is the main loss of the model, and the model can technically train using only this, although it will not learn visibility estimation and convergence will be slow.

On the model's visibility estimates, we apply a cross entropy loss:

$$\mathcal{L}_{\text{ce}} = \mathbf{V}^* \log \mathbf{V} + (1 - \mathbf{V}^*) \log(1 - \mathbf{V}). \tag{2}$$

We find it accelerates convergence to directly supervise the score maps to peak in the correct location (i.e., the location of the true correspondence):

$$\mathcal{L}_{\text{score}} = -\log(\exp(c_i)/\sum_{j}\exp(c_j))1\{\mathbf{V}^* \neq 0\}, \tag{3}$$

where c_j represents the match score at pixel j, and i is pixel index with the true correspondence, and $1\{\mathbf{V}^* \neq 0\}$ selects indices where the target is visible.

3.7   Test-Time Trajectory Linking

At test time, it is often desirable to generate correspondences over longer timespans than the training sequence length T. To generate these longer trajectories, we may repeat inference starting from any timestep along the estimated trajectory, treating (x_t, y_t) as the new (x_1, y_1), and thereby "continuing" the trajectory up to (x_{t+T}, y_{t+T}). However, doing this naively (e.g., always continuing from the last timestep), can quickly cause tracking to drift. In particular, it is crucial to avoid continuing the trajectory from a timestep where the target is occluded. Otherwise, the model will switch to tracking the occluder. To avoid these identity switches, we make use of our visibility estimates, and seek a late timestep whose visibility score is high. This allows the model to skip past frames where the target was momentarily occluded, as long as the temporal span of the occlusion is less than the temporal span of the model (T). We initialize a visibility threshold conservatively at 0.99, and decrease it in increments of 0.01 until a valid selection is found. To lock the model into tracking the "original" target, we simply re-use the original $\mathbf{F}^0$ across all re-initializations.

4   Implementation Details

CNN. Our CNN uses the "BasicEncoder" architecture from the official RAFT codebase [33]. This architecture has a 7×7 convolution with stride 2, then 6 residual blocks with kernel size 3×3, then a final convolution with kernel size 1×1. The CNN has an output dimension of $C = 256$.

Local correlation pyramids. We use four levels in our correlation pyramids, with radius 3, yielding four 7×7 correlation patches per timestep.

MLP-Mixer. The input to the MLP-Mixer is a sequence of displacements, features, and correlation pyramids. The per-timestep inputs are flattened, then treated as a sequence of vectors (i.e., "tokens") for the MLP-Mixer. We use the MLP-Mixer architecture exactly as described in the original paper; at the end of the model there is a mean over the sequence dimension, followed by a linear layer that maps to a channel size of $T \cdot (C + 2)$.

Updates. We reshape the MLP-Mixer's outputs into a sequence of feature updates and a sequence of coordinate updates, and apply them with addition. We train and test with 6 updates.

Visibility. We use a linear layer to map the last update iteration's pixel-level feature sequence into visibility logits.

Training. We train with a batch size of 4, distributed across four GPUs. At training time, we use a resolution of 368×512. For each element of the batch, (after applying data augmentation,) we randomly sample 128 trajectories which begin in-bounds and un-occluded. We train for 100,000 steps, with a learning rate of 3e−4 with a 1-cycle schedule [27], using the AdamW optimizer. Training takes approximately 2 days on four GeForce RTX 2080s.

Hyperparameters. We use $T = 8$ (timesteps considered simultaneously by the model), and $K = 6$ (update iterations). The model can in general be trained for any T, but we found that the model was more difficult to train at $T = 32$, likely because the complexity of trajectories grows rapidly with their length under our model, as there is no weight sharing across time. On the other hand, the temporal sensitivity allows our model to learn more complex temporal priors. We found that $K > 6$ performs similar to $K = 6$. Although we train the model at a spatial stride of 8, this may be changed at test time; we find that a stride of 4 works best on our (high-resolution) test datasets.

Complexity. *Speed:* When the number of targets is small enough to fit on a GPU (e.g., 256 targets for a 12G GPU), our model is faster than RAFT (200 ms vs. 2000 ms at 480×1024). RAFT is comparatively slow because (1) it is too memory-heavy to compute all frames' flows in parallel, so we must run it $T - 1$ times, and (2) it attempts to track all pixels instead of a given set of targets. When the number of targets is too large to fit on a GPU (in parallel), our model processes them in batches, and in this case PIPs may be slower than RAFT. *Memory:* Our model's memory scales primarily with $T \cdot N$, where N is the number of particles being tracked, due to the iterated MLP-Mixer which consumes a T-length sequence of features per particle.

5   Experiments

We train our model in a modified version of FlyingThings [20], which we name FlyingThings++ (discussed more below). We evaluate our model on tracking objects in FlyingThings++, tracking vehicles and pedestrians in KITTI [7], tracking heads in a crowd in CroHD [30], and finally, propagating keypoints in animal videos in BADJA [1]. We visualize trajectory estimates in DAVIS videos in Fig. 1, to illustrate the method's generality, and visualize the estimates against ground truth in Figs. 3 and 4. In the supplementary we include video visualizations of our results. All of our experiments evaluate the same PIP model—we do not customize any parameters for the individual test domains.

5.1   Training Data: FlyingThings++

To train our model, we created a synthetic dataset called FlyingThings++, based on FlyingThings [20]. The original FlyingThings is typically used in combination with other flow datasets to train optical flow models. We chose FlyingThings because (1) its visuals and motions are extremely complex, which gives hope of generalizing to other data, and (2) it provides 10-frame videos with ground-truth forward and backward optical flow, and instance masks, from which we can mine accurate multi-frame trajectories.

To create multi-frame trajectories, we chain the flows forward, and then discard chains which (i) fail a forward-backward consistency check, (ii) leave the image bounds, or (iii) shift from one instance ID to another. This leaves a sparse set of 8-frame trajectories, which cover approximately 30% of the pixels of the first frame. These checks ensure that the trajectories are accurate, but leave us with a library of trajectories where the target is visible on every timestep. Therefore, it is necessary to add *new occlusions* on top of the video. We do this on-the-fly during batching: for each FlyingThings video in the batch, we randomly sample an object from an alternate FlyingThings video, paste it directly on top of the current video, overwriting the pixels within its mask on each frame. We then update the ground-truth to reflect the occluded area on each frame, as well as update the trajectory list to include the trajectories of the added object.

Combining all videos with at least 256 valid 8-frame trajectories, we obtain a total of 13085 training videos, and 2542 test videos. To expand the breadth of the training set, we augment the data on-the-fly with random color and brightness changes, random scale changes, crops which randomly shift across time, random Gaussian blur, and random horizontal and vertical flips.

5.2   Baselines

In our experiments we consider the following baselines.

Recurrent All-Pairs Field Transforms (RAFT) [32] represents the state-of-the-art in optical flow estimation, where a high resolution flow field is refined through iterative updates, based on lookups from a 4D cost volume constructed between all pairs of pixels. Similar to our method, RAFT has been trained on FlyingThings (including occlusions and out-of-bounds motions), but only has a 2-frame temporal span. To generate multi-frame trajectories with RAFT at test time, we compute flow with all consecutive pairs of frames, and then compute flow chains at the pixels queried on the first frame. To continue chains that travel out of bounds, we clamp the coordinates to the image bounds and sample at the edge of the flow map.

DINO [4] is a vision transformer (ViT-S [5] with patch size 8) trained on ImageNet with a self-supervision objective based on a knowledge distillation setup that builds invariance to image augmentations. To use this model for multi-frame correspondence, we use the original work's code for instance tracking, which uses nearest neighbor between the initial frame and the current frame, as well as nearest-neighbor between consecutive frames, and a strategy to restrict matches to a local neighborhood around previous matches. We report results with and without this "windowing" strategy.

Contrastive Random Walk (CRW) [11] treats the video as a space-time graph, with edges containing transition probabilities of a random walk, and computes long-range correspondences by walking across the graph. The model learns correspondences between pixels from different frames by optimizing an objective that encourages correspondences to be cycle-consistent across time (i.e., forward-backward consistency), including across frame skips. This method tracks in a similar way to DINO.

Memory-Augmented Self-supervised Tracker (MAST) [17] learns correspondences between features by reconstructing the target frame with linear combinations of reference frames. At test time the correspondences are predicted autoregressively. The model is trained on OxUvA [36] and YouTube-VOS [42]

Video Frame-level Similarity (VFS) [41] learns an encoder that produces frame-level embeddings which are similar within a video, and dissimilar across videos. This model is trained on Kinetics-400 [14].

ImageNet ResNet [9] is a ResNet50 supervised for classification with ImageNet labels, and evaluated the same way as DINO.

5.3   Trajectory Estimation in FlyingThings++

Using 8-frame videos from the FlyingThings++ test set as input, we estimate trajectories for all pixels for which we have ground-truth, and evaluate the average distance between each estimated trajectory and its corresponding ground truth, averaging over all 8 timesteps. We are especially interested in measuring how our model's performance compares with the baselines when the target gets occluded or flies out of frame. We use a crop size of 384×512, which puts many trajectories flying out of image bounds. For this evaluation, since occlusions are extremely common, we count a trajectory as "visible" if at least half of its timesteps are visible, and count it as "occluded" otherwise.

We compare our model against DINO [4], representing the state-of-the-art for feature matching, and RAFT [32], representing the state-of-the-art for flow. Table 1 shows the results across the different evaluations on the test set. DINO struggles overall, likely because of the rapid motions, and performs worse on

Table 1. Trajectory error in FlyingThings++. PIP trajectories are more robust to occlusions

Method	Vis.	Occ.
DINO [4]	40.68	77.76
RAFT [32]	24.32	46.73
PIPs (ours)	**15.54**	**36.67**

Table 2. Trajectory error in KITTI. PIP and RAFT trajectories are similar; DINO lags behind both

Method	Vis.	Occ.
DINO [4]	13.33	13.45
RAFT [32]	**4.03**	6.79
PIPs (ours)	4.40	**5.56**

Table 3. Trajectory error in CroHD. PIP trajectories achieve better accuracy overall

Method	Vis.	Occ.
DINO [4]	22.50	26.06
RAFT [32]	7.91	13.04
PIPs (ours)	**5.16**	**7.56**

occluded pixels than on visible ones. This makes sense because during occlusions DINO cannot make any matches. RAFT obtains reasonable accuracy for visible pixels (considering the speed of the motion in this data), but its errors drastically increase for the heavily-occluded trajectories. We have also re-trained RAFT in this data and its performance did not improve, likely because these are *multi-timestep* occlusions, which chaining-based methods cannot accommodate. Inspecting the results manually, we see that RAFT's trajectories often drift off the targets and follow the occluders, which makes sense because during occluded timesteps the flow field does not contain the targets. Our model, in contrast, is able to locate the targets after they re-emerge from occlusions, and inpaint the missing portions of the trajectories, leading to better performance overall.

5.4 Trajectory Estimation in KITTI

We evaluate on an 8-frame point trajectory dataset that we created from the "tracking" subset of the KITTI [7] urban scenes benchmark. The data is at 10 FPS, and we use this framerate as-is. We use videos from sequences 0000–0009, which include mostly vehicles, as well as 0017 and 0019, which include mostly pedestrians. To create 8-frame trajectories, we sample a 3D box annotation that has at least 8 valid timesteps, compute the mean LiDAR point within the box on the first timestep, transform it in 3D to its corresponding location on every other step, and project this location into pixel coordinates. We approximate visibility/occlusion labels in this data by checking if another object crosses in front of the target. We resize the frames to 320×512.

Table 2 shows the results. RAFT performs slightly better than PIPs for targets that stay visible, but PIPs performs slightly better for targets that undergo occlusions. DINO's error is much higher. In this data, the motions are relatively slow, and we find that DINO's trajectories are only coarsely tracking the targets, likely because of the low-resolution features in that model. Qualitative results for our model are shown in Fig. 3-middle.

5.5 Trajectory Estimation in CroHD

We evaluate on the Crowd of Heads Dataset (CroHD) [30], which consists of high-resolution (1080×1920) videos of crowds, with annotations tracking the heads of people in the crowd. We evaluate on 8-frame sequences extracted from the dataset. We subsample the frames in the original dataset so that the FPS is reduced by a factor of 3. We use a resolution of 768×1280 for PIPs and RAFT, and 512×768 for DINO (since otherwise it exceeds our 24G GPU memory). We filter out targets whose motion is below a threshold distance, and split the evaluation between targets that stay visible and those that undergo occlusions (according to the visibility annotations in the data). The results are shown in Table 3, and Fig. 3-right. In this data, PIP trajectories outperform RAFT and DINO by a wide margin, in both visibility conditions. In this data, DINO likely struggles because the targets are all so similar to one another.

Fig. 3. Qualitative results in FlyingThings++ (left), KITTI (middle), and CroHD (right). We visualize a video with the mean of its RGB. We trace the PIP trajectories in pink-to-yellow, and show ground truth in blue-to-green. FlyingThings++ is chaotic, but training on this data allows our model to generalize (Color figure online).

5.6   Keypoint Propagation in BADJA

BADJA [1] is a dataset of animal videos with keypoint annotations. These videos overlap with the DAVIS dataset [22], but include keypoint annotations. Keypoint annotations exist on approximately 1/5 frames, and the standard evaluation is Percentage of Correct Keypoint-Transfer (PCK-T), where keypoints are provided on a reference image, and the goal is to propagate these annotations to other frames. A keypoint transfer is considered correct if it is within a distance of $0.2\sqrt{A}$ from the true pixel coordinate, where A is the area of the ground-truth segmentation mask on the frame. We note that some existing methods test on a simplified version of this keypoint propagation task, where the ground-truth segmentation is available on every frame of the video [44,45]. Here, we focus on the harder setting, where the ground-truth mask is unknown. We also note that feature-matching methods often constrain their correspondences to a local spatial window around the previous frame's match [4]. We therefore report additional baseline results using the qualifier "Windowed", but we focus PIPs on the un-constrained version of the problem, where keypoints need to be propagated from frame 1 to every other frame, with no other knowledge about motion or position. We test at a resolution of 320×512. We have observed that higher accuracy is possible (for many methods) at higher resolution, but this puts some models beyond the memory capacity of our GPUs.

Table 4 shows the results of the BADJA evaluation. On four of the seven videos, our model produces the best keypoint tracking accuracy, as well as the best on average by a margin of 9 points. DINO [4] obtains the best accuracy in the remaining videos, though its widest margin over our model is just 3 points. Interestingly, windowing helps DINO (and other baselines) in some videos but

Table 4. PCK-T in BADJA. In this evaluation, keypoints are initialized in the first frame of the video, and are propagated to the end of the video; PCK-T measures the accuracy of this propagation. In each column, we bold the best result, and underline the second-best. Above the middle bar, we give methods a spatial window (marked "Win.") to constrain how they propagate labels, which is a common strategy in existing work. Our method wins in most videos, but DINO performs well also

Method	Bear	Camel	Cows	Dog-a	Dog	Horse-h	Horse-l	Avg.
Win. DINO [4]	**77.9**	69.8	**83.7**	<u>17.2</u>	<u>46.0</u>	29.1	50.8	<u>53.5</u>
Win. ImageNet ResNet [9]	70.7	65.3	71.7	6.9	27.6	20.5	49.7	44.6
Win. CRW [11]	63.2	<u>75.9</u>	77.0	6.9	32.8	20.5	22.0	42.6
Win. VFS [41]	63.9	74.6	76.2	6.9	35.1	27.2	40.3	46.3
Win. MAST [17]	35.7	39.5	42.0	10.3	8.6	12.6	14.7	23.3
Win. RAFT [32]	64.6	65.6	69.5	3.4	38.5	33.8	28.8	43.5
DINO [4]	75.0	59.2	70.6	10.3	**47.1**	35.1	<u>56.0</u>	50.5
ImageNet ResNet [9]	65.4	53.4	52.4	0.0	23.0	19.2	27.2	34.4
CRW [11]	66.1	67.2	64.7	6.9	33.9	25.8	27.2	41.7
VFS [41]	64.3	62.7	71.9	10.3	35.6	33.8	33.5	44.6
MAST [17]	51.8	52.0	57.5	3.4	5.7	7.3	34.0	30.2
RAFT [32]	64.6	65.6	69.5	13.8	39.1	<u>37.1</u>	29.3	45.6
PIPs (ours)	<u>76.3</u>	**81.6**	<u>83.2</u>	**34.2**	44.0	**57.4**	**59.5**	**62.3**

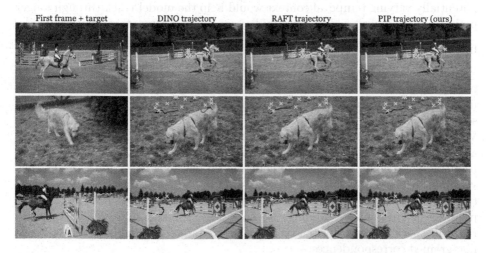

Fig. 4. Comparison with baselines in BADJA, on videos with occlusions. For each method, we trace the estimated trajectory with a pink-to-yellow colormap. The sparse ground truth is visualized with cyan × marks. In the first video, the target (on the dog's tail) leaves the image bounds then returns into view. In the second video, the target (on the horse's leg) is momentarily occluded, causing RAFT to lose track entirely. For a more detailed view, please watch the supplementary video.

not in others, perhaps because of the types of motions in DAVIS. We note that DAVIS has an object-centric bias (i.e., the target usually stays near the center of the frame), which translation-sensitive methods like DINO can exploit, since their features encode image position embeddings; RAFT and PIPs track more generally. In Fig. 4 we visualize trajectories on targets that undergo momentary occlusions, illustrating how DINO tracks only coarsely, and how RAFT loses track after the occlusion, while PIPs stay on target.

5.7 Limitations

Our model has two main limitations. First is our unique extreme tradeoff, of spatial awareness for temporal awareness. Although this maximizes the power of the temporal prior in the model, it discards information that could be shared between trajectories. We are indeed surprised that single-particle tracking performs as well as it does, considering that spatial smoothness is known to be essential for accurate optical flow estimation. Extending our architecture to concurrent estimation of multiple point trajectories is a direct avenue for future work.

Our second main limitation stems from the MLP-Mixer. Due to this architecture choice, our model is not recurrent across time. Although longer trajectories can be produced by re-initializing our inference at the tail of an initial trajectory, our model will lose the target if it stays occluded beyond the model's temporal window. We have tried models that are convolutional across time, and that use self-attention across the sequence length, but these did not perform as well as the MLP-Mixer on our FlyingThings++ tests. Taking advantage of longer and potentially varying temporal context would help the model track through longer periods of ambiguity, and potentially leverage longer-range temporal priors.

6 Conclusion

We propose Persistent Independent Particles (PIPs), a method for multi-frame point trajectory estimation through occlusions. Our method combines cost volumes and iterative inference with a deep temporal network, which jointly reasons about location and appearance of visual entities across multiple timesteps. We argue that optical flow, particle videos, and feature matches cover different areas in the spectrum of pixel-level correspondence tasks. Particle videos benefit from temporal context, which matching-based methods lack, and can also survive multi-frame occlusions, which is missing in flow-based methods. Given how tremendously useful optical flow and feature matching have been for driving progress in video understanding, we hope the proposed multi-frame trajectories will spark interest in architectures and datasets designed for longer-range fine-grained correspondences.

Acknowledgement. This material is based upon work supported by Toyota Research Institute (TRI), US Army contract W911NF20D0002, a DARPA Young Investigator Award, an NSF CAREER award, an AFOSR Young Investigator Award, and DARPA Machine Common Sense. Any opinions, findings and conclusions or recommendations expressed in this material are those of the authors and do not necessarily reflect the views of the United States Army or the United States Air Force.

References

1. Biggs, B., Roddick, T., Fitzgibbon, A., Cipolla, R.: Creatures great and SMAL: recovering the shape and motion of animals from video. In: Jawahar, C.V., Li, H., Mori, G., Schindler, K. (eds.) ACCV 2018. LNCS, vol. 11365, pp. 3–19. Springer, Cham (2019). https://doi.org/10.1007/978-3-030-20873-8_1
2. Bregler, C., Hertzmann, A., Biermann, H.: Recovering non-rigid 3D shape from image streams. In: Proceedings IEEE Conference on Computer Vision and Pattern Recognition, CVPR 2000 (Cat. No. PR00662), vol. 2, pp. 690–696 (2000)
3. Brox, T., Malik, J.: Large displacement optical flow: descriptor matching in variational motion estimation. IEEE Trans. Pattern Anal. Mach. Intell. **33**, 500–513 (2011)
4. Caron, M., et al.: Emerging properties in self-supervised vision transformers. In: ICCV (2021)
5. Dosovitskiy, A., et al.: An image is worth 16x16 words: Transformers for image recognition at scale. In: ICLR (2021)
6. Dosovitskiy, A., et al.: FlowNet: learning optical flow with convolutional networks. In: ICCV, pp. 2758–2766 (2015)
7. Geiger, A., Lenz, P., Stiller, C., Urtasun, R.: Vision meets robotics: the KITTI dataset. Int. J. Rob. Res. (IJRR) **32**, 1231–1237 (2013)
8. Germain, H., Lepetit, V., Bourmaud, G.: Visual correspondence hallucination: towards geometric reasoning. In: ICLR (2022)
9. He, K., Zhang, X., Ren, S., Sun, J.: Deep residual learning for image recognition. In: Proceedings of the IEEE Conference on Computer Vision and Pattern Recognition, pp. 770–778 (2016)
10. Ilg, E., Mayer, N., Saikia, T., Keuper, M., Dosovitskiy, A., Brox, T.: FlowNet 2.0: evolution of optical flow estimation with deep networks. In: CVPR (2017)
11. Jabri, A., Owens, A., Efros, A.A.: Space-time correspondence as a contrastive random walk. In: Advances in Neural Information Processing Systems (2020)
12. Janai, J., Güney, F., Ranjan, A., Black, M., Geiger, A.: Unsupervised learning of multi-frame optical flow with occlusions. In: Ferrari, V., Hebert, M., Sminchisescu, C., Weiss, Y. (eds.) ECCV 2018. LNCS, vol. 11220, pp. 713–731. Springer, Cham (2018). https://doi.org/10.1007/978-3-030-01270-0_42
13. Jiang, W., Trulls, E., Hosang, J., Tagliasacchi, A., Yi, K.M.: COTR: correspondence transformer for matching across images. In: ICCV (2021)
14. Kay, W., et al.: The kinetics human action video dataset. arXiv:1705.06950 (2017)
15. Kong, C., Lucey, S.: Deep non-rigid structure from motion with missing data. IEEE Trans. Pattern Anal. Mach. Intell. **43**(12), 4365–4377 (2021)
16. Lai, Z., Xie, W.: Self-supervised learning for video correspondence flow. In: BMVC (2019)
17. Lai, Z., Lu, E., Xie, W.: MAST: a memory-augmented self-supervised tracker. In: CVPR (2020)
18. Lucas, B.D., Kanade, T., et al.: An iterative image registration technique with an application to stereo vision, vol. 81. Vancouver (1981)
19. Matthews, L., Ishikawa, T., Baker, S.: The template update problem. IEEE Trans. Pattern Anal. Mach. Intell. **26**(6), 810–815 (2004)
20. Mayer, N., et al.: A large dataset to train convolutional networks for disparity, optical flow, and scene flow estimation. In: CVPR (2016)
21. Novotny, D., Ravi, N., Graham, B., Neverova, N., Vedaldi, A.: C3DPO: canonical 3D pose networks for non-rigid structure from motion. In: Proceedings of the IEEE International Conference on Computer Vision (2019)

22. Pont-Tuset, J., Perazzi, F., Caelles, S., Arbeláez, P., Sorkine-Hornung, A., Van Gool, L.: The 2017 DAVIS challenge on video object segmentation. arXiv:1704.00675 (2017)
23. Ren, Z., Gallo, O., Sun, D., Yang, M.H., Sudderth, E.B., Kautz, J.: A fusion approach for multi-frame optical flow estimation. In: Proceedings of the IEEE Winter Conference on Applications of Computer Vision (WACV) (2019)
24. Salgado, A., Sánchez, J.: Temporal constraints in large optical flow estimation. In: Moreno Díaz, R., Pichler, F., Quesada Arencibia, A. (eds.) EUROCAST 2007. LNCS, vol. 4739, pp. 709–716. Springer, Heidelberg (2007). https://doi.org/10.1007/978-3-540-75867-9_89
25. Sand, P., Teller, S.: Particle video: long-range motion estimation using point trajectories. In: CVPR, vol. 2, pp. 2195–2202 (2006)
26. Sidenbladh, H., Black, M.J., Fleet, D.J.: Stochastic tracking of 3D human figures using 2D image motion. In: Vernon, D. (ed.) ECCV 2000. LNCS, vol. 1843, pp. 702–718. Springer, Heidelberg (2000). https://doi.org/10.1007/3-540-45053-X_45
27. Smith, L.N., Topin, N.: Super-convergence: very fast training of neural networks using large learning rates. In: Artificial Intelligence and Machine Learning for Multi-Domain Operations Applications, vol. 11006, p. 1100612. International Society for Optics and Photonics (2019)
28. Sun, D., Yang, X., Liu, M.Y., Kautz, J.: PWC-Net: CNNs for optical flow using pyramid, warping, and cost volume. In: CVPR (2018)
29. Sundaram, N., Brox, T., Keutzer, K.: Dense point trajectories by GPU-accelerated large displacement optical flow. In: Daniilidis, K., Maragos, P., Paragios, N. (eds.) ECCV 2010. LNCS, vol. 6311, pp. 438–451. Springer, Heidelberg (2010). https://doi.org/10.1007/978-3-642-15549-9_32
30. Sundararaman, R., De Almeida Braga, C., Marchand, E., Pettre, J.: Tracking pedestrian heads in dense crowd. In: CVPR, pp. 3865–3875 (2021)
31. Taketomi, T., Uchiyama, H., Ikeda, S.: Visual slam algorithms: a survey from 2010 to 2016. IPSJ Trans. Comput. Vis. Appl. 9(1), 1–11 (2017)
32. Teed, Z., Deng, J.: RAFT: recurrent all-pairs field transforms for optical flow. In: Vedaldi, A., Bischof, H., Brox, T., Frahm, J.-M. (eds.) ECCV 2020. LNCS, vol. 12347, pp. 402–419. Springer, Cham (2020). https://doi.org/10.1007/978-3-030-58536-5_24
33. Teed, Z., Deng, J.: RAFT: recurrent all-pairs field transforms for optical flow (2020). https://github.com/princeton-vl/RAFT
34. Tolstikhin, I.O., et al.: MLP-mixer: an all-MLP architecture for vision. ArXiv abs/2105.01601 (2021)
35. Tomasi, C., Kanade, T.: Detection and tracking of point. Int. J. Comput. Vis. 9, 137–154 (1991)
36. Valmadre, J., et al.: Long-term tracking in the wild: a benchmark. In: Ferrari, V., Hebert, M., Sminchisescu, C., Weiss, Y. (eds.) ECCV 2018. LNCS, vol. 11207, pp. 692–707. Springer, Cham (2018). https://doi.org/10.1007/978-3-030-01219-9_41
37. Vaswani, A., et al.: Attention is all you need. In: Advances in Neural Information Processing Systems, pp. 5998–6008 (2017)
38. Wang, Q., Zhou, X., Hariharan, B., Snavely, N.: Learning feature descriptors using camera pose supervision. In: Vedaldi, A., Bischof, H., Brox, T., Frahm, J.-M. (eds.) ECCV 2020. LNCS, vol. 12346, pp. 757–774. Springer, Cham (2020). https://doi.org/10.1007/978-3-030-58452-8_44
39. Wang, X., Jabri, A., Efros, A.A.: Learning correspondence from the cycle-consistency of time. In: CVPR (2019)

40. Wiles, O., Ehrhardt, S., Zisserman, A.: Co-attention for conditioned image matching. In: CVPR (2021)
41. Xu, J., Wang, X.: Rethinking self-supervised correspondence learning: a video frame-level similarity perspective. In: Proceedings of the IEEE/CVF International Conference on Computer Vision (ICCV), pp. 10075–10085, October 2021
42. Xu, N., et al.: YouTube-VOS: sequence-to-sequence video object segmentation. In: Ferrari, V., Hebert, M., Sminchisescu, C., Weiss, Y. (eds.) ECCV 2018. LNCS, vol. 11209, pp. 603–619. Springer, Cham (2018). https://doi.org/10.1007/978-3-030-01228-1_36
43. Yang, C., Lamdouar, H., Lu, E., Zisserman, A., Xie, W.: Self-supervised video object segmentation by motion grouping. In: ICCV (2021)
44. Yang, G., et al.: LASR: learning articulated shape reconstruction from a monocular video. In: Proceedings of the IEEE/CVF Conference on Computer Vision and Pattern Recognition, pp. 15980–15989 (2021)
45. Yang, G., et al.: ViSER: video-specific surface embeddings for articulated 3D shape reconstruction. In: NeurIPS (2021)
46. Zhao, T., Nevatia, R.: Tracking multiple humans in crowded environment. In: Proceedings of the 2004 IEEE Computer Society Conference on Computer Vision and Pattern Recognition, CVPR 2004, vol. 2, p. II. IEEE (2004)

Tracking Objects as Pixel-Wise Distributions

Zelin Zhao[1]🆔, Ze Wu[2]🆔, Yueqing Zhuang[2]🆔, Boxun Li[2]🆔,
and Jiaya Jia[1,3](✉)🆔

[1] The Chinese University of Hong Kong, Hong Kong, China
leojia@cse.cuhk.edu.hk
[2] MEGVII Technology, Beijing, China
[3] SmartMore, Hong Kong, China

Abstract. Multi-object tracking (MOT) requires detecting and associating objects through frames. Unlike tracking via detected bounding
boxes or center points, we propose tracking objects as pixel-wise distributions. We instantiate this idea on a transformer-based architecture
named P3AFormer, with pixel-wise propagation, prediction, and association. P3AFormer propagates pixel-wise features guided by flow information to pass messages between frames. Further, P3AFormer adopts
a meta-architecture to produce multi-scale object feature maps. During inference, a pixel-wise association procedure is proposed to recover
object connections through frames based on the pixel-wise prediction.
P3AFormer yields 81.2% in terms of MOTA on the MOT17 benchmark
– highest among all transformer networks to reach 80% MOTA in literature. P3AFormer also outperforms state-of-the-arts on the MOT20 and
KITTI benchmarks. The code is at https://github.com/dvlab-research/
ECCV22-P3AFormer-Tracking-Objects-as-Pixel-wise-Distributions.

Keywords: Multi-object tracking · Transformer · Pixel-wise tracking

1 Introduction

Multi-Object Tracking (MOT) is a long-standing challenging problem in computer vision, which aims to predict the trajectories of objects in a video. Prior
work investigates the tracking paradigms [2,63,76,80], optimizes the association procedures [25,75] and learns the motion models [52,54]. Recently, with

---

The work was done when Zelin Zhao took internship at SmartMore.

Supplementary Information The online version contains supplementary material
available at https://doi.org/10.1007/978-3-031-20047-2_5.

Fig. 1. Comparison of concurrent transformer-based MOT approaches on the MOT17-val dataset. Each row corresponds to one method. (a) MOTR [71] occasionally fails to detect the small objects. (b) TransCenter [68] has a lot of ID-switches (indicated by blue circles) when the small objects are occluded. (c) Our proposed P3AFormer can robustly track the small objects under occlusion.

the powerful transformers deployed in image classification [15, 35] and object detection [4, 35, 82], concurrent work applies transformers to multi-object tracking [11, 51, 68, 71]. Albeit the promising results, we note that the power of the transformer still has much room to explore.

As shown in Fig. 1, current transformer-based MOT architectures MOTR [71] and TransCenter [68] still face challenges in detecting small objects and handling occlusions. Representing objects via pixel-wise distributions and conducting pixel-wise associations might alleviate these issues for the following reasons. First, pixel-wise information may help overcome occlusion based on low-level clues [44, 45, 57]. Moreover, recent transformer architecture demonstrates strong performance in pixel-wise prediction [8, 9, 35]. From another perspective, pixel-wise prediction preserves more low-confident details, which can improve tracking robustness [75].

We propose a transformer approach, called P3AFormer, to conduct pixel-wise propagation, prediction, and association. P3AFormer propagates information between frames via the dense feature propagation technique [83], exploiting context information to resist occlusion. To produce robust pixel-level distribution for each object, P3AFormer adopts the meta-architecture [8,9], which generates object proposals and object-centric heatmaps. Masked attention [8] is adopted to pursue localized tracking results and avoid background noise. Further, P3AFormer employs a multi-scale pixel-wise association procedure to recover object IDs robustly. Ablation studies demonstrate the effectiveness of these lines of improvement.

Besides these pixel-wise techniques, we consider a few whistles and bells during the training of P3AFormer. First, we use Hungarian matching [4] (different from direct mapping) to enhance detection accuracy. Second, inspired by the empirical findings of YOLOX [22], we use strong data augmentation, namely mosaic augmentation, in the training procedure of P3AFormer. Further, P3AFormer preserves all low-confident predictions [75] to ensure strong association.

We submit our results to the MOT17 test server and obtain 81.2% MOTA and 78.1% IDF1, outperforming all previous work. On the MOT20 benchmark, we report test accuracy of 78.1% MOTA and 76.4% IDF1, surpassing existing transformer-based work by a large margin. We further validate our approach on the KITTI dataset. It outperforms state-of-the-art methods. Besides, we validate the generalization of the pixel-wise techniques on other MOT frameworks and find that these pixel-wise techniques generalize well to other paradigms.

2   Related Work

2.1   Transformer-Based Multiple-object Tracking

We first discuss concurrent transformer-based MOT approaches. Track-Former [41] applies the vanilla transformer to the MOT domain and progressively handles newly appeared tracks. TransTrack [51] and MOTR [71] take similar approaches to update the track queries from frames. They explore a tracking-by-attention scheme, while we propose to track objects as pixel-wise distributions. TransCenter [68] conducts association via center offset prediction. It emphasizes a similar concept of dense query representation. However, the model design and tracking schemes are different from ours. TransMOT [11] is a recent architecture to augment the transformer with spatial-temporal graphs. It is noted that our P3AFormer does not use graph attention. We validate different paradigms and model components in experiments to support the design choices of our method.

2.2   Conventional Multi-object Tracking

The widely used MOT framework is tracking-by-detection [1,2,20,40,53,63,75, 76]. DeepSORT [63] leverages the bounding box overlap and appearance features from the neural network to associate bounding boxes predicted by an off-the-shelf detector [47]. Yang et al. [53] propose a graph-based formulation to link detected objects. Other work tries different formulations. For example, Yu et al. [65] formulate MOT into a decision-making problem in Markov Decision Processes (MDP). CenterTrack [80] tracks objects through predicted center off-sets. Besides, it is also investigated to reduce post-processing overhead by joint detection and tracking [5,38,61]. Another line of work [25,29,46] leverages graph neural networks to learn the temporal object relations.

2.3 Transformer Revolution

Transformer architectures achieved great success in natural language processing (NLP) [14,56]. Recently, transformer demonstrated strong performance in various vision tasks, such as image classification [15,35,55,67], object detection [4,82], segmentation [8,9,66], 3d recognition [60] and pose estimation [31, 32]. The seminal work [4] proposes a simple framework DETR for end-to-end object detection. MaskFormer [9] utilizes a meta-architecture to generate pixel embeddings and object proposals via transformers jointly. Previous transformers use masks in attention to restrict attention region [56] or force the computation to be local [35,77].

2.4 Video Object Detection

Tracking by detection paradigm requires accurate object detection and robust feature learning from videos [27,64]. Zhu et al. [83] propose dense feature propagation to aggregate features from nearby frames. The follow-up work [81] improves aggregation and keyframe scheduling. The MEGA model [7] combines messages from different frames on local and global scales. These methods do not consider video object detection with transformers. TransVOD [79] proposes aggregating the transformer output queries from different frames via a temporal query encoder. TransVOD cannot be directly applied to our setting because it is not an online algorithm and does not make pixel-wise predictions.

2.5 Pixel-Wise Techniques

Pixel-wise techniques have been proven effective in various applications in computer vision. Dense fusion [57] and pixel-wise voting network [18,44] are proposed to overcome occlusions in the object pose estimation [19]. DPT [45] uses a dense prediction transformer for monocular depth estimation and semantic segmentation. Pyramid vision transformer [59] replaces convolutional neural networks by attention to dense prediction tasks. Yuan et al. [70] presents a high-resolution transformer for human pose estimation. Our P3AFormer, instead, explores the power of pixel-wise techniques in the MOT domain.

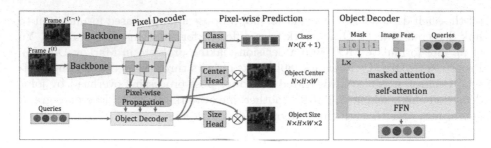

Fig. 2. Diagram of P3AFormer model. (**Left**) The backbone encodes the input images, and the pixel decoder produces pixel-level multi-frame feature embeddings. Then the object decoder predicts latent object features, which are passed through several MLP heads to produce class distribution and the pixel-wise representations for object center and size. (**Right**) The detailed structure of the object decoder. It uses masked attention, self-attention, and feed-forward networks (FFN) to update the query embedding. The add and normalization layers are omitted in this figure for simplicity.

3   Pixel-Wise Propagation, Prediction and Association

Different from tracking objects via bounding boxes [1, 51, 75] or as points [68, 80], we propose to track objects as pixel-wise distributions. Specifically, P3AFormer first extracts features from each single frame (Sect. 3.1), summarizes features from different frames via pixel-wise feature propagation (Sect. 3.2) and predicts pixel-wise object distributions via an object decoder (Sect. 3.3). The training targets are listed in Sect. 3.4. During inference, P3AFormer conducts pixel-wise association (Sect. 3.5) to build tracks from object distributions.

3.1   Single-Frame Feature Extraction

As shown on the top-left of Fig. 2, P3AFormer uses a backbone to generate latent features and a pixel decoder to produce pixel-wise heatmaps. The details are as follows.

Backbone. The input to the P3AFormer model is a set of continuous frames from a video. For simplicity and following previous work [68, 80], we take two consecutive frames $\mathcal{I}^{(t-1)}$ and $\mathcal{I}^{(t)}$ as input. A backbone generates low-resolution features $\mathbf{F}^{(t)} \in \mathbb{R}^{d \times H_\mathbf{F} \times W_\mathbf{F}}$ from the input image $\mathcal{I}^{(t)}$, where d is the feature dimension, $H_\mathbf{F}$ and $W_\mathbf{F}$ are the height and width of the extracted feature maps. Another backbone (sharing weight with the first backbone) extracts the previous-frame feature $\mathbf{F}^{(t-1)}$ from $\mathcal{I}^{(t-1)}$.

Pixel Decoder. P3AFormer uses the pixel decoder [9], which is a transformer decoder, to up-sample the features $\mathbf{F}^{(t)}$ and generate per-pixel representation $\mathbf{P}_l^{(t)}$ where l is the current decoding level. The pixel encoder is also applied to the previous-frame feature $\mathbf{F}^{(t-1)}$ to get the pixel-wise feature $\mathbf{P}_l^{(t-1)}$. In our work, we use a multi-scale deformable attention transformer [82] as the pixel decoder.

3.2   Pixel-Wise Feature Propagation

Extracting temporal context from nearby frames is very important in MOT [63, 71,80]. We use the pixel-wise flow-guided feature propagation [83] to summarize features between frames (shown in the middle-left of Fig. 2). Formally, given a flow network Φ [16], the flow guidance can be represented as $\Phi(\mathcal{I}^{(t-1)}, \mathcal{I}^{(t)})$. After that, a bilinear warping function $\mathcal{W}$ [83] transforms the previous-frame feature to align with the current feature as

$$\mathbf{P}_l^{(t-1)->(t)} = \mathcal{W}(\mathbf{P}_l^{(t-1)}, \Phi(\mathcal{I}^{(t-1)}, \mathcal{I}^{(t)})). \tag{1}$$

We then compute the fused feature as

$$\bar{\mathbf{P}}_l^{(t)} = \mathbf{P}_l^{(t)} + w^{(t-1)->(t)}\mathbf{P}_l^{(t-1)->(t)}, \tag{2}$$

where the weight $w^{(t-1)->(t)}$ is the pixel-wise cosine similarity [83] between the warped feature $\mathbf{P}_l^{(t-1)->(t)}$ and the reference feature $\mathbf{P}_l^{(t)}$. The pixel-wise cosine similarity function is provided in the supplementary file for reference. The shape of $\mathbf{P}_l$ is denoted as $H_{P_l} \times W_{P_l} \times d$.

3.3   Pixel-Wise Predictions

P3AFormer uses a transformer-based object decoder to generate object proposals. The object proposals are combined with the pixel-wise embeddings to get pixel-wise object distributions. As shown in the right part of Fig. 2, the object decoder follows the standard transformer [4,56], which transforms N learnable positional embeddings $\mathbf{Q}_l \in \mathbb{R}^{N \times d}$ using L attention layers.

Since an image from an MOT dataset [12,13] often involves a large number of small objects, local features around the objects are often more important than features at long range [76]. Inspired by the recent discovery [8] that masked attention [8,56,77] can promote localized feature learning, P3AFormer uses masked attention in each layer of the object decoder. The mask matrix $\mathbf{M}_l$ is initialized as an all-zero matrix, and it is determined by the center heatmaps at the previous level (presented in Eq. (5)). The standard masked attention [8,56,77] can be denoted as

$$\mathbf{X}_l = \text{softmax}\left(\mathbf{M}_{l-1} + \mathbf{Q}_l \mathbf{K}_l^T\right), \mathbf{V}_l + \mathbf{X}_{l-1}, \tag{3}$$

where X_l is the hidden query feature at layer l while the query feature is computed by a linear mapping from the hidden query feature of $\mathbf{Q}_l = f_Q(\mathbf{X}_{l-1})$. The key feature matrix $\mathbf{K}_l \in \mathbb{R}^{H_{P_l} W_{P_l} \times d}$ and the value feature matrix $\mathbf{V}_l \in \mathbb{R}^{H_{P_l} W_{P_l} \times d}$ are derived from the image feature as $\mathbf{K}_l = f_K(\bar{\mathbf{P}}_l), \mathbf{V}_l = f_V(\bar{\mathbf{P}}_l)$.

These functions f_Q, f_K and f_V are all linear transformations. As shown in the right part of Fig. 2, after the masked attention, the hidden query feature passes through the standard self-attention and feed-forward networks. Please refer to [9,56] for these operator details.

At each level, the query embeddings are decoded via three MLP heads to get three embeddings corresponding to object class $\mathcal{E}_l^{cls} = \mathrm{MLP}_{cls}(\mathbf{Q}_l) \in \mathbb{R}^{N \times d}$, the object center $\mathcal{E}_l^{ctr} = \mathrm{MLP}_{ctr}(\mathbf{Q}_l) \in \mathbb{R}^{N \times d}$, and the size of the object $\mathcal{E}_l^{sz} = \mathrm{MLP}_{sz}(\mathbf{Q}_l) \in \mathbb{R}^{N \times d \times 2}$. The hidden dimension of the object size embedding is doubled because the bounding box size is represented in two dimensions (x- and y-axis). Given the full-image representation $\bar{\mathbf{P}}_l$ and the object-centric embeddings $\mathcal{E}_l^{ctr}$ and $\mathcal{E}_l^{sz}$, we compute the center heatmaps $c_l \in \mathbb{R}^{N \times H_{P_l} \times W_{P_l}}$ and size maps $s_l \in \mathbb{R}^{N \times H_{P_l} \times W_{P_l} \times 2}$ via dot products as

$$
\begin{aligned}
c_l[i, h, w] &= \mathrm{sigmoid}(\bar{\mathbf{P}}_l[h, w, :] \cdot \mathcal{E}_l^{ctr}[i, :]), \\
s_l[i, h, w, j] &= \mathrm{sigmoid}(\bar{\mathbf{P}}_l[h, w, :] \cdot \mathcal{E}_l^{sz}[i, :, j]).
\end{aligned}
\tag{4}
$$

After getting the center heatmaps, the attention mask corresponding to i-th object and position (x, y) is updated as

$$
\mathbf{M}_{l-1}(i, x, y) = \begin{cases} 0, & \text{if } c_{l-1}[i, x, y] > 0.5, \\ -\infty, & \text{otherwise.} \end{cases}
\tag{5}
$$

Such a mask restricts the attention to the local region around the object center, much benefiting the tracking performance (as shown in Sect. 4.4).

3.4   Training Targets

P3AFormer leverages the bipartite Hungarian matching [4,82] to match N predicted objects to K ground-true objects. During classification, the unmatched object classes are set to an additional category called "no object" ($\varnothing$). Following MaskFormer [9], we adopt a pixel-wise metric (instead of bounding boxes) in the Hungarian matching.

First, we construct the ground-true heatmap h_l^i for an object via a Gaussian function where the Gaussian center is at the object center, and the Gaussian radius is proportional to the object size [68,80]. Given the predicted center heatmaps $\hat{h}_l^i$, class distribution $\hat{p}_l^i$ of the ith object, and the corresponding ground true center heatmaps h_l^i and object class c_l^i, we compute the association cost between the prediction and the ground truth via the pixel-wise cost function of

$$
\mathcal{L}_{pixel-wise} = \sum_l \sum_i \left(-\log \hat{p}_l^i(c_l^i) + \mathbf{1}_{c_l^i \neq \varnothing} |\hat{h}_l^i - h_l^i| \right).
\tag{6}
$$

P3AFormer further computes three losses given the matching between predictions and ground-true objects: (1) cross-entropy loss between the predicted and ground-true classes; (2) focal loss [80] between the predicted center heatmaps and ground-true center heatmaps; (3) size loss computed by the $L1$ loss between predicted and ground true size. The final loss is a weighted form of these three losses summarized for all levels.

3.5   Pixel-Wise Association

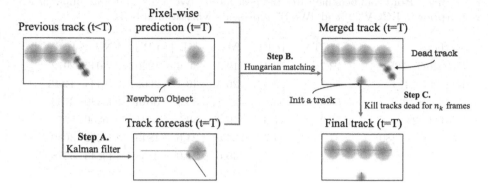

Fig. 3. Pixel-wise association scheme in P3AFormer. One object is represented as a pixel-wise distribution, denoted by spheres with the radial gradient change in this figure. We use one arrow and spheres on the arrow to denote a track. **Step A:** P3AFormer feeds the previous track into the Kalman filter [42] to produce the track forecast. **Step B:** A Hungarian algorithm matches predictions and the track forecast based on a pixel-wise cost function (Eq. (6)). P3AFormer initializes a new track if a newborn object is detected. **Step C:** The dead tracks are removed when an object is occluded or moves out of the image, and the final track is obtained.

After representing objects as a pixel-wise distribution, P3AFormer adopts a pixel association procedure to recover object tracks across frames. This procedure is conducted from the first frame ($t = 0$) to the current frame ($t = T$) in a frame-by-frame manner, which means P3AFormer is an online tracker.

We sketch the association procedure at the timestep $t = T$ in Fig. 3. A track τ_k corresponds to an object with a unique ID k. We store into τ_k the bounding boxes τ_k.`bbox` (recovered by the predicted center and size), the score τ_k.`score` (the peak value in the center heatmap), predicted class τ_k.`class` and the center heatmap τ_k.`heatmap`.

In **step A**, We use the Kalman Filter [42,75] to predict the location of objects in the current frame ($t = T$) based on previous center locations ($t < T$). The heatmaps are translated along with the forecast movement of the object center via bilinear warping. **Step B** uses the Hungarian algorithm to match the pixel-wise prediction with the track forecast. P3AFormer only matches objects under the same category and omits the "no-object" category. The association cost for Hungarian matching is the L1 distance between a track's forecast heatmap and an object's predicted heatmap. We accept a matching if the association cost between the matched track and prediction is smaller than a threshold η_m. A new track $\tau_{k'}$ would be initialized for an untracked object k' if its confidence $\tau_{k'}$.`score` is larger than η_s. In **step C**, the dead tracks that are not matched with any prediction for n_k frames are killed. All the above thresholds η_m, η_s, and η_k are hyper-parameters detailed in Sect. 4.2 and we provide more algorithm details in the supplementary file.

Table 1. Results on the MOT17 test set. We list transformer-based approaches on bottom of the table and others above. The numbers are from original papers released by authors. **Bold** numbers indicates the best model. We use † to denote unpublished work (prior to ECCV'22) and "W&B" represents whistles and bells.

Methods	MOTA ↑	IDF1 ↑	MT ↑	ML ↓	FP ↓	FN ↓	IDSW ↓
FairMOT [76]	73.7	72.3	19.5	36.6	12201	248047	2072
LSST17 [21]	54.7	62.3	20.4	40.1	26091	228434	**1243**
Tracktor v2 [1]	56.5	55.1	21.1	35.3	**8866**	235449	3763
GMOT [29]	50.2	47.0	19.3	32.7	29316	246200	5273
CenterTrack [80]	67.8	64.7	34.6	24.6	18498	160332	3039
QuasiDense [43]	68.7	66.3	40.6	21.9	26589	146643	3378
SiamMOT [49]	65.9	63.3	34.6	23.9	14076	200672	2583
PermaTrack [54]	73.8	68.9	43.8	17.2	28998	115104	3699
CorrTracker [58]	76.5	73.6	47.6	12.7	29808	99510	3369
ByteTrack† [75]	80.3	77.3	53.2	14.5	25491	**83721**	2196
MOTR† [71]	73.4	68.6	42.9	19.1	27939	119589	2439
TransTrack† [51]	74.5	63.9	46.8	**11.3**	28323	112137	3663
TransCenter† [68]	73.2	62.2	40.8	18.5	23112	123738	4614
TransMOT† [11]	76.7	75.1	51.0	16.4	36231	93150	2346
P3AFormer	69.2	69.0	34.8	28.8	18621	152421	2769
P3AFormer (+W&B)	**81.2**	**78.1**	**54.5**	13.2	17281	86861	1893

4   Experiments

P3AFormer accomplishes superior results to previous MOT approaches on three public benchmarks. We then ablate each component of the P3AFormer to demonstrate the effectiveness of the pixel-wise techniques. After that, we generalize the proposed pixel-wise techniques to other MOT frameworks.

4.1   Datasets

MOT17 [12]. The MOT17 dataset is focused on multiple persons tracking in crowded scenes. It has 14 video sequences in total and seven sequences for testing. The MOT17 dataset is the most popular dataset to benchmark MOT approaches [40, 63, 68, 71, 75]. Following previous work [75, 80] during validation, we split the MOT17 datasets into two sets. We use the first split for training and the second for validation. We denote this validation dataset as MOT17-val for convenience.

Table 2. Results on the MOT20 test set. The transformer-based approaches are the last three ones. We use **bold** numbers to indicate the best approach. We use † to denote unpublished work (prior to ECCV'22) and "W&B" represents whistles and bells.

Methods	MOTA ↑	IDF1 ↑	MT ↑	ML ↓	FP ↓	FN ↓	IDs ↓
MLT [74]	48.9	54.6	30.9	22.1	45660	216803	2187
FairMOT [76]	61.8	67.3	68.8	7.6	103440	88901	5243
CorrTracker [58]	65.2	69.1	66.4	8.9	79429	95855	5183
Semi-TCL [30]	65.2	70.1	61.3	10.5	61209	114709	4139
CSTrack [33]	66.6	68.6	50.4	15.5	**25404**	144358	3196
GSDT [61]	67.1	67.5	53.1	13.2	31913	135409	3131
SiamMOT [49]	67.1	69.1	49.0	16.3	–	–	–
RelationTrack [69]	67.2	70.5	62.2	8.9	61134	104597	4243
SOTMOT [78]	68.6	71.4	64.9	9.7	57064	101154	4209
ByteTrack [75]	77.8	75.2	69.2	9.5	26249	87594	**1223**
TransTrack [51]	65.0	59.4	50.1	13.4	27197	150197	3608
TransCenter [68]	61.9	50.4	49.4	15.5	45895	146347	4653
P3AFormer	60.3	56.2	50.4	13.5	43221	157564	4522
P3AFormer (+W&B)	**78.1**	**76.4**	**70.5**	**7.4**	25413	**86510**	1332

The best model selected during validation is trained on the full MOT17 dataset and is submitted to the test server under the "private detection" setting. The main metrics are MOTA, IDF1, MT, ML, FP, FN, and IDSW, and we refer the readers to [12] for details of these metrics. For MOT17, we add CrowdHuman [48], Cityperson [73], and ETHZ [17] into the training sets following [68,75]. When training on an image instead of a video with no neighboring frames, the P3AFormer model replicates it and takes two identical images as input.

MOT20 [13]. The MOT20 dataset consists of eight new sequences in crowded scenes. We train on the MOT20 training split with the same hyper-parameters as the MOT17 dataset. We submit our inferred tracks to the public server of MOT20 [13] under the "private detection" protocol. The evaluation metrics are the same as MOT17.

KITTI [23]. The KITTI tracking benchmark contains annotations for eight different classes while only two classes "car" and "pedestrian" are evaluated [54, 80]. Twenty-one training sequences and 29 test sequences are presented in the KITTI benchmark. We split the training sequences into halves for training and validation following [80]. Besides the common metrics, KITTI uses an additional metric of HOTA [39] to balance the effect of detection and association.

4.2   Implementation Details

Backbone. We mainly use ResNet [26] and Swin-Transformer [35] as the backbone in P3AFormer. For ResNet, we use the ResNet-50 [26] configuration. For Swin-Transformer, we use the Swin-B backbone [35]. We use Swin-B in all final models submitted to the leaderboards and ResNet-50 for validation experiments. The hidden feature dimension is $d = 128$.

Pixel Decoder. We adopt the deformable DETR decoder [82] as the multi-scale pixel-wise decoder. Specifically, we use six deformable attention layers to generate feature maps, and the resolutions are the same as Mask2Former [8]. We have in total $L = 3$ layers of feature maps. We add sinusoidal positional and learnable scale-level embedding to the feature maps following [9].

Pixel-Wise Feature Propagation. During feature propagation, we use the simple version of FlowNet [16,83] pre-trained on the Flying Chairs [16] dataset. The generated flow field is scaled to match the resolution of feature maps with bilinear interpolation.

Object Decoder. The object decoder also has $L = 3$ layers. We adopt $N = 100$ queries, which are initialized as all-zeros and are learnable embeddings [8] during training. No dropout [50] is adopted since it would deteriorate the performance of the meta architecture [8].

Pixel-Wise Association. The thresholds in the pixel-wise association are $\eta_m = 0.65$ and $\eta_s = 0.80$ on all benchmarks. We found that the P3AFormer model is robust under a wide range of thresholds (see supplementary). The lost tracks are deleted if they do not appear after $n_k = 30$ frames.

Training Process. The input image is of shape 1440×800 for MOT17/MOT20 and 1280×384 for KITTI. Following [22,75], we use data augmentation, such as Mosaic [3] and Mixup [36,72]. We use AdamW [37] with an initial learning rate of 6×10^{-5}. We adopt the poly learning rate schedule [6] with weight decay 1×10^{-4}. The full training procedure lasts for 200 epochs. The P3AFormer models are all trained with eight Tesla V100 GPUs. The specific configurations of the losses are provided in the supplementary. The run-time analysis of different models is provided in the supplementary.

4.3   Comparisons on Public Benchmarks

We first compare the P3AFormer model with several baselines on the MOT17 test sets, and the results are presented in Table 1. With whistles and bells, P3AFormer outperforms all previous approaches on the two major metrics of MOTA and IDF1. Besides, P3AFormer surpasses the concurrent unpublished transformer-based approaches by a large margin (4.5% MOTA and 3.0% IDF1). P3AFormer outperforms the strong unpublished baseline ByteTrack [75] while

Table 3. Results on the KITTI test split. We show results of two classes "car" and "person" on top and bottom splits. The numbers are from [54]. We use **bold** numbers to indicate the best approach of each class.

Classes	Methods	HOTA ↑	MOTA ↑	MT ↑	PT ↓	ML ↓
Car	MASS [28]	68.3	84.6	74.0	23.1	2.9
	IMMDP [65]	68.7	82.8	60.3	27.5	12.2
	AB3D [62]	69.8	83.5	67.1	21.5	11.4
	TuSimple [10]	71.6	86.3	71.1	22.0	6.9
	SMAT [24]	71.9	83.6	62.8	31.2	6.0
	TrackMPNN [46]	72.3	87.3	84.5	13.4	**2.2**
	CenterTrack [80]	73.0	88.8	82.2	15.4	2.5
	PermaTrack [54]	78.0	**91.3**	85.7	11.7	2.6
	P3AFormer	**78.4**	91.2	**86.5**	**10.9**	2.3
Person	AB3D [62]	35.6	38.9	17.2	41.6	41.2
	TuSimple [10]	45.9	57.6	30.6	44.3	25.1
	TrackMPNN [46]	39.4	52.1	35.1	46.1	18.9
	CenterTrack [80]	40.4	53.8	35.4	43.3	21.3
	PermTrack [54]	48.6	66.0	48.8	35.4	15.8
	P3AFormer	**49.0**	**67.7**	**49.1**	**33.2**	**14.5**

our model differs from theirs. Further, our association procedure does not involve additional training parameters, unlike those of [29,68,71,80].

We also report results on the MOT20 test server in Table 2. Again, P3AFormer demonstrates superior performance with whistles and bells. It outperforms SOTA methods [49,58,76,78] and even the unpublished work [69,75]. Besides, P3AFormer outperforms the concurrent transformer-based work by a large margin (13.1% MOTA and 17.0% IDF1). It achieves the best results on this leaderboard.

A comparison between P3AFormer and the baselines on the KITTI dataset is given in Table 3. Our work outperforms all baselines on two object classes. Notably, P3AFormer surpasses the strong baseline PermaTrack [54] that leverages additional synthetic training data to overcome occlusions. Intriguingly, our P3AFormer does not need those additional training data.

4.4 Effectiveness of Pixel-Wise Techniques

We decouple the P3AFormer's pixel-wise techniques and validate the contribution of each part. We use "Pro." to denote the pixel-wise feature propagation, "Pre." to denote pixel-wise prediction, and "Ass." to denote the pixel-wise association. The details of the ablated models are in the supplementary file.

The results are presented in Table 4. We also report the detection mean average precision (mAP [34]). The results are much worse when removing all

Fig. 4. Visualization of center heatmaps and tracking results of P3AFormer on `MOT17-val`. Each row corresponds to one video. The center heatmaps of different objects are put together into one frame and are best viewed on the screen.

pixel-wise techniques (the first row of Table 4). Compared to the last row, the incomplete system yields 9.2% mAP, 10.1% MOTA, and 9.2% IDF1 lower results.

When we remove the pixel-wise propagation or pixel-wise prediction (2nd and 3rd rows of Table 4), the results are worse in terms of the detection mAP. Finally, we try different combinations of pixel-wise techniques (4th and 5th rows of Table 4). These combinations improve the tracking performance.

4.5   Influence of Training Techniques

P3AFormer also incorporates several techniques for training transformers. The results are presented in Table 5. We use "Mask." to represent mask attention – it is beneficial to detection (0.3 mAP) and association (1.3% IDF1). We then verify the effect of mixing datasets (CrowdHuman [48], Cityperson [73] and ETHZ [17]) by comparison with only using MOT17 dataset (denoted as "w/o

Table 4. Comparison of the pixel-wise techniques on `MOT17-val`. Please refer to Sect. 4.4 for more details.

Methods	mAP ↑	MOTA ↑	IDF1 ↑
w/o All	39.1	68.3	66.8
Pro	43.5	73.6	73.2
Pre	42.1	72.8	74.5
Pre.+Ass	41.9	71.8	74.0
Pro.+Pre	48.3	69.1	72.3
Pro.+Pre.+Ass	48.3	78.4	76.0

Table 5. Ablation of the whistles and bells on the `MOT17-val` (see Sect. 4.5).

Methods	mAP ↑	MOTA ↑	IDF1 ↑
w/o All	46.1	71.3	72.1
w/o Mask	48.0	71.4	74.7
w/o Mix	47.8	76.6	74.8
w/o Mosiac	46.7	74.0	71.9
w/o LQ	47.9	77.6	75.1
w/o Bbox	48.3	79.1	74.8
With All	48.3	78.4	76.0

Table 6. Generalization of pixel-wise techniques to other trackers (refer to Sect. 4.6) on the `MOT17-val`. The validation results of P3AFormer are provided at the bottom for reference.

Methods	MOTA ↑	IDF1 ↑	MT ↑	ML ↓	FP ↓	FN ↓	IDSW ↓
Tractor [1]	61.9	64.7	35.3	21.4	323	42454	326
Tractor [1] + Pro	63.3	67.1	37.5	20.4	310	40930	279
Tractor [1] + Pro. + Pre.	64.6	69.3	38.1	17.9	287	39523	238
Tractor [1] + Pro. + Pre. + Ass	73.1	72.3	45.0	16.9	224	30000	208
P3AFormer	78.9	76.3	54.3	13.6	216	23462	193

Mix." in Table 5). It is also clear that using external datasets improves detection and tracking performance. Besides, we notice that using Mosaic augmentation (4th row of Table 5), using learnable query (5th row in Table 5) and connecting all bounding boxes (6th row in Table 5) all slightly improve P3AFormer.

4.6   Generalizing to Other Trackers

Although our pixel-wise techniques are implemented on the transformer structure, one can apply the pixel-wise techniques to other trackers. We consider the tracking-by-detection tracker Tractor [1], which is based on Faster R-CNN [47] with a camera motion model and a re-ID network.

First, we apply pixel-wise feature propagation to Tractor. Second, we change the output shape of faster-RCNN to predict pixel-wise information. After that, we remove the association procedure of the Tractor and replace it with our dense association scheme. More details are included in this generalization experiment in the supplementary file. The results of the above models are presented in Table 6. It is clear that tracking objects as pixel-wise distributions also improves CNN-based frameworks.

4.7 Visualization of Results

Visualization of tracking results in comparison to several transformer-based approaches is provided in Fig. 1. The P3AFormer can robustly track small objects without many ID switches. Besides, we provide the visualization of center heatmaps and tracking results of P3AFormer in Fig. 4. Even when the objects are heavily occluded, the predicted pixel-wise distribution can provide useful clues to recover the relationship between objects.

5 Conclusion

In this paper, we have presented the P3AFormer, which tracks objects as pixel-wise distributions. First, P3AFormer adopts dense feature propagation to build connections through frames. Second, P3AFormer generates multi-level heatmaps to preserve detailed information from the input images. Finally, the P3AFormer exploits pixel-wise predictions during the association procedure, making the association more robust.

P3AFormer obtains state-of-the-art results on three public benchmarks of MOT17, MOT20, and KITTI. P3AFormer demonstrates strong robustness against occlusion and outperforms concurrent transformer-based frameworks significantly. The proposed pixel-wise techniques can be applied to other trackers and may motivate broader exploration of transformers in future work. We will also study the transformer architecture and make it more efficient to satisfy the real-time tracking requirement.

References

1. Bergmann, P., Meinhardt, T., Leal-Taixe, L.: Tracking without bells and whistles. In: Proceedings of the IEEE/CVF International Conference on Computer Vision, pp. 941–951 (2019)
2. Bewley, A., Ge, Z., Ott, L., Ramos, F., Upcroft, B.: Simple online and realtime tracking. In: 2016 IEEE International Conference on Image Processing (ICIP), pp. 3464–3468. IEEE (2016)
3. Bochkovskiy, A., Wang, C.Y., Liao, H.Y.M.: YOLOv4: optimal speed and accuracy of object detection. arXiv preprint arXiv:2004.10934 (2020)
4. Carion, N., Massa, F., Synnaeve, G., Usunier, N., Kirillov, A., Zagoruyko, S.: End-to-end object detection with transformers. In: Vedaldi, A., Bischof, H., Brox, T., Frahm, J.-M. (eds.) ECCV 2020. LNCS, vol. 12346, pp. 213–229. Springer, Cham (2020). https://doi.org/10.1007/978-3-030-58452-8_13
5. Chaabane, M., Zhang, P., Beveridge, J.R., O'Hara, S.: Deft: detection embeddings for tracking. arXiv preprint arXiv:2102.02267 (2021)
6. Chen, L.C., Papandreou, G., Kokkinos, I., Murphy, K., Yuille, A.L.: DeepLab: semantic image segmentation with deep convolutional nets, atrous convolution, and fully connected CRFs. IEEE Trans. Pattern Anal. Mach. Intell. 40(4), 834–848 (2017)

7. Chen, Y., Cao, Y., Hu, H., Wang, L.: Memory enhanced global-local aggregation for video object detection. In: Proceedings of the IEEE/CVF Conference on Computer Vision and Pattern Recognition (CVPR), June 2020

8. Cheng, B., Misra, I., Schwing, A.G., Kirillov, A., Girdhar, R.: Masked-attention mask transformer for universal image segmentation. arXiv preprint arXiv:2112.01527 (2021)

9. Cheng, B., Schwing, A., Kirillov, A.: Per-pixel classification is not all you need for semantic segmentation. In: Advances in Neural Information Processing Systems, vol. 34 (2021)

10. Choi, W.: Near-online multi-target tracking with aggregated local flow descriptor. In: Proceedings of the IEEE International Conference on Computer Vision, pp. 3029–3037 (2015)

11. Chu, P., Wang, J., You, Q., Ling, H., Liu, Z.: TransMOT: spatial-temporal graph transformer for multiple object tracking. arXiv preprint arXiv:2104.00194 (2021)

12. Dendorfer, P., et al.: MOTchallenge: a benchmark for single-camera multiple target tracking. Int. J. Comput. Vision **129**(4), 845–881 (2021)

13. Dendorfer, P., et al.: MOT20: a benchmark for multi object tracking in crowded scenes. arXiv preprint arXiv:2003.09003 (2020)

14. Devlin, J., Chang, M.W., Lee, K., Toutanova, K.: BERT: pre-training of deep bidirectional transformers for language understanding. arXiv preprint arXiv:1810.04805 (2018)

15. Dosovitskiy, A., et al.: An image is worth 16×16 words: transformers for image recognition at scale. arXiv preprint arXiv:2010.11929 (2020)

16. Dosovitskiy, A., et al.: FlowNet: learning optical flow with convolutional networks. In: Proceedings of the IEEE International Conference on Computer Vision, pp. 2758–2766 (2015)

17. Ess, A., Leibe, B., Schindler, K., Van Gool, L.: A mobile vision system for robust multi-person tracking. In: 2008 IEEE Conference on Computer Vision and Pattern Recognition, pp. 1–8. IEEE (2008)

18. Fan, Z., et al.: Object level depth reconstruction for category level 6D object pose estimation from monocular RGB image (2022)

19. Fan, Z., et al.: Object level depth reconstruction for category level 6d object pose estimation from monocular RGB image. arXiv preprint arXiv:2204.01586 (2022)

20. Feichtenhofer, C., Pinz, A., Zisserman, A.: Detect to track and track to detect. In: Proceedings of the IEEE International Conference on Computer Vision, pp. 3038–3046 (2017)

21. Feng, W., Hu, Z., Wu, W., Yan, J., Ouyang, W.: Multi-object tracking with multiple cues and switcher-aware classification. arXiv preprint arXiv:1901.06129 (2019)

22. Ge, Z., Liu, S., Wang, F., Li, Z., Sun, J.: YOLOX: exceeding YOLO series in 2021. arXiv preprint arXiv:2107.08430 (2021)

23. Geiger, A., Lenz, P., Stiller, C., Urtasun, R.: Vision meets robotics: the KITTI dataset. Int. J. Rob. Res. **32**(11), 1231–1237 (2013)

24. Gonzalez, N.F., Ospina, A., Calvez, P.: SMAT: smart multiple affinity metrics for multiple object tracking. In: Campilho, A., Karray, F., Wang, Z. (eds.) ICIAR 2020. LNCS, vol. 12132, pp. 48–62. Springer, Cham (2020). https://doi.org/10.1007/978-3-030-50516-5_5

25. He, J., Huang, Z., Wang, N., Zhang, Z.: Learnable graph matching: incorporating graph partitioning with deep feature learning for multiple object tracking. In: Proceedings of the IEEE/CVF Conference on Computer Vision and Pattern Recognition, pp. 5299–5309 (2021)

26. He, K., Zhang, X., Ren, S., Sun, J.: Deep residual learning for image recognition. In: Proceedings of the IEEE Conference on Computer Vision and Pattern Recognition, pp. 770–778 (2016)
27. Huang, Z., Zhang, T., Heng, W., Shi, B., Zhou, S.: Real-time intermediate flow estimation for video frame interpolation. In: Proceedings of the European Conference on Computer Vision (ECCV) (2022)
28. Karunasekera, H., Wang, H., Zhang, H.: Multiple object tracking with attention to appearance, structure, motion and size. IEEE Access **7**, 104423–104434 (2019)
29. Li, J., Gao, X., Jiang, T.: Graph networks for multiple object tracking. In: Proceedings of the IEEE/CVF Winter Conference on Applications of Computer Vision, pp. 719–728 (2020)
30. Li, W., Xiong, Y., Yang, S., Xu, M., Wang, Y., Xia, W.: Semi-TCL: semi-supervised track contrastive representation learning. arXiv preprint arXiv:2107.02396 (2021)
31. Li, W., Liu, H., Ding, R., Liu, M., Wang, P., Yang, W.: Exploiting temporal contexts with strided transformer for 3D human pose estimation. IEEE Trans. Multimedia (2022)
32. Li, W., Liu, H., Tang, H., Wang, P., Van Gool, L.: MHFormer: multi-hypothesis transformer for 3D human pose estimation. In: Proceedings of the IEEE/CVF Conference on Computer Vision and Pattern Recognition, pp. 13147–13156 (2022)
33. Liang, C., et al.: Rethinking the competition between detection and ReID in multi-object tracking. arXiv preprint arXiv:2010.12138 (2020)
34. Lin, T.-Y., et al.: Microsoft COCO: common objects in context. In: Fleet, D., Pajdla, T., Schiele, B., Tuytelaars, T. (eds.) ECCV 2014. LNCS, vol. 8693, pp. 740–755. Springer, Cham (2014). https://doi.org/10.1007/978-3-319-10602-1_48
35. Liu, Z., et al.: Swin transformer: hierarchical vision transformer using shifted windows. In: Proceedings of the IEEE/CVF International Conference on Computer Vision, pp. 10012–10022 (2021)
36. Liu, Z., et al.: Unveiling the power of mixup for stronger classifiers. arXiv preprint arXiv:2103.13027 (2021)
37. Loshchilov, I., Hutter, F.: Decoupled weight decay regularization. arXiv preprint arXiv:1711.05101 (2017)
38. Lu, Z., Rathod, V., Votel, R., Huang, J.: RetinaTrack: online single stage joint detection and tracking. In: Proceedings of the IEEE/CVF Conference on Computer Vision and Pattern Recognition, pp. 14668–14678 (2020)
39. Luiten, J., et al.: HOTA: a higher order metric for evaluating multi-object tracking. Int. J. Comput. Vision **129**(2), 548–578 (2021)
40. Luo, W., Xing, J., Milan, A., Zhang, X., Liu, W., Kim, T.K.: Multiple object tracking: a literature review. Artif. Intell. **293**, 103448 (2021)
41. Meinhardt, T., Kirillov, A., Leal-Taixe, L., Feichtenhofer, C.: TrackFormer: multi-object tracking with transformers. arXiv preprint arXiv:2101.02702 (2021)
42. Meinhold, R.J., Singpurwalla, N.D.: Understanding the Kalman filter. Am. Stat. **37**(2), 123–127 (1983)
43. Pang, J., et al.: Quasi-dense similarity learning for multiple object tracking. In: Proceedings of the IEEE/CVF Conference on Computer Vision and Pattern Recognition, pp. 164–173 (2021)
44. Peng, S., Liu, Y., Huang, Q., Zhou, X., Bao, H.: PVNet: pixel-wise voting network for 6DoF pose estimation. In: Proceedings of the IEEE/CVF Conference on Computer Vision and Pattern Recognition, pp. 4561–4570 (2019)
45. Ranftl, R., Bochkovskiy, A., Koltun, V.: Vision transformers for dense prediction. In: Proceedings of the IEEE/CVF International Conference on Computer Vision, pp. 12179–12188 (2021)

46. Rangesh, A., Maheshwari, P., Gebre, M., Mhatre, S., Ramezani, V., Trivedi, M.M.: TrackMPNN: a message passing graph neural architecture for multi-object tracking. arXiv preprint arXiv:2101.04206 (2021)
47. Ren, S., He, K., Girshick, R., Sun, J.: Faster R-CNN: towards real-time object detection with region proposal networks. In: Advances in Neural Information Processing Systems, vol. 28 (2015)
48. Shao, S., et al.: CrowdHuman: a benchmark for detecting human in a crowd. arXiv preprint arXiv:1805.00123 (2018)
49. Shuai, B., Berneshawi, A., Li, X., Modolo, D., Tighe, J.: SiamMOT: Siamese multi-object tracking. In: Proceedings of the IEEE/CVF Conference on Computer Vision and Pattern Recognition, pp. 12372–12382 (2021)
50. Srivastava, N., Hinton, G., Krizhevsky, A., Sutskever, I., Salakhutdinov, R.: Dropout: a simple way to prevent neural networks from overfitting. J. Mach. Learn. Res. **15**(1), 1929–1958 (2014)
51. Sun, P., et al.: TransTrack: multiple object tracking with transformer. arXiv preprint arXiv:2012.15460 (2020)
52. Sun, S., Akhtar, N., Song, X., Song, H., Mian, A., Shah, M.: Simultaneous detection and tracking with motion modelling for multiple object tracking. In: Vedaldi, A., Bischof, H., Brox, T., Frahm, J.-M. (eds.) ECCV 2020. LNCS, vol. 12369, pp. 626–643. Springer, Cham (2020). https://doi.org/10.1007/978-3-030-58586-0_37
53. Tang, S., Andriluka, M., Andres, B., Schiele, B.: Multiple people tracking by lifted multicut and person re-identification. In: Proceedings of the IEEE Conference on Computer Vision and Pattern Recognition, pp. 3539–3548 (2017)
54. Tokmakov, P., Li, J., Burgard, W., Gaidon, A.: Learning to track with object permanence. In: Proceedings of the IEEE/CVF International Conference on Computer Vision, pp. 10860–10869 (2021)
55. Tu, Z., et al.: MaxViT: multi-axis vision transformer. arXiv preprint arXiv:2204.01697 (2022)
56. Vaswani, A., et al.: Attention is all you need. In: Advances in Neural Information Processing Systems, vol. 30 (2017)
57. Wang, C., et al.: DenseFusion: 6D object pose estimation by iterative dense fusion. In: Proceedings of the IEEE/CVF Conference on Computer Vision and Pattern Recognition, pp. 3343–3352 (2019)
58. Wang, Q., Zheng, Y., Pan, P., Xu, Y.: Multiple object tracking with correlation learning. In: Proceedings of the IEEE/CVF Conference on Computer Vision and Pattern Recognition, pp. 3876–3886 (2021)
59. Wang, W., et al.: Pyramid vision transformer: a versatile backbone for dense prediction without convolutions. In: Proceedings of the IEEE/CVF International Conference on Computer Vision (ICCV), pp. 568–578, October 2021
60. Wang, X., et al.: MVSTER: epipolar transformer for efficient multi-view stereo. arXiv preprint arXiv:2204.07346 (2022)
61. Wang, Y., Kitani, K., Weng, X.: Joint object detection and multi-object tracking with graph neural networks. In: 2021 IEEE International Conference on Robotics and Automation (ICRA), pp. 13708–13715. IEEE (2021)
62. Weng, X., Kitani, K.: A baseline for 3D multi-object tracking. arXiv preprint arXiv:1907.03961 1(2), 6 (2019)
63. Wojke, N., Bewley, A., Paulus, D.: Simple online and realtime tracking with a deep association metric. In: 2017 IEEE International Conference on Image Processing (ICIP), pp. 3645–3649. IEEE (2017)
64. Wu, W., et al.: End-to-end video text spotting with transformer. arXiv preprint arXiv:2203.10539 (2022)

65. Xiang, Y., Alahi, A., Savarese, S.: Learning to track: online multi-object tracking by decision making. In: Proceedings of the IEEE International Conference on Computer Vision, pp. 4705–4713 (2015)
66. Xie, E., Wang, W., Yu, Z., Anandkumar, A., Alvarez, J.M., Luo, P.: SegFormer: simple and efficient design for semantic segmentation with transformers. In: Advances in Neural Information Processing Systems, vol. 34 (2021)
67. Xu, R., Xiang, H., Tu, Z., Xia, X., Yang, M.H., Ma, J.: V2X-ViT: vehicle-to-everything cooperative perception with vision transformer. arXiv preprint arXiv:2203.10638 (2022)
68. Xu, Y., Ban, Y., Delorme, G., Gan, C., Rus, D., Alameda-Pineda, X.: TransCenter: transformers with dense queries for multiple-object tracking. arXiv preprint arXiv:2103.15145 (2021)
69. Yu, E., Li, Z., Han, S., Wang, H.: RelationTrack: relation-aware multiple object tracking with decoupled representation. IEEE Trans. Multimedia (2022)
70. Yuan, Y., et al.: HRFormer: high-resolution transformer for dense prediction. arXiv preprint arXiv:2110.09408 (2021)
71. Zeng, F., Dong, B., Wang, T., Zhang, X., Wei, Y.: MOTR: end-to-end multiple-object tracking with transformer. arXiv preprint arXiv:2105.03247 (2021)
72. Zhang, H., Cisse, M., Dauphin, Y.N., Lopez-Paz, D.: mixup: beyond empirical risk minimization. arXiv preprint arXiv:1710.09412 (2017)
73. Zhang, S., Benenson, R., Schiele, B.: CityPersons: a diverse dataset for pedestrian detection. In: Proceedings of the IEEE Conference on Computer Vision and Pattern Recognition, pp. 3213–3221 (2017)
74. Zhang, Y., et al.: Multiplex labeling graph for near-online tracking in crowded scenes. IEEE Internet Things J. **7**(9), 7892–7902 (2020). https://doi.org/10.1109/JIOT.2020.2996609
75. Zhang, Y., et al.: ByteTrack: multi-object tracking by associating every detection box. arXiv preprint arXiv:2110.06864 (2021)
76. Zhang, Y., Wang, C., Wang, X., Zeng, W., Liu, W.: FairMOT: on the fairness of detection and re-identification in multiple object tracking. Int. J. Comput. Vision **129**(11), 3069–3087 (2021)
77. Zhao, Z., Samel, K., Chen, B., et al.: ProTo: program-guided transformer for program-guided tasks. In: Advances in Neural Information Processing Systems, vol. 34 (2021)
78. Zheng, L., Tang, M., Chen, Y., Zhu, G., Wang, J., Lu, H.: Improving multiple object tracking with single object tracking. In: Proceedings of the IEEE/CVF Conference on Computer Vision and Pattern Recognition, pp. 2453–2462 (2021)
79. Zhou, Q., et al.: TransVOD: end-to-end video object detection with spatial-temporal transformers. arXiv preprint arXiv:2201.05047 (2022)
80. Zhou, X., Koltun, V., Krähenbühl, P.: Tracking objects as points. In: Vedaldi, A., Bischof, H., Brox, T., Frahm, J.-M. (eds.) ECCV 2020. LNCS, vol. 12349, pp. 474–490. Springer, Cham (2020). https://doi.org/10.1007/978-3-030-58548-8_28
81. Zhu, X., Dai, J., Yuan, L., Wei, Y.: Towards high performance video object detection. In: Proceedings of the IEEE Conference on Computer Vision and Pattern Recognition, pp. 7210–7218 (2018)
82. Zhu, X., Su, W., Lu, L., Li, B., Wang, X., Dai, J.: Deformable DETR: deformable transformers for end-to-end object detection. arXiv preprint arXiv:2010.04159 (2020)
83. Zhu, X., Wang, Y., Dai, J., Yuan, L., Wei, Y.: Flow-guided feature aggregation for video object detection. In: Proceedings of the IEEE International Conference on Computer Vision, pp. 408–417 (2017)

CMT: Context-Matching-Guided Transformer for 3D Tracking in Point Clouds

Zhiyang Guo[1], Yunyao Mao[1], Wengang Zhou[1,2]($\boxtimes$), Min Wang[2], and Houqiang Li[1,2]($\boxtimes$)

[1] CAS Key Laboratory of Technology in GIPAS, EEIS Department, University of Science and Technology of China, Hefei, China
{guozhiyang,myy2016}@mail.ustc.edu.cn
{zhwg,lihq}@ustc.edu.cn
[2] Institute of Artificial Intelligence, Hefei Comprehensive National Science Center, Hefei, China

Abstract. How to effectively match the target template features with the search area is the core problem in point-cloud-based 3D single object tracking. However, in the literature, most of the methods focus on devising sophisticated matching modules at point-level, while overlooking the rich spatial context information of points. To this end, we propose **C**ontext-**M**atching-Guided **T**ransformer (**CMT**), a Siamese tracking paradigm for 3D single object tracking. In this work, we first leverage the local distribution of points to construct a horizontally rotation-invariant contextual descriptor for both the template and the search area. Then, a novel matching strategy based on shifted windows is designed for such descriptors to effectively measure the template-search contextual similarity. Furthermore, we introduce a target-specific transformer and a spatial-aware orientation encoder to exploit the target-aware information in the most contextually relevant template points, thereby enhancing the search feature for a better target proposal. We conduct extensive experiments to verify the merits of our proposed CMT and report a series of new state-of-the-art records on three widely-adopted datasets.

Keywords: 3D single object tracking · Point clouds · Context match

1 Introduction

As an essential task for autonomous driving vehicles and intelligent robotics, 3D single object tracking (SOT) has attracted substantial attention in the past few years. Different from 2D SOT that is developed on images, 3D SOT is generally performed with point clouds data. Although the recent development of deep neural networks [13,19,37] has led to the surge of 2D SOT algorithms [2,10,26,27,39], it is still non-trivial to apply these 2D methods in 3D

Supplementary Information The online version contains supplementary material available at https://doi.org/10.1007/978-3-031-20047-2_6.

space, especially when it comes to the sparse 3D point clouds. In general, the point-cloud-based 3D SOT methods [15,17,33,46] follow the Siamese tracking paradigm [1], which has exhibited great success in RGB images. Notably, the pioneering work P2B [33] proposes the first end-to-end 3D object tracker based on template-search comparison and voting-based region proposal generation. The following work BAT [46] introduces BoxCloud feature representation and a box-aware feature fusion module to make the tracker robust to the sparse and incomplete point clouds.

Despite the significant advance, the state-of-the-art 3D trackers still suffer from non-trivial defects. Specifically, in BAT [46], the BoxCloud feature is not only exploited to facilitate the template-search comparison, but also leveraged in target proposal feature aggregation. However, in the box-aware feature fusion module of BAT, all the features belonging to different template points are simply concatenated and processed with multi-layer perceptrons (MLPs) and max-pooling, which struggles to capture useful target information from multiple template points. Moreover, the pairwise distance calculation relying only on BoxCloud may lead to mismatch for targets that are less distinctive in shape and size, since BoxCloud features merely focus on the relative position of the individual point inside a bounding box, but lack the awareness of spatial context.

Another issue lies in PointNet++ [32], as it is exploited as the backbone network for most of the existing point cloud trackers. Instead of adopting explicit T-Nets to realize geometric transformation invariance as in PointNet [31], PointNet++ achieves invariance through data augmentation. However, in 3D SOT, such geometric transformation invariance is hard to learn from data, which degrades the quality of the extracted feature when the target rotates during tracking. Subsequent modules based on the backbone feature, such as the template-search comparison, are inevitably affected.

To address the above issues, we propose a novel Context-Matching-Guided Transformer (CMT) for robust 3D SOT. Specifically, a descriptor invariant to horizontal rotations is developed for each point to describe its spatial context. Meanwhile, to effectively measure the similarity of such descriptors between points in the template and search area, we design a context matching strategy based on shifted windows. The proposed fine-grained context matching is combined with the efficient BoxCloud comparison [46] to

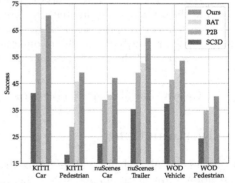

Fig. 1. Our method (CMT) significantly outperforms representative point cloud trackers [17,33,46] on multiple benchmarks.

form successive coarse-to-fine matching stages. The most relevant template points are thereby selected to be fused with each search point accordingly. Instead of simply using MLPs for template-search feature fusion, we develop a target-specific transformer to make the best of the target-aware information.

Furthermore, we introduce a spatial-aware orientation encoder after the transformer to integrate information from eight spatial orientations. Finally, a region proposal network (RPN) used in [33,46] is exploited to generate the 3D target proposal. We evaluate our method on three prevalent 3D SOT benchmarks, including KITTI [16], nuScenes [5] and Waymo Open Dataset (WOD) [35]. As shown in Fig. 1, our method sets a series of state-of-the-art records.

Our main contributions can be summarized as follows:

- We introduce a horizontally rotation-invariant descriptor for contextual description, and design a shifted-window matching strategy to effectively measure the spatial contextual similarity between points.
- We propose a context-matching-guided transformer for 3D object tracking, and present an elegant view of how to integrate point contextual cues and target-aware information into the feature of the search area.
- We conduct extensive experiments to validate the merits of our method, and show promising improvements on several prevalent benchmarks.

2 Related Works

2.1 2D Siamese Tracking

Recent years have witnessed the great development of 2D SOT approaches. Within these approaches, the Siamese tracking paradigm has demonstrated its advantages over the traditional discriminative correlation filter [4,11,12,20,21]. Specifically, a Siamese tracker is composed of two branches (*i.e.*, the template and the search area) with a shared feature extraction network to project RGB frames into an implicit feature space. The tracking task is then formulated as a feature matching problem. Following the pioneering work SiamFC [1], many Siamese trackers [8,18,26,27,39,42,47] have proved their competitiveness. In recent state-of-the-art RGB trackers [2,7,38,43], the Siamese network is still employed as a basic paradigm.

2.2 3D Single Object Tracking

Early 3D SOT methods [3,24,25,28,30] mainly focus on the RGB-D tracking scenario. As a pioneer in point cloud tracking, SC3D [17] generates candidates for template-search comparison by the Kalman filtering and introduces a shape completion network to retain geometric information in point features. However, SC3D is time-consuming and not end-to-end trainable. P2B [33] is proposed as the first end-to-end point cloud tracker based on pair-wise feature comparison and voting-based region proposal. It enhances search feature with target information in template and adapts SiamRPN [27] to 3D cases, thereby achieving significant performance improvement. 3D-SiamRPN [15] is another tracker inspired by SiamRPN and exhibits good generalization ability. MLVSNet [40] performs Hough voting on multi-level features to retain more useful information. BAT [46] presents a box-aware feature named BoxCloud that is robust to sparseness and incompleteness of point clouds. Benefiting from BoxCloud comparison and feature fusion, BAT exhibits state-of-the-art performance in point cloud SOT. V2B [22] builds a Siamese voxel-to-BEV tracker that regresses target center from the dense bird's eye view (BEV) feature map in an anchor-free manner. Nevertheless, none of these methods pays attention to the fine-grained template-search matching other than the calculation of some feature distance.

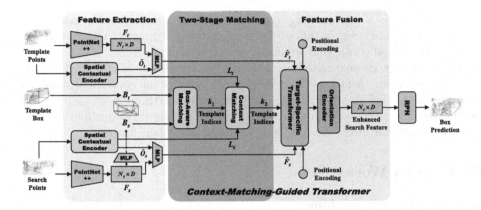

Fig. 2. Pipeline of the proposed CMT tracker. Multiple features are fed into the context-matching-guided transformer for template-search matching and context-aware feature fusion. Finally, a 3D RPN is exploited to generate the target proposal.

2.3   Transformer for Point Cloud Analysis

Since the proposal of transformer [37], such networks using attention mechanism for global awareness have achieved great success in both natural language processing and computer vision [6,13,29]. Recently, many methods [7,38,43] in 2D SOT also shed light on the transformer and show excellent performance. In the 3D domain, Point Transformer [45] is proposed with the vector attention mechanism, improving the performance in point cloud classification and segmentation tasks. Only a few works apply transformer in point cloud SOT. PTT [34] utilizes transformer in voting and proposal generation stage of P2B [33], but does not improve the quality of template-search feature augmentation. LTTR [9] employs transformer framework for feature fusion, but the reported performance is not satisfying due to the design of scalar attention. To this end, we propose a target-specific transformer guided by context matching for feature enhancement, which achieves significant performance improvement in point cloud SOT.

3   Method

Given the initial template point cloud P_t of a target, our CMT tracker localizes it with an input search point cloud P_s for each frame and outputs a 3D bounding box. As depicted in Fig. 2, the proposed method includes three main steps: feature extraction, two-stage template-search matching, and context-aware feature fusion. We will elaborate them in the following sections.

3.1   Feature Extraction

For efficient subsequent processing, four types of features are obtained for template and search point clouds, respectively: 1) *seed feature* denoted by $F_t = \{f_t^i \in \mathbb{R}^D\}_{i=1}^{N_t}$ and $F_s = \{f_s^i \in \mathbb{R}^D\}_{i=1}^{N_s}$ (N_t and N_s are the numbers of extracted seed points); 2) *BoxCloud feature* denoted by $B_t = \{b_t^i \in \mathbb{R}^9\}_{i=1}^{N_t}$ and $B_s = \{b_s^i \in \mathbb{R}^9\}_{i=1}^{N_s}$; 3) *local contextual descriptor* denoted by $L_t = \{l_t^i \in \mathbb{R}^{k_c \times 3}\}_{i=1}^{N_t}$ and $L_s = \{l_s^i \in \mathbb{R}^{k_c \times 3}\}_{i=1}^{N_s}$; 4) *orientational contextual feature* denoted by $\widetilde{O}_t = \{\tilde{o}_t^i \in \mathbb{R}^3\}_{i=1}^{N_t}$ and $\widetilde{O}_s = \{\tilde{o}_s^i \in \mathbb{R}^3\}_{i=1}^{N_s}$. Among them, F_t and F_s are extracted by a shared PointNet++ [32]. B depicts the distances from a point to the corners and center of the target bounding box [46]. Specifically, B_t is calculated directly from the template bounding box, while B_s is predicted by an MLP under the supervision of the ground-truth bounding box. The latter two features are produced by the spatial contextual encoder to describe the local context.

Spatial Contextual Encoder (SCE). In tracking, the rotations of targets are usually inevitable. However, many features directly learned from the input points are orientation-sensitive. Networks like PointNet++ [32] achieve geometric transforming invariance through data augmentation, which is difficult to recreate in 3D tracking. BoxCloud proposed in [46] is an interpretable feature invariant to rotations, since it measures the distance between a point and the 3D bounding box. Nevertheless, BoxCloud only focuses on individual points, ignoring the rich contextual information carried by the distribution of nearby points. To this end, we propose a spatial contextual encoder (SCE) to produce point-wise features with the following attributes: 1) invariant to horizontal rotations commonly encountered in 3D SOT; 2) able to effectively describe the spatial context of a point; 3) highly interpretable and easily inferred from point coordinates.

As illustrated in Fig. 3(a), the input point coordinates are first fed into two polar transform blocks to construct the *local contextual descriptor* $L = \{l^i \in \mathbb{R}^{k_c \times 3}\}_{i=1}^{N}$ and the *octant contextual descriptor* $O = \{o^i \in \mathbb{R}^{8 \times 3}\}_{i=1}^{N}$. Both l and o are a set of polar vectors representing the spatial context. The only difference between them is the way of selecting neighboring points. Local polar transform block searches for k_c nearest neighbors, while octant polar transform block looks for the nearest neighbor in each of eight octants, which is more informative than a set of homogeneous points in only a few directions.

For a point i, after selecting its k ($k = k_c$ for local and $k = 8$ for octant) neighbors based on Euclidean distance, the 3D polar vectors expressed by $\{\rho_j^i = (r_j^i, \alpha_j^i, \beta_j^i)\}_{j=1}^{k}$ are obtained using the following formulas [14]:

$$r_j^i = \sqrt{{x_j^i}^2 + {y_j^i}^2 + {z_j^i}^2}, \tag{1}$$

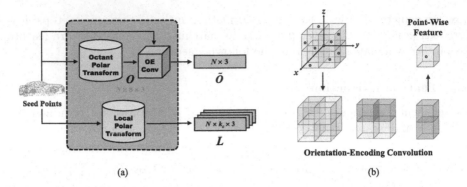

Fig. 3. (a) Architecture of spatial contextual encoder (SCE). Octant contextual descriptor O and local contextual descriptor L are extracted using different ways of selecting neighboring points. O is then further integrated by orientation-encoding convolution to produce the orientational contextual feature $\tilde{O}$. **(b) Illustration of orientation encoder (OE).** A three-stage convolution along each of three axes is performed successively on the features of neighbors from all eight octants.

$$\alpha_j^i = \arctan \frac{y_j^i}{x_j^i} - \arctan \frac{\bar{y}^i}{\bar{x}^i},\tag{2}$$

$$\beta_j^i = \arctan \frac{z_j^i}{\sqrt{x_j^i{}^2 + y_j^i{}^2}} - \arctan \frac{\bar{z}^i}{\sqrt{\bar{x}^i{}^2 + \bar{y}^i{}^2}},\tag{3}$$

where (x_j^i, y_j^i, z_j^i) is the relative coordinate of neighbor j in the Cartesian coordinate system with point i as the origin, and $(\bar{x}^i, \bar{y}^i, \bar{z}^i)$ denotes the mean values of neighboring relative coordinate, which is termed as center-of-mass point. Benefiting from the introduction of mass center, the polar vectors remain unchanged when point clouds rotate around z-axis in a 3D Cartesian coordinate system. Center-of-mass point can also effectively reduce the randomness caused by the downsampling before and reflect the general picture of the spatial context [14].

Due to the non-differentiable selecting operation in template-search comparison, we use the directly calculated $l = (\rho_1, \rho_2, \cdots, \rho_{kc}) \in \mathbb{R}^{k_c \times 3}$ to be a criteria in the context matching module, which is further discussed in Sect. 3.2. Moreover, in order to make use of such informative rotation-invariant feature in target proposal, we further process $o \in \mathbb{R}^{8 \times 3}$ with orientation-encoding convolution [23] to integrate information from all eight directions (Fig. 3(b)), which is detailed interpreted in Sect. 3.3. After that, the output $\tilde{o} \in \mathbb{R}^3$ is fed into MLPs along with the seed feature $f \in \mathbb{R}^D$ to produce $\hat{f} \in \mathbb{R}^D$.

3.2 Two-Stage Template-Search Matching

Template-search matching is a fundamental operation in Siamese trackers. Instead of comparing the distance between seed features, we introduce a more promising method composed of two stages: box-aware and context matching.

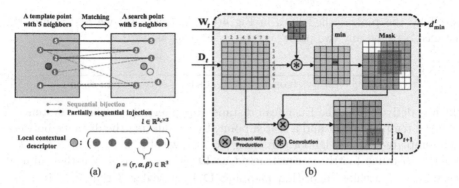

Fig. 4. (a) **An exemplified 2D illustration of good template-search matching.**
In both template and search area, there exist 5 neighbors sorted by their distances to
the center seed. Due to target moving or noise, the nearest point in template disappears
in search area (dashed point), and a new point (No. 4) appears in exchange. In this case,
the reasonable matching (black solid lines) has misalignment with some points ignored.
(b) **Illustration of shifted-window context matching.** Rows and columns of $\mathbf{D}_t$
refer to template and search neighbors, respectively. At every stage, the masked output
$\mathbf{D}_{t+1}$ serves as the input of the next stage, until all the windows are used. For $k_c = 8$
here, the sizes of two windows are set to 3 and 2. After two stages of convolutions,
two matching pairs are found: template $(3, 4, 5)$ and search $(4, 5, 6)$, template $(6, 7)$ and
search $(7, 8)$. Finally, the seed-wise contextual distance is calculated as $\hat{d} = d^1_{\min} + d^2_{\min}$.

Box-Aware Matching. Considering the success of BoxCloud comparison in
BAT [46], we first adopt a box-aware matching based on pairwise L_2 distance
between the BoxCloud B_t and B_s. Thereby k_1 nearest template points are
selected for each search point. Box-aware matching is effective for extremely
sparse point clouds, where meaningful neighboring points can hardly be found.
However, template-search matching relying only on BoxCloud may lead to mismatch for targets that are less distinctive in shape and size (*e.g.*, cyclists), since
BoxCloud features focus on the relative position of the individual point inside a
bounding box, yet ignoring the spatial context. Therefore, in our work, the box-
aware matching acts as a robust and efficient base for the following fine-grained
context matching. In this way, two stages of matching benefit from each other.
Shifted-Window Context Matching. Among the k_1 template points selected
for each search point by the coarse box-aware matching, we adopt the context
matching to further select k_2 template points in a fine-grained manner using the
local contextual descriptors l_t and $l_s \in \mathbb{R}^{k_c \times 3}$. Therefore, it becomes a problem how to exploit these two sets of polar vectors to describe the similarity
or distance between two points' local contexts. Points selection is not a differentiable operation, and there is no supervision available here. Therefore, no
learnable parameters can be introduced, which means the comparison is directly
performed between $2 \times k_c$ polar vectors. However, we cannot calculate the summation of distances directly between vectors in l_t and l_s, since the sequential
bijection between the neighbors sorted by distance is unreasonable, as is illus-

trated by the pink dashed lines in Fig. 4(a). In this case, we first define the distance between any two polar vectors ρ_m and ρ_n as

$$d_{mn} \triangleq \sqrt{r_m^2 + r_n^2 - 2r_m r_n \left(\cos\beta_m \cos\beta_n \cos\left(\alpha_m - \alpha_n\right) + \sin\beta_m \sin\beta_n\right)}, \quad (4)$$

which is derived from the Euclidean distance in spherical coordinate system.

For a template point and a search point, by calculating the distance between each template-search neighbor pair using Eq. (4), we obtain $d_{mn}, \forall m, n \in [1, k_c]$, and the distance matrix is constructed as $\mathbf{D} = (d_{mn})_{k_c \times k_c}$. We then aim at designing a matching algorithm mapping $\mathbf{D}$ to a scalar $\hat{d}$ that describes the distance between two distributions of neighbors. Considering the intrinsic defect of bijective matching that some of the matched pairs are meaningless due to target moving or noise, we propose the shifted-window matching strategy based on the assumption that partially sequential injective correspondences exist in similar spatial contexts, with noise points inserted between them (Fig. 4(a)).

As illustrated in Fig. 4(b), given a distance matrix $\mathbf{D}_{k_c \times k_c}$, a series of identity matrices (windows) denoted by $\{\mathbf{W}_t\}$ are generated with empirical sizes $S = \{s_t\}$ according to k_c. For example, when $k_c = 16$, we set $S = \{4, 3, 3\}$, which indicates that 10 of the neighbors have partially sequential injective matching solution, while the remaining 6 neighbors are considered as noise. Then we perform a 2D convolution on $\mathbf{D}_1 = \mathbf{D}$ using $\mathbf{W}_1$ as the kernel. The result is a distance map for different partial matchings, and its minimum element is denoted by $d_{\min}^1$. After that, we mask $\mathbf{D}_1$ to construct $\mathbf{D}_2$, so that only the top-left and bottom-right area of the window producing $d_{\min}^1$ is available for the next convolution using $\mathbf{W}_2$. The masking operation prevents unreasonable crossed matching. For example, once template neighbors $(3, 4, 5)$ have already been matched with search neighbors $(4, 5, 6)$, in no case should template neighbors 1 and 2 be matched with search neighbors 7 or 8. During convolutions for $t = 2, 3, \cdots$, if no area is available in $\mathbf{D}_t$ after masking, $d_{\min}^t$ is set to $d_{\max}^1$ to show that this is not a good matching. After finishing convolutions with all $\mathbf{W}_t$, we define that $\hat{d} = \sum_t d_{\min}^t$. Once $\hat{d}$ is obtained for all template-search pairs, k_2 contextually nearest template points are selected for each search point as the result of this matching stage.

3.3   Matching-Guided Feature Fusion

After the coarse-to-fine matching, we develop a target-specific transformer to perform feature fusion among the matched template-search pairs to exploit the target-aware information for a better target proposal. Then a spatial-aware orientation encoder is introduced to further enhance the attentional feature by integrating spatial information from all directions.

Target-Specific Transformer. As shown in Fig. 5, we adopt the vector attention mechanism [44] to enhance the search feature with attention to relevant template feature that contains potential target information useful for region proposal. Given the template feature $\widehat{F}_t = \left\{\hat{f}_t^i\right\}_{i=1}^{N_t}$, the search feature $\widehat{F}_s = \left\{\hat{f}_s^i\right\}_{i=1}^{N_s}$

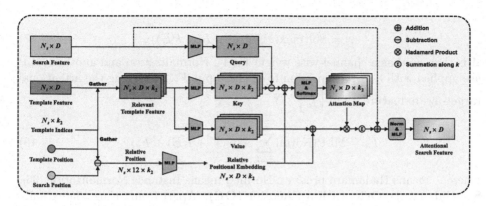

Fig. 5. Illustration of the target-specific transformer. k_2 relevant template points are gathered and aggregated with each search point. The positional encoding is learned from 3D coordinates and 9D BoxCloud. Note that the dimensionality of embedding space is set to be the same as that of the input feature space (D).

and k_2 relevant template indices for each search point selected by box-aware and context matching, the relevant template features $\widehat{F}_t^* = \left\{ \left\{ \hat{f}_{t,i}^j \right\}_{j=1}^{k_2} \right\}_{i=1}^{N_s}$ are first gathered. Then with three different MLPs, the embedding Q (Query) is generated from $\widehat{F}_s$, while K (Key) and V (Value) are generated from $\widehat{F}_t^*$.

Generally, the standard transformer uses scalar dot-product attention to obtain the relationship (attention map) between Q and K expressed as $A = \text{Softmax}(Q^T K)$. Instead of that, we adopt the subtraction operation with an extra MLP to improve the fitting ability:

$$A = \text{Softmax}(\text{MLP}(Q - K)). \tag{5}$$

It is reported in [45] that such vector attention is more suitable for point clouds than scalar attention, since it supports adaptive modulation of individual feature channels in V, rather than a shared scalar weight.

Positional Encoding. Positional encoding plays an important role in transformer. For point clouds, 3D coordinates themselves are naturally suitable for positional encoding. Meanwhile, the success of BoxCloud [46] implies that, the manually crafted 9D feature indicating a point's distance to the bounding box can be another candidate. Therefore, we integrate point coordinates and Box-Cloud feature to generate a trainable relative positional encoding expressed as

$$PE = \text{MLP}\left((P_s, B_s) - (P_t^*, B_t^*)\right), \tag{6}$$

where P_t^* and B_t^* are the coordinates and BoxCloud feature of k_2 relevant template points for each search point, and $(\cdot, \cdot)$ denotes the concatenation operation. We follow [45] to add PE to both $(Q - K)$ and V, since position encoding is important for both attention generation and feature transformation. Thereby Eq. (5) can be rewritten as

$$A = \text{Softmax}(\text{MLP}(Q - K + PE)). \tag{7}$$

A is then used as a channel-wise weight for V. Normalization and another MLP are applied with a skip connection from the input $\widehat{F}_s$, producing the attentional target-aware feature $\widehat{F}_a = \left\{ \hat{f}_a^i \right\}_{i=1}^{N_s}$:

$$\widehat{F}_a = \text{MLP}(\text{Norm}(\sum_{j=1}^{k_2} A \odot (V + PE) + F_s)), \tag{8}$$

where $\odot$ means Hadamard product; $\text{Norm}(\cdot)$ means Instance Normalization [36]. **Spatial-Aware Orientation Encoder (OE).** Apart from fusing contextually nearby f_t into f_s, we also introduce an orientation encoder (OE) that aggregates features from spatially nearby seeds. As illustrated in Fig. 3(b), OE first adopts stacked 8-neighborhood (S8N) search to find the nearest neighbor in each of the eight octants partitioned by three axes. If no point exists in some octant within a searching radius, the center point is duplicated as the nearest neighbor of itself. Then we perform a three-stage orientation-encoding convolution [23] on $\hat{f}_a$ of all eight neighbors along each of three axes successively. After squeezing, the output feature vector has the same size as $\hat{f}_a$. In OE, several orientation-encoding convolution blocks are stacked for a more extensive spatial awareness.

4   Experiments

4.1   Experimental Settings

Datasets. To evaluate our tracker, we conduct experiments on three datasets of point clouds scanned by LiDAR sensors, *i.e.*, KITTI [16], nuScenes [5] and WOD [35]. The KITTI dataset contains 21 outdoor scenes and 8 types of targets, and we follow [17] to set up the training, valid and test splits. The nuScenes dataset contains 1000 driving scenes across 23 target classes, and we train the models on the *train_track* split of its training set and test on its validation set. For WOD, we extract tracklets from its detection dataset to produce a SOT dataset with three target classes (Vehicle, Pedestrian and Cyclist). To alleviate the issue of extreme class imbalance, we use 10% of the Vehicle and Pedestrian samples to match the magnitude of Cyclist samples for a fair comparison.

Metrics. We follow [17,33,46] to use one-pass evaluation (OPE) [41], measuring *Success* and *Precision* of trackers. Specifically, given a predicted and a ground-truth 3D bounding box, *Success* is defined as the AUC (area under curve) for the percentage of frames where the IoU (intersection over union) between two boxes is within a given threshold as the threshold varies from 0 to 1. *Precision* is defined as the AUC for the percentage of frames where distance between two boxes' centers is within a given threshold as the threshold varies from 0 to 2 m.

Implementation Details. For training, the loss of our tracker is set to $\mathcal{L} = \mathcal{L}_{bc} + \mathcal{L}_{rpn}$ to count both the Huber loss for BoxCloud [46] and the region-proposal loss [33]. During both training and testing, the search area is formed by

Table 1. Performance (Success/Precision) comparison on the KITTI, nuScenes and WOD benchmarks. Bold denotes the best performance.

KITTI

Category	Car	Pedestrian	Van	Cyclist	Average
Frames	6424	6088	1248	308	14068
SC3D [17]	41.3/57.9	18.2/37.8	40.4/47.0	41.5 / 70.4	31.2/48.5
P2B [33]	56.2/72.8	28.7/49.6	40.8/48.4	32.1/44.7	42.4/60.0
3D-SiamRPN [15]	58.2/76.2	35.2/56.2	45.7/52.9	36.2/49.0	46.7/64.9
MLVSNet [40]	56.0/74.0	34.1/61.1	52.0/61.4	34.3/44.5	45.7/66.6
BAT [46]	65.4/78.9	45.7/74.5	52.4/**67.0**	33.7/45.4	55.0/75.2
V2B [22]	70.5/81.3	48.3/73.5	50.1/58.0	40.8/49.7	58.4/75.2
PTT [34]	67.8/81.8	44.9/72.0	43.6/52.5	37.2/47.3	55.1/74.2
LTTR [0]	65.0/77.1	33.2/56.8	35.8/45.6	**66.2/89.9**	48.7/65.8
CMT (Ours)	**70.5/81.9**	**49.1/75.5**	**54.1**/64.1	55.1/82.4	**59.4/77.6**

nuScenes

Category	Car	Truck	Trailer	Bus	Average
Frames	64159	13587	3352	2953	84051
SC3D [17]	22.3/21.9	30.7/27.7	35.3/28.1	29.4/24.1	24.4/23.2
P2B [33]	38.8/43.2	43.0/41.6	49.0/40.1	33.0/27.4	39.7/42.2
BAT [46]	40.7/43.3	45.3/42.6	52.6/44.9	35.4/28.0	41.8/42.7
V2B[*] [22]	36.5/38.8	40.8/36.7	48.2/39.9	31.4/26.1	37.5/38.1
PTT [34]	40.2/45.8	46.5/46.7	51.7/46.5	39.4/36.7	41.6/45.7
CMT (Ours)	**47.0/51.7**	**52.5/52.5**	**62.0/58.2**	**46.3/42.9**	**48.5/51.8**

Waymo open dataset

Category	Vehicle	Pedestrian	Cyclist	Average
Frames	142664	58497	13340	214501
SC3D[*] [17]	37.4/46.0	24.4/37.7	26.3/36.5	33.2/43.1
P2B[*] [33]	46.4/53.9	34.8/54.4	31.5/47.8	42.3/53.7
BAT[*] [46]	50.4/57.6	36.2/56.3	32.6/50.7	45.4/56.8
CMT (Ours)	**53.5/62.1**	**40.2/62.2**	**34.1/53.1**	**48.7/61.6**

[*] Reproduced with the official code provided by the authors.

enlarging the previous predicted bounding box, and the template is updated for each frame by merging the points inside the first (ground-truth) and the previous predicted box. For template-search matching, we set $k_1 = 16$ for box-aware stage and $k_c = 16$, $k_2 = 4$ for contextual stage. Our model is trained in an end-to-end manner with batch size 192 for 60 epochs using Adam optimizer. Other hyperparameters are consistent with the settings of [46]. All the experiments are conducted using NVIDIA GTX 1080Ti GPUs.

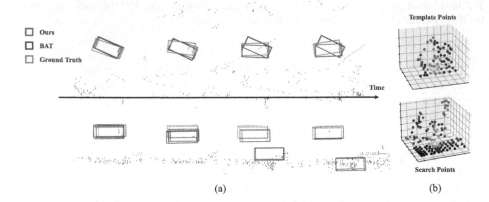

(a)   (b)

Fig. 6. (a) Advantage cases of our method compared with BAT on KITTI-Car. The upper tracklet belongs to a scene where the target car is turning a corner, and the lower tracklet targets another car in the same scene. **(b) Visualization of context matching.** The blue and the green points are a template and a search seed, respectively, surrounded by their k_c nearest neighbors with lighter colors.

4.2   Comparison Results

Comparison with State-of-the-Art Methods. We compare our tracker with existing 3D SOT methods [9,15,17,22,33,34,40,46] on the KITTI dataset. Tracking on nuScenes and WOD is more challenging, since much more distractors exist in a frame. For these two datasets, some methods are not included, since they are either not competitive enough against our baseline BAT [46], or do not provide open source code and have only reported their results on KITTI.

Table 1 summarizes the results on all three datasets. Our method shows significant advantage over the competitors on most categories on KITTI and all categories on nuScenes and WOD. For nuScenes, CMT even outperforms BAT by over 16% in Success and 21% in Precision on average. Notably, some methods [22,34] work well on the car category of KITTI, but struggle in other categories. In contrast, with the carefully-designed context-matching-guided transformer, CMT well adapts to different scales of samples with promising results.

Visualization and Qualitative Analysis. As shown in Fig. 6(a), we visualize CMT and BAT [46] on the car category of KITTI. In the upper case, the target car is turning a corner. Our CMT tracker captures the rotation accurately, while BAT makes mistakes in the orientation of bounding box. In the lower case, BAT fails to keep tracking due to a distractor, but our method works well consistently. We also visualize a case of template-search matching in Fig. 6(b). Despite the difference in point quantity and the existence of noise (in this case, plenty of ground points are included in the search area), our method can capture the contextual similarity between template and search area, mark the two seed points as relevant and aggregate their features for a better target proposal, which is mainly attributed to our design of context encoding and matching strategy.

Table 2. Results of different ablations. In the bottom part, our baseline BAT and the best results of CMT are presented.

	Method	Success	Precision
Components	BAT + Context Matching	46.8	44.5
	BAT + Transformer	48.7	49.2
	BAT + Transformer + OE	49.9	50.7
	CMT without $\widetilde{O}$	51.6	52.0
Inputs of transformer	P & B as feature	50.2	50.7
	P as PE, B as feature	51.7	51.9
	P as PE without B	50.9	51.3
	B as PE without P	51.5	51.6
Baseline & Best	BAT	45.3	42.6
	CMT (Ours)	**52.5**	**52.5**

4.3 Ablation Study

In order to validate the design of our CMT tracker, we conduct comprehensive ablative experiments on the truck class of nuScenes, which is much larger than any category of KITTI and can produce more stable results.

Effectiveness of Components. To illustrate the effectiveness of the components in CMT tracker, four ablative settings are applied: 1) BAT + Context Matching: we enhance BAT with our two-stage template-search matching module; 2) BAT + Transformer: instead of BAFF [46], we use the transformer for feature fusion; 3) BAT + Transformer + OE: everything in CMT is used except context matching; 4) CMT without $\widetilde{O}$: the orientational contextual feature is not integrated. As shown in the upper part of Table 2, BAT equipped with our context matching module defeats the original BAT, which confirms that a better template-search matching helps to improve the quality of proposal feature. Moreover, the result of CMT without $\widetilde{O}$ implies that the proposed spatial contextual encoder can mine useful clues in the orientational context of points, and the third setting further proves the effectiveness of our orientation encoder.

The Choice of k_c and k_1 k_c decides the number of neighbors that we use to construct L in the spatial contextual encoder. A larger k_c means a more extensive contextual awareness and additional computational overhead caused by a larger-scale context matching problem. Moreover, a global context matching is quite expensive. Therefore, we only compare k_1 template points selected by box-aware matching for each search seed. That means with a larger k_1, the context matching plays a more important role and the overhead is also increased.

According to the experiment results in Fig. 7(a), when k_c is too small, the constructed local contextual descriptor is not discriminative enough for matching. The performance also declines when $k_c = 20$, probably because more noise points are included and the designed shifted windows fail to filter all of them out. Meanwhile, Fig. 7(b) demonstrates that performance is improved when we

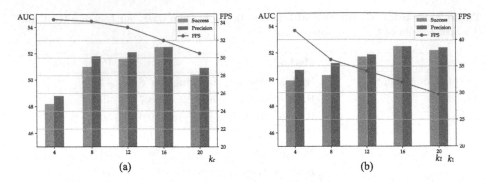

Fig. 7. (a) Comparison between choices of k_c ($k_1 = 16$)**.** Specific window sizes are designed for each k_c. **(b) Comparison between choices of** k_1 ($k_c = 16$)**.** Note that when $k_1 = 4$, the context matching module is not working since k_2 is also 4.

set a larger k_1, which further indicates the effectiveness of context matching on the basis of box-aware matching. In general, the best performance is achieved with the setting $k_c = k_1 = 16$. Besides, k_1's effect to the inference speed is larger than k_c's. However, considering the performance improvement, the drop of FPS from 41.7 ($k_1 = 4$) to 32 ($k_1 = 16$) is acceptable since it is still real-time level.

Inputs of Transformer. The feature aggregation submodule in [46] takes the 3D coordinates P and the 9D BoxCloud B as part of the input features, while in our transformer, P and B are concatenated to learn a trainable positional encoding (PE). Taking these into consideration, we test different settings for the inputs of the transformer, including 1) P and B as feature without PE; 2) P as PE while B as feature; 3) P as PE without using B; 4) B as PE without using P. As shown in the middle part of Table 2, the absence of PE leads to a slump in performance, while the introduction of B significantly improves the performance, especially when B plays the role of PE along with P, which demonstrates that BoxCloud contains useful information for location discrimination.

5   Conclusions

In this paper, we propose a context-matching-guided transformer (CMT) tracker for 3D SOT on LiDAR-based point clouds. A horizontally rotation-invariant spatial contextual descriptor, as well as a novel shifted-window matching strategy, is designed to effectively measure the contextual similarity between the template and the search area. Then we introduce a transformer to aggregate the target-aware information from the most contextually relevant template points into the search area with vector attention mechanism. Furthermore, we develop an orientation encoder to integrate spatial information from all directions. Extensive experiments on KITTI, nuScenes and WOD demonstrate that our tracker achieves promising improvement compared with previous state-of-the-art methods.

Acknowledgements.. This work was supported by the National Natural Science Foundation of China under Contract U20A20183, 61836011 and 62021001. It was also supported by the GPU cluster built by MCC Lab of Information Science and Technology Institution, USTC.

References

1. Bertinetto, L., Valmadre, J., Henriques, J.F., Vedaldi, A., Torr, P.H.S.: Fully-convolutional Siamese networks for object tracking. In: Hua, G., Jégou, H. (eds.) ECCV 2016. LNCS, vol. 9914, pp. 850–865. Springer, Cham (2016). https://doi.org/10.1007/978-3-319-48881-3_56
2. Bhat, G., Danelljan, M., Gool, L.V., Timofte, R.: Learning discriminative model prediction for tracking. In: Proceedings of the IEEE International Conference on Computer Vision, pp. 6182–6191 (2019)
3. Bibi, A., Zhang, T., Ghanem, B.: 3D part-based sparse tracker with automatic synchronization and registration. In: Proceedings of the IEEE Conference on Computer Vision and Pattern Recognition, pp. 1439–1448 (2016)
4. Bolme, D.S., Beveridge, J.R., Draper, B.A., Lui, Y.M.: Visual object tracking using adaptive correlation filters. In: Proceedings of the IEEE Conference on Computer Vision and Pattern Recognition, pp. 2544–2550 (2010)
5. Caesar, H., et al.: nuScenes: a multimodal dataset for autonomous driving. In: Proceedings of the IEEE Conference on Computer Vision and Pattern Recognition, pp. 11621–11631 (2020)
6. Carion, N., Massa, F., Synnaeve, G., Usunier, N., Kirillov, A., Zagoruyko, S.: End-to-end object detection with transformers. In: Vedaldi, A., Bischof, H., Brox, T., Frahm, J.-M. (eds.) ECCV 2020. LNCS, vol. 12346, pp. 213–229. Springer, Cham (2020). https://doi.org/10.1007/978-3-030-58452-8_13
7. Chen, X., Yan, B., Zhu, J., Wang, D., Yang, X., Lu, H.: Transformer tracking. In: Proceedings of the IEEE Conference on Computer Vision and Pattern Recognition, pp. 8126–8135 (2021)
8. Chen, Z., Zhong, B., Li, G., Zhang, S., Ji, R.: Siamese box adaptive network for visual tracking. In: Proceedings of the IEEE Conference on Computer Vision and Pattern Recognition, pp. 6667–6676 (2020)
9. Cui, Y., Fang, Z., Shan, J., Gu, Z., Zhou, S.: 3D object tracking with transformer. arXiv preprint arXiv:2110.14921 (2021)
10. Danelljan, M., Bhat, G., Khan, F.S., Felsberg, M.: ATOM: accurate tracking by overlap maximization. In: Proceedings of the IEEE Conference on Computer Vision and Pattern Recognition, pp. 4660–4669 (2019)
11. Danelljan, M., Häger, G., Khan, F., Felsberg, M.: Accurate scale estimation for robust visual tracking. In: Proceedings of the British Machine Vision Conference (2014)
12. Danelljan, M., Khan, F.S., Felsberg, M., Van de Weijer, J.: Adaptive color attributes for real-time visual tracking. In: Proceedings of the IEEE Conference on Computer Vision and Pattern Recognition, pp. 1090–1097 (2014)
13. Dosovitskiy, A., et al.: An image is worth 16×16 words: transformers for image recognition at scale. arXiv preprint arXiv:2010.11929 (2020)
14. Fan, S., Dong, Q., Zhu, F., Lv, Y., Ye, P., Wang, F.Y.: SCF-Net: learning spatial contextual features for large-scale point cloud segmentation. In: Proceedings of the IEEE Conference on Computer Vision and Pattern Recognition, pp. 14504–14513 (2021)

15. Fang, Z., Zhou, S., Cui, Y., Scherer, S.: 3D-SiamRPN: an end-to-end learning method for real-time 3D single object tracking using raw point cloud. IEEE Sens. J. **21**(4), 4995–5011 (2020)
16. Geiger, A., Lenz, P., Urtasun, R.: Are we ready for autonomous driving? The KITTI vision benchmark suite. In: Proceedings of the IEEE Conference on Computer Vision and Pattern Recognition, pp. 3354–3361 (2012)
17. Giancola, S., Zarzar, J., Ghanem, B.: Leveraging shape completion for 3D Siamese tracking. In: Proceedings of the IEEE Conference on Computer Vision and Pattern Recognition, pp. 1359–1368 (2019)
18. Guo, D., Wang, J., Cui, Y., Wang, Z., Chen, S.: SiamCAR: Siamese fully convolutional classification and regression for visual tracking. In: Proceedings of the IEEE Conference on Computer Vision and Pattern Recognition, pp. 6269–6277 (2020)
19. He, K., Zhang, X., Ren, S., Sun, J.: Deep residual learning for image recognition. In: Proceedings of the IEEE Conference on Computer Vision and Pattern Recognition, pp. 770–778 (2016)
20. Henriques, J.F., Caseiro, R., Martins, P., Batista, J.: Exploiting the circulant structure of tracking-by-detection with Kernels. In: Fitzgibbon, A., Lazebnik, S., Perona, P., Sato, Y., Schmid, C. (eds.) ECCV 2012. LNCS, vol. 7575, pp. 702–715. Springer, Heidelberg (2012). https://doi.org/10.1007/978-3-642-33765-9_50
21. Henriques, J.F., Caseiro, R., Martins, P., Batista, J.: High-speed tracking with kernelized correlation filters. IEEE Trans. Pattern Anal. Mach. Intell. **37**(3), 583–596 (2014)
22. Hui, L., Wang, L., Cheng, M., Xie, J., Yang, J.: 3D Siamese voxel-to-BEV tracker for sparse point clouds. Adv. Neural Inf. Process. Syst. **34**, 28714–28727 (2021)
23. Jiang, M., Wu, Y., Zhao, T., Zhao, Z., Lu, C.: PointSIFT: a SIFT-like network module for 3D point cloud semantic segmentation. arXiv preprint arXiv:1807.00652 (2018)
24. Kart, U., Kamarainen, J.K., Matas, J.: How to make an RGBD tracker? In: Proceedings of the European Conference on Computer Vision Workshops (2018)
25. Kart, U., Lukezic, A., Kristan, M., Kamarainen, J.K., Matas, J.: Object tracking by reconstruction with view-specific discriminative correlation filters. In: Proceedings of the IEEE Conference on Computer Vision and Pattern Recognition, pp. 1339–1348 (2019)
26. Li, B., Wu, W., Wang, Q., Zhang, F., Xing, J., Yan, J.: SiamRPN++: evolution of Siamese visual tracking with very deep networks. In: Proceedings of the IEEE Conference on Computer Vision and Pattern Recognition, pp. 4282–4291 (2019)
27. Li, B., Yan, J., Wu, W., Zhu, Z., Hu, X.: High performance visual tracking with Siamese region proposal network. In: Proceedings of the IEEE Conference on Computer Vision and Pattern Recognition, pp. 8971–8980 (2018)
28. Liu, Y., Jing, X.Y., Nie, J., Gao, H., Liu, J., Jiang, G.P.: Context-aware three-dimensional mean-shift with occlusion handling for robust object tracking in RGB-D videos. IEEE Trans. Multimedia **21**(3), 664–677 (2018)
29. Liu, Z., et al.: Swin transformer: hierarchical vision transformer using shifted windows. In: Proceedings of the IEEE International Conference on Computer Vision, pp. 10012–10022 (2021)
30. Pieropan, A., Bergström, N., Ishikawa, M., Kjellström, H.: Robust 3D tracking of unknown objects. In: IEEE International Conference on Robotics and Automation, pp. 2410–2417. IEEE (2015)
31. Qi, C.R., Su, H., Mo, K., Guibas, L.J.: PointNet: deep learning on point sets for 3D classification and segmentation. In: Proceedings of the IEEE Conference on Computer Vision and Pattern Recognition, pp. 652–660 (2017)

32. Qi, C.R., Yi, L., Su, H., Guibas, L.J.: PointNet++: deep hierarchical feature learning on point sets in a metric space. In: Advances in Neural Information Processing Systems, vol. 30 (2017)
33. Qi, H., Feng, C., Cao, Z., Zhao, F., Xiao, Y.: P2B: point-to-box network for 3D object tracking in point clouds. In: Proceedings of the IEEE Conference on Computer Vision and Pattern Recognition, pp. 6329–6338 (2020)
34. Shan, J., Zhou, S., Fang, Z., Cui, Y.: PTT: point-track-transformer module for 3D single object tracking in point clouds. In: IEEE International Conference on Intelligent Robots and Systems, pp. 1310–1316 (2021)
35. Sun, P., et al.: Scalability in perception for autonomous driving: waymo open dataset. In: Proceedings of the IEEE Conference on Computer Vision and Pattern Recognition, pp. 2446–2454 (2020)
36. Ulyanov, D., Vedaldi, A., Lempitsky, V.: Instance normalization: the missing ingredient for fast stylization. arXiv preprint arXiv:1607.08022 (2016)
37. Vaswani, A., et al.: Attention is all you need. In: Advances in Neural Information Processing Systems, pp. 5998–6008 (2017)
38. Wang, N., Zhou, W., Wang, J., Li, H.: Transformer meets tracker: exploiting temporal context for robust visual tracking. In: Proceedings of the IEEE Conference on Computer Vision and Pattern Recognition, pp. 1571–1580 (2021)
39. Wang, Q., Zhang, L., Bertinetto, L., Hu, W., Torr, P.H.: Fast online object tracking and segmentation: a unifying approach. In: Proceedings of the IEEE Conference on Computer Vision and Pattern Recognition, pp. 1328–1338 (2019)
40. Wang, Z., Xie, Q., Lai, Y.K., Wu, J., Long, K., Wang, J.: MLVSNet: multi-level voting Siamese network for 3D visual tracking. In: Proceedings of the IEEE International Conference on Computer Vision, pp. 3101–3110 (2021)
41. Wu, Y., Lim, J., Yang, M.H.: Online object tracking: a benchmark. In: Proceedings of the IEEE Conference on Computer Vision and Pattern Recognition, pp. 2411–2418 (2013)
42. Xu, Y., Wang, Z., Li, Z., Yuan, Y., Yu, G.: SiamFC++: towards robust and accurate visual tracking with target estimation guidelines. In: Proceedings of the AAAI Conference on Artificial Intelligence, vol. 34, pp. 12549–12556 (2020)
43. Yan, B., Peng, H., Fu, J., Wang, D., Lu, H.: Learning spatio-temporal transformer for visual tracking. In: Proceedings of the IEEE International Conference on Computer Vision, pp. 10448–10457 (2021)
44. Zhao, H., Jia, J., Koltun, V.: Exploring self-attention for image recognition. In: Proceedings of the IEEE Conference on Computer Vision and Pattern Recognition, pp. 10076–10085 (2020)
45. Zhao, H., Jiang, L., Jia, J., Torr, P., Koltun, V.: Point transformer. In: Proceedings of the IEEE International Conference on Computer Vision, pp. 16259–16268 (2021)
46. Zheng, C., et al.: Box-aware feature enhancement for single object tracking on point clouds. In: Proceedings of the IEEE International Conference on Computer Vision, pp. 13199–13208 (2021)
47. Zhu, Z., Wang, Q., Li, B., Wu, W., Yan, J., Hu, W.: Distractor-aware Siamese networks for visual object tracking. In: Proceedings of the European Conference on Computer Vision, pp. 101–117 (2018)

Towards Generic 3D Tracking in RGBD Videos: Benchmark and Baseline

Jinyu Yang[1,2], Zhongqun Zhang[2], Zhe Li[1], Hyung Jin Chang[2],
Aleš Leonardis[2], and Feng Zheng[1(✉)]

[1] Department of Computer Science and Engineering, Southern University of Science
and Technology, Shenzhen, China
f.zheng@ieee.org
[2] University of Birmingham, Birmingham, UK

Abstract. Tracking in 3D scenes is gaining momentum because of
its numerous applications in robotics, autonomous driving, and scene
understanding. Currently, 3D tracking is limited to specific model-based
approaches involving point clouds, which impedes 3D trackers from
applying in natural 3D scenes. RGBD sensors provide a more reasonable and acceptable solution for 3D object tracking due to their readily available synchronised color and depth information. Thus, in this
paper, we investigate a novel problem: is it possible to track a generic
(class-agnostic) 3D object in RGBD videos and predict 3D bounding
boxes of the object of interest? To inspire research on this topic, we
newly construct a standard benchmark for generic 3D object tracking,
'Track-it-in-3D', which contains 300 RGBD video sequences with dense
3D annotations and corresponding evaluation protocols. Furthermore,
we propose an effective tracking baseline to estimate 3D bounding boxes
for arbitrary objects in RGBD videos, by fusing appearance and spatial
information effectively. Resources are available on https://github.com/
yjybuaa/Track-it-in-3D.

Keywords: Object tracking · 3D object tracking · RGBD data

1 Introduction

Object tracking is to distinguish an arbitrary object from a video, given only
the object location in the first frame. 3D object tracking, which can estimate
not only the location but also the 3D size of objects, has a broader spectrum
of practical applications involving augmented reality [27], autonomous driving
[20], scene understanding [32] and robotic manipulation [7,21].

However, current state-of-the-art 3D trackers are mostly point cloud-based
and highly rely on geometric information to estimate the shape of objects. In
fact, LiDAR sensors are quite expensive, and the sparsity and disorder of the

---

Supplementary Information The online version contains supplementary material
available at https://doi.org/10.1007/978-3-031-20047-2_7.

Fig. 1. Examples of RGBD videos in our benchmark dataset. Each video is annotated with the object's per-frame 3D bounding box. Video sequences are captured towards 3D tracking challenges, e.g., (1) similar objects and occlusion; (2) small-sized object; (3) deformation; (4) symmetric object and partial occlusion; (5) dark scene and camera motion; (6) outdoor scenario.

point cloud impose great challenges on identifying target objects from backgrounds. Whilst, compared with point clouds, the ignored color cues are more informative for computing appearance features which are widely used to distinguish the target object from backgrounds. In addition, similar to LiDAR, depth information captured by low-cost sensors such as Kinect can also provide geometric information to estimate the shape of targets for most natural tracking scenarios. Moreover, it is easy to get the synchronised color channels from such cameras. Even for modelling target appearance, the depth information can be used to resolve tracking failures in cases of, e.g., distractors or rotation [3,12], due to its insensitivity to the variations in color, illumination, rotation angle, and scale. Therefore, a RGB+D fusion framework is a more reasonable and acceptable solution for 3D object tracking. On the one hand, appearance information in RGB channels and geometry information from the depth channel are two complementary data sources. On the other hand, the 3D coordinate of the object, with the spatial information given by depth information in 3D scenes, is more practical on real-world applications.

In addition, current state-of-the-art 3D tracking methods are mostly model-based: the trackers can track the target due to their discriminative ability to recognise targets' categories. For instance, P2B [24] trains the network on human and vehicle data to handle the challenges dedicated in human and vehicle categories respectively. However, object tracking is in essence a class-agnostic task that should track anything regardless of the object category. Moreover, in autonomous driving applications, the target objects are mostly rigid and placed on the ground so that 3D BBox is set as 4DoF (Degree-of-Freedom) or 7DoF for convenience. As a result, the precise 3D description of arbitrary objects is still unavailable which is desirable for generic 3D object tracking.

To this end, in this paper, we propose a novel task for 3D object tracking: given the real 3D BBox description of the target object in the first frame of RGBD videos, we aim to estimate the 3D BBox of it in the subsequent frames. To ensure the generic characteristic of object tracking, we collect a diverse RGBD video dataset for this task. The proposed *Track-it-in-3D* contains 300 video sequences with per-frame 3D annotations. The targets and scenarios are designed with a diverse range to avoid the semantic classification of specific targets. Specifically, the 3D BBox is freely rotating to fit the object's shape and orientation, which breaks the limitation of application scenarios. We provide some representative examples in Fig. 1. In addition, providing the input of RGB and depth data jointly provides new inspirations on how to leverage multi-modal information. Therefore, we propose a strong baseline, which for the first time realises tracking by 3D cross-correlation through dedicated RGBD fusion.

Our contributions are three-fold:

- We propose generic 3D object tracking in RGBD videos for the first time, which aims to realise class-agnostic 3D tracking in complex scenarios.
- We generate the benchmark *Track-it-in-3D*, which is, to the best of our knowledge, the first benchmark for generic 3D object tracking. With dense 3D BBox annotations and corresponding evaluation protocols provided, it contains 300 RGBD videos covering multiple tracking challenges.
- We introduce a strong baseline, *TrackIt3D*, for generic 3D object tracking, which handles 3D tracking difficulties by RGBD fusion and 3D cross-correlation. Extensive evaluations are given for in-depth analysis.

2   Related Work

3D Single Object Tracking. In 3D tracking, the task is defined as getting a 3D BBox in a video sequence given the object template of the first frame. In general, 3D single object tracking is still constrained by tracking on raw point clouds. SC3D [11] extends the 2D to 3D Siamese tracker on point clouds for the first time, in which exhaustive search is used to generate candidates. P2B [24] is proposed to solve the drawbacks of SC3D by importing VoteNet to construct the point-based correlation. Also, the 3D region proposal network (RPN) is utilised to obtain the object proposals. However, the ambiguities among part-aware features weaken the tracking performance severely. After that, BAT [33] is proposed to directly infer the BBox by box-aware feature enhancement, which is the first to use box information. Recent works make multiple attempts with the image prior [34], multi-level features [29], or transformers [8] to handle these problems, but the performances remain low with only point cloud provided. On the other hand, current RGBD tracking follows 2D BBox settings [14–16], while there were works devoted to predicting the 2D BBox in 3D view. In 2016, Bibi *et al.* developed 3D-T [3] which used 3D BBox with particle filter for RGBD tracking. In 2018, OTR [12] generated 3D BBox to model appearance changes during out-of-plane rotation. But they only generated incomplete 3D BBoxes in a rough level and served for 2D predictions.

Related Datasets and Benchmarks. There are four publicly available RGBD video datasets for tracking: *Princeton Tracking Benchmark* (PTB) [26], *Spatio-Temporal Consistency* dataset (STC) [30], *Color and Depth Tracking Benchmark*

(CDTB) [19] and *DepthTrack* [31]. We observe that they strictly follow the 2D mode with both input and output as axis-aligned BBoxes. Whereas in 3D tracking, LiDAR is the most popular sensor due to distant view and insensitivity to ambient light variations. The commonly used benchmarks on the 3D tracking task are *KITTI* [10] and *NuScenes* [4]. KITTI contains 21 outdoor scenes and 8 types of targets. NuScenes is more challenging, containing 1000 driving scenes across 23 object classes with annotated 3D BBoxes. With respect to their volume, the data diversity remains poor with focusing on driving scenarios and restraining methods to track objects in point clouds.

3   Proposed Benchmark: *Track-it-in-3D*

3.1   Problem Formulation

In current 3D tracking [24,33], the 3D BBox is represented as $(x, y, z, w, h, l, \theta) \in R^7$, in which (x, y, z) represents the target center and (w, h, l) represents the target size. There is only one parameter θ indicating rotation because the roll and pitch deviations are usually aligned to the road in autonomous driving scenarios. Notice that any BBox is amodal (covering the entire object even if only part of it is visible). The current 3D tracking task is to compare the point clouds of the given template BBox (P_t) with that of the search area candidates (P_s) and get the prediction of BBox. Therefore, the tracking process is formulated as:

$$Track : (P_t, P_s) \rightarrow (x, y, z, \theta).$$

In most cases, because the target size is fixed, the final output only gives a prediction of the target center (x, y, z) and rotation angle θ.

Differing from the existing 3D tracking in point clouds, we explore a more flexible and generic 3D tracking mode. We formulate the new task as:

$$Track : B_t \rightarrow (x, y, z, w, h, l, \alpha, \beta, \gamma),$$

in which B_t is the template 3D BBox given in the first frame, (x, y, z) indicates the target position, (w, h, l) indicates the target scale, and (α, β, γ) indicates the target rotation angle. Specifically, this tracking problem predicts a rotated 3D BBox to best match the initial target.

3.2   Dataset Construction

Video Collection. We collect the videos with *Microsoft Kinect V2* and *Intel RealSense SR300* for different depth ranges. We aim to provide a diverse set of groundtruthed synchronised color and depth sequences for generic 3D tracking, in which diversity is of priority. To this end, we carefully inspect each sequence among all candidate data for the availability and challenge for generic 3D tracking. Examples of some representative sequences are shown in Fig. 1. Finally, *Track-it-in-3D* comprises a total of 300 sequences with the data split as such:

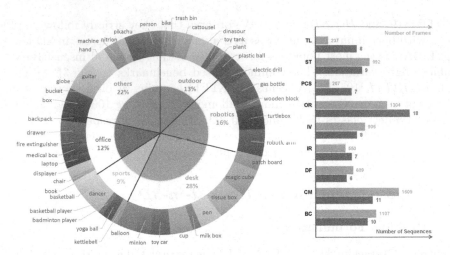

Fig. 2. Distribution of the object, scenarios and challenges in all test frames. Left: The inner pie-chart shows the distribution of the scenarios; The outside ring graph shows our target objects. Right: Brown histogram shows the attribute distribution on frame level; Green histogram shows the attribute distribution on sequence level. (Color figure online)

250 sequences (32,343 frames) for training, and 50 sequences (6,224 frames) for testing. All the videos are captured at 30 fps. We do not provide a further partition to leave users with the freedom of the training/validation split. We provide the distribution of scenarios and objects in our test set in Fig. 2. We keep our test set compact but diverse for a fair and effective evaluation.

Attribute Definition. Based on characteristics of the aforementioned problem, we annotate all the frames with 9 attributes to analyse how different kinds of challenges influence the tracking performance: Background Clutter (BC), Camera Motion (CM), Deformation (DF), In-plane Rotation (IR), Illumination Variation (IV), Out-of-plane Rotation (OR), Similar Targets (ST), Target Loss (TL) and Point Cloud Sparsity (PCS). Among them, background clutter, similar targets, and illumination variation are close related to depth favorable scenarios. In addition, point cloud sparsity, in-plane rotation and out-of-plane rotation are specifically challenging to 3D scenes. Unlike existing attributes in 3D tracking datasets, we are the first 3D dataset to provide detailed visual attributes according to both objects and scenarios. Distribution of attributes is given in Fig. 2. For detailed description of the attributes, please refer to the supplementary.

Data Annotation. For annotation, we manually annotate each target object in the video sequences with per-frame rotated 3D BBox on our modified version of SUSTechPoints tool [17]. We follow this principle for data annotation: given an initial target description (3D BBox) in a video, if the target appears in the

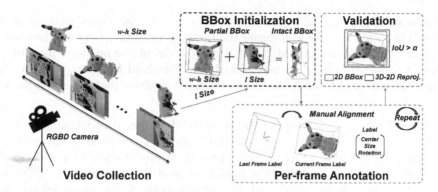

Fig. 3. Steps of our data annotation strategy. *BBox Initialisation:* We complete the size of the initial BBox from multi-view partial BBoxes. *Per-frame Annotation:* Similar to the tracking pipeline, annotators align the last-frame BBox with the current-frame object and record the label. *Validation:* We re-project the 3D BBox to image and generate 2D BBox. By computing the IoU between the re-projected 2D BBox with annotated 2D BBox, the accuracy of 3D annotation can be verified.

subsequent frames, we will edit the 3D BBox to tightly covering the whole target; otherwise, we will maintain the BBox state from the adjacent frame, and annotate the current frame with a "target loss" label. To guarantee annotation accuracy, we adopt a three-stage annotation strategy: 1) *BBox initialisation:* we firstly go through the whole sequences to best describe the target size (w, h, l) and give an initial 3D BBox. For example, we may not get precise length l_p in the first frame, but we can get precise width w_p and height h_p with an estimated length l_e of the target. Then we will go through the whole video to find the frame best showing the precise length l_p of the target, duplicate the 3D box to the first frame, and finally fine-tune the 3D box to get a precise length l_p for the target. 2) *Per-frame annotation:* an annotator edits the initial BBox in the subsequent frames to make the BBox best fit the target; the annotator can change the BBox's location and angle, and size if necessary (for cases like deformable objects) in this stage; 3) *Validation:* the authors finally check the annotation frame by frame to verify the annotation accuracy. The annotation workflow is shown in Fig. 3, which ensures high-quality annotation BBoxes in 3D scenes. Under such strategy, we can obtain the intact target BBox of the target in the specific frame, while it is tightest to fit the object with containing the real target size information in 3D space. We also evaluate our annotation accuracy with projection and sampling, please refer to the supplementary material.

3.3   Evaluation Protocols

To judge the quality of 3D tracking, measures are designed to reflect the 3D BBox tracking performance. Therefore, we follow the One Pass Evaluation (OPE) and the standard evaluation protocols to calculate the object center bias and 3D IoU accuracy. In the following, we present our evaluation protocols.

Precision Plot. One widely used evaluation metric for object tracking is the center bias, which is used to measure the Euclidean distance between the centers of predicted BBox and groundtruth BBox. We present the precision plots of the trackers averaged over all sequences with the threshold from 0 m to 0.5 m. We obtain the area-under-curve (AUC) of a tracker's precision plot as its "Precision".

Success Plot. As we propose the rotated 3D BBox description in the 3D tracking scenes, 3D Intersection-over-Union (IoU) is essential to measure the tracking accuracy. According to [9], we provide the IoU measure for general 3D-oriented boxes based on the Sutherland-Hodgman Polygon clipping algorithm. We firstly clip each face as the convex polygon between the predicted box and the groundtruth box. Then, the IoU is computed from the volume of the intersection and the volume of the union of two boxes by swapping the two boxes. AUC in success plot of IoU between groundtruth and predicted BBox is defined as "Success". For details, we refer readers to [1,9].

3.4 Comparison with Related Tasks

As shown in Fig. 4, we compare our 3D object tracking in RGBD videos with related tasks [10,25,28,31]. Compared to current *3D object tracking in point clouds* [10], we provide corresponding synchronised color information besides point clouds. Furthermore, instead of tracking with (x, y, z, θ), which only describes the location of the target center and one-dimensional rotation, we require a more flexible bounding box to better fit the object. Similarly, *3D object detection* [25] is to classify objects in image level, which also places all objects on the plane and cannot give a precise description for genric objects *e.g.*, suspended or sloping objects. Compared to *RGBD tracking*, [31] which remains on tracking the object within 2D settings, our proposed task requires a more detailed description of the object in the spatial domain. In addition, *6D pose tracking* [28] focuses on describing the pose of specific objects, which is heavily model-based. Different from existing tasks, 3D single object tracking (SOT) in RGBD videos is more challenging, in which the objects, scenarios, and annotations are more diverse and flexible. A detailed comparison of the proposed *Track-it-in-3d* with representative datasets from related tasks is summarised in Table 1. Although the proposed dataset is not prominent on volume compared to existing datasets, it can represent characteristics of the 3D tracking more effectively: 1) It achieves a high diversity for class-agnostic 3D tracking with covering indoor and outdoor scenarios, class-agnostic target objects and freely rotated 3D target annotation. 2) It provides a more effective way to track objects in 3D scenes with providing synchronised RGB and depth information.

Table 1. Comparison with related datasets. I = Indoor, O = Outdoor. We are the first dataset that provides 3D annotations for dynamic objects to realise generic 3D single object tracking in natural scenes.

Dataset	Type	Task	Modality	Sequence	Frame	Label	Class	Scenario	Dynamic
DepthTrack [31]	Video	RGBD tracking	RGB+D	200	294K	2D	46	I,O	✓
SUN-RGBD [25]	Image	3D detection	RGB+D	–	10K	3D	63	I	✗
Objectron [1]	Video	3D detection	RGB	14,819	4M	3D	9	I,O	✗
NOCS [28]	Image	Pose tracking	RGB+D	–	300K	3D	6	I,O	✗
KITTI [10]	Video	3D tracking	PC	21	15K	3D	8	O	✓
NuScenes [4]	Video	3D tracking	PC	1,000	40K	3D	23	O	✓
Track-it-in-3D	Video	3D tracking	RGB+D	300	36K	3D	144	I,O	✓

Fig. 4. Samples from related tasks and corresponding datasets, which basically show the object/scenario/annotation styles. a) KITTI [10], b) SUN-RGBD [25], c) Depth-Track [31], d) NOCS [28].

4 Proposed Baseline: *TrackIt3D*

Sole RGB based and point cloud based trackers already exist, and they perform well in specific cases respectively. Here, we propose a generic 3D tracker, namely *TrackIt3D*, which fuses the RGB and depth information in a seamless way. In this section, we first describe the overall network architecture, including the main components, then illustrate our implementation details.

4.1 Network Architecture

The input of our network is two frames from an RGBD video, defined as a target template frame and a search area frame respectively. The goal is simplified to localise the template target in the search area per frame. Our network consists of three main modules as shown in Fig. 5. We first design a Siamese RGBD Fusion Network to fuse the surface information (RGB Info.) and the spatial information (XYZ Info.) together. Next, the 3D Cross-Correlation Network is proposed to merge the template information into the search area. Finally, the fused feature is fed into the VoteNet module [22] to yield 3D BBox and confidence scores via the proposed BBox Loss and IoU Loss.

Siamese RGBD Fusion Network. The key idea of our fusion network is to enable surface information and spatial information to complement each other. To better exploit the spatial information of the depth map, we convert the

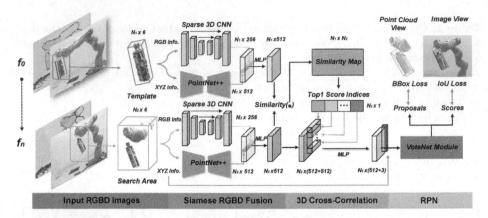

Fig. 5. Overview of our baseline TrackIt3D. The target gas bottle is moving with the robotic arm, tied by a transparent rope. The inputs are pixels and points of the template and search area, with the number of $N1$ and $N2$ respectively. The Siamese RGBD Fusion Network fuses the surface information (RGB Info.) and the spatial information (XYZ Info.). The Cross-Correlation Network learns the similarity between the template and the search area features. We use the BBox Loss and IoU Loss to enforce the VoteNet module [22] to yield the 3D BBox and corresponding confidence scores.

depth image to a point cloud. Given the RGBD template t and search area s, our network first associates each point to its corresponding image pixel based on projection onto the image plane using the known camera intrinsic parameters. The obtained pairs P of template and search area are then downsampled to $P^t \in \mathbb{R}^{N_1 \times 6}$ and $P^s \in \mathbb{R}^{N_2 \times 6}$ separately. Every pair P is represented as (x, y, z, R, G, B), in which (x, y, z) indicates the target spatial information and (R, G, B) indicates the surface information. We adopt an encoder-decoder structure with skip connections constructed by sparse 3D CNN [6], to extract the pixel-wise feature map $f^t_{rgb} \in \mathbb{R}^{N_1 \times 256}$ and $f^s_{rgb} \in \mathbb{R}^{N_2 \times 256}$ from the sparse surface pixels. We also implement a variant of the PointNet++ [23] architecture, with adding a decoder with skip connections to generate dense point-wise feature maps $f^t_{xyz} \in \mathbb{R}^{N_1 \times 512}$ and $f^s_{xyz} \in \mathbb{R}^{N_2 \times 512}$. The output feature maps of sparse 3D CNN and Pointnet++ are then concatenated and fed to a MLP network to generate the fused feature maps $f^t \in \mathbb{R}^{N_1 \times 512}$ and $f^s \in \mathbb{R}^{N_2 \times 512}$.

3D Cross-Correlation Network. Learning to track arbitrary objects can be addressed by similarity matching [2]. Following this, our 3D cross-correlation network learns to conduct a reliable similarity between the template features and the search area features. Different from unordered point sets [24], our points are in order because of pixel and point alignment, so that we can do similarity matching directly over 3D feature maps. As shown in Fig. 5, after obtaining the fused feature maps of the template and search area, we can compute the similarity map $Sim \in \mathbb{R}^{N_1 \times N_2}$ between f^t and f^s using the cosine distance. The column i in Sim means the similarity score of each feature in f^t to the ith feature in f^s. We then find the top score of i column, which represents the most similar template feature to the ith search feature. After getting all top score indices, we search the template feature by the index in f^t and then concatenate it with the corresponding feature in f^s, yielding a feature map of size $N_2 \times (512+512)$. Then we feed it into an MLP network to obtain the final feature map $f \in \mathbb{R}^{N_1 \times 512}$. The point-wise feature map f and the corresponding 3D position of each point are fed to the VoteNet module to obtain the final 3D BBox.

Loss Function. We train our network with the following loss function:

$$\mathcal{L}_{\text{total}} = \lambda_1 \mathcal{L}_{\text{reg}} + \lambda_2 \mathcal{L}_{\text{bbox}} + \lambda_3 \mathcal{L}_{\text{IoU}}. \tag{1}$$

Following [22], a shared voting module is used to predict the coordinate offset between points and target center. The predicted 3D offset is supervised by Vote loss $\mathcal{L}_{\text{reg}}$, which enforces the network to produce potential centers of the object. BBox loss $\mathcal{L}_{\text{bbox}}$ is designed to pull the K proposal BBoxes closer to the groundtruth BBox. Our 3D groundtruth BBox is defined by $\bar{B} = [\bar{x}, \bar{y}, \bar{z}, \bar{w}, \bar{h}, \bar{l}, \bar{q}]$, in which quaternion q represents the rotation. The BBox loss is computed via Huber (smooth-L1) loss:

$$\mathcal{L}_{\text{bbox}} = \frac{1}{K} \sum_i^K \left\| B_i - \bar{B}_i \right\|_1. \tag{2}$$

IoU loss $\mathcal{L}_{\text{IoU}}$ aims to ensure that the confidence score S_k approximates the IoU between proposals and groundtruth BBox. Following [9], we compute the IoU between the two 3D BBoxes based on the Sutherland-Hodgman Polygon clipping algorithm. The loss function is written as follow:

$$\mathcal{L}_{\text{IoU}} = \frac{1}{K} \sum_{i=1}^K \left\| IoU_k - S_k \right\|_1. \tag{3}$$

4.2 Implementation Details

Architecture. For our network, we downsample the points and pixels for template and search area to $N_1 = 512$ and $N_2 = 1024$. The cluster parameter in the VoteNet module is $K = 64$. The coefficients for the loss terms are $\lambda_1 = 1$, $\lambda_2 = 0.5$ and $\lambda_3 = 0.5$.

Training Phase. We train our model using the training set discussed in Sect. 3.2 which consists of RGBD videos and 3D object bounding box annotations. 1) *Template and Search Area:* we randomly sample RGBD image pairs from all the videos with a maximum gap of 10 frames. In each pair, the first image will serve as the template and the second will be the search area. The template is generated by cropping pixels and points inside the first given 3D BBox and we enlarge the second BBox by 4 times in each direction and collect pixels and points inside to generate the search area. 2) *3D Deformation:* to handle the shape variation of the target, we generate the augmented data for each pair by enlarging, shrinking, or changing some part of the point cloud following [5]. 3) The learning rate is 0.001, the batch size is 50, Adam [13] is adopted as an optimiser and trained for a total of 120 epochs. The learning rate decreased by 5 times after 50 epochs.

Inference Phase. During the inference, we also use the proposed dataset in Sect. 3.2. Different from the training phase, we track a target across all RGBD frames in a video. The given 3D BBox will be used to crop the template area, and the search area of the current frame is generated by enlarging (by 4 times in each direction) the predicted 3D BBox in the last frame and collecting the pixels and points in it.

5   Experiments

5.1   Benchmark Settings

As our proposed *TrackIt3D* is the first tracker designed for generic 3D tracking, we evaluate some representative 3D trackers based on point clouds for comparison. The compared trackers are SC3D [11], P2B [24], and BAT [33]. For model-based 3D trackers, we evaluate their default pre-trained models and the models finetuned on our proposed training set (if the model is trainable). Experiments are run on a single NVIDIA Tesla V100S GPU 32GB.

5.2   Benchmark Results

Overall Results. Table 2 gives the comparison results of 3D trackers. Our method achieves the highest score compared to the existing ones, in terms of both Success (31.1%) and Precision (35.0%). With dedicated combination of color and depth modalities, TrackIt3D is capable to distinguish the object in the RGB domain and makes good predictions of 3D BBox in the point cloud domain. It is worth noting that the SC3D, which performs worse on KITTI compared with P2B and BAT, shows a better performance on our test set even without finetuning on the proposed training set. The reason is that SC3D aims to compare the similarity between the template and 3D target proposals, while P2B and BAT utilise VoteNet to vote an object center, which tends to learn the center location based on strong category-related priors. We use their car-based model for testing. Therefore, when facing the class-agnostic tracking sequences, the sole VoteNet is not enough for center prediction. The P2B and BAT show remarkable improvements after finetuning on our training set. However, they still suffer low scores because the threshold of the center error is around 0.5m in our proposed dataset, while it is 2 m in KITTI [10]. In addition, they can only regress an axis-aligned BBox while we get a 9DoF BBox which contributes to a higher IoU score. We show the precision and success plots in Fig. 6.

Table 2. Quantitative comparison between our method and state-of-the-art methods. Our method outperforms the compared models by a large margin on our *Track-it-in-3d* test set. Speed is also listed and "_ft" means the method is finetuned on our training dataset. **Bold** denotes the best performance.

Tracker	SC3D [11]	P2B [24]	P2B_ft [24]	BAT [33]	BAT_ft [33]	TrackIt3D
Success	9.2%	4.2%	9.4%	2.5%	2.5%	**31.1%**
Precision	6.8%	1.1%	8.4%	0.8%	4.7%	**35.0%**
Speed(FPS)	0.51	23.78	21.25	**28.17**	25.08	6.95

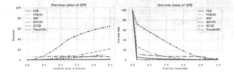 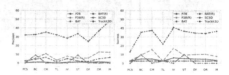

Fig. 6. The Success and Precision plots of the compared trackers and the proposed *TrackIt3D*.

Fig. 7. Optimal Precision (left) and Success (right) scores over the visual attributes.

Figure 8 shows several representative samples of results comparing our *TrackIt3D* with finetuned P2B. As shown, unlike P2B which only gives an axis-aligned estimation of the target object, our *TrackIt3D* can also distinguish the target orientation and track the target rotation. Specifically, row a) shows a scene with similar objects, in which P2B fails in total while our method can accurately track the target object. Besides, our method is more robust to challenging cases like object rotation and deformation, as shown in rows b) and c), due to its strong discriminative ability based on RGBD fusion. Moreover, row d) gives an outdoor scenario under low illumination, where it is difficult to locate the object, but our method shows a good estimation. The last row gives a failed case in which the target is severely occluded by a plant, both *TrackIt3D* and P2B fail due to their lack of a re-detection mechanism.

Attribute-Based Results. Per-attribute results are reported in Fig. 7. Although the overall performance is low, we can obtain informative analysis from the per-attribute result. Our method obviously outperforms the compared models in all attributes, especially in in-plane rotation and illumination variation. Clearly, the superior performance of our RGBD fusion over point cloud is evident. However, *TrackIt3D*'s success score degrades severely on the point cloud sparsity and target loss, indicating that it still need improvement on long-term discriminative ability and target localisation under little spatial information. Despite that, it is worth noting that the finetuned P2B performs well under in-camera motion and illumination variation, while SC3D beats the other trackers on background clutter and similar targets.

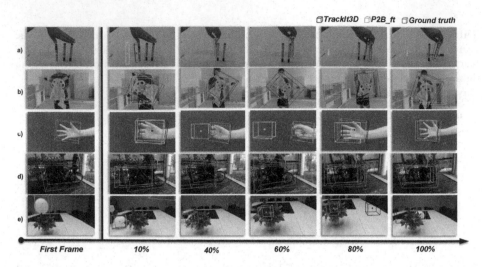

Fig. 8. Qualitative results of our baseline *TrackIt3D* compared with the fine-tuned *P2B*. We can observe our baseline's advantage over P2B in many challenge scenarios, *e.g.*, a) similar objects, b) rotation, c) deformation and d) dark scene. The last row is a failed case when the object is fully occluded.

Table 3. Performance of the RGBD variant of original 3D point cloud tracker, and P2B++ and BAT++ have been finetuned on our training dataset.

Tracker	P2B++ [24]	BAT++ [33]	TrackIt3D
Success	24.5%	18.1%	31.1%
Precision	28.2%	26.0%	35.0%

5.3 Ablation Study

Effectiveness of RGBD Fusion. To validate the effectiveness of the proposed RGBD fusion on 3D tracking, we apply it on P2B and BAT to instead their original heads and obtains corresponding variants P2B++ and BAT++. Table 3 shows the comparison between the variants with the RGBD fusion head and our *TrackIt3D*. Specifically, there are striking improvements (at least 15.1% and 19.8%) in terms of Success and Precision compared with the finetuned P2B and BAT, which proves that the RGBD fusion boosts the performance of point cloud voting models. Also, performance of BAT++ is lower that the P2B++ due to its strong object prior with fixed size.

Different Ways for 3D Cross-Correlation. Besides our default settings in Sect. 4.1, we consider other possible ways for 3D cross-correlation, *e.g.*, 2D correlation [18], which is commonly used in 2D tracking, instead of 3D correlation. The left section in Fig. 9 shows how we implement 2D correlation. Surprisingly,

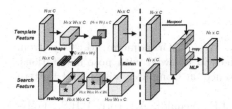

Fig. 9. Different ways for 3D cross-correlation. The left part is following 2D tracking pipeline. The right part is without calculating similarity map. ∗ means convolution operation.

Table 4. Different ways for 3D cross-correlation (xcorr.). Methods for similarity learning between search features and template following 2D tracking method are illustrated in Fig. 9.

Ways for 3D xcorr.	Success	Precision
Our default setting	**31.1%**	35.0%
w/ 2D xcorr. setting	28.3%	**38.4%**
w/o similarity map	30.9%	33.1%
w/o template feature	7.0%	5.0%

results in Table. 4 show that the 2D correlation setting outweighs our 3D correlation on Precision, although it gives a lower Success. This may reveal that the 2D-based method is more robust to estimate an accurate target center, while it is weaker on 3D BBox prediction as it omits the spatial correlation in 3D space. We also try to remove the similarity map and template feature, as shown in the right part of Fig. 9. The performance degrades without using the two parts. Specifically, once removing the template feature, Success and Precision degrade with 7% and 5%, which proves that the tracker loses the discriminative ability without the reference feature.

6 Conclusions

In this paper, we investigate a novel topic to track generic objects with 3D rotated BBox in RGBD videos. We first construct a novel benchmark *Track-it-in-3D* with 300 RGBD videos for training and testing, which covers diverse objects and challenging scenarios in 3D scenes. Also, this benchmark enables generic 3D tracking in complex scenarios with novel target annotation and performance evaluation. Furthermore, we propose an end-to-end method *TrackIt3D* for tracking class-agnostic 3D objects. With effective RGBD fusion and 3D cross-correlation, our baseline shows superior performance on this challenging task. We hope this work will facilitate further research on generic 3D tracking.

Acknowledgment. This work is supported by the National Natural Science Foundation of China under Grant No. 61972188 and 62122035. Z.Z. was supported by China Scholarship Council (CSC) Grant No. 202208060266. H.C. was supported by Institute of Information and communications Technology Planning and evaluation (IITP) grant funded by the Korea government (MSIT) (2021-0-00537, Visual common sense through self-supervised learning for restoration of invisible parts in images). A.L. was supported in part by the Engineering and Physical Sciences Research Council (grant number EP/S032487/1).

References

1. Ahmadyan, A., Zhang, L., Ablavatski, A., Wei, J., Grundmann, M.: Objectron: a large scale dataset of object-centric videos in the wild with pose annotations. In: Proceedings of the IEEE/CVF Conference on Computer Vision and Pattern Recognition, pp. 7822–7831 (2021)
2. Bertinetto, L., Valmadre, J., Henriques, J.F., Vedaldi, A., Torr, P.H.S.: Fully-convolutional Siamese networks for object tracking. In: Hua, G., Jégou, H. (eds.) ECCV 2016. LNCS, vol. 9914, pp. 850–865. Springer, Cham (2016). https://doi.org/10.1007/978-3-319-48881-3_56
3. Bibi, A., Zhang, T., Ghanem, B.: 3D part-based sparse tracker with automatic synchronization and registration. In: Proceedings of the IEEE Conference on Computer Vision and Pattern Recognition, pp. 1439–1448 (2016)
4. Caesar, H., et al.: nuscenes: a multimodal dataset for autonomous driving. In: Proceedings of the IEEE/CVF Conference on Computer Vision and Pattern Recognition, pp. 11621–11631 (2020)
5. Chen, W., Jia, X., Chang, H.J., Duan, J., Shen, L., Leonardis, A.: FS-Net: fast shape-based network for category-level 6d object pose estimation with decoupled rotation mechanism. In: Proceedings of the IEEE/CVF Conference on Computer Vision and Pattern Recognition, pp. 1581–1590 (2021)
6. Choy, C., Gwak, J., Savarese, S.: 4D spatio-temporal convnets: Minkowski convolutional neural networks. In: Proceedings of the IEEE/CVF Conference on Computer Vision and Pattern Recognition, pp. 3075–3084 (2019)
7. Comport, A.I., Marchand, É., Chaumette, F.: Robust model-based tracking for robot vision. In: 2004 IEEE/RSJ International Conference on Intelligent Robots and Systems (IROS)(IEEE Cat. No. 04CH37566), vol. 1, pp. 692–697. IEEE (2004)
8. Cui, Y., Fang, Z., Shan, J., Gu, Z., Zhou, S.: 3D object tracking with transformer. arXiv preprint arXiv:2110.14921 (2021)
9. Ericson, C.: Real-Time Collision Detection. CRC Press, Boca Raton (2004)
10. Geiger, A., Lenz, P., Urtasun, R.: Are we ready for autonomous driving? The Kitti vision benchmark suite. In: 2012 IEEE Conference on Computer Vision and Pattern Recognition, pp. 3354–3361. IEEE (2012)
11. Giancola, S., Zarzar, J., Ghanem, B.: Leveraging shape completion for 3D Siamese tracking. In: Proceedings of the IEEE/CVF Conference on Computer Vision and Pattern Recognition (CVPR), June 2019
12. Kart, U., Lukezic, A., Kristan, M., Kamarainen, J.K., Matas, J.: Object tracking by reconstruction with view-specific discriminative correlation filters. In: Proceedings of the IEEE/CVF Conference on Computer Vision and Pattern Recognition, pp. 1339–1348 (2019)
13. Kingma, D.P., Ba, J.: Adam: a method for stochastic optimization. arXiv preprint arXiv:1412.6980 (2014)
14. Kristan, M., et al.: The eighth visual object tracking VOT2020 challenge results. In: Bartoli, A., Fusiello, A. (eds.) ECCV 2020. LNCS, vol. 12539, pp. 547–601. Springer, Cham (2020). https://doi.org/10.1007/978-3-030-68238-5_39
15. Kristan, M., et al.: The seventh visual object tracking VOT2019 challenge results. In: Proceedings of the IEEE/CVF International Conference on Computer Vision Workshops (2019)
16. Kristan, M., et al.: The ninth visual object tracking vot2021 challenge results. In: Proceedings of the IEEE/CVF International Conference on Computer Vision, pp. 2711–2738 (2021)

17. Li, E., Wang, S., Li, C., Li, D., Wu, X., Hao, Q.: SUSTech points: a portable 3D point cloud interactive annotation platform system. In: 2020 IEEE Intelligent Vehicles Symposium (IV), pp. 1108–1115 (2020). https://doi.org/10.1109/IV47402.2020.9304562
18. Liao, B., Wang, C., Wang, Y., Wang, Y., Yin, J.: PG-Net: pixel to global matching network for visual tracking. In: Vedaldi, A., Bischof, H., Brox, T., Frahm, J.-M. (eds.) ECCV 2020. LNCS, vol. 12367, pp. 429–444. Springer, Cham (2020). https://doi.org/10.1007/978-3-030-58542-6_26
19. Lukezic, A., et al.: CDTB: a color and depth visual object tracking dataset and benchmark. In: Proceedings of the IEEE/CVF International Conference on Computer Vision, pp. 10013–10022 (2019)
20. Luo, W., Yang, B., Urtasun, R.: Fast and furious: real time end-to-end 3D detection, tracking and motion forecasting with a single convolutional net. In: Proceedings of the IEEE Conference on Computer Vision and Pattern Recognition, pp. 3569–3577 (2018)
21. Machida, E., Cao, M., Murao, T., Hashimoto, H.: Human motion tracking of mobile robot with Kinect 3D sensor. In: 2012 Proceedings of SICE Annual Conference (SICE), pp. 2207–2211. IEEE (2012)
22. Qi, C.R., Litany, O., He, K., Guibas, L.J.: Deep hough voting for 3D object detection in point clouds. In: Proceedings of the IEEE/CVF International Conference on Computer Vision, pp. 9277–9286 (2019)
23. Qi, C.R., Yi, L., Su, H., Guibas, L.J.: Pointnet++: deep hierarchical feature learning on point sets in a metric space. arXiv preprint arXiv:1706.02413 (2017)
24. Qi, H., Feng, C., Cao, Z., Zhao, F., Xiao, Y.: P2b: point-to-box network for 3D object tracking in point clouds. In: Proceedings of the IEEE/CVF Conference on Computer Vision and Pattern Recognition (CVPR), June 2020
25. Song, S., Lichtenberg, S.P., Xiao, J.: SUN RGB-D: A RGB-D scene understanding benchmark suite. In: Proceedings of the IEEE Conference on Computer Vision and Pattern Recognition, pp. 567–576 (2015)
26. Song, S., Xiao, J.: Tracking revisited using RGBD camera: unified benchmark and baselines. In: Proceedings of the IEEE International Conference on Computer Vision, pp. 233–240 (2013)
27. Taylor, C., McNicholas, R., Cosker, D.: Towards an egocentric framework for rigid and articulated object tracking in virtual reality. In: 2020 IEEE Conference on Virtual Reality and 3D User Interfaces Abstracts and Workshops (VRW), pp. 354–359 (2020). https://doi.org/10.1109/VRW50115.2020.00077
28. Wang, H., Sridhar, S., Huang, J., Valentin, J., Song, S., Guibas, L.J.: Normalized object coordinate space for category-level 6D object pose and size estimation. In: The IEEE Conference on Computer Vision and Pattern Recognition (CVPR), June 2019
29. Wang, Z., Xie, Q., Lai, Y.K., Wu, J., Long, K., Wang, J.: MLVSNet: multi-level voting Siamese network for 3D visual tracking. In: Proceedings of the IEEE/CVF International Conference on Computer Vision, pp. 3101–3110 (2021)
30. Xiao, J., Stolkin, R., Gao, Y., Leonardis, A.: Robust fusion of color and depth data for RGB-D target tracking using adaptive range-invariant depth models and spatio-temporal consistency constraints. IEEE Trans. Cybern. 48(8), 2485–2499 (2017)
31. Yan, S., Yang, J., Kapyla, J., Zheng, F., Leonardis, A., Kamarainen, J.K.: DepthTrack: unveiling the power of RGBD tracking. In: Proceedings of the IEEE/CVF International Conference on Computer Vision, pp. 10725–10733 (2021)

32. Yan, X., Zheng, C., Li, Z., Wang, S., Cui, S.: PointASNL: robust point clouds processing using nonlocal neural networks with adaptive sampling. In: Proceedings of the IEEE/CVF Conference on Computer Vision and Pattern Recognition, pp. 5589–5598 (2020)
33. Zheng, C., et al.: Box-aware feature enhancement for single object tracking on point clouds. In: Proceedings of the IEEE/CVF International Conference on Computer Vision, pp. 13199–13208 (2021)
34. Zou, H., et al.: F-Siamese tracker: a frustum-based double Siamese network for 3D single object tracking. In: 2020 IEEE/RSJ International Conference on Intelligent Robots and Systems (IROS), pp. 8133–8139. IEEE (2020)

Hierarchical Latent Structure for Multi-modal Vehicle Trajectory Forecasting

Dooseop Choi[✉] and KyoungWook Min

Artificial Intelligence Research Laboratory, ETRI, Daejeon, South Korea
{d1024.choi,kwmin92}@etri.re.kr

Abstract. Variational autoencoder (VAE) has widely been utilized for modeling data distributions because it is theoretically elegant, easy to train, and has nice manifold representations. However, when applied to image reconstruction and synthesis tasks, VAE shows the limitation that the generated sample tends to be blurry. We observe that a similar problem, in which the generated trajectory is located between adjacent lanes, often arises in VAE-based trajectory forecasting models. To mitigate this problem, we introduce a hierarchical latent structure into the VAE-based forecasting model. Based on the assumption that the trajectory distribution can be approximated as a mixture of simple distributions (or modes), the low-level latent variable is employed to model each mode of the mixture and the high-level latent variable is employed to represent the weights for the modes. To model each mode accurately, we condition the low-level latent variable using two lane-level context vectors computed in novel ways, one corresponds to vehicle-lane interaction and the other to vehicle-vehicle interaction. The context vectors are also used to model the weights via the proposed mode selection network. To evaluate our forecasting model, we use two large-scale real-world datasets. Experimental results show that our model is not only capable of generating clear multi-modal trajectory distributions but also outperforms the state-of-the-art (SOTA) models in terms of prediction accuracy. Our code is available at https://github.com/d1024choi/HLSTrajForecast.

1 Introduction

Trajectory forecasting has long been a great interest in autonomous driving since accurate predictions of future trajectories of traffic agents are essential for the safe motion planning of an autonomous vehicle (AV). Many approaches have been proposed for trajectory forecasting in the literature and remarkable progress has been made in recent years. The recent trend in trajectory forecasting is to predict multiple possible trajectories for each agent in the traffic scene. This

Supplementary Information The online version contains supplementary material available at https://doi.org/10.1007/978-3-031-20047-2_8.

is because human drivers' future behavior is uncertain, and consequently, the future motion of the agent naturally exhibits a multi-modal distribution.

Latent variable models, such as variational autoencoders (VAEs) [18] and generative adversarial networks (GANs) [13], have been used for modeling the distribution over the agents' future trajectories. Using latent variables, trajectory forecasting models can learn to capture agent-agent and agent-space interactions from data, and consequently, generate future trajectories that are compliant with the input scene contexts.

VAEs have been applied in many machine learning applications, including image synthesis [15,32], language modeling [3,33], and trajectory forecasting [5, 20] because they are theoretically elegant, easy to train, and have nice manifold representations. One of the limitations of VAEs is that the generated sample tends to be blurry (especially in image reconstruction and synthesis tasks) [36]. We found from our experiments that a similar problem often arises in VAE-based trajectory forecasting models. More specifically, it is often found that the generated trajectory is located between adjacent lanes as illustrated in Fig. 1. These false positive motion forecasts can cause uncomfortable rides for the AV with plenty of sudden brakes and steering changes [6]. In the rest of this paper, we will refer to this problem as *mode blur* as instance-level lanes are closely related to the modes of the trajectory distribution [16]. Mode blur is also found in the recent SOTA model [8] as shown in supplementary materials.

Many approaches have been proposed to mitigate the blurry sample generation problem primarily for image reconstruction or synthesis tasks. In this paper, we introduce a hierarchical latent structure into a VAE-based forecasting model to mitigate mode blur. Based on the assumption that the trajectory distribution can be approximated as a mixture of simple distributions (or modes), the low-level latent variable is employed to model each mode of the mixture and the high-level latent variable is employed to represent the weights for the modes. As a result, the forecasting model is capable of generating clear multi-modal trajectory distributions. To model each mode accurately, we condition the low-level latent variable using two lane-level context vectors (one corresponds to vehicle-lane interaction (VLI) and the other to vehicle-vehicle interaction (V2I)) computed in novel ways. The context vectors are also used to model the weights via the proposed mode selection network. Lastly, we also introduce two techniques to further improve the prediction performance of our model: 1) positional data preprocessing and 2) GAN-based regularization. The preprocessing is introduced based on the fact that vehicles moving along a lane usually try to be parallel to the tangent vector of the lane. The regularization is intended to ensure that the proposed model generates trajectories that match the shape of the lanes well.

In summary, our contributions are the followings:

- The hierarchical latent structure is introduced in the VAE-based forecasting model to mitigate mode blur.
- Two context vectors (one corresponds to the VLI and the other to the V2I) calculated in novel ways are proposed for lane-level scene contexts.

- Positional data preprocessing and GAN-based regularization are introduced to further improve the prediction performance.
- Our forecasting model outperforms the SOTA models in terms of prediction accuracy on two large-scale real-world datasets.

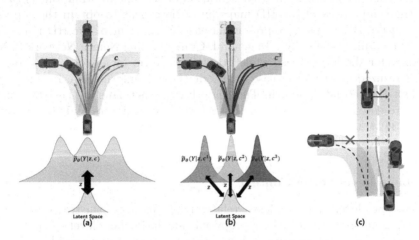

Fig. 1. Mode blur in trajectory forecasting and our approach. (a) Generated trajectories tend to locate between adjacent lanes. (b) We let a latent variable model each mode of the trajectory distribution to mitigate mode blur. (c) The target vehicle (red) takes into account not only its reference lane (red dashed line) but also the surrounding lanes (black dashed lines) and the surrounding vehicles. Only the surrounding vehicles within a certain distance from the reference lanes (green lines with arrows) influences the future motion of the target vehicle. (Color figure online)

2   Related Works

2.1   Limitations of VAEs

The VAE framework has been used to explicitly learn data distributions. The models based on the VAE framework learn mappings from samples in a dataset to points in a latent space and generate plausible samples from variables drawn from the latent space. The VAE-based generative models are known to suffer from two problems: 1) posterior collapse (that the models ignore the latent variable when generating samples) and 2) blurry sample generation. To mitigate the problems, many approaches have been proposed in the literature, primarily for image reconstruction or synthesis tasks [11,14,15,17,27,28,32,35]. In trajectory forecasting, some researchers [5,30] have employed the techniques for the mitigation of the posterior collapse. To mitigate the blurry sample generation, [2] proposed a "best-of-many" sample objective that leads to accurate and diverse trajectory generation.

2.2   Forecasting with Lane Geometry

Because the movement of vehicles on the road is greatly restricted by the lane geometry, many works have been proposed to utilize the lane information provided by High-Definition (HD) maps [5,9,10,12,16,22,23,25,26,30]. There are two types of approaches to the representation of the lane information: 1) rasterizing the components of the HD maps on a 2D canvas to obtain the top-view images of the HD maps, 2) representing each component of the HD maps as a series of coordinates of points. In general, Convolutional Neural Network (CNN) is utilized for the former case while Long Short-Term Memory (LSTM) or 1D-CNN is utilized for the latter case to encode the lane information. In this paper, we adopt the second approach. The centerline of each lane in the HD maps is first represented as a series of equally-spaced 2D coordinates and then encoded by an LSTM network. The ability to handle individual lanes in the HD maps allows us to calculate lane-level scene contexts.

2.3   Lane-Level Scene Context

Since instance-level lanes are closely related to the modes of the trajectory distribution, recent works [10,16,23,25] proposed calculating lane-level scene contexts and using them for generating trajectories. Our work shares the idea with the previous works. However, ours differs from them in the way it calculates the lane-level scene contexts, which leads to significant gains in the prediction performance. Instead of considering only a single lane for a lane-level scene context, we also take into account surrounding lanes along with their relative importance. The relative importance is calculated based on the past motion of the target vehicle, thus reflecting the vehicle-lane interaction. In addition, for the interaction between the target vehicle and surrounding vehicles, we consider only the surrounding vehicles within a certain distance from the reference lane as illustrated in Fig. 1c. This approach shows improved prediction performance compared to the existing approaches that consider either all neighbors [25] or only the most relevant neighbor [16]. This result is consistent with the observation that only a subset of surrounding vehicles is indeed relevant when predicting the future trajectory of the target vehicle [21].

3   Proposed Method

In this section, we present the details of our trajectory forecasting model.

3.1   Problem Formulation

Assume that there are N vehicles in the traffic scene. We aim to generate plausible trajectory distributions $p(\mathbf{Y}_i|\mathbf{X}_i, \mathcal{C}_i)$ for the vehicles $\{V_i\}_{i=1}^{N}$. Here, $\mathbf{X}_i = \mathbf{p}_i^{(t-H:t)}$ denotes the positional history of V_i for the previous H timesteps at time t, $\mathbf{Y}_i = \mathbf{p}_i^{(t+1:t+T)}$ denotes the future positions of V_i for the next T

timesteps, and $\mathcal{C}_i$ denotes additional scene information available to V_i. For $\mathcal{C}_i$, we use the positional histories of the surrounding vehicles $\{\mathbf{X}_j\}_{j=1,j\neq i}^{N}$ and the lane candidates $\mathbf{L}^{(1:M)}$ available for V_i at time t, where $\mathbf{L}^m = \mathbf{l}_{1,\ldots,F}^m$ denotes the F equally spaced coordinate points on the centerline of the m-th lane. Finally, we note that every positional information is expressed in the coordinate frame defined by V_i's current position and heading. According to [16], $p(\mathbf{Y}_i|\mathbf{X}_i,\mathcal{C}_i)$ can be re-written as

$$p(\mathbf{Y}_i|\mathbf{X}_i,\mathcal{C}_i) = \sum_{m=1}^{M} \underbrace{p(\mathbf{Y}_i|E_m,\mathbf{X}_i,\mathcal{C}_i)}_{\text{mode}}\underbrace{p(E_m|\mathbf{X}_i,\mathcal{C}_i)}_{\text{weight}}, \tag{1}$$

where E_m denotes the event that $\mathbf{L}^m$ becomes the reference lane for V_i. Equation 1 shows that the trajectory distribution can be expressed as a weighted sum of the distributions which we call *modes*. The fact that the modes are usually much simpler than the overall distribution inspired us to model each mode through a latent variable, and sample trajectories from the modes in proportion to their weights as illustrated in Fig. 1b.

3.2 Forecasting Model with Hierarchical Latent Structure

We introduce two latent variables $\mathbf{z}_l \in \mathbb{R}^D$ and $\mathbf{z}_h \in \mathbb{R}^M$ to model the modes and the weights for the modes in Eq. 1. With the low-level latent variable $\mathbf{z}_l$, our forecasting model defines $p(\mathbf{Y}_i|E_m,\mathbf{X}_i,\mathcal{C}_i)$ by using the decoder network $p_\theta(\mathbf{Y}_i|\mathbf{z}_l,\mathbf{X}_i,\mathcal{C}_i^m)$ and the prior network $p_\gamma(\mathbf{z}_l|\mathbf{X}_i,\mathcal{C}_i^m)$ based on

$$p(\mathbf{Y}_i|E_m,\mathbf{X}_i,\mathcal{C}_i) = \int_{\mathbf{z}_l} p(\mathbf{Y}_i|\mathbf{z}_l,\mathbf{X}_i,\mathcal{C}_i^m)p(\mathbf{z}_l|\mathbf{X}_i,\mathcal{C}_i^m)d\mathbf{z}_l, \tag{2}$$

where $\mathcal{C}_i^m \subset \mathcal{C}_i$ denotes the scene information relevant to $\mathbf{L}^m$. To train our forecasting model, we employ the conditional VAE framework [31] and optimize the following modified ELBO objective [14]:

$$\mathcal{L}_{ELBO} = -\mathbb{E}_{\mathbf{z}_l \sim q_\phi}[\log p_\theta(\mathbf{Y}_i|\mathbf{z}_l,\mathbf{X}_i,\mathcal{C}_i^m)]$$
$$+ \beta KL(q_\phi(\mathbf{z}_l|\mathbf{Y}_i,\mathbf{X}_i,\mathcal{C}_i^m)||p_\gamma(\mathbf{z}_l|\mathbf{X}_i,\mathcal{C}_i^m)), \tag{3}$$

where β is a constant and $q_\phi(\mathbf{z}_l|\mathbf{Y}_i,\mathbf{X}_i,\mathcal{C}_i^m)$ is the approximated posterior network. The weights for the modes $p(E_m|\mathbf{X}_i,\mathcal{C}_i)$ are modeled by the high-level latent variable $\mathbf{z}_h$, which is output of the proposed mode selection network $\mathbf{z}_h = f_\varphi(\mathbf{X}_i,\mathcal{C}_i^{(1:M)})$.

As shown in Eq. 3 and the definition of the mode selection network, the performance of our forecasting model is dependent on how the lane-level scene information $\mathcal{C}_i^m$ is utilized along with $\mathbf{X}_i$ for defining the lane-level scene context. One can consider two interactions for the lane-level scene context: the VLI and V2I. This is because the future motion of the vehicle is highly restricted not only by the vehicle's motion history but also by the motion histories of the surrounding vehicles and the lane geometry of the road. For the VLI, the existing works [10,16,23,25] considered only the reference lane. For the V2I, [16] considered only one vehicle most relevant to the reference lane, while the others considered all vehicles. In this paper, we present novel ways of defining the two interactions. For the VLI, instead of considering only the reference lane, we also take into account surrounding lanes along with their relative importance, which is calculated based on the target vehicle's motion history. The V2I is encoded through a GNN by considering only surrounding vehicles within a certain distance from the reference lane. Our approach is based on the fact that human drivers often pay attention to surrounding lanes and vehicles occupying the surrounding lanes when driving along the reference lane. Driving behaviors such as lane changes and overtaking are examples.

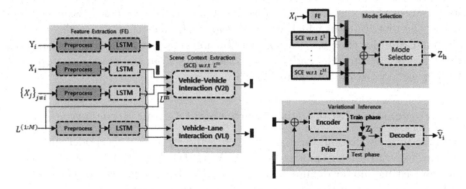

Fig. 2. Overall architecture of our forecasting model. To generate K future trajectories of V_i, lane-level scene context vectors $\{\mathbf{c}_i^m\}_{m=1}^M$, each of which corresponds to one of $\mathbf{L}^{(1:M)}$, are first calculated via scene context extraction module. Next, $\{w_m\}_{m=1}^M$ (w_m denotes the probability that V_i will drive along $\mathbf{L}^m$ in the future) are calculated by using $\mathbf{z}_h$. Finally, $\lfloor K \times w_m \rfloor$ out of K future trajectories are generated by the decoder network using $\mathbf{c}_i^m$ and $\mathbf{z}_l$.

3.3   Proposed Network Structure

We show in Fig. 2 the overall architecture of our forecasting model. In the following sections, we describe the details of our model.

Feature Extraction Module: Three LSTM networks are used to encode the positional data $\{\mathbf{X}_a\}_{a=1}^N$, $\mathbf{Y}_i$, and $\mathbf{L}^{(1:M)}$, respectively. The last hidden state vector of the networks is used for the encoding result. Before the encoding process, we preprocess the positional data. For the vehicles, we calculate the speed and heading at each timestep and concatenate the sequential speed and heading data to the original data along the data dimension. As a result, $\{\mathbf{X}_a\}_{a=1}^N$ and $\mathbf{Y}_i$ have the data dimension of size 4 (x-position, y-position, speed, and heading).

For the lanes, at each coordinate point, we calculate the tangent vector and the direction of the tangent vector. The sequential tangential and directional data are concatenated to the original data along the data dimension. As a result, $\mathbf{L}^{(1:M)}$ have the data dimension of size 5 (2D position vector, 2D tangent vector, and direction). We introduce the preprocessing step to make our model better infer the future positions of the target vehicle with the historical speed and heading records and the tangential data, based on that vehicles moving along a lane usually try to be parallel to the tangent vector of the lane. As shown in Table 1, the prediction performance of our model is improved due to the preprocessing step. In the rest of this paper, we use a tilde symbol at the top of a variable to indicate that it is the result of the encoding process. For example, the encoding result of $\mathbf{X}_i$ is expressed as $\tilde{\mathbf{X}}_i$.

Scene Context Extraction Module: Two lane-level context vectors are calculated in this stage. Assume that $\mathbf{L}^m$ is the reference lane for V_i. The context vector $\mathbf{a}_i^m$ for the VLI is calculated as follows:

$$\mathbf{a}_i^m = [\tilde{\mathbf{L}}^m; \sum_{l=1, l \neq m}^{M} \alpha_l \tilde{\mathbf{L}}^l], \tag{4}$$

where $\{\alpha_l\}_{l=1}^M$ are the weights calculated through the attention operation [1] between $\tilde{\mathbf{X}}_i$ and $\tilde{\mathbf{L}}^{(1:M)}$ and the semi-colon denotes the concatenation operation. α_l represents the relative importance of the surrounding lane L^l compared to the reference lane under the consideration of the past motion of V_i. As a result, our model can generate plausible trajectories for the vehicles that drive paying attention to multiple lanes. For example, suppose that the vehicle is changing its lane from L^m to L^l. α_l will be close to 1 and $\mathbf{a}_i^m$ can be approximated as $[\tilde{\mathbf{L}}^m; \tilde{\mathbf{L}}^l]$, thus, our model can generate plausible trajectories corresponding to the lane change. We show in supplementary materials how the target vehicle interacts with the surrounding lanes of the reference lane using some driving scenarios.

To model the interaction between V_i and its surrounding vehicles $\{V_j\}_{j \neq i}$, we use a GNN. As we mentioned, only the surrounding vehicles within a certain distance from the reference lane are considered for the interaction; see Fig. 1c. Let $\mathcal{N}_i^m$ denote the set of the vehicles including V_i and its select neighbors. The context vector $\mathbf{b}_i^m$ for the V2I is calculated as follows:

$$\mathbf{m}_{j \to i} = \mathrm{MLP}([\mathbf{p}_j^t - \mathbf{p}_i^t; \mathbf{h}_i^k; \mathbf{h}_j^k]), \tag{5}$$

$$\mathbf{o}_i = \sum_{j \in \mathcal{N}_i^m, j \neq i} \mathbf{m}_{j \to i}, \tag{6}$$

$$\mathbf{h}_i^{k+1} = \mathrm{GRU}(\mathbf{o}_i, \mathbf{h}_i^k), \tag{7}$$

$$\mathbf{b}_i^m = \sum_{j \in \mathcal{N}_i^m, j \neq i} \mathbf{h}_j^{K-1}, \tag{8}$$

where $\mathbf{h}^0 = \tilde{\mathbf{X}}$ for all vehicles in $\mathcal{N}_i^m$. The message passing from V_j to V_i is defined in Eq. 5 and all messages coming to V_i are aggregated by the sum operation as shown in Eq. 6. After the K rounds of the message passing, the hidden feature vector $\mathbf{h}_j^{K-1}$ represents not only the motion history of V_j but also the history of the interaction between V_j and the others. The distance threshold τ for $\mathcal{N}_i^m$ plays the important role in the performance improvement. We explore the choice of τ value and empirically find that the best performance is achieved with $\tau = 5$ meters (the distance between two nearby lane centerlines in straight roads is around 5 m). Finally, note that we use the zero vector for $\mathbf{b}_i^m$ when $\mathcal{N}_i^m$ has the target vehicle only.

Mode Selection Network: The weights for the modes of the trajectory distribution are calculated by the mode selection network $\mathbf{z}_h = f_\varphi(\mathbf{X}_i, \mathcal{C}_i^{(1:M)})$. As instance-level lanes are closely related to the modes, it can be assumed that there are M modes, each corresponding to one of $\mathbf{L}^{(1:M)}$. We calculate the weights from the lane-level scene context vectors $\mathbf{c}_i^m = [\tilde{\mathbf{X}}_i; \mathbf{a}_i^m; \mathbf{b}_i^m]$ which condense the information about the modes:

$$\mathbf{z}_h = \mathrm{MLP}_{f_\varphi}([\mathbf{c}_i^1; ...; \mathbf{c}_i^M]) \in \mathbb{R}^M. \tag{9}$$

The softmax operation is applied to $\mathbf{z}_h$ to get the final weights $\{w_m\}_{m=1}^M$. Let $\mathbf{z}_h^{SM}$ denote the result of applying the softmax operation to $\mathbf{z}_h$. w_m is equal to the m-th element of $\mathbf{z}_h^{SM}$. The lane-level scene context vector is the core feature vector for our encoder, prior, and decoder networks as described in the next section.

Encoder, Prior, and Decoder: The approximated posterior $q_\phi(\mathbf{z}_l|\mathbf{Y}_i, \mathbf{X}_i, \mathcal{C}_i^m)$, also known as encoder or recognition network, is implemented as MLPs with the encoding of the future trajectory and the lane-level scene context vector as inputs:

$$\mu_e, \sigma_e = \mathrm{MLP}_{q_\phi}([\tilde{\mathbf{Y}}_i; \mathbf{c}_i^m]), \tag{10}$$

where μ_e and σ_e are the mean and standard deviation vectors, respectively. The encoder is utilized in the training phase only because $\mathbf{Y}_i$ is not available in the inference phase. The prior $p_\gamma(\mathbf{z}_l|\mathbf{X}_i, \mathcal{C}_i^m)$ is also implemented as MLPs with the context vector as input:

$$\mu_p, \sigma_p = \mathrm{MLP}_{p_\gamma}(\mathbf{c}_i^m), \tag{11}$$

where μ_p and σ_p are the mean and standard deviation vectors, respectively. The latent variable $\mathbf{z}_l$ is sampled from (μ_e, σ_e) via the re-parameterization trick [18] during the training and from (μ_p, σ_p) during the inference.

The decoder network generates the prediction of the future trajectory, $\hat{\mathbf{Y}}_i$, via an LSTM network as follows:

$$\mathbf{e}_i^t = \mathrm{MLP}_{emb}(\hat{\mathbf{p}}_i^t), \tag{12}$$

$$\mathbf{h}_i^{t+1} = \mathrm{LSTM}([\mathbf{e}_i^t; \mathbf{c}_i^m; \mathbf{z}_l], \mathbf{h}_i^t), \tag{13}$$

$$\hat{\mathbf{p}}_i^{t+1} = \text{MLP}_{dec}(\mathbf{h}_i^{t+1}), \tag{14}$$

where we initialize $\hat{\mathbf{p}}_i^0$ and $\mathbf{h}_i^0$ as the last observed position of V_i and the zero-vector, respectively.

3.4   Regularization Through GAN

To generate more clear image samples, [19] proposed a method that combines VAE and GAN. Based on the observation that the discriminator network implicitly learns a rich similarity metric for images, the typical element-wise reconstruction metric (e.g., L_2-distance) in the ELBO objective is replaced with a feature-wise metric expressed in the discriminator. In this paper, we also propose training our forecasting model with a discriminator network simultaneously. However, we don't replace the element-wise reconstruction metric with the feature-wise metric since the characteristic of trajectory data is quite different from that of images. We instead use the discriminator to regularize our forecasting model during the training so that the trajectories generated by our model well match the shape of the reference lane.

The proposed discriminator network is defined as follows:

$$s = D(\mathbf{Y}_i, \mathbf{L}^m) = \text{MLP}_{dis}([\tilde{\mathbf{Y}}_i; \tilde{\mathbf{L}}^m]) \in \mathbb{R}^1. \tag{15}$$

We explored different choices for the encoding of the inputs to the discriminator network and observed that the following approaches improve the prediction performance: 1) $\tilde{\mathbf{Y}}_i$ is the result of encoding $[\mathbf{Y}_i; \Delta\mathbf{Y}_i]$ through an LSTM network where $\Delta\mathbf{Y}_i = \Delta\mathbf{p}_i^{(t+1:t+T)}$, $\Delta\mathbf{p}_i^t = \mathbf{p}_i^t - \mathbf{l}_f^m$, and $\mathbf{l}_f^m$ is the coordinate point of $\mathbf{L}^m$ closest to $\mathbf{p}_i^t$, 2) $\tilde{\mathbf{L}}^m$ is from the feature extraction module. We also observed that generating trajectories for the GAN objective ($\mathcal{L}_{GAN}$ defined in Eq. 18) from both the encoder and prior yields better prediction performance, which is consistent with the observations in [19]. However, not back-propagating the error signal from the GAN objective to the encoder and prior does not lead to the performance improvement, which is not consistent with the observations in [19].

3.5   Training Details

The proposed model is trained by optimizing the following objective:

$$\mathcal{L} = \mathcal{L}_{ELBO} + \alpha\mathcal{L}_{BCE} + \kappa\mathcal{L}_{GAN}. \tag{16}$$

Here, $\mathcal{L}_{BCE}$ is the binary cross entropy loss for the mode selection network and is defined as follows:

$$\mathcal{L}_{BCE} = \text{BCE}(\mathbf{g}^m, \texttt{softmax}(\mathbf{z}_h)), \tag{17}$$

where $\mathbf{g}^m$ is the one-hot vector indicating the index of the lane, in which the target vehicle traveled in the future timesteps, among the M candidate lanes. $\mathcal{L}_{GAN}$ is the typical adversarial loss defined as follows:

$$\mathcal{L}_{GAN} = \mathbb{E}_{\mathbf{Y} \sim p_{data}}[\log D(\mathbf{Y}, \mathbf{L})] + \mathbb{E}_{\mathbf{z} \sim p_z}[\log(1 - D(G(\mathbf{z}), \mathbf{L}))], \tag{18}$$

where G denotes our forecasting model. The hyper-parameters (α, κ) in Eq. 16 and β in Eq. 3 are set to 1, 0.01, and 0.5, respectively. More details can be found in supplementary materials.

3.6   Inference

Future trajectories for the target vehicle are generated from the modes based on their weights. Assume that K trajectories need to be generated for V_i. $\lfloor K \times w_m \rfloor$ out of K future trajectories are generated by the decoder network using $\mathbf{c}_i^m$ and $\mathbf{z}_l$. In the end, a total of K trajectories can be generated from $\{\mathbf{c}_i^m\}_{m=1}^{M}$ since $\sum_{m=1}^{M} w_m = 1$.

4   Experiments

4.1   Dataset

Two large-scale real-world datasets, Argoverse Forecasting [7] and nuScenes [4], are used to evaluate the prediction performance of our model. Both provide 2D or 3D annotations of road agents, track IDs of agents, and HD map data. nuScenes includes 1000 scenes, each 20 s in length. A 6-s future trajectory is predicted from a 2-s past trajectory for each target vehicle. Argoverse Forecasting is the dataset for the trajectory prediction task. It provides more than 300K scenarios, each 5 s in length. A 3-s future trajectory is predicted from a 2-s past trajectory for each target vehicle. Argoverse Forecasting and nuScenes publicly release only training and validation sets. Following the existing works [16,30], we use the validation set for the test. For the training, we use the training set only.

4.2   Evaluation Metric

For the quantitative evaluation of our forecasting model, we employ two popular metrics, average displacement error (ADE) and final displacement error (FDE), defined as follows:

$$ADE(\hat{\mathbf{Y}}, \mathbf{Y}) = \frac{1}{T} \sum_{t=1}^{T} ||\hat{\mathbf{p}}^t - \mathbf{p}^t||_2, \tag{19}$$

$$FDE(\hat{\mathbf{Y}}, \mathbf{Y}) = ||\hat{\mathbf{p}}^T - \mathbf{p}^T||_2, \tag{20}$$

where $\mathbf{Y}$ and $\hat{\mathbf{Y}}$ respectively denote the ground-truth trajectory and its prediction. In the rest of this paper, we denote ADE_K and FDE_K as the minimum of ADE and FDE among the K generated trajectories, respectively. It is worth noting that ADE_1 and FDE_1 metrics shown in the tables presented in the later sections represent the average quality of the trajectories generated for $\mathbf{Y}$. Our derivation can be found in the supplementary materials. On the other hand, ADE_K and FDE_K represent the quality of the trajectory closest to the ground-truth among the K generated trajectories. We will call $ADE_{K \geq 12}$ and $FDE_{K \geq 12}$ metrics in the tables the *best quality* in the rest of this paper. According to [5], the average quality and the best quality are complementary and evaluate the precision and coverage of the predicted trajectory distributions, respectively.

Table 1. Ablation study conducted on nuScenes.

Model	PDP	VLI	V2I	GAN	ADE_1/FDE_1	ADE_{15}/FDE_{15}
M1	✗	✗	✗	✗	3.15/7.53	0.95/1.82
M2	✔	✗	✗	✗	3.03/7.22	0.93/1.80
M3	✔	✔	✗	✗	2.91/7.00	0.94/1.82
M4	✔	✔	✔	✗	2.67/6.38	0.91/1.77
M5	✔	✔	✔	✔	**2.64/6.32**	**0.89/1.72**

(a)

Model	ADE_1/FDE_1	ADE_{15}/FDE_{15}
Ours ($\tau = 1$)	2.66/**6.31**	0.92/1.76
Ours ($\tau = 5$)	**2.64**/6.32	**0.89/1.72**
Ours ($\tau = 10$)	2.65/6.34	0.95/1.84
Ours+All	2.67/6.34	1.00/1.98
Ours+Rel	2.75/6.52	0.91/1.77

(b)

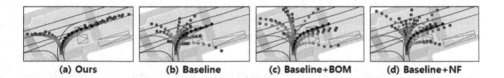

(a) Ours   (b) Baseline   (c) Baseline+BOM   (d) Baseline+NF

Fig. 3. Mode blur example.

4.3   Ablation Study

Performance Gain Over Baseline. In Table 1a, we present the contributions of each idea to the performance gain over a baseline. **M1** denotes the baseline that does not use the positional data preprocessing (PDP), VLI, V2I, and GAN regularization proposed in this paper. We can see from the table that the average quality of the generated trajectories is improved by both the PDP and the VLI (**M1** v.s. **M2** v.s. **M3**). The improvement due to the VLI is consistent with the observation in [16] that consideration of multiple lane candidates is more helpful than using a single best lane candidate in predicting the future trajectory. Both the average quality and the best quality are much improved by the V2I (**M3** v.s. **M4**). The accurate trajectory prediction for the vehicles waiting for traffic lights is the most representative case of the performance improvement by the V2I. Due to the past movement of the neighboring vehicles waiting for the traffic light,

Table 2. Quantitative comparison on nuScenes.

Model	ADE_1	FDE_1	ADE_5	FDE_5	ADE_{10}	FDE_{10}	ADE_{15}	FDE_{15}
CoverNet [26]	3.87	9.26	1.96	–	1.48	–	–	–
Trajectron++ [30]	–	9.52	1.88	–	1.51	–	–	–
AgentFormer [34]	–	–	1.86	3.89	1.45	2.86	–	–
ALAN [25]	4.67	10.0	1.77	_3.32_	_1.10_	**1.66**	–	–
LaPred [16]	_3.51_	_8.12_	_1.53_	3.37	1.12	2.39	1.10	2.34
MHA-JAM [24]	3.69	8.57	1.81	3.72	1.24	2.21	_1.03_	**1.7**
Ours	$\mathbf{2.64}_{0.87\downarrow}$	$\mathbf{6.32}_{1.8\downarrow}$	$\mathbf{1.33}_{0.2\downarrow}$	$\mathbf{2.92}_{0.4\downarrow}$	$\mathbf{1.04}_{0.06\downarrow}$	$\underline{2.15}_{0.49\uparrow}$	$\mathbf{0.89}_{0.14\downarrow}$	$\underline{1.72}_{0.02\uparrow}$

Table 3. Quantitative comparison on Argoverse Forecasting.

Model	ADE_1	FDE_1	ADE_5	FDE_5	ADE_6	FDE_6	ADE_{12}	FDE_{12}
DESIRE [20]	2.38	4.64	1.17	2.06	1.09	1.89	0.90	1.45
R2P2 [29]	3.02	5.41	1.49	2.54	1.40	2.35	1.11	1.77
VectorNet [12]	1.66	3.67	–	–	–	–	–	–
LaneAttention [23]	_1.46_	_3.27_	–	–	1.05	2.06	–	–
LaPred [16]	1.48	3.29	_0.76_	_1.55_	_0.71_	_1.44_	_0.60_	_1.15_
Ours	$\mathbf{1.44}_{0.02\downarrow}$	$\mathbf{3.15}_{0.12\downarrow}$	$\mathbf{0.70}_{0.06\downarrow}$	$\mathbf{1.35}_{0.2\downarrow}$	$\mathbf{0.65}_{0.06\downarrow}$	$\mathbf{1.24}_{0.2\downarrow}$	$\mathbf{0.51}_{0.09\downarrow}$	$\mathbf{0.85}_{0.3\downarrow}$

our model can easily conclude that the target vehicle will also be waiting for the traffic light. Finally, the prediction performance is further improved by the GAN regularization (**M4** v.s. **M5**). As seen in Eq. 15, our discriminator uses a future trajectory along with the reference lane to discriminate between fake trajectories and real trajectories.

Effect of Surrounding Vehicle Selection Mechanism. In Table 1b, we show the effect of the surrounding vehicle selection mechanism on the prediction performance of our model. Here, **Ours** (τ) denotes our model in which only the surrounding vehicles within τ meters from the reference lane are considered. **Ours+Rel** and **Ours+All** denote our model in which the most relevant vehicle and all the vehicles are considered, respectively. We can see from the table that **Ours** with $\tau = 5$ shows the best performance. This result demonstrates that considering only surrounding vehicles within a certain distance from the reference lane is effective in modeling the V2I from a lane-level perspective.

Hierarchical Latent Structure. We show in Fig. 3 the generated trajectories for a particular scenario to demonstrate how helpful the introduction of the hierarchical latent structure would be for the mitigation of mode blur. In the figure, **Baseline** denotes the VAE-based forecasting model in which a latent variable is trained to model the trajectory distribution. **Baseline+BOM** and **Baseline+NF** respectively denote **Baseline** trained with the best-of-many (BOM) sample objective [2] and normalizing flows (NF) [28]. We introduce NF since the blurry sample generation is often attributed to the limited capability of the

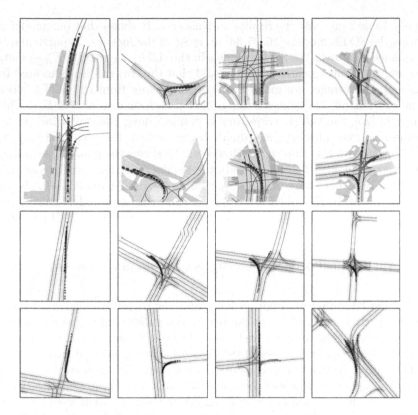

Fig. 4. Trajectory prediction examples of our forecasting model on nuScenes (the first and second rows) and Argoverse Forecasting (the third and fourth rows).

approximated posterior [15] and NF is a powerful framework for building flexible approximated posterior distributions [17]. In the figure, gray and black circles indicate historical and future positions, respectively. Squares with colors indicate the predictions of the future positions. Time is encoded in the rainbow color map ranging from red (0 s) to blue (6 s). Red solid lines indicate the centerlines of the candidate lanes. For the scenario, fifteen trajectories were generated. We can see in the figure that the proposed model generates trajectories that are aligned with the lane candidates. In contrast, neither normalizing flows nor BOM objective can help a lot for the mitigation of mode blur.

4.4 Performance Evaluation

Quantitative Evaluation. We compare our forecasting model with the existing models objectively. The results are shown in Table 2 and 3. Note that the bold and underline indicate the best and second-best performance, respectively. The values in the subscript indicate the performance gain over the second-best or loss over the best. Finally, the values in the table are from the corresponding papers and [16]. Table 2 presents the results on Nuscenes. It shows that our model out-performs the SOTA models [16, 25, 34] on most of the metrics. In particular, the performance gains over the SOTA models in the $ADE_{K \leq 5}$ and $FDE_{K \leq 5}$ metrics are significant. Consequently, it can be said that the trajectories generated from our model, on average, are more accurate than those from the SOTA models. On the other hand, [25] shows the significant performance on FDE_{10}. This is because, in [25], the vehicle trajectory is defined along the centerlines in a 2D curvilinear normal-tangential coordinate frame, so that the predicted trajectory is well aligned with the centerlines. However, [25] shows the poorest performance in the average quality. Table 3 presents the results on Argoverse Forecasting. It is seen that our forecasting model outperforms the SOTA models [16, 23] on all the metrics. The ADE_{12} and FDE_{12} results show that our model achieves much better performance in the best quality compared to the models. However, the performance gain over the second-best model in the average quality is not sig-nificant. In short, our forecasting model exhibits remarkable performance in the average and best quality on the two large-scale real-world datasets.

Qualitative Evaluation. Figure 4 illustrates the trajectories generated by our model for particular scenarios in the test dataset. Note that fifteen and twelve trajectories were generated for each scenario in nuScenes and Argoverse Fore-casting, respectively. We can see in the figure that the generated trajectories are well distributed along admissible routes. In addition, the shape of the generated trajectory matches the shape of the candidate lane well. These results verify that the trajectory distribution is nicely modeled by the two latent variables condi-tioned by the proposed lane-level scene context vectors. It is noticeable that our model can generate plausible trajectories for the driving behaviors that require simultaneous consideration of multiple lanes. The first and third figures in the first column show the scenario where the target vehicle has just started changing lanes, and the second shows the scenario where the target vehicle is in the middle of a lane change. For both scenarios, our model generates plausible trajectories corresponding to both changing lanes and returning back to its lane. Finally, the last figure in the first column shows the scenario where the target vehicle is in the middle of a right turn. Our model well captures the motion ambiguity of the vehicle that can keep a lane or change lanes.

5   Conclusions

In this paper, we proposed a VAE-based trajectory forecasting model that exploits the hierarchical latent structure. The hierarchy in the latent space was introduced to the forecasting model to mitigate mode blur by modeling the modes of the trajectory distribution and the weights for the modes separately. For the accurate modeling of the modes and weights, we introduced two lane-level context vectors calculated in novel ways, one corresponds to the VLI and the other to the V2I. The prediction performance of the model was further improved by the two techniques, positional data preprocessing and GAN-based regularization, introduced in this paper. Our experiments on two large-scale real-world datasets demonstrated that the model is not only capable of generating clear multi-modal trajectory distributions but also outperforms the SOTA models in terms of prediction accuracy.

Acknowledgment. This research work was supported by the Institute of Information & Communications Technology Planning & Evaluation (IITP) grant funded by the Korean government (MSIP) (No. 2020-0-00002, Development of standard SW platform-based autonomous driving technology to solve social problems of mobility and safety for public transport-marginalized communities)

References

1. Bahdanau, D., Cho, K., Bengio, Y.: Neural machine translation by jointly learning to align and translate. In: International Conference on Learning Representation (2015)
2. Bhattacharyya, A., Schiele, B., Fritz, M.: Accurate and diverse sampling of sequences based on a best-of-many sample objective. In: IEEE Conference on Computer Vision and Pattern Recognition (2018)
3. Bowman, S.R., Vilnis, L., Vinyals, O., Dai, A.M., Jozefowicz, R., Bengio, S.: Generating sentences from a continuous space. arXiv:1511.06349 (2015)
4. Caesar, H., et al.: nuScenes: a multimodal dataset for autonomous driving. In: IEEE Conference on Computer Vision and Pattern Recognition (2020)
5. Casas, S., Gulino, C., Suo, S., Luo, K., Liao, R., Urtasun, R.: Implicit latent variable model for scene-consistent motion forecasting. In: Vedaldi, A., Bischof, H., Brox, T., Frahm, J.-M. (eds.) ECCV 2020. LNCS, vol. 12368, pp. 624–641. Springer, Cham (2020). https://doi.org/10.1007/978-3-030-58592-1_37
6. Casas, S., Gulino, C., Suo, S., Urtasun, R.: The importance of prior knowledge in precise multimodal prediction. In: International Conference on Intelligent Robots and Systems (2020)
7. Chang, M.F., et al.: Argoverse: 3D tracking and forecasting with rich maps. In: IEEE Conference on Computer Vision and Pattern Recognition (2019)
8. Cui, A., Sadat, A., Casas, S., Liao, R., Urtasun, R.: Lookout: diverse multi-future prediction and planning for self-driving. In: International Conference on Computer Vision (2021)
9. Cui, H., et al.: Multimodal trajectory predictions for autonomous driving using deep convolutional networks. In: IEEE International Conference on Robotics and Automation (2019)
10. Fang, L., Jiang, Q., Shi, J., Zhou, B.: TPNet: trajectory proposal network for motion prediction. In: IEEE Conference on Computer Vision and Pattern Recognition (2020)
11. Fu, H., Li, C., Liu, X., Gao, J., Celikyilmaz, A., Carin, L.: Cyclical annealing schedule: a simple approach to mitigating KL vanishing. In: NAACL (2019)
12. Gao, J., et al.: VectorNet: encoding HD maps and agent dynamics from vectorized representation. In: IEEE Conference on Computer Vision and Pattern Recognition (2020)
13. Goodfellow, I., et al.: Generative adversarial nets. In: Advances in Neural Information Processing System (2014)

14. Higgins, I., et al.: beta-VAE: learning basic visual concepts with a constrained variational framework. In: International Conference on Learning and Representation (2017)
15. Huang, H., Li, Z., He, R., Sun, Z., Tan, T.: IntroVAE: introspective variational autoencoders for photographic image synthesis. In: Advances in Neural Information Processing System (2018)
16. Kim, B., et al.: LaPred: lane-aware prediction of multi-modal future trajectories of dynamic agents. In: IEEE Conference on Computer Vision Pattern Recognition (2021)
17. Kingma, D.P., Salimans, T., Jozefowicz, R., Chen, X., Sutskever, I., Welling, M.: Improved variational inference with inverse autoregressive flow. In: Advances in Neural Information Processing System (2016)
18. Kingma, D.P., Welling, M.: Auto-encoding variational Bayes. arXiv:1312.6114 (2013)
19. Larsen, A.B.L., Sonderby, S.K., Larochelle, H., Winther, O.: Autoencoding beyond pixels using a learned similarity metric. In: International Conference on Learning Representation (2016)
20. Lee, N., Choi, W., Vernaza, P., Choy, C.B., Torr, P.H.S., Chan, M.: Desire: Distant future prediction in dynamic scenes with interacting agents. In: IEEE Conference on Computer Vision on Pattern Recognition (2017)
21. Li, J., Yang, F., Ma, H., Malla, S., Tomizuka, M., Choi, C.: Rain: reinforced hybrid attention inference network for motion forecasting. In: Interantional Conference on Computer Vision (2021)
22. Liang, M., et al.: learning lane graph representations for motion forecasting. In: Vedaldi, A., Bischof, H., Brox, T., Frahm, J.-M. (eds.) ECCV 2020. LNCS, vol. 12347, pp. 541–556. Springer, Cham (2020). https://doi.org/10.1007/978-3-030-58536-5_32
23. Luo, C., Sun, L., Dabiri, D., Yuille, A.: Probabilistic multi-modal trajectory prediction with lane attention for autonomous vehicles. In: IEEE Conference on Intelligent Robots System (2020)
24. Messaoud, K., Deo, N., Trivedi, M.M., Nashashibi, F.: Trajectory prediction for autonomous driving based on multi-head attention with joint agent-map representation. arXiv:2005.02545 (2020)
25. Narayanan, S., Moslemi, R., Pittaluga, F., Liu, B., Chandraker, M.: Divide-and-conquer for lane-aware diverse trajectory prediction. In: IEEE Conference on Computer Vision and Pattern Recognition (2021)
26. P-Minh, T., Grigore, E.C., Boulton, F.A., Beijbom, O., Wolff, E.M.: CoverNet: multimodal behavior prediction using trajectory sets. In: IEEE Conference on Computer Vision and Pattern Recognition (2020)
27. Razavi, A., Oord, A., Poole, B., Vinyals, O.: Preventing posterior collapse with delta-VAEs. In: International Conference on Learning Representation (2019)
28. Rezende, D.J., Mohamad, S.: Variational inference with normalizing flows. In: International Conference on Machine Learning (2015)
29. Rhinehart, N., Kitani, K.M., Vernaza, P.: R2p2: a reparameterized pushforward policy for diverse, precise generative path forecasting. In: European Conference on Computer Vision (2018)
30. Salzmann, T., Ivanovic, B., Chakravarty, P., Pavone, M.: Trajectron++: dynamically-feasible trajectory forecasting with heterogeneous data. In: Vedaldi, A., Bischof, H., Brox, T., Frahm, J.-M. (eds.) ECCV 2020. LNCS, vol. 12363, pp. 683–700. Springer, Cham (2020). https://doi.org/10.1007/978-3-030-58523-5_40

31. Sohn, K., Lee, H., Yan, X.: Learning structured output representation using deep conditional generative models. In: Advances in Neural Information Processing System (2015)
32. Vahdat, A., Kautz, J.: NVAE: a deep hierarchical variational autoencoder. In: Advances in Neural Information Processing System (2020)
33. Yang, Z., Hu, Z., Salakhutdinov, R., B.-Kirkpatrick, T.: Improved variational autoencoders for text modeling using dilated convolutions. In: International Conference on Machine Learning (2017)
34. Yuan, Y., Weng, X., Ou, Y., Kitani, K.: AgentFormer: agent-aware transformers for socio-temporal multi-agent forecasting. arXiv:2103.14023 (2021)
35. Zhao, S., Song, J., Ermon, S.: InfoVAE: information maximizing variational autoencoders. In: arXiv:1706.02262 (2017)
36. Zhao, S., Song, J., Ermon, S.: Towards a deeper understanding of variational autoencoding models. In: arXiv:1702.08658v1 (2017)

AiATrack: Attention in Attention for Transformer Visual Tracking

Shenyuan Gao[1]([✉]), Chunluan Zhou[2], Chao Ma[3], Xinggang Wang[1],
and Junsong Yuan[4]

[1] Huazhong University of Science and Technology, Wuhan, China
shenyuangao@gmail.com, xgwang@hust.edu.cn
[2] Wormpex AI Research, Bellevue, USA
czhou002@e.ntu.edu.sg
[3] Shanghai Jiao Tong University, Shanghai, China
chaoma@sjtu.edu.cn
[4] State University of New York at Buffalo, Buffalo, USA
jsyuan@buffalo.edu

Abstract. Transformer trackers have achieved impressive advancements recently, where the attention mechanism plays an important role. However, the independent correlation computation in the attention mechanism could result in noisy and ambiguous attention weights, which inhibits further performance improvement. To address this issue, we propose an attention in attention (AiA) module, which enhances appropriate correlations and suppresses erroneous ones by seeking consensus among all correlation vectors. Our AiA module can be readily applied to both self-attention blocks and cross-attention blocks to facilitate feature aggregation and information propagation for visual tracking. Moreover, we propose a streamlined Transformer tracking framework, dubbed AiATrack, by introducing efficient feature reuse and target-background embeddings to make full use of temporal references. Experiments show that our tracker achieves state-of-the-art performance on six tracking benchmarks while running at a real-time speed. Code and models are publicly available at https://github.com/Little-Podi/AiATrack.

Keywords: Visual tracking · Attention mechanism · Vision transformer

1 Introduction

Visual tracking is one of the fundamental tasks in computer vision. It has gained increasing attention because of its wide range of applications [18,35]. Given a target with bounding box annotation in the initial frame of a video, the objective

Supplementary Information The online version contains supplementary material available at https://doi.org/10.1007/978-3-031-20047-2_9.

of visual tracking is to localize the target in successive frames. Over the past few years, Siamese trackers [2,31,32,58], which regards the visual tracking task as a one-shot matching problem, have gained enormous popularity. Recently, several trackers [6,8,48,51,52,54] have explored the application of the Transformer [47] architecture and achieved promising performance.

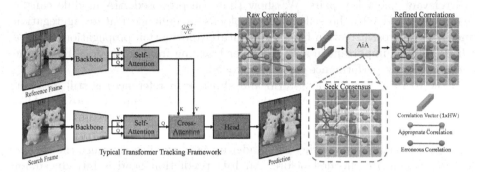

Fig. 1. Motivation of the proposed method. The left part of the figure shows a typical Transformer tracking framework. On the right, the nodes denote features at different positions in a feature map. These nodes serve as queries and keys for a self-attention block. The links between nodes represent the correlations between queries and keys in the attention mechanism. Some correlations of the green node is erroneous since it is linked to the nodes at irrelevant positions. By applying the proposed module to the raw correlations, we can seek consensus from the correlations of other nodes (*e.g.* the brown node) that can provide supporting cues for the appropriate correlations. By this means, the quality of the correlations can be refined. (Color figure online)

The crucial components in a typical Transformer tracking framework [8,48, 54] are the attention blocks. As shown in Fig. 1, the feature representations of the reference frame and search frame are enhanced via self-attention blocks, and the correlations between them are bridged via cross-attention blocks for target prediction in the search frame. The Transformer attention [47] takes queries and a set of key-value pairs as input and outputs linear combinations of values with weights determined by the correlations between queries and the corresponding keys. The correlation map is computed by the scaled dot products between queries and keys. However, the correlation of each query-key pair is computed independently, which ignores the correlations of other query-key pairs. This could introduce erroneous correlations due to imperfect feature representations or the existence of distracting image patches in a background clutter scene, resulting in noisy and ambiguous attention weights as visualized in Fig. 4.

To address the aforementioned issue, we propose a novel attention in attention (AiA) module, which extends the conventional attention [47] by inserting an inner attention module. The introduced inner attention module is designed to refine the correlations by seeking consensus among all correlation vectors. The motivation of the AiA module is illustrated in Fig. 1. Usually, if a key has a high correlation with a query, some of its neighboring keys will also have relatively high correlations with that query. Otherwise, the correlation might be noise. Motivated by this, we introduce the inner attention module to utilize these informative cues. Specifically, the inner attention module takes the raw correlations as queries, keys, and values and adjusts them to enhance the appropriate correlations of relevant query-key pairs and suppress the erroneous correlations of irrelevant query-key pairs. We show that the proposed AiA module can be readily inserted into the self-attention blocks to enhance feature aggregation and into the cross-attention block to facilitate information propagation, both of which are very important in a Transformer tracking framework. As a result, the overall tracking performance can be improved.

How to introduce the long-term and short-term references is still an open problem for visual tracking. With the proposed AiA module, we present AiA-Track, a streamlined Transformer framework for visual tracking. Unlike previous practices [19,48,52,56], which need an extra computational cost to process the selected reference frame during the model update, we directly reuse the cached features which are encoded before. An IoU prediction head is introduced for selecting high-quality short-term references. Moreover, we introduce learnable target-background embeddings to distinguish the target from the background while preserving the contextual information. With these designs, the proposed AiATrack can efficiently update short-term references and effectively exploit the long-term and short-term references for visual tracking.

We verify the effectiveness of our method by conducting comprehensive experiments on six prevailing benchmarks covering various kinds of tracking scenarios. Without bells and whistles, the proposed AiATrack sets new state-of-the-art results on these benchmarks with a real-time speed of 38 frames per second (fps).

In summary, the main contributions of our work are three-fold:

- We propose a novel attention in attention (AiA) module, which can mitigate noise and ambiguity in the conventional attention mechanism [47] and improve tracking performance by a notable margin.
- We present a neat Transformer tracking framework with the reuse of encoded features and the introduction of target-background embeddings to efficiently and effectively leverage temporal references.
- We perform extensive experiments and analyses to validate the effectiveness of our designs. The proposed AiATrack achieves state-of-the-art performance on six widely used benchmarks.

2   Related Work

2.1   Visual Tracking

Recently, Transformer [47] has shown impressive performance in computer vision [7,14,59]. It aggregates information from sequential inputs to capture global context by an attention mechanism. Some efforts [19,21,55] have been made to introduce the attention structure to visual tracking. Recently, several works [6, 8,48,51,52,54] apply Transformer architecture to visual tracking. Despite their impressive performance, the potential of Transformer trackers is still limited by the conventional attention mechanism. To this end, we propose a novel attention module, namely, attention in attention (AiA), to further unveil the power of Transformer trackers.

How to adapt the model to the appearance change during tracking has also been investigated by previous works [3,4,10,11,19,48,52,56]. A straightforward solution is to update the reference features by generation [56] or ensemble [19,48,52]. However, most of these methods need to resize the reference frame and re-encode the reference features, which may sacrifice computational efficiency. Following discriminative correlation filter (DCF) method [24], another family of approaches [3,11] optimize the network parameters during the inference. However, they need sophisticated optimization strategies with a sparse update to meet real-time requirements. In contrast, we present a new framework that can efficiently reuse the encoded features. Moreover, a target-background embedding assignment mechanism is also introduced. Different from [20,30,53], our target-background embeddings are directly introduced to distinguish the target and background regions and provide rich contextual cues.

2.2   Attention Mechanism

Represented by non-local operation [49] and Transformer attention [47], attention mechanism has rapidly received great popularity over the past few years. Recently, Transformer attention has been introduced to computer vision as a competitive architecture [7,14,59]. In vision tasks, it usually acts as a dynamic information aggregator in spatial and temporal domains. There are some works [26,27] that focus on solving existing issues in the conventional attention mechanism. Unlike these, in this paper, we try to address the noise and ambiguity issue in conventional attention mechanism by seeking consensus among correlations with a global receptive field.

2.3   Correlation as Feature

Treating correlations as features has been explored by several previous works [4,5,9,33,38,42–45]. In this paper, we use correlations to refer to the matching results of the pixels or regions. They can be obtained by squared difference, cosine similarity, inner product, *etc.* Several efforts have been made to recalibrate the raw correlations by processing them as features through hand-crafted algorithms [5,44] or learnable blocks [4,9,33,38,42,43]. To our best knowledge, we introduce this insight to the attention mechanism for the first time, making it a unified block for feature aggregation and information propagation in Transformer visual tracking.

3   Method

3.1   Attention in Attention

To present our attention in attention module, we first briefly revisit the conventional attention block in vision [7,14]. As illustrated in Fig. 2(a), it takes a query and a set of key-value pairs as input and produces an output which is a weighted sum of the values. The weights assigned to the values are computed by taking the softmax of the scaled dot products between the query and the corresponding keys. Denote queries, keys and values by $\mathbf{Q}, \mathbf{K}, \mathbf{V} \in \mathbb{R}^{HW \times C}$ respectively. The conventional attention can be formulated as

$$\text{ConvenAttn}(\mathbf{Q}, \mathbf{K}, \mathbf{V}) = (\text{Softmax}\left(\frac{\bar{\mathbf{Q}}\bar{\mathbf{K}}^{\mathbf{T}}}{\sqrt{C}}\right) \bar{\mathbf{V}})\mathbf{W_o} \qquad (1)$$

where $\bar{\mathbf{Q}} = \mathbf{Q}\mathbf{W_q}$, $\bar{\mathbf{K}} = \mathbf{K}\mathbf{W_k}$, $\bar{\mathbf{V}} = \mathbf{V}\mathbf{W_v}$ are different linear transformations. Here, $\mathbf{W_q}$, $\mathbf{W_k}$, $\mathbf{W_v}$ and $\mathbf{W_o}$ denote the linear transform weights for queries, keys, values, and outputs, respectively.

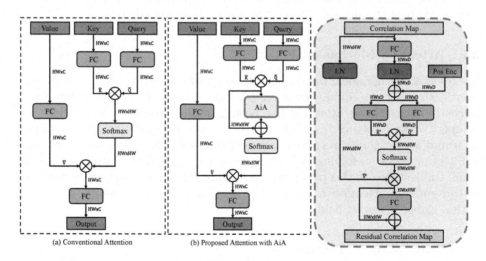

Fig. 2. Structures of conventional attention and the proposed attention in attention (AiA) module. $\otimes$ denotes matrix multiplication and $\oplus$ denotes element-wise addition. The numbers beside arrows are feature dimensions which do not include the batch size. Matrix transpose operations are omitted for brevity.

However, in the conventional attention block, the correlation of each query-key pair in the correlation map $\mathbf{M} = \frac{\bar{\mathbf{Q}}\bar{\mathbf{K}}^{\mathbf{T}}}{\sqrt{C}} \in \mathbb{R}^{HW \times HW}$ is computed independently, which ignores the correlations of other query-key pairs. This correlation computation procedure may introduce erroneous correlations due to imperfect feature representations or the existence of distracting image patches in a background clutter scene. These erroneous correlations could result in noisy and ambiguous attentions as visualized in Fig. 4. They may unfavorably affect the feature aggregation in self-attention and the information propagation in cross-attention, leading to sub-optimal performance for a Transformer tracker.

To address the aforementioned problem, we propose a novel attention in attention (AiA) module to improve the quality of the correlation map $\mathbf{M}$. Usually, if a key has a high correlation with a query, some of its neighboring keys will also have relatively high correlations with that query. Otherwise, the correlation might be a noise. Motivated by this, we introduce the AiA module to utilize the informative cues among the correlations in $\mathbf{M}$. The proposed AiA module seeks the correlation consistency around each key to enhance the appropriate correlations of relevant query-key pairs and suppress the erroneous correlations of irrelevant query-key pairs.

Specifically, we introduce another attention module to refine the correlation map $\mathbf{M}$ before the softmax operation as illustrated in Fig. 2(b). As the newly introduced attention module is inserted into the conventional attention block, we call it an inner attention module, forming an attention in attention structure. The inner attention module itself is a variant of the conventional attention. We consider columns in $\mathbf{M}$ as a sequence of correlation vectors which are taken as queries $\mathbf{Q}'$, keys $\mathbf{K}'$ and values $\mathbf{V}'$ by the inner attention module to output a residual correlation map.

Given the input $\mathbf{Q}'$, $\mathbf{K}'$ and $\mathbf{V}'$, we first generate transformed queries $\bar{\mathbf{Q}}'$ and keys $\bar{\mathbf{K}}'$ as illustrated in the right block of Fig. 2(b). To be specific, a linear transformation is first applied to reduce the dimensions of $\mathbf{Q}'$ and $\mathbf{K}'$ to $HW \times D$ ($D \ll HW$) for computational efficiency. After normalization [1], we add 2-dimensional sinusoidal encoding [7,14] to provide positional cues. Then, $\bar{\mathbf{Q}}'$ and $\bar{\mathbf{K}}'$ are generated by two different linear transformations. We also normalize $\mathbf{V}'$ to generate the normalized correlation vectors $\bar{\mathbf{V}}'$, $i.e.\, \bar{\mathbf{V}}' = \text{LayerNorm}(\mathbf{V}')$. With $\bar{\mathbf{Q}}'$, $\bar{\mathbf{K}}'$ and $\bar{\mathbf{V}}'$, the inner attention module generates a residual correlation map by

$$\text{InnerAttn}(\mathbf{M}) = \left(\text{Softmax}\left(\frac{\bar{\mathbf{Q}}'\bar{\mathbf{K}}'^{\mathbf{T}}}{\sqrt{D}}\right)\bar{\mathbf{V}}'\right)(1 + \mathbf{W}_\mathbf{o}') \tag{2}$$

where $\mathbf{W}_\mathbf{o}'$ denotes linear transform weights for adjusting the aggregated correlations together with an identical connection.

Essentially, for each correlation vector in the correlation map $\mathbf{M}$, the AiA module generates its residual correlation vector by aggregating the raw correlation vectors. It can be seen as seeking consensus among the correlations with a global receptive field. With the residual correlation map, our attention block with AiA module can be formulated as

$$\text{AttninAttn}(\mathbf{Q}, \mathbf{K}, \mathbf{V}) = (\text{Softmax}(\mathbf{M} + \text{InnerAttn}(\mathbf{M}))\bar{\mathbf{V}})\mathbf{W}_\mathbf{o} \tag{3}$$

For a multi-head attention block, we share the parameters of the AiA module between the parallel attention heads. It is worth noting that our AiA module can be readily inserted into both self-attenion and cross-attention blocks in a Transformer tracking framework.

3.2 Proposed Framework

With the proposed AiA module, we design a simple yet effective Transformer framework for visual tracking, dubbed AiATrack. Our tracker is comprised of a network backbone, a Transformer architecture, and two prediction heads as illustrated in Fig. 3. Given the search frame, the initial frame is taken as a long-term reference and an ensemble of several intermediate frames are taken as short-term references. The features of the long-term and short-term references and the search frame are extracted by the network backbone and then reinforced by the Transformer encoder. We also introduce learnable target-background embeddings to distinguish the target from background regions. The Transformer decoder propagates the reference features as well as the target-background embedding maps to the search frame. The output of the Transformer is then fed to a target prediction head and an IoU prediction head for target localization and short-term reference update, respectively.

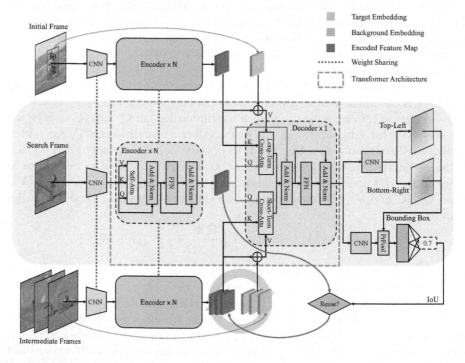

Fig. 3. Overview of the proposed Transformer tracking framework. The self-attention and cross-attention blocks are all equipped with the proposed AiA module. Note that only the components on the light green background need to be computed during the inference phase as described in Sect. 3.3 (Color figure online).

Transformer Architecture. The Transformer encoder is adopted to reinforce the features extracted by the convolutional backbone. For the search frame, we flatten its features to obtain a sequence of feature vectors and add sinusoidal positional encoding as in [7]. The sequence of feature vectors is then taken by the Transformer encoder as its input. The Transformer encoder consists of several layer stacks, each of which is made up of a multi-head self-attention block and a feed-forward network. The self-attention block serves to capture the dependencies among all feature vectors to enhance the original features, and is equipped with the proposed AiA module. Similarly, this procedure is applied independently to the features of the reference frames using the same encoder.

The Transformer decoder propagates the reference information from the long-term and short-term references to the search frame. Different from the classical Transformer decoder [47], we remove the self-attention block for simplicity and introduce a two-branch cross-attention design as shown in Fig. 3 to retrieve the target-background information from long-term and short-term references. The long-term branch is responsible for retrieving reference information from the initial frame. Since the initial frame has the most reliable annotation of the tracking target, it is crucial for robust visual tracking. However, as the appearance of the target and the background change through the video, the reference information from the long-term branch may not be up-to-date. This could cause tracker drift in some scenes. To address this problem, we introduce the short-term branch to utilize the information from the frames that are closer to the current frame. The cross-attention blocks of the two branches have the identical structure following the query-key-value design in the vanilla transformer [47]. We take the features of the search frame as queries and the features of the reference frames as keys. The values are generated by combining the reference features with target-background embedding maps, which will be described below. We also insert our AiA module into cross-attention for better reference information propagation.

Target-Background Embeddings. To indicate the target and background regions while preserving the contextual information, we introduce a target embedding $\mathcal{E}^{tgt} \in \mathbb{R}^C$ and a background embedding $\mathcal{E}^{bg} \in \mathbb{R}^C$, both of which are learnable. With $\mathcal{E}^{tgt}$ and $\mathcal{E}^{bg}$, we generate target-background embedding maps $\mathcal{E} \in \mathbb{R}^{HW \times C}$ for the reference frames with a negligible computational cost. Let's consider a location p in a $H \times W$ grid, the embedding assignment is formulated as

$$\mathcal{E}(p) = \begin{cases} \mathcal{E}^{tgt} & \text{if } p \text{ falls in the target region} \\ \mathcal{E}^{bg} & \text{otherwise} \end{cases} \tag{4}$$

Afterward, we attach the target-background embedding maps to the reference features and feed them to cross-attention blocks as values. The target-background embedding maps enrich the reused appearance features by providing contextual cues.

Prediction Heads. As described above, our tracker has two prediction heads. The target prediction head is adopted from [52]. Specifically, the decoded features are fed into a two-branch fully-convolutional network which outputs two probability maps for the top-left and the bottom-right corners of the target bounding box. The predicted box coordinates are then obtained by computing the expectations of the probability distributions of the two corners.

To adapt the model to the appearance change during tracking, the tracker needs to keep the short-term references up-to-date by selecting reliable references which contain the target. Moreover, considering our embedding assignment mechanism in Eq. 4, the bounding box of the selected reference frame should be as accurate as possible. Inspired by IoU-Net [28] and ATOM [11], for each predicted bounding box, we estimate its IoU with the ground truth via an IoU prediction head. The features inside the predicted bounding box are passed to a Precise RoI Pooling layer whose output is taken by a fully connected network to produce an IoU prediction. The predicted IoU is then used to determine whether to include the search frame as a new short-term reference.

We train the two prediction heads jointly. The loss of target prediction is defined by the combination of GIoU loss [41] and L1 loss between the predicted bounding box and the ground truth. The training examples of the IoU prediction head are generated by sampling bounding boxes around the ground truths. The loss of IoU prediction is defined by mean squared error. We refer readers to the supplementary material for more details about training.

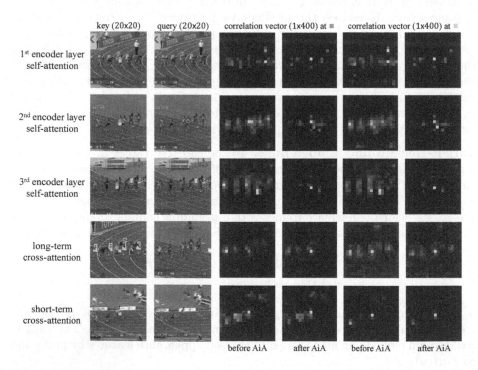

Fig. 4. Visualization of the effect of the proposed AiA module. We visualize several representative correlation vectors before and after the refinement by the AiA module. The visualized correlation vectors are reshaped according to the spatial positions of queries. We select the correlation vectors of keys corresponding to the target object regions in the first column. It can be observed that the erroneous correlations are effectively suppressed and the appropriate ones are enhanced with the AiA module.

3.3 Tracking with AiATrack

Given the initial frame with ground truth annotation, we initialize the tracker by cropping the initial frame as long-term and short-term references and pre-computing their features and target-background embedding maps. For each subsequent frame, we estimate the IoU score of the bounding box predicted by target prediction head for model update. The update procedure is more efficient than the previous practices [19,48,52], as we directly reuse the encoded features. Specifically, if the estimated IoU score of the predicted bounding box is higher than the pre-defined threshold, we generate the target-background embedding map for the current search frame and store the embedding map in a memory cache together with its encoded features. For each new-coming frame, we uniformly sample several short-term reference frames and concatenate their features and embedding maps from the memory cache to update the short term reference ensemble. The latest reference frame in the memory cache is always sampled as it is closest to the current search frame. The oldest reference frame in the memory cache will be popped out if the maximum cache size is reached.

Table 1. State-of-the-art comparison on LaSOT, TrackingNet, and GOT-10k. The best two results are shown in red and blue, respectively. All the trackers listed above adopt ResNet-50 pre-trained on ImageNet-1k as network backbone and the results on GOT-10k are obtained without additional training data for fair comparison.

Tracker	Source	LaSOT [17]			TrackingNet [40]			GOT-10k [25]		
		AUC	P_{Norm}	P	AUC	P_{Norm}	P	AO	$SR_{0.75}$	$SR_{0.5}$
AiATrack	Ours	69.0	79.4	73.8	82.7	87.8	80.4	69.6	63.2	80.0
STARK-ST50 [52]	ICCV2021	66.4	76.3	71.2	81.3	86.1	78.1	68.0	62.3	77.7
KeepTrack [36]	ICCV2021	67.1	77.2	70.2	–	–	–	–	–	–
DTT [54]	ICCV2021	60.1	–	–	79.6	85.0	78.9	63.4	51.4	74.9
TransT [8]	CVPR2021	64.9	73.8	69.0	81.4	86.7	80.3	67.1	60.9	76.8
TrDiMP [48]	CVPR2021	63.9	–	61.4	78.4	83.3	73.1	67.1	58.3	77.7
TrSiam [48]	CVPR2021	62.4	–	60.0	78.1	82.9	72.7	66.0	57.1	76.6
KYS [4]	ECCV2020	55.4	63.3	–	74.0	80.0	68.8	63.6	51.5	75.1
Ocean-online [58]	ECCV2020	56.0	65.1	56.6	–	–	–	61.1	47.3	72.1
Ocean-offline [58]	ECCV2020	52.6	–	52.6	–	–	–	59.2	–	69.5
PrDiMP50 [12]	CVPR2020	59.8	68.8	60.8	75.8	81.6	70.4	63.4	54.3	73.8
SiamAttn [55]	CVPR2020	56.0	64.8	–	75.2	81.7	–	–	–	–
DiMP50 [3]	ICCV2019	56.9	65.0	56.7	74.0	80.1	68.7	61.1	49.2	71.7
SiamRPN++ [31]	CVPR2019	49.6	56.9	49.1	73.3	80.0	69.4	51.7	32.5	61.6

4 Experiments

4.1 Implementation Details

Our experiments are conducted with NVIDIA GeForce RTX 2080 Ti. We adopt ResNet-50 [22] as network backbone which is initialized by the parameters pre-trained on ImageNet-1k [13]. We crop a search patch which is 5^2 times of the target box area from the search frame and resize it to a resolution of 320×320 pixels. The same cropping procedure is also applied to the reference frames. The cropped patches are then down-sampled by the network backbone with a stride of 16. The Transformer encoder consists of 3 layer stacks and the Transformer decoder consists of only 1 layer. The multi-head attention blocks in our tracker have 4 heads with channel width of 256. The inner AiA module reduces the channel dimension of queries and keys to 64. The FFN blocks have 1024 hidden units. Each branch of the target prediction head is comprised of 5 Conv-BN-ReLU layers. The IoU prediction head consists of 3 Conv-BN-ReLU layers, a PrPool [28] layer with pooling size of 3×3 and 2 fully connected layers.

4.2   Results and Comparisons

We compare our tracker with several state-of-the-art trackers on three prevailing large-scale benchmarks (LaSOT [17], TrackingNet and [40] and GOT-10k [25]) and three commonly used small-scale datasets (NfS30 [29], OTB100 [50] and UAV123 [39]). The results are summarized in Table 1 and Table 2.

LaSOT. LaSOT [17] is a densely annotated large-scale dataset, containing 1400 long-term video sequences. As shown in Table 1, our approach outperforms the previous best tracker KeepTrack [36] by 1.9% in area-under-the-curve (AUC) and 3.6% in precision while running much faster (see Table 2). We also provide an attribute-based evaluation in Fig. 5 for further analysis. Our method achieves the best performance on all attribute splits. The results demonstrate the promising potential of our approach for long-term visual tracking.

Table 2. State-of-the-art comparison on commonly used small-scale datasets in terms of AUC score. The best two results are shown in red and blue.

Tracker	SiamRPN++ [31]	PrDiMP50 [12]	TransT [8]	STARK-ST50 [52]	KeepTrack [36]	AiATrack (Ours)
NfS30 [29]	50.2	63.5	65.7	65.2	66.4	67.9
OTB100 [50]	69.6	69.6	69.4	68.5	70.9	69.6
UAV123 [39]	61.3	68.0	69.1	69.1	69.7	70.6
Speed (fps)	35	30	50	42	18	38

TrackingNet. TrackingNet [40] is a large-scale short-term tracking benchmark. It provides 511 testing video sequences without publicly available ground truths. Our performance reported in Table 1 is obtained from the online evaluation server. Our approach achieve 82.7% in AUC score and 87.8% in normalized precision score, surpassing all previously published trackers. It demonstrates that our approach is also very competitive for short-term tracking scenarios.

GOT-10k. To ensure zero overlaps of object classes between training and testing, we follow the one-shot protocol of GOT-10k [25] and only train our model

Fig. 5. Attribute-based evaluation on LaSOT in terms of AUC score. Our tracker achieves the best performance on all attribute splits while making a significant improvement in various kinds of scenarios such as background clutter, camera motion, and deformation. Axes of each attribute have been normalized.

with the specified subset. The testing ground truths are also withheld and our result is evaluated by the official server. As demonstrated in Table 1, our tracker improves all metrics by a large margin, *e.g.* 2.3% in success rate compared with STARK [52] and TrDiMP [48], which indicates that our tracker also has a good generalization ability to the objects of unseen classes.

NfS30. Need for Speed (NfS) [29] is a dataset that contains 100 videos with fast-moving objects. We evaluate the proposed tracker on its commonly used version NfS30. As reported in Table 2, our tracker improves the AUC score by 2.7% over STARK [52] and performs the best among the benchmarked trackers.

OTB100. Object Tracking Benchmark (OTB) [50] is a pioneering benchmark for evaluating visual tracking algorithms. However, in recent years, it has been noted that this benchmark has become highly saturated [36,48,52]. Still, the results in Table 2 show that our method can achieve comparable performance with state-of-the-art trackers.

UAV123. Finally, we report our results on UAV123 [39] which includes 123 video sequences captured from a low-altitude unmanned aerial vehicle perspective. As shown in Table 2, our tracker outperforms KeepTrack [36] by 0.9% and is suitable for UAV tracking scenarios.

4.3 Ablation Studies

To validate the importance of the proposed components in our tracker, we conduct ablation studies on LaSOT testing set and its new extension set [16], totaling 430 diverse videos. We summarize the results in Table 3, Table 4 and Table 5.

Target-Background Embeddings. In our tracking framework, the reference frames not only contain features from target regions but also include a large proportion of features from background regions. We implement three variants of our method to demonstrate the necessity of keeping the context and the importance of the proposed target-background embeddings. As shown in the 1st part of Table 3, we start from the variant (a), which is the implementation of the proposed tracking framework with both the target-background embeddings and the AiA module removed. Based on the variant (a), the variant (b) further discards the reference features of background regions with a mask. The variant (c) attaches the target-background embeddings to the reference features. Compared with the variant (a), the performance of the variant (b) drops drastically, which suggests that context is helpful for visual tracking. With the proposed target-background embeddings, the variant (c) can consistently improve the performance over the variant (a) in all metrics. This is because the proposed target-background embeddings further provide cues for distinguishing the target and background regions while preserving the contextual information.

Long-Term and Short-Term Branch. As discussed in Sect. 3.2, it is important to utilize an independent short-term reference branch to deal with the appearance change during tracking. To validate this, we implement a variant (d) by removing the short-term branch from the variant (c). We also implement a variant (e) by adopting a single cross-attention branch instead of the proposed two-branch design for the variant (c). Note that we keep the IoU prediction head for these two variants during training to eliminate the possible effect of IoU prediction on feature representation learning. From the 2nd part of Table 3, we can observe that the performance of variant (d) is worse than variant (c), which suggests the necessity of using short-term references. Meanwhile, compared with variant (c), the performance of variant (e) also drops, which validates the necessity to use two separate branches for the long-term and short-term references. This is because the relatively unreliable short-term references may disturb the robust long-term reference and therefore degrade its contribution.

Table 3. Ablative experiments about different components in the proposed tracker. We use † to denote the basic framework and ‡ to denote our final model with AiA. The best results in each part of the table are marked in **bold**.

	Modification	LaSOT [17]			LaSOT$_{Ext}$ [16]		
		AUC	P$_{Norm}$	P	AUC	P$_{Norm}$	P
1st	(a) none	65.8	75.8	69.5	44.5	51.5	50.5
	(b) mask	64.3	72.7	66.6	42.8	50.1	48.8
	(c) embed†	**67.0**	**77.0**	**71.3**	**44.7**	**52.7**	**51.5**
2nd	(d) w/o short refer	66.5	76.3	70.7	44.5	51.8	50.6
	(e) w/o branch split	63.8	72.9	66.7	42.7	50.3	48.6
	(c) w/ both†	**67.0**	**77.0**	**71.3**	**44.7**	**52.7**	**51.5**
3rd	(c) w/o AiA†	67.0	77.0	71.3	44.7	52.7	51.5
	(f) AiA in self-attn	68.6	78.7	72.9	46.2	**54.4**	53.4
	(g) AiA in cross-attn	67.5	77.9	71.8	46.2	54.2	53.3
	(h) w/o pos in both	68.0	78.2	72.7	46.2	54.0	53.0
	(i) AiA in both‡	**68.7**	**79.3**	**73.7**	**46.8**	**54.4**	**54.2**

Effectiveness of the AiA Module. We explore several ways of applying the proposed AiA module to the proposed Transformer tracking framework.

The variant (f) inserts the AiA module into self-attention blocks in the Transformer encoder. Compared with the variant (c), the performance can be greatly improved on the two subsets of LaSOT. The variant (g) inserts the AiA module into the cross-attention blocks in the Transformer decoder, which also brings a consistent improvement. These two variants demonstrate that the AiA module generalizes well to both self-attention blocks and cross-attention blocks. When we apply the AiA module to both self-attention blocks and cross-attention blocks, *i.e.* the final model (i), the performance on the two subsets of LaSOT can be improved by 1.7–2.7% in all metrics compared with the basic framework (c).

Recall that we introduce positional encoding to the proposed AiA module (see Fig. 2). To verify its importance, we implement a variant (h) by removing positional encoding from the variant (i). We can observe that the performance drops accordingly. This validates the necessity of positional encoding, as it provides spatial cues for consensus seeking in the AiA module. More analysis about the components of the AiA module are provided in the supplementary material.

Superiority of the AiA Module. One may concern that the performance gain of the AiA module is brought by purely adding extra parameters. Thus, we design two other variants to demonstrate the superiority of the proposed module.

First, we implement a variant of our basic framework where each Attention-Add-Norm block is replaced by two cascaded ones. From the comparison of the first two rows in Table 4, we can observe that simply increasing the number of attention blocks in our tracking framework does not help much, which demonstrates that our AiA module can further unveil the potential of the tracker.

We also implement a variant of our final model by replacing the proposed inner attention with a convolutional bottleneck [22], which is designed to have a similar computational cost. From the comparison of the last two rows in Table 4, we can observe that inserting a convolutional bottleneck can also bring positive effects, which suggests the necessity of correlation refinement. However, the convolutional bottleneck can only perform a fixed aggregation in each local neighborhood, while our AiA module has a global receptive field with dynamic weights determined by the interaction among correlation vectors. As a result, our AiA module can seek consensus more flexibly and further boost the performance.

Visualization Perspective. In Fig. 4, we visualize correlation maps from the perspective of keys. This is because we consider the correlations of one key with queries as a correlation vector. Thus, the AiA module performs refinement by

Table 4. Superiority comparison with the tracking performance and the running speed.

Modification	Correlation Refinement	LaSOT [17]			LaSOT$_{Ext}$ [16]			Speed (fps)
		AUC	P$_{Norm}$	P	AUC	P$_{Norm}$	P	
w/o AiA[†]	✗	67.0	77.0	71.3	44.7	52.7	51.5	44
w/o AiA cascade		67.1	77.0	71.7	44.6	52.9	51.6	40
conv in both	✓	67.9	78.2	72.8	46.0	53.4	52.8	39
AiA in both[‡]		**68.7**	**79.3**	**73.7**	**46.8**	**54.4**	**54.2**	38

Table 5. Impact of ensemble size in terms of AUC score and the running speed. All of our ablative experiments are conducted with ensemble size as 3 by default.

Ensemble Size	1	2	3	4	5	6	10
LaSOT [17]	66.8	68.1	68.7	**69.0**	68.2	68.6	68.9
LaSOT$_{Ext}$ [16]	44.9	46.3	46.8	46.2	47.4	**47.7**	47.1
Speed (fps)	39	39	38	38	38	38	34

seeking consensus among the correlation vectors of keys. Actually, refining the correlations from the perspective of queries also works well, achieving 68.5% in AUC score on LaSOT.

Short-Term Reference Ensemble. We also study the impact of the ensemble size in the short-term branch. Table 5 shows that by increasing the ensemble size from 1 to 3, the performance can be stably improved. Further increasing the ensemble size does not help much and has little impact on the running speed.

5   Conclusion

In this paper, we present an attention in attention (AiA) module to improve the attention mechanism for Transformer visual tracking. The proposed AiA module can effectively enhance appropriate correlations and suppress erroneous ones by seeking consensus among all correlation vectors. Moreover, we present a streamlined Transformer tracking framework, dubbed AiATrack, by introducing efficient feature reuse and embedding assignment mechanisms to fully utilize temporal references. Extensive experiments demonstrate the superiority of the proposed method. We believe that the proposed AiA module could also be beneficial in other related tasks where the Transformer architecture can be applied to perform feature aggregation and information propagation, such as video object segmentation [15,30,34,53], video object detection [23] and multi-object tracking [37,46,57].

Acknowledgment.. This work is supported in part by National Key R&D Program of China No. 2021YFC3340802, National Science Foundation Grant CNS1951952 and National Natural Science Foundation of China Grant 61906119.

References

1. Ba, J.L., Kiros, J.R., Hinton, G.E.: Layer normalization. arXiv preprint arXiv: 1607.06450 (2016)
2. Bertinetto, L., Valmadre, J., Henriques, J.F., Vedaldi, A., Torr, P.H.: Fully-convolutional Siamese networks for object tracking. In: European Conference on Computer Vision, pp. 850–865. Springer (2016). https://doi.org/10.1007/978-3-319-48881-3_56

3. Bhat, G., Danelljan, M., Gool, L.V., Timofte, R.: Learning discriminative model prediction for tracking. In: Proceedings of the IEEE/CVF International Conference on Computer Vision, pp. 6182–6191 (2019)
4. Bhat, G., Danelljan, M., Van Gool, L., Timofte, R.: Know your surroundings: exploiting scene information for object tracking. In: Vedaldi, A., Bischof, H., Brox, T., Frahm, J.-M. (eds.) ECCV 2020. LNCS, vol. 12368, pp. 205–221. Springer, Cham (2020). https://doi.org/10.1007/978-3-030-58592-1_13
5. Bian, J., Lin, W.Y., Matsushita, Y., Yeung, S.K., Nguyen, T.D., Cheng, M.M.: GMS: grid-based motion statistics for fast, ultra-robust feature correspondence. In: Proceedings of the IEEE Conference on Computer Vision and Pattern Recognition, pp. 4181–4190 (2017)
6. Cao, Z., Fu, C., Ye, J., Li, B., Li, Y.: HiFT: hierarchical feature transformer for aerial tracking. In: Proceedings of the IEEE/CVF International Conference on Computer Vision, pp. 15457–15466 (2021)
7. Carion, N., Massa, F., Synnaeve, G., Usunier, N., Kirillov, A., Zagoruyko, S.: End-to-end object detection with transformers. In: Vedaldi, A., Bischof, H., Brox, T., Frahm, J.-M. (eds.) ECCV 2020. LNCS, vol. 12346, pp. 213–229. Springer, Cham (2020). https://doi.org/10.1007/978-3-030-58452-8_13
8. Chen, X., Yan, B., Zhu, J., Wang, D., Yang, X., Lu, H.: Transformer tracking. In: Proceedings of the IEEE/CVF Conference on Computer Vision and Pattern Recognition, pp. 8126–8135 (2021)
9. Cho, S., Hong, S., Jeon, S., Lee, Y., Sohn, K., Kim, S.: CATs: cost aggregation transformers for visual correspondence. Adv. Neural Inf. Process. Syst. **34**, 9011–9023 (2021)
10. Dai, K., Zhang, Y., Wang, D., Li, J., Lu, H., Yang, X.: High-performance long-term tracking with meta-updater. In: Proceedings of the IEEE/CVF Conference on Computer Vision and Pattern Recognition, pp. 6298–6307 (2020)
11. Danelljan, M., Bhat, G., Khan, F.S., Felsberg, M.: Atom: accurate tracking by overlap maximization. In: Proceedings of the IEEE/CVF Conference on Computer Vision and Pattern Recognition, pp. 4660–4669 (2019)
12. Danelljan, M., Gool, L.V., Timofte, R.: Probabilistic regression for visual tracking. In: Proceedings of the IEEE/CVF Conference on Computer Vision and Pattern Recognition, pp. 7183–7192 (2020)
13. Deng, J., Dong, W., Socher, R., Li, L.J., Li, K., Fei-Fei, L.: ImageNet: a large-scale hierarchical image database. In: 2009 IEEE Conference on Computer Vision and Pattern Recognition, pp. 248–255. IEEE (2009)
14. Dosovitskiy, A., et al.: An image is worth 16 × 16 words: transformers for image recognition at scale. arXiv preprint arXiv:2010.11929 (2020)
15. Duke, B., Ahmed, A., Wolf, C., Aarabi, P., Taylor, G.W.: SSTVOS: sparse spatiotemporal transformers for video object segmentation. In: Proceedings of the IEEE/CVF Conference on Computer Vision and Pattern Recognition, pp. 5912–5921 (2021)
16. Fan, H., et al.: Lasot: a high-quality large-scale single object tracking benchmark. Int. J. Comput. Vis. **129**(2), 439–461 (2021). https://doi.org/10.1007/s11263-020-01387-y
17. Fan, H., et al.: LaSOT: a high-quality benchmark for large-scale single object tracking. In: Proceedings of the IEEE/CVF Conference on Computer Vision and Pattern Recognition, pp. 5374–5383 (2019)
18. Fiaz, M., Mahmood, A., Javed, S., Jung, S.K.: Handcrafted and deep trackers: recent visual object tracking approaches and trends. ACM Comput. Surv. (CSUR) **52**(2), 1–44 (2019)

19. Fu, Z., Liu, Q., Fu, Z., Wang, Y.: STMTrack: template-free visual tracking with space-time memory networks. In: Proceedings of the IEEE/CVF Conference on Computer Vision and Pattern Recognition, pp. 13774–13783 (2021)
20. Ge, W., Lu, X., Shen, J.: Video object segmentation using global and instance embedding learning. In: Proceedings of the IEEE/CVF Conference on Computer Vision and Pattern Recognition, pp. 16836–16845 (2021)
21. Guo, D., Shao, Y., Cui, Y., Wang, Z., Zhang, L., Shen, C.: Graph attention tracking. In: Proceedings of the IEEE/CVF Conference on Computer Vision and Pattern Recognition, pp. 9543–9552 (2021)
22. He, K., Zhang, X., Ren, S., Sun, J.: Deep residual learning for image recognition. In: Proceedings of the IEEE Conference on Computer Vision and Pattern Recognition, pp. 770–778 (2016)
23. He, L., et al.: End-to-end video object detection with spatial-temporal transformers. In: Proceedings of the 29th ACM International Conference on Multimedia, pp. 1507–1516 (2021)
24. Henriques, J.F., Caseiro, R., Martins, P., Batista, J.: High-speed tracking with kernelized correlation filters. IEEE Trans. Pattern Anal. Mach. Intell. **37**(3), 583–596 (2014)
25. Huang, L., Zhao, X., Huang, K.: Got-10k: a large high-diversity benchmark for generic object tracking in the wild. IEEE Trans. Pattern Anal. Mach. Intell. **43**(5), 1562–1577 (2019)
26. Huang, L., Wang, W., Chen, J., Wei, X.Y.: Attention on attention for image captioning. In: Proceedings of the IEEE/CVF International Conference on Computer Vision, pp. 4634–4643 (2019)
27. Huang, Z., Wang, X., Huang, L., Huang, C., Wei, Y., Liu, W.: CCNet: criss-cross attention for semantic segmentation. In: Proceedings of the IEEE/CVF International Conference on Computer Vision, pp. 603–612 (2019)
28. Jiang, B., Luo, R., Mao, J., Xiao, T., Jiang, Y.: Acquisition of localization confidence for accurate object detection. In: Proceedings of the European Conference on Computer Vision (ECCV), pp. 784–799 (2018)
29. Galoogahi, H.K., Fagg, A., Huang, C., Ramanan, D., Lucey, S.: Need for speed: a benchmark for higher frame rate object tracking. In: Proceedings of the IEEE International Conference on Computer Vision, pp. 1125–1134 (2017)
30. Lan, M., Zhang, J., He, F., Zhang, L.: Siamese network with interactive transformer for video object segmentation. arXiv preprint arXiv:2112.13983 (2021)
31. Li, B., Wu, W., Wang, Q., Zhang, F., Xing, J., Yan, J.: SiamRPN++: evolution of Siamese visual tracking with very deep networks. In: Proceedings of the IEEE/CVF Conference on Computer Vision and Pattern Recognition, pp. 4282–4291 (2019)
32. Li, B., Yan, J., Wu, W., Zhu, Z., Hu, X.: High performance visual tracking with Siamese region proposal network. In: Proceedings of the IEEE Conference on Computer Vision and Pattern Recognition, pp. 8971–8980 (2018)
33. Li, S., Han, K., Costain, T.W., Howard-Jenkins, H., Prisacariu, V.: Correspondence networks with adaptive neighbourhood consensus. In: Proceedings of the IEEE/CVF Conference on Computer Vision and Pattern Recognition, pp. 10196–10205 (2020)
34. Mao, Y., Wang, N., Zhou, W., Li, H.: Joint inductive and transductive learning for video object segmentation. In: Proceedings of the IEEE/CVF International Conference on Computer Vision, pp. 9670–9679 (2021)
35. Marvasti-Zadeh, S.M., Cheng, L., Ghanei-Yakhdan, H., Kasaei, S.: Deep learning for visual tracking: a comprehensive survey. IEEE Trans. Intell. Transp. Syst. (2021)

36. Mayer, C., Danelljan, M., Paudel, D.P., Van Gool, L.: Learning target candidate association to keep track of what not to track. In: Proceedings of the IEEE/CVF International Conference on Computer Vision, pp. 13444–13454 (2021)
37. Meinhardt, T., Kirillov, A., Leal-Taixe, L., Feichtenhofer, C.: Trackformer: multi-object tracking with transformers. arXiv preprint arXiv:2101.02702 (2021)
38. Min, J., Cho, M.: Convolutional Hough matching networks. In: Proceedings of the IEEE/CVF Conference on Computer Vision and Pattern Recognition, pp. 2940–2950 (2021)
39. Mueller, M., Smith, N., Ghanem, B.: A benchmark and simulator for UAV tracking. In: Leibe, B., Matas, J., Sebe, N., Welling, M. (eds.) ECCV 2016. LNCS, vol. 9905, pp. 445–461. Springer, Cham (2016). https://doi.org/10.1007/978-3-319-46448-0_27
40. Muller, M., Bibi, A., Giancola, S., Alsubaihi, S., Ghanem, B.: TrackingNet: a large-scale dataset and benchmark for object tracking in the wild. In: Proceedings of the European Conference on Computer Vision (ECCV), pp. 300–317 (2018)
41. Rezatofighi, H., Tsoi, N., Gwak, J., Sadeghian, A., Reid, I., Savarese, S.: Generalized intersection over union: a metric and a loss for bounding box regression. In: Proceedings of the IEEE/CVF Conference on Computer Vision and Pattern Recognition, pp. 658–666 (2019)
42. Rocco, I., Arandjelović, R., Sivic, J.: Efficient neighbourhood consensus networks via submanifold sparse convolutions. In: Vedaldi, A., Bischof, H., Brox, T., Frahm, J.-M. (eds.) ECCV 2020. LNCS, vol. 12354, pp. 605–621. Springer, Cham (2020). https://doi.org/10.1007/978-3-030-58545-7_35
43. Rocco, I., Cimpoi, M., Arandjelović, R., Torii, A., Pajdla, T., Sivic, J.: Neighbourhood consensus networks. Adv. Neural Inf. Process. Syst. **31** (2018)
44. Sattler, T., Leibe, B., Kobbelt, L.: SCRAMSAC: improving RANSAC's efficiency with a spatial consistency filter. In: 2009 IEEE 12th International Conference on Computer Vision, pp. 2090–2097. IEEE (2009)
45. Shechtman, E., Irani, M.: Matching local self-similarities across images and videos. In: 2007 IEEE Conference on Computer Vision and Pattern Recognition, pp. 1–8. IEEE (2007)
46. Sun, P., et al.: TransTrack: multiple object tracking with transformer. arXiv preprint arXiv:2012.15460 (2020)
47. Vaswani, A., et al.: Attention is all you need. Adv. Neural Inf. Process. Syst. **30** (2017)
48. Wang, N., Zhou, W., Wang, J., Li, H.: Transformer meets tracker: exploiting temporal context for robust visual tracking. In: Proceedings of the IEEE/CVF Conference on Computer Vision and Pattern Recognition, pp. 1571–1580 (2021)
49. Wang, X., Girshick, R., Gupta, A., He, K.: Non-local neural networks. In: Proceedings of the IEEE Conference on Computer Vision and Pattern Recognition, pp. 7794–7803 (2018)
50. Wu, Y., Lim, J., Yang, M.: Object tracking benchmark. IEEE Trans. Pattern Anal. Mach. Intell. **37**(9), 1834–1848 (2015)
51. Xing, D., Evangeliou, N., Tsoukalas, A., Tzes, A.: Siamese transformer pyramid networks for real-time UAV tracking. In: Proceedings of the IEEE/CVF Winter Conference on Applications of Computer Vision, pp. 2139–2148 (2022)
52. Yan, B., Peng, H., Fu, J., Wang, D., Lu, H.: Learning spatio-temporal transformer for visual tracking. In: Proceedings of the IEEE/CVF International Conference on Computer Vision, pp. 10448–10457 (2021)
53. Yang, Z., Wei, Y., Yang, Y.: Associating objects with transformers for video object segmentation. Adv. Neural Inf. Process. Syst. **34** (2021)

54. Yu, B., et al.: High-performance discriminative tracking with transformers. In: Proceedings of the IEEE/CVF International Conference on Computer Vision, pp. 9856–9865 (2021)
55. Yu, Y., Xiong, Y., Huang, W., Scott, M.R.: Deformable Siamese attention networks for visual object tracking. In: Proceedings of the IEEE/CVF Conference on Computer Vision and Pattern Recognition, pp. 6728–6737 (2020)
56. Zhang, L., Gonzalez-Garcia, A., Weijer, J.V.d., Danelljan, M., Khan, F.S.: Learning the model update for Siamese trackers. In: Proceedings of the IEEE/CVF International Conference on Computer Vision, pp. 4010–4019 (2019)
57. Zhang, Y., et al.: ByteTrack: multi-object tracking by associating every detection box. arXiv preprint arXiv:2110.06864 (2021)
58. Zhang, Z., Peng, H., Fu, J., Li, B., Hu, W.: Ocean: object-aware anchor-free tracking. In: Vedaldi, A., Bischof, H., Brox, T., Frahm, J.-M. (eds.) ECCV 2020. LNCS, vol. 12366, pp. 771–787. Springer, Cham (2020). https://doi.org/10.1007/978-3-030-58589-1_46
59. Zhu, X., Su, W., Lu, L., Li, B., Wang, X., Dai, J.: Deformable DETR: deformable transformers for end-to-end object detection. arXiv preprint arXiv:2010.04159 (2020)

Disentangling Architecture and Training
for Optical Flow

Deqing Sun(iD), Charles Herrmann(✉)(iD), Fitsum Reda(iD), Michael Rubinstein(iD),
David J. Fleet(iD), and William T. Freeman

Google Research, Mountain View, USA
irwinherrmann@google.com

Abstract. How important are training details and datasets to recent
optical flow architectures like RAFT? And do they generalize? To explore
these questions, rather than develop a new architecture, we revisit three
prominent architectures, PWC-Net, IRR-PWC and RAFT, with a common set of modern training techniques and datasets, and observe significant performance gains, demonstrating the importance and generality
of these training details. Our newly trained PWC-Net and IRR-PWC
show surprisingly large improvements, up to 30% versus original published results on Sintel and KITTI 2015 benchmarks. Our newly trained
RAFT obtains an Fl-all score of 4.31% on KITTI 2015 and an avg. rank of
1.7 for end-point error on Middlebury. Our results demonstrate the benefits of separating the contributions of architectures, training techniques
and datasets when analyzing performance gains of optical flow methods.
Our source code is available at https://autoflow-google.github.io.

Keywords: Optical flow · Architecture · Training · Evaluation

1 Introduction

The field of optical flow has witnessed rapid progress in recent years, driven
largely by deep learning. FlowNet [10] first demonstrated the potential of deep
learning for optical flow, while PWC-Net [45] was the first model to eclipse classical flow techniques. The widely-acclaimed RAFT model [48] reduced error rates
on common benchmarks by up to 30% versus state-of-the-art baselines, outperforming PWC-Net by a wide margin. RAFT quickly became the predominant
architecture for optical flow [20,28,31,38,51,54,55,62] and related tasks [24,49].

The success of RAFT has been attributed primarily to its novel architecture,
including its multi-scale all-pairs cost volume, its recurrent update operator, and
its up-sampling module. Meanwhile, other factors like training procedures and

---

D. Sun and C. Herrmann—Equal technical contribution.

D. Sun—Project lead.

Supplementary Information The online version contains supplementary material
available at https://doi.org/10.1007/978-3-031-20047-2_10.

S. Avidan et al. (Eds.): ECCV 2022, LNCS 13682, pp. 165–182, 2022.
https://doi.org/10.1007/978-3-031-20047-2_10

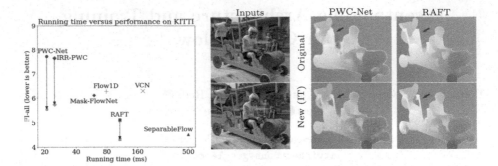

Fig. 1. Left: Large improvements with newly trained PWC-Net, IRR-PWC and RAFT (left: originally published results in blue; results of our newly trained models in red). Right: Visual comparison on a Davis sequence between the original [46] and our newly trained PWC-Net-it and RAFT-it, shows improved flow details, e.g. the hole between the cart and the person at the back. The newly trained PWC-Net-it recovers the hole between the cart and the front person better than RAFT. (Color figure online)

datasets have also evolved, and may play important roles. In this work, we pose the question: How much do training techniques of recent methods like RAFT contribute to their impressive performance? And, importantly, can these training innovations similarly improve the performance of other architectures?

We begin by revisiting the 2018 PWC-Net [45], and investigate the impact of datasets and training techniques for both pre-training and fine-tuning. We show that, even with such a relatively "old" model, by employing recent datasets and advances in training, and without any changes to the originally proposed architecture, one can obtain substantial performance gains, outperforming more recent models [55,64] and resolving finer-grained details of flow fields (see, e.g., Fig. 1 and Table 1). We further show that the same enhancements yield similar performance gains when applied to IRR-PWC, a prominent variant of PWC-Net that is closely related to RAFT. Indeed, these insights also yield an improved version of RAFT, which obtains competitive results on Sintel, KITTI, and VIPER while setting a new state of the art on Middlebury. We denote architectures trained with this new training by adding "-it" after the architecture name; for example, our newly trained RAFT will be abbreviated as RAFT-it.

We make the following contributions:

- We show that newly trained PWC-Net (PWC-Net-it), using ingredients from recent training techniques (gradient clipping, OneCycle learning rate, and long training) and modern datasets (AutoFlow), yields surprisingly competitive results on Sintel and KITTI benchmarks.
- These same techniques also deliver sizeable performance gains with two other prominent models, IRR-PWC and RAFT. Our newly trained RAFT (RAFT-it) is more accurate than all published optical flow methods on KITTI 2015.
- We perform a thorough ablation study on pre-training and fine-tuning to understand which ingredients are key to these performance improvements and how they are manifesting.

Table 1. Results of 2-frame methods on public benchmarks (AEPE↓ for Sintel and Fl-all↓ for KITTI). **Bold** indicates the best number and underline the second-best. The running time is for 448×1024 resolution input (*reported in paper); the differences will be larger for higher resolution (*c.f.* Table 6). Newly trained PWC-Net, IRR-PWC and RAFT are substantially more accurate than their predecessors. With improved training protocols, PWC-Net-it and IRR-PWC-it are more accurate than some recent methods [55,56] on KITTI 2015 while being about 3× faster in inference.

Method	Sintel.clean	Sintel.final	KITTI	Running time
PWC-Net [45]	3.86	5.13	9.60%	30 ms*
PWC-Net+ [46]	3.45	4.60	7.72%	30 ms*
PWC-Net-it (Ours)	2.31	3.69	5.54%	**21 ms**
IRR-PWC [17]	3.84	4.58	7.65%	180 ms*
IRR-PWC-it (Ours)	2.19	3.55	5.73%	25 ms
RAFT [48]	1.94	3.18	5.10%	94 ms*
RAFT-A [44]	2.01	3.14	4.78%	107 ms
RAFT-it (Ours)	1.55	2.90	**4.31%**	107 ms
HD^3 [58]	4.79	4.67	6.55%	100 ms*
VCN [57]	2.81	4.40	6.30%	180 ms*
Mask-FlowNet [64]	2.52	4.14	6.11%	60 ms*
DICL [52]	2.12	3.44	6.31%	–
Flow1D [55]	2.24	3.81	6.27%	79 ms*
RAFT+AOIR [31]	1.85	3.17	5.07%	10^4 ms*
CSFlow [38]	1.63	3.03	5.00%	200 ms*
SeparableFlow [62]	**1.50**	**2.67**	4.51%	250ms*

- The newly trained PWC-Net and IRR-PWC produce visually good results on 4K Davis input images, making them an appealing option for applications that require fast inference with low memory overhead.

2   Previous Work

Deep Models for Optical Flow. FlowNet [10] was the first model to demonstrate the potential of deep learning for optical flow, and inspired various new architectures. FlowNet2 [18] stacked basic models to improve model capacity and performance, while SpyNet [34] used an image pyramid and warping to build a compact model. PWC-Net [45] used classical optical flow principles (e.g., [3,43,47]) to build an effective model, which has since seen widespread use [2,8,19,22,35,41,63,65]. The concurrent LiteFlowNet [16] used similar ideas to build a lightweight network. TVNet [11] took a different approach with classical flow principles by unrolling the optimization iterations of the TV-L1 method [61].

Many architectures have used a pyramid structure. IRR-PWC [17] introduced iterative refinement, reusing the same flow decoder module at different pyramidal levels. VCN [56] used a 4D cost volume that is easily adapted to stereo and optical flow. HD^3 [58] modeled flow uncertainty hierarchically. MaskFlowNet [64] jointly modeled occlusion and optical flow. Improvements brought by each model over the previous SOTA was often within 5% on Sintel (c.f., Table 1).

A recent, notable architecture, RAFT [48], built a full cost volume and performs recurrent refinements at a single resolution. RAFT achieved a significant improvement over previous models on Sintel and KITTI benchmarks, and became a starting point for numerous new variants [20,28,31,38,51,54,55,62]. To reduce the memory cost of the all-pairs cost volume, Flow1D used 1D self-attention with 1D search, with minimal performance drop while enabling application to 4K video inputs [55]. SeparableFlow used a non-local aggregation module for cost aggregation, yielding substantial performance gains [62].

Recent research on optical flow has focused on architectural innovations. Nevertheless, most new optical flow papers combine new architectures with changes in training procedures and datasets. As such, it can be hard to identify which factors are responsible for the performance gains. In this paper, we take a different approach, instead we examine the effects of different ingredients of modern training techniques and datasets, but with established architectures. The results and findings are surprising. Our newly trained PWC-Net and IRR-PWC are more accurate than Flow1D while being almost 3× faster in inference, and our newly trained RAFT is more accurate than all published optical flow methods on KITTI 2015 while being more than 2× faster in inference than the previous best SeparableFlow.

Datasets for Optical Flow. For pre-training the predominant dataset is FlyingChairs [10]. Ilg et al. [18] introduced a dataset schedule that uses FlyingChairs and FlyingThings3D [30] sequentially. This remains a standard way to pre-train models. Sun et al. [44] proposed a new dataset, AutoFlow, which learns rendering hyperparameters and shows moderate improvements over the FlyingChairs and FlyingThings3D in pre-training PWC-Net and RAFT. For fine-tuning, the limited training data from Sintel and KITTI are often combined with additional datasets, such as HD1K [23] and VIPER [36], to improve generalization. In this paper, we show that PWC-Net and its variant, IRR-PWC, obtain competitive results when pre-trained on AutoFlow and fine-tuned using recent techniques.

Training Techniques for Optical Flow. While different papers tend to adopt slightly different training techniques and implementation details, some have examined the impact of recent training techniques on older architectures. Ilg et al. [18] found that using dataset scheduling can improve the pre-training results of FlowNetS and FlowNetC. Sun et al. [46] obtained better fine-tuning results with FlowNetS and FlowNetC on Sintel by using improved data augmentation and learning rate disruption; they also improved on the initial PWC-Net [45] by using additional datasets. Sun et al. [44] reported better pre-training results for PWC-Net but did not investigate fine-tuning. Here, with PWC-Net, IRR-PWC and RAFT, we show significantly better fine-tuning results.

Self-supervised Learning for Optical Flow. Significant progress has been achieved with self-supervised learning for optical flow [21,25,26,32,40,60], focusing more on the loss than model architecture. UFlow [21] systematically studied a set of key components for self-supervised optical flow, including both model elements and training techniques. Their study used PWC-Net as the main backbone. Here we focus on training techniques and datasets, systematically studying three prominent models to identify factors that generalize across models. FOAL introduces a meta learning approach for online adaptation [59].

Similar study on other vision tasks. The field of classification has also started to more closely examine whether performance improvements in recent papers come from the model architecture or training details. Both [15] and [53] examined modern training techniques on ResNet-50 [14] and observed significant performance improvements on ImageNet [7], improving top-1 precision from 76.?? in 2015, to 79.3 in 2018, and finally to 80.4 in 2021. These gains have come solely from improved training details, namely, from augmentations, optimizers, learning rate schedules, and regularization. The introduction of vision transformers (ViT) [9] also led to a series of papers [39,50] on improved training strategies, substantially improving performance from the initial accuracy of 76.5 up to 81.8.

Other recent papers took a related but slightly different direction, simultaneously modernizing both the training details and architectural elements but cleanly ablating and analyzing the improvements. Bello *et al.* [4] included an improved training procedure as well as exploration of squeeze-and-excite and different layer changes. Liu *et al.* [27] used recent training details and iteratively improves ResNet with modern network design elements, improving the accuracy from 76.2 to 82.0, which is competitive with similarly sized state-of-the-art models. While these papers mainly studied a single model and often involved modifying the backbone, we investigate three different models to understand key factors that apply to different models, and the trade-offs between models.

3   Approach and Results

Our goal is to understand which innovations in training techniques, principally from RAFT, play a major role in the impressive performance of modern optical flow methods, and to what extent they generalize well to different architectures. To this end, we decouple the contributions of architecture, training techniques, and dataset, and perform comparisons by changing one variable at a time. More specifically, we revisit PWC-Net, IRR-PWC and RAFT with the recently improved training techniques and datasets. We perform ablations on various factors including pre-training, fine-tuning, training duration, memory requirements and inference speed.

3.1   Models Evaluated

The first model we evaluate is PWC-Net, the design of which was inspired by three classical optical flow principles, namely pyramids, warping, and cost volumes. These inductive biases make the network effective, efficient, and compact compared to prior work. IRR-PWC [17] introduces iterative refinement and shares the optical flow estimation network weights among different pyramid levels. The number of iterative refinement steps for IRR-PWC is the number of pyramid levels. RAFT is closely related to IRR but enables an arbitrarily large number of refinement iterations. It has several novel network design elements, such as the recurrent refinement unit and convex upsampling module. Notably, RAFT eschews the pyramidal refinement structure, instead using an all-pairs cost volume at a single resolution.

Memory Usage. For an $H \times W$ input image, the memory cost for constructing the cost volume in RAFT is $\mathcal{O}((HW)^2 D)$, where D is the number of feature channels (constant, typically 256 for RAFT and ≤ 192 for PWC-Net and IRR-PWC). To reduce the memory cost for high-resolution inputs, Flow1D constructs a 1D cost volume with cost of $\mathcal{O}(HW(H+W)D)$. By comparison, the memory needed for the cost volume in PWC-Net and IRR-PWC is $\mathcal{O}(HWD(2d+1)^2)$, where the constant d is the search radius at each pyramid level (default 4). Note that $(2d+1)^2 \ll H+W \ll HW$ for high-resolution inputs; this is particularly important for 4K videos, which are becoming increasingly popular. We empirically compare memory usage at different resolutions in Table 6.

3.2   Pre-training

Typical Training Recipes. A typical training pipeline trains models first on the FlyingChairs dataset, followed by fine-tuning on the FlyingThings3D dataset, and then further fine-tuning using a mixture of datasets, including small amount of training data for the Sintel and KITTI benchmarks.

Since the introduction of PWC-Net in 2018, new training techniques and datasets have been proposed. As shown in [46], better training techniques and new datasets improve the pre-training performance of PWC-Net. We investigate how PWC-Net and IRR-PWC performs with the same pre-training procedure, and whether the procedure can be further improved.

Table 2 summaries the results of pre-training PWC-Net, IRR-PWC and RAFT using different datasets and techniques. (To save space, we omit some results for PWC-Net and RAFT and refer readers to [44].) We further perform an ablation study on several key design choices using PWC-Net, shown in Table 3. To reduce the effects of random initialization, we independently train the model six times, and report the results of the best run. While the original IRR-PWC computes bidirectional optical flow and jointly reasons about occlusion, we test a lightweight implementation without these elements [17].

Pre-training Datasets. Pre-training using AutoFlow results in significantly better results than FlyingChairs for PWC-Net, IRR-PWC and RAFT. Figure 2 visually compares the results by two PWC-Net models on Davis [33], and Middlebury [1] sequences. PWC-Net trained on AutoFlow better recovers fine motion details (top) and produces coherent motion for the foreground objects (bottom).

First frame   PWC-Net (FlyingChairs)   PWC-Net (AutoFlow)

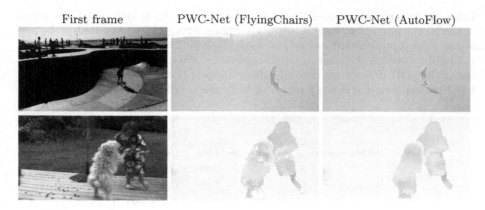

Fig. 2. Visual results of PWC-Net pre-trained using FlyingChairs and AutoFlow on Davis and Middlebury input images. PWC-Net trained using AutoFlow recovers fine details between the legs (top) and coherent motion for the girl and the dog (bottom).

Gradient Clipping. Gradient clipping is a heuristic to avoid cliff structures for recurrent neural networks [13]. The update operator of RAFT uses a GRU block that is similar to the LSTM block. Thus, RAFT training uses gradient clipping to avoid exploding gradients. Gradient clipping also improves the performance of PWC-Net and IRR-PWC substantially and results in more stable training. Removing gradient clipping from RAFT results in moderate performance degradation. We perform an ablation study on the threshold of gradient clipping and find that the training is robust to this parameter (Table 3).

Learning Rate Schedule. Before RAFT, nearly all optical flow models have been trained using a piecewise learning rate, with optional learning rate disruption. RAFT uses a OneCycle learning rate schedule, which starts from a small learning rate, linearly increases to the peak learning rate, and then linearly decreases to the starting learning rate. Using the OneCycle learning rate improves the performance of all three models (Table 2). Moving the position of the peak toward the origin slightly improves the performance (Table 3). Note that, for other published models, those that use gradient clipping and the OneCycle learning rate, *e.g.*, Flow1D and SeparableFlow, are generally better than those that do not, *e.g.*, VCN and MaskFlowNet. It would be interesting, though outside the scope of this paper, to investigate the performance of VCN and MaskFlowNet with recent techniques and datasets.

Training Iterations. PWC-Net and IRR-PWC need large numbers of training iterations. At the same number of training iterations, IRR-PWC is consistently more accurate than PWC-Net. This is encouraging because we can perform an ablation study using fewer iterations and then use the best setup to train the model using more iterations. One appealing feature of RAFT is its fast convergence, but we find that using more training iterations also improves RAFT. Note

Table 2. Pre-training results for PWC-Net, IRR-PWC, RAFT and some recent methods. The metric for Sintel is average end-point error (AEPE) and F-all is the percentage of outliers averaged over all ground truth pixels. Lower is better for both AEPE and F-all. "-" means the same as the row above. C+T stands for the FlyingChairs and FlyingThings3D dataset schedule. Gradient clipping (GC), OneCycle learning rate, AutoFlow and longer training improve all three models consistently.

Model	Dataset	GC	LR	Iters	Sintel		KITTI	
					clean	final	F-all	AEPE
PWC-Net	FlyingChairs	✗	Piecewise	1.2M	3.89	4.79	42.81%	13.59
–	–	–	–	3.2M	2.99	4.21	38.49%	10.7
–	AutoFlow	✓	OneCycle	1.2M	2.43	3.05	18.74%	6.41
–	–	–	–	3.2M	2.17	2.91	17.25%	5.76
–	–	–	–	6.2M	2.10	2.81	16.29%	5.55
IRR-PWC	FlyingChairs	✗	Piecewise	1.2M	4.3	5.09	44.06%	15.5
–	AutoFlow	–	–	–	3.01	4.11	26.95%	9.01
–	–	✓	–	–	2.42	3.29	18.31%	6.31
–	–	–	OneCycle	–	2.24	2.93	17.87%	6.02
–	–	–	–	3.2M	2.06	2.85	15.55%	5.14
–	–	–	-	6.2M	1.93	2.76	15.20%	5.05
RAFT	FlyingChairs	✗	Piecewise	0.2M	2.64	4.04	32.52%	10.01
–	AutoFlow	–	–	–	2.57	3.36	19.92%	5.96
–	–	✓	–	–	2.44	3.20	17.95%	5.49
–	–	–	OneCycle	–	2.08	2.75	15.32%	4.66
–	–	–	–	0.8M	1.95	2.57	13.82%	4.23
–	–	–	–	3.2M	1.74	2.41	13.41%	4.18
VCN	C+T	✗	Piecewise	0.22M	2.21	3.62	25.10%	8.36
MaskFlowNet	–	–	–	1.7M	2.25	3.61	23.14%	–
Flow1D	–	✓	OneCycle	0.2M	1.98	3.27	22.95%	6.69
SeparableFlow	–	–	–	0.2M	1.30	2.59	15.90%	4.60

that 3.2M iterations for RAFT takes about 11 days while 6.2M iterations take PWC and IRR-PWC about 6 days to finish (using 6 P100 GPUs). It is interesting that all three models show no sign of over-fitting after so many iterations.

Other Training Details. We further test the effect of weight decay, random erasing and vertical flipping. As shown in Table 3, the training is robust to the hyperparameter settings for the weight decay, random erasing and vertical flipping.

Recipes for Pre-training. Using AutoFlow, gradient clipping, the OneCycle learning rate and long training consistently improves the pre-training results for PWC-Net, IRR-PWC and RAFT. It is feasible to use short training to evaluate design choices and then use longer training times for the best performance.

Table 3. More ablation studies on pre-training PWC-Net using 1.2M training steps. Default settings are underlined. Pre-training is robust to moderate variations on the parameters settings for these training details.

Experiment	Parameter	Sintel		KITTI	
		clean	final	F-all	AEPE
Gradient clipping threshold	0.5	2.37	3.12	18.46%	6.14
	1.0	2.43	3.05	18.74%	6.41
	2.0	2.60	3.31	21.25%	7.73
Peak of OneCycle LR	0.1	2.38	3.04	17.35%	5.77
	0.2	2.43	3.05	18.74%	6.41
	0.3	2.35	3.08	19.39%	6.66
Weight decay	0	2.43	3.05	18.74%	6.41
	1e-8	2.31	3.09	18.07%	6.14
	1e-7	2.46	3.17	18.10%	6.17
Vertical flip probability	0	2.43	3.05	18.74%	6.41
	0.1	2.38	3.08	18.64%	6.14
Random erasing probability	0	2.43	3.05	18.74%	6.41
	0.5	2.46	3.13	17.39%	5.78

3.3 Fine-Tuning

To analyze fine-tuning, we use the training/validation split for Sintel proposed in Lv *et al.* [29], where the sets have different motion distributions (Fig. 3), and the training/validation split for KITTI proposed in Yang and Ramanan [56]. We follow [44] and use five datasets, Sintel [5] (0.4), KITTI [12] (0.2), VIPER [37] (0.2), HD1K [23] (0.08), and FlyingThings3D [30] (0.12), where the number indicates the sampling probability. We perform an ablation study on PWC-Net, and then apply the selected training protocol to IRR-PWC and RAFT.

Training Techniques. Table 4 summarizes the results of the ablation study on PWC-Net. Better initialization tends to lead to better fine-tuning results, especially on the KITTI dataset. For the same initialization, longer training yields more accurate results on the held-out validation set.

Removing gradient clipping results in a significant performance drop on the validation sets, and switching from the OneCycle to the piecewise learning rate results in moderate performance degradation too. We further experiment with adding the AutoFlow data to the fine-tuning process, and observe improvements for both PWC-Net and IRR-PWC on the Sintel validation set, and a small drop in performance on the KITTI validation set. Adding AutoFlow yields just a small improvement for RAFT on Sintel (we discuss this result again below with the in-distribution fine-tuning experiment).

Table 4. Ablation study on fine-tuning on Sintel and KITTI using the training/validation split for Sintel from [29] and for KITTI from [56]. GC stands for gradient clipping and () indicates training errors. 0M for fine-tuning means that no fine-tuning has been done (initialization). S,K,H,T,V and A denote Sintel, KITTI, FlyingThings3D, HD1K, VIPER and AutoFlow datasets, respectively. Better initialization, more training steps and adding AutoFlow improve the performance.

Model	Data	Init	Ft	Sintel				KITTI 2015			
				Training		Validation		Training		Validation	
				Clean	Final	Clean	Final	F-all	AEPE	F-all	AEPE
PWC-Net	SKHTV	1.2M	1.2M	(1.04)	(1.45)	3.58	3.88	(5.58%)	(1.44)	6.23%	1.92
–	–	3.2M	–	(1.05)	(1.55)	2.95	3.61	(5.44%)	(1.40)	6.13%	1.80
–	–	6.2M	–	(0.97)	(1.42)	3.09	3.65	(4.99%)	(1.31)	5.61%	1.62
No GC	–	–	–	(1.82)	(2.43)	4.51	4.98	(11.77%)	(3.06)	11.87%	3.79
Piecewise	–	–	–	(1.08)	(1.62)	3.32	3.77	(5.49%)	(1.42)	5.90%	1.78
PWC-Net	SKHTV	6.2M	0M	1.78	2.55	3.33	3.83	16.50%	5.58	15.45%	5.44
–	–	–	6.2M	(0.74)	(1.08)	2.79	3.52	(3.96%)	(1.08)	4.76%	1.52
–	+A	–	–	(0.80)	(1.19)	2.76	3.25	(4.10%)	(1.12)	4.89%	1.57
IRR-PWC	SKHTV	6.2M	0M	1.58	2.49	3.27	3.79	15.4%	5.05	14.3%	5.02
–	–	–	6.2M	(0.98)	(1.47)	2.85	3.50	(4.52%)	(1.21)	5.37%	1.59
–	+A	–	–	(1.01)	(1.49)	2.64	3.28	(4.86%)	(1.29)	5.39%	1.56
RAFT	SKHTV	3.2M	0M	1.40	2.31	2.88	3.38	13.57%	4.19	12.74%	4.13
–	–	–	1.2M	(0.66)	(1.14)	1.96	2.81	(3.55%)	(1.04)	3.96%	1.41
–	+A	–	–	(0.74)	(1.15)	2.00	2.76	(3.86%)	(1.09)	4.08%	1.39

Model Comparison. Among the three models, RAFT has the best accuracy on the validation set. The initialization of RAFT is almost as accurate as the fine-tuned PWC-Net on the Sintel.final validation set using the training/validation split [29]. While IRR-PWC has higher training errors on Sintel than PWC-Net, the validation errors of the two models are similar. IRR-PWC has slightly worse performance on the KITTI validation set than PWC-Net.

In-Distribution Fine-Tuning. The training and validation subsets for Sintel proposed by Lv *et al.* [29] have different motion distributions; the validation set has more middle-to-large range motion, as shown in Fig. 3. To examine the performance of fine-tuning when the training and validation sets have similar distributions, we perform fine-tuning experiments using another split by [56]. As summarized in Table 5, PWC-Net has lower errors than RAFT on the Sintel validation set. As shown in Fig. 3, both the training and validation sets by [56] concentrate on small motions, suggesting that RAFT is good at generalization to out-of-distribution large motion for the Lv *et al.* split. This generalization behavior likely explains why adding AutoFlow [44] does not significantly help RAFT in the experiment above. The result also suggests that PWC-Net may be a good option for applications dealing with small motions, *e.g.*, the hole between the cart and the man in the front in Fig. 1.

Table 5. In-distribution fine-tuning using the training/validation split [56] for Sintel. The training and validation sets share similar motion distributions (*c.f.*Fig. 3).

	Sintel				KITTI 2015			
	Training		Validation		Training		Validation	
	Clean	Final	Clean	Final	F-all	AEPE	F-all	AEPE
PWC-Net	2.06	2.67	2.24	3.23	16.50%	5.58	15.45%	5.44
PWC-Net-ft	(1.30)	(1.67)	1.18	1.74	(4.21%)	(1.14)	5.10%	1.51
IRR-PWC	1.87	2.53	2.09	3.44	15.4%	5.05	14.3%	5.02
IRR-PWC-ft	(1.34)	(1.88)	1.55	2.31	(4.94%)	(1.29)	5.42%	1.65
RAFT	1.74	2.24	1.74	2.91	13.57%	4.19	12.74%	4.13
RAFT-ft	(1.14)	(1.70)	1.37	2.14	(5.06%)	(1.61)	5.01%	1.40

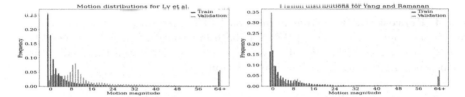

Fig. 3. Motion distributions for the Lv *et al.* [29] (left) and Yang and Ramanan [56] (right) training/validation splits. There is a mismatch between training and validation distributions for the Lv split, making it suitable for out-of-distribution fine-tuning test, while the other split is more suitable for in-distribution test.

Recipes for Fine-Tuning. Using better initialization and long training times helps fine-tuning. Both gradient clipping and the OneCycle learning rate help fine-tuning. Adding AutoFlow may help with generalization of the models.

3.4 Benchmark Results

We next apply the fine-tuning protocols above, with the full training sets from KITTI and Sintel, and then test the fine-tuned models on the public test sets. Table 1 summarizes the 2-frame results of previously published PWC-Net, IRR-PWC, and RAFT, our newly trained models, and several recent methods.

MPI Sintel. Our newly trained PWC-Net-it and IRR-PWC-it are substantially better than the respective, published models, with up to a 1 pixel reduction in average end-point error (AEPE) on the Sintel benchmark. As shown in Fig. 4, PWC-Net-it can much better recover fine motion details than the published one [46]. PWC-Net-it and IRR-PWC-it are even more accurate than some recent models [55,56,64] on the more challenging final pass, while being about 3× faster during inference.

Our newly trained RAFT-it is moderately better than the published RAFT [44,48]. Among all published 2-frame methods it is only less accurate

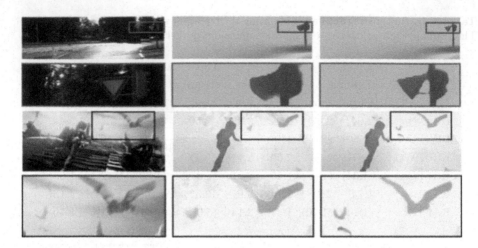

Fig. 4. Representative visual results on KITTI and Sintel test sets by the original [46] and our newly trained PWC-Net (both fine-tuned). Our newly trained PWC-Net can better recover fine details, *e.g.*, the traffic sign (top) and the small birds and the dragon's right wing (green is correct, bottom).

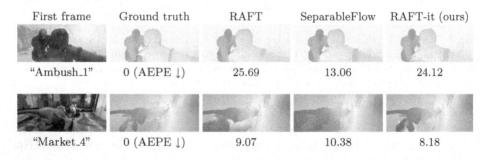

First frame	Ground truth	RAFT	SeparableFlow	RAFT-it (ours)
"Ambush_1"	0 (AEPE ↓)	25.69	13.06	24.12
"Market_4"	0 (AEPE ↓)	9.07	10.38	8.18

Fig. 5. Visual comparison on two challenging sequences from the Sintel test set. All 2-frame methods make large errors due to heavy snow on "Ambush_1", while RAFT models have larger errors. For the fast moving dragon under motion blur in "Market_4", the newly trained RAFT-it can better resolve the foreground motion from the background than SeparableFlow and the previously trained RAFT [44].

than SeparableFlow [62] while being more than 2× faster in inference. Figure 5 visually compares SeparableFlow and our newly trained RAFT on two challenging sequences from Sintel test. RAFT-it makes a larger error on "Ambush_1" under heavy snow, but it correctly predicts the motion of the dragon and the background on "Market_4". To some degree, these comparisons with recent methods compare the effect of innovations on architecture with training techniques, suggesting that there may be large gains for innovations on training techniques.

KITTI 2015. The newly trained PWC-Net-it and IRR-it are substantially better than the respective, published models, with more than 2 percent reduction in average outlier percentage (Fl-all) on the KITTI 2015 benchmark. Both are also more accurate than some more recent models [31,55,56,64].

Middlebury. At the time of writing, our newly trained RAFT-it is ranked first on Middlebury for both end-point and angular errors, with the avg. rank being 1.7 and 3.9, respectively. It is the first deep learning based approach to outperform traditional methods on Middlebury, such as NNF-Local [6] (avg. rank 5.8 and 7.4), which had been the top-performing method since 2013.

VIPER. Our newly trained RAFT-it obtains 73.6 for the mean weighted area under the curve (WAUC) over all conditions, *v.s.* 69.5 by RAFT_RVC [42].

3.5 Higher-Resolution Input, Inference Time and Memory

We perform qualitative evaluations on 2K and 4K resolution inputs from Davis [33]. For 2K, all models produce similarly high quality flow fields, please see the supplementals for images. In Fig. 6, we present optical flow results for the newly trained IRR-PWC-it and PWC-Net-it on 4K DAVIS samples. Overall, the flows are comparable, with IRR-PWC-it showing slightly better motion smoothness on the jumping dog (top row in Fig. 6).

Table 6 presents a comparison of inference times and memory consumption on an NVIDIA V100 GPU. To account for initial kernel loading, we report the average of 100 runs. For each model, we test three spatial sizes: 1024×448 (1K), 1920×1080 (Full HD/2K), and 3840×2160 (4K). PWC-Net and IRR-PWC show comparable inference time. RAFT, in contrast, is 4.3× and 14.4× slower in 1K and 2K, respectively. In terms of memory, PWC-Net and IRR-PWC , again, show comparable performance. The increase in memory usage from 1K to 2K is almost linear for PWC-Net and IRR-PWC. On the other hand, RAFT uses more memory. Its footprint grows almost quadratically, by 3.8×, from 1K to 2K, and at 4K resolution, RAFT leads to out-of-memory (OOM).

First frame   PWC-it   IRR-it

Fig. 6. Visual results on **Davis 4K**. We show only PWC-Net-it and IRR-PWC-it results since RAFT runs out of memory on the 16GB GPU.

Table 6. Inference time and memory usage for 1024×448, Full HD (1920×1080) and 4K (3840×2160) frame sizes, averaged over 100 runs on an NVIDIA V100 GPU.

	Inference time (msec)↓			Peak memory (GB)↓		
	1024×448	Full HD	4K	1024 × 448	Full HD	4K
PWC-Net	20.61	28.77	63.31	1.478	2.886	7.610
IRR-PWC	24.71	33.67	57.59	1.435	2.902	8.578
RAFT	107.38	499.63	n/a	2.551	9.673	OOM

3.6 Discussion

What Makes RAFT Better than PWC-Net? Our results show that several factors contribute to the performance gap between the published RAFT (5.10% Fl-all on KITTI 2015, see Table 1) and PWC-Net (7.72%) methods, including training techniques, datasets and architecture innovations. Recent training techniques and datasets significantly improve PWC-Net (5.54%) and IRR-PWC (5.73%). The newly trained models are competitive with published RAFT (5.10%) performance while maintaining their advantages in speed and memory requirements during inference. These insights also yield a newly trained RAFT-it model that sets a new state of the art on Middlebury at the time of writing. We conclude that innovations on training techniques and datasets are another fruitful path to performance gains, for both old and new optical flow architectures. After compensating for the differences in training techniques and datasets, we can identify the true performance gap between PWC-Net and RAFT that is solely due to architecture innovations (5.54% vs. 4.31% Fl-all on KITTI 2015). Future work should examine which specific architecture elements of RAFT are critical, and whether they may be transferable to other models.

No Model to Rule All. Our study also shows that there are several factors to consider when choosing an optical flow model, including flow accuracy, training time, inference time, memory cost and application scenarios. RAFT has the highest accuracy and faster convergence in training, but is slower at test time and has a high memory footprint. PWC-Net and IRR-PWC are more appealing for applications that require fast inference, low memory cost and high-resolution input. PWC-Net may be suitable for applications with small motions. Every model entails trade-offs between different requirements; no single model is superior on all metrics. Thus, researchers may wish to focus on specific metrics for improvement, thereby providing practitioners with more options.

4   Conclusions

We have evaluated three prominent optical flow architectures with improved training protocols and observed surprising and significant performance gains. The newly trained PWC-Net-it and IRR-PWC-it are more accurate than the more recent Flow1D model on KITTI 2015, while being about 3× faster during inference. Our newly trained RAFT-it sets a new state of the art and is the first deep learning approach to outperform traditional methods on the Middlebury benchmark. These results demonstrate the benefits of decoupling the contributions of model architectures, training techniques, and datasets to understand the sources of performance gains.

References

1. Baker, S., Scharstein, D., Lewis, J.P., Roth, S., Black, M.J., Szeliski, R.: A database and evaluation methodology for optical flow. IJCV **9**, 1–31 (2011)
2. Bao, W., Lai, W.S., Ma, C., Zhang, X., Gao, Z., Yang, M.H.: Depth-aware video frame interpolation. In: Proceedings of the IEEE/CVF Conference on Computer Vision and Pattern Recognition, pp. 3703–3712 (2019)
3. Barron, J., Fleet, D., Beauchemin, S.: Performance of optical flow techniques. IJCV **12**, 43–77 (1994)
4. Bello, I., et al.: Revisiting resnets: improved training and scaling strategies. Adv. Neural Inf. Process. Syst. **34**, 1–14 (2021)
5. Butler, D.J., Wulff, J., Stanley, G.B., Black, M.J.: A naturalistic open source movie for optical flow evaluation. In: Fitzgibbon, A., Lazebnik, S., Perona, P., Sato, Y., Schmid, C. (eds.) ECCV 2012. LNCS, vol. 7577, pp. 611–625. Springer, Heidelberg (2012). https://doi.org/10.1007/978-3-642-33783-3_44
6. Chen, Z., Jin, H., Lin, Z., Cohen, S., Wu, Y.: Large displacement optical flow from nearest neighbor fields. In: CVPR, pp. 2443–2450 (2013)
7. Deng, J., Dong, W., Socher, R., Li, L.J., Li, K., Fei-Fei, L.: Imagenet: a large-scale hierarchical image database. In: CVPR, pp. 248–255. IEEE (2009)
8. Djelouah, A., Campos, J., Schaub-Meyer, S., Schroers, C.: Neural inter-frame compression for video coding. In: CVPR, pp. 6421–6429 (2019)
9. Dosovitskiy, A., et al.: An image is worth 16×16 words: transformers for image recognition at scale. arXiv preprint arXiv:2010.11929 (2020)
10. Dosovitskiy, A., et al.: FlowNet: learning optical flow with convolutional networks. In: Proceedings of ICCV (2015)
11. Fan, L., Huang, W., Gan, C., Ermon, S., Gong, B., Huang, J.: End-to-end learning of motion representation for video understanding. In: Proceedings of CVPR (2018)
12. Geiger, A., Lenz, P., Urtasun, R.: Are we ready for autonomous driving? the kitti vision benchmark suite. In: Proceedings of CVPR, pp. 3354–3361. IEEE (2012)
13. Goodfellow, I., Bengio, Y., Courville, A.: Deep Learning. MIT press, Cambridge (2016)
14. He, K., Zhang, X., Ren, S., Sun, J.: Deep residual learning for image recognition. In: Proceedings of the IEEE Conference on Computer Vision and Pattern Recognition, pp. 770–778 (2016)
15. He, T., Zhang, Z., Zhang, H., Zhang, Z., Xie, J., Li, M.: Bag of tricks for image classification with convolutional neural networks. In: Proceedings of the IEEE/CVF Conference on Computer Vision and Pattern Recognition, pp. 558–567 (2019)
16. Hui, T.W., Tang, X., Change Loy, C.: Liteflownet: a lightweight convolutional neural network for optical flow estimation. In: Proceedings of CVPR (2018)
17. Hur, J., Roth, S.: Iterative residual refinement for joint optical flow and occlusion estimation. In: Proceedings of CVPR, pp. 5754–5763 (2019). https://github.com/visinf/irr/blob/master/models/pwcnet/_irr.py

18. Ilg, E., Mayer, N., Saikia, T., Keuper, M., Dosovitskiy, A., Brox, T.: FlowNet 2.0: evolution of optical flow estimation with deep networks. In: Proceedings of CVPR (2017)
19. Jiang, H., Sun, D., Jampani, V., Yang, M.H., Learned-Miller, E., Kautz, J.: Super SloMo: high quality estimation of multiple intermediate frames for video interpolation. In: Proceedings of CVPR (2018)
20. Jiang, S., Campbell, D., Lu, Y., Li, H., Hartley, R.: Learning to estimate hidden motions with global motion aggregation. In: Proceedings of the IEEE/CVF International Conference on Computer Vision, pp. 9772–9781 (2021)
21. Jonschkowski, R., Stone, A., Barron, J.T., Gordon, A., Konolige, K., Angelova, A.: What matters in unsupervised optical flow. In: Vedaldi, A., Bischof, H., Brox, T., Frahm, J.-M. (eds.) ECCV 2020. LNCS, vol. 12347, pp. 557–572. Springer, Cham (2020). https://doi.org/10.1007/978-3-030-58536-5_33
22. Kim, D., Woo, S., Lee, J.Y., Kweon, I.S.: Deep video inpainting. In: CVPR, pp. 5792–5801 (2019)
23. Kondermann, D., et al.: The hci benchmark suite: stereo and flow ground truth with uncertainties for urban autonomous driving. In: CVPR Workshops, pp. 19–28 (2016)
24. Lipson, L., Teed, Z., Deng, J.: Raft-stereo: multilevel recurrent field transforms for stereo matching. In: 3DV, pp. 218–227. IEEE (2021)
25. Liu, L., et al.: Learning by analogy: reliable supervision from transformations for unsupervised optical flow estimation. In: CVPR, pp. 6489–6498 (2020)
26. Liu, P., Lyu, M., King, I., Xu, J.: Selflow: self-supervised learning of optical flow. In: The IEEE Conference on Computer Vision and Pattern Recognition (CVPR) (2019)
27. Liu, Z., Mao, H., Wu, C.Y., Feichtenhofer, C., Darrell, T., Xie, S.: A convnet for the 2020s. arXiv preprint arXiv:2201.03545 (2022)
28. Luo, A., Yang, F., Luo, K., Li, X., Fan, H., Liu, S.: Learning optical flow with adaptive graph reasoning. arXiv preprint arXiv:2202.03857 (2022)
29. Lv, Z., Kim, K., Troccoli, A., Sun, D., Rehg, J.M., Kautz, J.: Learning rigidity in dynamic scenes with a moving camera for 3D motion field estimation. In: Ferrari, V., Hebert, M., Sminchisescu, C., Weiss, Y. (eds.) ECCV 2018. LNCS, vol. 11209, pp. 484–501. Springer, Cham (2018). https://doi.org/10.1007/978-3-030-01228-1_29
30. Mayer, N., et al.: A large dataset to train convolutional networks for disparity, optical flow, and scene flow estimation. In: Proceedings of CVPR (2016)
31. Mehl, L., Beschle, C., Barth, A., Bruhn, A.: An anisotropic selection scheme for variational optical flow methods with order-adaptive regularisation. In: Elmoataz, A., Fadili, J., Quéau, Y., Rabin, J., Simon, L. (eds.) SSVM 2021. LNCS, vol. 12679, pp. 140–152. Springer, Cham (2021). https://doi.org/10.1007/978-3-030-75549-2_12
32. Meister, S., Hur, J., Roth, S.: Unflow: unsupervised learning of optical flow with a bidirectional census loss. In: AAAI (2018)
33. Perazzi, F., Pont-Tuset, J., McWilliams, B., Van Gool, L., Gross, M., Sorkine-Hornung, A.: A benchmark dataset and evaluation methodology for video object segmentation. In: CVPR (2016)
34. Ranjan, A., Black, M.J.: Optical flow estimation using a spatial pyramid network. In: Proceedings of CVPR (2017)
35. Ranjan, A., et al.: Competitive collaboration: joint unsupervised learning of depth, camera motion, optical flow and motion segmentation. In: CVPR, pp. 12240–12249 (2019)

36. Richter, S.R., Hayder, Z., Koltun, V.: Playing for benchmarks. In: Proceedings of the IEEE International Conference on Computer Vision, pp. 2213–2222 (2017)
37. Richter, S.R., Hayder, Z., Koltun, V.: Playing for benchmarks. In: IEEE International Conference on Computer Vision, ICCV 2017, Venice, Italy, 22–29 October 2017, pp. 2232–2241 (2017). https://doi.org/10.1109/ICCV.2017.243
38. Shi, H., Zhou, Y., Yang, K., Yin, X., Wang, K.: Csflow: learning optical flow via cross strip correlation for autonomous driving. arXiv preprint arXiv:2202.00909 (2022)
39. Steiner, A., Kolesnikov, A., Zhai, X., Wightman, R., Uszkoreit, J., Beyer, L.: How to train your vit? data, augmentation, and regularization in vision transformers. arXiv preprint arXiv:2106.10270 (2021)
40. Stone, A., Maurer, D., Ayvaci, A., Angelova, A., Jonschkowski, R.: Smurf: self-teaching multi-frame unsupervised raft with full-image warping. In: CVPR, pp. 3887–3896 (2021)
41. Stroud, J., Ross, D., Sun, C., Deng, J., Sukthankar, R.: D3d: distilled 3d networks for video action recognition. In: CVPR, pp. 625–634 (2020)
42. Sun, D., et al.: TF-RAFT: a tensorflow implementation of raft. In: ECCV Robust Vision Challenge Workshop (2020)
43. Sun, D., Roth, S., Black, M.J.: Secrets of optical flow estimation and their principles. In: CVPR, pp. 2432–2439. IEEE (2010)
44. Sun, D., et al.: Autoflow: learning a better training set for optical flow. In: CVPR (2021)
45. Sun, D., Yang, X., Liu, M.Y., Kautz, J.: Pwc-net: Cnns for optical flow using pyramid, warping, and cost volume. In: CVPR (2018)
46. Sun, D., Yang, X., Liu, M.Y., Kautz, J.: Models matter, so does training: an empirical study of cnns for optical flow estimation. IEEE TPAMI **42**, 1408–1423 (2019)
47. Szeliski, R.: Computer Vision: Algorithms and Applications. Springer, Heidelberg (2010). https://doi.org/10.1007/978-1-84882-935-0
48. Teed, Z., Deng, J.: RAFT: recurrent all-pairs field transforms for optical flow. In: Vedaldi, A., Bischof, H., Brox, T., Frahm, J.-M. (eds.) ECCV 2020. LNCS, vol. 12347, pp. 402–419. Springer, Cham (2020). https://doi.org/10.1007/978-3-030-58536-5_24
49. Teed, Z., Deng, J.: Raft-3d: scene flow using rigid-motion embeddings. In: CVPR, pp. 8375–8384 (2021)
50. Touvron, H., Cord, M., Douze, M., Massa, F., Sablayrolles, A., Jégou, H.: Training data-efficient image transformers & distillation through attention. In: International Conference on Machine Learning, pp. 10347–10357. PMLR (2021)
51. Wan, Z., Mao, Y., Dai, Y.: Praflow_rvc: pyramid recurrent all-pairs field transforms for optical flow estimation in robust vision challenge 2020. arXiv preprint arXiv:2009.06360 (2020)
52. Wang, J., Zhong, Y., Dai, Y., Zhang, K., Ji, P., Li, H.: Displacement-invariant matching cost learning for accurate optical flow estimation. Adv. Neural Inf. Process. Syst. **33**, 15220–15231 (2020)
53. Wightman, R., Touvron, H., Jégou, H.: Resnet strikes back: an improved training procedure in timm. arXiv preprint arXiv:2110.00476 (2021)
54. Xiao, T., et al.: Learnable Cost Volume Using the Cayley Representation. In: Vedaldi, A., Bischof, H., Brox, T., Frahm, J.-M. (eds.) ECCV 2020. LNCS, vol. 12354, pp. 483–499. Springer, Cham (2020). https://doi.org/10.1007/978-3-030-58545-7_28

55. Xu, H., Yang, J., Cai, J., Zhang, J., Tong, X.: High-resolution optical flow from 1d attention and correlation. In: ICCV (2021)
56. Yang, G., Ramanan, D.: Volumetric correspondence networks for optical flow. In: NeurIPS, vol. 32, pp. 794–805 (2019)
57. Yang, G., Zhao, H., Shi, J., Deng, Z., Jia, J.: SegStereo: exploiting semantic information for disparity estimation. In: Ferrari, V., Hebert, M., Sminchisescu, C., Weiss, Y. (eds.) ECCV 2018. LNCS, vol. 11211, pp. 660–676. Springer, Cham (2018). https://doi.org/10.1007/978-3-030-01234-2_39
58. Yin, Z., Darrell, T., Yu, F.: Hierarchical discrete distribution decomposition for match density estimation. In: The IEEE Conference on Computer Vision and Pattern Recognition (CVPR) (2019)
59. Yu, H., et al.: Foal: fast online adaptive learning for cardiac motion estimation. In: CVPR, pp. 4313–4323 (2020)
60. Yu, J.J., Harley, A.W., Derpanis, K.G.: Back to basics: unsupervised learning of optical flow via brightness constancy and motion smoothness. In: Hua, G., Jégou, H. (eds.) ECCV 2016. LNCS, vol. 9915, pp. 3–10. Springer, Cham (2016). https://doi.org/10.1007/978-3-319-49409-8_1
61. Zach, C., Pock, T., Bischof, H.: A duality based approach for realtime tv-l 1 optical flow. In: DAGM (2007)
62. Zhang, F., Woodford, O.J., Prisacariu, V.A., Torr, P.H.: Separable flow: learning motion cost volumes for optical flow estimation. In: Proceedings of the IEEE/CVF International Conference on Computer Vision, pp. 10807–10817 (2021)
63. Zhao, H., Gan, C., Ma, W.C., Torralba, A.: The sound of motions. In: CVPR, pp. 1735–1744 (2019)
64. Zhao, S., Sheng, Y., Dong, Y., Chang, E.I.C., Xu, Y.: Maskflownet: asymmetric feature matching with learnable occlusion mask. In: Proceedings of the IEEE Conference on Computer Vision and Pattern Recognition (CVPR) (2020)
65. Zhao, X., Pang, Y., Zhang, L., Lu, H., Zhang, L.: Suppress and balance: a simple gated network for salient object detection. In: Vedaldi, A., Bischof, H., Brox, T., Frahm, J.-M. (eds.) ECCV 2020. LNCS, vol. 12347, pp. 35–51. Springer, Cham (2020). https://doi.org/10.1007/978-3-030-58536-5_3

A Perturbation-Constrained Adversarial Attack for Evaluating the Robustness of Optical Flow

Jenny Schmalfuss(✉)🆔, Philipp Scholze🆔, and Andrés Bruhn🆔

Institute for Visualization and Interactive Systems, University of Stuttgart, Stuttgart, Germany
{jenny.schmalfuss,andres.bruhn}@vis.uni-stuttgart.de,
philipp.scholze@simtech.uni-stuttgart.de

Abstract. Recent optical flow methods are almost exclusively judged in terms of accuracy, while their robustness is often neglected. Although adversarial attacks offer a useful tool to perform such an analysis, current attacks on optical flow methods focus on real-world attacking scenarios rather than a *worst case* robustness assessment. Hence, in this work, we propose a novel adversarial attack—the Perturbation-Constrained Flow Attack (PCFA)—that emphasizes destructivity over applicability as a real-world attack. PCFA is a global attack that optimizes adversarial perturbations to shift the predicted flow towards a specified target flow, while keeping the L_2 norm of the perturbation below a chosen bound. Our experiments demonstrate PCFA's applicability in white- and black-box settings, and show it finds stronger adversarial samples than previous attacks. Based on these strong samples, we provide the first joint ranking of optical flow methods considering both prediction quality and adversarial robustness, which reveals state-of-the-art methods to be particularly vulnerable. Code is available at https://github.com/cv-stuttgart/PCFA.

Keywords: Optical flow · Robustness · Global adversarial attack · L_2 constrained perturbation

1 Introduction

Optical flow describes the apparent motion between subsequent frames of an image sequence. It has numerous applications ranging from action recognition [42] and video processing [46] to robot navigation [53] and epidemic spread analysis [34]. Over the past decade, the quality of optical flow methods has improved dramatically due to methodological advances: While early optical flow methods were mostly variational [4,6,7,16,36], today's top methods are based on neural networks [17,19,29,37,39,49,50,52].

Supplementary Information The online version contains supplementary material available at https://doi.org/10.1007/978-3-031-20047-2_11.

Fig. 1. Robustness evaluation for RAFT [39]. Our Perturbation-Constrained Flow Attack trains flow-erasing *perturbations* δ_t, whose L_2 *norm* is controlled via ε_2.

Up to date, theses methodological advances are mainly driven by the quality scores on a few major benchmarks [2,3,9,14,18,23] that measure how well the calculated flow matches a known ground truth. Given that optical flow is also used in the context of medical applications [40,51] and autonomous driving [10,45], it is surprising that robustness plays only a subordinated role in the development of new methods. In fact, robustness is rarely assessed in the literature and only few methods were developed with robustness as explicit goal [4,21,22,35,43].

A possible explanation for this blind spot is the ambiguity of the term *robustness* as well as its challenging quantification for optical flow methods. In this work we therefore focus on an improved measure for quantifying the robustness by means of adversarial attacks. Our choice is motivated by the recently demonstrated vulnerability of optical flow networks to malicious input changes [30]. This vulnerability clearly suggests that adversarial robustness should complement the qualitative performance when evaluating optical flow methods.

Adversarial attacks for optical flow are a very recent field of research with only two attacks available so far. While Ranjan *et al.* [30] proposed a local attack in terms of a patch-based approach, Schrodi *et al.* [32] introduced a global attack inspired by attacks for classification. This raises the question whether these two attacks are sufficiently strong to meaningfully measure adversarial robustness. Answering it is difficult, as clear definitions for *attack strength* and *adversarial robustness* are currently missing in the context of optical flow.

In the context of classification, however, these quantities are already defined. There, adversarial networks aim to find small perturbations to the input that lead to its misclassification [15]. Hence, stronger attacks need smaller input perturbations to cause an incorrect class. While classification networks output a finite amount of discrete classes, optical flow methods predict a field of 2D flow vectors. Using a small perturbation makes it unlikely that one can create an arbitrarily large deviation from the unperturbed flow. Therefore, a sensible definition for a strong attack is "an attack that finds the most destructive adversarial perturbation from all perturbations under a specified bound".

This subtle change in the definition of attack strength for optical flow significantly influences the attack design: For a strong attack, an efficient way to bound the input perturbation is required; see Fig. 1. Previous attacks for optical flow either lack effective bounds for their adversarial perturbations [32], or provide a weak adversarial attack [30] to enable real-world applicability. More effective attacks are therefore required for a rigorous quantification of adversarial robustness for optical flow. In this context, we make the following contributions:

1. We formalize a generic *threat model* for optical flow attacks and propose measures for *attack strength* and *adversarial robustness*, to improve the comparability of robustness evaluations and among adversarial attacks.
2. We present the *Perturbation-Constrained Flow Attack (PCFA)*, a strong, global adversarial attack for optical flow that is able to limit the perturbation's L_2 norm to remain within a chosen bound.
3. With PCFA, we generate *joint* and *universal* global perturbations.
4. We experimentally demonstrate that PCFA finds *stronger adversarial samples* and is therefore better suited to quantify adversarial robustness than previous optical flow attacks.
5. We provide the first *ranking* of current optical flow methods that combines their *prediction quality* on benchmarks [9,23] with their *adversarial robustness* measured by the strongest configuration of PCFA.

2   Related Work

In the following, we mainly focus on related work in the field of optical flow. Thereby, we cover the assessment of robustness, the use of adversarial attacks as well as the design of neural networks. Further related work, also including adversarial attacks for classification, is discussed in our short review in Sect. 3.

Robustness Assessment for Optical Flow. For assessing the robustness of optical flow methods, different concepts have been proposed in the literature. On the one hand, early optical flow methods investigated robustness with regard to outliers [4], noise [6,8] or illumination changes [43]. On the other hand, the Robust Vision Challenge[1] quantifies robustness as the generalization of a method's qualitative performance across datasets. In contrast, our work relies on a different concept. We consider *adversarial robustness* [15,38], which is motivated by the Lipschitz continuity of functions. The Lipschitz constant is frequently used as a robustness measure for neural networks, where a small Lipschitz constant implies that the output does only change to the same extend as the input. While finding the exact Lipschitz constant for a neural network is NP-hard [44], bounding it is feasible. For upper bounds on the Lipschitz constant, analytic architecture-dependent considerations are required that are generally difficult – especially for such diverse architectures as in current flow networks. In contrast, finding lower bounds is possible by performing adversarial attacks [11]. Hence, this work uses adversarial attacks to quantify robustness. Thereby, we aim to find input perturbations that cause particularly strong output changes.

Adversarial Attacks for Optical Flow. To the best of our knowledge, there are only two works that propose adversarial attacks tailored to optical flow networks.

---

[1] http://www.robustvision.net/.

Ranjan et al. [30] developed the first adversarial attack, which causes wrong flow predictions by placing a colorful circular patch in both input frames. To be applicable in the real world, their patches are trained with many constraints (e.g. location and rotation invariances, patches are circular, coherent regions), which comes at the cost of a reduced attack strength. Recently, Schrodi et al. [32] introduced a less constrained global attack on optical flow. It is based on the I-FGSM [20] attack for classification that was developed for speed rather than attack strength and does not effectively limit the perturbation size[2]. Both attacks have their own merits, i.e. speed or real world applicability, but are consequently not fully suitable for a rigorous robustness assessement. In contrast, our novel PCFA has a different purpose: Unlike previous attacks, it does not compromise attack strength, thus enabling an effective robustness quantification.

In the context of vision problems similar to optical flow, Wong et al. [47] successfully attacked stereo networks with I-FGSM [20] and its momentum variant MI-FGSM [13]. Moreover, Anand et al. [1] proposed an approach to secure optical flow networks for action recognition against adversarial patch attacks by a preceding filtering step that detects, removes and inpaints the attacked location.

Neural Networks for Optical Flow. Regarding neural networks for optical flow, related work is given by those approaches for which we later on evaluate the robustness, i.e. the methods in [17,19,29,37,39]. These approaches are representatives of the following three classes of networks: classical, pyramidal and recurrent networks. *Classical networks* such as FlowNet2 [17] rely on a stacked encoder-decoder architecture with a dedicated feature extractor and a subsequent correlation layer. More advanced *pyramidal networks* such as SpyNet [29] and PWCNet [37] estimate the optical flow in coarse-to-fine manner using initializations from coarser levels, by warping either the input frames or the extracted features. Finally, state-of-the-art *recurrent networks* such as RAFT [39] and GMA [19] perform iterative updates that rely on a sampling-based hierarchical cost volume. Thereby GMA additionally considers globally aggregated motion features to improve the performance at occlusions.

3   Adversarial Attacks: Foundations and Notations

Adversarial attacks uncovered the brittle performance of neural networks on slightly modified input images, so called *adversarial samples* [15,38]. Different ways to train adversarial samples exist, which lead to different attack types. *Targeted attacks* perturb the input to induce a specified target output. Compared to *untargeted attacks*, they are considered the better choice for strong attacks, since they can simulate the former ones by running attacks on all possible targets and taking the most successful perturbation [11]. *Global attacks* [11,13,15,20]

---

[2] FGSM [15] and I-FGSM [20] limit the perturbation size below ε_∞ by performing only so many steps of a fixed step size τ, that exceeding the norm bound is impossible. To this end, the number of steps is fixed to $N = \lfloor \frac{\varepsilon_\infty}{\tau} \rfloor$, which comes down to a one-shot optimization. Additionally, this "early stopping" reduces the attack strength as it prevents optimizing in the vicinity of the bound.

allow any pixel of the image to be disturbed within a norm bound, while *patch attacks* [5,30] perturb only pixels within a certain neighborhood. So called *universal perturbations* are particularly transferable and have a degrading effect on multiple images rather than being optimized for a single one [12,24,30,32,33]. As they affect a class of input images, their effect on a single image is often weaker.

Since adversarial attacks were first used in the context of classification networks [15,38], many concepts go back to this field. Hence, we briefly review those attacks before we discuss attacks for optical flow in more detail.

Classification. Szegedy *et al.* [38] provided the first optimization formulation for a targeted adversarial attack to find a small perturbation $\delta \in \mathbb{R}^m$ to the input $x \in \mathbb{R}^m$, such that a classifier $\mathcal{C}$ outputs the incorrect label t:

$$\min \|\delta\|_2 \quad \text{s.t.} \quad \mathcal{C}(x + \delta) = t, \quad \text{and} \quad x + \delta \subset [0,1]^m. \tag{1}$$

Many adversarial attacks were proposed to solve problem (1), with varying focus and applicability [5,11,13,15,20]. Among them, the following two methods are most relevant to our work: The Fast Gradient Sign Method (FGSM) [15] method is used for a fast generation of adversarial samples; More recent variations include multiple iterations [20] and momentum [13]. In contrast, the C&W attack [11] emphasizes perturbation destructivity by encouraging the target over all other labels in the optimization (1), while minimizing the adversarial perturbation's L_2 norm. For a broader overview of classification attacks, we refer to the review article of Xu *et al.* [48].

Optical Flow. Given two subsequent frames $\mathcal{I}_t$ and $\mathcal{I}_{t+1} \in \mathbb{R}^I$ of an image sequence, optical flow describes the apparent motion of corresponding pixels in terms of a displacement vector field over the image domain $I = M \times N \times C$, where C is the number of channels per frame. Subsequently, we specify three flow fields: the *ground truth* flow field $f^g = (u^g, v^g) \in \mathbb{R}^{M \times N \times 2}$, the *unattacked* or *initial optical flow* $f \in \mathbb{R}^{M \times N \times 2}$ that comes from a given flow network with two input frames, and the *perturbed* or *adversarial flow* $\check{f} \in \mathbb{R}^{M \times N \times 2}$ from the same network after adding adversarial perturbations $\delta_t, \delta_{t+1} \in \mathbb{R}^I$ to the inputs.

The *local* Patch Attack by Ranjan *et al.* [30] optimizes universal patches

$$\underset{\delta}{\operatorname{argmin}} \; \mathcal{L}(\check{f}, f^t) \quad \text{s.t.} \quad \delta_t = \delta_{t+1} = \delta, \quad \delta \text{ is patch} \quad \text{and} \quad \delta \in [0,1]^I \tag{2}$$

over multiple frames. The cosine similarity serves as loss function $\mathcal{L}$ to minimize the angle between $\check{f}$ and f^t, targeting the negative initial flow $f^t = -f$. To make the circular perturbations location and rotation invariant, the respective transformations are applied before adding the perturbation to the frames.

In contrast, the *global* flow attack by Schrodi *et al.* [32] uses J steps of I-FGSM [20] to generate adversarial perturbations $\|\delta_t, \delta_{t+1}\|_\infty \leq \varepsilon_\infty$ for single frames as

$$\delta_z^{(j+1)} = \delta_z^{(j)} - \frac{\varepsilon_\infty}{J} \cdot \operatorname{sgn}(\nabla_{\mathcal{I}_z + \delta_z^{(j)}} \mathcal{L}(\check{f}, f^t)), \quad z = t, t+1, \quad j = 1, \dots, J. \tag{3}$$

For universal perturbations, it uses the loss function and training from [30].

While we also develop a global attack like [32], we do not base it on I-FGSM variants as they quickly generate non-optimal perturbations. Instead, we develop a novel attack for optical flow, and explicitly optimize it for attack strength.

4   A Global Perturbation-Constrained Adversarial Attack for Optical Flow Networks

As motivated in the introduction, strong flow attacks require refined notions for *attack strength* and *adversarial robustness*, which are discussed first. Based on these refined notions, we present the Perturbation-Constrained Flow Attack (PCFA) that optimizes for strong adversarial perturbations while keeping their L_2 norm under a specified bound. Moreover, with joint and universal perturbations we discuss different perturbation types for optical flow attacks.

4.1   Attack Strength and Adversarial Robustness for Optical Flow

In the context of classification networks, a strong adversarial sample is one that causes a misclassification while being small, see Problem (1). As optical flow methods do not produce discrete classes but flow fields $f \in \mathbb{R}^{M \times N \times 2}$, significantly larger adversarial perturbations δ_t, δ_{t+1} would be required to induce a specific target flow f^t. Further it is unclear whether a method *can* output a certain target. What can be controlled, however, is the perturbation size. Therefore, a useful *threat model for optical flow* is one that limits the perturbation size to ε and minimizes the distance between attacked flow and target at the same time:

$$\underset{\delta_t, \delta_{t+1}}{\mathrm{argmin}}\ \mathcal{L}(\check{f}, f^t)\ \text{ s.t. }\ \|\delta_t, \delta_{t+1}\| \leq \varepsilon,\ \ \mathcal{I}_z + \delta_z \in [0,1]^I,\ \ z = t, t+1. \quad (4)$$

Because the used norms and bounds are generic in this formulation, previous flow attacks fit into this framework: The Patch Attack by Ranjan *et al.* [30] poses a L_0 bound on the patch by limiting the patch size, while the I-FGSM flow attack by Schrodi *et al.* [32] can be seen as a L_∞ bound on the perturbation.

Quantifying Attack Strength. Given that two attacks use the same targets, norms and bounds, they are fully comparable in terms of effectiveness. For stronger attacks, the adversarial flow $\check{f}$ has a better resemblance to the target f^t. As the average endpoint error AEE (see Eq. (7)) is widely used to quantify distances between optical flow fields, we propose to quantify *attack strength* as

$$\mathrm{AEE}(\check{f}, f^t)\ \text{ for }\ \|\delta_t, \delta_{t+1}\| \leq \varepsilon\ \ =\ \ \text{Attack Strength.}$$

Quantifying Adversarial Robustness. To assess the general robustness of a given method, the specific target is of minor importance. A robust method should not produce a largely different flow prediction for slightly changed input frames, which makes the distance between adversarial flow $\check{f}$ and unattacked flow f a meaningful metric. This distance is small for robust methods and can be quantified with the AEE. Therefore we propose to quantify the *adversarial robustness* for optical flow as

$$\text{AEE}(\check{f}, f) \quad \text{for} \quad \|\delta_t, \delta_{t+1}\| \leq \varepsilon \quad = \quad \text{Adversarial Robustness.}$$

This definition of adversarial robustness does intentionally not include a comparison to the ground truth flow f^g as in [29,32] for two reasons. First, a ground truth comparison measures the flow quality, which should be kept separate from robustness because these quantities likely hinder each other [41]. Secondly, changed frame pairs will have another ground truth, but it is unclear what this ground truth for the attacked frame pairs looks like. While constructing a pseudo ground truth for patch attacks can be possible[3], the required ground truth modifications for global attacks are in general unknown. For those reasons, we suggest to report quality metrics and adversarial robustness separately.

4.2 The Perturbation-Constrained Flow Attack

Starting with the threat model for optical flow (4), we opt for global perturbations to generate strong adversarial samples. To obtain a differentiable formulation, the perturbation is bounded in the L_2 norm. Our *Perturbation-Constrained Flow Attack (PCFA)* then solves the inequality-constrained optimization

$$\underset{\delta_t, \delta_{t+1}}{\text{argmin}} \, \mathcal{L}(\check{f}, f^t) \quad \text{s.t.} \quad \|\delta_t, \delta_{t+1}\|_2 \leq \varepsilon_2 \sqrt{2I}, \quad \mathcal{I}_z + \delta_z \in [0,1]^I, \quad z = t, t+1. \quad (5)$$

We use the additional factor $\sqrt{2I}$ to make the perturbation bound independent of the image size $I = M \times N \times C$. This way, $\varepsilon_2 = 0.01$ signifies an average distortion of 1% of the frames' color range per pixel. To solve (5), four aspects need consideration: (i) How to implement the inequality constraint $\|\delta_t, \delta_{t+1}\|_2 \leq \varepsilon \sqrt{2I}$, (ii) how to choose the loss function $\mathcal{L}$, (iii) how to choose the target f^t and (iv) how to ensure the box constraint $\mathcal{I}_z + \delta_z \in [0,1]^I$, $z = t, t+1$.

Inequality Constraint. We use a penalty method with exact penalty function [27] to transform the inequality-constrained problem (5) into the following unconstrained optimization problem for $\hat{\delta} = \delta_t, \delta_{t+1}$:

$$\underset{\hat{\delta}}{\text{argmin}} \, \phi(\hat{\delta}, \mu), \quad \phi(\hat{\delta}, \mu) = \mathcal{L}(\check{f}, f^t) + \mu |c(\hat{\delta})|. \quad (6)$$

The penalty function c linearly penalizes deviations from the constraint $\|\hat{\delta}\|_2 \leq \hat{\varepsilon}_2 = \varepsilon_2 \sqrt{2I}$ and is otherwise zero: $c(\hat{\delta}) = \max(0, \|\hat{\delta}\|_2 - \hat{\varepsilon}_2) = \text{ReLU}(\|\hat{\delta}\|_2 - \hat{\varepsilon}_2)$. If the penalty parameter $\mu \in \mathbb{R}$ approaches infinity, the unconstrained problem (6) will take its minimum within the specified constraint. In practice, it is sufficient to choose μ large. The selected exact penalty function ϕ is nonsmooth at $\|\hat{\delta}\|_2 = \hat{\varepsilon}_2$, which makes its optimization potentially problematic. However, formulating

---

[3] Ranjan *et al.* [30] generate a pseudo ground truth for their attack with static patches by prescribing a zero-flow at the patch locations.

the problem with a smooth penalty function would require to solve a series of optimization problems and is therefore computationally expensive [27]. We solve (6) directly with the L-BFGS [26] optimizer, which worked well in practice. Moreover, in our implementation we use the squared quantities $\|\hat{\delta}\|_2^2 \leq \hat{\varepsilon}_2^2$ for the constraint to avoid a pole in the derivative of $\|\hat{\delta}\|_2$ at $\hat{\delta} = 0$.

Loss Functions. The loss function $\mathcal{L}$ should quantify the proximity of adversarial and target flow. The *average endpoint error (AEE)* is a classical measure to quantify the quality of optical flow as

$$\text{AEE}(\check{f}, f^t) = \frac{1}{MN} \sum_{i \in M \times N} \|\check{f}_i - f_i^t\|_2 \,. \tag{7}$$

However, its derivative is undefined if single components of the adversarial- and target flow coincide, i.e. $\check{f}_i = f_i^t$. In practice, we rarely observed problems for reasonably small perturbations bounds $\hat{\varepsilon}_2$, which prevent a perfect matching. The *mean squared error (MSE)* circumvents this issue due to its squared norm

$$\text{MSE}(\check{f}, f^t) = \frac{1}{MN} \sum_{i \in M \times N} \|\check{f}_i - f_i^t\|_2^2 \,, \tag{8}$$

but is less robust to outliers as deviations are penalized quadratically. Previous optical flow attacks [30,32] use the *cosine similarity (CS)*

$$\text{CS}(\check{f}, f^t) = \frac{1}{MN} \sum_{i \in M \times N} \frac{\langle \check{f}_i, f_i^t \rangle}{\|\check{f}_i\|_2 \cdot \|f_i^t\|_2} \,. \tag{9}$$

Since this loss only measures angular deviations between flows, it fails to train adversarial perturbation where the adversarial flow or the target are zero.

Target Flows. In principle, any flow field can serve as target flow. Ranjan *et al.* [30] flip the flow direction for a *negative-flow attack* $f^t = -f$. However, this target strongly depends on the initial flow direction. As input agnostic alternative, we propose the *zero-flow attack* with $f^t = 0$. It is especially useful to train universal perturbations that are effective on multiple frames.

Ensuring the Box Constraint. During the optimization, the perturbed frames should remain within the allowed value range, e.g. return a valid color value. All previous flow attacks use *clipping* that crops the perturbed frames to their allowed range after adding δ_t, δ_{t+1}. The *change of variables (COV)* [11] is an alternative approach that optimizes over the auxiliary variables w_t, w_{t+1} instead of δ_t, δ_{t+1} as

$$\delta_z = \frac{1}{2}(\tanh(w_z) + 1) - \mathcal{I}_z \,, \quad z = t, t+1 \,. \tag{10}$$

This optimizes $w_t, w_{t+1} \in [-\infty, \infty]^I$, and afterwards maps them into the allowed range $[0, 1]^I$ for the perturbed frames. Our evaluation considers both approaches.

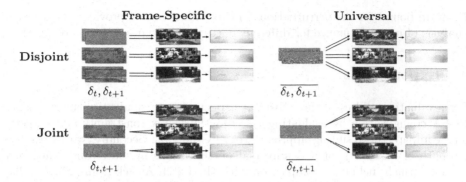

Fig. 2. Illustration of the differences between *disjoint* and *joint* as well as *frame-specific* and *universal* adversarial perturbations for attacking optical flow networks.

Table 1. Comparison of adversarial optical flow attacks, configurations as stated in the respective publications. *Clip* = Clipping, A = AAE, M = MSE, C = CS.

Attack	Type	$\|\delta\|_*$	Perturbation Types				Losses	Box Constr.
			δ_t, δ_{t+1}	$\delta_{t,t+1}$	$\overline{\delta_t, \delta_{t+1}}$	$\overline{\delta_{t,t+1}}$		
Patch Att. [30]	Patch	L_0	–	–	–	✓	C	Clip
I-FGSM [32]	Global	L_∞	✓	–	✓	–	C	Clip
PCFA (ours)	Global	L_2	✓	✓	✓	✓	A, M, C	Clip, COV

4.3 Joint and Universal Adversarial Perturbations

Out of the box, the optimization problem (6) holds for *disjoint* perturbations, resulting in two perturbations δ_t, δ_{t+1} for an input frame pair $\mathcal{I}_t, \mathcal{I}_{t+1}$. Let us now discuss optimizing *joint perturbations* for both input frames and *universal perturbations* for multiple input pairs; their difference is illustrated in Fig. 2. By at-tacking both frames or several frame pairs simultaneously, these perturbations have to fulfill more constraints and hence typically offer a weaker performance.

Joint Adversarial Perturbations. In case of *joint* adversarial perturbations, a common perturbation $\delta_{t,t+1}$ is added to both input frames. In its current formulation, the COV box constraint is only possible for disjoint perturbations.

Universal Adversarial Perturbations. Training *universal* instead of *frame-specific* perturbations is straightforward using our optimization (6). Additional projection operations to ensure the norm bound as in other schemes [12, 24, 30, 32, 33] are unnecessary, because PCFA directly optimizes perturbations of limited size. Similar to [33], we refine adversarial perturbations on minibatches. With this scheme, we train disjoint $\overline{\delta_t, \delta_{t+1}}$ and joint $\overline{\delta_{t,t+1}}$ universal perturbations.

4.4 Design Overview and Comparison to Literature

Table 1 summarizes our method design-wise and compares it to the other optical flow attacks from the literature. PCFA is the first attack that allows an effective

L_2 norm bound for the perturbation. In the evaluation, we provide an extensive analysis of its performance for different perturbation types, losses and targets.

5 Experiments

Our evaluation addresses three distinct aspects: First, we identify the strongest PCFA configuration by evaluating loss functions, box constraints and targets, and compare the resulting approach to I-FGSM [32]. Secondly, we assess the strength of PCFA's joint and universal perturbations in white- and black box attacks, which includes a comparison with the Patch Attack from [29]. Finally, based on PCFA's strongest configuration, we perform a common evaluation of optical flow methods regarding estimation quality *and* adversarial robustness.

At https://github.com/cv-stuttgart/PCFA we provide our PCFA implementation in PyTorch [28]. It is evaluated it with implementations of FlowNet2 [17] from [31], PWCNet [37], SpyNet [29] from [25], RAFT [39] and GMA [19] on the datasets KITTI 2015 [23] and MPI-Sintel final [9]. A full list of parameters and configurations for all experiments is in the supplementary material, Table A1.

5.1 Generating Strong Perturbations for Individual Frame Pairs

In the following we consider *disjoint non-universal* perturbations δ_t, δ_{t+1} on the KITTI test dataset. This allows us to (i) identify the strongest PCFA configuration, to (ii) show that PCFA can be used to target specific flows, and to (iii) compare its strength to I-FGSM [32]. We solve PCFA from Eq. (6) with 20 L-BFGS [26] steps per frame pair.

Loss and Box Constraint. Table 2 summarizes the attack strength $\text{AEE}(\check{f}, f^t)$ for all combinations of losses and box constraints on the targets $f^t \in \{0, -f\}$ with $\varepsilon_2 = 5 \cdot 10^{-3}$ for RAFT. Compared to clipping, the change of variables (COV) always yields a stronger attack, i.e. a smaller distance to the target when using the same loss. Despite its problematic derivative, the average endpoint error (AEE) reliably outperforms the other losses, while the cosine similarity (CS) that is used in all previous flow attacks [30,32] performs worst. Also, the CS loss fails on the zero-flow target where perturbations keep their initial values (*cf.* Supp. Table A2). Since AEE with COV yields the strongest attack independent of the target, we select this configuration for the remaining experiments.

Table 2. PCFA attack strength $\text{AEE}(\check{f}, f^t)$ on the KITTI test dataset for different *loss functions*, *targets* and *box constraints* on RAFT. Small values indicate strong attacks.

	$f^t = 0$			$f^t = -f$		
	AEE	MSE	CS	AEE	MSE	CS
Clipping	3.76	10.51	32.37	22.48	38.57	129.44
COV	**3.54**	7.46	32.37	**18.84**	34.82	86.00

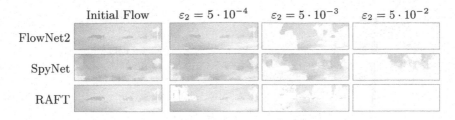

Fig. 3. Visual comparison of PCFA with zero-flow target on different *optical flow methods* for increasing *perturbation sizes* ε_2. White pixels represent zero flow.

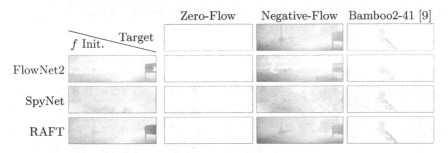

Fig. 4. Visual comparison of PCFA attacked flows with different *targets* for multiple *optical flow methods*. Choosing $\varepsilon_2 = 10^{-1}$ allows to come close to the respective target.

Targets. Next, we investigate how well PCFA can induce a given target flow for different perturbation sizes. Figure 1 depicts the perturbed input frames, normalized adversarial perturbations and resulting flow fields for a zero-flow attack with increasing perturbation size on RAFT. Similarly, Fig. 3 and Supp. Fig. A1 show resulting flow fields for the other networks. Evidently, a perturbation with larger L_2 norm ε_2 reaches a better resemblance between the adversarial flow prediction and the all-white zero-flow target. This is expected, as larger deviations in the input should result in larger output changes. However, it is remarkable that changing color values by 5% on average ($\varepsilon_2 = 5 \cdot 10^{-2}$) suffices to erase the predicted motion. Moreover, not only the zero-flow but also other targets can be induced with PCFA. This is illustrated in Fig. 4 and Supp. Fig. A2. Note that the final proximity to the target mainly depends on its initial distance to the predicted flow field, as close targets are easier to reach.

Comparison of PCFA and I-FGSM. Next, we compare the performance of PCFA and I-FGSM [32] on all networks over a range of perturbations $\varepsilon_2 \in \{5 \cdot 10^{-4}, 10^{-3}, 5 \cdot 10^{-3}, 10^{-2}, 5 \cdot 10^{-2}\}$. We configure I-FGSM as in [32] and iterate until ε_2 is reached, even though it still optimizes for L_∞. Figure 5 shows the attack strength over the average perturbation norm, Supp. Fig. A3 the corresponding adversarial robustness. While small perturbations δ_t, δ_{t+1} hardly minimize the distance between adversarial and zero-target flow in Fig. 5, large perturbations produce almost perfect target matches with a distance of 0. For each tested optical flow network (color coded) our PCFA (solid) achieves smaller

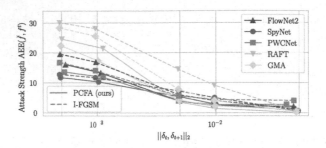

Fig. 5. *Attack strength* with zero-flow target over *perturbation size*, for *PCFA* (solid) and *I-FGSM* [32] (dashed) on different flow networks. Smaller is stronger.

Table 3. Zero-target proximity for different *perturbations*, examples in Supp. Fig. A4.

Perturbation Type		FlowNet2	SypNet	PWCNet	RAFT	GMA
Frame-Specific	δ_t, δ_{t+1}	**3.22**	**4.54**	4.28	**3.76**	**3.59**
	$\delta_{t,t+1}$	4.16	5.84	**3.82**	5.35	4.78
Universal	$\overline{\delta_t, \delta_{t+1}}$	22.03	14.57	19.13	28.88	28.49
	$\overline{\delta_{t,t+1}}$	**20.49**	**14.19**	**18.99**	**28.53**	**27.17**

distances than I-FGSM (dashed) – independent of the perturbation size. Hence, PCFA is the global attack of choice to generate strong disjoint image-specific perturbations for optical flow networks.

5.2   Joint and Universal Perturbations

Next we investigate PCFA's potential to generate more general, i.e. joint and universal, perturbations. Moreover, to assess the transferability of network-specific joint universal perturbations, we apply them to all tested networks.

Joint and Universal Perturbations (White Box). In the white box setting, the perturbations are trained and tested on the same model and data. We evaluate the attack strength of perturbation types as target proximity $\text{AEE}(\check{f}, f^t)$ for a zero-flow attack with $\varepsilon_2 = 5 \cdot 10^{-3}$ trained on the KITTI test dataset. For comparability, clipping is used as COV only works for disjoint perturbations. In Table 3, frame-specific perturbations clearly show a better target resemblance than universal ones for all networks, as they are optimized for frame-specific destructivity rather than transferability. Further, disjoint perturbations are more effective than joint ones when they are frame-specific. However, for universal perturbations the situation is reversed. This is surprising as disjoint perturbations can adapt to both inputs, which should allow an even better target match. While joint perturbations might add static structures to simulate zero-flow, we reproduced this observation also for a negative-flow target (*cf.* Supp. Table A3).

Table 4. Transferability of KITTI universal perturbations between *training* and *test* dataset and between different *networks*, measured as adversarial robustness AEE($\check{f}, f$). Large values denote a better transferability, smaller values indicate higher robustness.

Test \ Train	FlowNet2	SpyNet	PWCNet	RAFT	GMA
FlowNet2 [17]	**3.29**	**2.69**	2.22	1.17	1.12
SpyNet [29]	0.60	2.25	0.57	0.46	0.42
PWCNet [37]	1.53	2.19	**2.99**	0.85	0.75
RAFT [39]	2.88	1.87	2.52	3.52	3.19
GMA [19]	3.12	2.14	2.97	**3.95**	**3.81**

Table 5. Adversarial robustness with universal perturbations from *Patch Attack* [30] and *PCFA*, with the setup from Table 4. Perturbations from the KITTI training set are applied to the generating network on the KITTI test set, *cf.* Fig. 6 for perturbations.

Attack	FlowNet2	SpyNet	PWCNet	RAFT	GMA
Patch Attack [30]	0.99	1.38	1.37	0.76	0.95
PCFA (ours)	**3.29**	**2.25**	**2.99**	**3.52**	**3.81**

Transferability of Adversarial Perturbations (Black Box). To conclude the PCFA assessment, we train universal joint perturbations in a black box manner. Per network, we optimize $\overline{\delta_{t,t+1}}$ for 25 epochs (batch size 4) on the *training* set, before they are applied to the *test* set for every network. Table 4 shows the adversarial robustness w.r.t. universal perturbations for KITTI (see Supp. Table A4 for Sintel). Here, we observe great differences between the transferability. While SpyNet's perturbation reliably disturbs the predictions for all networks, perturbations for RAFT or GMA mutually cause strong deviations but hardly affect other networks. Figure 6 and Supp. Fig. A5 further suggest that networks with transferable perturbations mainly consider well generalizing, robust features. In contrast, fine-scaled, non-transferable patterns only affect today's top methods RAFT and GMA. Finally, we compare the effectiveness of the global PCFA to the Patch Attack by Ranjan *et al.* [30] with a diameter of 102 pixels in Table 5. As both attack setups perturb a similar amount of information per frame (see supplementary material for details), this supports the initial conjecture that fewer constraints help to increase PCFA's effectiveness.

5.3   Evaluating Quality and Robustness for Optical Flow Methods

Finally, we jointly evaluate the optical flow quality and adversarial robustness. For quality, we take the official scores from KITTI and Sintel. For robustness, we apply PCFA's strongest configuration (Sect. 5.1, δ_t, δ_{t+1} with AAE and COV) and report the deviation from the initial flow on the respective test datasets for a zero-flow target, $\varepsilon_2 = 5 \cdot 10^{-3}$. Figure 7 visualizes quality and adversarial robustness on different axes. On both datasets, we observe methods with good

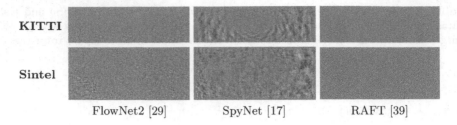

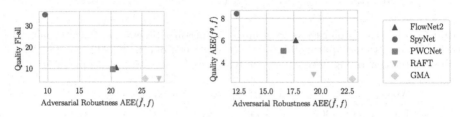

Fig. 6. Normalized *universal perturbations* for different network architectures learned from the respective training datasets. Top row: KITTI. Bottom row: Sintel.

Fig. 7. Joint evaluation of optical flow methods by *prediction quality* and *adversarial robustness* on KITTI (left) and Sintel (right), more attacks in Supp. Figure A6.

robustness (low adversarial robustness scores) to rank bad in terms of quality (high error) and vice versa. Further, we can identify methods with similar scores: Current networks like RAFT and GMA (recurrent) have good quality but little robustness, FlowNet2 (encoder-decoder) and PWCNet (feature pyramid) balance both, and SpyNet (image pyramid) leads in robustness but has the worst quality. These results indicate that flow networks are subject to a trade-off between accuracy and robustness [41], which also sheds new light on the development of high-accuracy methods that cannot sustain their top rank w.r.t. robustness.

6   Conclusions

This work describes the Perturbation-Constrained Flow Attack (PCFA), a novel global adversarial attack designed for a rigorous adversarial robustness assessment of optical flow networks. In contrast to previous flow attacks, PCFA finds more destructive adversarial perturbations and effectively limits their L_2 norm, which renders it particularly suitable for comparing the robustness of neural networks. Our experimental analysis clearly shows that high quality flow methods are not automatically robust. In fact, these methods seem to be particularly vulnerable to PCFA's perturbations. Therefore, we strongly encourage the research community to treat robustness with equal importance as quality and report both metrics for optical flow methods. With PCFA we not only provide a systematic tool to do so, but with our formal definition of adversarial robustness we also provide a general concept that allows to compare both methods and attacks.

Acknowledgments. Funded by the Deutsche Forschungsgemeinschaft (DFG, German Research Foundation) – Project-ID 251654672 – TRR 161 (B04). The International Max Planck Research School for Intelligent Systems supports J.S.

References

1. Anand, A.P., Gokul, H., Srinivasan, H., Vijay, P., Vijayaraghavan, V.: Adversarial patch defense for optical flow networks in video action recognition. In: Proceedings of the IEEE International Conference on Machine Learning and Applications (ICMLA), pp. 1289–1296 (2020)
2. Baker, S., Scharstein, D., Lewis, J.P., Roth, S., Black, M.J., Szeliski, R.: A database and evaluation methodology for optical flow. Int. J. Comput. Vis. **92**(1), 1–31 (2011)
3. Barron, J.L., Fleet, D.J., Beauchemin, S.S.: Performance of optical flow techniques. Int. J. Comput. Vis. **12**, 43–77 (1994)
4. Black, M.J., Anandan, P.: A framework for the robust estimation of optical flow. In: Proceedings of the IEEE International Conference on Computer Vision (ICCV), pp. 231–236 (1993)
5. Brown, T.B., Mané, D., Roy, A., Abadi, M., Gilmer, J.: Adversarial patch. In: arXiv preprint. arXiv:1712 (2018)
6. Brox, T., Bruhn, A., Papenberg, N., Weickert, J.: High accuracy optical flow estimation based on a theory for warping. In: Proceedings of European Conference on Computer Vision (ECCV), pp. 25–36 (2004)
7. Brox, T., Malik, J.: Large displacement optical flow: descriptor matching in variational motion estimation. IEEE Trans. Pattern Anal. Mach. Intell. **33**(3), 500–513 (2011)
8. Bruhn, A., Weickert, J., Schnörr, C.: Lucas/Kanade meets Horn/Schunck: combining local and global optic flow methods. Int. J. Comput. Vis. **61**(3), 211–231 (2005)
9. Butler, D.J., Wulff, J., Stanley, G.B., Black, M.J.: A naturalistic open source movie for optical flow evaluation. In: Proceedings of European Conference on Computer Vision (ECCV), pp. 611–625 (2012)
10. Capito, L., Ozguner, U., Redmill, K.: Optical flow based visual potential field for autonomous driving. In: IEEE Intelligent Vehicles Symposium (IV), pp. 885–891 (2020)
11. Carlini, N., Wagner, D.: Towards evaluating the robustness of neural networks. In: Proceedings of the IEEE Symposium on Security and Privacy (SP), pp. 39–57 (2017)
12. Deng, Y., Karam, L.J.: Universal adversarial attack via enhanced projected gradient descent. In: Proceedings of the IEEE International Conference on Image Processing (ICIP), pp. 1241–1245 (2020)
13. Dong, Y., et al.: Boosting adversarial attacks with momentum. In: Proceedings of the IEEE/CVF Conference on Computer Vision and Pattern Recognition (CVPR) (2018)
14. Geiger, A., Lenz, P., Urtasun, R.: Are we ready for autonomous driving? The KITTI vision benchmark suite. In: Proceedings of the IEEE Conference on Computer Vision and Pattern Recognition (CVPR) (2012)
15. Goodfellow, I.J., Shlens, J., Szegedy, C.: Explaining and harnessing adversarial examples. arXiv:1412.6572 (2014)

16. Horn, B.K.P., Schunck, B.G.: Determining optical flow. Artif. Intell. **17**(1–3), 185–203 (1981)
17. Ilg, E., Mayer, N., Saikia, T., Keuper, M., Dosovitskiy, A., Brox, T.: FlowNet 2.0: evolution of optical flow estimation with deep networks. In: Proceedings of the IEEE/CVF Conference on Computer Vision and Pattern Recognition (CVPR) (2017)
18. Janai, J., Güney, F., Wulff, J., Black, M., Geiger, A.: Slow Flow: exploiting high-speed cameras for accurate and diverse optical flow reference data. In: Proceedings of the IEEE/CVF Conference on Computer Vision and Pattern Recognition (CVPR), pp. 1406–1416 (2017)
19. Jiang, S., Campbell, D., Lu, Y., Li, H., Hartley, R.: Learning to estimate hidden motions with global motion aggregation. In: Proceedings of the IEEE/CVF International Conference on Computer Vision (ICCV), pp. 9772–9781 (2021)
20. Kurakin, A., Goodfellow, I., Bengio, S.: Adversarial machine learning at scale. arXiv: 6110.1236 (2017)
21. Li, R., Tan, R.T., Cheong, L.-F.: Robust optical flow in rainy scenes. In: Ferrari, V., Hebert, M., Sminchisescu, C., Weiss, Y. (eds.) ECCV 2018. LNCS, vol. 11219, pp. 299–317. Springer, Cham (2018). https://doi.org/10.1007/978-3-030-01267-0_18
22. Liu, C., Yuen, J., Torralba, A.: SIFT flow: dense correspondence across scenes and its applications. IEEE Trans. Pattern Anal. Mach. Intell. **33**(5), 978–994 (2010)
23. Menze, M., Heipke, C., Geiger, A.: Joint 3D estimation of vehicles and scene flow. In: Proceedings of the ISPRS Workshop on Image Sequence Analysis (ISA) (2015)
24. Moosavi-Dezfooli, S.M., Fawzi, A., Fawzi, O., Frossard, P.: Universal adversarial perturbations. In: Proceedings of the IEEE/CVF Conference on Computer Vision and Pattern Recognition (CVPR) (2017)
25. Niklaus, S.: A reimplementation of SPyNet using PyTorch (2018). https://github.com/sniklaus/pytorch-spynet
26. Nocedal, J.: Updating quasi-Newton matrices with limited storage. Math. Comput. **35**(151), 773–782 (1980)
27. Nocedal, J., Wright, S.J.: Numerical Optimization, 2nd edn. Springer, New York (2006). https://doi.org/10.1007/978-0-387-40065-5
28. Paszke, A., et al.: PyTorch: an imperative style, high-performance deep learning library. In: Proceedings of the Conference on Neural Information Processing Systems (NeurIPS), pp. 8024–8035 (2019)
29. Ranjan, A., Black, M.J.: Optical flow estimation using a spatial pyramid network. In: Proceedings of the IEEE/CVF Conference on Computer Vision and Pattern Recognition (CVPR) (2017)
30. Ranjan, A., Janai, J., Geiger, A., Black, M.J.: Attacking optical flow. In: Proceedings of the IEEE/CVF International Conference on Computer Vision (ICCV) (2019)
31. Reda, F., Pottorff, R., Barker, J., Catanzaro, B.: flownet2-pytorch: Pytorch implementation of FlowNet 2.0: evolution of optical flow estimation with deep networks (2017). https://github.com/NVIDIA/flownet2-pytorch
32. Schrodi, S., Saikia, T., Brox, T.: Towards understanding adversarial robustness of optical flow networks. In: Proceedings of the IEEE/CVF Conference on Computer Vision and Pattern Recognition (CVPR), pp. 8916–8924 (2022)
33. Shafahi, A., Najibi, M., Xu, Z., Dickerson, J., Davis, L.S., Goldstein, T.: Universal adversarial training. Proc. AAAI Conf. Artif. Intell. **34**(04), 5636–5643 (2020)
34. Stegmaier, T., Oellingrath, E., Himmel, M., Fraas, S.: Differences in epidemic spread patterns of norovirus and influenza seasons of Germany: an application of optical flow analysis in epidemiology. Nat. Res. Sci. Rep. **10**(1), 1–14 (2020)

35. Stein, F.: Efficient computation of optical flow using the census transform. In: Proceedings of the German Conference on Pattern Recognition (DAGM), pp. 79–86 (2004)
36. Sun, D., Roth, S., Black, M.: Secrets of optical flow estimation and their principles. In: Proceedings of the IEEE Conference on Computer Vision and Pattern Recognition (CVPR), pp. 2432–2499 (2010)
37. Sun, D., Yang, X., Liu, M.Y., Kautz, J.: PWC-Net: CNNs for optical flow using pyramid, warping, and cost volume. In: Proceeding of the IEEE/CVF Conference on Computer Vision and Pattern Recognition (CVPR) (2018)
38. Szegedy, C., et al.: Intriguing properties of neural networks. In: Proceedings of the International Conference on Learning Representations (ICLR) (2014)
39. Teed, Z., Deng, J.: RAFT: recurrent all-pairs field transforms for optical flow. In: Proceedings of the European Conference on Computer Vision (ECCV), pp. 402–419 (2020)
40. Tehrani, A., Mirzaei, M., Rivaz, H.: Semi-supervised training of optical flow convolutional neural networks in ultrasound elastography. In: Proceedings of the International Conference on Medical Image Computing and Computer-Assisted Intervention (MICCAI), pp. 504–513 (2020)
41. Tsipras, D., Santurkar, S., Engstrom, L., Turner, A., Madry, A.: Robustness may be at odds with accuracy. In: Proceedings of the International Conference on Learning Representations (ICLR) (2019)
42. Ullah, A., Muhammad, K., Del Ser, J., Baik, S.W., de Albuquerque, V.H.C.: Activity recognition using temporal optical flow convolutional features and multilayer LSTM. IEEE Trans. Ind. Electr. **66**(12), 9692–9702 (2019)
43. van de Weijer, J., Gevers, T.: Robust optical flow from photometric invariants. In: Proceedings of th IEEE International Conference on Image Processing (ICIP), vol. 3, pp. 1835–1838 (2004)
44. Virmaux, A., Scaman, K.: Lipschitz regularity of deep neural networks: analysis and efficient estimation. In: Proc. Conference on Neural Information Processing Systems (NeurIPS) (2018)
45. Wang, H., Cai, P., Fan, R., Sun, Y., Liu, M.: End-to-end interactive prediction and planning with optical flow distillation for autonomous driving. In: Proceedings of the IEEE/CVF Conference on Computer Vision and Pattern Recognition Workshops (CVPR-W), pp. 2229–2238 (2021)
46. Wang, L., Guo, Y., Liu, L., Lin, Z., Deng, X., An, W.: Deep video super-resolution using HR optical flow estimation. IEEE Trans. Image Process. **29**, 4323–4336 (2020)
47. Wong, A., Mundhra, M., Soatto, S.: Stereopagnosia: fooling stereo networks with adversarial perturbations. Proc AAAI Conf. Artif. Intell. **35**(4), 2879–2888 (2021)
48. Xu, H., et al.: Adversarial attacks and defenses in images, graphs and text: a review. Int. J. AOF Automat. Comput. **17**(2), 151–178 (2020)
49. Yang, G., Ramanan, D.: Volumetric correspondence networks for optical flow. In: Proceedings of Conference on Neural Information Processing Systems (NeurIPS), pp. 794–805 (2019)
50. Yin, Z., Darrell, T., Yu, F.: Hierarchical discrete distribution decomposition for match density estimation. In: Proceedings of the IEEE/CVF Conference on Computer Vision and Pattern Recognition (CVPR), pp. 6044–6053 (2019)
51. Yu, H., Chen, X., Shi, H., Chen, T., Huang, T.S., Sun, S.: Motion pyramid networks for accurate and efficient cardiac motion estimation. In: Proceedings of the International Conference on Medical Image Computing and Computer-Assisted Intervention (MICCAI), pp. 436–446 (2020)

52. Zhang, F., Woodford, O., Prisacariu, V., Torr, P.: Separable flow: Learning motion cost volumes for optical flow estimation. In: Proceedings of the IEEE/CVF International Conference on Computer Vision (ICCV), pp. 10807–10817 (2021)
53. Zhang, T., Zhang, H., Li, Y., Nakamura, Y., Zhang, L.: Flowfusion: dynamic dense RGB-D SLAM based on optical flow. In: Proc, IEEE International Conference on Robotics and Automation (ICRA), pp. 7322–7328 (2020)

Robust Landmark-Based Stent Tracking in X-ray Fluoroscopy

Luojie Huang[1]ⓘ, Yikang Liu[2]ⓘ, Li Chen[3], Eric Z. Chen[2], Xiao Chen[2], and Shanhui Sun[2](✉)

[1] Johns Hopkins University, Baltimore, MD, USA
[2] United Imaging Intelligence, Cambridge, MA, USA
shanhui.sun@uii-ai.com
[3] University of Washington, Seattle, WA, USA

Abstract. In clinical procedures of angioplasty (i.e., open clogged coronary arteries), devices such as balloons and stents need to be placed and expanded in arteries under the guidance of X-ray fluoroscopy. Due to the limitation of X-ray dose, the resulting images are often noisy. To check the correct placement of these devices, typically multiple motion-compensated frames are averaged to enhance the view. Therefore, device tracking is a necessary procedure for this purpose. Even though angioplasty devices are designed to have radiopaque markers for the ease of tracking, current methods struggle to deliver satisfactory results due to the small marker size and complex scenes in angioplasty. In this paper, we propose an end-to-end deep learning framework for single stent tracking, which consists of three hierarchical modules: a U-Net for landmark detection, a ResNet for stent proposal and feature extraction, and a graph convolutional neural network for stent tracking that temporally aggregates both spatial information and appearance features. The experiments show that our method performs significantly better in detection compared with the state-of-the-art point-based tracking models. In addition, its fast inference speed satisfies clinical requirements.

Keywords: Stent enhancement · Landmark tracking · Graph neural network

1 Introduction

Coronary artery disease (CAD) is one of the primary causes of death in most developed countries [19]. The current state-of-the-art treatment option

---

L. Huang and L. Chen—Work was done during an internship at United Imaging Intelligence America.

Supplementary Information The online version contains supplementary material available at https://doi.org/10.1007/978-3-031-20047-2_12.

for blocked coronary arteries is the percutaneous coronary intervention (PCI) (Fig. 1). During this minimally invasive procedure, a catheter with a tiny balloon (the tracked dark object in Fig. 1c) at the tip is put into a blood vessel and guided to the blocked coronary artery. Once the catheter arrives at the right place, the balloon is inflated to push the artery open, restoring room for blood flow. In most cases, a stent, which is a tiny tube of wire mesh (Fig. 1), is also placed in the blocked artery after the procedure to support the artery walls and prevent them from re-narrowing. Intraoperative X ray fluoroscopy is commonly used to check the location of stent/balloon before expansion. However, stent visibility is often limited (Fig. 1a and c) under X-ray because the minimal level radiation dose out of safety concerns. Furthermore, stents keep moving rapidly with heartbeat and breathing in the complicated environment of patients' anatomy.

Compared to other physical approaches, such as invasive imaging or increasing radiation dose, a more cost-effective solution is to enhance the stent appearance through image processing (a.k.a., digital stent enhancement), as shown in Fig. 1b and d. A common method is to track the stent motion, separate the stent layer from the background layer, and average the stent layers from multiple frames after motion compensation. Stent tracking is achieved by tracking two radiopaque balloon markers that locate at two ends of the stent (Fig. 1).

Stent tracking for enhancement remains quite challenging due to multiple reasons. First, the balloon markers are very small compared to the whole field of view (FOV) while the movements are large. Second, the scenes in PCI procedures are very complex: organs and other devices can form a noisy background and 3D organs and devices can be projected into different 2D images from different angles. Third, stent enhancement requires high localization accuracy and low false positives. Fourth, fast tracking speed is needed to meet the clinical requirements (e.g., 15 fps for a 512×512 video). Fifth, data annotations are limited just like other medical imaging applications.

Current stent tracking methods lie under the tracking-by-detection category and assume only one stent presents in the FOV. They first detect all possible radiopaque balloon marker from each frame, and then identify the target stent track based on motion smoothness [2,3] or consistency score [14,23]. However, these methods are prone to large detection and tracking errors caused by strong false alarms. Deep learning techniques dramatically improve detection and tracking accuracy. However, it is difficult to apply these techniques to the stent tracking problem because of the small object size and complex PCI scenes and overfitting issue on small dataset. Therefore, we tackle the above issues by incorporating some basic prior knowledge into our framework design. For example, the stent has distinctive hierarchical features: two dark markers that can be detected by low-level features and complicated patterns between the marker pairs, such as wire, mesh and balloon tubes, to be recognized from high-level semantic analysis. Additionally, the association of marker pairs in different frames requires long temporal dimension reasoning to tolerate inaccurate detections in certain frames with limited image quality. Moreover, most deep learning

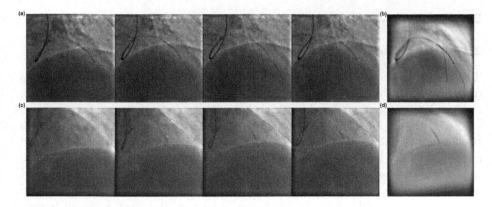

Fig. 1. Examples of stent tracking with the proposed method (a,c) and stent enhancement based on the tracking results (b,d). (a) and (c) show four frames from a video.

frameworks for keypoint tracking problems (such as human pose tracking) train detection and tracking modules separately. However, it is generally harder to detect small markers from a single X-ray image than keypoints from natural images due to the limited object features and complex background.

Therefore, we propose an end-to-end trainable deep learning framework that consists of three hierarchical modules: a landmark detection module, which is a U-Net [21] trained with small patches to detect potential balloon markers with local features; a stent proposal and feature extraction module, which is a ResNet [11] trained with larger stent patches to extract high-level features located between detected marker pairs; and a stent tracking module, which is a graph convolutional neural network (GCN) to associate marker pairs across frames using the combination of extracted features and spatial information. Our ablation study demonstrated that end-to-end learning of the whole framework can greatly benefit the performance of final stent tracking. For example, detector can be boosted by incorporating the feedback from trackers by learning to suppress some false positives that cause bad outcome in trackers.

In summary, the major contributions of this paper are as follows: 1) We propose the first deep learning method, to our best knowledge, to address the single stent tracking problem in PCI X-ray fluoroscopy. 2) To handle the challenge of tracking small stents in complex video background, we propose an end-to-end hierarchical deep learning architecture that exploits both local landmarks and general stent features by CNN backbones and achieves spatiotemporal associations using a GCN model. 3) We test the proposed method and several other state-of-the-art (SOTA) models on both public and private datasets, with hundreds of X-ray fluoroscopy videos, data of a scale that has not been reported before. The proposed method shows superior landmark detection, as well as frame-wise stent tracking performance.

2   Related Work

2.1   Digital Stent Enhancement

The digital stent enhancement (DSE) algorithm typically follows a bottom-up design and can be generally divided in to 4 main steps: landmark detection, landmark tracking, frame registration, and enhanced stent display.

First, the region of interest needs to be located from each frame. Due to the limited visibility of stent and large appearance variation between folded and expanded stents, it is challenging to extract the stent directly. Instead, potential landmarks such as the radiopaque balloon marker pairs at two ends of the stent or the guidewire in between is more commonly used to indicate the location of the stent. Throughout the X-ray image sequence, the stent location is constantly changing with cardiac and breathing motions. Based on the landmark candidates, the most promising track needs to be identified to associate the target stent across frames. Next, frames can be registered based on motion inferred by the landmark trajectory. The motion compensation is often performed by aligning tracked landmarks together using rigid registration [7,15] or elastic registration [2]. To enhance stent visualization, the stent layer is extracted while the background is suppressed [8].

2.2   Balloon Marker Detection

Two markers on the balloon used to deliver the stent are considered the most prominent feature of the stent structure due to the consistent ball shape and radio-opacity from high absorption coefficient. Various strategies are previously studied to achieve efficient balloon marker detection.

Conventional image processing methods are applied, including match filtering or blob detection, to extract candidate markers from the X-ray image. Bismuth et al. [3] proposed a method involving a priori knowledge and dark top hat preprocessing to detect potential markers from local minimum selection. Blob detectors [13,18,23] locate markers by differentiating regions with unique characteristics from neighborhood, such as brightness or color. However, the extremely small size of balloon markers and common noises from the background, such as guidewire tips, Sharp bone edges and other marker-like structure, make those methods prone to a high false positive rate.

Learning-based methods are also proposed to incorporate more extended context information for better markers localization. Lu et al. [14] used probabilistic boosting trees combining joint local context of each marker pair as classifiers to detect markers. Chabi et al. [6] detected potential markers based on adaptive threshold and refined detections by excluding non-mask area using various machine learning classifiers, including k-nearest neighbor, naive Bayesian classifier, support vector machine and linear discriminant analysis. Vernikouskaya et al. [21] employed U-Net, a popular encoder-decoder like CNN designed specifically for medical images, to segment markers and catheter shafts during pulmonary vein isolation as binary masks. The maker segmentation performances from the above methods are still limited by the super imbalance between foreground and background areas. Moreover, all the candidate refinements only focus on considering more local context information at single frame, while the temporal correlation has never been exploited to enhance the classifiers.

In our work, balloon marker detection is considered as a heatmap regression task, which has shown superior performances in other landmark detection applications, such as face recognition [25], human pose estimation [20] and landmark detection in various medical images [1,10]. To obtain potential markers, we use U-Net as the heatmap regression model, which represents each landmark as a 2D Gaussian distribution for more accurate localization.

2.3 Graph Based Object Tracking

Given the set of marker candidates across X-ray image sequence, either a priori motion information [3] or a heuristic temporal coherence analysis [14], which calculates consistency score between frames base on predefined criteria, is used to identify the most prominent landmark trajectory. Wang et al. [23] proposed a offline tracking algorithm as graph optimization problem, by constructing a trellis graph with all the potential marker pairs and then employed the Viterbi algorithm to search the optimal path across frame from the graph. Similar graph models are also applied to other general object tracking tasks [5,16,22] as min-cost flow optimization problem. However, these static graph models will fail when the information contained by nodes or edges is not representative enough or outdated. Brasó et al. [4] demonstrated superior results in multiple object tracking by constructing a dynamical graph of object detections and updating node and edge features using GCN.

In this work, we first interpret the whole video into a graph, where the nodes are associated with encoded appearance features of potential stent from marker pair detections and edges are temporal coherency across frames. A graph neural network is trained as a node classification model to update both node and edge features via message passing. The stent tracking is achieve by learning both context and temporal information.

To our knowledge, the proposed CNN-GCN based DSE algorithm is the first deep learning model to achieve robust balloon marker tracking and 2D stent visual enhancement by incorporating both extended context and temporal information.

3 Approach

In this work, we propose an effective end-to-end trainable framework for landmark based stent/balloon tracking (Fig. 2) with a hierarchical design: a U-Net based landmark detection module that generates a heatmap to localize marker candidates with local features, a ResNet based stent proposal and feature extraction module to extract global stent features in a larger context, and a GCN based stent tracking module to identify the real stent by temporally reasoning with stent features and marker locations.

3.1 Landmark Detection

In landmark based stent/balloon detection, each candidate object is represented by a detected landmark pair: $\mathcal{O}_i = (\mathcal{D}_{i1}^L, \mathcal{D}_{i2}^L)$. The first step is to detect landmarks from each frame using a U-Net [21]. In contrast to conventional object detection, the major challenge of landmark detection is the highly unbalanced foreground/background ratio, as landmarks are commonly tiny dots of few pixels compared to the frame size. Therefore, we treat landmark detection as a heatmap regression problem and pretrain the detector with smaller positive landmark patches, thus to increase fore-to-background ratio. The input video $\mathbf{V} \in \mathbb{R}^{T \times H \times W \times C}$ is fed into the landmark detector (U-Net) that generates heatmaps $\mathbf{H} \in \mathbb{R}^{T \times H \times W}$, where detected landmarks are represented as 2D Gaussian distributed points. From a predicted heatmap, peak points are extracted as landmark detections, represented as 2D coordinates and a confidence score: $\mathcal{D}_i^L = (x_i^L, y_i^L, s_i^L)$. During training, an false negative regularization (Sect. 3.4) is implemented to further enforce the detector to focus on landmarks.

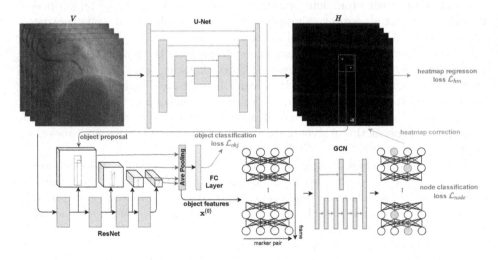

Fig. 2. The proposed end-to-end deep learning framework for stent tracking.

With an ideal landmark detection, the target stents can be directly located by landmarks and tracked over time with simple temporal association. However, due to the lack of extended context information for perfect landmark localization, the landmark detector is inevitably limited by a high false positive rate which further hinders stent tracking. Hence, we proposed a delicate pipeline to simultaneously refine object detection and tracking.

3.2 Stent Proposal and Feature Extraction

Given a set of landmark detections $\mathcal{D}_t^L$ at frame (t), candidate objects can be formed by all possible combination of landmark pairs $\mathcal{O}_t = \{(\mathcal{D}_{ti}^L, \mathcal{D}_{tj}^L) \mid$

$\mathcal{D}_{ti}^L, \mathcal{D}_{tj}^L \in \mathcal{D}_t^L\}$, where $\mathcal{D}_{ti}^L, \mathcal{D}_{tj}^L$ denote the ith and jth Landmark Detections in $\mathcal{D}_t^L$ at frame (t). As the landmark pair is always located at two ends of the corresponding object, We can assign a confidence score to the candidate object using the average of landmark confidence scores:

$$S_i^{\mathcal{O}} = \frac{1}{2}(S_{i1}^L + S_{i2}^L). \tag{1}$$

We can generate a rectangular bounding box for the object based on the landmark locations, of which the center is the middle point of the landmark pair and side lengths are the distance between the landmarks along the corresponding axis. A ResNet is used to extract appearance features of candidate objects. The outputs of ResNet at multiple levels within the corresponding bounding boxes were averaged and stored into a D-dimension feature vector $\mathbf{x}^{(0)} \in \mathbb{R}^D$ for each candidate object, which are used later in GCN for temporal reasoning (Fig. 2). In addition, to facilitate feature learning with a deep supervision, we feed the feature vector into a fully-connected layer and use a weighted cross-entropy loss ($\mathcal{L}_{obj}$ in Eq. 9) between the its outputs and labels indicating if the proposed bounding box contains the object of interests.

3.3 Stent Tracking

With the object candidates at every frame, we first construct an undirected graph $\mathcal{G} = (\mathcal{V}, \mathcal{E})$ across all frames, where vertices $\mathcal{V}$ represent candidate objects proposed by detected landmark pairs and edges $\mathcal{E}$ are full connections of candidate objects between adjacent frames. Every object at frame t is connected with all the candidate objects at frame $(t-1)$ and frame $(t+1)$.

The attributes of vertices are the appearance feature vectors $\mathbf{x}^{(0)}$ extracted from the feature extractor. The edge weights in the initial graph are calculated as a weighted combination of object confidence scores and the spatial similarity by comparing sizes, rotations and locations of objects:

$$\mathbf{w}_{i,j} = \frac{S_i^{\mathcal{O}} + S_j^{\mathcal{O}}}{2}(\alpha_1 IoU(\mathcal{O}_i, \mathcal{O}_j) + \alpha_2 AL(\mathcal{O}_i, \mathcal{O}_j)), \tag{2}$$

where α_1, α_2 are weighting factors, $IoU(\cdot)$ is the IoU between object bounding boxes and $AL(\cdot)$ measures the objects similarity by comparing angles and lengths of the landmark pair vector, defined as:

$$AL(\mathcal{O}_i, \mathcal{O}_j)) = \max(0, \frac{|\boldsymbol{v}_i \cdot \boldsymbol{v}_j|}{|\boldsymbol{v}_i||\boldsymbol{v}_j|} - \frac{||\boldsymbol{v}_i| - |\boldsymbol{v}_j||}{\sqrt{|\boldsymbol{v}_i||\boldsymbol{v}_j|}}). \tag{3}$$

Here, $\boldsymbol{v}_i, \boldsymbol{v}_j$ are the 2D vectors between landmark pairs of $\mathcal{O}_i$ and $\mathcal{O}_j$.

The initialized graph is a powerful representation of the whole video for object tracking, as the appearance features are embedded into vertices and spatiotemporal relations are embedded in the edge weights. To track objects over time, we perform node classification on the graph using a GCN, which identifies the tracked objects at different frames as positive nodes of a corresponding object class while false object detections and untracked objects are classified as negative nodes.

The tracking model is a GCN with a full connected bypass (Fig. 2). The GCN branch consists of a weighted graph convolution layer (wGCL) [12] and two edge convolution layers (ECLs) [24]. Weighted graph convolution layer with self-loop is defined as:

$$\mathbf{x}_i = \mathbf{\Theta} \sum_{j \in \mathcal{N}(i) \cup \{i\}} \frac{\mathbf{w}_{j,i}}{\hat{d}_i} \mathbf{x}_j^{(0)}, \tag{4}$$

with a normalization term $\hat{d}_i = 1 + \sum_{j \in \mathcal{N}(i)} \mathbf{w}_{j,i}$, where $\mathbf{w}_{j,i}$ denotes the edge weight between node j and node i.

Within an edge convolution layer, the edge features are first updated by a FC layer with the features of corresponding vertices pairs connected with each edge:

$$\mathbf{e}_{i,j} = h_{\mathbf{\Theta}}(\mathbf{x}_i, \mathbf{x}_j), \tag{5}$$

where $h_{\mathbf{\Theta}}$ is a nonlinear function with learnable parameters $\mathbf{\Theta}$. Then, ECL updates node features by the summation of updated edge features associated with all the edges emanating from each vertex:

$$\mathbf{x}_i^{EC} = \sum_{j \in \mathcal{N}(i)} \mathbf{e}_{i,j}. \tag{6}$$

The GCN branch effectively updates features of candidate objects by most similar objects from adjacent frames. Moreover, a sequence of convolution layers enables information propagation from even further frames. However, node features solely updated from the GCN are susceptible to noisy neighborhood. For example, if the target object is missed by the upstream detection at a certain frame, such errors would propagate to nearby frames and thus worsen general tracking performance. Therefore, we add a simple parallel FC bypass to the GCN branch. In the FC bypass, all the node features are updated independently without influence from connected nodes:

$$\mathbf{x}_i^{FC} = h_{\mathbf{\Theta}}(\mathbf{x}_i^{(0)}). \tag{7}$$

In the last layer, node features from the GCN branch $\mathbf{x}^{EC}$ are enhance by the FC bypass outputs $\mathbf{x}^{FC}$ for robust object tracking.

Heatmap correction GCN results are then used to correct the heatmaps generated in landmark detection. Specifically, we multiply heatmap values in the a $w \times w$ window centered around a detected landmark with the maximum probability of the graph nodes containing the marker. In this way, the landmark detector can ignore the false positives that can be easily rejected by the GCN model and increase detection sensitivity.

3.4   Training

The landmark detector was trained as a heatmap regression model. Since landmark detection results are used for object proposal, feature extraction, and graph construction, missed landmark would cause irreversible corruption to tracking as the missed object cannot be recovered, while false positives can be filtered out during object proposal or node classification. We used a modified cost term $\mathcal{L}_{hm}$ to ensure fewer false negatives, defined as:

$$\mathcal{L}_{hm} = \frac{\lambda_1}{N}\sum_{i=0}^{N}(y_i - \hat{y}_i)^2 + \frac{\lambda_2}{N}\sum_{i=0}^{N}(ReLU(y_i - \hat{y}_i))^2, \tag{8}$$

where λ_1, λ_2 are weighting factors, y_i, $\hat{y}_i$ are pixel intensities from ground truth and predicted heatmap (corrected by GCN outputs), respectively.

The feature extractor and GCN tracking model are trained as classification problems. We use weighted cross entropy as the cost function to handle the unbalanced labels (most object candidates are negative), which is defined as $-\sum_{i=1}^{C} w_i p_i \log(\hat{p}_i)$, where p, $\hat{p}$ denote the ground truth and predicted object/node class, respectively, and w_i is the predefined weight for class i.

Taken together, the total loss for end-to-end training is

$$\mathcal{L} = \mathcal{L}_{hm} + \alpha\mathcal{L}_{obj} + \beta\mathcal{L}_{node}, \tag{9}$$

where $\mathcal{L}_{obj}$ and $\mathcal{L}_{node}$ are weighted cross entropy losses for object classification and node classification respectively.

4   Experiments

4.1   Datasets

Our in-house stent dataset consists of 4,480 videos (128,029 frames of 512 × 512 8-bit frames) acquired during PCI procedures. The data acquisition was approved by Institutional Review Boards. For in-house videos, the landmarks are radiopaque balloon marker pairs located at two ends of the stent (Fig. 1). There are 114,352 marker pairs in the dataset, which were manually annotated by trained experts. The dataset was split into training, validation, and testing set with a 8:1:1 ratio, which resulted in 3584 videos (103892 frames), 448 videos (12990 frames), and 448 videos (11147 frames) respectively.

In addition, to verify generalization of our method, we included a public dataset in our experiment. The transcatheter aortic valve implantation (TAVI) dataset is a public intraoperative aortography X-ray imaging dataset including 35 videos of 1000 × 1000 pixels 8-bit frames. The original dataset consisted of 11 keypoint annotations including 4 anatomical landmarks, 4 catheter landmarks and 3 additional background landmarks. TAVI is different from PCI procedure but it contains landmark pairs: Catheter Proximal (CP) and Catheter Tip (CT) whose constellations are similar to the stents. We excluded irrelevant landmarks resulting the final TAVI dataset contains 2,652 frames from 26 videos. The TAVI dataset was randomly divided into a training set with 2,027 images from 18 videos and a test set with 625 images from 8 videos. We ran K-fold (k = 5) cross-validation for all models on both private dataset and the TAVI dataset, and the detailed results are reported in the Supplementary Materials.

4.2   Comparative Models

To demonstrate the efficacy of our algorithm, we compared it with several SOTA models on both datasets. First, we selected two coordinate regression models, ResNet V2 [11] and MobileNet V2 [17]. Such regression models detect landmarks in each frame by predicting the landmark center coordinates, which have shown superior performance regressing TAVI catheter landmarks in [9]. Moreover, we include a center based multi-object tracking (MOT) model, Center-Track [27], with two most powerful backbones: DLA-34 [26] and MobileNet V2. CenterTrack detects objects as heatmap regression of centers and simultaneously tracks objects over time by predicting the translations of center points between adjacent frames. CenterTrack has demonstrated extraordinary performance on various MOT benchmark datasets.

4.3   Evaluation Metrics

As our final goal is to enhance the stents by aligning landmark points across frames, detection success rate and localization accuracy are the most important factors to ensure high-quality enhancement. To compare the landmark prediction performance, we use the following detection and localization metrics for evaluation. For detection performance, we used *Precision*, *Recall*, F_1 and *Accuracy*. Landmark locations extracted from heatmaps were paired with the closest ground truth(GT) greedily. A stent prediction was matched if distances of its both landmarks to paired GT were smaller than 5pxs(in-house) or 15pxs(TAVI).

$$Precision = \frac{TP}{TP+FP}; \quad Recall = \frac{TP}{TP+FN}$$
$$F_1 = \frac{2 \cdot TP}{2 \cdot TP + FN + FP}; \quad Accuracy = \frac{TP+TN}{TP+FN+TN+FP}$$

On the successfully detected landmarks, we also evaluated landmark localization accuracy using pixel-wise MAE and RMSE:

$$MAE = \frac{1}{N} \sum_{i=1}^{N} |p_i - \hat{p}_i|; \quad RMSE = \sqrt{\frac{1}{N} \sum_{i=1}^{N} (p_i - \hat{p}_i)^2},$$

where p_i, $\hat{p}_i$ denote predicted and ground truth landmark coordinates.

4.4   Implementation Details

All deep learning models were implemented with PyTorch and run on NVIDIA V100. For the proposed method, the marker detection module was pre-trained on 128×128 image patches, and then the whole model was trained on 10-frame video clips. We used Adam optimizer with a learning rate of 1e–5. For the coordinates regression models, we follow the multi-task learning schemes provided by Danilov et al. [9], using Binary Cross Entropy for the classification branch and Log-Cosh loss for the regression branch, optimized with Adam with a learning rate of 1e–5. Similarly for CenterTrack, we trained the models based on the configuration described in the original publication. The major modification we made was to remove the branch of object bounding box size regression since we do not need the landmark size estimation for our task. We used the focal loss for heatmap regression and L1 loss for offset regression, optimized with Adam with learning rate 1.25e–4. Please see the supplementary material for more details on hyperparameters.

Table 1. Evaluations on **In-house Dataset**. CR means coordinate regression model, and CT means CenterNet. ↑ indicates that higher is better, ↓ indicates that lower is better.

Model		Detection				Localization	
Type	Backbone	Precision↑	Recall↑	F1↑	Accuracy↑	MAE↓	RMSE↓
CR	MobileNetV2	0.620	0.557	0.587	0.415	1.172	1.283
	ResNetV2	0.618	0.604	0.611	0.440	1.064	1.125
CT	MobileNetV2	0.485	0.932	0.638	0.469	0.455	0.837
	DLA34	0.591	**0.936**	0.725	0.568	**0.398**	**0.748**
Ours		**0.907**	0.908	**0.908**	**0.831**	0.597	0.963

Table 2. Evaluations on **TAVI Dataset**.

Model		Detection				Localization	
Type	Backbone	Precision↑	Recall↑	F1↑	Accuracy↑	MAE↓	RMSE↓
CR	MobileNetV2	0.839	0.735	0.784	0.644	12.904	14.129
	ResNetV2	0.857	0.846	0.851	0.741	11.571	12.490
CT	MobileNetV2	0.785	**0.961**	0.864	0.761	**5.100**	**6.159**
	DLA34	0.868	0.930	0.898	0.815	5.418	6.357
Ours		**0.918**	0.957	**0.938**	**0.882**	5.975	6.831

5   Results and Discussion

5.1   Main Results

Table 1 and Table 2 list the results of proposed model and baseline models on the in-house dataset and the public TAVI dataset[1]. The results are consistent on both datasets. In terms of detection, our framework significantly outperforms

---

[1] Example of stent tracking and enhancement comparisons are included in the Supplementary Materials.

the prior state of the art on both datasets. Firstly, tracking models generally excels pure detection models as the additional temporal information is helpful to enhance landmark detection. Another major limitation of the coordinate regression models is that the number of detections is always fixed. Therefore, some targeted landmarks can be easily overwhelmed by strong background noises in coordinate regressor, resulting in a common trend of lower *recall*. On the contrary, heatmap regression models have the flexibility to predict more possible landmarks as long as the desired features are identified from the image. This would help achieve higher recall but also resulting in a large number of false positive landmark detections, indicated as the worse CenterTrack *precision* values compared to coordinate regressors. To solve this issue, in our framework design, we introduced both additional spatial information and temporal information to refine the noisy preliminary detections.

As tracking models, the proposed model shows a remarkable detection margin over CenterTrack. The results demonstrate the effectiveness of our two major innovation in the framework: stent proposal and GCN-based tracking. Instead of tracking multiple landmarks as individual points as in CenterTrack, our model enhanced the isolated detections by introducing stent proposal stage. The feature of possible stents patches between candidate landmark pairs enables the model to enhance landmarks learning and context relationship between landmark pairs. Moreover, as a pure local tracking model, landmarks association of CenterTrack is limited to adjacent frames, where the landmark association is simply learnt as spatial displacements. The information propagation of our multi-layer GCN model enables stent feature nodes in graph, with the combination of both spatial and appearance features, to interact with other nodes in longer time range. We will further prove the effectiveness of our designs in the following ablation studies.

To compare two datasets, our in-house dataset includes more videos with more complicated background compared to the TAVI dataset, which makes the stent tracking a more challenge task for all models, with more likely false positive detections. From the results, we could observe the notable declines in in-house dataset detection metrics, especially in *precision*, for each model compared to TAVI's. However, the *precision* of our framework only dropped from 0.918 to 0.907, which indicates that our framework is more robust to suppress false positives and maintain high accuracy detection in more complex PCI scenes. This robustness advantage is a good reflection of our hierarchical landmark and stent feature extraction efficacy at the stent proposal stage. Even though more complicated background would cause confusion to individual landmark detection, our model can still successfully target the desired landmark pairs by identifying the prominent stent feature in between.

As for localization evaluation, the MAE and MSE values we got from TAVI is about 10 times larger than our own dataset. This is because, firstly, the original frame size is significantly larger than our data; secondly, the landmarks in TAVI, CP and CD, are also about 10 times larger than our landmarks. For example, the CD landmarks are more of a dim blob rather than a single opaque point as in our dataset. To compare the results among models, heatmap regression models perform generally better than coordinate regression models, as the numerical regression still remain an quite arbitrary task for CNN model and localization accuracy would be diminished during the single downsampling path in regressors. CenterTrack achieves the lowest MAE and MSE errors on both datasets. The high accurate localization of CenterTrack is realized by both sophisticated model architecture and the additional two-channel output branch specifically designed for localization offsets regression. The cost for the localization accuracy improvement is computational complexity and time (CenterTrack-DLA34: 10.1 FPS). As for our model, the localization solely depends on the heatmap regression from the faster U-Net (21.7 FPS). We have not tried to add any localization refinement design for the framework efficiency. On our dataset, the mean MAE value at 0.597 is already sufficient for our final stent enhancement task. Further localization refinement with the sacrifice of time would not cause any noticeable improvements. However, we want to note that our framework is very flexible that the current U-Net backbone can be replaced by any other delicate heatmap regression models, if a more accurate localization is necessary for an application.

Table 3. Ablation study on **In-house Dataset**.

Model	Detection				Localization	
	Precision↑	Recall↑	F1↑	Accuracy↑	MAE↓	RMSE↓
Detection only	0.551	**0.918**	0.688	0.525	**0.596**	0.998
Detection refinement	**0.927**	0.532	0.677	0.511	0.598	**0.946**
Separate learning	0.893	0.872	0.883	0.790	**0.596**	0.955
Ours	0.907	0.908	**0.908**	**0.831**	0.597	0.963

5.2   Ablation Studies

The proposed end-to-end learning framework consists of three major modules: heatmap regression based landmark detection (U-Net), landmark-conditioned stent proposal and feature extraction (ResNet), and stent tracking GCN. To demonstrate the benefits of our framework design, we ablated the main components of stent proposal ResNet and stent tracking GCN, as well as the end-to-end learning regime.

Detection only directly utilizes the U-Net to detect individual landmarks at each frame. This model only needs separate frames as inputs and individual landmark locations as supervision.

Detection refinement improves landmark detections in the heatmap prediction from the U-Net backbone and filters false positives by incorporating additional spatial information of the stent between candidate landmarks using a ResNet patch classifier. This two-step model also only requires single frame inputs and no temporal association is used.

Separate Learning includes all three proposed major modules (landmark detection, stent proposal and stent tracking). Instead of simply filtering out false stent patches by the CNN model, this model first uses the convolution layers from well-trained patch classification ResNet to extract feature vectors from candidate stent patches. Then, the features are reconstructed into stent graph and fed into the GCN model for stent tracking over frames. The final model outputs would be the tracked stents at each frame of the input video. However, this three-step approach is achieved by training each model independently: U-Net for landmark detection, ResNet for stents patch classification and GCN for stent tracking.

The ablation study results are shown in Table 3. Our full end-to-end model performs significantly better than the baselines in the detection task. The standalone U-Net yields a very high false positive rate (44.9%) as it is difficult for this model to learn meaningful features to differentiate small landmarks from dark spot noises in the background.

In the detection refinement results, the stent patch classifier significantly reduced the false positives from U-Net predictions, as *precision* surged to 92.7%. However, simply applying the patch classifier to the U-Net outputs would also filter out true stent patches with weaker patch features, resulting in a large drop in *recall*. The above results indicate a trade-off between *precision* and *recall* while applying spatial information based models.

The results of separate learning demonstrate that incorporating GCN temporal stent tracking improved recall and maintained the high precision from detection refinement, resulting in a boost in overall detection accuracy. False negatives are effectively suppressed by the information propagation mechanism in GCN, which helps to enhance the feature of weak but true stent nodes with nearby strong stent nodes in both space and time.

Compared with the separate three-stage learning model, our proposed end-to-end model achieved further improvements in all detection evaluation metrics and reached a better balance between *precision* and *recall*. Although different components of our framework have their specific tasks along the detection and tracking process, the end-to-end learning brings extra benefits, especially by optimizing the data flow between modules. For example, the back-propagated gradients from GCN can also guide the convolutional layers at stent proposal to extract better patch features that would be fed into GCN.

In regard to localization accuracy, all baseline models and the final model show similar performance, as we used the same U-Net backbone for all experiments. The MAE and RMSE values fluctuate within 0.002 and 0.052, which we believe are only from experimental uncertainty and would not have a sensible influence on the final stent enhancement task. For many multi-task learning models on limited data, there is conventionally a trade-off between excellency on specific metrics and good overall performance. The results suggest that the complicated multi-task learning of our end-to-end model would both maintain high localization accuracy and improve detection.

6   Conclusion

In this work, we proposed a novel end-to-end CNN-GCN framework for stent landmarks detection and tracking. The model includes three major modules: (1)

U-Net based heatmap regression for landmark candidate detection, (2) a ResNet for landmark-conditioned stent proposal and feature extraction, and (3) residual-GCN based stent tracking. We compared the proposed model with SOTA coordinate regression models and multi-object tracking models. Our experiments demonstrated that the proposed model remarkably outperformed previous SOTA models in stent detection. We further discussed the flexibility of the proposed framework to accommodate new heatmap regression backbones to overcome the current localization limitations. The ablation experiments showed the benefits of our novel designs in stent proposal ResNet, stent tracking GCN, and end-to-end learning scheme.

References

1. Bier, B., et al.: X-ray-transform invariant anatomical landmark detection for pelvic trauma surgery. In: Frangi, A.F., Schnabel, J.A., Davatzikos, C., Alberola-López, C., Fichtinger, G. (eds.) MICCAI 2018. LNCS, vol. 11073, pp. 55–63. Springer, Cham (2018). https://doi.org/10.1007/978-3-030-00937-3_7
2. Bismuth, V., Vaillant, R.: Elastic registration for stent enhancement in X-ray image sequences. In: 2008 15th IEEE International Conference on Image Processing, pp. 2400–2403 (2008). https://doi.org/10.1109/ICIP.2008.4712276
3. Bismuth, V., Vaillant, R., Funck, F., Guillard, N., Najman, L.: A comprehensive study of stent visualization enhancement in X-ray images by image processing means. Med. Image Anal. **15**(4), 565–576 (2011)
4. Braso, G., Leal-Taixe, L.: Learning a neural solver for multiple object tracking. In: 2020 IEEE/CVF Conference on Computer Vision and Pattern Recognition (CVPR), pp. 6246–6256. IEEE, Seattle, WA, USA. June 2020
5. Butt, A.A., Collins, R.T.: Multi-target Tracking by Lagrangian Relaxation to Min-cost Network Flow. In: 2013 IEEE Conference on Computer Vision and Pattern Recognition, pp. 1846–1853. IEEE, Portland, OR, June 2013
6. Chabi, N., Beuing, O., Preim, B., Saalfeld, S.: Automatic stent and catheter marker detection in X-ray fluoroscopy using adaptive thresholding and classification. Curr. Direct. Biomed. Eng. **6** (2020)
7. Close, R.A., Abbey, C.K., Whiting, J.S.: Improved localization of coronary stents using layer decomposition. Comput. Aided Surg. **7**(2), 84–89 (2002). Jan
8. Close, R.A., Abbey, C.K., Whiting, J.S.: Improved localization of coronary stents using layer decomposition. Comput. Aided Surg. **7**(2), 84–89 (2002). https://doi.org/10.3109/10929080209146019
9. Danilov, V.V., et al.: Aortography keypoint tracking for transcatheter aortic valve implantation based on multi-task learning. Front. Cardiovasc. Med. **8** (2021)
10. Ghesu, F., et al.: An artificial agent for anatomical landmark detection in medical images. In: Ourselin, S., Joskowicz, L., Sabuncu, M.R., Unal, G., Wells, W. (eds.) MICCAI 2016. LNCS, vol. 9902, pp. 229–237. Springer, Cham (2016). https://doi.org/10.1007/978-3-319-46726-9_27
11. He, K., Zhang, X., Ren, S., Sun, J.: Identity mappings in deep residual networks. In: Leibe, B., Matas, J., Sebe, N., Welling, M. (eds.) ECCV 2016. LNCS, vol. 9908, pp. 630–645. Springer, Cham (2016). https://doi.org/10.1007/978-3-319-46493-0_38
12. Kipf, T.N., Welling, M.: Semi-supervised classification with graph convolutional networks. In: ICLR 2017, pp. 24–26 (2017)

13. Lindeberg, T.: Feature detection with automatic scale selection. Int. J. Comput. Vision **30**(2), 79–116 (1998). https://doi.org/10.1023/A:1008045108935

14. Lu, X., Chen, T., Comaniciu, D.: Robust discriminative wire structure modeling with application to stent enhancement in fluoroscopy. In: CVPR 2011, pp. 1121–1127 (2011)

15. Mishell, J.M., Vakharia, K.T., Ports, T.A., Yeghiazarians, Y., Michaels, A.D.: Determination of adequate coronary stent expansion using StentBoost, a novel fluoroscopic image processing technique. Catheter. Cardiovasc. Interv. **69**(1), 84–93 (2007)

16. Pirsiavash, H., Ramanan, D., Fowlkes, C.C.: Globally-optimal greedy algorithms for tracking a variable number of objects. In: CVPR 2011, pp. 1201–1208, June 2011

17. Sandler, M., Howard, A.G., Zhu, M., Zhmoginov, A., Chen, L.C.: Mobilenetv 2: inverted residuals and linear bottlenecks. In: 2018 IEEE/CVF Conference on Computer Vision and Pattern Recognition, pp. 4510–4520 (2018)

18. Schoonenberg, G., Lelong, P., Florent, R., Wink, O., ter Haar Romeny, B.: The effect of automated marker detection on in vivo volumetric stent reconstruction. In: Metaxas, D., Axel, L., Fichtinger, G., Székely, G. (eds.) MICCAI 2008. LNCS, vol. 5242, pp. 87–94. Springer, Heidelberg (2008). https://doi.org/10.1007/978-3-540-85990-1_11

19. Shao, C., Wang, J., Tian, J., Tang, Y.: Coronary Artery Disease: From Mechanism to Clinical Practice. In: Wang, M. (ed.) Coronary Artery Disease: Therapeutics and Drug Discovery. AEMB, vol. 1177, pp. 1–36. Springer, Singapore (2020). https://doi.org/10.1007/978-981-15-2517-9_1

20. Toshev, A., Szegedy, C.: DeepPose: human pose estimation via deep neural networks. In: 2014 IEEE Conference on Computer Vision and Pattern Recognition. pp. 1653–1660. Columbus, OH, USA, June 2014

21. Vernikouskaya, I., Bertsche, D., Dahme, T., Rasche, V.: Cryo-balloon catheter localization in X-ray fluoroscopy using U-net. Int. J. Comput. Assist. Radiol. Surg. **16**(8), 1255–1262 (2021)

22. Wang, B., Wang, G., Chan, K.L., Wang, L.: Tracklet association with Online target-specific metric learning. In: 2014 IEEE Conference on Computer Vision and Pattern Recognition, pp. 1234–1241. IEEE, Columbus, OH, USA, June 2014

23. Wang, Y., Chen, T., Wang, P., Rohkohl, C., Comaniciu, D.: Automatic localization of balloon markers and guidewire in rotational fluoroscopy with application to 3d stent reconstruction. In: Computer Vision - ECCV 2012, pp. 428–441 (2012)

24. Wang, Y., Sun, Y., Liu, Z., Sarma, S.E., Bronstein, M.M., Solomon, J.M.: Dynamic Graph CNN for Learning on Point Clouds. ACM Trans. Graph. **38**(5), 146:1–146:12 (Oct 2019)

25. Wu, Y., Ji, Q.: Facial landmark detection: a literature survey. Int. J. Comput. Vision **127**(2), 115–142 (2019)

26. Yu, F., Wang, D., Shelhamer, E., Darrell, T.: Deep layer aggregation. In: 2018 IEEE/CVF Conference on Computer Vision and Pattern Recognition, pp. 2403–2412 (2018)

27. Zhou, X., Koltun, V., Krähenbühl, P.: Tracking objects as points. In: Vedaldi, A., Bischof, H., Brox, T., Frahm, J.-M. (eds.) ECCV 2020. LNCS, vol. 12349, pp. 474–490. Springer, Cham (2020). https://doi.org/10.1007/978-3-030-58548-8_28

Social ODE: Multi-agent Trajectory Forecasting with Neural Ordinary Differential Equations

Song Wen[✉], Hao Wang, and Dimitris Metaxas

Rutgers University, New Brunswick, USA
song.wen@rutgers.edu, dnm@cs.rutgers.edu

Abstract. Multi-agent trajectory forecasting has recently attracted a lot of attention due to its widespread applications including autonomous driving. Most previous methods use RNNs or Transformers to model agent dynamics in the temporal dimension and social pooling or GNNs to model interactions with other agents; these approaches usually fail to learn the underlying continuous temporal dynamics and agent interactions explicitly. To address these problems, we propose Social ODE which explicitly models temporal agent dynamics and agent interactions. Our approach leverages Neural ODEs to model continuous temporal dynamics, and incorporates distance, interaction intensity, and aggressiveness estimation into agent interaction modeling in latent space. We show in extensive experiments that our Social ODE approach compares favorably with state-of-the-art, and more importantly, can successfully avoid sudden obstacles and effectively control the motion of the agent, while previous methods often fail in such cases.

Keywords: Multi-agent modeling · Ordinary differential equations · Social ODEs

1 Introduction

The goal of multi-agent trajectory forecasting is to estimate future agent trajectories given historical trajectories of multiple agents. It has drawn much attention because of its widespread applications such as autonomous driving, urban data mining, path planning and traffic flow forecasting.

Multi-agent trajectory forecasting is a challenging problem because agent interactions (relational dimension) and underlying agent temporal dynamics (temporal dimension) jointly affect each agent in a nonlinear and complex way. By modeling the relational and temporal dimensions, previous deep learning approaches have shown to be promising. They often use graphs, social pooling, or spatial Transformers to model the relational dimension, while they apply RNNs or temporal Transformers to encode the temporal dimension. However, these methods usually fail to learn the underlying continuous temporal dynamics and the agent interactions with other agents explicitly. For example, spatial

© The Author(s), under exclusive license to Springer Nature Switzerland AG 2022
S. Avidan et al. (Eds.): ECCV 2022, LNCS 13682, pp. 217–233, 2022.
https://doi.org/10.1007/978-3-031-20047-2_13

Transformers estimate the attention between any two agents, but the attention can not explain how one agent affects the other and does not incorporate agent information explicitly, such as distance with other agents. Moreover, RNNs recurrently update the hidden state discretely as shown in Fig. 1a, which is a limitation, because the agent trajectory is continuous as shown in Fig. 1b. These modeling limitations often lead to inaccurate and unsatisfactory results, such as reduced forecasting accuracy and collisions among agents.

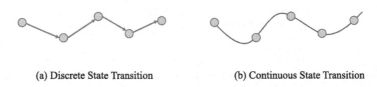

(a) Discrete State Transition   (b) Continuous State Transition

Fig. 1. Differences between discrete state transitions and continuous state transitions

To overcome the above limitations by previous methodologies, we propose Social ODE to explicitly model nonlinear agent interactions and agent temporal dynamics. In our Social ODE framework, the next position of each agent is determined based on the previous position and velocity. The agent's position and velocity are affected by other agents. For example, when we drive a vehicle (agent), if another vehicle approaches dangerously close, we tend to decrease or increase our vehicle's velocity and potentially change direction. Additionally, the distance between vehicles and the driver's driving habits determine how the vehicle's velocity changes. To incorporate into our Social ODE these real-world agent behaviors, we encode in latent space the real-world trajectories and we model them based on an Ordinary Differential Equation as follows:

$$\frac{dh(t)}{dt} = g(h(t), t), \ h(t) = h(0) + \int_0^t g(h, t)dt, \tag{1}$$

where h(t) is the state of the agent's latent trajectory at time t. Therefore, $g(h, t)$ models the current state and the nonlinear interactions with other agents.

The proposed Social ODE is an encoder-decoder architecture based on VAEs, where the encoder projects an agent's historical trajectories to latent space and the decoder recovers the historical trajectories and forecasts future agent trajectories using the latent space representation. To model and learn the agent's continuous latent trajectory from the historical trajectories, we use a Neural ODE that learns the underlying temporal dynamics of the agent's continuous trajectory. The agent's temporal dynamics are determined by the current state and the agent's interactions with other agents. To model the agent interactions explicitly (relational dimension), we decouple them into three components: distance, interaction intensity, and aggressiveness information. All three are multiplied to model their impact on the temporal dynamics of each agent. Because our Social ODE models the relational and temporal dimensions explicitly, an agent can also avoid collisions with other agents. In addition, using repellers and attractors, we can modify an agent's ODE to model more effectively an agent's trajectory, behavior (e.g., courageous) and goals.

The main contributions of our paper are the following:

Model an Agent's Trajectory Relational and Temporal Dimensions Explicitly: Our proposed Social ODE framework models the temporal dimension using a Neural ODE to learn an agent's trajectory continuous temporal dynamics in latent space, which are determined by the agent's current state and the interactions with other agents. We model agent interactions using the following three variables: distance with other agents, agent interaction intensity, and agent aggressiveness.

Effective Agent Trajectory Control Without Retraining: We demonstrate how to modify the ODE to effectively control the trajectory of an agent using attractors and repellers. This allows the modification of an agent's trajectory without retraining. Using our approach we can model dynamic environments where new obstacles and attractors can appear dynamically.

Extensive Experimental Study: We conduct extensive experiments on several datasets by comparing our Social ODE methodology with other state-of-the-art approaches. We demonstrate that our Social ODE achieves improved accuracy on complex trajectory forecasting. We demonstrate its effectiveness in reducing agent collision rates in dynamic environments without retraining.

2   Related Work

Neural Ordinary Differential Equations. In [3], Neural ODE, a new class of deep learning model is proposed, which is a continuous-time neural network by solving ODEs. Following their work in modeling continuous-time sequences, Latent ODE [23] is proposed to model the irregularly-sampled time series. ODE2VAE [29] models high-dimensional sequences by a latent second order ODE. Dupont et al. propose Augmented neural ODE [5] to make the model more expressive by preserving the topology of the input space. To model non-continuous observations using Neural ODEs, Brouwer et al. propose GRU-ODE-Bayes [4]. Moreover, [6,13,14,20,22,28] analyze and adapt Neural ODEs in other applications such as density estimation. [19,25,27] apply Neural ODEs in trajectory modeling or planning. Grunbacher et al. analyze the verification of Neural ODEs [9,10]. Park et al. generate continuous-time video by Neural ODE [21].

Inspired by these approaches, we propose Social ODE based on Latent ODE to model the realistic trajectory and underlying temporal dynamics of the latent trajectory. Similar to Latent ODE, our model also implements trajectory interpolation and extrapolation. The difference is that our model encodes the agent interactions in the ordinary differential equation.

Multi-agent Trajectory Forecasting. Social LSTM [1] is proposed by Alahi et al., which applies social pooling in the hidden state of LSTM. Following

Social LSTM, Gupta et al. propose Social GAN [12], which uses global social pooling and GAN to generate a trajectory consistent with the input. Graph-VRNN [26] proposed by Sun et al. adopt graph network and RNN to model the relational dimension. Kipf et al. represent underlying agent interaction in latent space by graph [15]. Based on their work, Graber develop dynamic neural relational inferece [8], instead of static relation in [15]. Trajectron++ [24] is a graph-structured model with LSTM and accounts for environmental information. EvolveGraph [18] forecasts the trajectory by dynamic relational reasoning by latent interaction graph. AgentFormer [30] proposes a novel Transformer to joint model social and temporal dimensions. Gu et al. propose DenseTNT [11] based on VectorNet [7] to encode all agent to vectors and graph.

Different from previous methods, our proposed Social ODE learns the underlying agent trajectory temporal dynamics in latent space using an ODE. The advantage of our approach is that it explicitly models the continuous-time agent trajectory which offers explainability. Besides, we model the relational dimension by incorporating agent distance, interaction intensity, and aggressiveness explicitly in the ODE.

3   Methodology

In this section, we first define the problem of trajectory forecasting. Then we present an overview of our proposed Social ODE and provide details of the formulation of the associated encoder, decoder, and loss function. Finally, we present agent trajectory control without retraining using Social ODEs.

3.1   Trajectory Forecasting

Multi-agent trajectory forecasting aims to estimate the future trajectories of multiple agents $\mathbf{X}_{T_h+1:T_h+T_f} = \{\mathbf{x}^i_{T_h+1}, \mathbf{x}^i_{T_h+2}, ..., \mathbf{x}^i_{T_h+T_f}, i = 1, ..., N\}$ simultaneously giving their historical trajectories $\mathbf{X}_{0:T_h} = \{\mathbf{x}^i_0, \mathbf{x}^i_1, ..., \mathbf{x}^i_{T_h}, i = 1, ..., N\}$, where N denotes the number of agents. T_h and T_f denote the historical and future trajectory temporal lengths, respectively. X_t denotes the state of all agents at time t and $\mathbf{x}^i_t$ denotes the state of agent i at time t, including its position and velocity.

3.2   Social ODE: Overview

Similar to Latent ODEs, which is a continuous-time, latent-variable method to model time series, our Social ODE is also an Encoder-Decoder architecture. As shown in Fig. 2, it concludes two components:

Encoder. It encodes the historical trajectory for each agent $\mathbf{X}^i_{0:T_h}$ into latent space. The encoder generates the initial state in latent space, which is set as the initial value for the ordinary differential equation. Different from a Latent ODE, we use a Spatio-Temporal Transformer as the encoder for improved learning.

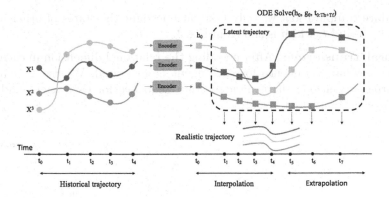

Fig. 2. Overview of the proposed Social ODE, which is composed of an encoder and a decoder. The encoder transfers the historical trajectory to latent space. The decoder first uses the ODE solver to generate a latent trajectory and then recover it back to a realistic trajectory. The output includes historical trajectory (interpolation) and future trajectory (extrapolation).

Decoder. It generates latent trajectories and decodes the latent vector back to the real-world state, i.e., the agent's trajectory position and velocity. After sampling the latent vector from the encoder, we design an ODE to model the agent's interactions in the decoder. The agent's interactions are modeled by incorporating distance, interaction intensity, and aggressiveness explicitly in the ODE, while we model the temporal dimension based on the current latent state. Using the initial state in latent space, we solve the ODE to generate latent trajectories. At the end of our approach, the latent trajectory is converted to a real-world trajectory.

Using our approach, an agent's trajectory i, is modeled as:

$$\mu_{h^i}, \sigma_{h^i} = g_{enc}(x^i_{0:T_h}, x^j_{0:T_h}), \; j \neq i \tag{2}$$

$$\mathbf{h}^i_0 \sim N(\mu_{h^i}, \sigma_{h^i}), \tag{3}$$

$$\mathbf{h}^i_0, \mathbf{h}^i_1, ..., \mathbf{h}^i_{T_h+T_f} = \text{ODESolve}(\mathbf{h}^i_0, g_\theta, t_{0:T_h+T_f}) \tag{4}$$

$$\text{each } \hat{x}^i_t \sim p(\hat{x}^i_t | \mathbf{h}^i_t), \tag{5}$$

where Eq. (2) is the encoder and Eqs. (3) to (5) model the decoder. ODESolver is the numerical ODE solver given equation $\frac{dh}{dt} = g_\theta$ with initial value $\mathbf{h}^i_0$.

3.3   Encoder: Spatio-Temporal Transformer

To encode the historical trajectory for each agent to latent vectors, we use a Spatio-Temporal Transformer for each agent and the architecture is shown in Fig. 3.

Spatial Transformer. It is used to encode the relational dimension. Because the state of agent i at time t is only affected by states of other agents before time

t, to reduce computation, we only take into account the states of other agents in time $t-1$ and t, which is shown in Fig. 3.

Temporal Transformer. After encoding the relational dimension in each time step, the new state sequence for each agent is generated. We use a Temporal Transformer to encode the generated state sequence for each agent and pool them to generate a latent vector.

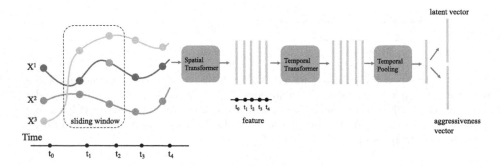

Fig. 3. The architecture of Spatio-Temporal Transformer. The figure shows that we apply Spatio-Temporal Transformer for trajectory X^1. When the red point is modeled, we improve the efficiency of the algorithm by using points only within the sliding window, which are states of other agents in the previous and current time steps.

3.4   Decoder

We use the decoder to recover the real-world trajectory from the initial value h_0. There are two steps in the decoder: solving an ODE and transferring the latent state to the real-world state.

In the Latent ODE model [3], after estimating the posterior $p(h_{t_0}|x_{0:t})$, the initial value h_{t_0} is sampled. These initial values are used to solve the corresponding ODE. However, the relational dimension is ignored in the standard Latent ODE formulation. To model agent interactions and improve agent prediction trajectory, we encode state sequences of each agent in the latent space and represent agent interaction in latent space using three variables: distance, interaction intensity and aggressiveness. We define the equation as:

$$\frac{dh_i(t)}{dt} = g_\theta(h_i(t), h_j(t)) \tag{6}$$

$$= \sum_{j \neq i} \frac{1}{||h_i - h_j||} k(i,j)a_i + f_\theta(h_i(t)), \tag{7}$$

where $h_i(t)$ denotes the latent vector of agent i in time t and g_θ is the derivative of the latent vector. Besides, $||h_i - h_j||$ denotes distance information between agent i and agent j, while $k(i,j)$ is the interaction intensity between two agents. a_i denotes the aggressiveness of agent i.

The agent interaction is modeled based on the following three components:

Interaction Intensity. It models how agent j affects the dynamics of agent i, which is denoted by $k(i, j)$. We concatenate the latent vectors of two agents (h_t^i and h_t^j) and the derivatives of two agents in the previous time step ($\frac{dh_t^i}{dt}$ and $\frac{dh_t^j}{dt}$), and apply a fully connected neural network to estimate $k(i, j)$.

Distance. It is obvious that the distance between two agents has a great influence on each other and the shorter distance between two agents means the greater influence. We represent this relationship explicitly in latent space, which is $\frac{1}{||h_i - h_j||}$, where i denotes the agent that is modeled and j denotes other agents. In latent space, the L2 distant $||h_i - h_j||$ of two agent contains realistic distance information. When agent j come to i, the dynamics of agent i are affected, so $\frac{dh_j(t)}{dt}$ becomes larger.

Aggressiveness. In real-world situations, some agents tend to refuse to avoid other agents and others do not. Therefore, besides the distant information, the aggressiveness of an agent should also be incorporated. The aggressiveness can also be learned from the historical trajectory of the agent. As shown in Fig. 3 we use other fully connected networks before generating a latent vector in the encoder to estimate the aggressiveness vector.

In the equation, interaction intensity, distance and aggressiveness are element-wise multiplied together as an agent interaction term. Besides agent interaction, the previous state is also essential to learning temporal dynamics. Similar to standard latent ODE, we use fully connected networks in the temporal modeling, which is denoted by $f_\theta(h_i(t))$ in Eq. (7). We add the agent interaction and feature of the current state together as the derivative of latent vector $h(t)$. By an ODE Solver, $h_{t_1}, h_{t_2}, .., h_{t_n}$ are estimated. Then we use fully connected neural networks to decode latent vectors to realistic states $x_{t_1}, x_{t_2}, .., x_{t_n}$ for each agent.

3.5   Loss Function

Because our method is based on the VAE model, we use the negative evidence lower bound (ELBO) in our loss function:

$$L_{elbo} = -E_{q_\phi(h_{t_0}|X_{0:T_h})}[\log p_\theta(X_{0:T_h}|h_{t_0})] + KL(q_\phi(h_{t_0}|X_{0:T_h})||p_\theta(h_{t_0})), \quad (8)$$

where $q_\phi(h_{t_0}|X)$ is the posterior distribution and $p_\theta(X_{0:T_h}|h_{t_0})$ denotes the interpolation period that recovers the historical trajectory.

Because ELBO only takes into account historical trajectories, the MSE loss is used to supervise prediction accuracy, which is the extrapolation period:

$$L_{mse} = \sum_i (\hat{y}_i - y_i)^2. \quad (9)$$

In training, the whole trajectory $X_{0:T_h+T_f}$ is input to the Social ODE. The output trajectory of input $X_{0:T_h+T_f}$ and input $X_{0:T_h}$ should be the same because they recover the same trajectory. Therefore, their latent vectors have the same distribution. Then we use another KL divergence as a loss function:

$$L_{kl} = KL(q_\phi(z_{t_0}|X_{0:T_h})||q_\phi(z_{t_0}|X_{0:T_h+T_f}))). \tag{10}$$

Consequently, the overall loss function is

$$L = L_{elbo} + L_{mse} + L_{kl} \tag{11}$$

3.6   Agent Controlling with Social ODE

Apart from forecasting future trajectories, our proposed Social ODE can also control a given agent's trajectory, by adding a term to the ODE based on repellers and attractors without the need for retraining. This control approach enables us to model real-world situations where obstacles (other agents) and agent goals can change in real-time and require the modification of the agent's trajectory.

Attractor and Repeller. Because our proposed Social ODE explicitly models the relational dimension, it is not hard to control an agent by modifying the relational dimension dynamically due to real-time changes in the other agents, obstacles and goals. We do this by adding terms modeling these changes as attractors and repellers. If we want to set one attractor (e.g., a location where the agent wants to reach), the ODE Eq. (7) can be modified as follows:

$$\frac{dh_i(t)}{dt} = \sum_{j \neq i} \frac{1}{||h_i - h_j||} k(i,j)a_i + f_\theta(h_i(t), t) - \lambda(h_i(t) - h_g), \tag{12}$$

where h_g denotes the latent vector of the attractor and λ is a positive coefficient.

We show below that this modeling of an attractor dynamically reduces the distance between the agent and the goal (attractor). The distance information in latent space between the agent and the attractor is modeled as $(h_i(t) - h_g)^2$. We can prove that this distance keeps getting smaller over time by examining its time derivative as follows:

$$\frac{d(h_i(t) - h_g)^2}{dt} = 2(h_i(t) - h_g) \times \frac{dh_i(t)}{dt} \tag{13}$$

$$= 2(h_i(t) - h_g)[\sum_{j \neq i} \frac{1}{||h_i - h_j||} k(i,j)a_i + f_\theta(h_i(t), t)] - 2\lambda(h_i(t) - h_g)^2.$$

Since λ is positive then the term is negative: $-2\lambda(h_i(t) - h_g)^2 < 0$. Therefore, if λ is large enough, $\frac{d(h_i(t)-h_g)^2}{dt} < 0$, which means the distance between the agent and the attractor decreases as time goes by.

Similarly, to add many attractors and repellers the ODE Eq. (12) is further modified as follows:

$$\frac{dh_i(t)}{dt} = \sum_{j \neq i} \frac{1}{||h_i - h_j||} k(i,j)a_i + f_\theta(h_i(t), t) + \sum_{n}(-\lambda_n(h_i(t) - h_g^n)) \tag{14}$$

$$+ \sum_{m}(\lambda_m(h_i(t) - h_g^m)),$$

where $(h^m)_g$ denotes the latent vector of a repeller and λ_m is a positive coefficient.

Adjusting Agent Interactions. To adjust the strength of agent interactions, we further modify the first two terms in Eq. (14) by introducing two new parameters β_1 and β_2 to adjust the dynamics of agent interactions as shown in the following equation. For example, if β_1 is small and β_2 is large, the agent will be more aggressive and take less into account the other close-by agents.

$$\beta_1 \sum_{j\neq i} \frac{1}{||h_i - h_j||} k(i,j)a_i + \beta_2 f_\theta(h_i(t)). \tag{15}$$

Agent Return to Desired Trajectory. We modeled obstacle avoidance (different from agent interactions) as repellers. However, the influence of repellers can make the agent deviate from the desired trajectory. In order to ensure the agent returns to the desired trajectory after obstacle avoidance, we add one more term to Eq. (14) as follows:

$$-\lambda \min_{\tilde{h}}(h_i(t) - \tilde{h}), \tag{16}$$

where $\tilde{h}_i(t)$ is the original trajectory prior to obstacle avoidance and the term $\min_{\tilde{h}}(h_i(t) - \tilde{h})$ is an attractor and ensures that the agent always returns to the closest point of the original trajectory.

After adding bother terms to Eq. (14) the final equation is:

$$\frac{dh_i(t)}{dt} = \sum_{j\neq i} \frac{1}{||h_i - h_j||} k(i,j)a_i + f_\theta(h_i(t),t) + \sum_n (-\lambda_n(h_i(t) - h_g^n)) \tag{17}$$
$$+ \sum_m (\lambda_m(h_i(t) - h_g^m)) - \lambda \min_{\tilde{h}}(h_i(t) - \tilde{h}),$$

4 Experiments

In this section, we present experimental results to evaluate the performance of our novel Social ODE framework. In Sects. 4.1 and 4.2, we present the training and test datasets and implementation details, respectively. Then we show comparison results with the state-of-the-art methods in Sect. 4.3. We present the agent control without the need for retraining in Sect. 4.4. Finally in Sect. 4.5, we conduct the ablation study.

4.1 Datasets

Our model is evaluated on the inD [2], rounD [17], and highD [16] traffic datasets. Those are datasets of naturalistic road user trajectories collected by a drone. For each dataset, 80% of the data are used for training and validation, and 20% are used for testing. We sample every 8 s as one instance and delete the case where some agents leave the area in the middle. In each trajectory, we sample one point every 0.4 s, so there are 20 points for agents which are present all the time. The trajectories in the first 4 s are used as input and those in the next 4 s are ground truth.

4.2   Implementation and Training Details

We normalize all the coordinates to range from 0 to 1. In the encoder module, the dimension of key, query and value is set to 128 and the number of heads is set to 8. Because there is no sequence information in the Spacial Transformer, positional encoding is only used in the Temporal Transformer. In the decoder module, the dimension of the latent vector is also 128. To model interaction intensity, a 512×128 fully connected network is used. We also use a 128×128 fully connected network to replace the last layer of the encoder to generate the aggressiveness vector. In the decoder process, there are two parts: interpolation and extrapolation. While inputting a historical trajectory $X_{0:T_h}$, our model will generate $\hat{X}_{0:T_h+T_f}$. The process of generating $\hat{X}_{0:T_h}$ is the interpolation, which is recovering the input like a VAE model, and that of $\hat{X}_{T_h+1:T_f}$ is the extrapolation, which estimates the prediction.

In the training phase, the Adam optimizer is used and the learning rate is set initially to 10^{-4}, which is then decayed by a factor of 0.5 when the loss comes to a plateau. We train the model on A100 GPUs using PyTorch.

4.3   Comparison Results

Evaluation Metric. We evaluated our model by ADE (Average Displacement Error), which is defined as

$$ADE = \frac{1}{T} \sum \|x_t^i - \hat{x}_t^i\|, \tag{18}$$

where x_t^i is the ground truth and $\hat{x}_t^i$ is the prediction in extrapolation. ADE is used to evaluate the mean square error between the ground truth and the prediction.

Baseline. We compare our Social ODE with several state-of-the-art methods: (1) Social LSTM [1]: Social pooling of hidden states in LSTM is used to model agent interactions. (2) Social GAN [12]: GAN is combined with LSTM encoder-decoder to judge whether the generated trajectory is similar to the realistic generated trajectory. (3) DenseTNT [11]: The graph is used to extract the relationship among different agents and each node in the graph is an agent's trajectory. (4) AgentFormer [30]: It is a Socio-Temporal Transformer encoder-decoder model to jointly extract the time dimension and social dimension. The codes of all the above methods have been published, so we directly train and evaluate these models on inD, roundD and highD traffic datasets.

As shown in Table 1, Social ODE achieves better performance than Social LSTM, Social GAN, and DenseTNT. We classify the trajectory into the 'curve' and 'straight' classes. From Table 1, if forecasting is for a long period of time, Social ODE always performs best in curved trajectories, which means Social ODE can deal better with complicated trajectories.

New Agents and Obstacles Dynamically Appearing. Most previous methods assume that the number of agents/obstacles does not change over time.

Table 1. Evaluation on inD, rounD and highD traffic datasets. The bold means best performance.

Method	Length	inD		highD		rounD	
		Straight	Curve	Straight	Curve	Straight	Curve
Social LSTM	2 s	0.2474	0.8537	0.2846	0.8347	0.2367	0.8986
Social GAN		0.2537	0.8236	0.2564	0.8977	0.2679	0.8876
DenseTNT		0.2367	**0.8046**	0.2465	0.8546	0.2268	0.8464
AgentFomer		**0.2346**	0.8124	**0.2368**	0.8263	**0.2140**	**0.8259**
Social ODE		0.2408	0.8147	0.2406	**0.8135**	0.2254	0.8357
Social LSTM	4 s	0.7973	3.1463	0.9525	3.5364	0.7268	2.6473
Social GAN		0.7861	3.1583	0.8367	3.4637	0.7483	2.6940
DenseTNT		0.7794	3.1578	0.7431	3.1778	0.6543	2.4764
AgentFomer		**0.7604**	3.1483	**0.6814**	3.1527	**0.5924**	2.4748
Social ODE		0.7728	**3.1417**	0.6873	**3.1509**	0.6005	**2.4738**
Social LSTM	8 s	2.7536	8.3456	2.4570	9.3365	2.5583	9.1346
Social GAN		2.6573	8.2478	2.3279	9.6437	2.9546	8.9446
DenseTNT		2.6644	8.1475	2.1345	9.3464	2.7854	8.4677
AgentFomer		**2.3474**	8.1457	**2.1167**	9.3258	**2.5337**	8.3464
Social ODE		2.6064	**8.1208**	2.1384	**9.3203**	2.6447	**8.3384**

However, in reality, some agents/obstacles may enter or leave during the course of a trajectory, which has a social influence on other agents. For example, in the autonomous driving scenario, the appearance of a pedestrian(s) close to or in front of the vehicle/agent can happen suddenly and the agent needs to change its trajectory. We conduct a set of experiments to show how the agent's trajectory is modified when a sudden obstacle appears. To model the sudden obstacle, we place a static and a moving obstacle in the predicted agent trajectory from the test dataset. Using our Social ODE approach we observe that the agent modifies the original trajectory to avoid the obstacle collision. In this experiment we test how one agent adapts its trajectory to sudden appearing obstacles, while the trajectories of the other agents are not modified and are kept constant. In our experiments we consider that a collision occurs when the distance between the agent and the obstacle is less than 0.5 m. Table 2 shows the collision rate of all methods. Social ODE achieves the lowest collision rate while avoiding the static or moving agent. Figure 4 shows some examples of the agent avoiding an obstacle using our approach. It demonstrates that our model can correctly extract the social relationship among agents and make agents realize that they should avoid other agents or obstacles although there are no similar cases in the training dataset.

4.4   Agent Controlling with Social ODE

In Sect. 3.6 we showed how our proposed Social ODE can control the agent's trajectory through Eq. (17). We conduct experiments to show how the use of the attractor (target) and the repeller (obstacles) affect the agent. All the experiments in this section are conducted during testing, without the need for retraining.

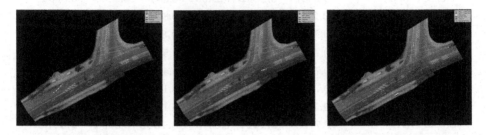

Fig. 4. Sudden obstacle visualization. In each image, the green trajectory is the ground truth and the white one is the predicted result. The black point is the sudden obstacle. The obstacle is placed in the ground truth trajectory. The white trajectory demonstrates that the agent successfully avoids the obstacle.

Table 2. Collision rate of different methods when introducing a sudden obstacle in the trajectory. Numbers in bold show the best performance.

Method	Social LSTM	Social GAN	DenseTNT	AgentFormer	Social ODE
Static obstacle	28.6%	29.6%	22.8%	28.4%	**8.8%**
Moving obstacle	32.4%	35.2%	32.6%	33.0%	**12.8%**

Target. In the test dataset, one point near the last trajectory point is set as the target. We represent the target in latent space using the encoder and use Eq. (17) to model the agent. λ is set from 0 to 10 and the reaching rate is computed within 8 s from the beginning of the trajectory. When $\lambda = 0$ then there is no target modeling within our Social ODE model. In this case reaching the target is defined when the distance between the agent and the target is less than 0.5 m. All other methods except denseTNT cannot use the target to control the agent. DenseTNT directly plans the path between the start point and the target and therefore can't be used for dynamic target or obstacle introduction like our approach. We therefore present results of target reaching using our method in Table 3, when λ changes. The results show that the larger the value of λ results in stronger attraction by the target.

Obstacle Avoidance and Return to the Agent Trajectory. In 4.3, showed how in our approach an agent can avoid an obstacle. However, after the target avoids a sudden obstacle, it should come back to the original trajectory assuming

Table 3. Reaching rate with different values of λ, if we dynamically set the target to be the last trajectory point, during agent movement. Bold numbers mean the best performance.

λ	0	2	4	6	8	10
Reaching rate	4.8%	8.6%	25.4%	43.6%	71.4%	**87.8%**

the target is not changed. We do some experiments to verify whether Eq. (17) can control an agent to avoid a sudden obstacle and return to the original trajectory. Similar to 4.4, we place a static obstacle in the predicted trajectory. Figure 5 shows that the agent can bypass the obstacle, similarly to how drivers react when encountering while driving a sudden obstacle. This is done without retraining and there is no similar case in the training dataset.

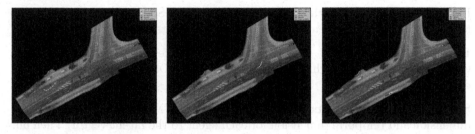

Fig. 5. Avoid the obstacle and return to the agent Trajectory. In each image, the green trajectory is the ground truth and the white is the predicted result. The black point is the sudden obstacle. The agent avoids the obstacle and returns to the original trajectory.

Obstacles and Targets. We also conducted experiments where we introduced obstacles and targets dynamically during an agent's trajectory and we showed modifications to the agent trajectory and the successful reaching of the target. Figure 6 demonstrates that the agent can avoid the obstacle and reach the target.

Adjusting the Relational Dimension. In Eq. (15), the β_1 and β_2 are parameters that can modify the effect of the relational dimension. Larger β_1 means the agent's trajectory tends to be affected more by other agents and larger β_2 means the agent's trajectory tends to keep its previous moving pattern. The results in Fig. 6b show the effect of those parameters on agent trajectories.

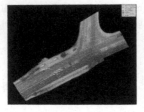 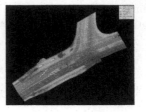

(a) Avoid obstacle and reach target   (b) Adjust the relational dimension

Fig. 6. (a) Avoid the obstacle and reach the target. The white trajectory is the output result of social ODE. The green one is the ground truth. The cyan point is the target and the black point is the obstacle. (b) Adjusting the relational dimension. White trajectory: $\beta_1 = 1$. Pink trajectory: $\beta_1 = 2$.

4.5   Ablation Study

In this section, we verify the design of the proposed Social ODE model. We do this by replacing components with similar components as follows.

Latent ODE Encoder + Our Decoder. We replace the decoder of the Latent ODE with our decoder, which enables the Latent ODE to model the relational dimension.

Social LSTM + Our Decoder. We use social LSTM to encode the relational dimension and temporal dimension for each agent to the latent vector. Then our decoder recovers the latent trajectory back to a realistic trajectory.

Our Encoder + Neural ODE. Our Spatio-temporal Transformer is used as the encoder, which generates the latent vector. The neural ODE decodes the latent vector to position and velocity.

Our Encoder + Social Pooling ODE. Our Spatio-temporal Transformer is used as the encoder to generate a latent vector. Instead of modeling the relational dimension by distance, interaction dynamics and aggressiveness, we use the social pooling from the Social LSTM model for latent vector in each time step.

The results are shown in Table 4. From the table, we can see that all the changes in our components result in a performance decrease, which means the design of our Social ODE is effective.

Table 4. Ablation Study: evaluation of changing some components on inD, rounD and highD traffic datasets. The forecasting length is 4 s. Bold depicts the best performance.

Method	inD		highD		rounD	
	Straight	Curve	Straight	Curve	Straight	Curve
Latent ODE + Our decoder	0.7732	3.2147	0.7886	3.3394	0.6373	2.5367
Social LSTM + Our decoder	0.7864	3.1584	0.7630	3.3256	0.6357	2.5774
Our encoder + Neural ODE	0.7925	3.1647	0.7974	3.2754	0.6438	2.6227
Our encoder + Social pooling ODE	0.7857	3.1594	0.7533	3.2740	0.6363	2.5830
Social ODE	**0.7728**	**3.1417**	**0.6873**	**3.1509**	**0.6005**	**2.4738**

5   Conclusion

In this paper, we present a Social ODE, which models and learns agent interaction and underlying temporal dynamics explicitly. To model the agent interaction, our Social ODE decouples it into three components: distance, interaction intensity and aggressiveness, all of which are multiplied to estimate the relational dimension. Meanwhile, the underlying temporal dynamics are learned by a Neural ODE in latent space, which includes agent interaction and the current state. We have validated the performance of Social ODE through extensive experiments using traffic datasets. Compared with previous schemes, our Social ODE is shown to achieve favorable performance in terms of forecasting accuracy. Social ODE can also allow the dynamic insertion of obstacles, targets and agents during the course of an agent's trajectory without *retraining*. As a result, our model achieves a lower collision rate when sudden obstacles occur in the trajectory and can control the agent motion by dynamically inserting attractors or repellers.

Acknowledgements. Research partially funded by research grants to Metaxas from NSF: 1951890, 2003874, 1703883, 1763523 and ARO MURI SCAN.

References

1. Alahi, A., Goel, K., Ramanathan, V., Robicquet, A., Fei-Fei, L., Savarese, S.: Social LSTM: human trajectory prediction in crowded spaces. In: Proceedings of the IEEE Conference on Computer Vision and Pattern Recognition, pp. 961–971 (2016)
2. Bock, J., Krajewski, R., Moers, T., Runde, S., Vater, L., Eckstein, L.: The IND dataset: a drone dataset of naturalistic road user trajectories at German intersections. In: 2020 IEEE Intelligent Vehicles Symposium (IV), pp. 1929–1934 (2020). https://doi.org/10.1109/IV47402.2020.9304839
3. Chen, R.T., Rubanova, Y., Bettencourt, J., Duvenaud, D.K.: Neural ordinary differential equations. In: 31st Proceedings of the Conference on Advances in Neural Information Processing Systems (2018)

4. De Brouwer, E., Simm, J., Arany, A., Moreau, Y.: GRU-ODE-Bayes: continuous modeling of sporadically-observed time series. In: Proceedings of the 32 International Conference on Advances in Neural Information Processing Systems (2019)
5. Dupont, E., Doucet, A., Teh, Y.W.: Augmented neural odes. In: Proceedings of the 32 International Conference on Advances in Neural Information Processing Systems (2019)
6. Durkan, C., Bekasov, A., Murray, I., Papamakarios, G.: Neural spline flows. In: Proceedings of the 32 International Conference on Advances in Neural Information Processing Systems (2019)
7. Gao, J., et al.: VectorNet: encoding HD maps and agent dynamics from vectorized representation. In: Proceedings of the IEEE/CVF Conference on Computer Vision and Pattern Recognition, pp. 11525–11533 (2020)
8. Graber, C., Schwing, A.: Dynamic neural relational inference for forecasting trajectories. In: Proceedings of the IEEE/CVF Conference on Computer Vision and Pattern Recognition Workshops, pp. 1018–1019 (2020)
9. Gruenbacher, S., et al.: GoTube: scalable stochastic verification of continuous-depth models. arXiv preprint arXaiv:2a107.08467 (2021)
10. Grunbacher, S., Hasani, R., Lechner, M., Cyranka, J., Smolka, S.A., Grosu, R.: On the verification of neural odes with stochastic guarantees. In: Proceedings of the AAAI Conference on Artificial Intelligence, vol. 35, pp. 11525–11535 (2021)
11. Gu, J., Sun, C., Zhao, H.: DenseTNT: end-to-end trajectory prediction from dense goal sets. In: Proceedings of the IEEE/CVF International Conference on Computer Vision, pp. 15303–15312 (2021)
12. Gupta, A., Johnson, J., Fei-Fei, L., Savarese, S., Alahi, A.: Social GAN: socially acceptable trajectories with generative adversarial networks. In: Proceedings of the IEEE Conference on Computer Vision and Pattern Recognition, pp. 2255–2264 (2018)
13. Hasani, R., Lechner, M., Amini, A., Rus, D., Grosu, R.: Liquid time-constant networks. arXiv preprint arXiv:2006.04439 (2020)
14. Jia, J., Benson, A.R.: Neural jump stochastic differential equations. In: 32nd Proceedings of the International Conference on Advances in Neural Information Processing Systems (2019)
15. Kipf, T., Fetaya, E., Wang, K.C., Welling, M., Zemel, R.: Neural relational inference for interacting systems. In: International Conference on Machine Learning, pp. 2688–2697. PMLR (2018)
16. Krajewski, R., Bock, J., Kloeker, L., Eckstein, L.: The highd dataset: A drone dataset of naturalistic vehicle trajectories on German highways for validation of highly automated driving systems. In: 2018 21st International Conference on Intelligent Transportation Systems (ITSC), pp. 2118–2125 (2018). https://doi.org/10.1109/ITSC.2018.8569552
17. Krajewski, R., Moers, T., Bock, J., Vater, L., Eckstein, L.: The round dataset: a drone dataset of road user trajectories at roundabouts in Germany. In: 2020 IEEE 23rd International Conference on Intelligent Transportation Systems (ITSC), pp. 1–6 (2020). https://doi.org/10.1109/ITSC45102.2020.9294728
18. Li, J., Yang, F., Tomizuka, M., Choi, C.: EvolveGraph: multi-agent trajectory prediction with dynamic relational reasoning. Adv. Neural. Inf. Process. Syst. **33**, 19783–19794 (2020)
19. Liang, Y., Ouyang, K., Yan, H., Wang, Y., Tong, Z., Zimmermann, R.: Modeling trajectories with neural ordinary differential equations. In: IJCAI, pp. 1498–1504 (2021)

20. Liebenwein, L., Hasani, R., Amini, A., Rus, D.: Sparse flows: pruning continuous-depth models. In: 34th Proceedings of the International Conference on Advances in Neural Information Processing Systems (2021)
21. Park, S., et al.: VID-ODE: continuous-time video generation with neural ordinary differential equation. In: Proceedings of the AAAI Conference on Artificial Intelligence, vol. 35, pp. 2412–2422 (2021)
22. Quaglino, A., Gallieri, M., Masci, J., Koutník, J.: SNODE: spectral discretization of neural odes for system identification. arXiv preprint arXiv:1906.07038 (2019)
23. Rubanova, Y., Chen, R.T., Duvenaud, D.K.: Latent ordinary differential equations for irregularly-sampled time series. In: 32nd Proceedings of the International Conference on Advances in Neural Information Processing Systems (2019)
24. Salzmann, Tim, Ivanovic, Boris, Chakravarty, Punarjay, Pavone, Marco: Trajectron++: dynamically-feasible trajectory forecasting with heterogeneous data. In: Vedaldi, Andrea, Bischof, Horst, Brox, Thomas, Frahm, Jan-Michael. (eds.) ECCV 2020. LNCS, vol. 12363, pp. 683–700. Springer, Cham (2020). https://doi.org/10.1007/978-3-030-58523-5_40
25. Shi, R., Morris, Q.: Segmenting hybrid trajectories using latent odes. In: International Conference on Machine Learning, pp. 9569–9579. PMLR (2021)
26. Sun, C., Karlsson, P., Wu, J., Tenenbaum, J.B., Murphy, K.: Stochastic prediction of multi-agent interactions from partial observations. arXiv preprint arXiv:1902.09641 (2019)
27. Vorbach, C., Hasani, R., Amini, A., Lechner, M., Rus, D.: Causal navigation by continuous-time neural networks. In: 34th Proceedings of the International Conference on Advances in Neural Information Processing Systems (2021)
28. Yan, H., Du, J., Tan, V.Y., Feng, J.: On robustness of neural ordinary differential equations. arXiv preprint arXiv:1910.05513 (2019)
29. Yildiz, C., Heinonen, M., Lahdesmaki, H.: ODE2VAE: deep generative second order odes with Bayesian neural networks. In: 32nd Proceedings of the Advances in Neural Information Processing Systems 2019)
30. AgentFormer: agent-aware transformers for socio-temporal multi-agent forecasting. In: Proceedings of the IEEE/CVF International Conference on Computer Vision, pp. 9813–9823 (2021)

Social-SSL: Self-supervised Cross-Sequence Representation Learning Based on Transformers for Multi-agent Trajectory Prediction

Li-Wu Tsao[1(✉)], Yan-Kai Wang[1], Hao-Siang Lin[1], Hong-Han Shuai[1], Lai-Kuan Wong[2], and Wen-Huang Cheng[1]

[1] National Yang Ming Chiao Tung University, Hsinchu, Taiwan
{ykwang.ee09g,mrfish.eic08g,hhshuai,whcheng}@nctu.edu.tw
[2] Multimedia University, Cyberjaya, Malaysia
lkwong@mmu.edu.my

Abstract. Earlier trajectory prediction approaches focus on ways of capturing sequential structures among pedestrians by using recurrent networks, which is known to have some limitations in capturing long sequence structures. To address this limitation, some recent works proposed Transformer-based architectures, which are built with attention mechanisms. However, these Transformer-based networks are trained end-to-end without capitalizing on the value of pre-training. In this work, we propose Social-SSL that captures cross-sequence trajectory structures via self-supervised pre-training, which plays a crucial role in improving both data efficiency and generalizability of Transformer networks for trajectory prediction. Specifically, Social-SSL models the interaction and motion patterns with three pretext tasks: interaction type prediction, closeness prediction, and masked cross-sequence to sequence pre-training. Comprehensive experiments show that Social-SSL outperforms the state-of-the-art methods by at least 12% and 20% on ETH/UCY and SDD datasets in terms of Average Displacement Error and Final Displacement Error (code available at https://github.com/Sigta678/Social-SSL.

Keywords: Trajectory prediction · Self-supervised learning · Transformer · Representation learning

1 Introduction

Human trajectory prediction plays a crucial role in path planning and collision avoidance for various applications, *e.g.*, autonomous driving and robot navigation [3, 18, 30, 35, 39]. The main challenges of trajectory prediction lie in the complexity of dynamic actions and multi-agent interactions. Early trajectory prediction works employed Kalman filter [11] and model-based methods [8, 13, 24, 42]

Supplementary Information The online version contains supplementary material available at https://doi.org/10.1007/978-3-031-20047-2_14.

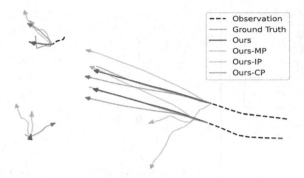

Fig. 1. An illustrative example on ZARA1 dataset. We design three pretexts, including IP (Interaction pretext), CP (Closeness pretext), and MP (Motion pretext). The figure demonstrates how three pretexts benefit the trajectory prediction. Ours-MP does not know how to correctly utilize the social representation, since there is not enough understanding of motion. Ours-IP tends to predict all trajectories pointing towards the upper left corner, since no interaction pretext guides the understanding of social behavior. Ours-CP established an inappropriate relationship between the far agent in the bottom left and the group of agents in the middle, making their predicted trajectories closer because no closeness pretext indicates the influence of mutual distance on social cues. Ours shows the effectiveness of three pretexts to maintain the agent's motion, capture the social pattern, and ignore the irrelevant social agents.

for learning dynamic actions of a single agent; Social Force models [8,15] learn to formulate human-like behaviors for goal navigation as classic interaction modeling. However, these hand-crafted approaches have difficulties dealing with complex multi-agent interactions in real-world applications.

Recent trajectory prediction approaches adopt data-driven techniques based on Recurrent Neural Networks (RNN) [21], with most methods utilizing Long-Short Term Memory (LSTM) [9] as their base model. Various mechanisms such as social pooling [1], conditional variational autoencoder [35], attention [2,33,34], visual semantics [19], and graph neural networks [10,14,17,28,35] are proposed to model the social interactions between the agents so that the generated trajectory represents reasonable routes. While RNN can effectively model the trajectory of an agent as a temporal sequence to capture the dynamic actions of the agent, it is known to be inefficient in memorizing information from long sequences or a large amount of spatial cues. Social-STGCNN [25] is one of the works that moves away from using RNN to represent the spatio-temporal relationship fully as a Graph Convolutional Network (GCN) [12]. Moreover, with the great success of Transformers [41], Transformer TF [6] and STAR [43] adopted Transformers for single-agent and multi-agent trajectory predictions. A new branch of study includes the joint modeling by considering both spatial and temporal sequence in one model. The idea is proposed by AgentFormer [44], which utilizes an extremely long sequence as a complicated cross-sequence to combine all the agent sequences into one via Transformers.

However, these previous works did not capitalize on the benefit of the pre-training strategy, which is a key mechanism that contributes to the success of Transformers in Natural Language Processing. Motivated by the idea of cross-

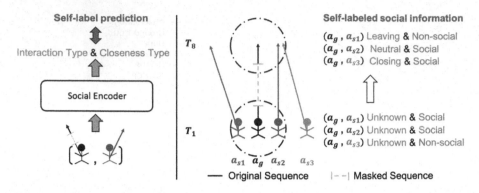

Fig. 2. Illustration of self-supervised cross-sequence representation learning. We propose to learn the interaction and motion patterns based on Transformer, using self-labeled social information and the masked section of a cross-sequence to extract representation without the complete sequence.

sequence that can model both spatial and temporal information, we propose Social-SSL, which is a self-supervised cross-sequence representation learning framework based on Transformers. As shown in Fig. 2, two social-related pretext tasks and a motion-related pretext task are proposed. Specifically, interaction type prediction and closeness prediction are designed to capture the inter-relation between the target agent and each of the social agents. Meanwhile, masked cross-sequence to sequence pre-training provides the understanding of intra-relation among the remaining sequence of the target agent. In our study, combining both the inter- and intra-relation into a cross-sequence representation is effective for crowded agent scenarios and can reduce the amount of data needed for fine-tuning. To the best of our knowledge, this is the first work that proposes the pre-training strategy on a social-related trajectory model.

The core contributions of Social-SSL are highlighted as follow:

- Two social-related pretext tasks for cross-sequence inter-relation learning; interaction type prediction and closeness prediction that learns the social interaction patterns between every pair of agents in the scene.
- A motion-related pretext task for cross-sequence intra-relation learning; the masked cross-sequence to sequence pre-training that learns the motion of a target agent from the non-masked section of its own sequence, and discover the inter-relation with its surrounding social agents via the cross-sequence structure.
- By capitalizing the advantage of self-supervised representation learning, Social-SSL achieves state-of-the-art results on trajectory prediction task, even when trained on a small amount of trajectory data. In addition, it can improve the generalizability of the trajectory prediction task.

2   Related Work

Human trajectories are heavily influenced by the social interaction among agents. With the rise of deep learning, the quality and the amount of data becomes more critical. Based on the importance of data, Social-LSTM [1] is a pioneering work that models social interaction for trajectory prediction via the concept of social pooling, which aggregates the hidden states among the nearby agents. Social-GAN [7] revises the pooling module to capture global information from all agents in the scene. SoPhie [33] proposes the idea of social attention that introduces an importance weight for each pair of agents. Different from previous works that utilize LSTM models, a recent line of studies introduced new ideas, such as graph attention networks [10, 14], for modelling the social interactions between pedestrians.

Since Transformer has its ability to handle the long-sequence problem well, using Transformers to solve the problem on trajectory prediction becomes more popular. For instance, Transformer TF [6] first introduced the use of Transformer for single-agent trajectory prediction. Capitalizing on the self-attention advantage of Transformer, STAR [43] introduced a Graph Transformer Network that models the spatial interaction on a Transformer-based graph convolution mechanism and memorizes the embeddings of each pedestrian via a temporal Transformer. Agent-Former [44] designed the spatio-temporal Transformer along with better multimodal properties, and used all the observable agent sequence in the scene to conduct a complicated cross-sequence input with end-to-end training. Unlike previous works, we introduce a novel approach on the spatio-temporal pre-training strategy under a deterministic setting. This makes better use of the sequence data by predicting the self-labeled social types and recovering the masked cross-sequence as the supervision for pre-training. Our studies show that Social-SSL can reduce the need for a large amount of training data and improve the generalizability of trajectory prediction task. To the best of our knowledge, our work is the first to consider trajectory forecasting in the self-supervised manner, introducing brand new tasks to embed the social representation into a basic Transformer [41] model.

3   Social-SSL

We introduce Social-SSL, a self-supervised cross-sequence representation learning framework via Transformer, to better capture the interaction and motion embeddings from the proposed pretext tasks. Since Transformers are data-hungry, i.e., require a large amount of training data, by creating the pretext tasks related to the downstream task whereby labels can be automatically generated, the data representation can be trained by using a huge amount of additional self-supervised label, rather than using only the downstream task label itself. In our study, these prior knowledge of social interaction and motion representations can be quickly transferred to the trajectory prediction task.

Figure 3 illustrates the architecture of our proposed Social-SSL. Given a paired sequence of the target agent and a social agent, which we called the cross-sequence in our work, the model is pre-trained using the cross-sequence

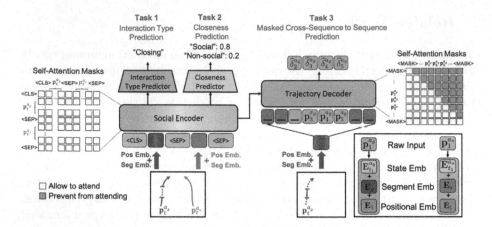

Fig. 3. The pre-training structure of Social-SSL. The input sequence for the encoder constitutes the masked sequence of the target agent a_g and the unmasked sequence of a social agent a_s, separated by <SEP>. <CLS> in front of the sequence aggregates the social representation from a_g and a_s. The red dotted line and the symbol "_" both represent <MASK> in the observation sequence of the target agent. The social-related pretext tasks, *i.e.*, interaction type recognition and closeness prediction, are designed to learn the social representation from the cross-sequence. The motion-related pretext task, *i.e.*, the masked cross-sequence to sequence pre-training, aims to learn to recover the target agent trajectory from its incomplete encoder sequence.

with three pretext tasks to model the feature representations from the aspect of social interaction and agent's motion.

In Social-SSL, we set our Social Encoder and Trajectory Decoder as a simple Transformer Encoder and Decoder, which is simple yet effective for pre-training tasks. Since these three pretext tasks are trained simultaneously and share the same parameters of Social Encoder, the Trajectory Decoder side with the masked cross-sequence to sequence task, is enforced to consider both intra- and inter-relations between agents via the target agent's motion and the influential social information from the Social Encoder respectively. After training on these pretext tasks, Social-SSL can model all the observed cross-sequences as spatio-temporal embeddings and implicitly provide useful social information when predicting the unknown sequence of future timestamps.

3.1 Preliminary

Problem Definition. Given a set of N agents $\mathcal{A} = \{a_j|\ 1 \leq j \leq N,\ j \in \mathbb{N}\}$ over a past time period $(1, 2, \cdots, t, \cdots, t_c)$, where t_c is the current timestamp, the observed positions of agent a_j are re-scaled to $[0,1]^2$ and can be represented as $(\mathbf{p}_1^{a_j}, \mathbf{p}_2^{a_j}, \cdots, \mathbf{p}_t^{a_j}, \cdots)$, where $\mathbf{p}_t^{a_j} = (x_t^{a_j}, y_t^{a_j})$ denotes the re-scaled position of agent a_j at time t. Since the model should focus on predicting the relative coordinates instead of absolute positions, we transform the absolute coordinates into the relative coordinates. Let $\boldsymbol{\delta}_t^{a_j} = (\delta_{x,t}^{a_j}, \delta_{y,t}^{a_j})$ denote the relative coordinates of agent a_j at time t, which can be calculated by $\boldsymbol{\delta}_t^{a_j} = \mathbf{p}_t^{a_j} - \mathbf{p}_{t-1}^{a_j}$.

In the pre-train phase, the Social Encoder is trained with the pretext tasks using only the observed trajectory (8 frames) of the training data to create the self-labeled social information. This setting ensures that our method can avoid memorizing the sequence information while fine-tuning on the trajectory prediction task. Meanwhile, both the interaction type predictor ($f_I(.)$) and closeness predictor ($f_C(.)$) adopt a 2-layer MLP, which plays the role of simple decoders.

Input Representation. The self-attention masks in Social Encoder allows the model to learn the social relationship from two observation sequences in a bidirectional spatio-temporal form. The hidden state corresponding to <CLS> is used as the aggregate representation of sequences a_g and a_s through self-attention for interaction type and closeness prediction tasks, denoted by $\mathbf{s}_f$. In other words, the social feature ($\mathbf{s}_f$) output by the Social Encoder at the <CLS> position, is used as the input by the interaction type predictor and closeness predictor, denoted as $f_I(\mathbf{s}_f)$ and $f_C(\mathbf{s}_f)$. The State Embeddings, Segment Embeddings, and Position Embeddings are combined as the encoder input with dimension d_{model} set to 256. The State Embeddings are represented by using a fully connected layer $\psi(.)$ that projects $(x_t^{a_j}, y_t^{a_j})$ into $\mathbb{R}^{256}$. The state definition for <CLS> is (1,0), <SEP> is (0,1), <MASK> is (0,0). This setting is based on the 2-dimension structure of the re-scaled position $(x_t^{a_j}, y_t^{a_j})$, which is between 0 and 1. Moreover, we use Segment Embeddings to differentiate the embeddings of the target agent (a_g) and its surrounding social agent (a_s) for the encoder input, where 0 and 1 represent the target and social agent respectively and are projected into $\mathbb{R}^{256}$. The Position Embeddings are the same as Transformer [41], which enforces the sequential structure in the self-attention operations.

3.2 Pretext Task

In this section, we present three pretext tasks for interaction and motion modeling: 1) interaction type prediction, 2) closeness prediction, and 3) masked cross-sequence to sequence prediction. For interaction type prediction and closeness prediction, Social-SSL learns to capture social information from the cross-sequence self-supervision with the Social Encoder. For masked cross-sequence to sequence prediction, the Trajectory Decoder of Social-SSL aims to predict the masked section of the target agent by utilizing the self-sequence and the important social relationships captured via Social Encoder. Also, by adding segment and positional embeddings, the sequence separation of two agents and spatio-temporal information are better captured from the pretext. In the following, we introduce the self-labeling mechanism to assign the label automatically for interaction type and closeness.

Task 1: Interaction Type Prediction. The idea of interaction type prediction comes from observing distance fluctuation between two agents, which can be an analogy to summarize the positive and negative sentiment from documents. For example, if a comment "good service" on a restaurant with this positive aspect term happens three times, and a comment "poor service" happens once, we might have an impression that this restaurant provides "good service". Based on this analogy, we sum up the frequency of both agents getting closer and the frequency of them leaving away to create two classes of "closing" and "leaving". In addition, the class "neutral," is used to represent cases where two agents are not apparent whether they are closing or leaving.

Specifically, let $I_t^{(a_g, a_s)}$ denote the indicator of the sign obtained from the change in distance between the target and the social agent, a_g and a_s at time t:

$$
I_t^{(a_g, a_s)} = \begin{cases} +1 & \text{if } d(\mathbf{p}_t^{a_g}, \mathbf{p}_t^{a_s}) - d(\mathbf{p}_{t-1}^{a_g}, \mathbf{p}_{t-1}^{a_s}) > 0, \\ -1 & \text{if } d(\mathbf{p}_t^{a_g}, \mathbf{p}_t^{a_s}) - d(\mathbf{p}_{t-1}^{a_g}, \mathbf{p}_{t-1}^{a_s}) < 0, \\ 0 & \text{otherwise}, \end{cases} \tag{1}
$$

where $d(.)$ is the Euclidean distance function. To track the trend of social relations, we summarize all the indicators within a period r^1 and determine the interaction type between two agents as follows.

$$
y_{inter}^{(a_g, a_s)} = \begin{cases} 1 \ (leaving) & \text{if } \sum_{t \in [t_c - r, t_c]} I_t > 0, \\ 2 \ (closing) & \text{if } \sum_{t \in [t_c - r, t_c]} I_t < 0, \\ 3 \ (neutral) & \text{otherwise}. \end{cases} \tag{2}
$$

The output of interaction type prediction denoted as $\hat{y}_{inter}^{(a_g, a_s)}$ is obtained by performing multi-class classification with cross-entropy as the loss function, L_I:

$$
L_I = - \sum_{i=1}^{3} P(y_{inter}^{(a_g, a_s)} = i) \log P(\hat{y}_{inter}^{(a_g, a_s)} = i). \tag{3}
$$

Task 2: Closeness Prediction. Intuitively, an agent near the target agent has more influence on the trajectory than an agent who is far away. The closeness prediction is used to capture this social characteristic. Specifically, we separate closeness prediction into sparse prediction and dense prediction, which could better adapt to different scenarios.

Sparse Prediction. At any time $t \in [1, t_c]$, if the distance between target agent a_g and social agent a_s is smaller than the distance threshold, d_{th}, we assign their closeness label as 1, otherwise 0:

$$
y_{close}^{(a_g, a_s)} = \begin{cases} 1 \ (nearby/social) & \text{if } \exists \ d(\mathbf{p}_t^{a_g}, \mathbf{p}_t^{a_s}) < d_{th}, \\ 0 \ (faraway/non - social) & \text{otherwise}. \end{cases} \tag{4}
$$

The sparse prediction as shown in Fig. 4, denoted as $\hat{y}_{cs}^{(a_g, a_s)}$, is performed using binary cross-entropy as the objective function, L_{CS}:

$$
L_{CS} = - \sum_{i=0}^{1} P(y_{close}^{(a_g, a_s)} = i) \log P(\hat{y}_{cs}^{(a_g, a_s)} = i). \tag{5}
$$

---

[1] In the experiments, r is set to half of the input length empirically (In Appendix).

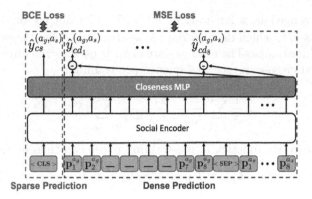

Fig. 4. Details for closeness pretext with sparse and dense prediction settings.

Dense Prediction. For dense prediction, we consider the precise distance between the target agent a_g and a social agent a_s, represented by the distance difference of the corresponding timestamps, denoted as $\widehat{y}_{cd_t}^{(a_g,a_s)}$ in Fig. 4. The objective function L_{CD} for guiding the dense prediction for closeness is formulated using mean square error as:

$$L_{CD} = \frac{1}{t_c}\sum_{t=1}^{t_c}(d(\mathbf{p}_t^{a_g},\mathbf{p}_t^{a_s}) \; - \; \widehat{y}_{cd_t}^{(a_g,a_s)})^2. \tag{6}$$

Finally, L_{CS} and L_{CD} are added together to form the total loss, L_C for the closeness prediction task.

Task 3: Masked Cross-Sequence to Sequence Prediction. The third pretext task is created by randomly masking a target agent's subsequence, and the model should learn to reconstruct the masked subsequence from the cross-sequence input. Since the ground truth of the masked subsequence is known before being masked, the model can be trained in a self-supervised learning manner. The advantages of this pretext task are three-fold. First, this mechanism enhances the representation of the target agent sequence. Simultaneously pre-training the Social Encoder and Trajectory Decoder enforces the model to capture the intra-relation by reconstructing the masked subsequence of the target agent on the decoder side. Second, the model learns a robust representation that can handle a sequence with missing parts, which may happen due to occlusion. Third, the model learns to consider not only the intra-relation of the target trajectory but also the social inter-relation among social agents when predicting the missing part of a sequence. If the sequence information from the target agent itself is not sufficient to reconstruct the masked subsequence, the social cues can provide additional assistance to constrain the reconstructed trajectory.

Specifically, t_{ms} and t_{me} are denoted as the start and the end of the randomly masked subsequence timestamps. We adopt the auto-regressive structure on the decoder to predict the trajectory during fine-tuning, where the self-attention masks are arranged in a left-to-right form [5]. The output of the decoder is represented as $\widehat{\delta}_i^{a_j}$, which denotes the reconstruction of the target sequence on the masked timestamps. The mean square error is used as the objective function for the masked cross-sequence to sequence pre-training:

$$L_{MSE} = \frac{1}{N} \sum_{j=1}^{N} \left(\frac{1}{t_{me} - t_{mo} + 1} \sum_{i=t_{ms}}^{t_{me}} (\delta_i^{a_j} - \widehat{\delta}_i^{a_j})^2 \right). \tag{7}$$

The overall objective function in pre-training phase can then be represented as:

$$L_{pre} = L_{MSE} + \lambda_I L_I + \lambda_C L_C, \tag{8}$$

where λ_I and λ_C are respectively the hyperparameters controlling the importance of the losses for interaction type prediction and closeness prediction.

It is worth noting that the masked language model is widely-used in NLP, e.g., BERT [4], MASS [40]. Different from the masked language model that only considers the context in the target sequence, the proposed Masked Cross-Sequence to Sequence Prediction also takes the sequence from other agents as the context. As such, the proposed pretext task helps the model learn the fine-grained social importance for predicting the masked subsequence.

4   Experiments

4.1   Experimental Setup

Datasets. We perform the comparisons on the benchmark datasets: ETH [31], UCY [16], and SDD [32]. These datasets are collected from the bird's eye view with many human interactions. Specifically, ETH is a small dataset which contains the ETH and HOTEL scenes with less than 4 and 8 pedestrians in each frame, respectively. UCY is a larger dataset which contains the ZARA1, ZARA2, and UNIV scenes, with each scene having more than 10 pedestrians. For the UNIV scene, most frames contains 20 to 40 pedestrians. On the other hand, SDD is a large-scale dataset containing pedestrians, bicyclists, and vehicles.

Settings. Follow the setting of prior works [7,25], we use leave-one-out training on ETH and UCY datasets. Different from ETH and UCY, SDD is commonly-used with the standard train-test split in prior works [29,33]. The experimental setting on the observable period is 8 frames and the prediction period is 12 frames. In the pre-training phase, we use only the observable period of the training set to avoid data leakage. When fine-tuning on the trajectory prediction task, the observable period of the training set remains as the input information, whereas the future period is used as the groundtruth in computing the MSE loss for guiding the trajectory prediction.

Metrics. Similar to prior works [2,7], we use Average Displacement Error (ADE) and Final Displacement Error (FDE) to evaluate the results. ADE reflects the reaction to abrupt change, while FDE reflects more on the long-term goal.

4.2   Implementation Details

Social-SSL uses 4 layers on both Transformer Encoder and Transformer Decoder, $d_{model} = 256$, and 16 attention heads. AdamW [22] optimizer is adopted for two phases; pretext task training and trajectory prediction fine-tuning.

Pretext Task Training: For each agent in a scene, we generate $N-1$ agent pairs for cross-sequence learning, with the purpose of enlarging the amount of self-supervision data. We set λ_I and λ_C to 1, with the learning rate of 3e–6, for the first 700 epochs. For the remaining 300 epochs, λ_I and λ_C are reduced to 0.01, with the learning rate set to 3e–7.

Fine-Tune on Trajectory Prediction: We fine-tune the weights of the Trajectory Decoder by freezing the Social Encoder, so that the embedded inter- and intra-relation can be preserved. Meanwhile, we add a Gumbel-Softmax to select the influential social agent for each target agent. The setting of learning rate is further discussed in our experimental study.

Inference on Tajectory Prediction: We perform auto-regressive decoding on the Trajectory Decoder by choosing the pair of cross-sequence from the result of Gumbel-Softmax. This produces our deterministic result for each target agent in the multi-agent scenario. The experiments are implemented using PyTorch on an RTX 2080 Ti GPU. The average results from 10 runs are reported.

Table 1. Comparison with state-of-the-art methods on ADE/FDE metrics. All the baselines are evaluated using only 1 sample. A lower ADE/FDE value indicates better performance. Social-SSL-S and Social-SSL-D indicate the closeness pretext using sparse and dense settings individually, and the combination of sparse and dense setting is Social-SSL.

Model	Venue	ETH	HOTEL	UNIV	ZARA1	ZARA2	AVG
Linear		1.33/2.94	0.39/0.72	0.82/1.59	0.62/1.21	0.77/1.48	0.79/1.59
Social-GAN [7]	CVPR'18	1.13/2.21	1.01/2.18	0.60/1.28	0.42/0.91	0.52/1.11	0.74/1.54
STGAT [10]	ICCV'19	0.88/1.66	0.56/1.15	0.52/1.13	0.41/0.91	**0.31**/0.68	0.54/1.11
Transformer TF [6]	ICPR'20	1.03/2.10	0.36/0.71	0.53/1.32	0.44/1.00	0.34/0.76	0.54/1.17
STAR [43]	ECCV'20	0.76/1.67	0.41/0.95	0.61/1.32	0.48/1.06	0.39/0.85	0.53/1.17
AgentFormer [44]	ICCV'21	0.99/1.96	0.37/0.76	0.64/1.34	0.46/1.00	0.38/0.84	0.57/1.18
Social-DPF [38]	AAAI'21	0.69/1.35	0.39/0.84	0.61/1.00	**0.40**/0.89	0.39/0.84	0.50/0.98
Social-SSL-S		**0.68/1.27**	0.26/0.47	0.55/1.02	0.43/0.85	0.34/0.67	0.45/0.86
Social-SSL-D		0.69/1.34	0.27/0.48	0.53/0.95	0.43/**0.84**	0.34/**0.65**	0.45/**0.85**
Social-SSL		0.69/1.37	**0.24/0.44**	**0.51/0.93**	0.42/**0.84**	0.34/0.67	**0.44/0.85**

4.3   Quantitative Results

Our proposed Social-SSL captures the deterministic social embeddings based on the self-supervision of interaction labels. To better transfer the pre-trained embeddings to the fine-tuning task, the deterministic evaluation is a better way to measure its performance. Table 1 shows the deterministic results of different baselines on ETH and UCY datasets. The results demonstrate that Social-SSL outperforms state-of-the-art methods by at least 12% in terms of ADE and FDE.

Compared with AgentFormer that uses a more "complicated" cross-sequence input structure via Transformer, we demonstrate the advantages of using "simple" cross-sequence with our pre-train strategy. From Table 1, Social-SSL emphasizes the potential disadvantage of AgentFormer under low sampling, while demonstrating the effectiveness of our proposed pretext tasks under deterministic setting with suitable supervision of cross-sequence.

Interestingly, the combination of sparse and dense settings in closeness pretext demonstrates that the social information learned by Social-SSL could better solve complex social situations with large amount of pedestrians in the scene, which indicates the improvement on the UNIV dataset. It is also worth noting that Social-SSL shows significant improvements on the HOTEL dataset, *i.e.*, at least 33% and 38% reduction in terms of ADE and FDE. Since HOTEL is the scene with 90-degree rotation change in trajectory direction, which is not seen in the other datasets, the performance of Social-SSL in this scenario could be attributed to the adoption of the self-supervised learning approach, which is known for its capability in improving generalizability [26,27].

Table 2. State-of-the-art performance comparison on SDD (Evaluated in pixels).

Model	Venue	Sampling	ADE/FDE
SoPhie [33]	CVPR'19	20	16.27/29.38
SimAug [20]	ECCV'20	20	10.27/19.71
PECNet [23]	ECCV'20	20	8.92/15.63
LB-EBM [29]	CVPR'21	20	8.87/15.61
SIT [36]	AAAI'22	20	8.59/15.27
Social-SSL		1	**6.63/12.23**

Table 2 shows that the proposed Social-SSL outperforms state-of-the-art methods by at least 23% and 20% in terms of ADE and FDE on SDD dataset. Please note that the results of the baselines here are obtained by sampling 20 times and selecting the best prediction since these models are multi-modal. Interestingly, although Social-SSL uses only 1 sample, it outperforms all the baselines. SDD is a more challenging large-scale dataset containing the complicated interactions among heterogeneous agents, *i.e.*, pedestrians, bicyclists, and vehicles. The baseline methods learn the interaction patterns from the supervision of trajectory prediction, which is an indirect way to model and capture social interaction among heterogeneous agents. In contrast, our pre-train strategy is able to capture not only the interaction among the pedestrians but also the social interaction across different types of agents from a large dataset, leading to better performance. This result exemplifies the advantage of pre-training.

Table 3. Comparison on a small amount of data training. We use the same amount of data for pre-training and fine-tuning with leave-one-out setting.

Method	Data amount	ETH	HOTEL	UNIV	ZARA1	ZARA2	AVG
Social-STGCNN [25]	10%	2.01/3.08	1.90/3.08	1.30/2.04	1.15/1.85	1.06/1.68	1.48/2.35
	100%	0.92/1.81	0.76/1.49	0.63/1.26	0.52/1.06	0.44/0.90	0.65/1.30
SGCN [37]	10%	1.33/2.63	0.90/1.69	0.81/1.53	0.69/1.27	0.66/1.23	0.88/1.67
	100%	0.86/1.76	0.57/1.12	0.61/1.23	0.49/1.01	0.36/0.75	0.58/1.17
Social-SSL	10%	**0.85/1.75**	**0.46/0.85**	**0.68/1.25**	**0.50/0.96**	**0.41/0.77**	**0.59/1.14**
	100%	**0.69/1.37**	**0.24/0.44**	**0.51/0.93**	**0.42/0.84**	**0.34/0.67**	**0.44/0.85**

Small Amount Data Training. Table 3 compares the performance of different methods trained on 10% and 100% data of the five datasets. We chose Social-STGCNN and SGCN as baseline comparisons because these methods claimed data efficiency on fewer amounts of data. On 10% data setting, Social-SSL outperforms Social-STGCNN and SGCN by at least 51% and 32% in terms of ADE and FDE. Also, the performance of Social-SSL using only 10% data is comparable to SGCN, demonstrating the effectiveness of our pre-train strategy.

4.4   Qualitative Results

Amount of Data for Fine-Tuning. Figure 5 demonstrates the advantage of our pre-training strategy. Using 100% of data for fine-tuning takes more time, and does not seem to perform better than using 1% of data after the learning rate decays. Interestingly, with only 1% data used for fine-tuning, the training can easily converge and reach good enough performance within a few epochs. This could be attributed to the effectiveness of the masked cross-sequence to sequence pre-training task. Since we pre-trained the Trajectory Decoder in a way that is closely related to the trajectory prediction task, the pre-train model itself can rapidly transfer the knowledge to downstream tasks with simple hints.

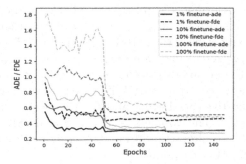

Fig. 5. Evaluation results using different amounts of data to fine-tune on HOTEL dataset. We set the initial learning rate as 3e-6 and the decay rate by 0.1 for every 50 epochs to better observe the convergence phenomenon. Please refer to Appendix for more evaluation details on other datasets.

 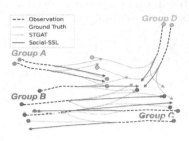

| (a) Multiple social interactions | (b) Multiple group behaviors |

Fig. 6. Visualization of results on ZARA1 and ZARA2 datasets. The endpoint of the arrow signifies the predicted final destination. In Fig. 6(b), we mark the start-point and end-point for each group with different colors and take off the background scene information for better observations. For simplicity, we only compare one baseline at a time. Please refer to Appendix for more visualization cases.

Multiple Social Interactions. Two agents in the middle of Fig. 6(b) shows that Social-STGCNN predicts one agent moves faster than the other. In contrast, Social-SSL is able to preserve the intra- and inter-relationship by embedding the "neutral" interaction type and cross-sequence to sequence representation, which maintains a better speed and distance between these two agents. For the agent at the upper left, Social-STGCNN predicts the agent moving towards the direction of the two agents in the middle. In contrast, Social-SSL predicts the leaving behavior precisely, based on the past trajectory. This shows the effectiveness of closeness pretext since the agent at the upper left is too far away to interact with the agents in the middle.

Multiple Group Behaviors. Figure 6(b) compares the performance of STGAT and Social-SSL in a multi-group case. It can be observed that STGAT can capture the social interactions within a group precisely, *e.g.*, parallel walking. However, there is still a performance gap between STGAT and our method. Specifically, STGAT regards each agent as a node and models their relationship as a complete graph, making it hard to control the trajectory of each agent in a complex social situation with multiple group behaviors. As observed, behavior of one group might affect the behaviors of other groups that are not close, leading to inferior performance. In contrast, Social-SSL predicts the target agent's trajectory via the most effective social agent and can thus aggregate their interaction into independent groups. The closeness pretext in Social-SSL ensures that agents who are too far away to interact, will not be considered, making each group's behavior independent of other groups.

4.5   Ablation Study

To further evaluate the contribution of each pretext task, we compare the performance of Social-SSL trained on different combinations of pretext tasks in Table 4.

Table 4. Ablation study on pretext tasks using SDD dataset (Evaluated in pixels).

	Description	Mask	Interaction	Closeness	Segment embedding	ADE/FDE
Ours-NPS	Single-agent baseline without pre-training				V	16.88/31.50
Ours-NPC	Cross-agent baseline without pre-training				V	26.46/48.45
Ours-MP	Social-SSL without motion-related pretext	V	V	V	V	26.81/46.72
Ours-SP	Social-SSL without social-related pretext	V			V	11.96/22.36
Ours-SP-SE	Ours-SP without segment embeddings	V				17.65/31.62
Ours-IP	Social-SSL without interaction pretext	V		V	V	11.27/20.94
Ours-CP	Social-SSL without closeness pretext	V	V		V	7.64/14.27
Ours-SE	Social-SSL without segment embeddings	V	V	V		9.23/17.75
Ours	Social-SSL	V	V	V	V	**6.63/12.23**

Ours-NPS is the baseline that uses the "plain" structure of Transformer encoder and decoder with an end-to-end training, which is the same as Transformer TF [6]. However, since a single-agent model does not consider social information, we extend this structure to cross-sequence without any pre-training (Ours-NPC). Result shows that the performance of Ours-NPC is worse than Ours-NPS, due to the complexity of the cross-sequence input structure, causing it unable to learn the social information directly, without any proper supervision. Moreover, the performance of purely adding the social-related pretext tasks (Ours-MP) is close to Ours-NPC. This is because the social-related pretext tasks only teach the model to understand the relation without asking the model to use the social context for predicting the trajectory. However, adding social pretext tasks and motion-related pretext improves Ours-SP by at least 45% in terms of ADE and FDE, demonstrating that the motion-related pretext (Ours-SP) plays an essential role in making social pretext tasks useful on the trajectory prediction task. Comparing results of the social-related pretexts, Ours-IP and Ours-CP, the interaction pretext is shown to be more important between the two social features. As expected, the closeness pretext plays a minor role in distinguishing which agent to be considered more. Results of Ours-SE and Ours-SP-SE show that segment embeddings are essential to enable the Trajectory Decoder to distinguish the target and social agents in the cross-sequence of the Social Encoder.

5   Conclusions

This work presents Social-SSL that employed self-supervised cross-sequence learning based on Transformers, to learn better representations for performing the downstream multi-agent trajectory prediction task. The pre-training tasks of Social-SSL enhance the inter- and intra-relationship for cross-sequence representation. By designing the pretext tasks of interaction type prediction and closeness prediction, along with masked cross-sequence to sequence pre-training, Social-SSL can handle the problem of missing values in the target sequence and capture informative social information from the cross-sequence simultaneously. Quantitative and qualitative experiments show that Social-SSL outperforms state-of-the-art approaches across the benchmark datasets. Future work includes extending

Social-SSL with multi-modality via architecture modifications and the design of new pretext tasks.

Acknowledgement. This work was supported in part by Ministry of Science and Technology of Taiwan under the grant numbers: MOST-109-2221-E-009-114-MY3, MOST-110-2221-E-A49-164, MOST-109-2223-E-009-002-MY3, MOST-110-2218-E-A49-018 and MOST-111-2634-F-007-002, as well as the partial support from QUAL-COMM TAIWAN UNIVERSTIV RESEARCH 2021 PROGRAM (NYCU). We are grateful to the National Center for High-performance Computing for computer time and facilities.

References

1. Alahi, A., et al.: Social LSTM: human trajectory prediction in crowded spaces. In: IEEE/CVF Conference on Computer Vision and Pattern Recognition (CVPR), pp. 961–971 (2016)
2. Amirian, J., et al.: Social ways: learning multi-modal distributions of pedestrian trajectories with GANs. In: IEEE/CVF Conference on Computer Vision and Pattern Recognition Workshops (CVPRW), pp. 2964–2972 (2019)
3. Choi, C., Choi, J.H., Li, J., Malla, S.: Shared cross-modal trajectory prediction for autonomous driving. In: Proceedings of the IEEE/CVF Conference on Computer Vision and Pattern Recognition (CVPR), pp. 244–253 (2021)
4. Devlin, J., et al.: BERT: pre-training of deep bidirectional transformers for language understanding. In: Proceedings of the 2019 Conference of the North American Chapter of the Association for Computational Linguistics: Human Language Technologies (NAACL-HLT), Volume 1 (Long and Short Papers), pp. 4171–4186 (2019)
5. Dong, L., et al.: Unified language model pre-training for natural language understanding and generation. In: Proceedings of the 33rd International Conference on Neural Information Processing Systems (NeurIPS), pp. 13063–13075 (2019)
6. Giuliari, F., Hasan, I., Cristani, M., Galasso, F.: Transformer networks for trajectory forecasting. In: 2020 25th International Conference on Pattern Recognition (ICPR), pp. 10335–10342. IEEE (2021)
7. Gupta, A., et al.: Social GAN: socially acceptable trajectories with generative adversarial networks. In: IEEE/CVF Conference on Computer Vision and Pattern Recognition (CVPR), pp. 2255–2264 (2018)
8. Helbing, D., et al.: Social force model for pedestrian dynamics. Phys. Rev. E **51**(5), 4282 (1995)
9. Hochreiter, S., et al.: Long short-term memory. Neural Comput. **9**(8), 1735–1780 (1997)
10. Huang, Y., et al.: STGAT: modeling spatial-temporal interactions for human trajectory prediction. In: IEEE/CVF International Conference on Computer Vision (ICCV), pp. 6271–6280 (2019)
11. Kalman, R.E.: A new approach to linear filtering and prediction problems. Trans. ASME-J. Basic Eng. **82**(Series D), 35–45 (1960)
12. Kipf, T.N., et al.: Semi-supervised classification with graph convolutional networks. In: International Conference on Learning Representations (ICLR) (2017)

13. Kitani, K.M., Ziebart, B.D., Bagnell, J.A., Hebert, M.: Activity forecasting. In: Fitzgibbon, A., Lazebnik, S., Perona, P., Sato, Y., Schmid, C. (eds.) ECCV 2012. LNCS, vol. 7575, pp. 201–214. Springer, Heidelberg (2012). https://doi.org/10. 1007/978-3-642-33765-9_15

14. Kosaraju, V., et al.: Social-BIGAT: multimodal trajectory forecasting using bicycle-GAN and graph attention networks. In: Advances in Neural Information Processing Systems (NeurIPS), pp. 137–146 (2019)

15. Kuderer, M., et al.: Feature-based prediction of trajectories for socially compliant navigation. In: Robotics: Science and Systems (2012)

16. Lerner, A., et al.: Crowds by example. Comput. Graph. Forum. **26**, 655–664. Wiley Online Library (2007)

17. Li, J., et al.: EvolveGraph: multi-agent trajectory prediction with dynamic relational reasoning. In: 34th Conference on Advances in Neural Information Processing Systems (NeurIPS) (2020)

18. Li, L.L., et al.: End-to-end contextual perception and prediction with interaction transformer. In: IEEE/RSJ International Conference on Intelligent Robots and Systems (IROS), pp. 5784–5791 (2020)

19. Liang, J., et al.: Peeking into the future: predicting future person activities and locations in videos. In: IEEE/CVF Conference on Computer Vision and Pattern Recognition (CVPR), pp. 5725–5734 (2019)

20. Liang, J., Jiang, L., Hauptmann, A.: *SimAug*: learning robust representations from simulation for trajectory prediction. In: Vedaldi, A., Bischof, H., Brox, T., Frahm, J.-M. (eds.) ECCV 2020. LNCS, vol. 12358, pp. 275–292. Springer, Cham (2020). https://doi.org/10.1007/978-3-030-58601-0_17

21. Lipton, Z.C., et al.: A critical review of recurrent neural networks for sequence learning. arXiv preprint arXiv:1506.00019 (2015)

22. Loshchilov, I., et al.: Decoupled weight decay regularization. In: International Conference on Learning Representations (ICLR) (2019)

23. Mangalam, K., et al.: It is not the journey but the destination: endpoint conditioned trajectory prediction. In: European Conference on Computer Vision (ECCV), pp. 759–776 (2020)

24. Møgelmose, A., et al.: Trajectory analysis and prediction for improved pedestrian safety: integrated framework and evaluations. In: IEEE Intelligent Vehicles Symposium (IV), pp. 330–335. IEEE (2015)

25. Mohamed, A., et al.: Social-STGCNN: a social spatio-temporal graph convolutional neural network for human trajectory prediction. In: IEEE/CVF Conference on Computer Vision and Pattern Recognition (CVPR), pp. 14424–14432 (2020)

26. Mohseni, S., et al.: Self-supervised learning for generalizable out-of-distribution detection. In: Proceedings of the AAAI Conference on Artificial Intelligence (AAAI)., vol. 34, pp. 5216–5223 (2020)

27. Mohsenvand, M.N., et al.: Contrastive representation learning for electroencephalogram classification. In: Proceedings of Machine Learning for Health, vol. 136, pp. 238–253. (PMLR) (2020)

28. Monti, A., et al.: Dag-Net: double attentive graph neural network for trajectory forecasting. In: 25th International Conference on Pattern Recognition (ICPR) (2020)

29. Pang, B., et al.: Trajectory prediction with latent belief energy-based model. In: Proceedings of the IEEE/CVF Conference on Computer Vision and Pattern Recognition (CVPR), pp. 11814–11824 (2021)

30. Park, S.H., et al.: Diverse and admissible trajectory forecasting through multimodal context understanding. In: Vedaldi, A., Bischof, H., Brox, T., Frahm, J.-M. (eds.) ECCV 2020. LNCS, vol. 12356, pp. 282–298. Springer, Cham (2020). https://doi.org/10.1007/978-3-030-58621-8_17

31. Pellegrini, S., et al.: You'll never walk alone: Modeling social behavior for multi-target tracking. In: IEEE/CVF 12th International Conference on Computer Vision (ICCV), pp. 261–268 (2009)

32. Robicquet, A., Sadeghian, A., Alahi, A., Savarese, S.: Learning social etiquette: human trajectory understanding in crowded scenes. In: Leibe, B., Matas, J., Sebe, N., Welling, M. (eds.) ECCV 2016. LNCS, vol. 9912, pp. 549–565. Springer, Cham (2016). https://doi.org/10.1007/978-3-319-46484-8_33

33. Sadeghian, A., et al.: Sophie: an attentive GAN For predicting paths compliant to social and physical constraints. In: IEEE/CVF Conference on Computer Vision and Pattern Recognition (CVPR), pp. 1349–1358 (2019)

34. Sadeghian, A., et al.: Car-Net: clairvoyant attentive recurrent network. In: Proceedings of the European Conference on Computer Vision (ECCV), pp. 151–167 (2018)

35. Salzmann, T., Ivanovic, B., Chakravarty, P., Pavone, M.: Trajectron++: dynamically-feasible trajectory forecasting with heterogeneous data. In: Vedaldi, A., Bischof, H., Brox, T., Frahm, J.-M. (eds.) ECCV 2020. LNCS, vol. 12363, pp. 683–700. Springer, Cham (2020). https://doi.org/10.1007/978-3-030-58523-5_40

36. Shi, L., et al.: Social interpretable tree for pedestrian trajectory prediction. In: AAAI Conference on Artificial Intelligence (AAAI) (2022)

37. Shi, L., et al.: SGCN: sparse graph convolution network for pedestrian trajectory prediction. In: Proceedings of the IEEE/CVF Conference on Computer Vision and Pattern Recognition (CVPR), pp. 8994–9003 (2021)

38. Shi, X., et al.: Social DPF: socially acceptable distribution prediction of futures. In: Proceedings of the AAAI Conference on Artificial Intelligence (AAAI), vol. 35, pp. 2550–2557 (2021)

39. Song, H., Ding, W., Chen, Y., Shen, S., Wang, M.Y., Chen, Q.: PiP: planning-informed trajectory prediction for autonomous driving. In: Vedaldi, A., Bischof, H., Brox, T., Frahm, J.-M. (eds.) ECCV 2020. LNCS, vol. 12366, pp. 598–614. Springer, Cham (2020). https://doi.org/10.1007/978-3-030-58589-1_36

40. Song, K., et al.: Mass: Masked sequence to sequence pre-training for language generation. In: International Conference on Machine Learning (ICML), pp. 5926–5936 (2019)

41. Vaswani, A., et al.: Attention is all you need. In: 31st Conference on Advances Neural Information Processing Systems (NIPS 2017), pp. 5998–6008 (2017)

42. Wang, J.M., et al.: Gaussian process dynamical models for human motion. IEEE Trans. Pattern Anal. Mach. Intell. **30**(2), 283–298 (2008)

43. Yu, C., Ma, X., Ren, J., Zhao, H., Yi, S.: Spatio-temporal graph transformer networks for pedestrian trajectory prediction. In: Vedaldi, A., Bischof, H., Brox, T., Frahm, J.-M. (eds.) ECCV 2020. LNCS, vol. 12357, pp. 507–523. Springer, Cham (2020). https://doi.org/10.1007/978-3-030-58610-2_30

44. Yuan, Y., Weng, X., Ou, Y., Kitani, K.M.: AgentFormer: agent-aware transformers for socio-temporal multi-agent forecasting. In: Proceedings of the IEEE/CVF International Conference on Computer Vision (ICCV), pp. 9813–9823 (2021)

Diverse Human Motion Prediction Guided by Multi-level Spatial-Temporal Anchors

Sirui Xu$^{(\boxtimes)}$, Yu-Xiong Wang, and Liang-Yan Gui

University of Illinois at Urbana-Champaign, Champaign, USA
{siruixu2,yxw,lgui}@illinois.edu

Abstract. Predicting diverse human motions given a sequence of historical poses has received increasing attention. Despite rapid progress, existing work captures the multi-modal nature of human motions primarily through likelihood-based sampling, where the mode collapse has been widely observed. In this paper, we propose a simple yet effective approach that disentangles randomly sampled codes with a *deterministic learnable component named anchors* to promote sample precision and diversity. Anchors are further factorized into spatial anchors and temporal anchors, which provide attractively *interpretable* control over spatial-temporal disparity. In principle, our spatial-temporal anchor-based sampling (STARS) can be applied to different motion predictors. Here we propose an interaction-enhanced spatial-temporal graph convolutional network (IE-STGCN) that encodes prior knowledge of human motions (*e.g.*, spatial locality), and incorporate the anchors into it. Extensive experiments demonstrate that our approach outperforms state of the art in both stochastic and deterministic prediction, suggesting it as a *unified* framework for modeling human motions. Our code and pretrained models are available at https://github.com/Sirui-Xu/STARS.

Keywords: Stochastic human motion prediction · Generative models · Graph neural networks

1 Introduction

Predicting the evolution of the surrounding physical world over time is an essential aspect of human intelligence. For example, in a seamless interaction, a robot is supposed to have some notion of how people move or act in the near future, conditioned on a series of historical movements. Human motion prediction has thus been widely used in computer vision and robotics, such as autonomous driving [54], character animation [62], robot navigation [59], motion tracking [48],

---

Y.-X. Wang and L.-Y. Gui—Contributed equally to this work.

Supplementary Information The online version contains supplementary material available at https://doi.org/10.1007/978-3-031-20047-2_15.

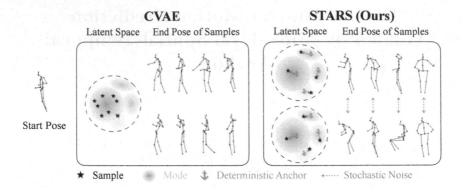

Fig. 1. Our Spatial-Temporal AnchoR-based Sampling (STARS) is able to *capture multiple modes*, thus facilitating diverse human motion prediction. **Left:** with the traditional generative models such as conditional variational autoencoders (CVAEs), the predicted motions are often concentrated in the major mode with less diversity (illustrated with 8 samples). **Right:** STARS is able to cover more modes, where motions in the same mode have similar characteristics but vary widely across modes. Here, we use 4 anchors to pinpoint different modes. With each anchor, we sample noise and generate 2 similar motions with slight variation in each mode

and human-robot interaction [7,34,35,38]. Owing to deep learning techniques, there has been significant progress over the past few years in modeling and predicting motions. Despite notable successes, forecasting human motions, especially over longer time horizons (*i.e.*, up to several seconds), is fundamentally challenging, because of the difficulty of modeling multi-modal motion dynamics and uncertainty of human conscious movements. Learning such uncertainty can, for example, help reduce the search space in motion tracking problems.

As a powerful tool, deep generative models are thus introduced for this purpose, where random codes from a prior distribution are employed to capture the multi-modal distribution of future human motions. However, current motion capture datasets are typically constructed in a way that there is *only a single ground truth future sequence* for each single historical sequence [30,60], which makes it difficult for generators to model the underlying multi-modal densities of future motion distribution. Indeed, in practice, generators tend to ignore differences in random codes and simply produce similar predictions. This is known as *mode collapse* – the samples are concentrated in the major mode, as depicted with a representative example in Fig. 1, which has been widely observed [72]. Recent work has alleviated this problem by explicitly promoting diversity in sampling using post-hoc diversity mappings [72], or through sequentially generating different body parts [51] to achieve combinatorial diversity. These techniques, however, induce additional modeling complexity, without guaranteeing that the diversity modeling accurately covers multiple plausible modes of human motions.

To this end, we propose a simple yet effective strategy – Multi-Level **S**patial-**T**emporal **A**ncho**R**-Based **S**ampling (STARS) – with the *key insight* that future motions are not completely random or independent of each other; they share some deterministic properties in line with physical laws and human body constraints, and continue trends of historical movements. For example, we may expect changes in velocity or direction to be shared deterministically among some future motions, whereas they might differ in the magnitude stochastically. Based on this observation, we disentangle latent codes in the generative model into a *stochastic* component (noise) and a *deterministic learnable* component named *anchors*. With this disentanglement, the diversity of predictions is jointly affected by random noise as well as anchors that are learned to be specialized for certain modes of future motion. In contrast, the diversity from traditional generative models is determined by solely independent noise, as depicted in Fig. 1. Now, on the one hand, random noise only accounts for modeling the uncertainty *within* the mode identified by the anchor, which reduces the burden of having to model the entire future diversity. On the other hand, the model can better capture deterministic states of multiple modes by directly optimizing the anchors, thereby reducing the modeling complexity.

Naturally, human motions exhibit variation in the spatial and temporal domains, and these two types of variation are comparatively independent. Inspired by this, we propose a further decomposition to *factorize anchors into spatial and temporal anchors*. Specifically, our designed spatial anchors capture future motion variation at the spatial level, but remain constant at the temporal level, and vice versa. Another appealing property of our approach is that, by introducing straightforward linear interpolation of spatial-temporal anchors, we achieve flexible and seamless control over the predictions (Fig. 6 and Fig. 7). Unlike low-level controls that combine motions of different body parts [51, 72], our work enables manipulation of future motions in the *native space* and *time*, which is an under-explored problem. Additionally, we propose a multi-level mechanism for spatial-temporal anchors to capture multi-scale modes of future motions.

As a key advantage, spatial-temporal anchors are compatible with any motion predictor. Here, we introduce an **I**nteraction-**E**nhanced **S**patial-**T**emporal **G**raph **C**ovolutional **N**etwork (IE-STGCN). This model encodes the spatial locality of human motion and achieves state-of-the-art performance as a motion predictor.

Our contributions can be summarized as follows. (1) We propose a novel anchor-based generative model that formulates sampling as learning deterministic anchors with likelihood sampling to better capture the multiple modes of human motions. (2) We propose a multi-level spatial-temporal decomposition of anchors for interpretable control over future motions. (3) We develop a spatial-temporal graph neural network with interaction enhancement to incorporate our anchor-based sampling. (4) We demonstrate that our approach, as a *unified* framework for modeling human motions, significantly outperforms state-of-the-art models in both diverse and deterministic human motion prediction.

2   Related Work

Deterministic Motion Prediction. Existing work on deterministic human motion forecasting predicts a single future motion based on a sequence of past poses [1,6,15,42,49], or video frames [11,71,74], or under the constraints of the scene context [8,12,25], by using recurrent neural networks (RNNs) [63], temporal convolutional networks (TCNs) [3], and graph neural networks (GNNs) [33] for sequence modeling. Common early trends involve the use of RNNs [20–22,31,65], which are limited in long-term temporal encoding due to error accumulation [18,53] and training difficulty [55]. Some recent attempts exploit GNNs [16,50] to encode poses from the spatial level, but such work still relies on RNNs [41], CNNs [14,39,40], or feed-forward networks [52] for temporal modeling. Recently, spatial-temporal graph convolutional networks (STGCNs) [61, 67,69] are proposed to jointly encode the spatial and temporal correlations with spatial-temporal graphs. Continuing this effort, we propose IE-STGCN, which additionally encodes inductive biases such as spatial locality into STGCNs.

Stochastic Motion Prediction. Stochastic human motion prediction is an emerging trend with the development of deep generative models such as variational autoencoders (VAEs) [32], generative adversarial networks (GANs) [19], and normalizing flows (NFs) [58]. Most existing work [2,4,26,37,43,64,66,73] produces various predictions from a set of codes independently sampled from a given distribution. As depicted in DLow [72], such likelihood-based sampling cannot produce enough diversity, as many samples are merely perturbations in the major mode. To overcome the issue, DLow employs a two-stage framework, using post-hoc mappings to shape the latent samples to improve the diversity. GSPS [51] generates different body parts in a sequential manner to achieve combinatorial diversity. Nevertheless, their explicit promotion of diversity induces additional complexity but does not directly enhance multi-mode capture. We introduce anchors that are comparatively easy to optimize, to locate deterministic components of motion modes and impose sample diversity.

Controllable Motion Prediction. Controllable motion prediction has been explored in computer graphics for virtual character generation [27,28,44]. In the prediction task, DLow [72] and GSPS [51] propose to control the predicted motion by separating upper and lower body parts, fixing one part while controlling the diversity of the other. In this paper, through the use of spatial-temporal anchors, we propose different but more natural controllability in native space and time. By varying and interpolating the spatial and temporal anchors, we achieve high-level control over the spatial and temporal variation, respectively.

Learnable Anchors. Our anchor-based sampling, *i.e.*, sampling with deterministic learnable codes, is inspired by work on leveraging predefined primitives and learnable codes for applications such as trajectory prediction [10,13,36,46,57], object detection [9,45], human pose estimation [68], and video representation learning [24]. Anchors usually refer to the *hypothesis* of predictions, such as box candidates with different shapes and locations in object detection [45]. In a similar spirit, anchors in the context of human motion prediction indicate assumptions about future movements. The difference is that the anchors here are *not hand-crafted or predefined* primitives; instead, they are latent codes learned from the data. In the meantime, we endow anchors with explainability *i.e.*, to describe the multi-level spatial-temporal variation of future motions.

3   Methodology

Problem Formulation. We denote the input motion sequence of length T_h as $\mathbf{X} = [\mathbf{x}_1, \mathbf{x}_2, \ldots, \mathbf{x}_{T_h}]^T$, where the 3D coordinates of V joints are used to describe each pose $\mathbf{x}_i \in \mathbb{R}^{V \times C^{(0)}}$. Here, we have $C^{(0)} = 3$. The K output sequences of length T_p are denoted as $\widehat{\mathbf{Y}}_1, \widehat{\mathbf{Y}}_2, \ldots, \widehat{\mathbf{Y}}_K$. We have access to a *single* ground truth future motion of length T_p as $\mathbf{Y}$. *Our objectives* are: (1) one of the K predictions is as close to the ground truth as possible; and (2) the K sequences are as diverse as possible, yet representing realistic future motions.

In this section, we first briefly review deep generative models, describe how they draw samples to generate multiple futures, and discuss their limitations (Sect. 3.1). We then detail our insights on STARS including anchor-based sampling and multi-level spatial-temporal anchors (Sect. 3.1 and Fig. 2). To model the human motion, we design an IE-STGCN and incorporate our spatial-temporal anchors into it (Sect. 3.2), as illustrated in Fig. 3.

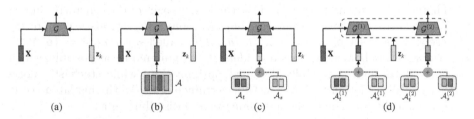

(a)   (b)   (c)   (d)

Fig. 2. Comparison of generative models without and with anchor-based sampling. Anchors and network parameters are jointly optimized. (a) Conventional generative model with only stochastic noise; (b) Generative model with deterministic anchor process: an anchor with Gaussian noise corresponds to a prediction; (c) Spatial-temporal compositional anchors: any pair of combined spatial and temporal anchors corresponds to a prediction; (d) Multi-level spatial-temporal anchors: anchors at different levels are combined for encoding multi-scale modes

3.1   Multi-level Spatial-Temporal Anchor-Based Sampling

Preliminaries: Deep Generative Models. There is a large body of work on the generation of multiple hypotheses with deep generative models, most of which learn a parametric probability distribution function explicitly or implicitly. Let $p(\mathbf{Y}|\mathbf{X})$ denote the distribution of the future human motion $\mathbf{Y}$ conditioned on the past sequence $\mathbf{X}$. With a latent variable $\mathbf{z} \in \mathcal{Z}$, the distribution can be reparameterized as $p(\mathbf{Y}|\mathbf{X}) = \int p(\mathbf{Y}|\mathbf{X}, \mathbf{z})p(\mathbf{z})d\mathbf{z}$, where $p(\mathbf{z})$ is often a Gaussian prior distribution. To generate a future motion sequence $\widehat{\mathbf{Y}}$, $\mathbf{z}$ is drawn from the given distribution $p(\mathbf{z})$, and then a deterministic generator $\mathcal{G} : \mathcal{Z} \times \mathcal{X} \rightarrow \mathcal{Y}$ is used for mapping, as illustrated in Fig. 2(a):

$$\mathbf{z} \sim p(\mathbf{z}), \ \widehat{\mathbf{Y}} = \mathcal{G}(\mathbf{z}, \mathbf{X}), \tag{1}$$

where $\mathcal{G}$ is a deep neural network parameterized by θ. The goal of generative modeling is to make the distribution $p_\theta(\widehat{\mathbf{Y}}|\mathbf{X})$ derived from the generator $\mathcal{G}$ close to the actual distribution $p(\mathbf{Y}|\mathbf{X})$.

To generate K diverse motion predictions, traditional approaches first independently sample a set of latent codes $Z = \{\mathbf{z}_1, \ldots, \mathbf{z}_K\}$ from a prior distribution $p(\mathbf{z})$. Although in theory, generative models are capable of covering different modes, they are not guaranteed to locate all the modes precisely, and mode collapse has been widely observed [70, 72].

Anchor-Based Sampling. To address this problem, we propose a simple yet effective sampling strategy. Our intuition is that the diversity in future motions could be characterized by: (1) deterministic component – across different actions performed by different subjects, there exist correlated or shareable changes in velocity, direction, movement patterns, etc., which naturally emerge and can be directly learned from data; and (2) stochastic component – given an action carried out by a subject, the magnitude of the changes exists which is stochastic.

Therefore, we disentangle the code in the latent space of the generative model into a *stochastic* component sampled from $p(\mathbf{z})$, and a *deterministic* component represented by a set of K *learnable parameters* called *anchors* $\mathcal{A} = \{\mathbf{a}_k\}_{k=1}^K$. Deterministic anchors are expected to identify as many modes as possible, which is achieved through a carefully designed optimization, while stochastic noise further specifies motion variation within certain modes. With this latent code disentanglement, we denote the new multi-modal distribution as

$$p_\theta(\widehat{\mathbf{Y}}|\mathbf{X}, \mathcal{A}) = \frac{1}{K} \sum_{k=1}^K \int p_\theta(\widehat{\mathbf{Y}}|\mathbf{X}, \mathbf{z}, \mathbf{a}_k)p(\mathbf{z})d\mathbf{z}. \tag{2}$$

Consequently, as illustrated in Fig. 2(b), suppose we select the k-th learned anchor $\mathbf{a}_k \in \mathcal{A}$, along with the randomly sampled noise $\mathbf{z} \in Z$, we can generate the prediction $\widehat{\mathbf{Y}}_k$ as,

$$\mathbf{z} \sim p(\mathbf{z}), \ \widehat{\mathbf{Y}}_k = \mathcal{G}(\mathbf{a}_k, \mathbf{z}, \mathbf{X}). \tag{3}$$

We can produce a total of K predictions if using each anchor once, though all anchors are not limited to being used or used only once. To incorporate anchors into the network, we find it effective to make simple additions between selected anchors and latent features, as shown in Fig. 3.

Spatial-Temporal Compositional Anchors. We observe that the diversity of future motions can be roughly divided into two types, namely *spatial variation*

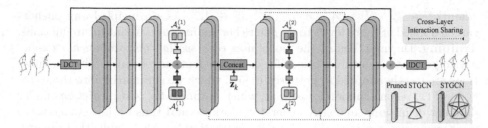

Fig. 3. Overview of our STARS w/ IE-STGCN framework. We combine the multi-level spatial-temporal anchors, the sampled noise, with the backbone IE-STGCN. To generate one of the predictions given a past motion, we draw noise $\mathbf{z}_k$, and add the selected spatial-temporal anchors to the latent feature at each level

and *temporal variation*, which are relatively independent. This sheds light on a feasible further decomposition of the K anchors into two types of learnable codes: spatial anchors $\mathcal{A}_s = \{\mathbf{a}_i^s\}_{i=1}^{K_s}$ and temporal anchors $\mathcal{A}_t = \{\mathbf{a}_j^t\}_{j=1}^{K_t}$, where $K = K_s \times K_t$. With this decomposition, we still can yield a total of $K_s \times K_t$ compositional anchors through *each pair of spatial-temporal anchors*. Note that the temporal anchors here, in fact, control the frequency variation of future motion sequences, since our temporal features are in the frequency domain, as we will demonstrate in Sect. 3.2. To be more specific, conceptually, all spatial anchors are set to be identical in the temporal dimension but characterize the variation of motion in the spatial dimension, taking control of the movement trends and directions. Meanwhile, all temporal anchors remain unchanged in the spatial dimension but differ in the temporal dimension, producing disparities in frequency to affect the movement speed.

To produce $\widehat{\mathbf{Y}}_k$, as depicted in Fig. 2(c), we sample $\mathbf{z}$ and select i-th spatial anchor $\mathbf{a}_i^s$ and j-th temporal anchor $\mathbf{a}_j^t$,

$$\mathbf{z} \sim p(\mathbf{z}), \ \widehat{\mathbf{Y}}_k = \mathcal{G}(\mathbf{a}_i^s + \mathbf{a}_j^t, \mathbf{z}, \mathbf{X}), \tag{4}$$

where $\mathbf{a}_i^s + \mathbf{a}_j^t$ is a spatial-temporal compositional anchor corresponding to an original anchor $\mathbf{a}_k$. Furthermore, motion control over spatial and temporal variation can be customized through these spatial-temporal anchors. For example, we can produce future motions with similar trends by fixing the spatial anchors while varying or interpolating the temporal anchors, as shown in Sect. 4.3.

Multi-level Spatial-Temporal Anchors. To further learn and capture multi-scale modes of future motions, we propose a multi-level mechanism to extend the spatial-temporal anchors. As an illustration, Fig. 2(d) shows a simple two-level case for this design. We introduce two different spatial-temporal anchor sets, $\{\mathcal{A}_t^{(1)}, \mathcal{A}_s^{(1)}\}$ and $\{\mathcal{A}_t^{(2)}, \mathcal{A}_s^{(2)}\}$, and assign them sequentially to different network parts $\mathcal{G}^{(1)}, \mathcal{G}^{(2)}$. Suppose (i, j) is a spatial-temporal index corresponding to the 1D index k, we can generate $\widehat{\mathbf{Y}}_k$ through a two-level process as

$$\mathbf{z} \sim p(\mathbf{z}), \ \widehat{\mathbf{Y}}_k = \mathcal{G}^{(2)}(\mathbf{a}_i^{s_2} + \mathbf{a}_j^{t_2}, \mathbf{z}, \mathcal{G}^{(1)}(\mathbf{a}_i^{s_1} + \mathbf{a}_j^{t_1}, \mathbf{X})), \tag{5}$$

where $a_i^{s_1} \in \mathcal{A}_s^{(1)}, a_j^{t_1} \in \mathcal{A}_t^{(1)}, a_i^{s_2} \in \mathcal{A}_s^{(2)}, a_j^{t_2} \in \mathcal{A}_t^{(2)}$. As a principled way, anchors can be applied at more levels to encode richer assumptions about future motions.

Training. During training, the model uses *each spatial-temporal anchor* explicitly to generate K future motions for each past motion sequence. The loss functions are mostly adopted as proposed in [51], which we summarize into three categories: (1) reconstruction losses that, which optimize *the best predictions* under different definitions among K generated motions, and thus optimize anchors to their own nearest modes; (2) a diversity-promoting loss that explicitly promotes pairwise distances in predictions, avoiding that anchors collapse to the same; and (3) motion constraint losses that encourage output movements to be realistic. All anchors are directly learned from the data via gradient descent. In the forward pass, we explicitly take *every* anchor $\mathbf{a}_i \in \mathcal{A} = \{\mathbf{a}_k\}_{k=1}^{K}$ as an additional input to the network and produce a total of K outputs. In the backward pass, each anchor is optimized *separately* based on its corresponding outputs and losses, while the backbone network is updated based on the *fused* losses from all outputs. This separate backward pass is automatically done via PyTorch [56]. Please refer to the supplementary material for more details.

3.2 Interaction-Enhanced Spatial-Temporal Graph Convolutional Network

In principle, our proposed anchor-based sampling permits flexible network architecture. Here, to incorporate our multi-level spatial-temporal anchors, we naturally represent motion sequences as spatial-temporal graphs (to be precise, spatial-frequency graphs), instead of the widely used spatial graphs [51,52]. Our approach builds upon the Discrete Cosine Transform (DCT) [51,52] to transform the motion into the frequency domain. Specifically, given a past motion $\mathbf{X}_{1:T_h} \in \mathbb{R}^{T_h \times V \times C^{(0)}}$, where each pose has V joints, we first replicate the last pose T_p times to get $\mathbf{X}_{1:T_h+T_p} = [\mathbf{x}_1, \mathbf{x}_2, \ldots, \mathbf{x}_{T_h}, \mathbf{x}_{T_h}, \ldots, \mathbf{x}_{T_h}]^T$. With predefined M basis $\mathbf{C} \in \mathbb{R}^{M \times (T_h+T_p)}$ for DCT, the motion is transformed as

$$\widetilde{\mathbf{X}} = \mathbf{C}\mathbf{X}_{1:T_h+T_p}. \tag{6}$$

We formulate $\widetilde{\mathbf{X}} \in \mathbb{R}^{M \times V \times C^{(0)}}$ in the 0-th layer and latent features in any l-th graph layer as spatial-temporal graphs $(\mathcal{V}^{(l)}, \mathcal{E}^{(l)})$ with $M \times V$ nodes. We specify the node i by 2D index (f_i, v_i) for joint v_i with frequency f_i component. The edge $(i, j) \in \mathcal{E}^{(l)}$ associated with the interaction between node i and node j is represented by $\mathbf{Adj}^{(l)}[i][j]$, where the adjacency matrix $\mathbf{Adj}^{(l)} \in \mathbb{R}^{MV \times MV}$ is learnable. We bottleneck spatial-temporal interactions as [61], by factorizing the adjacency matrix into the product of low-rank spatial and temporal matrices $\mathbf{Adj}^{(l)} = \mathbf{Adj}_s^{(l)} \mathbf{Adj}_f^{(l)}$. The spatial adjacency matrix $\mathbf{Adj}_s^{(l)} \in \mathbb{R}^{MV \times MV}$ connects only nodes with the same frequency. And the frequency adjacency matrix $\mathbf{Adj}_f^{(l)} \in \mathbb{R}^{MV \times MV}$ is merely responsible for the interplay between the nodes representing the same joint.

The spatial-temporal graph can be conveniently encoded by a graph convolutional network (GCN). Given a set of trainable weights $\mathbf{W}^{(l)} \in \mathbb{R}^{C^{(l)} \times C^{(l+1)}}$ and activation function $\sigma(\cdot)$, such as ReLU, a spatial-temporal graph convolutional layer projects the input from $C^{(l)}$ to $C^{(l+1)}$ dimensions by

$$\mathbf{H}_k^{(l+1)} = \sigma(\mathbf{Adj}^{(l)}\mathbf{H}_k^{(l)}\mathbf{W}^{(l)}) = \sigma(\mathbf{Adj}_s^{(l)}\mathbf{Adj}_f^{(l)}\mathbf{H}_k^{(l)}\mathbf{W}^{(l)}), \qquad (7)$$

where $\mathbf{H}_k^{(l)} \in \mathbb{R}^{MV \times C^{(l)}}$ denotes the latent feature of the prediction $\widehat{\mathbf{Y}}_k$ at l-th layer. The backbone consists of multiple graph convolutional layers. After generating predicted DCT coefficients $\widetilde{\mathbf{Y}}_k \in \mathbb{R}^{M \times V \times C^{(L)}}$ reshaped from $\mathbf{H}_k^{(L)}$, where $C^{(L)} = 3$, we recover $\widehat{\mathbf{Y}}_k$ via Inverse DCT (IDCT) as

$$\widehat{\mathbf{Y}}_k = (\mathbf{C}^\top \widetilde{\mathbf{Y}}_k)_{T_h+1:T_h+T_p}, \qquad (8)$$

where the last T_p frames of the recovered sequence represent future poses.

Conceptually, interactions between spatial-temporal nodes should be relatively invariant across layers, and different interactions should not be equally important. For example, we would expect constraints and dependencies between "left arm" and "left forearm," while the movements of "head" and "left forearm" are relatively independent. We consider it redundant to construct a *complete* spatial-temporal graph for each layer *independently*. Therefore, we introduce cross-layer interaction sharing to share parameters between graphs in different layers, and spatial interaction pruning to prune the complete graph.

Cross-Layer Interaction Sharing. Much care has been taken into employing learnable interactions between spatial nodes across all graph layers [52,61,67]. We consider the spatial relationship to be relatively unchanged. Empirically, we find that sharing the adjacency matrix at intervals of one layer is effective. As shown in Fig. 3, we set $\mathbf{Adj}_s^{(4)} = \mathbf{Adj}_s^{(6)} = \mathbf{Adj}_s^{(8)}$ and $\mathbf{Adj}_s^{(5)} = \mathbf{Adj}_s^{(7)}$.

Spatial Interaction Pruning. To emphasize the physical relationships and constraints between spatial joints, we prune the spatial connections $\widehat{\mathbf{Adj}}_s^{(l)} = \mathbf{M}_s \odot \mathbf{Adj}_s^{(l)}$ in every graph layer l using a predefined mask $\mathbf{M}_s$, where $\odot$ is an element-wise product. Inspired by [47], we emphasize spatial locality based on skeletal connections and mirror symmetry tendencies. We denote our proposed predefined mask matrix as

$$\mathbf{M}_s[i][j] = \begin{cases} 1, & v_i \text{ and } v_j \text{ are physically connected, } f_i = f_j \\ 1, & v_i \text{ and } v_j \text{ are mirror-symmetric, } f_i = f_j \\ 0, & \text{otherwise.} \end{cases} \qquad (9)$$

Finally, our architecture consists of four original **STGCNs** without spatial pruning and four **Pruned STGCNs**, as illustrated in Fig. 3. Please refer to the supplementary material for more information of the architecture.

4   Experiments

4.1   Experimental Setup for Diverse Prediction

Datasets. We perform evaluation on two motion capture datasets, Human3.6M [30] and HumanEva-I [60]. Human3.6M consists of 11 subjects and 3.6 million frames 50 Hz. Following [51,72], we use a 17-joint skeleton representation and train our model to predict 100 future frames given 25 past frames without global translation. We train on five subjects (S1, S5, S6, S7, and S8) and test on two subjects (S9 and S11). HumanEva-I contains 3 subjects recorded 60 Hz. Following [51,72], the pose is represented by 15 joints. We use the official train/test split [60]. The model forecasts 60 future frames given 15 past frames.

Metrics. For a fair comparison, we measure the diversity and accuracy of the predictions according to the evaluation metrics in [2,51,70,72]. (1) **Average Pairwise Distance (APD)**: average ℓ_2 distance between all prediction pairs, defined as $\frac{1}{K(K-1)} \sum_{i=1}^{K} \sum_{j \neq i}^{K} \|\widehat{\mathbf{Y}}_i - \widehat{\mathbf{Y}}_j\|_2$. (2) **Average Displacement Error (ADE)**: average ℓ_2 distance over the time between the ground truth and the closest prediction, computed as $\frac{1}{T_p} \min_k \|\widehat{\mathbf{Y}}_k - \mathbf{Y}\|_2$. (3) **Final Displacement Error (FDE)**: ℓ_2 distance of the last frame between the ground truth and the closest prediction, defined as $\min_k \|\widehat{\mathbf{Y}}_k[T_p] - \mathbf{Y}[T_p]\|_2$. To measure the ability to produce multi-modal predictions, we also report multi-modal versions of ADE and FDE. We define the multi-modal ground truth [70] as $\{\mathbf{Y}_n\}_{n=1}^{N}$, which is clustered based on historical pose distances, representing possible multi-modal future motions. The detail of multi-modal ground truth is in the supplementary material. (4) **Multi-Modal ADE (MMADE)**: the average displacement error between the predictions and the multi-modal ground truth, denoted as $\frac{1}{NT_p} \sum_{n=1}^{N} \min_k \|\widehat{\mathbf{Y}}_k - \mathbf{Y}_n\|_2$. (5) **Multi-Modal FDE (MMFDE)**: the final displacement error between the predictions and the multi-modal ground truth, denoted as $\frac{1}{N} \sum_{n=1}^{N} \min_k \|\widehat{\mathbf{Y}}_k[T_p] - \mathbf{Y}_n[T_p]\|_2$. All metrics here are in *meters*.

Baselines. To evaluate our stochastic motion prediction method, we consider two types of baselines: (1) Stochastic methods, including CVAE-based methods, **Pose-Knows** [64] and **MT-VAE** [66], as well as CGAN-based methods, **HP-GAN** [4]; (2) Diversity promoting methods, including **Best-of-Many** [5], **GMVAE** [17], **DeLiGAN** [23], **DSF** [70], **DLow** [72], **MOJO** [75], and **GSPS** [51].

Implementation Details. The backbone consists of 8 GCN layers. We perform spatial pruning on 4 GCN layers (denoted as 'Pruned'). The remaining 4 layers are not pruned. In each layer, we use batch normalization [29] and residual connections. We add K spatial-temporal compositional anchors at layers 4 and 6, and perform random sampling at the layer 5. Here, $K = 50$ unless otherwise specified. For Human3.6M, the model is trained for 500 epochs, with a batch size of 16 and 5000 training instances per epoch. For HumanEva-I, the model is trained for 500 epochs, with a batch size of 16 and 2000 training instances per epoch. Additional implementation details are provided in the supplementary material.

4.2   Quantitative Results and Ablation of Diverse Prediction

We compare our method with the baselines in Table 1 on Human3.6M and HumanEva-I. We produce one prediction using *each spatial-temporal anchor* for a total of 50 predictions, which is consistent with the literature [51,72]. For all metrics, our method consistently outperforms all baselines on both datasets.

Table 1. Quantitative results on Human3.6M and HumanEva-I for $K = 50$. Our model significantly outperforms all stochastic prediction baselines on all metrics. The results of baselines are reported from [51, 72, 75]

Method	Human3.6M [30]					HumanEva-I [60]				
	APD ↑	ADE ↓	FDE ↓	MMADE ↓	MMFDE ↓	APD ↑	ADE ↓	FDE ↓	MMADE ↓	MMFDE ↓
Pose-Knows [64]	6.723	0.461	0.560	0.522	0.569	2.308	0.269	0.296	0.384	0.375
MT-VAE [66]	0.403	0.457	0.595	0.716	0.883	0.021	0.345	0.403	0.518	0.577
HP-GAN [4]	7.214	0.858	0.867	0.847	0.858	1.139	0.772	0.749	0.776	0.769
BoM [5]	6.265	0.448	0.533	0.514	0.544	2.846	0.271	0.279	0.373	0.351
GMVAE [17]	6.769	0.461	0.555	0.524	0.566	2.443	0.305	0.345	0.408	0.410
DeLiGAN [23]	6.509	0.483	0.534	0.520	0.545	2.177	0.306	0.322	0.385	0.371
DSF [70]	9.330	0.493	0.592	0.550	0.599	4.538	0.273	0.290	0.364	0.340
DLow [72]	11.741	0.425	0.518	0.495	0.531	4.855	0.251	0.268	0.362	0.339
MOJO [75]	12.579	0.412	0.514	0.497	0.538	4.181	0.234	0.244	0.369	0.347
GSPS [51]	14.757	0.389	0.496	0.476	0.525	5.825	0.233	0.244	0.343	0.331
STARS (Ours)	**15.884**	**0.358**	**0.445**	**0.442**	**0.471**	**6.031**	**0.217**	**0.241**	**0.328**	**0.321**

Table 2. Ablation study on Human3.6M and HumanEva-I for $K = 50$. We compare the following 4 cases: (I) 50 original anchors; (II) 2 temporal anchors and 25 spatial anchors; (III) 50 spatial-temporal compositional anchors from 5 temporal anchors and 10 spatial anchors; (IV) 50 spatial-temporal compositional anchors for both levels

# of anchors	Human3.6M [30]					HumanEva-I [60]				
	APD ↑	ADE ↓	FDE ↓	MMADE ↓	MMFDE ↓	APD ↑	ADE ↓	FDE ↓	MMADE ↓	MMFDE ↓
(I) 50	**16.974**	0.363	0.447	0.444	0.473	**7.786**	0.221	0.249	**0.327**	**0.321**
(II) 2 × 25	16.303	0.356	**0.442**	0.440	0.468	5.254	0.224	0.253	0.337	0.331
(III) 5 × 10	13.681	**0.355**	**0.442**	**0.439**	**0.467**	6.199	0.226	0.255	0.334	0.330
(IV) (5 × 10) × 2	15.884	0.358	0.445	0.442	0.471	6.031	**0.217**	**0.241**	0.328	**0.321**

Methods such as GMVAE [17] and DeLiGAN [23] have relatively low accuracy (ADE, FDE, MMADE, and MMFDE) and diversity (APD), since they still follow a pure random sampling. Methods such as DSF [70], DLow [72] and GSPS [51] explicitly promote diversity by introducing assumptions in the latent codes or directly in the generation process. Instead, we propose to use anchors to locate diverse modes directly learned from the data, which is more effective.

Effectiveness of Multi-level Spatial-Temporal Anchors. As shown in Table 2, compared with not using spatial-temporal decoupling (I), using it (II and III) leads to relatively lower diversity, but facilitates mode capture and results in higher accuracy on Human3.6M. Applying the multi-level mechanism (IV) improves diversity, but sacrifices a little accuracy on Human3.6M. By contrast, we observe improvements in both diversity and accuracy on HumanEva-I. The results suggest that there is an intrinsic trade-off between diversity and accuracy. Higher diversity indicates that the model has a better chance of covering multiple modes. However, when the diversity exceeds a certain level, the trade-off between diversity and accuracy becomes noticeable.

Impact of Number of Anchors and Samples. We investigate the effect of two important hyperparameters on the model, $i.e.$, the number of anchors and

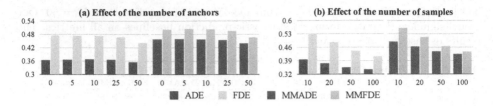

Fig. 4. Ablation study on Human3.6M. We report ADE, MMADE, FDE, and MMFDE, comparing settings with different numbers of anchors and samples

Table 3. Ablation study on Human3.6M for $K = 100$. We demonstrate the generalizability of our anchor-based sampling. For a fair comparison, we add single-level anchor-based sampling to GSPS [51] and IE-STGCN, without changing any other design and without using spatial-temporal decomposition. We observe that our anchor-based sampling mechanism consistently improves diversity and accuracy for both approaches. Meanwhile, our backbone is more lightweight but performs better

Backbone	Parameter	Random sampling					Single-level anchor-based sampling (Ours)				
		APD ↑	ADE ↓	FDE ↓	MMADE ↓	MMFDE ↓	APD ↑	ADE ↓	FDE ↓	MMADE ↓	MMFDE ↓
GSPS [51]	1.30M	14.751	0.369	0.462	0.455	0.491	19.022	0.364	0.443	0.443	0.465
IE-STGCN (Ours)	0.29M	11.701	0.352	0.445	0.443	0.476	14.554	0.344	0.411	0.423	0.436

the number of samples. As illustrated in Fig. 4(a), we fix the number of samples to 50 and compare the results when the number of anchors varies within $0, 5, 10, 25, 50$. The results show that more anchors enable the model to better capture the major modes (ADE, FDE) and also other modes (MMADE, MMFDE). In Fig. 4(b), we vary the sample size to be $10, 20, 50, 100$ and keep the number of anchors the same as the number of samples. The results show that the larger the number of samples is, the easier it is for a sample to approach the ground truth.

Generalizability of Anchor-Based Sampling. In Table 3, we demonstrate that our anchor-based sampling is *model-agnostic* and can be inserted as a *plug-and-play* module into different motion predictors. Concretely, we apply our anchor-based sampling to the baseline method GSPS [51], which also achieves consistent improvements under every metric, with improvements in terms of diversity and multi-modal accuracy being particularly evident. For simplicity, this evaluation uses simple single-level anchors, but the improvements are pronounced. We would also like to emphasize that the total number of parameters in our IE-STGCN predictor is only **22%** of that in GSPS.

4.3   Qualitative Results of Diverse Prediction

We visualize the start pose, the end pose of the ground truth future motions, and the end pose of 10 motion samples in Fig. 5. The qualitative comparisons support the ADE results in Table 1 that our best predicted samples are closer to the ground truth. In Fig. 6 and Fig. 7, we provide the predicted sequences sampled every ten frames. As mentioned before, our spatial-temporal anchors provide a new form of control over spatial-temporal aspects. With the same temporal anchor, the motion frequencies are similar, but the motion patterns are different. Conversely, if we control the spatial anchors to be the same, the motion trends are similar, but the speed might be different. We show a smooth control through the linear interpolation of spatial-temporal anchors in Fig. 7. The new interpolated anchors produce some interesting and valid pose sequences. And smooth changes in spatial trend and temporal velocity can be observed.

4.4 Effectiveness on Deterministic Prediction

Our model can be easily extended to deterministic prediction by specifying $K = 1$. Without diverse sampling, we retrain two deterministic prediction model variants. IE-STGCN-Short dedicated to short-term prediction and IE-STGCN-

Fig. 5. Visualization of end poses on Human3.6M. We show the historical poses in red and black skeletons, and the predicted end poses with purple and green. As highlighted by the red and blue dashed boxes, the best predictions of our method are closer to the ground truth than the state-of-the-art baseline GSPS [51]

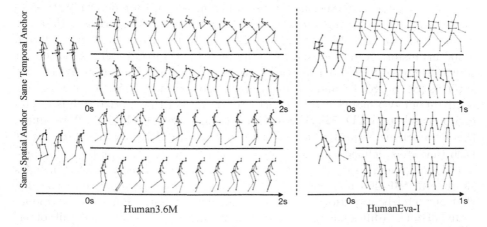

Fig. 6. Visualization of controllable motion prediction on Human3.6M and HumanEva-I. We control different trends and speeds of motions by controlling spatial and temporal anchors. For example, the third and fourth rows have similar motion trends, but the motion in the third row is faster

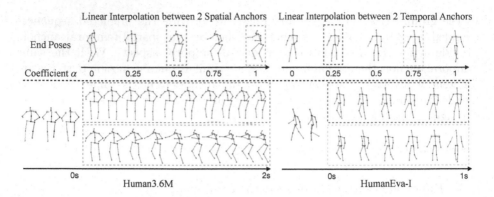

Fig. 7. Linear interpolation of anchors. We seamlessly control different trends and speeds of future motions by linear interpolation of spatial and temporal anchors. Specifically, given two anchors $\mathbf{a}_1$ and $\mathbf{a}_2$ and a coefficient α, we produce predictions from the interpolated anchor formulated as $(1 - \alpha)\mathbf{a}_1 + \alpha\mathbf{a}_2$

Table 4. Quantitative results on Human3.6M for $K = 1$. Both our long-term and short-term deterministic models significantly outperform all deterministic baselines

Method	Short-term prediction				Long-term prediction			
	80	*160*	*320*	*400*	*560*	*720*	*880*	*1000*
LTD [52]	11.2	23.3	47.9	59.3	79.9	94.3	106.1	113.3
STS-GCN [61]	13.5	27.7	54.4	65.8	85.0	98.3	108.9	117.0
MSR-GCN [16]	11.3	24.3	50.8	61.9	80.0	93.8	105.5	112.9
IE-STGCN-Short (Ours)	**9.7**	**21.2**	**44.5**	**55.5**	77.1	91.1	102.6	110.1
IE-STGCN-Long (Ours)	10.0	21.8	45.7	56.9	**75.8**	**89.3**	**100.8**	**108.4**

Long for long-term prediction. We use different settings for deterministic prediction, following existing work [16,52,61] and for fair comparisons. Here, we evaluate on Human3.6M and use the 22-joint skeleton representations. Given a 400 ms historical motion sequence, the model generates a 400 ms motion for short-term prediction and a 1000 ms motion for long-term prediction. We use five subjects (S1, S6, S7, S8 and S9) for training and a subject 5 (S5) for testing. We compare our two model variants with recent state-of-the-art deterministic prediction baselines: **LTD** [52], **STS-GCN** [61], and **MSR-GCN** [16]. We evaluate this by reporting Mean Per Joint Position Error (MPJPE) [30] in *millimeter* at each time step, defined as $\frac{1}{V}\sum_{i=1}^{V} \|\widehat{\mathbf{y}}_t[i] - \mathbf{y}_t[i]\|_2$, where $\widehat{\mathbf{y}}_t[i]$ and $\mathbf{y}_t[i]$ are produced and ground truth 3D positions of the i-th joint at time t. Table 4 includes short-term (80~400 ms) and long-term (560~1000 ms) comparisons, showing that our models outperform the baseline models on both short-term and long-term horizons. Additional experimental results and implementation details of our two deterministic prediction models are provided in the supplementary material.

5   Conclusion

In this paper, we present a simple yet effective approach, STARS, to predict multiple plausible and diverse future motions. And our spatial-temporal anchors enable novel controllable motion prediction. To incorporate our spatial-temporal anchors, we propose a novel motion predictor IE-STGCN. Extensive experiments on Human3.6M and HumanEva-I show the state-of-the-art performance of our unified approach for both diverse and deterministic motion predictions. In the future, we will consider human-scene interaction and investigate the integration of our predictor into human-robot interaction systems.

Acknowledgement. This work was supported in part by NSF Grant 2106825, the Jump ARCHES endowment through the Health Care Engineering Systems Center, the New Frontiers Initiative, the National Center for Supercomputing Applications (NCSA) at the University of Illinois at Urbana-Champaign through the NCSA Fellows program, and the IBM-Illinois Discovery Accelerator Institute.

References

1. Aksan, E., Kaufmann, M., Hilliges, O.: Structured prediction helps 3D human motion modelling. In: Proceedings of the IEEE/CVF International Conference on Computer Vision, pp. 7144–7153 (2019)
2. Aliakbarian, S., Saleh, F.S., Salzmann, M., Petersson, L., Gould, S.: A stochastic conditioning scheme for diverse human motion prediction. In: Proceedings of the IEEE/CVF Conference on Computer Vision and Pattern Recognition, pp. 5223–5232 (2020)
3. Bai, S., Kolter, J.Z., Koltun, V.: An empirical evaluation of generic convolutional and recurrent networks for sequence modeling. arXiv preprint arXiv:1803.01271 (2018)
4. Barsoum, E., Kender, J.R., Liu, Z.: HP-GAN: Probabilistic 3D Human Motion Prediction via GAN. In: IEEE/CVF Conference on Computer Vision and Pattern Recognition Workshops, pp. 1418–1427 (2018)
5. Bhattacharyya, A., Schiele, B., Fritz, M.: Accurate and diverse sampling of sequences based on a "best of many" sample objective. In: Proceedings of the IEEE Conference on Computer Vision and Pattern Recognition, pp. 8485–8493 (2018)
6. Butepage, J., Black, M.J., Kragic, D., Kjellstrom, H.: Deep representation learning for human motion prediction and classification. In: Proceedings of the IEEE Conference on Computer Vision and Pattern Recognition, pp. 6158–6166 (2017)
7. Bütepage, J., Kjellström, H., Kragic, D.: Anticipating many futures: Online human motion prediction and generation for human-robot interaction. In: IEEE International Conference on Robotics and Automation, pp. 4563–4570 (2018)
8. Cao, Z., et al.: Long-Term human motion prediction with scene context. In: Vedaldi, A., Bischof, H., Brox, T., Frahm, J.-M. (eds.) ECCV 2020. LNCS, vol. 12346, pp. 387–404. Springer, Cham (2020). https://doi.org/10.1007/978-3-030-58452-8_23

9. Carion, N., Massa, F., Synnaeve, G., Usunier, N., Kirillov, A., Zagoruyko, S.: End-to-end object detection with transformers. In: Vedaldi, A., Bischof, H., Brox, T., Frahm, J.-M. (eds.) ECCV 2020. LNCS, vol. 12346, pp. 213–229. Springer, Cham (2020). https://doi.org/10.1007/978-3-030-58452-8_13

10. Chai, Y., Sapp, B., Bansal, M., Anguelov, D.: Multipath: Multiple probabilistic anchor trajectory hypotheses for behavior prediction. arXiv preprint arXiv:1910.05449 (2019)

11. Chao, Y.W., Yang, J., Price, B., Cohen, S., Deng, J.: Forecasting human dynamics from static images. In: Proceedings of the IEEE Conference on Computer Vision and Pattern Recognition, pp. 548–556 (2017)

12. Corona, E., Pumarola, A., Alenya, G., Moreno-Noguer, F.: Context-aware human motion prediction. In: Proceedings of the IEEE/CVF Conference on Computer Vision and Pattern Recognition, pp. 6992–7001 (2020)

13. Cui, H., et al.: Multimodal trajectory predictions for autonomous driving using deep convolutional networks. In: International Conference on Robotics and Automation, pp. 2090–2096 (2019)

14. Cui, Q., Sun, H.: Towards accurate 3D human motion prediction from incomplete observations. In: Proceedings of the IEEE/CVF Conference on Computer Vision and Pattern Recognition. pp. 4801–4810 (2021)

15. Cui, Q., Sun, H., Yang, F.: Learning dynamic relationships for 3D human motion prediction. In: Proceedings of the IEEE/CVF Conference on Computer Vision and Pattern Recognition, pp. 6519–6527 (2020)

16. Dang, L., Nie, Y., Long, C., Zhang, Q., Li, G.: MSR-GCN: multi-scale residual graph convolution networks for human motion prediction. In: Proceedings of the IEEE/CVF International Conference on Computer Vision, pp. 11467–11476 (2021)

17. Dilokthanakul, N., et al.: Deep unsupervised clustering with Gaussian mixture variational autoencoders. arXiv preprint arXiv:1611.02648 (2016)

18. Fragkiadaki, K., Levine, S., Felsen, P., Malik, J.: Recurrent network models for human dynamics. In: Proceedings of the IEEE/CVF International Conference on Computer Vision, pp. 4346–4354 (2015)

19. Goodfellow, I., et al.: Generative adversarial nets. In: 27th Proceedings of the International Conference on Advances in Neural Information Processing Systems (2014)

20. Gui, L.Y., Wang, Y.X., Liang, X., Moura, J.M.F.: Adversarial geometry-aware human motion prediction. In: European Conference on Computer Vision, pp. 786–803 (2018)

21. Gui, L.Y., Wang, Y.X., Ramanan, D., Moura, J.M.F.: Few-shot human motion prediction via meta-learning. In: European Conference on Computer Vision, pp. 432–450 (2018)

22. Gui, L.Y., Zhang, K., Wang, Y.X., Liang, X., Moura, J.M.F., Veloso, M.: Teaching robots to predict human motion. In: 2018 IEEE/RSJ International Conference on Intelligent Robots and Systems, pp. 562–567 (2018)

23. Gurumurthy, S., Kiran Sarvadevabhatla, R., Venkatesh Babu, R.: DeLiGAN : generative adversarial networks for diverse and limited data. In: Proceedings of the IEEE Conference on Computer Vision and Pattern Recognition, pp. 166–174 (2017)

24. Han, T., Xie, W., Zisserman, A.: Memory-augmented dense predictive coding for video representation learning. In: European Conference on Computer Vision, pp. 312–329 (2020)

25. Hassan, M., et al.: Stochastic scene-aware motion prediction. In: Proceedings of the International Conference on Computer Vision, pp. 11374–11384 (2021)

26. Hernandez, A., Gall, J., Moreno-Noguer, F.: Human motion prediction via spatio-temporal inpainting. In: Proceedings of the IEEE/CVF International Conference on Computer Vision, pp. 7134–7143 (2019)
27. Holden, D., Komura, T., Saito, J.: Phase-functioned neural networks for character control. ACM Trans. Graph. **36**, 1–13 (2017)
28. Holden, D., Saito, J., Komura, T.: A deep learning framework for character motion synthesis and editing. ACM Trans. Graph. **35**, 1–11 (2016)
29. Ioffe, S., Szegedy, C.: Batch normalization: accelerating deep network training by reducing internal covariate shift. In: International Conference on Machine Learning, pp. 448–456. PMLR (2015)
30. Ionescu, C., Papava, D., Olaru, V., Sminchisescu, C.: Human3. 6M: large scale datasets and predictive methods for 3D human sensing in natural environments. IEEE Trans. Pattern Anal. Mach. Intell. **36**(7), 1325–1339 (2013)
31. Jain, A., Zamir, A.R., Savarese, S., Saxena, A.: Structural-RNN: deep learning on spatio-temporal graphs. In: Proceedings of the IEEE Conference on Computer Vision and Pattern Recognition, pp. 5308–5317 (2016)
32. Kingma, D.P., Ba, J.: Adam: A method for stochastic optimization. arXiv preprint arXiv:1412.6980 (2014)
33. Kipf, T.N., Welling, M.: Semi-supervised classification with graph convolutional networks. arXiv preprint arXiv:1609.02907 (2016)
34. Koppula, H.S., Saxena, A.: Anticipating human activities using object affordances for reactive robotic response. IEEE Trans. Pattern Anal. Mach. Intell. **38**(1), 14–29 (2016)
35. Koppula, H.S., Saxena, A.: Anticipating human activities for reactive robotic response. In: IEEE/RSJ International Conference on Intelligent Robots and Systems, pp. 2071–2071 (2013)
36. Kothari, P., Sifringer, B., Alahi, A.: Interpretable social anchors for human trajectory forecasting in crowds. In: Proceedings of the IEEE/CVF Conference on Computer Vision and Pattern Recognition, pp. 15551–15561 (2021)
37. Kundu, J.N., Gor, M., Babu, R.V.: BiHMP-GAN: Bidirectional 3D human motion prediction GAN. In: Proceedings of the AAAI Conference on Artificial Intelligence, vol. 33, pp. 8553–8560 (2019)
38. Lasota, P.A., Shah, J.A.: A multiple-predictor approach to human motion prediction. In: IEEE International Conference on Robotics and Automation, pp. 2300–2307 (2017)
39. Lebailly, T., Kiciroglu, S., Salzmann, M., Fua, P., Wang, W.: Motion prediction using temporal inception module. In: Proceedings of the Asian Conference on Computer Vision (2020)
40. Li, C., Zhang, Z., Lee, W.S., Lee, G.H.: Convolutional sequence to sequence model for human dynamics. In: Proceedings of the IEEE Conference on Computer Vision and Pattern Recognition, pp. 5226–5234 (2018)
41. Li, M., Chen, S., Zhao, Y., Zhang, Y., Wang, Y., Tian, Q.: Dynamic multiscale graph neural networks for 3D skeleton based human motion prediction. In: Proceedings of the IEEE/CVF Conference on Computer Vision and Pattern Recognition, pp. 214–223 (2020)
42. Li, X., Li, H., Joo, H., Liu, Y., Sheikh, Y.: Structure from recurrent motion: From rigidity to recurrency. In: Proceedings of the IEEE Conference on Computer Vision and Pattern Recognition, pp. 3032–3040 (2018)
43. Lin, X., Amer, M.R.: Human motion modeling using DVGANs. arXiv preprint arXiv:1804.10652 (2018)

44. Ling, H.Y., Zinno, F., Cheng, G., Van De Panne, M.: Character controllers using motion VAEs. ACM Trans. Graph. **39**(4), 40–1 (2020)
45. Lui, W., et al.: SSD: single shot multibox detector. In: Leibe, B., Matas, J., Sebe, N., Welling, M. (eds.) ECCV 2016. LNCS, vol. 9905, pp. 21–37. Springer, Cham (2016). https://doi.org/10.1007/978-3-319-46448-0_2
46. Liu, Y., Zhang, J., Fang, L., Jiang, Q., Zhou, B.: Multimodal motion prediction with stacked transformers. In: Proceedings of the IEEE/CVF Conference on Computer Vision and Pattern Recognition, pp. 7577–7586 (2021)
47. Liu, Z., et al.: Motion prediction using trajectory cues. In: Proceedings of the IEEE/CVF International Conference on Computer Vision, pp. 13299–13308 (2021)
48. Luber, M., Stork, J.A., Tipaldi, G.D., Arras, K.O.: People tracking with human motion predictions from social forces. In: IEEE International Conference on Robotics and Automation, pp. 464–469 (2010)
49. Lyu, K., Liu, Z., Wu, S., Chen, H., Zhang, X., Yin, Y.: Learning human motion prediction via stochastic differential equations. In: Proceedings of ACM International Conference on Multimedia, pp. 4976–4984 (2021)
50. Mao, W., Liu, M., Salzmann, M.: History repeats itself: human motion prediction via motion attention. In: Vedaldi, A., Bischof, H., Brox, T., Frahm, J.-M. (eds.) ECCV 2020. LNCS, vol. 12359, pp. 474–489. Springer, Cham (2020). https://doi.org/10.1007/978-3-030-58568-6_28
51. Mao, W., Liu, M., Salzmann, M.: Generating smooth pose sequences for diverse human motion prediction. In: Proceedings of the IEEE/CVF International Conference on Computer Vision, pp. 13309–13318 (2021)
52. Mao, W., Liu, M., Salzmann, M., Li, H.: Learning trajectory dependencies for human motion prediction. In: Proceedings of the IEEE/CVF International Conference on Computer Vision, pp. 9489–9497 (2019)
53. Martinez, J., Black, M.J., Romero, J.: On human motion prediction using recurrent neural networks. In: Proceedings of the IEEE Conference on Computer Vision and Pattern Recognition, pp. 2891–2900 (2017)
54. Paden, B., Cáp, M., Yong, S.Z., Yershov, D.S., Frazzoli, E.: A survey of motion planning and control techniques for self-driving urban vehicles. IEEE Trans. Intell. Veh. **1**, 33–55 (2016)
55. Pascanu, R., Mikolov, T., Bengio, Y.: On the difficulty of training recurrent neural networks. In: International Conference on Machine Learning, pp. 1310–1318. PMLR (2013)
56. Paszke, A., et al.: PyTorch: an imperative style, high-performance deep learning library. In: 32nd Proceedings of the International Conference on Advances in Neural Information Processing Systems (2019)
57. Phan-Minh, T., Grigore, E.C., Boulton, F.A., Beijbom, O., Wolff, E.M.: CoverNet: multimodal behavior prediction using trajectory sets. In: Proceedings of the IEEE/CVF Conference on Computer Vision and Pattern Recognition, pp. 14074–14083 (2020)
58. Rezende, D., Mohamed, S.: Variational inference with normalizing flows. In: International Conference on Machine Learning, pp. 1530–1538. PMLR (2015)
59. Rudenko, A., Palmieri, L., Arras, K.O.: Joint long-term prediction of human motion using a planning-based social force approach. In: IEEE International Conference on Robotics and Automation, pp. 4571–4577 (2018)

60. Sigal, L., Balan, A.O., Black, M.J., HumanEva: synchronized video and motion capture dataset and baseline algorithm for evaluation of articulated human motion: HumanEva: synchronized video and motion capture dataset and baseline algorithm for evaluation of articulated human motion. Int. J. Comput. Vision **87**(1), 4–27 (2010)
61. Sofianos, T., Sampieri, A., Franco, L., Galasso, F.: Space-Time-Separable Graph Convolutional Network for pose forecasting. In: Proceedings of the IEEE/CVF International Conference on Computer Vision, pp. 11209–11218 (2021)
62. Starke, S., Zhao, Y., Zinno, F., Komura, T.: Neural animation layering for synthesizing martial arts movements. ACM Trans. Graphi. **40**, 1–16 (2021)
63. Sutskever, I., Martens, J., Hinton, G.: Generating text with recurrent neural networks. In: International Conference on Machine Learning, pp. 1017–1024 (2011)
64. Walker, J., Marino, K., Gupta, A., Hebert, M.: The pose knows: Video forecasting by generating pose futures. In: Proceedings of the IEEE International Conference on Computer Vision, pp. 3332–3341 (2017)
65. Wang, B., Adeli, E., Chiu, H.k., Huang, D.A., Niebles, J.C.: Imitation learning for human pose prediction. In: Proceedings of the IEEE/CVF International Conference on Computer Vision, pp. 7124–7133 (2019)
66. Yan, X., et al.: MT-VAE: learning motion transformations to generate multimodal human dynamics. In: European Conference on Computer Vision, pp. 276–293 (2018)
67. Yan, Z., Zhai, D.H., Xia, Y.: DMS-GCN: dynamic mutiscale spatiotemporal graph convolutional networks for human motion prediction. arXiv preprint arXiv:2112.10365 (2021)
68. Yang, Y., Ramanan, D.: Articulated pose estimation with flexible mixtures-of-parts. In: Proceedings of the IEEE Conference on Computer Vision and Pattern Recognition, pp. 1385–1392 (2011)
69. Yu, B., Yin, H., Zhu, Z.: Spatio-temporal graph convolutional networks: a deep learning framework for traffic forecasting. arXiv preprint arXiv:1709.04875 (2017)
70. Yuan, Y., Kitani, K.: Diverse trajectory forecasting with determinantal point processes. arXiv preprint arXiv:1907.04967 (2019)
71. Yuan, Y., Kitani, K.: Ego-pose estimation and forecasting as real-time PD control. In: Proceedings of the IEEE International Conference on Computer Vision, pp. 10082–10092 (2019)
72. Yuan, Y., Kitani, K.: DLow: diversifying latent flows for diverse human motion prediction. In: Vedaldi, A., Bischof, H., Brox, T., Frahm, J.-M. (eds.) ECCV 2020. LNCS, vol. 12354, pp. 346–364. Springer, Cham (2020). https://doi.org/10.1007/978-3-030-58545-7_20
73. Yuan, Y., Kitani, K.: Residual force control for agile human behavior imitation and extended motion synthesis. Adv. Neural. Inf. Process. Syst. **33**, 21763–21774 (2020)
74. Zhang, J.Y., Felsen, P., Kanazawa, A., Malik, J.: Predicting 3D human dynamics from video. In: Proceedings of the IEEE/CVF International Conference on Computer Vision, pp. 7114–7123 (2019)
75. Zhang, Y., Black, M.J., Tang, S.: We are more than our joints: predicting how 3D bodies move. In: Proceedings of the IEEE/CVF Conference on Computer Vision and Pattern Recognition, pp. 3372–3382 (2021)

Learning Pedestrian Group Representations for Multi-modal Trajectory Prediction

Inhwan Bae⬝, Jin-Hwi Park⬝, and Hae-Con Jeon⁽✉⁾⬝

AI Graduate School, GIST, Gwangju, South Korea
{inhwanbae,jinhwipark}@gm.gist.ac.kr, haegonj@gist.ac.kr

Abstract. Modeling the dynamics of people walking is a problem of long-standing interest in computer vision. Many previous works involving pedestrian trajectory prediction define a particular set of individual actions to implicitly model group actions. In this paper, we present a novel architecture named GP-Graph which has collective group representations for effective pedestrian trajectory prediction in crowded environments, and is compatible with all types of existing approaches. A key idea of GP-Graph is to model both individual-wise and group-wise relations as graph representations. To do this, GP-Graph first learns to assign each pedestrian into the most likely behavior group. Using this assignment information, GP-Graph then forms both intra- and inter-group interactions as graphs, accounting for human-human relations within a group and group-group relations, respectively. To be specific, for the intra-group interaction, we mask pedestrian graph edges out of an associated group. We also propose group pooling&unpooling operations to represent a group with multiple pedestrians as one graph node. Lastly, GP-Graph infers a probability map for socially-acceptable future trajectories from the integrated features of both group interactions. Moreover, we introduce a group-level latent vector sampling to ensure collective inferences over a set of possible future trajectories. Extensive experiments are conducted to validate the effectiveness of our architec ture, which demonstrates consistent performance improvements with publicly available benchmarks. Code is publicly available at https://github.com/inhwanbae/GPGraph.

Keywords: Pedestrian trajectory prediction · Group representation

1 Introduction

Pedestrian trajectory prediction attempts to forecast the socially-acceptable future paths of people based on their past movement patterns. These behavior patterns often depend on each pedestrian's surrounding environments, as well as collaborative movement, mimicking a group leader, or collision avoidance. Collaborative movement, one of the most frequent patterns, occurs when several

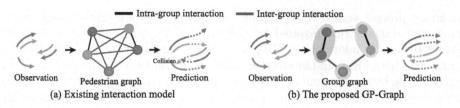

Fig. 1. Comparison of existing agent-agent interaction graphs and the proposed group-aware GP-Graph. To capture social interactions, (a) existing pedestrian trajectory prediction models each pedestrian on a graph node. Since the pedestrian graph is a complete graph, it is difficult to capture the group's movement because it becomes overly complex in a crowded scene. (b) GP-Graph is directly able to learn an intra-/inter-group interaction while keeping the agent-wise structure.

colleagues form a group and move together. Computational social scientists estimate that up to 70% of the people in a crowd will form groups [40,48]. They also gather surrounding information and have the same destination [40]. Such groups have characteristics that are distinguishable from those of individuals, maintain rather stable formations, and even provide important cues that can be used for future trajectory prediction [48,78].

Pioneering works in human trajectory forecasting model the group movement by assigning additional hand-crafted terms as energy potentials [41,47,66]. These works account for the presence of other group members and physics-based attractive forces, which are only valid between the same group members. In recent works, convolutional neural networks (CNNs) and graph neural networks (GNNs) show impressive progress modeling the social interactions, including traveling together and collision avoidance [1,2,17,39,54]. Nevertheless, trajectory prediction is still a challenging problem because of the complexity of implicitly learning individual and group behavior at once.

There are several attempts that explicitly encode the group coherence behaviors by assigning hidden states of LSTM with a summation of other agents' states, multiplied by a binary group indicator function [6]. However, existing studies have a critical problem when it comes to capturing the group interaction. Since their forecasting models focus more on individuals, the group features are shared at the individual node as illustrated in Fig. 1(a). Although this approach can conceptually capture group movement behavior, it is difficult for the learning-based methods to represent it because of the overwhelming number of edges for the individual interactions. And, this problem is increasingly difficult in crowded environments.

To address this issue, we propose a novel general architecture for pedestrian trajectory prediction: GrouP-Graph (GP-Graph). As illustrated in Fig. 1(b), our GP-Graph captures intra-(members in a group) and inter-group interactions by disentangling input pedestrian graphs. Specifically, our GP-Graph first learns to assign each pedestrian into the most likely behavior group. The group indices of each pedestrian are generated using a pairwise distance matrix. To make the indexing process end-to-end trainable, we introduce a straight-through group back-propagation trick inspired by the Straight-Through estimator [5,21,35]. Using the group information, GP-graph then transforms the input pedestrian graph into both intra- and inter-group interaction graphs. We construct the intra-group graph by masking out edges of the input pedestrian graph for unassociated group members. For the inter-group graph, we propose group pooling&unpooling operations to represent a group with multiple members as one graph node. By applying these processes, GP-Graph architecture has three advantages: (1) It reduces the complexity of trajectory prediction which is caused by the different social behaviors of individuals, by modeling group interactions. (2) It alleviates inherent scene bias by considering the huge number of unseen pedestrian graph nodes between the training and test environments, as discussed in [8]. (3) It offers a graph augmentation effect with pedestrian node grouping.

Next, through weight sharing with baseline trajectory predictors, we force a hierarchy representation from both the input pedestrian graph and the disentangled interactions. This representation is used to infer a probability map for socially-acceptable future trajectories after passing through our group integration module. In addition, we introduce a group-level latent vector sampling to ensure collective inferences over a set of plausible future trajectories.

To the best of our knowledge, this is the first model that literally pools pedestrian colleagues into one group node to efficiently capture group motion behaviors, and learns pedestrian grouping in an end-to-end manner. Furthermore, GP-Graph has the best performance on various datasets among existing methods when unifying with GNN-based models, and it can be integrated with all types of trajectory prediction models, achieving consistent improvements. We also provide extensive ablation studies to analyze and evaluate our GP-Graph.

2   Related Works

2.1   Trajectory Prediction

Earlier works [18,38,42,66] model human motions in crowds using hand-crafted functions to describe attractive and repulsive forces. Since then, pedestrian trajectory prediction has been advanced by research interest in computer vision. Such research leverages the impressive capacity of CNNs which can capture social interactions between surrounding pedestrians. One pioneering work is Social-LSTM [1], which introduces a social pooling mechanism considering a neighbor's hidden state information inside a spatial grid. Much of the emphasis in subsequent research has been to add human-environment interactions from a surveillance view perspective [11,23,33,37,49,52,58,59,61,75]. Instead of taking environmental information into account, some methods directly share hidden states of agents between other interactive agents [17,50,64]. In particular, Social-GAN [17] takes the interactions via max-pooling in all neighborhood features in the scene, and Social-Attention [64] introduces an attention mechanism to impose a relative importance on neighbors and performs a weighted aggregation for the features.

In terms of graph notations, each pedestrian and their social relations can be represented as a node and an edge, respectively. When predicting pedestrian trajectories, graph representation is used to model social interactions with graph convolutional networks (GCNs) [2,22,39,59], graph attention networks (GATs) [3,19,23,32,54,63], and transformers [16,69,70]. Usually, these approaches infer future paths through recurrent estimations [1,9,16,17,26,50,74] or extrapolations [2,31,39,54]. Other types of relevant research are based on probabilistic inferences for multi-modal trajectory prediction using Gaussian modeling [1,2,30,39,54,55,65,69], generative models [11,17,19,23,49,58,75], and a conditional variational autoencoder [9,20,26,27,29,36,50,60]. We note that these approaches focus only on learning implicit representations for group behaviors from agent-agent interactions.

2.2   Group-Aware Representation

Contextual and spatial information can be derived from group-aware representations of agent dynamics. To accomplish this, one of the group-aware approaches is social grouping, which describes agents in groups that move differently than independent agents.

In early approaches [24,76,77], pedestrians can be divided into several groups based on behavior patterns. To represent the collective activities of agents in a supervised manner, a work in [41] exploits conditional random fields (CRF) to jointly predict the future trajectories of pedestrians and their group membership. Yamaguchi *et al.* [66] harness distance, speed, and overlap time to train a linear SVM to classify whether two pedestrians are in the same group or not. In contrast, a work in [14] proposes automatic detection for small groups of individuals using a bottom-up hierarchical clustering with speed and proximity features.

Group-aware predictors recognize the affiliations and relations of individual agents, and encode their proper reactions to moving groups. Several physics-based techniques represent group relations by adding attractive forces among group members [40,41,44,46,51,56,66]. Although a dominant learning paradigm [1,4,43,62,73] implicitly learns intra- and inter-group coherency, only two works in [6,12] explicitly define group information. To be specific, one [6] identifies pedestrians walking together in the crowd using a coherent filtering algorithm [77], and utilizes the group information in a social pooling layer to share their hidden states. Another work [12] proposes a generative adversarial model (GAN)-based trajectory model, jointly learning informative latent features for simultaneous pedestrian trajectory forecasting and group detection. These approaches only learn individual-level interactions within a group, but do not encode their affiliated groups and future paths at the same time. Unlike them, our GP-Graph aggregates a group-group relation via a novel group pooling in the proposed end-to-end trainable architecture without any supervision.

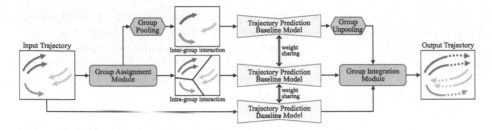

Fig. 2. An overview of our GP-Graph architecture. Starting with graph-structured trajectories for N pedestrians, we first estimate grouping information with the Group Assignment Module. We then generate both intra-/inter-group interaction graphs by masking out unrelated nodes and by performing pedestrian group pooling. The weight-shared trajectory prediction model takes the three types of graphs and capture group-aware social interactions. Group pooling operators are then applied to encode agent-wise features from group-wise features, and then fed into the Group Integration Module to estimate the probability distribution for future trajectory prediction.

2.3   Graph Node Pooling

Pooling operations are used for features extracted from grid data, like images, as well as graph-structured data. However, there is no geographic proximity or order information in the graph nodes that existing pooling operations require. As alternative methods, three types of graph pooling are introduced: topology-based pooling [10,45], global pooling [15,72], and hierarchical pooling [7,13,68]. These approaches are designed for general graph structures. However, since human behavior prediction has time-variant and generative properties, it is no possible to leverage the advantages of these pooling operations for this task.

3   Proposed Method

In this work, we focus on how group awareness in crowds is formed for pedestrian trajectory prediction. We start with a definition of a pedestrian graph and trajectory prediction in Sect. 3.1. We then introduce our end-to-end learnable pedestrian group assignment technique in Sect. 3.2. Using group index information and our novel pedestrian group pooling&unpooling operations, we construct a group hierarchy representation of pedestrian graphs in Sect. 3.3. The overall architecture of our GP-Graph is illustrated in Fig. 2.

3.1   Problem Definition

Pedestrian trajectory prediction can be defined as a sequential inference task made observations for all agents in a scene. Suppose that N is the number of pedestrians in a scene, the history trajectory of each pedestrian $n \in [1,...,N]$ can be represented as $\boldsymbol{X}_n = \{(x_n^t, y_n^t) \mid t \in [1,...,T_{obs}]\}$, where the (x_n^t, y_n^t) is the 2D spatial coordinate of a pedestrian n at specific time t. Similarly, the ground truth future trajectory of pedestrian n can be defined as $Y_n = \{(x_n^t, y_n^t) \mid t \in [T_{obs}+1, ..., T_{pred}]\}$.

The social interactions are modeled from the past trajectories of other pedestrians. In general, the pedestrian graph $\mathcal{G}_{ped} = (\mathcal{V}_{ped}, \mathcal{E}_{ped})$ refers to a set of pedestrian nodes $\mathcal{V}_{ped} = \{X_n \mid n \in [1, ..., N]\}$ and edges on their pairwise social interaction $\mathcal{E}_{ped} = \{e_{i,j} \mid i, j \in [1, ..., N]\}$. The trajectory prediction process forecasts their future sequences based on their past trajectory and the social interaction as:

$$\widehat{Y} = F_\theta (X, \mathcal{G}_{ped}) \tag{1}$$

where $\widehat{Y} = \{\widehat{Y}_n \mid n \in [1, ..., N]\}$ denotes the estimated future trajectories of all pedestrians in a scene, and $F_\theta(\cdot)$ is the trajectory generation network.

3.2 Learning the Trajectory Grouping Network

Our goal in this work is to encode powerful group-wise features beyond existing agent-wise social interaction aggregation models to achieve highly accurate human trajectory prediction. The group-wise features represent group members in input scenes as single nodes, making pedestrian graphs simpler. We use a U-Net architecture with pooling layers to encode the features on graphs. By reducing the number of nodes through the pooling layers in the U-Net, higher-level group-wise features can be obtained. After that, agent-wise features are recovered through unpooling operations.

Unlike conventional pooling&unpooling operators working on grid-structured data, like images, it is not feasible to apply them to graph-structured data. Some earlier works to handle this issue [7,13]. The works focus on capturing global information by removing relatively redundant nodes using a graph pooling, and restoring the original shapes by adding dummy nodes from a graph unpooling if needed. However, in pedestrian trajectory prediction, each node must keep its identity index information and describe the dynamic property of the group behavior in scenes. For that, we present pedestrian graph-oriented group pooling&unpooling methods. We note that it is the first work to exploit the pedestrian index itself as a group representation.

Learning Pedestrian Grouping.   First of all, we estimate grouping information to which the pedestrian belongs using a Group Assignment Module. Using the history trajectory of each pedestrian, we measure the feature similarity among all pedestrian pairs based on their L_2 distance. With this pairwise distance, we pick out all pairs of pedestrians that are likely to be a colleague (affiliated with same group). The pairwise distance matrix D and a set of colleagues indices Υ are defined as:

$$D_{i,j} = \|F_\phi(X_i) - F_\phi(X_j)\| \quad \text{for} \ \ i, j \in [1, ..., N], \tag{2}$$

$$\Upsilon = \{\text{pair}(i, j) \mid i, j \in [1, ..., N], \ i \neq j, \ D_{i,j} \leq \pi\}, \tag{3}$$

where $F_\phi(\cdot)$ is a learnable convolutional layer and π is a learnable thresholding parameter.

Next, using the pairwise colleague set Υ, we arrange the colleague members in associated groups and assign their group index. We make a group index set G, which is formulated as follows:

$$G = \left\{ G_k \mid G_k = \bigcup_{(i,j) \in \Upsilon} \{i, j\}, \quad G_a \cap G_b = \varnothing \text{ for } a \neq b \right\} \tag{4}$$

where G_k denotes the k-th group and is the union of each pair set (i, j). This information is used as important prior knowledge in the subsequent pedestrian group pooling and unpooling operators.

Pedestrian Group Pooling. Based on the group behavior property that group members gather surrounding information and share behavioral patterns, we group the pedestrian nodes, where the corresponding node's features are aggregated into one node. The aggregated group features are then stacked for subsequent social interaction capturing modules (*i.e.*GNNs). Here, the most representative feature for each pedestrian node is selected via an average pooling. With the feature, we can model the group-wise graph structures, which have much fewer number of nodes than the input pedestrian graph, as will be demonstrated in Sec. 4.3. We define the pooled group-wise trajectory feature Z as follows:

$$Z = \{ Z_k \mid k \in [1, ..., K] \}, \qquad Z_k = \frac{1}{|G_k|} \sum_{i \in G_k} X_i, \tag{5}$$

where K is the total group numbers in G.

Pedestrian Group Unpooling. Next, we upscale the group-wise graph structures back to their original size by using an unpooling operation. This enables each pedestrian trajectory to be forecast with output agent-wise feature fusion information. In existing methods [7,13], zero vector nodes are appended into the group features during unpooling. The output of the convolution process on the zero vector nodes fails to exhibit the group properties. To alleviate this issue, we duplicate the group features and then assign them into nodes for all the relevant group members so that they have identical group behavior information. The pedestrian group unpooling operator can be formulated as follows:

$$\overline{X} = \{ \overline{X}_n \mid n \in [1, ..., N] \}, \qquad \overline{X}_n = Z_k \quad \text{where } n \in G_k, \tag{6}$$

where $\overline{X}$ is the agent-wise trajectory feature reconstructed from Z, having the same order of pedestrian indices as in X.

Straight-Through Group Estimator. A major hurdle, when training the group assignment module in Eq. (4) which is a sampling function, is that index information is not treated as learnable parameters. Accordingly, the group index cannot be trained using standard backpropagation algorithms. The reason is why the existing methods utilize separate training steps from main trajectory prediction networks for the group detection task.

We tackle this problem by introducing a Straight-through (ST) trick, inspired by the biased path derivative estimators in [5,21,35]. Instead of making the

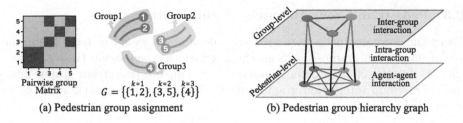

(a) Pedestrian group assignment   (b) Pedestrian group hierarchy graph

Fig. 3. An illustration of our pedestrian group assignment method using a pairwise group probability matrix A. With a group index set G, a pedestrian group hierarchy is constructed based on three types of interaction graphs.

discrete index set G_k differentiable, we separate the forward pass and backward pass of the group assignment module in the training process. Our intuition for constructing the backward pass is that group members have similar features with closer pairwise distance between colleagues.

In the forward pass, we perform our group pooling over both pedestrian features and the group index from the input trajectory and estimated group assignment information, respectively. For the backward pass, we propose group-wise continuous relaxed features to approximate the group indexing process. We compute the probability that a pair of pedestrians belongs to the same group using the proposed differentiable binary thresholding function $\frac{1}{1+\exp(x-\pi)}$, and apply it on the pairwise distance matrix D. We then measure the normalized probability A of the summation of all neighbors' probability. Lastly, we compute a new pedestrian trajectory feature X' by aggregating features between group members through the matrix multiplication of X and A as follows:

$$A_{i,j} = \frac{\frac{1}{1+\exp\left(\frac{D_{i,j}-\pi}{\tau}\right)}}{\sum_{i=1}^{N}\left(\frac{1}{1+\exp\left(\frac{D_{i,j}-\pi}{\tau}\right)}\right)} \quad \text{for } i,j \in [1,...,N], \tag{7}$$

$$X' = \langle X - XA \rangle + XA, \tag{8}$$

where τ is the temperature of the sigmoid function and $\langle \cdot \rangle$ is the *detach* (in PyTorch) or *stop gradient* (in Tensorflow) function which prevents the back-propagation.

For further explanation of Eq. (8), we replace the input of pedestrian group pooling module X with a new pedestrian trajectory feature X' in implementation. To be specific, we can remove XA in the forward pass, allowing us to compute a loss for the trajectory feature X. In contrast, due to the stop gradient $\langle \cdot \rangle$, the loss is only backpropagated to XA in the backward pass. To this end, we can train both the convolutional layer F_ϕ and the learnable threshold parameter π which are used for the computation of the pairwise distance matrix D and the construction of group index set G, respectively.

3.3   Pedestrian Group Hierarchy Architecture

Using the estimated pedestrian grouping information, we reconstruct the initial social interaction graph $\mathcal{G}_{ped}$ in an efficient form for pedestrian trajectory prediction. Instead of the existing complex and complete pedestrian graph, intra- and inter-group interaction graphs capture the group-ware social relation, as illustrated in Fig. 3

Intra-group Interaction Graph.   We design a pedestrian interaction graph that captures relations between members affiliated with the same group. The intra-group interaction graph $\mathcal{G}_{member} = (\mathcal{V}_{ped}, \mathcal{E}_{member})$ consists of a set of pedestrian nodes $\mathcal{V}_{ped}$ and edges on their pairwise social interaction of group members $\mathcal{E}_{member} = \{e_{i,j} \,|\, i,j \in [1,...,N], k \in [1,...,K], \{i,j\} \subset G_k\}$. Through this graph representation, pedestrian nodes can learn social norms of internal collision avoidance between group members while maintaining their own formations and on-going directions.

Inter-group Interaction Graph.   Inter-group interactions (group-group relation) are indispensable to learn social norms between groups as well. To take various group behaviors such as following a leading group, avoiding collisions and joining a new group, we create an inter-group interaction graph $\mathcal{G}_{group} = (\mathcal{V}_{group}, \mathcal{E}_{group})$. Here, nodes refer to each group's features $\mathcal{V}_{group} = \{\overline{X}_k \,|\, k \in [1,...,K]\}$ generated with our pedestrian group pooling operation, and edges mean the pairwise group-group interactions $\mathcal{E}_{group} = \{\overline{e}_{p,q} \,|\, p,q \in [1,...,K]\}$.

Group Integration Network.   We incorporate the social interactions as a form of group hierarchy into well-designed existing trajectory prediction baseline models in Fig. 3(b). Meaningful features can be extracted by feeding a different type of graph-structured data into the same baseline model. Here, the baseline models share their weights to reduce the amount of parameters while enriching the augmentation effect. Afterward, the output features from the baseline models are aggregated agent-wise, and are then used to predict the probability map of future trajectories using our group integration module. The generated output trajectory $\widehat{Y}$ with the group integration network F_ψ is formulated as:

$$\widehat{Y} = F_\psi \big(\underbrace{F_\theta(X, \mathcal{G}_{ped})}_{\text{Agent-wise GNN}}, \ \underbrace{F_\theta(X, \mathcal{G}_{member})}_{\text{Intra-group GNN}}, \ \underbrace{F_\theta(\overline{X}, \mathcal{G}_{group})}_{\text{Inter-group GNN}} \big). \tag{9}$$

Group-Level Latent Vector Sampling.   To infer the multi-modal future paths of pedestrians, an additional random latent vector is introduced with an input observation path. This latent vector becomes a factor, determining a person's choice of behavior patterns, such as acceleration/deceleration and turning to right/left. There are two ways to adopt this latent vector in trajectory generation: (1) Scene-level sampling [17] where everyone in the scene shares one latent vector, unifying the behavior patterns of all pedestrians in a scene (*e.g.,* all pedestrians are slow down); (2) Pedestrian-level sampling [50] that allocates the different latent vectors for each pedestrian, but forces the pedestrians to have different patterns, where the group behavior property is lost.

We propose a group-level latent vector sampling method as a compromise of the two ways. We use the group information estimated from the GP-Graph to share the latent vector between groups. If two people are not associated with the same group, an independent random noise is assigned as a latent vector. In this way, it is possible to sample a multi-modal trajectory, which is independent of other groups members and follows associated group behaviors. The effectiveness of the group-level sampling is visualized in Sect. 4.3.

3.4 Implementation Details

To validate the generality of our GP-Graph, we incorporate it into four state-of-the-art baselines: three different GNN-based baseline methods including 3TGCNN (GCN-based) [39], SGCN (GAT-based) [54] and STAR (Transformer-based) [69], and one non-GNN model, PECNet [36]. We simply replace their trajectory prediction parts with ours. We additionally embed our agent/intra-/inter-graphs on the baseline networks, and compute integrated output trajectories to obtain the group-aware prediction.

For our proposed modules, we initialize the learnable parameter π as one, which cut the total number of nodes moderately down by half, with the group pooling in the initial training step. Other learnable parameters such as F_θ, F_ϕ and F_ψ are randomly initialized. We set the hyperparameter τ to 0.1 to give the binary thresholding function a steep slope.

To train the GP-Graph architecture, we use the same training hyperparameters (e.g., batch size, train epochs, learning rate, learning rate decay), loss functions, and optimizers of the baseline models. We note that we do not use additional group labels for an apple-to-apple comparison with the baseline models. Our group assignment module is trained to estimate effective groups for trajectory prediction in an unsupervised manner. Thanks to our powerful Straight-Through Group Estimator, it accomplish promising results over other supervised group detection networks [7] that require additional group labels.

4 Experiments

In this section, we conduct comprehensive experiments to verify how the grouping strategy contributes to pedestrian trajectory prediction. We first briefly describe our experimental setup (Sect. 4.1). We then provide comparison results with various baseline models for both group detection and trajectory prediction (Sect. 4.3 and Sect. 4.2). We lastly conduct an extensive ablation study to demonstrate the effect of each component of our method (Sect. 4.4).

4.1 Experimental Setup

Datasets.   We evaluate the effectiveness of our GP-Graph by incorporating it into several baseline models and check the performance improvement on public datasets: ETH [42], UCY [28], Stanford Drone Dataset (SDD) [47], and the

Table 1. Comparison between GP-Graph architecture and the vanilla agent-wise interaction graph for four state-of-the-art multi-modal trajectory prediction models, Social-STGCNN [39], SGCN [54], STAR [69] and PECNet [36]. The models are evaluated on the ETH [42], UCY [28], SDD [47] and GCS [67] datasets. Gain: performance improvement w.r.t FDE over the baseline models, Unit for ADE and FDE: meter, **Bold**: Best.

	STGCNN				GP-Graph-STGCNN					SGCN				GP-Graph-SGCN				
	ADE↓	FDE↓	COL↓	TCC↑	ADE↓	FDE↓	COL↓	TCC↑	Gain↑	ADE↓	FDE↓	COL↓	TCC↑	ADE↓	FDE↓	COL↓	TCC↑	Gain↑
ETH	0.73	1.21	1.80	0.47	**0.48**	**0.77**	1.15	0.63	36.4%	0.63	1.03	1.69	0.55	**0.43**	**0.63**	1.35	**0.65**	38.8%
HOTEL	0.41	0.68	3.94	0.28	**0.24**	**0.40**	2.00	0.32	41.2%	0.32	0.55	2.52	0.29	**0.18**	**0.30**	0.66	**0.35**	45.5%
UNIV	0.49	0.91	9.69	0.63	**0.29**	**0.47**	7.54	0.77	48.4%	0.37	0.70	6.85	0.69	**0.24**	**0.42**	5.52	**0.80**	40.0%
ZARA1	0.33	0.52	2.54	0.71	**0.24**	**0.40**	2.13	0.82	23.1%	0.29	0.53	0.79	0.74	**0.17**	**0.31**	0.62	**0.86**	41.5%
ZARA2	0.30	0.48	7.15	0.39	**0.23**	**0.40**	3.80	0.49	16.7%	0.25	0.45	2.23	0.49	**0.15**	**0.29**	1.44	**0.56**	35.6%
AVG	0.45	0.76	5.02	0.50	**0.29**	**0.49**	3.32	0.60	35.5%	0.37	0.65	2.82	0.55	**0.23**	**0.39**	1.92	**0.64**	40.0%
SDD	20.8	33.2	6.79	0.47	10.6	20.5	4.36	0.67	38.3%	25.0	41.5	4.45	0.57	**15.7**	**32.5**	2.59	**0.60**	21.7%
GCS	14.7	23.9	3.92	0.70	11.5	19.3	1.24	0.73	19.2%	11.2	20.7	1.45	0.78	**7.8**	**13.7**	0.67	**0.79**	33.8%

	STAR				GP-Graph-STAR					PECNet				GP-Graph-PECNet				
	ADE↓	FDE↓	COL↓	TCC↑	ADE↓	FDE↓	COL↓	TCC↑	Gain↑	ADE↓	FDE↓	COL↓	TCC↑	ADE↓	FDE↓	COL↓	TCC↑	Gain↑
ETH	**0.36**	0.65	1.46	0.72	0.37	**0.58**	0.88	0.77	11.0%	0.64	1.13	3.08	0.58	**0.56**	**0.82**	2.38	0.59	27.3%
HOTEL	0.17	0.36	1.51	**0.32**	0.16	0.24	1.46	0.31	32.2%	0.22	0.38	5.69	0.33	**0.18**	**0.26**	3.45	0.34	32.1%
UNIV	**0.31**	0.62	1.95	0.69	0.31	0.57	1.65	0.73	7.4%	0.35	0.57	3.80	0.75	**0.31**	**0.46**	2.89	0.77	19.5%
ZARA1	0.26	0.55	1.55	0.73	**0.24**	**0.44**	1.39	0.82	20.3%	0.25	0.45	2.99	0.80	**0.23**	**0.40**	2.57	0.82	11.7%
ZARA2	0.22	0.46	1.46	**0.50**	0.21	0.39	1.27	0.46	14.3%	0.18	0.31	4.91	0.55	**0.17**	**0.27**	2.92	0.58	13.0%
AVG	**0.26**	0.53	1.59	0.59	0.26	**0.44**	1.33	0.62	15.7%	0.33	0.60	4.09	0.61	**0.29**	**0.44**	2.84	0.62	26.4%
SDD	14.9	28.2	0.72	0.59	13.7	25.2	0.35	0.61	10.4%	10.0	15.8	**0.22**	0.64	9.1	13.8	0.23	**0.65**	12.7%
GCS	15.6	31.8	1.79	**0.80**	14.9	30.3	0.81	0.80	4.8%	17.1	29.3	0.20	0.71	14.2	23.9	0.19	0.72	18.4%

Grand Central Station (GCS) [67] datasets. The ETH & UCY datasets contain five unique scenes (ETH, Hotel, Univ, Zara1 and Zara2) with 1,536 pedestrians, and the official leave-one-out strategy is used to train and to validate the models. SDD consists of various types of objects with a birds-eye view, and GCS shows highly congested pedestrian walking scenes. We use the standard training and evaluation protocol [17,19,36,39,50,54] in which the first 3.2 s (8 frames) are observed and next 4.8 s (12 frames) are used for a ground truth trajectory. Additionally, two scenes (Seq-eth, Seq-hotel) of the ETH datasets provide ground-truth group labels. We use them to evaluate how accurately our GP-Graph groups individual pedestrians.

Evaluation Protocols. For multi-modal human trajectory prediction, we follow a standard evaluation manner, in Social-GAN [17], generating 20 samples based on predicted probabilistic distributions, and then choosing the best sample to measure the evaluation metrics. We use same evaluation metrics of previous works [1,17,34,61] for future trajectory prediction. Average Displacement Error (ADE) computes the Euclidean distance between a prediction and ground-truth trajectory, while Final Displacement Error (FDE) computes the Euclidean distance between an end-point of prediction and ground-truth. Collision rate (COL) checks the percentage of test cases where the predicted trajectories of different agents run into collisions, and Temporal Correlation Coefficient (TCC) measures the Pearson correlation coefficient of motion patterns between a predicted and ground-truth trajectory. We use both ADE and FDE as accuracy measures, and both COL and TCC as reliability measures in our group-wise prediction. For the COL metric, we average a set of collision ratios over the 20 multi-modal samples.

Table 2. Comparison of GP-Graph on SGCN with other state-of-the-art group detection models (Precision/Recall). For fair comparison, the evaluation results are directly referred from [6,12]. S: Use a loss for supervision, **Bold**: Best, <u>Underline</u>: Second best.

		Shao et al. [53]	Zanotto et al. [71]	Yamaguchi et al. [66]	Ge et al. [14]	Solera et al. [57]	Fernando et al. [12]	GP-Graph	GP-Graph+S
Seq-eth	PW↑	44.5/**87.0**	79.0/82.0	72.9/78.0	80.7/80.7	91.1/83.4	<u>91.3</u>/83.5	**91.7**/82.1	91.1/<u>84.1</u>
	GM↑	69.3/68.2	– / –	60.6/76.4	87.0/84.2	<u>91.3</u>/**94.2**	**92.5**/**94.2**	86.9/86.8	**92.5**/<u>91.3</u>
Seq-hotel	PW↑	51.5/90.4	81.0/91.0	83.7/93.9	88.9/89.3	89.1/91.9	90.2/<u>93.1</u>	**91.5**/80.1	<u>90.4</u>/**93.3**
	GM↑	67.3/64.1	– / –	84.0/51.2	89.2/90.9	<u>97.3</u>/**97.7**	**97.5**/**97.7**	84.5/80.0	96.1/<u>96.0</u>

For grouping measures, we use precision and recall values based on two popular metrics, proposed in prior works [6,12]: A group pair score (PW) measures the ratio between group pairs that disagree on their cluster membership, and all possible pairs in a scene. A Group-MITRE score (GM) is a ratio of the minimum number of links for group members and fake counterparts for pedestrians who are not affiliated with any group.

4.2 Quantitative Results

Evaluation on Trajectory Prediction. We first compare our GP-Graph with conventional agent-wise prediction models on the trajectory prediction benchmarks. As reported in Table 1, our GP-Graph achieves consistent performance improvements on all the baseline models. Additionally, our group-aware prediction also reduces the collision rate between agents, and shows analogous motion patterns with its ground truth by capturing the group movement behavior well. The results demonstrate that the trajectory prediction models benefit from the group-awareness cue of our group assignment module.

Evaluation on Group Estimation. We also compare the grouping ability of our GP-Graph with that of state-of-the-art models in Table 2. Our group assignment module trained in an unsupervised manner achieves superior results in the PW precision in both scenes, but shows relatively low recall values over the baseline models.

There are various group interaction scenarios in both scenes, and we found that our model sometimes fails to assign pedestrians into one large group when either a person joins the group or the group splits into both sides to avoid a collision. In this situation, while forecasting agent-wise trajectories, it is advantageous to divide the group into sub-groups or singletons, letting them have different behavior patterns. Although false-negative group links sometimes occur during the group estimation because of this, it is not a big issue for trajectory prediction.

To measure the maximum capability of our group estimator, we additionally carry out an experiment with a supervision loss to reduce the false-negative group links. We use a binary cross-entropy loss between the distance matrix and the ground-truth group label. As shown in Table 2, the performance is comparable to the state-of-the art group estimation models with respect to the PW and GM metrics. This indicates that our learning trajectory grouping network can properly assign groups without needing complex clustering algorithms.

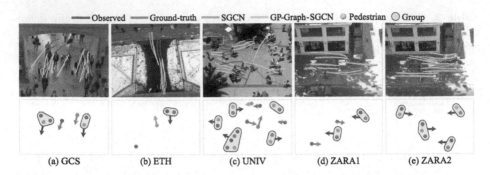

Fig. 4. (Top): Examples of pedestrian trajectory prediction results. (Bottom): Examples of group estimation results on ETH/UCY datasets [28,42].

4.3 Qualitative Results

Trajectory Visualization. In Fig. 4, we visualize some prediction results of GP-Graph and other methods. Since GP-Graph estimates the group-aware representations and captures both intra-/inter-group interactions, the predicted trajectories are closer to socially-acceptable trajectories and forms more stable behaviors between group members than those of the comparison models. Figure 4 also shows the pedestrians forming a group with our group assignment module. GP-Graph uses movement patterns and proximity information to properly create a group node for pedestrians who will take the same behaviors and walking directions in the future. This simplifies complex pedestrian graphs and eliminates potential errors associated with the collision avoidance between colleagues.

Group-Level Latent Vector Sampling. To demonstrate the effectiveness of the group-level latent vector sampling strategy, we compare ours with two previous strategies: scene-level and pedestrian-level sampling in Fig. 5. Even though the probability maps of pedestrians are well predicted with the estimated group information (Fig. 5(a)), its limitation still remains. For example, all sampled trajectories in the probability distributions lean toward the same directions (Fig. 5(b)) or are scattered with different patterns even within group members, which leads to collisions between colleagues (Fig. 5(c)). Our GP-Graph

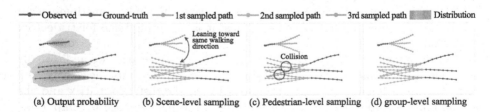

Fig. 5. (a) Visualization of predicted trajectory distribution in ZARA1 scene. (b–d) Examples of three sampled trajectories with scene-level, pedestrian-level, and group-level latent vector sampling strategy.

Table 3. Ablation study of various pooling&unpooling operations on SGCN [54] (FDE/COL/TCC). In the case of our Pedestrian Group Pooling&Unpooling, we additionally provide experimental results using the ground-truth group labels (Oracle). **Bold**: Best, <u>Underline</u>: Second best.

	ETH	HOTEL	UNIV	ZARA1	ZARA2	AVG
w/o Pool&Unpool	1.03 / 1.69 / 0.55	0.55 / 2.52 / 0.29	0.70 / <u>6.85</u> / 0.69	0.53 / 1.79 / 0.74	0.45 / <u>2.23</u> / 0.49	0.65 / 3.02 / 0.55
gPool&gUnpool [13]	0.73 / 1.88 / <u>0.66</u>	0.44 / 1.78 / **0.35**	<u>0.44</u> / 7.67 / <u>0.78</u>	<u>0.35</u> / <u>1.14</u> / <u>0.84</u>	<u>0.30</u> / 2.30 / <u>0.52</u>	<u>0.45</u> / <u>2.96</u> / <u>0.63</u>
SAGPool&gUnpool [25]	0.77 / 1.15 / 0.63	0.40 / 2.00 / <u>0.32</u>	0.47 / 7.54 / 0.77	0.40 / 2.13 / 0.82	0.40 / 3.80 / 0.49	0.49 / 3.32 / 0.60
Group Pool&Unpool	<u>0.63</u> / 1.35 / 0.65	<u>0.30</u> / <u>0.66</u> / **0.35**	**0.42** / **5.52** / **0.80**	**0.31** / **0.62** / **0.86**	**0.29** / **1.44** / **0.56**	**0.39** / **1.92** / **0.64**
+Oracle group label	**0.62** / <u>1.27</u> / **0.67**	**0.28** / **0.61** / **0.35**	– / – / –	– / – / –	– / – / –	– / – / –

with the proposed group-level sampling strategy predicts the collaborative walking trajectories of associated group members, which is independent of other groups (Fig. 5(d)).

4.4 Ablation Study

Pooling&Unpooling. To check the effectiveness of the proposed group pooling&unpooling layers, we compare it with different pooling methods including gPool [13] and SAGPool [25] with respect to FDE, COL and TCC. gPool proposes a top-k pooling by employing a projection vector to compute a rank score for each node. SAGpool is similar to the gPool method, but encodes topology information in a self-attention manner. As shown in Table 3, for both gPool and SAGPool, pedestrian features are lost via the pooling operations on unimportant nodes. By contrast, our pooling approach focuses on group representations of the pedestrian graph structure because it is optimized to capture group-related patterns.

Group Hierarchy Graph. We examine each component of the group hierarchy graph in Table 4. Both intra-/inter-group interaction graphs show a noticeable performance improvement compared to the baseline models, and the inter-group graph with our group pooling operation has the most important role in performance improvement (variants 1 to 4). The best performances can be achieved when all three types of interaction graphs are used with a weight-shared baseline model, which takes full advantage of graph augmentations (variants 4 and 5).

Grouping Method. We introduce a learnable threshold parameter π on the group assignment module in Eq. (2) because in practice the total number of groups in a scene can change according to the trajectory feature of the input pedestrian node. To highlight the importance of π, we test a fixed ratio group pooling with a node reduction ratio of 50%. As expected, the learnable threshold shows lower errors than the fixed ratio of group pooling (variants 5 and 6). This means that it is effective to guarantee the variability of group numbers, since the number can vary even when the same number of pedestrians exists in a scene.

Additionally, we report results for the group-level latent vector sampling strategy (variants 5 and 7). Since the ADE and FDE metrics are based on best-

Table 4. Ablation study (ADE/FDE). AW, MB, GP, WS, FG and GS respectively denote agent-wise pedestrian graph, intra-group member graph, inter-group graph, weight sharing among different interaction graph, fixed ratio node reduction of grouping and group-level latent vector sampling respectively. All tests are performed on SGCN. **Bold**: Best, <u>Underline</u>: Second best.

Varient ID	Components						Performance					
	AW	MB	GP	WS	FG	GS	ETH	HOTEL	UNIV	ZARA1	ZARA2	AVG
1	–	✓	–	–	–	–	0.45/0.74	0.26/0.48	0.39/0.66	0.28/0.48	0.23/0.41	0.32/0.55
2	–	–	✓	–	–	–	0.47/0.80	**0.17** / <u>0.31</u>	0.26/0.48	<u>0.18</u>/0.34	<u>0.16</u> / **0.29**	0.25/0.44
3	–	✓	✓	✓	–	–	**0.43** / <u>0.69</u>	0.20/0.37	0.25/0.47	0.19/0.35	0.17/<u>0.32</u>	0.25/0.44
4	✓	✓	✓	–	–	–	<u>0.44</u>/0.75	<u>0.18</u>/**0.30**	**0.23** / <u>0.43</u>	<u>0.18</u>/<u>0.33</u>	<u>0.16</u>/0.29	<u>0.24</u>/<u>0.42</u>
5	✓	✓	✓	✓	–	–	**0.43** / **0.63**	<u>0.18</u>/**0.30**	<u>0.24</u>/**0.42**	0.17/**0.31**	0.15/**0.29**	**0.23** / **0.39**
6	✓	✓	✓	✓	✓	–	0.55/0.87	0.24/<u>0.31</u>	0.42/0.82	0.30/0.56	0.22/0.35	0.35/0.58
7	✓	✓	✓	✓	–	✓	**0.43** / **0.63**	<u>0.18</u> / **0.30**	<u>0.24</u> / **0.42**	**0.17**/**0.31**	0.15 / **0.29**	**0.23** / **0.39**

of-many strategies, there is no difference with respect to numerical performance. However, it allows each group to keep their own behavior patterns, and to represent independency between groups, as in Fig. 5.

5   Conclusion

In this paper, we present a GP-Graph architecture for learning group-aware motion representations. We model group behaviors in crowded scenes by proposing a group hierarchy graph using novel pedestrian group pooling&unpooling operations. We use them for our group assignment module and straight-forward group estimation trick. Based on the GP-Graph, we introduce a multi-modal trajectory prediction framework that can attend intra-/inter group interaction features to capture human-human interactions as well as group-group interactions. Experiments demonstrate that our method significantly improves performance on challenging pedestrian trajectory prediction datasets.

Acknowledgement. This work is in part supported by the Institute of Information & communications Technology Planning & Evaluation (IITP) (No. 2019-0-01842, Artificial Intelligence Graduate School Program (GIST), No. 2021-0-02068, Artificial Intelligence Innovation Hub), the National Research Foundation of Korea (NRF) (No. 2020R1C1C1012635) grant funded by the Korea government (MSIT), Vehicles AI Convergence Research & Development Program through the National IT Industry Promotion Agency of Korea (NIPA) funded by the Ministry of Science and ICT (No. S1602-20-1001), the GIST-MIT Collaboration grant and AI-based GIST Research Scientist Project funded by the GIST in 2022.

References

1. Alahi, A., Goel, K., Ramanathan, V., Robicquet, A., Fei-Fei, L., Savarese, S.: Social LSTM: human trajectory prediction in crowded spaces. In: Proceedings of IEEE Conference on Computer Vision and Pattern Recognition (CVPR) (2016)

2. Bae, I., Jeon, H.G.: Disentangled multi-relational graph convolutional network for pedestrian trajectory prediction. In: Proceedings of the AAAI Conference on Artificial Intelligence (AAAI) (2021)
3. Bae, I., Park, J.H., Jeon, H.G.: Non-probability sampling network for stochastic human trajectory prediction. In: Proceedings of IEEE Conference on Computer Vision and Pattern Recognition (CVPR) (2022)
4. Bartoli, F., Lisanti, G., Ballan, L., Del Bimbo, A.: Context-aware trajectory prediction. In: 2018 24th International Conference on Pattern Recognition (ICPR) (2018)
5. Bengio, Y., Léonard, N., Courville, A.: Estimating or propagating gradients through stochastic neurons for conditional computation. arXiv preprint arXiv:1308.3432 (2013)
6. Bisagno, N., Zhang, B., Conci, N.: Group LSTM: group trajectory prediction in crowded scenarios. In: Leal-Taixé, L., Roth, S. (eds.) ECCV 2018. LNCS, vol. 11131, pp. 213–225. Springer, Cham (2019). https://doi.org/10.1007/978-3-030-11015-4_18
7. Cangea, C., Velickovic, P., Jovanovic, N., Kipf, T., Lio', P.: Towards sparse hierarchical graph classifiers. arXiv preprint arXiv:1811.01287 (2018)
8. Chen, G., Li, J., Lu, J., Zhou, J.: Human trajectory prediction via counterfactual analysis. In: Proceedings of International Conference on Computer Vision (ICCV) (2021)
9. Chen, G., Li, J., Zhou, N., Ren, L., Lu, J.: Personalized trajectory prediction via distribution discrimination. In: Proceedings of International Conference on Computer Vision (ICCV) (2021)
10. Defferrard, M., Bresson, X., Vandergheynst, P.: Convolutional neural networks on graphs with fast localized spectral filtering. In: Proceedings of the Neural Information Processing Systems (NeurIPS) (2016)
11. Dendorfer, P., Elflein, S., Leal-Taixé, L.: MG-GAN: a multi-generator model preventing out-of-distribution samples in pedestrian trajectory prediction. In: Proceedings of International Conference on Computer Vision (ICCV) (2021)
12. Fernando, T., Denman, S., Sridharan, S., Fookes, C.: GD-GAN: generative adversarial networks for trajectory prediction and group detection in crowds. In: Proceedings of Asian Conference on Computer Vision (ACCV) (2018)
13. Gao, H., Ji, S.: Graph U-Nets. In: Proceedings of the International Conference on Machine Learning (ICML) (2019)
14. Ge, W., Collins, R.T., Ruback, R.B.: Vision-based analysis of small groups in pedestrian crowds. IEEE Transactions on Pattern Analysis and Machine Intelligence (TPAMI) (2012)
15. Gilmer, J., Schoenholz, S.S., Riley, P.F., Vinyals, O., Dahl, G.E.: Neural message passing for quantum chemistry. In: Proceedings of the International Conference on Machine Learning (ICML) (2017)
16. Gu, T., et al.: Stochastic trajectory prediction via motion indeterminacy diffusion. In: Proceedings of IEEE Conference on Computer Vision and Pattern Recognition (CVPR) (2022)
17. Gupta, A., Johnson, J., Fei-Fei, L., Savarese, S., Alahi, A.: Social GAN: socially acceptable trajectories with generative adversarial networks. In: Proceedings of IEEE Conference on Computer Vision and Pattern Recognition (CVPR) (2018)
18. Helbing, D., Molnar, P.: Social force model for pedestrian dynamics. Phys. Rev. E 51(5), 4282 (1995)

19. Huang, Y., Bi, H., Li, Z., Mao, T., Wang, Z.: STGAT: modeling spatial-temporal interactions for human trajectory prediction. In: Proceedings of International Conference on Computer Vision (ICCV) (2019)
20. Ivanovic, B., Pavone, M.: The trajectron: probabilistic multi-agent trajectory modeling with dynamic spatiotemporal graphs. In: Proceedings of International Conference on Computer Vision (ICCV) (2019)
21. Jang, E., Gu, S., Poole, B.: Categorical reparameterization with Gumbel-Softmax. International Conference on Learning Representations (ICLR) (2017)
22. Kipf, T.N., Welling, M.: Semi-supervised classification with graph convolutional networks. In: International Conference on Learning Representations (ICLR) (2017)
23. Kosaraju, V., Sadeghian, A., Martín-Martín, R., Reid, I., Rezatofighi, H., Savarese, S.: Social-BiGAT: multimodal trajectory forecasting using bicycle-GAN and graph attention networks. In: Proceedings of the Neural Information Processing Systems (NeurIPS) (2019)
24. Lawal, I.A., Poiesi, F., Anguita, D., Cavallaro, A.: Support vector motion clustering. IEEE Trans. Circ. Syst. Video Technol. (TCSVT) **27**, 2395–2408 (2017)
25. Lee, J., Lee, I., Kang, J.: Self-attention graph pooling. In: Proceedings of the International Conference on Machine Learning (ICML) (2019)
26. Lee, M., Sohn, S.S., Moon, S., Yoon, S., Kapadia, M., Pavlovic, V.: Muse-VAE: multi-scale VAE for environment-aware long term trajectory prediction. In: Proceedings of IEEE Conference on Computer Vision and Pattern Recognition (CVPR) (2022)
27. Lee, N., Choi, W., Vernaza, P., Choy, C.B., Torr, P.H.S., Chandraker, M.: Desire: distant future prediction in dynamic scenes with interacting agents. In: Proceedings of IEEE Conference on Computer Vision and Pattern Recognition (CVPR) (2017)
28. Lerner, A., Chrysanthou, Y., Lischinski, D.: Crowds by example. Comput. Graph. Forum **26**(3), 655–664 (2007)
29. Li, J., Ma, H., Tomizuka, M.: Conditional generative neural system for probabilistic trajectory prediction. In: Proceedings of IEEE International Conference on Intelligent Robots and Systems (IROS) (2019)
30. Li, J., Yang, F., Tomizuka, M., Choi, C.: EvolveGraph: multi-agent trajectory prediction with dynamic relational reasoning. In: Proceedings of the Neural Information Processing Systems (NeurIPS) (2020)
31. Li, S., Zhou, Y., Yi, J., Gall, J.: Spatial-temporal consistency network for low-latency trajectory forecasting. In: Proceedings of International Conference on Computer Vision (ICCV) (2021)
32. Liang, J., Jiang, L., Murphy, K., Yu, T., Hauptmann, A.: The garden of forking paths: Towards multi-future trajectory prediction. In: Proceedings of IEEE Conference on Computer Vision and Pattern Recognition (CVPR) (2020)
33. Liang, J., Jiang, L., Niebles, J.C., Hauptmann, A.G., Fei-Fei, L.: Peeking into the future: predicting future person activities and locations in videos. In: Proceedings of IEEE Conference on Computer Vision and Pattern Recognition (CVPR) (2019)
34. Liu, Y., Yan, Q., Alahi, A.: Social NCE: contrastive learning of socially-aware motion representations. In: Proceedings of International Conference on Computer Vision (ICCV) (2021)
35. Maddison, C.J., Mnih, A., Teh, Y.W.: The concrete distribution: a continuous relaxation of discrete random variables. In: International Conference on Learning Representations (ICLR) (2017)
36. Mangalam, K., et al.: It is not the journey but the destination: endpoint conditioned trajectory prediction. In: Vedaldi, A., Bischof, H., Brox, T., Frahm, J.-M. (eds.)

ECCV 2020. LNCS, vol. 12347, pp. 759–776. Springer, Cham (2020). https://doi. org/10.1007/978-3-030-58536-5_45

37. Marchetti, F., Becattini, F., Seidenari, L., Bimbo, A.D.: Mantra: memory augmented networks for multiple trajectory prediction. In: Proceedings of IEEE Conference on Computer Vision and Pattern Recognition (CVPR) (2020)

38. Mehran, R., Oyama, A., Shah, M.: Abnormal crowd behavior detection using social force model. In: Proceedings of IEEE Conference on Computer Vision and Pattern Recognition (CVPR) (2009)

39. Mohamed, A., Qian, K., Elhoseiny, M., Claudel, C.: Social-STGCNN: a social spatio-temporal graph convolutional neural network for human trajectory prediction. In: Proceedings of IEEE Conference on Computer Vision and Pattern Recognition (CVPR) (2020)

40. Moussaïd, M., Perozo, N., Garnier, S., Helbing, D., Theraulaz, G.: The Walking Behaviour of Pedestrian Social Groups and Its Impact on Crowd Dynamics. Public Library of Science One (2010)

41. Pellegrini, S., Ess, A., Van Gool, L.: Improving data association by joint modeling of pedestrian trajectories and groupings. In: Daniilidis, K., Maragos, P., Paragios, N. (eds.) ECCV 2010. LNCS, vol. 6311, pp. 452–465. Springer, Heidelberg (2010). https://doi.org/10.1007/978-3-642-15549-9_33

42. Pellegrini, S., Ess, A., Schindler, K., Van Gool, L.: You'll never walk alone: modeling social behavior for multi-target tracking. In: Proceedings of International Conference on Computer Vision (ICCV) (2009)

43. Pfeiffer, M., Paolo, G., Sommer, H., Nieto, J.I., Siegwart, R.Y., Cadena, C.: A data-driven model for interaction-aware pedestrian motion prediction in object cluttered environments. In: Proceedings of IEEE International Conference on Robotics and Automation (ICRA) (2018)

44. Qiu, F., Hu, X.: Modeling group structures in pedestrian crowd simulation. Simul. Model. Pract. Theory **18**(2), 190–205 (2010)

45. Rhee, S., Seo, S., Kim, S.: Hybrid approach of relation network and localized graph convolutional filtering for breast cancer subtype classification. In: Proceedings of the Twenty-Seventh International Joint Conference on Artificial Intelligencev (IJCAI) (2018)

46. Robicquet, A., Sadeghian, A., Alahi, A., Savarese, S.: Learning social etiquette: human trajectory understanding in crowded scenes. In: Leibe, B., Matas, J., Sebe, N., Welling, M. (eds.) ECCV 2016. LNCS, vol. 9912, pp. 549–565. Springer, Cham (2016). https://doi.org/10.1007/978-3-319-46484-8_33

47. Robicquet, A., Sadeghian, A., Alahi, A., Savarese, S.: Learning social etiquette: human trajectory understanding in crowded scenes. In: Leibe, B., Matas, J., Sebe, N., Welling, M. (eds.) ECCV 2016. LNCS, vol. 9912, pp. 549–565. Springer, Cham (2016). https://doi.org/10.1007/978-3-319-46484-8_33

48. Rudenko, A., Palmieri, L., Lilienthal, A.J., Arras, K.O.: Human motion prediction under social grouping constraints. In: Proceedings of IEEE International Conference on Intelligent Robots and Systems (IROS) (2018)

49. Sadeghian, A., Kosaraju, V., Sadeghian, A., Hirose, N., Rezatofighi, H., Savarese, S.: Sophie: an attentive GAN for predicting paths compliant to social and physical constraints. In: Proceedings of IEEE Conference on Computer Vision and Pattern Recognition (CVPR) (2019)

50. Salzmann, T., Ivanovic, B., Chakravarty, P., Pavone, M.: Trajectron++: Dynamically-feasible trajectory forecasting with heterogeneous data. In: Proceedings of European Conference on Computer Vision (ECCV) (2020)

51. Seitz, M., Köster, G., Pfaffinger, A.: Pedestrian group behavior in a cellular automaton. In: Weidmann, U., Kirsch, U., Schreckenberg, M. (eds.) Pedestrian and Evacuation Dynamics 2012, pp. 807–814. Springer, Cham (2014). https://doi.org/10.1007/978-3-319-02447-9_67

52. Shafiee, N., Padir, T., Elhamifar, E.: Introvert: Human trajectory prediction via conditional 3d attention. In: Proceedings of IEEE Conference on Computer Vision and Pattern Recognition (CVPR) (2021)

53. Shao, J., Loy, C.C., Wang, X.: Scene-independent group profiling in crowd. In: Proceedings of IEEE Conference on Computer Vision and Pattern Recognition (CVPR) (2014)

54. Shi, L., et al.: SGCN: sparse graph convolution network for pedestrian trajectory prediction. In: Proceedings of IEEE Conference on Computer Vision and Pattern Recognition (CVPR) (2021)

55. Shi, X., et al.: Multimodal interaction-aware trajectory prediction in crowded space. In: Proceedings of the AAAI Conference on Artificial Intelligence (AAAI) (2020)

56. Singh, H., Arter, R., Dodd, L., Langston, P., Lester, E., Drury, J.: Modelling subgroup behaviour in crowd dynamics dem simulation. Appl. Math. Model. **33**(12), 4408–4423 (2009)

57. Solera, F., Calderara, S., Cucchiara, R.: Socially constrained structural learning for groups detection in crowd. IEEE Trans. Pattern Anal. Mach. Intell. **38**, 995–1008 (2016)

58. Sun, H., Zhao, Z., He, Z.: Reciprocal learning networks for human trajectory prediction. In: Proceedings of IEEE Conference on Computer Vision and Pattern Recognition (CVPR) (2020)

59. Sun, J., Jiang, Q., Lu, C.: Recursive social behavior graph for trajectory prediction. In: Proceedings of IEEE Conference on Computer Vision and Pattern Recognition (CVPR) (2020)

60. Sun, J., Li, Y., Fang, H.S., Lu, C.: Three steps to multimodal trajectory prediction: Modality clustering, classification and synthesis. In: Proceedings of International Conference on Computer Vision (ICCV) (2021)

61. Tao, C., Jiang, Q., Duan, L., Luo, P.: Dynamic and static context-aware LSTM for multi-agent motion prediction. In: Vedaldi, A., Bischof, H., Brox, T., Frahm, J.-M. (eds.) ECCV 2020. LNCS, vol. 12366, pp. 547–563. Springer, Cham (2020). https://doi.org/10.1007/978-3-030-58589-1_33

62. Varshneya, D., Srinivasaraghavan, G.: Human trajectory prediction using spatially aware deep attention models. arXiv preprint arXiv:1705.09436 (2017)

63. Veličković, P., Cucurull, G., Casanova, A., Romero, A., Liò, P., Bengio, Y.: Graph attention networks. In: International Conference on Learning Representations (ICLR) (2018)

64. Vemula, A., Muelling, K., Oh, J.: Social attention: modeling attention in human crowds. In: Proceedings of IEEE International Conference on Robotics and Automation (ICRA) (2018)

65. Xu, Y., Wang, L., Wang, Y., Fu, Y.: Adaptive trajectory prediction via transferable GNN. In: Proceedings of IEEE Conference on Computer Vision and Pattern Recognition (CVPR) (2022)

66. Yamaguchi, K., Berg, A.C., Ortiz, L.E., Berg, T.L.: Who are you with and where are you going? In: Proceedings of IEEE Conference on Computer Vision and Pattern Recognition (CVPR) (2011)

67. Yi, S., Li, H., Wang, X.: Understanding pedestrian behaviors from stationary crowd groups. In: Proceedings of IEEE Conference on Computer Vision and Pattern Recognition (CVPR) (2015)

68. Ying, Z., You, J., Morris, C., Ren, X., Hamilton, W., Leskovec, J.: Hierarchical graph representation learning with differentiable pooling. In: Proceedings of the Neural Information Processing Systems (NeurIPS) (2018)
69. Yu, C., Ma, X., Ren, J., Zhao, H., Yi, S.: Spatio-temporal graph transformer networks for pedestrian trajectory prediction. In: Vedaldi, A., Bischof, H., Brox, T., Frahm, J.-M. (eds.) ECCV 2020. LNCS, vol. 12357, pp. 507–523. Springer, Cham (2020). https://doi.org/10.1007/978-3-030-58610-2_30
70. Yuan, Y., Weng, X., Ou, Y., Kitani, K.: AgentFormer: agent-aware transformers for socio-temporal multi-agent forecasting. In: Proceedings of International Conference on Computer Vision (ICCV) (2021)
71. Zanotto, M., Bazzani, L., Cristani, M., Murino, V.: Online Bayesian nonparametrics for group detection. In: Proceedings of British Machine Vision Conference (BMVC) (2012)
72. Zhang, M., Cui, Z., Neumann, M., Chen, Y.: An end-to-end deep learning architecture for graph classification. In: Proceedings of the AAAI Conference on Artificial Intelligence (AAAI) (2018)
73. Zhang, P., Ouyang, W., Zhang, P., Xue, J., Zheng, N.: SR-LSTM: state refinement for LSTM towards pedestrian trajectory prediction. In: Proceedings of IEEE Conference on Computer Vision and Pattern Recognition (CVPR) (2019)
74. Zhao, H., Wildes, R.P.: Where are you heading? dynamic trajectory prediction with expert goal examples. In: Proceedings of International Conference on Computer Vision (ICCV) (2021)
75. Zhao, T., et al.: Multi-agent tensor fusion for contextual trajectory prediction. In: Proceedings of IEEE Conference on Computer Vision and Pattern Recognition (CVPR) (2019)
76. Zhong, J., Cai, W., Luo, L., Yin, H.: Learning behavior patterns from video: a data-driven framework for agent-based crowd modeling. In: Proceedings of the 2015 International Conference on Autonomous Agents and Multiagent Systems (AAMAS) (2015)
77. Zhou, B., Tang, X., Wang, X.: Coherent filtering: Detecting coherent motions from crowd clutters. In: Proceedings of European Conference on Computer Vision (ECCV) (2012)
78. Zhou, B., Wang, X., Tang, X.: Understanding collective crowd behaviors: learning a mixture model of dynamic pedestrian-agents. In: Proceedings of IEEE Conference on Computer Vision and Pattern Recognition (CVPR) (2012)

Sequential Multi-view Fusion Network for Fast LiDAR Point Motion Estimation

Gang Zhang[2], Xiaoyan Li[1(✉)], and Zhenhua Wang[3]

[1] Beijing Municipal Key Lab of Multimedia and Intelligent Software Technology, Beijing Artificial Intelligence Institute, Faculty of Information Technology, Beijing University of Technology, Beijing 100124, China
hblixy2@gmail.com
[2] Damo Academy, Alibaba Group, Hangzhou, China
[3] Cenozoic Robot, Lanzhou, China

Abstract. The LiDAR point motion estimation, including motion state prediction and velocity estimation, is crucial for understanding a dynamic scene in autonomous driving. Recent 2D projection-based methods run in real-time by applying the well-optimized 2D convolution networks on either the bird's-eye view (BEV) or the range view (RV) but suffer from lower accuracy due to information loss during the 2D projection. Thus, we propose a novel sequential multi-view fusion network (SMVF), composed of a BEV branch and an RV branch, in charge of encoding the motion information and spatial information, respectively. By looking from distinct views and integrating with the original LiDAR point features, the SMVF produces a comprehensive motion prediction, while keeping its efficiency. Moreover, to generalize the motion estimation well to the objects with fewer training samples, we propose a sequential instance copy-paste (SICP) for generating realistic LiDAR sequences for these objects. The experiments on the SemanticKITTI moving object segmentation (MOS) and Waymo scene flow benchmarks demonstrate that our SMVF outperforms all existing methods by a large margin.

Keywords: Motion state prediction · Velocity estimation · Multi-view fusion · Generalization of motion estimation

1 Introduction

Based on the 3D point clouds captured at consecutive time steps, the motion estimation aims at describing which parts of the scene are moving and where they are moving to. It is a combination of moving object segmentation and scene flow estimation, which are highly related and can be given by a single inference. The motion estimation provides a low-level understanding of a dynamic scene

---

Supplementary Information The online version contains supplementary material available at https://doi.org/10.1007/978-3-031-20047-2_17.

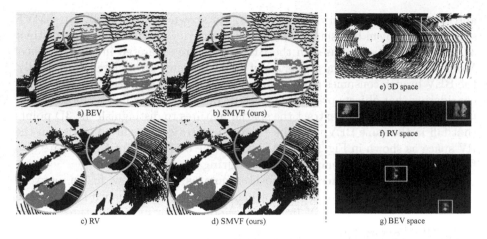

Fig. 1. The left part shows that the previous single-view methods frequently confuse points projected to the same or nearby 2D grids (a,c), while our SMVF solves the problem (b,d). The predicted moving points are shown in red, while the stationary ones are shown in black. The right part shows two moving pedestrians with almost the same velocity in the 3D space (e), while their trajectories are distorted in the RV space (f) but consistent in the BEV space (g). The red pedestrians are in the current scan and the green ones are in the history scan.

that not only benefits downstream tasks, such as object trajectory prediction, object tracking, simultaneous localization and mapping (SLAM), *etc.*, but also remedies for undetected objects in the perception system. Therefore, an accurate, fast, and well-generalized motion estimation algorithm is crucial for real-world applications, *e.g.* autonomous driving. Previous methods are grouped as point-based methods, sparse voxel-based methods, and 2D projection-based methods.

The point-based methods, including FlowNet3D [14], FlowNet3D++ [24], MeteorNet [15], and HPLFlowNet [9], directly process the raw unordered 3D points. These methods extract motion information by searching the spatiotemporal neighborhoods, which is both memory and computation inefficient. Thus, these methods are rarely used in real-world autonomous driving systems. To reduce the memory and computation costs, the sparse voxel-based methods [4,18] quantize a sequence of the LiDAR points into sparse voxels, and apply convolution operations on these non-empty voxels along spatial and temporal dimensions. However, they are still too computationally expensive to run in real-time.

The 2D projection-based methods first project the 3D points onto a 2D plane, such as bird's-eye view (BEV) [10,25] or range view (RV) [3,6], to generate a sequence of 2D pseudo images, where existing optical flow methods [5,17,19] of the 2D image domain can be applied. Generally, these methods achieve real-time inference speed but have lower accuracy due to the 2D projection information loss as shown in Fig. 1(a,c).

For accurate and fast LiDAR point motion estimation, it is argued that the deficiencies of the 2D projection-based paradigms can be remedied by division and cooperation between different views. As shown in Fig. 1(b,d), our SMVF solves this problem by using the proposed multi-view features since the distinct 3D points that are confused in the BEV space are separated in the RV space. Moreover, in this work, the properties of different views are explored. Specifically, the BEV branch consumes multiple LiDAR scans for motion features extraction, considering that objects primarily move on the BEV plane. The RV branch only uses the current scan to extract the spatial features to distinguish the 3D points that fall in the same BEV grid, since the object trajectories are distorted in the RV space as shown in Fig. 1(e–g). Moreover, the original point features are also fused to alleviate other information loss during the 2D projection.

In this work, we present a novel sequential multi-view fusion network (SMVF), which consists of two complementary branches, namely a BEV branch and an RV branch. The BEV branch is responsible for motion features extraction according to a sequence of consecutive LiDAR scans, while the RV branch extracts complementary spatial features only from the current scan. Finally, the motion and spatial features are fused with the 3D point features to acquire per-point motion estimation. Besides, the sequential instance copy-paste (SICP) is designed to generate and insert object trajectories into a sequence of LiDAR scans to mimic the real data and further improve the generalization ability of a motion estimator. Our contributions include:

- The SMVF is designed for accurate and fast LiDAR point motion estimation by fusing motion features from the BEV and spatial features from the RV.
- The SICP is proposed to generalize the motion estimation well to the objects with fewer training samples.
- Our SMVF currently ranks **1st** on the SemanticKITTI MOS leaderboard and Waymo scene flow benchmark, running 13 ms on NVIDIA RTX 2080Ti GPU with TensorRT [22] FP16 inference mode.

2   Related Work

Point motion estimation, including moving object segmentation (MOS) and scene flow estimation, can not only benefit the downstream tasks, such as tracking and SLAM, but also serve as a powerful basis for planning when the object detection and tracking systems fail in the presence of undetected objects.

Moving Object Segmentation (MOS). In this task, each 3D point is classified as moving or stationary. SpSequenceNet [18] divides the 3D space uniformly into structured voxels, and then a cross-frame global attention module and a cross-frame local interpolation module operating on these sparse voxels are proposed to capture spatial and temporal information. Recently, Chen *et al.* [3] project the 3D points to the RV, and generate the 2D residual distance images between the current frame and history frames to provide motion information. Different from the previous voxel-based methods, the 2D projection-based methods support real-time perception and are easily deployed on an autonomous vehicle.

Scene Flow Estimation. In this work, the scene flow estimation refers to predicting the velocity for each 3D point instead of each BEV grid. To achieve this goal, a series of point-based methods are proposed. FlowNet3D [14] adopts the time-consuming farthest point sampling (FPS) for downsampling points, and ball query for spatiotemporal neighbor searching. MeteorNet [15] proposes a direct grouping and a chained-flow grouping to determine the spatiotemporal neighborhoods. Inspired by Bilateral Convolution Layers (BCL), HPLFlowNet [9] proposes DownBCL, UpBCL, and CorrBCL that restore the spatial relationship of points to accelerate the FlowNet3D. These point-based methods can preserve and exploit the information from raw point clouds, but they are computation and memory inefficient. Recently, the FastFlow3D [10] fuses the BEV motion features and the point features for real-time scene flow estimation. However, the point features cannot be fully digested by a shared MLP and fail to compensate for the aforementioned projection information loss. Therefore, the FastFlow3D may classify the stationary points as moving.

Other Spatiotemporal Encoding Methods. Other methods that also exploit the spatiotemporal information are introduced for inspiration. For multi-scan LiDAR semantic segmentation, Minkowski CNN [4] projects 3D points into voxels and applies a novel 4D spatiotemporal convolution along both 3D spatial and 1D temporal dimensions. Duerr *et al.* [6] project the input point clouds onto the RV and propose a novel temporal memory alignment strategy to align features between adjacent frames. For object trajectory prediction, the RV-FuseNet [11] consumes multiple LiDAR scans in the RV space and predicts object trajectory on the BEV plane. MVFuseNet [12] fuses the features from the multi-scan BEV and multi-scan RV branches to form the new BEV features for the latter prediction. In contrast to RV-FuseNet and MVFuseNet, our SMVF conducts motion estimation on 3D points instead of BEV grids. Moreover, our SMVF illustrates the complementary properties of the two views, which is not discussed before.

3 Approach

The sequential multi-view fusion network (SMVF) is proposed for LiDAR point motion estimation, as shown in Fig. 2. The SMVF encodes the features in a multi-view manner: the bird's-eye view (BEV) branch takes a sequence of consecutive LiDAR scans as input for motion information extraction; the range view (RV) branch only uses the current LiDAR scan to extract spatial information for distinguishing nearby points; finally, the features of the point clouds and the two views are fused for per-point motion prediction. Moreover, the sequential instance copy-paste (SICP) is designed to augment more training samples.

The problem definition, multi-view feature encoding paradigm, sequential instance copy-paste, and the overall optimization objectives are illustrated in Sects. 3.1, 3.2, 3.3, and 3.4, respectively.

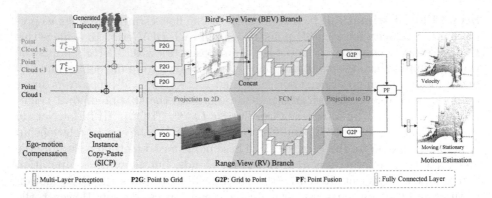

Fig. 2. Overview of the SMVF. First, the input sequential point clouds are adjusted by ego-motion compensation and augmented by the sequential instance copy-paste. Then, efficient and effective feature extraction is achieved by looking from the BEV and RV with 2D FCNs. Finally, features from the original points and the two branches are fused in 3D space to produce per-point motion predictions. Note that the multi-layer perception (MLP) of each LiDAR frame has shared parameters.

3.1   Problem Definition

Point motion estimation is an integration of scene flow estimation and moving object segmentation. A motion estimator $\mathcal{M}$ takes a sequence of 3D point clouds $\{\boldsymbol{p}_t^j\}$, $\{\boldsymbol{p}_{t-1}^j\}$, ..., $\{\boldsymbol{p}_{t-k}^j\}$ as inputs (where t is a constant denoting the time stamp, and $k+1$ is the size of the time window, and $j = 1, \ldots, N$ denotes the index of the point in a scan with N points), and outputs a set of motion vectors $\{\boldsymbol{m}_t^j\}$ at time t, as the following,

$$\mathcal{M}(\{\boldsymbol{p}_t^j\}, \{\boldsymbol{p}_{t-1}^j\}, \ldots, \{\boldsymbol{p}_{t-k}^j\}) = \{\boldsymbol{m}_t^j\}, \tag{1}$$

where the motion vector $\boldsymbol{m}_t^j = (v_x, v_y, v_z, m)$ corresponding to the point $\boldsymbol{p}_t^j$ includes the velocities (v_x, v_y, v_z) of the point $\boldsymbol{p}_t^j$ in each axis, and a binary variable m, indicating whether the point is moving ($m = 1$) or not ($m = 0$).

3.2   Multi-view Feature Encoding

The proposed SMVF exploits the multi-view projection-based paradigm for efficient and effective feature encoding. Since object movements in autonomous driving are mostly present on the x-y plane, the BEV that squeezes the z-axis is adequate for encoding temporal motion information. However, there are spatial confusions between points that are projected to the same or nearby BEV grid. Thus, the RV encoding of the current LiDAR scan is required for complementing the spatial information. Both BEV and RV branches have a similar three-step process, including 1) projection to the 2D space (P2G), 2) feature extraction with a fully convolutional network (FCN), and 3) projection back to the 3D

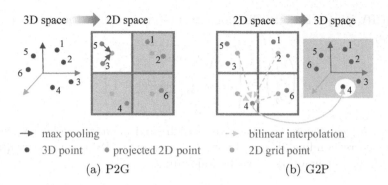

3D space ➡ 2D space   2D space ➡ 3D space

(a) P2G   (b) G2P

➡ max pooling   ⇢ bilinear interpolation
• 3D point   • projected 2D point   • 2D grid point

Fig. 3. An illustration of Point to Grid (a) and Grid to Point (b) operations. The white area shows the targets of interest in the output space.

space (G2P). For the BEV branch, each LiDAR frame is projected to the BEV grid separately.

Ego-Motion Compensation. Each LiDAR scan is described by its local coordinate system. The proposed method transforms the history LiDAR scans $(t-1, \ldots, t-k)$ to the coordinates of the current scan (t), to avoid specious motion estimation caused by ego-motion. The k consecutive relative transformations are represented as transformation matrices $T_{t-1}^t, \ldots, T_{t-k}^t$ ($T_i^t \in \mathbb{R}^{4 \times 4}$), and assumed to be known following the common practice.

Point to Grid (P2G). The Point to Grid (P2G) operation transforms the 3D point features to the 2D grid feature maps (*e.g.* BEV, RV), as shown in Fig. 3a. Each frame of consecutive LiDAR scans applies the same P2G operation separately. Thus, we only illustrate the P2G of the current scan t. The jth 3D point of the current scan t is $\boldsymbol{p}_t^j = (x_j, y_j, z_j)$, which is first projected onto the 2D grid to acquire the corresponding 2D coordinates (u_j, v_j). Then the features $\mathcal{F}_{j,c}^{3D}$ of 3D points that fall in the same 2D grid (h, w), namely $\lfloor u_j \rfloor = h$ and $\lfloor v_j \rfloor = w$, are aggregated by max-pooling to form the 2D grid features $\mathcal{F}_{h,w,c}^{2D}$,

$$\mathcal{F}_{h,w,c}^{2D} = \max_{\forall j \text{ s.t. } \lfloor u_j \rfloor = h, \lfloor v_j \rfloor = w} \mathcal{F}_{j,c}^{3D}. \tag{2}$$

Both BEV and RV are 2D representations. They use a similar P2G operation and just differ in the way of 2D projection. For the BEV projection, it projects the 3D point onto the x-y plane that is discretized by using a rectangular 2D grid $(x_{min}, y_{min}, x_{max}, y_{max})$ with the predefined width W_{bev} and height H_{bev}. The corresponding 2D coordinates on the BEV are formulated as

$$\begin{pmatrix} u_j \\ v_j \end{pmatrix} = \begin{pmatrix} \frac{x_j - x_{min}}{x_{max} - x_{min}} \times W_{bev} \\ \frac{y_j - y_{min}}{y_{max} - y_{min}} \times H_{bev} \end{pmatrix}. \tag{3}$$

For the RV projection, the 3D point is first mapped to the spherical space (r_j, θ_j, ϕ_j),

$$\begin{pmatrix} r_j \\ \theta_j \\ \phi_j \end{pmatrix} = \begin{pmatrix} \sqrt{x_j^2 + y_j^2 + z_j^2} \\ \arcsin\left(\frac{z_j}{\sqrt{x_j^2 + y_j^2 + z_j^2}}\right) \\ \arctan2(y_j, x_j) \end{pmatrix}, \tag{4}$$

where r_j, θ_j, ϕ_j denote the distance, zenith, and azimuth angle, respectively. Then, its corresponding 2D coordinates (u_j, v_j) on the RV are given by quantizing θ_j and ϕ_j but ignoring r_j as the following,

$$\begin{pmatrix} u_j \\ v_j \end{pmatrix} = \begin{pmatrix} \frac{1}{2}(1 - \phi_j \pi^{-1}) W_{rv} \\ \left[1 - (\theta_j + f_{up}) f^{-1}\right] H_{rv} \end{pmatrix}, \tag{5}$$

where $f = f_{up} + f_{down}$ is the LiDAR vertical field-of-view, and W_{rv} and H_{rv} are the width and height of the RV.

Fully Convolutional Network (FCN). For efficiency, both BEV and RV branches adopt a similar 2D fully convolutional network (FCN) to extract meaningful features. The RV branch only takes the current LiDAR scan as input to provide spatial information and the input size of RV is $C \times H_{rv} \times W_{rv}$, where C denotes the number of feature channels. For the BEV branch, the features from consecutive LiDAR scans are concatenated to form a $(kC + C) \times H_{bev} \times W_{bev}$ input tensor, where k denotes the number of history LiDAR scans. The detailed architecture of the FCN can be seen in the supplementary material.

Grid to Point (G2P). On the contrary to the Point to Grid (P2G) operation, the Grid to Point (G2P) operation transfers the features from the 2D grid to the 3D point for the latter point-level prediction, as shown in Fig. 3b. The features of the jth 3D point p_t^j can be obtained by bilinear interpolation within the four-neighbor grids of its corresponding 2D position (u_j, v_j) as follows,

$$\mathcal{F}_{j,c}^{3D} = \sum_{p=0}^{1} \sum_{q=0}^{1} \omega_{p,q,j} \mathcal{F}_{\lfloor u_j \rfloor + p, \lfloor v_j \rfloor + q, c}^{2D}, \tag{6}$$

where $\omega_{p,q,j} = (1 - |u_j - (\lfloor u_j \rfloor + p)|)(1 - |v_j - (\lfloor v_j \rfloor + q)|)$ denotes the bilinear interpolation weight. The neighbor grids beyond the 2D grid range are regarded as all zeros.

Point Fusion. The point fusion (PF) module fuses the features from the 3D points and the projected features from the BEV and RV to form a final per-point estimation. The PF serves as a mid-fusion module and allows end-to-end training of the proposed SMVF. For efficiency, it only adopts a feature concatenation operation and two MLP layers for feature fusion. Finally, two additional fully connected (FC) layers predict the velocity and segmentation results, respectively. By using this simple fusion module, the network automatically learns motion information from the BEV branch, spatial information from the RV branch, and other complementary information from the original point clouds.

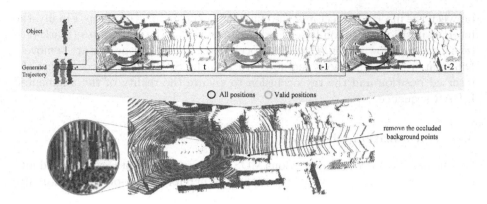

Fig. 4. Overview of the proposed sequential instance copy-paste (SICP). The augmented LiDAR sequence is shown with all scans overlapped. Note that all LiDAR scans have been compensated with ego-motion.

3.3 Sequential Instance Copy-Paste

The motion estimator usually presents lower confidence on the objects with fewer or even no training samples (*e.g. cyclist, dog, toy car*). Inspired by the previous 3D detection methods [13,26] that adopt the instance copy-paste strategy to improve the performance of rare classes (*e.g. pedestrian* and *cyclist*), we extend the instance copy-paste from a single frame to multiple frames as shown in Fig. 4. First, it constructs an object bank, consisting of the objects cropped from their original LiDAR scans according to the annotated 3D bounding boxes. Then, it uniformly samples a category and an object from this category. Finally, an object trajectory is generated by inserting this object to the LiDAR sequence.

Specifically, the object is assumed to be moving along its 3D bounding box heading yaw with a random sampled velocity $\tilde{v}$ on the x-y plane. The velocities $\tilde{v}_x$, $\tilde{v}_y$ of an inserted object are formulated by

$$\begin{pmatrix} \tilde{v}_x \\ \tilde{v}_y \end{pmatrix} = \begin{pmatrix} \tilde{v}\cos(yaw) \\ \tilde{v}\sin(yaw) \end{pmatrix}. \tag{7}$$

$\tilde{v}$ is sampled uniformly within a predefined range of each category and the object is moving backward when $\tilde{v}$ is negative. Its speed $\tilde{v}_z$ along the z-axis is calculated by ensuring that the object is moving on the ground.

Then, the position of an inserted object trajectory is determined by first filtering out the infeasible positions and then randomly sampling from the remaining candidates. The inserted object has a distance $\tilde{r}_k$ to the sensor in its original LiDAR scan. Given that the LiDAR point density is changed across different distances, the candidate positions in the tth scan are kept, only when their distance to the sensor are the same as $\tilde{r}_k$ (marked as a black circle in Fig. 4). Then, the corresponding positions in the history LiDAR scans can be derived from the above velocity $(\tilde{v}_x, \tilde{v}_y, \tilde{v}_z)$. A candidate position of the trajectory is filtered out if the inserted object cannot be placed on the ground or there is occlusion between the inserted object and the existing objects in any time step. Finally, the inserted position is randomly selected from the remaining candidates (marked as transparent yellow in Fig. 4) and the occluded background points are removed. Different from the previous methods [13, 26], the SICP specially considers the inserted position and the ray occlusion to ensure the reality of the augmented LiDAR sequence.

3.4 Optimization Objectives

For the moving object segmentation (MOS) task, the 3D points are classified into two categories, namely moving or stationary. Therefore, we apply the commonly-used cross-entropy (CE) loss, which can be formulated as,

$$\mathcal{L}_{CE} = -\frac{1}{N} \sum_{n=1}^{N} \sum_{c=1}^{C} y_n^c \log(\hat{y}_n^c), \tag{8}$$

where y_n^c ($y_n^c \in \{0,1\}$) and $\hat{y}_n^c$ ($\hat{y}_n^c \in [0,1]$) are the ground-truth label and the predicted probability of the cth class on the nth point. To facilitate more accurate classification on hard samples, another loss term $\mathcal{L}_{CE}^{20\%}$ only considers the top 20% points with higher losses. In addition, the Lovász-Softmax loss [2] $\mathcal{L}_{LS}$ is also adopted to directly optimize the Intersection over Union (IoU) metric. The total loss function for the MOS task is defined as

$$\mathcal{L}_{mos} = \mathcal{L}_{CE} + 4\mathcal{L}_{CE}^{20\%} + 3\mathcal{L}_{LS}. \tag{9}$$

For the scene flow estimation task, the L_2 error between the ground-truth velocities $\tilde{v}_n$ and the predicted velocities v_n is used as the following,

$$\mathcal{L}_{sf} = \frac{1}{N} \sum_{n=1}^{N} ||v_n - \tilde{v}_n||_2. \tag{10}$$

If a dataset simultaneously provides benchmarks of the two tasks, $\mathcal{L}_{mos}$ and $\mathcal{L}_{sf}$ are both adopted for the guidance of corresponding predictions.

4   Experiments

We conduct ablation studies and evaluate the performance of the proposed SMVF on the SemanticKITTI [1] benchmark for moving object segmentation and the Waymo Open Dataset [10] for scene flow estimation.

4.1 Datasets and Evaluation Metrics

SemanticKITTI. The SemanticKITTI [1] derives from the odometry dataset of the KITTI Vision Benchmark [8]. It contains 43,552 360° LiDAR scans from 22 sequences collected in a city of Germany. The training set (19,130 scans) consists of sequences from 00 to 10 except 08, and the sequence 08 (4,071 scans) is used for validation. The rest sequences (20,351 scans) from 11 to 21 are only provided with LiDAR point clouds and are used for the online leaderboard. This dataset is labeled with 28 classes. For the moving object segmentation (MOS) task, the same splits for training, validation, and test sets are used, while all classes are reorganized into only two types: moving and non-moving/static [3].

As the official guidance [3] suggests, we adopt the Intersection over Union (IoU) [7] on the **moving** class to evaluate the proposed SMVF and its competitors. It can be formulated as

$$IoU = \frac{TP}{TP + FP + FN},$$ (11)

where TP, FP, and FN correspond to the true positive, false positive, and false negative of the **moving** points.

Waymo Open Dataset. The Waymo Open Dataset is a large-scale dataset for autonomous driving perception across a diverse and rich domain [10, 20]. The scene flow labels are generated by leveraging the human-annotated tracked 3D objects in this dataset [20]. The training split consists of 800 run segments containing 158,081 frames in total, while the validation split contains 200 run segments with 39,987 frames.

The commonly-used metrics for scene flow estimation are the mean L_2 error of point-wise flow and the percentage of predictions with L_2 error below a given threshold [14, 23]. Considering that objects in autonomous driving have different speed distributions dictated by the object category (*e.g.* *vehicle*, *pedestrian*), prediction performances delineated by the object category are also reported.

4.2   Experimental Setup

Network Setup. The input point features contain x, y, z, *intensity*, r, Δx and Δy, where Δx and Δy denote the offsets to the corresponding BEV grid center. For the Waymo Open Dataset, *elongation* is used as an additional feature. As shown in Fig. 2, the first MLP layer of each LiDAR frame has shared parameters and outputs 64 feature channels, which the following P2G operation transforms to the BEV and RV feature maps, respectively. Both BEV and RV branches utilize a similar 2D FCN network with three down-sampling and two up-sampling stages, but the RV does not apply down-sampling along the height dimension. The PF module with only two MLP layers takes features from the three sources as inputs and outputs 64 feature channels. Finally, two FC layers are used for motion state prediction and scene flow estimation, respectively.

Data Augmentation. During training, we apply the widely-used data augmentation strategies, including random rotation around the z-axis, random global scale sampled from $[0.95, 1.05]$, random flipping along x and y axes, and random Gaussian noise $\mathcal{N}(0, 0.02)$. Besides, the proposed SICP is adopted.

4.3   Results on the SemanticKITTI

Moving object segmentation is evaluated on the SemanticKITTI. The 3D space is set to be within $[-50, 50]$m for the x and y axes and $[-2, 4]$m for the z-axis. For the BEV branch, the input resolutions are $W_{bev} = 512$ and $H_{bev} = 512$. For the RV branch, the input resolutions are $W_{rv} = 2048$ and $H_{rv} = 64$. Our SMVF is trained from scratch for 48 epochs with a batch size of 24, taking around 15 h on 8 NVIDIA RTX 2080Ti GPUs. Stochastic gradient descent (SGD) serves as the optimizer with a weight decay of 0.001 and a learning rate initialized to 0.02, which is decayed by 0.1 every 10 epochs.

Table 1. Moving object segmentation results on the SemanticKITTI validation and test set. k denotes the number of history LiDAR scans. * means the re-implementation based on its official code. "TRT16" means the TensorRT FP16 inference.

Method	k	val IoU	test IoU	Runtime
KPConv [21]	1	–	60.9	168 ms
SpSequenceNet [18]	1	–	43.2	450 ms
Chen *et al.* [3]	1	59.9	52.0	24.3 ms
SMVF [ours]	1	**75.1**	**72.1**	**21.8 ms**
Chen *et al.* [3]	8	66.5	62.5	24.8 ms
MotionNet* [25]	4	67.8	62.6	78.9 ms
SMVF [ours]	2	**76.9**	**75.9**	**24.3 ms**
SMVF [ours]; TRT16	2	**77.0**	**75.9**	**13 ms**

Comparison with the State of the Art. All methods are evaluated on the SemanticKITTI validation and test set with the official evaluation code. In Table 1, our SMVF outperforms the previous methods by remarkable margins. By utilizing the current LiDAR scan and one history LiDAR scan ($k = 1$), the point-based KPConv [21] and the sparse voxel-based SpSequenceNet [18] are ×7.7 and ×20.6 slower than our SMVF, respectively, and they also perform worse with -11.2 and -28.9 IoU drops on the test set, respectively. Chen *et al.* [3] ($k = 8$) based on the RV representation, runs as fast as our SMVF ($k = 2$), but it performs much worse with -10.4 and -13.4 IoU drops on the validation and test set, respectively. We re-implement the BEV-based MotionNet [25] on the SemanticKITTI based on its official code. For a fair comparison, the scope and partition of the 3D space are the same as our SMVF, while it divides 20 bins along the z-axis. The point-level prediction is acquired by its corresponding BEV grid prediction. Our SMVF ($k = 2$) outperforms the MotionNet on both IoU metric and inference speed. There are three primary reasons: 1) the Motion-Net is a BEV-based method that cannot distinguish the 3D points on the same BEV grid; 2) the MotionNet encodes the BEV features by the binary voxels that lead to information loss; 3) the MotionNet adopts a expensive spatiotemporal network to extract motion information. Besides, our SMVF can be easily deployed with TensorRT FP16 inference mode and runs only 13 ms, supporting real-time perception tasks in autonomous driving. **Ablation Studies.** The settings for the multi-view framework and the number of history LiDAR scans are evaluated on the SemanticKITTI validation set. As shown in Table 2, we can discover that: 1) the BEV branch is more suitable for extracting motion information than the RV branch (a,c and b,d); 2) the multi-view framework performs better than the single-view one (a,b and c,d); 3) based on our SMVF, the RV branch does not need to extract temporal information (d,e); 4) the segmentation performance rises up when more history LiDAR scans ($k \leqslant 2$) are incorporated, but the performance saturates when $k > 2$ (f,d,g,h).

Table 2. Ablative analysis on the SemanticKITTI validation set. "-": the branch is not applied. "multi": the branch takes multiple LiDAR scans as input. "single": the branch only uses the current LiDAR scan. k: the number of history LiDAR scans.

(a) Multi-view framework.

	BEV	RV	k	IoU	Runtime
a)	-	multi	2	63.8	**14.4 ms**
b)	single	multi	2	66.5	22.3 ms
c)	multi	-	2	73.5	15.9 ms
d)	multi	single	2	**76.9**	24.3 ms
e)	multi	multi	2	76.7	28.1 ms

(b) Number of history LiDAR scans.

	BEV	RV	k	IoU	Runtime
f)	multi	single	1	75.1	**21.8 ms**
d)	multi	single	2	**76.9**	24.3 ms
g)	multi	single	3	76.8	26.5 ms
h)	multi	single	4	**76.9**	29.0 ms

4.4 Results on the Waymo Open Dataset

The scene flow estimation task is conducted on the Waymo Open Dataset. The same configuration as FastFlow3D [10] is adopted. The 3D space is limited to $[-85, 85]$m for the x and y axes and $[-3, 3]$m for the z-axis. For the BEV branch, the input resolutions are $W_{bev} = 512$ and $H_{bev} = 512$. For the RV branch, the input resolutions are $W_{rv} = 2560$ and $H_{rv} = 64$. The proposed SMVF is trained from scratch for 24 epochs with a batch size of 24, taking around 40 h on 8 NVIDIA RTX 2080Ti GPUs. The optimizer is AdamW [16] with a weight decay of 0.001 and an initial learning rate of 0.002, which is decayed by 0.1 every 10 epochs. The SICP constructs the object bank on the training split by the annotated 3D bounding boxes and it inserts 10 object trajectories into each training sample consisting of $k + 1$ LiDAR scans.

Comparison with the State of the Art. As shown in Table 3, the point-based FlowNet3D [14] over-fits on the stationary class, and our SMVF surpasses it by a large margin for all the other metrics, while our SMVF runs ×5.7 faster. Compared with the FastFlow3D [10], our SMVF achieves higher performance especially for the mean L_2 error and the percentage of predictions with L_2 error $\leqslant 1.0$m/s. Besides, our SMVF shows obvious superiority for *Background* and the

Table 3. Scene flow performance comparison on the validation split of the Waymo Open Dataset. k denotes the number of history LiDAR scans. * means the re-implementation based on its official code. A: All. M: Moving. S: Stationary.

Method	k	SICP	Metric	Vehicle			Pedestrian			Cyclist			Background	Runtime
				A	M	S	A	M	S	A	M	S		
FlowNet3D* [14]	1		mean (m/s) ↓	1.90	7.25	**0.04**	0.92	1.34	**0.09**	3.49	3.94	**0.09**	**0.00**	172 ms
			⩽ 0.1 m/s ↑	67.4%	0.0%	90.9%	24.3%	0.0%	**72.9%**	9.2%	0.0%	79.3%	99.9%	
			⩽ 1.0 m/s ↑	75.9%	7.0%	**99.9%**	44.0%	17.3%	99.9%	12.6%	1.1%	99.9%	99.9%	
FastFlow3D [10]	1		mean (m/s) ↓	0.18	0.54	0.05	0.25	0.32	0.10	0.51	0.57	0.10	0.07	32.5 ms
			⩽ 0.1 m/s ↑	70.0%	11.6%	90.2%	**33.0%**	**14.0%**	71.4%	13.4%	4.8%	78.0%	95.7%	
			⩽ 1.0 m/s ↑	97.7%	92.8%	99.4%	96.7%	95.4%	99.4%	89.5%	88.2%	99.6%	96.7%	
SMVF [ours]	1		mean (m/s) ↓	0.17	0.51	0.05	**0.23**	0.29	0.11	0.38	0.42	0.10	0.028	**30 ms**
			⩽ 0.1 m/s ↑	67.7%	10.6%	90.4%	30.1%	13.3%	68.6%	14.6%	6.7%	75.1%	98.9%	
			⩽ 1.0 m/s ↑	**97.9%**	**92.9%**	99.6%	**98.2%**	**97.5%**	99.6%	95.6%	95.1%	99.7%	99.5%	
SMVF [ours]	1	✓	mean (m/s) ↓	**0.16**	**0.46**	0.05	**0.23**	**0.28**	0.11	**0.35**	**0.38**	0.11	0.028	**30 ms**
			⩽ 0.1 m/s ↑	67.8%	10.2%	89.8%	29.4%	11.7%	67.9%	**15.3%**	**7.7%**	73.2%	99.0%	
			⩽ 1.0 m/s ↑	**97.9%**	92.8%	99.7%	98.1%	97.4%	99.5%	**97.0%**	**96.8%**	99.3%	99.5%	
MotionNet* [25]	4		mean (m/s) ↓	0.20	0.64	**0.04**	0.20	0.25	**0.10**	0.35	0.38	**0.09**	0.05	79.1 ms
			⩽ 0.1 m/s ↑	68.8%	8.9%	89.7%	34.8%	17.6%	69.4%	15.6%	7.3%	77.2%	97.2%	
			⩽ 1.0 m/s ↑	97.5%	90.5%	**99.8%**	98.8%	98.3%	**99.8%**	96.4%	95.9%	**99.9%**	97.9%	
MotionNet* [25]	4	✓	mean (m/s) ↓	0.19	0.61	**0.04**	0.20	**0.24**	**0.10**	0.31	0.34	**0.09**	0.05	79.1 ms
			⩽ 0.1 m/s ↑	69.0%	9.0%	**89.9%**	34.4%	16.7%	69.7%	16.5%	8.2%	78.0%	96.9%	
			⩽ 1.0 m/s ↑	97.3%	90.1%	**99.8%**	98.8%	98.3%	**99.8%**	97.8%	97.5%	**99.9%**	97.6%	
SMVF [ours]	4	✓	mean (m/s) ↓	**0.14**	**0.41**	**0.04**	**0.19**	**0.24**	**0.10**	**0.29**	**0.31**	**0.09**	**0.027**	38.4 ms
			⩽ 0.1 m/s ↑	**69.6%**	**12.1%**	89.6%	**35.5%**	**18.2%**	**70.0%**	**19.1%**	**11.2%**	**78.2%**	**99.2%**	
			⩽ 1.0 m/s ↑	**98.5%**	**94.7%**	**99.8%**	**98.9%**	**98.4%**	99.7%	**97.9%**	**97.6%**	99.8%	**99.6%**	

Table 4. Multi-view framework analysis on the validation split of the Waymo Open Dataset with $k = 1$. A: All. M: Moving. S: Stationary.

	BEV	RV	Metric	Vehicle			Pedestrian			Cyclist			Background	Runtime
				A	M	S	A	M	S	A	M	S		
a)	multi	–	Mean (m/s) ↓	0.18	0.53	**0.05**	0.24	0.30	0.12	0.40	0.44	**0.10**	0.04	17.0 ms
			⩽ 0.1 m/s ↑	67.6%	9.7%	87.9%	**30.5%**	12.3%	66.9%	14.7%	6.7%	**75.1%**	97.5%	
			⩽ 1.0 m/s ↑	97.7%	92.2%	**99.7%**	**98.2%**	97.3%	99.6%	94.6%	94.0%	99.6%	98.3%	
b)	–	multi	mean (m/s) ↓	0.70	2.48	0.08	0.58	0.77	0.19	1.45	1.62	0.18	**0.028**	**16.5 ms**
			⩽ 0.1 m/s ↑	64.8%	2.5%	86.6%	22.6%	3.48%	60.7%	8.29%	1.19%	62.2%	97.9%	
			⩽ 1.0 m/s ↑	86.9%	52.3%	99.0%	77.6%	67.7%	97.3%	52.6%	46.6%	98.3%	98.9%	
c)	multi	single	mean (m/s) ↓	**0.17**	**0.51**	**0.05**	**0.23**	**0.29**	**0.11**	**0.38**	**0.42**	**0.10**	0.028	30 ms
			⩽ 0.1 m/s ↑	67.7%	**10.6%**	**90.4%**	30.1%	**13.3%**	**68.6%**	14.6%	6.7%	**75.1%**	98.9%	
			⩽ 1.0 m/s ↑	**97.9%**	**92.9%**	99.6%	**98.2%**	**97.5%**	99.6%	**95.6%**	**95.1%**	**99.7%**	**99.5%**	
d)	multi	multi	mean (m/s) ↓	**0.17**	0.52	**0.05**	0.24	0.30	0.12	0.39	**0.42**	0.11	**0.028**	34.8 ms
			⩽ 0.1 m/s ↑	**67.8%**	9.81%	88.1%	29.9%	12.0%	65.6%	**15.1%**	**7.24%**	74.4%	**99.0%**	
			⩽ 1.0 m/s ↑	**97.9%**	92.8%	**99.7%**	**98.2%**	**97.5%**	99.6%	94.8%	94.3%	99.1%	**99.5%**	

class with fewer training samples (*e.g. Cyclist*), demonstrating its generalization ability for various classes. We also re-implement the BEV-based MotionNet [25] based on its official code and assign the predicted BEV grid velocities to the corresponding LiDAR points. The scope and partition of the 3D space are the same as our SMVF, while it divides 20 bins along the z-axis. Our SMVF outperforms the MotionNet on most metrics and inference speed for the same reason in Sect. 4.3. Moreover, we integrate the proposed SICP into the MotionNet and SMVF, respectively, and it improves the performance across all categories, especially *Cyclist* that has fewer training samples.

Ablation Studies. The ablative analysis of the multi-view framework on the Waymo Open Dataset is shown in Table 4. All methods here do not adopt the proposed SICP. Compared with the BEV-only model, the performance of the RV-only model drops drastically on the moving points (a,b). Moreover, when the multi-view fusion framework is adopted, the performance drops, if the RV branch uses multiple LiDAR scans instead of a single scan (c,d). These observations are similar to those of the SemanticKITTI in Table 2. It proves that the distorted object trajectories in the RV space are not helpful for extracting motion information, while a single LiDAR scan in the RV space is enough to compensate for the spatial information loss in the BEV space. More ablation studies can be found in the supplementary material.

Table 5. Generalization of scene flow on the validation split of the Waymo Open Dataset with $k = 1$.

Method	SICP			Cyclist			Pedestrain		
				Mean error (m/s)↓			Mean error (m/s)↓		
				A	M	S	A	M	S
FastFlow3D [10]			Supervised	0.51	0.57	0.10	0.25	0.32	0.10
			Stationary	1.13	1.24	**0.06**	0.90	1.30	0.10
			Ignored	0.83	0.93	**0.06**	0.88	1.25	0.10
SMVF			Supervised	0.38	0.42	0.10	**0.23**	0.29	0.11
			Stationary	0.49	0.54	0.10	0.79	1.15	**0.09**
			Ignored	0.47	0.53	0.10	0.57	0.80	**0.09**
SMVF	✓		Supervised	0.35	0.38	0.11	**0.23**	**0.28**	0.11
			Stationary	0.35	**0.37**	0.11	0.70	1.01	**0.09**
			Ignored	**0.34**	**0.37**	0.11	0.36	0.48	0.10

Generalization of Scene Flow. As illustrated in FastFlow3D [10], the point-level ground-truth velocities are obtained by the tracked 3D bounding boxes. However, some objects (*e.g. dog, toy car*) do not have any annotated 3D bounding boxes. For a reliable autonomous driving system, the ability to predict accurate motion velocity should generalize well to these objects, even though they are treated to be "stationary" or "ignored" during training. To quantitatively evaluate the generalization ability, we selectively ablate the categories for *pedestrian* and *cyclist* during training in two ways: 1) "stationary" treats the ablated category to be stationary; 2) "ignored" treats the ablated category to be ignored. On the Waymo Open Dataset, the number of *cyclist* samples is much fewer than that of *pedestrian* samples. Generally, the objects (*e.g. dog, toy car*) that have no annotated 3D bounding boxes have a limited number of samples, similar to or even fewer than that of the *cyclist*. As shown in Table 5, we can discover that: 1) the performance gets better when the ablated category is labeled as "ignored" rather than "stationary"; 2) our SMVF shows a much stronger generalization ability than the FastFlow3D; 3) the proposed SICP significantly improves the performance for the two categories. It indicates that the SICP can be used to generate reliable training samples for these unlabeled objects and promotes the model to be comparable with that in the supervised manner.

5   Conclusion

A novel SMVF is proposed for fast LiDAR point motion estimation, where features from the 3D points, the BEV, and the RV are assigned complementary roles and fused for accurate prediction. The SICP is designed to augment the training LiDAR sequences and improve the generalization ability for the category with fewer training samples. Experimental results on the SemanticKITTI dataset and the Waymo Open Dataset demonstrate the effectiveness and superiority of the proposed components. It can be observed that the information loss during the 2D projection can be remedied by using the multi-view fusion framework and the BEV branch is more suitable for extracting motion features, while the RV can be used to provide the complementary spatial information.

References

1. Behley, J., et al.: SemanticKITTI: a dataset for semantic scene understanding of lidar sequences. In: Proceedings of the IEEE/CVF International Conference on Computer Vision, pp. 9297–9307 (2019)
2. Berman, M., Triki, A.R., Blaschko, M.B.: The lovász-softmax loss: a tractable surrogate for the optimization of the intersection-over-union measure in neural networks. In: Proceedings of the IEEE Conference on Computer Vision and Pattern Recognition, pp. 4413–4421 (2018)
3. Chen, X., et al.: Moving object segmentation in 3d lidar data: a learning-based approach exploiting sequential data. IEEE Robot. Autom. Lett. **6**(4), 6529–6536 (2021)
4. Choy, C., Gwak, J., Savarese, S.: 4D spatio-temporal convNets: Minkowski convolutional neural networks. In: Proceedings of the IEEE/CVF Conference on Computer Vision and Pattern Recognition, pp. 3075–3084 (2019)
5. Dosovitskiy, A., et al.: FlowNet: learning optical flow with convolutional networks. In: Proceedings of the IEEE International Conference on Computer Vision, pp. 2758–2766 (2015)
6. Duerr, F., Pfaller, M., Weigel, H., Beyerer, J.: Lidar-based recurrent 3d semantic segmentation with temporal memory alignment. In: 2020 International Conference on 3D Vision (3DV), pp. 781–790. IEEE (2020)
7. Everingham, M., Van Gool, L., Williams, C.K., Winn, J., Zisserman, A.: The pascal visual object classes (VOC) challenge. Int. J. Comput. Vision **88**(2), 303–338 (2010)
8. Geiger, A., Lenz, P., Urtasun, R.: Are we ready for autonomous driving? the KITTI vision benchmark suite. In: 2012 IEEE Conference on Computer Vision and Pattern Recognition, pp. 3354–3361. IEEE (2012)
9. Gu, X., Wang, Y., Wu, C., Lee, Y.J., Wang, P.: HplflowNet: Hierarchical permutohedral lattice flowNet for scene flow estimation on large-scale point clouds. In: Proceedings of the IEEE/CVF Conference on Computer Vision and Pattern Recognition, pp. 3254–3263 (2019)

10. Jund, P., Sweeney, C., Abdo, N., Chen, Z., Shlens, J.: Scalable scene flow from point clouds in the real world. IEEE Robot. Autom. Lett. (99):1 (2021)
11. Laddha, A., Gautam, S., Meyer, G.P., Vallespi-Gonzalez, C., Wellington, C.K.: RV-FuseNet: range view based fusion of time-series lidar data for joint 3d object detection and motion forecasting. In: 2021 IEEE/RSJ International Conference on Intelligent Robots and Systems (IROS), pp. 7060–7066. IEEE (2020)
12. Laddha, A., Gautam, S., Palombo, S., Pandey, S., Vallespi-Gonzalez, C.: MvfuseNet: Improving end-to-end object detection and motion forecasting through multi-view fusion of lidar data. In: Proceedings of the IEEE/CVF Conference on Computer Vision and Pattern Recognition, pp. 2865–2874 (2021)
13. Lang, A.H., Vora, S., Caesar, H., Zhou, L., Yang, J., Beijbom, O.: PointPillars: fast encoders for object detection from point clouds. In: Proceedings of the IEEE/CVF Conference on Computer Vision and Pattern Recognition, pp. 12697–12705 (2019)
14. Liu, X., Qi, C.R., Guibas, L.J.:FlowNet3D: learning scene flow in 3D point clouds. In: Proceedings of the IEEE/CVF Conference on Computer Vision and Pattern Recognition, pp. 529–537 (2019)
15. Liu, X., Yan, M., Bohg, J.: MeteorNet: deep learning on dynamic 3D point cloud sequences. In: Proceedings of the IEEE/CVF International Conference on Computer Vision, pp. 9246–9255 (2019)
16. Loshchilov, I., Hutter, F.: Decoupled weight decay regularization. arXiv preprint arXiv:1711.05101 (2017)
17. Ranjan, A., Black, M.J.: Optical flow estimation using a spatial pyramid network. In: Proceedings of the IEEE Conference on Computer Vision and Pattern Recognition, pp. 4161–4170 (2017)
18. Shi, H., Lin, G., Wang, H., Hung, T.Y., Wang, Z.: SpSequenceNet:: semantic segmentation network on 4d point clouds. In: Proceedings of the IEEE/CVF Conference on Computer Vision and Pattern Recognition, pp. 4574–4583 (2020)
19. Sun, D., Yang, X., Liu, M.Y., Kautz, J.: PWC-Net : CNNs for optical flow using pyramid, warping, and cost volume. In: Proceedings of the IEEE Conference on Computer Vision and Pattern Recognition, pp. 8934–8943 (2018)
20. Sun, P., et al.: Scalability in perception for autonomous driving: Waymo open dataset. In: Proceedings of the IEEE/CVF Conference on Computer Vision and Pattern Recognition, pp. 2446–2454 (2020)
21. Thomas, H., Qi, C.R., Deschaud, J.E., Marcotegui, B., Goulette, F., Guibas, L.J.: KPConv: flexible and deformable convolution for point clouds. In: Proceedings of the IEEE/CVF International Conference on Computer Vision, pp. 6411–6420 (2019)
22. Vanholder, H.: Efficient inference with TensorRT. In: GPU Technology Conference. vol. 1, p. 2 (2016)
23. Wang, S., Suo, S., Ma, W.C., Pokrovsky, A., Urtasun, R.: Deep parametric continuous convolutional neural networks. In: Proceedings of the IEEE Conference on Computer Vision and Pattern Recognition, pp. 2589–2597 (2018)
24. Wang, Z., Li, S., Howard-Jenkins, H., Prisacariu, V., Chen, M.: Flownet3d++: Geometric losses for deep scene flow estimation. In: Proceedings of the IEEE/CVF Winter Conference on Applications of Computer Vision, pp. 91–98 (2020)
25. Wu, P., Chen, S., Metaxas, D.N.: MotionNet: joint perception and motion prediction for autonomous driving based on bird's eye view maps. In: Proceedings of the IEEE/CVF Conference on Computer Vision and Pattern Recognition, pp. 11385–11395 (2020)
26. Yan, Y., Mao, Y., Li, B.: Second: sparsely embedded convolutional detection. Sensors 18(10), 3337 (2018)

E-Graph: Minimal Solution for Rigid Rotation with Extensibility Graphs

Yanyan Li[1,2]($\boxtimes$)(iD) and Federico Tombari[1,3](iD)

[1] Technical University of Munich, Munich, Germany
yanyan.li@tum.de, tombari@in.tum.de
[2] Meta-Bounds Tech, Shenzhen, China
[3] Google, Zurich, Switzerland

Abstract. Minimal solutions for relative rotation and translation estimation tasks have been explored in different scenarios, typically relying on the so-called co-visibility graphs. However, how to build direct rotation relationships between two frames without overlap is still an open topic, which, if solved, could greatly improve the accuracy of visual odometry. In this paper, a new minimal solution is proposed to solve relative rotation estimation between two images without overlapping areas by exploiting a new graph structure, which we call Extensibility Graph (E-Graph). Differently from a co-visibility graph, high-level landmarks, including vanishing directions and plane normals, are stored in our E-Graph, which are geometrically extensible. Based on E-Graph, the rotation estimation problem becomes simpler and more elegant, as it can deal with pure rotational motion and requires fewer assumptions, e.g. Manhattan/Atlanta World, planar/vertical motion. Finally, we embed our rotation estimation strategy into a complete camera tracking and mapping system which obtains 6-DoF camera poses and a dense 3D mesh model. Extensive experiments on public benchmarks demonstrate that the proposed method achieves state-of-the-art tracking performance.

1 Introduction

Camera pose estimation is a long-standing problem in computer vision as a key step in algorithms for visual odometry, Simultaneous Localization and Mapping (SLAM) and related applications in robotics, augmented reality, autonomous driving (to name a few). As part of the camera pose estimation problem, the minimal case [40] provides an estimate of whether the problem can be solved and how many elements are required to obtain a reliable estimate. According to the input data type and scenarios, different solutions [1,9,15,28] were proposed, most of which became very popular in the computer vision and robotic community, such as the seven-point [1] and five-point [28] approaches. A typical limitation of traditional pose estimation solutions based on the minimal case [1,9,28,31] is that

Supplementary Information The online version contains supplementary material available at https://doi.org/10.1007/978-3-031-20047-2_18.

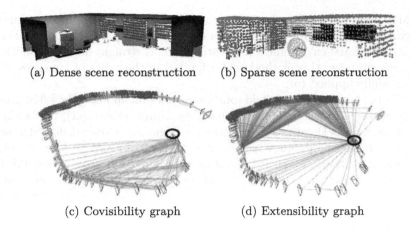

(a) Dense scene reconstruction   (b) Sparse scene reconstruction

(c) Covisibility graph   (d) Extensibility graph

Fig. 1. Dense (a) and sparse (b) scene reconstruction of the office-room scene from the ICL dataset [10] obtained by the proposed method. (c) and (d): keyframes (in blue) and connected frames are linked with green and red lines, respectively, to build up the proposed covisibility and extensibility graphs. The black ellipses denote the start points of the camera trajectory. (Color figure online)

both rotation and translation estimation rely on the co-visibility features between two frames, this having as a consequence that the length of an edge between two nodes is often relatively short. Therefore, tracking errors tend to accumulate easily based on a frame-to-frame or frame-to-keyframe strategy. To solve this issue, more advanced tracking systems [3, 26] with optimization solutions, including local and global bundle adjustment approaches, were exploited to refine poses from minimal solutions. Loop Closure is a common algorithm used in feature-based [24] and direct [7] methods to remove drift. However, it also requires the camera to revisit the same place, which is a limiting assumption in many scenarios.

Compared with point features, lines and planes require more computation to be extracted and described. Early multi-feature SLAM systems [8] use them to increase the number of features to combat low-textured scenes. After that, co-planar, parallel and perpendicular relationships were explored [18,20,39] to add more constraints in the optimization module, still following a similar tracking strategy as ORBSLAM [25] or DSO [36] for the initial pose estimation.

Different to the tightly coupled estimation strategy, some works [43] proposed to decouple the 6-DoF pose estimation into rotation and translation estimation aiming to achieve a more accurate rotation estimation, based on the idea that pose drift is mainly caused by the rotation component [14]. At the same time, based on an estimated rotation matrix [31], only two points are required to compute the translation motion, leading to more robustness in low-textured regions.

The Manhattan World (MW) [43] and Atlanta World (AW) [13] assumptions introduce stronger constraints since they require a single orthogonal scene, or a scene with a unified vertical direction. Unlike loop closure that removes drift by detecting trajectory loops, the assumption of MW and AW is introduced for indoor tracking scenarios [14,19] to improve the accuracy of camera pose estimation, since most indoor artificial environments follow this assumption. MW and AW improve accuracy when the main structure of the scene has orthogonal elements However, since this assumption requires the observation of vertical/orthogonal environmental features (such as straight lines or planes), the SLAM system using this method is also limited in the types of scenarios it can be successfully applied to.

In this paper we propose a rigid rotation estimation approach based on a novel graph structure, which we dub Extensibility Graph (E-Graph), for landmark association in RGB-D data. Our approach is designed to reduce drift and improve the overall trajectory accuracy in spite of loop closure or MW/AW assumptions. Benefiting of E-Graph, the drift-free rotation estimation problem is simplified to the alignment problem of rotating coordinate systems. Importantly, our rotation step does not need overlaps between two frames by making use of vanishing directions of lines and plane normals in the scene, hence can relate a higher number of keyframes with respect to standard co-visibility graphs, with benefits in terms of accuracy and robustness in presence of pure rotational motions.

In addition, we develop a complete tracking and dense mapping system base on the proposed E-Graph and rotation estimation strategies, which we demonstrate to outperform state-of-the-art SLAM approaches [3, 20, 26, 38]. To summarize, the main contributions of this paper are as follows: i) a new perspective for reducing drift is proposed based on our novel graph structure, E-Graph, which connects keyframes across long distances; ii) a novel drift-free rotation alignment solution between two frames without overlapping areas based on E-Graph; iii) a complete SLAM system based on the two previous contributions to improve robustness and accuracy in pose estimation and mapping. The proposed approach is evaluated on common benchmarks such as ICL [10] and TUM-RGBD [33], demonstrating an improved performance compared to the state of the art.

2   Related Work

By making the assumption of planar motion [9], two-view relative pose estimation is implemented based on a single affine correspondence. Point features are common geometric features used in VO and SLAM [3] systems. To remove the drift from point-based front ends, different types of back ends are explored in tracking methods. Loop closing is an important module to remove drift, which happens when the system recognizes that a place [6, 23] has been visited before. After closing the loop, associated keyframes in the covisibility graph will be adjusted. Benefiting of loop closure and optimization modules, ORB-SLAM series [3, 26] organize the keyframes efficiently, which provides robust support for tracking tasks. Different from sparse point features used in ORB-SLAM, BAD-SLAM [32] implements a direct bundle adjustment formulation supported by GPU processing.

However, in indoor environments, to cover texture-less regions that have few point features, more geometric features are merged into the front end of systems. At the early stage, methods build re-projection error functions for lines and planes. CPA-SLAM [22] makes use of photometric and plane re-projection terms to estimate the camera pose. Based on estimated camera poses, detected planes are merged together with a global plane model. Similar to our method, CPA-SLAM and KDP-SLAM [11] can build constraints between non-overlapping frames. However those constraints are used to build heavy optimization targets instead of improving the efficiency. Furthermore, the relationship between parallel lines (vanishing points) and perpendicular planes is explored in [17,41]. Based on the regularities of those structural features, they obtain a more accurate performance. Instead of exploring the parallel/perpendicular relationships between lines/planes, [18,30] make use of constraints between co-planar points and lines in the optimization module.

Those regularities aim to build constraints between local features, [14,20] introduce global constraints by modeling the environment as a special shape, like MW and AW. The MW assumption is suitable for a cuboid scenario, which is supposed to be built by orthogonal elements. Based on this assumption, those methods estimate each frame's rotation between the frame and the Manhattan world directly, which is useful to avoid drift between frames in those scenes. L-SLAM [14] groups normal vectors of each pixel into an orthogonal coordinate by projecting them into a Gaussian Sphere [43] and tracks the coordinate axes to compute the relative rotation motion. Similar to the main idea of L-SLAM, [15] provides a RGB-D compass by using a single line and plane. Since the line lies on the plane, the underlying assumption of the system is the MW-based rotation estimation method. However, the limitation of this strategy is also very obvious, that it works only in Manhattan environments. Based on ORB-SLAM2 [26], Structure-SLAM [19,20] merges the MW assumption with keyframe-based tracking, to improve the robustness of the system in non-MW indoor scenes, which refine decoupled camera pose by using a frame-to-model strategy. Compared with MW-based tracking methods, our approach is less sensitive to the structure of environments.

3 Minimal Case in Orientation Estimation

Commonly, the 6-DoF Euclidean Transform $T \in SE(3)$ defines motions as a set of rotation $R \in SO(3)$ and translation $\mathbf{t} \in \mathbb{R}^3$. Based on point correspondences, camera pose estimation can be defined as,

$$\mathbf{P}' = R\mathbf{P} + \mathbf{t} \tag{1}$$

where $\mathbf{P}'$ and $\mathbf{P}$ are 3D correspondences, and $[R, \mathbf{t}]$ defines the relative motion between two cameras. For monocular sensors, their image normalized representations are $\mathbf{X}'_c$ and $\mathbf{X}_c$,

$$\mathbf{X}'_c = \alpha(R\mathbf{X}_c + \gamma\mathbf{t}) \tag{2}$$

where α and γ are depth-related parameters. After multiplying (2) by $\mathbf{X}'^T_c[\mathbf{t}]_x$, we can obtain the classic essential matrix equation,

$$\mathbf{X}'^T_c E\mathbf{X}_c = 0 \tag{3}$$

where $E = [\mathbf{t}]_x R$ and $[\mathbf{t}]_x$ is the skew symmetric matrix formed by $\mathbf{t}$.

For RGB-D sensors, the task is simplified since the absolute depth information is directly provided by sensors. Equation (3) can be solved by using 3 non-collinear correspondences only [29], although the distance between two frames is supposed to be kept small to extract enough correspondences.

3.1   Minimal Solution for Rotation

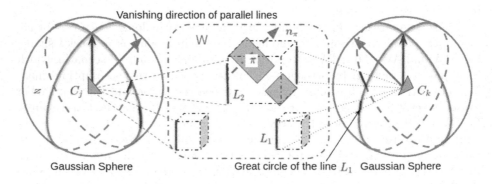

Fig. 2. Minimal case of rotation estimation in EG

Different from traditional methods based on co-visibility graphs, the proposed method decouples rotation and translation estimation into two separate stages. Moreover, the rotation estimation task does not require feature correspondences. As shown in Fig. 2, non-parallel direction vectors $\mathbf{v}_m, m \in [0, 1, \ldots, n]$ are detected in the camera coordinate C_j, where $\mathbf{v}_m^j = [_x v_{m,y}^j \ v_{m,z}^j \ v_m^j]^T$. In Euclidean 3D space, the size of a finite and linearly independent set of vectors is less then four. According to the Gram-Schmidt orthogonalization process, we can obtain an orthogonal set $S = [\mathbf{u}_0, \mathbf{u}_1, \mathbf{u}_2]$,

$$
\begin{aligned}
\mathbf{u}_0 &= \mathbf{v}_0^j \\
\mathbf{u}_1 &= \mathbf{v}_1^j - proj_{[\mathbf{v}_0^j]}(\mathbf{v}_1^j) \\
\mathbf{u}_2 &= \mathbf{v}_2^j - proj_{[\mathbf{v}_0^j]}(\mathbf{v}_2^j) - proj_{[\mathbf{v}_1^j]}(\mathbf{v}_2^j)
\end{aligned}
\tag{4}
$$

by using the projection operator $proj_{[\mathbf{u}]}(\mathbf{v}) = \frac{<\mathbf{u},\mathbf{v}>}{<\mathbf{u},\mathbf{v}>}\mathbf{u}$, where $< \mathbf{u}, \mathbf{v} >$ shows the inner product of the vectors $\mathbf{u}$ and $\mathbf{v}$. Furthermore, we obtain the normalized vectors $\mathbf{e}_0$, $\mathbf{e}_1$ and $\mathbf{e}_2$ via $\mathbf{e}_m = \frac{\mathbf{u}_m}{||\mathbf{u}_m||}$.

For the Euclidean space $\mathbb{R}^3$, the relevant orthonormal basis set based on the detected direction vectors is $(\mathbf{e}_0, \mathbf{e}_1, \mathbf{e}_2)$. In the jth camera coordinate, the orthonormal set is detected as $(\mathbf{e}_0, \mathbf{e}_1, \mathbf{e}_2)$, while $(\mathbf{e}_0^*, \mathbf{e}_1^*, \mathbf{e}_2^*)$ in the kth camera coordinate.

Therefore, from the perspective of the orthonormal set, those j^{th} and k^{th} coordinates are represented as $[\mathbf{e}_0, \mathbf{e}_1, \mathbf{e}_2]^T$ and $[\mathbf{e}_0^*, \mathbf{e}_1^*, \mathbf{e}_2^*]^T$, respectively.

Given $\begin{bmatrix} \mathbf{e}_0^T \\ \mathbf{e}_1^T \\ \mathbf{e}_2^T \end{bmatrix}$ $[\mathbf{e}_0, \mathbf{e}_1, \mathbf{e}_2]$ is the identity matrix, the matrix $[\mathbf{e}_0, \mathbf{e}_1, \mathbf{e}_2]$ is an
orthogonal matrix and the columns of $[\mathbf{e}_0, \mathbf{e}_1, \mathbf{e}_2]^T$ are orthonormal vectors as
well, which can be used to build the orthonomal basis set of the jth camera
coordinate. Therefore, in $\mathbb{R}^3$ an arbitrary vector $\mathbf{x}$ can be represented by two
orthonormal sets, $(\mathbf{e}_0, \mathbf{e}_1, \mathbf{e}_2)^T$ and $(\mathbf{e}_0^*, \mathbf{e}_1^*, \mathbf{e}_2^*)^T$, independently,

$$\mathbf{x} = (\mathbf{e}_0, \mathbf{e}_1, \mathbf{e}_2)^T (x_0, x_1, x_2)^T \\ = (\mathbf{e}_0^*, \mathbf{e}_1^*, \mathbf{e}_2^*)^T (x_0^*, x_1^*, x_2^*)^T \tag{5}$$

Finally, $(x_0, x_1, x_2)^T = (\mathbf{e}_0, \mathbf{e}_1, \mathbf{e}_2)(\mathbf{e}_0^*, \mathbf{e}_1^*, \mathbf{e}_2^*)^T (x_0^*, x_1^*, x_2^*)^T$ where the rotation motion $R_{c_j c_k}$ from camera k to camera j is $[\mathbf{e}_0, \mathbf{e}_1, \mathbf{e}_2][\mathbf{e}_0^*, \mathbf{e}_1^*, \mathbf{e}_2^*]^T$.

Two-Observation Case. In the spatial case where two linearly independent
direction vectors are detected, $\mathbf{u}_2$ can be achieved by the cross product process
of $\mathbf{u}_0$ and $\mathbf{u}_1$. Obviously, the new set $[\mathbf{u}_0, \mathbf{u}_1, \mathbf{u}_0 \times \mathbf{u}_1]$ maintains the orthogonal
property, which is the minimal solution for relative pose estimation problems.

Orthogonal-Observation Case. As discussed in Sect. 2, the MW assumption
is enforced mostly by SLAM/VO methods designed to work indoor [14,15,19,
38], achieving particularly good results when the MW assumption holds. When
the observation vectors $\mathbf{v}_m^j$ are orthogonal, the projection operation between
different vectors is zero and the proposed method degenerates to a multi-MW
case,

$$R_{c_j c_k} = R_{c_j M_i} R_{c_k M_i}^T \\ = [\frac{\mathbf{v}_0^j}{||\mathbf{v}_0^j||}, \frac{\mathbf{v}_1^j}{||\mathbf{v}_1^j||}, \frac{\mathbf{v}_2^j}{||\mathbf{v}_2^j||}][\frac{\mathbf{v}_0^k}{||\mathbf{v}_0^k||}, \frac{\mathbf{v}_1^k}{||\mathbf{v}_1^k||}, \frac{\mathbf{v}_2^k}{||\mathbf{v}_2^k||}]^T. \tag{6}$$

For single-MW scenarios, a global orthogonal set can be obtained by every
frame, therefore $R_{c_j w}$, from world to camera C_j, can be computed by $R_{c_j M} R_{c_0 M}^T$,
here $R_{c_0 w}$ is an identity matrix.

Compared with the visual compass [15] method making use of a combination of line and plane features from MW [14] to estimate camera rotation, our
graph is more robust and flexible. Furthermore, compared to [31] that generates
four rotation candidates after aligning two frames' vanishing points, our method
not only leverages plane features, but also solves the ambiguity regarding the
directions of the vanishing points [31].

After the relative rotation pose estimation step between two frames, in case
of no overlap between them, we need to make use of their neighboring frames to
compute translation vectors. Note that only two correspondences are required
in translation estimation by making use of Eq. 3, which is particularly suited
to deal with scenes and environments characterized by different texture types
compared to traditional approaches [3,26].

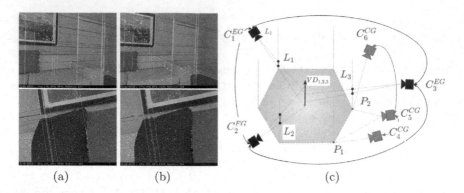

(a)   (b)   (c)

Fig. 3. Vanishing point detection and rotation connection examples. (a) Detection results of J-Linkage. (b) Refined results by our system. (c) E-Graph (black) and co-visibility graph (red). (Color figure online)

4   Extensibility Graph (E-Graph)

As shown in Fig. 3(c), the E-Graph method builds rotation connections (edges) between frames $[C_1^{EG}, C_2^{EG}, C_3^{EG}]$ that share global directions instead of any low-level correspondences (like points and lines). At the same time, no connection between C_4^{CG} and C_6^{CG} can be made since these frames have no co-visible features within the co-visibility graph. The proposed connection strategy will be detailed in the following subsections.

4.1   Landmarks from a RGB-D Frame

Similar to the co-visibility graph, the proposed graph is also a topological representation of scenes. The difference is that the proposed graph is built based on the scene structure rather than on overlapping parts between frames. The distance between connected frames in a co-visibility graph tends to be small (see Fig. 3) since two frames that are distant from each other rarely overlap, leading to the pose of the current frame being estimated based on the last frame or last keyframes only. The issue can be alleviated by using global bundle adjustment and loop closure modules, although they bring in intensive computation and trajectory constraints (e.g. need to re-visit a certain area).

In our graph $\mathscr{G} = [\mathcal{N}_c, \mathcal{N}_{lm}, \mathscr{E}]$ frames and landmarks are regarded as nodes $\mathcal{N}_c$ and $\mathcal{N}_{lm}$ respectively, while $\mathscr{E}$ represents the edges among connected frames. Note that landmarks are border-less planes and vanishing directions, e.g. $VD_{1,2,3}$, of lines detected in multiple views. In particular, an edge is established between two frames every time two or more structural elements are matched across them.

Features and Landmarks. Vanishing directions are estimated from parallel lines detected by a joint 2D-3D process, where LSD [35] is used to extract 2D line features from RGB images. Meanwhile, AHP [5] is carried out to extract plane features from depth maps.

Firstly, as shown in Fig. 3(a), we make use of the J-Linkage algorithm to classify detected 2D lines into different groups of parallel lines as described in [34]. However, there are still outliers left based on the 2D process. To solve this issue, we take advantage of depth maps to check the directions of lines in each group by using RANSAC to detect the best direction vector VD_n to represent the group S_n.

As for planar landmarks, we make use of the Hessian ($\boldsymbol{\pi} = (\mathbf{n}^\pi, d^\pi)$) to represent a plane detected from the ith frame, where $\mathbf{n}^\pi$ denotes the normal vector and d^π represents the distance between the camera center and this plane, which is transferred to world coordinates via the initial pose T_{wc_i}.

4.2   Data Association

After generating vanishing directions and planes, we now explain how to initialize and update them.

Initialization. Combined with the first keyframe Kf_0, detected planes and optimized vanishing directions are used to initialize the E-Graph. The camera pose T_0 of Kf_0 is set as the world coordinate for landmarks in the E-Graph. Planes π_i measured by Kf_0 are transferred to the graph directly as,

$$\mathcal{G}_0 = [\mathcal{N}_{c_0}, \mathcal{N}_{lm_0}, \mathcal{E}_0] \tag{7}$$

where $\mathcal{N}_{c_0}$ is Kf_0 and $\mathcal{E}_0$ has no edges yet. $\mathcal{N}_{lm_0}$ contains $[\pi_i, VD_i, PD_j]$, where VD_i and PD_j refer to two different types of 3D lines detected in the RGB-D frame: the former refers to lines that are parallel to at least another 3D line, the latter to lines that are not parallel to any line. The first type of lines can generate vanishing directions VD_i in a single view, which are stored into the graph directly, similarly to planes. In addition, lines that do not have parallel lines detected in this RGB-D frame are marked as potential vanishing direction PD_j. In case parallel lines will be detected in successive frames, these lines will also be transferred to VD_j, otherwise, they are removed from the E-Graph.

Landmarks Fusion. For each new input frame we need to extract vectors $\mathbf{n}^\pi$, VD and PD from the current frame. After rotating VD_i^c to the world coordinate frame as VD_i^w, if the direction between VD_i^c is parallel to $VD_k^w, k \in [0, \dots, m]$, where m is the number of vanishing directions saved in E-Graph, VD_i^c is then associated to the graph. To solve the unsure issues [31] of vanishing directions, we will unify the direction during the association process by using

$$\tilde{VD}_i^c = \begin{cases} VD_i^c & (|norm(VD_i^w \cdot VD_k^w) - 1| < th_{vd}) \\ -VD_i^c & (|norm(VD_i^w \cdot VD_k^w) + 1| < th_{vd}) \end{cases} \tag{8}$$

where $norm(\cdot)$ shows a dot product between two normalized vectors and $|\cdot|$ is the absolute difference. th_{vd} is a threshold to check the angle distance between two vectors. To include additional graph connections, we also try to associate

PD_j^c with VD_k^w and PD_k^w. If new pairs can be made at this stage, the associated PD vectors are transferred to the vanishing directions and fused into the graph.

Since the vanishing direction is independent from translation motion, VD_i^w, the vanishing direction in the world coordinate can be obtained as

$$VD_i^w = R_{wc} VD_i^c \tag{9}$$

where R_{wc} is the rotation motion from the camera coordinate frame to the world coordinate frame.

In certain indoor scenes, e.g. a corridor or hallway, when a robot moves along the wall, an extended planar region is detected across multiple views, with most of these views encompassing no overlap. To address this issue, we extract the normal vector $[n_x^c, n_y^c, n_z^c]$ of the plane in the camera coordinate, which can be fused into the world coordinate in the same way as the vanishing directions.

Edge Connection. In E-Graph, all landmarks come from keyframes that follow the decision mechanisms of a feature-based SLAM system [20, 24], which we summarize in the following. A new keyframe is detected if it satisfies one of the following two conditions: 1) 20 frames have passed from the last keyframe; 2) the current frame tracks less than 85% points and lines correspondences with the last keyframe. Furthermore, when the current frame detects a new plane or a new vanishing direction, the frame is considered as a new keyframe. In addition, new landmarks connected to this keyframe are also merged into the graph at this stage.

By sequentially processing keyframes, if more than two pairs of matched landmarks are observed between two keyframes, an edge will be created to connect the respective two graph nodes. As shown in Fig. 2, C_j and C_k detect the plane π and the same vanishing point generated by L_1 and L_2. Notably, even if these two frames do not have any correspondence, they can still be connected in our E-Graph.

5   Experiments

In this section, the proposed system is evaluated on different indoor benchmarks: ICL-NUIM [10] and TUM RGB-D [33]. ICL-NUIM [10] contains eight synthetic sequences recorded in two scenarios (living room and office room). TUM RGB-D [33] is recorded in real scenarios and includes varied sequences in terms of texture, scene size, presence of moving objects, etc.

Rotation Estimation. The proposed rotation algorithm is compared with other state-of-the-art orientation estimation approaches. Compass [15] makes use of a single line and plane. OPRE [43] and GOME [12] estimate the distribution of surface normal vectors based on depth maps. OLRE [2] and ROVE [16] take advantage of vanishing directions for rotation estimation. Importantly, Compass, GOME, OLRE, OPRE, and P-SLAM [20] are all based on the MW assumption, while our method, ORB-SLAM2 [25] and ROVE are designed for general scenes.

Translation Estimation. Since the rotation of the current frame is estimated from a keyframe that may not be overlapping with the current frame, we follow the 3D translation estimation model [20,26] to estimate the translation **t** based on the predicted rotation. In this module, re-projection errors from point-line-plane feature correspondences are used to build a target optimization function, $\mathbf{t} = argmin(\sum_{j=0}^{n} e_{i,j}^{\pi} \Lambda^{\pi} e_{i,j}^{\pi} + e_{i,j}^{L} \Lambda^{L} e_{i,j}^{L} + e_{i,j}^{P} \Lambda^{L} e_{i,j}^{P})$, where e^{π}, e^{L} and e^{P} are re-projection error functions for planes, lines and points, respectively. The target function is optimized by using the Levenberg-Marquardt method. The translation is compared with the following state-of-the-art methods. ORB-SLAM2 [26] and ORB-SLAM3 [3] are popular keypoint-based SLAM systems. In our experiments, for fairness of comparison the loop closure is removed to reduce the effect of the back-ends. SP-SLAM [39] additionally uses points and planes in the tracking and optimization modules based on ORB-SLAM2. P-SLAM [19] assumes the indoor environments as MW, and includes a refinement module to make the tracking process more robust. Moreover, we also compare our system with GPU-based methods, including BadSLAM [32] and BundleFusion [4].

Dense Mapping. In this paper, a mapping module is implemented to reconstruct unknown environments in sparse and dense types. The sparse map is reconstructed by the point-line-plane features extracted from keyframes, which supports a frame-to-map pose refinement step. Since sparse maps cannot provide enough information for robots, our system also generates a dense mesh map incrementally based on CPU. When a new keyframe is generated from the tracking thread, we make use of the estimated camera pose and the RGB-D pair to build a dense TSDF model based on [27,42]. After that, the marching cubes method [21] is exploited to extract the surface from voxels.

Metrics. The metrics used in our experiments include absolute trajectory error (ATE), absolute rotation error (ARE), and relative pose error (RPE) that shows the difference in relative motion between two pairs of poses to evaluate the tracking process. Our results are reported in Table 2 and obtained on an Intel Core @i7-8700 CPU @3.20 GHz and without any use of GPU resources.

5.1   ICL NUIM Dataset

As shown in Table 1, the proposed method outperforms other MW-based and feature-based methods in terms of average rotation error. In *office room* sequences, OPRE and P-SLAM also perform well since orthogonal planar features can be found in the environment. However, in *office room 0*, parts of the camera movement only contain a single plane and some lines, leading to performance degradation, while our method achieves robust orientation tracking by taking advantage of a set of non-parallel planes and lines.

Furthermore, we compare the translation results against two feature-based methods as shown in Table 2. The first four sequences are related to a living room scenario, while the remaining sequences are from an office scenario. All methods obtain good results in *living room 0* where the camera moves back and forth

Table 1. Comparison of the average value of the absolute rotation error (degrees) on ICL-NUIM and TUM RGB-D structural benchmarks. The best result for each sequence is bolded. × shows that the method fails to track the orientation.

Sequence	Ours	Compass [15]	OPRE [43]	GOME [12]	ROVE [16]	OLRE [2]	ORB2 [26]	P-SLAM [20]
office room 0	**0.11**	0.37	0.18	5.12	29.11	6.71	0.40	0.57
office room 1	**0.22**	0.37	0.32	×	34.98	×	2.30	**0.22**
office room 2	0.39	0.38	0.33	6.67	60.54	10.91	0.51	**0.29**
office room 3	0.24	0.38	**0.21**	5.57	10.67	3.41	0.30	**0.21**
living room 0	0.44	**0.31**	×	×	×	×	0.97	0.36
living room 1	**0.24**	0.38	0.97	8.56	26.74	3.72	0.22	0.26
living room 2	0.36	**0.34**	0.49	8.15	39.71	4.21	0.83	0.44
living room 3	0.36	0.35	1.34	×	×	×	0.42	**0.27**
$f3\_stru\_notex$	4.46	1.96	3.01	4.07	×	11.22	×	4.71
$f3\_stru\_tex$	**0.60**	2.92	3.81	4.71	13.73	8.21	0.63	2.83
$f3\_l\_cabinet$	**1.45**	2.04	36.34	3.74	28.41	38.12	2.79	2.55
$f3\_cabinet$	2.47	2.48	2.42	2.59	×	×	5.45	**1.18**

between the two parallel walls. P-SLAM detects a good MW model, and ORB-SLAM3 also observes enough features, benefiting from paintings hanging on the wall and small furniture. Compared with the living room, the office room has many low-textured regions. The performance of feature-based algorithms is not as good as in the living room scenes, especially in *office room 1* and *office room 3*.

Table 2. Comparison in terms of translation RMSE (m) for ICL-NUIM and TUM RGB-D sequences. × means that the system fails in the tracking process.

Sequence	Ours	P-SLAM [20]	ORB-SLAM3 [3]
office room 0	**0.014**	0.068	0.035
office room 1	**0.013**	0.020	0.091
office room 2	0.020	0.011	**0.010**
office room 3	**0.011**	0.012	0.096
living room 0	0.008	**0.006**	**0.006**
living room 1	**0.006**	0.015	0.206
living room 2	**0.017**	0.020	0.018
living room 3	0.021	**0.012**	0.019
$f1\_360$	0.114	×	**0.108**
$f1\_room$	**0.095**	×	×
$f2\_rpy$	**0.002**	0.154	0.003
$f2\_xyz$	**0.003**	0.009	0.004
$f3\_l\_o\_house$	0.012	0.122	**0.009**
$f3\_stru\_notex$	**0.017**	0.025	×
$f3\_l\_cabinet$	**0.058**	0.071	0.072

To analyze the relationship between rotation and translation results of different methods, absolute translation and rotation errors on the *office room 0* sequence are presented in Fig. 4. When the camera moves to the ceiling, the number of detected features decreases, then an interesting phenomenon is witnessed (see also Fig. 4(a)): the tracking error of feature-based systems quickly and drastically increases, then gradually fades as the number of features increases. At the same time, our method and P-SLAM exhibit a more robust performance when they face this challenge. An important difference is that, while P-SLAM underperforms due to the non-rigid MW scene, our method's performance is accurate thanks to the use of the E-Graph, which demonstrates to be more flexible than MW-based paradigms.

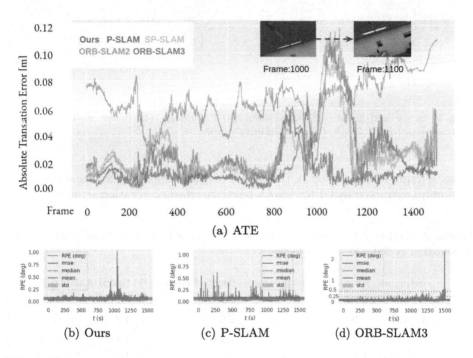

Fig. 4. Comparison of the proposed system against state-of-the-art methods in the *office room 0* sequence of ICL NUIM in terms of mean/average absolute translation errors (top) and rotation errors (bottom).

5.2   TUM RGB-D

Different types of sequences are included from the TUM RGB-D benchmark, which aims to test general indoor scenes with low-textured scenes and sharp rotational motions. *f1_360, f1_room, f2_rpy* and *f2_xyz* are recorded in real office scenes, but the camera's rotation motion changes sharply especially in the first sequence. *f3_Lo_house, f3_sn_near* and *f3_Lcabinet* contain more structural information, where *f3_sn_near* is built on two white corners, and *f3_Lcabinet* records several movements around the white cabinet. Table 1 shows that ROVE, OLRE and ORB-SLAM2 have problems in low/non-textured regions. In *f3_Lcabinet* that

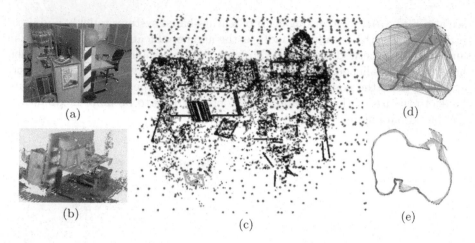

Fig. 5. Scene and graphs of *f3_Lo_house*. (a) 2D image, (b) dense mesh model, (c) sparse map, (d) E-Graph, (e) co-visibilitity graph.

is not a rigid MW environment, the quality of depth maps is noisy, the surface normal maps extracted by OPRE have a negative effect on rotation estimation.

Table 3. ATE RMSE results (cm) on the TUM RGB-D dataset. Results for Bundle-Fusion and BadSLAM are taken from [32]

Sequence	Ours CPU	BundleFusion [4] GPU	ElasticFusion [37] GPU	BadSLAM [32] GPU
f1_desk	1.0	1.6	2.0	1.7
f2_xyz	0.7	1.1	1.1	1.1
f3_office	1.4	2.2	3.6	1.7

For structural sequences listed in Table 1, P-SLAM shows stable performance. In Table 2, general scenes are added as a comparison. As listed in Table 2, the keypoint-based method [3] cannot achieve robust results in *f3_sn_near*, i.e. , a textureless scenario, while the MW-based method [20] has problems when the scene structure breaks the MW assumption, by reporting a low performance in *f2_rpy* and *f3_Lo_house*, and even losing track in *f1_360* and *f1_room*. Therefore, the proposed method shows more robust performances in different types of scenarios, compared with MW-based systems [15,20] and feature-based approaches [3,26]. Furthermore, compared with GPU-based systems, our system only works on limited computation sources. As shown in Fig. 5, *f3_Lo_house* is used to compare E-Graph and co-visibility graph. As clearly shown, E-Graph allows connecting more distant keyframes than a co-visibility graph. When two keyframes can be connected together, drifting phenomena can more easily be limited, in a similar

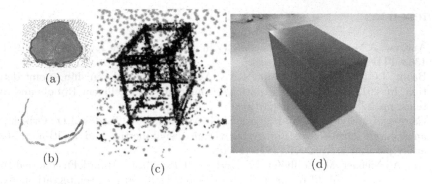

Fig. 6. Scene and graph of *f3_cabinet*. (a) E-Graph, (b) trajectory from ORB-SLAM3, (c) sparse map, (d) 2D image.

way to the underlying idea behind loop closure. The cabinet scene is also a difficult sequence for point-based methods (see Fig. 6(b)) since point features are concentrated in a few boundary regions. However, our method can deal with this type of scene where the same plane is observed in a number of frames.

6   Conclusion

This paper proposed a new graph structure, E-Graph, to reduce tracking drift based on plane normals and vanishing directions in a scene, which can be used to build a rotation connection between two frames without visual overlap. The advantage of this idea is that rotation errors that occur between two frames have small or no effect on this relative rotation estimation step. Based on the proposed graph, a minimal solution is presented, that shows that two landmarks and two correspondences can be used to solve the relative camera pose. Therefore, the proposed method is better suited for texture-less scenes compared with traditional minimal solutions based on co-visible features. However, the proposed method also has limitations. Compared with point-based systems, our approach requires more types of features. Furthermore, since we need vanishing directions and plane vectors, the method is more suitable for man-made scenes.

Feature Work. The E-Graph is a new tool to establish connections across frames and keyframes. An interesting topic for future exploration is considering a covisibility graph and our graph together to revisit pose estimation and obtain further improvements in drift removal.

Acknowledgment. We gratefully acknowledge Xin Li, Keisuke Tateno, Nicolas Brasch and Dr. Liang Zhao for the helpful discussion.

References

1. Andrew, A.M.: Multiple view geometry in computer vision. Kybernetes **30**(9/10), 1333–1341 (2001)
2. Bazin, J.C., Pollefeys, M.: 3-line RANSAC for orthogonal vanishing point detection. In: 2012 IEEE/RSJ International Conference on Intelligent Robots and Systems, pp. 4282–4287. IEEE (2012)
3. Campos, C., Elvira, R., Rodríguez, J.J.G., Montiel, J.M., Tardós, J.D.: Orb-slam3: an accurate open-source library for visual, visual-inertial and multi-map slam. arXiv preprint arXiv:2007.11898 (2020)
4. Dai, A., Nießner, M., Zollhöfer, M., Izadi, S., Theobalt, C.: BundleFusion: real-time globally consistent 3d reconstruction using on-the-fly surface reintegration. ACM Trans. Graph. **36**(4), 1 (2017)
5. Feng, C., Taguchi, Y., Kamat, V.R.: fast plane extraction in organized point clouds using agglomerative hierarchical clustering. In: 2014 IEEE International Conference on Robotics and Automation (ICRA), pp. 6218–6225. IEEE (2014)
6. Galvez-López, D., Tardos, J.D.: Bags of binary words for fast place recognition in image sequences. IEEE Trans. Rob. **28**(5), 1188–1197 (2012). https://doi.org/10.1109/TRO.2012.2197158
7. Gao, X., Wang, R., Demmel, N., Cremers, D.: LDSO: direct sparse odometry with loop closure. In: 2018 IEEE/RSJ International Conference on Intelligent Robots and Systems (IROS), pp. 2198–2204. IEEE (2018)
8. Gomez-Ojeda, R., Moreno, F.A., Zuniga-Noël, D., Scaramuzza, D., Gonzalez-Jimenez, J.: PL-Slam: a stereo slam system through the combination of points and line segments. IEEE Trans. Rob. **35**(3), 734–746 (2019)
9. Guan, B., Zhao, J., Li, Z., Sun, F., Fraundorfer, F.: Minimal solutions for relative pose with a single affine correspondence. In: Proceedings of the IEEE/CVF Conference on Computer Vision and Pattern Recognition, pp. 1929–1938 (2020)
10. Handa, A., Whelan, T., McDonald, J., Davison, A.: A Benchmark for RGB-D Visual Odometry, 3D Reconstruction and SLAM. In: IEEE International Conference on Robotics and Automation (2014)
11. Hsiao, M., Westman, E., Zhang, G., Kaess, M.: Keyframe-based dense planar slam. In: 2017 IEEE International Conference on Robotics and Automation (ICRA), pp. 5110–5117 (2017). https://doi.org/10.1109/ICRA.2017.7989597
12. Joo, K., Oh, T.H., Kim, J., Kweon, I.S.: Globally optimal manhattan frame estimation in real-time. In: Proceedings of the IEEE Conference on Computer Vision and Pattern Recognition, pp. 1763–1771 (2016)
13. Joo, K., Oh, T.H., Rameau, F., Bazin, J.C., Kweon, I.S.: Linear RGB-D SLAM for Atlanta world. In: 2020 IEEE International Conference on Robotics and Automation (ICRA), pp. 1077–1083. IEEE (2020)
14. Kim, P., Coltin, B., Jin Kim, H.: Linear RGB-D SLAM for planar environments. In: Proceedings of the European Conference on Computer Vision (ECCV), pp. 333–348 (2018)
15. Kim, P., Coltin, B., Kim, H.J.: Indoor RGB-D compass from a single line and plane. In: Proceedings of the IEEE Conference on Computer Vision and Pattern Recognition, pp. 4673–4680 (2018)
16. Lee, J.K., Yoon, K.J.: Real-time joint estimation of camera orientation and vanishing points. In: Proceedings of the IEEE Conference on Computer Vision and Pattern Recognition, pp. 1866–1874 (2015)

17. Li, H., Xing, Y., Zhao, J., Bazin, J., Liu, Z., Liu, Y.: Leveraging structural regularity of Atlanta world for monocular slam. In: 2019 International Conference on Robotics and Automation (ICRA), pp. 2412–2418 (2019). https://doi.org/10.1109/ICRA.2019.8793716

18. Li, X., Li, Y., Pınar Örnek, E., Lin, J., Tombari, F.: Co-planar parametrization for stereo-slam and visual-inertial odometry. arXiv e-prints, arXiv-2009 (2020)

19. Li, Y., Brasch, N., Wang, Y., Navab, N., Tombari, F.: Structure-slam: Low-drift monocular slam in indoor environments. IEEE Rob. Autom. Lett. **5**(4), 6583–6590 (2020)

20. Li, Y., Yunus, R., Brasch, N., Navab, N., Tombari, F.: RGB-D SLAM with structural regularities. In: 2021 IEEE International Conference on Robotics and Automation (ICRA) (2021)

21. Lorensen, W.E., Cline, H.E.: Marching cubes: a high resolution 3d surface construction algorithm. ACM SIGGRAPh Comput. Graph. **21**(4), 163–169 (1987)

22. Ma, L., Kerl, C., Stückler, J., Cremers, D.: CPA-SLAM: consistent plane-model alignment for direct RGB-d slam. In: 2016 IEEE International Conference on Robotics and Automation (ICRA), pp. 1285–1291 (2016). https://doi.org/10.1109/ICRA.2016.7487260

23. Mei, C., Sibley, G., Newman, P.: Closing loops without places. In: 2010 IEEE/RSJ International Conference on Intelligent Robots and Systems, pp. 3738–3744. IEEE (2010)

24. Mur-Artal, Raúl, M.J.M.M., Tardós, J.D.: ORB-SLAM: a versatile and accurate monocular SLAM system. IEEE Trans. Robot. **31**(5), 1147–1163 (2015). https://doi.org/10.1109/TRO.2015.2463671

25. Mur-Artal, R., Montiel, J.M.M., Tardos, J.D.: ORB-SLAM: a versatile and accurate monocular slam system. IEEE Trans. Rob. **31**(5), 1147–1163 (2015)

26. Mur-Artal, R., Tardós, J.D.: ORB-SLAM2: an open-source SLAM system for monocular, stereo and RGB-D cameras. IEEE Trans. Rob. **33**(5), 1255–1262 (2017). https://doi.org/10.1109/TRO.2017.2705103

27. Nießner, M., Zollhöfer, M., Izadi, S., Stamminger, M.: Real-time 3D reconstruction at scale using voxel hashing. ACM Trans. Graph. **32**(6), 1–11 (2013)

28. Nistér, D.: An efficient solution to the five-point relative pose problem. IEEE Trans. Pattern Anal. Mach. Intell. **26**(6), 756–770 (2004)

29. Pomerleau, F., Colas, F., Siegwart, R.: A review of point cloud registration algorithms for mobile robotics. Found. Trends in Rob. **4**(1), 1–104 (2015)

30. Rosinol, A., Sattler, T., Pollefeys, M., Carlone, L.: Incremental visual-inertial 3d mesh generation with structural regularities. In: 2019 International Conference on Robotics and Automation (ICRA), pp. 8220–8226. IEEE (2019)

31. Salaün, Y., Marlet, R., Monasse, P.: Robust and accurate line- and/or point-based pose estimation without manhattan assumptions. In: Leibe, B., Matas, J., Sebe, N., Welling, M. (eds.) ECCV 2016. LNCS, vol. 9911, pp. 801–818. Springer, Cham (2016). https://doi.org/10.1007/978-3-319-46478-7_49

32. Schöps, T., Sattler, T., Pollefeys, M.: Bad slam: Bundle adjusted direct RGB-D SLAM. In: 2019 IEEE/CVF Conference on Computer Vision and Pattern Recognition (CVPR), pp. 134–144 (2019). https://doi.org/10.1109/CVPR.2019.00022

33. Sturm, J., Engelhard, N., Endres, F., Burgard, W., Cremers, D.: A benchmark for the evaluation of RGB-D SLAM systems. In: IEEE International Conference on Intelligent Robots and Systems (2012)

34. Tardif, J.P.: Non-iterative approach for fast and accurate vanishing point detection. In: 2009 IEEE 12th International Conference on Computer Vision, pp. 1250–1257. IEEE (2009)

35. Von Gioi, R.G., Jakubowicz, J., Morel, J.M., Randall, G.: LSD: a fast line segment detector with a false detection control. IEEE Trans. Pattern Anal. Mach. Intell. **32**(4), 722–732 (2010)
36. Wang, R., Schworer, M., Cremers, D.: Stereo DSO: large-scale direct sparse visual odometry with stereo cameras. In: Proceedings of the IEEE International Conference on Computer Vision, pp. 3903–3911 (2017)
37. Whelan, T., Leutenegger, S., Salas-Moreno, R., Glocker, B., Davison, A.: Elastic-Fusion: dense SLAM without a pose graph. In: Conference on Robotics: Science and Systems (2015)
38. Yunus, R., Li, Y., Tombari, F.: Manhattanslam: robust planar tracking and mapping leveraging mixture of Manhattan frames. arXiv preprint arXiv:2103.15068 (2021)
39. Zhang, X., Wang, W., Qi, X., Liao, Z., Wei, R.: Point-plane SLAM using supposed planes for indoor environments. Sensors **19**(17), 3795 (2019)
40. Zhao, J., Kneip, L., He, Y., Ma, J.: Minimal case relative pose computation using ray-point-ray features. IEEE Trans. Pattern Anal. Mach. Intell. **42**(5), 1176–1190 (2019)
41. Zhou, H., Zou, D., Pei, L., Ying, R., Liu, P., Yu, W.: Structslam: visual SLAM with building structure lines. IEEE Trans. Veh. Technol. **64**(4), 1364–1375 (2015). https://doi.org/10.1109/TVT.2015.2388780
42. Zhou, Q.Y., Koltun, V.: Dense scene reconstruction with points of interest. ACM Trans. Graph. **32**(4), 1–8 (2013)
43. Zhou, Y., Kneip, L., Rodriguez, C., Li, H.: Divide and conquer: efficient density-based tracking of 3D sensors in manhattan worlds. In: Lai, S.-H., Lepetit, V., Nishino, K., Sato, Y. (eds.) ACCV 2016. LNCS, vol. 10115, pp. 3–19. Springer, Cham (2017). https://doi.org/10.1007/978-3-319-54193-8_1

Point Cloud Compression with Range Image-Based Entropy Model for Autonomous Driving

Sukai Wang[1,4] and Ming Liu[1,2,3]([⊠])

[1] The Hong Kong University of Science and Technology, Hong Kong SAR, China
{swangcy,eelium}@ust.hk
[2] The Hong Kong University of Science and Technology (Guangzhou), Nansha,
Guangzhou 511400, Guangdong, China
[3] HKUST Shenzhen-Hong Kong Collaborative Innovation Research Institute,
Futian, Shenzhen, China
[4] Clear Water Bay Institute of Autonomous Driving, Hong Kong SAR, China

Abstract. For autonomous driving systems, the storage cost and transmission speed of the large-scale point clouds become an important bottleneck because of their large volume. In this paper, we propose a range image-based three-stage framework to compress the scanning LiDAR's point clouds using the entropy model. In our three-stage framework, we refine the coarser range image by converting the regression problem into the limited classification problem to improve the performance of generating accurate point clouds. And in the feature extraction part, we propose a novel attention Conv layer to fuse the voxel-based 3D features in the 2D range image. Compared with the Octree-based compression methods, the range image compression with the entropy model performs better in the autonomous driving scene. Experiments on LiDARs with different lines and in different scenarios show that our proposed compression scheme outperforms the state-of-the-art approaches in reconstruction quality and downstream tasks by a wide margin.

Keywords: Point cloud compression · Entropy encoding · Autonomous driving

1 Introduction

Point clouds from scanning LiDARs are to be used in the downstream tasks in the autonomous systems, such as localization [26], detection [42], global mapping [46], etc. In autonomous vehicles, point clouds are required to be transmitted to the server for data recording or backup, or be stored for mapping. The large amount of

---

Supplementary Information The online version contains supplementary material available at https://doi.org/10.1007/978-3-031-20047-2_19.

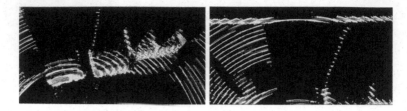

Fig. 1. The comparison of our reconstructed point cloud in red points with the baseline reconstructed point cloud in cyan points. On the left are boxes and to the right is a wall. (Color figure online)

precision point cloud data from high-frequency scanning LiDAR may cause storage and transmission problems, especially when the network is unstable. Thus, point cloud compression has attracted many people's research attention [3,13,24].

Large-scale outdoor LiDAR point clouds have the characteristics of large-area coverage, unstructured organization, and huge volume in Cartesian space. Thus, the compression performance is not satisfactory when using the ordinary methods of compressing files to compress the XYZ data. There are two common representations, octree and range image, to make the point cloud more structured. The octree, which divides the three-dimensional space into eight parts recursively, has been widely used to progressively compress point cloud data [15,20,27]. However, octree focuses on structural characteristics and does not eliminate redundancy. It is also inefficient to use the octree method for encoding when the high-precision requirement must be satisfied in the LiDAR point cloud data for autonomous mobile robots. For the range image, the point cloud can be projected into a 2D arrangement, and the shape of the 2D range image is fixed when the point cloud is collected from the scanning LiDAR.

Researchers have focused on using existing image and video encoders to compress the range image [16,25,36,39]. However, these methods are limited in several ways. Traditional image or video encoding algorithms, designed for encoding integer pixel values, will cause significant distortion when encoding floating-point LiDAR data. Additionally, the range image is characterized by sharp edges and homogeneous regions with nearly constant values because of the object geometry. Encoding the range image with traditional techniques, for instance, the block-based discrete cosine transform (DCT) [48] followed by coarse quantization, will result in significant encoding errors at the sharp edges. Moreover, image-based compression methods do not make use of the 3D characteristics of point clouds, while it is inefficient to use existing image-based prediction techniques to remove the redundancy in LiDAR data. Another problem of the traditional compression methods based on the quantization of point clouds is that the reconstructed point cloud will show a wave-like shape from the bird's-eye-view. For example, in Fig. 1, the cyan points are the reconstructed point cloud from the baseline range image-based method [43] using a quantizer. The wavy appearance is extremely obvious in a plane. To solve this issue, we are motivated to refine the quantized point cloud to improve the reconstruction quality.

Wang *et al.* [43] introduced several data encoding algorithms, such as BZip2, LZ4, arithmetic coding, etc. Among all these algorithms, the arithmetic coding is the most popular choice in learning-based compression methods [13,21,24,40], because its differentiable version is open-source and implemented with pytorch [19]. Besides, the probability model in the algorithm can be easily obtained by a neural network. Tree-based methods [13,24] used voxelized point clouds by octree and predicted the occupancy code of each voxel in the tree. Inspired by that, we propose a three-stage coarse-to-fine framework. By transferring the regression problem to the classification problem, we can use a neural network to predict the probability of the quantized occupancy code for compression.

In this paper, we propose a three-stage framework to compress single-frame large-scale dense point clouds from a mechanical-scanning LiDAR. The first stage projects the point cloud into the 2D range image, and then segments the whole point cloud into ground points and non-ground points. The points are quantized to be the coarse points with a large-error quantization module. The second stage is to refine the coarse points to finer points, by enhancing the accuracy of the non-ground points as a classification problem, and then apply arithmetic coding to encode the probability of each point in the entropy model. The last stage refines the finer point cloud to the accurate points, and makes the reconstructed point cloud more similar to the original point cloud.

To the best of our knowledge, this is the first method that explores the idea of using an end-to-end range image-based entropy network for intra-frame compression. With the 3D feature extracted from sparse voxels and the 2D attention-based fusion module, the reconstructed point cloud can obtain much higher quality within less volume compared with the state-of-the-art methods. The major contributions of the paper are summarized as follows.

- We propose a novel three-stage entropy model-based compression framework, to apply the differentiable arithmetic coding in the range image-based method, by transferring the regression problem to the classification problem.
- We introduce a geometry-aware attention layer to replace the 2D convolutional layer in the 3D-2D feature fusion part, to improve the performance of high-resolution processing in the range image.
- The experiment results show that our compression framework yields better performance than the state-of-the-art methods in terms of compression ratio, reconstruction quality, and the performance of downstream tasks.

2   Related Works

2.1   Point Cloud Compression Frameworks

According to the representation types of point cloud, compression algorithms can be roughly divided into tree-based and range image-based compression.

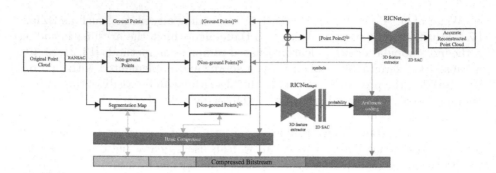

Fig. 2. The overall architecture of our proposed three-stage compression framework. Stage 0 consists of the ground extraction and quantization pre-processing, the stage 1 is an entropy model $RICNet_{stage1}$ for occupancy probability prediction, and the stage 2 is a refinement module $RICNet_{stage2}$ which is used during decompression. The encoding and decoding of the bitstream are totally lossless.

Tree-Based Compression: For tree-based compression, Wang *et al.* [41] introduced the voxel representation for sparse point cloud to utilize the geometry information. From the highest root depth level to the lowest leaf depth level, the size of the voxel gradually decreases. The accuracy of the voxel-based point cloud is determined by the size of the leaf voxel [24]. For the traditional algorithm, the MPEG group developed a geometry-based point cloud compression, G-PCC [10,11,28], as a standard compression library. For the learning-based method, VoxelContext-Net [24] and OctSqueeze [13] are two state-of-the-art octree-based methods, but without open-source code. The proposed networks predict the occupancy probability of each voxel in the octree, and apply arithmetic coding to encode the probability with the ground truth symbol.

Range Image-Based Compression: To transform the 3D point cloud into 2D image, Houshiar *et al.*. [12] project 3D points onto three panorama images, and Ahn *et al.*. [1] projected the point cloud into a range image with the geometry information. Then they compressed the 2D images using an image compression method [39]. Clustering is another common method used in range image compression. Sun *et al.* [31,32] first clustered the point cloud into several segments, and then used traditional compression algorithms, such as BZiP2 [29], to encode the residual of the ground truth points with the clustering centers. Wang *et al.* [43] proposed an open-source baseline method for range image-based compression framework, which can choose uniform or non-uniform compression after obtaining the clustering result. However, all of these range image-based compression methods are based on hand-crafted techniques and thus cannot be optimized in an end-to-end network with a large amount of unsupervised point cloud data. Thus, in this paper, we propose an unsupervised end-to-end framework, to encode and refine the point cloud with the entropy model.

2.2 3D and 2D Feature Extractors

PointNet [22] and PointNet++ [23] are two widely used point-wise feature extraction backbones for 3D point clouds. PointNet concatenates all points and learns global features, and PointNet++ can extract the local features by grouping the neighbors of each point. The 3D sparse convolution (SPConv) [9] and the MinkowskiEngine [4] are the two latest 3D feature extraction backbones with 3D convolution, pooling, unpooling, and broadcasting operations for sparse voxel tensors. In this work, we choose MinkowskiEngine as our 3D backbones after comparing the performance of different network backbones.

SqueezeSeg [45] and PointSeg [44] use the FireConv and FireDeconv modules to extract the 2D features from a range image and output pixel-wise segmentation results for autonomous driving. Attention networks [37] and graph attention networks [38] are used widely in context-related tasks. In our 2D feature extraction module, a geometry-aware scan-attentive convolutional block is used to fuse the 3D features to smooth the final results.

3 Our Approach

3.1 System Overview

In this paper, we propose a three-stage entropy model-based point cloud compression framework, which is shown in Fig. 2. The first stage is for basic coarse point cloud creation and storage, the second and third stages use the neural network iteratively, $RICNet_{stage1}$ and $RICNet_{stage2}$, for point cloud refinement. The output of $RICNet_{stage1}$ helps to generate the compressed bitstream from arithmetic coding. There are two quantization modules, Q_1 and Q_2, which have different quantization accuracies, q_1 and q_2 respectively, with q_1 larger than q_2. The non-ground points of the stage 0 output have accuracy q_1, and the whole point cloud of the stage 1 output has an accuracy of q_2.

The input of our framework is the range image collected from scanning LiDAR, and each point in the point cloud can be converted from the row and column indexes with the depth of each pixel. If we collect the disordered point cloud at the beginning, we can project the point cloud into the range image, and then use the range image to create an ordered point cloud.

In the stage 0, the segmentation map M, ground points P_g and non-ground points P_{ng} are extracted from the original point cloud by the traditional RANSAC algorithm [43]. Note that a small difference in the segmentation module will only have a very limited impact on the compression rate, which can be ignored. The ground points are quantized with Q_2, $[P_g]^{Q_2} = \lfloor P_g/q_2 \rceil * q_2$, where $\lfloor \rceil$ represents a rounding operation, $[P]^Q$ means the original complete point cloud P is quantized with the quantization module Q, and the non-ground points P_{ng} are quantized with Q_1 and Q_2, and named $[P_{ng}]^{Q_1}$ and $[P_{ng}]^{Q_2}$ respectively. The ground points are easier for compression compared with the non-ground points because they are denser and well-organized. Thus, in the stage 1, $RICNet_{stage1}$ only predicts the probability distribution of the non-ground points $[P_{ng}]^{Q_2}$. The differentiable arithmetic coding [19] takes as input the probability with the occupancy symbol, and outputs the encoded bitstream. In the decompression process, the stage 1 will recover the point cloud with accuracy q_2 losslessly. Stage 2 is trained with the ground truth point cloud and only works in the decompression process. In the stage 2, the point cloud with quantized module Q_2, $[P]^{Q_2}$, is fed into RICNet$_{stage2}$ to get the final accurate reconstructed point cloud.

During compression, the M, $[P_g]^{Q_2}$, and $[P_{ng}]^{Q_1}$ are encoded by a basic compressor, and the distribution occupancy symbols are encoded by the entropy coding. All of these coding and decoding processes are losslessly. Based on the comparative results given in [43], we choose BZip2 as our basic compressor.

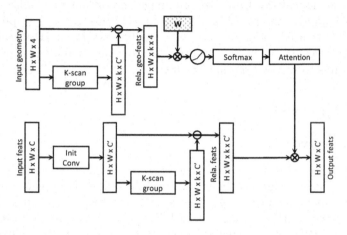

Fig. 3. Our proposed SAC block. The shadow **W** block is the added weights for attention calculation. The K-scan group block groups the neighbors of each point in the same LiDAR scan.

3.2 Network Architecture

RICNet$_{stage1}$ and RICNet$_{stage2}$ are two similar 3D-2D feature fusion networks with the same network architecture, for point cloud refinement. These two networks take as input the coarse points and output the probability of the occupancy code of the refined points. In the stage 1, the output is fed into the arithmetic coding for entropy encoding; in the stage 2, the output can output the final accurate reconstructed point cloud as a refinement module. The 3D feature extractor and 2D attention block in RICNet$_{stage1}$ and RICNet$_{stage2}$ are the same, but the weights are not shared.

3D Feature Extractor: We implement the Minkowski convolutional UNet backbone [4] as our 3D feature extraction module. It is an open-source auto-differentiation library for high-dimensional sparse tensors. The encoder-decoder

3D UNet architecture is similar to the well-known 2D UNet for point-wise prediction, including four convolutional layers and four transposed convolutional layers. The encoder can reduce the spatial dimensions and increase the feature channels, and the skip connection can directly fast-forward the high-resolution features from the encoder to the decoder. The input features are the concatenated point depths with the Cartesian XYZ coordinates, and the output features are the point-wise features.

2D Scan-Attentive Feature Extractor: Owing to the features of different points in the same voxel obtained from the 3D extractor being the same, the 3D features can be seen as the global features. Inspired by GCN [38] and scan-based geometry features in range images used in SLAM [47], we devise the **S**can-**A**ttentive **C**onv (SAC) block to integrate the geometry information of the neighbors of each pixel. Our proposed 2D feature extraction module can fuse the 3D features in the 2D range image, which consists of two SAC blocks after the 3D feature extractor.

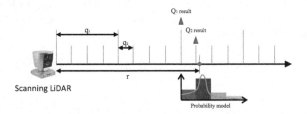

Fig. 4. Toy example of the two quantizers' combination relationship. The red point is the target point, with depth r. The quantized points after Q_1 and Q_2 are labeled. The residual is calculated by quantized depth $-r$. The probability distribution predicted from the RICNet$_{stage1}$ is fed into the arithmetic encoder to encode the ground truth occupancy label ([0, 1, 0, 0] in this example). (Color figure online)

The details of the SAC block are shown in Fig. 3. After obtaining the input features, let F_{in} be the input of a SAC block, $F_{in} \in \mathbb{R}^{H \times W \times C}$, where H and W are the height and width of the range image respectively, and C is the number of channels. After the quantization, the points in single scan have obvious geometric characteristics. Thus, for each pixel p_i, we only group $2k$ neighbors (adjacent pixels) in the scan s, $\{q_j, |i-j| \leq k\}$, where $\{s, i\}, \{s, j\}$ are the pixel coordinates and k is the kernel size ($k = 3$ in experiments). Because range images have sharp edges, the values of adjacent pixels may vary greatly. We would like to pay more attention to the features of the adjacent pixels that are not too far away, and ignore the points in different objects. We first obtain the relative geometry features $\Delta G = G_p - G_q$ and relative input features $\Delta F = Conv_{init}(F_p) - Conv_{init}(F_q)$, where $\Delta G = \{(r, x, y, z)\} \in \mathbb{R}^4$, r is the depth of the points, $Conv_{init}$ is an initial convolutional layer with kernel size 3 and out channels C', and $\Delta F \in \mathbb{R}^{C'}$. To calculate the important coefficients between the grouped pixels and the object point, a weight-shared linear transformation with weight matrix $\mathbf{W} \in \mathbb{R}^{4 \times C'}$ is applied to every pixel. The attention coefficient between pixel p_i and its neighbors can be calculated:

$$\alpha = \text{softmax}(\mathbf{LeakyReLU}(\mathbf{W}\Delta G)). \tag{1}$$

Then, the relative features of the neighbors ΔF are multiplied with the attention, and the sum of the neighbors' geometry-attentive features is the output of our SAC block.

Occupancy Head and Refinement Head: We propose an occupancy head for RICNet$_{stage1}$ and a refinement head for RICNet$_{stage2}$. The output of the occupancy head is the probability of each occupancy code for entropy encoding, and the output of the refinement head is the residual of the Q_2 quantized point cloud for accurate point cloud reconstruction.

Figure 4 shows a toy example of a point in red and its ground truth occupancy label in the stage 0 and stage 1. Q_1 result corresponds to the coarse point, and Q_2 result corresponds to the finer point, in Fig. 2. For point $p_{\{i,j\}}$ in the range image with depth r, the residual between the quantized point from the two quantizers and the ground truth points:

$$res^{Q_1}_{\{i,j\}} = [p]^{Q_1} - r = \lfloor \frac{r}{q_1} \rceil * q_1 - r \in (-\frac{q_1}{2}, \frac{-q_1}{2}], \tag{2}$$

$$res^{Q_2}_{\{i,j\}} = [p]^{Q_2} - r = \lfloor \frac{r}{q_2} \rceil * q_2 - r \in (-\frac{q_2}{2}, \frac{-q_2}{2}], \tag{3}$$

and the length of the occupancy label in the stage 1 for arithmetic coding can be calculated as

$$\text{len}(O) = (\lceil \frac{q_1}{2}/q_2 \rceil) * 2 + 1 \geq \lceil res^{Q_1}_{\{i,j\}}/res^{Q_2}_{\{i,j\}} \rceil. \tag{4}$$

Equation 4 helps to ensure the occupancy label contains all possible conditions when q_1 cannot be divided by q_2. Thus, in the stage 1, the occupancy head outputs the probability prediction

$$occ_{pred} = \text{softmax}(Conv(F)), \tag{5}$$

where $Conv$ is the 1D convolutional layer with out channels len(O).

In the stage 2, since the absolute ground truth residual of every point is less than $q_2/2$, the refinement head predicts a sigmoid residual with q_2 gain:

$$res_{pred} = \text{sigmoid}(Conv(F)) * q_2 - q_2/2, \tag{6}$$

where $Conv$ has one out channel as the limited residual. In this way, we can ensure the maximum error of the reconstructed point cloud does not exceed $q_2/2$.

3.3   Network Learning

The training of our network is unsupervised, with the real-world point cloud only. $RICNet_{stage1}$ is an entropy model with the classification output. The loss function in this stage consists of three parts: an l2-regression loss for the residual between the predicted range image and the original range image, a cross entropy loss for classification in the occupancy label, and an entropy loss for end-to-end encoding the bitrate from the differentiable arithmetic coding algorithm. And in $RICNet_{stage2}$, only the mean square error loss of the residual is counted. Thus, the total loss is

$$\mathcal{L} = \mathcal{L}^{S_1} + \mathcal{L}^{S_2} = \mathcal{L}^{S_1}_{MSE} + \mathcal{L}_{CE} + \mathcal{L}_{BPP} + \mathcal{L}^{S_2}_{MSE}.$$

More specifically, to calculate the predicted point cloud in the stage 1, the classification probability can be converted to the regression residual by accumulating each occupancy location with its probability.

3.4   Compression and Decompression

During compression and decompression, our method can keep the number of points constant, and the only lossy part in our framework is the second quantizer Q_2. The first quantizer is restricted by the ground truth occupancy label, and the maximum error of each pixel in the range image will be less than $q_2/2$. All encoding and decoding processes can be fully lossless in compression and decompression. $RICNet_{stage1}$ takes as input the probability model with the ground truth label of the occupancy label and outputs the compressed bitstream during data encoding. It decodes the ground truth occupancy losslessly using the predicted probability model and the encoded bitstream. Meanwhile, $RICNet_{stage2}$ only works during the decompression as a refinement module.

4   Experiments

4.1   Datasets

We evaluate our proposed compression framework on three real-world point cloud datasets, KITTI [7], Oxford [17], and Campus16 [43]. The KITTI dataset is collected from a Velodyne-HDL64 LiDAR with 64 scans. The city scene in the KITTI raw-data dataset is evaluated in reconstruction quality experiments, and the KITTI detection dataset is evaluated in the detection downstream task experiments. The Oxford dataset is collected from the Velodyne-HDL32 LiDAR with 32 LiDAR scans. The point clouds collected from the left-hand LiDAR are used for training and testing. Meanwhile, the Campus16 dataset is shared by Wang et al. [43], who collected from a Velodyne-VLP16 LiDAR with 16 scans. All three datasets are split into training (2,000 frames), validation (1,000 frames) and testing (1000 frames) sets. The shapes of the range images on three datasets are [64, 2000], [32, 2250], and [16, 1800], respectively. All of the experimental results are evaluated on the testing dataset.

4.2   Evaluation Metrics

To evaluate the degree of compression, we apply bit-per-point (BPP) and compression ratio (CR) as two evaluation metrics. This is because we only consider the geometric compression of the point cloud, and the original points have float32 x, y, and z, CR equals $(32 * 3)$/BPP.

To evaluate the reconstruction quality, we calculate the Chamfer distance (CD) [6,14], F_1 score, point-to-point PSNR, and point-to-plane peak signal-to-noise ratio (PSNR) [18,34], where the voxel size of the F_1 score is set as 0.02 m, and the peak constant values of the two PSNR metrics are set as 59.70 m [2]. The definition and the other settings are the same as the corresponding cited papers. The chamfer distance and the PSNR are all symmetric for the original point cloud and the reconstructed point cloud. We then choose the average of these two bi-directional results as the final results.

Table 1. Compression ratio and reconstruction quality vs. different network architectures. The bold font highlights the best results. PSNR1 is the point-to-point PSNR, and PSNR2 is the point-to-plane PSNR.

3D	2D	Attention	Bpp ↓	CD ↓	F1 score ↑	PSNR1 ↑	PSNR2 ↑
×	SqueezeSeg	×	2.65	0.0367	0.285	67.48	72.53
PointNet++	XSolidBrush	×	2.46	0.0283	0.421	68.41	75.19
Minkowski	×	×	2.38	0.0265	0.467	69.74	75.36
Minkowski	2D Conv	×	2.26	0.027	0.466	69.54	75.28
Minkowski	2D Attentive Conv (SAC)	**2.25**	**0.0255**	**0.508**	**69.86**	**75.39**

Table 2. BPP ↓ results of different architectures and quantizer combination ratios. The bold font highlights the best results.

BPP	0.2	0.3	0.4	0.5	0.6
w/o Stage 0 & 1	2.27	2.27	2.27	2.27	2.27
w/o Stage 0	2.04	1.97	2.1	2.14	2.18
Ours	2.04	**1.92**	2.08	2.09	2.13

To utilize our compression and decompression framework in an autonomous driving system, the performance degradation after using the reconstructed point cloud is also important. In this paper, we evaluate the bounding box average precision (AP) [5,30] for 3D object detection, and the absolute trajectory error (ATE) and the relative pose error (RPE) [49] for simultaneous localization and mapping (SLAM) using the reconstructed point clouds.

4.3   Ablation Study

In this section, we perform ablation studies on compression frameworks and network architectures. The reconstruction quality and compression ratio are evaluated over different 3D and 2D network modules, and only the compression ratio is evaluated over different quantizer combinations.

Three-Stage Architecture. In this section, we evaluate the BPP when the first quantizer uses different quantization accuracy q_1, and proves the significance of stage 0 and stage 1 in our proposed three-stage framework. In the experiments, we first guarantee that the accuracy of the second quantizer is always 0.1, and change the accuracy of the first quantizer to 0.2, 0.3, 0.4, 0.5, and 0.6. When the first quantizer changes from finer to coarser, the bitstream length of the non-ground points encoded by the basic compressor changes from long to short, but the bitstream length of the arithmetic coding will grow because the probability results become worse simultaneously. The BPP results in Table 2 show that the compression performance of our stage 1 entropy model is best when $q1/q2 = 3$. When we remove stage 0 and stage 1 from our three-stage architecture, RICNet_{stage1} is replaced with the basic compressor BZiP2, and the point cloud will be quantized with $q_2 = 0.1$. In addition, when we remove stage 0 only, the input of RICNet_{stage1} changes to the whole point cloud rather than the non-ground points. The experimental results in Table 2 show that our hierarchical range image entropy model is better than the traditional encoding, and only using the non-ground points can remove the interference of ground points, especially in the low-precision quantization situation.

Network Architectures. In this section, we test and compare different well-known 3D and 2D feature extractors for point-wise tasks from the point cloud or pixel-wise tasks from the range image:

- SqueezeSeg [44,45]: We implement the SqueezeSeg twice to replace RICNet, and the heads of the two networks are changed to be the same as the occupancy head and refinement head in RICNet_{stage1} and RICNet_{stage2}, respectively.
- PointNet++ [22,23]: Consists of four down-sampling layers (set abstraction modules), and four up-sampling layers (feature propogation modules) with the skip connections.
- Our Minkowski UNet architecture [4]: The Minkowski UNet14 is implemented as the 3D feature extractor. The network architecture performs quickly and well on the point-wise segmentation tasks.
- 2D Conv: We replace the two SAC blocks in the 2D module with two 2D Conv layers with kernel size 3.

Table 1 shows the comparative results of different network architectures. The bottom row is the setting in our proposed RICNet. From the first three rows, we can find that the Minkowski encoder-decoder architecture performs best when the network only has a single 2D or 3D feature extractor. The fourth row shows that using the single 2D feature fusion with 2D convolutional layers, the network performs better, with a 0.12 BPP improvement in the stage 1. However, the performance of stage 2 remains unchanged. And with our proposed 2D attentive convolutional layer, the BPP metric shows a further 0.01 improvement, and our refinement model in the stage 2 can predict the point cloud with better reconstruction quality.

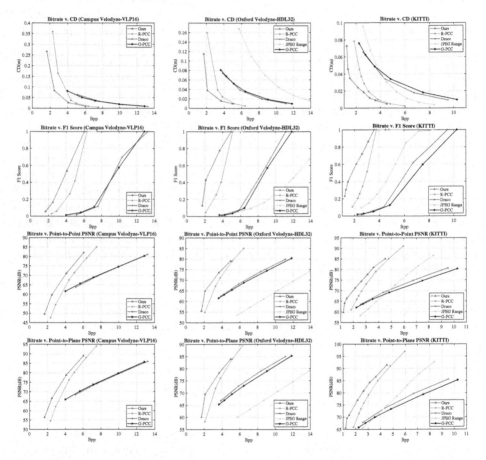

Fig. 5. Quantitative results on KITTI city dataset. Bit-per-point *vs.* symmetric Chamfer distance ($\downarrow$), F1 score (with $\tau_{geo} = 0.02$ m) ($\uparrow$), and point-to-plane PSNR (with $r = 59.70$) ($\uparrow$) are shown from top to bottom. The left column is the campus point clouds collected from a Velodyne-VLP16, the middle column is the Oxford dataset collected from a Velodyne-HDL32, and the right column is the KITTI dataset collected from a Velodyne-HDL64.

4.4   Comparative Results

In this section, we compare our RICNet with the baseline point cloud compression frameworks: Google Draco [8], G-PCC [11,28], JPEG Range [25,39] (using FPEG2000 for range image compression), and R-PCC [43]. In R-PCC implementation, we only evaluate and compare the uniform compression framework for equal comparison.

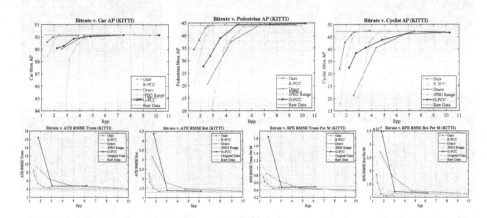

Fig. 6. Quantitative results of the 3D object detection (first row) and SLAM (second row) using reconstructed point cloud. The 3D object detection task is using pre-trained PointPillar from OpenPCDet [33] on the KITTI detection dataset. Car, pedestrian, and cyclist bounding box AP are evaluated from left to right in the first row. The SLAM is using A-LOAM [35] on the KITTI odometry dataset (seq 00).

Reconstruction Quality in Different Datasets. Figure 5 shows the quantitative results of our proposed method with the baseline methods on the KITTI, Oxford, and Campus datasets. The results show that our RICNet shows a large improvement in the low-BPP compression, which means it can generate a better refined point cloud from the low-precision point cloud from stage 1. At the same time, the bitrate and reconstruction quality of the range image-based methods are better than the tree-based methods, which means that the range image presentation is efficient enough for compression. In high-accuracy compression situations, our method becomes closer to R-PCC. This is because the error from LiDAR collection and the uneven surfaces of the objects will infer the geometric feature learning when the quantization accuracy of the first quantizer is high. It is also hard to use the irregular learned features to recover the original point cloud.

Downstream Tasks. In this section, we evaluate the performance of the downstream tasks (3D object detection and SLAM) using the reconstructed point

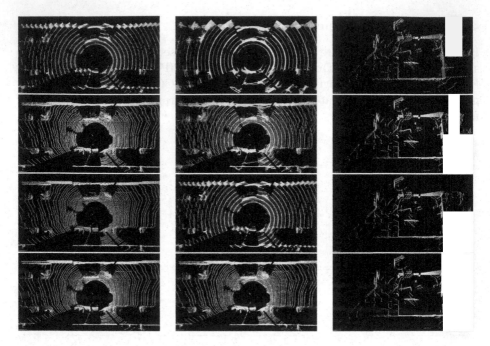

Fig. 7. The qualitative results of our predicted point cloud with the baseline quantized point cloud and ground truth point cloud. From top to bottom, the red points are the predicted point clouds of $RICNet_{stage1}$, $RICNet_{stage1}$, $RICNet_{stage2}$, and $RICNet_{stage2}$, respectively; the cyan points are the baseline quantized point cloud using the first quantizer Q_1, ground truth point cloud, the quantized point cloud using Q_2, and ground truth point cloud, respectively. The left column is the KITTI dataset with the two quantizers $q_1 = 0.3$ m, $q_2 = 0.1$ m, while in the middle column $q_1 = 1.5$ m, $q_2 = 0.5$ m. The right column is the Campus dataset with $q_1 = 0.3$ m, $q_2 = 0.1$ m. (Color figure online)

cloud. In Fig. 6, the first row shows the evaluation results of the 3D object detection, and the second row shows the comparative SLAM results with the baseline methods. Similar to the experimental results of reconstruction quality, the performance in the low-BPP compression situation shows obvious improvements in the downstream tasks too. The lossless threshold of our proposed method is lower than that of the other baseline methods. Since our learning-based method can learn more features from the structured point regions and reconstruct them better, our method has advantages in the downstream tasks for autonomous driving system implementation.

4.5   Qualitative Results

From the quantitative results, we illustrate the advantages of our method in terms of reconstruction quality and downstream tasks. And in Fig. 7, we show the comparative bird's-eye-view image of the predicted point cloud with the ground-truth point cloud and the baseline quantized point cloud in the stage 1. It shows the outstanding prediction and refinement ability of our proposed network, whether using a high-precision quantized point cloud or a low-precision point cloud. And it is also robust for point clouds of different densities, which are collected from different LiDARs. In structured locations and environments especially, such as walls, the predicted points are almost the same as the real points.

5 Conclusion

Our proposed unsupervised end-to-end three-stage compression framework with RICNet outperforms the state-of-the-art methods not only in terms of the reconstruction quality but also in downstream tasks. The experimental results show that our compression framework can bring great improvement in low-precision quantization situations, and the network can learn and reconstruct the structured point regions better. The drawback of our framework is that our method can only compose point clouds collected from a scanning LiDAR. The bottleneck of all range image-based point cloud compression frameworks is the error caused by point cloud projection.

Acknowledgment. This work was supported by Zhongshan Science and Technology Bureau Fund, under project 2020AG002, Foshan-HKUST Project no. FSUST20-SHCIRI06C, and the Project of Hetao Shenzhen-Hong Kong Science and Technology Innovation Cooperation Zone(HZQB-KCZYB-2020083), awarded to Prof. Ming Liu. (Corresponding author: Ming Liu)

References

1. Ahn, J.K., Lee, K.Y., Sim, J.Y., Kim, C.S.: Large-scale 3d point cloud compression using adaptive radial distance prediction in hybrid coordinate domains. IEEE J. Sel. Topics Signal Process. **9**(3), 422–434 (2014)
2. Biswas, S., Liu, J., Wong, K., Wang, S., Urtasun, R.: Muscle: multi sweep compression of lidar using deep entropy models. arXiv preprint arXiv:2011.07590 (2020)
3. Cao, C., Preda, M., Zaharia, T.: 3D point cloud compression: a survey. In: The 24th International Conference on 3D Web Technology, pp. 1–9 (2019)
4. Choy, C., Gwak, J., Savarese, S.: 4D spatio-temporal convnets: minkowski convolutional neural networks. In: Proceedings of the IEEE Conference on Computer Vision and Pattern Recognition, pp. 3075–3084 (2019)
5. Everingham, M., Van Gool, L., Williams, C.K., Winn, J., Zisserman, A.: The pascal visual object classes (voc) challenge. Int. J. Comput. Vision **88**(2), 303–338 (2010)
6. Fan, H., Su, H., Guibas, L.J.: A point set generation network for 3D object reconstruction from a single image. In: Proceedings of the IEEE Conference on Computer Vision and Pattern Recognition, pp. 605–613 (2017)
7. Geiger, A., Lenz, P., Stiller, C., Urtasun, R.: Vision meets robotics: the kitti dataset. Int. J. Rob. Res. **32**(11), 1231–1237 (2013)
8. Google: Draco: 3D Data Compression (2018). https://github.com/google/draco

9. Graham, B., Engelcke, M., van der Maaten, L.: 3D semantic segmentation with submanifold sparse convolutional networks. In: CVPR (2018)
10. Graziosi, D., Nakagami, O., Kuma, S., Zaghetto, A., Suzuki, T., Tabatabai, A.: An overview of ongoing point cloud compression standardization activities: Video-based (v-pcc) and geometry-based (g-pcc). APSIPA Trans. Signal Inf. Process. **9** (2020)
11. Group, M.· MPEG G-PCC TMC13 (2020). https://github.com/MPEGGroup/mpeg-pcc-tmc13
12. Houshiar, H., Nuchter, A.: 3D point cloud compression using conventional image compression for efficient data transmission. In: XXV International Conference on Information (2015)
13. Huang, L., Wang, S., Wong, K., Liu, J., Urtasun, R.: Octsqueeze: octree-structured entropy model for lidar compression. In: Proceedings of the IEEE/CVF Conference on Computer Vision and Pattern Recognition, pp. 1313–1323 (2020)
14. Huang, T., Liu, Y.: 3D point cloud geometry compression on deep learning. In: Proceedings of the 27th ACM International Conference on Multimedia, pp. 890–898 (2019)
15. Koh, N., Jayaraman, P.K., Zheng, J.: Parallel point cloud compression using truncated octree. In: 2020 International Conference on Cyberworlds (CW), pp. 1–8. IEEE (2020)
16. Korshunov, P., Ebrahimi, T.: Context-dependent jpeg backward-compatible high-dynamic range image compression. Optical Eng. **52**(10), 102006 (2013)
17. Maddern, W., Pascoe, G., Linegar, C., Newman, P.: 1 Year, 1000 km: the oxford RobotCar Dataset. Int. J. Rob. Res. (IJRR) **36**(1), 3–15 (2017). https://doi.org/10.1177/0278364916679498
18. Mekuria, R., Laserre, S., Tulvan, C.: Performance assessment of point cloud compression. In: 2017 IEEE Visual Communications and Image Processing (VCIP), pp. 1–4. IEEE (2017)
19. Mentzer, F., Agustsson, E., Tschannen, M., Timofte, R., Van Gool, L.: Practical full resolution learned lossless image compression. In: Proceedings of the IEEE Conference on Computer Vision and Pattern Recognition (CVPR) (2019)
20. Morell, V., Orts, S., Cazorla, M., Garcia-Rodriguez, J.: Geometric 3D point cloud compression. Pattern Recogn. Lett. **50**, 55–62 (2014)
21. Nguyen, D.T., Quach, M., Valenzise, G., Duhamel, P.: Multiscale deep context modeling for lossless point cloud geometry compression. In: 2021 IEEE International Conference on Multimedia & Expo Workshops (ICMEW), pp. 1–6. IEEE (2021)
22. Qi, C.R., Su, H., Mo, K., Guibas, L.J.: Pointnet: deep learning on point sets for 3D classification and segmentation. In: Proceedings of the IEEE Conference on Computer Vision and Pattern Recognition, pp. 652–660 (2017)
23. Qi, C.R., Yi, L., Su, H., Guibas, L.J.: Pointnet++: deep hierarchical feature learning on point sets in a metric space. arXiv preprint arXiv:1706.02413 (2017)
24. Que, Z., Lu, G., Xu, D.: Voxelcontext-net: an octree based framework for point cloud compression. In: Proceedings of the IEEE/CVF Conference on Computer Vision and Pattern Recognition, pp. 6042–6051 (2021)
25. Rabbani, M.: Jpeg 2000: image compression fundamentals, standards and practice. J. Electron. Imaging **11**(2), 286 (2002)
26. Rozenberszki, D., Majdik, A.L.: Lol: lidar-only odometry and localization in 3D point cloud maps. In: 2020 IEEE International Conference on Robotics and Automation (ICRA), pp. 4379–4385. IEEE (2020)

27. Schnabel, R., Klein, R.: Octree-based point-cloud compression. In: PBG@ SIG-GRAPH, pp. 111–120 (2006)
28. Schwarz, S., et al.: Emerging mpeg standards for point cloud compression. IEEE J. Emerg. Sel. Topics Circ. Syst. **9**(1), 133–148 (2018)
29. Seward, J.: bzip2 and libbzip2 (1996). http://www.bzip.orgbzip.org
30. Sun, P., et al.: Scalability in perception for autonomous driving: waymo open dataset. In: Proceedings of the IEEE/CVF Conference on Computer Vision and Pattern Recognition, pp. 2446–2454 (2020)
31. Sun, X., Wang, S., Liu, M.: A novel coding architecture for multi-line lidar point clouds based on clustering and convolutional lstm network. IEEE Trans. Intell. Transp. Syst. **23**, 2190–2201 (2020)
32. Sun, X., Wang, S., Wang, M., Wang, Z., Liu, M.: A novel coding architecture for lidar point cloud sequence. IEEE Rob. Autom. Lett. **5**(4), 5637–5644 (2020)
33. Team, O.D.: Openpcdet: an open-source toolbox for 3D object detection from point clouds (2020). https://github.com/open-mmlab/OpenPCDet
34. Tian, D., Ochimizu, H., Feng, C., Cohen, R., Vetro, A.: Geometric distortion metrics for point cloud compression. In: 2017 IEEE International Conference on Image Processing (ICIP), pp. 3460–3464. IEEE (2017)
35. Tong Qin, S.C.: Advanced implementation of loam (2019). https://github.com/HKUST-Aerial-Robotics/A-LOAM
36. Tu, C., Takeuchi, E., Miyajima, C., Takeda, K.: Compressing continuous point cloud data using image compression methods. In: 2016 IEEE 19th International Conference on Intelligent Transportation Systems (ITSC), pp. 1712–1719. IEEE (2016)
37. Vaswani, A., et al.: Attention is all you need. Adv. Neural Inf. Process. Syst. **30**, 5998–6008 (2017)
38. Veličković, P., Cucurull, G., Casanova, A., Romero, A., Lio, P., Bengio, Y.: Graph attention networks. arXiv preprint arXiv:1710.10903 (2017)
39. Wallace, G.K.: The jpeg still picture compression standard. IEEE Trans. Cons. Electron. **38**(1), xviii-xxxiv (1992)
40. Wang, J., Ding, D., Li, Z., Ma, Z.: Multiscale point cloud geometry compression. In: 2021 Data Compression Conference (DCC), pp. 73–82. IEEE (2021)
41. Wang, J., Zhu, H., Ma, Z., Chen, T., Liu, H., Shen, Q.: Learned point cloud geometry compression. arXiv preprint arXiv:1909.12037 (2019)
42. Wang, S., Cai, P., Wang, L., Liu, M.: Ditnet: end-to-end 3D object detection and track id assignment in spatio-temporal world. IEEE Rob. Autom. Lett. **6**(2), 3397–3404 (2021)
43. Wang, S., Jiao, J., Cai, P., Liu, M.: R-pcc: a baseline for range image-based point cloud compression. arXiv preprint arXiv:2109.07717 (2021)
44. Wang, Y., Shi, T., Yun, P., Tai, L., Liu, M.: Pointseg: real-time semantic segmentation based on 3D lidar point cloud. arXiv preprint arXiv:1807.06288 (2018)
45. Wu, B., Wan, A., Yue, X., Keutzer, K.: Squeezeseg: convolutional neural nets with recurrent crf for real-time road-object segmentation from 3D lidar point cloud. In: 2018 IEEE International Conference on Robotics and Automation (ICRA), pp. 1887–1893. IEEE (2018)
46. Ye, H., Chen, Y., Liu, M.: Tightly coupled 3D lidar inertial odometry and mapping. In: 2019 International Conference on Robotics and Automation (ICRA), pp. 3144–3150. IEEE (2019)
47. Zhang, J., Singh, S.: Loam: lidar odometry and mapping in real-time. In: Robotics: Science and Systems, vol. 2 (2014)

48. Zhang, X., Wan, W., An, X.: Clustering and DCT based color point cloud compression. J. Signal Process. Syst. **86**(1), 41–49 (2017)
49. Zhang, Z., Scaramuzza, D.: A tutorial on quantitative trajectory evaluation for visual (-inertial) odometry. In: 2018 IEEE/RSJ International Conference on Intelligent Robots and Systems (IROS), pp. 7244–7251. IEEE (2018)

Joint Feature Learning and Relation Modeling for Tracking: A One-Stream Framework

Botao Ye[1,2], Hong Chang[1,2(✉)], Bingpeng Ma[2], Shiguang Shan[1,2], and Xilin Chen[1,2]

[1] Key Lab of Intelligent Information Processing of Chinese Academy of Sciences (CAS), Institute of Computing Technology, CAS, Beijing 100190, China
botao.ye@vipl.ict.ac.cn, {changhong,sgshan,xlchen}@ict.ac.cn
[2] University of Chinese Academy of Sciences, Beijing 100049, China
bpma@ucas.ac.cn

Abstract. The current popular two-stream, two-stage tracking framework extracts the template and the search region features separately and then performs relation modeling, thus the extracted features lack the awareness of the target and have limited target-background discriminability. To tackle the above issue, we propose a novel *one-stream tracking* (OSTrack) framework that unifies feature learning and relation modeling by bridging the template-search image pairs with bidirectional information flows. In this way, discriminative target-oriented features can be dynamically extracted by mutual guidance. Since no extra heavy relation modeling module is needed and the implementation is highly parallelized, the proposed tracker runs at a fast speed. To further improve the inference efficiency, an in-network candidate early elimination module is proposed based on the strong similarity prior calculated in the one-stream framework. As a unified framework, OSTrack achieves state-of-the-art performance on multiple benchmarks, in particular, it shows impressive results on the one-shot tracking benchmark GOT-10k, *i.e.,*, achieving 73.7% AO, improving the existing best result (SwinTrack) by 4.3%. Besides, our method maintains a good performance-speed trade-off and shows faster convergence. The code and models are available at https://github.com/botaoye/OSTrack.

1 Introduction

Visual object tracking (VOT) aims at localizing an arbitrary target in each video frame, given only its initial appearance. The *continuously changing* and *arbitrary* nature of the target poses a challenge to learn a target appearance model that can effectively discriminate the specified target from the background. Current mainstream trackers typically address this problem with a common *two-stream*

Supplementary Information The online version contains supplementary material available at https://doi.org/10.1007/978-3-031-20047-2_20.

and *two-stage* pipeline, which means that the features of the template and the search region are separately extracted (two-stream), and the whole process is divided into two sequential steps: feature extraction and relation modeling (two-stage). Such a natural pipeline employs the strategy of "divide-and-conquer" and achieves remarkable success in terms of tracking performance.

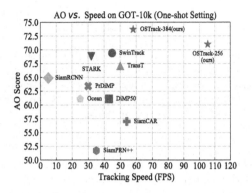

Fig. 1. A comparison of AO and speed of state-of-the-art trackers on GOT-10k under one-shot setting. Our OSTrack-384 sets a new SOTA of 73.7% AO on GOT-10k, showing impressive one-shot tracking performance. OSTrack-256 runs at 105.4 FPS while still outperforming all previous trackers.

However, the separation of feature extraction and relation modeling suffers from the following limitations. Firstly, the feature extracted by the vanilla two-stream two-stage framework is unaware of the target. In other words, the extracted feature for each image is determined after off-line training, since there is no interaction between the template and the search region. This is against with the continuously changing and arbitrary nature of the target, leading to limited target-background discriminative power. On some occasions when the category of the target object is not involved in the training dataset (*i.e.*,, one-shot tracking), the above problems are particularly serious. Secondly, the two-stream, two-stage framework is vulnerable to the performance-speed dilemma. According to the computation burden of the feature fusion module, two different strategies are commonly utilized. The first type, shown in Fig. 2(a), simply adopts one single operator like cross-correlation [1,23] or discriminative correlation filter [2,6], which is efficient but less effective since the simple linear operation leads to discriminative information loss [4]. The second type, shown in Fig. 2(b), addresses the information loss by complicated non-linear interaction (Transformer [38]), but is less efficient due to a large number of parameters and the use of iterative refinement (*e.g.*,, for each search image, STARK-S50 [43] takes 7.5 ms for the feature extraction and 14.1 ms for relation modeling on an RTX2080Ti GPU).

In this work, we set out to address the aforementioned problems via a unified *one-stream one-stage* tracking framework. The core insight of the one-stream framework is to bridge a free information flow between the template and search region at the early stage (*i.e.*,, the raw image pair), thus extracting target-oriented features and avoiding the loss of discriminative information. Specifically, we concatenate the flattened template and search region and feed them into staked self-attention layers [38] (widely used Vision Transformer (ViT) [10] is chosen in our implementation), and the produced search region features can be directly used for target classification and regression without further matching. The staked self-attention operations enable iteratively feature matching between the template and the search region, thus allowing mutual guidance for target-oriented feature extraction. Therefore, both template and search region features can be extracted dynamically with strong discriminative power. Additionally, the proposed framework achieves a good balance between performance and speed because the concatenation of the template and the search region makes the one-stream framework highly parallelizable and does not require additional heavy relational modeling networks.

Moreover, the proposed one-stream framework provides a strong prior about the similarity of the target and each part of the search region (*i.e.*, candidates) as shown in Fig. 4, which means that the model can identify background regions even at the early stage. This phenomenon verifies the effectiveness of the one-stream framework and motivates us to propose an in-network *early candidate elimination* module for progressively identifying and discarding the candidates belonging to the background in a timely manner. The proposed candidate elimination module not only significantly boosts the inference speed, but also avoids the negative impact of uninformative background regions on feature matching.

Despite its simple structure, the proposed trackers achieve impressive performance and set a new state-of-the-art (SOTA) on multiple benchmarks. Moreover, it maintains adorable inference efficiency and shows faster convergence compared to SOTA Transformer based trackers. As shown in Fig. 1, our method achieves a good balance between the accuracy and inference speed.

The main contributions of this work are three-fold: (1) We propose a simple, neat, and effective one-stream, one-stage tracking framework by combining the feature extraction and relation modeling. (2) Motivated by the prior of the early acquired similarity score between the target and each part of the search region, an in-network early candidate elimination module is proposed for decreasing the inference time. (3) We perform comprehensive experiments to verify that the one-stream framework outperforms the previous SOTA two-stream trackers in terms of performance, inference speed, and convergence speed. The resulting tracker OSTrack sets a new state-of-the-art on multiple tracking benchmarks.

2   Related Work

In this section, we briefly review different tracking pipelines, as well as the adaptive inference methods related to our early candidate elimination module.

Tracking Pipelines. Based on the different computational burdens of feature extraction and relation modeling networks, we compare our method with two different two-stream two-stage archetypes in Fig. 2. Earlier Siamese trackers [1,23,46] and discriminative trackers [2,6] belong to Fig. 2(a). They first extract the features of the template and the search region separately by a CNN backbone [15,20], which shares the same structure and parameters. Then, a lightweight relation modeling network (e.g.,, the cross-correlation layer [1,22] in Siamese trackers and correlation filter [3,16] in discriminative trackers) takes responsibility to fuse these features for the subsequent state estimation task. However, the template feature cannot be adjusted according to the search region feature in these methods. Such a shallow and unidirectional relation modeling strategy may be insufficient for information interaction. Recently, stacked Transformer layers [38] are introduced for better relation modeling. These methods belong to Fig. 2(b) where the relation modeling module is relatively heavy and enables bi-directional information interaction. TransT [4] proposes to stack a series of self-attention and cross-attention layers for iterative feature fusion. STARK [43] concatenates the pre-extracted template and search region features and feeds them into multiple self-attention layers. The bi-directional heavy structure brings performance gain but inevitably slows down the inference speed. Differently, our one-stream one-stage design belongs to Fig. 2(c). For the first time, we seamlessly combine feature extraction and relation modeling into a unified pipeline. The proposed method provides free information flow between the template and search region with minor computation costs. It not only generates target-oriented features by mutual guidance but also is efficient in terms of both training and testing time.

Adaptive Inference. Our early candidate elimination module can be seen as a progressive process of adaptively discarding potential background regions based on the similarity between the target and the search region. One related topic is the adaptive inference [24,33,44] in vision transformers, which is proposed to accelerate the computation of ViT. DynamicViT [33] trains extra control gates with the Gumbel-softmax trick to discard tokens during inference. Instead of directly discarding non-informative tokens, EViT [24] fuses them to avoid

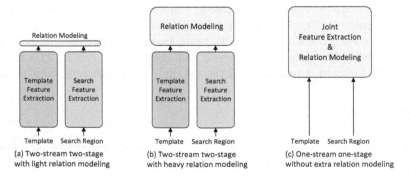

Fig. 2. Three different taxonomies of tracking pipeline. The height of each rectangular represents the relative model size.

potential information loss. These works are tightly coupled with the classification task and are therefore not suitable for tracking. Instead, we treat each token as a target candidate and then discard the candidates that are least similar to the target by means of a free similarity score calculated by the self-attention operation. To the best of our knowledge, this is the first work that attempts to eliminate potential background candidates within the tracking network.

3   Method

This section describes the proposed one-stream tracker (OSTrack). The input image pairs are fed into a ViT backbone for simultaneous feature extraction and relation modeling, and the resulting search region features are directly adopted for subsequent target classification and regression. An overview of the model is shown in Fig. 3(a).

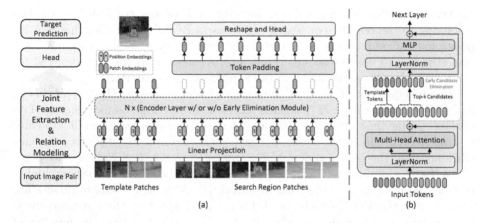

Fig. 3. (a) The overall framework of the proposed one-stream framework. The template and search region are split, flattened, and linear projected. Image embeddings are then concatenated and fed into Transformer encoder layers for joint feature extraction and relation modeling. (b) The structure of the encoder layer with early candidate elimination module, which is insert after the multi-head attention operation [38].

3.1   Joint Feature Extraction and Relation Modeling

We propose to combine the feature extraction and relation modeling modules and construct a free information flow between the contents of the template and the search region. The global contextual modeling capacity of self-attention [38] operation perfectly fits our goal, therefore, vanilla ViT [10] is selected as the main body of OSTrack. Adopting the existing Vision Transformer architecture also provides a bunch of publicly available pre-trained models [14,36], freeing us from the time-consuming pre-training stage. The input of OSTrack is a pair of images, namely, the template image patch $z \in \mathbb{R}^{3 \times H_z \times W_z}$ and the search region patch $x \in \mathbb{R}^{3 \times H_x \times W_x}$. They are first split and flattened into sequences of patches $z_p \in \mathbb{R}^{N_z \times (3 \cdot P^2)}$ and $x_p \in \mathbb{R}^{N_x \times (3 \cdot P^2)}$, where $P \times P$ is the resolution of each patch, and $N_z = H_z W_z / P^2$, $N_x = H_x W_x / P^2$ are the number of patches of template and search region respectively. After that, a trainable linear projection layer with parameter E is used to project z_p and x_p into D dimension latent space as in Eq. 1 and Eq. 2, and the output of this projection is commonly called patch embeddings [10]. Learnable 1D position embeddings P_z and P_x are added to the patch embeddings of the template and search region separately to produce the final template token embeddings $H_z^0 \in \mathbb{R}^{N_z \times D}$ and search region token embeddings $H_x^0 \in \mathbb{R}^{N_x \times D}$.

$$H_z^0 = \left[z_p^1 E; z_p^2 E; \cdots ; z_p^{N_z} E \right] + P_z, \quad E \in \mathbb{R}^{(3 \cdot P^2) \times D}, P_z \in \mathbb{R}^{N_z \times D} \quad (1)$$

$$H_x^0 = \left[x_p^1 E; x_p^2 E; \cdots ; x_p^{N_z} E \right] + P_x, \quad P_x \in \mathbb{R}^{N_x \times D} \quad (2)$$

To verify whether adding addition identity embeddings (to indicate a token belonging to the template or search region as in BERT [9]) or adopting relative positional embeddings are beneficial to the performance, we also conduct ablation studies and observe no significant improvement, thus they are omitted for simplicity (details can be found in the supplementary material).

Token sequences H_z^0 and H_x^0 are then concatenated as $H_{zx}^0 = [H_z^0; H_x^0]$, and the resulting vector H_{zx}^0 is then fed into several Transformer encoder layers [10]. Unlike the vanilla ViT [10], we insert the proposed early candidate eliminating module into some of encoder layers as shown in Fig. 3(b) for inference efficiency, and the technical details are presented in Sec. 3.2. Notably, adopting the self-attention of concatenated features makes the whole framework highly parallelized compared to the cross-attention [4]. Although template images are also fed into the ViT for each search frame, the impact on the inference speed is minor due to the highly parallel structure and the fact that the number of template tokens is small compared to the number of search region tokens.

Analysis. From the perspective of the self-attention mechanism [38], we further analyze the intrinsic reasons why the proposed framework is able to realize simultaneous feature extraction and relation modeling. The output of self-attention operation A in our approach can be written as:

$$A = \text{Softmax}\left(\frac{Q K^\top}{\sqrt{d_k}} \right) \cdot V = \text{Softmax}\left(\frac{[Q_z; Q_x][K_z; K_x]^\top}{\sqrt{d_k}} \right) \cdot [V_z; V_x], \quad (3)$$

where Q, K, and V are query, key and value matrices separately. The subscripts z and x denote matrix items belonging to the template and search region. The calculation of attention weights in Eq. 3 can be expanded to:

$$\text{Softmax}\left(\frac{[\boldsymbol{Q}_z; \boldsymbol{Q}_x][\boldsymbol{K}_z; \boldsymbol{K}_x]^\top}{\sqrt{d_k}}\right) = \text{Softmax}\left(\frac{[\boldsymbol{Q}_z\boldsymbol{K}_z^\top, \boldsymbol{Q}_z\boldsymbol{K}_x^\top; \boldsymbol{Q}_x\boldsymbol{K}_z^\top, \boldsymbol{Q}_x\boldsymbol{K}_x^\top]}{\sqrt{d_k}}\right)$$

$$\triangleq [\boldsymbol{W}_{zz}, \boldsymbol{W}_{zx}; \boldsymbol{W}_{xz}, \boldsymbol{W}_{xx}],$$

$$(4)$$

where $\boldsymbol{W}_{zx}$ is a measure of similarity between the template and the search region, and the rest are similar. The output $\boldsymbol{A}$ can be further written as:

$$\boldsymbol{A} = [\boldsymbol{W}_{zz}\boldsymbol{V}_z + \boldsymbol{W}_{zx}\boldsymbol{V}_x; \boldsymbol{W}_{xz}\boldsymbol{V}_z + \boldsymbol{W}_{xx}\boldsymbol{V}_x]. \tag{5}$$

In the right part of Eq. 5, $\boldsymbol{W}_{xz}\boldsymbol{V}_z$ is responsible for aggregating the iter-image feature (relation modeling) and $\boldsymbol{W}_{xx}\boldsymbol{V}_x$ aggregating the intra-image feature (feature extraction) based on the similarity of different image parts. Therefore, the feature extraction and relation modeling can be done with a self-attention operation. Moreover, Eq. 5 also constructs a bi-direction information flow that allows mutual guidance of target-oriented feature extraction through the similarity learning.

Comparisons with Two-Stream Transformer Fusion Trackers. 1) Previous two-stream Transformer fusion trackers [4, 25] all adopt a Siamese framework, where the features of the template and search region are separately extracted first, and the Transformer layer is only adopted to fuse the extracted features. Therefore, the extracted features of these methods are not adaptive and may lose some discriminative information, which is irreparable. In contrast, OSTrack directly concatenates linearly projected template and search region images at the first stage, so feature extraction and relation modeling are seamlessly integrated and target-oriented features can be extracted through the mutual guidance of the template and the search region. 2) Previous Transformer fusion trackers only employ ImageNet [8] pre-trained backbone networks [15, 27] and leave Transformer layers randomly initialized, which degrades the convergence speed, while OSTrack benefits from pre-trained ViT models for faster convergence. 3) The one-stream framework provides the possibility of identifying and discarding useless background regions for further improving the model performance and inference speed as presented in Sect. 3.2.

3.2   Early Candidate Elimination

Each token of the search region can be regarded as a target candidate and each template token can be considered as a part of the target object. Previous trackers keep all candidates during feature extraction and relation modeling, while background regions are not identified until the final output of the network (*i.e.,*, classification score map). However, our one-stream framework provides a strong prior on the similarity between the target and each candidate. As shown in Fig. 4, the attention weights of the search region highlight the foreground objects in the early stage of ViT (*e.g.,*, layer 4), and then progressively focus on

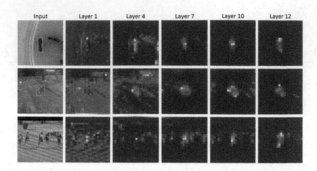

Fig. 4. Visualization of the attention weights of search region corresponding to the center part of template after different ViT layers, the green rectangles indicate target objects. It can be seen as an estimate of the similarity between the target and each position of the search region. (Color figure online)

the target. This property makes it possible to progressively identify and eliminate candidates belonging to the background regions inside the network. Therefore, we propose an early candidate elimination module that progressively eliminates candidates belonging to the background in the early stages of ViT to lighten the computational burden and avoid the negative impact of noisy background regions on feature learning.

Candidate Elimination. Recall that the self-attention operation in ViT can be seen as a spatial aggregation of tokens with normalized importances [38], which is measured by the dot product similarity between each token pair. Specifically, each template token $h_z^i, 1 \leq i \leq N_z$ is calculated as:

$$h_z^i = \text{Softmax}\left(\frac{q_i \cdot [K_z; K_x]^\top}{\sqrt{d}}\right) \cdot V = [w_z^i; w_x^i] \cdot V, \tag{6}$$

where q_i, K_z, K_x and V denote the query vector of token h_z^i, the key matrix corresponding to the template, the key matrix corresponding to the search region and the value matrix. The attention weight w_x^i determines the similarity between the template part h_z^i and all search region tokens (candidates). The $j-th$ item ($1 \leq j \leq n$, n is the number of input search region tokens) of w_x^i determines the similarity between h_z^i and the $j-th$ candidate. However, the input templates usually include background regions that introduce noise when calculating the similarity between the target and each candidate. Therefore, instead of summing up the similarity of each candidate to all template parts w_x^i, $i = 1, \ldots, N_z$, we take $w_x^\phi, \phi = \lfloor \frac{W_z}{2} \rfloor + W_z \cdot \lfloor \frac{H_z}{2} \rfloor$ ($\phi - th$ token corresponding to the center part of the original template image) as the representative similarity. This is fairly reasonable as the center template part has aggregated enough information through self-attention to represent the target. In the supplementary, we compare the effect of different template token choices. Considering that multi-head self-attention is used in ViT, there are multiple similarity scores $w_x^\phi(m)$, where $m = 1, \ldots, M$ and M is the total number of attention heads [38]. We average the similarity scores of all heads by $\overline{\boldsymbol{w}}_x^\phi = \sum_{m=1}^M \boldsymbol{w}_x^\phi(m)/M$, which serves as the final similarity score of the target and each candidate. One candidate is more likely to be a background region if its similarity score with the target is relatively small. Therefore, we only keep the candidates corresponding to the k largest (top-k) elements in $\overline{\boldsymbol{w}}_x^\phi$ (k is a hyperparameter, and we define the token keeping ratio as $\rho = k/n$), while the remaining candidates are eliminated. The proposed candidate elimination module is inserted after the multi-head attention operation [38] in the encoder layer, which is illustrated in Fig. 3(b). In addition, the original order of all remaining candidates is recorded so that it can be recovered in the final stage.

Candidate Restoration. The aforementioned candidate elimination module disrupts the original order of the candidates, making it impossible to reshape the candidate sequence back into the feature map as described in Sect. 3.3, so we restore the original order of the remaining candidates and then pad the missing positions. Since the discarded candidates belong to the irrelevant background regions, they will not affect the classification and regression tasks. In other words, they just act as placeholders for the reshaping operation. Therefore, we first restore the order of the remaining candidates and then zero-pad in between them.

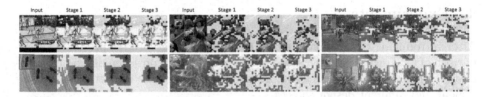

Fig. 5. Visualization of the progressive early candidate elimination process. The main body of "Input" is the search region image, and the upper left corner shows the corresponding template image. The Green rectangles indicate target objects and the masked regions represent the discarded candidates. The results show that our method can gradually identify and discard the candidates belonging to the background regions.(Color figure online)

Visualization. To further investigate the behavior of the early candidate elimination module, we visualize the progressive process in Fig. 5. By iteratively discarding the irrelevant tokens in the search region, OSTrack not only largely lightens the computation burden but also avoids the negative impact of noisy background regions on feature learning.

3.3 Head and Loss

We first re-interpret the padded sequence of search region tokens to a 2D spatial feature map and then feed it into a fully convolutional network (FCN), which consists of L stacked Conv-BN-ReLU layers for each output. Outputs of the FCN contrain the target classification score map $\boldsymbol{P} \in [0,1]^{\frac{H_x}{P} \times \frac{W_x}{P}}$, the local offset $\boldsymbol{O} \in [0,1)^{2 \times \frac{H_x}{P} \times \frac{W_x}{P}}$ to compensate the discretization error caused by reduced resolution and the normalized bounding box size (*i.e.*, width and height) $\boldsymbol{S} \in [0,1]^{2 \times \frac{H_x}{P} \times \frac{W_x}{P}}$. The position with highest classification score is considered to be target position, *i.e.*, $(x_d, y_d) = \arg\max_{(x,y)} \boldsymbol{P}_{xy}$ and the finial target bounding box is obtained as:

$$(x, y, w, h) = (x_d + \boldsymbol{O}(0, x_d, y_d), y_d + \boldsymbol{O}(1, x_d, y_d), \boldsymbol{S}(0, x_d, y_d), \boldsymbol{S}(1, x_d, y_d)). \quad (7)$$

During training, both classification and regression losses are used. We adopt the weighted focal loss [21] for classification (see the supplementary for more details). With the predicted bounding box, ℓ_1 loss and the generalized IoU loss [34] are employed for bounding box regression. Finally, the overall loss function is:

$$L_{track} = L_{cls} + \lambda_{iou} L_{iou} + \lambda_{L_1} L_1, \quad (8)$$

where $\lambda_{iou} = 2$ and $\lambda_{L_1} = 5$ are the regularization parameters in our experiments as in [43].

4   Experiments

After introducing the implementation details, this section first presents a comparison of OSTrack with other state-of-the-art methods on seven different benchmarks. Then, ablation studies are provided to analyze the impact of each component and different design choices.

4.1   Implementation Details

Our trackers are implemented in Python using PyTorch. The models are trained on 4 NVIDIA A100 GPUs and the inference speed is tested on a single NVIDIA RTX2080Ti GPU.

Model. The vanilla ViT-Base [10] model pre-trained with MAE [14] is adopted as the backbone for joint feature extraction and relation modeling. The head is a lightweight FCN, consisting of 4 stacked Conv-BN-ReLU layers for each of three outputs. The keeping ratio ρ of each candidate elimination module is set as 0.7, and a total of three candidate elimination modules are inserted at layers 4, 7, and 10 of ViT respectively, following [33]. We present two variants with different input image pair resolution for showing the scalability of OSTrack:

- **OSTrack-256.** Template: 128×128 pixels; Search region: 256×256 pixels.
- **OSTrack-384.** Template: 192×192 pixels; Search region: 384×384 pixels.

Training. The training splits of COCO [26], LaSOT [12], GOT-10k [17] (1k forbidden sequences from GOT-10k training set are removed following the convention [43]) and TrackingNet [31] are used for training. Common data augmentations including horizontal flip and brightness jittering are used in training. Each GPU holds 32 image pairs, resulting in a total batch size of 128. We train the model with AdamW optimizer [28], set the weight decay to 10^{-4}, the initial learning rate for the backbone to 4×10^{-5} and other parameters to 4×10^{-4}, respectively. The total training epochs are set to 300 with 60k image pairs per epoch and we decrease the learning rate by a factor of 10 after 240 epochs.

Inference. During inference, Hanning window penalty is adopted to utilize positional prior in tracking following the common practice [4,46]. Specifically, we simply multiply the classification map P by the Hanning window with the same size, and the box with the highest score after multiplication will be selected as the tracking result.

4.2 Comparison with State-of-the-Arts

To demonstrate the effectiveness of the proposed models, we compare them with state-of-the-art (SOTA) trackers on seven different benchmarks.

GOT-10k. GOT-10k [17] test set employs the one-shot tracking rule, *i.e.,*, it requires the trackers to be trained only on the GOT-10k training split, and the object classes between train and test splits are not overlapped. We follow this protocol to train our model and evaluate the results by submitting them to the

Table 1. Comparison with state-of-the-arts on four large-scale benchmarks: LaSOT, LaSOT$_{ext}$, TrackingNet and GOT-10k. The best two results are shown in red and **blue** fonts.

Method	Source	LaSOT [12]			LaSOT$_{ext}$ [11]			TrackingNet [31]			GOT-10k* [17]		
		AUC	P$_{Norm}$	P	AUC	P$_{Norm}$	P	AUC	P$_{Norm}$	P	AO	SR$_{0.5}$	SR$_{0.75}$
SiamFC [1]	ECCVW16	33.6	42.0	33.9	23.0	31.1	26.9	57.1	66.3	53.3	34.8	35.3	9.8
MDNet [32]	CVPR16	39.7	46.0	37.3	27.9	34.9	31.8	60.6	70.5	56.5	29.9	30.3	9.9
ECO [7]	ICCV17	32.4	33.8	30.1	22.0	25.2	24.0	55.4	61.8	49.2	31.6	30.9	11.1
SiamPRN++ [22]	CVPR19	49.6	56.9	49.1	34.0	41.6	39.6	73.3	80.0	69.4	51.7	61.6	32.5
DiMP [2]	ICCV19	56.9	65.0	56.7	39.2	47.6	45.1	74.0	80.1	68.7	61.1	71.7	49.2
SiamR-CNN [39]	CVPR20	64.8	72.2	-	-	-	-	81.2	85.4	80.0	64.9	72.8	59.7
MAMLTrack [40]	CVPR20	52.3	-	-	-	-	-	75.7	82.2	72.5	-	-	-
LTMU [5]	CVPR20	57.2	-	57.2	41.4	49.9	47.3	-	-	-	-	-	-
Ocean [46]	ECCV20	56.0	65.1	56.6	-	-	-	-	-	-	61.1	72.1	47.3
TrDiMP [41]	CVPR21	63.9	-	61.4	-	-	-	78.4	83.3	73.1	67.1	77.7	58.3
TransT [4]	CVPR21	64.9	73.8	69.0	-	-	-	81.4	86.7	80.3	67.1	76.8	60.9
AutoMatch [45]	ICCV21	58.3	-	59.9	-	-	-	76.0	-	72.6	65.2	76.6	54.3
STARK [43]	ICCV21	67.1	77.0	-	-	-	-	82.0	86.9	-	68.8	78.1	64.1
KeepTrack [29]	ICCV21	67.1	77.2	70.2	**48.2**	-	-	-	-	-	-	-	-
SwinTrack-B [25]	arXiv21	**69.6**	78.6	74.1	47.6	**58.2**	**54.1**	82.5	87.0	80.4	69.4	78.0	64.3
OSTrack-256	Ours	69.1	**78.7**	**75.2**	47.4	57.3	53.3	**83.1**	**87.8**	**82.0**	**71.0**	**80.4**	**68.2**
OSTrack-384	Ours	71.1	81.1	77.6	50.5	61.3	57.6	83.9	88.5	83.2	73.7	83.2	70.8

We add the symbol * to GOT-10k if the corresponding models are trained following the one-shot protocol, otherwise they are trained with all training data.

Table 2. Comparison with state-of-the-arts on three benchmarks: NFS [19], UAV123 [30] and TNL2K [42]. AUC(%) scores are reported. The best two results are shown in red and **blue** fonts.

	SiamFC [1]	RT-MDNet [18]	ECO [7]	Ocean [46]	ATOM [6]	DiMP50 [2]	STMTrack [13]	TransT [4]	STARK [43]	OSTrack -256	OSTrack -384
NFS	37.7	43.3	52.2	49.4	58.3	61.8	-	65.3	**66.2**	64.7	66.5
UAV123	46.8	52.8	53.5	57.4	63.2	64.3	64.7	68.1	68.2	**68.3**	70.7
TNL2K	29.5	-	32.6	38.4	40.1	44.7	-	50.7		**54.3**	55.9

official evaluation server. As reported in Table 1, OSTrack-384 and OSTrack-256 outperform SwinTrack-B [25] by 1.6% and 4.3% in AO. The $SR_{0.75}$ score of OSTrack-384 reaches 70.8%, outperforming SwinTrack-B by 6.5%, which verifies the capability of our trackers in both accurate target-background discrimination and bounding box regression. Moreover, the high performance on this one-shot tracking benchmark demonstrates that our one-stream tracking framework can extract more discriminative features for unseen classes by mutual guidance.

LaSOT. LaSOT [12] is a challenging large-scale long-term tracking benchmark, which contains 280 videos for testing. We compare the result of the OSTrack with previous SOTA trackers in Table 1. The results show that the proposed tracker with smaller input resolution, i.e.,, OSTrack-256, already obtains comparable performance with SwinTrack-B [25]. Besides, OSTrack-256 runs at a fast inference speed of 105.4 FPS, being 2x faster than SwinTrack-B (52 FPS), which indicates that OSTrack achieves an excellent balance between accuracy and inference speed. By increasing the input resolution, OSTrack-384 further improves the AUC on LaSOT to 71.1% and sets a new state-of-the-art.

Table 3. The effect of our proposed early candidate elimination module on the inference speed, MACs and tracking performance on LaSOT, GOT-10k and TrackingNet benchmarks, and w/o and w/ denote the models with or without early candidate elimination module separately.

Input Resolution	FPS w/o	FPS w/	MACs (G) w/o	MACs (G) w/	LaSOT AUC (%) w/o	LaSOT AUC (%) w/	TrackingNet AUC (%) w/o	TrackingNet AUC (%) w/	GOT-10k* AO (%) w/o	GOT-10k* AO (%) w/
256x256	93.1	105.4(+13.2%)	29.0	21.5(-25.9%)	68.7	69.1(+0.4)	82.9	83.1(+0.2)	71.0	71.0(+0.0)
384x384	41.4	58.1(+40.3%)	65.3	48.3(-26.0%)	71.0	71.1(+0.1)	83.5	83.9(+0.4)	73.5	73.7(+0.2)

TrackingNet. The TrackingNet [31] benchmark contains 511 sequences for testing, which covers diverse target classes. Table 1 shows that OSTrack-256 and OSTrack-384 surpass SwinTrack-B [25] by 0.6% and 1.4% in AUC separately. Moreover, both models are faster than SwinTrack-B.

LaSOT$_{ext}$. LaSOT$_{ext}$ [11] is a recently released extension of LaSOT, which consists of 150 extra videos from 15 object classes. Table 1 presents the results. Previous SOTA tracker KeepTrack [29] designs a complex association network and runs at 18.3 FPS. In contrast, our simple one-stream tracker OSTrack-256 shows slightly lower performance but runs at 105.4 FPS. OSTrack-384 sets a new state-of-the-art AUC score of 50.5% while runs in 58.1 FPS, which is 2.3% higher in AUC score and 3x faster in speed.

NFS, UAV123 and TNL2K. We also evaluate our tracker on three additional benchmarks: NFS [19], UAV123 [30] and TNL2K [42] includes 100, 123, and 700 video sequences, separately. The results in Table 2 show that OSTrack-384 achieves the best performance on all three benchmarks, demonstrating the strong generalizability of OSTrack.

4.3 Ablation Study and Analysis

The Effect of Early Candidate Elimination Module. Table 1 shows that increasing the input resolution of the input image pairs can bring significant performance gain. However, the quadratic complexity with respect to the input resolution makes simply increasing the input resolution unaffordable in inference time. The proposed early candidate elimination module addresses the above problem well. We present the effect of the early candidate elimination module from the aspects of inference speed (FPS), multiply-accumulate computations (MACs), and tracking performance on multiple benchmarks in Table 3. The effect on different input search region resolutions is also presented. Table 3 shows that the early candidate elimination module can significantly decrease the calculation and increase the inference speed, while slightly boosting the performance in most cases. This demonstrates that the proposed module alleviates the negative impact brought by the noisy background regions on feature learning. For example, adding the early candidate elimination module in OSTrack-256 decreases the MACs by 25.9% and increases the tracking speed by 13.2%, and the LaSOT AUC is increased by 0.4%. Furthermore, larger input resolution benefits more from this module, *e.g.*,, OSTrack-384 shows a 40.3% increase in speed.

Table 4. The effect of different pre-training methods. All the models are trained without the early candidate elimination module.

Trackers	LaSOT			TrackingNet			GOT-10k		
	Success	P_{Norm}	P	Success	P_{Norm}	P	AO	$SR_{0.5}$	$SR_{0.75}$
No pre-training	60.4	70.0	62.8	77.5	83.0	73.8	62.7	72.8	53.7
ImageNet-1k	66.1	75.8	70.6	82.0	86.7	80.1	69.7	79.0	65.6
ImageNet-21k	66.9	76.3	71.2	82.4	86.9	80.1	70.2	80.7	65.4
MAE	**68.7**	**78.1**	**74.6**	**82.9**	**87.5**	**81.6**	**73.6**	**83.0**	**71.7**

Different Pre-Training Methods. While previous Transformer fusion trackers [4,25,43] random initialize the weights of Transformer layers, our joint feature learning and relation modeling module can directly benefit from the pre-trained weights. We further investigate the effect of different pre-training methods on the tracking performance by comparing four different pre-training strategies:

354   B. Ye et al.

no pre-training; ImageNet-1k [8] pre-trained model provided by [37]; ImageNet-21k [35] pre-trained model provided by [36]; unsupervised pre-training model MAE [14]. As the results in Table 4 show, pre-training is necessary for the model weights initialization. Interestingly, we also observe that the unsupervised pre-training method MAE brings better tracking performance than the supervised pre-training ones using ImageNet. We hope this can inspire the community for designing better pre-training strategies tailored for the tracking task.

Aligned Comparison with SOTA Two-stream Trackers. One may wonder whether the performance gain is brought by the proposed one-stream structure or purely by the superiority of ViT. We thus compare our method with two SOTA two-stream Transformer fusion trackers [25,43] by eliminating the influencing factors of backbone and head structure. To be specific, we align two previous SOTA two-stream trackers (STRAK-S [43] and SwinTrack [25]) with ours for fair comparison as follows: replacing their backbones with the same pre-trained ViT and setting the same input resolution, head structure, and training objective as OSTrack-256. The remaining experimental settings are kept the same as in the original paper. As shown in Table 5, our re-implemented two-stream trackers show comparable or stronger performance compared to the initially published performance, but still lag behind OSTrack, which demonstrates the effectiveness of our one-stream structure. We also observe that OSTrack significantly outperforms the previous two-stream trackers on the one-shot benchmark GOT-10k, which further proves the advantage of our one-stream framework in the challenging scenario. Actually, the discriminative power of features extracted by the two-stream framework is limited since the object classes in the testing set are completely different from the training set. Whereas, by iterative interaction between the features of the template and search region, OSTrack can extract more discriminative features through mutual guidance.

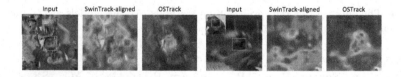

Fig. 6. Visualization of discriminative regions (*i.e.*,, activation maps) of backbone features extracted by OSTrack and two-stream tracker (SwinTrack-aligned).

Table 5. Comparison with re-implemented previous SOTA trackers aligned with OSTrack. Here OSTrack is trained without the early candidate elimination module for fair comparison and "aligned" denotes that the backbone, head, loss and input resolution are kept the same as OSTrack.

Trackers	LaSOT			TrackingNet			GOT-10k*			FPS	Traing Pairs($\times 10^6$)
	Success	P_{Norm}	P	Success	P_{Norm}	P	AO	$SR_{0.5}$	$SR_{0.75}$		
STARK-aligned	67.6	76.3	72.8	82.6	87.4	81.5	68.8	78.4	65.6	52.9	30
SwinTrack-aligned	68.0	77.6	73.9	**82.9**	**87.6**	**81.6**	69.5	79.2	65.0	67.5	39.3
OSTrack	**68.7**	**78.1**	**74.6**	**82.9**	87.5	**81.6**	**71.0**	**80.3**	**68.2**	**93.1**	**18**

Different from the two-stream SOTA trackers, OSTrack neglects the extra heavy relation modeling module while still keeping the high parallelism of joint feature extraction and relation modeling module. Therefore, when the same backbone network is adopted, the proposed one-stream framework is much faster than STARK (40.2 FPS faster) and SwinTrack (25.6 FPS faster). Besides, OSTrack requires fewer training image pairs to converge.

Discriminative Region Visualization. To better illustrate the effectiveness of the proposed one-stream tracker, we visualize the discriminative regions of the backbone features extracted by OSTrack and a SOTA two-stream tracker (SwinTrack-aligned) in Fig. 6. As can be observed, due to the lack of target awareness, features extracted by the backbone of SwinTrack-aligned show limited target-background discriminative power and may lose some important target information (*e.g.*,, head and helmet in Fig. 6), which is irreparable. In contrast, OSTrack can extract discriminative target-oriented features, since the proposed early fusion mechanism enables relation modeling between the template and search region at the first stage.

5 Conclusion

This work proposes a simple, neat, and high-performance one-stream tracking framework based on Vision Transformer, which breaks out of the Siamese-like pipeline. The proposed tracker combines the feature extraction and relation modeling tasks, and shows a good balance between performance and inference speed. In addition, we further propose an early candidate elimination module that progressively discards search region tokens belonging to background regions, which significantly boosts the tracking inference speed. Extensive experiments show that the proposed one-stream trackers perform much better than previous methods on multiple benchmarks, especially under the one-shot protocol. We expect this work can attract more attention to the one-stream tracking framework.

Acknowledgment. This work is partially supported by Natural Science Foundation of China (NSFC): 61976203 and 61876171. Thanks Zhipeng Zhang for his helpful suggestions.

References

1. Bertinetto, L., Valmadre, J., Henriques, J.F., Vedaldi, A., Torr, P.H.S.: Fully-convolutional Siamese networks for object tracking. In: Hua, G., Jégou, H. (eds.) ECCV 2016. LNCS, vol. 9914, pp. 850–865. Springer, Cham (2016). https://doi.org/10.1007/978-3-319-48881-3_56
2. Bhat, G., Danelljan, M., Gool, L.V., Timofte, R.: Learning discriminative model prediction for tracking. In: ICCV, pp. 6182–6191 (2019)
3. Bolme, D.S., Beveridge, J.R., Draper, B.A., Lui, Y.M.: Visual object tracking using adaptive correlation filters. In: CVPR, pp. 2544–2550 (2010)
4. Chen, X., Yan, B., Zhu, J., Wang, D., Yang, X., Lu, H.: Transformer tracking. In: CVPR, pp. 8126–8135 (2021)

5. Dai, K., Zhang, Y., Wang, D., Li, J., Lu, H., Yang, X.: High-performance long-term tracking with meta-updater. In: CVPR, pp. 6298–6307 (2020)
6. Danelljan, M., Bhat, G., Khan, F.S., Felsberg, M.: Atom: accurate tracking by overlap maximization. In: CVPR, pp. 4660–4669 (2019)
7. Danelljan, M., Bhat, G., Shahbaz Khan, F., Felsberg, M.: ECO: efficient convolution operators for tracking. In: CVPR, pp. 6638–6646 (2017)
8. Deng, J., Dong, W., Socher, R., Li, L.J., Li, K., Fei-Fei, L.: ImageNet: a large-scale hierarchical image database. In: CVPR, pp. 248–255 (2009)
9. Devlin, J., Chang, M.W., Lee, K., Toutanova, K.: BERT: pre-training of deep bidirectional transformers for language understanding. In: NAACL, pp. 4171–4186 (2019)
10. Dosovitskiy, A., et al.: An image is worth 16 x 16 words: transformers for image recognition at scale. In: ICLR (2021)
11. Fan, H., et al.: LaSOT: a high-quality large-scale single object tracking benchmark. IJCV **129**(2), 439–461 (2021)
12. Fan, H., et al.: LaSOT: a high-quality benchmark for large-scale single object tracking. In: CVPR, pp. 5374–5383 (2019)
13. Fu, Z., Liu, Q., Fu, Z., Wang, Y.: STMTrack: template-free visual tracking with space-time memory networks. In: CVPR, pp. 13774–13783 (2021)
14. He, K., Chen, X., Xie, S., Li, Y., Dollár, P., Girshick, R.: Masked autoencoders are scalable vision learners. arXiv preprint arXiv:2111.06377 (2021)
15. He, K., Zhang, X., Ren, S., Sun, J.: Deep residual learning for image recognition. In: CVPR, pp. 770–778 (2016)
16. Henriques, J.F., Caseiro, R., Martins, P., Batista, J.: High-speed tracking with kernelized correlation filters. TPAMI **37**(3), 583–596 (2014)
17. Huang, L., Zhao, X., Huang, K.: Got-10k: a large high-diversity benchmark for generic object tracking in the wild. TPAMI **43**(5), 1562–1577 (2019)
18. Jung, I., Son, J., Baek, M., Han, B.: Real-time mdnet. In: ECCV, pp. 83–98 (2018)
19. Kiani Galoogahi, H., Fagg, A., Huang, C., Ramanan, D., Lucey, S.: Need for speed: a benchmark for higher frame rate object tracking. In: ICCV, pp. 1125–1134 (2017)
20. Krizhevsky, A., Sutskever, I., Hinton, G.E.: ImageNet classification with deep convolutional neural networks. In: NeurIPS, vol. 25 (2012)
21. Law, H., Deng, J.: CornerNet: Detecting objects as paired keypoints. In: ECCV, pp. 734–750 (2018)
22. Li, B., Wu, W., Wang, Q., Zhang, F., Xing, J., Yan, J.: SiamRPN++: evolution of Siamese visual tracking with very deep networks. In: CVPR, pp. 4282–4291 (2019)
23. Li, B., Yan, J., Wu, W., Zhu, Z., Hu, X.: High performance visual tracking with Siamese region proposal network. In: CVPR, pp. 8971–8980 (2018)
24. Liang, Y., GE, C., Tong, Z., Song, Y., Wang, J., Xie, P.: EViT: expediting vision transformers via token reorganizations. In: ICLR (2022)
25. Lin, L., Fan, H., Xu, Y., Ling, H.: SwinTrack: a simple and strong baseline for transformer tracking. arXiv preprint arXiv:2112.00995 (2021)
26. Lin, T.Y., et al.: Microsoft coco: common objects in context. In: ECCV, pp. 740–755 (2014)
27. Liu, Z., et al.: Swin transformer: hierarchical vision transformer using shifted windows. In: ICCV, pp. 10012–10022 (2021)
28. Loshchilov, I., Hutter, F.: Decoupled weight decay regularization. In: ICLR (2018)
29. Mayer, C., Danelljan, M., Paudel, D.P., Van Gool, L.: Learning target candidate association to keep track of what not to track. In: ICCV, pp. 13444–13454 (2021)
30. Mueller, M., Smith, N., Ghanem, B.: A benchmark and simulator for UAV tracking. In: ECCV, pp. 445–461 (2016)

31. Muller, M., Bibi, A., Giancola, S., Alsubaihi, S., Ghanem, B.: TrackingNet: a large-scale dataset and benchmark for object tracking in the wild. In: ECCV, pp. 300–317 (2018)
32. Nam, H., Han, B.: Learning multi-domain convolutional neural networks for visual tracking. In: CVPR, pp. 4293–4302 (2016)
33. Rao, Y., Zhao, W., Liu, B., Lu, J., Zhou, J., Hsieh, C.J.: DynamicViT: efficient vision transformers with dynamic token sparsification. In: NeurIPS, vol. 34 (2021)
34. Rezatofighi, H., Tsoi, N., Gwak, J., Sadeghian, A., Reid, I., Savarese, S.: Generalized intersection over union: a metric and a loss for bounding box regression. In: CVPR, pp. 658–666 (2019)
35. Ridnik, T., Ben-Baruch, E., Noy, A., Zelnik-Manor, L.: ImageNet-21k pretraining for the masses. arXiv preprint arXiv:2104.10972 (2021)
36. Steiner, A., Kolesnikov, A., Zhai, X., Wightman, R., Uszkoreit, J., Beyer, L.: How to train your ViT? data, augmentation, and regularization in vision transformers. arXiv preprint arXiv:2106.10270 (2021)
37. Touvron, H., Cord, M., Douze, M., Massa, F., Sablayrolles, A., Jégou, H.: Training data-efficient image transformers & distillation through attention. In: ICML, pp. 10347–10357 (2021)
38. Vaswani, A., et al.: Attention is all you need. In: NeurIPS, pp. 5998–6008 (2017)
39. Voigtlaender, P., Luiten, J., Torr, P.H., Leibe, B.: Siam R-CNN: visual tracking by re-detection. In: CVPR, pp. 6578–6588 (2020)
40. Wang, G., Luo, C., Sun, X., Xiong, Z., Zeng, W.: Tracking by instance detection: a meta-learning approach. In: CVPR, pp. 6288–6297 (2020)
41. Wang, N., Zhou, W., Wang, J., Li, H.: Transformer meets tracker: exploiting temporal context for robust visual tracking. In: CVPR, pp. 1571–1580 (2021)
42. Wang, X., et al.: Towards more flexible and accurate object tracking with natural language: algorithms and benchmark. In: CVPR, pp. 13763–13773 (2021)
43. Yan, B., Peng, H., Fu, J., Wang, D., Lu, H.: Learning Spatio-temporal transformer for visual tracking. In: ICCV, pp. 10448–10457 (2021)
44. Yin, H., Vahdat, A., Alvarez, J., Mallya, A., Kautz, J., Molchanov, P.: AdaViT: adaptive tokens for efficient vision transformer. arXiv preprint arXiv:2112.07658 (2021)
45. Zhang, Z., Liu, Y., Wang, X., Li, B., Hu, W.: Learn to match: automatic matching network design for visual tracking. In: ICCV, pp. 13339–13348 (2021)
46. Zhang, Z., Peng, H., Fu, J., Li, B., Hu, W.: Ocean: object-aware anchor-free tracking. In: ECCV, pp. 771–787 (2020)

MotionCLIP: Exposing Human Motion Generation to CLIP Space

Guy Tevet[✉], Brian Gordon, Amir Hertz, Amit H. Bermano,
and Daniel Cohen-Or

Tel Aviv University, Tel Aviv, Israel
{guytevet,briangordon}@mail.tau.ac.il

Abstract. We introduce MotionCLIP, a 3D human motion auto-encoder featuring a latent embedding that is disentangled, well behaved, and supports highly semantic textual descriptions. MotionCLIP gains its unique power by aligning its latent space with that of the Contrastive Language-Image Pre-training (CLIP) model. Aligning the human motion manifold to CLIP space implicitly infuses the extremely rich semantic knowledge of CLIP into the manifold. In particular, it helps continuity by placing semantically similar motions close to one another, and disentanglement, which is inherited from the CLIP-space structure. MotionCLIP comprises a transformer-based motion auto-encoder, trained to reconstruct motion while being aligned to its text label's position in CLIP-space. We further leverage CLIP's unique visual understanding and inject an even stronger signal through aligning motion to rendered frames in a self-supervised manner. We show that although CLIP has never seen the motion domain, MotionCLIP offers unprecedented text-to-motion abilities, allowing out-of-domain actions, disentangled editing, and abstract language specification. For example, the text prompt "couch" is decoded into a sitting down motion, due to lingual similarity, and the prompt "Spiderman" results in a web-swinging-like solution that is far from seen during training. In addition, we show how the introduced latent space can be leveraged for motion interpolation, editing and recognition (See our project page: https://guytevet.github.io/motionclip-page/.

1 Introduction

Human motion generation includes the intuitive description, editing, and generation of 3D sequences of human poses. It is relevant to many applications that require virtual or robotic characters. Motion generation is, however, a challenging task. Perhaps the most challenging aspect is the limited availability of data, which is expensive to acquire and to label. Recent years have brought larger

---

G. Tevet and B. Gordon—The authors contributed equally.

Supplementary Information The online version contains supplementary material available at https://doi.org/10.1007/978-3-031-20047-2_21.

"Usain Bolt"   "Swan lake"

"Gollum"   "Spiderman in action!"

Fig. 1. Motions generated by MotionCLIP conditioned on different cultural references. MotionCLIP exploits the rich knowledge encapsulated in pre-trained language-images model (CLIP) and projects the human motion manifold over its latent space.

sets of motion capture acquisitions [?9], sometimes sorted by classes [21,25] or even labeled with free text [35,37]. Yet, it seems that while this data may span a significant part of human motion, it is not enough for machine learning algorithms to understand the semantics of the motion manifold, and it is definitely not descriptive enough for natural language usage. Hence, neural models trained using labeled motion data [2,24,28,33,48] do not generalize well to the full richness of the human motion manifold, nor to the natural language describing it.

In this work, we introduce MotionCLIP, a 3D motion auto-encoder that induces a latent embedding that is disentangled, well behaved, and supports highly semantic and elaborate descriptions. To this end, we employ CLIP [38], a large scale visual-textual embedding model. Our key insight is that even though CLIP has not been trained on the motion domain what-so-ever, we can inherit much of its latent space's virtue by enforcing its powerful and semantic structure onto the motion domain. To do this, we train a transformer-based [43] auto-encoder that is aligned to the latent space of CLIP, using existing motion textual labels. In other words, we train an encoder to find the proper embedding of an input sequence in CLIP space, and a decoder that generates the most fitting motion to a given CLIP space latent code. To further improve the alignment with CLIP-space, we also leverage CLIP's visual encoder, and synthetically render frames to guide the alignment in a self-supervised manner (see Fig. 2). As we demonstrate, this step is crucial for out-of-domain generalization, since it allows finer-grained description of the motion, unattainable using text.

The merit of aligning the human motion manifold to CLIP space is two-fold: First, combining the geometric motion domain with lingual semantics benefits the semantic description of motion. As we show, this benefits tasks such as text-to-motion and motion style transfer. More importantly however, we show that this alignment benefits the motion latent space itself, infusing it with semantic knowledge and inherited disentanglement. Indeed, our latent space demonstrates unprecedented compositionality of independent actions, semantic interpolation between actions, and even natural and linear latent-space based editing.

As mentioned above, the textual and visual CLIP encoders offer the semantic description of motion. In this aspect, our model demonstrates never

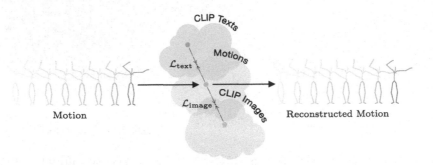

Fig. 2. MotionCLIP overview. A motion auto-encoder is trained to simultaneously reconstruct motion sequences while aligning their latent representation with corresponding texts and images representations in CLIP space.

-before-seen capabilities for the field of motion generation. For example, motion can be specified using arbitrary natural language, through abstract scene or intent descriptions instead of the motion directly, or even through pop-culture references. For example, the CLIP embedding for the phrase "wings" is decoded into a flapping motion like a bird, and "Williams sisters" into a tennis serve, since these terms are encoded close to motion seen during training, thanks to CLIP's semantic understanding. Through the compositionality induced by the latent space, the aforementioned process also yields clearly unseen motions, such as the iconic web-swinging gesture that is produced for the input "Spiderman" (see this and other culture references in Fig. 1). Our model also naturally extents to other downstream tasks. In this aspect, we depict motion interpolation to depict latent smoothness, editing to demonstrate disentanglement, and action recognition to point out the semantic structure of our latent space. For all these applications, we show comparable or preferable results either through metrics or a user study, even though each task is compared against a method that was designed especially for it. Using the action recognition benchmark, we also justify our design choices with an ablation study.

2 Related Work

2.1 Guided Human Motion Generation

One means to guide motion generation is to condition on another domain. An immediate, but limited, choice is conditioning on *action* classes. ACTOR [33] and Action2Motion [14] suggested learning this multi-modal distribution from existing action recognition datasets using Conditional Variational-Autoencoder (CVAE) [42] architectures. MUGL [28] model followed with elaborated Conditional Gaussian-Mixture-VAE [6] that supports up to 120 classes and multi-person generation, based on the NTU-RGBD-120 dataset [25].

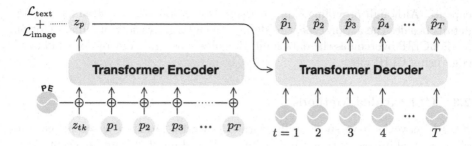

Fig. 3. Motion Auto-Encoder. A transformer encoder is trained to project a motion sequence $p_{1:T}$ into a latent vector z_p in CLIP latent space. Simultaneously, a transformer decoder is trained to recover the motion by attending to z_p.

Motion can be conditioned on other domains. For example, recent works [3, 23] generated dance moves conditioned on music and the motion prefix. Edwards et al. [8] generated facial expressions to fit a speaking audio sequence.

A more straightforward approach to control motion is using another motion. In particular, for style transfer applications. Holden et al. [18] suggested to code style using the latent code's Gram matrix, inspired by Gatys et al. [12]. Aberman et al. [1] injected style attributes using a dedicated temporal-invariant AdaIN layer [20]. Recently, Wen et al. [47] encoded style in the latent code of Normalizing Flow generative model [7]. We show that MotionCLIP also encodes style in its latent representation, without making any preliminary assumptions or using a dedicated architecture.

2.2 Text-to-Motion

The KIT dataset [35] provides about 11 h of motion capture sequences, each sequence paired with a sentence explicitly describing the action performed. KIT sentences describe the action type, direction and sometimes speed, but lacks details about the style of the motion, and not including abstract descriptions of motion. Current text-to-motion research is heavily based on KIT. Plappert et al. [36] learned text-to-motion and motion-to-text using seq2seq RNN-based architecture. Yamada et al. [48] learned those two mappings by simultaneously training text and motion auto-encoders while binding their latent spaces using text and motion pairs. Lin et al. [24] further improved trajectory prediction by adding a dedicated layer. Ahuja et al. [2] introduced JL2P model, which got improved results with respect to nuanced concepts of the text, namely velocity, trajectory and action type. They learned joint motion-text latent space and apply training curriculum to ease optimization. Concurrent to our work, Petrovich et al. [34] and Guo et al. [13] encourage diverse generation using VAE based models [22], yet not generalizing outside of the limited available data.

More recently, BABEL dataset [37] provided per-frame textual labels ordered in 260 classes to the larger AMASS dataset [29], including about 40 h of motion capture. Although providing explicit description of the action, often lacking any details besides the action type, this data spans a larger variety of human motion. MotionCLIP overcomes the data limitations by leveraging out-of-domain knowledge using CLIP [38].

2.3 CLIP Aided Methods

Neural networks have successfully learned powerful latent representations coupling natural images with natural language describing it [17,39]. A recent example is CLIP [38], a model coupling images and text in deep latent space using a constructive objective [4,16]. By training over hundred millions of images and their captions, CLIP gained a rich semantic latent representation for visual content. This expressive representation enables high quality image generation and editing, controlled by natural language [10,11,31]. Even more so, this model has shown that connecting the visual and textual worlds also benefits purely visual tasks [44], simply by providing a well-behaved, semantically structured, latent space.

Closer to our method are works that utilize the richness of CLIP outside the imagery domain. In the 3D domain, CLIP's latent space provides a useful objective that enables semantic manipulation [30,40,45] where the domain gap is closed by a neural rendering. CLIP is even adopted in temporal domains [9,15,27] that utilize large datasets of video sequences that are paired with text and audio. Unlike these works that focus on classification and retrieval, we introduce a generative approach that utilizes limited amount of human motion sequences that are paired with text.

More recently, CLIP was used for motion applications. CLIP-Actor [49] is using CLIP representation to query motions from BABEL. The motions in that case are represented by their attached textual labels. AvatarCLIP [19] used CLIP as a loss term for direct motion optimization, where the motion is represented by rendered poses. Contrary to their claim, MotionCLIP shows that motions can be successfully encoded-to and decoded-from CLIP space.

3 Method

Our goal is learning a semantic and disentangled motion representation that will serve as a basis for generation and editing tasks. To this end, we need to learn not only the mapping to this representation (encoding), but also the mapping back to explicit motion (decoding).

Our training process is illustrated in Fig. 2. We train a transformer-based motion auto-encoder, while aligning the latent motion manifold to CLIP joint representation. We do so using (i) a *Text Loss*, connecting motion representations to the CLIP embedding of their text labels, and (ii) an *Image Loss*, connecting motion representations to CLIP embedding of rendered images that depict the motion visually.

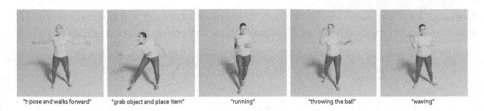

"t-pose and walks forward"   "grab object and place item"   "running"   "throwing the ball"   "waving"

Fig. 4. A sample of the rendered frames and their text description used during training.

At inference time, semantic editing applications can be performed in latent space. For example, to perform style transfer, we find a latent vector representing the style, and simply add it to the content motion representation and decode the result back into motion. Similarly, to classify an action, we can simply encode it into the latent space, and see to which of the class text embedding it is closest. Furthermore, we use the CLIP text encoder to perform text-to-motion - An input text is decoded using the text encoder then directly decoded by our motion decoder. The implementation of these and other applications is detailed in Sect. 4.

We represent motion sequences using the SMPL body model [26]. A sequence of length T denoted $p_{1:T}$ such that $p_i \in \mathbb{R}^{24 \times 6}$ defines orientations in 6D representation [50] for global body orientation and 23 SMPL joints, at the ith frame. The mesh vertices locations $v_{1:T}$ are calculated according to SMPL specifications with $\beta = 0$ and a neutral-gender body model following Petrovich et al. [33].

To project the motion manifold into the latent space, we learn a transformer-based auto-encoder [43], adapted to the motion domain [23,33,46]. Motion-CLIP's architecture is detailed in Fig. 3.

Transformer Encoder. E, Maps a motion sequence $p_{1:T}$ to its latent representation z_p. The sequence is embedded into the encoder's dimension by applying linear projection for each frame separately, then adding standard positional embedding. The embedded sequence is the input to the transformer encoder, together with additional learned prefix token z_{tk}. The latent representation, z_p is the first output (the rest of the sequence is dropped out). Explicitly, $z_p = E(z_{tk}, p_{1:T})$.

Transformer Decoder. D, predicts a motion sequence $\hat{p}_{1:T}$ given a latent representation z_p. This representation is fed to the transformer as key and value, while the query sequence is simply the positional encoding of $1:T$. The transformer outputs a representation for each frame, which is then mapped to pose space using a linear projection. Explicitly, $\hat{p}_{1:T} = D(z_p)$. We further use a differentiable SMPL layer to get the mesh vertices locations, $\hat{v}_{1:T}$.

Losses. This auto-encoder is trained to represent motion via reconstruction $L2$ losses on joint orientations, joint velocities and vertices locations. Explicitly,

$$\mathcal{L}_{\text{recon}} = \frac{1}{|p|T} \sum_{i=1}^{T} \|p_i - \hat{p}_i\|^2 + \frac{1}{|v|T} \sum_{i=1}^{T} \|v_i - \hat{v}_i\|^2$$
$$+ \frac{1}{|p|(T-1)} \sum_{i=1}^{T-1} \|(p_{i+1} - p_i) - (\hat{p}_{i+1} - \hat{p}_i)\|^2 \tag{1}$$

Given text-motion and image-motion pairs, $(p_{1:T}, t)$, $(p_{1:T}, s)$ correspondingly, we attach the motion representation to the text and image representations using cosine distance,

$$\mathcal{L}_{\text{text}} = 1 - \cos(CLIP_{\text{text}}(t), z_p) \tag{2}$$

and

$$\mathcal{L}_{\text{image}} = 1 - \cos(CLIP_{\text{image}}(s), z_p) \tag{3}$$

The motion-text pairs can be derived from labeled motion dataset, whereas the images can be achieved by rendering a single pose from a motion sequence, to a synthetic image s, in an unsupervised manner (More details in Sect. 4).

Overall, the loss objective of MotionCLIP is defined,

$$\mathcal{L} = \mathcal{L}_{\text{recon}} + \lambda_{\text{text}} \mathcal{L}_{\text{text}} + \lambda_{\text{image}} \mathcal{L}_{\text{image}} \tag{4}$$

4   Results

To evaluate MotionCLIP, we consider its two main advantages. In Sect. 4.2, we inspect MotionCLIP's ability to convert text into motion. Since the motion's latent space is aligned to that of CLIP, we use CLIP's pretrained text encoder to process input text, and convert the resulting latent embedding into motion using MotionCLIP's decoder. We compare our results to the state-of-the-art and report clear preference for both seen and unseen generation. We also show comparable performance to state-of-the-art style transfer work simply by adding the style as a word to the text prompt. Lastly, we exploit CLIP expert lingual understanding to convert abstract text into corresponding, and sometimes unexpected, motion.

In Sects. 4.3 and 4.4 we focus on the resulting auto-encoder, and the properties of its latent-space. We inspect its smoothness and disentanglement by (1) conducting ablation study using established quantitative evaluation, and (2) demonstrating various applications. Smoothness is shown through well-behaved interpolations, even between distant motion. Disentanglement is demonstrated using latent space arithmetic; by adding and subtracting various motion embeddings, we achieve compositionality and semantic editing. Lastly, we leverage our latent structure to perform action recognition over the trained encoder. The latter setting is also used for ablation study. In the following, we first lay out the data used, and other general settings.

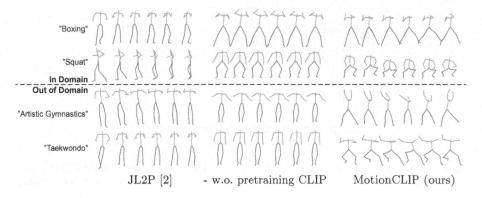

Fig. 5. In- and Out-of-domain Qualitative results for MotionCLIP with and without CLIP pretraining. MotionCLIP (right) performs better for in-domain motions than out-of-domain, and in any case better than JL2P and MotionCLIP ablated variant.

4.1 General Settings

We train our model on the BABEL dataset [37]. It comprises about 40 h of motion capture data, represented with the SMPL body model [26]. The motions are annotated with per-frame textual labels, and is categorized into one of 260 action classes. We down sample the data to 30 frames per-second and cut it into sequences of length 60. We get a single textual label per sequence by listing all actions in a given sequence, then concatenating them to a single string. Finally, we choose for each motion sequence a random frame to be rendered using the *Blender* software and the SMPL-X add-on [32] (See Fig. 4). This process outputs triplets of (motion, text, synthetic image) which are used for training.

We train a transformer auto-encoder with 8 layers for each encoder and decoder as described in Sect. 3. We align it with the *CLIP-ViT-B/32* frozen model. Out of the data triplets, the text-motion pairs are used for the *text loss* and image-motion pairs for the *image loss*. Both λ values are set to 0.01 throughout our experiments.[1]

4.2 Text-to-Motion

Text-to-motion is performed at inference time, using the CLIP text encoder and MotionCLIP decoder, without any further training. Even though not directly trained for this task, MotionCLIP shows unprecedented performance in text-to-motion, dealing with explicit descriptions, subtle nuances and abstract language.

Actions. We start by demonstrating the capabilities of MotionCLIP to generate explicit actions - both seen and unseen in training. We compare our model to JL2P [2] trained on BABEL and two ablated variants of MotionCLIP:(1) without CLIP pre-training (in this case, the text encoder is trained from scratch together

---

[1] https://github.com/GuyTevet/MotionCLIP.

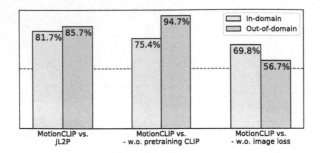

Fig. 6. Action generation from text - user study. The bars depict MotionCLIP's preference score vs. each of the other models (when compared side-by-side). The dashed line marks 50% (i.e. equally preferred models). MotionCLIP is clearly preferred by the users over JL2P [2] and our two ablated variants.

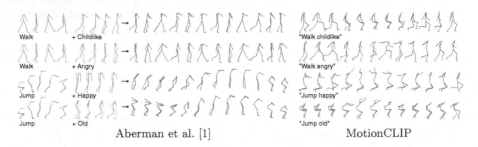

Fig. 7. Style generation. Left: style transfer by Aberman et al. [1], conditioned on action (green) and style (orange) motions. Right: MotionCLIP generating style from plain text input. (Color figure online)

with MotionCLIP, as in JL2P) and (2) without CLIP image loss (i.e. using text loss only). We distinguish between in-domain and out-of-domain actions by conducting a user study[2] using two different text sets: (1) The *in-domain set* comprises of BABEL-60 class names. (2) the *Out-of-domain set* includes textual labels that do not appear in any of the training labels. We construct this set from the list of Olympic sports that are disjoint to BABEL. Figure 6 shows that MotionCLIP is clearly preferred by the users over JL2P and the MotionCLIP variant without pretraining CLIP. Figure 5 further demonstrates that while MotionCLIP generates better motions for in-domain examples, for the out-of-domain set, it is not only the highest quality model, but often the only model that is not mode-collapsed, and generates a valid result. Figure 12 qualitatively shows the effect of text and image CLIP losses on the generation quality. In the Supplementary Materials, we present a variety of sports generated by MotionCLIP, as used in the user-study. Even though this is not a curated list, the motion created according to all 30 depicted text prompts resembles the requested actions.

---

[2] 30 unique users, each was asked 12 questions.

Styles. We investigate MotionCLIP's ability to represent motion style, without being explicitly trained for it. We compare the results produced by MotionCLIP to the style transfer model by Aberman et al. [1]. The latter receives two input motion sequences, one indicating content and the other style, and combines them through a dedicated architecture, explicitly trained to disentangle style and content from a single sequence. In contrast, we simply feed MotionCLIP with the action and style textual names (e.g. "walk proud"). We show to users[3] the outputs of the two models side-by-side and ask them to choose which one presents both style and/or action better (See Fig. 7). Even though Aberman et al. was trained specifically for this task and gets the actual motions as an input, rather then text, Table 1 shows comparable results for the two models, with an expected favor toward Aberman et al. This, of course, also means that MotionCLIP allows expressing style with free text, and does not require an exemplar motion to describe it. Such novel free text style augmentations are demonstrated in Fig. 8.

Fig. 8. MotionCLIP expresses the style described as a free text.

Table 1. Style generation - user study (preference score side-by-side). We compare our style + action generation from text, to those of Aberman et al. [1] which gets style and content motions as input. Interestingly, although not trained to generate style, our model wins twice and break even once

	Aberman et al. [1]	MotionCLIP
Happy	31.3%	**68.7%**
Proud	**86.4%**	13.6%
Angry	43.5%	**56.5%**
Childlike	**57.6%**	42.4%
Depressed	**74.2%**	25.8%
Drunk	**50%**	**50%**
Old	**57.7%**	42.3%
Heavy	**85.2%**	14.8%
Average	**62.1%**	37.9%

[3] 55 unique users, each was asked 4 questions.

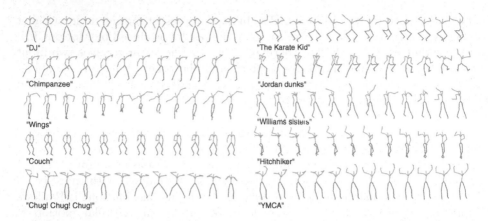

"DJ"

"Chimpanzee"

"Wings"

"Couch"

"Chug! Chug! Chug!"

"The Karate Kid"

"Jordan dunks"

"Williams sisters"

"Hitchhiker"

"YMCA"

Fig. 9. Abstract language. MotionCLIP generates the signature motions of culture figures and phrases.

Abstract Language. One of the most exciting capabilities of MotionCLIP is generating motion given text that doesn't explicitly describe motion. This includes obvious linguistic connections, such as the act of sitting down, produced from the input text "couch". Other, more surprising examples include mimicking the signature moves of famous real and fictional figures, like *Usain Bolt* and *The Karate Kid*, and other cultural references like the famous ballet performance of *Swan Lake* and the *YMCA* dance (Figs. 1 and 9). These results include motions definitely not seen during training (e.g., Spiderman in Fig. 1), which strongly indicates how well the motion manifold is aligned to CLIP space.

4.3 Motion Manifold Evaluation

Accuracy Metric. Following ACTOR [33] we use the *accuracy* metric to evaluate MotionCLIP's latent space. To this end, we use the UESTC action recognition dataset [21], including $25K$ motion sequences annotated with 40 action classes. This data was not seen during MotionCLIP training, hence, this is a zero-shot evaluation for our model. We encode the validation set motions, and collect their mean and standard deviation. Using these statistics, we sample new motions for each class according to the class distribution found in the test set. Then, we decode the sampled motions and feed the result to an action recognition model (pre-trained on UESTC, as reported by ACTOR). In Table 2, we use the accuracy metric to ablate CLIP losses, and examine 2-layered GRU [5] backbone, in addition to our reported Transformer backbone. The results imply that although failing in text-to-motion (Fig. 12), GRU provides smoother latent space.

Interpolation. As can be seen in Fig. 10, the linear interpolation between two latent codes yields semantic transitions between motions in both time and space.

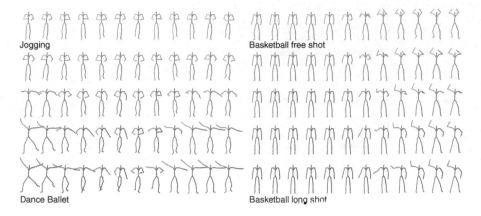

Jogging

Basketball free shot

Dance Ballet

Basketball long shot

Fig. 10. Latent space motion interpolation. MotionCLIP enables semantic interpolation between two motions.

Table 2. Accuracy metric. We report the Top-5 accuracy of a pre-trained action recognition model [33] trained on the UESTC dataset [21] for ablated variants of MotionCLIP. This dataset was not seen during training, hence, it provides zero-shot evaluation for our latent space. The results surprisingly indicate that GRU backbone yields smoother latent space, although failing in the text-to-motion task.

	Transformer	GRU
MotionCLIP	$63.5\% \pm 0.7$	$73.3\% \pm 0.8$
- w.o. image loss	$69\% \pm 0.8$	$62.9\% \pm 0.9$
- w.o. text loss	$63.5\% \pm 0.7$	$75.6\% \pm 0.8$
- w.o. pretraing CLIP	$45.1\% \pm 1$	$66.2\% \pm 0.8$
ACTOR [33]	$99.2\% \pm 0.1$	
Real	$98.8\% \pm 0.2$	

This is a strong indication to the smoothness of this representation. Here, the source and target motions (top and bottom respectively) are sampled from the validation set, and between them three transitions are evenly sampled from the linear trajectory between the two representations, and decoded by MotionCLIP.

4.4 Motion Manifold Applications

It is already well established that the CLIP space is smooth and expressive. We demonstrate its merits also exist in the aligned motion manifold, through the following experiments.

Latent-Based Editing. To demonstrate how disentangled and uniform MotionCLIP latent space is, we experiment with latent-space arithmetic to edit motion (see Fig. 11). As can be seen, these linear operations allow motion compositionality - the upper body action can be decomposed from the lower body one,

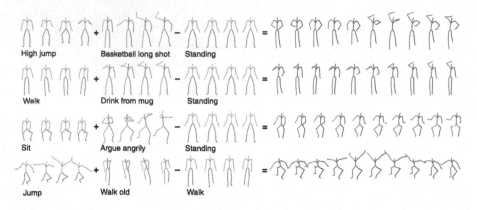

Fig. 11. Latent space motion editing. MotionCLIP enables semantic editing in latent space. Here we demonstrate two applications (1) upper and lower body action compositions (top two examples) and (2) style transfer (the two examples at the bottom).

Table 3. Action recognition. Using MotionCLIP together with CLIP text encoder for classification yields performance marginally close to 2s-AGCN [41] dedicated architecture on the BABEL-60 benchmark.

	Top-1 acc.	Top-5 acc.
MotionCLIP	40.9%	57.71%
- w.o. image loss	35.05%	50.26%
- w.o. text loss	4.54%	18.37%
2s-AGCN [41]	41.14%	73.18%

and recomposed with another lower body performance. In addition, Style can be added by simply adding the vector of the style name embedding. These two properties potentially enable intuitive and semantic editing even for novice users.

Action Recognition. Finally, we further demonstrate how well our latent spaces is semantically structured. We show how combined with the CLIP text encoder, MotionCLIP encoder can be used for action recognition. We follow BABEL 60-classes benchmark and train the model with BABEL class names instead of the raw text. At inference, we measure the cosine distance of a given motion sequence to all 60 class name encodings and apply softmax, as suggested originally for image classification [38]. In Table 3, we compare Top-1 and Top-5 accuracy of MotionCLIP classifier to 2s-AGCN classifier [41], as reported by Punnakkal et al. [37]. As can be seen, this is another example where our framework performs similarly to dedicated state-of-the-art methods, even though Motion-CLIP was not designed for it.

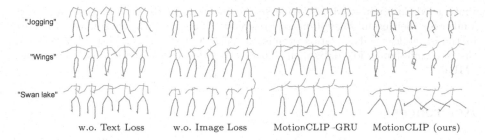

"Jogging"

"Wings"

"Swan lake"

w.o. Text Loss   w.o. Image Loss   MotionCLIP -GRU   MotionCLIP (ours)

Fig. 12. Ablation study on the loss term and backbone. By training with both losses, CLIP text and CLIP image, MotionCLIP can better generate motions for challenging text inputs.

5   Conclusions

We have presented a motion generation network that leverages the knowledge encapsulated in CLIP, allowing intuitive operations, such as text conditioned motion generation and editing. As demonstrated, training an auto-encoder on the available motion data alone struggles to generalize well, possibly due to data quality or the complexity of the domain. Nonetheless, we see that the same auto-encoder with the same data can lead to a significantly better understanding of the motion manifold and its semantics, merely by aligning it to a well-behaved knowledge-rich latent space. We restress the fascinating fact that even though CLIP has never seen anything from the motion domain, or any other temporal signal, its latent structure naturally induces semantics and disentanglement. This succeeds even though the connection between CLIP's latent space and the motion manifold is through sparse and inaccurate textual labeling. In essence, the alignment scheme transfers semantics by encouraging the encoder to place semantically similar samples closer together. Similarly, it induces the disentanglement built into the CLIP space, as can be seen, for example, in our latent-space arithmetic experiments. Of course, MotionCLIP has its limitations, opening several novel research opportunities. It struggles to understand directions, (e.g. left, right and counter-clockwise), to capture some styles (such as heavy and proud), and is of course not consistent for out-of-domain cultural reference examples (e.g., it fails to produce *Cristiano Ronaldo*'s goal celebration, and *Superman*'s signature pose). In addition, we observe that text-to-motion generation provide substandard global position and orientation, and leave it to a future work. Nonetheless, we believe MotionCLIP is an important step toward intuitive motion generation. Knowledge-rich disentangled latent spaces have already proven themselves as a flexible tool to novice users in other fields, such as facial images. In the future, we would like to further explore how powerful large-scale latent spaces could be leveraged to benefit additional domains.

Acknowledgements. We thank and appreciate the early collaboration on the problem with our colleagues Nefeli Andreou, Yiorgos Chrysanthou and Nikos Athanasiou, that fueled and motivated our research. We thank Sigal Raab, Rinon Gal and Yael Vinker for their useful suggestions and references. This research was supported in part by the Israel Science Foundation (grants no. 2492/20 and 3441/21), Len Blavatnik and the Blavatnik family foundation, and The Tel Aviv University Innovation Laboratories (TILabs).

References

1. Aberman, K., Weng, Y., Lischinski, D., Cohen-Or, D., Chen, B.: Unpaired motion style transfer from video to animation. ACM Trans. Graph. (TOG) **39**(4), 64-1 (2020)
2. Ahuja, C., Morency, L.P.: Language2Pose: natural language grounded pose forecasting. In: 2019 International Conference on 3D Vision (3DV), pp. 719–728. IEEE (2019)
3. Aristidou, A., Yiannakidis, A., Aberman, K., Cohen-Or, D., Shamir, A., Chrysanthou, Y.: Rhythm is a dancer: music-driven motion synthesis with global structure. IEEE Trans. Visual. Comput. Graph. (2022)
4. Chen, T., Kornblith, S., Norouzi, M., Hinton, G.: A simple framework for contrastive learning of visual representations. In: International Conference on Machine Learning, pp. 1597–1607. PMLR (2020)
5. Cho, K., et al.: Learning phrase representations using RNN encoder-decoder for statistical machine translation. arXiv preprint arXiv:1406.1078 (2014)
6. Dilokthanakul, N., et al.: Deep unsupervised clustering with Gaussian mixture variational autoencoders. arXiv preprint arXiv:1611.02648 (2016)
7. Dinh, L., Krueger, D., Bengio, Y.: Nice: non-linear independent components estimation. arXiv preprint arXiv:1410.8516 (2014)
8. Edwards, P., Landreth, C., Fiume, E., Singh, K.: Jali: an animator-centric viseme model for expressive lip synchronization. ACM Trans. graph. (TOG) **35**(4), 1–11 (2016)
9. Fang, H., Xiong, P., Xu, L., Chen, Y.: Clip2Video: mastering video-text retrieval via image clip. arXiv preprint arXiv:2106.11097 (2021)
10. Frans, K., Soros, L., Witkowski, O.: ClipDraw: exploring text-to-drawing synthesis through language-image encoders. arXiv preprint arXiv:2106.14843 (2021)
11. Gal, R., Patashnik, O., Maron, H., Chechik, G., Cohen-Or, D.: StyleGAN-NADA: clip-guided domain adaptation of image generators. arXiv preprint arXiv:2108.00946 (2021)
12. Gatys, L.A., Ecker, A.S., Bethge, M.: Image style transfer using convolutional neural networks. In: Proceedings of the IEEE Conference on Computer Vision and Pattern Recognition (CVPR), June 2016
13. Guo, C., et al.: Generating diverse and natural 3D human motions from text. In: Proceedings of the IEEE/CVF Conference on Computer Vision and Pattern Recognition (CVPR), pp. 5152–5161, June 2022
14. Guo, C., et al.: Action2Motion: conditioned generation of 3D human motions. In: Proceedings of the 28th ACM International Conference on Multimedia, pp. 2021–2029 (2020)
15. Guzhov, A., Raue, F., Hees, J., Dengel, A.: AudioClip: extending clip to image, text and audio. In: ICASSP 2022–2022 IEEE International Conference on Acoustics, Speech and Signal Processing (ICASSP), pp. 976–980. IEEE (2022)

16. Hadsell, R., Chopra, S., LeCun, Y.: Dimensionality reduction by learning an invariant mapping. In: 2006 IEEE Computer Society Conference on Computer Vision and Pattern Recognition (CVPR 2006), vol. 2, pp. 1735–1742. IEEE (2006)

17. He, X., Peng, Y.: Fine-grained image classification via combining vision and language. In: Proceedings of the IEEE Conference on Computer Vision and Pattern Recognition, pp. 5994–6002 (2017)

18. Holden, D., Saito, J., Komura, T.: A deep learning framework for character motion synthesis and editing. ACM Trans. Graph. (TOG) **35**(4), 1–11 (2016)

19. Hong, F., Zhang, M., Pan, L., Cai, Z., Yang, L., Liu, Z.: AvatarClip: zero-shot text-driven generation and animation of 3d avatars. ACM Trans. Graph. (TOG) **41**(4), 1–19 (2022). https://doi.org/10.1145/3528223.3530094

20. Huang, X., Belongie, S.: Arbitrary style transfer in real-time with adaptive instance normalization. In: Proceedings of the IEEE International Conference on Computer Vision, pp. 1501–1510 (2017)

21. Ji, Y., Xu, F., Yang, Y., Shen, F., Shen, H.T., Zheng, W.S.: A large-scale RGB-D database for arbitrary-view human action recognition. In: Proceedings of the 26th ACM international Conference on Multimedia, pp. 1510–1518 (2018)

22. Kingma, D.P., Welling, M.: Auto-encoding variational Bayes. arXiv preprint arXiv:1312.6114 (2013)

23. Li, R., Yang, S., Ross, D.A., Kanazawa, A.: AI choreographer: music conditioned 3D dance generation with AIST++. In: The IEEE International Conference on Computer Vision (ICCV) (2021)

24. Lin, A.S., Wu, L., Corona, R., Tai, K., Huang, Q., Mooney, R.J.: Generating animated videos of human activities from natural language descriptions. Learning **2018**, 1 (2018)

25. Liu, J., Shahroudy, A., Perez, M., Wang, G., Duan, L.Y., Kot, A.C.: NTU RGB+D 120: a large-scale benchmark for 3D human activity understanding. IEEE Trans. Pattern Anal. Mach. Intell. **42**(10), 2684–2701 (2019)

26. Loper, M., Mahmood, N., Romero, J., Pons-Moll, G., Black, M.J.: SMPL: a skinned multi-person linear model. ACM Trans. Graph. (TOG) **34**(6), 1–16 (2015)

27. Luo, H., et al.: CLIP4Clip: an empirical study of clip for end to end video clip retrieval. arXiv preprint arXiv:2104.08860 (2021)

28. Maheshwari, S., Gupta, D., Sarvadevabhatla, R.K.: MUGL: large scale multi person conditional action generation with locomotion. In: Proceedings of the IEEE/CVF Winter Conference on Applications of Computer Vision, pp. 257–265 (2022)

29. Mahmood, N., Ghorbani, N., Troje, N.F., Pons-Moll, G., Black, M.J.: AMASS: archive of motion capture as surface shapes. In: International Conference on Computer Vision, pp. 5442–5451, October 2019

30. Michel, O., Bar-On, R., Liu, R., Benaim, S., Hanocka, R.: Text2Mesh: text-driven neural stylization for meshes. In: Proceedings of the IEEE/CVF Conference on Computer Vision and Pattern Recognition, pp. 13492–13502 (2022)

31. Patashnik, O., Wu, Z., Shechtman, E., Cohen-Or, D., Lischinski, D.: StyleClip: text-driven manipulation of styleGAN imagery. In: Proceedings of the IEEE/CVF International Conference on Computer Vision, pp. 2085–2094 (2021)

32. Pavlakos, G., et al.: Expressive body capture: 3D hands, face, and body from a single image. In: Proceedings IEEE Conf. on Computer Vision and Pattern Recognition (CVPR), pp. 10975–10985 (2019)

33. Petrovich, M., Black, M.J., Varol, G.: Action-conditioned 3D human motion synthesis with transformer VAE. In: International Conference on Computer Vision (ICCV), pp. 10985–10995, October 2021

34. Petrovich, M., Black, M.J., Varol, G.: TEMOS: generating diverse human motions from textual descriptions. In: European Conference on Computer Vision (ECCV) (2022)
35. Plappert, M., Mandery, C., Asfour, T.: The kit motion-language dataset. Big Data **4**(4), 236–252 (2016)
36. Plappert, M., Mandery, C., Asfour, T.: Learning a bidirectional mapping between human whole-body motion and natural language using deep recurrent neural networks. Robot. Auton. Syst. **109**, 13–26 (2018)
37. Punnakkal, A.R., Chandrasekaran, A., Athanasiou, N., Quiros-Ramirez, A., Black, M.J.: BABEL: bodies, action and behavior with English labels. In: Proceedings IEEE/CVF Conference on Computer Vision and Pattern Recognition (CVPR), pp. 722–731, June 2021
38. Radford, A., et al.: Learning transferable visual models from natural language supervision. In: International Conference on Machine Learning, pp. 8748–8763. PMLR (2021)
39. Ramesh, A., et al.: Zero-shot text-to-image generation. In: International Conference on Machine Learning, pp. 8821–8831. PMLR (2021)
40. Sanghi, A., et al.: Clip-forge: towards zero-shot text-to-shape generation. In: Proceedings of the IEEE/CVF Conference on Computer Vision and Pattern Recognition, pp. 18603–18613 (2022)
41. Shi, L., Zhang, Y., Cheng, J., Lu, H.: Two-stream adaptive graph convolutional networks for skeleton-based action recognition. In: Proceedings of the IEEE/CVF Conference on Computer Vision and Pattern Recognition, pp. 12026–12035 (2019)
42. Sohn, K., Lee, H., Yan, X.: Learning structured output representation using deep conditional generative models. In: Advances in Neural Information Processing Systems, vol. 28 (2015)
43. Vaswani, A., et al.: Attention is all you need. In: Advances in Neural Information Processing Systems, vol. 30 (2017)
44. Vinker, Y., et al.: ClipASSO: semantically-aware object sketching. arXiv preprint arXiv:2202.05822 (2022)
45. Wang, C., Chai, M., He, M., Chen, D., Liao, J.: Clip-NERF: text-and-image driven manipulation of neural radiance fields. In: Proceedings of the IEEE/CVF Conference on Computer Vision and Pattern Recognition, pp. 3835–3844 (2022)
46. Wang, J., Xu, H., Narasimhan, M., Wang, X.: Multi-person 3D motion prediction with multi-range transformers. In: Advances in Neural Information Processing Systems, vol. 34 (2021)
47. Wen, Y.H., Yang, Z., Fu, H., Gao, L., Sun, Y., Liu, Y.J.: Autoregressive stylized motion synthesis with generative flow. In: Proceedings of the IEEE/CVF Conference on Computer Vision and Pattern Recognition, pp. 13612–13621 (2021)
48. Yamada, T., Matsunaga, H., Ogata, T.: Paired recurrent autoencoders for bidirectional translation between robot actions and linguistic descriptions. IEEE Robot. Autom. Lett. **3**(4), 3441–3448 (2018)
49. Youwang, K., Ji-Yeon, K., Oh, T.H.: Clip-Actor: text-driven recommendation and stylization for animating human meshes (2022)
50. Zhou, Y., Barnes, C., Lu, J., Yang, J., Li, H.: On the continuity of rotation representations in neural networks. In: Proceedings of the IEEE/CVF Conference on Computer Vision and Pattern Recognition, pp. 5745–5753 (2019)

Backbone is All Your Need: A Simplified Architecture for Visual Object Tracking

Boyu Chen[1]📵, Peixia Li[1]📵, Lei Bai[2(✉)]📵, Lei Qiao[3], Qiuhong Shen[3], Bo Li[3], Weihao Gan[3], Wei Wu[3], and Wanli Ouyang[1,2]📵

[1] The University of Sydney, SenseTime Computer Vision Group, Camperdown, Australia
[2] Shanghai AI Laboratory, Shanghai, China
bailei@pjlab.org.cn
[3] SenseTime, Hong Kong, China

Abstract. Exploiting a general-purpose neural architecture to replace hand-wired designs or inductive biases has recently drawn extensive interest. However, existing tracking approaches rely on customized submodules and need prior knowledge for architecture selection, hindering the development of tracking in a more general system. This paper presents a Simplified Tracking architecture (SimTrack) by leveraging a transformer backbone for joint feature extraction and interaction. Unlike existing Siamese trackers, we serialize the input images and concatenate them directly before the one-branch backbone. Feature interaction in the backbone helps to remove well-designed interaction modules and produce a more efficient and effective framework. To reduce the information loss from down-sampling in vision transformers, we further propose a foveal window strategy, providing more diverse input patches with acceptable computational costs. Our SimTrack improves the baseline with 2.5%/2.6% AUC gains on LaSOT/TNL2K and gets results competitive with other specialized tracking algorithms without bells and whistles. The source codes are available at https://github.com/LPXTT/SimTrack.

1 Introduction

Visual Object Tracking (VOT) [7,11,29,52] aims to localize the specified target in a video, which is a fundamental yet challenging task in computer vision. Siamese network is a representative paradigm in visual object tracking [1,26,27,51], which usually consists of a Siamese backbone for feature extraction, an interactive head (e.g., naive correlation [1]) for modeling the relationship between the *exemplar* and *search*, and a predictor for generating the target localization. Recently, transformer [9,44,51] has been introduced as a more powerful

---

B. Chen and P. Li—Equal contribution.

Supplementary Information The online version contains supplementary material available at https://doi.org/10.1007/978-3-031-20047-2_22.

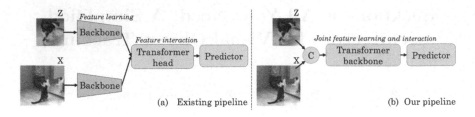

Fig. 1. The pipeline of existing transformer trackers (a) and ours (b). A transformer backbone is used to create a simple and generic framework for tracking.

interactive head to Siamese-based trackers for providing information interaction, as shown in Fig. 1(a), and pushes the accuracy to a new level.

While effective, these transformer heads are highly customized and meticulously designed, making it difficult to incorporate them into a more general system or generalize to a wide variety of intelligence tasks. On the other hand, transformers have recently shown an excellent capability to simplify frameworks for computer vision tasks, like object detection [8] and object segmentation [56]. Owning to the superior model capacity of transformers, the sub-modules and processes with task-specific prior knowledge can be removed by adequately leveraging transformers to a specific task. Producing a task-agnostic network can not only get a more simplified framework but also help the community move towards a general-purpose neural architecture, which is an appealing trend [23,58]. However, as observed in this paper, exploiting the transformer to produce a simple and generic framework is not investigated in existing VOT approaches.

With the observation above, this paper advocates a Simplified Tracking (Sim-Track) paradigm by leveraging a transformer backbone for joint feature learning and interaction, shown as Fig. 1(b). Specifically, we serialize the *exemplar* (Z) and *search* (X) images as multiple tokens at the beginning and send them together to our transformer backbone. Then, the *search* features from the transformer backbone are directly used for target localization through the predictor without any interaction module. Like existing backbones, our transformer backbone can also be pre-trained on other vision tasks, *e.g.* classification, providing stronger initialization for VOT. Moreover, our SimTrack brings multiple new benefits for visual object tracking. (1) Our SimTrack is a simpler and more generic framework with fewer sub-modules and less reliance on prior knowledge about the VOT task. The transformer backbone is a one-branch backbone instead of a Siamese network, consistent with the backbones used in many vision tasks, e.g., image classification [15,21,40,49], object detection [38], semantic segmentation [20,53], depth estimation [25,43], *etc.* (2) The attention mechanism in our transformer backbone facilitates a multi-level and more comprehensive interaction between the *exemplar* and *search* features. In this way, the backbone features for the *search* and *exemplar* image will be dependent on each other in every transformer block, resulting in a designated *exemplar(search)*-sensitive rather than general *search(exemplar)* feature, which is the hidden factor for the

effectiveness of the seemingly simple transformer backbone. (3) Removing transformer head reduces training expenses. On one hand, the SimTrack can reach
the same training loss or testing accuracy with only half training epochs as
the baseline model because information interaction happens in a well-initialized
transformer backbone instead of a randomly-initialized transformer head. On
the other hand, although adding information interaction in backbone will bring
additional computation, the additional computation is generally smaller than
that from a transformer head. (4) According to extensive experiments, Sim-
Track can get more accurate results with appropriate initialization than other
transformer-based trackers using the same transformer as Siamese backbone.

   While the transformer-based backbone is capable of achieving sufficient feature learning and interaction between the *exemplar* and *search* jointly, the
down-sampling operation may cause unavoidable information loss for VOT,
which is a localization task and requires more object visual details instead of
only abstract/semantic visual concepts. To reduce the adverse effects of down-
sampling, we further present a foveal window strategy inspired by fovea centralis.
The fovea centralis is a small central region in the eyes, enabling human eyes
to capture more useful information from the central part of vision area. In our
paper, the centre area in the *exemplar* image contains more target-relevant
information and needs more attention accordingly. Therefore, we add a foveal
window at the central area to produce more diverse target patches, making the
patch sampling frequencies around the image centre higher than those around
the image border and improving the tracking performance.

   In conclusion, our contributions are summarized as follows:

- We propose SimTrack, a Simplified Tracking architecture that feeds the serialized *exemplar* and *search* into a transformer backbone for joint feature
  learning and interaction. Compared with the existing Siamese tracking architecture, SimTrack only has the one-branch backbone and removes the existing
  interaction head, leading to a simpler framework with more powerful learning
  ability.
- We propose a foveal window strategy to remedy the information loss caused
  by the down-sampling in SimTrack, which helps the transformer backbone
  capture more details in important *exemplar* image areas.
- Extensive experiments on multiple datasets show the effectiveness of our
  method. Our SimTrack achieves state-of-the-art performances with 70.5%
  AUC on LaSOT [12], 55.6% AUC on TNL2K [48], 83.4% AUC on TrackingNet [35], 69.8% AO on GOT-10k [22] and 71.2% on UAV123 [34].

2   Related Work

2.1   Vision Transformer

Vaswani *et.al.* [42] originally proposed transformer and applied it in the machine
translation task. The key character of the transformer is the self-attention
mechanism which learns the dependencies of all input tokens and captures the

global information in sequential data. Thanks to significantly more paralleliza-
tion and competitive performance, transformer becomes a prevailing architecture
in both language modeling [14,37] and vision community [5,6,15,41]. The first
convolution-free vision transformer, ViT [15], splits input images into fixed-size
patches, which are converted to multiple 1D input tokens. All these tokens are
concatenated with a class token and sent into a transformer encoder. After the
encoder, the class token is used for image classification. Later, DeiT [41] introduces a distillation strategy to help transformers reduce the reliance on huge
training data. For object detection, DETR [4] treats the task as a sequential prediction problem and achieves promising performance. To reduce the long training
time of DETR, deformable DETR [57] replaces the global attention to adaptive
local attention and speeds up the training process. Besides, transformer has
also shown their powerful potential in other research topics like self-supervised
learning [10,33], multi-module learning [24,36], *etc.*

2.2   Visual Object Tracking

Siamese networks is a widely-used two-branch architecture in a surge of tracking
algorithms. Previous works [1,11,18,27,28,39,46,50,59] based on Siamese Networks [3] formulate VOT as a similarity matching problem and conduct the interaction through cross-correlation. Concretely, SiameseFC [1] utilize the response
map from cross-correlation between the *exemplar* and *search* features for target
localization. The highest score on the response map generally indicts the target
position. In stead of directly getting the target position through the response
map, SiamRPN [27] and the follow-ups [11,18,52,59] send the response map to
Region Proposal Network (RPN) [38] to get a more accurate localization and
scale estimation. Later, GAT [16] and AutoMatch [54] tried to replace the global
cross-correlation with more effective structure to improve model performance.
Recently, there have been several notable transformer trackers [9,44,51] which
introduce the transformer to tracking framework for stronger information interaction and achieve compelling results.

All the above-mentioned works introduce interaction between the *exemplar*
and *search* frames after the backbones. A recent work [17] adds multiple interaction modellers inside the backbone through hand-designed sub-modules. Our
SimTrack also moves information interaction to the backbone but has the following fundamental differences. First, our SimTrack is a more generic and straightforward framework without using Siamese architecture or well-designed interaction modules, which are both used in [17] and all above Siamese-based methods.
Second, our SimTrack utilizes pre-trained vision transformers for the interaction
instead of training the interaction module from scratch. Third, the interaction
between the *exemplar* and *search* exists in each block of our backbone. In contrast, the interaction modules are only added at the end of several blocks in [17].
Fourth, there is only information flow from the *exemplar* feature to the *search*
feature in [17], while ours has bidirectional information interaction between the
exemplar and *search* features.

3 Proposed Method

Our SimTrack consists of a transformer backbone and a predictor, as shown in Fig. 2 (b). The transformer backbone is used for feature extraction and information interaction between the *exemplar* and *search* features, guiding the network to learn a target-relevant *search* feature. After passing the backbone, the output features corresponding to the *search* area are sent to a corner predictor for target localization. For better understanding, we will first introduce our baseline model in Sect. 3.1, which replaces the CNN backbone of STARK-S [51] with a transformer backbone, and then show details of our SimTrack in Sect. 3.2 and the foveal window strategy for improving SimTrack in Sect. 3.3.

3.1 Baseline Model

STARK-S has no extra post-processing during inference, which is consistent with our initial purpose to simplify the tracking framework. We replace the backbone of STARK-S [51] from Res50 [21] to ViT [15] to get our baseline model STARK-SV. Like other transformer-based trackers, the pipeline of STARK-SV is shown in Fig. 1 (a). Given a video, we treat the first frame with ground truth target box as *exemplar* frame. According to the target box, we crop an *exemplar* $\mathbf{Z} \in \mathbb{R}^{H_z \times W_z \times 3}$ from the first frame, where (H_z, W_z) is the input resolution of $\mathbf{Z}$. All following frames $\mathbf{X} \in \mathbb{R}^{H_x \times W_x \times 3}$ are the *search* frames.

Image Serialization. The two input images are serialized into input sequences before the backbone. Specifically, similar to current vision transformers [15, 41], we reshape the images $\mathbf{Z} \in \mathbb{R}^{H_z \times W_z \times 3}$ and $\mathbf{X} \in \mathbb{R}^{H_x \times W_x \times 3}$ into two sequences of flattened 2D patches $\mathbf{Z_p} \in \mathbb{R}^{N_z \times (P^2 \cdot 3)}$ and $\mathbf{X_p} \in \mathbb{R}^{N_x \times (P^2 \cdot 3)}$, where (P, P) is the patch resolution, $N_z = H_z W_z / P^2$ and $N_x = H_x W_x / P^2$ are patch number of the *exemplar* and *search* images. The 2D patches are mapped to 1D tokens with C dimensions through a linear projection. After adding the 1D tokens with positional embedding [42], we get the input sequences of the backbone, including the *exemplar* sequence $e^0 \in \mathbb{R}^{N_z \times C}$ and the *search* sequence $s^0 \in \mathbb{R}^{N_x \times C}$.

Feature Extraction with Backbone. The transformer backbone consists of L layers. We utilize e^l and s^l to represent the input *exemplar* and *search* sequences of the $(l+1)_{th}$ layer, $l = 0, ..., L-1$. The forward process of the *exemplar* feature in one layer can be written as:

$$e^* = e^l + Att(LN(e^l)),$$
$$e^{l+1} = e^* + FFN(LN(e^*)), \tag{1}$$

where FFN is a feed forward network, LN denotes Layernorm and Att is self-attention module [42] (we remove LN in the following functions for simplify),

$$Att(e^l) = softmax \left(\frac{(e^l W_Q)(e^l W_K)^T}{\sqrt{d}} \right) (e^l W_V), \tag{2}$$

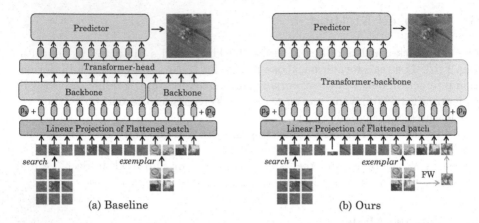

Fig. 2. The pipeline of the baseline model (a) and our proposed SimTrack (b). 'FW' in (b) denotes foveal window, p_s and p_e are position embedding of the *search* and *exemplar* tokens. In (b), a transformer backbone is utilized to replace the Siamese backbone and transformer head in (a). Both *exemplar* and *search* images in (b) are serialized into input sequences, which are sent to the transformer backbone for joint feature extraction and interaction. Finally, the target-relevant search feature is used for target localization through a predictor.

where $1/\sqrt{d}$ is the scaling factor, $W_Q \in \mathbb{R}^{C \times D}$, $W_K \in \mathbb{R}^{C \times D}$, $W_V \in \mathbb{R}^{C \times D}$ are project metrics to convert input sequence to *query*, *key* and *value*. Generally, multi-head self-attention [42] is adopted to replace self-attention in Eq. (1). For simplicity and better understanding, we use the self-attention module in our descriptions. As we can see, the feature extraction of e^l only considers *exemplar* information. The feed forward process of s^l is the same as e^l. After passing the input into the backbone, we get the output *exemplar* sequence e^L and the output *search* sequence s^L.

Feature Interaction with Transformer Head. The features $e^L \in \mathbb{R}^{N_z \times D}$ and $s^L \in \mathbb{R}^{N_x \times D}$ interact with each other in the transformer head. We refer readers to STARK-S [51] for more details of the transformer head in our baseline models.

Target Localization with Predictor. After transformer head, we get a target-relevant *search* feature $s^{L*} \in \mathbb{R}^{N_x \times D^*}$, which is reshaped to $\frac{H_x}{s} \times \frac{W_x}{s} \times D^*$ and sent to a corner predictor. The corner predictor outputs two probability maps for the top-left and bottom-right corners of the target box.

During offline training, a pair of images within a pre-defined frame range in a video are randomly selected to serve as the *exemplar* and *search* frame. After getting the predicted box b_i on the *search* frame, the whole network is trained through ℓ_1 loss and generalized IoU loss [4],

$$L = \lambda_{iou} L_{iou}(b_i, b_i^*) + \lambda_{L_1} L_1(b_i, b_i^*), \tag{3}$$

where b_i^* is the ground truth box, λ_{iou} and λ_{L_1} are loss weights, L_{iou} is generalized IoU loss and L_1 is the ℓ_1 loss.

3.2 Simplified Tracking Framework

Our key idea is replacing the Siamese backbone and transformer head in the baseline model with a unified transformer backbone, as shown in Fig. 2 (b). For STARK-S, the function of the backbone is to provide a strong feature extraction. The transformer head is responsible for information interaction between the *exemplar* and *search* features. In our SimTrack, only a transformer backbone is needed for joint feature and interaction learning. In the following, we show how to apply vision transformer as a powerful backbone to VOT successfully and create a more simplified framework. The input of our transformer backbone is also a pair of images, the *exemplar* image $\mathbf{Z} \in \mathbb{R}^{H_z \times W_z \times 3}$ and the *search* image $\mathbf{X} \in \mathbb{R}^{H_x \times W_x \times 3}$. Similarly, we first serialize the two images to input sequences $e^0 \in \mathbb{R}^{N_z \times C}$ and $s^0 \in \mathbb{R}^{N_x \times C}$ as mentioned above.

Joint Feature Extraction and Interaction with Transformer Backbone. Different from the baseline model, we directly concatenate e^0 and s^0 along the first dimension and send them to the transformer backbone together. The feed forward process of $(l+1)_{th}$ layer is:

$$\begin{bmatrix} e^* \\ s^* \end{bmatrix} = \begin{bmatrix} e^l \\ s^l \end{bmatrix} + Att\left(\begin{bmatrix} e^l \\ s^l \end{bmatrix}\right),$$
$$\begin{bmatrix} e^{l+1} \\ s^{l+1} \end{bmatrix} = \begin{bmatrix} e^* \\ s^* \end{bmatrix} + FFN\left(\begin{bmatrix} e^* \\ s^* \end{bmatrix}\right). \tag{4}$$

The symbol of layer normalization is removed in Eq. (4) for simplify. The main difference between Eqs. (1) and (4) is the computation in $Att(.)$,

$$Att\left(\begin{bmatrix} e^l \\ s^l \end{bmatrix}\right) = softmax\left(\begin{bmatrix} a(e^l, e^l), a(e^l, s^l) \\ a(s^l, e^l), a(s^l, s^l) \end{bmatrix}\right)\left(\begin{bmatrix} e^l W_V \\ s^l W_V \end{bmatrix}\right), \tag{5}$$

where $a(x, y) = (xW_Q)(yW_K)^T/\sqrt{d}$. After converting Eq. (5), the *exemplar* attention $Att(e^l)$ and the *search* attention $Att(s^l)$ are,

$$Att(e^l) = softmax\left([a(e^l, e^l), a(e^l, s^l)]\right)\left[e^l W_V, s^l W_V\right]^T,$$
$$Att(s^l) = softmax\left([a(s^l, e^l), a(s^l, s^l)]\right)\left[e^l W_V, s^l W_V\right]^T. \tag{6}$$

In the baseline model, the feature extraction of the *exemplar* and *search* features are independent with each other as shown in Eq. (2). While, in our transformer backbone, the feature learning of *exemplar* and *search* images influence each other through $a(e^l, s^l)$ and $a(s^l, e^l)$ in Eq. (6). $Att(e^l)$ contains information from s^l and vice verse. The information interaction between the *exemplar* and *search* features exists in every layer of our transformer backbone, so there is no need to add additional interaction module after the backbone. We directly send the output *search* feature s^L to the predictor for target localization.

Distinguishable Position Embedding. It is a general paradigm to seamlessly transfer networks pre-trained from the classification task to provide a stronger initialization for VOT. In our method, we also initialize our transformer backbone with pre-trained parameters. For the *search* image, the input size (224×224) is the same with that in general vision transformers [15,41], so the pre-trained position embedding p_0 can be directly used for the *search* image ($p_s = p_0$). However, the *exemplar* image is smaller than the *search* image, so the pre-trained position embedding can not fit well for the *exemplar* image. Besides, using the same pre-trained position embedding for both images provides the backbone with no information to distinguish the two images. To solve the issue, we add a learnable position embedding $p_e \in \mathbb{R}^{N_z \times D}$ to the *exemplar* feature, which is calculated by the spatial position (i, j) of the patch and the ratio R_{ij} of the target area in this patch (as depicted in Fig. 3 (b)),

$$p_e = FCs(i, j, R_{ij}),$$ (7)

where p_e denotes the position embedding of the *exemplar* feature, FCs are two fully connected layers. After obtaining the position embedding p_e and p_s, we add them to the embedding vectors. The resulting sequences of embedding vectors serve as inputs to the transformer backbone.

3.3   Foveal Window Strategy

The *exemplar* image contains the target in the center and a small amount of background around the target. The down-sampling process may divide the important target region into different parts. To provide the transformer backbone with more detailed target information, we further propose a foveal window strategy on the *exemplar* image to produce more diverse target patches with acceptable com-

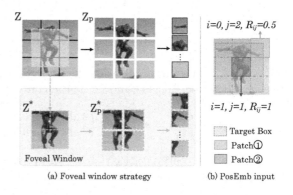

(a) Foveal window strategy   (b) PosEmb input

Fig. 3. (a) the foveal window strategy and (b) getting the inputs of FCs in Eq. (7)

putational costs. As shown in the second row of Fig. 3(a), we crop a smaller region $\mathbf{Z}^* \in \mathbb{R}^{H_z^* \times W_z^* \times 3}$ in the center of the *exemplar* image and serialize $\mathbf{Z}^*$ into image patches $\mathbf{Z_p^*} \in \mathbb{R}^{N_z^* \times (P^2 \cdot 3)}$, where $N_z^* = H_x^* W_x^* / P^2$. The partitioning lines on $\mathbf{Z}^*$ are located in the center of those on the *exemplar* image $\mathbf{Z}$, so as to ensure that the foveal patches $\mathbf{Z_p^*}$ contain different target information with the original patches $\mathbf{Z_p}$. After getting the foveal patches $\mathbf{Z_p^*}$, we calculate their position embedding according to Eq. (7). Then, we map $\mathbf{Z_p^*}$ with the same linear projection as $\mathbf{Z_p}$ and add the mapped feature with the position embedding to get the foveal sequence e^{0*}. Finally, the input of transformer backbone includes the *search* sequence s^0, the *exemplar* sequence e^0 and the foveal sequence e^{0*}. The *exemplar* image is small in VOT, so the token number in e^0 and e^{0*} are modest as well.

4 Experiments

4.1 Implementation Details

Model. We evaluate our method on vision transformer [36] and produce three variants of SimTrack: Sim-B/32, Sim-B/16, and Sim-L/14 with the ViT base, base, and large model [15] as the backbone, respectively, where input images are split into 32×32, 16×16 and 14×14 patches, correspondingly. All parameters in the backbone are initialized with pre-trained parameters from the vision branch of CLIP [36]. For better comparison with other trackers, we add another variant Sim-B/16* with fewer FLOPs than Sim-B/16. In Sim-B/16*, we remove the last four layers in the transformer backbone to reduce computation costs. The predictor is exactly the same as that in STARK-S [51].

Training. Our SimTrack is implemented with Python 3.6.9 on PyTorch 1.8.1. All experiments are conducted on a server with 8 16GB V100 GPUs. The same as STARK-S, we train our models with training-splits of LaSOT [12], GOT-10K [22], COCO2017 [30], and TrackingNet [35] for experiments on all testing datasets except for GOT-10k_Test. For GOT-10k_Test, we follow the official requirements and only use the *train* set of GOT-10k for model training. In Sim-B/32, we set the input sizes of *exemplar* and *search* images as 128×128 and 320×320, corresponding to 2^2 and 5^2 times of the target bounding box, because the larger stride 32 makes the output features having a smaller size. Too small output size has a negative effect on target localization. In Sim-B/16, the input sizes are 112×112 and 224×224, corresponding to 2^2 and 4^2 times of the target bounding box. For Sim-L/14, the *exemplar* input size is reduced to 84×84 (1.5^2 times of target bounding box) to reduce computation costs. Without the special declaration, all other experiments use the same input sizes as Sim-B/16. The size of the cropped image for the foveal window is 64×64. All other training details are the same with STARK-S [51] and shown in the supplementary materials.

Inference. Like STARK-S [51], there is no extra post-processing for all SimTrack models. The inference pipeline only consists of a forward pass and coordinate transformation process. The input sizes of *exemplar* and *search* images are consistent with those during offline training. Our Sim-B/16 can run in real-time at more than 40 fps.

4.2 State-of-the-art Comparisons

We compare our SimTrack with other trackers on five datasets, including LaSOT [12], TNL2K [48], TrackingNet [35], UAV123 [34] and GOT-10k [22].

Table 1. Performance comparisons with state-of-the-art trackers on the *test* set of LaSOT [12], TNL2K [48] and TrackingNet [35]. 'Size' means the size of *search* image, 'FLOPs' shows the computation costs of backbone and transformer head. For methods without transformer head, 'FLOPs' shows the computation costs from the backbone. AUC, P_{norm} and P are AUC, normalized precision and precision. Sim-B/16* denotes removing the last four layers of the transformer-backbone in Sim-B/16 to reduce FLOPs. Trackers shown with ◊ have online update modules. Red, green and blue fonts indicate the top-3 methods.

Methods	Net	Size	FLOPs	LaSOT		TNL2K		TrackingNet	
				AUC	P_{norm}	AUC	P	AUC	P
SiamFC [1]	AlexNet	255	4.9G	33.6	42.0	29.5	28.6	57.1	66.3
ATOM [13] ◊	ResNet18	288	3.0G	51.5	57.6	40.1	39.2	70.3	64.8
DiMP [2] ◊	ResNet50	288	5.4G	56.9	65.0	44.7	43.4	74.0	68.7
SiamRPN++ [26]	ResNet50	255	7.8G	49.6	56.9	41.3	41.2	73.3	69.4
SiamFC++ [50]	GoogleNet	303	15.8G	54.4	56.9	38.6	36.9	75.4	70.5
Ocean [55] ◊	ResNet50	255	7.8G	56.0	65.0	38.4	37.7	70.3	68.8
SiamBAN [11]	ResNet50	255	12.1G	51.4	52.1	41.0	41.7	-	-
SiamAtt [52]	ResNet50	255	7.8G	56.0	64.8	-	-	75.2	-
TransT [9]	ResNet50	256	29.3G	64.9	73.8	50.7	51.7	81.4	80.3
TrDiMP [45] ◊	ResNet50	352	18.2G	63.9	-	-	-	78.4	73.1
KeepTrack [32] ◊	ResNet50	464	28.7G	67.1	77.2	-	-	-	-
AutoMatch [54]	ResNet50	-	-	58.3	-	47.2	43.5	76.0	72.6
TransInMo* [17]	ResNet50	255	16.9G	65.7	76.0	52.0	52.7	-	-
STARK-S [51]	ResNet50	320	15.6G	65.8	-	-	-	80.3	-
STARK-ST [51] ◊	ResNet101	320	28.0G	67.1	77.0	-	-	82.0	86.9
Sim-B/32	ViT-B/32	320	11.5G	66.2	76.1	51.1	48.1	79.1	83.9
Sim-B/16*	ViT-B/16*	224	14.7G	68.7	77.5	53.7	52.6	81.5	86.0
Sim-B/16	ViT-B/16	224	25.0G	69.3	78.5	54.8	53.8	82.3	86.5
Sim-L/14	ViT-L/14	224	95.4G	70.5	79.7	55.6	55.7	83.4	87.4

LaSOT is a large-scale dataset with 1400 long videos in total. The *test* set of LaSOT [12] consists of 280 sequences. Table 1 shows the AUC and normalized precision scores (P_{norm}) of all compared trackers. Our SimTrack can get a competitive or even better performance compared with state-of-the-art trackers. Our Sim-B/16* outperforms all compared trackers with a simpler framework and lower computation costs. Our Sim-B/16 achieves a new state-of-the-art result, 69.3% AUC score and 78.5% normalized precision score, with acceptable computation costs. After using the larger model ViT-L/14, our Sim-L/14 can get a much higher performance, 70.5% AUC score and 79.7% normalized precision score. We are the first to exploit such a large model and demonstrate its effectiveness in visual object tracking.

Table 2. Performance comparisons on UAV123 [34] dataset. *Red*, *green* and *blue* fonts indicate the top-3 methods.

	SiamFC [1]	SiamRPN [27]	SiamFC++ [50]	DiMP [2]	TrDiMP [45]	TransT [9]	Ours ViT-B/16	Ours ViT-L/14
AUC↑	48.5	55.7	63.1	65.4	67.5	68.1	69.8	71.2
Pre↑	64.8	71.0	76.9	85.6	87.2	87.6	89.6	91.6

Table 3. Experimental results on GOT-10k_Test [22] dataset.

	SiamFC [1]	SiamRPN [27]	SiamFC++ [50]	DiMP [2]	TrDiMP [45]	STARK-s [51]	Ours ViT-B/16	Ours ViT-L/14
AO↑	34.8	46.3	59.5	61.1	67.1	67.2	68.6	69.8
$SR_{0.5}$ ↑	35.3	40.4	69.5	71.7	77.7	76.1	78.9	78.8
$SR_{0.75}$ ↑	9.8	14.4	47.9	49.2	58.3	61.2	62.4	66.0

TNL2K is a recently published datasets which composes of 3000 sequences. We evaluate our SimTrack on the *test* set with 700 videos. From Table 1, SimTrack performs the best among all compared trackers. The model with ViT-B/16 exceeds 2.8 AUC points than the highest AUC score (52.0%) of all compared trackers. Leveraging a larger model can further improve the AUC score to 55.6%.

TrackingNet is another large-scale dataset consists of 511 videos in the *test* set. The *test* dataset is not publicly available, so results should be submitted to an online server for performance evaluation. Compared with the other trackers with complicated interaction modules, our SimTrack is a more simple and generic framework, yet achieves competitive performance. By leveraging a larger model, Sim-L/14 outperforms all compared trackers including those with online update.

UAV123 provides 123 aerial videos captured from a UAV platform. In Table 2, two versions of our method both achieve better AUC scores (69.8 and 71.2) than the highest AUC score (68.1) of all compared algorithms.

GOT-10k requires training trackers with only the *train* subset and testing models through an evaluation server. We follow this policy for all experiments on GOT-10k. As shown in Table 3, our tracker with ViT-B/16 obtains the best performance. When leveraging a larger model ViT-L/14, our model can further improve the performance to 69.8 AUC score.

4.3 Ablation Study and Analysis

Simplified Framework *vs.* **STARK-SV**. To remove concerns about backbone, we compare our method with the baseline tracker STARK-SV [51] using the same backbone architecture. In Table 4, our design can consistently get significant performance gains with similar or even fewer computation costs. Our three

Table 4. Ablation study about our simplified framework and the baseline model STARK-S [51]. 'FLOPs' shows computation costs of different methods, AUC, P_{norm} and P respectively denote AUC, normalized precision and precision.

Backbone		FLOPs	LaSOT			TNL2K	
			AUC↑	P_{norm}↑	P↑	AUC↑	P↑
STARK-SV	ViT-B/32	13.3G	62.5	72.1	64.0	48.0	44.0
Ours	ViT-B/32	11.5G	66.2(+3.7)	76.1(+4.0)	68.8(+4.8)	51.1(+3.1)	48.1(+4.1)
STARK-SV	ViT-B/16	25.6G	66.8	75.7	70.6	52.2	51.1
Ours	ViT-B/16	23.4G	69.3(+2.5)	78.5(+2.8)	74.0(+3.4)	54.8(+2.6)	53.8(+2.7)
STARK-SV	ViT-L/14	95.6G	69.2	78.2	74.3	54.0	54.1
Ours	ViT-L/14	95.4G	70.5(+1.3)	79.7(+1.5)	76.2(+1.9)	55.6(+1.6)	55.7(+1.6)

Table 5. The AUC/Pre scores of Sim-Track (with ViT-B/16 as backbone) when using different pre-training weights.

Table 6. The training loss and AUC (on LaSOT) in the Y-axis for different training epochs (X-axis).

#Num		①	②	③	④	⑤
Pretrain		DeiT	Moco	SLIP	CLIP	MAE
LaSOT	AUC	66.9	66.4	67.6	69.3	70.3
	Prec	70.3	69.4	71.0	74.0	75.5
TNL2K	AUC	51.9	51.9	53.4	54.8	55.7
	Prec	49.6	49.4	51.8	53.8	55.8

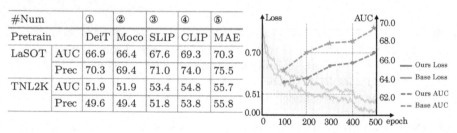

variations with ViT-B/32, ViT-B/16 and ViT-L/14 as backbone outperforms STARK-SV for 3.7/3.1, 2.5/2.6 and 1.3/1.6 AUC points on LaSOT/TNL2K dataset, respectively, demonstrating the effectiveness and efficiency of our method.

Training Loss & Accuracy. In Fig. 6, we show the training losses and AUC scores of the baseline model STARK-SV and our method 'Ours' on the LaSOT dataset. Both the two trackers utilize ViT-B/16 as the backbone. We can see that 'Ours' uses fewer training epochs to get the same training loss with STARK-SV. When training models for the same epochs, 'Ours' can get lower training losses than STARK-SV. In terms of testing accuracy, training our model for 200 epochs is enough to get the same AUC score (66.8% *vs.* 66.8%) with the baseline model trained for 500 epochs. We think the main reason is 'Ours' does not have a randomly initialized transformer head. The transformer head without pre-training needs more training epochs to get a good performance.

Results with Other Transformer Backbones. We evaluate our framework with Swin Transformer [31] and Pyramid Vision Transformer (PVT) [47]. For Swin Transformer, we made a necessary adaption, considering the shifted window strategy. We remove the $a(e^l, s^l)$ and $s^l W_V$ in the first function of Eq.(6),

Table 7. The AUC scores and FLOPs of SimTrack using PVT and Swin-Transformer as backbone on LaSOT and UAV123 dataset.

	DiMP	TrDiMP	TransT	STARK-S	**PVT-M**	**Swin-B**
FLOPs	5.4G	18.2G	29.3G	15.6G	**8.9G**	**15.0G**
LaSOT	56.9	63.9	64.9	65.8	**66.6**	**68.3**
UAV123	65.4	67.5	68.1	68.2	**68.5**	**69.4**

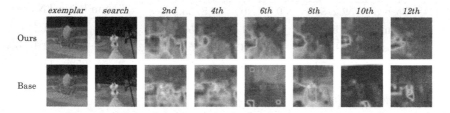

Fig. 4. The images in different columns are the *exemplar* image, *search* image, target-relevant attention maps from the $2nd, 4th, 6th, 8th, 10th, 12th(last)$ layer of the transformer backbone. Details can be found in supplementary materials.

which has less influence according to our experiments (from 69.3% to 69.1% AUC score on LaSOT for SimTrack-ViT). The attention of each *search* token is calculated with the tokens inside the local window and those from *exemplar* features. During attention calculation, the *exemplar* features are pooled to the size of the local window. For PVT, we reduce the reduction ratio of SRA module for the *exemplar* by half, to keep a reasonable *exemplar* size. In the Table 7, Sim-Track with PVT-Medium is denoted as PVT-M and SimTrack with Swin-Base is denoted as Swin-B. PVT-M gets comparable AUC scores with fewer FLOPs, and Swin-B has higher AUC scores with similar FLOPs to STARK-S on both datasets, demonstrating the good generalization of our SimTrack.

Different Pre-Training. We evaluate our SimTrack when using ViT-B/16 as backbone and initializing the backbone with parameters pre-trained with several recent methods, including DeiT [41], MOCO-V3 [10], SLIP [33], CLIP [36], and MAE [19]. From Table 5, all of these versions achieve competitive performance with state-of-the-art trackers on the two datasets. However, the pre-trained parameters from MAE show the best performance, suggesting that appropriate parameter initialization is helpful to the training of SimTrack.

Component-Wise Analysis. To prove the efficiency of our method, we perform a component-wise analysis on the TNL2K [48] benchmark, as shown in Table 8. The 'Base' means STARK-SV with ViT-B/16, which obtains an AUC score of 52.2. In ②, '+Sim' indicates using our SimTrack framework without adding the distinguishable position embedding or foveal window strategy. It brings significant gains, *i.e.* 1.3/1.4 point in terms of AUC/Pre score, and verifies the effectiveness of our framework. Adding our position embedding helps

Table 8. Component-wise analysis. AUC/Pre scores are reported respectively. The results demonstrate that each component is important in our framework.

#Num	Com	TNL2K↑
①	Base	52.2/51.1
②	+Sim	53.5/52.5
③	+PosEm	54.0/53.1
④	+FW	54.8/53.8

Table 9. The influence of introducing decoders in SimTrack. With sufficient interaction in the transformer backbone, decoder becomes redundant for SimTrack.

#Num	Dec	TNL2K↑
①	0	54.8/53.8
②	1	54.8/54.2
③	3	54.6/54.0
④	6	54.7/54.3

Table 10. Analysis of information interaction ratio in backbone. ① is ours with interaction in 100% blocks. ② and ③ reduce the number of interaction blocks to 50% and 25%.

#Num	Ratio	TNL2K↑
①	100%	54.8/53.8
②	50%	52.3/50.4
③	25%	49.8/46.2

model performs slightly better (③ *vs.* ②). Furthermore, the foveal window strategy brings an improvement of 0.8 point on AUC score in ④. This shows using more detailed target patches at the beginning contributes to improving accuracy.

Decoder Number. We analyze the necessity of introducing transformer decoders in our SimTrack. Specifically, we add a transformer decoder at the end of our backbone for further information interaction. In the decoder, the *search* features from the backbone are used to get *query* values. The *exemplar* features are adopt to calculate *key* and *value*. Through changing the layer number of the decoder from 0 to 6, the performance changes less. This shows another information interaction module is unnecessary in our framework, because our transformer backbone can provide enough information interaction between the *search* and *exemplar* features.

Dense or Sparse Information Interaction. The information interaction between the *exemplar* and *search* features exist in all twelve blocks in our Sim-B/16, shown as ① in Table 10. In ②, we only enable the interaction in the $2nd, 4th, 6th, 8th, 10th$ and $12th$ block, removing half of the interaction in ①. As we can see, using less information interaction leads to 2.5 points AUC drop. When we further reduce half interaction in ②, the AUC score drops another 2.5 points in ③. The experiments show that comprehension information interaction helps to improve the tracking performance in SimTrack (Table 9).

Visualization. Figure 4 shows the target-relevant area in the search region for different layers. Our architecture can gradually and quickly focus on the designated target and keep following the target in the following layers. The visualization maps show that the Siamese backbone in 'base' tends to learn general-object sensitive features instead of designated-target sensitive features and no information interaction hinders the backbone from 'sensing' the target during feature learning. By contrast, 'Ours' can produce designated-target sensitive features thanks to the information interaction from the first block to the last block.

5   Conclusions

This work presents SimTrack, a simple yet effective framework for visual object tracking. By leveraging a transformer backbone for joint feature learning and information interaction, our approach streamlines the tracking pipeline and eliminates most of the specialization in current tracking methods. While it obtains compelling results against well-established baselines on five tracking benchmarks, both architecture and training techniques can be optimized for further performance improvements

Acknowledgments. This work was supported by the Australian Research Council Grant DP200103223, Australian Medical Research Future Fund MRFAI000085, CRC-P Smart Material Recovery Facility (SMRF) - Curby Soft Plastics, and CRC-P ARIA - Bionic Visual-Spatial Prosthesis for the Blind.

References

1. Bertinetto, L., Valmadre, J., Henriques, J.F., Vedaldi, A., Torr, P.H.S.: Fully-convolutional Siamese networks for object tracking. In: Hua, G., Jégou, H. (eds.) ECCV 2016. LNCS, vol. 9914, pp. 850–865. Springer, Cham (2016). https://doi.org/10.1007/978-3-319-48881-3_56
2. Bhat, G., Danelljan, M., Gool, L.V., Timofte, R.: Learning discriminative model prediction for tracking. In: ICCV (2019)
3. Bromley, J., Guyon, I., Lecun, Y., Säckinger, E., Shah, R.: Signature verification using a Siamese time delay neural network. In: NeurIPS, pp. 737–744 (1993)
4. Carion, N., Massa, F., Synnaeve, G., Usunier, N., Kirillov, A., Zagoruyko, S.: End-to-end object detection with transformers. In: Vedaldi, A., Bischof, H., Brox, T., Frahm, J.-M. (eds.) ECCV 2020. LNCS, vol. 12346, pp. 213–229. Springer, Cham (2020). https://doi.org/10.1007/978-3-030-58452-8_13
5. Chen, B., et al.: PSVIT: better vision transformer via token pooling and attention sharing. arXiv preprint arXiv:2108.03428 (2021)
6. Chen, B., et al.: GLIT: neural architecture search for global and local image transformer. In: ICCV (2021)
7. Chen, B., Wang, D., Li, P., Wang, S., Lu, H.: Real-time 'actor-critic' tracking. In: Ferrari, V., Hebert, M., Sminchisescu, C., Weiss, Y. (eds.) ECCV 2018. LNCS, vol. 11211, pp. 328–345. Springer, Cham (2018). https://doi.org/10.1007/978-3-030-01234-2_20
8. Chen, T., Saxena, S., Li, L., Fleet, D.J., Hinton, G.: Pix2seq: a language modeling framework for object detection. arXiv preprint arXiv:2109.10852 (2021)
9. Chen, X., Yan, B., Zhu, J., Wang, D., Yang, X., Lu, H.: Transformer tracking. In: CVPR (2021)
10. Chen, X., Xie, S., He, K.: An empirical study of training self-supervised vision transformers. In: ICCV (2021)
11. Chen, Z., Zhong, B., Li, G., Zhang, S., Ji, R.: Siamese box adaptive network for visual tracking. In: CVPR (2020)
12. Choi, J., Kwon, J., Lee, K.M.: Deep meta learning for real-time visual tracking based on target-specific feature space. CoRR abs/1712.09153 (2017)

13. Danelljan, M., Bhat, G., Khan, F.S., Felsberg, M.: ATOM: accurate tracking by overlap maximization. In: CVPR (2019)
14. Devlin, J., Chang, M.W., Lee, K., Toutanova, K.: Bert: Pre-training of deep bidirectional transformers for language understanding. arXiv preprint arXiv:1810.04805 (2018)
15. Dosovitskiy, A., et al.: An image is worth 16×16 words: transformers for image recognition at scale. arXiv preprint arXiv:2010.11929 (2020)
16. Guo, D., Shao, Y., Cui, Y., Wang, Z., Zhang, L., Shen, C.: Graph attention tracking. In: CVPR (2021)
17. Guo, M., et al.: Learning target-aware representation for visual tracking via informative interactions. arXiv preprint arXiv:2201.02526 (2022)
18. Guo, Q., Feng, W., Zhou, C., Huang, R., Wan, L., Wang, S.: Learning dynamic Siamese network for visual object tracking. In: Proceedings of the IEEE International Conference on Computer Vision, pp. 1763–1771 (2017)
19. He, K., Chen, X., Xie, S., Li, Y., Dollár, P., Girshick, R.: Masked autoencoders are scalable vision learners. In: CVPR (2022)
20. He, K., Gkioxari, G., Dollár, P., Girshick, R.: Mask R-CNN. In: ICCV (2017)
21. He, K., Zhang, X., Ren, S., Sun, J.: Deep residual learning for image recognition. In: CVPR (2016)
22. Huang, L., Zhao, X., Huang, K.: Got-10k: a large high-diversity benchmark for generic object tracking in the wild. CoRR abs/1810.11981 (2018)
23. Jaegle, A., et al.: Perceiver IO: a general architecture for structured inputs & outputs. arXiv preprint arXiv:2107.14795 (2021)
24. Kamath, A., Singh, M., LeCun, Y., Synnaeve, G., Misra, I., Carion, N.: Mdetr-modulated detection for end-to-end multi-modal understanding. In: ICCV (2021)
25. Laina, I., Rupprecht, C., Belagiannis, V., Tombari, F., Navab, N.: Deeper depth prediction with fully convolutional residual networks. In: 2016 Fourth International Conference on 3D Vision (3DV), pp. 239–248. IEEE (2016)
26. Li, B., Wu, W., Wang, Q., Zhang, F., Xing, J., Yan, J.: SiamRPN++: evolution of Siamese visual tracking with very deep networks. In: CVPR (2019)
27. Li, B., Yan, J., Wu, W., Zhu, Z., Hu, X.: High performance visual tracking with Siamese region proposal network. In: CVPR (2018)
28. Li, P., Chen, B., Ouyang, W., Wang, D., Yang, X., Lu, H.: GradNet: gradient-guided network for visual object tracking. In: ICCV (2019)
29. Li, P., Wang, D., Wang, L., Lu, H.: Deep visual tracking: review and experimental comparison. Pattern Recogn. **76**, 323–338 (2018)
30. Lin, T.-Y., et al.: Microsoft COCO: common objects in context. In: Fleet, D., Pajdla, T., Schiele, B., Tuytelaars, T. (eds.) ECCV 2014. LNCS, vol. 8693, pp. 740–755. Springer, Cham (2014). https://doi.org/10.1007/978-3-319-10602-1_48
31. Liu, Z., Lin, Y., Cao, Y., Hu, H., Wei, Y., Zhang, Z., Lin, S., Guo, B.: Swin transformer: hierarchical vision transformer using shifted windows. In: ICCV (2021)
32. Mayer, C., Danelljan, M., Paudel, D.P., Van Gool, L.: Learning target candidate association to keep track of what not to track. In: ICCV (2021)
33. Mu, N., Kirillov, A., Wagner, D., Xie, S.: Slip: self-supervision meets language-image pre-training. arXiv preprint arXiv:2112.12750 (2021)
34. Mueller, M., Smith, N., Ghanem, B.: A benchmark and simulator for UAV tracking. In: Leibe, B., Matas, J., Sebe, N., Welling, M. (eds.) ECCV 2016. LNCS, vol. 9905, pp. 445–461. Springer, Cham (2016). https://doi.org/10.1007/978-3-319-46448-0_27

35. Müller, M., Bibi, A., Giancola, S., Alsubaihi, S., Ghanem, B.: TrackingNet: a large-scale dataset and benchmark for object tracking in the wild. In: Ferrari, V., Hebert, M., Sminchisescu, C., Weiss, Y. (eds.) ECCV 2018. LNCS, vol. 11205, pp. 310–327. Springer, Cham (2018). https://doi.org/10.1007/978-3-030-01246-5_19

36. Radford, A., et al.: Learning transferable visual models from natural language supervision. In: ICML (2021)

37. Radford, A., Narasimhan, K., Salimans, T., Sutskever, I.: Improving language understanding by generative pre-training (2018)

38. Ren, S., He, K., Girshick, R., Sun, J.: Faster R-CNN: towards real-time object detection with region proposal networks. Adv. Neural. Inf. Process. Syst. **28**, 1–9 (2015)

39. Shen, Q., et al.: Unsupervised learning of accurate Siamese tracking. In: CVPR (2022)

40. Tang, S., Chen, D., Bai, L., Liu, K., Ge, Y., Ouyang, W.: Mutual CRF-GNN for few-shot learning. In: CVPR (2021)

41. Touvron, H., Cord, M., Douze, M., Massa, F., Sablayrolles, A., Jégou, H.: Training data-efficient image transformers & distillation through attention. In: ICML (2021)

42. Vaswani, A., et al.: Attention is all you need. In: NeurIPS, vol. 30 (2017)

43. Wang, L., Zhang, J., Wang, O., Lin, Z., Lu, H.: SDC-depth: semantic divide-and-conquer network for monocular depth estimation. In: CVPR (2020)

44. Wang, N., Zhou, W., Wang, J., Li, H.: Transformer meets tracker: exploiting temporal context for robust visual tracking. In: CVPR (2021)

45. Wang, N., Zhou, W., Wang, J., Li, H.: Transformer meets tracker: exploiting temporal context for robust visual tracking. In: ICCV (2021)

46. Wang, Q., Zhang, L., Bertinetto, L., Hu, W., Torr, P.H.S.: Fast online object tracking and segmentation: a unifying approach. In: CVPR (2019)

47. Wang, W., et al.: Pyramid vision transformer: a versatile backbone for dense prediction without convolutions. In: ICCV (2021)

48. Wang, X., et al.: Towards more flexible and accurate object tracking with natural language: algorithms and benchmark. In: CVPR (2021)

49. Wang, Y., et al.: Revisiting the transferability of supervised pretraining: an MLP perspective. In: CVPR (2022)

50. Xu, Y., Wang, Z., Li, Z., Ye, Y., Yu, G.: SiamFC++: towards robust and accurate visual tracking with target estimation guidelines. In: AAAI (2020)

51. Yan, B., Peng, H., Fu, J., Wang, D., Lu, H.: Learning spatio-temporal transformer for visual tracking. arXiv preprint arXiv:2103.17154 (2021)

52. Yu, Y., Xiong, Y., Huang, W., Scott, M.R.: Deformable Siamese attention networks for visual object tracking. In: CVPR (2020)

53. Zhang, Z., et al.: Joint task-recursive learning for semantic segmentation and depth estimation. In: Ferrari, V., Hebert, M., Sminchisescu, C., Weiss, Y. (eds.) ECCV 2018. LNCS, vol. 11214, pp. 238–255. Springer, Cham (2018). https://doi.org/10.1007/978-3-030-01249-6_15

54. Zhang, Z., Liu, Y., Wang, X., Li, B., Hu, W.: Learn to match: automatic matching network design for visual tracking. In: ICCV (2021)

55. Zhang, Z., Peng, H., Fu, J., Li, B., Hu, W.: Ocean: object-aware anchor-free tracking. In: Vedaldi, A., Bischof, H., Brox, T., Frahm, J.-M. (eds.) ECCV 2020. LNCS, vol. 12366, pp. 771–787. Springer, Cham (2020). https://doi.org/10.1007/978-3-030-58589-1_46

56. Zheng, S., et al.: Rethinking semantic segmentation from a sequence-to-sequence perspective with transformers. In: CVPR (2021)

57. Zhu, X., Su, W., Lu, L., Li, B., Wang, X., Dai, J.: Deformable DETR: deformable transformers for end-to-end object detection. arXiv preprint arXiv:2010.04159 (2020)
58. Zhu, X., et al.: Uni-perceiver: pre-training unified architecture for generic perception for zero-shot and few-shot tasks. arXiv preprint arXiv:2112.01522 (2021)
59. Zhu, Z., et al.: Distractor-aware Siamese networks for visual object tracking. In: Ferrari, V., Hebert, M., Sminchisescu, C., Weiss, Y. (eds.) ECCV 2018. LNCS, vol. 11213, pp. 103–119. Springer, Cham (2018). https://doi.org/10.1007/978-3-030-01240-3_7

Aware of the History: Trajectory Forecasting with the Local Behavior Data

Yiqi Zhong[1] , Zhenyang Ni[2] , Siheng Chen[2(✉)] , and Ulrich Neumann[1]

[1] Department of Computer Science, University of Southern California, Los Angeles, CA 90089, USA
{yiqizhon,uneumann}@usc.edu
[2] Cooperative Medianet Innovation Center (CMIC), Shanghai Jiao Tong University, Shanghai, China
{0107nzy,sihengc}@sjtu.edu.cn

Abstract. The historical trajectories previously passing through a location may help infer the future trajectory of an agent currently at this location. Despite great improvements in trajectory forecasting with the guidance of high-definition maps, only a few works have explored such local historical information. In this work, we re-introduce this information as a new type of input data for trajectory forecasting systems: the *local behavior data*, which we conceptualize as a collection of location-specific historical trajectories. *Local behavior data* helps the systems emphasize the prediction locality and better understand the impact of static map objects on moving agents. We propose a novel local-behavior-aware (LBA) prediction framework that improves forecasting accuracy by fusing information from observed trajectories, HD maps, and local behavior data. Also, where such historical data is insufficient or unavailable, we employ a local-behavior-free (LBF) prediction framework, which adopts a knowledge-distillation-based architecture to infer the impact of missing data. Extensive experiments demonstrate that upgrading existing methods with these two frameworks significantly improves their performances. Especially, the LBA framework boosts the SOTA methods' performance on the nuScenes dataset by at least 14% for the $K = 1$ metrics. Code is at https://github.com/Kay1794/LocalBehavior-based-trajectory-prediction.

Keywords: Trajectory forecasting · Historical data · Knowledge-distillation

1 Introduction

Trajectory forecasting aims to predict an agent's future trajectory based on its past trajectory and surrounding scene information. This task is essential in a

Supplementary Information The online version contains supplementary material available at https://doi.org/10.1007/978-3-031-20047-2_23.

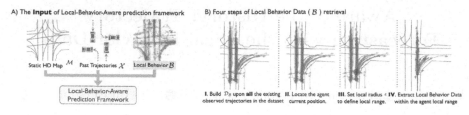

Fig. 1. A) Compared to previous works that mostly rely on HD maps and agents' past trajectories, we additionally input the local behavior data to the prediction framework. B) For agents to be predicted in the scene, we follow these steps to retrieve their local behavior data for the framework input composition.

variety of applications, including self-driving cars [27], surveillance systems [8], robotics [2], and human behavior analysis [36]. Prior prediction systems primarily use deep-learning-based models (e.g., LSTM, temporal convolutions) to exploit limited information such as past trajectories [1,21,30]. Recent efforts also reveal that forecasting ability will improve as more scene information is introduced into the input. One type of scene information, for example, is the past trajectories of a target agent's neighboring agents. To date, many graph-neural-network-based methods have explored the potential of agents' motion features and interactive motion relations to improve predictions [20,35,42]. Recently, high-definition (HD) maps are incorporated as an additional type of scene information [9,11,13,23,41] to provide geometric priors.

Besides the widely used HD maps and agents' past trajectories, we propose a novel Local-Behavior-Aware (LBA) prediction framework that takes a new type of scene information as the input, which we term as *local behavior data*. The local behavior data is defined as a collection of historical trajectories at an agent's current location. Figure 1 (A) shows the three components of the LBA framework input. Taking local behavior data as the input brings two benefits to the task. First, the data provides location-specific motion patterns, which helps the model effectively narrow down the search space for future trajectories. Most of the existing prediction models solely rely on the features learned from the static HD map to infer such information [10,13,15]. In comparison, taking local behavior data as the input immediately equips the model with this information, making the model more tractable and robust. Second, local behavior data provides complementary information to augment static maps into dynamic behavioral maps. The map prior in the current literature is limited to static geometric information. The rich dynamic information brought by this new input would help the model better understand the impact of map objects on moving agents.

Many car companies and navigation apps are collecting such local behavior data. Yet, sometimes this data is insufficient or is yet to be gathered (e.g. when a self-driving car explores new areas). Therefore, we further propose a Local-Behavior-Free (LBF) prediction framework that only takes the current agents' observed trajectories and HD maps as the input, when the local behavior data is unavailable. Inspired by recent development in knowledge distillation, we use our pre-trained LBA prediction framework as the teacher network during the training phase. This teacher network guides the LBF student network in inferring the features of the absent local behavior data. The intuition behind this design is that a traffic agent's movement at a particular location is confined to a limited number of possibilities. The teacher network essentially provides the ground truth of the movement pattern, making it plausible for the student network to learn the inference of the pattern given the current scene information.

LBA and LBF frameworks both have strong generalizability to be adopted by a wide range of existing trajectory forecasting methods. In Sects. 4.2 and 5.2, we showcase the implementation methodology on how to upgrade existing systems to the LBA/LBF framework respectively. We then implement and validate the two frameworks based on three state-of-the-art trajectory forecasting methods, P2T [9], LaneGCN [23], and DenseTNT [15].

In summary, this work has three major contributions to the literature:

- We propose a Local-Behavior-Aware prediction framework. It enables most of the existing methods to incorporate the local behavior data, a new type of system input which contains the local historical information.
- We further introduce a Local-Behavior-Free prediction framework, which adopts a knowledge-distillation-based architecture to infer local behavioral information when it is temporarily unavailable.
- We conduct extensive experiments on published benchmarks (Argoverse [6], nuScenes [3]), and validate that upgrading the SOTA methods to LBA/LBF frameworks consistently improves their performances by significant margins on various metrics. Especially, the LBA framework improves the SOTA methods on the nuScenes dataset by at least 14% on the K=1 metrics.

2   Related Work

2.1   Historical Behaviors in Trajectory Forecasting

Historical behaviors are very helpful to trajectory forecasting since they reveal the motion pattern of agents. Several previous works have made significant progress in this direction by adopting memory-based designs. MANTRA [28] uses the observed past trajectories and the map as the key to query the possible hidden features of future trajectories. Similarly, Zhao et al. [45] build an expert repository to retrieve the possible destinations by matching the current trajectory with the ones in the repository. MemoNet [40] also considers memorizing the destinations of each agent and first applies the memory mechanism to multi-agent trajectory forecasting. Compared to those memory-based methods, our work: i) regards the historical behaviors as system inputs to benefit the task from the perspective of enriching scene information; ii) directly uses geometric coordinates to query related historical information which emphasizes the data locality and is more interpretable and robust.

2.2   Scene Representation in Trajectory Forecasting

To use a new type of scene information in systems requires fusing it with existing scene information sources. After reviewing how scene information is encoded in previous methods, we see two main types of scene representations: 1) rasterized-image-based representations [5,20], 2) graph-based representations [11,12,23,39]. Rasterized-image-based representations render static HD maps and motion data into a birds' eye view (BEV) image, using various colors to represent different objects. Systems with this scene representation tend to use standard convolutional neural networks (CNNs) backbones to extract scene features [5,9,13,20,31]. These methods transform scenes into image coordinates systems.

Graph-based scene representations become popular with the recent development of graph learning [34] and attention mechanism [37]. These methods build a graph that can be either directional or non-directional, and use techniques such as graph neural network (GNN) [34] or attention-based operations [37] to enable the interaction among map objects and agents. The nodes are the semantic map objects, e.g., lane segments and agents. The edges are defined by heuristics, which can be the spatial distances between the two nodes or the semantic labels of the two nodes. Systems using graph-based scene representations [11,12,15,23,44] independently encode each map object to make the graph more informative. Graph-based scene representations have an outstanding information fusion capability and are substantially explored recently.

Other methods that do not strictly fall into the above two categories can share some properties with one or both of them. For example, TPCN [41] uses point cloud representations for the scene and does not manually specify the interaction structures. Yet, by using PointNet++ [32] to aggregate each point's neighborhood information, TPCN still technically defines local complete subgraphs for the scene where each point is a node connected with its neighbors.

To show the generalizability of the proposed frameworks, in this work we introduce an implementation methodology for upgrading forecasting systems that use either rasterized-image-based or graph-based scene representations to the LBA and LBF frameworks in Sects. 4.2 and 5.2 respectively.

2.3   Knowledge Distillation

Our LBF framework is inspired by the recent study of knowledge distillation (KD). Knowledge distillation is a technique that compresses a larger teacher network to a smaller student network by urging the student to mimic the teacher at the intermediate feature or output level [19]. KD is widely used for various tasks, including object detection [7,16], semantic segmentation [18,25] and tracking [26]. Its usage is still being explored. For example, researchers start to use KD for collaborative perception tasks [22]. In our work, the proposed LBF framework uses KD in the trajectory forecasting task. Compared to previous works that pay more attention to model compression, we seek to compress the volume of input data. We use the offline framework as the teacher network, which takes each agent's local behavior data as the input along with HD maps and the agents' observed trajectories, while the student network (i.e., the online framework) only uses the later two data modalities as the input without requiring local behavior data. Our experiments show that KD-based information compression significantly boosts the performance of trajectory forecasting.

3   Formulation of Local Behavior

In trajectory forecasting, the observed trajectories of the agents previously passing through a location may help infer the future trajectory of an agent currently at the location. In this work, we collect such historical information and reformulate it to make it become one of the inputs for the trajectory forecasting system. We name this new type of scene information as the *local behavior data*. In this section, we introduce its formulation and the methodology about how to retrieve such data from existing datasets.

Consider a trajectory forecasting dataset with S scenes and the pth scene has K_p agents. The observed trajectory and ground truth future trajectory of agent i in scene p are denoted respectively as $\mathbf{X}^{(i,p)}$ and $\mathbf{Y}^{(i,p)}$, where $\mathbf{X}^{(i,p)} \in \mathbb{R}^{\mathbf{T}^- \times 2}$ and $\mathbf{Y}^{(i,p)} \in \mathbb{R}^{\mathbf{T}^+ \times 2}$. Each $\mathbf{X}^{(i,p)}$ or $\mathbf{Y}^{(i,p)}$ consists of two-dimensional coordinates at $\mathbf{T}^-$ or $\mathbf{T}^+$ timestamps. Note that the coordinate system used for the trajectories is the global coordinate system aligned with the global geometric map. In this work, we specifically denote two special items in $\mathbf{X}^{(i,p)}$. We use $\mathbf{X}_1^{(i,p)} \in \mathbb{R}^2$ to represent the location of agent i in scene s at the *first* timestamp, i.e., the first observed location of the agent. Accordingly, we use $\mathbf{X}_{\mathbf{T}^-}^{(i,p)} \in \mathbb{R}^2$ to denote the agent location at timestamp $\mathbf{T}^-$, i.e., its current location. By gathering all the observed trajectories in this dataset, we build a behavior database $\mathcal{D}_\mathcal{B} = \{\mathbf{X}^{(i,p)}, p \in \{1, 2, \cdots, S\}, i \in \{1, 2, \cdots, K_p\}\}_{i,p}$. We can query the local behavior from $\mathcal{D}_\mathcal{B}$; namely, the local behavior data of agent i in scene p is

$$\mathcal{B}_\epsilon^{(i,p)} = \{\mathbf{X}^{(j,q)} \mid \left\| \mathbf{X}_{\mathbf{T}^-}^{(i,p)} - \mathbf{X}_1^{(j,q)} \right\|_2 < \epsilon, \mathbf{X}^{(j,q)} \in \mathcal{D}_\mathcal{B}\}, \tag{1}$$

where ϵ is an adjustable hyper-parameter defining the radius of the neighboring area of a location. The *size of* $\mathcal{B}_\epsilon^{(i,p)}$ refers to the number of observed trajectories in $\mathcal{B}_\epsilon^{(i,p)}$. Figure 1 (B) shows the steps to query local behavior data from $\mathcal{D}_\mathcal{B}$.

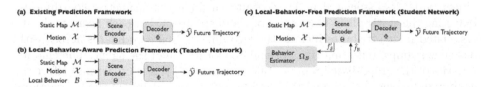

Fig. 2. General pipelines of: (a) the baseline model that uses HD map data and observed trajectory data, which is typical for SOTA trajectory forecasting systems; (b) the LBA framework that takes local behavior data as an extra input; (c) the LBF framework that uses estimated local behavior features during the inference phase. (c) has fewer constraints in the use cases compared to (b).

4   Local-Behavior-Aware Prediction

In real life, local behavior data has been widely collected by navigation apps and car companies. To use such data to benefit the trajectory forecasting task, we propose a Local-Behavior-Aware (LBA) prediction framework. In this section, we first demonstrate the generic pipeline of the LBA prediction framework and its major components. Then, we introduce the implementation strategy of the framework which especially emphasizes the representation of local behavior data and its corresponding scene encoder design.

4.1   Framework Pipeline

Like a typical prediction framework pipeline adopted by previous works [11,20, 31] (see Fig. 2 (a)), our LBA framework follows an encoder-decoder structure (see Fig. 2 (b)). The encoder Θ extracts features from multiple scene information sources. Then, the subsequent decoder Φ generates the predicted future trajectories $\widehat{\mathcal{Y}}$ based on the scene features.

The main difference between LBA and previous frameworks is the design of the encoder Θ. Our scene encoder involves two steps: 1) scene modeling, which assembles data from all three sources to generate a comprehensive representation of the current scene, and 2) scene feature extraction, which extracts the high-dimensional features from the generated scene representation. The way to represent a scene would largely determine the inner structure of a scene encoder.

In the current literature, the two most frequently used scene representations are **graph**-based and **rasterized-image**-based representations. To show that most of the existing forecasting systems can be upgraded to fit the proposed LBA prediction framework, we will describe the implementation strategies for the graph-based and rasterized-image-based systems.

4.2   Implementation

Graph-Based Systems. The existing graph-based systems represent the whole scene information into a scene graph $G(V, E)$, where V is the node set that contains both the map object node set $V_{\mathcal{M}}$ and the agent node sets $V_{\mathcal{X}}$, and E is the edge set that reflects the internal interactions between nodes. For each map object node, its associated node attributes include the geometric coordinates, reflecting the static physical location of the map object. For each agent node, its associated node attributes include the two-dimensional coordinates across various time-stamps, reflecting the movement information of the agent. The characteristics of the graph-based representation are that i) it is compact and effective, leading to an efficient system; ii) it enables effective modeling of the interactions among objects (both map objects and agents) in the scene, which is crucial for understanding complicated dynamic relations in traffic scenarios.

To implement the graph-based LBA prediction system, we emphasize the strategy of incorporating local behavior data into the scene graph and enabling the feature interaction between local behavior data and other nodes.

Representation of Local Behavior Data. Given the ith agent in the pth scene, we can query its specific local behavior data $\mathcal{B}_e^{(i,p)}$ from the behavior database $\mathcal{D}_\mathcal{B}$. For each individual observed trajectory in $\mathcal{B}_e^{(i,p)}$, we create a local behavior node. This step results in a local behavior node set $V_\mathcal{B}$, which has the same size as the local behavior data.

Scene Encoder. As demonstrated in Fig. 3, the scene encoder of the LBA graph-based systems includes the scene graph initialization, individual node feature extraction, and interactive node feature extraction. To initialize the local-behavior-aware scene graph $G'(V', E)$, we add the local behavior node set to the original graph $G(V, E)$, where the updated node set is $V' = V \cup V_\mathcal{B}$ and the updated edge set is $E' = E \cup \{(v_m, v_n) | v_m \in V', v_n \in V_\mathcal{B}\}_{m,n}$. With this graph, the local behavior data will participate in the feature interaction procedure (some methods may further update the edge set based on the node distance [15,22,43]). The output of the scene encoder $f_\mathcal{S}$ will also be local-behavior-aware. We use three feature encoders $(\Theta_\mathcal{M}, \Theta_\mathcal{X}, \Theta_\mathcal{B})$ to extract the features of map objects $f_\mathcal{M}$, agents' observed trajectories $f_\mathcal{X}$, and the local behavior data $f_\mathcal{B}$, respectively. Here each scene node will obtain its corresponding node features individually. To capture internal interactions, we use an interaction module $\mathcal{I}$, which is either GNN-based or attention-based, depending on the design of the original system. The interaction module aggregates information from all three scene components.

The architecture of $\Theta_\mathcal{M}$, $\Theta_\mathcal{X}$ and $\mathcal{I}$ can remain unchanged from the original system structure for our implementation. As for $\Theta_\mathcal{B}$, since each independent behavior data is essentially an observed trajectory, we can directly adopt the structure of the trajectory encoder $\Theta_\mathcal{X}$ in the system as our behavior encoder structure. We can also use simple encoder structures, such as multi-layer perceptrons (MLPs), to keep the system light-weight.

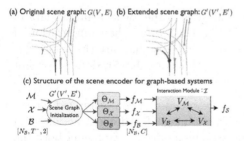

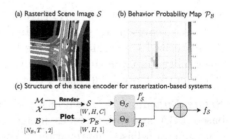

Fig. 3. Scene encoder implementation for graph-based systems. In (c): i) $V_\mathcal{B}, V_\mathcal{X}, V_\mathcal{M} \subseteq V'$ are respectively the behavior node set, motion node set, and map node set; ii) $N_\mathcal{B}$ is the size of the local behavior data; iii) C is the feature channel; iv) each trajectory in the local behavior data is encoded independently.

Fig. 4. Scene encoder implementation for rasterized-image-based systems. (a) is generated with P2T's [9] official code. In (c): features of the rasterized scene image and the local behavior are concatenated channel-wise to generate the final output features.

Rasterized-Image-Based Systems. Rasterized-image-based systems represent the whole scene information as a rasterized scene image (see an example in Fig. 4). The rasterized scene image reflects the HD map objects (junctions, lanes) and the agent trajectory information as BEV images with various colors according to their semantic labels. This representation method essentially transforms a global coordinate system into an image coordinate system, where each location on the map can be represented by a pixel coordinate. The main characteristic of rasterization-based representations is that they can leverage established CNN backbones, such as ResNet [17], to extract image features.

To implement the rasterized-image-based LBA prediction system, we need to render local behavior data to an image that has the same coordinate system with the original scene image, which ensures consistency and compatibility.

Representation of Local Behavior Data. We seek to render local behavior data into a *behavior probability map* $\mathcal{P}_\mathcal{B}$. It is an image whose pixel value reflects an agent's moving probability from the current pixel to another pixel in the image. For the ith agent at the pth scene, $\mathcal{P}_\mathcal{B}^{(i,p)}$ is formulated as a single channel image of size $(H, W, 1)$ that shares the same coordinate system with the rasterized scene image, where W, H are the width and the height of $\mathcal{P}_\mathcal{B}$. To generate such a behavior probability map, we initialize each pixel value in the image $\mathcal{P}_\mathcal{B}^{(i,p)}(x, y)$ to be 0. We then enumerate each trajectory $f_\mathcal{X} \in \mathcal{B}_\epsilon^{(i,p)}$ and add the corresponding information into $\mathcal{P}_\mathcal{B}^{(i,p)}(x, y)$ by adding 1 to the pixel value once each trajectory covers that pixel. In the end, we normalize $\mathcal{P}_\mathcal{B}^{(i,p)}$ by dividing every pixel by the maximum value of the pixels, specifically

$$\mathcal{P}_\mathcal{B}^{(i,p)}(x, y) = \frac{\mathcal{P}_\mathcal{B}^{(i,p)}(x, y)}{\max(\mathcal{P}_\mathcal{B}^{(i,p)}(x, y))}, \tag{2}$$

where $0 \leq x < W, 0 \leq y < H$. Figure 4 (b) illustrates the local behavior data of the agent represented as a red rectangle in Fig. 4 (a). Since the configuration of the rasterized scene image and the behavior probability map are the same, this probability map indicates how likely, according to local behavior data, the agent at the current pixel will pass a certain pixel on the scene image.

Scene Encoder. As shown in Fig. 4, the scene encoder of the rasterized image-based LBA systems includes image rendering, image feature extraction, and concatenation-based aggregation. To achieve scene modeling, we render both the rasterized scene image and the behavior probability map. To comprehensively extract scene features, we use two separate encoders, $\Theta_\mathcal{S}$, which extracts features from the rasterized scene image $\mathcal{S}$, and $\Theta_\mathcal{B}$, which extracts features from the behavior probability map $\mathcal{P}_\mathcal{B}$. The architecture of $\Theta_\mathcal{S}$ can remain identical with the one in the original systems. To implement $\Theta_\mathcal{B}$, we can adopt any established images' feature extraction networks, such as ResNet [17]. Afterwards, the output of the two encoders will be concatenated channel-wise to build the output of the scene encoder, which is now local-behavior-aware.

5   Local-Behavior-Free Prediction

As mentioned in Sect. 1, there will be scenarios where the local behavior data is yet to be gathered or insufficient. To handle such situations, we propose a Local-Behavior-Free (LBF) prediction framework based on knowledge distillation.

The training of the LBF prediction framework follows a teacher-student structure. The teacher network is implemented using the LBA framework introduced in Sect. 4, which uses local behavior data as the third input; while the student network only takes static HD map information and the agents' observed trajectories as the input. The knowledge-distillation-based training strategy enhances the training of the LBF prediction framework by urging the student network to imitate the teacher network in the intermediate feature levels when processing the same data samples.

The intuition behind this design is that given a specific location, the number of possible movement patterns of an traffic agent is limited. With the guidance from the teacher network that is trained on local behavior data, it is feasible for the student network to learn the reasoning of the movement pattern based on the static map objects and agents' observed trajectories.

5.1   Framework Pipeline

The LBF framework includes a teacher network and a student network. See Fig. 2 (b), (c). The teacher network follows the LBA framework. For the student network, we remove the input stream of local behavior data in the LBA framework and add a behavior estimator Ω_B to the pipeline. Ω_B takes the intermediate scene features f'_S from the scene encoder Θ as the input, and outputs the estimated local behavior features $\widehat{f}_B$. Note that f'_S is not involved with local behavioral information. Next, we let $\widehat{f}_B$ join the scene encoder along with f'_S for the final feature generation. The scene encoder outputs the updated f_S, which contains the estimated local behavioral information, to the decoder Φ. The decoder then processes f_S and generates the predicted future trajectories $\widehat{\mathcal{Y}}$. The core step of the LBF student network is to link the behavior estimator and the scene encoder.

5.2   Implementation

Like Sect. 4.2, this section introduces the implementation of the student networks in the LBF prediction framework based on two scene representations.

Graph-Based Systems. In the teacher network (the LBA prediction system), the local behavior data goes through an encoder to obtain behavior features f_B. In the student network (the LBF version), we use a behavior estimator Ω_B to estimate the behavior features even when the original local behavior data is not available. We implement the behavior estimator Ω_B by a graph neural network. Its input includes the features of the map objects f_M and the features of the agents' observed trajectories f_X, which include all scene information in hand. It outputs the estimated behavior features $\widehat{f_B}$. After $f_{\mathcal{M}}$ and $f_{\mathcal{X}}$ are interacted in the interaction module, we aggregate its output $\widehat{f_S'}$ and the estimated behavior features $\widehat{f_B}$ in a fusion module Ψ to form the final scene feature f_S. We implement Ψ by an attention-based network. The pipeline of this procedure is shown in Fig. 5. During training, the estimated behavior features $\widehat{f_B}$ in the student network can be supervised by the behavior features f_B in the teacher network through a knowledge-distillation loss.

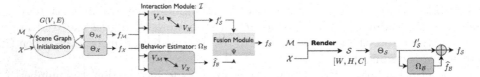

Fig. 5. Local-Behavior-Free implementation for graph-based systems. During training, $\widehat{f_B}$ and f_S can be supervised by the corresponding features from the teacher network.

Fig. 6.   Local-Behavior-Free implementation for rasterization-based systems.

Rasterized-image-based Systems. In the teacher network (the LBA prediction system), the behavior probability map leads to behavior features f_B. In the student network (the LBF version), we use a behavior estimator Ω_B to estimate such behavior features even the behavior probability map is not available. We implement the behavior estimator Ω_B by a CNN-based network. Its input is the output of the scene encoder Θ_S, which is the intermediate scene feature f_S'. Its output is the estimated behavior features $\widehat{f_B}$. We then concatenate $\widehat{f_B}$ and f_S' to form the final scene feature f_S. The pipeline of this procedure is shown in Fig. 6. During training, the estimated behavior features $\widehat{f_B}$ in the student network can be supervised by the behavior features f_B in the teacher network through a knowledge-distillation loss.

Note that both graph-based and rasterized-image-based LBF systems follow the same design rationale: estimating local behavior data based on the other known scene information. The difference between the two types of systems is in the fusion step. In the graph-based system, we use a trainable fusion module; and in the rasterized-image-based system, since the scene image and the behavior probability map share the same coordinate system, we simply concatenate them.

5.3 Training with Knowledge Distillation

To train such a teacher-student framework, we pre-train an LBA prediction network as the teacher network, and then use the intermediate features from the teacher network as the supervision signals to guide the training of the student network. We consider features from the teacher network that are leveraged to guide the student network training as $\mathbf{F}_t$ and the corresponding features from the student network as $\mathbf{F}_s$. Note that $\mathbf{F}_s$ may include but are not limited to the reconstructed local behavior features and the scene encoder's outputs.

The training loss thereafter contains the trajectory forecasting loss $\mathcal{L}_{pred}$, which is defined by the original system and identical with the training loss of the teacher network as well as a KD loss. In this work, we use ℓ_2 loss as the KD loss and set λ_{kd} as the adjustable weight of the KD loss. The overall loss function aggregates the loss over all the samples; that is,

$$\mathcal{L} = \Sigma_i \left(\lambda_{kd} \left\| \mathbf{F}_s^i - \widehat{\mathbf{F}}_t^i \right\|_2 + \mathcal{L}_{pred}^i \right). \tag{3}$$

6   Experiments

6.1   Experimental Setup

Datasets. We consider two widely used trajectory forecasting benchmarks, *nuScenes* [3] and *Argoverse* [6]. *nuScenes* collected 1000 scenes. Each scene is 20s long with a sampling rate 2 Hz. The instances for trajectory forecasting tasks were split into train, validation and test splits, which respectively entail 32186, 8560 and 9041 instances. Each agent in the instances had 2s' observed trajectories and the ground truth of 6s' future trajectories. *Argoverse* collected over 30K scenarios. Each scenario is sampled 10 Hz. The train/ val/ test splits had 205942/ 39472/ 78143 sequences respectively. Each agent in the scene had 2s' observed trajectories and the ground-truth of 3s' future trajectories.

Database Construction. To evaluate local-behavior-aware (LBA) framework without ground-truth data leakage, we only use the 2s' observed trajectories of all agents in each data split to build the behavior database $\mathcal{D}_B$ for each corresponding phase (e.g. testing phase only uses the test split). For the local-behavior-free (LBF) framework, we only use the observed trajectories from the training split during the training phase. Please see appendix for detailed information of behavior database construction.

Metrics. We adopt three widely used metrics for quantitative evaluation: minimum average displacement error among K predictions (minADE$_K$), minimum final displacement error among K predictions (minFDE$_K$) and the missing rate (MR). minADE evaluates the minimum average prediction error of all timestamps among the predicted K trajectories; minFDE is the minimum error of the final position among the K predictions; MR$_K$ is the ratio of agents whose minFDE$_K$ is larger than 2.0 m.

6.2   Implementation Details

We pick three SOTA trajectory forecasting methods: LaneGCN [23], DenseTNT [15] and P2T [9], and adapt them to our behavior-aware framework. We use their official code packages as the implementation start code. The baseline performances in Tables 1 and 2 are reproduced by ourselves for variables controlling.

LaneGCN and DenseTNT are graph-based methods. We use stacked linear residual blocks mentioned in [23] as our behavior encoder $E_\mathcal{B}$ for both methods. In the LBF prediction, we use attention based architecture to implement the behavior estimator $\Omega_\mathcal{B}$ as well as the auxiliary fusion module Ψ.

P2T is a rasterization-based method. We use *behavioral probability map* to represent the local behavior data, and ResNet [17] as the encoder backbone to extract features from the behavioral probability map. For the LBF prediction, we use three 1D Convolutional Layers to implement the behavior estimator $\Omega_\mathcal{B}$.

To train the network, we adopt the hyper-parameter configuration from each method's official instructions. More implementation details are in the appendix.

6.3   Evaluation

We evaluate LaneGCN and P2T on nuScenes (see the quantitative results in Table 1). For Argoverse, we evaluate LaneGCN and DenseTNT (see Table 2). We also show the qualitative evaluation in Fig. 7.

In all experiments, when upgraded to either the LBA or LBF framework, the baseline methods significantly improve in performance. Unconventionally, our proposed frameworks bring consistent improvements to various models (P2T, LaneGCN, DenseTNT) across **all** metrics. This is a substantive progress compared to previous methods, because SOTA methods [12,14,41,43] usually only show improvements in one or some metrics but not all metrics. Furthermore, on both datasets, the gains brought by local behavior data are consistently larger on $K = 1$ metrics than on other metrics. This may result from the raise of average performance of the worst prediction among K predictions, as local behavior data efficiently narrows down the solution search space (explained in Sect. 1).

Table 1. Evaluation results on nuScenes [3] dataset test split.

Method	Framework	minADE$_1$	minFDE$_1$	minADE$_{10}$	minFDE$_{10}$
P2T [9]	Baseline	4.60	10.80	1.17	2.15
	LBA	3.78 ↓ 18%	9.25 ↓ 14%	1.08 ↓ 8%	2.04 ↓ 5%
	LBF	4.04 ↓ 12%	9.54 ↓ 12%	1.15 ↓ 2%	2.11 ↓ 2%
LaneGCN [23]	Baseline	6.17	12.34	1.82	2.98
	LBA	2.72 ↓ 56%	6.78 ↓ 45%	0.95 ↓ 48%	1.85 ↓ 38%
	LBF	5.58 ↓ 10%	11.47 ↓ 7%	1.67 ↓ 8%	2.66 ↓ 11%

Interestingly, the prediction performance of the LBF framework occasionally surpasses that of the LBA framework, even though the LBF framework lacks local behavior data input. Table 2 shows an example of this case, with the LaneGCN results on Argoverse. Our educated conjecture is that sometimes the LBF framework enjoys more data representativeness thanks to the reconstructed behavioral features; whereas, in the meantime, the LBA framework may be using pre-gathered local behavior data of a small size in its testing phase.

Besides the comparison with the baselines, we also show the comparison with the other published works on the benchmarks; see Tables 3 and 4.

Table 2. Evaluation results on Argoverse [6] dataset test split.

Method	Framework	minADE$_1$	minFDE$_1$	minADE$_6$	minFDE$_6$
LaneGCN [23]	Baseline	1.74	3.89	0.87	1.37
	LBA	1.64 ↓ 6%	3.61 ↓ 7%	0.84 ↓ 3%	1.30 ↓ 5%
	LBF	1.61 ↓ 7%	3.54 ↓ 9%	0.85 ↓ 2%	1.31 ↓ 4%
DenseTNT [15]	Baseline	1.70	3.72	0.90	1.33
	LBA	1.65 ↓ 3%	3.57 ↓ 4%	0.88 ↓ 2%	1.26 ↓ 5%
	LBF	1.67 ↓ 2%	3.63 ↓ 2%	0.89 ↓ 2%	1.29 ↓ 3%

Table 3. nuScenes benchmark comparison.

Method	minADE$_{10}$	MR$_5$	MR$_{10}$	minFDE$_1$
P2T [9]	1.16	64%	46%	10.50
MHA-JAM [29]	1.24	59%	46%	8.57
SGNet [38]	1.40	67%	52%	9.25
Trajectron++ [33]	1.51	70%	57%	9.52
M-SCOUT [4]	1.92	78%	78%	9.29
GOHOME [12]	1.15	57%	47%	6.99
P2T-LBA	1.08	57%	41%	9.25
P2T-LBF	1.15	61%	46%	9.37
LaneGCN-LBA	0.95	49%	36%	6.78
LaneGCN-LBF	1.67	75%	68%	11.47

Table 4. Argoverse benchmark comparison.

Method	minADE$_1$	minADE$_6$	Brier-FDE$_6$
LaneRCNN [43]	1.69	0.90	2.15
DenseTNT [15]	1.68	0.88	1.98
GOHOME [12]	1.69	0.94	1.98
MMTransformer [24]	1.77	0.84	2.03
LaneGCN [23]	1.71	0.87	2.06
LaneGCN-LBA	1.64	0.84	2.00
LaneGCN-LBF	1.61	0.85	2.00
DenseTNT-LBA	1.65	0.88	1.93
DenseTNT-LBF	1.67	0.89	1.96

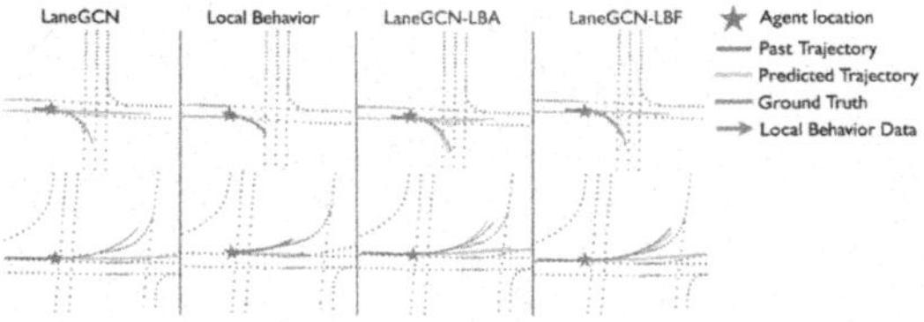

Fig. 7. LaneGCN qualitative results on Argoverse val split.

Table 5. minFDE$_1$ of LaneGCN on Argoverse val split among agents having different sizes of local behavior data.

Size	% of agents	Baseline	LBA
$[0, 4)$	24%	3.33	3.36
$[4, 8)$	14%	3.25	3.19 ↓ 2%
$[8, 12)$	10%	3.22	3.13 ↓ 3%
$[12, 16)$	9%	3.00	2.87 ↓ 4%
$[16, \infty)$	43%	2.66	2.60 ↓ 2%

6.4   Ablation Study

We conduct the ablation study on the hyper-parameters regarding local behavior data generation and our prediction frameworks.

Local Behavior Data Size. Regarding the relationship between prediction performance and the local behavior data size of each agent, Table 5 shows: when there is few local behavior data, prediction is not as accurate as the baseline; but, even a small size of local behavior data can improve the prediction.

Local Range ϵ. The adjustable parameter ϵ defines the local radius (see Sect. 3). See Table 6 for the impact of ϵ on LaneGCN performance with Argoverse test split. When ϵ increases, the performance of the LBA framework first go up but later go down. It matches our intuition that a large ϵ will introduce distractions. The LBF framework, however, shows less confusion brought by the pre-trained LBA network, demonstrating stronger robustness to ϵ.

Knowledge Distillation Parameters. We study the impact of knowledge-distillation-related parameters, i.e., the loss weight λ_{kd} and the number of times that intermediate features are involved in the KD loss (denoted as KD times). See the results in Table 7. Detailed information about the choices of intermediate features is in the appendix. We see that firstly, the knowledge distillation structure does help the framework infer the impact of local behavior data. The framework, across all parameter settings in Table 7, outperforms the baseline method (in Table 2, row 1) and the model without KD loss (in Table 7, row 1). Secondly, the comparatively similar results across all the settings show that the LBF framework is relatively robust to the KD hyper-parameters.

Table 6. Impact of the behavioral data's local range. A larger ϵ brings a larger size of local behavior data, but when ϵ is too large, it can also introduce confusion due to the loss of the data locality.

Framework	ϵ	minADE$_1$	minFDE$_1$
LBA	0.5 m	1.64	3.61
	1.0 m	1.62	3.58
	1.5 m	1.71	3.86
LBF	0.5 m	1.61	3.54
	1.0 m	1.62	3.57
	1.5 m	1.63	3.59

Table 7. Impact of the number of times that KD supervision gets applied in the training phase and the weight of the KD loss.

KD times	λ_{kd}	minADE$_1$	minFDE$_1$
N/A	0	1.68	3.72
2	1	1.62	3.57
2	1.5	**1.61**	**3.54**
2	2	1.62	3.56
1	1.5	1.64	3.61
3	1.5	1.61	3.56

7   Conclusion

In this work, we re-introduce the local historical trajectories as a new type of data input to the trajectory forecasting task, referred as *local behavior data*. To adapt to this new data input and fully exploit its value, we propose a behavior-*aware* framework and a behavior-*free* framework for trajectory forecasting. The behavior-free framework, especially, adopts a knowledge-distillation architecture to estimate the impact of local behavior data. Extensive experiments on published benchmarks validate that the proposed frameworks significantly improve the performances of SOTA methods on prevalent metrics.

Limitations. Local historical information reveals local motion patterns with high fidelity, but there are always outliers. For use cases of great safety concerns (e.g. autonomous driving), historical data may provide good reference but should not be the only reference. Also, the motion patterns of a certain location can vary over time. To optimize the benefits of the LBA and LBF framework, future research should explore the historical data gathering strategies.

Acknowledgements. National Natural Science Foundation of China under Grant 62171276, the Science and Technology Commission of Shanghai Municipal under Grant 21511100900, CCF-DiDi GAIA Research Collaboration Plan 202112 and CALT 2021-01.

References

1. Alahi, A., Goel, K., Ramanathan, V., Robicquet, A., Fei-Fei, I., Savarese, S.: Social LSTM: human trajectory prediction in crowded spaces. In: Proceedings of the IEEE Conference On Computer Vision and Pattern Recognition, pp. 961–971 (2016)
2. Bennewitz, M., Burgard, W., Thrun, S.: Learning motion patterns of persons for mobile service robots. In: Proceedings 2002 IEEE International Conference on Robotics and Automation (Cat. No. 02CH37292), vol. 4, pp. 3601–3606. IEEE (2002)
3. Caesar, H., et al.: nuscenes: A multimodal dataset for autonomous driving. In: Proceedings of the IEEE/CVF Conference on Computer Vision and Pattern Recognition, pp. 11621–11631 (2020)
4. Carrasco, S., Llorca, D.F., Sotelo, M.Á.: SCOUT: socially-consistent and understandable graph attention network for trajectory prediction of vehicles and VRUs. arXiv preprint arXiv:2102.06361 (2021)
5. Casas, S., Luo, W., Urtasun, R.: Intentnet: learning to predict intention from raw sensor data. In: Conference on Robot Learning, pp. 947–956. PMLR (2018)
6. Chang, M.F., et al.: Argoverse: 3d tracking and forecasting with rich maps. In: Proceedings of the IEEE/CVF Conference on Computer Vision and Pattern Recognition, pp. 8748–8757 (2019)
7. Chen, G., Choi, W., Yu, X., Han, T., Chandraker, M.: Learning efficient object detection models with knowledge distillation. Adv. Neural. Inf. Process. Syst. **30**, 1–10 (2017)
8. De Leege, A., van Paassen, M., Mulder, M.: A machine learning approach to trajectory prediction. In: AIAA Guidance, Navigation, and Control (GNC) Conference, p. 4782 (2013)
9. Deo, N., Trivedi, M.M.: Trajectory forecasts in unknown environments conditioned on grid-based plans. arXiv preprint arXiv:2001.00735 (2020)
10. Deo, N., Wolff, E., Beijbom, O.: Multimodal trajectory prediction conditioned on lane-graph traversals. In: 5th Annual Conference on Robot Learning (2021)
11. Gao, J., et al.: VectorNet: Encoding HD maps and agent dynamics from vectorized representation. In: Proceedings of the IEEE/CVF Conference on Computer Vision and Pattern Recognition, pp. 11525–11533 (2020)
12. Gilles, T., Sabatini, S., Tsishkou, D., Stanciulescu, B., Moutarde, F.: Gohome: graph-oriented heatmap output for future motion estimation. arXiv preprint arXiv:2109.01827 (2021)
13. Gilles, T., Sabatini, S., Tsishkou, D., Stanciulescu, B., Moutarde, F.: Home: heatmap output for future motion estimation. arXiv preprint arXiv:2105.10968 (2021)

14. Gilles, T., Sabatini, S., Tsishkou, D., Stanciulescu, B., Moutarde, F.: Thomas: trajectory heatmap output with learned multi-agent sampling. arXiv:2110.06607 (2021)
15. Gu, J., Sun, C., Zhao, H.: DenseTNT: end-to-end trajectory prediction from dense goal sets. In: Proceedings of the IEEE/CVF International Conference on Computer Vision, pp. 15303–15312 (2021)
16. Hao, Y., Fu, Y., Jiang, Y.G., Tian, Q.: An end-to-end architecture for class-incremental object detection with knowledge distillation. In: 2019 IEEE International Conference on Multimedia and Expo (ICME), pp. 1–6. IEEE (2019)
17. He, K., Zhang, X., Ren, S., Sun, J.: Deep residual learning for image recognition. In: Proceedings of the IEEE Conference on Computer Vision and Pattern Recognition, pp. 770–778 (2016)
18. He, T., Shen, C., Tian, Z., Gong, D., Sun, C., Yan, Y.: Knowledge adaptation for efficient semantic segmentation. In: Proceedings of the IEEE/CVF Conference on Computer Vision and Pattern Recognition, pp. 578–587 (2019)
19. Hinton, G., Vinyals, O., Dean, J.: Distilling the knowledge in a neural network. arXiv preprint arXiv:1503.02531 (2015)
20. Hu, Y., Chen, S., Zhang, Y., Gu, X.: Collaborative motion prediction via neural motion message passing. In: Proceedings of the IEEE/CVF Conference on Computer Vision and Pattern Recognition, pp. 6319–6328 (2020)
21. Kim, B., Kang, C.M., Kim, J., Lee, S.H., Chung, C.C., Choi, J.W.: Probabilistic vehicle trajectory prediction over occupancy grid map via recurrent neural network. In: 2017 IEEE 20th International Conference on Intelligent Transportation Systems (ITSC), pp. 399–404. IEEE (2017)
22. Li, Y., Ren, S., Wu, P., Chen, S., Feng, C., Zhang, W.: Learning distilled collaboration graph for multi-agent perception. arXiv preprint arXiv:2111.00643 (2021)
23. Liang, M., et al.: Learning lane graph representations for motion forecasting. In: Vedaldi, A., Bischof, H., Brox, T., Frahm, J.-M. (eds.) ECCV 2020. LNCS, vol. 12347, pp. 541–556. Springer, Cham (2020). https://doi.org/10.1007/978-3-030-58536-5_32
24. Liu, Y., Zhang, J., Fang, L., Jiang, Q., Zhou, B.: Multimodal motion prediction with stacked transformers. In: Proceedings of the IEEE/CVF Conference on Computer Vision and Pattern Recognition, pp. 7577–7586 (2021)
25. Liu, Y., Chen, K., Liu, C., Qin, Z., Luo, Z., Wang, J.: Structured knowledge distillation for semantic segmentation. In: Proceedings of the IEEE/CVF Conference on Computer Vision and Pattern Recognition, pp. 2604–2613 (2019)
26. Liu, Y., Dong, X., Lu, X., Khan, F.S., Shen, J., Hoi, S.: Teacher-students knowledge distillation for Siamese trackers. arXiv preprint arXiv:1907.10586 (2019)
27. Luo, Y., Cai, P., Bera, A., Hsu, D., Lee, W.S., Manocha, D.: PORCA: modeling and planning for autonomous driving among many pedestrians. IEEE Robot. Autom. Lett. 3(4), 3418–3425 (2018)
28. Marchetti, F., Becattini, F., Seidenari, L., Bimbo, A.D.: MANTRA: memory augmented networks for multiple trajectory prediction. In: Proceedings of the IEEE/CVF Conference on Computer Vision and Pattern Recognition, pp. 7143–7152 (2020)
29. Messaoud, K., Deo, N., Trivedi, M.M., Nashashibi, F.: Trajectory prediction for autonomous driving based on multi-head attention with joint agent-map representation. arXiv preprint arXiv:2005.02545 (2020)
30. Nikhil, N., Morris, B.T.: Convolutional neural network for trajectory prediction. In: Leal-Taixé, L., Roth, S. (eds.) ECCV 2018. LNCS, vol. 11131, pp. 186–196. Springer, Cham (2019). https://doi.org/10.1007/978-3-030-11015-4_16

31. Phan-Minh, T., Grigore, E.C., Boulton, F.A., Beijbom, O., Wolff, E.M.: Cover-Net: multimodal behavior prediction using trajectory sets. In: Proceedings of the IEEE/CVF Conference on Computer Vision and Pattern Recognition, pp. 14074–14083 (2020)
32. Qi, C.R., Yi, L., Su, H., Guibas, L.J.: PointNet++: deep hierarchical feature learning on point sets in a metric space. arXiv preprint arXiv:1706.02413 (2017)
33. Salzmann, T., Ivanovic, B., Chakravarty, P., Pavone, M.: Trajectron++: dynamically-feasible trajectory forecasting with heterogeneous data. In: Vedaldi, A., Bischof, H., Brox, T., Frahm, J.-M. (eds.) ECCV 2020. LNCS, vol. 12363, pp. 683–700. Springer, Cham (2020). https://doi.org/10.1007/978-3-030-58523-5_40
34. Scarselli, F., Gori, M., Tsoi, A.C., Hagenbuchner, M., Monfardini, G.: The graph neural network model. IEEE Trans. Neural Netw. **20**(1), 61–80 (2008)
35. Sun, C., Karlsson, P., Wu, J., Tenenbaum, J.B., Murphy, K.: Stochastic prediction of multi-agent interactions from partial observations. arXiv preprint arXiv:1902.09641 (2019)
36. Sun, C., Shrivastava, A., Vondrick, C., Sukthankar, R., Murphy, K., Schmid, C.: Relational action forecasting. In: Proceedings of the IEEE/CVF Conference on Computer Vision and Pattern Recognition, pp. 273–283 (2019)
37. Vaswani, A., et al.: Attention is all you need. In: Advances in Neural Information Processing Systems, pp. 5998–6008 (2017)
38. Wang, C., Wang, Y., Xu, M., Crandall, D.J.: Stepwise goal-driven networks for trajectory prediction. arXiv preprint arXiv:2103.14107 (2021)
39. Xu, C., Li, M., Ni, Z., Zhang, Y., Chen, S.: GroupNet: multiscale hypergraph neural networks for trajectory prediction with relational reasoning. In: Proceedings of the IEEE/CVF Conference on Computer Vision and Pattern Recognition, pp. 6498–6507 (2022)
40. Xu, C., Mao, W., Zhang, W., Chen, S.: Remember intentions: retrospective-memory-based trajectory prediction. In: Proceedings of the IEEE/CVF Conference on Computer Vision and Pattern Recognition, pp. 6488–6497 (2022)
41. Ye, M., Cao, T., Chen, Q.: TPCN: temporal point cloud networks for motion forecasting. In: Proceedings of the IEEE/CVF Conference on Computer Vision and Pattern Recognition, pp. 11318–11327 (2021)
42. Yu, C., Ma, X., Ren, J., Zhao, H., Yi, S.: Spatio-temporal graph transformer networks for pedestrian trajectory prediction. In: Vedaldi, A., Bischof, H., Brox, T., Frahm, J.-M. (eds.) ECCV 2020. LNCS, vol. 12357, pp. 507–523. Springer, Cham (2020). https://doi.org/10.1007/978-3-030-58610-2_30
43. Zeng, W., Liang, M., Liao, R., Urtasun, R.: LanerCNN: distributed representations for graph-centric motion forecasting. arXiv preprint arXiv:2101.06653 (2021)
44. Zhao, H., et al.: Tnt: Target-driven trajectory prediction. arXiv preprint arXiv:2008.08294 (2020)
45. Zhao, H., Wildes, R.P.: Where are you heading? Dynamic trajectory prediction with expert goal examples. In: Proceedings of the IEEE/CVF International Conference on Computer Vision, pp. 7629–7638 (2021)

Optical Flow Training Under Limited Label Budget via Active Learning

Shuai Yuan(✉), Xian Sun, Hannah Kim, Shuzhi Yu,
and Carlo Tomasi

Duke University, Durham, NC 27708, USA
{shuai,hannah,shuzhiyu,tomasi}@cs.duke.edu, xian.sun@duke.edu

Abstract. Supervised training of optical flow predictors generally yields better accuracy than unsupervised training. However, the improved performance comes at an often high annotation cost. Semi-supervised training trades off accuracy against annotation cost. We use a simple yet effective semi-supervised training method to show that even a small fraction of labels can improve flow accuracy by a significant margin over unsupervised training. In addition, we propose active learning methods based on simple heuristics to further reduce the number of labels required to achieve the same target accuracy. Our experiments on both synthetic and real optical flow datasets show that our semi-supervised networks generally need around 50% of the labels to achieve close to full-label accuracy, and only around 20% with active learning on Sintel. We also analyze and show insights on the factors that may influence active learning performance. Code is available at https://github.com/duke-vision/optical-flow-active-learning-release.

Keywords: Optical flow · Active learning · Label efficiency

1 Introduction

The estimation of optical flow is a very important but challenging task in computer vision with broad applications including video understanding [7], video editing [9], object tracking [1], and autonomous driving [34].

Inspired by the successes of deep CNNs in various computer vision tasks [12, 23], much recent work has modeled optical flow estimation in the framework of supervised learning, and has proposed several networks of increasingly high performance on benchmark datasets [5,14,15,38,47,49,60]. Ground-truth labels provide a strong supervision signal when training these networks. However, ground-truth optical flow annotations are especially hard and expensive to obtain. Thus, many methods use synthetic data in training, since ground-truth

Supplementary Information The online version contains supplementary material available at https://doi.org/10.1007/978-3-031-20047-2_24.

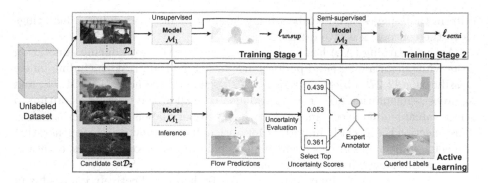

Fig. 1. Overview of our active learning framework for the semi-supervised training.

labels can be generated as part of data synthesis. Nevertheless, it is still an open question whether synthetic data are an adequate proxy for real data.

Another way to circumvent label scarcity is unsupervised training, which does not require any labels at all. Instead, it relies on unsupervised loss measures that enforce exact or approximate constraints that correct outputs should satisfy. Common losses used in unsupervised optical flow estimation are the photometric loss, which penalizes large color differences between corresponding points, and the smoothness loss, which penalizes abrupt spatial changes in the flow field [17, 18,28,29,33,40]. While unsupervised methods allow training on large datasets from the application domain, their performance is still far from ideal because the assumed constraints do not always hold. For instance, the photometric loss works poorly with non-Lambertian surfaces or in occlusion regions [52], while the smoothness loss fails near motion discontinuities [21].

Semi-supervised training can be a way to combine the advantages of both supervised and unsupervised training for optical flow models. The idea is simple, and amounts to training the network with a mix of labeled and unlabeled data. This is possible because we can charge different losses (supervised or unsupervised) to different samples depending on whether they are labeled or not.

The trade-off between performance and labeling cost is of interest in real practice, since it describes the marginal benefit that can be accrued at the price of a unit of labeling effort. However, little work has focused on the semi-supervised training of optical flow. Existing methods have tried to improve flow estimates given an available, partially labeled dataset [24,45,57]. Other work uses semi-supervised training to address specific problem conditions, *e.g.*, foggy scenes [56].

In contrast, we are particularly interested in label efficiency, that is, in the performance improvement gained as the fraction of labeled samples increases from 0 ("unsupervised") to 1 ("supervised"). Specifically, we use a simple yet effective semi-supervised algorithm and show that the model error drops significantly as soon as a small fraction of the samples are labeled. This suggests that even a modest labeling budget can lead to a significant performance boost.

Given a specific labeling budget, an important related question is how to determine which part of the dataset to label. A simple method is random sampling, but it is possible to do better. Specifically, we propose and evaluate criteria that suggest whose labels bring larger benefits in training. This brings us to the concept of active learning.

Active Learning (AL) has been shown to be effective in reducing annotation costs while maintaining good performance in many vision tasks including image classification [2,27], object detection [4,42], semantic segmentation [31,44], and instance segmentation [51]. The general idea is to allow the training algorithm to select valuable unlabeled samples for which to query labels for further training. This selection is especially important for optical flow estimation, since generating labels for additional samples incurs high costs in terms of computation, curation, and sometimes even hand annotations.

While annotating individual flow vectors by hand is effectively impossible in practice, annotation can be and often is done by hand at a higher level and, even so, is costly. For instance, in KITTI 2015 [34], correspondences between points on CAD models of moving cars are annotated by hand so that dense optical flow can be inferred for these cars. In addition, nonrigid objects such as pedestrians or bicyclists are manually masked out, and so are errors in the flow and disparity masks inferred from LiDAR and GPS/IMU measurements and from stereo depth estimation. This is still manual annotation and curation, painstaking and expensive. Some amount of curation, at the very least, is necessary for most high-quality training sets with real imagery, and the methods we propose aim to reduce the need for this type of work, and to make the products of whatever manual work is left more effective. To the best of our knowledge, we are the first to study active learning as a way to moderate the high annotation costs for optical flow estimation.

As illustrated in Fig. 1, our training pipeline (top part of the diagram) includes an unsupervised first stage and a semi-supervised second stage. We split our unlabeled dataset to two sets, one ($\mathcal{D}_1$) used to pre-train an unsupervised model $\mathcal{M}_1$ and the other ($\mathcal{D}_2$) used as the *candidate* set, from which samples are selected to query labels from expert annotators. After training model $\mathcal{M}_1$ on $\mathcal{D}_1$ in Stage 1, we estimate flow for all the samples in $\mathcal{D}_2$ and score each of them based on our active learning criteria. We query for labels for top-scoring samples and add these to $\mathcal{D}_2$ for further semi-supervised training in Stage 2. In this paper, we show that using active learning to query labels can help further reduce the number of labels required to achieve a given performance target in semi-supervised training.

In summary, our contributions are as follows.

- We show on several synthetic and real-life datasets that the performance from unsupervised training of optical flow estimators can be improved significantly as soon as a relatively small fraction of labels are added for semi-supervised training.
- To the best of our knowledge, we are the first to explore active learning as a way to save annotation cost for optical flow estimation, and our novel pipeline can be used directly in real practice.
- We set up the new problem of semi-supervised training of optical flow under certain label ratio constraints. We anticipate follow-up research to propose better methods for this problem.

2 Related Work

Supervised Optical Flow. Supervised methods use deep networks to learn the mapping from image pairs to the corresponding optical flow by minimizing the supervised loss, namely, some distance measure between computed and true flow. FlowNet [5] used a multi-scale encoder-decoder structure with skip connections between same-scale layers. Following this framework, many networks have been proposed to decrease both model size and error. Traditional ideas or heuristics have been introduced into the network, including image pyramid in SPyNet [38], feature pyramid, warping, and cost volume in PWC-Net [47] and LiteFlowNet [14]. Iterative decoder modules have also been explored as a way to reduce model size while retaining accuracy in IRR-PWC [15] and RAFT [49]. The latter built the network based on full-pair correlations and has led to many follow-up models that have achieved the state-of-the-art performance [60].

Unsupervised Optical Flow. Recent research has focused on the unsupervised learning of optical flow as a compromise between label availability and model performance. Initial work on this topic proposed to train FlowNet-like networks using surrogate loss terms, namely photometric loss and smoothness loss [18,40]. As found by many papers, flow at occlusion region is especially challenging for unsupervised networks [52]. Thus, much research focused on solving the occlusion problem via occlusion masks [52], bi-directional consistency [33], multi-frame consistency [17,41], and self-supervised teacher-student models [29,59]. ARFlow [28] integrated a second forward pass using transformed inputs for augmentation and has achieved the state-of-the-art unsupervised performance. Multi-frame unsupervised models have also been investigated [17,46].

Semi-supervised Training in Vision. Semi-supervised training targets applications where partial labels are available. Early approaches in image classification [11,25,35,43] utilize label propagation with regularization and augmentation based on the belief that nearby data points tend to have similar class labels. A more recent class of methods train on unlabeled samples with pseudo-labels [26,55] predicted by a supervised trained network trained with labeled samples. Similar teacher-student models have also been explored [30,48].

Although widely explored in many other vision tasks, there is little work on semi-supervised optical flow. Some early work utilized semi-supervised learning to achieve comparable flow accuracy to the supervised methods [24,24,45,57]. Others applied semi-supervised methods to tackle specific cases of optical flow, such as dense foggy scenes [56] and ultrasound elastography [50]. In contrast, we focus on label efficiency for optical flow estimation: Instead of proposing semi-supervised networks that focus on improving benchmark performances by adding external unlabeled data, we are more focused on the trade-off between performance and label ratio given a fixed dataset.

Active Learning in Vision. Active Learning (AL) aims to maximize model performance with the least amount of labeled data by keeping a human in the training loop. The general idea is to make the model actively select the most valuable unlabeled samples and query the human for labels which are used in the next stage of training. There are two main categories, namely, uncertainty-based (select samples based on some pre-defined uncertainty metric) [6,8,13,20], and distribution-based (query representative samples of sufficient diversity) [37,54].

Active learning has achieved extensive success in various fields in computer vision, including image classification [2,27], object detection [4,42], semantic segmentation [31,44], and instance segmentation [51]. However, the concept has received little attention in optical flow estimation where acquiring labels is especially difficult. To the best of our knowledge, we are the first to apply active learning to optical flow estimation to reduce annotation cost.

3   Method

As we are among the first to explore active learning as a way to tackle the high annotation costs in optical flow training, we start from simple yet effective methods to implement our ideas. This section describes our semi-supervised training method (Sect. 3.1), active learning heuristics (Sect. 3.2), and network structure and loss functions (Sect. 3.3).

3.1   Semi-supervised Training

Given a partially labeled data set, we implement the semi-supervised training by charging a supervised loss to the labeled samples and an unsupervised loss to the unlabeled ones. Specifically, the semi-supervised loss for each sample x is

$$\ell_{\text{semi}}(x) = \begin{cases} \ell_{\text{unsup}}(x), & \text{if } x \text{ is unlabeled,} \\ \alpha\ell_{\text{sup}}(x), & \text{otherwise} \end{cases} \tag{1}$$

where $\alpha > 0$ is a balancing weight. We do not include the unsupervised loss for labeled samples (although in principle this is also an option) to avoid any conflict between the two losses, especially on occlusion and motion boundary regions.

Thus, the final loss of the data set $\mathcal{D} = \mathcal{D}^u \cup \mathcal{D}^l$ is

$$\mathcal{L}_{\text{semi}} = \sum_{x \in \mathcal{D}} \ell_{\text{semi}}(x) = \sum_{x \in \mathcal{D}^u} \ell_{\text{unsup}}(x) + \alpha \sum_{x \in \mathcal{D}^l} \ell_{\text{sup}}(x), \tag{2}$$

where $\mathcal{D}^u$ and $\mathcal{D}^l$ are the unlabeled and labeled sets. We define the *label ratio* as $r = |\mathcal{D}^l|/|\mathcal{D}|$. During training, we randomly shuffle the training set $\mathcal{D}$, so that each batch of data has a mix of labeled and unlabeled samples.

3.2   Active Learning Heuristics

Figure 1 shows a general overview of our active learning framework. After pre-training our model on unlabeled data (Stage 1), we invoke an active learning algorithm to determine samples to be labeled for further training. Specifically, we first use the pre-trained model to infer flow on the samples of another disjoint unlabeled data set (the *candidate* set) and select a fraction of the samples to be labeled, based on some criterion. After obtaining those labels, we continue to train the model on the partially labeled candidate set using the semi-supervised loss (Stage 2). Note that in this second stage, we do not include the unlabeled data used in pre-training (see ablation study in Sect. 4.5). By allowing the model to actively select samples to query labels, we expect the model to achieve the best possible performance under a fixed ratio of label queries (the "label budget").

So, what criteria should be used for selecting samples to be labeled? Many so-called uncertainty-based methods for active learning algorithms for image classification or segmentation use the soft-max scores to compute how confident the model is about a particular output. However, optical flow estimation is a regression problem, not a classification problem, so soft-max scores are typically not available, and would be in any case difficult to calibrate.

Instead, we select samples for labelling based on heuristics specific to the optical flow problem. For example, the photometric loss is low for good predictions. In addition, unsupervised flow estimation performs poorly at occlusion regions and motion discontinuities. These considerations suggest the following heuristic metrics to flag points for which unsupervised estimates of flow are poor:

- *Photo loss*: the photometric loss used in training.
- *Occ ratio*: the ratio of occlusion pixels in the frame, with occlusion estimated by consistency check of forward and backward flows [33].
- *Flow grad norm*: the magnitude of gradients of the estimated flow field as in [16] averaged across the frame, used to indicate the presence of motion boundaries.

We experiment with three active learning methods, each using one of the metrics above. When querying labels for a given label ratio r, we first compute the metric for each sample in the candidate set, and then sort and pick the samples with largest uncertainties as our queries.

3.3 Network Structure and Loss Functions

Network Structure. We adopt the unsupervised state-of-the-art, ARFlow [28], as our base network, which is basically a lightweight variant of PWC-Net [47]. PWC-Net-based structures have been shown to be successful in both supervised and unsupervised settings, so it is a good fit for our hybrid semi-supervised training. We do not choose RAFT because it has been mostly proven to work well in the supervised setting, while our setting (Sect. 4.4) is much closer to the unsupervised one (see appendix for details).

Each sample is a triple $x = (I_1, I_2, U_{12})$ where $I_1, I_2 \in \mathbb{R}^{h \times w \times 3}$ are the two input frames and U_{12} is the true optical flow (set as "None" for unlabeled samples). The network estimates a multi-scale forward flow field $f(I_1, I_2) = \{\hat{U}_{12}^{(2)}, \hat{U}_{12}^{(3)}, \cdots, \hat{U}_{12}^{(6)}\}$, where the output $\hat{U}_{12}^{(l)}$ at scale l has dimension $\frac{h}{2^l} \times \frac{w}{2^l} \times 2$. The finest estimated scale is $\hat{U}_{12}^{(2)}$, which is up-sampled to yield the final output.

Unsupervised Loss. For unsupervised loss $\ell_{\text{unsup}}(\boldsymbol{x})$ we follow ARFlow [28], which includes a photometric loss $\ell_{\text{ph}}(\boldsymbol{x})$, a smoothness loss $\ell_{\text{sm}}(\boldsymbol{x})$, and an augmentation loss $\ell_{\text{aug}}(\boldsymbol{x})$:

$$\ell_{\text{unsup}}(\boldsymbol{x}) = \ell_{\text{ph}}(\boldsymbol{x}) + \lambda_{\text{sm}}\ell_{\text{sm}}(\boldsymbol{x}) + \lambda_{\text{aug}}\ell_{\text{aug}}(\boldsymbol{x}). \tag{3}$$

Specifically, given the sample $\boldsymbol{x}$, we first estimate both forward and backward flow, $\hat{U}_{12}^{(l)}$ and $\hat{U}_{21}^{(l)}$, and then apply forward-backward consistency check [33] to estimate their corresponding occlusion masks, $\hat{O}_{12}^{(l)}$ and $\hat{O}_{21}^{(l)}$.

To compute the photometric loss, we first warp the frames by $\hat{I}_1^{(l)}(\boldsymbol{p}) = I_2^{(l)}(\boldsymbol{p} + \hat{U}_{12}^{(l)}(\boldsymbol{p}))$, where $I_2^{(l)}$ is I_2 down-sampled to the l-th scale and $\boldsymbol{p}$ denotes pixel coordinates at that scale. The occlusion-aware photometric loss at each scale can be then defined as

$$\ell_{\text{ph}}^{(l)}(\boldsymbol{x}) = \sum_{i=1}^{3} c_i \, \rho_i(\hat{I}_1^{(l)}, I_1^{(l)}, \hat{O}_{12}^{(l)}) \tag{4}$$

where ρ_1, ρ_2, ρ_3 are three distance measures with the estimated occlusion region filtered out in computation. As proposed in [28], these three measures are the L_1-norm, structural similarity (SSIM) [53], and the ternary census loss [33], respectively, weighted by c_i.

The edge-aware smoothness loss of each scale l is computed using the second-order derivatives:

$$\ell_{\text{sm}}^{(l)}(\boldsymbol{x}) = \frac{1}{2|\Omega^{(l)}|} \sum_{z \in \{x,y\}} \sum_{\boldsymbol{p} \in \Omega^{(l)}} \left\| \frac{\partial^2 \hat{U}_{12}^{(l)}(\boldsymbol{p})}{\partial z^2} \right\|_1 e^{-\delta \left\| \frac{\partial I_1(\boldsymbol{p})}{\partial z} \right\|_1}, \tag{5}$$

where $\delta = 10$ is a scaling parameter, and $\Omega^{(l)}$ denotes the set of pixel coordinates on the l-th scale.

We combine the losses of each scale linearly using weights $w_{\text{ph}}^{(l)}$ and $w_{\text{sm}}^{(l)}$ by

$$\ell_{\text{ph}}(\boldsymbol{x}) = \sum_{l=2}^{6} w_{\text{ph}}^{(l)} \ell_{\text{ph}}^{(l)}(\boldsymbol{x}), \quad \ell_{\text{sm}}(\boldsymbol{x}) = \sum_{l=2}^{6} w_{\text{sm}}^{(l)} \ell_{\text{sm}}^{(l)}(\boldsymbol{x}). \tag{6}$$

We also include the photometric and smoothness loss for the backward temporal direction, which is not shown here for conciseness.

After the first forward pass of the network, ARFlow also conducts an additional forward pass on input images transformed with random spatial, appearance, and occlusion transformations to mimic online augmentation. The augmentation loss $\ell_{\text{aug}}(\boldsymbol{x})$ is then computed based on the consistency between outputs before and after the transformation. See [28] for details.

Supervised Loss. For supervised loss $\ell_{\text{sup}}(\boldsymbol{x})$, we apply the multi-scale robust L_1-norm

$$\ell_{\text{sup}}(\boldsymbol{x}) = \sum_{l=2}^{6} \frac{w_{\text{sup}}^{(l)}}{|\Omega^{(l)}|} \sum_{\boldsymbol{p} \in \Omega^{(l)}} (\|\hat{U}_{12}^{(l)}(\boldsymbol{p}) - U_{12}^{(l)}(\boldsymbol{p})\|_1 + \epsilon)^q, \tag{7}$$

where $U_{12}^{(l)}$ is the down-sampled true flow to the l-th scale. A small ϵ and $q < 1$ is included to penalize less on outliers. We set $\epsilon = 0.01$ and $q = 0.4$ as in [47].

Semi-supervised Loss. The semi-supervised loss is computed by Eq. (1).

4   Experimental Results

4.1   Datasets

As most optical flow methods, we train and evaluate our method on Fly-ingChairs [5], FlyingThings3D [32], Sintel [3], and KITTI [10,34] datasets. Apart from the labeled datasets, raw Sintel and KITTI frames with no labels are also available and often used in recent unsupervised work [28,29,39,58]. As common practice, we have excluded the labeled samples from the raw Sintel and KITTI datasets.

In our experiments, we also split our own train and validation set on Sintel and KITTI. We split Sintel clean and final passes by scenes to 1,082 training samples and 1,000 validation samples. For KITTI, we put the first 150 samples in each of 2015 and 2012 set as our training set, yielding 300 training samples and 94 validation samples. A summary of our data splits is in the appendix.

4.2   Implementation Details

We implement the model in PyTorch [36], and all experiments share the same hyper-parameters as follows. Training uses the Adam optimizer [22] with $\beta_1 = 0.9$, $\beta_2 = 0.999$ and batch size 8. The balancing weight α in Eq. (1) is set as 1. The weights of each unsupervised loss term in Eq. (3) are $\lambda_{sm} = 50$ for Sintel and $\lambda_{sm} = 75$ otherwise; and $\lambda_{aug} = 0.2$ unless otherwise stated. The weights of different distance measures in Eq. (4) are set as $(c_1, c_2, c_3) = (0.15, 0.85, 0)$ in the first 50k iterations and $(c_1, c_2, c_3) = (0, 0, 1)$ in the rest as in ARFlow [28].

The supervised weights $w_{sup}^{(l)}$ for scales $l = 2, 3, \cdots, 6$ in Eq. (7) are 0.32, 0.08, 0.02, 0.01, 0.005 as in PWC-Net [47]. The photometric weights $w_{ph}^{(l)}$ in Eq. (6) are 1, 1, 1, 1, 0, and the smoothness weights $w_{sm}^{(l)}$ in Eq. (6) are 1, 0, 0, 0, 0.

For data augmentation, we include random cropping, random rescaling, horizontal flipping, and appearance transformations (brightness, contrast, saturation, hue, Gaussian blur). Please refer to the appendix for more details.

4.3   Semi-supervised Training Settings

The goal of this first experiment is to see how the validation error changes as we gradually increase the label ratio r from 0 (unsupervised) to 1 (supervised). We are specifically interested in the changing error rate, which reflects the marginal gain of a unit of labeling effort.

We ensure that all experiments on the same dataset have exactly the same setting except the label ratio r for fair comparison. For each experiment, the labeled set is sampled uniformly. We experiment on all four datasets independently using label ratio $r \in \{0, 0.05, 0.1, 0.2, 0.4, 0.6, 0.8, 1\}$ with settings below.

FlyingChairs and FlyingThings3D. As a simple toy experiment, we split the labeled and unlabeled sets randomly and train using the semi-supervised loss. We train for 1,000k iterations with a fixed learning rate $\eta = 0.0001$.

Sintel. Unlike the two large datasets above, Sintel only has ground-truth labels for 2,082 clean and final samples, which is too small to train a flow model effectively on its own. Thus, the single-stage schedule above may not apply well.

Instead, as is common practice in many unsupervised methods, we first pre-train the network using the large Sintel raw movie set in an unsupervised way. Subsequently, as the second stage, we apply semi-supervised training with different label ratios on our training split of clean and final samples. Note that we compute the label ratio r as the ratio of labeled samples only in our second-stage train split, which does not include the unlabeled raw data samples in the first stage. This is because the label ratio would otherwise become too small (thus less informative) since the number of raw data far exceeds clean and final data.

We train the first stage using learning rate $\eta = 0.0001$ for 500k iterations, while the second stage starts with $\eta = 0.0001$, which is cut by half at 400, 600, and 800 epochs, and ends at 1,000 epochs. Following ARFlow [28], we turn off the augmentation loss by assigning $\lambda_{aug} = 0$ in the first stage.

KITTI. We apply a similar two-stage schedule to KITTI. We first pre-train the network using KITTI raw sequences with unsupervised loss. Subsequently, we assign labels to our train split of the KITTI 2015/2012 set with a given label ratio by random sampling and then run the semi-supervised training. The learning rate schedule is the same as that for Sintel above.

4.4   Active Learning Settings

The second part of experiments is on active learning, where we show that allowing the model to select which samples to label can help reduce the error.

We mainly experiment on Sintel and KITTI since they are close to real data. Since active learning is a multi-stage process (which needs a pre-trained model to query labels for the next stages), it fits well with the two-stage semi-supervised settings described in Sect. 4.3. Thus, we use those settings with labels queried totally at random as our baseline. In comparison, we show that using the three active learning heuristics described in Sect. 3.2 to query labels can yield better results than random sampling. We try small label ratios $r \in \{0.05, 0.1, 0.2\}$ since the semi-supervised training performance starts to saturate at larger label ratios.

4.5   Main Results

Semi-supervised Training. We first experiment with the semi-supervised training with different label ratios across four commonly used flow datasets. As shown in Fig. 2, the model validation error drops significantly at low label

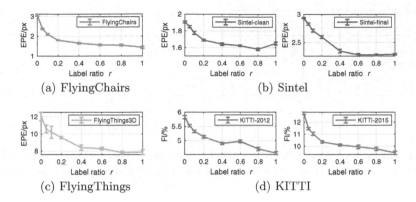

(a) FlyingChairs   (b) Sintel

(c) FlyingThings   (d) KITTI

Fig. 2. Model validation errors of the semi-supervised training with different label ratios. 'EPE': End-Point Error, 'Fl': Flow error percentage.

ratios and tends to saturate once an adequate amount of labels are used. This supports our hypothesis that even a few labels can help improve performance significantly.

Another observation is that the errors for FlyingChairs, FlyingThings3D, and Sintel saturate at around 50% labeling, whereas KITTI keeps improving slowly at high label ratios. One explanation for this discrepancy may involve the amount of repetitive information in the dataset: Sintel consists of video sequences with 20–50 frames that are very similar to each other, while KITTI consists of individually-selected frame pairs independent from the other pairs.

Active Learning. Our active learning results are shown in Fig. 3. We compare the validation errors for our three active learning criteria against the baseline setting, in which the labeled samples are selected randomly. To better illustrate the scale of the differences, we add two horizontal lines to indicate totally unsupervised and supervised errors as the "upper" and "lower" bound, respectively.

The Sintel results (Fig. 3a) show that all our three active learning algorithms can improve the baseline errors by large margins. Notably, our active learning algorithms can achieve close to supervised performance with only 20% labeling. This number is around 50% without active learning.

The KITTI results (Fig. 3b) show slight improvements with active learning. Among our three algorithms, "occ ratio" works consistently better than random sampling, especially at a very small label ratio $r = 0.05$. We discuss the reason why our active learning methods help less on KITTI at the end of this chapter.

Among our three active learning heuristics, "occ ratio" has the best performance overall and is therefore selected as our final criterion. Note that the occlusion ratio is computed via a forward-backward consistency check, so it captures not only real occlusions but also inconsistent flow estimates.

Benchmark Testing. We also show results on the official benchmark test sets. Qualitative examples are also included in the appendix. As is shown in Table 1,

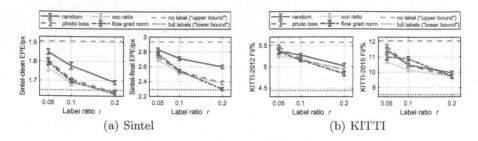

(a) Sintel   (b) KITTI

Fig. 3. Validation errors of different active learning algorithms compared with random sampling (baseline); pseudo error bars obtained by taking the standard deviations in the last 50 epochs.

compared with the backbone ARFlow [28] and two other top unsupervised estimators [19,29], our Sintel test EPEs improve significantly even when we utilize a very small fraction (5–20%) of labels in training. This holds true for both clean and final passes, as well as occluded and non-occluded pixels. To indicate the scale of improvements, our semi-supervised results are even comparable to the supervised IRR-PWC [15], which has a similar PWC-Net-based structure, even if we only use 20% of the Sintel labels. We also include the state-of-the-art RAFT [15] results to get a sense of the overall picture.

In addition, Table 1 also shows that our active learning method works favorably against the baseline ("rand"). We found that our active learning method ("occ") may overly sample the same scenes (*e.g.,* "ambush"), so we also test an alternative ("occ-2x") to balance the queried samples. Specifically, we select a double number of samples with top uncertainties and then randomly sample a half from them to query labels. This helps diversify our selected samples when the label ratio is very small. Our active learning methods perform comparably or better than the baseline, especially on the realistic final pass.

Table 2 shows our benchmark testing results on KITTI. Consistent with our findings on Sintel, our semi-supervised methods are significantly better than the compared unsupervised state-of-the-art methods, and close to the supervised IRR-PWC [15], even if we only use a very small fraction (5–20%) of labels. In addition, our active learning method also works consistently better than the baseline for all tested label ratios, especially on the harder KITTI-2015 set.

Ablation Study on Settings of Stage 2. We try different active learning schedules in Stage 2 and show our current setting works the best. We report the Sintel final EPE for different Stage 2 settings with label ratio $r = 0.1$. In Table 3, the first row is our current Stage 2 setting, *i.e.,* semi-supervised training on the partial labeled train set. The second row refers to supervised training only on the labeled part of train set, without the unsupervised samples. The third row considers also including the unlabeled raw data (used in Stage 1) in the Stage 2 semi-supervised training. We can see that our current setting works significantly better than the two alternatives. The second setting works poorly due to overfitting on the very small labeled set, which means that the unlabeled

Table 1. Sintel benchmark results (EPE/px). Metrics evaluated at 'all' (all pixels), 'noc' (non-occlusions), and 'occ' (occlusions). The key metrics (used to sort on the official website) are underlined. Parenthesis means evaluation data used in training. For all metrics, lower is better.

Label ratio r	Method	Train Clean all	Final all	Test Clean all	noc	occ	Final all	noc	occ
$r = 0$	SelFlow [29]	(2.88)	(3.87)	6.56	2.67	38.30	6.57	3.12	34.72
	UFlow [19]	(2.50)	(3.39)	5.21	2.04	31.06	6.50	3.08	34.40
	ARFlow [28]	(2.79)	(3.73)	**4.78**	**1.91**	**28.26**	**5.89**	**2.73**	**31.60**
$r = 0.05$	Ours(rand)	(2.09)	(2.99)	4.04	1.52	24.65	5.49	2.62	28.86
	Ours(occ)	(1.95)	(2.38)	4.11	1.63	**24.39**	**5.28**	**2.49**	**28.03**
	Ours(occ-2x)	(1.94)	(2.55)	**3.96**	**1.45**	24.42	5.35	2.50	28.58
$r = 0.1$	Ours(rand)	(2.36)	(3.18)	**3.91**	**1.47**	**23.82**	5.21	2.46	27.66
	Ours(occ)	(1.64)	(1.98)	4.28	1.68	25.49	5.31	**2.44**	28.68
	Ours(occ-2x)	(1.75)	(2.30)	4.06	1.63	23.94	**5.09**	2.49	**26.31**
$r = 0.2$	Ours(rand)	(2.17)	(2.93)	3.89	1.56	**22.86**	5.20	2.50	27.19
	Ours(occ)	(1.35)	(1.63)	4.36	1.86	24.76	5.09	2.45	26.69
	Ours(occ-2x)	(1.57)	(2.05)	**3.79**	**1.44**	23.02	**4.62**	**2.07**	**25.38**
$r = 1$	PWC-Net [47]	(2.02)	(2.08)	4.39	1.72	26.17	5.04	2.45	26.22
	IRR-PWC [15]	(1.92)	(2.51)	3.84	1.47	23.22	4.58	2.15	24.36
	RAFT [49]	(0.77)	(1.27)	**1.61**	**0.62**	**9.65**	**2.86**	**1.41**	**14.68**

(Left margin labels: unsup / semi-sup / sup)

part of the train split helps prevent overfitting. The third setting also fails due to the excessive amount of unlabeled data used in Stage 2, which overwhelms the small portion of supervised signal from queried labels.

Model Analysis and Visualization. Table 4(a) shows which Sintel samples are selected by different active learning methods. As shown in the left-most column, the pre-trained model after Stage 1 generally has high EPEs (top 20% shown in the figure) on four scenes, namely "ambush", "cave", "market", and "temple". The random baseline tends to select a bit of every scene, whereas all our three active learning algorithms query scenes with high EPEs for labels. This confirms that our active learning criteria capture samples that are especially challenging to the current model, which explains the success of active learning.

We also analyze the relationships between our criteria and model errors through correlation matrices visualized by heat maps in Figs. 4(b) and 4(c). We can see that the sample errors in Sintel generally have high correlations with all three score values, whereas in KITTI the correlations are much smaller. Also, the "occ ratio" score generally has the highest correlation with sample errors among the three proposed methods. All these observations are consistent with our active

Table 2. KITTI benchmark results (EPE/px and Fl/%). Metrics evaluated at 'all' (all pixels, default for EPE), 'noc' (non-occlusions), 'bg' (background), and 'fg' (foreground). Key metrics (used to sort on the official website) are underlined. '()' means evaluation data used in training. '-' means unavailable. For all metrics, lower is better.

Label ratio r	Method	Train		Test					
		2012	2015	2012		2015			
		EPE	EPE	Fl-noc	EPE	Fl-all	Fl-noc	Fl-bg	Fl-fg
unsup $r = 0$	SelFlow [29]	(1.69)	(4.84)	4.31	2.2	14.19	9.65	12.68	21.74
	UFlow [19]	(1.68)	(2.71)	4.26	1.9	11.13	8.41	9.78	17.87
	ARFlow [28]	(1.44)	(2.85)	-	1.8	11.80	-	-	-
semi-sup $r = 0.05$	Ours(rand)	(1.25)	(2.61)	3.90	1.6	9.77	6.99	8.33	17.02
	Ours(occ)	(1.22)	(2.29)	3.90	**1.5**	**9.65**	**6.94**	**8.20**	**16.91**
$r = 0.1$	Ours(rand)	(1.21)	(2.56)	3.75	1.5	9.51	6.69	8.01	17.01
	Ours(occ)	(1.21)	(1.98)	**3.74**	1.5	**8.96**	**6.28**	**7.74**	**15.04**
$r = 0.2$	Ours(rand)	(1.16)	(2.10)	3.50	1.5	8.38	**5.68**	7.37	**13.44**
	Ours(occ)	(1.13)	(1.73)	**3.49**	1.5	**8.30**	5.69	**7.25**	13.53
sup $r = 1$	PWC-Net [47]	(1.45)	(2.16)	4.22	1.7	9.60	6.12	9.66	9.31
	IRR-PWC [15]	-	(1.63)	3.21	1.6	7.65	4.86	7.68	7.52
	RAFT [49]	-	(0.63)	-	-	**5.10**	**3.07**	**4.74**	**6.87**

Table 3. Ablation study: different Stage 2 settings. Sintel final validation EPE, label ratio $r = 0.1$. Standard deviations from the last 50 epoches. * denotes current setting.

Data split [Loss]	Method			
	Random	Photo loss	Occ ratio	Flow grad norm
Train [semi-sup]*	**2.71(±0.02)**	**2.54(±0.02)**	**2.52(±0.02)**	**2.54(±0.02)**
Train [sup]	2.82(±0.01)	2.82(±0.01)	2.59(±0.01)	2.77(±0.01)
Raw+train [semi-sup]	3.13(±0.04)	3.09(±0.05)	3.15(±0.06)	3.07(±0.05)

learning validation results. Thus, we posit that the correlation between uncertainty values and sample errors can be a good indicator in designing effective active learning criteria.

Discussion on Factors That May Influence Active Learning

- **Pattern Homogeneity**: Based on our validation results in Fig. 3, active learning seems more effective on Sintel than on KITTI. This may be because KITTI samples are relatively more homogeneous in terms of motion patterns. Unlike the Sintel movie sequences, which contain arbitrary motions of various scales, driving scenes in KITTI exhibit a clear *looming motion* caused by the dominant forward motion of the vehicle that carries the camera. Specif-

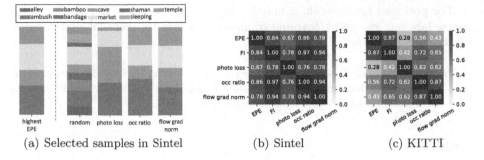

(a) Selected samples in Sintel   (b) Sintel   (c) KITTI

Fig. 4. (a) Sintel samples selected by different methods ($r = 0.2$), grouped by scenes; and correlation matrices with sample errors for Sintel (b) and KITTI (c).

Fig. 5. An example for the information mismatch problem. Data from KITTI-2015, frame 79 (Fl=19.35%), with the third largest "occ ratio" score: (a) superposed input images; (b) estimated occlusion map; (c) flow prediction; (d) flow ground truth.

ically, Sintel has extremely hard scenes like "ambush" as well as extremely easy scenes like "sleeping". This large variation of difficulty makes it possible to select outstandingly helpful samples and labels. In contrast, since KITTI motions are more patterned and homogeneous, any selection tends to make little difference with respect to random sampling.

- **Label Region Mismatch**: KITTI only has sparse labels, *i.e.*, only a part of the image pixels have labels. This is crucial because our active learning criteria are computed over the whole frame, so there is a mismatch between the support of our criteria and the KITTI labels. Specifically, the sparse labels may not cover the problematic regions found by our criteria. One example is shown in Fig. 5. The sky region has bad predictions due to lack of texture, and the "occ ratio" method captures the inconsistent flow there by highlighting the sky region. However, the ground-truth labels do not cover the sky region, so having this sample labeled does not help much in training.

5   Conclusion

In this paper, we first analyzed the trade-off between model performance and label ratio using a simple yet effective semi-supervised optical flow network and found that the unsupervised performance can be significantly improved even with a small fraction of labels. We then explored active learning as a way to further improve the performance and reduce annotation costs. Our active learning method works consistently better than baseline on Sintel and KITTI datasets.

For potential future work, it may be interesting to explore how to deal with sparse labels in the active learning framework or how to query labels by region rather than full frame.

Acknowledgments. This material is based upon work supported by the National Science Foundation under Grant No. 1909821 and by the Intelligence Advanced Research Projects Agency under contract number 2021-21040700001.

References

1. Aslani, S., Mahdavi-Nasab, H.: Optical flow based moving object detection and tracking for traffic surveillance. Int. J. Elect. Comput. Energ. Electron. Commun. Eng. **7**(9), 1252–1256 (2013)
2. Beluch, W.H., Genewein, T., Nürnberger, A., Köhler, J.M.: The power of ensembles for active learning in image classification. In: Proceedings of the IEEE Conference on Computer Vision and Pattern Recognition, pp. 9368–9377 (2018)
3. Butler, D.J., Wulff, J., Stanley, G.B., Black, M.J.: A naturalistic open source movie for optical flow evaluation. In: Fitzgibbon, A., Lazebnik, S., Perona, P., Sato, Y., Schmid, C. (eds.) ECCV 2012. LNCS, vol. 7577, pp. 611–625. Springer, Heidelberg (2012). https://doi.org/10.1007/978-3-642-33783-3_44
4. Choi, J., Elezi, I., Lee, H.J., Farabet, C., Alvarez, J.M.: Active learning for deep object detection via probabilistic modeling. In: Proceedings of the IEEE International Conference on Computer Vision (2021)
5. Dosovitskiy, A., et al.: FlowNet: learning optical flow with convolutional networks. In: Proceedings of the IEEE International Conference on Computer Vision, pp. 2758–2766 (2015)
6. Ebrahimi, S., Elhoseiny, M., Darrell, T., Rohrbach, M.: Uncertainty-guided continual learning with Bayesian neural networks. In: International Conference on Learning Representations (2020)
7. Fan, L., Huang, W., Gan, C., Ermon, S., Gong, B., Huang, J.: End-to-end learning of motion representation for video understanding. In: Proceedings of the IEEE Conference on Computer Vision and Pattern Recognition, pp. 6016–6025 (2018)
8. Gal, Y., Islam, R., Ghahramani, Z.: Deep Bayesian active learning with image data. In: Proceedings of the International Conference on Machine Learning, pp. 1183–1192. PMLR (2017)
9. Gao, C., Saraf, A., Huang, J.-B., Kopf, J.: Flow-edge guided video completion. In: Vedaldi, A., Bischof, H., Brox, T., Frahm, J.-M. (eds.) ECCV 2020. LNCS, vol. 12357, pp. 713–729. Springer, Cham (2020). https://doi.org/10.1007/978-3-030-58610-2_42
10. Geiger, A., Lenz, P., Stiller, C., Urtasun, R.: Vision meets robotics: the kitti dataset. Int. J. Robot. Res. **32**(11), 1231–1237 (2013)
11. Grandvalet, Y., Bengio, Y.: Semi-supervised learning by entropy minimization. In: Advances in Neural Information Processing Systems, vol. 17. MIT Press (2005)
12. He, K., Zhang, X., Ren, S., Sun, J.: Deep residual learning for image recognition. In: Proceedings of the IEEE Conference on Computer Vision and Pattern Recognition, pp. 770–778 (2016)
13. Houlsby, N., Huszár, F., Ghahramani, Z., Lengyel, M.: Bayesian active learning for classification and preference learning. arXiv preprint arXiv:1112.5745 (2011)

14. Hui, T.W., Tang, X., Change Loy, C.: LiteflowNet: a lightweight convolutional neural network for optical flow estimation. In: Proceedings of the IEEE Conference on Computer Vision and Pattern Recognition, pp. 8981–8989 (2018)
15. Hur, J., Roth, S.: Iterative residual refinement for joint optical flow and occlusion estimation. In: Proceedings of the IEEE Conference on Computer Vision and Pattern Recognition, pp. 5754–5763 (2019)
16. Ilg, E., Saikia, T., Keuper, M., Brox, T.: Occlusions, motion and depth boundaries with a generic network for disparity, optical flow or scene flow estimation. In: Proceedings of the European Conference on Computer Vision, pp. 614–630 (2018)
17. Janai, J., Guney, F., Ranjan, A., Black, M., Geiger, A.: Unsupervised learning of multi-frame optical flow with occlusions. In: Proceedings of the European Conference on Computer Vision, pp. 690–706 (2018)
18. Yu, J.J., Harley, A.W., Derpanis, K.G.: Back to basics: unsupervised learning of optical flow via brightness constancy and motion smoothness. In: Hua, G., Jégou, H. (eds.) Computer Vision – ECCV 2016 Workshops. LNCS, vol. 9915, pp. 3–10. Springer, Cham (2016). https://doi.org/10.1007/978-3-319-49409-8_1
19. Jonschkowski, R., Stone, A., Barron, J.T., Gordon, A., Konolige, K., Angelova, A.: What matters in unsupervised optical flow. In: Vedaldi, A., Bischof, H., Brox, T., Frahm, J.-M. (eds.) ECCV 2020. LNCS, vol. 12347, pp. 557–572. Springer, Cham (2020). https://doi.org/10.1007/978-3-030-58536-5_33
20. Kapoor, A., Grauman, K., Urtasun, R., Darrell, T.: Active learning with gaussian processes for object categorization. In: Proceedings of the IEEE International Conference on Computer Vision, pp. 1–8. IEEE (2007)
21. Kim, H.H., Yu, S., Tomasi, C.: Joint detection of motion boundaries and occlusions. In: British Machine Vision Conference (2021)
22. Kingma, D.P., Ba, J.: Adam: a method for stochastic optimization. In: International Conference on Learning Representations (2014)
23. Krizhevsky, A., Sutskever, I., Hinton, G.E.: ImageNet classification with deep convolutional neural networks. In: Advances in Neural Information Processing Systems, pp. 1097–1105 (2012)
24. Lai, W.S., Huang, J.B., Yang, M.H.: Semi-supervised learning for optical flow with generative adversarial networks. In: Advances in Neural Information Processing Systems, pp. 353–363 (2017)
25. Laine, S., Aila, T.: Temporal ensembling for semi-supervised learning. In: International Conference on Learning Representations (2017)
26. Lee, D.H., et al.: Pseudo-label: the simple and efficient semi-supervised learning method for deep neural networks. In: Workshop on challenges in representation learning, ICML, vol. 3, p. 896 (2013)
27. Li, X., Guo, Y.: Adaptive active learning for image classification. In: Proceedings of the IEEE Conference on Computer Vision and Pattern Recognition, pp. 859–866 (2013)
28. Liu, L., et al.: Learning by analogy: Reliable supervision from transformations for unsupervised optical flow estimation. In: Proceedings of the IEEE Conference on Computer Vision and Pattern Recognition, pp. 6489–6498 (2020)
29. Liu, P., Lyu, M., King, I., Xu, J.: Selflow: self-supervised learning of optical flow. In: Proceedings of the IEEE Conference on Computer Vision and Pattern Recognition, pp. 4571–4580 (2019)
30. Liu, Y., Chen, K., Liu, C., Qin, Z., Luo, Z., Wang, J.: Structured knowledge distillation for semantic segmentation. In: Proceedings of the IEEE Conference on Computer Vision and Pattern Recognition, pp. 2604–2613 (2019)

31. Mackowiak, R., Lenz, P., Ghori, O., Diego, F., Lange, O., Rother, C.: Cereals-cost-effective region-based active learning for semantic segmentation. In: British Machine Vision Conference (2018)
32. Mayer, N., Ilg, E., Häusser, P., Fischer, P., Cremers, D., Dosovitskiy, A., Brox, T.: A large dataset to train convolutional networks for disparity, optical flow, and scene flow estimation. In: Proceedings of the IEEE International Conference on Computer Vision (2016). arXiv:1512.02134
33. Meister, S., Hur, J., Roth, S.: UnFlow: unsupervised learning of optical flow with a bidirectional census loss. In: Proceedings of the AAAI Conference on Artificial Intelligence (2018)
34. Menze, M., Geiger, A.: Object scene flow for autonomous vehicles. In: Proceedings of the IEEE Conference on Computer Vision and Pattern Recognition (2015)
35. Miyato, T., Maeda, S.I., Koyama, M., Ishii, S.: Virtual adversarial training: a regularization method for supervised and semi-supervised learning. IEEE Trans. Pattern Anal. Mach. Intell. **41**(08), 1979–1993 (2019)
36. Paszke, A., et al.: Pytorch: an imperative style, high-performance deep learning library. In: Advances in Neural Information Processing Systems, pp. 8024–8035. Curran Associates, Inc. (2019)
37. Paul, S., Bappy, J.H., Roy-Chowdhury, A.K.: Non-uniform subset selection for active learning in structured data. In: Proceedings of the IEEE Conference on Computer Vision and Pattern Recognition, pp. 6846–6855 (2017)
38. Ranjan, A., Black, M.J.: Optical flow estimation using a spatial pyramid network. In: Proceedings of the IEEE Conference on Computer Vision and Pattern Recognition, pp. 4161–4170 (2017)
39. Ranjan, A., et al.: Competitive collaboration: Joint unsupervised learning of depth, camera motion, optical flow and motion segmentation. In: Proceedings of the IEEE Conference on Computer Vision and Pattern Recognition, pp. 12240–12249 (2019)
40. Ren, Z., Yan, J., Ni, B., Liu, B., Yang, X., Zha, H.: Unsupervised deep learning for optical flow estimation. In: Proceedings of the AAAI Conference on Artificial Intelligence (2017)
41. Ren, Z., Gallo, O., Sun, D., Yang, M.H., Sudderth, E.B., Kautz, J.: A fusion approach for multi-frame optical flow estimation. In: Winter Conference on Applications of Computer Vision, pp. 2077–2086. IEEE (2019)
42. Roy, S., Unmesh, A., Namboodiri, V.P.: Deep active learning for object detection. In: British Machine Vision Conference, vol. 362, p. 91 (2018)
43. Sajjadi, M., Javanmardi, M., Tasdizen, T.: Regularization with stochastic transformations and perturbations for deep semi-supervised learning. Adv. Neural. Inf. Process. Syst. **29**, 1–10 (2016)
44. Siddiqui, Y., Valentin, J., Nießner, M.: Viewal: Active learning with viewpoint entropy for semantic segmentation. In: Proceedings of the IEEE Conference on Computer Vision and Pattern Recognition, pp. 9433–9443 (2020)
45. Song, X., Zhao, Y., Yang, J., Lan, C., Zeng, W.: FPCR-net: feature pyramidal correlation and residual reconstruction for semi-supervised optical flow estimation. arXiv preprint arXiv:2001.06171 (2020)
46. Stone, A., Maurer, D., Ayvaci, A., Angelova, A., Jonschkowski, R.: SMURF: self-teaching multi-frame unsupervised raft with full-image warping. In: Proceedings of the IEEE Conference on Computer Vision and Pattern Recognition, pp. 3887–3896 (2021)
47. Sun, D., Yang, X., Liu, M.Y., Kautz, J.: PWC-net: CNNs for optical flow using pyramid, warping, and cost volume. In: Proceedings of the IEEE Conference on Computer Vision and Pattern Recognition, pp. 8934–8943 (2018)

48. Tarvainen, A., Valpola, H.: Mean teachers are better role models: weight-averaged consistency targets improve semi-supervised deep learning results. Adv. Neural. Inf. Process. Syst. **30**, 1–10 (2017)

49. Teed, Z., Deng, J.: RAFT: recurrent all-pairs field transforms for optical flow. In: Vedaldi, A., Bischof, H., Brox, T., Frahm, J.-M. (eds.) ECCV 2020. LNCS, vol. 12347, pp. 402–419. Springer, Cham (2020). https://doi.org/10.1007/978-3-030-58536-5_24

50. K. Z. Tehrani, A., Mirzaei, M., Rivaz, H.: Semi-supervised training of optical flow convolutional neural networks in ultrasound elastography. In: Martel, A.L., et al. (eds.) MICCAI 2020. LNCS, vol. 12263, pp. 504–513. Springer, Cham (2020). https://doi.org/10.1007/978-3-030-59716-0_48

51. Wang, R., Wang, X.Z., Kwong, S., Xu, C.: Incorporating diversity and informativeness in multiple-instance active learning. IEEE Trans. Fuzzy Syst. **25**(6), 1460–1475 (2017)

52. Wang, Y., Yang, Y., Yang, Z., Zhao, L., Wang, P., Xu, W.: Occlusion aware unsupervised learning of optical flow. In: Proceedings of the IEEE Conference on Computer Vision and Pattern Recognition, pp. 4884–4893 (2018)

53. Wang, Z., Bovik, A.C., Sheikh, H.R., Simoncelli, E.P.: Image quality assessment: from error visibility to structural similarity. IEEE Trans. Image Process. **13**(4), 600–612 (2004)

54. Wei, K., Iyer, R., Bilmes, J.: Submodularity in data subset selection and active learning. In: Proceedings of the International Conference on Machine Learning, pp. 1954–1963. PMLR (2015)

55. Xie, Q., Luong, M.T., Hovy, E., Le, Q.V.: Self-training with noisy student improves imagenet classification. In: Proceedings of the IEEE Conference on Computer Vision and Pattern Recognition, pp. 10687–10698 (2020)

56. Yan, W., Sharma, A., Tan, R.T.: Optical flow in dense foggy scenes using semi-supervised learning. In: Proceedings of the IEEE Conference on Computer Vision and Pattern Recognition, pp. 13259–13268 (2020)

57. Yang, Y., Soatto, S.: Conditional prior networks for optical flow. In: Ferrari, V., Hebert, M., Sminchisescu, C., Weiss, Y. (eds.) ECCV 2018. LNCS, vol. 11219, pp. 282–298. Springer, Cham (2018). https://doi.org/10.1007/978-3-030-01267-0_17

58. Yin, Z., Shi, J.: GeoNet: unsupervised learning of dense depth, optical flow and camera pose. In: Proceedings of the IEEE Conference on Computer Vision and Pattern Recognition, pp. 1983–1992 (2018)

59. Yu, H., Chen, X., Shi, H., Chen, T., Huang, T.S., Sun, S.: Motion pyramid networks for accurate and efficient cardiac motion estimation. In: Martel, A.L., et al. (eds.) MICCAI 2020. LNCS, vol. 12266, pp. 436–446. Springer, Cham (2020). https://doi.org/10.1007/978-3-030-59725-2_42

60. Zhang, F., Woodford, O.J., Prisacariu, V.A., Torr, P.H.: Separable flow: learning motion cost volumes for optical flow estimation. In: Proceedings of the IEEE International Conference on Computer Vision, pp. 10807–10817 (2021)

Hierarchical Feature Embedding
for Visual Tracking

Zhixiong Pi[1], Weitao Wan[2], Chong Sun[2], Changxin Gao[1], Nong Sang[1(✉)],
and Chen Li[2]

[1] Key Laboratory of Image Processing and Intelligent Control, School of Artificial
Intelligence and Automation, Huazhong University of Science and Technology,
Wuhan, China
nsang@hust.edu.cn
[2] WeChat, Tencent, Shenzhen, China

Abstract. Features extracted by existing tracking methods may contain instance- and category-level information. However, it usually occurs that either instance- or category-level information uncontrollably dominates the feature embeddings depending on the training data distribution, since the two types of information are not explicitly modeled. A more favorable way is to produce features that emphasize both types of information in visual tracking. To achieve this, we propose a hierarchical feature embedding model which separately learns the instance and category information, and progressively embeds them.

We develop the instance-aware and category-aware modules that collaborate from different semantic levels to produce discriminative and robust feature embeddings. The instance-aware module concentrates on the instance level in which the inter-video contrastive learning mechanism is adopted to facilitate inter-instance separability and intra-instance compactness. However, it is challenging to force the intra-instance compactness by using instance-level information alone because of the prevailing appearance changes of the instance in visual tracking. To tackle this problem, the category-aware module is employed to summarize high-level category information which remains robust despite instance-level appearance changes. As such, intra-instance compactness can be effectively improved by jointly leveraging the instance- and category-aware modules. Experimental results on various benchmarks demonstrate the proposed method performs favorably against the state-of-the-arts. The code is available on https://github.com/zxgravity/CIA.

Keywords: Instance-level · Category-level · Visual tracking

This work was done while Zhixiong Pi was an intern at Tencent.

Supplementary Information The online version contains supplementary material available at https://doi.org/10.1007/978-3-031-20047-2_25.

S. Avidan et al. (Eds.): ECCV 2022, LNCS 13682, pp. 428–445, 2022.
https://doi.org/10.1007/978-3-031-20047-2_25

1   Introduction

Visual object tracking is a fundamental computer vision task, which is widely used in surveillance, automatic drive, and video analysis, to name a few. With the initial target location annotated, the visual tracking algorithms attempt to identify and localize the target object continuously in a video sequence.

Benefiting from the powerful deep neural network, Siamese networks [1,12, 18,19] and discriminative modules [2,6,7] have improved the performance significantly. Among these methods, robust target representation learning plays an important role in boosting tracking performance. However, existing tracking methods mainly have two limitations, *i.e.*, the absence of category awareness and the uncontrollable dominance of either instance or category information

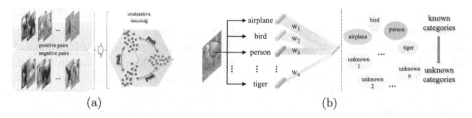

(a)   (b)

Fig. 1. Illustration of the instance-level and category-level awareness. (a) The model learns the feature embedding that pushes away different instances through contrastive learning. (b) In order to maintain intra-category compactness, the model is trained to produce features from a handful of known categories and generalize to cluster the unknown ones.

In visual tracking, it is crucial to learn feature embeddings that not only have inter-instance distinction but also have intra-category consistency. Existing tracking methods focus on modeling the discriminative instance features while ignoring the category information modeling. A typical idea of such methods is to learn the instance-specific features by forcing the model to increase the response on the foreground and suppressing that on the background in each frame. However, suppressing the background response may not be effective since many background features are semantically meaningless. Other existing trackers, like DaSiamRPN [43], focus on the distractors by using the hard negative mining method. Similarly, DiMP [2] suppresses the influence of the easy negative samples by masking out the loss from the areas with low response. We argue that it can stabilize target features and improve tracking performance further by modeling category information properly. A simple manner to encode category information in the backbone features is to introduce an additional category loss, leading to the multi-task learning problem. However, there are numerous categories in visual tracking. Explicit category information learning via straightforward multi-task training is sub-optimal, as learned category information is difficult to generalize to the unknown categories with limited annotated categories in the training set.

According to the experimental analysis in current Siamese trackers [2,19], though the category factor is not explicitly considered, the learned features do contain a certain amount of category information. However, the importance of the instance and category information is not properly regularized, which is susceptible to the training data distribution. For example, more category cues are learned when the training data has fewer intra-category distractions, and vice versa. The unconstrained feature learning process increases the overfitting risk making the model to highlight either the instance or the category information.

To overcome these difficulties, we propose to hierarchically embed the instance and category information by explicitly modeling the instance and category cues in a progressive manner during the feature learning process Fig. 1. We propose the instance-aware and category-aware modules that contribute to producing discriminative and robust feature embeddings from different semantic levels. The instance-aware module, which concentrates on a fine-grained semantic level, employs the proposed video-level contrastive learning mechanism exploiting rich inter-video cues to facilitate inter-instance separability and intra-instance compactness. In this module, we extend the InfoNCE [27] loss to learn an instance feature extractor. Then the instance-level information is effectively embedded into the backbone features through a novel angle modulation strategy which modulates the vectorial angles in the feature space, producing the instance-aware features. To improve intra-instance compactness in spite of instance appearance changes in the sequence, the category-aware module is employed to summarize high-level category information which remains robust although the instance-level appearance can change dramatically. Furthermore, the proposed method can generalize to unknown categories by incorporating a transformer-based dictionary learning approach. We summarize our contributions as follows:

- We propose a novel cross-video training paradigm based on the video-level contrastive learning. The positive and negative training pairs are constructed across videos, which can sufficiently mine the potential of instance distinction of the tracker. Furthermore, we introduce an auxiliary task in visual tracking which employs the momentum contrast to improve the performance.
- We propose the instance-aware module and category-aware module to extract the features with better inter-instance separability and intra-instance compactness. We achieve more understandable feature learning by explicitly encoding the instance and category information with supervision signals.
- We conduct the experiments based on both the ResNet18 and ResNet50 backbones. The ablation studies demonstrate the effectiveness of both the instance- and category-aware modules. The proposed tracker performs favorably against the state-of-the-arts.

2   Related Work

Generic visual object tracking algorithms have achieved remarkable improvement in recent years. Because of its high accuracy and efficiency, the Siamese network based trackers [1,12,13,18,19,29,35] have gained widespread attention. SINT [28] firstly introduces the Siamese network in the visual tracking task.

Hereafter, many siamese based trackers are proposed. For locating targets more precisely, The bounding box regression head is integrated in SiamRPN [19], adapting to the scale and ratio changes. SiamMask [35] further improves the localization precision by predicting the target mask. Another way of boosting performance is to exploit the potential of the deep network for the tracking task. With the random shifting augmentation, trackers with very deep networks [18,40] are successfully proposed. In spite of the remarkable improvement brought by the better output formats and the deep backbones, the lack of online updating prevents the trackers from adapting to the target appearance changes, especially in the long-term sequences. To improve the tracking robustness, ATOM [6] designs a fast online updating method in the inference process to overcome the appearance changes. Then, the online updating method is improved by a meta-learning based updating module [2]. Considering the case of very confusing distractors, the appearance model is unreliable sometimes. To this end, KYS [3] and KeepTrack [24] extract the context information to suppress the confusing distractors. Recently, benefiting from the transformer, the visual tracking accuracy rises significantly. Some trackers integrate the transformer modules into the siamese network to mine the spatial and temporal context information [33,39] or promote the power of the matching head [5].

Despite the competitive performance of the existing trackers, it remains challenging to learn the reliable instance-specific features. Zhu *et al.* [43] improve the instance representation by adding positive and hard negative pairs with data augmentation and using hard negative mining. Wang *et al.* [32] use forward-backward tracking to construct sample pairs and train the tracker with the consistency loss. However, these methods still cannot exploit the instance information sufficiently. Different from them, we follow the idea from He *et al.* [14], that more negative sample pairs can improve the contrastive learning. We construct the sample pairs between the images in the same mini-batch, where the images from the different video sequences. We can construct negative and positive pairs between the different sequences and inside the same sequence. The negative pairs are much more than the positive pairs. Then, we train the tracker via the momentum contrastive learning.

Generic visual tracking needs recognizing and localizing the target annotated in the initial frame without the category information. We observe that the category information, if provided, can stabilize the tracking process. To the best of our knowledge, there are barely any previous works discussing the influence of the category information in generic visual tracking. SA-Siam [13] combines the responses from the semantic network and the appearance network to improve the tracking precision. The semantic network is pretrained on the ImageNet [8] dataset, and the parameters are then fixed, which can be viewed as a model with the category awareness. However, the pretrained semantic network in the SA-Siam model is optimized for the ImageNet classification task, which leads to suboptimal performance in the generic visual tracking task. In contrast, the proposed category-aware module is jointly optimized with the other parts of the tracker for the generic visual tracking task. We demonstrate experimentally that the proposed category-aware module can effectively improve intra-category compactness and stabilize the features of the target instance.

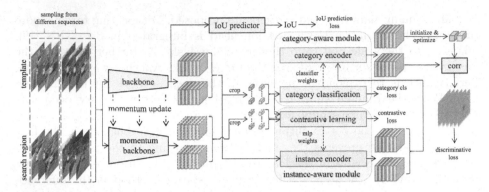

Fig. 2. The pipeline of our approach. The inputs are the frames sampled from video sequences. The features extracted from different sequences are colored with orange and blue, respectively. 'corr' represents the correlation operator. We encode the instance and category information in a progressive manner. The instance encoder integrates instance-aware information into the backbone features. The category encoder then integrates category-aware information into preceding instance-aware features.

3   Our Approach

In this section, we first briefly summarize the proposed algorithm considering hierarchical feature embeddings. Then, we introduce the details about the instance-aware module which exploits the proposed video-level momentum contrastive learning algorithm to highlight the instance separability ability. Last but not least, the category-aware module, which models the stable category information in the feature embedding, is detailed.

3.1   Overview

The pipeline of our algorithm is illustrated in Fig. 2. Inspired by MoCo [14], we introduce a momentum key update mechanism for the contrastive learning formula. Thus, our architecture contains both the prototype and momentum backbones, wherein both backbones share the same architectures containing the template and the search region branches. In each training iteration, we randomly obtain samples from several sequences, and equally split the samples in each sequence as the template and search region samples. The samples are processed by both the prototype and momentum backbones to obtain the intermediate feature representations. Then they are fed into the IoU predictor, as well as the instance-aware module for further computation. As is defined in the previous Siamese trackers [19,43], the feature maps corresponding to the template and search region are named as the template and search region features, respectively. The IoU predictor is implemented following DiMP [2], and it is used to predict the IoU values between the groundtruth and the bounding boxes sampled around.

For the instance-aware module, we crop the intermediate features corresponding to the object regions and generate a group of sample pairs based on the cropped feature maps. In each sequence, we sample three template and three target features. Thus we have $6 \times 6 = 36$ positive sample pairs. Sample pairs from any two different sequences are regarded as negative pairs. These sample pairs are utilized as the inputs of the contrastive learning module which produces the instance-specific features. The instance encoder takes the instance-specific features and the prototype backbone features as the inputs, and produces the features with instance-level discrimination.

The category-aware module, which takes the computed instance-aware features as inputs, consists of two sub-modules, *i.e.*, the category encoder module and category classification module. Trained from the samples annotated with a handful of known categories, the weight parameters in the category classification module contain rich category encoding information. These weight parameters are regarded as the dictionary atoms and fed into the category encoder module. Then the instance-aware features are modulated with the dictionary, generating the instance- and category-aware target representations. The generated features are then fed into the model optimizer and correlation module following [2]. As shown in Fig. 2, altogether 4 losses are used to optimize the proposed model, including the IoU prediction loss, the category classification loss, the contrastive loss, and the discriminative loss. Among these losses, the definitions of the IoU prediction loss and the discriminative loss are the same as those in DiMP [2]. We employ the cross entropy loss as the category classification loss and extend the InfoNCE [27] loss to make it more suitable for the video-level contrast.

3.2   Instance-Aware Module

In this paper, we explicitly model the instance-level discrimination information considering both the intra- and inter-sequence training samples. A novel

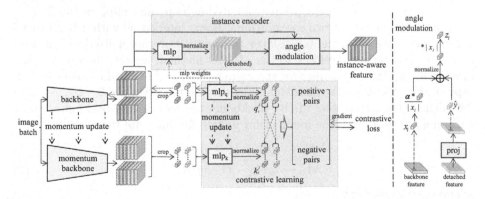

Fig. 3. Our instance-aware module. The module consists of the contrastive learning and the instance encoder. The detail of the angle modulation in the instance encoder is also illustrated at the right of this figure. The orange dash arrows annotate the gradient flows of the contrastive learning. The green and purple dash lines represent the two samples of a sample pair are from the same or the different sequences, respectively.

instance-aware module is proposed, which consists of the video-level contrastive learning module and the instance encoder. The brief pipeline of the instance-aware module is illustrated in Fig. 3, which will be detailed in this section.

Video-Level Contrastive Learning In the existing tracking algorithms, the positive and negative samples are generated from the same video sequence, wherein the annotated objects are consistently regarded as positive samples. In such methods, the rich inter-video instance level discrimination information is ignored. Different from the previous implementations, we propose the video-level contrastive learning algorithm, where the annotated object in one video sequence can be regarded as a positive or negative sample in the training pipeline.

The constrasive learning algorithm [14] is a self-supervised method, which learns the feature representations without the need for annotated samples. Given a set of keys $\{k_0, k_1, ..., k_i, ..., k_I\}$ of a dictionary and a query encoder q, we use k_d to denote the matched key of q. The constrasive learning algorithm tries to increase similarity between q and k_d, whilst suppressing the similarity between q and k_i $(i \neq d)$. InfoNCE loss is exploited to achieve this goal:

$$\mathcal{L}_{\text{con}} = -\log\frac{\exp(q^\top k_d/\tau)}{\sum_i \exp(q^\top k_i/\tau)}, \tag{1}$$

where τ is the temperature hyper-parameter.

The original implementation regards samples from the same image as positive training pairs, and regards samples from different images as negative pairs. We extend the constrasive learning method considering the temporal consistency in the video sequence. In our method, we use q_i^j and k_i^j to denote the query and key features for contrastive learning, respectively, where $i \in [1, ..., M]$ denotes sequence index, $j \in [1, ..., N]$ is sample index within each sequence. As is illustrated in Fig. 3, the cropped features in both the upper and lower branches are fed into two multi-layer perceptions (denoted as mlp_q and mlp_k in the figure), each of which consists of two convolutional layers interleaved with a ReLU activation. The outputs of the multi-layer perceptions are normalized to generate q_i^j and k_i^j respectively. Similar to the MOCO method, we also incorporate the momentum update mechanism for the momentum backbone and multi-layer perception mlp_k to ensure the consistent encoders for the keys. Let $\mathcal{B}_q$, $\mathcal{B}_k$, $\mathcal{M}_q$ and $\mathcal{M}_k$ denote the parameters of the backbone, the momentum backbone, mlp_q, and mlp_k, respectively. The momentum update formulas are therefore

$$\mathcal{B}_k \leftarrow \eta\mathcal{B}_k + (1 - \eta)\mathcal{B}_q$$
$$\mathcal{M}_k \leftarrow \eta\mathcal{M}_k + (1 - \eta)\mathcal{M}_q, \tag{2}$$

where η is the momentum factor.

Based on our extended constrasive learning method, the extended InfoNCE (named as InfoNCE-V in this paper) loss can be rewriten as

$$\mathcal{L}_{\text{con}} = -\log\frac{\sum_i \sum_{j,f} \exp(q_i^j k_i^f/\tau)}{\sum_{i,l}^{i\neq l} \sum_{j,f} \exp(q_i^j k_l^f/\tau)}, \tag{3}$$

which tries to increase the similarity between targets in the same video, whilst suppressing the similarity between targets in different videos. This simple implementation enables our method to simultaneously exploit the cross-video instance training pairs, facilitating the learning of more discriminative features. Compared with InfoNCE, InfoNCE-V allows the positive pair generation between the identical target from different frames in a sequence, supervising our model to cluster samples of the same instance and pushes the different instances away.

Instance Encoder Directly exploiting the features output by mlp_q for target/background classification is suboptimal, as it contains limited category information. The features are susceptible to the drastic appearance changes of the target object. As is described in many recognition papers [9,21], the angle between two feature vectors is crucial to perform instance level discrimination. Inspired by this, we propose the novel angle modulation module to properly embed the instance discrimination information into the backbone features. As illustrated in Fig. 3, the model parameters of mlp_q is copied to mlp, which outputs the instance discriminative convolution feature map sharing the same size with the input feature (feature padding is considered). We use X to denote the backbone feature, then the output feature Y is computed as $Y = mlp(X)$. Let x_i and y_i denote the feature vector extracted in the i-th position of X and Y respectively, the modulated feature vector z_i is computed as

$$\hat{x}_i = \frac{\alpha * x_i}{|x_i|}, \hat{y}_i = \frac{y_i}{|y_i|} \tag{4}$$

$$z_i = |x_i| * \frac{\hat{x}_i + \hat{y}_i}{|\hat{x}_i + \hat{y}_i|}, \tag{5}$$

where $|.|$ represents the norm of a vector. The learned parameter α controls the modulation strength. More instance discriminative information will be embedded into z_i with a smaller α. By modulating all the elements of the backbone features, we obtain the instance-aware features.

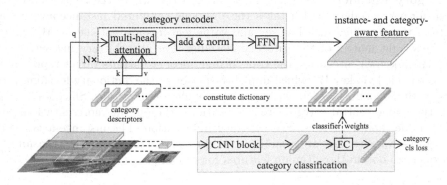

Fig. 4. Our category-aware module. The classifier weights serve as the category descriptors to represent the input features.

3.3 Category-Aware Module

The aforementioned instance-aware features concentrate on the instance discrimination information, which are less robust to the target appearance changes. Further improvement can be achieved by exploiting the categorical information of the instances. Motivated by this, we propose a novel category-aware module on top of the instance aware module to achieve hierarchical feature embedding. The category-aware module consists of the category classification and the category encoder, the details of which are illustrated in Fig. 4.

Category Classification. In the visual tracking task, the so-called classification process means distinguishing the foreground target from the background distractors. To avoid confusion, we define the recognition of the target category as the *category classification* in this paper. In several visual tracking datasets (*e.g.*, LaSOT [10]), each sequence is annotated with one category label. The straightforward way to utilize the category information is to add another branch for category classification, introducing the multi-task training strategy. In our work, we introduce one convolutional block in the category classification module to extract the features, which are then flattened and fed into a fully connected layer for category classification. As is shown in Fig. 4, we adopt the cross entropy loss as the category classification loss $\mathcal{L}_{\mathrm{cls}}$. The parameters of the fully connected layer construct the classifier weights. Assuming there are C known categories, the classifier weights W can be decomposed into C vectors $[w_1, ..., w_c]$, each of which can be viewed as the stable central representation for the corresponding category. During training, the tracker learns to classify the target into these known categories. In the experiments, we further discuss the extreme case where the number of known category C is 0. It is worth noting that directly exploiting multi-task learning mechanism cannot ensure satisfactory performance, as the learned features can hardly be generated to other categories. We further introduce the category encoder module to address this issue.

Category Encoder. The category encoder is essentially the concatenated N transformer encoders, which takes the previous computed instance-aware feature as the query feature. The key and value features are both set as W, which is the weight matrix of the category classifier. For an arbitrary instance with known/unknown categories, the transformer encoder outputs target representations encoded via key W, which implicitly performs the dictionary learning process with its column vectors $w_1, ..., w_C$ as the dictionary atoms. Since $w_1, ..., w_C$ are the stable central category representations, the output representations are also stable representations with category information. The instance-aware and category-aware features are combined (via the residual module in the transformer encoder) to obtain the ultimate features for tracking.

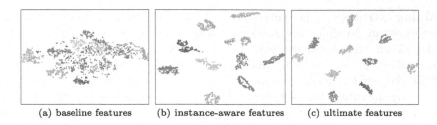

(a) baseline features   (b) instance-aware features   (c) ultimate features

Fig. 5. Visualization results of (a) baseline, (b) instance-aware, and (c) ultimate features with t-SNE [23]. Compared with the baseline features, the instance-aware features have better inter-instance separability. In the ultimate features, the intra-instance compactness is further strengthened.

3.4 Visualization

We visualize the instance-aware and category-aware features of some targets with the t-SNE [23] algorithm in Fig. 5. The baseline features are extracted by DiMP18. The instance-aware features and the ultimate features are from our CIA18. The instance-aware module produces the instance-aware features which are then enriched by the category-aware module to obtain the ultimate features. The distributions of the baseline, instance-aware, and ultimate features are shown in subfigures (a), (b), and (c) of Fig. 5, respectively. Despite the competitive performance, the instance discrimination of DiMP [2] is unsatisfactory. As subfigure (a) shows, it is hard to split the features of different instances. In contrast, the instance-aware module mines the instance discrimination effectively. After integrating the instance-aware module, the features can be split as subfigure (b) illustrates. The category-aware module can stabilize the target features. As shown in subfigure (c), the intra-instance compactness is further strengthened in the ultimate features, compared to the instance-aware features.

4 Experimental Results

4.1 Implementation Details

Network Architecture. We conduct experiments with the DiMP [2] being the baseline. Our modules are integrated into the baseline trackers DiMP18 [2] and SuperDiMP [2] to obtain our **C**ategory- and **I**nstance-**A**ware (CIA) trackers CIA18 and CIA50. The size of the template image is the same as the search region image. For CIA18 and CIA50, the area of the input image is 5 times and 6 times that of the corresponding target box, respectively. The architecture of the momentum backbone is the same as the feature extraction backbone (*i.e.*, the prototype backbone). The mlp in the instance-aware module consists of a 3×3 convolutional layer, a ReLU activation, and a 1×1 convolutional layer. The projector ('proj' in Fig. 3) in the angle modulation is composed of two 1×1 convolutional layers with a ReLU activation between them. In the category-aware module, the number of the transformer encoder is $N = 3$. The CNN block of the category classification has the same architecture as the layer4 of ResNet.

Training stratagy. The parameters of the proposed instance-aware and category-aware modules are randomly initialized. Then, we train the whole model in an end-to-end manner. The training datasets are GOT-10K [15], TrackingNet [26], COCO [20], and LaSOT [10]. Labeled 70 categories of the LaSOT [10] are the known categories. The samples without category labels are ignored by the category classification. The model is trained on the training video sequences for 50 epochs with an Adam solver with a learning rate decay of 0.2 every 15 epochs. Each epoch includes 2000 iterations. In one batch, we sample images from 64 sequences with 6 random frames in each. There are 4 losses in total, including the contrastive loss $\mathcal{L}_{con}$, the category classification loss $\mathcal{L}_{cls}$, the discriminative loss $\mathcal{L}_{dis}$, and the IoU prediction loss $\mathcal{L}_{iou}$. The final loss is:

$$\mathcal{L}_{all} = \mathcal{L}_{con} + \mathcal{L}_{cls} + \mathcal{L}_{dis} + \mathcal{L}_{iou}. \tag{6}$$

$\mathcal{L}_{dis}$ and $\mathcal{L}_{iou}$ are from [2]. We refer the readers to [2] for mor details. $\mathcal{L}_{con}$ is our InfoNCE-V loss defined in Eq. 3. $\mathcal{L}_{cls}$ is the cross entropy loss. The parameters of the momentum backbone and the mlp_k are not updated based on the gradients. Instead, they are initialized by the parameters of the backbone and the mlp_q, and updated via the momentum updating as the Formula 2 lists.

Testing. During the testing phase, we do not need the contrastive learning and category classification parts. The backbone is used to extract the features of the template and the search regions. The template is cropped from the initial frame. We use data augmentation to expand the template, and initialize the template filter according to these augmented images. The template filter is updated during the testing process, like [2] does. For encoding the instance-aware information, we copy the parameters of the mlp_q as those of the mlp in the instance encoder. The padding operation is used for the convolutional layers in the mlp to keep the feature resolution unchanged. The category descriptors remain fixed during the testing phase for encoding the category-aware information. We evaluate our method on various public benchmarks. Our CIA18 and CIA50 run about 43 and 30 fps on one TITAN X GPU, which achieves real-time tracking.

4.2 Ablation Study

We conduct the ablation studies on the OTB100 [37] and the LaSOT [10] datasets. The results of the ablation studies are reported in Table 1. The notations 'CC', 'CE', 'CL', and 'IE' represent category classification, category encoder, contrastive learning, and instance encoder, respectively. If we add the category classification (CC) alone, we obtain minor improvement based on either DiMP18 [2] or SuperDiMP [2] baseline. To utilize the known category information better, we further integrate the category encoder (CE) into the baselines. When adding the category classification (CC) together with the category encoder (CE), we observe a significant improvement. The performance of DiMP18 [2] and SuperDiMP [2] are improved by 3.3% and 1.7% on the LaSOT dataset, respectively. To demonstrate the effectiveness of the instance-aware module, we evaluate the performance of integrating the contrastive learning (CL) and the instance

Table 1. The AUC scores (%) of the ablation studies on OTB100 and LaSOT datasets.

baseline	+CC	+CE	+CL	+IE	AUC on OTB100	AUC on LaSOT
DiMP18	-	-	-	-	66.0	53.5
	✓	-	-	-	66.7	54.0
	✓	✓	-	-	68.1	56.8
	-	-	✓	-	68.4	57.0
	-	-	✓	✓	68.6	57.8
	✓	✓	✓	✓	**70.1**	**59.2**
SuperDiMP	-	-	-	-	70.1	63.1
	✓	-	-	-	69.7	63.8
	✓	✓	-	-	70.4	64.0
	-	-	✓	-	70.5	64.3
	-	-	✓	✓	70.8	65.1
	✓	✓	✓	✓	**71.3**	**66.2**

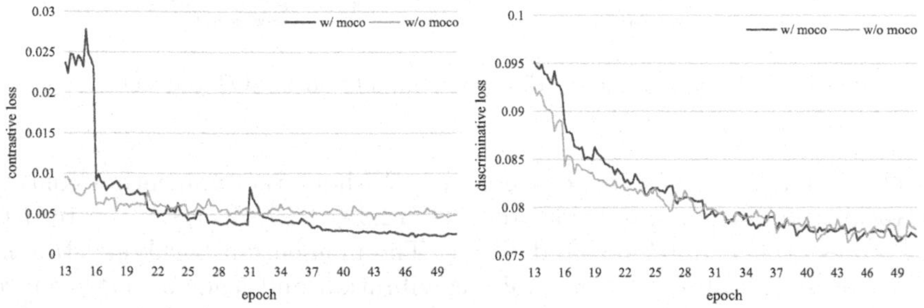

Fig. 6. Contrastive loss and discriminative loss of using momentum update or not.

encoder (IE). The contrastive learning (CL) can enrich the instance information, which improves the performance of DiMP18 from 66.0% and 53.5% to 68.4% and 57% AUC scores on the OTB100 and the LaSOT datasets, respectively. Based on the DiMP18 [2] with the contrastive learning, the instance encoder (IE) can further improve the AUC scores. The best performance is achieved by using both the complete category-aware module and the instance-aware module. By integrating the proposed modules into DiMP18 [2] and SuperDiMP [2], we obtain the CIA18 and CIA50 trackers, respectively. CIA18 achieves 70.1% and 59.2% AUC scores on the OTB100 and the LaSOT datasets. CIA50 obtains 71.3% and 66.2% AUC scores on the OTB100 and LaSOT datasets, respectively.

We also compare the training strategies of using momentum contrast or not based on our CIA18. Without momentum contrast, we use the same backbone to extract the features of the sample pairs for the contrastive learning. Figure 6 illustrates the losses of the two training strategies, which validates that momen-

Table 2. Influence of the category information.

	CIA18 w/ category	CIA18 w/o category	CIA50 w/ category	CIA50 w/o category
AUC on OTB100	70.1	69.7	71.3	71.2
AUC on LaSOT	59.2	58.5	66.2	65.7

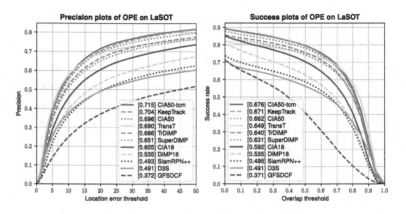

Fig. 7. Precision and overlap success plots on LaSOT dataset.

tum contrast facilitates better convergence. Without the momentum contrast, the tracking performance degrades to 65.8%(4.3%↓)/57.4%(1.8%↓) in terms of AUC scores on OTB100/LaSOT datasets. The momentum backbone stabilizes features of queue, prevents from training vibration and leads a better convergence. It is worth noting that we adopt the momentum contrast as an auxiliary task in the supervised learning process. This is the reason why it can work well with relatively small batch size.

For exploring the influences of the category information, we train our trackers without any known categories, and compare with the performance in Table 2. In this case, the dictionary of the category encoder is initialized randomly and trained with only the discriminative loss. Without any known category, our trackers can also achieve remarkable performance. The known category information can further stabilize the feature extraction and improve the performance.

4.3 State-of-the-Art Comparisons

Results on LaSOT [10]. Figure 7 illustrates the tracking results of the top-performing trackers. On the LaSOT, our CIA50 performs favorably against the state-of-the-arts. After integrating the target candidate matching (tcm) post-processing, like KeepTrack, our CIA50-tcm achieves a 67.6% AUC score, setting a new state-of-the-art record.

Table 3. State-of-the-art comparison on TrackingNet test set. The color red and blue notate the best and the second best result, respectively.

	C-RPN [11]	ATOM [6]	D3S [22]	SiamRPN ++ [18]	DiMP 50 [2]	KYS [3]	SiamFC ++ [38]	PrDiMP 50 [7]	TrDiMP [34]	TransT [5]	CIA 18	CIA 50
Success	66.9	70.3	72.8	73.3	74.0	74.0	75.4	75.8	78.4	81.4	74.5	**79.2**
N.Prec	74.6	77.1	76.8	80.0	80.1	80.0	80.0	81.6	83.3	86.7	80.7	**84.5**
Prec	61.9	64.8	66.4	69.4	68.7	68.8	70.5	70.4	73.1	80.3	69.5	**75.1**

Results on TrackingNet [26]. We evaluate the trackers on the TrackingNet dataset with the online evaluation server. The tracking performance are shown in Table 3. Our CIA50 achieves a success score of 79.2% and a normalized precision score of 84.5%. Our CIA18 performs better than the ResNet18 based tracker ATOM with 4.2% success score.

Results on OTB100 [37], **UAV123** [25], **and NFS** [16]. The results on the OTB100, UAV123 and NFS datasets are shown in Table 4. On the OTB100 and NFS datasets, our tracker CIA50 performs the best, surpassing the recent methods KeepTrack, STARK and TrDiMP. Compared with the ResNet18 based trackers like DiMP18, our CIA18 outperforms it on all 3 datasets.

Table 4. State-of-the-art comparisons on OTB100, UAV123, and NFS. The color red and blue notate the best and the second best result.

	DiMP 18 [2]	TransT [5]	PrDiMP 50 [7]	SiamRPN ++ [18]	Super DiMP [2]	TrSiam [34]	TrDiMP [34]	STARK [39]	Keep Track [24]	CIA 18	CIA 50
OTB [37]	66.0	69.4	69.6	69.6	70.1	70.3	70.8	68.1	**70.9**	70.1	71.3
UAV [25]	64.3	**69.1**	68.0	61.3	67.7	67.4	67.5	68.2	69.7	66.0	68.9
NFS [16]	61.0	65.7	63.5	50.2	64.8	65.8	**66.5**	66.2	66.4	63.2	66.7

Results on GOT-10K [15]. The performance is evaluated on the 180 test video sequences. Table 5 shows the state-of-the-arts comparison results. Our tracker CIA50 achieves a 67.9% AO score, which is 1.8% higher than SuperDiMP.

Results on VOT2020 [17]. The state-of-the-art comparisons on the VOT2020 dataset are shown in Table 6. We compare the bounding box prediction results. Our trackers can achieve competitive performance.

Table 5. State-of-the-art comparison on GOT-10K test set. The color red and blue notate the best and the second best result, respectively.

	SPM [31]	DiMP 18 [2]	SiamFC ++ [38]	D3S [22]	Ocean [41]	DCFST [42]	Siam RCNN [30]	Super DiMP [2]	TrDiMP [34]	TransT [5]	CIA 18	CIA 50
AO	51.3	57.9	59.5	59.7	61.1	63.8	64.9	66.1	67.1	**67.1**	60.4	67.9
$SR_{0.50}$	59.3	67.2	69.5	67.6	72.1	75.3	72.8	77.2	**77.7**	76.8	71.4	79.0
$SR_{0.75}$	35.9	44.6	47.9	46.2	47.3	49.8	59.7	58.7	58.3	60.9	48.3	**60.3**

Table 6. State-of-the-art comparisons on VOT2020. The color red and **blue** notate the best and the second best results.

	SiamFC [1]	ATOM [6]	DiMP50 [2]	UPDT [4]	SuperDiMP [2]	STARK [39]	CIA18	CIA50
EAO(↑)	0.179	0.271	0.274	0.278	0.305	**0.308**	0.278	0.309
A(↑)	0.418	0.462	0.457	0.465	0.477	**0.478**	0.462	0.481
R(↑)	0.502	0.734	0.740	0.755	**0.786**	0.799	0.739	0.782

Results on TNL2K [36]. We evaluate the trackers on the recently proposed TNL2K dataset containing 700 challenging test videos. The comparison results are shown in Fig. 8. Our tracker CIA50 achieves the best performance.

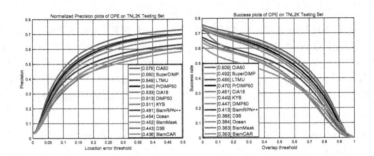

Fig. 8. Normalized precision plots and overlap success plots on TNL2K dataset.

5 Conclusions

In this paper, we propose a novel framework for visual tracking based on instance-level and category-level hierarchical feature embedding. The proposed model extracts deep features by exploiting both intra and inter-video sequences, exploiting richer information for instance discrimination and category generalization. The proposed instance-aware module improves instance discrimination by introducing the contrastive learning method and a novel angel modulation approach to embed the instance information. The category-aware module is developed to generalize the categorical information to unknown categories and enhance categorical consistency, producing stable category descriptors. The instance-aware and category-aware modules are jointly optimized through end-to-end training, achieving the feature embedding that highlights inter-instance separability and intra-instance compactness. Extensive experiments on various benchmarks verify that the proposed method performs favourably against the state-of-the-arts.

Acknowledgement. This work is supported in part by the National Natural Science Foundation of China under Grant 61433007, Grant 61271328, and Grant 62106149.

References

1. Bertinetto, L., Valmadre, J., Henriques, J.F., Vedaldi, A., Torr, P.H.S.: Fully-convolutional Siamese networks for object tracking. In: Hua, G., Jégou, H. (eds.) ECCV 2016. LNCS, vol. 9914, pp. 850–865. Springer, Cham (2016). https://doi.org/10.1007/978-3-319-48881-3_56
2. Bhat, G., Danelljan, M., Gool, L.V., Timofte, R.: Learning discriminative model prediction for tracking. In: ICCV (2019)
3. Bhat, G., Danelljan, M., Van Gool, L., Timofte, R.: Know your surroundings: exploiting scene information for object tracking. In: Vedaldi, A., Bischof, H., Brox, T., Frahm, J.-M. (eds.) ECCV 2020. LNCS, vol. 12368, pp. 205–221. Springer, Cham (2020). https://doi.org/10.1007/978-3-030-58592-1_13
4. Bhat, G., Johnander, J., Danelljan, M., Khan, F.S., Felsberg, M.: Unveiling the power of deep tracking. In: Ferrari, V., Hebert, M., Sminchisescu, C., Weiss, Y. (eds.) ECCV 2018. LNCS, vol. 11206, pp. 493–509. Springer, Cham (2018). https://doi.org/10.1007/978-3-030-01216-8_30
5. Chen, X., Yan, B., Zhu, J., Wang, D., Yang, X., Lu, H.: Transformer tracking. In: CVPR (2021)
6. Danelljan, M., Bhat, G., Khan, F.S., Felsberg, M.: Atom: accurate tracking by overlap maximization. In: CVPR (2019)
7. Danelljan, M., Gool, L.V., Timofte, R.: Probabilistic regression for visual tracking. In: CVPR (2020)
8. Deng, J., Dong, W., Socher, R., Li, L.J., Li, K., Fei-Fei, L.: ImageNet: a large-scale hierarchical image database. In: CVPR (2009)
9. Deng, J., Guo, J., Xue, N., Zafeiriou, S.: ArcFace: additive angular margin loss for deep face recognition. In: CVPR (2019)
10. Fan, H., et al.: LaSOT: a high-quality benchmark for large-scale single object tracking. In: CVPR (2019)
11. Fan, H., Ling, H.: Siamese cascaded region proposal networks for real-time visual tracking. In: CVPR (2019)
12. Guo, D., Wang, J., Cui, Y., Wang, Z., Chen, S.: SiamCAR: Siamese fully convolutional classification and regression for visual tracking. In: CVPR (2020)
13. He, A., Luo, C., Tian, X., Zeng, W.: A twofold siamese network for real-time object tracking. In: CVPR (2018)
14. He, K., Fan, H., Wu, Y., Xie, S., Girshick, R.: Momentum contrast for unsupervised visual representation learning. In: CVPR (2020)
15. Huang, L., Zhao, X., Huang, K.: Got-10k: A large high-diversity benchmark for generic object tracking in the wild. IEEE Trans. Pattern Anal. Mach. Intell. **43**(5), 1562–1577 (2021). https://doi.org/10.1109/TPAMI.2019.2957464
16. Kiani Galoogahi, H., Fagg, A., Huang, C., Ramanan, D., Lucey, S.: Need for speed: A benchmark for higher frame rate object tracking. In: ICCV (2017)
17. Kristan, M., et al.: The eighth visual object tracking vot2020 challenge results. In: Bartoli, A., Fusiello, A. (eds.) ECCV 2020. LNCS, vol. 12539, pp. 547–601. Springer, Cham (2020). https://doi.org/10.1007/978-3-030-68238-5_39
18. Li, B., Wu, W., Wang, Q., Zhang, F., Xing, J., Yan, J.: SiamRPN++: evolution of Siamese visual tracking with very deep networks. In: CVPR (2019)
19. Li, B., Yan, J., Wu, W., Zhu, Z., Hu, X.: High performance visual tracking with Siamese region proposal network. In: CVPR (2018)
20. Lin, T.-Y., et al.: Microsoft COCO: common objects in context. In: Fleet, D., Pajdla, T., Schiele, B., Tuytelaars, T. (eds.) ECCV 2014. LNCS, vol. 8693, pp. 740–755. Springer, Cham (2014). https://doi.org/10.1007/978-3-319-10602-1_48

21. Liu, W., Wen, Y., Yu, Z., Li, M., Raj, B., Song, L.: SphereFace: deep hypersphere embedding for face recognition. In: CVPR (2017)
22. Lukezic, A., Matas, J., Kristan, M.: D3s - a discriminative single shot segmentation tracker. In: CVPR (2020)
23. Van der Maaten, L., Hinton, G.: Visualizing data using T-SNE. J. Mach. Learn. Res. **9**(11), 2579–2605 (2008)
24. Mayer, C., Danelljan, M., Paudel, D.P., Van Gool, L.: Learning target candidate association to keep track of what not to track. In: ICCV (2021)
25. Mueller, M., Smith, N., Ghanem, B.: A benchmark and simulator for UAV tracking. In: Leibe, B., Matas, J., Sebe, N., Welling, M. (eds.) ECCV 2016. LNCS, vol. 9905, pp. 445–461. Springer, Cham (2016). https://doi.org/10.1007/978-3-319-46448-0_27
26. Müller, M., Bibi, A., Giancola, S., Alsubaihi, S., Ghanem, B.: TrackingNet: a large-scale dataset and benchmark for object tracking in the wild. In: Ferrari, V., Hebert, M., Sminchisescu, C., Weiss, Y. (eds.) ECCV 2018. LNCS, vol. 11205, pp. 310–327. Springer, Cham (2018). https://doi.org/10.1007/978-3-030-01246-5_19
27. Oord, A.v.d., Li, Y., Vinyals, O.: Representation learning with contrastive predictive coding. arXiv preprint arXiv:1807.03748 (2018)
28. Tao, R., Gavves, E., Smeulders, A.W.: Siamese instance search for tracking. In: CVPR (2016)
29. Valmadre, J., Bertinetto, L., Henriques, J., Vedaldi, A., Torr, P.H.S.: End-to-end representation learning for correlation filter based tracking. In: CVPR (2017)
30. Voigtlaender, P., Luiten, J., Torr, P.H., Leibe, B.: Siam R-CNN: visual tracking by re-detection. In: CVPR (2020)
31. Wang, G., Luo, C., Xiong, Z., Zeng, W.: SPM-tracker: series-parallel matching for real-time visual object tracking. In: CVPR (2019)
32. Wang, N., Song, Y., Ma, C., Zhou, W., Liu, W., Li, H.: Unsupervised deep tracking. In: CVPR (2019)
33. Wang, N., Zhou, W., Wang, J., Li, H.: Transformer meets tracker: Exploiting temporal context for robust visual tracking. In: CVPR (2021)
34. Wang, N., Zhou, W., Wang, J., Li, H.: Transformer meets tracker: exploiting temporal context for robust visual tracking. In: CVPR (2021)
35. Wang, Q., Zhang, L., Bertinetto, L., Hu, W., Torr, P.H.: Fast online object tracking and segmentation: a unifying approach. In: CVPR (2019)
36. Wang, X., et al.: Towards more flexible and accurate object tracking with natural language: algorithms and benchmark. In: CVPR (2021)
37. Wu, Y., Lim, J., Yang, M.H.: Object tracking benchmark. IEEE Trans. Pattern Anal. Mach. Intell. **37**(9), 1834–1848 (2015)
38. Xu, Y., Wang, Z., Li, Z., Yuan, Y., Yu, G.: SiamFC++: towards robust and accurate visual tracking with target estimation guidelines. In: AAAI (2020)
39. Yan, B., Peng, H., Fu, J., Wang, D., Lu, H.: Learning spatio-temporal transformer for visual tracking. In: ICCV (2021)
40. Zhang, Z., Peng, H.: Deeper and wider Siamese networks for real-time visual tracking. In: CVPR (2019)
41. Zhang, Z., Peng, H., Fu, J., Li, B., Hu, W.: Ocean: object-aware anchor-free tracking. In: Vedaldi, A., Bischof, H., Brox, T., Frahm, J.-M. (eds.) ECCV 2020. LNCS, vol. 12366, pp. 771–787. Springer, Cham (2020). https://doi.org/10.1007/978-3-030-58589-1_46
42. Zheng, L., Tang, M., Chen, Y., Wang, J., Lu, H.: Learning feature embeddings for discriminant model based tracking. In: Vedaldi, A., Bischof, H., Brox, T., Frahm,

J.-M. (eds.) Chen, Y., Wang, J., Lu, H.: Learning feature embeddings for discriminant model based tracking. In: ECCV (2020). LNCS, vol. 12360, pp. 759–775. Springer, Cham (2020). https://doi.org/10.1007/978-3-030-58555-6_45

43. Zhu, Z., Wang, Q., Li, B., Wu, W., Yan, J., Hu, W.: Distractor-aware Siamese networks for visual object tracking. In: Ferrari, V., Hebert, M., Sminchisescu, C., Weiss, Y. (eds.) ECCV 2018. LNCS, vol. 11213, pp. 103–119. Springer, Cham (2018). https://doi.org/10.1007/978-3-030-01240-3_7

Tackling Background Distraction in Video Object Segmentation

Suhwan Cho[1], Heansung Lee[1], Minhyeok Lee[1], Chaewon Park[1],
Sungjun Jang[1], Minjung Kim[1], and Sangyoun Lee[1,2(✉)]

[1] Yonsei University, Seoul, South Korea
syleee@yonsei.ac.kr
[2] Korea Institute of Science and Technology (KIST), Seoul, South Korea

Abstract. Semi-supervised video object segmentation (VOS) aims to densely track certain designated objects in videos. One of the main challenges in this task is the existence of background distractors that appear similar to the target objects. We propose three novel strategies to suppress such distractors: 1) a spatio-temporally diversified template construction scheme to obtain generalized properties of the target objects; 2) a learnable distance-scoring function to exclude spatially-distant distractors by exploiting the temporal consistency between two consecutive frames; 3) swap-and-attach augmentation to force each object to have unique features by providing training samples containing entangled objects. On all public benchmark datasets, our model achieves a comparable performance to contemporary state-of-the-art approaches, even with real-time performance. Qualitative results also demonstrate the superiority of our approach over existing methods. We believe our approach will be widely used for future VOS research. Code and models are available at https://github.com/suhwan-cho/TBD.

Keywords: Video object segmentation · Metric learning · Temporal consistency · Video data augmentation

1 Introduction

Video object segmentation (VOS) aims to keep tracking certain designated objects within an entire given video at the pixel level. Depending on the type of guidance provided with regard to the target objects, VOS can be divided into semi-supervised VOS, unsupervised VOS, referring VOS, and other subcategories. We focus on the semi-supervised setting, in which densely-annotated objects are provided in the initial frame of a video. Given its diverse applicability, semi-supervised VOS has recently attracted extensive attention in many vision fields such as autonomous driving, video editing, and video surveillance.

In semi-supervised VOS, one of the main challenges is the existence of background distractors that have a similar appearance to the target objects. As comparing visual properties is a fundamental technique to detect and track the designated objects, visual distractions can severely lower the reliability of

S. Avidan et al. (Eds.): ECCV 2022, LNCS 13682, pp. 446–462, 2022.
https://doi.org/10.1007/978-3-031-20047-2_26

a system. We propose three novel strategies to suppress the negative influence of background distractions in VOS: 1) a spatio-temporally diversified template construction scheme to prepare various object properties for reliable and stable prediction; 2) a learnable distance-scoring function to consider the temporal consistency of a video; 3) swap-and-attach data augmentation to provide hard training samples showing severe occlusions.

As VOS is a pixel-level classification task that requires fine-grained information, most feature matching-based approaches including VideoMatch [12] and RANet [36] adopt pixel-level fine matching. While this approach is popular owing to its superior ability to capture details, it also has the shortcoming of easily causing noise. Given that each element in its template has small receptive fields, it is very susceptible to background distractors. To address this issue, we propose a novel way to construct a coarse matching template by compressing the fine matching template considering the probability of each pixel location. Unlike the fine matching template, each element in the coarse matching template covers large receptive fields that are dynamically defined based on past predictions. By employing fine matching and coarse matching simultaneously, more stable predictions can be obtained thanks to improved spatial diversity. In addition, to construct various templates exploiting multiple temporal properties in a video, we operate multiple templates that are independently built and updated based on their own strategies. The proposed spatio-temporally diversified template construction enables the model to capture local details while simultaneously obtaining a clear distinction between foreground and background as well as learning the ability to utilize various time-specific properties.

While visual information is important, exploiting temporal consistency between adjacent frames is also important for a robust VOS. To leverage the temporal consistency of a video, FEELVOS [34] and CFBI [41] apply a square window when transferring the reference frame information to the query frame. RMNet [38] reduces the search area based on the coarsely predicted segmentation mask of the query frame. These hard windowing methods, which totally exclude the non-candidates, are effective for capturing the locality of a video, but as the size of a window is a discrete value, a human-tuning process is required for setting the hyper-parameters, which makes the solution less elegant and incomplete. To overcome this issue, we propose a learnable distance-scoring function that takes the distance between two pixels of consecutive frames as its input and simply outputs a spatial distance score from 0 to 1. When transferring the information from a reference frame pixel to a query frame pixel, it outputs a low score for distant pixels and vice versa.

We also propose a novel data augmentation technique for VOS, termed swap-and-attach augmentation. By simply swapping the objects between multiple sequences and attaching the swapped objects on the frames, realistic video data with severe occlusions can be simulated. As this creates training snippets containing multiple entangled objects, the model can learn strong feature representations to force each object to have unique features. Furthermore, it generalizes the model by dramatically increasing the amount of VOS training data, which is scarce as compared to other vision tasks.

We validate the effectiveness of our method by evaluating it on three public VOS benchmark datasets, i.e., DAVIS 2016 [28], DAVIS 2017 [29], and YouTube-VOS 2018 [40] datasets. On all datasets, our method achieves a competitive performance compared to the current state-of-the-art methods while maintaining a real-time inference speed. In particular, in complex scenarios that have background distractors, our approach is proven to be much more effective than state-of-the-art solutions. Note that all our experiments are implemented on a single GeForce RTX 2080 Ti GPU, which makes our method much more accessible than other state-of-the-art methods, which require powerful hardware resources. We believe our proposed three novel strategies will be widely used for future VOS research.

Our main contributions can be summarized as follows:

- We introduce a spatio-temporally diversified template construction mechanism to prepare diverse features for stable and robust feature matching.
- We propose an end-to-end learnable distance-scoring function to fully exploit the temporal consistency between two consecutive frames in a video.
- We present swap-and-attach augmentation to learn a strong VOS model by ensuring the diversity of training data and simulating occluded samples.
- Our proposed approach achieves a competitive performance on the DAVIS and YouTube-VOS datasets, while maintaining a real-time performance.

2   Related Work

Feature Similarity Matching. Contemporary VOS methods track and segment the designated objects based on the similarity of the embedded features. Given that semi-supervised VOS is a pixel-level classification task, pixel-level fine matching is adopted in most cases. PML [3] learns a pixel-wise embedding using the nearest neighbor classifier. VideoMatch [12] produces foreground and background similarity maps using a soft matching layer. Extending these works, FEELVOS [34] and CFBI [41] exploit global matching and local matching to obtain long-term and short-term appearance information. RANet [36] maximizes the use of similarity maps from feature similarity matching by ranking and selecting conformable feature maps as per their importance. To fully exploit the information extracted from all previous frames, STM [27] adopts a memory network by defining the past frames with object masks as external memory and the current frame as the query. The query and the memory are densely matched in feature space, covering all the space-time pixel locations. Extended from STM, KMN [31] proposes memory-to-query matching to reduce background distractions when transferring the memorized information by applying a 2D Gaussian kernel. EGMN [25] exploits an episodic memory network where frames are stored as nodes so that cross-frame correlations can be captured effectively. These memory-based methods achieve admirable performance but face a serious issue: the size of memory increases over time, and therefore, they are not efficient for long videos. To address this, GC [19] stores and updates a key-value mapping instead of storing all the key and value features of the past frames.

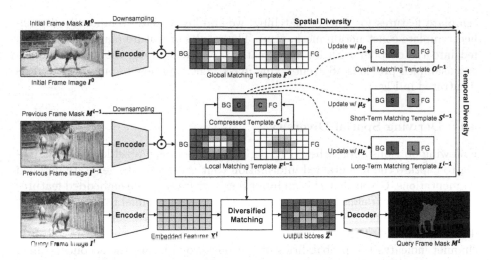

Fig. 1. Architecture of our proposed method. The templates for feature similarity matching are independently constructed and updated as per their own objectives. The spatial diversity and temporal diversity of the templates are represented horizontally and vertically, respectively. Several components, e.g., skip connections and mask propagation, are omitted for better clarification of the overall architecture.

AFB-URR [21] introduces an adaptive feature bank update scheme to efficiently discard obsolete features and absorb new features based on a pre-defined policy.

Leveraging Temporal Consistency. As a video shares some common properties between the consecutive frames, there are several VOS methods that leverage this temporal consistency of a video. FEELVOS and CFBI apply a fixed-sized square window for a local feature similarity matching. When transferring information from the previous adjacent frame to the query frame, each query frame pixel can only refer to the region within a square window centered on the spatial location of that pixel. Similarly, RMNet [38] also reduces the search area by applying a square window. An optical flow model first coarsely predicts the segmentation mask of the query frame by warping the previous frame segmentation mask. Then, a square window is generated and applied based on the coarsely predicted query frame segmentation mask. These hard windowing methods are effective at leveraging the temporal consistency of a video, but as the size of a window is a discrete value, it needs a human-tuning process and is also not end-to-end learnable.

3 Approach

In our framework, frames in a video sequence are segmented using the ground truth segmentation mask given in the initial frame. Mask prediction is performed based on feature similarity between the embedded features. To prepare various template features for feature matching, we employ a spatio-temporally diversified template construction mechanism. The results of feature matching are then fed into the decoder with low-level features extracted from the encoder and a downsampled previous adjacent frame mask. The overview of our framework is illustrated in Fig. 1.

3.1   Deriving Spatial Diversity

Following previous approaches [6, 12, 34, 36, 41], we employ pixel-level fine matching to capture the fine-grained information that is essential to generate detailed segmentations. Given that I^i is an input image at frame i, the embedded features for that frame are defined as $X^i \in [-1, 1]^{C \times H \times W}$ after channel L2 normalization. The provided or predicted segmentation mask and its downsampled version are denoted as $M^i \in [0, 1]^{2 \times H0 \times W0}$ and $m^i \in [0, 1]^{2 \times H \times W}$, respectively. The first channel indicates the probabilities of the background, and the second channel indicates those of a foreground object. Using X^i and m^i, we define the pixel-level fine matching template $F^i \in [-1, 1]^{C \times H \times W}$ as

$$F^i_{BG} = X^i \odot m^i_0$$
$$F^i_{FG} = X^i \odot m^i_1 \, , \tag{1}$$

where $\odot$ denotes the Hadamard product and m^i_0 and m^i_1 denote the first and second channels of m^i, respectively.

Fine matching is effective at capturing the details that are inherent at the pixel-level, but thereafter, is susceptible to background distractors that have a similar appearance to a foreground object. In order to obtain more general features for an object and its background, i.e., to obtain spatial diversity, we propose coarse matching to complement the fine matching. Unlike the fine matching template whose receptive fields are small and local, the receptive fields of the coarse matching template are dynamically defined covering a large range. Therefore, coarse matching is able to obtain a clear distinction between foreground and background because outlier features are less likely to negatively affect the feature similarity matching scores.

To design the coarse matching template, we first build a compressed template $C^i \in [-1, 1]^{C \times 1 \times 1}$ that indicates the normalized mean features of X^i weighted by the probabilities of each class in every spatial location. By using pre-computed F^i, it can be summarized as

$$C^i_{BG} = \mathcal{N}\left(\mathcal{S}\left(X^i \odot m^i_0\right)\right) = \mathcal{N}\left(\mathcal{S}\left(F^i_{BG}\right)\right)$$
$$C^i_{FG} = \mathcal{N}\left(\mathcal{S}\left(X^i \odot m^i_1\right)\right) = \mathcal{N}\left(\mathcal{S}\left(F^i_{FG}\right)\right) \, , \tag{2}$$

where $\mathcal{S}$ and $\mathcal{N}$ indicate channel-wise summation and channel L2 normalization, respectively. The compressed template is used to build various coarse matching templates according to respective strategies that are pre-defined based on certain objectives to exploit various temporal characteristics.

3.2   Deriving Temporal Diversity

As much as spatial diversity is effective to enrich the semantic information of the embedded features, utilizing temporal diversity is also important considering the nature of a video. When constructing the fine matching templates, we use the initial frame to exploit accurate information and the previous adjacent frame to leverage the most related information, similar to FEELVOS [34], CFBI [41], and BMVOS [6]. Those matching templates are defined as the global matching template and local matching template, respectively.

As opposed to the fine matching template whose elements contain their unique positional information, the features in the compressed template do not contain any positional information because it only has a single spatial location. Therefore, it is able to integrate multiple compressed templates of historic frames based on specific goals. Using this, we build temporally diversified coarse matching templates to fully exploit various time-specific properties of a video. We define the coarse matching templates as follows: 1) an overall matching template that memorizes the general features along an entire video; 2) a short-term matching template that is built by paying more attention to temporally-near frames; 3) a long-term matching template that is built by paying more attention to temporally-distant frames. Assuming frame i is the current frame being processed, the overall matching template $O^i \in [-1,1]^{C \times 1 \times 1}$, short-term matching template $S^i \in [-1,1]^{C \times 1 \times 1}$, and long-term matching template $L^i \in [-1,1]^{C \times 1 \times 1}$ are defined as follows.

$$\mu_{O,BG} = \Sigma_{k=0}^{i-1} \mathcal{S}\left(m_0^k\right) / \Sigma_{k=0}^{i} \mathcal{S}\left(m_0^k\right)$$

$$\mu_{O,FG} = \Sigma_{k=0}^{i-1} \mathcal{S}\left(m_1^k\right) / \Sigma_{k=0}^{i} \mathcal{S}\left(m_1^k\right)$$

$$O_{BG}^i = \mathcal{N}\left(\mu_{O,BG} O_{BG}^{i-1} + (1 - \mu_{O,BG}) C_{BG}^i\right)$$

$$O_{FG}^i = \mathcal{N}\left(\mu_{O,FG} O_{FG}^{i-1} + (1 - \mu_{O,FG}) C_{FG}^i\right) \tag{3}$$

$$S_{BG}^i = \mathcal{N}\left(\mu_{S,BG} S_{BG}^{i-1} + (1 - \mu_{S,BG}) C_{BG}^i\right)$$

$$S_{FG}^i = \mathcal{N}\left(\mu_{S,FG} S_{FG}^{i-1} + (1 - \mu_{S,FG}) C_{FG}^i\right) \tag{4}$$

$$L_{BG}^i = \mathcal{N}\left(\mu_{L,BG} L_{BG}^{i-1} + (1 - \mu_{L,BG}) C_{BG}^i\right)$$

$$L_{FG}^i = \mathcal{N}\left(\mu_{L,FG} L_{FG}^{i-1} + (1 - \mu_{L,FG}) C_{FG}^i\right) \tag{5}$$

Considering that the compressed template is a channel normalized vector, taking the average over two vectors will generate a vector with a scale lower than 1, if two vectors have different directions. Therefore, the scale of the coarse matching templates will keep decreasing over time, which will lead to a scale-vanishing problem that engenders low confidence in the coarse matching. To prevent this, we apply channel re-normalization after every template update step to maintain the scale of the coarse matching templates at 1. The inertia values for short-term matching and long-term matching, i.e., μ_S and μ_L, are learnable parameters and trained during the network training stage. To press

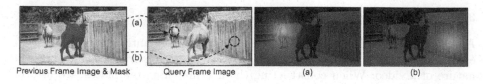

Previous Frame Image & Mask   Query Frame Image   (a)   (b)

Fig. 2. Visualized information transfer flow for local matching when spatial distance scoring is applied. The information of each reference frame pixel is weighted by a distance score that indicates how close two pixels are spatially.

the values to be trained for respective objectives, we set the initial values to $\frac{1}{1+exp(1)}$ and $\frac{1}{1+exp(-1)}$, respectively. At the initial frame, all μ values are set to 0 because there is no previous frame.

3.3   Diversified Feature Similarity Matching

Assuming frame i is the query frame, the spatio-temporally diversified templates, i.e., global matching template F^0, local matching template F^{i-1}, overall matching template O^{i-1}, short-term matching template S^{i-1}, and long-term matching template L^{i-1}, are compared to the query frame embedded features X^i. Given that a feature similarity matching template has a size of $C \times M \times N$, taking a matrix inner product along the channel dimension with X^i will output a similarity map with the size of $MN \times HW$. By taking query-wise maximum operation and reshaping, a score map with the size of $H \times W$ can be obtained for each template and class. As there are five different matching templates consisting of foreground and background, the output scores of feature similarity matching are defined as $Z^i \in [-1, 1]^{10 \times H \times W}$. These scores are fed into a decoder as an input, to provide visually derived information that can specify the target object.

3.4   Spatial Distance Scoring

As described before, the feature similarity matching operates in a non-local manner, which excludes the importance of temporal consistency of a video. However, adjacent frames in a video sequence are strongly dependent on each other, and therefore, are predominantly local. To exploit this locality of VOS, FEELVOS [34] and CFBI [41] restrict the search area by applying a square window for every spatial location when transferring the previous adjacent frame information to the query frame. Similarly, RMNet [38] reduces the search area under a hard square that is generated by warping the previous frame mask using a pre-trained optical flow model. These hard windowing methods are effective at capturing the temporal consistency of a video, but as the size of a window is a discrete value, it needs a human-tuning process, which makes the solution less elegant and complete.

   To obtain temporal consistency automatically without any human-tuning process, we propose an end-to-end learnable distance-scoring function that takes

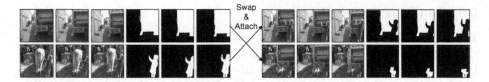

Fig. 3. Example video sequences before and after applying swap-and-attach data augmentation method.

a spatial distance between two pixels as its input and simply outputs a distance score from 0 to 1. When performing local matching with the previous frame, we first calculate a distance matrix that comprises of the spatial distance of every previous adjacent frame pixel location p and query frame pixel location q based on Euclidean distance as

$$d = \sqrt{(p_x - q_x)^2 + (p_y - q_y)^2},$$ (6)

where p_x, p_y, q_x, and q_y are x, y coordinates of p and q. Then, by independently applying the distance-scoring function to every single element in the matrix, spatial distance score D can be obtained as

$$D = f(d; \mathrm{w}) = Sigmoid\left(\mathrm{w}_2 * \max\left(0, \mathrm{w}_1 * \mathrm{d}\right)\right),$$ (7)

where f is the distance-scoring function and w indicates learnable parameters of f. By multiplying the spatial distance scores to feature similarity scores obtained from the local matching, the spatial distance as well as the feature distance can be reflected in the similarity matching scores. Figure 2 shows the information transfer flow when applying spatial distance scoring. As information transfer is adjusted by spatial distance scores between two pixels, temporal consistency between adjacent frames can be effectively considered.

3.5 Swap-and-Attach Augmentation

As annotating video data in a pixel level is extremely laborious, VOS data is not sufficient compared to other computer vision tasks. To increase the amount of VOS training data, we propose a swap-and-attach data augmentation method. In Fig. 3, we show some example sequences when applying swap-and-attach augmentation. During the network training stage, each video sequence of a single batch exchanges its information with another video sequence of a different batch. The objects from multiple frames are jointly swapped between different sequences and attached on respective frames. As this process does not harm the temporal consistency of each video sequence, the generated video sequences are also realistic and have temporal connectivity between the consecutive frames. The swap-and-attach augmentation has two main advantages. First, as the amount of training data is dramatically increased, the model can be much more generalized. Second, as the objects may be severely occluded by the attached objects, the model can learn strong feature representations to force each object to have unique features.

3.6 Implementation Details

Encoder. We take the DenseNet-121 [13] architecture as our encoder. To initialize the model with rich feature representations, we use the ImageNet [17] pretrained version. As the highest-level features extracted from original DenseNet-121 have low resolution, we skip the last block to use a higher feature resolution.

Decoder. Taking processed features from the encoder and cues from feature matching module, the decoder generates the final segmentation. To better exploit the locality of VOS, m^{i-1} is fed into the decoder when predicting frame i. As Z^i and m^{i-1} have a small spatial size compared to the required output size, low-level features extracted from the encoder are also fed into the middle of the decoder via skip connections. For fast decoding, a channel-reducing deconvolutional layer [43] is added after every skip connection as in CRVOS [5]. To obtain rich feature representations, we adopt CBAM [37] after every deconvolutional layer.

3.7 Network Training

Following most state-of-the-art methods [10,21,27,31,38], we simulate training samples using static image dataset, COCO [23], to obtain sufficient training data. After pre-training the network using static images, either the DAVIS 2017 [29] training set or YouTube-VOS 2018 [40] training set is used for the main training depending on the testing dataset. From a video sequence, we randomly crop 384×384 patches from 10 consecutive frames jointly. If the first frame does not contain any object, the cropping is repeated until it contains at least one object. After that, a single designated object is defined as a foreground object and other objects are considered as background. Similar to CFBI [41], if the number of foreground pixels is not enough, that sequence is not used for network training to prevent the model from being biased to background attributes. We use cross-entropy loss and Adam optimizer [16] with a learning rate of 1e-4 without learning rate decay. During the network training, the backbone encoder is frozen and all batch normalization layers [14] are disabled. The swap-and-attach augmentation is applied with a probability of 20%.

4 Experiments

In this section, we first describe the datasets and evaluation metrics used in this study in Sect. 4.1. Each component of our proposed approach is validated in Sect. 4.2. Quantitative and qualitative comparison with state-of-the-art methods can be found in Sect. 4.3 and Sect. 4.4, respectively. Our method is abbreviated as TBD.

4.1 Experimental Setup

Datasets. The task of semi-supervised VOS is associated with two popular benchmark datasets, i.e., DAVIS [28,29] and YouTube-VOS [40] datasets. DAVIS

Table 1. Ablation study on the proposed components. G, L, O, and T indicate the use of global, local, overall, and short-term & long-term matching templates, respectively. DS, HW, and Size denote spatial distance scoring, hard windowing, and window size for the hard windowing (the distance between the center point and side of a window). Aug indicates the use of swap-and-attach augmentation. The models are tested on the DAVIS 2017 validation set.

Version	G	L	O	T	DS	HW	Size	Aug	$\mathcal{G}_M$	$\mathcal{J}_M$	$\mathcal{F}_M$
I	✓	✓			✓		-	✓	77.2	75.3	79.1
II		✓	✓		✓		-	✓	72.7	70.2	75.2
III	✓	✓	✓		✓		-	✓	79.1	76.7	81.6
IV	✓	✓		✓	✓		-	✓	78.7	76.7	80.7
V	✓	✓	✓	✓			-	✓	78.8	76.7	80.9
VI	✓	✓	✓	✓		✓	1	✓	79.2	76.9	81.5
VII	✓	✓	✓	✓		✓	2	✓	79.3	76.9	81.8
VIII	✓	✓	✓	✓		✓	4	✓	79.9	77.4	82.5
IX	✓	✓	✓	✓		✓	8	✓	78.5	76.3	80.7
X	✓	✓	✓	✓	✓		-		78.6	76.1	81.2
XI	✓	✓	✓	✓	✓		-	✓	80.0	77.6	82.3

2016 consists of 30 videos in the training set and 20 videos in the validation set. DAVIS 2017 comprises 60 videos in the training set, 30 videos in the validation set, and 30 videos in the test-dev set. Each video is 24 fps and all frames are annotated. YouTube-VOS 2018 is the largest dataset for VOS, containing 3,471 videos in the training set and 474 videos in the validation set. All videos are 30 fps, annotated every five frames.

Evaluation Metrics. We use the standard evaluation metrics for VOS. The predicted segmentation masks with hard labels are evaluated using region accuracy and contour accuracy. Region accuracy $\mathcal{J}$ can be obtained by computing the number of pixels in the intersection between the predicted segmentation mask and the ground truth segmentation mask and then dividing it by the size of their union. Contour accuracy $\mathcal{F}$ can be obtained using the same process but is evaluated only on the object boundaries. The overall accuracy $\mathcal{G}$ is the average of the $\mathcal{J}$ and $\mathcal{F}$ measures.

4.2 Analysis

Spatio-Temporal Diversity of Template. To capture the local keypoints while perceiving the global tendencies, we employ a fine matching template and coarse matching template simultaneously. In addition, we build each template using multiple sub-templates to exploit various temporal properties. In Table 1, various model versions with different template construction schemes are compared. As can be seen, a joint use of fine matching and coarse matching significantly improves the performance compared to when each one is used individually. The use of diverse temporal properties is also quantitatively validated

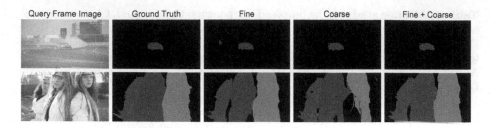

Fig. 4. Qualitative comparison of various model versions with different spatial template construction schemes. Fine and coarse indicate the use of fine matching and coarse matching, respectively.

to be effective. In Fig. 4, we compare the results of various model versions with different spatial diversities of a feature matching template. As can be seen, fine matching is effective for capturing local details (second sequence), but thereafter, is susceptible to visual distractions as it misses the global tendencies (first sequence). By contrast, coarse matching can capture the general features for an object (first sequence), but is not able to capture the details of the objects (second sequence). By using fine and coarse matching methods simultaneously, their respective advantages can be effectively leveraged.

Spatial Distance Scoring. In order to capture the temporal consistency between consecutive frames in a video without a human-tuning process, we present a novel spatial distance scoring method by learning a distance-scoring function that takes a spatial distance between two pixels as its input and outputs a naive distance score. According to Table 1, our proposed spatial distance scoring method is more effective than hard windowing method used in FEELVOS [34] and CFBI [41], even without the need for manual tuning. We also visualize a fully-trained

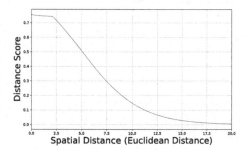

Fig. 5. Visualized input and output of a fully-trained distance-scoring function. Spatial distance indicates the Euclidean distance between two pixels after feature embedding.

distance-scoring function to confirm that it really works. As can be seen in Fig. 5, the fully-trained distance-scoring function outputs a high distance score when two pixels are spatially near, and vice versa, which accords with the expected behavior.

Swap-and-Attach Augmentation. Our proposed swap-and-attach augmentation is also demonstrated to be effective through a quantitative evaluation in Table 1. Simply swapping and attaching the objects of different batches brings 1.4% improvement on a $\mathcal{G}$ score, as it increases the amount of training data and provides hard training samples that contain some severe occlusions.

Table 2. Quantitative evaluation on the DAVIS datasets. OL denotes online learning. (+S) denotes the use of static image datasets during the network training.

Method	OL	fps	2016 val			2017 val			2017 test-dev		
			$\mathcal{G}_M$	$\mathcal{J}_M$	$\mathcal{F}_M$	$\mathcal{G}_M$	$\mathcal{J}_M$	$\mathcal{F}_M$	$\mathcal{G}_M$	$\mathcal{J}_M$	$\mathcal{F}_M$
STCNN (+S) [39]		0.26	83.8	83.8	83.8	61.7	58.7	64.6	-	-	-
FEELVOS (+S) [34]		2.22	81.7	80.3	83.1	69.1	65.9	72.3	54.4	51.2	57.5
DMM-Net (+S) [44]		-	-	-	-	70.7	68.1	73.3	-	-	-
AGSS-VOS (+S) [22]		10.0	-	-	-	67.4	64.9	69.9	57.2	54.8	59.7
RANet (+S) [36]		30.3	85.5	85.5	85.4	65.7	63.2	68.2	55.3	53.4	57.2
DTN (+S) [45]		14.3	83.6	83.7	83.5	67.4	64.2	70.6	-	-	-
STM (+S) [27]		6.25	86.5	84.8	<u>88.1</u>	71.6	69.2	74.0	-	-	-
DIPNet (+S) [11]		0.92	86.1	85.8	86.4	68.5	65.3	71.6	55.2	-	-
LWL (+S) [1]	✓	14.0	-	-	-	74.3	72.2	76.3	-	-	-
CFBI (+S) [41]		5.56	86.1	85.3	86.9	74.9	72.1	77.7	-	-	-
GC (+S) [19]		25.0	86.6	<u>87.6</u>	85.7	71.4	69.3	73.5	-	-	-
KMN (+S) [31]		8.33	<u>87.6</u>	87.1	<u>88.1</u>	76.0	74.2	77.8	-	-	-
AFB-URR (+S) [21]		4.00	-	-	-	74.6	73.0	76.1	-	-	-
STG-Net (+S) [24]		-	85.7	85.4	86.0	74.7	71.5	77.9	<u>63.1</u>	<u>59.7</u>	<u>66.5</u>
RMNet (+S) [38]		11.9	81.5	80.6	82.3	75.0	72.8	77.2	-	-	-
LCM (+S) [10]		8.47	-	-	-	75.2	73.1	77.2	-	-	-
SSTVOS (+S) [8]		-	-	-	-	78.4	75.4	81.4	-	-	-
HMMN (+S) [32]		10.0	**89.4**	**88.2**	**90.6**	**80.4**	**77.7**	**83.1**	-	-	-
TBD (+S)		**50.1**	86.8	87.5	86.2	<u>80.0</u>	<u>77.6</u>	<u>82.3</u>	**69.4**	**66.6**	**72.2**
AGSS-VOS [22]		10.0	-	-	-	66.6	63.4	69.8	54.3	51.5	57.1
RANet [36]		30.3	-	73.2	-	-	-	-	-	-	-
STM [27]		6.25	-	-	-	43.0	38.1	47.9	-	-	-
FRTM [30]	✓	21.9	81.7	-	-	68.8	66.4	71.2	-	-	-
TVOS [46]		37.0	-	-	-	72.3	69.9	74.7	<u>63.1</u>	58.8	<u>67.4</u>
JOINT [26]	✓	4.00	-	-	-	**78.6**	**76.0**	**81.2**	-	-	-
BMVOS [6]		<u>45.9</u>	<u>82.2</u>	<u>82.9</u>	<u>81.4</u>	72.7	70.7	74.7	62.7	<u>60.7</u>	64.7
TBD		**50.1**	**84.3**	**85.2**	**83.4**	<u>75.2</u>	<u>73.2</u>	<u>77.2</u>	**66.0**	**63.1**	**68.9**

4.3 Quantitative Results

DAVIS. We present a quantitative comparison of our proposed method with state-of-the art methods on the DAVIS 2016 [28] and DAVIS 2017 [29] datasets in Table 2. For all methods, inference speed is calculated on the DAVIS 2016 validation set with the 480p resolution. TBD shows competitive performance on all datasets, even maintaining a real-time inference speed. Compared to the real-time methods faster than 24 fps (DAVIS default setting), it outperforms all existing methods by a significant margin.

YouTube-VOS. In Table 3, our method is compared to state-of-the-art methods on the YouTube-VOS 2018 validation set. Gen. indicates the generalization gap

Table 3. Quantitative evaluation on the YouTube-VOS 2018 validation set. OL denotes online learning and (+S) denotes the use of static image datasets during the network training. Gen. denotes the generalization gap between seen and unseen categories.

Method	OL	fps	$\mathcal{G}_M$	$\mathcal{J}_S$	$\mathcal{J}_U$	$\mathcal{F}_S$	$\mathcal{F}_U$	Gen.
DMM-Net (+S) [44]		12.0	51.7	58.3	41.6	60.7	46.3	15.6
STM (+S) [27]		-	79.4	79.7	72.8	84.2	80.9	5.10
SAT (+S) [2]		39.0	63.6	67.1	55.3	70.2	61.7	10.2
LWL (+S) [1]	✓	-	81.5	80.4	76.4	84.9	84.4	2.25
EGMN (+S) [25]		-	80.2	80.7	74.0	85.1	80.9	5.45
CFBI (+S) [41]		-	81.4	81.1	75.3	85.8	83.4	4.10
GC (+S) [19]		-	73.2	72.6	68.9	75.6	75.7	<u>1.80</u>
KMN (+S) [31]		-	81.4	81.4	75.3	85.6	83.3	4.20
AFB-URR (+S) [21]		-	79.6	78.8	74.1	83.1	82.6	2.60
STG-Net (+S) [24]		6.00	73.0	72.7	69.1	75.2	74.9	1.95
RMNet (+S) [38]		-	81.5	82.1	75.7	85.7	82.4	4.85
LCM (+S) [10]		-	82.0	<u>82.2</u>	75.7	86.7	83.4	4.90
GIEL (+S) [9]		-	80.6	80.7	75.0	85.0	81.9	4.40
SwiftNet (+S) [35]		-	77.8	77.8	72.3	81.8	79.5	3.90
SSTVOS (+S) [8]		-	81.7	81.2	76.0	-	-	-
JOINT (+S) [26]	✓	-	<u>83.1</u>	81.5	**78.7**	85.9	**86.5**	1.10
HMMN (+S) [32]		-	82.6	82.1	76.8	<u>87.0</u>	84.6	3.85
AOT-T (+S) [42]		<u>41.0</u>	80.2	80.1	74.0	84.5	82.2	4.20
SwinB-AOT-L (+S) [42]		9.30	**84.5**	**84.3**	<u>77.9</u>	**89.3**	<u>86.4</u>	4.65
STCN (+S) [4]		-	83.0	81.9	<u>77.9</u>	86.5	85.7	2.40
TBD (+S)		30.4	80.5	79.4	75.5	83.8	83.2	2.25
RVOS [33]		22.7	56.8	63.6	45.5	67.2	51.0	17.2
A-GAME [15]		-	66.1	67.8	60.8	-	-	-
AGSS-VOS [22]		12.5	71.3	71.3	65.5	76.2	73.1	4.45
CapsuleVOS [7]		13.5	62.3	67.3	53.7	68.1	59.9	10.9
STM [27]		-	68.2	-	-	-	-	-
FRTM [30]	✓	-	72.1	72.3	65.9	76.2	74.1	4.25
TVOS [46]		37.0	67.8	67.1	63.0	69.4	71.6	**0.95**
STM-cycle [20]		**43.0**	69.9	71.7	61.4	75.8	70.4	7.85
BMVOS [6]		28.0	<u>73.9</u>	<u>73.5</u>	<u>68.5</u>	<u>77.4</u>	<u>76.0</u>	3.20
TBD		30.4	**77.8**	**77.4**	**72.7**	**81.2**	**79.9**	<u>3.00</u>

proposed in MAST [18]. In order to capture small objects, we use the 720p resolution if a target object contains less than 1,000 pixels; if not, we use the 480p resolution. The experimental results indicate TBD is comparable to other competitive methods, while showing a fast inference speed of 30.4 fps.

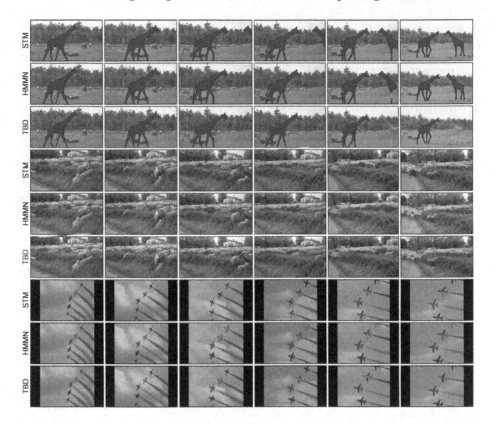

Fig. 6. Qualitative evaluation of TBD obtained by comparing it to other state-of-the-art methods.

4.4 Qualitative Results

In Fig. 6, we qualitatively compare our method to state-of-the-art STM [27] and HMMN [32]. As can be seen, TBD predicts more stable outputs compared to other methods, thanks to its diverse feature similarity matching templates and spatial distance scoring. Exceptional temporal consistency and robustness against occlusion can also be observed.

5   Conclusion

We introduce a spatio-temporally diversified template construction scheme for robust and stable VOS. In addition, a spatial distance scoring method with a learnable distance-scoring function and a novel swap-and-attach augmentation method are proposed. On public benchmark datasets, our approach achieves a comparable performance to the current state-of-the-art solutions while maintaining a real-time inference speed. We believe our approach will be widely used for future VOS research and various fields in computer vision.

Acknowledgement. This research was supported by R&D program for Advanced Integrated-intelligence for Identification (AIID) through the National Research Foundation of KOREA (NRF) funded by Ministry of Science and ICT (NRF-2018M3 E3A1057289) and the KIST Institutional Program (Project No.2E31051-21-203).

References

1. Bhat, G., et al.: Learning what to learn for video object segmentation. In: Vedaldi, A., Bischof, H., Brox, T., Frahm, J.-M. (eds.) ECCV 2020. LNCS, vol. 12347, pp. 777–794. Springer, Cham (2020). https://doi.org/10.1007/978-3-030-58536-5_46
2. Chen, X., Li, Z., Yuan, Y., Yu, G., Shen, J., Qi, D.: State-aware tracker for real-time video object segmentation. In: Proceedings of the IEEE/CVF Conference on Computer Vision and Pattern Recognition, pp. 9384–9393 (2020)
3. Chen, Y., Pont-Tuset, J., Montes, A., Van Gool, L.: Blazingly fast video object segmentation with pixel-wise metric learning. In: Proceedings of the IEEE Conference on Computer Vision and Pattern Recognition, pp. 1189–1198 (2018)
4. Cheng, H.K., Tai, Y.W., Tang, C.K.: Rethinking space-time networks with improved memory coverage for efficient video object segmentation. Adv. Neural. Inf. Process. Syst. **34**, 1–14 (2021)
5. Cho, S., Cho, M., Chung, T.y., Lee, H., Lee, S.: CRVOS: clue refining network for video object segmentation. In: 2020 IEEE International Conference on Image Processing (ICIP), pp. 2301–2305. IEEE (2020)
6. Cho, S., Lee, H., Kim, M., Jang, S., Lee, S.: Pixel-level bijective matching for video object segmentation. arXiv preprint arXiv:2110.01644 (2021)
7. Duarte, K., Rawat, Y.S., Shah, M.: CapsuleVOS: semi-supervised video object segmentation using capsule routing. In: Proceedings of the IEEE/CVF International Conference on Computer Vision, pp. 8480–8489 (2019)
8. Duke, B., Ahmed, A., Wolf, C., Aarabi, P., Taylor, G.W.: SSTVOS: sparse spatiotemporal transformers for video object segmentation. In: Proceedings of the IEEE/CVF Conference on Computer Vision and Pattern Recognition. pp. 5912–5921 (2021)
9. Ge, W., Lu, X., Shen, J.: Video object segmentation using global and instance embedding learning. In: Proceedings of the IEEE/CVF Conference on Computer Vision and Pattern Recognition. pp. 16836–16845 (2021)
10. Hu, L., Zhang, P., Zhang, B., Pan, P., Xu, Y., Jin, R.: Learning position and target consistency for memory-based video object segmentation. In: Proceedings of the IEEE/CVF Conference on Computer Vision and Pattern Recognition. pp. 4144–4154 (2021)
11. Hu, P., Liu, J., Wang, G., Ablavsky, V., Saenko, K., Sclaroff, S.: Dipnet: Dynamic identity propagation network for video object segmentation. In: Proceedings of the IEEE/CVF Winter Conference on Applications of Computer Vision. pp. 1904–1913 (2020)
12. Hu, Y.T., Huang, J.B., Schwing, A.G.: Videomatch: Matching based video object segmentation. In: Proceedings of the European conference on computer vision (ECCV). pp. 54–70 (2018)
13. Huang, G., Liu, Z., Van Der Maaten, L., Weinberger, K.Q.: Densely connected convolutional networks. In: Proceedings of the IEEE conference on computer vision and pattern recognition. pp. 4700–4708 (2017)
14. Ioffe, S., Szegedy, C.: Batch normalization: Accelerating deep network training by reducing internal covariate shift. arXiv preprint arXiv:1502.03167 (2015)

15. Johnander, J., Danelljan, M., Brissman, E., Khan, F.S., Felsberg, M.: A generative appearance model for end-to-end video object segmentation. In: Proceedings of the IEEE Conference on Computer Vision and Pattern Recognition. pp. 8953–8962 (2019)
16. Kingma, D.P., Ba, J.: Adam: A method for stochastic optimization. arXiv preprint arXiv:1412.6980 (2014)
17. Krizhevsky, A., Sutskever, I., Hinton, G.E.: Imagenet classification with deep convolutional neural networks. Commun. ACM **60**(6), 84–90 (2017)
18. Lai, Z., Lu, E., Xie, W.: Mast: A memory-augmented self-supervised tracker. In: Proceedings of the IEEE/CVF Conference on Computer Vision and Pattern Recognition. pp. 6479–6488 (2020)
19. Li, Y., Shen, Z., Shan, Y.: Fast video object segmentation using the global context module. In: European Conference on Computer Vision. pp. 735–750. Springer (2020)
20. Li, Y., Xu, N., Peng, J., See, J., Lin, W.: Delving into the cyclic mechanism in semi-supervised video object segmentation. arXiv preprint arXiv:2010.12176 (2020)
21. Liang, Y., Li, X., Jafari, N., Chen, Q.: Video object segmentation with adaptive feature bank and uncertain-region refinement. arXiv preprint arXiv:2010.07958 (2020)
22. Lin, H., Qi, X., Jia, J.: AGSS-VOS: attention guided single-shot video object segmentation. In: Proceedings of the IEEE International Conference on Computer Vision, pp. 3949–3957 (2019)
23. Lin, T.-Y., et al.: Microsoft COCO: common objects in context. In: Fleet, D., Pajdla, T., Schiele, B., Tuytelaars, T. (eds.) ECCV 2014. LNCS, vol. 8693, pp. 740–755. Springer, Cham (2014). https://doi.org/10.1007/978-3-319-10602-1_48
24. Liu, D., Xu, S., Liu, X.Y., Xu, Z., Wei, W., Zhou, P.: Spatiotemporal graph neural network based mask reconstruction for video object segmentation. In: Proceedings of the AAAI Conference on Artificial Intelligence, vol. 35, pp. 2100–2108 (2021)
25. Lu, X., Wang, W., Danelljan, M., Zhou, T., Shen, J., Van Gool, L.: Video object segmentation with episodic graph memory networks. In: Vedaldi, A., Bischof, H., Brox, T., Frahm, J.-M. (eds.) ECCV 2020. LNCS, vol. 12348, pp. 661–679. Springer, Cham (2020). https://doi.org/10.1007/978-3-030-58580-8_39
26. Mao, Y., Wang, N., Zhou, W., Li, H.: Joint inductive and transductive learning for video object segmentation. In: Proceedings of the IEEE/CVF International Conference on Computer Vision, pp. 9670–9679 (2021)
27. Oh, S.W., Lee, J.Y., Xu, N., Kim, S.J.: Video object segmentation using space-time memory networks. In: Proceedings of the IEEE International Conference on Computer Vision, pp. 9226–9235 (2019)
28. Perazzi, F., Pont-Tuset, J., McWilliams, B., Van Gool, L., Gross, M., Sorkine-Hornung, A.: A benchmark dataset and evaluation methodology for video object segmentation. In: Proceedings of the IEEE Conference on Computer Vision and Pattern Recognition, pp. 724–732 (2016)
29. Pont-Tuset, J., Perazzi, F., Caelles, S., Arbeláez, P., Sorkine-Hornung, A., Van Gool, L.: The 2017 Davis challenge on video object segmentation. arXiv:1704.00675 (2017)
30. Robinson, A., Lawin, F.J., Danelljan, M., Khan, F.S., Felsberg, M.: Learning fast and robust target models for video object segmentation. In: Proceedings of the IEEE/CVF Conference on Computer Vision and Pattern Recognition, pp. 7406–7415 (2020)

31. Seong, H., Hyun, J., Kim, E.: Kernelized memory network for video object segmentation. In: Vedaldi, A., Bischof, H., Brox, T., Frahm, J.-M. (eds.) ECCV 2020. LNCS, vol. 12367, pp. 629–645. Springer, Cham (2020). https://doi.org/10.1007/978-3-030-58542-6_38
32. Seong, H., Oh, S.W., Lee, J.Y., Lee, S., Lee, S., Kim, E.: Hierarchical memory matching network for video object segmentation. In: Proceedings of the IEEE/CVF International Conference on Computer Vision, pp. 12889–12898 (2021)
33. Ventura, C., Bellver, M., Girbau, A., Salvador, A., Marques, F., Giro-i Nieto, X.: RVOS: end-to-end recurrent network for video object segmentation. In: Proceedings of the IEEE/CVF Conference on Computer Vision and Pattern Recognition, pp. 5277–5286 (2019)
34. Voigtlaender, P., Chai, Y., Schroff, F., Adam, H., Leibe, B., Chen, L.C.: FEELVOS: fast end-to-end embedding learning for video object segmentation. In: Proceedings of the IEEE Conference on Computer Vision and Pattern Recognition, pp. 9481–9490 (2019)
35. Wang, H., Jiang, X., Ren, H., Hu, Y., Bai, S.: SwiftNet: real-time video object segmentation. In: Proceedings of the IEEE/CVF Conference on Computer Vision and Pattern Recognition, pp. 1296–1305 (2021)
36. Wang, Z., Xu, J., Liu, L., Zhu, F., Shao, L.: RANET: ranking attention network for fast video object segmentation. In: Proceedings of the IEEE International Conference on Computer Vision, pp. 3978–3987 (2019)
37. Woo, S., Park, J., Lee, J.-Y., Kweon, I.S.: CBAM: convolutional block attention module. In: Ferrari, V., Hebert, M., Sminchisescu, C., Weiss, Y. (eds.) ECCV 2018. LNCS, vol. 11211, pp. 3–19. Springer, Cham (2018). https://doi.org/10.1007/978-3-030-01234-2_1
38. Xie, H., Yao, H., Zhou, S., Zhang, S., Sun, W.: Efficient regional memory network for video object segmentation. In: Proceedings of the IEEE/CVF Conference on Computer Vision and Pattern Recognition, pp. 1286–1295 (2021)
39. Xu, K., Wen, L., Li, G., Bo, L., Huang, Q.: Spatiotemporal CNN for video object segmentation. In: Proceedings of the IEEE/CVF Conference on Computer Vision and Pattern Recognition, pp. 1379–1388 (2019)
40. Xu, N., Yang, L., Fan, Y., Yue, D., Liang, Y., Yang, J., Huang, T.: YouTube-VOS: a large-scale video object segmentation benchmark. arXiv preprint arXiv:1809.03327 (2018)
41. Yang, Z., Wei, Y., Yang, Y.: Collaborative video object segmentation by foreground-background integration. arXiv preprint arXiv:2003.08333 (2020)
42. Yang, Z., Wei, Y., Yang, Y.: Associating objects with transformers for video object segmentation. Adv. Neural. Inf. Process. Syst. 34, 1–11 (2021)
43. Zeiler, M.D., Taylor, G.W., Fergus, R.: Adaptive deconvolutional networks for mid and high level feature learning. In: 2011 International Conference on Computer Vision, pp. 2018–2025. IEEE (2011)
44. Zeng, X., Liao, R., Gu, L., Xiong, Y., Fidler, S., Urtasun, R.: DMM-Net: differentiable mask-matching network for video object segmentation. In: Proceedings of the IEEE/CVF International Conference on Computer Vision, pp. 3929–3938 (2019)
45. Zhang, L., Lin, Z., Zhang, J., Lu, H., He, Y.: Fast video object segmentation via dynamic targeting network. In: Proceedings of the IEEE/CVF International Conference on Computer Vision, pp. 5582–5591 (2019)
46. Zhang, Y., Wu, Z., Peng, H., Lin, S.: A transductive approach for video object segmentation. In: Proceedings of the IEEE/CVF Conference on Computer Vision and Pattern Recognition, pp. 6949–6958 (2020)

Social-Implicit: Rethinking Trajectory Prediction Evaluation and The Effectiveness of Implicit Maximum Likelihood Estimation

Abduallah Mohamed[1(✉)], Deyao Zhu[2], Warren Vu[1], Mohamed Elhoseiny[2], and Christian Claudel[1]

[1] The University of Texas, Austin, USA
{abduallah.mohamed,warren.vu,christian.claudel}@utexas.edu
[2] KAUST, Thuwal, Saudi Arabia
{deyao.zhu,mohamed.elhoseiny}@kaust.edu.sa

Abstract. Best-of-N (BoN) Average Displacement Error (ADE)/ Final Displacement Error (FDE) is the most used metric for evaluating trajectory prediction models. Yet, the BoN does not quantify the whole generated samples, resulting in an incomplete view of the model's prediction quality and performance. We propose a new metric, Average Mahalanobis Distance (AMD) to tackle this issue. AMD is a metric that quantifies how close the whole generated samples are to the ground truth. We also introduce the Average Maximum Eigenvalue (AMV) metric that quantifies the overall spread of the predictions. Our metrics are validated empirically by showing that the ADE/FDE is not sensitive to distribution shifts, giving a biased sense of accuracy, unlike the AMD/AMV metrics. We introduce the usage of Implicit Maximum Likelihood Estimation (IMLE) as a replacement for traditional generative models to train our model, Social-Implicit. IMLE training mechanism aligns with AMD/AMV objective of predicting trajectories that are close to the ground truth with a tight spread. Social-Implicit is a memory efficient deep model with only 5.8K parameters that runs in real time of 580 Hz and achieves competitive results (Code: https://github.com/abduallahmohamed/Social-Implicit/).

Keywords: Motion prediction · Motion forecasting · Deep Graph CNNs · Evaluation · Trajectory forecasting

1 Introduction

Trajectory prediction is an essential component for multiple applications, such as autonomous driving [4,5,16,28,35], augmented reality [18,34], and

---

M. Elhoseiny C. Claudel—Equal advising.

Supplementary Information The online version contains supplementary material available at https://doi.org/10.1007/978-3-031-20047-2_27.

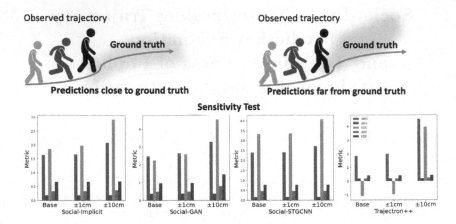

Fig. 1. The current BoN ADE/FDE metrics are not sensitive to the predicted distribution. The BoN ADE/FDE only focuses on the closest sample to the ground truth. We can see for both the green and red predictions, the BoN ADE/FDE stays the same. On the other hand, the proposed AMD/AMV metrics changes based on how close the whole predicted distribution and it is spread with respect to the ground truth. This makes the AMD/AMV a better metric to evaluate the predictions. (Color figure online)

robotics [2,19]. Typically, solving this problem requires a generative model to predict the future agent's trajectories. Though there are plenty of deep models and design architectures that tackle this problem, the evaluation method used is being questioned. Typically, two metrics are used to evaluate the trajectory predictions models. The first one is Average Displacement Error (ADE) [24] which is the average L_2 distance between the predicted and ground truth trajectories. Lower ADE values means that the overall predicted trajectory is close to the ground truth. The other metric is the Final Displacement Error (FDE) [1], which is an L_2 distance between the two final predicted and ground truth locations. In other terms, it describes if the predicted agent reaches its last goal or not. Also, the lower the FDE is, the better the model in not accumulating errors during the predictions. This issue of accumulating errors, resulting in a higher FDE was noticed in prior works that used recurrent based architectures. Prior works introduced the idea of a full CNN based architecture [23] to solve this error accumulation behavior.

Yet, this ADE/FDE metric remains unsuitable for generative models. Generative models predict multiple samples of future trajectories, implicitly forming a predicted distribution. This generative behavior is suitable for the problem, as the motion of an agent or pedestrian can be a multi-modal with possible future trajectories. In order to use the ADE/FDE in generative settings, the works of [1,8] introduced the concept of Best-of-N (BoN). BoN technique chooses from N samples the closest sample to the ground truth and calculates the ADE/FDE metric on it. This has a main issue of ignoring the set of generated samples.

A model might generate an outlier sample that is luckily close enough to the ground truth, while the other samples are way off from the ground truth. This approach also fails in real-life applications, as there is a lack in the assessment of the predictions. Some important components, such as motion planning and collision avoidance, need a complete view of the predictions. Another issue we noticed that the recent models [20,22,30,37] which are state-of-the-art based on the ADE/FDE metric only differ by 1 cm ADE and few centimeters FDE on the ETH [24] and UCY [14] datasets, one of the most commonly used datasets in this area. The 1 cm difference between a previous SOTA model and the next one is so subtle and tiny that it can be an annotation error or an outlier sampling. Thus, there is a need for a new metric that can evaluate the whole predicted samples and have a sense of where the whole generated distribution is regarding the ground truth. Also, there is a need to quantify the uncertainty of the generated samples giving a view regarding the confidence of the model, something that is needed in real-life applications. For this, we introduce the usage of Mahalanobis Distance [21] as a metric in this domain. We introduce two metrics, the Average Mahalanobis Distance (AMD) which evaluates how close a generated distribution is with respect to the ground truth, and the Average Maximum Eigenvalue (AMV) that evaluates the confidence of the predictions. The AMD quantifies how close a ground truth point is to a predicted distribution in a sense of standard deviation units. Also, AMD connects with χ^2 distribution, helping us to determine the confidence of our predictions when the generated distribution degree of freedom is known. The AMV depends on the maximum magnitude of the eigenvalues of the covariance matrix of the predicted distribution. It quantifies the spread of the prediction. Thus, we can tell if a model is more confident than another model by using it. So, our goal is to achieve a model that generates a distribution which is close to the ground truth and has a small spread of samples around the ground truth. This aim leads us to rethink the nature of generative models used in training motion prediction models. We can classify the used generative techniques into parametric and non-parametric ones. Parametric ones use Maximum Likelihood Estimation (MLE) to model the predicted trajectories as Gaussian or Gaussian Mixture Models (GMM). Generative Adversarial Networks (GANs) [7] is an examples of non-parametric distributions. These approaches learn the distribution of the observed trajectories in order to generate the future ones. Yet, the primary goal of trajectory prediction models is the generated samples themselves. The MLE needs plenty of samples to converge, something we do not have in practice. While the GANs rely on the design of the discriminator and VAEs need to optimize the Evidence Lower Bound (ELBO). So, we needed a generative approach that only focuses on the generated samples and does not come with extra hassles. In this work, we show that Implicit Maximum Likelihood Estimation (IMLE) technique is an effective alternative to these approaches. IMLE focuses directly on the predicted trajectories, simplifying the optimization function. By using IMLE to train our introduced model Social-Implicit, the predicted trajectories improve in terms of quality and accuracy in comparison with prior works. Social-Implicit is a memory efficient deep model with only 5.8K parameters almost 55x less than the closest SOTA and runs in real-time almost 8.5x faster than the closest SOTA. This work is organized as follows: We start by literature review of recent relative works. Then we formulate the motion prediction problem, followed by an introduction and discussion for both new metrics AMD and AMV. Then we introduce the Trajectory Conditioned IMLE mechanism used in training our model Social-Implicit. We follow this by explaining the architecture of Social-Implicit. Lastly, we analyze the results of the new metrics on our model and recent SOTA ones accompanied with a sensitivity analysis.

2   Literature Review

Trajectory Forecasting Models. Recent works have proposed various models to forecast future trajectories. Based on their output formats, they can be roughly grouped into two categories. Explicitly modeling the future as a parametric distribution, or implicitly modeling the future as a non-parametric distribution. In the first category, methods model the future explicitly as continuous or discrete distribution [1,3,4,13,17,23,26,27,30,32,36–38]. For example, S-LSTM [1] and S-STGCNN [23] use Gaussian distribution to model the future trajectory that are trained by Maximum Likelihood Estimation (MLE). Gaussian distribution is single-mode and cannot catch the multi-modality of the future. To tackle this issue, PRECOG [27], Trajectron++ [30], ExpertTraj [37], and AgentFormer [36] learn a latent behavior distribution, which can be either discrete [30,37] or continuous [27,36], to represent the agent multi-modality intent. In these works, the predicted Gaussian distribution is generated conditioned on the sampled latent intent. This type of method is usually based on Conditional VAE [31]. Besides continuous distributions like Gaussian methods like MTP [4] and LaneGCN [17] use a discrete distribution to represent the future. These methods predict a fixed number of deterministic trajectories as the future candidates and use a categorical distribution to model their possibilities. In the second category, some methods model the future distribution in an implicit way. For example, S-GAN [8], SoPhie [29], S-BiGAT [11] and DiversityGAN [9] follows a Conditional GAN [6] architecture. Instead of generating a distribution as the model output they predict a deterministic trajectory that is conditioned on a random sampled noise and is trained by an adversarial loss mechanism. Our proposed method Social-Implicit models the future distribution implicitly by training it using IMLE [15] avoiding additional hassles like the discriminator in a GAN training mechanism.

Trajectory Forecasting Metrics. Most of the trajectory forecasting methods are evaluated by the metric Average Displacement Error (ADE) [24] or Final Displacement Error (FDE) [1]. These two metrics are based on the L_2 distance of the whole temporal horizon (ADE) or the last time step (FDE) between the prediction and the ground truth trajectory. When the model generates a distribution as the output, the Best-of-N trick [8] is applied to evaluate the best trajectory only from N sampled predictions. The mean ADE/FDE can be also used to evaluate the predictions, it is mostly suitable in single modality predictions and when

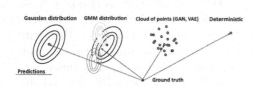

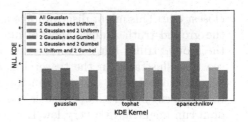

Fig. 2. Different motion prediction models output. The Gaussian and GMM are examples of parametric models. The GAN and VAE are examples of non-parametric models. The last category is a deterministic model output. A unified metric is needed to evaluate all of these models.

Fig. 3. Different mixture models NLL KDE vs the choice of the KDE Kernel. The lower the better. We also notice that the results vary depending on the kernel.

the predictions are close to a Gaussian distribution. In multi-modality, when for example the predictions are contradictory to each other (turning left, turning right) the mean ADE/FDE will fail because it is deterministic in nature. Another way to evaluate the distribution quality is Kernel Density Estimate (KDE), first used in [10]. KDE fits a kernel-based distribution from the prediction samples and estimates the negative log-likelihood of the ground truth as the evaluated score. Quehl et al. [25] propose a synthesized metric that is a weighted sum of different similarity metrics to alleviate the metric bias. But their metric is only suitable for deterministic models. We propose two new metrics Average Mahalanobis Distance (AMD) and Average Maximum Eigenvalue (AMV) that are a better alternative for the BoN ADE/FDE in evaluating the predictions.

3   The Average Mahalanobis Distance (AMD) Metric

We define the problem of trajectory prediction as follows: Given an observed trajectories of N agents across a sequence of observed time steps T_o, the goal is to predict the next T_p prediction time steps. The observed trajectories contain P points, where each point indicates the spatial location of an agent. In the pedestrian trajectory prediction problems the P is a 2D Cartesian locations (x,y). We denote the set of observation to be $d_o = \{p_t|\ t \in T_o\}$ and the set of predictions to be $d_p = \{p_t|\ t \in T_p\}$.

To highlight the issue in the current BoN ADE/FDE, we start with Fig. 2 that illustrates the different types prediction models outputs. For deterministic models, it is straightforward to compute the ADE/FDE metrics defined in Eq. 1. But for generative models, the ADE/FDE is being computed by the BoN approach. The BoN works by sampling N (usually 20) samples, selecting the closest sample to the ground truth, then using this sample to calculate the ADE/FDE. We can criticize this BoN approach in multiple aspects. The major concern is that it does not quantify the whole generated samples and only focuses on the closest one. This might disadvantage a model with a density that is surrounding the ground truth against another model with a density that is completely off the ground truth, but has one sample that is close to the ground truth. We can see this illustrated in the teaser Fig. 1. We base the other concern that with this method of BoN, one can run the metric a couple of times, getting a result that is 1 cm better than another model. In some extreme cases, a lucky random run might have a very low BoN ADE/FDE. The work of [10] noticed this issue and introduced the usage of A Kernel Density Estimate (KDE) defined in Eq. 1. The KDE is a kernel based tool that gets a non-parametric representation of the predictions' probability density. Then, the negative log likelihood of the ground truth is calculated and reported in logarithmic units (nats). Yet, there is a mix of limitations and concerns with the KDE metric. The main concern is that the KDE metric is sensitive to the choice of a kernel under the settings of low number of samples, which is the case in real-life datasets. Figure 3 illustrates the different choices of the kernel used in the KDE versus a variety of mixtures of distributions. We notice that when a Gaussian kernel is being used; it does not differentiate between different samples and might favour a model with a full GMM output in comparison with other outputs. We also notice, we might get a mixed results whenever a different choice of kernel is being used, such as with tophat kernel versus a Gaussian kernel. The work of [10] was using KDE metrics with a Gaussian kernel. The other limitation of the KDE kernel is that it does not contain analytical properties that are easy to interpret. This limitation is because of the non-parametric nature of the KDE. Such properties of interest might be the probability moments and the confidence intervals.

$$\text{ADE} = \frac{1}{N \times T_p} \sum_{n \in N} \sum_{t \in T_p} \|\hat{p}_t^n - p_t^n\|_2, \ \text{FDE} = \frac{1}{N} \sum_{n \in N} \|\hat{p}_{T_p}^n - p_{T_p}^n\|_2, \ \text{KDE} = \frac{-1}{N \times T_p} \sum_{n \in N} \sum_{t \in T_p} \log \text{KDE}(\hat{p}_t^n, p_t^n) \tag{1}$$

where p_t^n is ground truth location of agent $n \in N$ at predicted time step $t \in T_p$ and $\hat{p}_t^n$ is the predicted location. The new metric needs to be parametric that allows further analysis and insensitive to the way it calculates the distance. Thus, we introduce the usage of Mahalanobis distance. Mahalanobis distance can measure how far a point from a distribution is, while correlating the distance with the variance of the predictions. It also has analytical properties that connect it with the Chi-square distribution, in which one can evaluate the confidence of the predictions. Lastly, it depends on Gaussian distribution, which allows further analysis of the predicted moments. The Mahalanobis distance (MD) is defined as: $M_D\left(\hat{\mu}, \hat{\Sigma}, p\right) = \sqrt{(p - \hat{\mu})^T \hat{\Sigma}^{-1} (p - \hat{\mu})}$. Where, $\hat{\mu}$ is the mean of the prediction, $\hat{\Sigma}$ is the variance of the predicted distribution and p is the ground truth location. Originally, Mahalanobis distance was not designed for a GMM distribution. Yet, the work of [33] extended MD into a GMM by formulating it as:

$$M_D\left(\hat{\mu}_{\text{GMM}}, \hat{G}, p\right) = \sqrt{(\hat{\mu}_{\text{GMM}} - p)^T \hat{G} (\hat{\mu}_{\text{GMM}} - p)} \tag{2}$$

where $\hat{G}$, the inverse covariances of each mixture components averaged and weighted probabilistically, is defined as: $\hat{G} = \frac{\sum_{k=1}^K \hat{\Sigma}_k^{-1} \hat{\pi}_k \int_{\hat{\mu}_{\text{GMM}}}^P p(x|k)dx}{\sum_{k=1}^K \hat{\pi}_k \int_{\hat{\mu}_{\text{GMM}}}^P p(x|k)dx}$, where

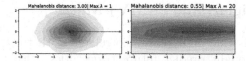 

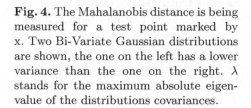

Fig. 4. The Mahalanobis distance is being measured for a test point marked by x. Two Bi-Variate Gaussian distributions are shown, the one on the left has a lower variance than the one on the right. λ stands for the maximum absolute eigenvalue of the distributions covariances.

Fig. 5. GMM fit exhibit an error and need a lot of samples to converge into the true mean, something might be a disadvantage to non-parametric models. At the 1000 samples mark, GMM starts to converge to the true mean and variance with stable MD.

K is the number of mixture components, $\hat{\pi}_k$ is the weight of the kth component and the mean of the GMM is defined as: $\hat{\mu}_{\text{GMM}} = \sum_{k=1}^{K} \hat{\pi}_k \hat{\mu}_k$. The integral term in $\hat{G}$ is tractable, as noted in [33]. We notice that if the GMM contains only one component, the G will be the $\hat{\Sigma}^{-1}$, thus the Tipping's MD is a more generalized version of the original MD. Our approach is the following, whatever distribution or output produced by a model, we fit into a GMM. A question will be raised regarding the number of optimal mixture components K. This can be easily solved by using the Bayesian information criterion (BIC): $\text{BIC} = m \ln n - 2 \ln \hat{L}_{\text{GMM}}$, where m is the number of parameters of the GMM model, n is the number of observed data points and $\hat{L}_{\text{GMM}}$ is the likelihood function of the model. The lower the BIC is the better the fitted GMM model representing the data points. The best GMM is chosen automatically based on the BIC. Looking into the reason for sampling from a model that is already predicting the mean and variance of trajectories such as [1,23], that we want to be fair. Fitting a GMM will carry out a sort of error, thus we want this error to be incorporated into all modes of measurements to have a unified metric. Figure 5 show this error.

Because a deterministic model does not have a variance, we need a representation of the error in the model. We can train the deterministic model multiple times and fit the predictions to a GMM. Another proposal is to calculate the ensemble mean and variance and directly apply the MD distance without the GMM fit. The later approach might have an error that is equivalent to the GMM fit error, making the metric more fair. In the supplementary, we discuss both cases. We believe that evaluating a deterministic model versus a generative model is an open question that needs a further research and it is a limitation similar to the KDE [10] limitation. Now, we define the Average Mahalanobis Distance (AMD):

$$\text{AMD} = \frac{1}{N \times T_p} \sum_{n \in N} \sum_{t \in T_p} M_D \left(\hat{\mu}_{\text{GMM},t}^n, \hat{G}_t^n, p_t^n \right) \tag{3}$$

4   The Average Maximum Eigenvalue (AMV) Metric

A major concern of the AMD metric is that it is highly correlated with the variance of the distribution. A model might predict future trajectories, with a huge on-practical variance having the ground truth close to the mean. This will lead to a very low AMD in comparison with another model with a higher variance. Another example is a model that predicts a huge variance that is in meters covering all the predicted points. This also will lead to an optimal AMD value. To counter this false behavior, we need our models to have a low AMD accompanied with a low variance aka a more certain model. Also, in practical application, we need to quantify the overall uncertainty of the predictions to have a holistic view of the performance. Thus, we introduce the usage of the eigenvalues of the covariance matrix. The largest magnitude eigenvalue of the covariance matrix is an indicator of the spread of the covariance matrix. Figure 4 illustrates two distributions, the one on the left has a smaller variance than the one on the right. We notice that the MD of a fixed point with respect to the left distribution is much higher when compared to the right distribution. Yet, the largest magnitude eigenvalue of the left distribution is way less than the right distribution, showing the spread of the predictions. So, to properly evaluate the models we need both of the AMD and a measurement of the spread. And as we discussed we can have a measurement of the spread directly from the prediction covariance matrix. Because of the framework we introduced in the AMD metric, we have a covariance matrix of the prediction. Something that was missing in the KDE metric. Now, we can introduce the AMV metric:

$$\text{AMV} = \frac{1}{N \times T_p} \sum_{n \in N} \sum_{t \in T_p} \lambda_1^{\downarrow}(\hat{\Sigma}_{\text{GMM},t}^n) \tag{4}$$

where $\lambda_1^{\downarrow}$ is the eigenvalue with the largest magnitude from the matrix eigenvalues. The $\hat{\Sigma}_{\text{GMM}}$ is the covariance matrix of the predicted GMM distribution defined as: $\hat{\Sigma}_{\text{GMM}} = \sum_{k=k}^{K} \hat{\pi}_k \hat{\Sigma}_k + \sum_{k=1}^{K} \hat{\pi}_k (\hat{\mu}_k - \hat{\mu}_{\text{GMM}})(\hat{\mu}_k - \hat{\mu}_{\text{GMM}})^T$. Thus, the AMV becomes a metric that evaluates the overall spread of the predicted trajectories. A model with low AMD will have a predicted distribution that is closer to the ground truth. And a model with low AMV will be more certain in their predictions. *Thus, a model with both low AMD/AMV average is preferred when compared with another model with a higher AMD/AMV average.* For this we use the $\frac{AMD+AMV}{2}$ as an indicator of a good model.

5   Trajectory Conditional Implicit Maximum Likelihood Estimation (IMLE) Mechanism

By induction from the goal of the AMD/AMV metric to have a model that generates samples that is close to the ground truth with low spread, we need a training mechanism that allows full control over the predicted samples as the main optimization goal. Typical training mechanism such as Maximum Likelihood Estimation (MLE) or its variants like maximizing evidence lower bound (ELBO) encourages the prediction samples to be close to some (ground truth) data sample. In this way, some data examples may be missed and lead to a mode dropping [15]. Other methods, such as GANs, need to introduce additional modules like the discriminator and their training is usually unstable and need to be carefully tuned to reach a proper Nash's equilibrium. The work of [15] introduced the concept of Implicit Maximum Likelihood Estimation (IMLE). IMLE encourages every target ground truth to be close to some predicted samples. Therefore, it leads to a predicted distribution that is better in covering the ground truth unlike MLE. IMLE trains a model via a simple mechanism: inject a noise into the model's input to predict multiple samples, select the one closest to the ground truth, and back propagate using this sample. Unlike other generative approaches, IMLE does not load the optimization objective with a specific training technique and keeps the training stable due to the simple distance-minimization-based optimization. Using IMLE as a training mechanism aligns with the AMD/AMV goals and focuses on the important product, the predicted output. Another point of view for IMLE is that it is a more advanced neural technique in comparison with estimation techniques such as Kalman filter where the process and measurement noises drive the model. We refer the reader to the original IMLE paper [15] for a further discussion. The training mechanism is shown in Alg.1:

Algorithm 1 Trajectory Conditional Implicit Maximum Likelihood Estimation (IMLE) algorithm

---

Require: The dataset $D = (d_o^i, d_p^i)_{i=1}^n$ and the model $\theta(.)$ with a sampling mechanism conditioned on the input

Require: Choose a proper loss function $\mathcal{L}(.)$ such as mean squared error or L_1

Initialize the model

  for $e = 1$ **to** Epochs **do**

    Pick a random batch (d_o, d_p) from D

    Draw i.i.d. samples $\tilde{d}_p^{\,1}, \ldots, \tilde{d}_p^{\,m}$ from $\theta(d_o)$

    $\sigma(i) \leftarrow \arg\min_i \mathcal{L}\left(d_p - \tilde{d}_p^{\,i}\right) \ \forall i \in m$

    $\theta \leftarrow \theta - \eta \nabla_\theta \sigma(i)$

  end for

  return θ

---

6 The Social-Implicit Model

In this section, we present the Social-Implicit model. The Social-Implicit is tiny in memory size with only 5.8K parameters with real run-time 588 Hz. The method comprises three concepts, Social-Zones, Social-Cell and Social-Loss.

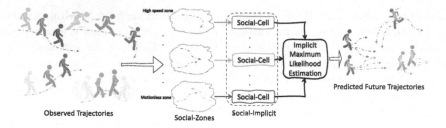

Fig. 6. Social-Implicit model concept. The Social-Zones cluster the observed trajectories based on their maximum observed speed. Then each Social-Zone is processed by a Social-Cell. The model is trained using IMLE.

The Social-Zones: The Social-Zones cluster the observed agents trajectories based on their maximum change of speed. The average pedestrian speed is 1.2 m/s [12]. We noticed that we can cluster the motion of pedestrians into four groups. The first group is the motion-less group, where the pedestrian is waiting at the traffic light as an example. This group's maximum speed change is between 0–0.01 m/s. While the second group is pedestrians with minimal motion, aka someone who is shaking in place or a group of pedestrians greeting each other, typically this group's maximum change of speed is between 0.01–0.1 m/s. The third group are pedestrians with an average walking speed, these pedestrians motion is between 0.1–1.2 m/s. The last group is the running pedestrians, typically with a speed above the 1.2 m/s average. When a deep model is trained on the stationary pedestrians alongside the faster ones, a bias towards the moving ones will exist in the predictions. This will force the model to predict the non-moving objects as moving ones. It is a sort of data imbalance, or in other terms, a zero(motionless)-inflated data issue. Hence, the concept of Social-Zones is needed to solve this issue. Empirically, we show that our model with the Social-Zones performs better than without it. The input to the Social-Zones is the observed trajectories and the output is clusters of pedestrians, each cluster is a graph of dimensions $P \times T_o \times N$ (Fig. 6).

The Social-Cell: The fundamental building unit of the Social-Implicit model is the Social-Cell. The Social-Cell is a 4 layers deep model that is simple and directly dealing with the spatio-temporal aspects of the observations. Figure 7 illustrates the structure of the Social-Cell. We notice the cell has two components, one that deals with each individual agent at a local level and one that deals with the whole agents at a global level. We generate the final output of the cell by combining the local and global streams via self-learning weights. Both local and global streams are two consecutive residually connected CNN layers. The first CNN is a spatial CNN, which creates an embedding of the spatial information of the observed agents. The second layer is a temporal CNN that treats the time aspect of the observed trajectories. It treats the time as a feature channel, allowing us to predict the next T_p time steps without using a recurrent

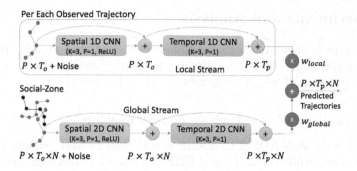

Fig. 7. Social-Cell model. The local and global stream has only two CNNs. P is the observed location, T_o and T_p is the observed and predicted time steps and N is the count of agents. Where K and P of the CNNs is the kernel and padding size.

network [23]. We found out that this simple architecture is as effective as much larger and complex models, resulting in a small memory size and real-run time capabilities. Each Social-Cell deals with a specific Social-Zone. The input is $P \times T_o \times N$ and the output is $P \times T_p \times N$. The operations are shown in Fig. 7.

The Social-Loss: The loss function of Social-Implicit exhibits several parts. The first part is the direct optimization objective of the IMLE mechanism that we discussed before. The second part is a triplet loss. This triplet loss considers the anchor to be the closest sample $\tilde{d}_p^1$ to the ground truth. The positive example is the next closest example $\tilde{d}_p^2$ to the ground truth. The negative example $\tilde{d}_p^m$ is the farthest sample from the ground truth. This helps in grouping the samples closer to the ground truth, resulting in a tighter distribution around the real trajectory. The last part of the loss is a geometric loss function that treats the predicted locations as a polygon. First, it ensures that the intra-distance between the predicted location matches the intra-distance between the ground truth locations. Second, it makes sure that the angles between the predicted points are the same as the angles between the ground truth points. It ensures that the predicted scene geometrically looks like the ground truth. We defines these losses in Eq. 5. The social aspects of the scene can be addressed beyond what we introduced which is an open research area.

$$\mathcal{L}_{\text{triplet}} = \|\tilde{d}_p^1 - \tilde{d}_p^2\|_1 - \|\tilde{d}_p^1 - \tilde{d}_p^m\|_1$$

$$\mathcal{L}_{\text{G-distance}} = \frac{1}{\frac{T_p(T_p-1)}{2}} \sum_{t \in T_p} \sum_{j \in T_p, j>t} \left\| \|p_t - p_j\|_2 - \|\tilde{p}_t - \tilde{p}_j\|_2 \right\|_1 \tag{5}$$

$$\mathcal{L}_{\text{G-angle}} = \frac{1}{\frac{T_p(T_p-1)}{2}} \sum_{t \in T_p} \sum_{j \in T_p, j>t} \left\| \angle(p_t, p_j) - \angle(\tilde{p}_t, \tilde{p}_j) \right\|_1$$

Thus we define the Social-Loss as:

$$\mathcal{L} = \|d_p - \tilde{d}_p^1\|_1 + \alpha_1 \mathcal{L}_{\text{triplet}} + \alpha_1 \mathcal{L}_{\text{G-distance}} + \alpha_3 \mathcal{L}_{\text{G-angle}} \tag{6}$$

where $\alpha_1 = 0.0001, \alpha_2 = 0.0001$ or $0.00001, \alpha_3 = 0.0001$.

7   Experiments and Analysis

We analyze the behavior of the metrics on common pedestrian motion prediction models in terms of overall performance and sensitivity analysis. Then we analyze our model in terms of design components and performance.

7.1   Metrics Sensitivity Analysis and Evaluation

We show that the BoN ADE/FDE metric is not sensitive to the change or shift in the distribution, while the AMD and KDE can quantify such a change. Figure 1 illustrates this concept. We tested different models by shifting their predicted samples using different amounts, specifically ±1 cm and ±10 cm. In all of the models, the BoN ADE/FDE metric did not change at all or had a very tiny subtle change. Unlike the metrics that measure the whole distribution, like AMD and KDE the shift of the predicted distribution is reflected into the metric. This concludes that the ADE/FDE metric is not sensitive to the change of the whole distribution, even on a tremendous change of 10 cm, which sometimes can define a new SOTA model over another. So, the BoN ADE/FDE metric is incapable of evaluating the whole predicted trajectories. Also, the AMV metric stayed the same, this was expected as only shifting the predictions does not change the variance. We notice that the KDE of Trajectron++ is -ve unlike other models because Trajectron++ output is a GMM distribution which is a bias in the KDE metric due to the kernel choice as we discussed earlier.

To evaluate the metrics quantitatively, we report the AMD/AMV, KDE and ADE/FDE metrics on different motion prediction models using the ETH/UCY datasets. We chose classic ones such as S-GAN [8] and S-STGCNN [23]. We also chose more recent ones such Trajectron++ [30] and ExpertTraj [37]. From Tab. 1 we notice that the last two models, which are considered SOTA, differ by a few centimetres on the ADE/FDE metric. Yet, when we evaluate both of them using the AMD/AMV metrics, we notice that Trajectron++ is performing much better than the ExpertTraj model. From the AMD/AMV metric, ExpertTraj generates a tight distribution that does not surround the ground truth, which results in a higher AMD unlike the Trajectron++. Though, both of ExpertTraj and Trajectron++ have very close ADE/FDE metrics, the quality of the whole predicted samples is completely different. Examining the results of our model, Social-Implicit, we see that it has the lowest AMD/AMV. By digesting the results, the ADE/FDE metric is not an indicative of the overall performance of the models which correlates with the aforementioned sensitivity analysis.

7.2   Ablation Study of Social-Implicit

We conduct an ablation study of the Social-Implicit components. Specifically, the Social-Zones and the Social-Loss. Table 2 illustrates the results. We noticed that the existence of the Social-Zones enhanced the AMD metric by almost 40%. It also led to a good AMV value, which enhanced the overall AMD/AMV performance. We notice that the triplet loss alone with the Social-Zones leads improves

Table 1. For all metrics, the lower the better. The results are on the ETH/UCY datasets. M is a non reported model. NaN is failed computation. ExpertTraj ADE/FDE were taken from their paper. We notice sometimes, even if a model has a low ADE/FDE the AMD/AMV contradicts this by evaluating the overall generated samples.

	ETH	Hotel	Univ	Zara1	Zara2	Mean	(AMD+AMV)/2
			ADE/ FDE				
			AMD/ AMV				
			KDE				
S-GAN [8]	0.81/1.52	0.72/1.61	0.60/1.26	0.34/0.69	0.42/0.84	0.58/1.18	
	3.94/0.373	2.59/0.384	2.37/0.440	1.79/0.355	1.66/0.254	2.47/0.361	1.42
	5.02	3.45	2.03	0.68	-0.03	2.23	
S-STGCNN [23]	0.64/1.11	0.49/0.85	0.44/0.79	0.34/0.53	0.30/0.48	0.44/0.75	
	3.73/0.094	1.67/0.297	3.31/0.060	1.65/0.149	1.57/0.103	2.39/0.104	1.26
	6.83	1.56	5.65	1.40	1.17	3.32	
Trajectron++ [30]	0.39/0.83	0.12/0.21	0.20/0.44	0.15/0.33	0.11/0.25	0.19/0.41	
	3.04/0.286	1.98/0.114	1.73/0.228	1.21/0.171	1.23/0.116	1.84/0.183	1.01
	1.34	-1.89	-1.08	-1.38	-2.43	**-1.09**	
ExpertTraj [37]	0.30/0.62	0.09/0.15	0.19/0.44	0.15/0.31	0.12/0.24	**0.17/0.35**	
	61.77/0.034	21.30/0.003	M/M	32.14/0.005	M/M	38.4/0.004	19.20
	NaN	NaN	M	NaN	M	NaN	
Social-Implicit(ours)	0.66/1.44	0.20/0.36	0.31/0.60	0.25/0.50	0.22/0.43	0.33/0.67	
	3.05/0.127	0.58/0.410	1.65/0.148	1.72/0.078	1.16/0.106	**1.63/0.174**	**0.90**
	5.08	0.59	1.67	1.24	0.69	1.85	

AMD/AMV. The effect of geometric angle loss is more than the geometric distance loss in improving the AMD/AMV. While both work better together.

Table 2. Ablation study of Social-Implicit components.

$\mathcal{L}_{\text{triplet}}$	$\mathcal{L}_{\text{G-distance}}$	$\mathcal{L}_{\text{G-angle}}$	Zones	AMD/KDE/AMV	AMD/AMV	ADE/FDE
				2.06/2.29/0.110	1.09	0.32/0.66
			✓	2.04/1.86/0.104	1.07	0.32/0.64
✓			✓	1.96/2.16/0.097	1.03	0.56/1.08
✓	✓		✓	2.13/2.32/0.092	1.11	0.32/0.62
✓		✓	✓	1.84/1.78/0.094	0.97	0.78/1.38
✓	✓	✓		2.29/2.76/0.090	1.16	0.35/0.71
✓	✓	✓	✓	1.63/1.85/0.174	**0.90**	0.33/0.67

7.3 Inference and Memory Analysis

Social-Implicit besides being the most accurate model when compared with other models on the AMD/AMV metrics, it is the smallest and the fastest in terms of parameters size and inference time. Table 3 shows these results. The closest SOTA is ExpertTraj which Social-Implicit is 55x smaller and 8.5x faster.

Table 3. Parameters counts and mean inference speed reported, benchmarked on the GTX1080Ti.

	Parameters count	Speed (s)
S-GAN [8]	46.3K (7.98x)	0.0968 (56.9x)
S-STGCNN [23]	7.6K (1.3x)	0.0020 (1.2x)
Trajectron++ [30]	128K (22.1x)	0.6044 (355.5x)
ExpertTraj [37]	323.3k (55.74x)	0.0144 (8.5x)
Social-Implicit (ours)	**5.8K**	**0.0017**

Table 4. Number of zones and their speed effect on our model accuracy.

#Zones	ADE/FDE	KDE	AMD/AMV	AVG
1	0.35/0.71	2.76	2.29/0.090	1.16
2	0.36/0.73	3.09	2.32/0.088	1.20
3	0.34/0.70	2.31	2.08/0.085	1.08
4@0.6 m/s	0.34/0.69	2.85	2.31/0.080	1.19
4@1.2 m/s	0.33/0.67	1.85	1.63/0.174	**0.90**

7.4 Social-Zones Ablation

Table 4 shows the ablation of the number of zones. Different zones affects the model's performance. Also, the model is sensitive to the zone's speeds. For example, when we changed the last zone from 1.2 m/s to 0.6 m/s the results changed. The 1.2 m/s reflects human average walking speed, thus the 0.6 m/s does not suit the data, hence it leads to poor performance in comparison with the 1.2 m/s.

7.5 Qualitative Results

In Fig. 8, we list two qualitative examples of our method and baseline models. In the first row, we see a pedestrian turns right at the end of the ground truth future. We notice that Social-Implicit and Trajectron++ cover the ground truth future well, whereas S-GAN and ExpertTraj give us an early turning prediction and concentrate away from the ground truth. The second row shows a zigzag walking pedestrian. Baseline models like S-STGCNN, Trajectron++, and ExpertTraj cannot generate good distributions to cover the ground truth trajectory, unlike ours and S-GAN. Although the prediction of ExpertTraj is close to the ground

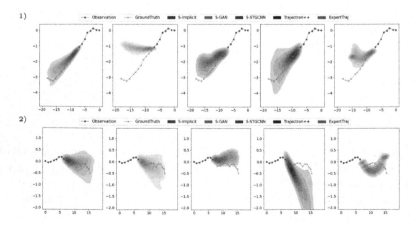

Fig. 8. Visualization of the predicted trajectories on the ETH/UCY datasets.

truth, ExpertTraj is over confident contradicting the ground truth. Qualitative results show that our predicted distribution are better.

8   Conclusions

We introduced the AMD and AMV metrics that evaluate the distribution generated by a trajectory prediction model. We showed that the BoN ADE/FDE metric gives out an inadequate evaluation of the generated distribution. Based on the objective of AMD/AMV metrics to have a model that generates samples that are close to the ground truth with a tight variance, we introduced the usage of IMLE to train our model, Social-Implicit. We showed that Social-Implicit is a memory efficient model that runs in real time and relies on several concepts such as Social-Zones, Social-Cell and Social-Loss to enhance the performance. Overall, we invite the motion prediction community to adapt the AMD/AMV to have a better evaluation of their methods.

References

1. Alahi, A., Goel, K., Ramanathan, V., Robicquet, A., Fei-Fei, L., Savarese, S.: Social LSTM: human trajectory prediction in crowded spaces. In: Proceedings of the IEEE Conference on Computer Vision and Pattern Recognition, pp. 961–971 (2016)
2. Bütepage, J., Kjellström, H., Kragic, D.: Anticipating many futures: online human motion prediction and generation for human-robot interaction. In: 2018 IEEE International Conference on Robotics and Automation (ICRA), pp. 4563–4570. IEEE (2018)
3. Chai, Y., Sapp, B., Bansal, M., Anguelov, D.: Multipath: multiple probabilistic anchor trajectory hypotheses for behavior prediction. arXiv preprint arXiv:1910.05449 (2019)
4. Cui, H., et al.: Multimodal trajectory predictions for autonomous driving using deep convolutional networks. In: 2019 International Conference on Robotics and Automation (ICRA), pp. 2090–2096. IEEE (2019)
5. Deo, N., Trivedi, M.M.: Convolutional social pooling for vehicle trajectory prediction. In: Proceedings of the IEEE Conference on Computer Vision and Pattern Recognition Workshops, pp. 1468–1476 (2018)
6. Gauthier, J.: Conditional generative adversarial nets for convolutional face generation. In: Class Project for Stanford CS231N: Convolutional Neural Networks for Visual Recognition, Winter semester 2014(5), 2 (2014)
7. Goodfellow, I., et al.: Generative adversarial nets. Adv. Neural. Inf. Process. Syst. 27, 1–10 (2014)
8. Gupta, A., Johnson, J., Fei-Fei, L., Savarese, S., Alahi, A.: Social GAN: socially acceptable trajectories with generative adversarial networks. In: Proceedings of the IEEE Conference on Computer Vision and Pattern Recognition, pp. 2255–2264 (2018)
9. Huang, X., et al.: DiversityGAN: diversity-aware vehicle motion prediction via latent semantic sampling. IEEE Robot. Autom. Lett. 5(4), 5089–5096 (2020)

10. Ivanovic, B., Pavone, M.: The trajectron: probabilistic multi-agent trajectory modeling with dynamic spatiotemporal graphs. In: Proceedings of the IEEE/CVF International Conference on Computer Vision, pp. 2375–2384 (2019)
11. Kosaraju, V., et al.: Social-BIGAT: multimodal trajectory forecasting using bicycle-GAN and graph attention networks. arXiv preprint arXiv:1907.03395 (2019)
12. Laplante, J.N., Kaeser, T.P.: The continuing evolution of pedestrian walking speed assumptions. Insti. Transp. Eng. ITE J. **74**(9), 32 (2004)
13. Lee, N., Choi, W., Vernaza, P., Choy, C.B., Torr, P.H., Chandraker, M.: Desire: distant future prediction in dynamic scenes with interacting agents. In: Proceedings of the IEEE Conference on Computer Vision and Pattern Recognition, pp. 336–345 (2017)
14. Lerner, A., Chrysanthou, Y., Lischinski, D.: Crowds by example. In: Computer Graphics Forum. vol. 26, pp. 655–664. Wiley Online Library (2007)
15. Li, K., Malik, J.: Implicit maximum likelihood estimation. arXiv preprint arXiv:1809.09087 (2018)
16. Li, X., Ying, X., Chuah, M.C.: Grip: graph-based interaction-aware trajectory prediction. In: 2019 IEEE Intelligent Transportation Systems Conference (ITSC), pp. 3960–3966. IEEE (2019)
17. Liang, M., et al.: Learning lane graph representations for motion forecasting. In: Vedaldi, A., Bischof, H., Brox, T., Frahm, J.-M. (eds.) ECCV 2020. LNCS, vol. 12347, pp. 541–556. Springer, Cham (2020). https://doi.org/10.1007/978-3-030-58536-5_32
18. Limmer, M., Forster, J., Baudach, D., Schüle, F., Schweiger, R., Lensch, H.P.: Robust deep-learning-based road-prediction for augmented reality navigation systems at night. In: 2016 IEEE 19th International Conference on Intelligent Transportation Systems (ITSC), pp. 1888–1895. IEEE (2016)
19. Liu, H., Wang, L.: Human motion prediction for human-robot collaboration. J. Manuf. Syst. **44**, 287–294 (2017)
20. Liu, Y., Yan, Q., Alahi, A.: Social NCE: contrastive learning of socially-aware motion representations. In: Proceedings of the IEEE/CVF International Conference on Computer Vision, pp. 15118–15129 (2021)
21. Mahalanobis, P.C.: On the generalized distance in statistics. National Institute of Science of India (1936)
22. Mangalam, K., An, Y., Girase, H., Malik, J.: From goals, waypoints & paths to long term human trajectory forecasting. In: Proceedings of International Conference on Computer Vision (ICCV), October 2021
23. Mohamed, A., Qian, K., Elhoseiny, M., Claudel, C.: Social-STGCNN: a social spatio-temporal graph convolutional neural network for human trajectory prediction. In: Proceedings of the IEEE/CVF Conference on Computer Vision and Pattern Recognition, pp. 14424–14432 (2020)
24. Pellegrini, S., Ess, A., Schindler, K., Van Gool, L.: You'll never walk alone: Modeling social behavior for multi-target tracking. In: 2009 IEEE 12th International Conference on Computer Vision, pp. 261–268. IEEE (2009)
25. Quehl, J., Hu, H., Taş, Ö.Ş., Rehder, E., Lauer, M.: How good is my prediction? Finding a similarity measure for trajectory prediction evaluation. In: 2017 IEEE 20th International Conference on Intelligent Transportation Systems (ITSC), pp. 1–6. IEEE (2017)
26. Rhinehart, N., Kitani, K.M., Vernaza, P.: R2P2: a reparameterized pushforward policy for diverse, precise generative path forecasting. In: Ferrari, V., Hebert, M.,

Sminchisescu, C., Weiss, Y. (eds.) ECCV 2018. LNCS, vol. 11217, pp. 794–811. Springer, Cham (2018). https://doi.org/10.1007/978-3-030-01261-8_47

27. Rhinehart, N., McAllister, R., Kitani, K., Levine, S.: PRECOG: prediction conditioned on goals in visual multi-agent settings. In: Proceedings of the IEEE/CVF International Conference on Computer Vision, pp. 2821–2830 (2019)

28. Rudenko, A., et al.: Human motion trajectory prediction: a survey. Int. J. Robot. Res. **39**(8), 895–935 (2020)

29. Sadeghian, A., Kosaraju, V., Sadeghian, A., Hirose, N., Rezatofighi, H., Savarese, S.: Sophie: an attentive GAN for predicting paths compliant to social and physical constraints. In: Proceedings of the IEEE/CVF Conference on Computer Vision and Pattern Recognition, pp. 1349–1358 (2019)

30. Salzmann, T., Ivanovic, B., Chakravarty, P., Pavone, M.: Trajectron++: dynamically-feasible trajectory forecasting with heterogeneous data. In: Vedaldi, A., Bischof, H., Brox, T., Frahm, J.-M. (eds.) ECCV 2020. LNCS, vol. 12363, pp. 683–700. Springer, Cham (2020), https://doi.org/10.1007/978-3-030-58523-5_40

31. Sohn, K., Lee, H., Yan, X.: Learning structured output representation using deep conditional generative models. Adv. Neural. Inf. Process. Syst. **28**, 3483–3491 (2015)

32. Tang, C., Salakhutdinov, R.R.: Multiple futures prediction. Adv. Neural. Inf. Process. Syst. **32**, 15424–15434 (2019)

33. Tipping, M.E.: Deriving cluster analytic distance functions from gaussian mixture models. In: 1999 Ninth International Conference on Artificial Neural Networks ICANN 1999. (Conf. Publ. No. 470), vol. 2, pp. 815–820. IET (1999)

34. Westphal, C.: Challenges in networking to support augmented reality and virtual reality. In: IEEE ICNC (2017)

35. Wu, P., Chen, S., Metaxas, D.N.: MotionNet: joint perception and motion prediction for autonomous driving based on bird's eye view maps. In: Proceedings of the IEEE/CVF Conference on Computer Vision and Pattern Recognition, pp. 11385–11395 (2020)

36. Yuan, Y., Weng, X., Ou, Y., Kitani, K.: Agentformer: Agent-aware transformers for socio-temporal multi-agent forecasting. arXiv preprint arXiv:2103.14023 (2021)

37. Zhao, H., Wildes, R.P.: Where are you heading? Dynamic trajectory prediction with expert goal examples. In: Proceedings of the IEEE/CVF International Conference on Computer Vision, pp. 7629–7638 (2021)

38. Zhu, D., Zahran, M., Li, L.E., Elhoseiny, M.: Motion forecasting with unlikelihood training in continuous space. In: 5th Annual Conference on Robot Learning (2021)

TEMOS: Generating Diverse Human Motions from Textual Descriptions

Mathis Petrovich[1,2]($\boxtimes$), Michael J. Black[2], and Gül Varol[1]

[1] LIGM, École des Ponts, Univ Gustave Eiffel, CNRS, Paris, France
[2] Max Planck Institute for Intelligent Systems, Tübingen, Germany
{mathis.petrovich,gul.varol}@enpc.fr, black@tue.mpg.de
https://mathis.petrovich.fr/temos/

Abstract. We address the problem of generating diverse 3D human motions from textual descriptions. This challenging task requires joint modeling of both modalities: understanding and extracting useful human-centric information from the text, and then generating plausible and realistic sequences of human poses. In contrast to most previous work which focuses on generating a single, deterministic, motion from a textual description, we design a variational approach that can produce *multiple* diverse human motions. We propose TEMOS, a text-conditioned generative model leveraging variational autoencoder (VAE) training with human motion data, in combination with a text encoder that produces distribution parameters compatible with the VAE latent space. We show the TEMOS framework can produce both skeleton-based animations as in prior work, as well more expressive SMPL body motions. We evaluate our approach on the KIT Motion-Language benchmark and, despite being relatively straightforward, demonstrate significant improvements over the state of the art. Code and models are available on our webpage.

1 Introduction

We explore the problem of generating 3D human motions, i.e., sequences of 3D poses, from natural language textual descriptions (in English in this paper). Generating text-conditioned human motions has numerous applications both for the virtual (e.g., game industry) and real worlds (e.g., controlling a robot with speech for personal physical assistance). For example, in the film and game industries, motion capture is often used to create special effects featuring humans. Motion capture is expensive, therefore technologies that automatically synthesize new motion data could save time and money.

Language represents a natural interface for people to interact with computers [18], and our work provides a foundational step towards creating human animations using natural language input. The problem of generating human motion

---

Supplementary Information The online version contains supplementary material available at https://doi.org/10.1007/978-3-031-20047-2_28.

S. Avidan et al. (Eds.): ECCV 2022, LNCS 13682, pp. 480–497, 2022.
https://doi.org/10.1007/978-3-031-20047-2_28

A man walks in a circle.
$z \in \mathcal{N}(0,1)$

A person stands, then walks a few steps, then stops again.
$z \in \mathcal{N}(0,1)$

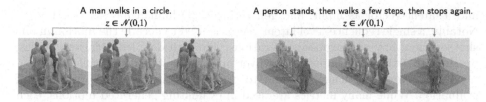

Fig. 1. Goal: Text-to-Motions (TEMOS) learns to synthesize human motion sequences conditioned on a textual description and a duration. SMPL pose sequences are generated by sampling from a single latent vector, z. Here, we illustrate the diversity of our motions on two sample texts, providing three generations per text input. Each image corresponds to a motion sequence where we visualize the root trajectory projected on the ground plane and the human poses at multiple equidistant time frames. The flow of time is shown with a color code where lighter blue denotes the past.

from free-form text, however, is relatively new since it relies on advances in both language modeling and human motion synthesis. Regarding the former, we build on advances in language modeling using transformers. In terms of human motion synthesis, much of the previous work has focused on generating motions conditioned on a single action label, not a sentence, e.g., [14,38]. Here we go further by encoding both the language and the motion using transformers in a joint latent space. The approach is relatively straightforward, yet achieves results that significantly outperform the latest state of the art. We perform extensive experiments and ablation studies to understand which design choices are critical.

Despite recent efforts in this area, most current methods generate only *one* output motion per text input [2,12,28]. That is, with the input "A man walks in a circle", these methods synthesize one motion. However, one description often can map to *multiple* ways of performing the actions, often due to ambiguities and lack of details, e.g., in our example, the size and the orientation of the circle are not specified. An ideal generative model should therefore be able to synthesize multiple sequences that respect the textual description while exploring the degrees of freedom to generate natural variations. While, in theory, the more precise the description becomes, the less space there is for diversity; it is a desirable property for natural language interfaces to manage intrinsic ambiguities of linguistic expressions [11]. In this paper, we propose a method that allows sampling from a distribution of human motions conditioned on natural language descriptions. Figure 1 illustrates multiple sampled motions generated from two input texts; check the project webpage [37] for video examples.

A key challenge is building models that are effective for temporal modeling. Most prior work employs autoregressive models that iteratively decode the next time frame given the past. These approaches may suffer from drift over time and often, eventually, produce static poses [34]. In contrast, sequence-level generative models encode an entire sequence and can exploit long-range context. In this work, we incorporate the powerful Transformer models [47], which have proven effective for various sequence modeling tasks [4,8]. We design a simple yet effective architecture, where both the motion and text are input to Transformer encoders before projecting them to a cross-modal joint space. Similarly, the motion decoder uses a Transformer architecture taking positional encodings and a latent vector as input, and generating a 3D human motion (see Fig. 2). Notably, a single sequence-level latent vector is used to decode the motion in one shot, without any autoregressive iterations. Through detailed ablation studies, we show that the main improvement over prior work stems from this design.

A well-known challenge common to generative models is the difficulty of evaluation. While many metrics are used in evaluating generated motions, each of them is limited. Consequently, in this work, we rely on both quantitative measures that compare against the ground truth motion data associated with each test description, and human perceptual studies to evaluate the perceived quality of the motions. The former is problematic particularly for this work, because it assumes one true motion per text, but our method produces multiple motions due to its probabilistic nature. We find that human judgment of motion quality is necessary for a full picture.

Moreover, the state of the art reports results on the task of future motion prediction. Specifically, Ghosh et al. [12] assume the first pose in the generated sequence is available from the ground truth. In contrast, we evaluate our method by synthesizing the full motion from scratch; i.e. without conditioning on the first, ground truth, frame. We provide results for various settings, e.g., comparing a random generation against the ground truth, or picking the best out of several generations. We outperform previous work even when sampling a single random generation, but the performance improves as we increase the number of generations and pick the best.

A further addition we make over existing text-to-motion approaches is to generate sequences of SMPL body models [30]. Unlike classical skeleton representations, the parametric SMPL model provides the body surface, which can support future research on motions that involve interaction with objects or the scene. Such skinned generations were considered in other work on unconstrained or action-conditioned generation [38,56]. Here, we demonstrate promising results for the text-conditioning scenario as well. The fact that the framework supports multiple body representations, illustrates its generality.

In summary, our contributions are the following: (i) We present Text-to-Motions (TEMOS), a novel cross-modal variational model that can produce diverse 3D human movements given textual descriptions in natural language. (ii) In our experiments, we provide an extensive ablation study of the model components and outperform the state of the art by a large margin both on standard metrics and through perceptual studies. (iii) We go beyond stick figure generations, and exploit the SMPL model for text-conditioned body surface synthesis, demonstrating qualitatively appealing results. The code and trained models are available on our project page [37].

2   Related Work

We provide a brief summary of relevant work on human motion synthesis and text-conditioned motion generation. While there is also work on facial motion generation [7,10,22,42], here we focus on articulated human bodies.

Human Motion Synthesis. While there is a large body of work focusing on future human motion prediction [3,5,15,36,53,56] and completion [9,16], here, we give an overview of methods that generate motions from scratch (i.e., no past or future observations). Generative models of human motion have been designed using GANs [1,29], VAEs [14,38], or normalizing flows [17,54]. In this work, we employ VAEs in the context of Transformer neural network architectures. Recent work suggest that VAEs are effective for human motion generation compared with GANs [14,38], while being easier to train.

Motion synthesis methods can be broadly divided into two categories: (i) unconstrained generation, which models the entire space of possible motions [50,55,57] and (ii) conditioned synthesis, which aims for controllability such as using music [25–27], speech [6,13], action [14,38], and text [1,2,12,28,29,44] conditioning. Generative models that synthesize unconstrained motions aim, by design, to sample from a distribution, allowing generation of diverse motions. However, they lack the ability to control the generation process. On the other hand, the conditioned synthesis can be further divided into two categories: deterministic [2,12,28] or probabilistic [1,14,25,26,29,38]. In this work, we focus on the latter, motivated by the fact that there are often multiple possible motions for a given condition.

Text-Conditioned Motion Generation. Recent work explores the advances in natural language modeling [8,35] to design sequence-to-sequence approaches to cast the text-to-motion task as a machine translation problem [1,28,40]. Others build joint cross-modal embeddings to map the text and motion to the same space [2,12,49], which has been a success in other research area [4,41,51,52].

Several methods use an impoverished body motion representation. For example, some do not model the global trajectory [40,49], making the motions unrealistic and ignoring the global movement description in the input text. Text2Action [1] uses a sequence-to-sequence model but only models the upper body motion. This is because Text2Action uses a semi-automatic approach to create training data from the MSR-VTT captioned video dataset [48], which contains frequently occluded lower bodies. They apply 2D pose estimation, lift the joints to 3D, and employ manual cleaning of the input text to make it generic.

Most other work uses 3D motion capture data [2,12,28,29]. DVGANs [29] adapt the CMU MoCap database [46] and Human3.6M [20,21] for the task of motion generation and completion, and they use the action labels as text-conditioning instead of categorical supervision. More recent works [2,12,28] employ the KIT Motion-Language dataset [39], which is also the focus of our work.

A key limitation of many state-of-the-art text-conditioned motion generation models is that they are deterministic [2,12]. These methods employ a shared cross-modal latent space approach. Ahuja et al. [2] employ word2vec text embeddings [35], while [12] uses the more recent BERT model [8].

Most similar to our work is Ghosh et al. [12], which builds on Language2Pose [2]. Our key difference is the integration of a variational approach for sampling a diverse set of motions from a single text. Our further improvements include the use of Transformers to encode motion sequences into a single embedding instead of the autoregressive approach in [12]. This allows us to encode distribution

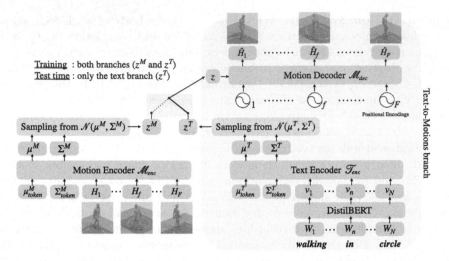

Fig. 2. Method overview: During training, we encode both the motion and text through their respective Transformer encoders, together with modal-specific learnable distribution tokens. The encoder outputs corresponding to these tokens provide Gaussian distribution parameters on which the KL losses are applied and a latent vector z is sampled. Reconstruction losses on the motion decoder outputs further provide supervision for both motion and text branches. In practice, our word embedding consists of a variational encoder that takes input from a pre-trained and frozen DistilBERT [43] model. Trainable layers are denoted in green, the inputs/outputs in brown. At test time, we only use the right branch, which goes from an input text to a diverse set of motions through the random sampling of the latent vector z^T on the cross-modal space. The output motion duration is determined by the number of positional encodings F.

parameters of the VAE as in [38], proving effective in our state-of-the-art results. Ghosh et al. [12] also encode the upper body and lower body separately, whereas our approach does not need such hand crafting.

3   Generating Multiple Motions from a Textual Description

In this section, we start by formulating the problem (Sect. 3.1). We then provide details on our model design (Sect. 3.2), as well as our training strategy (Sect. 3.3).

3.1   Task Definition

Given a sentence describing a motion, the goal is to generate various sequences of 3D human poses and trajectories that match the textual input. Next, we describe the representation for the text and motion data.

Textual description represents a written natural language sentence (e.g., in English) that describes what and how a human motion is performed. The sentence can include various levels of detail: a precise sequence of actions such as

"A human walks two steps and then stops" or a more ambiguous description such as *"A man walks in a circle"*. The data structure is a sequence of words $W_{1:N} = W_1, \ldots, W_N$ from the English vocabulary.

3D human motion is defined as a sequence of human poses $H_{1:F} = H_1, \ldots, H_F$, where F denotes the number of time frames. Each pose H_f corresponds to a representation of the articulated human body. In this work, we employ two types of body motion representations: one based on skeletons, one based on SMPL [30]. First, to enable a comparison with the state of the art, we follow the rotation-invariant skeleton representation from Holden et al. [19], which is used in the previous work we compare with [2,12]. Second, we incorporate the parametric SMPL representation by encoding the global root trajectory of the body and parent-relative joint rotations in 6D representation [58]. We provide detailed formulations for both motion representations in Appendix B.

More generally, a human motion can be represented by a sequence of F poses each with p dimensions, so that at frame f, we have $H_f \in \mathbb{R}^p$. Our goal is, given a textual description $W_{1:N}$, to sample from a distribution of plausible motions $H_{1:F}$ and to generate multiple hypotheses.

3.2   TEMOS Model Architecture

Following [2], we learn a joint latent space between the two modalities: motion and text (see Fig. 2). To incorporate generative modeling in such an approach, we employ a VAE [24] formulation that requires architectural changes. We further employ Transformers [47] to obtain sequence-level embeddings both for the text and motion data. Next, we describe the two encoders for motion and text, followed by the motion decoder.

Motion and Text Encoders. We have two encoders for representing motion $\mathcal{M}_{enc}$ and text $\mathcal{T}_{enc}$ in a joint space. The encoders are designed to be as symmetric as possible across the two modalities. To this end, we adapt the ACTOR [38] Transformer-based VAE motion encoder by making it class-agnostic (i.e., removing action conditioning). This encoder takes as input a sequence of vectors of arbitrary length, as well as learnable *distribution tokens*. The outputs corresponding to the distribution tokens are treated as Gaussian distribution parameters μ and Σ of the sequence-level latent space. Using the reparameterization trick [24], we sample a latent vector $z \in \mathbb{R}^d$ from this distribution (see Fig. 2). The latent space dimensionality d is set to 256 in our experiments.

For the motion encoder $\mathcal{M}_{enc}$, the input sequence of vectors is $H_{1:F}$, representing the poses. For the text encoder $\mathcal{T}_{enc}$, the inputs are word embeddings for $W_{1:N}$ obtained from a pretrained language model DistilBERT [43]. We freeze the weights of DistilBERT unless stated otherwise.

Motion Decoder. The motion decoder $\mathcal{M}_{dec}$ is a Transformer decoder (as in ACTOR [38], but without the bias token to make it class agnostic), so that given a latent vector z and a duration F, we generate a 3D human motion sequence $\widehat{H}_{1:F}$ non-autoregressively from a single latent vector. Note that such approach does not require masks in self-attention, and tends to provide a globally consistent motion. The latent vector is obtained from one of the two encoders during training (described next, in Sect. 3.3), and the duration is represented as a sequence of positional encodings in the form of sinusoidal functions. We note that our model can produce variable durations, which is another source of diversity (see supplementary video [37]).

3.3   Training Strategy

For our cross-modal neural network training, we sample a batch of text-motion pairs at each training iteration. In summary, both input modalities go through their respective encoders, and both encoded vectors go through the motion decoder to reconstruct the 3D poses. This means we have one branch that is text-to-motion and another branch that is an autoencoder for motion-to-motion (see Fig. 2). At test time, we only use the text-to-motion branch. This approach proved effective in previous work [2]. Here, we first briefly describe the loss terms to train this model *probabilistically*. Then, we provide implementation details.

Given a ground-truth pair consisting of human motion $H_{1:F}$ and textual description $W_{1:N}$, we use (i) two reconstruction losses – one per modality, (ii) KL divergence losses comparing each modality against Gaussion priors, (iii) KL divergence losses, as well as a cross-modal embedding similarity loss to compare the two modalities to each other.

Reconstruction Losses ($\mathcal{L}_R$). We obtain $\widehat{H}_{1:F}^M$ and $\widehat{H}_{1:F}^T$ by inputting the motion embedding and text embedding to the decoder, respectively. We compare these motion reconstructions to the ground-truth human motion $H_{1:F}$ via:

$$\mathcal{L}_R = \mathcal{L}_1(H_{1:F}, \widehat{H}_{1:F}^M) + \mathcal{L}_1(H_{1:F}, \widehat{H}_{1:F}^T) \tag{1}$$

where $\mathcal{L}_1$ denotes the smooth L1 loss.

KL Losses ($\mathcal{L}_{KL}$). To enforce the two modalities to be close to each other in the latent space, we minimize the Kullback-Leibler (KL) divergences between the distributions of the text embedding $\phi^T = \mathcal{N}(\mu^T, \Sigma^T)$ and the motion embedding $\phi^M = \mathcal{N}(\mu^M, \Sigma^M)$. To regularize the shared latent space, we encourage each distribution to be similar to a normal distribution $\psi = \mathcal{N}(0, I)$ (as in standard VAE formulations). Thus we obtain four terms:

$$\mathcal{L}_{KL} = KL(\phi^T, \phi^M) + KL(\phi^M, \phi^T) \\ + KL(\phi^T, \psi) + KL(\phi^M, \psi). \tag{2}$$

Cross-modal Embedding Similarity Loss ($\mathcal{L}_E$). After sampling the text embedding $z^T \sim \mathcal{N}(\mu^T, \Sigma^T)$ and the motion embedding $z^M \sim \mathcal{N}(\mu^M, \Sigma^M)$ from the two encoders, we also constrain them to be as close as possible to each other, with the following loss term (i.e., loss between the cross-modal embeddings):

$$\mathcal{L}_E = \mathcal{L}_1(z^T, z^M). \tag{3}$$

The resulting total loss is defined as a weighted sum of the three terms: $\mathcal{L} = \mathcal{L}_R + \lambda_{KL}\mathcal{L}_{KL} + \lambda_E\mathcal{L}_E$. We empirically set λ_{KL} and λ_E to 10^{-5}, and provide ablations. While some of the loss terms may appear redundant, we experimentally validate each term.

Implementation Details. We train our models for 1000 epochs with the AdamW optimizer [23,31] using a fixed learning rate of 10^{-4}. Our minibatch size is set to 32. Our Transformer encoders and decoders consist of 6 layers for both motion and text encoders, as well the motion decoder. Ablations about these hyperparameters are presented in Appendix A.

At training time, we input the full motion sequence, i.e., a variable number of frames for each training sample. At inference time, we can specify the desired duration F (see supplementary video [37]); however, we provide quantitative metrics with known ground-truth motion duration.

4 Experiments

We first present the data and performance measures used in our experiments (Sect. 4.1). Next, we compare to previous work (Sect. 4.2) and present an ablation study (Sect. 4.3). Then, we demonstrate our results with the SMPL model (Sect. 4.4). Finally, we discuss limitations (Sect. 4.5).

4.1 Data and Evaluation Metrics

KIT Motion-Language [39] dataset (KIT) provides raw motion capture (MoCap) data, as well as processed data using the Master Motor Map (MMM) framework [45]. The motions comprise a collection of subsets of the KIT Whole-Body Human Motion Database [33] and of the CMU Graphics Lab Motion Capture Database [46]. The dataset consists of 3911 motion sequences with 6353 sequence-level description annotations, with 9.5 words per description on average. We use the same splits as in Language2Pose [2] by extracting 1784 training, 566 validation and 587 test motions (some motions do not have corresponding descriptions). As the model from Ghosh et al. [12] produce only 520 sequences in the test set (instead of 587), for a fair comparison we evaluate all methods with this subset, which we will refer to as the test set. If the same motion sequence corresponds to multiple descriptions, we randomly choose one of these descriptions at each training iteration, while we evaluate the method on the first description. Recent state-of-the-art methods on text-conditioned motion synthesis employ this dataset, by first converting the MMM axis-angle data into 21 xyz coordinates and downsampling the sequences 100 Hz to 12.5 Hz. We do the same procedure, and follow the training and test splits explained above to compare methods. Additionally, we find correspondences from the KIT sequences to the AMASS MoCap collection [32] to obtain the motions in SMPL body format. We note that this procedure resulted in a subset of 2888 annotated motion sequences, as some sequences have not been processed in AMASS. We refer to this data as KIT$_{SMPL}$.

Evaluation Metrics. We follow the performance measures employed in Language2Pose [2] and Ghosh et al. [12] for quantitative evaluations. In particular, we report Average Positional Error (APE) and Average Variance Error (AVE) metrics. However, we note that the results in [12] do not match the ones in [2] due to lack of evaluation code from [2]. We identified minor issues with the evaluation code of [12] (more details in Appendix C); therefore, we reimplement our own evaluation. Moreover, we introduce several modifications (which we believe make the metrics more interpretable): in contrast to [2,12], we compute the root joint metric by using the joint coordinates only (and not on velocities for x and y axes) and all the metrics are computed without standardizing the data (i.e., mean subtraction and division by standard deviation). Our motivation for this is to remain in the coordinate space since the metrics are *positional*. Note that the KIT data in the MMM format is canonicalized to the same body shape. We perform most of our experiments with this data format to remain comparable to the state of the art. We report results with the SMPL body format separately since the skeletons are not perfectly compatible (see Appendix A.5). Finally, we convert our low-fps generations (12 Hz) to the original frame-rate of KIT (100 Hz) via linear interpolation on coordinates and report the error comparing to this original ground truth. We display the error in meters.

As discussed in Sect. 1, the evaluation is suboptimal because it assumes one ground truth motion per text; however, our focus is to generate multiple different motions. The KIT test set is insufficient to design distribution-based metrics such as FID, since there are not enough motions for the same text (see Appendix E. for statistics). We therefore report the performance of generating a single sample, as well as generating multiple and evaluating the closest sample to the ground truth. We rely on additional perceptual studies to assess the correctness of multiple generations, which is described in Appendix C.

4.2   Comparison to the State of the Art

Quantitative. We compare with the state-of-the-art text-conditioned motion generation methods [2,12,28] on the test set of the KIT dataset (as defined in 4.1). To obtain motions for these three methods, we use their publicly available codes (note that all three give the ground truth initial frame as input to their generations). We summarize the main results in Table 1. Our TEMOS approach substantially outperforms on all metrics, except APE on local joints. As pointed by [2,12], the most difficult metric that better differentiates improvements on this dataset is the APE on the root joint, and we obtain significant improvements on this metric. Moreover, we sample a random latent vector for reporting the results for TEMOS; however, as we will show next in Sect. 4.3, if we sample more, we are more likely to find the motion closer to the ground truth.

Qualitative. We further provide qualitative comparisons in Fig. 4 with the state of the art. We show sample generations for Lin et al. [28], JL2P [2], and Ghosh et al. [12]. The motions from our TEMOS model reflect the semantic content of the input text better than the others across a variety of samples. Furthermore, we

Table 1. State-of-the-art comparison: We compare our method with recent works [2,12,28], on the KIT Motion-Language dataset [39] and obtain significant improvements on most metrics (values in meters) even if we are sampling a random motion per text conditioning for our model.

Methods	Average Positional Error ↓				Average Variance Error ↓			
	root joint	global traj.	mean local	mean global	root joint	global traj.	mean local	mean global
Lin et al. [28]	1.966	1.956	0.105	1.969	0.790	0.789	0.007	0.791
JL2P [2]	1.622	1.616	0.097	1.630	0.669	0.669	0.006	0.672
Ghosh et al. [12]	1.291	1.242	0.206	1.294	0.564	0.548	0.024	0.563
TEMOS (ours)	0.963	0.955	0.104	0.076	0.445	0.445	0.005	0.448

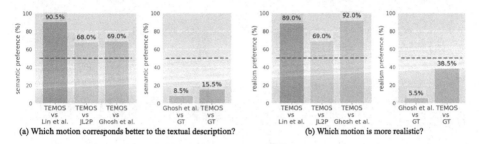

(a) Which motion corresponds better to the textual description?   (b) Which motion is more realistic?

Fig. 3. Perceptual study: (a) We ask users which motion corresponds better to the input text between two displayed samples generated from model A vs model B. (b) We ask other users which motion is more realistic without showing the textual description. We report the percentage for which the users show a preference for A. The red dashed line denotes the 50% level (equal preference). On the left of both studies, our generations from TEMOS were rated better than the previous work of Lin et al. [28], JL2P [2], and Ghosh et al. [12]. On the right of both studies, we compare against the ground truth (GT) and see that our motions are rated as better than the GT 15.5% and 38.5% of the time, whereas Ghosh et al. [12] are at 8.5% and 5.5%.

observe that while [28] generates overly smooth motions, JL2P has lots of foot sliding. [12], on the other hand, synthesizes unrealistic motions due to exaggerated foot contacts (and even extremely elongated limbs such as in 3rd column, 3rd row of Fig. 4). Our generations are the most realistic among all. Further visualizations are provided in the supplementary video [37].

Perceptual Study. These conclusions are further justified by two human perceptual studies that evaluate which methods are preferred in terms of semantics (correspondence to the text) or in terms of realism. For the first study, we displayed a pair of motions (with a randomly swapped order in each display) and a description of the motion, and asked Amazon Mechanical Turk (AMT) workers the question: "Which motion corresponds better to the textual description?". We collected answers for 100 randomly sampled test descriptions, showing each description to multiple workers. For the second study, we asked another set of AMT workers the question: "Which motion is more realistic?" without showing the description. We give more details on our perceptual studies in Appendix C.

The resulting ranking between our method and each of the state-of-the-art methods [2,12,28] is reported in Fig. 3. We see that humans perceive our motions

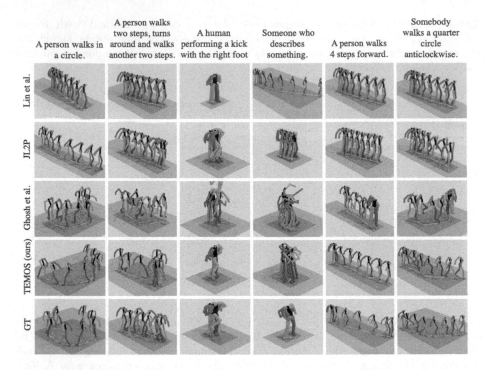

Fig. 4. Qualitative comparison to the state of the art: We qualitatively compare the generations from our TEMOS model with the recent state-of-the-art methods and the ground truth (GT). We present different textual queries in columns, and different methods in rows. Overall, our generations better match semantically to the textual descriptions. We further overcome several limitations with the prior work, such as over-smooth motions in Lin et al. [28], foot sliding in J2LP [2], and exaggerated foot contacts in Ghosh et al. [12], which can better be viewed in our supplementary video [37].

as better matching the descriptions compared to all three state-of-the-art methods, especially significantly outperforming Lin et al. [28] (users preferred TEMOS over [28] 90.5% of the time). For the more competitive and more recent Ghosh et al. [12] method, we ask users to compare their generations against the ground truth. We do the same for our generations and see that users preferred our motions over the ground truth 15.5% of the time where the ones from Ghosh et al. [12] are preferred only 8.5% of the time. Our generations are also clearly preferred in terms of realism over the three methods. Our motions are realistic enough that they are preferred to real motion capture data 38.5% of the time, as compared to 5.5% of the time for Ghosh et al. [12].

4.3   Ablation Study

In this section, we evaluate the influence of several components of our framework in a controlled setting.

Table 2. Variational vs deterministic models: We first provide the performance of the deterministic version of our model. We then report results with several settings using our variational model: (i) generating a single motion per text to compare against the ground truth (either randomly or using a zero-vector representing the mean of the Gaussian latent space), and (ii) generating 10 motions per text, each compared against the ground truth separately (either averaging the metrics or taking the motion with the best metric). As expected, TEMOS is able to produce multiple hypotheses where the best candidates improve the metrics.

Model	Sampling	Average Positional Error ↓				Average Variance Error ↓			
		root joint	global traj.	mean local	mean global	root joint	global traj.	mean local	mean global
Deterministic	n/a	1.175	1.165	0.106	1.188	0.514	0.513	0.005	0.516
Variational	1 sample, $z = 0$	1.005	0.997	0.104	1.020	0.443	0.442	0.005	0.446
Variational	1 random sample	0.963	0.955	0.104	0.976	0.445	0.445	0.005	0.448
Variational	10 random avg	1.001	0.993	0.104	1.015	0.451	0.451	0.005	0.454
Variational	10 random best	**0.784**	**0.774**	0.104	**0.802**	**0.392**	**0.391**	0.005	**0.395**

Variational Design. First, we 'turn off' the variational property of our generative model and synthesize a single motion per text. Instead of two learnable distribution tokens as in Fig. 2, we use one learnable *embedding* token from which we directly obtain the latent vector using the corresponding encoder output (hence removing sampling). We removed all the KL losses such that the model becomes deterministic, and keep the embedding similarity loss to learn the joint latent space. In Table 2, we report performance metrics with this approach and see that we already obtain competitive performance with the deterministic version of our model, demonstrating the improvements from our temporal sequence modeling approach compared to previous works.

As noted earlier, our variational model can produce multiple generations for the same text, and a single random sample may not necessarily match the ground truth. In Table 2, we report results for one generation from a random z noise vector, or generating from the zero-vector that represents the mean of the latent space ($z = \mathbf{0}$); both perform similarly. To assess the performance with multiple generations, we randomly sample 10 latent vectors per text, and provide two evaluations. First, we compare each of the 10 generations to the single ground truth, and average over all generations (10 random avg). Second, we record the performance of the motion that best matches to the ground truth out of the 10 generations (10 random best). As expected, Table 2 shows improvements with the latter (see Appendix A.5 for more values for the number of latent vectors).

Architectural and Loss Components. Next, we investigate which component is most responsible for the performance improvement over the state of the art, since even the deterministic variant of our model outperforms previous works. Table 3 reports the performance by removing one component at each row. The APE root joint performance drops from 0.96 to i) 1.44 using GRUs instead of Transformers; ii) 1.18 without the motion encoder (using only one KL loss); iii) 1.09 without the cross-modal embedding loss; iv) 1.05 without the Gaussian priors; v) 0.99 without the cross-modal KL losses. Note that the cross-modal framework originates from JL2P [2]. While we observe slight improvement with each of the cross-modal terms, we notice that the model performance is already satis-

Table 3. Architectural and loss study: We conclude that the most critical component is the Transformer architecture, as opposed to a recurrent one (i.e., GRU). While the additional losses are helpful, they bring relatively minor improvements.

Arch $\mathcal{L}_{KL}$	$\mathcal{L}_E$	Average Positional Error ↓				Average Variance Error ↓			
		root joint	glob traj	mean loc	mean glob	root joint	glob traj	mean loc	mean glob
GRU $KL(\phi^T,\phi^M) + KL(\phi^M,\phi^T) + KL(\phi^T,\psi) + KL(\phi^M,\psi)$	✓	1.443	1.433	0.105	1.451	0.600	0.599	0.007	0.601
Transf $KL(\phi^T,\psi)$ w/out $\mathcal{M}_{enc}$	✗	1.178	1.168	0.106	1.189	0.506	0.505	0.006	0.508
Transf $KL(\phi^T,\phi^M) + KL(\phi^M,\phi^T) + KL(\phi^T,\psi) + KL(\phi^M,\psi)$	✗	1.091	1.083	0.107	1.104	0.449	0.448	0.005	0.451
Transf $KL(\phi^T,\psi) + KL(\phi^M,\psi)$ w/out cross-modal KL losses ✗		1.080	1.071	0.107	1.095	0.453	0.452	0.005	0.456
Transf $KL(\phi^T,\psi) + KL(\phi^M,\psi)$ w/out cross-modal KL losses ✓		0.993	0.983	0.105	1.006	0.461	0.460	0.005	0.463
Transf $KL(\phi^T,\phi^M) + KL(\phi^M,\phi^T)$ w/out Gaussian priors	✓	1.049	1.039	0.108	1.065	0.472	0.471	0.005	0.475
Transf $KL(\phi^T,\phi^M) + KL(\phi^M,\phi^T) + KL(\phi^T,\psi) + KL(\phi^M,\psi)$	✓	**0.963**	**0.955**	**0.104**	**0.976**	**0.445**	**0.445**	**0.005**	**0.448**

Table 4. Language model finetuning: We experiment with finetuning the language model (LM) parameters (i.e., DistilBERT [43]) end-to-end with our motion-language cross-modal framework, and do not observe improvements. Here 'Frozen' refers to not updating the LM parameters.

LM params	Average Positional Error ↓				Average Variance Error ↓			
	root joint	global traj.	mean local	mean global	root joint	global traj.	mean local	mean global
Finetuned	1.402	1.393	0.113	1.414	0.559	0.558	0.006	0.562
Frozen	0.963	0.955	0.104	0.976	0.445	0.445	0.005	0.448

factory even without the motion encoder. We therefore conclude that the main improvement stems from the improved non-autoregressive Transformer architecture, and removing each of the other components (4 KL loss terms, motion encoder, embedding similarity) also slightly degrades performance.

Language Model Finetuning. As explained in Sect. 3.2, we do not update the language model parameters during training, which are from the pretrained DistilBERT [43]. We measure the performance with and without finetuning in Table 4 and conclude that freezing performs better while being more efficient. We note that we already introduce additional layers through our text encoder (see Fig. 2), which may be sufficient to adapt the embeddings to our specific motion description domain. We provide an additional experiment with larger language models in Appendix A.4.

4.4 Generating Skinned Motions

We evaluate the variant of our model which uses the parametric SMPL representation to generate full body meshes. The quantitative performance metrics on KIT$_{SMPL}$ test set can be found in Appendix A.5. We provide qualitative examples in Fig. 5 to illustrate the diversity of our generations for a given text. For each text, we present 2 random samples. Each column shows a different text input. For all the visualization renderings in this paper, the camera is fixed and the bodies are sampled evenly across time. Moreover, the forward direction of the first frame is always facing the same canonical direction. Our observation is that the model can generate multiple plausible motions corresponding to the same

A person walks two steps, turns around and walks another two steps. A person performs a squat. A person stands, then walks a few steps, then stops again. A person walking in a circle to the right. A human performing a kick with the right foot. A person goes backward on his tiptoes.

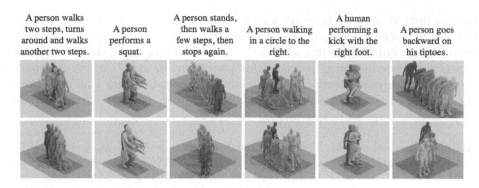

Fig. 5. Qualitative evaluation of the diversity: We display two motion generations for each description. Our model shows certain diversity among different generations while respecting the textual description.

text, exploring the degrees of freedom remaining from ambiguities in the language description. On the other hand, if the text describes a precise action, such as 'A person performs a squat' the diversity is reduced. The results are better seen as movies; see supplementary video [37], where we also display other effects such as generating variable durations, and interpolating in the latent space.

4.5   Limitations

Our model has several limitations. Firstly, the vocabulary of the KIT data is relatively small with 1263 unique words compared to the full open-vocabulary setting of natural language, and are dominated by locomotive motions. We therefore expect our model to suffer from out-of-distribution descriptions. Moreover, we do not have a principled way of measuring the diversity of our models since the training does not include multiple motions for the exact same text. Secondly, we notice that if the input text contains typos (e.g., 'wals' instead of 'walks'), TEMOS might drastically fail, suggesting that a preprocessing step to correct them beforehand might be needed. Finally, our method cannot scale up to very long motions (such as walking for several minutes) due to the quadratic memory cost.

5   Conclusion

In this work, we introduced a variational approach to generate diverse 3D human motions given textual descriptions in the form of natural language. In contrast to previous methods, our approach considers the intrinsically ambiguous nature of language and generates multiple plausible motions respecting the textual description, rather than deterministically producing only one. We obtain state-of-the-art results on the widely used KIT Motion-Language benchmark, outperforming prior work by a large margin both in quantitative experiments and perceptual studies. Our improvements are mainly from the architecture design of incorporating sequence modeling via Transformers. Furthermore, we employ full body meshes instead of only skeletons. Future work should focus on explicit modeling of contacts and integrating physics knowledge. Another interesting direction is to explore duration estimation for the generated motions. While we do not expect any immediate negative societal impact from our work, we note that with the potential advancement of fake visual data generation, a risk may arise from the integration of our model in the applications that animate existing people without their consent, raising privacy concerns.

Acknowledgement.. This work was granted access to the HPC resources of IDRIS under the allocation 2021-AD011012129R1 made by GENCI. GV acknowledges the ANR project CorVis ANR-21-CE23-0003-01, and research gifts from Google and Adobe. The authors would like to thank Monika Wysoczanska, Georgy Ponimatkin, Romain Loiseau, Lucas Ventura and Margaux Lasselin for their feedbacks, Tsvetelina Alexiadis and Taylor McConnell for helping with the perceptual study, and Anindita Ghosh for helping with the evaluation details on the KIT dataset.
    Disclosure: https://files.is.tue.mpg.de/black/CoI_ECCV_2022.txt

References

1. Ahn, H., Ha, T., Choi, Y., Yoo, H., Oh, S.: Text2Action: generative adversarial synthesis from language to action. In: International Conference on Robotics and Automation (ICRA) (2018)
2. Ahuja, C., Morency, L.P.: Language2Pose: natural language grounded pose forecasting. In: International Conference on 3D Vision (3DV) (2019)
3. Aksan, E., Kaufmann, M., Hilliges, O.: Structured prediction helps 3D human motion modelling. In: International Conference on Computer Vision (ICCV) (2019)
4. Bain, M., Nagrani, A., Varol, G., Zisserman, A.: Frozen in time: a joint video and image encoder for end-to-end retrieval. In: International Conference on Computer Vision (ICCV) (2021)
5. Barsoum, E., Kender, J., Liu, Z.: HP-GAN: probabilistic 3D human motion prediction via GAN. In: Computer Vision and Pattern Recognition Workshops (CVPRW) (2018)
6. Bhattacharya, U., Childs, E., Rewkowski, N., Manocha, D.: Speech2Affective Gestures: Synthesizing Co-Speech Gestures with Generative Adversarial Affective Expression Learning (2021)
7. Cudeiro, D., Bolkart, T., Laidlaw, C., Ranjan, A., Black, M.: Capture, learning, and synthesis of 3D speaking styles. In: Computer Vision and Pattern Recognition (CVPR) (2019)
8. Devlin, J., Chang, M.W., Lee, K., Toutanova, K.: BERT: pre-training of deep bidirectional transformers for language understanding. In: North American Chapter of the Association for Computational Linguistics (NAACL) (2019)
9. Duan, Y., et al.: Single-shot motion completion with transformer. arXiv preprint arXiv:2103.00776 (2021)
10. Fan, Y., Lin, Z., Saito, J., Wang, W., Komura, T.: FaceFormer: speech-driven 3D facial animation with transformers. In: Computer Vision and Pattern Recognition (CVPR) (2022)
11. Gao, T., Dontcheva, M., Adar, E., Liu, Z., Karahalios, K.G.: DataTone: managing ambiguity in natural language interfaces for data visualization. In: ACM Symposium on User Interface Software & Technology (2015)

12. Ghosh, A., Cheema, N., Oguz, C., Theobalt, C., Slusallek, P.: Synthesis of compositional animations from textual descriptions. In: International Conference on Computer Vision (ICCV) (2021)
13. Ginosar, S., Bar, A., Kohavi, G., Chan, C., Owens, A., Malik, J.: Learning individual styles of conversational gesture. In: Computer Vision and Pattern Recognition (CVPR) (2019)
14. Guo, C., et al.: Action2Motion: conditioned generation of 3D human motions. In: ACM International Conference on Multimedia (ACMMM) (2020)
15. Habibie, I., Holden, D., Schwarz, J., Yearsley, J., Komura, T.: A recurrent variational autoencoder for human motion synthesis. In: British Machine Vision Conference (BMVC) (2017)
16. Harvey, F.G., Yurick, M., Nowrouzezahrai, D., Pal, C.: Robust motion in-betweening. ACM Trans. Graph. (TOG) **39**, 60–61 (2020)
17. Henter, G.E., Alexanderson, S., Beskow, J.: MoGlow: probabilistic and controllable motion synthesis using normalising flows. ACM Trans. Graph. (TOG) **39**, 1–14 (2020)
18. Hill, I.: Natural language versus computer language. In: Designing for Human-Computer Communication (1983)
19. Holden, D., Saito, J., Komura, T.: A deep learning framework for character motion synthesis and editing. ACM Trans. Graph. (TOG) **35**, 1–14 (2016)
20. Ionescu, C., Li, F., Sminchisescu, C.: Latent structured models for human pose estimation. In: International Conference on Computer Vision (ICCV) (2011)
21. Ionescu, C., Papava, D., Olaru, V., Sminchisescu, C.: Human36M: large scale datasets and predictive methods for 3D human sensing in natural environments. Trans. Pattern Anal. Mach. Intell. (TPAMI). **36**, 1325–1349 (2014)
22. Karras, T., Aila, T., Laine, S., Herva, A., Lehtinen, J.: Audio-driven facial animation by joint end-to-end learning of pose and emotion. ACM Trans. Graph. (TOG) **36**, 1–2 (2017)
23. Kingma, D.P., Ba, J.: Adam: a method for stochastic optimization. In: International Conference on Learning Representations (ICLR) (2015)
24. Kingma, D.P., Welling, M.: Auto-encoding variational Bayes. In: International Conference on Learning Representations (ICLR) (2014)
25. Lee, H.Y., et al.: Dancing to music. In: Neural Information Processing Systems (NeurIPS) (2019)
26. Li, J., et al.: Learning to generate diverse dance motions with transformer. arXiv preprint arXiv:2008.08171 (2020)
27. Li, R., Yang, S., Ross, D.A., Kanazawa, A.: AI choreographer: Music conditioned 3D dance generation with AIST++. In: International Conference on Computer Vision (ICCV) (2021)
28. Lin, A.S., Wu, L., Corona, R., Tai, K., Huang, Q., Mooney, R.J.: Generating animated videos of human activities from natural language descriptions. In: Visually Grounded Interaction and Language (ViGIL) NeurIPS Workshop (2018)
29. Lin, X., Amer, M.: Human motion modeling using DVGANs. arXiv preprint arXiv:1804.10652 (2018)
30. Loper, M., Mahmood, N., Romero, J., Pons-Moll, G., Black, M.J.: SMPL: a skinned multi-person linear model. ACM Trans. Graph. (TOG) **34**, 1–6 (2015)
31. Loshchilov, I., Hutter, F.: Decoupled weight decay regularization. In: International Conference on Learning Representations (ICLR) (2019)
32. Mahmood, N., Ghorbani, N., Troje, N.F., Pons-Moll, G., Black, M.J.: AMASS: archive of motion capture as surface shapes. In: International Conference on Computer Vision (ICCV) (2019)

33. Mandery, C., Terlemez, O., Do, M., Vahrenkamp, N., Asfour, T.: The kit whole-body human motion database. In: International Conference on Advanced Robotics (ICAR) (2015)
34. Martinez, J., Black, M.J., Romero, J.: On human motion prediction using recurrent neural networks. In: Computer Vision and Pattern Recognition (CVPR) (2017)
35. Mikolov, T., Sutskever, I., Chen, K., Corrado, G.S., Dean, J.: Distributed representations of words and phrases and their compositionality. In: Neural Information Processing Systems (NeurIPS) (2013)
36. Pavllo, D., Grangier, D., Auli, M.: QuaterNet: A quaternion-based recurrent model for human motion. In: British Machine Vision Conference (BMVC) (2018)
37. Petrovich, M., Black, M.J., Varol, G.: TEMOS project page: generating diverse human motions from textual descriptions. https://mathis.petrovich.fr/temos/
38. Petrovich, M., Black, M.J., Varol, G.: Action-conditioned 3D human motion synthesis with transformer VAE. In: International Conference on Computer Vision (ICCV) (2021)
39. Plappert, M., Mandery, C., Asfour, T.: The KIT motion-language dataset. Big Data. **4**, 236–252 (2016)
40. Plappert, M., Mandery, C., Asfour, T.: Learning a bidirectional mapping between human whole-body motion and natural language using deep recurrent neural networks. Robot. Auton. Syst. **109**, 13–26 (2018)
41. Radford, A., et al.: Learning transferable visual models from natural language supervision. In: International Conference on Machine Learning (ICML) (2021)
42. Richard, A., Zollhöfer, M., Wen, Y., de la Torre, F., Sheikh, Y.: Meshtalk: 3D face animation from speech using cross-modality disentanglement. In: International Conference on Computer Vision (ICCV) (2021)
43. Sanh, V., Debut, L., Chaumond, J., Wolf, T.: DistilBERT, a distilled version of BERT: smaller, faster, cheaper and lighter. arXiv preprint arXiv:1910.01108 (2019)
44. Saunders, B., Camgoz, N.C., Bowden, R.: Mixed SIGNals: sign language production via a mixture of motion primitives. In: International Conference on Computer Vision (ICCV) (2021)
45. Terlemez, O., Ulbrich, S., Mandery, C., Do, M., Vahrenkamp, N., Asfour, T.: Master motor map (MMM) - framework and toolkit for capturing, representing, and reproducing human motion on humanoid robots. In: International Conference on Humanoid Robots (2014)
46. University, C.M.: CMU MoCap Dataset
47. Vaswani, A., et al.: Attention is all you need. In: Neural Information Processing Systems (NeurIPS) (2017)
48. Xu, J., Mei, T., Yao, T., Rui, Y.: MSR-VTT: a large video description dataset for bridging video and language. In: Computer Vision and Pattern Recognition (CVPR) (2016)
49. Yamada, T., Matsunaga, H., Ogata, T.: Paired recurrent autoencoders for bidirectional translation between robot actions and linguistic descriptions. Robot. Auton. Lett. **3**, 441–448 (2018)
50. Yan, S., Li, Z., Xiong, Y., Yan, H., Lin, D.: Convolutional sequence generation for skeleton-based action synthesis. In: International Conference on Computer Vision (ICCV) (2019)
51. Yang, J., et al.: Unified contrastive learning in image-text-label space. In: Computer Vision and Pattern Recognition (CVPR) (2022)
52. Yuan, L., et al.: Florence: a new foundation model for computer vision. arXiv preprint arXiv:2111.11432 (2021)

53. Yuan, Y., Kitani, K.: DLow: diversifying latent flows for diverse human motion prediction. In: Vedaldi, A., Bischof, H., Brox, T., Frahm, J.-M. (eds.) ECCV 2020. LNCS, vol. 12354, pp. 346–364. Springer, Cham (2020). https://doi.org/10.1007/978-3-030-58545-7_20

54. Zanfir, A., Bazavan, E.G., Xu, H., Freeman, W.T., Sukthankar, R., Sminchisescu, C.: Weakly supervised 3d human pose and shape reconstruction with normalizing flows. In: Vedaldi, A., Bischof, H., Brox, T., Frahm, J.-M. (eds.) ECCV 2020. LNCS, vol. 12351, pp. 465–481. Springer, Cham (2020). https://doi.org/10.1007/978-3-030-58539-6_28

55. Zhang, Y., Black, M.J., Tang, S.: Perpetual motion: generating unbounded human motion. arXiv preprint arXiv:2007.13886 (2020)

56. Zhang, Y., Black, M.J., Tang, S.: We are more than our joints: predicting how 3D bodies move. In: Computer Vision and Pattern Recognition (CVPR) (2021)

57. Zhao, R., Su, H., Ji, Q.: Bayesian adversarial human motion synthesis. In: Computer Vision and Pattern Recognition (CVPR) (2020)

58. Zhou, Y., Barnes, C., Lu, J., Yang, J., Li, H.: On the continuity of rotation representations in neural networks. In: Computer Vision and Pattern Recognition (CVPR) (2019)

Tracking Every Thing in the Wild

Siyuan Li, Martin Danelljan, Henghui Ding, Thomas E. Huang,
and Fisher Yu[✉]

Computer Vision Lab, ETH Zürich, Zürich, Switzerland
i@yf.io
http://vis.xyz/pub/tet

Abstract. Current multi-category Multiple Object Tracking (MOT)
metrics use class labels to group tracking results for per-class evaluation. Similarly, MOT methods typically only associate objects with the
same class predictions. These two prevalent strategies in MOT implicitly assume that the classification performance is near-perfect. However,
this is far from the case in recent large-scale MOT datasets, which contain large numbers of classes with many rare or semantically similar
categories. Therefore, the resulting inaccurate classification leads to sub-
optimal tracking and inadequate benchmarking of trackers. We address
these issues by disentangling classification from tracking. We introduce
a new metric, Track Every Thing Accuracy (TETA), breaking tracking
measurement into three sub-factors: localization, association, and classification, allowing comprehensive benchmarking of tracking performance
even under inaccurate classification. TETA also deals with the challenging incomplete annotation problem in large-scale tracking datasets. We
further introduce a Track Every Thing tracker (TETer), that performs
association using Class Exemplar Matching (CEM). Our experiments
show that TETA evaluates trackers more comprehensively, and TETer
achieves significant improvements on the challenging large-scale datasets
BDD100K and TAO compared to the state-of-the-art.

Keywords: Large-scale Long-tailed MOT · Class exemplar matching ·
TETA Metric

1 Introduction

Multiple Object Tracking (MOT) aims to estimate the trajectory of objects in
a video sequence. While common MOT benchmarks [10,14,29] only consider
tracking objects from very few pre-defined categories, *e.g.*, pedestrian and car,
the number of categories of interest in the real world is overwhelming. Although
the recent extension of MOT to a large number of categories [8,46] may seem
trivial, it raises profound questions about the definition and formulation of the
problem itself, which are yet to be addressed by the community.

Supplementary Information The online version contains supplementary material
available at https://doi.org/10.1007/978-3-031-20047-2_29.

Which is the better tracker?

Tracker A   Tracker B

Fig. 1. Tracking results from two different trackers (A and B). The same color means the same track. Tracker A gets 0 score in terms of the MOTA [3], IDF1 [39], and HOTA [27] metrics, while the tracker B gets 33 for first two and 44 for HOTA

In Fig. 1, we show tracking results from two different trackers on the same video sequence. Tracker A tracks the object perfectly, but with a slightly incorrect classification on a fine-grained level. Tracker B classifies the object perfectly but does not track the object at all. *Which one is the better tracker?* The mMOTA [3] metric gives a 0 score for tracker A and a score of 33 for tracker B. The above example raises an interesting question: *Is tracking still meaningful if the class prediction is wrong?* In many cases, the trajectories of wrongly classified or even unknown objects are still valuable. For instance, an autonomous vehicle may occasionally track a van as a bus, but the estimated trajectory can equally well be used for path planning and collision avoidance.

Current MOT models and metrics [2,3,27,39,40,47] are mainly designed for single-category multiple object tracking. When extending MOT to the large-scale multi-category scenarios, they simply adopt the same single-category metrics and models by treating each class independently. The models first detect and classify each object, and then the association is only done between objects of the same class. Similarly, the metrics use class labels to group tracking results and evaluate each class separately. This implicitly assumes that the classification is good enough since it is the prerequisite for conducting association and evaluating tracking performance.

The aforementioned near-perfect classification accuracy is mostly valid on benchmarks consisting of only a handful of common categories, such as humans and cars. However, it does not hold when MOT extends to a large number of categories with many rare or semantically similar classes. The classification itself becomes a very challenging task on imbalanced large-scale datasets such as LVIS [15]. Also, it is difficult to distinguish similar fine-grained classes because of the naturally existing class hierarchy, *e.g.*, the bus and van in Fig. 1. Besides, many objects do not belong to any predefined category in real-world settings. Thus, treating every class independently without accounting for the inaccuracy in classification leads to inadequate benchmarking and non-desired tracking behavior. To expand tracking to a more general scenario, we propose that classification should be disentangled from tracking, in both evaluation and model design, for multi-category MOT. To achieve this, we design a new metric, Track Every Thing Accuracy (TETA), and a new model, Track Every Thing tracker (TETer).

The proposed TETA metric disentangles classification performance from tracking. Instead of using the predicted class labels to group per-class tracking results, we use location with the help of local cluster evaluation. We treat each

Fig. 2. CEM can be trained with large-scale datasets and directly employed for tracking

ground truth bounding box of the target class as the anchor of each cluster and group prediction results inside each cluster to evaluate the localization and association performance. Our local clusters enable us to evaluate tracks even when the class prediction is wrong. Furthermore, the local cluster evaluation makes TETA competent to deal with incomplete annotations, which are common in datasets with a large number of classes, such as TAO [8].

Our TETer follows an *Associate-Every-Thing (AET)* strategy. Instead of associating objects in the same class, we associate every object in neighboring frames. The AET strategy frees association from the challenging classification/detection issue under large-scale long-tailed settings. However, despite wholly disregarding the class information during association, we propose a new way of leveraging it, which is robust to classification errors. We introduce Class Exemplar Matching (CEM), where the learned class exemplars incorporate valuable class information in a soft manner. In this way, we effectively exploit semantic supervision on large-scale detection datasets while not relying on the often incorrect classification output. CEM can be seamlessly incorporated into existing MOT methods and consistently improve performance. Moreover, our tracking strategy enables us to correct the per-frame class predictions using rich temporal information (Fig. 2).

We analyze our methods on the newly introduced large-scale multi-category tracking datasets, TAO [8] and BDD100K [46]. Our comprehensive analysis show that our metric evaluate trackers more comprehensively and achieve better cross dataset consistency despite incomplete annotations. Moreover, our tracker achieves state-of-the-art performance on TAO and BDD100K, both when using previously established metrics and the proposed TETA.

2   Related Work

Multi-Object Tracking (MOT) aims to track multiple objects in video sequences. Earlier methods follow a track-first paradigm, which do not rely on classification during tracking [1,34,35]. Some utilize LiDAR data with model-free detection [11,17,32] or point cloud segmentation [42,43]. Others [31,33,34] first segment the scene [12], which enables tracking of generic objects. Recently, the most common paradigm for MOT is tracking-by-detection, focusing on learning better appearance features to strengthen association [20,23,26,28,30,45], modeling the displacement of each tracked object [2,37,47], or using a graph-based approach [5,41]. Previous MOT approaches mostly focus on benchmarks with a few common categories, while recent works [9,24] study the MOT in open-set settings where the goal is to track and segment any objects regardless of their categories. Those methods use a class agnostic trained detector or RPN network to generate object proposals, while classification is essential in many applications, *e.g.*, video analysis. The close-set settings with large-scale, long-tailed datasets are severely under-explored. We study the MOT in such a scenario, identifying issues and proposing solutions in both model design and evaluation metric.

MOT Metrics often evaluate both detection and association performance. Multi-Object Tracking Accuracy (MOTA) [3] was first introduced to unify the two measures. MOTA performs matching on the detection level and measures association performance by counting the number of identity switches. IDF1 [39] and Track-mAP instead performs matching on the trajectory level. Recently, Higher-Order Tracking Accuracy (HOTA) [27] was proposed to fairly balance both components by computing a separate score for each. Liu et al. [24] proposes a recall-based evaluation to extend MOT into open-world settings. All above metrics do not independently access the classification performance, making them unsuitable for large-scale multi-category MOT. TETA extends HOTA by further breaking down detection into localization and classification, enabling TETA to evaluate association despite classification failures. Furthermore, current metrics have issues when evaluating trackers on non-exhaustively annotated datasets such as TAO, which TETA can handle.

3   Tracking-Every-Thing Metric

Here we introduce the Track Every Thing Accuracy (TETA) metric. We first discuss how classification is handled in current metrics and the incomplete annotation problem in Sect. 3.1. Then, we formulate TETA in Sect. 3.2 to address the existing issues.

3.1   Limitations for Large-scale MOT Evaluation

How to Handle Classification. How to evaluate classification in MOT is an important but under-explored problem. MOT metrics such as MOTA [3], IDF1 [39], and HOTA [27] are designed for the single category MOT. When extending to multiple classes, they require trackers to predict a class label for each object, then they group tracking results based on the labels and evaluate each class separately. However, the wrong classification happens frequently in long-tailed scenarios, which leads to failures in the grouping based on class labels, and the tracking performance will not be evaluated even if the tracker localizes and tracks the object perfectly as shown in Fig. 1.

One simple solution is to ignore classification and evaluate every object class-agnostically. However, large vocabulary datasets often follow long-tailed distributions where few classes dominate the dataset. Ignoring class information leads to the evaluation being dominated by those classes, resulting in trackers' performance in tracking rare classes being negligible. The class-aware HOTA proposes to use a geometric mean between with classification confidence and HOTA, which requires

Fig. 3. Left: TAO ground truth sample. TAO is partially annotated. **Right**: Corresponding prediction from the best tracker AOA [13] ranked by TAO metric. AOA generates many low confidence bounding boxes, making it difficult to use in practice

the trackers to output the class probability distribution, while most only output the final categories. Moreover, it still cannot access classification independently.

Incomplete Annotations. MOT metrics such as MOTA [3], IDF1 [39], and HOTA [27] are designed for datasets with exhaustive annotations of every object. However, it is prohibitively expensive to annotate every object when constructing large-scale datasets with many categories. The TAO dataset contains over 800 categories, but most of them are not exhaustively annotated (see Fig. 3). Incomplete annotations pose a new challenge: *how can we identify and penalize false positive (FP) predictions?* MOTA, IDF1, and HOTA metrics treat every unmatched prediction as FP, but this falsely penalizes correct predictions with no corresponding annotations. On the other hand, TAO metric [8] adopts the same federated evaluation strategy as the LVIS [15] dataset and does not penalize categories if there is no ground-truth information about their presence or absence. This strategy inadvertently rewards a large number of false positives. In Fig. 3, we visualize predictions from the best tracker on TAO. Since TAO does not punish most false positives, trackers are incentivized to generate many low confidence tracks to increase the chances that objects from rare categories get tracked, making their results difficult to be used in practice. Also, this makes TAO a game-able metric. We show a simple copying and pasting trick that can drastically improve the TAO metric's score in Sect. 5.1. A similar issue is also observed in the LVIS mAP metric [7].

3.2 Tracking-Every-Thing Accuracy (TETA)

TETA builds upon the HOTA [27] metric, while extending it to better deal with multiple categories and incomplete annotations. TETA consists of three parts: a localization score, an association score, and a classification score, which enable us to evaluate the different aspects of each tracker properly.

Local Cluster Evaluation. We design the local clusters to deal with incomplete annotations and disentangle classification from large-scale tracking evaluation. The main challenge for evaluation with incomplete annotations is determining false positives. We propose local cluster evaluation to strike a balance between false-penalizing or the non-penalizing phenomenon as discussed in 3.1. We have observed that even though we do not have exhaustive annotations, we can still identify a specific type of false positives with high confidence. Unlike

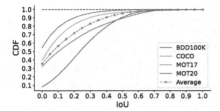

Fig. 4. Left: Inter-object overlap in real datasets. We compute the cumulative probability of ground truth bounding boxes that have different level of IoU overlaps in four different datasets with exhaustive annotations along with their average. Extreme inter-object overlap is very rare in real data. **Right**: Local cluster evaluation. TPL, FPL, and GT are the true positive localization, false positive localization, and ground truth, respectively. We create a cluster for each ground truth bounding box based on the IoU similarities. For evaluation, we only consider predictions inside each cluster. The predictions that do not belong to any cluster will be Ignored

previous metrics, we only consider predictions within local clusters. We view each ground truth bounding box as an anchor point of a cluster and assign each prediction to the closest anchor points within an IoU margin of r. The predictions inside the clusters not chosen as matched true positives are considered false positives. Figure 4 shows the inter-object overlap in popular object detection and tracking datasets, which indicates extreme inter-object overlap is rare in the real world. If we set the r to 0.7 or higher, there is less than 1% chances that we make mistakes even in highly crowded dataset like MOT20.

To avoid false punishments, we ignore the predictions that are not assigned to any clusters during evaluation. This process is illustrated in Fig. 4. The margin r of the clusters can be set according to different scenarios. The bigger the r is, the more conservative the metric is regarding choosing false positives. Also, it means fewer false punishments. If the dataset is super crowded and lacks annotation, we can select a higher r to avoid false punishment. The local cluster design also allows us to disentangle classification. For evaluation of a particular class, we evaluate predictions that are assigned to clusters with ground truth bounding boxes of that class. Since the per class result grouping is done using location instead of classification. Thus, within each local cluster, we are able to evaluate the tracking performance even if the class predictions are wrong.

Localization Score. The localization score measures the localization performance of a tracker. A true positive candidate $b \in$ TPL is a prediction box (pBox) that has an IoU higher than a localization threshold α with a ground truth box (gBox). We use the Hungarian algorithm [19] to choose the final matched TPL that optimizes both localization and association scores. The chosen assignment represents the best-localized tracks. A false negative localization (FNL) is a gBox that is not matched to any other pBox. A false positive localization (FPL) is defined based on each cluster. If a pBox is in a cluster but is not matched to any ground truth, it is a false positive. The localization score is computed using the Jaccard Index,

$$\text{LocA} = \frac{|\text{TPL}|}{|\text{TPL}| + |\text{FPL}| + |\text{FNL}|}. \tag{1}$$

Association Score. Our association score follows the definition of HOTA but redefines true positive associations (TPA), false negative associations (FNA), and false positive associations (FPA) to be based on each b. The association score of b is

$$\text{AssocA}(b) = \frac{|\text{TPA}(b)|}{|\text{TPA}(b)| + |\text{FPA}(b)| + |\text{FNA}(b)|}. \tag{2}$$

The final association score is the average over all TPLs,

$$\text{AssocA} = \frac{1}{|\text{TPL}|} \sum_{b \in \text{TPL}} \text{AssocA}(b). \tag{3}$$

Classification Score. The classification score reflects the pure performance of the classifier in each tracker. Unlike all other tracking metrics where classification performance is entangled with tracking performance, our metric makes it an independent score. We only consider the well-matched TPL, where α is at least 0.5. The classification score is defined for each class. The true positive classification (TPC) for certain class c is defined as

$$\text{TPC}(c) = \{b | b \in \text{TPL} \ \wedge \ \text{pc}(b) = \text{gc}(b) = c\}, \tag{4}$$

where $\text{pc}(b)$ is the class ID of b and $\text{gc}(b)$ is the class ID of the ground truth that is matched to b. This set includes all TPL that have the same predicted class as the corresponding ground truth. The false negative classification for class c is defined as

$$\text{FNC}(c) = \{b | b \in \text{TPL} \ \wedge \ \text{pc}(b) \neq c \wedge \text{gc}(b) = c\}, \tag{5}$$

which includes all TPL that have incorrect class predictions with ground truth class c. The false positive classification for class c is defined as

$$\text{FPC}(c) = \{b | b \in \text{TPL} \ \wedge \ \text{pc}(b) = c \wedge \text{gc}(b) \neq c\} \tag{6}$$

which includes all TPL with class c but is matched to an incorrect ground truth class. If the dataset is fully annotated, the $b \in P$, which includes TPL and the predictions outside clusters. Full annotations indicate that the predictions that are far away from gBox wrongly classify background or other classes as c. The final classification score is

$$\text{ClsA} = \frac{|\text{TPC}|}{|\text{TPC}| + |\text{FPC}| + |\text{FNC}|}. \tag{7}$$

Combined Score. HOTA uses geometric mean to balance detection and association. However, the geometric mean becomes zero if any term is zero. If the classification performance of a tracker is close to zero, *e.g.* due to a long-tail class distribution, it will completely dominate the final tracking metric if computed as a geometric mean. Therefore, we use an arithmetic mean to compute the final score:

$$\text{TETA} = \frac{\text{LocA} + \text{AssocA} + \text{ClsA}}{3}. \tag{8}$$

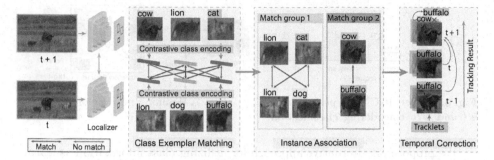

Fig. 5. Association protocol of TETer. For every pair of frames, we first compute and match the class exemplars for each localized object to determine potential matching candidates. Then, we perform instance association to determine the final matches. Finally, we use rich temporal information to correct classification errors in each frame

Besides, since different applications focus on different aspects, we encourage users to look at each subfactor based on the needs instead of focusing on a single score.

4   Tracking-Every-Thing Tracker

We here introduce our Tracking Every Thing tracker (TETer). TETer aims to discover every foreground object, associate, and classify them across time. The full pipeline is shown in Fig. 5.

4.1   Class-Agnostic Localization (CAL)

To track every thing, we first need to localize them. However, object detectors struggle on large-scale, long-tailed datasets, especially for rare categories. Interestingly, when decoupling localization and classification in common object detectors, we find that the detector can still localize rare or even novel objects well. Figure 6 shows a comparison of the object detector's performance with and without considering classification on the TAO validation set. When we do not consider class predictions during evaluation, the performance of the detector is stable across rare, common, and frequent classes. This strongly suggests that the bottleneck in detection performance lies in the classifier. With this in mind, we replace the commonly used intra-class non-maximum suppression (NMS) using class confidence with a class-agnostic counterpart to better localize every object in the wild.

4.2   Associating Every Thing

Association is often done by considering a single or a combination of cues, *e.g.*, location, appearance, and class. Learning motion priors under large-scale, long-tailed settings is challenging since the motion patterns are irregular among classes. Moreover, there are also many objects in the real world that are not in any predefined categories. In contrast, objects in different categories usually have very different appearances. Thus, we adopt appearance similarity as our primary cue.

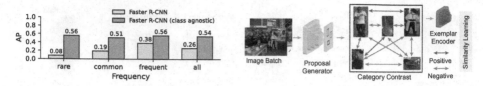

Fig. 6. Faster R-CNN's performance w/ and w/o considering classification

Fig. 7. Training pipeline of CEM

We propose an alternative approach for utilizing class information as feature clues during association. Instead of trusting the class predictions from object detectors and using them as hard prior, we learn class exemplars by directly contrasting samples from different categories. This enables us to compute similarity scores for pairs of objects at the category-level, which can better deal with semantically similar classes compared to discrete class labels. During association, we use the class exemplars to determine potential matching candidates for each object. This process can be thought of as using class information as soft prior. Therefore, it can integrate fine-grained cues required for classification (*e.g.* the difference between a big red bus and a red truck), which are difficult to learn for the purely class-agnostic appearance embedding.

Class Exemplar Matching (CEM). The training pipeline based on a two-stage detector is shown in Fig. 7. The Region Proposal Network (RPN) computes all the Region of Interest (RoI) proposals from the input images. Then, we use RoI align to extract the feature maps from the multi-scale feature outputs. The feature maps are used as input for the exemplar encoder to learn category similarity. The exemplar encoder generates class exemplars for each RoI. We assign category labels to each RoI with a localization threshold α. If a RoI has an IoU higher than α (in our case, $\alpha = 0.7$) with a ground truth box, then we assign the corresponding category label to the RoI. Positive samples are RoIs from the same category, and negative samples are those from different categories.

We adapt the SupCon loss [18] and propose an unbiased supervised contrastive loss (U-SupCon):

$$\mathcal{L}_C = -\sum_{q \in Q} \frac{1}{|Q^+(q)|} \sum_{q^+ \in Q^+(q)} \log \frac{\exp(\mathrm{sim}(q, q^+)/\tau)}{\mathrm{PosD}(q) + \sum_{q^- \in Q^-} \exp(\mathrm{sim}(q, q^-)/\tau)}, \quad (9)$$

$$\mathrm{PosD}(q) = \frac{1}{|Q^+(q))|} \sum_{q^+ \in Q^+} \exp(\mathrm{sim}(q, q^+)/\tau), \quad (10)$$

where Q is the set of class generated from a random sampled image batch, $Q^+(q)$ is the set of all positive samples to q, $Q^-(q)$ is the set of all negative samples to q, $\mathrm{sim}(\cdot)$ denotes cosine similarity, and τ is a temperature parameter. We set τ to 0.07. We add the $\mathrm{PosD}(q)$ to prevent the varying lower bound of the SupCon loss when training with detection proposals, where the number of positive samples is consistently changing.

Association Strategy. For a query object q in a tracklet, we find a group of candidates by comparing their class exemplars. Specifically, assume we have the class exemplar q_c for the query object q in frame t, and a set of detected objects D in frame $t + 1$ and their class exemplars $d_c \in D_c$. We compute the similarities between q_c and D_c and select candidates with high similarity. This gives us a candidate list $C = \{d \mid \text{sim}(q_c, d_c) > \delta, d \in D\}$. δ is set to 0.5.

To determine the final match from the candidate list, any existing association method can be used. Thus, CEM can be readily used to replace existing hard prior-based matching. For our final model TETer, we further utilize quasi-dense similarity learning [36] to learn instance features for instance-level association. We compute instance-level matching scores with each candidate from C using bidirectional softmax and cosine similarity. We take the candidate with the maximum score and if the score is larger than β, then it is a successful match. We set β to 0.5.

Temporal Class Correction (TCC). The AET strategy allows us to correct the classification using rich temporal information. If we track an object, we assume the class label to be consistent across the entire track. We use a simple majority vote to correct the per-frame class predictions.

5   Experiments

We conduct analyses of different evaluation metrics and investigate the effectiveness of our new tracking method on TAO [8] and BDD100K [46]. TAO provides videos and tracking labels for both common and rare objects with over 800 object classes. Although BDD100K for driving scenes has fewer labeled categories, some, like trains, are much less frequent than common objects such as cars. In this section, we first compare different metrics with TETA. Then we evaluate the proposed TETer on different datasets and plug CEM into existing tracking methods to demonstrate its generalizability.

Implementation Details. For the object detector, we use Faster R-CNN [38] with Feature Pyramid Network (FPN) [22]. We use ResNet-101 as backbone on TAO, same as TAO baseline [8], and use ResNet-50 as backone on BDD100K, same as the QDTrack [36]. On TAO, we train our model on a combination of LVISv0.5 [15] and the COCO dataset using repeat factor sampling. The repeat factor is set to 0.001. We use the SGD optimizer with a learning rate of 0.02 and adopt the step policy for learning rate decay, momentum, and weight decay are set to 0.9 and 0.0001. We train our model for 24 epoch in total and learning rate is decreased at 16 and 22 epoch. For TETer with SwinT backbone [25], we use 3x schedule used by mmdetection [6]. For TETer-HTC, we use the HTC-X101-MS-DCN detector from [21]. On BDD100K, we load the same object detector weights from QDTrack [36] and fine-tune the exemplar encoder with on BDD100K Detection dataset with other weights frozen. For each image, we sample a maximum of 256 object proposals. For more details, please refer to the supplemental materials.

5.1   Metric Analysis

Cross Dataset Consistency. A good metric should correlate with real world tracking performance. Although we face difficulties in incomplete annotations,

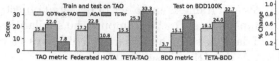 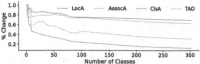

Fig. 8. Left: We pre-train models on TAO (incomplete annotations) and directly test them on BDD (complete annotations) with the default BDD metric (IDF1). We omit MOTA as its value range is $(-\infty, 1]$, which is inconsistent with other metrics. **Right**: Percentage change in score of each metric as number of evaluation classes increases

this principle for metric design should not change. For instance, a tracker designed for tracking objects belonging to hundreds of categories on TAO should also work well on new video sequences that contain a subset of those categories. We evaluate this by using the BDD100K dataset, which has seven out of eight of its categories overlapped with TAO. We treat BDD100K as the new video sequences in the real world to test two trackers: QDTrack-TAO [36], which is optimized for the TAO metric, and our tracker, which is optimized for TETA. We only evaluate on the overlapped categories, which also contains exhaustive annotations for every object.

As shown in Fig. 8 (Left), the tracker selected by the TAO metric overly optimizes for the incomplete TAO dataset setting, which does not generalize well to BDD100K. In comparison, the tracker selected by TETA generalizes well to BDD100K. Our metric gives the same ranking on the complete annotations setting with the default BDD100K IDF1 metric despite facing the difficulties of ranking trackers under incomplete annotations.

Comprehensively Analyze Trackers. Correctly understanding different aspects of trackers is crucial for designing trackers for various scenarios. For example, it is important for an autonomous vehicle to detect and understand the trajectory of every object to avoid collision, but slightly wrong classification may not be as critical. In this experiment, we evaluate the effect of the number of classes on metric scores on the TAO validation set. We use the same tracking predictions but merge the class predictions by sorting the classes in descending order based on the number of instances and combining the last n classes. For example for $n = 2$, we merge all classes besides humans (the most frequent class) into a single class and only evaluate on two classes. We sample several n between 1 (single class) and 302 (all classes) and evaluate on each set of classes.

The result is shown in Fig. 8 (Right). Although the trajectory predictions are the same, the score produced by the TAO metric drops significantly as the number of classes increases. As the TAO metric entangles classification and tracking into a single metric, this makes it hard to determine which part of the tracker went wrong. On the other hand, with TETA, we can separately investigate different aspects. While the classification performance follows the same trend as the TAO metric, the localization and association scores are still stable. This allows us to instantly understand that the degradation is due to classification.

Cheating TAO Track mAP Metric. Figure 9 shows a copy & paste trick that can boost the TAO track mAP. We simply copy and paste existing trajectories

(a) Original   (b) After copy & paste

Table 1. The table shows the comparison between TAO track mAP and TETA with a simple copy & paste trick for the sequence in Fig. 9

Fig. 9. Copy & paste strategy to cheat the TAO track mAP. (a) tracking result from our tracker, which incorrectly classifies the deer as a goat. (b) copying and pasting existing tracks with low confidence class predictions from the object detector

TAO track mAP	AP↑	AP$_{50}$ ↑	AP$_{75}$ ↑	AR ↑
Before copy	0	0	0	0
After copy	62.9	75.2	50.5	62.9
Federated HOTA	HOTA ↑	DetA ↑	AssA ↑	-
Before copy	4.2	3.0	5.9	-
After copy	68.7	75.7	62.8	-
TETA (ours)	TETA ↑	LocA ↑	AssocA ↑	ClsA ↑
Before copy	47.6	80.1	59.6	3.2
After copy	13.8	3.3	10.2	27.9

Table 2. Results on TAO

Method	TETA	LocA	AssocA	ClsA
SORT [4]	24.845	48.13	14.32	12.08
Tracktor [2]	24.15	47.41	12.96	12.08
DeepSORT [44]	25.98	48.35	17.52	12.09
AOA [13]	25.27	23.40	30.56	**21.86**
Tracktor++ [2]	27.97	49.04	22.81	12.05
QDTrack [36]	30.00	50.53	27.36	12.11
TETer	**33.25**	**51.58**	**35.02**	13.16
QDTrack-SwinT	31.22	51.32	27.27	15.06
TETer-SwinT	**34.61**	**52.10**	**36.71**	15.03
QDTrack-HTC	32.79	56.21	27.43	14.73
TETer-HTC	**36.85**	**57.53**	**37.53**	**15.70**

Table 3. Results on BDD100K

Method	Split	mMOTA	mIDF1	TETA	LocA	AssocA	ClsA
DeepSORT [44]	val	35.2	49.3	48.03	46.36	46.69	51.04
QDTrack [36]	val	36.6	51.6	47.84	45.86	48.47	49.20
TETer	val	**39.1**	**53.3**	**50.83**	**47.16**	**52.89**	**52.44**
DeepSORT [44]	test	34.0	50.2	46.75	45.26	47.04	47.93
QDTrack [36]	test	35.7	52.3	49.17	**47.19**	50.93	49.38
TETer	test	**37.4**	**53.3**	**50.42**	46.99	**53.56**	**50.71**

with low confidence class predictions from the object detector without additional training. As shown in Table 1, TAO track mAP and Federated HOTA metric increase drastically from 0 to 62.9 and 4.2 to 68.7. In comparison, TETA drops from 47.6 to 13.8, which suggests the trick does not work on TETA. Moreover, we can clearly see consequences brought by copy & paste. The localization score drops sharply as copy & paste generates a lot of false positive localizations. On the other hand, the trick only improves the classification performance.

5.2 TAO Tracking Results

We provide a thorough comparison of TETer against competing methods on the TAO validation set in Table 2 using our TETA metric. We set the margin r of local clusters to 0.5 since we observe the TAO dataset is not crowded, and this choice gives a proper balance between non-penalizing and over-penalizing FPs. We also include results of other margins in the supplemental material. For this experiment, we only use the predefined 302 categories without considering the unknown classes. We allow each tracker maximum outputs 50 predictions per image. We use the same FasterRCNN detectors with class-agnostic NMS

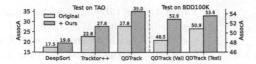

Fig. 10. Shows comparison of DeepSORT [16], Tracktor++ [2], and QDTrack [36] with w/ and w/o our CEM module on TAO and BDD100K datasets. CEM consistently improves association performance of all methods

Table 4. Shows comparison with different components of TETer on the TAO open set using our TETA metrics

Components	Known				Unknown		
	TETA	LocA	AssocA	ClsA	TETA	LocA	AssocA
QDTrack [36]	28.89	46.60	27.76	12.37	19.89	32.25	27.42
+ CAL	30.00	50.53	27.36	12.11	20.85	36.06	26.50
+ CEM	32.86	51.55	35.00	12.06	24.00	37.38	34.61
+ TCC	33.25	51.55	35.00	13.16	24.00	37.38	34.61

for all methods except AOA [13]. Despite the increased difficulty introduced by the large number of categories, TETer outperforms all other methods, providing consistent improvements in TETA, LocA, and AssocA. In particular, TETer improves TETA of QDTrack [36] by over 3 points and AssocA by over 7 points.

We also compare our method to AOA [13], the winner of the ECCV 2020 TAO challenge, using the publicly available predictions[1]. AOA combines multiple state-of-the-art few-shot detection and object ReID models that are trained using additional external datasets, which enables it to obtain very strong classification performance. However, as it is optimized using the TAO metric, it makes excessive false positive predictions, which are punished by TETA. Additionally, TETer achieves better association performance without using external datasets.

5.3 BDD100K Tracking Results

We provide evaluation results on both the BDD100K validation and test sets in Table 3. We first evaluate each tracker using the established CLEAR MOT metrics, including MOTA, MOTP, and IDF1, each averaged over every class. Without bells and whistles, TETer can obtain performance gains across all three metrics compared to QDTrack [36] on both sets, achieving state-of-the-art performances. In particular, TETer improves the mMOTA and mIDF1 of QDTrack by 2.5 and 1.7 points on the validation set and 1.7 and 1 points on the test set. We also show evaluation results using TETA. TETer again obtains consistent performance gains across all metrics. On both validation and test sets, TETer can improve AssocA of QDTrack by over 2.5 points.

5.4 Generalizability of CEM

To demonstrate the generalizability of our CEM module, we further apply CEM to other MOT methods to replace existing hard prior-based matching. We compare three methods, DeepSORT [44], Tracktor++ [2], and QDTrack [36], with and without CEM across both TAO and BDD100K. The results are shown in Fig. 10. On the TAO validation set, adding CEM results in at least 2 points of improvement in AssocA across all methods. In particular, CEM can improve AssocA of

---

[1] https://github.com/feiaxyt/Winner_ECCV20_TAO.

QDTrack by 7 points. On both BDD100K validation and test sets, CEM can obtain over 2.5 points of improvement in AssocA of QDTrack. This shows our CEM module can be applied to various popular MOT methods and achieve consistent improvements in association by better exploiting class information.

5.5   Ablation Study

We conduct ablation studies on TAO and BDD100K. We investigate the importance of our proposed modules on both predefined and unknown categories. For TAO, we use their split for known and unknown (free-form) classes. For unknown split, we only report the LocA and AssocA.

Tracking Components.   We evaluate the contributions of each component of TETer on the TAO open set using TETA in Table 4. When we replace the class-dependent intra-class NMS from the object detector with a class-agnostic NMS, we can improve LocA by over 3 points on both known objects and unknown objects. Adding CEM drastically improves its AssocA by over 7 points on known objects and 8 points on unknown objects. Further, using temporal class correction can improve ClsA by over 1 point.

Comparison of using class information.   We compare different ways of utilizing class information during association on the validation set of BDD100K and TAO in Table 5. The baseline protocol follows the AET strategy and performs class-agnostic association with pure instance appearance features described in Sect. 4.2. We then add different class prior on top of the AET baseline to study their effectiveness. Softmax use class labels as hard prior and associate objects within the same class. This strategy leads to a severe downgrade in the tracking performance, especially for the TAO dataset.

Alternatively, we use the out-of-the-shelf word embeddings to incorporate class information. The semantically similar classes should be closer in the word embedding space. This way transfers the hard class labels to soft ones. We utilize the BERT model to embed the class names to replace our CEM. While the performance is slightly better than using softmax predictions, it is inferior to the CEM. Our CEM is the only method capable of effectively utilizing semantic

Table 5. Comparing different ways of using class information. AET Baseline associates every objects without using any class information. Softmax indicates association happens only within the same class. BERT indicates using BERT word embeddings to group candidates for association

Class	BDD100K val			TAO val
	mMOTA	mIDF1	AssocA	AssocA
AET Baseline	37.3	52.6	52.0	33.5
Softmax	36.6 (-0.7)	51.6 (-0.2)	48.9 (-0.2)	27.4 (-6.1)
BERT	37.2 (-0.1)	52.6	52.0	27.8 (-5.7)
CEM	**39.1** ($+1.8$)	**53.3** ($+0.7$)	**52.9** ($+0.9$)	**35.0** ($+1.5$)

information to improve the association by outperforming the AET baseline on large-scale long-tailed datasets.

6   Conclusion

We present a new metric TETA and a new model TETer for tracking every thing in the wild. TETA and TETer disentangle classification from evaluation and model design for the long-tailed MOT. TETA can evaluate trackers more comprehensively and better deal with incomplete annotation issues in large-scale tracking datasets. TETer disentangles the unreliable classifier from both detection and association, resulting in a better tracker which outperforms existing state-of-the-art trackers on large-scale MOT datasets, TAO and BDD100K. The core component of TETer, CEM, can be used as a drop-in module for existing tracking methods and boost their performance.

Acknowledgement. Special thanks go to Ruolan Xiang for her help in editing the paper.

References

1. Athar, A., Mahadevan, S., Ošep, A., Leal-Taixé, L., Leibe, B.: STEm-Seg: Spatio-Temporal embeddings for instance segmentation in videos. In: Vedaldi, A., Bischof, H., Brox, T., Frahm, J.-M. (eds.) ECCV 2020. LNCS, vol. 12356, pp. 158–177. Springer, Cham (2020). https://doi.org/10.1007/978-3-030-58621-8_10
2. Bergmann, P., Meinhardt, T., Leal-Taixe, L.: Tracking without bells and whistles. In: Proceedings of the IEEE/CVF International Conference on Computer Vision, pp. 941–951 (2019)
3. Bernardin, K., Stiefelhagen, R.: Evaluating multiple object tracking performance: the clear mot metrics. EURASIP J. Image Video Process. **2008**, 1–10 (2008)
4. Bewley, A., Ge, Z., Ott, L., Ramos, F., Upcroft, B.: Simple online and realtime tracking. In: 2016 IEEE international conference on image processing (ICIP), pp. 3464–3468. IEEE (2016)
5. Brasó, G., Leal-Taixé, L.: Learning a neural solver for multiple object tracking. In: Proceedings of the IEEE/CVF Conference on Computer Vision and Pattern Recognition, pp. 6247–6257 (2020)
6. Chen, K., et al.: MMDetection: open MMLab detection toolbox and benchmark. arXiv preprint arXiv:1906.07155 (2019)
7. Dave, A., Dollár, P., Ramanan, D., Kirillov, A., Girshick, R.: Evaluating large-vocabulary object detectors: The devil is in the details. arXiv preprint arXiv:2102.01066 (2021)
8. Dave, A., Khurana, T., Tokmakov, P., Schmid, C., Ramanan, D.: TAO: a large-scale benchmark for tracking any object. In: Vedaldi, A., Bischof, H., Brox, T., Frahm, J.-M. (eds.) ECCV 2020. LNCS, vol. 12350, pp. 436–454. Springer, Cham (2020). https://doi.org/10.1007/978-3-030-58558-7_26
9. Dave, A., Tokmakov, P., Ramanan, D.: Towards segmenting anything that moves. In: Proceedings of the IEEE/CVF International Conference on Computer Vision Workshops (2019)

10. Dendorfer, P., et al.: Mot20: A benchmark for multi object tracking in crowded scenes. arXiv preprint arXiv:2003.09003 (2020)
11. Dewan, A., Caselitz, T., Tipaldi, G.D., Burgard, W.: Motion-based detection and tracking in 3d lidar scans. In: 2016 IEEE International Conference on Robotics and Automation (ICRA), pp. 4508–4513 (2016). https://doi.org/10.1109/ICRA.2016.7487649
12. Ding, H., Jiang, X., Shuai, B., Liu, A.Q., Wang, G.: Context contrasted feature and gated multi-scale aggregation for scene segmentation. In: Proceedings of the IEEE Conference on Computer Vision And Pattern Recognition, pp. 2393–2402 (2018)
13. Du, F., Xu, B., Tang, J., Zhang, Y., Wang, F., Li, H.: 1st place solution to ECCV-TAO-2020: detect and represent any object for tracking. arXiv preprint arXiv:2101.08040 (2021)
14. Geiger, A., Lenz, P., Stiller, C., Urtasun, R.: Vision meets robotics: the KITTI dataset. Int. J. Robot. Res. **32**(11), 1231–1237 (2013)
15. Gupta, A., Dollar, P., Girshick, R.: Lvis: A dataset for large vocabulary instance segmentation. In: Proceedings of the IEEE/CVF Conference on Computer Vision and Pattern Recognition, pp. 5356–5364 (2019)
16. He, K., Zhang, X., Ren, S., Sun, J.: Deep residual learning for image recognition. In: Proceedings of the IEEE Conference on Computer Vision and Pattern Recognition, pp. 770–778 (2016)
17. Kaestner, R., Maye, J., Pilat, Y., Siegwart, R.: Generative object detection and tracking in 3d range data. In: 2012 IEEE International Conference on Robotics and Automation, pp. 3075–3081. IEEE (2012)
18. Khosla, P., et al.: Supervised contrastive learning. arXiv preprint arXiv:2004.11362 (2020)
19. Kuhn, H.W.: The Hungarian method for the assignment problem. Naval Res. Logist. Q. **2**(1–2), 83–97 (1955). https://doi.org/10.1002/nav.3800020109. https://onlinelibrary.wiley.com/doi/abs/10.1002/nav.3800020109
20. Leal-Taixé, L., Canton-Ferrer, C., Schindler, K.: Learning by tracking: Siamese CNN for robust target association. In: Proceedings of the IEEE Conference on Computer Vision and Pattern Recognition Workshops, pp. 33–40 (2016)
21. Li, Y., Wang, T., Kang, B., Tang, S., Wang, C., Li, J., Feng, J.: Overcoming classifier imbalance for long-tail object detection with balanced group softmax. In: Proceedings of the IEEE/CVF Conference on Computer Vision and Pattern Recognition, pp. 10991–11000 (2020)
22. Lin, T.Y., Dollár, P., Girshick, R.B., He, K., Hariharan, B., Belongie, S.J.: Feature pyramid networks for object detection. In: 2017 IEEE Conference on Computer Vision and Pattern Recognition (CVPR), pp. 936–944 (2017)
23. Liu, Q., Chu, Q., Liu, B., Yu, N.: GSM: graph similarity model for multi-object tracking. In: IJCAI, pp. 530–536 (2020)
24. Liu, Y., et al.: Opening up open-world tracking. arXiv preprint arXiv:2104.11221 (2021)
25. Liu, Z., et al.: Swin transformer: hierarchical vision transformer using shifted windows. In: Proceedings of the IEEE/CVF International Conference on Computer Vision, pp. 10012–10022 (2021)
26. Lu, Z., Rathod, V., Votel, R., Huang, J.: RetinaTrack: online single stage joint detection and tracking. In: Proceedings of the IEEE/CVF Conference on Computer Vision and Pattern Recognition, pp. 14668–14678 (2020)
27. Luiten, J., et al.: HOTA: a higher order metric for evaluating multi-object tracking. Int. J. Comput. Vision **129**(2), 548–578 (2021)

28. Meinhardt, T., Kirillov, A., Leal-Taixe, L., Feichtenhofer, C.: Trackformer: multi-object tracking with transformers. arXiv preprint arXiv:2101.02702 (2021)
29. Milan, A., Leal-Taixé, L., Reid, I., Roth, S., Schindler, K.: Mot16: a benchmark for multi-object tracking. arXiv preprint arXiv:1603.00831 (2016)
30. Milan, A., Rezatofighi, S.H., Dick, A., Reid, I., Schindler, K.: Online multi-target tracking using recurrent neural networks. In: Thirty-First AAAI Conference on Artificial Intelligence (2017)
31. Mitzel, D., Leibe, B.: Taking mobile multi-object tracking to the next level: people, unknown objects, and carried items. In: Fitzgibbon, A., Lazebnik, S., Perona, P., Sato, Y., Schmid, C. (eds.) ECCV 2012. LNCS, vol. 7576, pp. 566–579. Springer, Heidelberg (2012). https://doi.org/10.1007/978-3-642-33715-4_41
32. Moosmann, F., Stiller, C.: Joint self-localization and tracking of generic objects in 3d range data. In: 2013 IEEE International Conference on Robotics and Automation, pp. 1146–1152 (2013). https://doi.org/10.1109/ICRA.2013.6630716
33. Ošep, A., Hermans, A., Engelmann, F., Klostermann, D., Mathias, M., Leibe, B.: Multi-scale object candidates for generic object tracking in street scenes. In: 2016 IEEE International Conference on Robotics and Automation (ICRA), pp. 3180–3187. IEEE (2016)
34. Ošep, A., Mehner, W., Voigtlaender, P., Leibe, B.: Track, then decide: category-agnostic vision-based multi-object tracking. In: 2018 IEEE International Conference on Robotics and Automation (ICRA), pp. 3494–3501. IEEE (2018)
35. Ošep, A., Voigtlaender, P., Luiten, J., Breuers, S., Leibe, B.: Large-scale object mining for object discovery from unlabeled video, pp. 5502–5508 (2019). https://doi.org/10.1109/ICRA.2019.8793683
36. Pang, J., Qiu, L., Li, X., Chen, H., Li, Q., Darrell, T., Yu, F.: Quasi-dense similarity learning for multiple object tracking. In: IEEE/CVF Conference on Computer Vision and Pattern Recognition, June 2021
37. Peng, J., et al.: Chained-tracker: chaining paired attentive regression results for end-to-end joint multiple-object detection and tracking. In: Vedaldi, A., Bischof, H., Brox, T., Frahm, J.-M. (eds.) ECCV 2020. LNCS, vol. 12349, pp. 145–161. Springer, Cham (2020). https://doi.org/10.1007/978-3-030-58548-8_9
38. Ren, S., He, K., Girshick, R., Sun, J.: Faster R-CNN: towards real-time object detection with region proposal networks. Adv. Neural. Inf. Process. Syst. **28**, 91–99 (2015)
39. Ristani, E., Solera, F., Zou, R., Cucchiara, R., Tomasi, C.: Performance measures and a data set for multi-target, multi-camera tracking. In: Hua, G., Jégou, H. (eds.) ECCV 2016. LNCS, vol. 9914, pp. 17–35. Springer, Cham (2016). https://doi.org/10.1007/978-3-319-48881-3_2
40. Russakovsky, O., et al.: ImageNet large scale visual recognition challenge. Int. J. Comput. Vision **115**(3), 211–252 (2015)
41. Schulter, S., Vernaza, P., Choi, W., Chandraker, M.: Deep network flow for multi-object tracking. In: Proceedings of the IEEE Conference on Computer Vision and Pattern Recognition, pp. 6951–6960 (2017)
42. Teichman, A., Levinson, J., Thrun, S.: Towards 3d object recognition via classification of arbitrary object tracks. In: 2011 IEEE International Conference on Robotics and Automation, pp. 4034–4041. IEEE (2011)
43. Teichman, A., Thrun, S.: Tracking-based semi-supervised learning. Int. J. Robot. Res. **31**(7), 804–818 (2012)
44. Wojke, N., Bewley, A., Paulus, D.: Simple online and realtime tracking with a deep association metric. In: 2017 IEEE International Conference on Image Processing (ICIP), pp. 3645–3649. IEEE (2017)

45. Yang, L., Fan, Y., Xu, N.: Video instance segmentation. In: Proceedings of the IEEE/CVF International Conference on Computer Vision, pp. 5188–5197 (2019)
46. Yu, F., et al.: BDD100K: a diverse driving dataset for heterogeneous multitask learning. In: IEEE/CVF Conference on Computer Vision and Pattern Recognition (CVPR), June 2020
47. Zhou, X., Koltun, V., Krähenbühl, P.: Tracking objects as points. In: Vedaldi, A., Bischof, H., Brox, T., Frahm, J.-M. (eds.) ECCV 2020. LNCS, vol. 12349, pp. 474–490. Springer, Cham (2020). https://doi.org/10.1007/978-3-030-58548-8_28

HULC: 3D HUman Motion Capture with Pose Manifold SampLing and Dense Contact Guidance

Soshi Shimada[1]([✉]), Vladislav Golyanik[1], Zhi Li[1], Patrick Pérez[2], Weipeng Xu[1], and Christian Theobalt[1]

[1] Max Planck Institute for Informatics, Saarland Informatics Campus, Saarbrücken, Germany
sshimada@mpi-inf.mpg.de
[2] Valeo.ai, Paris, France

Abstract. Marker-less monocular 3D human motion capture (MoCap) with scene interactions is a challenging research topic relevant for extended reality, robotics and virtual avatar generation. Due to the inherent depth ambiguity of monocular settings, 3D motions captured with existing methods often contain severe artefacts such as incorrect body-scene inter-penetrations, jitter and body floating. To tackle these issues, we propose HULC, a new approach for 3D human MoCap which is aware of the scene geometry. HULC estimates 3D poses and dense body-environment surface contacts for improved 3D localisations, as well as the absolute scale of the subject. Furthermore, we introduce a 3D pose trajectory optimisation based on a novel pose manifold sampling that resolves erroneous body-environment inter-penetrations. Although the proposed method requires less structured inputs compared to existing scene-aware monocular MoCap algorithms, it produces more physically-plausible poses: HULC significantly and consistently outperforms the existing approaches in various experiments and on different metrics. Project page: https://vcai.mpi-inf.mpg.de/projects/HULC/.

Keywords: 3D Human MoCap · Dense contact estimations · Sampling

1 Introduction

3D human motion capture (MoCap) from a single colour camera received a lot of attention over the past years [1,5,6,9,15,16,19–23,27–31,33,35–37,40,45,49–51,56,57,63]. Its applications range from mixed and augmented reality, to movie production and game development, to immersive virtual communication and telepresence. MoCap techniques that not only focus on humans *in a vacuum* but also account for the scene environment—this encompasses awareness of

Supplementary Information The online version contains supplementary material available at https://doi.org/10.1007/978-3-031-20047-2_30.

the physics or constraints due to the underlying scene geometry— are coming increasingly into focus [11,38,39,46,47,58,60,61].

Taking into account interactions between the human and the environment in MoCap poses many challenges, as not only articulations and global translation of the subject must be accurate, but also contacts between the human and the scene need to be plausible. A misestimation of only a few parameters, such as a 3D translation, can lead to reconstruction artefacts that contradict physical reality (e.g., body-environment penetrations or body floating). On the other hand, known human-scene contacts can serve as reliable boundary conditions for improved 3D pose estimation and localisation. While several algorithms merely consider human interactions with a ground plane [38,39,46,47,60], a few other methods also account for the contacts and interactions with the more general 3D environment [11,61]. However, due to the depth ambiguity of the monocular setting, their estimated subject's root translations can be inaccurate, which can create implausible body-environment collisions. Next, they employ a body-environment collision penalty as a soft constraint. Therefore, the convergence of the optimisation to a bad local minima can also cause unnatural body-environment collisions. This paper addresses the limitations of the current works and proposes a new 3D **HU**man MoCap framework with pose manifold samp**L**ing and guidance by body-scene **C**ontacts, abbreviated as HULC. It improves over other monocular 3D human MoCap methods that consider constraints from 3D scene priors [11,61]. Unlike existing works, HULC estimates contacts not only on the human body surface but also on the environment surface for the improved global 3D translation estimations. Next, HULC introduces a pose manifold sampling-based optimisation to obtain plausible 3D poses while handling the severe body-environment collisions in a *hard manner*. Our approach regresses more accurate 3D motions respecting scene constraints while requiring less-structured inputs (*i.e.*, an RGB image sequence and a point cloud of the static background scene) compared to the related monocular scene-aware methods [11,61] that require a complete mesh and images. HULC returns physically-plausible motions, an absolute scale of the subject and dense contact labels both on a human template surface model and the environment.

Table 1. Overview of inputs and outputs of different methods. "τ" and "env. contacts" denote global translation and environment contacts, respectively. "*" stands for sparse marker contact labels

Approach	Inputs	Outputs				
		bodypose	τ	absolute scale	bodycontacts	env. contacts
PROX [31]	RGB + scene mesh	✓	✓	✗	✗	✗
PROX-D [11]	RGB(D) + scene mesh	✓	✓	✗	✗	✗
LEMO [61]	RGB(D) + scene mesh	✓	✓	✗	✓*	✗
HULC (ours)	RGB + scene point cloud	✓	✓	✓	✓	✓

HULC features several innovations which in interplay enable its functionality, *i.e.*, 1) a new learned implicit function-based dense contact label estimator for humans and the general 3D scene environment, and 2) a new pose optimiser for scene-aware pose estimation based on a pose manifold sampling policy. The first component allows us to jointly estimate the absolute subject's scale and its highly accurate root 3D translations. The second component prevents severe body-scene collisions and acts as a hard constraint, in contrast to widely-used soft collision losses [11,26]. To train the dense contact estimation networks, we also annotate contact labels on a large scale synthetic daily motion dataset: GTA-IM [2]. To summarise, our primary technical contributions are as follows:

- A new 3D MoCap framework with simultaneous 3D human pose localisation and body scale estimation guided by estimated contacts. It is the first method that regresses the dense body and environment contact labels from an RGB sequence and a point cloud of the scene using an implicit function (Sect. 3.1).
- A new pose optimisation approach with a novel pose manifold sampling yielding better results by imposing hard constraints on incorrect body-environment interactions (Sect. 3.2).
- Large-scale body contact annotations on the GTA-IM dataset [2] that provides synthetic 3D human motions in a variety of scenes (Fig. 1 and Sect. 4).

We report quantitative results, including an ablative study, which show that HULC outperforms existing methods in 3D accuracy and on physical plausibility metrics (Sect. 5). See our video for qualitative comparisons.

2   Related Works

Most monocular MoCap approaches estimate 3D poses alone or along with the body shape from an input image or video [1, 5, 6, 9, 9, 13, 15, 16, 19, 20, 22, 23, 27, 28, 31, 33, 35, 36, 40, 45, 49–51, 56, 57, 62, 63]. Some methods also estimate 3D translation of the subject in addition to the 3D poses [21, 29, 30, 37]. Fieraru *et al.* [8] propose a multi-person 3D reconstruction method considering human-human interactions. Another algorithm class incorporates an explicit physics model into MoCap and avoids environmental collisions [39, 46, 47, 59]. These methods consider interactions with only a flat ground plane or a stick-like object [25], unlike our HULC, that can work with arbitrary scene geometry.

Awareness of human-scene contacts is helpful for the estimation and synthesis [10, 53] of plausible 3D human motions. Some existing works regress sparse joint contacts on a kinematic skeleton [25, 38, 39, 46, 47, 64] or sparse markers [61]. A few approaches forecast contacts on a dense human mesh surface [12, 32]. Hassan *et al.* [12] place a human in a 3D scene considering the semantic information and dense human body contact labels. Müller *et al.*. [32] propose a dataset with discrete annotations for self-contacts on the human body. Consequently, they apply a self-contact loss for more plausible final 3D poses. Unlike the existing works, our algorithm estimates vertex-wise dense contact labels on the human body surface from an RGB input only. Along with that, it also regresses dense contact labels on the environment given the scene point cloud along with the RGB sequence. The simultaneous estimation of the body and scene contacts allows HULC to disambiguate the depth and scale of the subject, although only a single camera view and a single scene point cloud are used as inputs.

Monocular MoCap with Scene Interactions. Among the scene-aware MoCap approaches [11, 38, 39, 46, 47, 60, 61], there are a few ones that consider human-environment interactions given a highly detailed scene geometry [11, 24, 61]. PROX (PROX-D) [11] estimates 3D motions given RGB (RGB-D) image, along with an input geometry provided as a signed distance field (SDF). Given an RGB(D) measurement and a mesh of the environment, LEMO [61] also

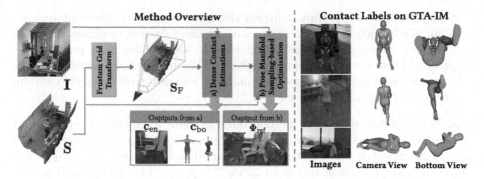

Fig. 1. (*Left*) Given image sequence **I**, scene point cloud **S** and its associated frustum voxel grid $\mathbf{S}_F$, HULC first predicts for each frame dense contact labels on the body $\mathbf{c}_{bo}$, and on the environment $\mathbf{c}_{en}$. It then refines initial, physically implausible and scale-ambiguous global 3D poses Φ_0 into the final ones Φ_{ref} in (b). Also see Fig. 2 for the details of stage (a) and (b). (*Right*) Example visualisations of our contact annotations (shown in green) on GTA-IM dataset [2]

produces geometry-aware global 3D human motions with an improved motion quality characterised by smoother transitions and robustness to occlusions thanks to the learned motion priors. These two algorithms require an RGB or RGB-D sequence with SDF (a 3D scan of the scene) or occlusion masks. In contrast, our HULC requires only an RGB image sequence and a point cloud of the scene; it returns dense contact labels on 1) the human body and 2) the environment, 3) global 3D human motion with translations and 4) absolute scale of the human body. See Table 1 for an overview of the characteristics. Compared to PROX and LEMO, HULC shows significantly-mitigated body-environment collisions.

Sampling-Based Human Pose Tracking. Several sampling-based human pose tracking algorithms were proposed. Some of them utilise particle-swarm optimisation [14,41,42]. Charles *et al.* [4] employ Parzen windows for 2D joints tracking. Similar to our HULC, Sharma *et al.* [44] generate 3D pose samples by a conditional variational autoencoder (VAE) [48] conditioned on 2D poses. In contrast, we utilise the learned pose manifold of VAE for sampling, which helps to avoid local minima and prevent body-scene collisions. Also, unlike [44], we sample around a latent vector obtained from the VAE's encoder to obtain poses that are plausible and similar to the input 3D pose.

3   Method

Given monocular video frames and a point cloud of the scene registered to the coordinate frame of the camera, our goal is to infer physically-plausible global 3D human poses along with dense contact labels on both body and environment surfaces. Our approach consists of two stages (Fig. 1):

– **Dense Body-environment contacts estimation**: Dense contact labels are predicted on body and scene surfaces using a learning-based approach with a pixel-aligned implicit representation inspired by [43] (Sect. 3.1);

- **Sampling-based optimisation on the pose manifold**: We combine sampling in a learned latent pose space with gradient descent to obtain the absolute scale of the subject and its global 3D pose, under hard guidance by predicted contacts. This approach significantly improves the accuracy of the estimated root translation and articulations, and mitigates incorrect environment penetrations. (Sect. 3.2).

Modelling and Notations. Our method takes as input a sequence $\mathbf{I} = \{\mathbf{I}_1, ..., \mathbf{I}_T\}$ of T successive video frames from a static camera with known intrinsics ($T = 5$ in our experiments). We detect a squared bounding box around the subject and resize the cropped image region to 225×225 pixels. The background scene's geometry that corresponds to the detected bounding box is represented by a single static point cloud $\mathbf{S} \in \mathbb{R}^{M \times 3}$ composed of M points aligned in the camera reference frame in an absolute scale. To model the 3D pose and human body surface, we employ the parametric model SMPL-X [34] (its gender-neutral version). This model defines the 3D body mesh as a differentiable function $\mathcal{M}(\boldsymbol{\tau}, \boldsymbol{\phi}, \boldsymbol{\theta}, \boldsymbol{\beta})$ of global root translation $\boldsymbol{\tau} \in \mathbb{R}^3$, global root orientation $\boldsymbol{\phi} \in \mathbb{R}^3$, root-relative pose $\boldsymbol{\theta} \in \mathbb{R}^{3K}$ of K joints and shape parameters $\boldsymbol{\beta} \in \mathbb{R}^{10}$ capturing body's identity. For efficiency, we downsample the original SMPL-X body mesh with over 10k vertices to $\mathbf{V} \in \mathbb{R}^{N \times 3}$, where $N = 655$. In the following, we denote $\mathbf{V} = \mathcal{M}(\boldsymbol{\Phi}, \boldsymbol{\beta})$, where $\boldsymbol{\Phi} = (\boldsymbol{\tau}, \boldsymbol{\phi}, \boldsymbol{\theta})$ denotes the kinematic state of the human skeleton, from which the global positions $\mathbf{X} \in \mathbb{R}^{K \times 3}$ of the $K = 21$ joints can be derived.

3.1   Contact Estimation in the Scene

We now describe our learning-based approach for contact labels estimation on the human body and environment surfaces; see Fig. 1-a) for an overview of this stage. The approach takes $\mathbf{I}$ and $\mathbf{S}$ as inputs. It comprises three fully-convolutional feature extractors, N_1, N_2 and N_3, and two fully-connected layer-based contact prediction networks, Ω_{bo} and Ω_{en}, for body and environment, respectively.

Network N_1 extracts from $\mathbf{I}$ a stack of visual features $\mathbf{f_I} \in \mathbb{R}^{32 \times 32 \times 256}$. The latent space features of N_1 are also fed to Ω_{bo} to predict the vector $\mathbf{c}_{\mathrm{bo}} \in [0, 1]^N$ of per-vertex contact probabilities on the *body* surface.

We also aim at estimating the corresponding contacts on the *environment* surface using an implicit function. To train a model that generalises well, we need to address two challenges: (i) No correspondence information between the scene points and the image pixels are given; (ii) Each scene contains a variable number of points. Accordingly, we convert the scene point cloud $\mathbf{S}$ into a frustum voxel grid $\mathbf{S}_{\mathrm{F}} \in \mathbb{R}^{32 \times 32 \times 256}$ (the third dimension corresponds to the discretised depth of the 3D space over 256 bins, please refer to our supplement for the details). This new representation is independent of the original point-cloud size and is aligned with the camera's view direction. The latter will allow us to leverage a pixel-aligned implicit function inspired by PIFu [43], which helps the networks figure out the correspondences between pixel and geometry information. More specifically, $\mathbf{S}_{\mathrm{F}}$ is fed into N_2, which returns scene features $\mathbf{f_S} \in \mathbb{R}^{32 \times 32 \times 256}$. The third encoder, N_3, ingests $\mathbf{f_I}$ and $\mathbf{f_S}$ concatenated along their third dimension

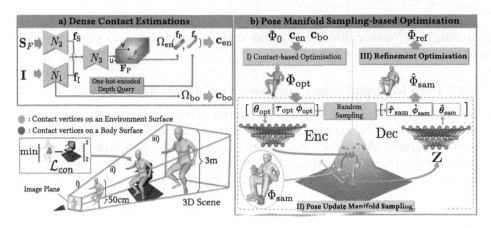

Fig. 2. Overview of a) dense contact estimation and b) pose manifold sampling-based optimisation. In b-II), we first generate samples around the mapping from θ_{opt} (orange arrows), and elite samples are then selected among them (yellow points). After resampling around the elite samples (yellow arrows), the best sample is selected (green point). The generated sample poses Φ_{sam} (in gray color at the bottom left in b-II)) from the sampled latent vectors are plausible and similar to Φ_{opt}. (***bottom left of the Figure***) Different body scale and depth combinations can be re-projected to the same image coordinates (i, ii and iii), *i.e.*, **scale-depth ambiguity**. To simultaneously estimate the accurate body scale and depth of the subject (ii), we combine the body-environment contact surface distance loss $\mathcal{L}_{\text{con}}$ with the 2D reprojection loss

and returns pixel-aligned features $\mathbf{F}_{\text{P}} \in \mathbb{R}^{32 \times 32 \times 64}$. Based on $\mathbf{F}_{\text{P}}$, Ω_{en} predicts the contact labels on the environment surface as follows. Given a 3D position in the scene, we extract the corresponding visual feature $\mathbf{f}_{\text{P}} \in \mathbb{R}^{64}$ at the (u, v)-position in the image space from $\mathbf{F}_{\text{P}}$ (via spacial bilinear interpolation), and query arbitrary depth with a one-hot vector $\mathbf{f}_{\text{z}} \in \mathbb{R}^{256}$. We next estimate the contact labels c_{en} as follows:

$$c_{\text{en}} = \Omega_{\text{en}}(\mathbf{f}_{\text{P}}, \mathbf{f}_{\text{z}}). \tag{1}$$

Given contact ground truths $\hat{\mathbf{c}}_{\text{bo}} \in \{0, 1\}^N$ and $\hat{\mathbf{c}}_{\text{en}} \in \{0, 1\}^M$ on the body and the environment, the five networks are trained with the following loss:

$$\mathcal{L}_{\text{labels}} = \|\mathbf{c}_{\text{en}} - \hat{\mathbf{c}}_{\text{en}}\|_2^2 + \lambda \, \text{BCE}(\mathbf{c}_{\text{bo}}, \hat{\mathbf{c}}_{\text{bo}}), \tag{2}$$

where BCE denotes the binary cross-entropy and $\lambda = 0.3$. We use BCE for the body because the ground-truth contacts on its surface are binary; the ℓ_2 loss is used for the environment, as sparse ground-truth contact labels are smoothed with a Gaussian kernel to obtain continuous signals. For further discussions of (2), please refer to our supplement. At test time, we only provide the 3D vertex positions of the environment to $\Omega_{\text{en}}(\cdot)$—to find the contact area on the scene point cloud—rather than all possible 3D sampling points as queries. This significantly accelerates the search of environmental contact labels while reducing the number of false-positive contact classifications. For more details of the network architecture, further discussions of the design choice and data pre-processing, please refer to our supplement.

3.2 Pose Manifold Sampling-based Optimisation

In the second stage of the approach, we aim at recovering an accurate global 3D trajectory of the subject as observed in the video sequence, see Fig. 2-(b) for the overview. An initial estimate Φ_0 is extracted for each input image using SMPLify-X [34]. Its root translation τ being subject to scale ambiguity, we propose to estimate it more accurately, along with the actual scale h of the person with respect to the original body model's height, under the guidance of the predicted body-environment contacts (**Contact-based Optimisation**). We then update the body trajectory and articulations in the scene, while mitigating the body-environment collisions with a new sampling-based optimisation on the pose manifold (**Sampling-based Trajectory Optimisation**). A subsequent refinement step yields the final global physically-plausible 3D motions.

I) Contact-Based Optimisation. Scale ambiguity is inherent to a monocular MoCap setting: Human bodies with different scale and depth combinations in 3D can be reprojected on the same positions in the image frame; see Fig. 2 and supplementary video for the schematic visualisation. Most existing algorithms that estimate global 3D translations of a subject either assume its known body scale [7,46,47] or use a statistical average body scale [30]. In the latter case, the estimated τ is often inaccurate and causes physically implausible body-environment penetrations. In contrast to the prior art, we simultaneously estimate τ and h by making use of the body-environment dense contact labels from the previous stage (Sect. 3.1).

For the given frame at time $t \in [1, T]$, we select the surface regions with $c_{en} > 0.5$ and $c_{bo} > 0.5$ as effective contacts and leverage them in our optimisation. Let us denote the corresponding index subsets of body vertices and scene points by $\mathcal{C}_{bo} \subset [1, N]$ and $\mathcal{C}_{en} \subset [1, M]$. The objective function for contact-based optimisation is defined as:

$$\mathcal{L}_{opt}(\tau, h) = \lambda_{2D}\mathcal{L}_{2D} + \lambda_{smooth}\mathcal{L}_{smooth} + \lambda_{con}\mathcal{L}_{con}, \tag{3}$$

where the reprojection $\mathcal{L}_{2D}$, the temporal smoothness $\mathcal{L}_{smooth}$ and the contact $\mathcal{L}_{con}$ losses weighted by empirically-set multipliers λ_{2D}, λ_{smooth} and λ_{con}, read:

$$\mathcal{L}_{2D} = \frac{1}{K}\sum_{k=1}^{K} w_k \left\| \Pi(\mathbf{X}_k) - \mathbf{p}_k \right\|_2^2, \tag{4}$$

$$\mathcal{L}_{smooth} = \left\| \tau - \tau_{prev} \right\|_2^2, \tag{5}$$

$$\mathcal{L}_{con} = \sum_{n \in \mathcal{C}_{bo}} \min_{m \in \mathcal{C}_{en}} \left\| \mathbf{V}_n - \mathbf{P}_m \right\|_2^2, \tag{6}$$

where $\mathbf{p}_k$ and w_k are the 2D detection in the image of the k-th body joint and its associated confidence, respectively, obtained by OpenPose [3]; Π is the perspective projection operator; τ_{prev} is the root translation estimated in the previous frame; $\mathbf{X}_k$, $\mathbf{V}_n$ and $\mathbf{P}_m$ are, respectively, the k-th 3D joint, the n-th body vertex ($n \in \mathcal{C}_{\text{bo}}$) and the m-th scene point ($m \in \mathcal{C}_{\text{en}}$). Note that the relative rotation and pose are taken from $\boldsymbol{\Phi}_0$. The body joints and vertices are obtained from $\mathcal{M}$ using τ and scaled with h. For $\mathcal{L}_{\text{con}}$, we use a directed Hausdorff measure [18] as a distance between the body and environment contact surfaces. The combination of $\mathcal{L}_{\text{con}}$ and $\mathcal{L}_{\text{2D}}$ is key to disambiguate τ and h (thus, resolving the monocular scale ambiguity). As a result of optimising (3) in frame t, we obtain $\boldsymbol{\Phi}_{\text{opt}}^t$, *i.e.*, the global 3D human motion with absolute body scale. We solve jointly on T frames and optimise for a single h for them.

II-a) Sampling-based Trajectory Optimisation. Although the poses $\boldsymbol{\Phi}_{\text{opt}}^t$, $t = 1 \cdots T$, estimated in the previous step yield much more accurate τ and h compared to existing monocular RGB based methods, incorrect body environment penetrations are still observable. This is because the gradient-based optimisation often gets stuck in bad local minima (see the supplementary video for a toy example illustrating this issue). To overcome this problem, we introduce an additional sampling-based optimisation that imposes hard penetration constraints, thus significantly mitigating physically-implausible collisions. The overview of this algorithm is as follows: (i) For each frame t, we first draw candidate poses around $\boldsymbol{\Phi}_{\text{opt}}^t$ with a sampling function $\mathcal{G}$; (ii) The quality of these samples is ranked by a function $\mathcal{E}$ that allows selecting the most promising ("elite") ones; samples with severe collisions are discarded; (iii) Using $\mathcal{G}$ and $\mathcal{E}$ again, we generate and select new samples around the elite ones. The details of these steps, $\mathcal{E}$ and $\mathcal{G}$, are elaborated next (dropping time index t for simplicity).

II-b) Generating Pose Samples. We aim to generate N_{sam} sample states $\boldsymbol{\Phi}_{\text{sam}}$ around the previously-estimated $\boldsymbol{\Phi}_{\text{opt}} = (\tau_{\text{opt}}, \phi_{\text{opt}}, \theta_{\text{opt}})$. To generate samples $(\tau_{\text{sam}}, \phi_{\text{sam}})$ for the global translation and orientation, with 3DoF each, we simply use a uniform distribution around $(\tau_{\text{opt}}, \phi_{\text{opt}})$; see our supplement for the details. However, naïvely generating the relative pose θ_{sam} in the same way around θ_{opt} is highly inefficient because (i) the body pose is high-dimensional and (ii) the randomly-sampled poses are not necessarily plausible. These reasons lead to an infeasible amount of generated samples required to find a plausible collision-free pose; which is intractable on standard graphics hardware. To tackle these issues, we resort to the pose manifold learned by VPoser [34], which is a VAE [17] trained on AMASS [26], *i.e.*, a dataset with many highly accurate MoCap sequences. Sampling is conducted in this VAE's latent space rather than in the kinematics pose space. Specifically, we first map θ_{opt} into a latent pose vector with the VAE's encoder $\text{Enc}(\cdot)$. Next, we sample latent vectors using a Gaussian distribution centered at this vector, with standard deviation σ (see Fig. 2-b). Each latent sample is then mapped through VAE's decoder $\text{Dec}(\cdot)$ into a pose that is combined with the original one on a per-joint basis. The complete sampling process reads:

$$\mathbf{Z} \sim \mathcal{N}\big(\text{Enc}(\theta_{\text{opt}}), \sigma\big), \quad \theta_{\text{sam}} = \mathbf{w} \circ \theta_{\text{opt}} + (1 - \mathbf{w}) \circ \text{Dec}(\mathbf{Z}), \tag{7}$$

where $\circ$ denotes Hadamard matrix product and $\mathbf{w} \in \mathbb{R}^{3K}$ is composed of the detection confidence values w_k, $k = 1 \cdots K$, obtained from OpenPose, each appearing three times (for each DoF of the joint). This confidence-based strategy allows weighting higher the joint angles obtained by sampling, if the image-based detections are less confident (*e.g.*, under occlusions). Conversely, significant modifications are not required for the joints with high confidence values.

Since the manifold learned by VAE is smooth, the poses derived from the latent vectors sampled around $\mathrm{Enc}(\boldsymbol{\theta}_{\mathrm{opt}})$ should be close to $\boldsymbol{\theta}_{\mathrm{opt}}$. Therefore, we empirically set $\boldsymbol{\sigma}$ to a small value (0.1). Compared to the naïve random sampling in the joint angle space, whose generated poses are not necessarily plausible, this pose sampling on the learned manifold significantly narrows down the solution space. Hence, a lot fewer samples are required to escape local minima. At the bottom left of Fig. 2-b contains examples (gray color) of $\boldsymbol{\Phi}_{\mathrm{sam}}$ ($N_{\mathrm{sam}} = 10$) overlayed onto $\boldsymbol{\Phi}_{\mathrm{opt}}$ (green). In the following, we refer to this sample generation process as function $\mathcal{G}(\cdot)$.

II-c) Sample Selection. The quality of the N_{sam} generated samples $\boldsymbol{\Phi}_{\mathrm{sam}}$ is evaluated using the following cost function:

$$\mathcal{L}_{\mathrm{sam}} = \mathcal{L}_{\mathrm{opt}} + \lambda_{\mathrm{sli}}\mathcal{L}_{\mathrm{sli}} + \lambda_{\mathrm{data}}\mathcal{L}_{\mathrm{data}}, \tag{8}$$

$$\mathcal{L}_{\mathrm{sli}} = \|\mathbf{V}_{\mathrm{c}} - \mathbf{V}_{\mathrm{c,pre}}\|_2^2, \tag{9}$$

$$\mathcal{L}_{\mathrm{data}} = \|\boldsymbol{\Phi}_{\mathrm{sam}} - \boldsymbol{\Phi}_{\mathrm{opt}}\|_2^2, \tag{10}$$

where $\mathcal{L}_{\mathrm{sli}}$ and $\mathcal{L}_{\mathrm{data}}$ are contact sliding loss and data loss, respectively, and $\mathcal{L}_{\mathrm{opt}}$ is the same as in (3) with the modification that the temporal consistency (5) applies to the whole $\boldsymbol{\Phi}_{\mathrm{sam}}$; $\mathbf{V}_{\mathrm{c}}$ and $\mathbf{V}_{\mathrm{c,pre}}$ are the body contact vertices (with vertex indices in $\mathcal{C}_{\mathrm{bo}}$) and their previous positions, respectively.

Among N_{sam} samples ordered according to their increasing $\mathcal{L}_{\mathrm{sam}}$ values, the selection function $\mathcal{E}_U(\cdot)$ first discards those causing stronger penetrations (in the sense that the amount of scene points inside a human body is above a threshold γ) and returns U first samples from the remaining ones. If no samples pass the collision test, we regenerate the new set of N_{sam} samples. This selection mechanism introduces the collision handling in a hard manner. After applying $\mathcal{E}_U(\cdot)$, with $U < N_{\mathrm{sam}}$, U elite samples are retained. Then, $\lfloor N_{\mathrm{sam}}/U \rfloor$ new samples are regenerated around every elite sample using $\mathcal{G}$. Among those, the one with minimum $\mathcal{L}_{\mathrm{sam}}$ value is retained as the final estimate. The sequence of obtained poses is temporally smoothed by Gaussian filtering to further remove jittering, which yields the global 3D motion $(\hat{\boldsymbol{\Phi}}_{\mathrm{sam}}^t)_{t=1}^T$ with significantly mitigated collisions.

III) Final Refinement. From the previous step, we obtained the sequence $\hat{\boldsymbol{\Phi}}_{\mathrm{sam}} = (\hat{\boldsymbol{\tau}}_{\mathrm{sam}}, \hat{\boldsymbol{\phi}}_{\mathrm{sam}}, \hat{\boldsymbol{\theta}}_{\mathrm{sam}})$ of kinematic states whose severe body-environment collisions are prevented as hard constraints. Starting from these states as initialisation, we perform a final gradient-based refinement using cost function $\mathcal{L}_{\mathrm{sam}}$ with $\hat{\boldsymbol{\Phi}}_{\mathrm{sam}}$ replacing $\boldsymbol{\Phi}_{\mathrm{opt}}$. The final sequence is denoted $(\boldsymbol{\Phi}_{\mathrm{ref}}^t)_{t=1}^T$.

4   Datasets with Contact Annotations

As there are no publicly-available large-scale datasets with images and corresponding human-scene contact annotations, we annotate several existing datasets.

GTA-IM [2] dataset contains various daily 3D motions. First, we fit SMPL-X model onto the 3D joint trajectories in GTA-IM. For each frame, we select contact vertices on the human mesh if: i) The Euclidean distance between the human body vertices on and the scene vertices are smaller than a certain threshold; ii) The velocity of the vertex is lower than a certain threshold. In total, we obtain the body surface contact annotations on $320k$ frames, which will be released for research purposes, see Fig. 1 for the examples of the annotated contact labels.

PROX dataset [11] contains scanned scene meshes, scene SDFs, RGB-D sequences, 3D human poses and shapes generated by fitting SMPL-X model onto the RGB-D sequences (considering collisions). We consider the body vertices, whose SDF values are lower than 5 cm, as contacts. We annotate the environment contacts by finding the vertices that are the nearest to the body contacts.

GPA dataset [54,55] contains multi-view image sequences of people interacting with various rigid 3D geometries, accurately reconstructed 3D scenes and 3D human motions obtained from VICON system [52] with 28 calibrated cameras. We fit SMPL-X on GPA to obtain the 3D shapes and compute the scene's SDFs to run other methods [11,12,61].

We extract from **GPA** 14 test sequences with 5 different subjects. We also split **PROX** [11] into training and test sequences. The training sequences of **PROX** and **GTA-IM** [2] are used to train the contact estimation networks. For further details of dataset and training, please refer to our supplement.

5   Evaluations

We compare our HULC with the most related scene-aware 3D MoCap algorithms, *i.e.*, PROX [11], PROX-D [11], POSA [12] and LEMO [61]. We also test SMPLify-X [34] which does not use scene constraints. The root translation of SMPLify-X is obtained from its estimated camera poses as done in [11]. To run LEMO [61] on the RGB sequence, we use SMPLify-X [34] to initialise it; we call this combination "LEMO (RGB)". We use the selected test sequences of GPA [54,55] and PROX [11] dataset for the quantitative and qualitative comparisons. To avoid redundancy, we downsample all the predictions to 10 fps except for the temporal consistency measurement (e_{smooth} in Table 4). Since the 3D poses in PROX dataset are prone to inaccuracies due to their human model fitting onto the RGB-D sequence, we use it only for reporting the body-scene penetrations (Table 4) and for qualitative comparisons.

5.1   Quantitative Results

We report 3D joint and vertex errors (Table 2), global translation and body scale estimation errors (Table 3), body-environment penetration and smoothness

Table 2. Comparisons of 3D error on GPA dataset [54,55]. "†" denotes that the occlusion masks for LEMO(RGB) were computed from GT 3D human mesh

	No Procrustes			Procrustes		
	MPJPE [mm]↓	PCK [%]↑	PVE [mm]↓	MPJPE [mm]↓	PCK [%]↑	PVE [mm]↓
Ours	**217.9**	**35.3**	**214.7**	**81.5**	**89.3**	**72.6**
Ours (w/o S)	221.3	34.5	217.2	82.6	**89.3**	73.1
Ours (w/o R)	240.8	31.9	237.3	83.1	86.6	73.6
Ours (w/o SR)	251.1	31.5	245.2	83.9	86.6	74.1
SMPLify-X [34]	550.0	10.0	549.1	84.7	85.9	74.1
PROX [11]	549.7	10.1	548.7	84.6	86.0	73.9
POSA [12]	552.2	10.1	550.9	85.5	85.6	74.5
LEMO (RGB) [61]	570.1	8.75	570.5	83.0	86.4	73.7
LEMO (RGB) [61]†	570.0	8.77	570.4	83.0	86.4	73.6

Table 3. Ablations and comparisons for global translations and absolute body length on GPA dataset

	global translation error [m] ↓	absolute bone length error [m]↓
Ours (+1m)	**0.242**	0.104
Ours (+3m)	0.244	**0.097**
Ours (+10m)	0.244	0.109
Baseline (+1m)	0.751	0.498
Baseline (+3m)	1.033	0.560
Baseline (+10m)	2.861	1.918
SMPLify-X [34]	0.527	0.156
PROX [11]	0.528	0.160
POSA [12]	0.545	0.136

Table 4. Comparisons of physical plausibility measures on GPA dataset [54,55] and PROX dataset [11]

		GPA Dataset		PROX Dataset
		Non penet. [%]↑	e_{smooth} ↓	Non penet. [%]↑
RGB	Ours	**99.4**	20.2	97.0
	Ours (w/o S)	97.6	28.1	93.8
	Ours (w/o R)	**99.4**	24.7	**97.1**
	Ours (w/o SR)	97.6	47.1	93.8
	SMPLify-X [34]	97.7	43.3	88.9
	PROX [11]	97.7	43.2	89.8
	LEMO (RGB) [61]	97.8	**19.9**	-
	POSA [12]	98.0	47.0	93.0
RGB-D	PROX-D [11]	-	-	94.2
	LEMO [61]	-	-	96.4

errors (Table 4) and ablations on the sampling-based optimisation component, *i.e.*, a) Manifold sampling vs. random sampling and b) Different number of sampling iterations in Fig. 3. "Ours (w/o S)" represents our method without the sampling optimisation component, *i.e.*, only the contact-based optimisation and refinement are applied (see Fig. 2-(b) and Sect. 3.2). "Ours (w/o R)" represents our method without the final refinement. "Ours (w/o SR)" denotes ours without the sampling and refinement. For a further ablation study and evaluation of contact label estimation networks, please see our supplement.

3D Joint and Vertex Errors. Table 2 compares the accuracy of 3D joint and vertex positions with and without Procrustes alignment. LEMO also requires human body occlusion masks on each frame. We compute them using the scene geometry and SMPLify-X [34] results. We also show another variant "LEMO (RGB)†" whose occlusion masks are computed using the ground-truth global 3D human mesh instead of SMPLify-X. Here, we report the standard 3D metrics, *i.e.*, mean per joint position error (MPJPE), percentage of correct keypoints (PCK) (@150mm) and mean per vertex error (PVE). Lower MPJPE and PVE represent more accurate 3D reconstructions, higher PCK indicates more accurate 3D joint positions.

On all these metrics, HULC outperforms other methods both with and without Procrustes. Notably, thanks to substantially more accurate global translations obtained from the contact-based optimisation (Sect. 3.2), HULC significantly reduces the MPJPE and PVE with a big margin, *i.e.*, $\approx 60\%$ error deduction in MPJPE and PVE w/o Procrustes compared to the second-best method. The ablative studies on Table 2 also indicate that both the sampling and refinement optimisations contribute to accurate 3D poses. Note that the sampling optimisation alone ("Ours (w/o R)") does not significantly reduce the error compared to "Ours (w/o SR)". This is because the sampling component prioritises removal of environment penetrations by introducing hard collision handling, which is the most important feature of this component. Therefore, the sampling component significantly contributes to reducing the environment collision as can be seen in Table 4 (discussed in the later paragraph). Applying the refinement after escaping from severe penetrations by the sampling optimisation further increases the 3D accuracy ("Ours" in Table 2) while significantly mitigating physically implausible body-environment penetrations (Table 4).

Global Translation and Body Scale Estimation. Table 3 reports global translation and body scale estimation errors for the ablation study of the contact-based optimisation (Sect. 3.2). More specifically, we evaluate the output Φ_{opt} obtained from the contact-based optimisation denoted "ours". We also show the optimisation result without using the contact loss term (6) ("Baseline"). The numbers next to the method names represent the initialisation offset from the ground-truth 3D translation position (*e.g.,* "+10m" indicates that the initial root position of the human body was placed at 10 meters away along the depth direction from the ground-truth root position when solving the optimisations).

Without the contact loss term—since global translation and body scale are jointly estimated in the optimisation—the baseline method suffers from *up-to-scale* issue (see Fig. 2). Hence, its results are significantly worse due to worse initialisations. In contrast, our contact-based optimisation disambiguates the scale and depth by localising the contact positions on the environment, which confirms HULC to be highly robust to bad initialisations. Compared to the RGB-based methods PROX, POSA and SMPLify-X, our contact-based optimisation result has $\approx 40\%$ smaller error in the absolute bone length, and $\approx 57\%$ smaller error in global translation, which also contributes to the reduced body-environment collisions as demonstrated in Table 4 (discussed in the next paragraph).

Plausibility Measurements. We also report the plausibility of the reconstructed 3D motions in Table 4. *Non penet.* measures the average ratio of non-penetrating body vertices into the environment over all frames. A higher value denotes fewer body-environment collisions in the sequence; e_{smooth} measures the temporal smoothness error proposed in [47]. Lower e_{smooth} indicates more temporally smooth 3D motions. On both GPA and PROX datasets, our full framework mitigates the collisions thanks to the manifold sampling-based optimisations (ours vs. ours (w/o S)). It also does so when compared to other related works as well. Notably, HULC shows the least amount of collisions even compared with RGBD-based methods on the PROX dataset. Finally, the proposed method also shows the significantly low e_{smooth} (on par with LEMO(RGB)) in this experiment.

More Ablations on Sampling-based Optimisation. In addition to the ablation studies reported in Tables 2, 3 and 4, we further assess the performance of the pose update manifold sampling step (Fig. 2-(b)-(II)) on GPA dataset [54,55], reporting the 3D error (MPJPE [mm]) measured in world frame. Note that we report MPJPE without the final refinement step to assess the importance of the manifold sampling approach. In Fig. 3-(a), we show the influence of the number N_{sam} of sam-

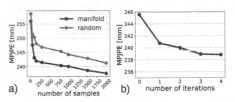

Fig. 3. (a) MPJPE [mm] comparison with different numbers of samples for the learned manifold sampling strategy vs. the naïve random sampling in the joint angle space of the kinematic skeleton.(b) MPJPE [mm] comparison with different numbers of iterations in the sampling strategy

ples on the performance of our manifold sampling strategy vs. a naïve random sampling with a uniform distribution in a kinematic skeleton frame. For the details of the naïve random sampling strategy, please refer to our supplement. In Fig. 3-(a), since the generated samples of the learned manifold return plausible pose samples, our pose manifold sampling strategy requires significantly fewer samples compared to the random sampling ($\sim$15× more samples are required for the random sampling to reach 243 [mm] error in MPJPE). This result strongly supports the importance of the learned manifold sampling. No more than 2000 samples can be generated due to the hardware memory capacity. In Fig. 3-(b), we report the influence of the number of generation-selection steps using functions $\mathcal{G}$ and $\mathcal{E}_U$ (with $U = 3$) introduced in Sect. 3.2, with $N_{\text{sam}} = 1000$ samples. No iteration stands for choosing the best sample from the first generated batch (hence no resampling), while one iteration is the variant described in Sect. 3.2. This first iteration sharply reduces the MPJPE, while the benefit of the additional iterations is less pronounced. Based on these observations, we use only one re-sampling iteration with 1000 samples in the previous experiments. Finally, we ablate the confidence value-based pose merging in Eq. (7), setting $N_{\text{sam}} = 1000$ and the number of iterations to 0. The measured MPJPE for with and without this confidence merging are 245.5 and 249.1, respectively.

5.2   Qualitative Results

Figure 4 summarises the qualitative comparisons on GPA and PROX datasets. HULC produces more physically-plausible global 3D poses with mitigated collisions, whereas the other methods show body-environment penetrations. Even compared with the RGB(D) approaches, HULC mitigates collisions (mind the red rectangles). For more qualitative results, please refer to our video.

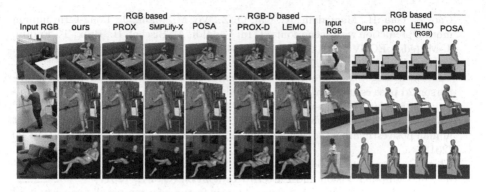

Fig. 4. The qualitative comparisons of our results with the related methods on PROX (left) and GPA dataset (right). Our RGB-based HULC shows fewer body-scene penetrations even when compared with RGB-D based methods; mind the red rectangles in the second row (Color figure online)

6 Concluding Remarks

Limitations. HULC requires the scene geometry aligned in a camera frame like other related works [11,12,61]. Also, HULC does not capture non-rigid deformations of scenes and bodies, although the body surface and some objects in the environment deform (*e.g.*, when sitting on a couch or lying in a bed). Moreover, since our algorithm relies on the initial root-relative pose obtained from an RGB-based MoCap algorithm, the subsequent steps can fail under severe occlusions. Although the estimated contact labels help to significantly reduce the 3D translation error, the estimated environment contacts contain observable false positives. These limitations can be tackled in the future.

Conclusion. We introduced *HULC*—the first RGB-based scene-aware MoCap algorithm that estimates and is guided by dense body-environment surface contact labels combined with a pose manifold sampling. HULC shows 60% smaller 3D-localisation errors compared to the previous methods. Furthermore, deep body-environment collisions are handled in hard manner in the pose manifold sampling-based optimisation, which significantly mitigates collisions with the scene. HULC shows the lowest collisions even compared with RGBD-based scene-aware methods.

Acknowledgement. The authors from MPII were supported by the ERC Consolidator Grant 4DRepLy (770784). We also acknowledge support from Valeo.

References

1. Bogo, F., Kanazawa, A., Lassner, C., Gehler, P., Romero, J., Black, M.J.: Keep it SMPL: automatic estimation of 3d human pose and shape from a single image. In: Leibe, B., Matas, J., Sebe, N., Welling, M. (eds.) ECCV 2016. LNCS, vol. 9909, pp. 561–578. Springer, Cham (2016). https://doi.org/10.1007/978-3-319-46454-1_34

2. Cao, Z., Gao, H., Mangalam, K., Cai, Q.-Z., Vo, M., Malik, J.: Long-term human motion prediction with scene context. In: Vedaldi, A., Bischof, H., Brox, T., Frahm, J.-M. (eds.) ECCV 2020. LNCS, vol. 12346, pp. 387–404. Springer, Cham (2020). https://doi.org/10.1007/978-3-030-58452-8_23
3. Cao, Z., Hidalgo, G., Simon, T., Wei, S.E., Sheikh, Y.: Openpose: realtime multi-person 2d pose estimation using part affinity fields. Transactions on Pattern Analysis and Machine Intelligence (TPAMI) (2019)
4. Charles, J., Pfister, T., Everingham, M., Zisserman, A.: Automatic and efficient human pose estimation for sign language videos. Int. J. Comput. Vision 110, 70–90 (2013)
5. Chen, C., Ramanan, D.: 3d human pose estimation = 2d pose estimation + matching. In: Computer Vision and Pattern Recognition (CVPR) (2017)
6. Choi, H., Moon, G., Lee, K.M.: Beyond static features for temporally consistent 3d human pose and shape from a video. In: Computer Vision and Pattern Recognition (CVPR) (2021)
7. Dabral, R., Shimada, S., Jain, A., Theobalt, C., Golyanik, V.: Gravity-aware monocular 3d human-object reconstruction. In: International Conference on Computer Vision (ICCV) (2021)
8. Fieraru, M., Zanfir, M., Oneata, E., Popa, A.I., Olaru, V., Sminchisescu, C.: Three-dimensional reconstruction of human interactions. In: Computer Vision and Pattern Recognition (CVPR) (2020)
9. Habibie, I., Xu, W., Mehta, D., Pons-Moll, G., Theobalt, C.: In the wild human pose estimation using explicit 2d features and intermediate 3d representations. In: Computer Vision and Pattern Recognition (CVPR) (2019)
10. Hassan, M., Ceylan, D., Villegas, R., Saito, J., Yang, J., Zhou, Y., Black, M.J.: Stochastic scene-aware motion prediction. In: International Conference on Computer Vision (ICCV) (2021)
11. Hassan, M., Choutas, V., Tzionas, D., Black, M.J.: Resolving 3D human pose ambiguities with 3D scene constraints. In: International Conference on Computer Vision (ICCV) (2019)
12. Hassan, M., Ghosh, P., Tesch, J., Tzionas, D., Black, M.J.: Populating 3D scenes by learning human-scene interaction. In: Computer Vision and Pattern Recognition (CVPR) (2021)
13. Jiang, W., Kolotouros, N., Pavlakos, G., Zhou, X., Daniilidis, K.: Coherent reconstruction of multiple humans from a single image. In: Computer Vision and Pattern Recognition (CVPR) (2020)
14. John, V., Trucco, E., McKenna, S.: Markerless human motion capture using charting and manifold constrained particle swarm optimisation. In: British Machine Vision Conference (BMVC) (2010)
15. Kanazawa, A., Black, M.J., Jacobs, D.W., Malik, J.: End-to-end recovery of human shape and pose. In: Computer Vision and Pattern Recognition (CVPR) (2018)
16. Kanazawa, A., Zhang, J.Y., Felsen, P., Malik, J.: Learning 3d human dynamics from video. In: Computer Vision and Pattern Recognition (CVPR) (2019)
17. Kingma, D.P., Welling, M.: Auto-encoding variational bayes. In: International Conference on Learning Representations (ICLR) (2014)
18. Knauer, C., Löffler, M., Scherfenberg, M., Wolle, T.: The directed hausdorff distance between imprecise point sets. In: International Symposium on Algorithms and Computation (ISAAC) (2009)
19. Kocabas, M., Athanasiou, N., Black, M.J.: Vibe: video inference for human body pose and shape estimation. In: Computer Vision and Pattern Recognition (CVPR) (2020)

20. Kocabas, M., Huang, C.H.P., Hilliges, O., Black, M.J.: PARE: part attention regressor for 3D human body estimation. In: International Conference on Computer Vision (ICCV) (2021)
21. Kocabas, M., Huang, C.H.P., Tesch, J., Müller, L., Hilliges, O., Black, M.J.: SPEC: seeing people in the wild with an estimated camera. In: International Conference on Computer Vision (ICCV) (2021)
22. Kolotouros, N., Pavlakos, G., Black, M.J., Daniilidis, K.: Learning to reconstruct 3d human pose and shape via model-fitting in the loop. In: International Conference on Computer Vision (ICCV) (2019)
23. Kolotouros, N., Pavlakos, G., Jayaraman, D., Daniilidis, K.: Probabilistic modeling for human mesh recovery. In: International Conference on Computer Vision (ICCV) (2021)
24. Li, Z., Shimada, S., Schiele, B., Theobalt, C., Golyanik, V.: Mocapdeform: monocular 3d human motion capture in deformable scenes. In: Arxiv (2022)
25. Li, Z., Sedlar, J., Carpentier, J., Laptev, I., Mansard, N., Sivic, J.: Estimating 3d motion and forces of person-object interactions from monocular video. In: Computer Vision and Pattern Recognition (CVPR) (2019)
26. Mahmood, N., Ghorbani, N., Troje, N.F., Pons-Moll, G., Black, M.J.: AMASS: archive of motion capture as surface shapes. In: International Conference on Computer Vision (ICCV) (2019)
27. Martinez, J., Hossain, R., Romero, J., Little, J.J.: A simple yet effective baseline for 3d human pose estimation. In: International Conference on Computer Vision (ICCV) (2017)
28. Mehta, D., et al.: Monocular 3d human pose estimation in the wild using improved CNN supervision. In: International Conference on 3D Vision (3DV) (2017)
29. Mehta, D., et al.: XNect: real-time multi-person 3d motion capture with a single RGB camera. ACM Trans. Graph. (TOG) **39**(4), 82–91 (2020)
30. Mehta, D., et al.: VNect: Real-time 3d human pose estimation with a single RGB camera. ACM Trans. Graph. (TOG) **36**(4), 1–4 (2017)
31. Moreno-Noguer, F.: 3d human pose estimation from a single image via distance matrix regression. In: Computer Vision and Pattern Recognition (CVPR) (2017)
32. Müller, L., Osman, A.A.A., Tang, S., Huang, C.H.P., Black, M.J.: On self-contact and human pose. In: Computer Vision and Pattern Recognition (CVPR) (2021)
33. Newell, A., Yang, K., Deng, J.: Stacked hourglass networks for human pose estimation. In: Leibe, B., Matas, J., Sebe, N., Welling, M. (eds.) ECCV 2016. LNCS, vol. 9912, pp. 483–499. Springer, Cham (2016). https://doi.org/10.1007/978-3-319-46484-8_29
34. Pavlakos, G., et al.: Expressive body capture: 3d hands, face, and body from a single image. In: Computer Vision and Pattern Recognition (CVPR) (2019)
35. Pavlakos, G., Zhou, X., Derpanis, K.G., Daniilidis, K.: Coarse-to-fine volumetric prediction for single-image 3D human pose. In: Computer Vision and Pattern Recognition (CVPR) (2017)
36. Pavlakos, G., Zhu, L., Zhou, X., Daniilidis, K.: Learning to estimate 3d human pose and shape from a single color image. In: Computer Vision and Pattern Recognition (CVPR) (2018)
37. Pavllo, D., Feichtenhofer, C., Grangier, D., Auli, M.: 3d human pose estimation in video with temporal convolutions and semi-supervised training. In: Computer Vision and Pattern Recognition (CVPR) (2019)
38. Rempe, D., Birdal, T., Hertzmann, A., Yang, J., Sridhar, S., Guibas, L.J.: Humor: 3d human motion model for robust pose estimation. In: International Conference on Computer Vision (ICCV) (2021)

39. Rempe, D., Guibas, L.J., Hertzmann, A., Russell, B., Villegas, R., Yang, J.: Contact and human dynamics from monocular video. In: Vedaldi, A., Bischof, H., Brox, T., Frahm, J.-M. (eds.) ECCV 2020. LNCS, vol. 12350, pp. 71–87. Springer, Cham (2020). https://doi.org/10.1007/978-3-030-58558-7_5

40. Rhodin, H., Salzmann, M., Fua, P.: Unsupervised geometry-aware representation for 3d human pose estimation. In: Ferrari, V., Hebert, M., Sminchisescu, C., Weiss, Y. (eds.) Unsupervised geometry-aware representation learning for 3d human pose estimatio. LNCS, vol. 11214, pp. 765–782. Springer, Cham (2018). https://doi.org/10.1007/978-3-030-01249-6_46

41. Saini, S., Rambli, D.R.B.A., Sulaiman, S.B., Zakaria, M.N.B.: Human pose tracking in low-dimensional subspace using manifold learning by charting. In: International Conference on Signal and Image Processing Applications (ICSIPA) (2013)

42. Saini, S., Rambli, D.R.B.A., Sulaiman, S.B., Zakaria, M.N.B., Rohkmah, S.: Markerless multi-view human motion tracking using manifold model learning by charting. Proc. Eng. **41**, 664–670 (2012)

43. Saito, S., Huang, Z., Natsume, R., Morishima, S., Kanazawa, A., Li, H.: PiFU: pixel-aligned implicit function for high-resolution clothed human digitization. In: International Conference on Computer Vision (ICCV) (2019)

44. Sharma, S., Varigonda, P.T., Bindal, P., Sharma, A., Jain, A.: Monocular 3d human pose estimation by generation and ordinal ranking. In: International Conference on Computer Vision (ICCV) (2019)

45. Shi, M.: Motionet: 3d human motion reconstruction from monocular video with skeleton consistency. ACM Trans. Graph. (TOG) **40**(1), 1–15 (2020)

46. Shimada, S., Golyanik, V., Xu, W., Pérez, P., Theobalt, C.: Neural monocular 3d human motion capture with physical awareness. ACM Trans. Graph. (TOG) **40**(4), 1–5 (2021)

47. Shimada, S., Golyanik, V., Xu, W., Theobalt, C.: PhysCAP: physically plausible monocular 3d motion capture in real time. ACM Trans. Graph. **39**(6), 1–6 (2020)

48. Sohn, K., Lee, H., Yan, X.: Learning structured output representation using deep conditional generative models. In: Advances in Neural Information Processing Systems (NIPS) (2015)

49. Sun, Y., Ye, Y., Liu, W., Gao, W., Fu, Y., Mei, T.: Human mesh recovery from monocular images via a skeleton-disentangled representation. In: International Conference on Computer Vision (ICCV) (2019)

50. Tekin, B., Katircioglu, I., Salzmann, M., Lepetit, V., Fua, P.: Structured prediction of 3d human pose with deep neural networks. In: British Machine Vision Conference (BMVC) (2016)

51. Tomè, D., Russell, C., Agapito, L.: Lifting from the deep: convolutional 3d pose estimation from a single image. In: Computer Vision and Pattern Recognition (CVPR) (2017)

52. Vicon blade. https://www.vicon.com/

53. Wang, J., Xu, H., Xu, J., Liu, S., Wang, X.: Synthesizing long-term 3d human motion and interaction in 3d scenes. In: Computer Vision and Pattern Recognition (CVPR) (2021)

54. Wang, Z., Chen, L., Rathore, S., Shin, D., Fowlkes, C.: Geometric pose affordance: 3d human pose with scene constraints. In: Arxiv (2019)

55. Wang, Z., Shin, D., Fowlkes, C.C.: Predicting camera viewpoint improves cross-dataset generalization for 3d human pose estimation. In: Bartoli, A., Fusiello, A. (eds.) ECCV 2020. LNCS, vol. 12536, pp. 523–540. Springer, Cham (2020). https://doi.org/10.1007/978-3-030-66096-3_36

56. Wei, X., Chai, J.: VideoMocap: modeling physically realistic human motion from monocular video sequences. ACM Trans. Graph. (TOG) **29**(4), 1–7 (2010)
57. Yang, W., Ouyang, W., Wang, X., Ren, J., Li, H., Wang, X.: 3d human pose estimation in the wild by adversarial learning. In: Computer Vision and Pattern Recognition (CVPR) (2018)
58. Yi, X., et al.: Physical inertial poser (PIP): physics-aware real-time human motion tracking from sparse inertial sensors. In: Computer Vision and Pattern Recognition (CVPR) (2022)
59. Yuan, Y., Wei, S.E., Simon, T., Kitani, K., Saragih, J.: SimPoE: simulated character control for 3d human pose estimation. In: Computer Vision and Pattern Recognition (CVPR) (2021)
60. Zanfir, A., Marinoiu, E., Sminchisescu, C.: Monocular 3d pose and shape estimation of multiple people in natural scenes - the importance of multiple scene constraints. In: Computer Vision and Pattern Recognition (CVPR) (2018)
61. Zhang, S., Zhang, Y., Bogo, F., Marc, P., Tang, S.: Learning motion priors for 4d human body capture in 3d scenes. In: International Conference on Computer Vision (ICCV), October 2021
62. Zhang, T., Huang, B., Wang, Y.: Object-occluded human shape and pose estimation from a single color image. In: Computer Vision and Pattern Recognition (CVPR) (2020)
63. Zhou, X., Huang, Q., Sun, X., Xue, X., Wei, Y.: Towards 3d human pose estimation in the wild: a weakly-supervised approach. In: International Conference on Computer Vision (ICCV) (2017)
64. Zou, Y., Yang, J., Ceylan, D., Zhang, J., Perazzi, F., Huang, J.B.: Reducing footskate in human motion reconstruction with ground contact constraints. In: Winter Conference on Applications of Computer Vision (WACV) (2020)

Towards Sequence-Level Training
for Visual Tracking

Minji Kim[1], Seungkwan Lee[3,4], Jungseul Ok[3], Bohyung Han[1,2],
and Minsu Cho[3(✉)]

[1] ECE, Seoul National University, Seoul, South Korea
[2] IPAI, Seoul National University, Seoul, South Korea
[3] POSTECH, Pohang, South Korea
`mscho@postech.ac.kr`
[4] Deeping Source Inc., Seoul, South Korea
`https://github.com/byminji/SLTtrack`

Abstract. Despite the extensive adoption of machine learning on the
task of visual object tracking, recent learning-based approaches have
largely overlooked the fact that visual tracking is a sequence-level task
in its nature; they rely heavily on frame-level training, which inevitably
induces inconsistency between training and testing in terms of both data
distributions and task objectives. This work introduces a sequence-level
training strategy for visual tracking based on reinforcement learning and
discusses how a sequence-level design of data sampling, learning objectives, and data augmentation can improve the accuracy and robustness of
tracking algorithms. Our experiments on standard benchmarks including
LaSOT, TrackingNet, and GOT-10k demonstrate that four representative tracking models, SiamRPN++, SiamAttn, TransT, and TrDiMP,
consistently improve by incorporating the proposed methods in training
without modifying architectures.

Keywords: Visual tracking · Sequence-level training · Reinforcement
learning

1 Introduction

Visual object tracking aims to estimate the spatial extent, *e.g.*, a bounding box,
of a target object over a sequence of video frames [23,30,34]. This task has been
drawing significant attention due to its wide range of applications including
visual surveillance, robotics, and autonomous driving [12,14]. Unlike standard
recognition tasks such as image classification and object detection, the class of
the target object is unknown and only its bounding box at the initial frame is

---

M. Kim S. Lee — These authors contributed equally to this work.

Supplementary Information The online version contains supplementary material
available at https://doi.org/10.1007/978-3-031-20047-2_31.

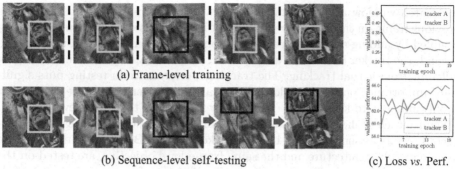

(a) Frame-level training

(b) Sequence-level self-testing

(c) Loss *vs.* Perf.

Fig. 1. Pitfall of frame-level training for visual tracking. Training a tracker to better localize a target in each of individual frames of (a) does not necessarily improve actual tracking in the sequence of (b). Green/red boxes indicate success/failure in localization. Due to the issue, inconsistency between the loss and the performance is often observed during training as shown in (c) where trackers, A and B, being frame-level trained are evaluated while the training loss (top) and the tracking performance of average overlap (bottom) are measured. After 10 epochs, A outperforms B in spite of higher losses. (Color figure online)

given for testing. Despite the long history of its study [30], object tracking in the wild still remains challenging due to appearance variation, occlusion, interference, distracting clutter, etc. To tackle the issues, recent methods increasingly rely on robust feature representations that are learned by deep neural networks with convolutions [1,2,19,21,25,43] and attention [4,32,39].

Although learning to track has been widely adopted in the research community, it is largely overlooked that visual tracking is essentially a *sequence-level* task; the estimated target state in the current frame is affected by the history of target states in the previous frames and also influences tracking results in the subsequent frames. For example, recent state-of-the-art methods [2,5,8,20,25,32,38,39,43] rely heavily on *frame-level* training, which encourages the trackers to better localize target objects in each frame through supervised learning. While it greatly improves the tracker by learning robust features for tracking, disregarding the sequential dependency across frames can lead to unexpected tracking failures. Let us assume a tracker that is trained with a typical frame-level training scheme using a set of annotated training videos; random pairs of a target template and a search frame are sampled from a video and the tracker is trained to best localize the target on the search frame independently for each pair. As shown in Fig. 1, now consider one of the training videos that contains a *hard* frame, where the tracker fails to localize the target object. Although the tracker is trained to perform almost perfectly on frame-level localization except for the hard frame (Fig. 1a), its sequence-level performance may turn out to be poor as it loses the target from the hard frame in actual tracking on the sequence (Fig. 1b).

This pitfall of frame-level training mainly stems from inconsistency between training and testing in terms of both *data distributions* and *task objectives*. First, the tracker observes data samples, *i.e.*, tracking situations, that significantly deviate from a real data distribution. That is, while in actual tracking the search window at each frame is determined based on the estimation at the previous frame, in the frame-level training it is not; the search window is typically sampled by adding a random transformation to the ground-truth bounding box. Second, the tracker learns with an objective, *i.e.*, a reward system, that is largely different from actual tracking. The tracking performance in testing puts significant importance on retaining localization accuracy over a sequence, whereas it is only immediate localization quality that matters in the frame-level training. The mismatch of the objectives between training and testing often leads to unexpected results as shown in Fig. 1c; two trackers, A and B, being trained with the same network architecture and the same frame-level objective, are tested on the GOT-10k validation split where the loss and the performance are measured[1]. While constantly yielding a higher loss, tracker A achieves better performance than tracker B after 10 epochs. Such inconsistency should be rectified for more robust tracking but has hardly been explored so far in the tracking community.

This work investigates the sequence-level training for visual object tracking and analyzes how the performance of a tracking algorithm improves by resolving the aforementioned inconsistency issues. Without adding any architectural components, we train a tracker end-to-end by simulating sequence-level tracking scenarios with a properly matching reward system in the framework of reinforcement learning (RL). Specifically, our tracker observes a sequence of frames sampled from an actual tracking trajectory and optimizes the objective based on the test-time metric such as the average overlap [16,34]. Our training strategy not only resolves the inconsistency in data distributions but also addresses the discrepancy in task objectives by teaching the tracker how its decision in the current frame affects future ones. Furthermore, this approach enables us to extend data augmentation to a temporal domain; on top of commonly-used data augmentation strategies in the spatial domain [23], we can simulate temporally-varying tracking scenarios for training, corresponding to videos with diverse object/camera motions (Sec. 3). Note that this new type of augmentation has not been available under the frame-level training of previous trackers. To sum up, the proposed sequence-level training allows a tracker to learn a robust strategy for realistic tracking scenarios by leveraging the simulated tracking samples, (*i.e.*, *sequence-level sampling*), the long-term objective (*i.e.*, *sequence-level objective*), and the data augmentation in the temporal domain (*i.e.*, *sequence-level augmentation*).

Our contributions are summarized as follows.

- We analyze the inherent drawbacks of frame-level training adopted in recent trackers, which motivate sequence-level training (SLT) for robust visual object tracking.
- We introduce an SLT strategy for visual tracking in an RL framework and propose an effective toolset of data sampling, training objectives, and data augmentation.
- We demonstrate the effectiveness of SLT using four recent trackers, SiamRPN++ [20], SiamAttn [39], TransT [4], and TrDiMP [32], and achieve

---

[1] Both trackers A and B adopt SiamRPN++ as their network architectures, but the backbone of tracker A is frozen in the early training stages.

competitive performance on the standard benchmarks, LaSOT [10], TrackingNet [24], and GOT-10k [16].

- We provide in-depth analyses of SLT by studying the effects of the sequence-level data sampling and the corresponding objective as well as the sequence-level data augmentation diversifying tracking episodes in a temporal domain.

2 Related Work

2.1 Visual Object Tracking (VOT)

There has been a large body of active research on VOT [18,23,30], which still remains one of the major topics in computer vision. Recent methods for VOT have greatly improved tracking performance based on deep learning with large-scale datasets [10,16,22,24,26,29]. Currently, state-of-the-art trackers are represented by two families of trackers: Siamese [1,4,20,21,39] and DiMP [2,7,8,32]. The Siamese trackers [1,20,21] rely heavily on an effective template-matching mechanism that is trained offline using large-scale datasets. While being fast and accurate in a short term, they tend to be vulnerable to long-term tracking due to the lack of online adaptability. Recent variants mitigate this limitation by updating template features during tracking [44,45] or using an attention mechanism to diversify the feature representation [39]. DiMP trackers [2,8,32] learn the online model predictor for target center regression and combine it with bounding box regression. Their model predictor, which is an iterative optimization-based neural module, is trained offline with a meta-learning-based objective and is used to build an online target model during tracking. Recently, Transformer-based architectures are adopted in both Siamese [4] and DiMP [32] trackers to enhance target feature representations.

Note that all of these state-of-the-art trackers are trained with frame-level objectives; it forces the model to take an instantaneous greedy decision at each frame, ignoring that the tracking errors accumulate over the sequence. In contrast, we study how to improve tracking by considering temporal dependency in the sequence of frames.

2.2 Reinforcement Learning for VOT

Our sequence-level training scheme is built on reinforcement learning (RL), which provides a natural framework for sequential decision-making on the problem with interactive temporal dependency. RL is not new in visual tracking and there exist several RL-based trackers [3,9,15,17,27,40–42]. Most of them [9,15,17,27] aim to assist tracking by learning an additional RL agent while considering both a given tracker and its input sequence as an environment. HP-Siam [9] uses RL to optimize hyper-parameters of the tracker such as scale step, penalty, and window weight. DRL-IS [27] and P-Track [17] learn a policy to decide the state transition of the tracker. EAST [15] uses RL to speed up tracking by learning to stop feed-forwarding frames through layers.

Only a few RL-based methods [3,40,41] learn the tracker itself as an RL agent, which performs actual tracking, e.g., estimating a target bounding box.

ADNet [40] formulates tracking as a discrete box adjustment problem, where at each time step the agent observes a current frame and a previous localization box and then decides discrete actions for adjusting the box. In a similar manner, ACT [3] learns to predict box transformation parameters in a continuous space of actions while PACNet [41] jointly learns both box estimation and state transition of the tracker. Their methods, however, require a specific form of output for training trackers in RL, e.g., the output of box transformation parameters [3,41] and pre-defined actions for box adjustment [40], and hardly exploit the advantage of RL training in a generic perspective. In contrast, we introduce a generic training strategy using RL and analyze its advantages over its frame-level counterpart, which is prevalent in recent state-of-the-art trackers. We advocate sequence-level training *per se* as the integral role of RL in tracking, showing that recent learnable trackers greatly benefit from RL-based training without additional components.

Regarding our effort to address the training-testing inconsistency, the most related work is [28], which tackles a similar problem in image captioning. It proposes self-critical sequence training (SCST), a form of the well-known REINFORCE [33] algorithm, to train image captioning models directly on NLP metrics. We build our sequence-level training scheme on SCST and adapt it for visual object tracking.

3   Our Approach

3.1   Sequence-Level Training (SLT)

Given a video $\mathbf{v} = (v_0, ..., v_T)$ of $T + 1$ frames and the ground-truth bounding box g_0 of the target object in the initial frame v_0, a tracker sequentially predicts a bounding box l_t of the target in each frame v_t, $t = 1, 2, ..., T$. The tracker, parameterized by θ, is modeled as a function π_θ that takes observation o_t and predicts l_t, i.e., $l_t = \pi_\theta(o_t)$, where o_t is the information available at time t including the video frames $(v_0, ..., v_t)$, the initial target bounding box g_0, and the previously estimated target states $(l_1, ..., l_{t-1})$. In online tracking, most trackers estimate the current state based only on the previous prediction l_{t-1} and the observation of the current frame v_t, e.g., searching for the optimal local window in v_t around l_{t-1}. The objective of a tracking algorithm is to maximize the *sequence-level* performance $r(\mathbf{l})$, where $\mathbf{l} = (l_1, ..., l_T)$ includes all the frames in a video and r is an evaluation metric, e.g., average overlap ratio [16,34].

Due to the sequential structure of the tracking process, its current decision l_t naturally affects the future ones $l_{t+1}, ..., l_T$. In the frame-level training, which is the de facto standard for recent methods [2,4,20,32,37,39], however, trackers do not simulate sequential target state estimation procedure in training. In other words, given each frame v_t, trackers are trained to localize the target object bounding box g_t from its random perturbation $\rho(g_t)$ instead of l_{t-1}, where ρ is a random perturbation function. Such a frame-level approximation, i.e., $l_{t-1} \approx \rho(g_t)$, requires additional hyper-parameters for ρ and, more importantly, introduces inconsistency of data distributions between training and test-

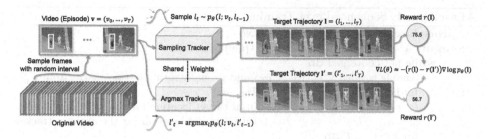

Fig. 2. Illustration of our sequence-level training framework. In training time, a video (episode), which is sampled from the original video with random intervals, is tracked twice by the sampling tracker and the argmax tracker. In this example, when a target person is fully occluded for a while, the argmax tracker mistakenly localizes the other person as the target due to its highest score in the occluded scene. In contrast, the sampling tracker stays nearby the previously estimated location (because of the random sampling) and successfully re-tracks the target object. In such a case, the reward becomes positive so that the sampled action is encouraged. In the opposite case, the reward becomes negative so that the sampled action is discouraged.

ing; the trackers have no opportunity to learn how the previous decision affects the current one in a real tracking scenario.

To overcome the limitation of frame-level training and capture the temporal dependency between decisions, we build our sequence-level training scheme based on RL. We simulate the tracker (agent) on a sequence of video frames, and directly optimize with respect to the test-time evaluation metric:

$$L(\theta) := -\mathbb{E}_{\mathbf{l} \sim \pi_\theta}[r(\mathbf{l})] . \tag{1}$$

Note that this *sequence-level objective* directly optimizes the real objective of tracking, and thus is a more natural way to train trackers than frame-level counterparts. This objective relieves the aforementioned issues in frame-level training; the tracker observes the real data distributions via *sequence-level sampling*, which draws samples from actual tracking trajectories and facilitates learning temporal dependency in tracking.

To directly optimize the task objective in (1), we employ the REINFORCE algorithm [33]. According to the algorithm, the expected gradient is computed as follows:

$$\nabla_\theta L(\theta) = -\mathbb{E}_{\mathbf{l} \sim \pi_\theta}[r(\mathbf{l})\nabla_\theta \log p_\theta(\mathbf{l})]. \tag{2}$$

In practice, the expected gradient is approximated by using a single Monte Carlo sample $\mathbf{l} = (l_1, ..., l_T)$ of sequential decisions from π_θ. For each training episode, the gradient is given by

$$\nabla_\theta L(\theta) \approx -r(\mathbf{l})\nabla_\theta \log p_\theta(\mathbf{l}). \tag{3}$$

To reduce the variance of gradient estimation, we adopt the self-critical sequence training (SCST) [28], which exploits the test-mode performance of the

---

Algorithm 1. Sequence-Level Training

1: **procedure** SEQUENCE-LEVEL TRAINING
    Input: A tracker parametrized by θ, training dataset Γ
2:    **while** not converged **do**
3:        Sample a video $\mathbf{v} = (v_0, ..., v_T)$ and ground-truth $\mathbf{g} = (g_0, ..., g_T)$ from Γ
4:        Initialize the tracker by using $\{v_0,\ g_0\}$
5:        $l_0 = g_0$ ▷ Initial target location for the sampling tracker
6:        $l'_0 = g_0$ ▷ Initial target location for the argmax tracker
7:        **for** $t \in 1, ..., T$ **do**
8:            $l_t = $ sample l from $p_\theta(l; v_t, l_{t-1})$
9:            $l'_t = \arg\max_l p_\theta(l; v_t, l'_{t-1})$
10:      **end for**
11:      $r = $ evaluate$(\{l_1, ..., l_T\}, \{g_1, ..., g_T\})$
12:      $r' = $ evaluate$(\{l'_1, ..., l'_T\}, \{g_1, ..., g_T\})$
13:      $L = -(r - r')\sum_{t=1}^{t=T} \log p_\theta(l_t; v_t, l_{t-1})$ ▷ (4)
14:      $\theta = \theta - \alpha\nabla_\theta L$ ▷ Update model parameters
15:    **end while**
16: **end procedure**

---

current model as a baseline for the reward. To be specific, we adopt two trackers sharing network parameters: a sampling tracker and an argmax tracker. During training, a video (episode) is played twice independently by both trackers. Given the probability distribution of actions, the sampling tracker decides the target bounding box stochastically while the argmax tracker selects the most confident one. If the agent obtains a higher reward from the sampling mode than the argmax mode, the resulting reward becomes positive to encourage the sampled actions. Otherwise, the agent receives a negative reward to suppress the sampled actions. In this way, we employ the SCST algorithm to train the tracker using the following gradient:

$$\nabla_\theta L(\theta) \approx -(r(\mathbf{l}) - r(\mathbf{l}'))\nabla_\theta \log p_\theta(\mathbf{l}), \tag{4}$$

where $r(\mathbf{l})$ and $r(\mathbf{l}')$ are rewards obtained from the current model by the sampling mode and the argmax mode during training, respectively. Such a REINFORCE-based training scheme is a certain realization of SLT and may be further improved by other RL-based algorithms. We illustrate the proposed sequence-level training pipeline in Fig. 2, and provide the pseudo-code in Algorithm 1.

3.2 Integration into Tracking Algorithms

We now present how to integrate the proposed SLT scheme into existing trackers. To demonstrate the effect of SLT, we adopt four representative trackers as our baselines: SiamRPN++ [20], SiamAttn [39], TransT [4], and TrDiMP [32]. In the following, we briefly describe each tracker and explain how it is trained.

SLT-SiamRPN++. SiamRPN++ [20] is a representative Siamese tracker based on the region proposal network (RPN) [11]. This method tracks the target object by repeatedly matching between feature embeddings of a template image and a search image [1]. Specifically, the tracker outputs confidence scores and box coordinates of N anchor boxes and performs greedy selection to choose the most confident one, where its box coordinates are selected as the estimation of the target location in the current frame. Since the current prediction for the target state, *i.e.*, position and size, determines the search area in the next frame, this decision not only influences the current frame but also will potentially affect predictions in the future. Thus, we reinforce the box selection procedure of SiamRPN++ with the proposed sequence-level training strategy to teach the tracker temporal dependencies.

Since our training method assumes that the target localization of the tracker is a stochastic action, we convert the greedy anchor selection of SiamRPN++ to become stochastic. Let $\mathbf{x} = (x_1, ..., x_N) \in \mathbb{R}^N$ denote the output anchor scores of SiamRPN++, where $N = a \times H \times W$ denotes the number of candidates in a score map with size of $H \times W$ and a anchor types. We define a categorical distribution $p(n)$ as follows:

$$p(n) = \frac{\exp(\sigma^{-1}(x_n))}{\sum_{m=1}^{N} \exp(\sigma^{-1}(x_m))}, \tag{5}$$

where σ^{-1} indicates the logit (inverse sigmoid) function. Since x_n is a normalized score whose value is between 0 and 1, we first apply the logit function before applying the softmax function. In training time, the tracker samples an anchor box from p for the current target localization. In test time, it selects the most confident anchor box deterministically as in the original SiamRPN++. For each training episode, the loss in the classification branch is given by

$$L = -(r(\mathbf{1}) - r(\mathbf{1}')) \sum_{t=1}^{T} \log p(n_t), \tag{6}$$

where $(r(\mathbf{1}) - r(\mathbf{1}'))$ is the self-critical reward (Sec. 3.1) and n_t is the sampled anchor box at frame t. The overall sequence-level training loss of SiamRPN++ is defined by combining the loss L for the classification branch and the ℓ_1 loss for the bounding-box regression branch [20], which is given by

$$L_{\text{siamrpn++}} = L + L_{\text{bbox}}. \tag{7}$$

SLT-SiamAttn. SiamAttn [39] is an extension of SiamRPN++ with an additional bounding box refinement module and a mask prediction module, along with attention modules for enhancing the feature representation. Similar to SiamRPN++, SiamAttn takes greedy anchor selection to choose the best target candidate among N anchor boxes from RPN. Once the box is chosen, SiamAttn additionally refines the bounding box using a deformable RoI pooling operation [6]. We thus use the same loss L for the classification branch. The overall sequence-level training loss of SiamAttn is to enhance the capability of target classification with SLT and increase the accuracy of localization modules with the help of sequence-level data sampling:

$$L_{\text{siamattn}} = L + \lambda_1 L_{\text{bbox}} + \lambda_2 L_{\text{refine-bbox}} + \lambda_3 L_{\text{mask}}, \tag{8}$$

where each loss term except for L follows [39]. The weight parameters are set as $\lambda_1 = 0.5$, $\lambda_2 = 0.5$, and $\lambda_3 = 0.2$.

SLT-TransT. TransT [4] adopts Transformer-like feature fusion networks into Siamese architecture and localizes the target object by computing attention between template vectors and search vectors. Unlike SiamRPN++ and SiamAttn, TransT has neither anchor points nor anchor boxes, and its prediction heads directly make N classification results and N normalized box estimations from fusion vectors corresponding to each position of the feature map, where $N = H \times W$ denotes the size of the feature map. We also take a categorical distribution $p(n)$ of equation (5) for N candidate vectors, and use the same loss L for the classification branch. The overall sequence-level training loss for TransT is:

$$L_{\text{transt}} = L + \lambda_4 L_{\text{bbox-L1}} + \lambda_5 L_{\text{bbox-GIoU}}, \tag{9}$$

where the box regression losses follow [4] and $\lambda_4 = 0.33$, $\lambda_5 = 0.13$ in our implementation.

SLT-TrDiMP. TrDiMP [32] is one of the state-of-the-art DiMP tracker using Transformer architectures. Its tracking procedure consists of two steps: target center prediction and bounding box regression. Given template samples generated from the initial frame, the model predictor generates a discriminative CNN kernel to convolve with the feature embedding from a search image for target response generation. The most confident location of the score map becomes the target center prediction, and starting from the randomly drawn candidate boxes around the location, the final bounding box estimation l_t is obtained from the IoU-Net-based box optimization [7,8].

For sequence-level training of TrDiMP, we convert the target center prediction into stochastic action by simply taking softmax on its score prediction. Let $\mathbf{y} = (y_1, ..., y_N) \in \mathbb{R}^N$ denotes the center prediction score of TrDiMP, where $N = H \times W$ means a number of candidates in a score map with a spatial size of $H \times W$. Now we define a categorical distribution $p(n)$ as follows:

$$p(n) = \frac{\exp(y_n)}{\sum_{m=1}^{N} \exp(y_m)}. \tag{10}$$

The loss for the center prediction module is same with L, and the overall sequence-level training loss for TrDiMP is:

$$L_{\text{trdimp}} = L + \lambda_6 L_{\text{iou-net}}, \tag{11}$$

where the loss term for IoU-Net follows [32] and λ_6 is set to 0.0025.

3.3 Sequence-Level Data Augmentation

Learning visual tracking in a sequence level naturally motivates sequence-level data augmentation that is conceptually incompatible with frame-level training. To improve the data quality and avoid the over-fitting problem of the networks, data augmentation strategies in a spatial domain such as geometric transformation, color perturbations, and blur, are widely adopted for convolutional trackers [23]. Conventional frame-level training, however, treats the training sequence merely as a group of independent images that need to be sampled and cropped, hardly considering the relationship between each image, thereby missing the potential effect of data augmentation towards the temporal domain. In contrast, our sequence-level training effectively benefits from exploring diverse changes in the temporal axis that can enrich the tracking scenarios, as well as the conventional data augmentation strategies in the spatial axis.

Among many possible ways of sequence-level augmentation, here we focus on a simple frame-interval augmentation, i.e., subsampling the training videos with different frame intervals. In our sequence-level augmentation setting, some episodes are sampled from the original video with random intervals as shown on the left side of Fig. 2. This scheme simulates dynamic visual differences along time steps and teaches the tracker to adapt to situations in which objects and/or cameras move faster. Diversifying the tracking scenarios in terms of frame rates makes the tracker improve or at least maintain the performance in general test videos. Experimental results in Sec. 4 show how our augmentation strategy affects the tracking performance. We believe that more advanced sequence-level augmentation strategies, e.g., temporal motion blur, may help sequence-level training further in general.

4 Experiments

This section presents the effectiveness of the proposed sequencel-level training using four baseline trackers, SiamRPN++ [20], SiamAttn [39], TransT [4], and TrDiMP [32], on three standard benchmarks, LaSOT [10], TrackingNet [24], and GOT-10k [16].

4.1 Implementation Details

As widely adopted in deep RL [13,28,40], we pre-train the trackers with supervised learning, which is done with frame-level training in our case, to stabilize and speed up the subsequent SLT. For each training iteration, k tracking episodes are randomly sampled from training datasets, where k is set to 8 for SiamRPN++, TransT, and TrDiMP and 12 for SiamAttn, respectively. Each episode is composed of T video frames and a single template frame and T is a hyper-parameter for training. For frame-interval augmentation, the interval is randomly chosen every time sampling the video frames and its maximum is set to 7 for SiamRPN++ and SiamAttn, and 10 for TransT and TrDiMP, respectively. We use the average overlap (AO) score for the reward function r in Eq. 6.

Many recent trackers have post-processing strategies based on geometric priors [2,4,20,32,39]. For example, SiamRPN++ has the cosine-window penalty and the shape penalty, which prevent drastic updates in target bounding box estimation. These penalties are typically not applied during frame-level training, which also brings inconsistency between training and testing. However, our sequence-level training also resolves this inconsistency problem. Note that x_n in Eq. 5 is the anchor score after post-processing.

The argmax and sampling trackers in our SLT framework share all weights for training, and our tracker behaves like the argmax tracker during inference. Thus, the additional memory cost is marginal in training, and the test-time efficiency of the original tracker is not affected by SLT. Our algorithm is implemented in Python using PyTorch with NVIDIA RTX A6000 2GPUs.

4.2 Training Dataset

For a fair comparison, we aligned the pre-training datasets for the baseline with the fine-tuning datasets for SLT as similar as possible. 1) For SiamRPN++, we adopt LaSOT, TrackingNet, and GOT-10k for both pre-training and fine-tuning. 2) Following the original paper, SiamAttn is trained on LaSOT, TrackingNet, COCO [22], and YouTube-VOS [35]. Since COCO is an image dataset, a data augmentation scheme such as shift, scale, and blur is adopted to extend the image to compose an episode. Note that the data augmentation strategy except for frame-interval augmentation is used only for COCO. 3) Finally, TransT and TrDiMP are both pre-trained using LaSOT, TrackingNet, GOT-10k, and COCO, as same as the original papers, and then fine-tuned on three video datasets, LaSOT, TrackingNet, and GOT-10k.

4.3 Evaluation

We compare the performance of SLT with four baseline trackers. Note that for a fair comparison, we strictly maintain the same test-time hyper-parameters for

Table 1. Performance of sequence-level training on LaSOT, TrackingNet, and GOT-10k.

Method		LaSOT		TrackingNet			GOT-10k		
		AUC (Δ)	P_{Norm}	AUC (Δ)	P_{Norm}	P	AO (Δ)	$SR_{0.5}$	$SR_{0.75}$
SiamRPN++	Base	51.0	60.3	68.2	78.3	68.9	49.5	58.0	30.5
	+SLT	58.4 (+7.4)	66.6	75.8 (+7.6)	81.0	71.3	62.1 (+12.6)	74.9	49.0
SiamAttn	Base	54.8	63.5	74.3	80.9	70.6	53.4	61.8	36.4
	+SLT	57.4 (+2.6)	66.2	76.9 (+2.6)	82.3	72.6	62.5 (+9.1)	75.4	50.2
TrDiMP	Base	63.3	72.3	78.1	83.3	73.1	67.1	77.4	58.5
	+SLT	64.4 (+1.1)	73.5	78.1 (+0.0)	83.1	73.1	67.5 (+0.4)	78.8	58.7
TransT	Base	64.2	73.7	81.1	86.8	80.1	66.2	75.5	58.7
	+SLT	66.8 (+2.6)	75.5	82.8 (+1.7)	87.5	81.4	67.5 (+1.3)	76.5	60.3

each method for all datasets. Only TrDiMP uses a different hyper-parameter setting for evaluation in LaSOT following the baseline paper [32].

LaSOT [10] is a recently published dataset that consists of 1,400 videos with more than 3.5M frames in total. This benchmark is widely used to measure the long-term capability of trackers. The average video length of LaSOT is more than 2,500 frames, and each sequence comprises various challenging attributes. The one-pass evaluation (OPE) protocol is used to measure the normalized precision (P_{Norm}) and the area under curve (AUC) of the success plot. Table 1 shows that the proposed method consistently improves all baseline trackers.

TrackingNet [24] is a large-scale dataset that provides 30K videos in training split and 511 videos in test split. We evaluate our trackers on the test split of TrackingNet through the evaluation server. Table 1 shows that our SLT improves the AUC score by 7.6%p, 2.6%p, and 1.7%p for SiamRPN++, SiamAttn, and TransT, respectively. It is noteworthy that the simple convolutional tracker SiamRPN++ shows competitive performance with SiamAttn with the power of SLT.

GOT-10k [16] is a large-scale dataset that contains 10k sequences for training and 180 videos for testing. For evaluation metrics, the average overlap (AO) and the success rate (SR) at overlap thresholds 0.5 and 0.75 are adopted. Following the evaluation protocol of GOT-10k, we retrain our models using only the GOT-10k train split and submit the tracking results to the evaluation server. Since the GOT-10k benchmark does not provide mask annotations, SLT-SiamAttn is trained without the mask branch. Table 1 shows that our SLT successfully improves all the baseline trackers in all evaluation metrics. Baseline models are reproduced using only the GOT-10k train split.

Comparison with SOTA Trackers. We compare the performance of the proposed SLT family with the other state-of-the-art trackers on LaSOT and TrackingNet as shown in Table 2 and 3. When compared to the recently proposed RL-based tracker PACNet [41], all four SLT trackers are showing superior performance by a large margin. SLT-TransT, which is our best model, achieves state-of-the-art performance in both benchmarks. Note that STARK-ST101 [37] uses deeper backbone (ResNet101) than TransT, which use ResNet50 backbone.

Table 2. Comparison with the state-of-the-art trackers on LaSOT.

	PACNet [41]	Ocean [43]	DiMP50 [2]	PrDiMP50 [8]	TransT [4]	STARK-ST50 [37]	STARK-ST101 [37]	SLT-SiamRPN++	SLT-SiamAttn	SLT-TrDiMP	SLT-TransT
AUC (%)	55.3	56.0	56.9	59.8	64.2	66.4	**67.1**	58.4	57.4	64.4	66.8
P_{Norm} (%)	62.8	65.1	64.3	68.0	73.7	76.3	**77.0**	66.6	66.2	73.5	75.5

Table 3. Comparison with the state-of-the-art trackers on TrackingNet.

	DiMP50 [2]	SiamFC++ [36]	MAML [31]	PrDiMP50 [8]	TransT [4]	STARK-ST50 [37]	STARK-ST101 [37]	SLT-SiamRPN++	SLT-SiamAttn	SLT-TrDiMP	SLT-TransT
AUC (%)	74.0	75.4	75.7	75.8	81.1	81.3	82.0	75.8	76.9	78.1	**82.8**
P_{Norm} (%)	80.1	80.0	82.2	81.6	86.8	86.1	86.9	81.0	82.3	83.1	**87.5**

Table 4. Comparison with the state-of-the-art trackers on GOT-10k. 'Add. data' denotes that trackers are trained using additional training datasets other than GOT-10k.

	Add. data	SiamFC++ [36]	DiMP50 [2]	Ocean [43]	PrDiMP50 [8]	TransT [4]	TrDiMP [32]	STARK-ST50 [37]	SLT-SiamRPN++	SLT-SiamAttn	SLT-TrDiMP	SLT-TransT
AO (%)		59.5	61.1	61.1	63.4	66.2	67.1	**68.0**	62.1	62.5	67.5	67.5
$SR_{0.5}$ (%)	-	69.5	71.7	72.1	73.8	75.5	77.4	77.7	74.9	75.4	**78.8**	76.5
$SR_{0.75}$ (%)		47.9	49.2	47.3	54.3	58.7	58.5	**62.3**	49.0	50.2	58.7	60.3
AO (%)	✓	-	60.4	-	65.2	71.9	68.6	71.5	56.9	62.8	69.0	**72.5**

SLT-TransT thus needs to be compared with STARK-ST50 for fairness. Table 4 also shows that both SLT-TrDiMP and SLT-TransT achieve comparable performance with state-of-the-art trackers on GOT-10k.

4.4   Analysis

We also analyze the effects of SLT using SiamRPN++ as the base tracker. The experimental analyses in this subsection are done on the *validation* split of GOT-10k and the *test* splits of LaSOT and TrackingNet.

Sequence-level Training Components. The benefit of SLT comes from sequence-level sampling, sequence-level objective, and sequence-level data augmentation. We validate the components of SLT by measuring the accuracy gains on the three benchmarks (Table 5) and performing an attribute-based analysis on LaSOT (Fig. 3).

Sequence-Level Sampling (SS). To measure the net effect of SS, we train a tracker with SS but use the frame-level objective. As shown at '+SS' in Table 5, by learning more accurate input data distribution, the tracker with SS outperforms the baseline with frame-level sampling by 4.1%p, 5.3%p, and 3.8%p, respectively, on the three benchmarks. SS allows the tracker to observe realistic appearance variations of target objects during tracking, making itself more robust to variations of aspect ratio, scale, rotation, and illumination (ARC, SC, R, IV) as seen in Fig. 3.

Sequence-Level Objective (SO). As shown at '+SS+SO' in Table 5, SO additionally improves the performance by 2.2%p, 1.5%p, and 3.6%p on three benchmarks, respectively. SO enables the tracker to reflect accumulated localization

Table 5. Effect of sequence-level training components.

Benchmark	SiamRPN++			
	Baseline	+SS (Δ)	+SS+SO (Δ)	+SS+SO+SA (Δ)
LaSOT (AUC)	51.0	55.1 (+4.1)	57.3 (+6.3)	58.4 (+7.4)
TrackingNet (AUC)	68.2	73.5 (+5.3)	75.0 (+6.8)	75.8 (+7.6)
GOT-10k (AO)	66.4	70.2 (+3.8)	73.8 (+7.4)	74.3 (+7.9)

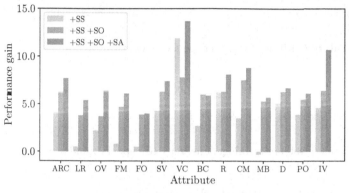

ARC: Aspect Ratio Change
LR: Low Resolution
OV: Out-of-View
FM: Fast Motion
FO: Full Occlusion
SV: Scale Variation
VC: Viewpoint Change
BC: Background Clutter
R: Rotation
CM: Camera Motion
MB: Motion Blur
D: Deformation
PO: Partial Occlusion
IV: Illumination Variation

Fig. 3. Benefits of sequence-level training components to individual attributes on the LaSOT dataset. The baseline tracker is SiamRPN++, and the y-axis is performance (AUC) gain compared with the baseline tracker.

errors, preventing it from losing the target in challenging situations such as full occlusion, background clutters, and motion blur (FO, BC, MB) as seen in Fig. 3.

Sequence-Level Augmentation (SA). As shown at '+SS+SO+SA' in Table 5, SA further improves the performance by 1.1%p, 0.8%p, and 0.5%p, respectively, resulting in the significant gain of SLT in total as 7.4%p, 7.6%p, and 7.9%p. The effectiveness of SA is also evident from the improvement in the overall attributes in Fig. 3.

To show that the frame-interval augmentation strategy of SA also potentially helps in adapting to videos with diverse frame rates, we set up tracking scenarios with lower frame rates (*i.e.*, faster motion). In the evaluation protocol, we track objects every ith frame only, skipping all the other frames; when the interval is 1, the evaluation protocol is the same as the original benchmark. Table 6 shows that the frame-interval augmentation strategy not only improves the performance in normal videos, but also makes the tracker more robust to videos with lower frame rates.

Length of Training Episodes. In training time, we randomly sample training episodes of pre-defined sequence length T. Learning temporal dependency may be affected by the length of training sequences. We thus experiment with varying T while fixing the sampled frame interval to 1. The best result is obtained with

Table 6. Effect of sequence-level augmentation (SA) in terms of video frame interval with the low frame rate protocol. The frame interval is denoted by i.

Method	SA	GOT-10k (AO)			LaSOT (AUC)			
		$i=1$	$i=2$	$i=3$	$i=1$	$i=2$	$i=3$	$i=4$
SiamRPN++	-	66.4	63.1	60.8	51.0	50.0	50.2	48.8
SLT-SiamRPN++	-	73.8	67.9	65.5	57.3	55.1	54.1	52.6
SLT-SiamRPN++	✓	74.3	70.8	67.8	58.4	56.9	56.2	54.6

Table 7. Effect of training sequence length.

Benchmark	Training sequence length (T)					
	1	4	8	16	24	32
GOT-10k (AO)	65.8	69.6	70.1	73.0	**73.8**	73.4

Table 8. Effect of frame-level pre-training. The zero (0) epoch stands for random initialization.

Method	Frame-level pre-training (epoch)				
	0	1	5	10	20
SiamRPN++	-	62.0	64.2	64.9	66.4
SLT-SiamRPN++	60.3	68.3	70.6	72.1	74.3

$T = 24$, as can be seen in Table 7. When $T = 1$, the performance does not improve over the pre-trained tracker.

Frame-level Pre-training. In our experiments, we perform SLT from a model pre-trained by frame-level training (FLT). We analyze the effect of warm-up FLT in Table 8, showing that it improves tracking performance indeed, and FLT with only a few epochs is sufficient for the warm-up. We also observed that the gain from SLT easily disappears by another few epochs of FLT (*i.e.*, FLT → SLT → FLT). In particular, the AO score of SiamRPN++ on the GOT-10k validation split reverted from 74.3% to 66.2% after 5 epochs of FLT. This indicates that SLT grants a unique gain, which FLT cannot provide.

For additional analysis and qualitative results, see the supplementary material.

5 Conclusion

We have proposed a novel sequence-level training strategy for visual object tracking to resolve the training-testing inconsistency problem of existing trackers. Unlike existing methods, it trains a tracker by actually tracking on a video and directly optimizing a tracking performance metric, boosting the generalization performance without modifying the model architecture. Experiments on SiamRPN++, SiamAttn, TransT, and TrDiMP trackers show that sequence-level sampling, objective, and augmentation are all effective in learning visual tracking.

Acknowledgement. This work was supported by Samsung Advanced Institute of Technology (Neural Processing Research Center), the NRF grants (No. 2021M3E5D2A01023887, No. 2022R1A2C3012210) and the IITP grants (No. 2021-0-01343, No. 2022-0-00959) funded by the Korea government (MSIT).

References

1. Bertinetto, L., Valmadre, J., Henriques, J.F., Vedaldi, A., Torr, P.H.S.: Fully-convolutional Siamese networks for object tracking. In: Hua, G., Jégou, H. (eds.) ECCV 2016. LNCS, vol. 9914, pp. 850–865. Springer, Cham (2016). https://doi.org/10.1007/978-3-319-48881-3_56
2. Bhat, G., Danelljan, M., Gool, L.V., Timofte, R.: Learning discriminative model prediction for tracking. In: ICCV (2019)
3. Chen, B., Wang, D., Li, P., Wang, S., Lu, H.: Real-time 'Actor-Critic' tracking. In: Ferrari, V., Hebert, M., Sminchisescu, C., Weiss, Y. (eds.) ECCV 2018. LNCS, vol. 11211, pp. 328–345. Springer, Cham (2018). https://doi.org/10.1007/978-3-030-01234-2_20
4. Chen, X., Yan, B., Zhu, J., Wang, D., Yang, X., Lu, H.: Transformer tracking. In: CVPR (2021)
5. Chen, Z., Zhong, B., Li, G., Zhang, S., Ji, R.: Siamese box adaptive network for visual tracking. In: CVPR (2020)
6. Dai, J., Qi, H., Xiong, Y., Li, Y., Zhang, G., Hu, H., Wei, Y.: Deformable convolutional networks. In: ICCV (2017)
7. Danelljan, M., Bhat, G., Khan, F.S., Felsberg, M.: Atom: accurate tracking by overlap maximization. In: CVPR (2019)
8. Danelljan, M., Gool, L.V., Timofte, R.: Probabilistic regression for visual tracking. In: CVPR (2020)
9. Dong, X., Shen, J., Wang, W., Liu, Y., Shao, L., Porikli, F.: Hyperparameter optimization for tracking with continuous deep q-learning. In: CVPR (2018)
10. Fan, H., et al.: LaSOT: a high-quality benchmark for large-scale single object tracking. In: CVPR (2019)
11. Girshick, R.: Fast R-CNN. In: ICCV (2015)
12. Henschel, R., Zou, Y., Rosenhahn, B.: Multiple people tracking using body and joint detections. In: CVPR (2019)
13. Hester, T., et al.: Deep q-learning from demonstrations. In: AAAI (2018)
14. Hu, H.N., et al.: Joint monocular 3d vehicle detection and tracking. In: ICCV (2019)
15. Huang, C., Lucey, S., Ramanan, D.: Learning policies for adaptive tracking with deep feature cascades. In: ICCV (2017)
16. Huang, L., Zhao, X., Huang, K.: Got-10k: a large high-diversity benchmark for generic object tracking in the wild. TPAMI. **43**, 1562–1577 (2019)
17. III, J.S.S., Ramanan, D.: Tracking as online decision-making: Learning a policy from streaming videos with reinforcement learning. In: ICCV (2017)

18. Javed, S., Danelljan, M., Khan, F.S., Khan, M.H., Felsberg, M., Matas, J.: Visual object tracking with discriminative filters and Siamese networks: a survey and outlook. arXiv preprint arXiv:2112.02838 (2021)
19. Jung, I., Son, J., Baek, M., Han, B.: Real-time MDNet. In: Ferrari, V., Hebert, M., Sminchisescu, C., Weiss, Y. (eds.) ECCV 2018. LNCS, vol. 11208, pp. 89–104. Springer, Cham (2018). https://doi.org/10.1007/978-3-030-01225-0_6
20. Li, B., Wu, W., Wang, Q., Zhang, F., Junliang Xing, J.Y.: SiamRPN++: evolution of Siamese visual tracking with very deep networks. In: CVPR (2019)
21. Li, B., Yan, J., Wu, W., Zhu, Z., Hu, X.: High performance visual tracking with Siamese region proposal network. In: CVPR (2018)
22. Lin, T.-Y., et al.: Microsoft COCO: common objects in context. In: Fleet, D., Pajdla, T., Schiele, B., Tuytelaars, T. (eds.) ECCV 2014. LNCS, vol. 8693, pp. 740–755. Springer, Cham (2014). https://doi.org/10.1007/978-3-319-10602-1_48
23. Marvasti-Zadeh, S.M., Cheng, L., Ghanei-Yakhdan, H., Kasaei, S.: Deep learning for visual tracking: a comprehensive survey. IEEE Transactions on Intelligent Transportation Systems (2021)
24. Müller, M., Bibi, A., Giancola, S., Alsubaihi, S., Ghanem, B.: TrackingNet: a large-scale dataset and benchmark for object tracking in the wild. In: Ferrari, V., Hebert, M., Sminchisescu, C., Weiss, Y. (eds.) ECCV 2018. LNCS, vol. 11205, pp. 310–327. Springer, Cham (2018). https://doi.org/10.1007/978-3-030-01246-5_19
25. Nam, H., Han, B.: Learning multi-domain convolutional neural networks for visual tracking. In: CVPR (2016)
26. Real, E., Shlens, J., Mazzocchi, S., Pan, X., Vanhoucke, V.: YouTube-boundingboxes: a large high-precision human-annotated data set for object detection in video. In: CVPR (2017)
27. Ren, L., Yuan, X., Lu, J., Yang, M., Zhou, J.: Deep reinforcement learning with iterative shift for visual tracking. In: Ferrari, V., Hebert, M., Sminchisescu, C., Weiss, Y. (eds.) ECCV 2018. LNCS, vol. 11213, pp. 697–713. Springer, Cham (2018). https://doi.org/10.1007/978-3-030-01240-3_42
28. Rennie, S.J., Marcheret, E., Mroueh, Y., Ross, J., Goel, V.: Self-critical sequence training for image captioning. In: CVPR (2017)
29. Russakovsky, O., et al.: ImageNet large scale visual recognition challenge. IJCV. 115, 211–252 (2015)
30. Smeulders, A.W., Chu, D.M., Cucchiara, R., Calderara, S., Dehghan, A., Shah, M.: Visual tracking: an experimental survey. TPAMI. 36, 1444–1468 (2013)
31. Wang, G., Luo, C., Sun, X., Xiong, Z., Zeng, W.: Tracking by instance detection: a meta-learning approach. In: CVPR (2020)
32. Wang, N., Zhou, W., Wang, J., Li, H.: Transformer meets tracker: exploiting temporal context for robust visual tracking. In: CVPR (2021)
33. Williams, R.J.: Simple statistical gradient-following algorithms for connectionist reinforcement learning. Mach. Learn. 8, 229–256 (1992)
34. Wu, Y., Lim, J., Yang, M.H.: Online object tracking: a benchmark. In: CVPR (2013)
35. Xu, N., et al.: YouTube-VOS: sequence-to-sequence video object segmentation. In: Ferrari, V., Hebert, M., Sminchisescu, C., Weiss, Y. (eds.) ECCV 2018. LNCS, vol. 11209, pp. 603–619. Springer, Cham (2018). https://doi.org/10.1007/978-3-030-01228-1_36
36. Xu, Y., Wang, Z., Li, Z., Yuan, Y., Yu, G.: SiamFC++: towards robust and accurate visual tracking with target estimation guidelines. In: CVPR (2020)
37. Yan, B., Peng, H., Fu, J., Wang, D., Lu, H.: Learning spatio-temporal transformer for visual tracking. In: ICCV (2021)

38. Yan, B., Zhang, X., Wang, D., Lu, H., Yang, X.: Alpha-Refine: boosting tracking performance by precise bounding box estimation. In: CVPR (2021)
39. Yu, Y., Xiong, Y., Huang, W., Scott, M.R.: Deformable Siamese attention networks for visual object tracking. In: CVPR (2020)
40. Yun, S., Choi, J., Yoo, Y., Yun, K., Young Choi, J.: Action-decision networks for visual tracking with deep reinforcement learning. In: CVPR (2017)
41. Zhang, D., Zheng, Z., Jia, R., Li, M.: Visual tracking via hierarchical deep reinforcement learning. In: AAAI (2021)
42. Zhang, W., et al.: Online decision based visual tracking via reinforcement learning. In: NIPS (2020)
43. Zhang, Z., Peng, H., Fu, J., Li, B., Hu, W.: Ocean: object-aware anchor-free tracking. In: Vedaldi, A., Bischof, H., Brox, T., Frahm, J.-M. (eds.) ECCV 2020. LNCS, vol. 12366, pp. 771–787. Springer, Cham (2020). https://doi.org/10.1007/978-3-030-58589-1_46
44. Zhang, Z., Gonzalez-Garcia, A., van de Weijer, J., Danelljan, M., Khan, F.S.: Learning the model update for Siamese trackers. In: ICCV (2019)
45. Zhu, Z., et al.: Distractor-aware Siamese networks for visual object tracking. In: Ferrari, V., Hebert, M., Sminchisescu, C., Weiss, Y. (eds.) ECCV 2018. LNCS, vol. 11213, pp. 103–119. Springer, Cham (2018). https://doi.org/10.1007/978-3-030-01240-3_7

Learned Monocular Depth Priors
in Visual-Inertial Initialization

Yunwen Zhou[✉], Abhishek Kar, Eric Turner, Adarsh Kowdle, Chao X. Guo,
Ryan C. DuToit, and Konstantine Tsotsos

Google AR, Mountain View, USA
{verse,abhiskar,elturner,adarshkowdle,chaoguo,
rdutoit,ktsotsos}@google.com

Abstract. Visual-inertial odometry (VIO) is the pose estimation backbone for most AR/VR and autonomous robotic systems today, in both
academia and industry. However, these systems are highly sensitive to
the initialization of key parameters such as sensor biases, gravity direction, and metric scale. In practical scenarios where high-parallax or variable acceleration assumptions are rarely met (e.g. hovering aerial robot,
smartphone AR user not gesticulating with phone), classical visual-
inertial initialization formulations often become ill-conditioned and/or
fail to meaningfully converge. In this paper we target visual-inertial initialization specifically for these low-excitation scenarios critical to in-
the-wild usage. We propose to circumvent the limitations of classical
visual-inertial structure-from-motion (SfM) initialization by incorporating a new learning-based measurement as a higher-level input. We leverage learned monocular depth images (mono-depth) to constrain the relative depth of features, and upgrade the mono-depths to metric scale
by jointly optimizing for their scales and shifts. Our experiments show a
significant improvement in problem conditioning compared to a classical
formulation for visual-inertial initialization, and demonstrate significant
accuracy and robustness improvements relative to the state-of-the-art
on public benchmarks, particularly under low-excitation scenarios. We
further extend this improvement to implementation within an existing
odometry system to illustrate the impact of our improved initialization
method on resulting tracking trajectories.

Keywords: Visual-inertial initialization · Monocular depth ·
Visual-inertial structure from motion

Supplementary Information The online version contains supplementary material
available at https://doi.org/10.1007/978-3-031-20047-2_32.

1   Introduction

Monocular visual-inertial odometry (VIO) enables accurate tracking of metric 3D position and orientation (pose) using just a monocular camera and inertial measurement unit (IMU) providing linear acceleration and rotational velocity. These techniques have unlocked an economical and near-ubiquitous solution for powering complex scene understanding in augmented or virtual reality (AR/VR) experiences (e.g. [15]) on commodity platforms (e.g., Google's ARCore and Apple's ARKit), alongside other robotic applications such as aerial delivery drones. A precondition of successful operation in these scenarios is successful (and accurate) initialization of key system parameters such as scale, initial velocity, accelerometer and gyro biases, and initial gravity direction. Poor initialization typically leads to tracking divergence, unacceptable transients, low-accuracy operation, or outright failures, especially of downstream modules (e.g. drone navigation software). Unfortunately, visual-inertial initialization routines

(a) **First Row:** Intensity image inputs. **Second Row:** Mono-depth images. **Third Row:** Metric-depth images, recovered after joint motion, scale, and shift optimization. Stable metric-depth is recovered after the optimization from initial inconsistent and inaccurate mono-depth. **Green Tracks on First Row:** Inlier feature-tracks for mono depth constraints. **Red Tracks on First Row:** Outlier feature-tracks due to temporally inconsistent associated mono-depth values (see Sec. 3.3)

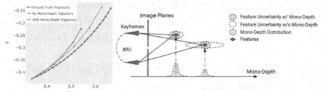

(b) **Left:** Initialization trajectory under a limited motion scenario in meters. Trajectory recovery is improved with tight coupling between VI-SFM and mono-depth (note incorrect scale in blue trajectory). **Right:** Mono-depth coupling improves problem conditioning, potentially reducing uncertainty of estimates and increasing accuracy.

Fig. 1. At top, demonstration of depth constraints over an initialization window. At bottom, demonstration of trajectories estimated with and without mono depth on the sequence shown at **top**, illustration of feature position uncertainty.

have a very common failure mode in these realistic scenarios: insufficient motion for the system's motion and calibration states to be unambiguously resolvable [29,33,35,47,60]. This occurs, for example, if the user of a phone-based AR game moves with very little parallax relative to the visible scene or when a drone must initialize while hovering. These are extremely common in practice. To improve VIO initialization in these scenarios on commodity hardware we must optimize for the total (user-visible) latency to initialization and accuracy of the resulting trajectories, while not violating real-time operation. For example, a phone-based AR user may expect a responsive ($< 500ms$) startup of their game, regardless of how they moved their phone, and without taking noticeable compute resources from the primary AR application.

Due to its impact, many recent works have focused on formulating fast and accurate initialization algorithms for robust monocular VIO [8,34,43,47,50,62]. These works rely on sparse visual feature tracks to constrain relative pose (up to scale) in the visual-inertial structure-from-motion (VI-SFM) problem. Under low parallax initialization scenarios, any classical depth estimation approach for these features in the VI-SFM problem will be susceptible to large uncertainty, such as in the sequence in Fig. 1a. This uncertainty (illustrated in Fig. 1b) makes the overall system ill-conditioned, often resulting in poor or failed initializations. This ambiguity is exacerbated if the inertial measurements lack enough variation to reliably recover metric scale [47].

Inspired by the robustness achievements of depth-enabled visual SLAM systems [13,17,48,59] and recent advances in generalized learning-based monocular depth (mono-depth) [51,52], we propose a novel formulation of monocular VIO initialization. We incorporate depth measurements from a mono-depth model directly into a classical VI-SFM framework as measurements. Our proposed method operates in real-time on a mobile phone and is able to accurately initialize in traditionally challenging low parallax or limited acceleration scenarios, *without* requiring an additional dedicated sensor for estimating depth (e.g. LiDAR, Time-of-Flight). Our primary contributions are:

- We apply learned monocular depth priors for VIO initialization. To the best of our knowledge, we are the first to leverage the power of learned depth for this problem through coupling with classical methods.
- We propose a novel residual function which tightly couples scale and shift invariant monocular depth measurements within a traditional VI-SFM formulation.
- We propose a gradient-based residual weighting function and an outlier rejection module to effectively deal with noisy depth predictions.
- We demonstrate robust and accurate initialization relative to the state-of-the-art on public benchmarks when embedded within an existing tracking system, particularly under low-excitation scenarios (i.e. when accelerometer readings or velocity do not significantly change across the initialization window). We achieve all of the above while maintaining real-time performance 10 Hz image streams on resource constrained devices.

2   Related Work

Visual-inertial odometry [31,53] is a well-studied problem in both the computer vision and robotics communities and many works [6,18,20,30,39,44,49,56,57] have focused specifically on accurate initial estimation of states required by the inertial sensor. These works can be roughly classified into two categories - 1) jointly solving a visual-inertial SFM problem directly in closed form or as a bundle adjustment problem [7,43,47] and 2) cascaded approaches which solve a pure visual SFM for up to scale pose followed by metric scale recovery using inertial observations [8,42,50,62]. Both approaches typically use a visual-inertial bundle adjustment (VI-BA) step to further refine their solution.

Feature-based visual odometry (VO) plays a key role in VIO initialization but often exhibits large uncertainty in low parallax and motion scenarios. Additionally, the VO prior requires enough non-zero inertial measurements for observing metric scale [47] to initialize VIO. A recent state-of-the-art method [8] (used as the initialization routine for the popular ORBSLAM3 system [6]) still requires around 2 s (10 Hz) to initialize and only succeeds with reasonable motion excitation. Our proposed method aims to initialize with lower (user-visible) latency (i.e. less data collection time) even in challenging low-motion scenarios. Some prior works have explored using higher order visual information such as lines [42] for increased system observability in monocular VIO. Additionally, RGB-D SLAM systems [13,17,48] have been tremendously successful in a number of domains (AR/VR, self driving cars, etc.) and can inherently initialize faster given direct metric depth observations. For example, [25] demonstrated that the inclusion of a depth sensor significantly reduces the required number of feature observations. However, in spite of their advantages, depth sensors can significantly increase the cost and/or complexity of a device. Our work is focused on improving VIO initialization for commodity devices equipped with only an IMU and single camera.

With the advent of deep learning, there has been significant interest in end-to-end learning for VIO [2,10,12,26,41,58]. However, the proposed methods often lack the explainability and modular nature of traditional VIO systems, have alternative end-goals (e.g. self supervised depth/optical flow/camera pose estimation), or are too expensive to operate on commodity hardware without custom accelerators. Moreover, end-to-end methods don't explicitly consider in-motion initialization and often benchmark on datasets with the trajectory starting at stationary point [5,22]. Prior works have also explored learning methods in purely inertial [9,28,46] or visual systems [4,36,54]. CodeVIO [61] demonstrated that incorporating a differentiable depth decoder into an existing VIO system (OpenVINS) [23] can improve tracking odometry accuracy. Note that CodeVIO does not tackle the VIO initialization problem and relies on tracking landmarks from already-initialized VIO. It uses the OpenVINS initialization solution which only initializes after observing enough IMU excitation following a static period. However, CodeVIO does demonstrate an effective and modular integration of learned priors within VIO and inspires us to deliver similar improvements to VIO initialization, while operating under realtime performance constraints.

3   Methodology

Our proposed system is composed of two modules as shown in Fig. 2: 1) monocular depth inference which infers (relative) depth from each RGB keyframe, and 2) a VIO initialization module which forms a visual-inertial structure-from-motion (VI-SFM) problem, with the relative depth constraints from the inferred monocular depth. This VI-SFM problem aims to estimate keyframe poses, velocity, and calibration states, which are then used as the initial condition for a full VIO system.

Like most VIO initialization algorithms [7,8,62], our VIO initialization consists of a closed-form solver, whose solution is then refined with visual-inertial bundle adjustment (VI-BA). In this section, we first briefly describe our mono-depth model. Then, we detail our contribution on employing mono-depth constraints in VI-BA refinement.

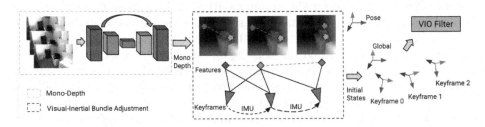

Fig. 2. Overall initialization diagram composed of monocular depth inference module running on each keyframe, and the visual-inertial bundle adjustment module. Initialized states are then fed into our VIO for tracking.

3.1   Light-Weight Monocular Depth Model

Our key contribution in this work is to incorporate prior-driven monocular depth constraints within a classical VIO initialization framework for better tracking initialization. For the final system to be practical, we require the mono-depth model to generalize to a wide variety of scenes and operate under a small compute budget. We follow recent state-of-the-art monocular depth estimation models [52] and train a lightweight mono-depth network. Specifically, we use the robust scale-shift invariant loss [52] alongside various edge-sensitive depth losses [45,52] and train a small UNet model on a variety of datasets including ScanNet [14], MannequinChallenge [45] as well as pseudo-ground truth disparity maps generated on the OpenImages [37] dataset using large pretrained publicly available models [52]. For datasets with metric depth ground truth (e.g. ScanNet), we also add a loose metric depth loss term (Charbonnier loss [3] between prediction and inverse metric depth) to inform the scale and shift priors in Eq. 5. We trained our model on gravity-aligned (or "upright") images to avoid having it learn depth maps for "sideways" images and better use its limited model capacity. Our final model is fast (Table 4), light-weight ($\sim 600K$ parameters) and predicts relative (inverse) depth maps as shown in Fig. 1a.

Given the scale-shift invariant nature of our training losses, the metric inverse depth, z, can be expressed as a scaled and shifted version of the model prediction, d, as $z = ad + b$, where a and b are the scale and shift parameters respectively. Moreover, as our model is trained on gravity aligned ("upright") images, we rotate the input image in 90-degree increments before inferring depth. Since only 45-degree accuracy is required to get the best rotation, for simplicity we use accelerometer measurements rotated through pre-calibrated IMU-camera extrinsics as an estimate of gravity in the camera frame.

3.2   VI-BA with Monocular Depth Constraints

We aim to solve for the following state parameters, $\mathcal{X}$, in our VI-BA problem

$$\mathcal{X} = [X_0; \dots; X_{N-1}; {}^{C_j}f_0; \dots; {}^{C_j}f_{M-1}; S_0; \dots; S_{N-1}] \tag{1}$$

where

- X_k represents the kth IMU keyframe state among N keyframes in total, which is $[q_k; p_k; v_k; b_k^a; b_k^\omega]$. q_k and p_k are the kth IMU keyframe pose parameterized as quarternion and translation w.r.t the global frame $\{G\}$ in which we assume the direction of gravity is known. v_k is the velocity in $\{G\}$ and b_k^a, b_k^ω are the accelerometer and gyro biases at the kth keyframes.
- ${}^{C_j}f_i$ represents the ith feature point parameterized in local inverse depth $[u_{ij}, v_{ij}, w_{ij}]^T$ with respect to the jth keyframe's camera coordinates. u_{ij} and v_{ij} lie on normalized image XY plane and w_{ij} is the inverse depth [11].
- $S_k = [a_k; b_k]$ following Sect. 3.1, which are scale and shift for recovering metric depth from the raw mono-depth at the kth keyframe.
- The IMU-camera extrinsics (q_C, p_C) and 3D-2D projection parameters $Proj(\cdot)$ are not estimated due to lack of information in such a small initialization window. We adopt pre-calibrated values as is customary.

We initialize the state $\mathcal{X}$ using a standard closed-form solver [43] for a VI-SFM problem formulated with reprojection error. Its formulation and derivation are presented in the supplemental material. Given keyframes $\mathcal{K}$, with up to scale and shift mono inverse depth, feature points $\mathcal{F}$, and $\mathcal{L}(\subset \mathcal{F})$ feature points with mono inverse depth measurements, the VI-BA minimizes the following objective function:

$$\hat{\mathcal{X}} = \underset{\mathcal{X}}{\arg\min} \underbrace{\sum_{(i,j)\in\mathcal{K}} \|r_{\mathcal{I}_{ij}}\|_{\Sigma_{ij}}^2}_{\text{Inertial Constraints}} + \underbrace{\sum_{i\in\mathcal{F}}\sum_{k\in\mathcal{K}} \rho(\|r_{\mathcal{F}_{ik}}\|_{\Sigma_{\mathcal{F}}}^2)}_{\text{Visual Constraints}}$$
$$+ \underbrace{\sum_{i\in\mathcal{L}}\sum_{k\in\mathcal{K}} \lambda_{ik}\rho(\|r_{\mathcal{L}_{ik}}\|^2)}_{\text{Mono-Depth Constraints}} + \underbrace{\|r_0\|_{\Sigma_0}^2 + \sum_{i\in\mathcal{K}} \|r_{S_i}\|_{\Sigma_S}^2}_{\text{Prior Constraints}} \tag{2}$$

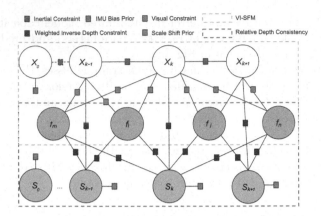

Fig. 3. A factor graph illustration of the VI-SFM depth refinement problem Eq. (2). Circled nodes represent $\mathcal{X}$ in Eq. (1) to be estimated. They are connected by constraints illustrated in the graph. The **pink dashed box** is the traditional VI-SFM problem. The **green dashed box** represents the new proposed constraints to maintain relative feature depth consistency across keyframes. Feature points and poses are constrained through the scale-shift parameters S.

where $r_{\mathcal{I}_{ij}}$ is the IMU preintegration residual error [19] corresponding to IMU measurements between two consecutive keyframes, $r_{\mathcal{F}_{ik}}$ is the standard visual reprojection residual resulting from subtracting a feature-point's pixel measurement from the projection of f_i into the kth keyframe [27], $r_{\mathcal{L}_{ik}}$ is an inverse depth temporal consistency residual for incorporating mono-depth, and $r_{\mathcal{S}_i}$ is a residual relative to a prior for scale and shift (Sect. 3.3). r_0 is a prior for the bias estimates of the $0th$ keyframe and Σ_0, Σ_{ij}, $\Sigma_{\mathcal{F}}$, $\Sigma_{\mathcal{S}}$ are the corresponding measurement covariance matrices. λ_{ik} is a scalar weight for each depth residual and $\rho(.)$ refers the huber-loss function [32].

The factor graph resulting from (2) is illustrated in Fig. 3. $(r_{\mathcal{I}_{ij}}, r_{\mathcal{F}_{ik}}, r_0)$ forms the traditional VI-SFM problem as highlighted in the pink dashed box. The following sections detail the proposed depth constraints $(r_{\mathcal{L}_{ik}}, r_{\mathcal{S}_i})$ which are grouped by green dashed box.

3.3   Weighted Mono-Depth Constraints

As illustrated in Fig. 3, depth constraints relate observed feature-point depth with that keyframe's scale-shift parameters, S_k. Hence only 2 additional parameters are needed to model the hundreds of mono-depth residual equations for each keyframe-landmark pair. As demonstrated in Sect. 4, this improves the system conditioning under motion restricted scenarios.

The depth constraints comprise three major components - the **residual function**, the **weight** for each residual and the **outlier rejection** module to reject inconsistent mono-depth measurements across keyframes.

Inverse Depth Residual Function. Inspired by the loss functions employed in monocular deep depth estimation [16], our proposed depth residual for keyframe k and feature point i takes the form of the *log* of the ratio between the measured depth scaled/shifted by $\boldsymbol{S}_k$ and the feature point's estimated depth:

$$r_{\mathcal{L}_{ik}} = \log\left((a_k d_{ik} + b_k) \cdot \Omega(^{C_j}\boldsymbol{f}_i, \boldsymbol{q}_j, \boldsymbol{p}_j, \boldsymbol{q}_k, \boldsymbol{p}_k)\right) \tag{3}$$

where $\Omega(\cdot)$ is the depth of the feature point i (which is parameterized with respect to keyframe j) in keyframe k. If $k = j$ then $\Omega(\cdot)$ can be simplified to w_{ij}^{-1}. This is how we tie mono-depth parameters to multiple features and poses to better constrain the problem. The derivation details for $\Omega(\cdot)$ are presented in supplemental material.

It is well known that this residual can lead to a degenerate solution of scale going to zero or a negative value [21]. To avoid this, we adopt the common technique of defining the scale parameter a_k as

$$a_k = \varepsilon + \log(e^{s_k} + 1) \tag{4}$$

where $\varepsilon = 10^{-5}$, which prevents a_k from being either negative or zero, allowing us to optimize s_k freely.

Scale-Shift Prior. Reiterating Sect. 3.1, the ML model is trained on certain metric depth datasets with a loss where the scale is supposed to be 1 and shift is 0. We define prior residuals for scale and shift at the ith frame as

$$\boldsymbol{r}_{\mathcal{S}_i} = \begin{bmatrix} 1 - a_i & -b_i \end{bmatrix}^T \tag{5}$$

Since metric depth is not observable from the ML model, in practice we assign a *very* large covariance $\Sigma_{\mathcal{S}}$ to these scale-shift priors terms (0.3 for scale, 0.2 for shift), which keeps parameters bounded to the regime in which model training occurred, and in degenerate situations such as zero-acceleration, allows us to converge to a sensible scale.

Figure 1a shows the effectiveness of the depth constraints and scale-shift priors. With them, we are able to upgrade the learned depth to metric level. The better-conditioned problem then yields a more accurate trajectory, illustrated in Fig. 1b.

Edge Awareness Weight. The ML model doesn't explicitly yield prediction uncertainty, however, we empirically observe the uncertainty is larger near depth edges and propose a loss weight, λ_{ik}, which modulates the residual with gradients of image I_k and depth D_k as follows

$$\lambda_{ik} = e^{-(\alpha|\nabla^2\Phi(I_k(u_{ik}, v_{ik}))| + |\nabla^2\Phi(D_k(u_{ik}, v_{ik}))|)} \tag{6}$$

where ∇^2 is the laplacian operator, $\Phi(\cdot)$ is a bilateral filter for sharpening image and depth edges, α is a hyperparameter for relative weighting of image/depth gradients and (u_{ik}, v_{ik}) is the pixel location of the feature point in keyframe k. This weight diminishes the effect of depth constraints on feature points near image/depth edges and favors non-edge regions where the depth and image gradients are in agreement.

Outlier Rejection for Depth Measurements. The weighting function Eq. (6) helps mitigate effects of erroneous mono-depth measurements at a given keyframe, but cannot reconcile inconsistency in depth measurements across keyframes. For a short initialization window ($< 2s$), keyframe images tend not to vary drastically. Given this, we expect the mono-depth output to not vary significantly as well (even though they are up to an unknown scale and shift). For example, if the mono-depth model predicts a feature point to have small depth w.r.t the rest of the scene in one keyframe but large depth in another, the mono-depth residuals for this given feature are likely to be unreliable and should not be included in the final optimization.

Algorithm 1. Outlier Depth Measurements Rejection

Input: Mono-depth residuals $r_{\mathcal{L}ik}, i \in \mathcal{L}, k \in \mathcal{K}$; thresholds $\sigma_{\min}, \sigma_{\max}$

Output: Set of inlier mono-depth residuals

1: $\sigma_{\mathcal{L}} \leftarrow \{\}$
2: **for** $i \in \mathcal{L}$ **do**
3:     Append $\sigma_i = \sqrt{\frac{\sum_k (r_{ik} - \hat{r}_i)}{N-1}}$ to $\sigma_{\mathcal{L}}$
4: **end for**
5: **if** percentile$(\sigma_{\mathcal{L}}, 25) > \sigma_{\max}$ **then**
        return $\{\}$
6: **else if** percentile$(\sigma_{\mathcal{L}}, 85) < \sigma_{\min}$ **then**
        return $\{r_{\mathcal{L}ik}, \forall i \in \mathcal{L}, \forall k \in \mathcal{K}\}$
7: **else**
        return $\{r_{\mathcal{L}ik} | \sigma_i < \text{percentile}(\sigma_{\mathcal{L}}, 85)\}$
8: **end if**

Thus, we devise an outlier-rejection scheme detailed in Algorithm 1. This algorithm first evaluates the standard deviations of residuals involving a given feature point, $\sigma_{\mathcal{L}} = \{\sigma_i, \forall i \in \mathcal{L}\}$. Then depending on the distribution of $\sigma_{\mathcal{L}}$ we choose the inlier set. (i) If the 25th percentile of $\sigma_{\mathcal{L}}$ is larger than a maximum threshold, we reject all mono-depth constraints. This scenario occurs when the ML inference is highly unstable and typically does not yeild useful constraints. (ii) When mono-depth constraints are generally self-consistent (the 85th percentile of $\sigma_{\mathcal{L}}$ is smaller than a minimum threshold) we accept all mono-depth constraints. (iii) In all other cases, we reject residuals corresponding to σ_i in upper 15th percentile of $\sigma_{\mathcal{L}}$, removing the least self-consistent constraints. Such a scenario is depicted in Sect. 1, where the mono-depth residuals involving red feature tracks are rejected.

In practice, we require an up-to-scale accurate estimate of camera pose and feature position to evaluate $r_{\mathcal{L}ik}$ for input to Algorithm 1. Therefore, we first solve the VI-BA without mono-depth (i.e., the pink rectangle portion of Fig. 3). Finally after convergence of the depth-less cost-function, we add the depth constraints as detailed in this section, and solve Eq. (2).

4   Experiments

We perform two sets of experiments on the popular EuRoC dataset [5], containing visual and inertial data from a micro air vehicle (MAV) along with accurate motion ground truth. To generate reliable correspondences for visual and mono-depth constraints, our front-end uses gyro measurements as a prior for frame-to-frame rotations following 2-pt RANSAC [55]. We first exhaustively evaluate VIO initialization performance on the whole trajectory by running our initialization routine in windows sampled throughout each trajectory in the dataset, which is commonly done in a variety initialization works [8,42,62]. Additionally, we also evaluate the effect of initialization on tracking performance by employing our method on a baseline similar to OpenVINS [23] in 10 s time windows distributed uniformly across datasets. In both cases, we compare against ground truth poses captured by a VICON system present in the dataset.

4.1   Exhaustive Initialization Evaluation

Following prior related initialization works [8,42,62], we exhaustively create VIO initialization events across the whole trajectory to evaluate performance across different motion and visual scenarios. For a fair comparison, we split each dataset into segments evenly and attempt to initialize all methods on the same set of segments. We collect poses from all successful initializations for the evaluation, **though note:** not all trials are successful due to internal validation steps of the respective algorithms and success does not necessarily mean that the initialization poses are **qualified** for tracking. Accuracy may be poor (measured by scale error or RMSE), in which case tracking may diverge.

Our baseline method consists of a closed-form initialization [43] followed by VI-BA [40] with only the VI-SFM portion of residuals present (pink rectangle in Fig. 3). We also compare against the state-of-the-art VI-initialization method Inertial-only [8], implementation of which is obtained from the open-sourced SLAM method [6]. Given N keyframes, Inertial-only uses up-to-scale visual odometry as the prior in a MAP framework to recover the metric scale, gravity vector, and IMU biases, followed by a VI-BA refinement step. Inertial-only's visual front-end performs RANSAC with PnP [38].

We configured all three methods to operate on 10Hz image streams following previous works [8,50,62]. We treat each image as a keyframe and use either 5 or 10 keyframes (KFs) for initialization. In the 5KFs setting, we split datasets into $0.8s$ initialization windows evenly. For practical applications, faster initialization is preferred. So we specifically highlight a 5KFs experiment to further exacerbate issues of insufficient baseline/motion, which are commonplace in deployment scenarios (e.g. MAVs, AR/VR). Other detailed experimental results for 10KFs under $10Hz/4Hz$ settings (also studied in [8]) are presented in the supplemental material.

We were able to generate 1078, 1545, 1547, initialization trajectories respectively for Inertial-only, baseline, and our proposed method over all EuRoC datasets from 1680 initialization attempts. The average initialization trajectory latency for the three methods were 0.592 s, 0.399 s, and 0.399 s respectively. For our 10KFs setting, we split datasets into $1.6s$ windows. We generated 571, 809, 815 initialization trajectories for the three methods with an average trajectory latency of 1.367, 0.897 and 0.897 from 839 initialization attempts. Since Inertial-only uses visual odometry as the prior, to better align with the resulting expectations across different methods, we rejected those trajectories with poor resulting reprojection error of each visual constraint for the baseline and our proposed method. We observed that Inertial-only had longer initialization latency and typically led to fewer successful initializations because it requires mean trajectory acceleration larger than 0.5% of gravity ($||\bar{a}|| > 0.005G$) as stated in [8].

To measure trajectory accuracy, we perform a $Sim(3)$ alignment against the ground truth trajectory to get scale error and position RMSE for each initialization. Since the global frames of the IMU sensor should be gravity-aligned, the gravity RMSE (in degrees) is computed from the global z axis angular deviation in the IMU frame. Following past work [8], we omit scale errors when the mean trajectory acceleration $||\bar{a}|| < 0.005G$, however gravity and position RMSE are still reported. Finally, we also empirically compute the condition number of the problem hessian in the most challenging of sequences (mean acceleration $||\bar{a}|| < 0.005G$) to evaluate problem conditioning with the added mono-depth constraints. We present our aggregated results for the 5KFs setting in Table 1. We significantly outperform state-of-the-art Inertial-only in all metrics, achieving on average a 43% reduction in scale error, 61% reduction in position RMSE, and 21% reduction in gravity RMSE for the challenging $5KF$ setting at an initialization latency of 0.4 s. Furthermore, our formulation leads to a lower condition number compared to the baseline, indicating improved problem conditioning.

To demonstrate the importance of the scale/shift priors, edge weighting, and outlier rejection introduced in this work, we present results of an ablation study in Table 2. This study shows each component significantly improves the overall performance of the system.

In Fig. 4, we plot the cumulative distributions for the metrics above for both the 10 KFs (top) and 5 KFs (bottom) settings. We can see that while we do better than the baseline and Inertial-only in the 10 KFs setting, the gains are greater in the more challenging 5 KFs setting with low-excitation, highlighting the benefit of the mono-depth residuals. In order to gain insights into where our method outperforms others, we visualize a dataset with trajectory color coded by acceleration magnitude and scale error for the various methods in Fig. 5. We outperform both Inertial-only and the baseline almost across the

Table 1. Exhaustive initialization benchmark results per dataset from Inertial-only, our baseline, and our proposed method using 5 KFs with 10 Hz image data. For each metric, lower is better.

Dataset	Scale Error (%) $\|\bar{a}\| > 0.005\,G$			Position RMSE (meters)			Gravity RMSE (degrees)			log(Condition Num) $\|\bar{a}\| < 0.005\,G$	
	Inertial-only	Baseline	Ours	Inertial-only	Baseline	Ours	Inertial-only	Baseline	Ours	Baseline	Ours
mh_01	41.34	43.65	**31.11**	0.047	0.035	**0.025**	**1.38**	2.43	1.82	13.97	**13.16**
mh_02	38.80	41.41	**34.98**	0.048	0.033	**0.026**	**1.33**	2.04	1.81	13.31	**12.50**
mh_03	57.44	59.09	**34.65**	0.145	0.091	**0.055**	3.09	3.73	**2.89**	13.83	**12.73**
mh_04	74.29	56.26	**48.40**	0.179	0.090	**0.075**	2.38	2.69	**2.31**	13.42	**11.27**
mh_05	70.35	54.64	**44.52**	0.145	0.078	**0.063**	**2.13**	2.77	2.30	13.66	**12.51**
v1_01	55.44	54.25	**25.59**	0.056	0.038	**0.021**	3.47	3.73	**3.36**	12.93	**11.43**
v1_02	56.86	45.12	**26.12**	0.106	0.069	**0.038**	3.77	3.86	**2.44**	13.26	**11.67**
v1_03	56.93	38.55	**20.01**	0.097	0.048	**0.025**	5.36	3.59	**2.37**	12.62	**12.03**
v2_01	42.40	40.84	**23.51**	0.035	0.026	**0.015**	1.49	1.78	**1.35**	13.45	**12.84**
v2_02	41.27	34.31	**19.33**	0.035	0.026	**0.015**	2.92	2.66	**1.96**	**12.20**	12.27
v2_03	59.64	36.42	**27.87**	0.116	0.044	**0.033**	4.10	2.81	**2.24**	13.30	**11.17**
Mean	54.07	45.87	**30.55**	0.092	0.053	**0.036**	2.86	2.92	**2.26**	13.27	**12.14**

Table 2. Aggregated exhaustive initialization benchmark ablation study of our proposed method using 5 KFs with 10 Hz image data for all EuRoC datasets. For each metric, lower is better.

Metrics	Ours	Ours w/o Prior	Ours w/o Weight	Ours w/o Outlier rejection	Ours w/o Everything
Scale error (%) $\|\bar{a}\| > 0.005G$	**31.23**	35.47	34.22	36.59	37.55
Position RMSE (meters)	**0.036**	0.041	0.041	0.039	0.044
Gravity RMSE (degrees)	**2.26**	2.53	2.46	2.46	2.57
log(Condition Num) $\|\bar{a}\| < 0.005G$	**12.14**	13.24	13.23	13.18	13.49

whole trajectory but more specifically so in low acceleration regions which are traditionally the hardest for classical VIO initialization methods. This further validates our hypothesis that the added mono-depth constraints condition the system better with direct (up to scale/shift) depth measurement priors in low-excitation scenarios, which is critical for today's practical applications of VIO.

4.2 Visual-Inertial Odometry Evaluation

To better illustrate our method's in-the-wild applicability, we conduct experiments quantifying the impact of our method when used in-the-loop with odometry. Considering the additional challenge of 5KFs initialization, we focus our experiments there instead of typical 10KFs [8] and evaluate the accuracy of final tracking trajectories. The evaluation is performed with a baseline similar to OpenVINS [23], which is a state-of-the art VIO system commonly used in compute-limited use-cases (e.g., mobile AR/VR, drones). Similar to 4.1, we create initialization events periodically but evaluate the tracking trajectories instead. We split the datasets evenly into 10s segments and initialize and perform VIO using the same 10s of information for both methods.

As in Sect. 4.1, our baseline is tracking initialized with VI-SFM only. We generated a total of 142 trajectories using our protocol over all EuRoC datasets for each method and report aggregated position and gravity RMSE for each dataset. The aggregated results are shown in Table 3 where we see an 84% improvement in position RMSE and 46% improvement in gravity RMSE over the baseline method. This suggests a significant expected improvement in downstream uses of odometry, such as rendering virtual content, depth estimation, or navigation.

Computation Cost. We ran our system on a Pixel4XL mobile phone using only CPU cores. The computation cost (in milliseconds) for different initializa-

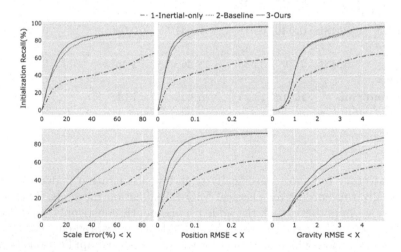

Fig. 4. Cumulative distribution plots for primary error metrics. **First row**: Results with 10 keyframes. **Second row**: Results with 5 keyframes. For each plot, the X axis denotes a threshold for error metric and the Y axis shows the fraction of initialization attempts with the respective error metric smaller than the threshold on the X axis. **Note:** 1) Improved gains in the 5KF (i.e. less motion) setting where mono-depth residuals show greater impact. 2) Recall doesn't converge to 100% due to initialization failures among attempts.

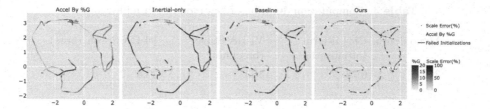

Fig. 5. Acceleration and scale error visualizations for the v2_01 dataset (best viewed in color). **Left:** Trajectory colored by acceleration magnitude as %G (lighter indicates low acceleration). **Right:** Segments of poses colored by scale error magnitude for each initialization window in the dataset (lighter is better). Segments colored black indicate failed initializations for the respective methods. We outperform other methods over the entire trajectory on scale error, especially in low acceleration regions, e.g. left side of the plot, where our method performs significantly better.

Table 3. Visual-inertial odometry benchmark results over all EuRoC datasets with and without mono-depth constraints used in initialization. VIO runs at 10 Hz and is initialized with 5KFs.

Dataset	Position RMSE (m)			Gravity RMSE (deg)		
	Baseline	Ours	Diff (%)	Baseline	Ours	Diff (%)
mh_01	1.560	**0.543**	−65.19	2.21	**1.55**	−29.86
mh_02	0.604	**0.071**	−88.24	1.65	**1.31**	−20.60
mh_03	2.466	**1.299**	−47.32	2.88	**2.29**	−20.48
mh_04	0.526	**0.124**	−76.42	2.01	**1.01**	−49.75
mh_05	3.204	**0.910**	−71.59	3.44	**1.88**	−45.34
v1_01	3.438	**0.082**	−97.61	4.66	**2.69**	−42.27
v1_02	2.846	**0.097**	−96.59	3.57	**1.22**	−65.82
v1_03	2.649	**0.059**	−97.77	3.19	**1.28**	−59.87
v2_01	1.824	**0.046**	−97.47	2.19	**1.08**	−50.68
v2_02	2.615	**0.060**	−97.70	3.42	**1.25**	−63.45
v2_03	2.939	**0.567**	−80.70	3.99	**2.06**	−48.37
Mean	2.243	**0.351**	−84.35	3.02	**1.61**	−46.68

tion modules is shown in Table 4. The closed-form initialization problem is solved using Eigen [24] and the subsequent VI-BA is solved with the Ceres Solver [1] using Levenberg-Marquardt. We run ML inference on the CPU in its own thread and hence achieve real-time performance (within $100ms$ for the $10Hz$ configuration) on a mobile phone. While we do observe that adding depth constraints increases the computational cost of the VI-SFM problem, we still improve in terms of overall initialization speed by producing a satisfactory solution with only 5KFs (**0.5 s of data**) as opposed to 10 KFs typically required by the baseline and Inertial-only.

Table 4. Computation duration of key modules in milliseconds.

Mono depth	Closed-form Initialization	VI-BA Solver (baseline)	VI-BA Solver (ours)
71.64	0.73	16.2	39.8

5 Conclusion

In this paper, we introduced a novel VIO initialization method leveraging learned monocular depth. We integrated the learned depth estimates, with alignment parameters, into a classical VI-SFM formulation. Through the learned image priors, our method gains significant robustness to typical degenerate motion configurations for VI-SFM, such as low parallax and low excitation (near-zero) acceleration. This method only requires a lightweight ML model and additional residuals (with associated states) to be added to a standard pipeline and does not significantly impact runtime, enabling application on mobile devices. Our experiments demonstrated significant improvements to accuracy, problem conditioning, and robustness relative to the state-of-the-art, even when significantly reducing the number of keyframes used and exacerbating the problem of low excitation. Our method could serve as a straightforward upgrade for most traditional pipelines. There are several key limitations and directions for future work to call out:

- We do not claim any direct upgrades to VI system observability. While the use of a prior on scale and shift and the training of the mono-depth network (assuming scale and shift being 1 and 0) may provide some direct scale information, our work's primary contribution is to problem conditioning and behaviour under *limited* motion, not *zero* motion.
- Mono-depth has generalization limitations due to biases in its training data, learning scheme, and model structure. It is crucial to note that we **did not re-train** our network for EuRoC. It was used *off the shelf* after training on general imagery which are very different from EuRoC. With a network trained specifically for the problem domain (or optimized in the loop at test time per initialization window) we expect an even greater improvement.

Acknowledgements. We thank Josh Hernandez and Maksym Dzitsiuk for their support in developing our real-time system implementation.

References

1. Agarwal, S., Mierle, K., Others: Ceres solver. https://ceres-solver.org
2. Almalioglu, Y., et al.: SelfVIO: self-supervised deep monocular visual-inertial odometry and depth estimation. CoRR abs/1911.09968 (2019). https://doi.org/arxiv.org/abs/1911.09968

3. Barron, J.T.: A general and adaptive robust loss function. In: Proceedings of the IEEE/CVF Conference on Computer Vision and Pattern Recognition, pp. 4331–4339 (2019)
4. Bloesch, M., Czarnowski, J., Clark, R., Leutenegger, S., Davison, A.J.: CodeSLAM-learning a compact, optimisable representation for dense visual slam. In: Proceedings of the IEEE/CVF Conference on Computer Vision and Pattern Recognition, pp. 2560–2568 (2018)
5. Burru, M., et al.: The EuRoC micro aerial vehicle datasets. Int. J. Robot. Res. **35**(10), 1157–1163 (2016)
6. Campos, C., Elvira, R., Rodríguez, J.J.G., Montiel, J.M., Tardós, J.D.: ORB-SLAM3: an accurate open-source library for visual, visual-inertial, and multimap slam. IEEE Trans. Robot. **37**(6), 1874–1890 (2021)
7. Campos, C., Montiel, J.M.M., Tardós, J.D.: Fast and robust initialization for visual-inertial SLAM. CoRR abs/1908.10653 (2019), https://doi.org/arxiv.org/abs/1908.10653
8. Campos, C., Montiel, J.M., Tardós, J.D.: Inertial-only optimization for visual-inertial initialization. In: 2020 IEEE International Conference on Robotics and Automation (ICRA), pp. 51–57. IEEE (2020)
9. Chen, C., Lu, X., Markham, A., Trigoni, N.: IONet: learning to cure the curse of drift in inertial odometry. In: Proceedings of the AAAI Conference on Artificial Intelligence (2018)
10. Chen, C., et al.: Selective sensor fusion for neural visual-inertial odometry. In: Proceedings of the IEEE/CVF Conference on Computer Vision and Pattern Recognition, pp. 10542–10551 (2019)
11. Civera, J., Davison, A.J., Montiel, J.M.: Inverse depth parametrization for monocular slam. IEEE Trans. Rob. **24**(5), 932–945 (2008)
12. Clark, R., Wang, S., Wen, H., Markham, A., Trigoni, N.: ViNet: visual-inertial odometry as a sequence-to-sequence learning problem. In: Proceedings of the AAAI Conference on Artificial Intelligence (2017)
13. Concha, A., Civera, J.: RGBDTAM: A cost-effective and accurate RGB-D tracking and mapping system. CoRR abs/1703.00754 (2017). https://doi.org/arxiv.org/abs/1703.00754
14. Dai, A., Chang, A.X., Savva, M., Halber, M., Funkhouser, T., Nießner, M.: ScanNet: richly-annotated 3d reconstructions of indoor scenes. In: Proceedings Computer Vision and Pattern Recognition (CVPR). IEEE (2017)
15. Du, R., et al.: DepthLab: real-time 3D interaction with depth maps for mobile augmented reality. In: Proceedings of the 33rd Annual ACM Symposium on User Interface Software and Technology, pp. 829–843 (2020)
16. Eigen, D., Puhrsch, C., Fergus, R.: Depth map prediction from a single image using a multi-scale deep network. CoRR abs/1406.2283 (2014). https://doi.org/arxiv.org/abs/1406.2283
17. Endres, F., Hess, J., Sturm, J., Cremers, D., Burgard, W.: 3-D mapping with an RGB-D camera. IEEE Trans. Rob. **30**(1), 177–187 (2013)
18. Fei, X., Soatto, S.: Xivo: an open-source software for visual-inertial odometry (2019). https://doi.org/github.com/ucla-vision/xivo
19. Forster, C., Carlone, L., Dellaert, F., Scaramuzza, D.: On-manifold preintegration theory for fast and accurate visual-inertial navigation. CoRR abs/1512.02363 (2015). https://doi.org/arxiv.org/abs/1512.02363
20. Forster, C., Pizzoli, M., Scaramuzza, D.: SVO: fast semi-direct monocular visual odometry. In: 2014 IEEE International Conference on Robotics and Automation (ICRA), pp. 15–22. IEEE (2014)

21. Garg, R., Wadhwa, N., Ansari, S., Barron, J.T.: Learning single camera depth estimation using dual-pixels. CoRR abs/1904.05822 (2019). https://doi.org/arxiv.org/abs/1904.05822

22. Geiger, A., Lenz, P., Stiller, C., Urtasun, R.: Vision meets robotics: the kitti dataset. Int. J. Rob. Res. (IJRR) **32**(11), 1231–1237 (2013)

23. Geneva, P., Eckenhoff, K., Lee, W., Yang, Y., Huang, G.: OpenVINS: a research platform for visual-inertial estimation. In: 2020 IEEE International Conference on Robotics and Automation (ICRA), pp. 4666–4672. IEEE (2020)

24. Guennebaud, G., Jacob, B., et al.: Eigen v3 (2010). https://eigen.tuxfamily.org

25. Guo, C.X., Roumeliotis, S.I.: IMU-RGBD camera 3D pose estimation and extrinsic calibration: observability analysis and consistency improvement. In: 2013 IEEE International Conference on Robotics and Automation, pp. 2935–2942 (2013). https://doi.org/10.1109/ICRA.2013.6630984

26. Han, L., Lin, Y., Du, G., Lian, S.: DeepVIO: self-supervised deep learning of monocular visual inertial odometry using 3D geometric constraints. In: 2019 IEEE/RSJ International Conference on Intelligent Robots and Systems (IROS), pp. 6906–6913. IEEE (2019)

27. Hartley, R.I., Zisserman, A.: Multiple View Geometry in Computer Vision, 2nd edn. Cambridge University Press, ISBN: 0521540518 (2004)

28. Herath, S., Yan, H., Furukawa, Y.: RoNIN: robust neural inertial navigation in the wild: benchmark, evaluations, and new methods. In: 2020 IEEE International Conference on Robotics and Automation (ICRA), pp. 3146–3152 (2020). https://doi.org/10.1109/ICRA40945.2020.9196860

29. Hernandez, J., Tsotsos, K., Soatto, S.: Observability, identifiability and sensitivity of vision-aided inertial navigation. In: 2015 IEEE International Conference on Robotics and Automation (ICRA), pp. 2319–2325. IEEE (2015)

30. Huai, Z., Huang, G.: Robocentric visual-inertial odometry. In: 2018 IEEE/RSJ International Conference on Intelligent Robots and Systems (IROS), pp. 6319–6326. IEEE (2018)

31. Huang, G.: Visual-inertial navigation: a concise review. In: 2019 International Conference on Robotics and Automation (ICRA), pp. 9572–9582 (2019). https://doi.org/10.1109/ICRA.2019.8793604

32. Huber, P.J.: Robust estimation of a location parameter. In: Kotz, S., Johnson, N.L. (eds.) Breakthroughs in statistics, pp. 492–518. Springer, New York (1992). https://doi.org/10.1007/978-1-4612-4380-9_35

33. Jones, E., Vedaldi, A., Soatto, S.: Inertial structure from motion with autocalibration. In: Workshop on Dynamical Vision, vol. 25, p. 11 (2007)

34. Kaiser, J., Martinelli, A., Fontana, F., Scaramuzza, D.: Simultaneous state initialization and gyroscope bias calibration in visual inertial aided navigation. IEEE Rob. Autom. Lett. **2**(1), 18–25 (2017). https://doi.org/10.1109/LRA.2016.2521413

35. Kelly, J., Sukhatme, G.S.: Visual-inertial sensor fusion: localization, mapping and sensor-to-sensor self-calibration. Int. J. Rob. Res. **30**(1), 56–79 (2011)

36. Kopf, J., Rong, X., Huang, J.B.: Robust consistent video depth estimation. In: IEEE/CVF Conference on Computer Vision and Pattern Recognition (2021)

37. Krasin, I., et al.: OpenImages: a public dataset for large-scale multi-label and multi-class image classification. Dataset available from https://storage.googleapis.com/openimages/web/index.html (2017)

38. Lepetit, V., Moreno-Noguer, F., Fua, P.: EPNP: an accurate o(n) solution to the PNP problem. Int. J. Computer Vis. **81**(2), 155 (2009)

39. Leutenegger, S., Lynen, S., Bosse, M., Siegwart, R., Furgale, P.: Keyframe-based visual-inertial odometry using nonlinear optimization. Int. J. Rob. Res. **34**(3), 314–334 (2015)
40. Leutenegger, S., Lynen, S., Bosse, M., Siegwart, R., Furgale, P.: Keyframe-based visual-inertial odometry using nonlinear optimization. Int. J. Rob. Res. **34**(3), 314–334 (2015)
41. Li, C., Waslander, S.L.: Towards end-to-end learning of visual inertial odometry with an EKF. In: 2020 17th Conference on Computer and Robot Vision (CRV), pp. 190–197. IEEE (2020)
42. Li, J., Bao, H., Zhang, G.: Rapid and robust monocular visual-inertial initialization with gravity estimation via vertical edges. In: 2019 IEEE/RSJ International Conference on Intelligent Robots and Systems (IROS), pp. 6230–6236 (2019). https://doi.org/10.1109/IROS40897.2019.8968456
43. Li, M., Mourikis, A.I.: A convex formulation for motion estimation using visual and inertial sensors. In: Proceedings of the Workshop on Multi-View Geometry, held in conjunction with RSS. Berkeley, CA, July 2014
44. Li, M., Mourikis, A.I.: High-precision, consistent EKF-based visual-inertial odometry. Int. J. Rob. Res. **32**(6), 690–711 (2013)
45. Li, Z., et al.: Learning the depths of moving people by watching frozen people. In: Proceedings of the IEEE Conference on Computer Vision and Pattern Recognition (CVPR) (2019)
46. Liu, W., et al.: TLIO: tight learned inertial odometry. IEEE Rob. Autom. Lett. **5**(4), 5653–5660 (2020)
47. Martinelli, A.: Closed-form solution of visual-inertial structure from motion. Int. J. Comput. Vision **106**(2), 138–152 (2014)
48. Mur-Artal, R., Tardós, J.D.: ORB-SLAM2: an open-source slam system for monocular, stereo, and RGB-D cameras. IEEE Trans. Rob. **33**(5), 1255–1262 (2017). https://doi.org/10.1109/TRO.2017.2705103
49. Qin, T., Li, P., Shen, S.: VINS-Mono: a robust and versatile monocular visual-inertial state estimator. CoRR abs/1708.03852 (2017). https://doi.org/arxiv.org/abs/1708.03852
50. Qin, T., Shen, S.: Robust initialization of monocular visual-inertial estimation on aerial robots. In: 2017 IEEE/RSJ International Conference on Intelligent Robots and Systems (IROS), pp. 4225–4232 (2017). https://doi.org/10.1109/IROS.2017.8206284
51. Ranftl, R., Bochkovskiy, A., Koltun, V.: Vision transformers for dense prediction. ArXiv preprint (2021)
52. Ranftl, R., Lasinger, K., Hafner, D., Schindler, K., Koltun, V.: Towards robust monocular depth estimation: mixing datasets for zero-shot cross-dataset transfer. IEEE Trans. Pattern Anal. Mach. Intell. (TPAMI) **44**(3), 1623–1637 (2020)
53. Scaramuzza, D., Fraundorfer, F.: Visual odometry [tutorial]. IEEE Rob. Autom. Mag. **18**(4), 80–92 (2011). https://doi.org/10.1109/MRA.2011.943233
54. Tang, C., Tan, P.: BA-Net: dense bundle adjustment networks. In: International Conference on Learning Representations (2018)
55. Troiani, C., Martinelli, A., Laugier, C., Scaramuzza, D.: 2-point-based outlier rejection for camera-IMU systems with applications to micro aerial vehicles. In: 2014 IEEE International Conference on Robotics and Automation (ICRA), pp. 5530–5536 (2014). https://doi.org/10.1109/ICRA.2014.6907672
56. Tsotsos, K., Chiuso, A., Soatto, S.: Robust inference for visual-inertial sensor fusion. In: 2015 IEEE International Conference on Robotics and Automation (ICRA), pp. 5203–5210. IEEE (2015)

57. Von Stumberg, L., Usenko, V., Cremers, D.: Direct sparse visual-inertial odometry using dynamic marginalization. In: 2018 IEEE International Conference on Robotics and Automation (ICRA), pp. 2510–2517. IEEE (2018)
58. Wang, S., Clark, R., Wen, H., Trigoni, N.: DeepVO: towards end-to-end visual odometry with deep recurrent convolutional neural networks. In: 2017 IEEE International Conference on Robotics and Automation (ICRA), pp. 2043–2050. IEEE (2017)
59. Whelan, T., Leutenegger, S., Salas-Moreno, R., Glocker, B., Davison, A.: Elasticfusion: dense slam without a pose graph. In: Robotics: Science and Systems (2015)
60. Wu, K.J., Guo, C.X., Georgiou, G., Roumeliotis, S.I.: Vins on wheels. In: 2017 IEEE International Conference on Robotics and Automation (ICRA), pp. 5155–5162. IEEE (2017)
61. Zuo, X., Merrill, N., Li, W., Liu, Y., Pollefeys, M., Huang, G.: Codevio: visual-inertial odometry with learned optimizable dense depth. In: 2021 IEEE International Conference on Robotics and Automation (ICRA), pp. 14382–14388. IEEE (2021)
62. Zuñiga-Noël, D., Moreno, F.A., Gonzalez-Jimenez, J.: An analytical solution to the IMU initialization problem for visual-inertial systems. IEEE Rob. Autom. Lett. 6(3), 6116–6122 (2021). https://doi.org/10.1109/LRA.2021.3091407

Robust Visual Tracking by Segmentation

Matthieu Paul$^{(\boxtimes)}$, Martin Danelljan, Christoph Mayer, and Luc Van Gool

Computer Vision Lab, ETH Zürich, Zürich, Switzerland
{paulma,damartin,chmayer,vangool}@vision.ee.ethz.ch

Abstract. Estimating the target extent poses a fundamental challenge in visual object tracking. Typically, trackers are *box-centric* and fully rely on a bounding box to define the target in the scene. In practice, objects often have complex shapes and are not aligned with the image axis. In these cases, bounding boxes do not provide an accurate description of the target and often contain a majority of background pixels. We propose a *segmentation-centric* tracking pipeline that not only produces a highly accurate segmentation mask, but also internally works with segmentation masks instead of bounding boxes. Thus, our tracker is able to better learn a target representation that clearly differentiates the target in the scene from background content. In order to achieve the necessary robustness for the challenging tracking scenario, we propose a separate instance localization component that is used to condition the segmentation decoder when producing the output mask. We infer a bounding box from the segmentation mask, validate our tracker on challenging tracking datasets and achieve the new state of the art on LaSOT with a success AUC score of 69.7%. Since most tracking datasets do not contain mask annotations, we cannot use them to evaluate predicted segmentation masks. Instead, we validate our segmentation quality on two popular video object segmentation datasets. The code and trained models are available at https://github.com/visionml/pytracking.

1 Introduction

Visual object tracking is the task of estimating the state of a target object for each frame in a video sequence. The target is solely characterized by its initial state in the video. Current approaches predominately characterize the state itself with a bounding box. However, this only gives a very coarse representation of the target in the image. In practice, objects often have complex shapes, undergo substantial deformations. Often, targets do not align well with the image axes, while most benchmarks use axis-aligned bounding boxes. In such cases, the majority of the image content inside the target's bounding box often consists of background regions which provide limited information about the object itself. In contrast, a segmentation mask precisely indicates the object's extent in the image (see Fig. 1 frames #1600 and #3200). Such information is vital in a variety of applications,

---

Supplementary Information The online version contains supplementary material available at https://doi.org/10.1007/978-3-031-20047-2_33.

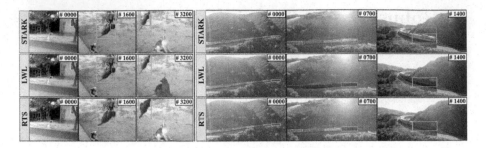

Fig. 1. Comparison between the VOT method Stark [55], the VOS method LWL [5] and our proposed method on two tracking sequences from the LaSOT [16] dataset. The ground-truth annotation (□) is shown in each frame for reference. Our approach is more robust and predicts a more accurate target representation.

including video analysis, video editing, and robotics. In this work, we therefore develop an approach for accurate and robust target object segmentation, even in the highly challenging tracking datasets [16,36].

While severely limiting the information about the target's state in the video, the aforementioned issues with the bounding box representation can itself lead to inaccurate bounding box predictions, or even tracking failure. To illustrate this, Fig. 1 shows two typical tracking sequences. The tracking method STARK [55] (first row) fails to regress bounding boxes that contain the entire object (#1600, #1400) or even starts tracking the wrong object (#0700). Conversely, segmentation masks are a better fit to differentiate pixels in the scene that belong to the background and the target. Therefore, a *segmentation-centric* tracking architecture designed to work internally with a segmentation mask of the target instead of a bounding box has the potential to learn better target representations, because it can clearly differentiate background from foreground regions in the scene.

A few recent tracking methods [47,54] have recognized the advantage of producing segmentation masks instead of bounding boxes as final output. However, these trackers are typically *bounding-box-centric* and the final segmentation mask is obtained by a separate *box-to-mask* post-processing network. These methods do not leverage the accurate target definition of segmentation masks to learn a more accurate and robust internal representation of the target.

In contrast, most Video Object Segmentation (VOS) methods [5,38] follow a *segmentation-centric* paradigm. However, these methods are not designed for the challenging tracking scenarios. Typical VOS sequences consist only of a few hundred frames [41] whereas multiple sequences of more than ten thousand frames exist in tracking datasets [16]. Due to this setup, VOS methods focus on producing highly accurate segmentation masks but are sensitive to distractors, substantial deformations and occlusions of the target object. Figure 1 shows two typical tracking sequences where the VOS method LWL [5] (second row) produces a fine-grained segmentation mask of the wrong object (#3200) or is unable to detect only the target within a crowd (#0700, #1400).

We propose *Robust Visual Tracking by Segmentation* (RTS), a unified tracking architecture capable of predicting accurate segmentation masks. To design a *segmentation-centric* approach, we take inspiration from the aforementioned LWL [5] method. However, to achieve robust and accurate segmentation on Visual Object Tracking (VOT) datasets, we introduce several new components. In particular, we propose an instance localization branch trained to predict a target appearance model, which allows occlusion detection and target identification even in cluttered scenes. The output of the instance localization branch is further used to condition the high-dimensional mask encoding. This allows the segmentation decoder to focus on the localized target, leading to a more robust mask prediction. Since our proposed method contains a segmentation and instance memory that need to be updated with previous tracking results, we design a memory management module. This module first assesses the prediction quality, decides whether the sample should enter the memory and, when necessary, triggers the model update.

Contributions. Our contributions are the following: **(i)** We propose a unified tracking architecture capable of predicting robust classification scores and accurate segmentation masks. We design separate feature spaces and memories to ensure optimal receptive fields and update rates for segmentation and instance localization. **(ii)** To produce a segmentation mask which agrees with the instance prediction, we design a fusion mechanism that conditions the segmentation decoder on the instance localization output and leads to more robust tracking performance. **(iii)** We introduce an effective inference procedure capable of fusing the instance localization output and mask encoding to ensure both robust and accurate tracking. **(iv)** We perform comprehensive evaluation and ablation studies of the proposed tracking pipeline on multiple popular tracking benchmarks. Our approach achieves the new state of the art on LaSOT with an *area-under-the-curve* (AUC) score of 69.7%.

2 Related Work

Visual Object Tracking. Over the years, research in the field of visual tracking has been accelerated by the introduction of new and challenging benchmarks, such as LaSOT [16], GOT-10k [24], and TrackingNet [37]. This led to the introduction of new paradigms in visual object tracking, based on DCFs, Siamese networks and Transformers.

One of the most popular type of approaches, DCF-based visual trackers [3,6,12,14,15,22,32,48,61] essentially solve an optimization problem to estimate the weights of the DCF that allow to distinguish foreground from background regions. The DCF is often referred to as the target appearance model and allows to localize the target in the video frame. More recent DCF approaches [3,14] enable end-to-end training by unrolling a fixed number of the optimization iterations during *offline* training.

Siamese tracking methods have gained in popularity due to their simplicity, speed and end-to-end trainability [2,20,21,28,29,43,44,50,62]. These trackers learn a similarity metric using only the initial video frame and its annotation that allows to clearly identify the target *offline*. Since no *online* learning component is involved, these trackers achieve high frame rates at the cost of limited *online* adaptability to changes of the target's appearance. Nonetheless, several methods have been proposed to overcome these issues [2, 28, 29, 44].

Very recently, Transformer-based trackers have achieved state-of-the-art performance on many datasets, often outperforming their rivals. This group of trackers typically uses a Transformer component in order to fuse information extracted from training and test frames. This produces discriminative features that allow to accurately localize and estimate the target in the scene [8, 34, 49, 55, 56].

Video Object Segmentation. Semi-supervised VOS is the task of classifying all pixels belonging to the target in each video frame, given only the segmentation mask of the target in the initial frame. The cost of annotating accurate segmentation masks is limiting the sequence length and number of videos contained in available VOS datasets. Despite the relatively small size of VOS datasets compared to other computer vision problems, new benchmarks such as Youtube-VOS [53] and DAVIS [41] accelerated the research progress in the last years.

Some methods rely on a learnt target detector [7, 33, 46], others learn how to propagate the segmentation mask across frames [25, 30, 40, 52]. Another group of methods uses feature matching techniques across one or multiple frames with or without using an explicit spatio-temporal memory [9, 23, 38, 45]. Recently, Bhat et al. [5] employed meta-learning approach, introducing an end-to-end trainable VOS architecture. In this approach, a few-shot learner predicts a learnable labels encoding. It generates and updates *online* the parameters of a segmentation target model that produces the mask encoding used to generate the final segmentation mask.

Joint Visual Tracking and Segmentation. A group of tracking methods have already identified the advantages of predicting a segmentation mask instead of a bounding box [31, 42, 47, 51, 54, 60]. Siam-RCNN is a box-centric tracker that uses a pretrained *box2seg* network to predict the segmentation mask given a bounding box prediction. In contrast, AlphaRefine represents a novel *box2seg* method that has been evaluated with many recent trackers such as SuperDiMP [14] and SiamRPN++ [28]. Further, Zhao et al. [60] focus on generating segmentation masks from bounding box annotations in videos using a spatio-temporal aggregation module to mine consistencies of the scene across multiple frames. Conversely, SiamMask [51] and D3S [31] are segmentation-centric trackers that produce a segmentation mask directly, without employing a *box2seg* module. In particular, SiamMask [51] is a fully-convolutional Siamese network with a separate branch which predicts binary segmentation masks supervised by a segmentation loss.

From a high-level view, the single-shot segmentation tracker D3S [31] is most related to our proposed method. Both methods employ two dedicated modules or branches; one for localization and one for segmentation. D3S adopts the target

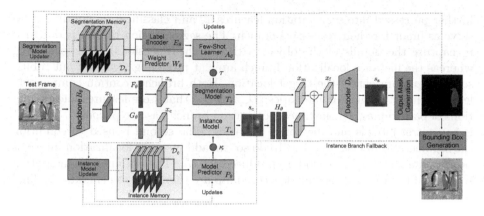

Fig. 2. Overview of our entire online tracking pipeline used for inference, see Sect. 3.1.

classification component of ATOM [12], requiring online optimization of weights in a two-layer CNN. In contrast, we learn online the weights of a DCF similar to DiMP [3]. For segmentation, D3S [31] propose a feature matching technique that matches test frame features with background and foreground features corresponding to the initial frame. In contrast, we adopt the few-shot learning based model prediction proposed in LWL [5] to produce accurate segmentation masks. Furthermore, D3S proposes to simply concatenate the outputs of both modules whereas we learn a localization encoding to condition the segmentation mask decoding based on the localization information. Compared to D3S, we update not only the instance localization but also the segmentation models and memories. Hence, our method integrates specific memory management components.

3 Method

3.1 Overview

Video object segmentation methods can produce high quality segmentation masks but are typically not robust enough for video object tracking. Robustness becomes vital for medium and long sequences, which are most prevalent in tracking datasets [16,36]. In such scenarios, the target object frequently undergoes substantial appearance changes. Occlusions and similarly looking objects are common. Hence, we propose to adapt a typical VOS approach with tracking components to increase its robustness. In particular, we base our approach on the Learning What to Learn (LWL) [5] method and design a novel and segmentation-centric tracking pipeline that estimates accurate object masks instead of bounding boxes. During inference, a segmentation mask is typically not provided in visual object tracking. Hence, we use STA [60] to generate a segmentation mask from the provided initial bounding box. An overview of our RTS method is shown in Fig. 2. Our pipeline consists of a backbone network, a segmentation branch, an instance localization branch and a segmentation decoder. For each video frame, the backbone first extracts a feature map x_b. These features are further processed into segmentation features x_s and classification features x_c to serve as input for their respective branch. The segmentation branch is designed to capture the details of the object with a high dimensional mask encoding, whereas the instance localization branch aims at providing a coarser but robust score map representing the target location. Both branches contain components learned online, trained on memories ($\mathcal{D}_s$ and $\mathcal{D}_c$) that store features and predictions of past frames. The instance localization branch has two purposes. The first is to control models and memories updating. The second is used to condition the segmentation mask decoder. To do so, we add instance localization information with a learnt score encoding produced by H_θ. The obtained segmentation scores and the raw instance model score map are then used to generate the final segmentation mask output.

3.2   Segmentation Branch

The architecture of the segmentation branch is adopted from LWL [5], and we briefly review it here. It consists of a segmentation sample memory $\mathcal{D}_s$, a label generator E_θ, a weight predictor W_θ, a few-shot learner A_θ and a segmentation model T_τ. The goal of the few-shot learner A_θ is producing the parameters τ of the segmentation model T_τ such that the obtained mask encoding x_m contains the information needed to compute the final segmentation mask of the target object. The label mask encodings used by the few-shot learner are predicted by the label generator E_θ.

The few-shot learner is formulated through the following optimization problem, which is unrolled through steepest descent iterations in the network

$$L_s(\tau) = \frac{1}{2} \sum_{(x_s, y_s) \in \mathcal{D}_s} \left\| W_\theta(y_s) \cdot (T_\tau(x_s) - E_\theta(y_s)) \right\|^2 + \frac{\lambda_s}{2} \|\tau\|^2, \qquad (1)$$

where $\mathcal{D}_s$ corresponds to the segmentation memory, x_s denotes the segmentation features, y_s the segmentation masks and λ_s is a learnable scalar regularization parameter. The weight predictor W_θ produces sample confidence weights for each spatial location in each memory sample. Applying the optimized model parameters τ^* within the segmentation model produces the mask encoding $x_m = T_{\tau^*}(x_s)$ for the segmentation features x_s.

LWL [5] feeds the mask encoding directly into the segmentation decoder to produce the segmentation mask. For long and challenging tracking sequences, only relying on the mask encoding may lead to an accurate segmentation mask, but often for the wrong object in the scene (see Fig. 1). Since LWL [5] is only able to identify the target to a certain degree in challenging tracking sequences, we propose to condition the mask encoding based on an instance localization representation, described next.

3.3   Instance Localization Branch

The segmentation branch can produce accurate masks but typically lacks the necessary robustness for tracking in medium or long-term sequences. Especially challenging are sequences where objects similar to the target appear, where the target object is occluded or vanishes from the scene for a short time. Therefore, we propose a dedicated branch for target instance localization, in order to robustly identify the target among distractors or to detect occlusions. A powerful tracking paradigm that learns a target-specific appearance model on both foreground and background information are discriminative correlation filters (DCF) [3,6,13,22]. These methods learn the weights of a filter that differentiates foreground from background pixels represented by a score map, where the maximal value corresponds to the target's center.

Similar to the segmentation branch, we propose an instance localization branch that consists of a sample memory $\mathcal{D}_c$ and a model predictor P_θ. The latter predicts the parameters κ of the instance model T_κ. The instance model is trained online to produce the target score map used to localize the target object. To obtain the instance model parameters κ we minimize the following loss function

$$L_c(\kappa) = \sum_{(x_c, y_c) \in \mathcal{D}_c} \left\| R(T_\kappa(x_c), y_c) \right\|^2 + \frac{\lambda_c}{2} \|\kappa\|^2, \tag{2}$$

where $\mathcal{D}_c$ corresponds to the instance memory containing the classification features x_c and the Gaussian labels y_c. R denotes the robust hinge-like loss [3] and λ_c is a fixed regularization parameter. To solve the optimization problem we apply the method from [3], which unrolls steepest descent iterations of the Gauss-Newton approximation of (2) to obtain the final model parameters κ^*. The score map can then be obtained with $s_c = T_{\kappa^*}(x_c)$ by evaluating the target model on the classification features x_c.

3.4 Instance-Conditional Segmentation Decoder

In video object segmentation the produced mask encoding is directly fed into the segmentation decoder to generate the segmentation mask. However, solely relying on the mask encoding is not robust enough for the challenging tracking scenario, see Fig. 1. Thus, we propose to integrate the instance localization information into the segmentation decoding procedure. In particular, we condition the mask encoding on a learned encoding of the instance localization score map.

First, we encode the raw score maps using a multi-layer Convolutional Neural Network (CNN) to learn a suitable representation. Secondly, we condition the mask encoding with the learned representation using element-wise addition. The entire conditioning procedure can be defined as $x_f = x_m + H_\theta(s_c)$, where H_θ denotes the CNN encoding the scores s_c, and x_m the mask encoding. The resulting features are then fed into the segmentation decoder that produces segmentation scores of the target object.

3.5 Jointly Learning Instance Localization and Segmentation

In this section, we describe our general training strategy and parameters. In particular, we further detail the segmentation and classification losses that we use for offline training.

Segmentation Loss. First, we randomly sample J frames from an annotated video sequence and sort them according to their frame IDs in increasing order to construct the training sequence $\mathcal{V} = \{(x_\mathrm{b}^j, y_\mathrm{s}^j, y_\mathrm{c}^j)\}_{j=0}^{J-1}$, where $x_\mathrm{b}^j = B_\theta(I^j)$ are the extracted features of the video frame I^j using the backbone B_θ, y_s^j is the corresponding segmentation mask and y_c^j denotes the Gaussian label at the target's center location. We start with entry $v_0 \in \mathcal{V}$ and store it in the segmentation $\mathcal{D}_\mathrm{s}$ and instance memory $\mathcal{D}_\mathrm{c}$ and obtain parameters τ^0 and κ^0 of the segmentation and instance model. We use these parameters to compute the segmentation loss for $v_1 \in \mathcal{V}$. Using the predicted segmentation mask, we update the segmentation model parameters to τ^1 but keep the instance model parameters fixed. Segmentation parameters typically need to be updated frequently to enable accurate segmentation. Conversely, we train the model predictor on a single frame only. The resulting instance model generalizes to multiple unseen future frames, ensuring robust target localization. The resulting segmentation loss for the entire sequence $\mathcal{V}$ can thus be described as follows

$$\mathcal{L}_\mathrm{s}^\mathrm{seq}(\theta; \mathcal{V}) = \sum_{j=1}^{J-1} \mathcal{L}_\mathrm{s}\left(D_\theta\left(T_{\tau^{j-1}}(x_\mathrm{s}^j) + H_\theta\left(T_{\kappa^0}(x_\mathrm{c}^j)\right)\right), y_\mathrm{s}^j\right), \qquad (3)$$

where $x_\mathrm{s} = F_\theta(x_\mathrm{b})$ and $x_\mathrm{c} = G_\theta(x_\mathrm{b})$ and $\mathcal{L}_\mathrm{s}$ is the Lovasz segmentation loss [1].

Classification Loss. Instead of training our tracker only with the segmentation loss, we add an auxiliary loss to ensure that the instance module produces score maps localizing the target via a Gaussian distribution. These score maps are essential to update the segmentation and instance memories and to generate the final output. As explained before, we use only the first training $v_0 \in \mathcal{V}$ to optimize the instance model parameters. To encourage fast convergence, we use not only the parameters corresponding to the final iteration N_iter of the optimization method $\kappa^0_{(N_\mathrm{iter})}$ explained in Sect. 3.3, but also all the intermediate parameters $\kappa^0_{(i)}$ of loss computation. The final target classification loss for the whole sequence $\mathcal{V}$ is defined as follows

$$\mathcal{L}_\mathrm{c}^\mathrm{seq}(\theta; \mathcal{V}) = \sum_{j=1}^{J-1} \left(\frac{1}{N_\mathrm{iter}} \sum_{i=0}^{N_\mathrm{iter}} \mathcal{L}_\mathrm{c}\left(T_{\kappa^0_{(i)}}(x_\mathrm{c}^j), y_\mathrm{c}^j\right) \right), \qquad (4)$$

where $\mathcal{L}_\mathrm{c}$ is the hinge loss defined in [3]. To train our tracker we combine the segmentation and classification losses using the scalar weight η and minimize both losses jointly

$$\mathcal{L}_\mathrm{tot}^\mathrm{seq}(\theta; \mathcal{V}) = \mathcal{L}_\mathrm{s}^\mathrm{seq}(\theta; \mathcal{V}) + \eta \cdot \mathcal{L}_\mathrm{c}^\mathrm{seq}(\theta; \mathcal{V}). \qquad (5)$$

Training Details. We use the train sets of LaSOT [16], GOT-10k [24], Youtube-VOS [53] and DAVIS [41]. For VOT datasets that only provide annotated bounding boxes we use these boxes and STA [60] to generate segmentation masks and treat them as ground truth annotations during training. STA [60] is trained separately on YouTube-VOS 2019 [53] and DAVIS 2017 [39]. For our model, we use ResNet-50 with pre-trained MaskRCNN weights as our backbone and initialize the segmentation model and decoder weights with the ones available from LWL [5]. We train for 200 epochs and sample 15'000 videos per epoch, which takes 96 h to train on a single Nvidia A100 GPU. We use the ADAM [26] optimizer with a learning rate decay of 0.2 at epochs 25, 115 and 160. We weigh the losses such that the segmentation loss is predominant but in the same range as the classification loss. We empirically choose $\eta = 10$. Further details about training and the network architecture are given in the appendix.

3.6   Inference

Memory Management and Model Updating. Our tracker consists of two different memory modules. A segmentation memory that stores segmentation features and predicted segmentation masks of previous frames. In contrast, an instance memory contains classification features and Gaussian labels marking the center location of the target in the predicted segmentation mask of the previous video frame. The quality of the predicted labels directly influences the localization and segmentation quality in future video frames. Hence, it is crucial to avoid contaminating the memory modules with predictions that do not correspond to the actual target. We propose the following strategy to keep the memory as clean as possible. (a) If the instance model is able to clearly localize the target (maximum value in the score map larger than $t_{s_c} = 0.3$) and the segmentation model constructs a valid segmentation mask (at least one pixel above $t_{s_s} = 0.5$) we update both memories with the current predictions and features. (b) If either the instance localization or segmentation fail to identify the target we omit updating the segmentation memory. (c) If only the segmentation mask fails to represent the target but the instance model can localize it, we update the instance memory only. (d) If instance localization fails we do not update either memory. Further, we trigger the few-shot learner and model predictor after 20 frames have passed, but only if the corresponding memory has been updated.

Final Mask Output Generation. We obtain the final segmentation mask by thresholding the segmentation decoder output. To obtain the bounding box required for standard tracking benchmarks, we report the smallest axis-aligned box that contains the entire estimated object mask.

Inference Details. We set the input image resolution such that the segmentation learner features have a resolution of 52×30 (stride 16), while the instance learner operates on features of size 26×15 (stride 32). The learning rate is set to 0.1 and 0.01 for the segmentation and instance learner respectively. We use a maximum buffer of 32 frames for the segmentation memory and 50 frames for the instance memory. We keep the samples corresponding to the initial frame in both memories and replace the oldest entries if the memory is full. We update both memories for the first 100 video frames and afterwards only after every 20^{nth} frame. We randomly augment the sample corresponding to the initial frame with vertical flip, random translation and blurring.

4   Evaluation

Our approach is developed within the PyTracking [11] framework. The implementation is done with PyTorch 1.9 with CUDA 11.1. Our model is evaluated on a single Nvidia GTX 2080Ti GPU. Our method achieves an average speed of 30 FPS on LaSOT [16]. Each number corresponds to the average of five runs with different random seeds.

4.1   Branch Ablation Study

For the ablation study, we analyze the impact of the instance branch on three datasets and present the results in Table 1. First, we report the performance of LWL [5] since we build upon it to design our final tracking pipeline. We use the network weights provided by Bhat *et al.* [5] and the corresponding inference settings. We input the same segmentation masks obtained from the initial bounding box for LWL as used for our method. We observe that LWL is not robust enough for challenging tracking scenarios. The second row in Table 1 corresponds to our method but we omit the proposed instance branch. Hence, we use the proposed inference components and settings and train the tracker as explained in Sect. 3.5, but with conditioning removed. We observe that even without the instance localization branch our tracker can achieve competitive performance on all three datasets (e.g +5.6% on LaSOT). Fully integrating the instance localization branch increases the performance even more (e.g +4.4 on LaSOT). Thus, we conclude that adapting the baseline method to the tracking domain improves the tracking performance. To boost the performance and achieve state-of-the-art results, an additional component able to increase the tracking robustness is required.

4.2   Inference Parameters

In this part, we ablate two key aspects of our inference strategy. First, we study the effect of relying on the instance branch if the segmentation decoder is unable to localize the target $(\max(s_s) < t_{s_s})$. Second, we study different values for t_{s_c} that determines whether the target is detected by the instance model, see Table 2.

If the segmentation branch cannot identify the target, using the instance branch improves tracking performance on all datasets (e.g +1.3% on UAV123).

Table 1. Comparison between our segmentation network baseline LWL and our pipeline, with and without Instance conditioning on different VOT datasets

Method	Seg. branch	Inst. branch	conditioning	LaSOT [16]			NFS [19]			UAV123 [36]		
				AUC	P	NP	AUC	P	NP	AUC	P	NP
LWL [5]	✓		–	59.7	60.6	63.3	61.5	75.1	76.9	59.7	78.8	71.4
RTS	✓		✗	65.3	68.5	71.5	65.8	84.0	85.0	65.2	85.6	78.8
RTS	✓		✓	69.7	73.7	76.2	65.4	82.8	84.0	67.6	89.4	81.6

Table 2. Ablation on inference strategies. The first column analyzes the effect of using the instance branch as fallback for target localization if the segmentation branch is unable to detect the target $(\max(s_s) < t_{s_s})$. The second column shows the impact of different confidence thresholds t_{s_c}

Inst. branch fallback	t_{s_c}	LaSOT [16]			NFS [19]			UAV123 [36]		
		AUC	P	NP	AUC	P	NP	AUC	P	NP
✗	0.30	69.3	73.1	75.9	65.3	82.7	84.0	66.3	87.2	80.4
✓	0.30	69.7	73.7	76.2	65.4	82.8	84.0	67.6	89.4	81.6
✓	0.20	68.6	72.3	75.0	65.3	82.7	83.9	67.0	88.7	80.7
✓	0.30	69.7	73.7	76.2	65.4	82.8	84.0	67.6	89.4	81.6
✓	0.40	69.1	72.7	75.6	63.3	79.7	81.7	67.1	89.1	80.7

Table 3. Comparison to the state of the art on the LaSOT [16] test set in terms of AUC score. The methods are ordered by AUC score

	RTS	ToMP 101 [34]	ToMP 50 [34]	Keep Track [35]	STARK ST-101 [55]	Alpha Refine [54]	TransT [8]	Siam R-CNN [47]	Tr DiMP [49]	Super DiMP [11]	STM Track [18]	Pr DiMP [14]	LWL [5]	DM Track [59]	LTMU [10]	DiMP [3]	Ocean [58]	D3S [31]
Precision	73.7	**73.5**	72.2	70.2	72.2	68.8	69.0	68.4	66.3	65.3	63.3	60.8	60.6	59.7	57.2	56.7	56.6	49.4
Norm. Prec	76.2	79.2	**78.0**	77.2	76.9	73.8	73.8	72.2	73.0	72.2	69.3	68.8	63.3	66.9	66.2	65.0	65.1	53.9
Success (AUC)	69.7	**68.5**	67.6	67.1	67.1	65.9	64.9	64.8	63.9	63.1	60.6	59.8	59.7	58.4	57.2	56.9	56.0	49.2
Δ AUC to Ours	–	1.2	2.1	2.6	2.6	3.8	4.8	4.9	5.8	6.6	9.1	9.9	10.0	11.3	12.5	12.8	13.7	20.5

Furthermore, Table 2 shows that our tracking pipeline achieves the best performance when setting $t_{s_c} = 0.3$ whereas smaller or larger values for t_{s_c} decrease the tracking accuracy. Hence, it is important to find a suitable trade-off between frequently updating the model and memory to quickly adapt to appearance changes and updating only rarely to avoid contaminating the memory and model based on wrong predictions.

4.3 Comparison to the State of the Art

Assessing segmentation accuracy on tracking datasets is not possible since only bounding box annotations are provided. Therefore, we compare our approach on six VOT benchmarks and validate the segmentation masks quality on two VOS datasets.

LaSOT [16]. We evaluate our method on the test set of the LaSOT dataset, consisting of 280 sequences with 2500 frames on average. Thus, the benchmark challenges the long term adaptability and robustness of trackers. Figure 3 shows the success plot reporting the overlap precision OP with respect to the overlap threshold T. Trackers are ranked by AUC score. In addition, Table 3 reports the precision and normalized precision for all compared methods. Our method outperforms the state-of-the-art ToMP-50 [34] and ToMP-101 [34] by large margins (+1.2% and +2.1% AUC respectively). Our method is not only as robust as KeepTrack (see the success plot for $T < 0.2$) but also estimates far more accurate bounding boxes than any tracker ($0.8 < T < 1.0$).

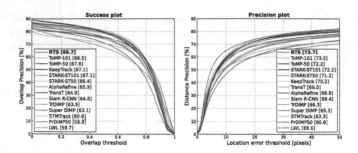

Fig. 3. Success (left) and Precision (right) plots on LaSOT [16] with other state-of-the-art methods. The AUCs for all methods are ordered and reported in the legend. Our method outperforms all existing approaches, both in Overlap Precision (left) and Distance Precision (right)

Table 4. Results on the GOT-10k validation set [24] in terms of Average Overlap (AO) and Success Rates (SR) for overlap thresholds of 0.5 and 0.75

	RTS	STA [60]	LWL [5]	PrDiMP-50 [14]	DiMP-50 [3]	SiamRPN++ [28]
$SR_{0.50}(\%)$	**94.5**	95.1	92.4	89.6	88.7	82.8
$SR_{0.75}(\%)$	**82.6**	85.2	82.2	72.8	68.8	–
$AO(\%)$	**85.2**	86.7	84.6	77.8	75.3	73.0

Table 5. Comparison to the state of the art on the TrackingNet [37] test set in terms of AUC scores, Precision and Normalized Precision

	RTS	ToMP 101 [34]	ToMP 50 [34]	Keep Track [35]	STARK ST101 [55]	STARK ST50 [55]	STA [60]	LWL [5]	TransT [8]	Siam R-CNN [47]	Alpha Refine [54]	STM Track [18]	DTT [56]	Tr DiMP [49]	Super DiMP [11]	Pr DiMP [14]	D3S [31]
Precision	79.4	78.9	78.6	73.8	–	–	79.1	78.4	80.3	**80.0**	78.3	76.7	78.9	73.1	73.3	70.4	66.4
Norm. Prec	86.0	86.4	86.2	83.5	86.9	86.1	84.7	84.4	**86.7**	85.4	85.6	85.1	85.0	83.3	83.5	81.6	76.8
Success (AUC)	81.6	81.5	81.2	78.1	82.0	81.3	81.2	80.7	81.4	81.2	80.5	80.3	79.6	78.4	78.1	75.8	72.8
Δ AUC to Ours	–	↑ 0.1	↑ 0.4	↑ 3.5	↓0.4	↑ 0.3	↑ 0.4	↑ 0.9	↑ 0.2	↑ 0.4	↑ 1.1	↑ 1.3	↑ 2.0	↑ 3.2	↑ 3.5	↑ 5.8	↑ 8.8

GOT-10k [24]. The large-scale GOT-10k dataset contains over 10.000 shorter sequences. Since we train our method on several datasets instead of only GOT-10k *train*, we evaluate it on the *val* set only, which consists of 180 short videos. We compile the results in Table 4. Our method ranks second for all metrics, falling between two VOS-oriented methods, +0.6% over LWL [5] and −1.5% behind STA [60]. Our tracker outperforms other trackers by a large margin.

TrackingNet [37]. We compare our approach on the test set of the TrackingNet dataset, consisting of 511 sequences. Table 5 shows the results obtained from the online evaluation server. Our method outperforms most of the existing approaches and ranks second in terms of AUC, close behind STARK-ST101 [55] which is based on a ResNet-101 backbone. Note that we outperform STARK-ST50 [55] that uses a ResNet-50 as backbone. Also, we achieve a higher precision score than other methods that produce a segmentation mask output such as LWL [5], STA [60], Alpha-Refine [54] and D3S [31].

Table 6. Comparison with state-of-the-art on the UAV123 [36] and NFS [19] datasets in terms of AUC score

	RTS	ToMP 101 [34]	ToMP 50 [34]	Keep Track [35]	CRACT [17]	STARK ST101 [55]	TrDiMP [49]	TransT [8]	STARK ST50 [55]	Super DiMP [11]	Pr DiMP [14]	STM Track [18]	Siam AttN [57]	Siam R-CNN [47]	KYS [4]	DiMP [3]	LWL [5]
UAV123	67.6	66.9	69.0	69.7	66.4	68.2	67.5	**69.1**	**69.1**	67.7	68.0	64.7	65.0	64.9	–	65.3	59.7
NFS	65.4	**66.7**	66.9	66.4	62.5	66.2	66.2	65.7	65.2	64.8	63.5	–	–	63.9	63.5	62.0	61.5

Table 7. Results on the VOT2020-ST [27] challenge in terms of Expected Average Overlap (EAO), Accuracy and Robustness

	RTS	STARK ST-50+AR [55]	STARK-ST-101- +AR [55]	LWL [27]	STA [60]	Ocean Plus [27]	Fast Ocean [27]	Alpha Refine [27]	RPT [27]	AFOD [27]	D3S [27]	STM [27]
Robustness	**0.845**	0.817	0.789	0.798	0.824	0.842	0.803	0.777	0.869	0.795	0.769	0.574
Accuracy	0.710	**0.759**	0.763	0.719	0.732	0.685	0.693	0.754	0.700	0.713	0.699	0.751
EAO	0.506	0.505	0.497	0.463	0.510	0.491	0.491	0.482	0.530	0.472	0.439	0.308
Δ EAO to Ours	–	0.001	0.009	0.043	↓0.004	0.015	0.045	0.024	↓0.024	0.034	0.067	0.198

UAV123 [36]. The UAV dataset consists of 123 test videos that contain small objects, target occlusion, and distractors. Small objects are particularly challenging in a segmentation setup. Table 6 shows the achieved results in terms of success AUC. Our method achieves competitive results on UAV123, close to TrDiMP [49] or SuperDiMP [11]. It outperforms LWL [5] by a large margin.

NFS [19]. The NFS dataset (30FPS version) contains 100 test videos with fast motions and challenging sequences with distractors. Our method achieves an AUC score that is only 1% below the current best method KeepTrack [35] while outperforming numerous other trackers, including STARK-ST50 [55] (+0.2) SuperDiMP [3] (+0.6) and PrDiMP [14] (+1.9).

VOT 2020 [27]. Finally, we evaluate our method on the VOT2020 short-term challenge. It consists of 60 videos and provides segmentation mask annotations. For the challenge, the multi-start protocol is used and the tracking performance is assessed based on accuracy and robustness. We compare with the top methods on the leader board and include more recent methods in Table 7. In this setup, our method ranks 2^{nth} in Robustness, thus outperforming most of the other methods. In particular, we achieve a higher EAO score than STARK [55], LWL [5], AlphaRefine [54] and D3S [31].

YouTube-VOS 2019 [53]. We use the validation set which consist of 507 sequences. They contain 91 object categories out of which 26 are *unseen* in the training set. The results presented in Table 8 were generated by an online server after uploading the raw results. On this benchmark, we want to validate the quality of the produced segmentation masks rather than to achieve the best accuracy possible. Hence, we use the same model weight as for VOT without further fine tuning.

When using the provided segmentation masks for initialization, we observe that our method performs slightly worse than LWL [5] and STA [60] ($-1.3\mathcal{G}$, $-0.9\mathcal{G}$) but still outperforms the VOS method STM [38] ($+0.5\ \mathcal{G}$). We conclude that our method can generate accurate segmentation masks. When using

Table 8. Results on the Youtube-VOS 2019 [53] and DAVIS 2017 [41] datasets. The table is split in two parts to separate methods using bounding box initialization or segmentation masks initialization, in order to enable a fair comparison

Method	YouTube-VOS 2019 [53]					DAVIS 2017 [41]		
	$\mathcal{G}$	$\mathcal{J}_{seen}$	$\mathcal{J}_{unseen}$	$\mathcal{F}_{seen}$	$\mathcal{F}_{unseen}$	$\mathcal{J}\&\mathcal{F}$	$\mathcal{J}$	$\mathcal{F}$
RTS	79.7	77.9	75.4	82.0	83.3	80.2	77.9	82.6
LWL [5]	81.0	79.6	76.4	83.8	84.2	81.6	79.1	84.1
STA [60]	80.6	–	–	–	–	–	–	–
STM [38]	79.2	79.6	73.0	83.6	80.6	81.8	79.2	84.3
RTS (Box)	70.8	71.1	65.2	74.0	72.8	72.6	69.4	75.8
LWL (Box) [5]	–	–	–	–	–	70.6	67.9	73.3
Siam-RCNN [47]	67.3	68.1	61.5	70.8	68.8	70.6	66.1	75.0
D3S [51]	–	–	–	–	–	60.8	57.8	63.8
SiamMask [31]	52.8	60.2	45.1	58.2	47.7	56.4	54.3	58.5

bounding boxes to predict both the initialization and segmentation masks, we outperform all other methods by a large margin. This confirms that even with our bounding-box initialization strategy, RTS produces accurate segmentation masks.

DAVIS 2017 [41]. Similarly, we compare our method on the validation set of DAVIS 2017 [41], which contains 30 sequences. We do not fine tune the model for this benchmark. The results are shown in Table 8 and confirm the observation made above that RTS is able to generate accurate segmentation masks. Our method is competitive in the mask-initialization setup. In the box-initialization setup however, our approach outperforms all other methods in $\mathcal{J}\&\mathcal{F}$, in particular the segmentation trackers like SiamMask [51] (+16.2) and D3S [31] (+11.8).

5   Conclusion

We introduced RTS, a robust, end-to-end trainable, segmentation-driven tracking method that is able to generate accurate segmentation masks. Compared to the traditional bounding box outputs of classical visual object trackers, segmentation masks enable a more accurate representation of the target's shape and extent. The proposed instance localization branch helps increasing the robustness of our tracker to enable reliable tracking even for long sequences of thousands of frames. Our method outperforms previous segmentation-driven tracking methods by a large margin, and it is competitive on several VOT benchmarks. In particular, we set a new state of the art on the challenging LaSOT [16] dataset with a success AUC of 69.7%. Competitive results on two VOS datasets confirm the high quality of the generated segmentation masks.

Acknowledgements. This work was partly supported by uniqFEED AG and the ETH Future Computing Laboratory (EFCL) financed by a gift from Huawei Technologies.

References

1. Berman, M., Triki, A.R., Blaschko, M.B.: The Lovász-softmax loss: a tractable surrogate for the optimization of the intersection-over-union measure in neural networks. In: Proceedings of the IEEE Conference on Computer Vision and Pattern Recognition (CVPR), June 2018
2. Bertinetto, L., Valmadre, J., Henriques, J.F., Vedaldi, A., Torr, P.H.S.: Fully-convolutional Siamese networks for object tracking. In: Hua, G., Jégou, H. (eds.) ECCV 2016. LNCS, vol. 9914, pp. 850–865. Springer, Cham (2016). https://doi.org/10.1007/978-3-319-48881-3_56
3. Bhat, G., Danelljan, M., Gool, L.V., Timofte, R.: Learning discriminative model prediction for tracking. In: Proceedings of the IEEE/CVF International Conference on Computer Vision (ICCV), October 2019
4. Bhat, G., Danelljan, M., Van Gool, L., Timofte, R.: Know your surroundings: exploiting scene information for object tracking. In: Vedaldi, A., Bischof, H., Brox, T., Frahm, J.-M. (eds.) ECCV 2020. LNCS, vol. 12368, pp. 205–221. Springer, Cham (2020). https://doi.org/10.1007/978-3-030-58592-1_13
5. Bhat, G., et al.: Learning what to learn for video object segmentation. In: Vedaldi, A., Bischof, H., Brox, T., Frahm, J.-M. (eds.) ECCV 2020. LNCS, vol. 12347, pp. 777–794. Springer, Cham (2020). https://doi.org/10.1007/978-3-030-58536-5_46
6. Bolme, D.S., Beveridge, J.R., Draper, B.A., Lui, Y.M.: Visual object tracking using adaptive correlation filters. In: CVPR (2010)
7. Caelles, S., Maninis, K.K., Pont-Tuset, J., Leal-Taixé, L., Cremers, D., Van Gool, L.: One-shot video object segmentation. In: Proceedings of the IEEE Conference on Computer Vision and Pattern Recognition, pp. 221–230 (2017)
8. Chen, X., Yan, B., Zhu, J., Wang, D., Yang, X., Lu, H.: Transformer tracking. In: Proceedings of the IEEE/CVF Conference on Computer Vision and Pattern Recognition (CVPR), June 2021
9. Chen, Y., Pont-Tuset, J., Montes, A., Van Gool, L.: Blazingly fast video object segmentation with pixel-wise metric learning. In: Proceedings of the IEEE Conference on Computer Vision and Pattern Recognition, pp. 1189–1198 (2018)
10. Dai, K., Zhang, Y., Wang, D., Li, J., Lu, H., Yang, X.: High-performance long-term tracking with meta-updater. In: Proceedings of the IEEE/CVF Conference on Computer Vision and Pattern Recognition (CVPR), June 2020
11. Danelljan, M., Bhat, G.: PyTracking: visual tracking library based on PyTorch (2019). http://github.com/visionml/pytracking
12. Danelljan, M., Bhat, G., Khan, F.S., Felsberg, M.: ATOM: accurate tracking by overlap maximization. In: Proceedings of the IEEE/CVF Conference on Computer Vision and Pattern Recognition (CVPR), June 2019
13. Danelljan, M., Bhat, G., Shahbaz Khan, F., Felsberg, M.: ECO: efficient convolution operators for tracking. In: Proceedings of the IEEE Conference on Computer Vision and Pattern Recognition (CVPR), June 2017
14. Danelljan, M., Gool, L.V., Timofte, R.: Probabilistic regression for visual tracking. In: CVPR (2020)

15. Danelljan, M., Robinson, A., Shahbaz Khan, F., Felsberg, M.: Beyond correlation filters: learning continuous convolution operators for visual tracking. In: Leibe, B., Matas, J., Sebe, N., Welling, M. (eds.) ECCV 2016. LNCS, vol. 9909, pp. 472–488. Springer, Cham (2016). https://doi.org/10.1007/978-3-319-46454-1_29

16. Fan, H., et al.: LaSOT: a high-quality benchmark for large-scale single object tracking. In: Proceedings of the IEEE/CVF Conference on Computer Vision and Pattern Recognition (CVPR), June 2019

17. Fan, H., Ling, H.: CRACT: cascaded regression-align-classification for robust visual tracking. arXiv preprint arXiv:2011.12483 (2020)

18. Fu, Z., Liu, Q., Fu, Z., Wang, Y.: STMTrack: template-free visual tracking with space-time memory networks. In: Proceedings of the IEEE/CVF Conference on Computer Vision and Pattern Recognition (CVPR), June 2021

19. Galoogahi, H.K., Fagg, A., Huang, C., Ramanan, D., Lucey, S.: Need for speed: a benchmark for higher frame rate object tracking. In: ICCV (2017)

20. Guo, Q., Feng, W., Zhou, C., Huang, R., Wan, L., Wang, S.: Learning dynamic Siamese network for visual object tracking. In: ICCV (2017)

21. He, A., Luo, C., Tian, X., Zeng, W.: Towards a better match in Siamese network based visual object tracker. In: Leal-Taixé, L., Roth, S. (eds.) ECCV 2018. LNCS, vol. 11129, pp. 132–147. Springer, Cham (2019). https://doi.org/10.1007/978-3-030-11009-3_7

22. Henriques, J.F., Caseiro, R., Martins, P., Batista, J.: High-speed tracking with kernelized correlation filters. IEEE Trans. Pattern Anal. Mach. Intell. (TPAMI) **37**(3), 583–596 (2015)

23. Hu, Y.-T., Huang, J.-B., Schwing, A.G.: VideoMatch: matching based video object segmentation. In: Ferrari, V., Hebert, M., Sminchisescu, C., Weiss, Y. (eds.) ECCV 2018. LNCS, vol. 11212, pp. 56–73. Springer, Cham (2018). https://doi.org/10.1007/978-3-030-01237-3_4

24. Huang, L., Zhao, X., Huang, K.: Got-10k: a large high-diversity benchmark for generic object tracking in the wild. IEEE Trans. Pattern Anal. Mach. Intell. (TPAMI) **43**(5), 1562–1577 (2021)

25. Khoreva, A., Benenson, R., Ilg, E., Brox, T., Schiele, B.: Lucid data dreaming for object tracking. In: The DAVIS Challenge on Video Object Segmentation (2017)

26. Kingma, D.P., Ba, J.: Adam: a method for stochastic optimization. In: Proceedings of the International Conference on Learning Representations (ICLR) (2014)

27. Kristan, M., et al.: The eighth visual object tracking VOT2020 challenge results. In: Bartoli, A., Fusiello, A. (eds.) ECCV 2020. LNCS, vol. 12539, pp. 547–601. Springer, Cham (2020). https://doi.org/10.1007/978-3-030-68238-5_39

28. Li, B., Wu, W., Wang, Q., Zhang, F., Xing, J., Yan, J.: SiamRPN++: evolution of Siamese visual tracking with very deep networks. In: Proceedings of the IEEE/CVF Conference on Computer Vision and Pattern Recognition (CVPR), June 2019

29. Li, B., Yan, J., Wu, W., Zhu, Z., Hu, X.: High performance visual tracking with Siamese region proposal network. In: Proceedings of the IEEE/CVF Conference on Computer Vision and Pattern Recognition (CVPR), June 2018

30. Li, X., Loy, C.C.: Video object segmentation with joint re-identification and attention-aware mask propagation. In: Ferrari, V., Hebert, M., Sminchisescu, C., Weiss, Y. (eds.) ECCV 2018. LNCS, vol. 11207, pp. 93–110. Springer, Cham (2018). https://doi.org/10.1007/978-3-030-01219-9_6

31. Lukezic, A., Matas, J., Kristan, M.: D3S - a discriminative single shot segmentation tracker. In: CVPR (2020)

32. Lukezic, A., Vojír, T., Zajc, L.C., Matas, J., Kristan, M.: Discriminative correlation filter tracker with channel and spatial reliability. Int. J. Comput. Vis. (IJCV) **126**(7), 671–688 (2018)

33. Maninis, K.K., et al.: Video object segmentation without temporal information. IEEE Trans. Pattern Anal. Mach. Intell. **41**(6), 1515–1530 (2018)

34. Mayer, C., et al.: Transforming model prediction for tracking. In: Proceedings of the IEEE/CVF Conference on Computer Vision and Pattern Recognition (CVPR), pp. 8731–8740, June 2022

35. Mayer, C., Danelljan, M., Paudel, D.P., Van Gool, L.: Learning target candidate association to keep track of what not to track. In: Proceedings of the IEEE/CVF International Conference on Computer Vision (ICCV), pp. 13444–13454, October 2021

36. Mueller, M., Smith, N., Ghanem, B.: A benchmark and simulator for UAV tracking. In: Leibe, B., Matas, J., Sebe, N., Welling, M. (eds.) ECCV 2016. LNCS, vol. 9905, pp. 115–101. Springer, Cham (2016). https://doi.org/10.1007/978-3-319-46448-0_27

37. Müller, M., Bibi, A., Giancola, S., Alsubaihi, S., Ghanem, B.: TrackingNet: a large-scale dataset and benchmark for object tracking in the wild. In: Ferrari, V., Hebert, M., Sminchisescu, C., Weiss, Y. (eds.) ECCV 2018. LNCS, vol. 11205, pp. 310–327. Springer, Cham (2018). https://doi.org/10.1007/978-3-030-01246-5_19

38. Oh, S.W., Lee, J.Y., Xu, N., Kim, S.J.: Video object segmentation using space-time memory networks. In: Proceedings of the IEEE/CVF International Conference on Computer Vision (ICCV), October 2019

39. Perazzi, F., Pont-Tuset, J., McWilliams, B., Van Gool, L., Gross, M., Sorkine-Hornung, A.: A benchmark dataset and evaluation methodology for video object segmentation. In: Computer Vision and Pattern Recognition (2016)

40. Perazzi, F., Khoreva, A., Benenson, R., Schiele, B., Sorkine-Hornung, A.: Learning video object segmentation from static images. In: Proceedings of the IEEE Conference on Computer Vision and Pattern Recognition, pp. 2663–2672 (2017)

41. Pont-Tuset, J., et al.: The 2017 Davis challenge on video object segmentation. arXiv:1704.00675 (2017)

42. Son, J., Jung, I., Park, K., Han, B.: Tracking-by-segmentation with online gradient boosting decision tree. In: Proceedings of the IEEE International Conference on Computer Vision (ICCV), December 2015

43. Tao, R., Gavves, E., Smeulders, A.W.M.: Siamese instance search for tracking. In: CVPR (2016)

44. Valmadre, J., Bertinetto, L., Henriques, J., Vedaldi, A., Torr, P.H.S.: End-to-end representation learning for correlation filter based tracking. In: Proceedings of the IEEE/CVF Conference on Computer Vision and Pattern Recognition (CVPR), July 2017

45. Voigtlaender, P., Chai, Y., Schroff, F., Adam, H., Leibe, B., Chen, L.C.: FEELVOS: fast end-to-end embedding learning for video object segmentation. In: Proceedings of the IEEE Conference on Computer Vision and Pattern Recognition, pp. 9481–9490 (2019)

46. Voigtlaender, P., Leibe, B.: Online adaptation of convolutional neural networks for video object segmentation. In: BMVC (2017)

47. Voigtlaender, P., Luiten, J., Torr, P.H., Leibe, B.: Siam R-CNN: visual tracking by re-detection. In: IEEE/CVF Conference on Computer Vision and Pattern Recognition (CVPR), June 2020

48. Wang, G., Luo, C., Sun, X., Xiong, Z., Zeng, W.: Tracking by instance detection: a meta-learning approach. In: Proceedings of the IEEE/CVF Conference on Computer Vision and Pattern Recognition (CVPR), June 2020
49. Wang, N., Zhou, W., Wang, J., Li, H.: Transformer meets tracker: exploiting temporal context for robust visual tracking. In: Proceedings of the IEEE/CVF Conference on Computer Vision and Pattern Recognition (CVPR), June 2021
50. Wang, Q., Teng, Z., Xing, J., Gao, J., Hu, W., Maybank, S.J.: Learning attentions: residual attentional Siamese network for high performance online visual tracking. In: CVPR (2018)
51. Wang, Q., Zhang, L., Bertinetto, L., Hu, W., Torr, P.H.: Fast online object tracking and segmentation: a unifying approach. In: Proceedings of the IEEE Conference on Computer Vision and Pattern Recognition (2019)
52. Wug Oh, S., Lee, J.Y., Sunkavalli, K., Joo Kim, S.: Fast video object segmentation by reference-guided mask propagation. In: Proceedings of the IEEE Conference on Computer Vision and Pattern Recognition, pp. 7376–7385 (2018)
53. Xu, N., et al.: YouTube-VOS: a large-scale video object segmentation benchmark (2018)
54. Yan, B., Wang, D., Lu, H., Yang, X.: Alpha-refine: boosting tracking performance by precise bounding box estimation. In: CVPR (2021)
55. Yan, B., Peng, H., Fu, J., Wang, D., Lu, H.: Learning spatio-temporal transformer for visual tracking. In: Proceedings of the IEEE/CVF International Conference on Computer Vision (ICCV), pp. 10448–10457, October 2021
56. Yu, B., et al.: High-performance discriminative tracking with transformers. In: Proceedings of the IEEE/CVF International Conference on Computer Vision (ICCV), pp. 9856–9865, October 2021
57. Yu, Y., Xiong, Y., Huang, W., Scott, M.R.: Deformable Siamese attention networks for visual object tracking. In: Proceedings of the IEEE/CVF Conference on Computer Vision and Pattern Recognition (CVPR), June 2020
58. Zhang, Z., Peng, H., Fu, J., Li, B., Hu, W.: Ocean: object-aware anchor-free tracking. In: Vedaldi, A., Bischof, H., Brox, T., Frahm, J.-M. (eds.) ECCV 2020. LNCS, vol. 12366, pp. 771–787. Springer, Cham (2020). https://doi.org/10.1007/978-3-030-58589-1_46
59. Zhang, Z., Zhong, B., Zhang, S., Tang, Z., Liu, X., Zhang, Z.: Distractor-aware fast tracking via dynamic convolutions and mot philosophy. In: Proceedings of the IEEE/CVF Conference on Computer Vision and Pattern Recognition (CVPR), June 2021
60. Zhao, B., Bhat, G., Danelljan, M., Van Gool, L., Timofte, R.: Generating masks from boxes by mining spatio-temporal consistencies in videos. In: Proceedings of the IEEE/CVF International Conference on Computer Vision (ICCV), pp. 13556–13566, October 2021
61. Zheng, L., Tang, M., Chen, Y., Wang, J., Lu, H.: Learning feature embeddings for discriminant model based tracking. In: Vedaldi, A., Bischof, H., Brox, T., Frahm, J.-M. (eds.) ECCV 2020. LNCS, vol. 12360, pp. 759–775. Springer, Cham (2020). https://doi.org/10.1007/978-3-030-58555-6_45
62. Zhu, Z., Wang, Q., Li, B., Wu, W., Yan, J., Hu, W.: Distractor-aware Siamese networks for visual object tracking. In: Ferrari, V., Hebert, M., Sminchisescu, C., Weiss, Y. (eds.) ECCV 2018. LNCS, vol. 11213, pp. 103–119. Springer, Cham (2018). https://doi.org/10.1007/978-3-030-01240-3_7

MeshLoc: Mesh-Based Visual Localization

Vojtech Panek[1,2(✉)] [ID], Zuzana Kukelova[3] [ID], and Torsten Sattler[2] [ID]

[1] Faculty of Electrical Engineering, Czech Technical University (CTU) in Prague, Prague, Czech Republic
vojtech.panek@cvut.cz
[2] Czech Institute of Informatics, Robotics and Cybernetics CTU in Prague, Prague, Czech Republic
[3] Visual Recognition Group, Faculty of Electrical Engineering CTU in Prague, Prague, Czech Republic

Abstract. Visual localization, *i.e.*, the problem of camera pose estimation, is a central component of applications such as autonomous robots and augmented reality systems. A dominant approach in the literature, shown to scale to large scenes and to handle complex illumination and seasonal changes, is based on local features extracted from images. The scene representation is a sparse Structure-from-Motion point cloud that is tied to a specific local feature. Switching to another feature type requires an expensive feature matching step between the database images used to construct the point cloud. In this work, we thus explore a more flexible alternative based on dense 3D meshes that does not require features matching between database images to build the scene representation. We show that this approach can achieve state-of-the-art results. We further show that surprisingly competitive results can be obtained when extracting features on renderings of these meshes, without any neural rendering stage, and even when rendering raw scene geometry without color or texture. Our results show that dense 3D model-based representations are a promising alternative to existing representations and point to interesting and challenging directions for future research.

Keywords: Visual localization · 3D meshes · Feature matching

1 Introduction

Visual localization is the problem of estimating the position and orientation, *i.e.*, the camera pose, from which the image was taken. Visual localization is a core component of intelligent systems such as self-driving cars [27] and other autonomous robots [40], augmented and virtual reality systems [42,45], as well as of applications such as human performance capture [26].

In terms of pose accuracy, most of the current state-of-the-art in visual localization is structure-based [11–14,16,28,59,61,65,69,74,79,92]. These approaches

Supplementary Information The online version contains supplementary material available at https://doi.org/10.1007/978-3-031-20047-2_34.

Fig. 1. Modern learned features such as Patch2Pix [94] are not only able to establish correspondences between real images (top-left), but are surprisingly good at matching between a real images and non-photo-realistic synthetic views (top-right: textured mesh, bottom-left: colored mesh, bottom-right: raw surface rendering). This observation motivates our investigation into using dense 3D meshes, rather than the Structure-from-Motion point clouds predominantly used in the literature

establish 2D-3D correspondences between pixels in a query image and 3D points in the scene. The resulting 2D-3D matches can in turn be used to estimate the camera pose, *e.g.*, by applying a minimal solver for the absolute pose problem [24,53] inside a modern RANSAC implementation [4–6,18,24,37]. The scene is either explicitly represented via a 3D model [28,29,38,39,59,62,63,65,79,92] or implicitly via the weights of a machine learning model [9–12,14–16,44,74,86].

Methods that explicitly represent the scene via a 3D model have been shown to scale to city-scale [63,79,92] and beyond [38], while being robust to illumination, weather, and seasonal changes [28,61,62,83]. These approaches typically use local features to establish the 2D-3D matches. The dominant 3D scene representation is a Structure-from-Motion (SfM) [1,70,76] model. Each 3D point in these sparse point clouds was triangulated from local features found in two or more database images. To enable 2D-3D matching between the query image and the 3D model, each 3D point is associated with its corresponding local features. While such approaches achieve state-of-the-art results, they are rather *inflexible*. Whenever a better type of local features becomes available, it is necessary to recompute the point cloud. Since the intrinsic calibrations and camera poses of the database images are available, it is sufficient to re-triangulate the scene rather than running SfM from scratch. Still, computing the necessary feature matches between database images can be highly time-consuming.

Often, it is possible to obtain a dense 3D model of the scene, *e.g.*, in the form of a mesh obtained via multi-view stereo [32,71], from depth data, from LiDAR, or from other sources such as digital elevation models [13,84]. Using a dense model instead of a sparse SfM point cloud offers more flexibility: rather than having to match features between database images to triangulate 3D scene points, one can simply obtain the corresponding 3D point from depth maps rendered from the model. Due to decades of progress in computer graphics research and development, even large 3D models can be rendered in less than a millisecond. Thus, feature matching and depth map rendering can both be done online without the need to pre-extract and store local features. This leads to the question whether one needs to store images at all or could render views of the model on demand. This in turn leads to the question how realistic these renderings need to be and thus which level of detail is required from the 3D models.

This paper investigates using dense 3D models instead of sparse SfM point clouds for feature-based visual localization. Concretely, the paper makes the following contributions: (1) we discuss how to design a dense 3D model-based localization pipeline and contrast this system to standard hierarchical localization systems. (2) we show that a very simple version of the pipeline can already achieve state-of-the-art results when using the original images and a 3D model that accurately aligns with these images. Our mesh-based framework reduces overhead in testing local features and feature matchers for visual localization tasks compared to SfM point cloud-based methods. (3) we show interesting and promising results when using non-photo-realistic renderings of the meshes instead of real images in our pipeline. In particular, we show that existing features, applied out-of-the-box without fine-tuning or re-training, perform surprisingly well when applied on renderings of the raw 3D scene geometry without any colors or textures (*cf.* Fig. 1). We believe that this result is interesting as it shows that standard local features can be used to match images and purely geometric 3D models, *e.g.*, laser or LiDAR scans. (4) our code and data are publicly available at https://github.com/tsattler/meshloc_release.

Related Work. One main family of state-of-the-art visual localization algorithms is based on local features [13,28,38,59,61,63,65,69,79–81,92]. These approaches commonly represent the scene as a sparse SfM point cloud, where each 3D point was triangulated from features extracted from the database images. At test time, they establish 2D-3D matches between pixels in a query image and 3D points in the scene model using descriptor matching. In order to scale to large scenes and handle complex illumination and seasonal changes, a hybrid approach is often used [28,29,60,67,80,81]: an image retrieval stage [2,85] is used to identify a small set of potentially relevant database images. Descriptor matching is then restricted to the 3D points visible in these images. We show that it is possible to achieve similar results using a mesh-based scene representation that allows researchers to more easily experiment with new types of features.

An alternative to explicitly representing the 3D scene geometry via a 3D model is to implicitly store information about the scene in the weights of a machine learning model. Examples include scene coordinate regression techniques [9,10,12,14–16,74,86], which regress 2D-3D matches rather than computing them via explicit descriptor matching, and absolute [33,34,47,73,89] and relative pose [3,22,36] regressors. Scene coordinate regressors achieve state-of-the-art results for small scenes [8], but have not yet shown strong performance in more challenging scenes. In contrast, absolute and relative pose regressors are currently not (yet) competitive to feature-based methods [68,95], even when using additional training images obtained via view synthesis [47,50,51].

Ours is not the first work to use a dense scene representation. Prior work has used dense Multi-View Stereo [72] and laser [50,51,75,80,81] point clouds as well as textured or colored meshes [13,48,93]. [48,50,51,72,75] render novel views of the scene to enable localization of images taken from viewpoints that differ strongly from the database images. Synthetic views of a scene, rendered from an estimated pose, can also be used for pose verification [80,81]. [47,48,93] rely on neural rendering techniques such as Neural Radiance Fields (NeRF's) [46,49] or image-to-image translation [96] while [50,72,75,93] rely on classical rendering techniques. Most related to our work are [13,93] as both use meshes for localization: given a rather accurate prior pose, provided manually, [93] render the scene from the estimated pose and match features between the real image and the rendering. This results in a set of 2D-3D matches used to refine the pose. While [93] start with poses close to the ground truth, we show that meshes can be used to localize images from scratch and describe a full pipeline for this task. While the city scene considered in [93] was captured by images, [13] consider localization in mountainous terrain, where only few database images are available. As it is impossible to compute an SfM point cloud from the sparsely distributed database images, they instead use a textured digital elevation model as their scene representation. They train local features to match images and this coarsely textured mesh, whereas we use learned features without re-training or fine-tuning. While [13] focus on coarse localization (on the level of hundreds of meters or even kilometers), we show that meshes can be used for centimeter-accurate localization. Compared to these prior works, we provide a detailed ablation study investigating how model and rendering quality impact the localization accuracy.

2   Feature-Based Localization via SfM Models

This section first reviews the general outline of state-of-the-art hierarchical structure-based localization pipelines. Section 3 then describes how such a pipeline can be adapted when using a dense instead of a sparse scene representation.

Stage 1: Image Retrieval. Given a set of database images, this stage identifies a few relevant reference views for a given query. This is commonly done via nearest neighbor search with image-level descriptors [2,25,55,85].

Stage 2: 2D-2D Feature Matching. This stage establishes feature matches between the query image and the top-k retrieved database images, which will be upgraded to 2D-3D correspondences in the next stage. It is common to use state-of-the-art learned local features [21,23,56,61,78,94]. Matches are established either by (exhaustive) feature matching, potentially followed by outlier filters such as Lowe's ratio test [41], or using learned matching strategies [57,58,61,94].

There are two representation choices for this stage: pre-compute the features for the database images or only store the photos and extract the features on-the-fly. The latter requires less storage at the price of run-time overhead. *E.g.*, storing SuperPoint [21] features for the Aachen Day-Night v1.1 dataset [66,67, 93] requires more than 25 GB while the images themselves take up only 7.5 GB (2.5 GB when reducing the image resolution to at most 800 pixels).

Stage 3: Lifting 2D-2D to 2D-3D Matches. For the i-th 3D scene point $\mathbf{p}_i \in \mathbb{R}^3$, each SfM point cloud stores a set $\{(\mathcal{I}_{i_1}, \mathbf{f}_{i_1}), \cdots (\mathcal{I}_{i_n}, \mathbf{f}_{i_n})\}$ of (image, feature) pairs. Here, a pair $(\mathcal{I}_{i_j}, \mathbf{f}_{i_j})$ denotes that feature $\mathbf{f}_{i_j}$ in image $\mathcal{I}_{i_j}$ was used to triangulate the 3D point position $\mathbf{p}_i$. If a feature in the query image matches $\mathbf{f}_{i_j}$ in database image $\mathcal{I}_{i_j}$, it thus also matches $\mathbf{p}_i$. Thus, 2D-3D matches are obtained by looking up 3D points corresponding to matching database features.

Stage 4: Pose Estimation. The last stage uses the resulting 2D-3D matches for camera pose estimation. It is common practice to use LO-RANSAC [17,24,37] for robust pose estimation. In each iteration, a P3P solver [53] generates pose hypotheses from a minimal set of three 2D-3D matches. Non-linear refinement over all inliers is used to optimize the pose, both inside and after LO-RANSAC.

Covisibility Filtering. Not all matching 3D points might be visible together. It is thus common to use a covisibility filter [38,39,60,64]: a SfM reconstruction defines the so-called visibility graph $\mathcal{G} = ((I, P), E)$ [39], a bipartite graph where one set of nodes I corresponds to the database images and the other set P to the 3D points. $\mathcal{G}$ contains an edge between an image node and a point node if the 3D point has a corresponding feature in the image. A set $M = \{(\mathbf{f}_i, \mathbf{p}_i)\}$ of 2D-3D matches defines a subgraph $\mathcal{G}(M)$ of $\mathcal{G}$. Each connected component of $\mathcal{G}(M)$ contains 3D points that are potentially visible together. Thus, pose estimation is done per connected component rather than over all matches [60,63].

3   Feature-Based Localization Without SfM Models

This paper aims to explore dense 3D scene models as an alternative to the sparse Structure-from-Motion (SfM) point clouds typically used in state-of-the-art feature-based visual localization approaches. Our motivation is three-fold:

(1) dense scene models are more flexible than SfM-based representations: SfM point clouds are specifically build for a given type of feature. If we want to use another type, *e.g.*, when evaluating the latest local feature from the literature, a new SfM point cloud needs to be build. Feature matches between the database images are required to triangulate SfM points. For medium-sized scenes, this matching process can take hours, for large scenes days or weeks. In contrast, once a dense 3D scene model is build, it can be used to directly provide the corresponding 3D point for (most of) the pixels in a database image by simply rendering a depth map. In turn, depth maps can be rendered highly efficiently

when using 3D meshes, *i.e.*, in a millisecond or less. Thus, there is only very little overhead when evaluating a new type of local features.

(2) dense scene models can be rather compact: at first glance, it seems that storing a dense model will be much less memory efficient than storing a sparse point cloud. However, our experiments show that we can achieve state-of-the-art results on the Aachen v1.1 dataset [66,67,93] using depth maps generated by a model that requires only 47 MB. This compares favorably to the 87 MB required to store the 2.3M 3D points and 15.9M corresponding database indices (for co-visibility filtering) for the SIFT-based SfM model provided by the dataset.

(3) as mentioned in Sect. 2, storing the original images and extracting features on demand requires less memory compared to directly storing the features. One intriguing possibility of dense scene representations is thus to not store images at all but to use rendered views for feature matching. Since dense representations such as meshes can be rendered in a millisecond or less, this rendering step introduces little run-time overhead. It can also help to further reduce memory requirements: *E.g.*, a textured model of the Aachen v1.1 [66,67,93] dataset requires around 837 MB compared to the more than 7 GB needed for storing the original database images (2.5 GB at reduced resolution). While synthetic images can also be rendered from sparse SfM point clouds [54,77], these approaches are in our experience orders of magnitude slower than rendering a 3D mesh.

The following describes the design choices one has when adapting the hierarchical localization pipeline from Sect. 2 to using dense scene representations.

Stage 1: Image Retrieval. We focus on exploring using dense representations for obtaining 2D-3D matches and do not make any changes to the retrieval stage. Naturally, use additional rendered views can be used to improve the retrieval performance [29,48,75]. As we are interested in comparing classical SfM-based and dense representations, we do not investigate this direction of research though.

Stage 2: 2D-2D Feature Matching. Algorithmically, there is no difference between matching features between real images and a real query image and a rendered view. Both cases result in a set of 2D-2D matches that can be upgraded to 2D-3D matches in the next stage. As such, we do not modify this stage. We employ state-of-the-art learned local features [21,23,56,61,78,94] and matching strategies [61]. We do not re-train any of the local features. Rather, we are interested in determining how well these features work out-of-the-box for non-photo-realistic images for different degrees of non-photo-realism, *i.e.*, textured 3D meshes, colored meshes where each vertex has a corresponding RGB color, and raw geometry without any color.

Stage 3: Lifting 2D-2D to 2D-3D Matches. In an SfM point cloud, each 3D point $\mathbf{p}_i$ has multiple corresponding features $\mathbf{f}_{i_1}, \cdots, \mathbf{f}_{i_n}$ from database images $\mathcal{I}_{i_1}, \cdots, \mathcal{I}_{i_n}$. Since the 2D feature positions are subject to noise, $\mathbf{p}_i$ will not precisely project to any of its corresponding features. $\mathbf{p}_i$ is computed such that it minimizes the sum of squared reprojection errors to these features, thus averaging out the noise in the 2D feature positions. If a query feature $\mathbf{q}$ matches to features $\mathbf{f}_{i_j}$ and $\mathbf{f}_{i_k}$ belonging to $\mathbf{p}_i$, we obtain a single 2D-3D match $(\mathbf{q}, \mathbf{p}_i)$.

When using a depth map obtained by rendering a dense model, each database feature $\mathbf{f}_{i_j}$ with a valid depth will have a corresponding 3D point $\mathbf{p}_{i_j}$. Each $\mathbf{p}_{i_j}$ will project precisely onto its corresponding feature, $i.e.$, the noise in the database feature positions is directly propagated to the 3D points. This implies that even though $\mathbf{f}_{i_1}, \cdots, \mathbf{f}_{i_n}$ are all noisy measurements of the same physical 3D point, the corresponding model points $\mathbf{p}_{i_1}, \cdots, \mathbf{p}_{i_n}$ will all be (slightly) different. If a query feature $\mathbf{q}$ matches to features $\mathbf{f}_{i_j}$ and $\mathbf{f}_{i_k}$, we thus obtain multiple (slightly) different 2D-3D matches $(\mathbf{q}, \mathbf{p}_{i_j})$ and $(\mathbf{q}, \mathbf{p}_{i_k})$.

There are two options to handle the resulting multi-matches: (1) we **simply use all individual matches**. This strategy is extremely simple to implement, but can also produce a large number of matches. For example, when using the top-50 retrieved images, each query feature $\mathbf{q}$ can produce up to 50 2D-3D correspondences. This in turn slows down RANSAC-based pose estimation. In addition, it can bias the pose estimation process towards finding poses that are consistent with features that produce more matches.

(2) we **merge multiple 2D-3D matches into a single 2D-3D match**: given a set $\mathcal{M}(\mathbf{q}) = \{(\mathbf{q}, \mathbf{p}_i)\}$ of 2D-3D matches obtained for a query feature $\mathbf{q}$, we estimate a single 3D point $\mathbf{p}$, resulting in a single 2D-3D correspondence $(\mathbf{q}, \mathbf{p})$. Since the set $\mathcal{M}(\mathbf{q})$ can contain wrong matches, we first try to find a consensus set using the database features $\{\mathbf{f}_i\}$ corresponding to the matching points. For each matching 3D point $\mathbf{p}_i$, we measure the reprojection error $w.r.t.$ to the database features and count the number of features for which the error is within a given threshold. The point with the largest number of such inliers[1] is then refined by optimizing its sum of squared reprojection errors $w.r.t.$ the inliers. If there is no point $\mathbf{p}_i$ with at least two inliers, we keep all matches from $\mathcal{M}(\mathbf{q})$. This approach thus aims at averaging out the noise in the database feature detections to obtain more precise 3D point locations.

Stage 4: Pose Estimation. Given a set of 2D-3D matches, we follow the same approach as in Sect. 2 for camera pose estimation. However, we need to adapt covisibility filtering and introduce a simple position averaging approach as a post-processing step after RANSAC-based pose estimation.

Covisibility Filtering. Dense scene representations do not directly provide the co-visibility relations encoded in the visibility graph $\mathcal{G}$ and we want to avoid computing matches between database images. Naturally, one could compute visibility relations between views using their depth maps. However, this approach is computationally expensive. A more efficient alternative is to define the visibility graph on-the-fly via shared matches with query features: the 3D points visible in views $\mathcal{I}_i$ and $\mathcal{I}_j$ are deemed co-visible if there exists at least one pair of matches

---

[1] We actually optimize a robust MSAC-like cost function [37] not the number of inliers.

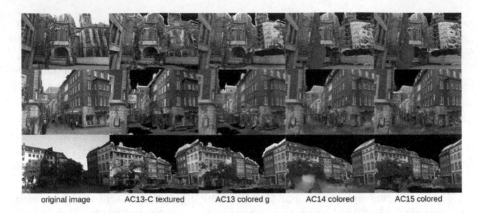

original image   AC13-C textured   AC13 colored g   AC14 colored   AC15 colored

Fig. 2. Examples of colored/textured renderings from the Aachen Day-Night v1.1 dataset [66,67,93]. We use meshes of different levels of detail (from coarsest to finest: *AC13-C, AC13, AC14,* and *AC15*) and different rendering styles: a textured 3D model (only for *AC13-C*) and meshes with per-vertex colors (*colored*). For reference, the leftmost column shows the corresponding original database image.

$(\mathbf{q}, \mathbf{f}_i)$, $(\mathbf{q}, \mathbf{f}_j)$ between a query feature $\mathbf{q}$ and features $\mathbf{f}_i \in \mathcal{I}_i$ and $\mathbf{f}_j \in \mathcal{I}_j$. In other words, the 3D points from two images are considered co-visible if at least one feature in the query image matches to a 3D point from each image.

Naturally, the 2D-2D matches (and the corresponding 2D-3D matches) define a set of connected components and we can perform pose estimation per component. However, the visibility relations computed on the fly are an approximation to the visibility relations encoded in $\mathcal{G}$: images $\mathcal{I}_i$ and $\mathcal{I}_j$ might not share 3D points, but can observe the same 3D points as image $\mathcal{I}_k$. In $\mathcal{G}(M)$, the 2D-3D matches found for images $\mathcal{I}_i$ and $\mathcal{I}_j$ thus belong to a single connected component. In the on-the-fly approximation, this connection might be missed, *e.g.*, if image $\mathcal{I}_k$ is not among the top-retrieved images. Covisibility filtering using the on-the-fly approximation might thus be too aggressive, resulting in an over-segmentation of the set of matches and a drop in localization performance.

Position Averaging. The output of pose estimation approach is a camera pose R, $\mathbf{c}$ and the 2D-3D matches that are inliers to that pose. Here, $R \in \mathbb{R}^{3 \times 3}$ is the rotation from global model coordinates to camera coordinates while $\mathbf{c} \in \mathbb{R}^3$ is the position of the camera in global coordinates. In our experience, the estimated rotation is often more accurate than the estimated position. We thus use a simple scheme to refine the position $\mathbf{c}$: we center a volume of side length $2 \cdot d_{\text{vol}}$ around the position $\mathbf{c}$. Inside the volume, we regularly sample new positions with a step size d_{step} in each direction. For each such position $\mathbf{c}_i$, we count the number I_i of inliers to the pose R, $\mathbf{c}_i$ and obtain a new position estimate $\mathbf{c}'$ as the weighted average $\mathbf{c}' = \frac{1}{\sum_i I_i} \sum_i I_i \cdot \mathbf{c}_i$. Intuitively, this approach is a simple but efficient way to handle poses with larger position uncertainty: for these poses, there will be multiple positions with a similar number of inliers and the resulting position

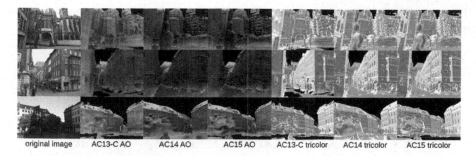

| original image | AC13-C AO | AC14 AO | AC15 AO | AC13-C tricolor | AC14 tricolor | AC15 tricolor |

Fig. 3. Example of raw geometry renderings for the Aachen Day-Night v1.1 dataset [66,67,93]. We use different rendering styles to generate synthetic views of the *raw scene geometry*: *ambient occlusion* [97] (AO) and illumination from three colored lights (*tricolor*). The leftmost column shows the corresponding original database image.

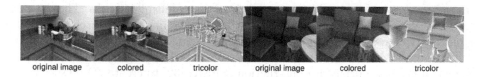

| original image | colored | tricolor | original image | colored | tricolor |

Fig. 4. Example renderings for the 12 scenes dataset [86].

c' will be closer to their average rather than the position with the largest number of inliers (which might be affected by noise in the features and 3D points). Note that this averaging strategy is not tied to using a dense scene representations.

4 Experimental Evaluation

We evaluate the localization pipeline described in Sect. 3 on two publicly available datasets commonly used to evaluate visual localization algorithms, Aachen Day-Night v1.1 [66,67,93] and 12 Scenes [86]. We use the Aachen Day-Night dataset to study the importance (or lack thereof) of the different components in the pipeline described Sect. 3. Using the original database images, we evaluate the approach using multiple learned local features [56,61,78,91,94] and 3D models of different levels of detail. We show that the proposed approach can reach state-of-the-art performance compared to the commonly used SfM-based scene representations. We further study using renderings instead of real images to obtain the 2D-2D matches in Stage 2 of the pipeline, using 3D meshes of different levels of quality and renderings of different levels of detail. A main result is that modern features are robust enough to match real photos against non-photo-realistic renderings of raw scene geometry, even though they were never trained for such a scenario, resulting in surprisingly accurate pose estimates.

Datasets. The Aachen Day-Night v1.1 dataset [66,67,93] contains 6,697 database images captured in the inner city of Aachen, Germany. All database

Table 1. Statistics for the 3D meshes used for experimental evaluation as well as rendering times for different rendering styles and resolutions

	Model	Style	Size [MB]	Vertices	Triangles	Render time [μs] 800 px	full res.
	AC13-C	textured	645	$1.4 \cdot 10^6$	$2.4 \cdot 10^6$	1143	1187
	AC13 C	tricolor	47	$1.4 \cdot 10^6$	$2.4 \cdot 10^6$	115	219
Aachen v1.1	AC13	colored	617	$14.8 \cdot 10^6$	$29.3 \cdot 10^6$	92	140
	AC13	tricolor	558	$14.8 \cdot 10^6$	$29.3 \cdot 10^6$	97	152
	AC14	colored	1234	$29.4 \cdot 10^6$	$58.7 \cdot 10^6$	100	139
	AC14	tricolor	1116	$29.4 \cdot 10^6$	$58.7 \cdot 10^6$	93	205
	AC15	colored	2805	$66.8 \cdot 10^6$	$133.5 \cdot 10^6$	98	137
	AC15	tricolor	2538	$66.8 \cdot 10^6$	$133.5 \cdot 10^6$	97	160

images were taken under daytime conditions over multiple months. The dataset also contains 824 daytime and 191 nighttime query images captured with multiple smartphones. We use only the more challenging night subset for evaluation.

To create dense 3D models for the Aachen Day-Night dataset, we use Screened Poisson Surface Reconstruction (SPSR) [32] to create 3D meshes from Multi-View Stereo [71] point clouds. We generate meshes of different levels of quality by varying the depth parameter of SPSR, controlling the maximum resolution of the Octree that is used to generate the final mesh. Each of the resulting meshes, AC13, AC14, and AC15 (corresponding to depths 13, 14, and 15, with larger depth values corresponding to more detailed models), has an RGB color associated to each of its vertices. We further generate a compressed version of AC13, denoted as AC13-C, using [31] and texture it using [88]. Figure 2 shows examples.

The 12 Scenes dataset [86] consists of 12 room-scale indoor scenes captured using RGB-D cameras, with ground truth poses created using RGB-D SLAM [20]. Each scene provides RGB-D query images, but we only use the RGB part for evaluation. The dataset further provides the colored meshes reconstructed using [20], where each vertex is associated with an RGB color, which we use for our experiments. Compared to the Aachen Day-Night dataset, the 12 Scenes dataset is "easier" in the sense that it only contains images taken by a single camera that is not too far away from the scene and under constant illumination conditions. Figure 4 shows example renderings.

For both datasets, we render depth maps and images from the meshes using an OpenGL-based rendering pipeline [87]. Besides rendering colored and textured meshes, we also experiment with raw geometry rendering. In the latter case, no colors or textures are stored, which reduces memory requirements. In order to be able to extract and match features, we rely on shading cues. We evaluate two shading strategies for the raw mesh geometry rendering: the first uses ambient occlusion [97] (AO) pre-computed in MeshLab [19]. The second one uses three colored light sources (tricolor) (*cf.* supp. mat. for details). Figs. 3

and 4 show example renderings. Statistics about the meshes and rendering times can be found in Table 1 for Aachen and in the supp. mat. for 12 Scenes.

This paper focuses on dense scene representations based on meshes. Hence, we refer to the pipeline from Sect. 3 as MeshLoc. A more modern dense scene representations are NeRFs [7,43,46,82,90]. Preliminary experiments with a recent NeRF implementation [49] resulted in realistic renderings for the 12 Scenes dataset [86]. Yet, we were not able to obtain useful depth maps. We attribute this to the fact that the NeRF representation can compensate for noisy occupancy estimates via the predicted color [52]. We thus leave a more detailed exploration of neural rendering strategies for future work. At the moment we use well-matured OpenGL-based rendering on standard 3D meshes, which is optimized for GPUs and achieves very fast rendering times (see Table 1). See Sect. 6 in supp. mat. for further discussion on use of NeRFs.

Experimental Setup. We evaluate multiple learned local features and matching strategies: SuperGlue [61] (SG) first extracts and matches SuperPoint [21] features before applying a learned matching strategy to filter outliers. While SG is based on explicitly detecting local features, LoFTR [78] and Patch2Pix [94] (P2P) densely match descriptors between pairs of images and extract matches from the resulting correlation volumes. Patch2Pix+SuperGlue (P2P+SG) uses the match refinement scheme from [94] to refine the keypoint coordinates of SuperGlue matches. For merging 2D-3D matches, we follow [94] and cluster 2D match positions in the query image to handle the fact that P2P and P2P+SG do not yield repeatable keypoints. The supp. mat. provides additional results with R2D2 [56] and CAPS [91] descriptors.

Following [8,30,66,74,83,86], we report the percentage of query images localized within X meters and Y degrees of their respective ground truth poses.

We use the LO-RANSAC [17,37] implementation from PoseLib [35] with a robust Cauchy loss for non-linear refinement (*cf.* supp. mat. for details).

Experiments on Aachen Day-Night. We first study the importance of the individual components of the MeshLoc pipeline. We evaluate the pipeline on real database images and on rendered views of different level of detail and quality. For the retrieval stage, we follow the literature [59,61,78,94] and use the top-50 retrieved database images/renderings based on NetVLAD [2] descriptors extracted from the real database and query images.

Studying the Individual Components of MeshLoc. Table 2 presents an ablation study for the individual components of the MeshLoc pipeline from Sect. 3. Namely, we evaluate combinations of using all available individual 2D-3D matches (I) or merging 2D-3D matches for each query features (M), using the approximate covisibility filter (C), and position averaging (PA). We also compare a baseline that triangulates 3D points from 2D-2D matches between the query image and multiple database images (T) rather than using depth maps.

Table 2. Ablation study on the Aachen Day-Night v1.1 dataset [66,67,93] using real images at reduced (max. side length 800 px) and full resolution (res.), and depth maps rendered using the AC13 model. We evaluate different strategies for obtaining 2D-3D matches (using all individual matches (I), merging matches (M), or triangulation (T)), with and without covisibility filtering (C), and with and without position averaging (PA) for various local features. We report the percentage of nighttime query images localized within 0.25m and 2°/0.5 m and 5°/5 m and 10° of the ground truth pose. For reference, we also report the corresponding results (from visuallocaliztion.net) obtained using SfM-based representations (last row). Best results per feature are marked in bold

res.	2D-3D	C	PA	SuperGlue (SG) [61]	LoFTR [78]	Patch2Pix [94]	Patch2Pix + SG [94]
	I			72.8/**93.2**/99.0	77.0/92.1/**99.5**	70.7/89.0/95.3	72.3/91.6/100.0
	I	✓		72.3/92.7/99.0	76.4/92.1/**99.5**	72.3/**91.1**/97.4	73.3/91.1/99.5
	I		✓	74.3/93.2/99.0	**78.5**/**93.2**/**99.5**	73.8/89.5/95.3	73.8/92.1/99.5
800	I	✓	✓	73.3/92.1/99.0	77.5/92.7/**99.5**	73.3/**91.1**/97.4	73.8/91.1/99.5
	M		✓	75.4/92.7/99.5	77.0/92.7/**99.5**	70.7/89.5/96.3	73.8/92.7/99.5
	M	✓	✓	75.4/91.6/99.5	75.4/92.1/99.5	69.6/89.0/97.4	72.8/**93.2**/**100.0**
	T		✓	72.3/90.1/97.9	73.3/90.6/98.4	63.9/83.8/94.8	70.7/90.6/97.4
	T	✓	✓	71.7/89.5/97.9	73.8/90.6/98.4	62.8/82.2/94.2	72.3/90.6/97.9
full	I		✓	**77.0**/92.1/99.0		74.3/90.1/96.3	74.3/92.1/99.5
SfM				**77.0**/90.6/**100.0**	**78.5**/90.6/99.0	72.3/88.5/**97.9**	**78.0**/90.6/99.0

As can be seen from the results of using down-scaled images (with maximum side length of 800 px), using 3D points obtained from the AC13 model depth maps typically leads to better results than triangulating 3D points. For triangulation, we only use database features that match to the query image. Compared to an SfM model, where features are matched between database images, this leads to fewer features that are used for triangulation per point and thus to less accurate points. Preliminary experiments confirmed that, as expected, the gap between using the 3D mesh and triangulation grows when retrieving fewer database images. Compared to SfM-based pipelines, which use covisibility filtering before RANSAC-based pose estimation, we observe that covisibility filtering typically decreases the pose accuracy of the MeshLoc pipeline due to its approximate nature. Again, preliminary results showed that the effect is more pronounced when using fewer retrieved database images (as the approximation becomes coarser). In contrast, position averaging (PA) typically gives a (slight) accuracy boost. We further observe that the simple baseline that uses all individual matches (I) often leads to similar or better results compared to merging 2D-3D matches (M). In the following, we thus focus on a simple version of MeshLoc, which uses individual matches (I) and PA, but not covisibility filtering.

Comparison with SfM-Based Representations. Table 2 also evaluates the simple variant of MeshLoc on full-resolution images and compares MeshLoc against the corresponding SfM-based results from visuallocalization.net. Note

Table 3. Ablation study on the Aachen Day-Night v1.1 dataset [66,67,93] using real images at reduced resolution (max. 800 px) and full resolution with depth maps rendered from 3D meshes of different levels of detail (*cf.* Table 1). We use a simple MeshLoc variant that uses individual matches and position averaging, but no covis. filtering

Feature	res.	AC13-C	AC13	AC14	AC15
SuperGlue [61]		74.3/92.7/99.5	74.3/93.2/99.0	71.7/91.6/99.0	72.8/92.7/99.5
LoFTR [78]	800	77.5/92.7/99.5	78.5/93.2/99.5	76.4/92.1/99.5	78.0/92.7/99.5
Patch2Pix [94]		71.7/88.0/95.3	73.8/89.5/95.3	67.0/85.9/95.8	72.3/89.0/96.3
Patch2Pix+SG [61,94]		74.9/92.1/99.5	73.8/92.1/99.5	73.8/90.1/99.0	75.4/91.1/99.5
SuperGlue [61]		77.0/92.1/99.5	77.0/92.1/99.0	75.4/91.1/99.0	76.4/92.1/99.0
Patch2Pix [94]	full	74.3/90.1/96.9	74.3/90.1/96.3	71.2/86.9/95.3	72.3/88.0/96.9
Patch2Pix+SG [61,94]		73.3/92.1/99.5	74.3/92.1/99.5	73.3/91.1/99.5	74.3/92.7/99.5

that we did not evaluate LoFTR on the full-resolution images due to the memory constraints of our GPU (NVIDIA GeForce RTX 3060, 12 GB RAM). The simple MeshLoc variant performs similarly well or slightly better than its SfM-based counterparts, with the exception of the finest pose threshold (0.25 m, 2°) for Patch2Pix+SG. This is despite the fact that SfM-based pipelines are significantly more complex and use additional information (feature matches between database images) that are expensive to compute. Moreover, MeshLoc requires less memory at only a small run-time overhead (see supp. mat.). Given its simplicity and ease of use, we thus believe that MeshLoc will be of interest to the community as it allows researchers to more easily prototype new features.

Mesh Level of Detail. Table 3 shows results obtained when using 3D meshes of different levels of detail (*cf.* Table 1). The gap between using the compact AC13-C model (47 MB to store the raw geometry) and the larger AC13 model (558 MB for the raw geometry) is rather small. While AC14 and AC15 offer more detailed geometry, they also contain artefacts in the form of blobs of geometry (*cf.* supp. mat.). Note that we did not optimize these models (besides parameter adjustments) and leave experiments with more accurate 3D models for future work. Overall the level of detail does not seem to be critical for MeshLoc.

Using Rendered Instead of Real Images. Next, we evaluate the MeshLoc pipeline using synthetic images rendered from the poses of the database images instead of real images. Table 4 shows results for various rendering settings, resulting in different levels of realism for the synthetic views. We focus on Super-Glue [61] and Patch2Pix + SuperGlue [61,94]. LoFTR performed similarly well or better than both on textured and colored renderings, but worse when rendering raw geometry (*cf.* supp. mat.).

As Table 4 shows, the pose accuracy gap between using real images and textured/colored renderings is rather small. This shows that advanced neural rendering techniques, *e.g.*, NeRFs [46], have only a limited potential to improve the

Table 4. Ablation study on the Aachen Day-Night v1.1 dataset [66,67,93] using images rendered at reduced resolution (max. 800 px) from 3D meshes of different levels of detail (*cf.* Tab. 1) and different rendering types (textured/colored, raw geometry with ambient occlusion (AO), raw geometry with tricolor shading (tricolor)). For reference, the rightmost column shows results obtained with real images on AC13. MeshLoc uses individual matches and position averaging, but no covisibility filtering

AC13-C:	textured	AO	tricolor	real
SuperGlue [61]	72.3/91.1/99.0	0.5/3.1/24.6	7.3/23.0/53.9	74.3/92.7/99.5
Patch2Pix+SG [61,94]	70.7/90.6/99.5	1.0/4.2/27.7	9.4/25.1/57.6	74.9/92.1/99.5
AC13:	colored	AO	tricolor	real
SuperGlue [61]	68.1/90.1/97.4	6.3/19.9/45.5	22.0/50.8/74.3	74.3/93.2/99.0
Patch2Pix+SG [61,94]	71.7/91.1/97.9	6.8/26.2/49.2	23.0/55.0/78.5	73.8/92.1/99.5
AC14:	colored	AO	tricolor	real
SuperGlue [61]	70.2/90.1/96.3	23.6/44.5/63.9	33.0/65.4/79.1	71.7/91.6/99.0
Patch2Pix+SG [61,94]	72.3/92.1/96.9	26.7/48.2/68.1	39.3/68.6/80.6	73.8/90.1/99.0
AC15:	colored	AO	tricolor	real
SuperGlue [61]	75.4/89.5/98.4	24.1/47.1/63.4	37.2/60.7/77.5	72.8/92.7/99.5
Patch2Pix+SG [61,94]	72.8/92.1/98.4	25.1/51.3/70.2	40.3/66.0/80.1	75.4/91.1/99.5

results. Rendering raw geometry results in significantly reduced performance since neither SuperGlue nor Patch2Pix+SG were trained on this setting. AO renderings lead to worse results compared to the tricolor scheme as the latter produces more sharp details (*cf.* Fig. 3). Patch2Pix+SuperGlue outperforms SuperGlue as it refines the keypoint detections used by SuperGlue on a per-match-basis [94], resulting in more accurate 2D positions and reducing the bias between positions in real and rendered images. Still, the results for the coarsest threshold (5 m, 10°) are surprisingly competitive. This indicates that there is quite some potential in matching real images against renderings of raw geometry, *e.g.*, for using dense models obtained from non-image sources (laser, LiDAR, depth, *etc.*.) for visual localization. Naturally, having more geometric detail leads to better results as it produces more fine-grained details in the renderings.

Experiments on 12 Scenes. The meshes provided by the 12 Scenes dataset [86] come from RGB-D SLAM. Compared to Aachen, where the meshes were created from the images, the alignment between geometry and image data is imperfect.

We follow [8], using the top-20 images retrieved using DenseVLAD [85] descriptors extracted from the original database images and the original pseudo ground-truth provided by the 12 Scenes dataset. The simple MeshLoc variant with SuperGlue, applied on real images, is able to localize 94.0% of all query images within 5 cm and 5° threshold on average over all 12 scenes. This is comparable to state-of-the-art methods such as Active Search [65], DSAC* [12], and DenseVLAD retrieval with R2D2 [56] features, which on average localize more than 99.0% of all queries within 5 cm and 5°. The drop is caused by a visible misalignment between the geometry and RGB images in some scenes, *e.g.*, apt2/living (see supp. mat. for visualizations), resulting in non-compensable errors in the 3D point positions. Using renderings of colored meshes respectively the tricolor scheme reduces the average percentages of localized images to 65.8% respectively 14.1%. Again, the color and geometry misalignment seems the main reason for the drop when rendering colored meshes, while we did not observed such a large gap for Aachen dataset (which has 3D meshes that better align with the images). Still, 99.6%/92.7%/36.0% of the images can be localized when using real images/colored renderings/tricolor renderings for a threshold of 7 cm and $7°$. These numbers further increase to 100%/99.1%/54.2% for 10 cm and $10°$. Overall, our results show that using dense 3D models leads to promising results and that these representations are a meaningful alternative to SfM point clouds. Please see the supp. mat. for more 12 Scenes results.

5   Conclusion

In this paper, we explored dense 3D model as an alternative scene representation to the SfM point clouds widely used by feature-based localization algorithms. We have discussed how to adapt existing hierarchical localization pipelines to dense 3D models. Extensive experiments show that a very simple version of the resulting MeshLoc pipeline is able to achieve state-of-the-art results. Compared to SfM-based representations, using a dense scene model does not require an extensive matching step between database images when switching to a new type of local features. Thus, MeshLoc allows researchers to more easily prototype new types of features. We have further shown that promising results can be obtained when using synthetic views rendered from the dense models rather than the original images, even without adapting the used features. This opens up new and interesting directions of future work, *e.g.*, more compact scene representations that still preserve geometric details, and training features for the challenging tasks of matching real images against raw scene geometry. The meshes obtained via classical approaches and classical, *i.e.*, non-neural, rendering techniques that are used in this paper thereby create strong baselines for learning-based follow-up work. The rendering approach also allows to use techniques such as database expansion and pose refinement, which were not included in this paper due to limited space. We released our code, meshes, and renderings.

Acknowledgement. This work was supported by the EU Horizon 2020 project RICAIP (grant agreement No. 857306), the European Regional Development Fund under project IMPACT (No. CZ.02.1.01/0.0/0.0/15_003/0000468), a Meta Reality Labs research award under project call 'Benchmarking City-Scale 3D Map Making with Mapillary Metropolis', the Grant Agency of the Czech Technical University in Prague (No. SGS21/119/OHK3/2T/13), the OP VVV funded project CZ.02.1.01/0.0/0.0/16 019/0000765 "Research Center for Informatics", and the ERC-CZ grant MSMT LL1901.

References

1. Agarwal, S., Snavely, N., Simon, I., Seitz, S., Szeliski, R.: Building Rome in a day. In: ICCV 2009, pp. 72–79 (2009)
2. Arandjelović, R., Gronat, P., Torii, A., Pajdla, T., Sivic, J.: NetVLAD: CNN architecture for weakly supervised place recognition. In: CVPR (2016)
3. Balntas, V., Li, S., Prisacariu, V.: RelocNet: continuous metric learning relocalisation using neural nets. In: Ferrari, V., Hebert, M., Sminchisescu, C., Weiss, Y. (eds.) Computer Vision – ECCV 2018. LNCS, vol. 11218, pp. 782–799. Springer, Cham (2018). https://doi.org/10.1007/978-3-030-01264-9_46
4. Barath, D., Ivashechkin, M., Matas, J.: Progressive NAPSAC: sampling from gradually growing neighborhoods. arXiv preprint arXiv:1906.02295 (2019)
5. Barath, D., Matas, J.: Graph-cut RANSAC. In: Proceedings of the IEEE Conference on Computer Vision and Pattern Recognition, pp. 6733–6741 (2018)
6. Barath, D., Noskova, J., Ivashechkin, M., Matas, J.: MAGSAC++, a fast, reliable and accurate robust estimator. In: Proceedings of the IEEE/CVF Conference on Computer Vision and Pattern Recognition, pp. 1304–1312 (2020)
7. Barron, J.T., Mildenhall, B., Tancik, M., Hedman, P., Martin-Brualla, R., Srinivasan, P.P.: Mip-NeRF: a multiscale representation for anti-aliasing neural radiance fields. In: 2021 IEEE/CVF International Conference on Computer Vision (ICCV), pp. 5835–5844 (2021)
8. Brachmann, E., Humenberger, M., Rother, C., Sattler, T.: On the limits of pseudo ground truth in visual camera re-localisation. In: Proceedings of the IEEE/CVF International Conference on Computer Vision, pp. 6218–6228 (2021)
9. Brachmann, E., Krull, A., Nowozin, S., Shotton, J., Michel, F., Gumhold, S., Rother, C.: DSAC - differentiable RANSAC for camera localization. In: CVPR (2017)
10. Brachmann, E., Rother, C.: Learning less is more - 6D camera localization via 3D surface regression. In: CVPR (2018)
11. Brachmann, E., Rother, C.: Expert sample consensus applied to camera relocalization. In: ICCV (2019)
12. Brachmann, E., Rother, C.: Visual camera re-localization from RGB and RGB-D images using DSAC. TPAMI 44, 5847–5865 (2021)
13. Brejcha, J., Lukáč, M., Hold-Geoffroy, Y., Wang, O., Čadík, M.: LandscapeAR: large scale outdoor augmented reality by matching photographs with terrain models using learned descriptors. In: Vedaldi, A., Bischof, H., Brox, T., Frahm, J.-M. (eds.) ECCV 2020. LNCS, vol. 12374, pp. 295–312. Springer, Cham (2020). https://doi.org/10.1007/978-3-030-58526-6_18
14. Cavallari, T., Bertinetto, L., Mukhoti, J., Torr, P., Golodetz, S.: Let's take this online: adapting scene coordinate regression network predictions for online RGB-D camera relocalisation. In: 3DV (2019)
15. Cavallari, T., Golodetz, S., Lord, N.A., Valentin, J., Di Stefano, L., Torr, P.H.S.: On-the-fly adaptation of regression forests for online camera relocalisation. In: CVPR (2017)
16. Cavallari, T., et al.: Real-time RGB-D camera pose estimation in novel scenes using a relocalisation cascade. TPAMI 42, 2465–2477 (2019)
17. Chum, O., Matas, J.: Randomized RANSAC with $T_{d,d}$ test. In: British Machine Vision Conference (BMVC) (2002)
18. Chum, O., Perdoch, M., Matas, J.: Geometric min-hashing: finding a (thick) needle in a haystack. In: ICCV (2007)

19. Cignoni, P., Callieri, M., Corsini, M., Dellepiane, M., Ganovelli, F., Ranzuglia, G.: MeshLab: an open-source mesh processing tool. In: Eurographics Italian Chapter Conference (2008)
20. Dai, A., Nießner, M., Zollöfer, M., Izadi, S., Theobalt, C.: BundleFusion: real-time globally consistent 3D reconstruction using on-the-fly surface re-integration. TOG **36**, 1 (2017)
21. DeTone, D., Malisiewicz, T., Rabinovich, A.: SuperPoint: self-supervised interest point detection and description. In: CVPR Workshops (2018)
22. Ding, M., Wang, Z., Sun, J., Shi, J., Luo, P.: CamNet: coarse-to-fine retrieval for camera re-localization. In: ICCV (2019)
23. Dusmanu, M., et al.: D2-Net: a trainable CNN for joint detection and description of local features. In: CVPR (2019)
24. Fischler, M.A., Bolles, R.C.: Random sampling consensus: a paradigm for model fitting with application to image analysis and automated cartography. CACM (1981)
25. Gordo, A., Almazan, J., Revaud, J., Larlus, D.: End-to-end learning of deep visual representations for image retrieval. Int. J. Comput. Vision **124**(2), 237–254 (2017)
26. Guzov, V., Mir, A., Sattler, T., Pons-Moll, G.: Human POSEitioning system (HPS): 3D human pose estimation and self-localization in large scenes from body-mounted sensors. In: Proceedings of the IEEE/CVF Conference on Computer Vision and Pattern Recognition, pp. 4318–4329 (2021)
27. Heng, L., et al.: Project AutoVision: localization and 3D scene perception for an autonomous vehicle with a multi-camera system. In: ICRA (2019)
28. Humenberger, M., et al.: Robust image retrieval-based visual localization using kapture. arXiv:2007.13867 (2020)
29. Irschara, A., Zach, C., Frahm, J.M., Bischof, H.: From structure-from-motion point clouds to fast location recognition. In: CVPR (2009)
30. Jafarzadeh, A., et al.: CrowdDriven: a new challenging dataset for outdoor visual localization. In: 2021 IEEE/CVF International Conference on Computer Vision (ICCV), pp. 9825–9835 (2021)
31. Jakob, W., Tarini, M., Panozzo, D., Sorkine-Hornung, O.: Instant field-aligned meshes. ACM Trans. Graph. **34**(6), 189–1 (2015)
32. Kazhdan, M., Hoppe, H.: Screened poisson surface reconstruction. ACM Trans. Graph. **32**(3) (2013)
33. Kendall, A., Cipolla, R.: Geometric loss functions for camera pose regression with deep learning. In: CVPR (2017)
34. Kendall, A., Grimes, M., Cipolla, R.: PoseNet: a convolutional network for real-time 6-DOF camera relocalization. In: ICCV (2015)
35. Larsson, V.: PoseLib - minimal solvers for camera pose estimation (2020). https://github.com/vlarsson/PoseLib
36. Laskar, Z., Melekhov, I., Kalia, S., Kannala, J.: Camera relocalization by computing pairwise relative poses using convolutional neural network. In: ICCV Workshops (2017)
37. Lebeda, K., Matas, J.E.S., Chum, O.: Fixing the locally optimized RANSAC. In: BMVC (2012)
38. Li, Y., Snavely, N., Huttenlocher, D., Fua, P.: Worldwide pose estimation using 3D point clouds. In: Fitzgibbon, A., Lazebnik, S., Perona, P., Sato, Y., Schmid, C. (eds.) ECCV 2012. LNCS, vol. 7572, pp. 15–29. Springer, Heidelberg (2012). https://doi.org/10.1007/978-3-642-33718-5_2
39. Li, Y., Snavely, N., Huttenlocher, D.P.: Location recognition using prioritized feature matching. In: Daniilidis, K., Maragos, P., Paragios, N. (eds.) ECCV 2010.

LNCS, vol. 6312, pp. 791–804. Springer, Heidelberg (2010). https://doi.org/10.1007/978-3-642-15552-9_57

40. Lim, H., Sinha, S.N., Cohen, M.F., Uyttendaele, M.: Real-time image-based 6-DOF localization in large-scale environments. In: CVPR (2012)

41. Lowe, D.G.: Distinctive image features from scale-invariant keypoints. IJCV **60**, 91–110 (2004)

42. Lynen, S., Sattler, T., Bosse, M., Hesch, J., Pollefeys, M., Siegwart, R.: Get out of my lab: large-scale, real-time visual-inertial localization. In: RSS (2015)

43. Martin-Brualla, R., Radwan, N., Sajjadi, M.S.M., Barron, J.T., Dosovitskiy, A., Duckworth, D.: NeRF in the wild: neural radiance fields for unconstrained photo collections. In: 2021 IEEE/CVF Conference on Computer Vision and Pattern Recognition (CVPR), pp. 7206–7215 (2021)

44. Massiceti, D., Krull, A., Brachmann, E., Rother, C., Torr, P.H.: Random forests versus neural networks - what's best for camera relocalization? In: ICRA (2017)

45. Middelberg, S., Sattler, T., Untzelmann, O., Kobbelt, L.: Scalable 6-DOF localization on mobile devices. In: Fleet, D., Pajdla, T., Schiele, B., Tuytelaars, T. (eds.) ECCV 2014. LNCS, vol. 8690, pp. 268–283. Springer, Cham (2014). https://doi.org/10.1007/978-3-319-10605-2_18

46. Mildenhall, B., Srinivasan, P.P., Tancik, M., Barron, J.T., Ramamoorthi, R., Ng, R.: NeRF: representing scenes as neural radiance fields for view synthesis. In: Vedaldi, A., Bischof, H., Brox, T., Frahm, J.-M. (eds.) ECCV 2020. LNCS, vol. 12346, pp. 405–421. Springer, Cham (2020). https://doi.org/10.1007/978-3-030-58452-8_24

47. Moreau, A., Piasco, N., Tsishkou, D., Stanciulescu, B., de La Fortelle, A.: LENS: localization enhanced by neRF synthesis. In: CoRL (2021)

48. Mueller, M.S., Sattler, T., Pollefeys, M., Jutzi, B.: Image-to-image translation for enhanced feature matching, image retrieval and visual localization. ISPRS Ann. Photogram. Remote Sens. Spatial Inf. Sci. (2019)

49. Müller, T., Evans, A., Schied, C., Keller, A.: Instant neural graphics primitives with a multiresolution hash encoding. ACM Trans. Graph. **41**(4), 102:1–102:15 (2022). https://doi.org/10.1145/3528223.3530127

50. Naseer, T., Burgard, W.: Deep regression for monocular camera-based 6-DoF global localization in outdoor environments. In: IEEE/RSJ International Conference on Intelligent Robots and Systems (IROS) (2017)

51. Ng, T., Rodriguez, A.L., Balntas, V., Mikolajczyk, K.: Reassessing the limitations of CNN methods for camera pose regression. CoRR abs/2108.07260 (2021)

52. Oechsle, M., Peng, S., Geiger, A.: UNISURF: unifying neural implicit surfaces and radiance fields for multi-view reconstruction. In: Proceedings of the IEEE/CVF International Conference on Computer Vision (ICCV) (2021)

53. Persson, M., Nordberg, K.: Lambda twist: an accurate fast robust perspective three point (P3P) solver. In: Ferrari, V., Hebert, M., Sminchisescu, C., Weiss, Y. (eds.) ECCV 2018. LNCS, vol. 11208, pp. 334–349. Springer, Cham (2018). https://doi.org/10.1007/978-3-030-01225-0_20

54. Pittaluga, F., Koppal, S.J., Kang, S.B., Sinha, S.N.: Revealing scenes by inverting structure from motion reconstructions. In: The IEEE Conference on Computer Vision and Pattern Recognition (CVPR) (2019)

55. Revaud, J., Almazán, J., Rezende, R.S., Souza, C.R.D.: Learning with average precision: training image retrieval with a listwise loss. In: Proceedings of the IEEE/CVF International Conference on Computer Vision, pp. 5107–5116 (2019)

56. Revaud, J., Weinzaepfel, P., de Souza, C.R., Humenberger, M.: R2D2: repeatable and reliable detector and descriptor. In: NeurIPS (2019)

57. Rocco, I., Arandjelović, R., Sivic, J.: Efficient neighbourhood consensus networks via submanifold sparse convolutions. In: Vedaldi, A., Bischof, H., Brox, T., Frahm, J.-M. (eds.) ECCV 2020. LNCS, vol. 12354, pp. 605–621. Springer, Cham (2020). https://doi.org/10.1007/978-3-030-58545-7_35

58. Rocco, I., Cimpoi, M., Arandjelović, R., Torii, A., Pajdla, T., Sivic, J.: Neighbourhood consensus networks. Adv. Neural Inf. Process. Syst. **31** (2018)

59. Sarlin, P.E., Cadena, C., Siegwart, R., Dymczyk, M.: From coarse to fine: robust hierarchical localization at large scale. In: CVPR (2019)

60. Sarlin, P.E., Debraine, F., Dymczyk, M., Siegwart, R., Cadena, C.: Leveraging deep visual descriptors for hierarchical efficient localization. In: Conference on Robot Learning (CoRL) (2018)

61. Sarlin, P.E., DeTone, D., Malisiewicz, T., Rabinovich, A.: SuperGlue: learning feature matching with graph neural networks. In: CVPR (2020)

62. Sarlin, P.E., et al.: Back to the feature: learning robust camera localization from pixels to pose. In: Proceedings of the IEEE/CVF Conference on Computer Vision and Pattern Recognition, pp. 3247–3257 (2021)

63. Sattler, T., Havlena, M., Radenovic, F., Schindler, K., Pollefeys, M.: Hyperpoints and fine vocabularies for large-scale location recognition. In: ICCV (2015)

64. Sattler, T., Leibe, B., Kobbelt, L.: Improving image-based localization by active correspondence search. In: Fitzgibbon, A., Lazebnik, S., Perona, P., Sato, Y., Schmid, C. (eds.) ECCV 2012. LNCS, vol. 7572, pp. 752–765. Springer, Heidelberg (2012). https://doi.org/10.1007/978-3-642-33718-5_54

65. Sattler, T., Leibe, B., Kobbelt, L.: Efficient & effective prioritized matching for large-scale image-based localization. PAMI **39**, 1744–1756 (2017)

66. Sattler, T., et al.: Benchmarking 6DOF urban visual localization in changing conditions. In: CVPR (2018)

67. Sattler, T., Weyand, T., Leibe, B., Kobbelt, L.: Image retrieval for image-based localization revisited. In: BMVC (2012)

68. Sattler, T., Zhou, Q., Pollefeys, M., Leal-Taixé, L.: Understanding the limitations of cnn-based absolute camera pose regression. In: CVPR (2019)

69. Schönberger, J.L., Pollefeys, M., Geiger, A., Sattler, T.: Semantic visual localization. In: CVPR (2018)

70. Schönberger, J.L., Frahm, J.M.: Structure-from-motion revisited. In: CVPR (2016)

71. Schönberger, J.L., Zheng, E., Frahm, J.-M., Pollefeys, M.: Pixelwise view selection for unstructured multi-view stereo. In: Leibe, B., Matas, J., Sebe, N., Welling, M. (eds.) ECCV 2016. LNCS, vol. 9907, pp. 501–518. Springer, Cham (2016). https://doi.org/10.1007/978-3-319-46487-9_31

72. Shan, Q., Wu, C., Curless, B., Furukawa, Y., Hernandez, C., Seitz, S.M.: Accurate geo-registration by ground-to-aerial image matching. In: 3DV (2014)

73. Shavit, Y., Ferens, R., Keller, Y.: Learning multi-scene absolute pose regression with transformers. In: ICCV (2021)

74. Shotton, J., Glocker, B., Zach, C., Izadi, S., Criminisi, A., Fitzgibbon, A.: Scene coordinate regression forests for camera relocalization in RGB-D images. In: CVPR (2013)

75. Sibbing, D., Sattler, T., Leibe, B., Kobbelt, L.: SIFT-realistic rendering. In: 3DV (2013)

76. Snavely, N., Seitz, S.M., Szeliski, R.: Modeling the world from internet photo collections. IJCV **80**, 189–210 (2008)

77. Song, Z., Chen, W., Campbell, D., Li, H.: Deep novel view synthesis from colored 3D point clouds. In: Vedaldi, A., Bischof, H., Brox, T., Frahm, J.-M. (eds.) ECCV

2020. LNCS, vol. 12369, pp. 1–17. Springer, Cham (2020). https://doi.org/10.1007/978-3-030-58586-0_1

78. Sun, J., Shen, Z., Wang, Y., Bao, H., Zhou, X.: Loftr: detector-free local feature matching with transformers. In: Proceedings of the IEEE/CVF Conference on Computer Vision and Pattern Recognition (CVPR) (2021)

79. Svärm, L., Enqvist, O., Kahl, F., Oskarsson, M.: City-scale localization for cameras with known vertical direction. PAMI **39**(7), 1455–1461 (2017)

80. Taira, H., et al.: InLoc: indoor visual localization with dense matching and view synthesis. In: CVPR (2018)

81. Taira, H., et al.: Is this the right place? geometric-semantic pose verification for indoor visual localization. In: The IEEE International Conference on Computer Vision (ICCV) (2019)

82. Tancik, M., et al.: Block-NeRF: scalable large scene neural view synthesis. ArXiv abs/2202.05263 (2022)

83. Toft, C., et al.: Long-term visual localization revisited. TPAMI 1 (2020). https://doi.org/10.1109/TPAMI.2020.3032010

84. Tomešek, J., Čadík, M., Brejcha, J.: CrossLocate: cross-modal large-scale visual geo-localization in natural environments using rendered modalities. In: 2022 IEEE/CVF Winter Conference on Applications of Computer Vision (WACV), pp. 2193–2202 (2022)

85. Torii, A., Arandjelović, R., Sivic, J., Okutomi, M., Pajdla, T.: 24/7 place recognition by view synthesis. In: CVPR (2015)

86. Valentin, J., et al.: Learning to navigate the energy landscape. In: 3DV (2016)

87. Waechter, M., Beljan, M., Fuhrmann, S., Moehrle, N., Kopf, J., Goesele, M.: Virtual rephotography: novel view prediction error for 3D Reconstruction. ACM Trans. Graph. **36**(1) (2017)

88. Waechter, M., Moehrle, N., Goesele, M.: Let there be color! large-scale texturing of 3D reconstructions. In: Fleet, D., Pajdla, T., Schiele, B., Tuytelaars, T. (eds.) ECCV 2014. LNCS, vol. 8693, pp. 836–850. Springer, Cham (2014). https://doi.org/10.1007/978-3-319-10602-1_54

89. Walch, F., Hazirbas, C., Leal-Taixé, L., Sattler, T., Hilsenbeck, S., Cremers, D.: Image-based localization using LSTMs for structured feature correlation. In: ICCV (2017)

90. Wang, Q., et al.: IBRNet: learning multi-view image-based rendering. In: 2021 IEEE/CVF Conference on Computer Vision and Pattern Recognition (CVPR), pp. 4688–4697 (2021)

91. Wang, Q., Zhou, X., Hariharan, B., Snavely, N.: Learning feature descriptors using camera pose supervision. arXiv:2004.13324 (2020)

92. Zeisl, B., Sattler, T., Pollefeys, M.: Camera pose voting for large-scale image-based localization. In: ICCV (2015)

93. Zhang, Z., Sattler, T., Scaramuzza, D.: Reference pose generation for long-term visual localization via learned features and view synthesis. IJCV **129**, 821–844 (2020)

94. Zhou, Q., Sattler, T., Leal-Taixe, L.: Patch2pix: epipolar-guided pixel-level correspondences. In: Proceedings of the IEEE/CVF Conference on Computer Vision and Pattern Recognition (CVPR) (2021)

95. Zhou, Q., Sattler, T., Pollefeys, M., Leal-Taixé, L.: To learn or not to learn: visual localization from essential matrices. In: ICRA (2019)

96. Zhu, J.Y., Park, T., Isola, P., Efros, A.A.: Unpaired image-to-image translation using cycle-consistent adversarial networks. In: ICCV (2017)

97. Zhukov, S., Iones, A., Kronin, G.: An ambient light illumination model. In: Rendering Techniques (1998)

S2F2: Single-Stage Flow Forecasting for Future Multiple Trajectories Prediction

Yu-Wen Chen$^{(\boxtimes)}$, Hsuan-Kung Yang, Chu-Chi Chiu, and Chun-Yi Lee

Elsa Lab, Department of Computer Science, National Tsing Hua University,
Hsinchu, Taiwan
{carrie,hellochick,chulie9710}@gapp.nthu.edu.tw

Abstract. In this work, we present a single-stage framework, named **S2F2**, for forecasting multiple human trajectories from raw video images by predicting future optical flows. S2F2 differs from the previous two-stage approaches in that it performs detection, Re-ID, and forecasting of multiple pedestrians at the same time. The architecture of S2F2 consists of two primary parts: (1) a *context feature extractor* responsible for extracting a shared latent feature embedding for performing detection and Re-ID, and (2) a *forecasting module* responsible for extracting a shared latent feature embedding for forecasting. The outputs of the two parts are then processed to generate the final predicted trajectories of pedestrians. Unlike previous approaches, the computational burden of S2F2 remains consistent even if the number of pedestrians grows. In order to fairly compare S2F2 against the other approaches, we designed a StaticMOT dataset that excludes video sequences involving egocentric motions. The experimental results demonstrate that S2F2 is able to outperform two conventional trajectory forecasting algorithms and a recent learning-based two-stage model, while maintaining tracking performance on par with the contemporary MOT models.

Keywords: Multiple trajectory forecasting · Optical flow estimation · Single-stage forecasting framework · S2F2

1 Introduction

Multiple pedestrian trajectory forecasting is the task of predicting future locations of pedestrians from video data, and has received increasing attention in recent years across a wide variety of domains. Foreseeing how a scene involving multiple objects will unfold over time is crucial for a number of applications, such as self-driving vehicles, service robots, and advanced surveillance systems.

In the past few years, multiple pedestrian trajectory forecasting from image sequences has been implemented as a two-stage process: (1) *the detection and*

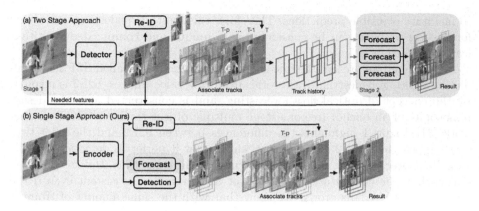

Fig. 1. A comparison between the two-stage approach and our one stage framework.

tracking stage, where targets in a single video frame are first located (i.e., detection), and then associated to existing trajectories (i.e., tracking) with or without the help of re-identification (Re-ID); and (2) *the forecasting stage*, where the previous trajectory of each person is fed into a forecasting model to predict its potential future locations over a short period of time. This branch of methods is referred to as the *two-stage approach* in this work, and is illustrated in Fig 1 (a). Among them, previous works concentrated only on the second stage, and utilized pre-processed bounding boxes and tracking histories [2,5,6,13,21,28]. Albeit effective, two-stage approaches inherently suffer from several limitations. First, their forecasting performances are constrained by the quality and correctness of the first stage. Second, despite that the first stage only processes the input in one pass, the second stage usually requires multiple passes of forecasting if the input image sequence contains multiple pedestrians [13,21,28].

In light of these shortcomings, a promising direction to explore is the use of a single-stage architecture. Single-stage architectures often possess favorable properties such as multitasking, fast inference speed, etc., and have recently been investigated in a wide range of other domains [19,22,24,27,31,32]. The advantages of these one-stage approaches usually come from the bottom-up design philosophy, where their feature maps are typically constructed from features of local regions, and optimized to encompass certain hierarchies of different scales if necessary. Such a design philosophy allows them to make multiple predictions in one shot, regardless of the number of target instances in an image. Despite their successes, the previous single-stage approaches are mostly designed for tasks involving only a single image frame. The multiple pedestrian trajectory forecasting task, however, requires temporal information encoded from multiple past frames, making previous single-stage architectures not readily applicable. As this problem setup has not been properly investigated, the challenges to be addressed are twofold. First, it requires various types of information (e.g., detection results, past trajectories, context features, etc.) to be concurrently encrypted to the latent features. Second, it necessitates temporal information to facilitate plausible predictions. Therefore, this multiple pedestrian trajectory forecasting problem can be considered as a unique and complicated multitask learning problem.

To this end, we present the first single-stage framework, called **S2F2**, for predicting multiple pedestrian trajectories from raw video images. S2F2 is inspired by the concept of optical flow forecasting, and is constructed atop the design philosophy of an anchor-free one-stage multiple object tracking (MOT) framework [31]. Figure 1 highlights the differences between S2F2 and the prior two stage approaches. S2F2 differs from them in that it performs detection, Re-ID, as well as forecasting of multiple pedestrians at the same time. Unlike two-stage approaches, the computational burden of S2F2 remains consistent even if the number of pedestrians grows. We show that with the same amount of training data, S2F2 is able to outperform two conventional trajectory forecasting algorithms and a recent learning-based two-stage model [21], while maintaining its tracking performance on par with the contemporary MOT models. The main contributions of this work are:

1. We present the first single-stage framework that jointly accomplishes tracking and forecasting of multiple pedestrians from raw video image frames.
2. We introduce a future flow decoder and a special loss function to enable the predictions of future optical flows without any additional labeled data.
3. We propose to leverage the predicted optical flow maps to assist in forecasting the trajectories of multiple pedestrians concurrently, within a consistent computational burden even if the number of pedestrians increases.

2   Related Work

The task of forecasting the trajectories of multiple pedestrians typically requires their track histories. To date, the existing methods [1,2,5,6,13,20,21,26,28] are all carried out in a two-stage fashion: (1) object detection and tracking, and (2) forecasting. The former stage is responsible for extracting features and associating bounding boxes, while the latter utilizes the information from the former to forecast their potential future locations. These two stages have been treated by these methods separately, instead of being integrated as a single model. In these methods, detection is usually based on the ground truths provided by the datasets [4,10,17,18,21,26], which offer continuously tracked bounding boxes or centers. On the other hand, forecasting is performed either based on the track histories alone [1,2,5,6,28], or with a combination of additional extracted context features [11,13,15,20,21,26]. Social-LSTM [1] introduces the concept of social interactions by proposing a technique called social pooling, which encodes the latent features of multiple trajectories through LSTMs for sharing the information of interactions among pedestrians in a scene. In order to make reasonable forecasts, some researchers proposed to further incorporate content or context features into their architectures [11,20,21], such as semantic segmentation [13], optical flow [20,21], human pose [26], ego motion [15,26], etc., and have demonstrated the effectiveness of them. Such additional features are extracted separately by distinct deep neural networks. Albeit effective, these two-stage methods suffer from the issues discussed in Sect. 1. Although single-stage forecasting has been attempted for point cloud based input data captured by lidars [12], there is no single-stage forecasting method that makes predictions based on raw RGB image frames.

3   Methodology

In this section, we first describe the problem formulation of this work. Then, we introduce the proposed S2F2 framework, followed by a detailed description of its various task modules.

3.1   Problem Formulation

Consider a sequence of raw RGB images from a static scene $\{I_0, I_1, ..., I_t\}$, where t represents the current timestep, our objective is to estimate and track the current and future locations of all pedestrians. Given the tracking information encoded from the previous images, the task of multiple pedestrian trajectory forecasting aims to infer a set of bounding boxes $B_t^i = \{b_t^i, b_{t+1}^i, b_{t+2}^i, ..., b_{t+n}^i\}$ for each identifiable person i in the current and the subsequent n image frames, where b_i^t denotes the bounding box of person i at timestep t.

3.2   Overview of the S2F2 Framework

Figure 2 illustrates an overview of the S2F2 framework. To accomplish trajectory forecasting for multiple pedestrians within a single stage, S2F2 employs two distinct modules in its architecture: (a) a *context feature extractor* for processing and encrypting the input RGB image frame of the current timestep t, and (b) a *forecasting module* for recurrently encoding the latent features and predicting the future optical flows, which are later exploited for deriving the future trajectories of the pedestrians in the image. Given a raw input image I_t, it is first processed by the backbone K of the context feature extractor to generate a feature embedding $\mathcal{X}_t$, which is used for three purposes: detection, Re-ID, and forecasting. To derive the future flow maps, the forecasting module takes $\mathcal{X}_t$ as its input, and leverages a set of gated recurrent units (GRUs) to generate a series of optical flow maps $\{f_{t+1}, f_{t+2}, ..., f_{t+n}\}$ for the subsequent n timesteps. These optical flow maps represent the estimated offsets of each pixel from I_t to I_{t+n}, and thus can be utilized to perform forward warping of the detection results to derive the future bounding boxes B_t^i for each identifiable person i in the scene, as depicted in Fig. 2 (highlighted as the blue bounding boxes). Finally, all the bounding boxes are processed by a tracking algorithm, and are associated into distinct tracks.

3.3   Context Feature Extractor

The context feature extractor of S2F2 inherits the design from FairMOT [31], in which an enhanced version of Deep Layer Aggregation (DLA) [32] is used

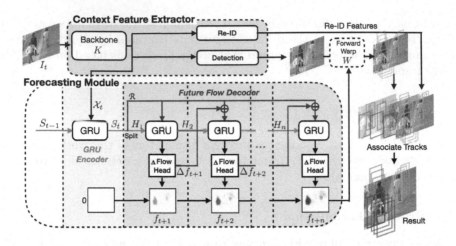

Fig. 2. The proposed S2F2 framework. Our model contains two modules: (a) a context feature extractor for processing I_t, and (b) a forecasting module for aggregating past features to predict future flow maps. Forecasting is accomplished by forward warping the detection results, followed by a tracking algorithm to associate them into tracks.

as the backbone to generate $\mathcal{X}_t$. Except for forwarding it to the forecasting module, the other two objectives of the context feature extractor is to utilize $\mathcal{X}_t$ to extract necessary features for the detection and Re-ID tasks. These two tasks are accomplished by four heads, including a heatmap head, an offset head, a size head, and a Re-ID head. These heads ensure that $\mathcal{X}_t$ can serve as an adequate representation of the locations and the appearances of the objects in I_t, and offer sufficient information for the forecasting module. We explain the functionality of each head in the following paragraphs.

– **Heatmap Head.** The heatmap head is responsible for estimating the locations of the centers of different bounding boxes in an input image.
– **Offset and Size Heads.** The function of the offset head is to precisely locate the objects, while the role of the size head is to estimate the height and width of the target bounding boxes.
– **Re-ID Head.** The function of this head is to extract features for generating a unique identifier for each person so as to track its bounding boxes across different frames.

3.4   Forecasting Module

The forecasting module is in charge of encoding temporal features based on $\mathcal{X}_t$, and predicting the future optical flow maps which are later used to derive the future trajectories. It contains an encoder and a decoder, which are depicted in Fig 2 and explained as follows.

GRU Encoder Block. The goal of the gated recurrent unit (GRU) encoder block is to generate an embedding S_t from $\mathcal{X}_t$. It is a single convolutional GRU (ConvGRU) [25]. At timestep t, $\mathcal{X}_t$ is passed into the ConvGRU along with the corresponding previous embedding S_{t-1} to derive the updated $S_t = GRU(S_{t-1}, \mathcal{X}_t)$. S_t can be considered as a summary of the past state embeddings up to t. Note that at $t = 1$, $\mathcal{X}_1$ is also utilized as the initial state embedding S_0.

Future Flow Decoder Block. The objective of the future flow decoder is to predict n residual future flow estimations $\{\Delta f_{t+1}, \Delta f_{t+2}, ..., \Delta f_{t+n}\}, \Delta f \in \mathbb{R}^{2 \times w \times h}$, where each estimation is an update direction used to update a fixed flow field initialized with zeros. More specifically, this decoder generates a set of future flow maps $F = \{f_{t+1}, f_{t+2}, ..., f_{t+n}\}$, where $f_{t+1} = \Delta f_{t+1} + f_t$. Each of the predicted flows in F has the same initial reference frame I_t (i.e., f_n is the optical flow from frame I_t to I_{t+n}, instead of $I_{t+(n-1)}$ to I_{t+n}). This design choice aims to avoid error accumulation while forming forecasting predictions. Similar to the encoder block, the decoder also contains a ConvGRU. It takes the state embedding S_t as its input, and splits S_t into a hidden state H_1 and an input R. They are then fed separately into the ConvGRU to generate the next hidden state $H_2 = GRU(H_1, R)$, which is utilized by a Δ *flow head* to produce Δf_{t+1}. This, in turn, is used to generate the subsequent input to the ConvGRU by concatenating Δf_{t+1} with R. The above procedure repeats n times, where each iteration stands for a timestep into the future.

To train the future flow decoder block, a loss function consisting of two parts are employed. The first part is a supervised loss for the centers of future bounding boxes, given by:

$$L_{Center} = \sum_{\tau=t+1}^{t+n} \sum_{i=1}^{K_\tau} \|c_\tau^i - \hat{c}_\tau^i\|_1 = \sum_{\tau=t+1}^{t+n} \sum_{i=1}^{K_\tau} \|c_\tau^i - (c_t^i + f_\tau(c_t^i))\|_1, \quad (1)$$

where f_τ is the estimated future flow, c_τ^i and $\hat{c}_\tau^i$ represent the centers of the annotated bounding box b_τ^i and the predicted bounding box $\hat{b}_\tau^i$ of pedestrian i at timestep τ, respectively, and K_τ denotes the number of pedestrians in the image at timestep τ. For each center c_τ, the forecasted center $\hat{c}_\tau$ can be inferred from f_τ, i.e., $\hat{c}_\tau = c_t + f_\tau(c_t)$. Please note that, instead of directly warping the entire frame I_t using f_τ, we only warp the centers of bounding boxes appeared at timestep t. This is because warping the entire frame may cause occlusions, and leave behind duplicate pixels. The second part further refines the flow maps and stabilizes the training process with the structural similarity index (SSIM) loss adopted in several unsupervised optical flow estimation works [7,16,23,29]:

$$L_{SSIM} = \sum_{\tau=t+1}^{t+n} SSIM\Big(I_t, W(I_\tau, f_\tau)\Big), \quad (2)$$

where $W(\cdot)$ is the backward warping operator, and the SSIM loss L_{SSIM} is obtained by calculating the similarities of the corresponding pixels between I_t and its warped frame I_τ.

3.5   Online Association with Forecasting Refinement

In order to enhance the tracking performance with the information provided from the forecasted results, we modify the original tracking algorithm of FairMOT [31] by not only considering the current bounding boxes b_t, but taking the bounding boxes $\hat{b}_t$ forecasted from the previous timestep $t-1$ into consideration. In the original design, only the bounding boxes predicted with confidence scores higher than a threshold δ are associated into tracks. However, this might result in missing objects and fragmented trajectories, since objects with low confidence scores are neglected (e.g., occluded objects) [30]. To alleviate this issue, we reduce the threshold value if the distance of any $\hat{c}_t$ and c_t is within a predefined range r, which can be formulated as:

$$\forall i \in K, \delta_i = \begin{cases} \delta/2, & \text{if } \exists \hat{c}_t, \|\hat{c}_t - c_t^i\|_1 < r \\ \delta, & \text{otherwise} \end{cases}, \tag{3}$$

where K denotes the number of pedestrians in I_t, and δ_i is the threshold for pedestrian i. This design allows the bounding boxes with lower confidence scores to be re-considered and associated if their previously forecasted locations are nearby. We examine the effectiveness of this design in Sect. 4.4.

3.6   Training Objective

We trained S2F2 in an end-to-end fashion by minimizing the following objective:

$$L_{all} = \frac{1}{e^{w_1}} L_{det} + \frac{1}{e^{w_2}} L_{id} + \frac{1}{e^{w_3}} L_{fut} + w_1 + w_2 + w_3, \tag{4}$$

where $L_{fut} = L_{Center} + L_{SSIM}$, w_1, w_2 and w_3 are learnable parameters, and L_{det} and L_{id} are the losses for the detection and Re-ID tasks, respectively. In Eq. (4), we modify the formulation of the uncertainty loss proposed in [9] to balance the detection, Re-ID, and forecasting tasks.

4   Experimental Results

In this section, we first briefly introduce the settings used for training and validation, then evaluate S2F2 in terms of its tracking and forecasting performance.

4.1   Data Curation for Forecasting Without Camera Movement

In this work, we examine the proposed S2F2 on the subset of the widely-adopted MOT17 and MOT20 Challenge Datasets [3,14]. The video sequences can be classified into two categories based on whether the ego-motion of the camera is involved. Image sequences with ego-motion are considered to be hard cases for the forecasting task, since additional designs may be required to handle the viewpoint movements. Some research works [17,21,26] focus on the image sequences from a first-person moving perspective, however, in our work, we concentrate on the model's capability of both tracking and forecasting, and thus the movements from the camera are not considered. As a result, we select a subset of video sequences from MOT17 and MOT20 without camera movement to form our dataset, named StaticMOT. The details of StaticMOT are shown in Table 1. We train and evaluate S2F2 on StaticMOT, with each sequence presented in Table 1 split into halves to form the training and validation sets, respectively.

Table 1. The video sequences contained in StaticMOT. Please note that 'Density' refers to the average number of pedestrians per frame.

Sequence	Frames	Density	Viewpoint	Sequence	Frames	Density	Viewpoint
MOT17 02	300	31.0	Eye level	MOT20-02	1390	72.7	Elevated
MOT17-04	525	45.3	Elevated	MOT20-03	1002	148.3	Elevated
MOT17-09	262	10.1	Eye level	MOT20-05	1657	226.6	Elevated
MOT20-01	214	62.1	Elevated	Average	764	126.8	–

4.2   Trajectory Forecasting Results

In this section, we compare our approach with two conventional trajectory forecasting algorithms and a recent learning-based method STED [21]. To fairly compare different methods, the pre-processed bounding boxes and the necessary past trajectories of the pedestrians are generated by S2F2 from the validation set of StaticMOT. Tracks that are not continuously detected for six frames are discarded, resulting in around 470, 000 tracks for evaluation. We predict three future frames, corresponding to around one second of forecasting into the future.

1) Baselines:

- **Constant Velocity & Constant Scale (CV-CS):** We adopt the simple constant velocity model, which is used widely as a baseline for trajectory forecasting models and as a motion model for MOT. We only use the previous three frames to compute the velocity, instead of the whole past history, as this setting delivers better performance.
- **Linear Kalman Filter (LKF)** [8]: LKF is one of the most popular motion models for MOT, and is widely used for tracking objects and predicting trajectories under noisy conditions. We use the implementation in [31], and use the last updated motion value for forecasting. Unlike CV-CS, all the previous bounding box locations of a tracked object are utilized.
- **STED** [21]: STED is a recent two-stage pedestrian forecasting model with a GRU based encoder-decoder architecture. Instead of encoding image features, it encodes pre-computed bounding box information along with features extracted from pre-generated optical flow to forecast future bounding boxes. We follow the original implementatio of STED, and train it on the ground truth tracks from the StaticMOT training set for 20 epochs.

2) Forecasting Metrics:

- **(ADE, FDE):** Average displacement error (ADE) is defined as the mean Euclidean distance between the predicted and ground-truth bounding box centroids for all predicted bounding boxes, and final displacement error (FDE) is defined similarly but only for the final timestep.
- **(AIOU, FIOU):** Average intersection-over-union (AIOU) is defined as the mean intersection-over-union (IOU) of the predicted and ground truth bounding boxes for all predicted boxes, and final intersection-over-union (FIOU) is the mean IOU for the bounding boxes at the final timestep.

Table 2. The forecasting results evaluated on the StaticMOT validation set. The latency reported is evaluated on an NVIDIA Tesla V100 GPU.

Model	ADE(↓)	FDE(↓)	AIOU(↑)	FIOU(↑)	Latency (ms)
CV	14.481	20.196	0.673	0.594	–
LKF	20.635	24.323	0.581	0.512	–
STED	16.928	23.761	0.654	0.570	623.480
Ours	**12.275**	**16.228**	**0.704**	**0.643**	**13.788**

Table 3. The detailed forecasting results evaluated on the StaticMOT validation set.

Sequences	Boxes	AIOU (↑)			ADE (↓)			FIOU (↑)			FDE (↓)		
Model	–	CV	LKF	Ours	CV	LKF	Ours	CV	LKF	Ours	CV	LKF	Ours
MOT17-02	4202	0.58	0.536	**0.602**	17.136	22.112	**16.171**	0.514	0.483	**0.544**	22.423	23.447	**20.656**
MOT17-04	19506	0.702	0.654	**0.724**	11.672	16.304	**10.802**	0.638	0.585	**0.677**	15.651	19.187	**13.631**
MOT17-09	1302	0.508	0.426	**0.58**	67.857	62.232	**52.954**	0.364	0.248	**0.488**	104.309	121.644	**72.297**
MOT20-01	6343	0.606	0.495	**0.656**	23.962	33.395	**18.59**	0.483	0.371	**0.559**	36.096	44.601	**26.683**
MOT20-02	49985	0.647	0.534	**0.676**	21.449	31.446	**18.428**	0.547	0.435	**0.591**	30.977	37.856	**25.2**
MOT20-03	103031	0.698	0.568	**0.727**	8.351	15.334	**7.007**	0.627	0.524	**0.672**	11.571	14.666	**9.231**
MOT20-05	286362	0.67	0.592	**0.703**	15.165	20.45	**12.811**	0.592	0.521	**0.643**	20.96	24.906	**16.805**
Average	67247	0.673	0.581	**0.704**	14.481	20.635	**12.275**	0.594	0.512	**0.643**	20.196	24.323	**16.228**

3) Quantitative Results: Table 2 shows the quantitative results in terms of ADE/FDE and AIOU/FIOU for all methods on StaticMOT. The latency of S2F2 and STED are also included for comparison. The latency is calculated for the forecasting part only, and is tested on sequence MOT20-05 with the largest pedestrian density. Please note that for STED, the time needed for precomputing optical flow is not included. It can be observed that, the proposed S2F2 outperforms all baselines, while running several times faster than STED. This is because STED requires feature extraction for every person in a scene. Another reason is that STED was designed for videos from the first person perspective, while the majority of StatcMOT are elevated sequences. Table 3 shows more detailed results on every sequence.

4) Qualitative Results: Figure 3 shows three examples of the successful scenarios selected and evaluated from our StaticMOT validation set. From the left to the right, the scenarios are: (1) a person behind two people walks away from the viewpoint, (2) a person moves to the right and takes a sharp turn due to the lockers in his way, and (3) a person makes a right turn to follow the crowd. In the first scenario, the person's bounding boxes from different timesteps become closer to each other due to the increase in their distances from the viewpoint. This can be forecasted by S2F2, but is unable to be correctly predicted by CV-CS. In the second scenario, CV-CS also fails to estimate the trajectory of the person. However, S2F2 incorporates features from the whole images, enabling it to anticipate the lockers in the person's way. In the third scenario, since S2F2 makes predictions for all objects concurrently based on a dense flow field, it is thus capable of capturing the spatial correlations between different objects, allowing it to forecast the future trajectory of the person by taking into account the behavior of the crowd. The failure scenarios are shown in Fig 4. From the left to the right, the scenarios are: (1) a person suddenly turns and runs to the

Fig. 3. Examples where the forecasting results made by S2F2 outperform CV-CS. From the left to the right, a pedestrian (1) walks away from the viewpoint, (2) makes a sharp turn due to the lockers in his way, and (3) makes a right turn to follow the crowd. The bounding boxes are highlighted in different colors to represent the ground truth (red), the past locations (white), and the predictions made by CV-CS (aqua) and those made by S2F2 (dark blue). The predictions are one second into the future. (Color figure online)

Table 4. A comparison between the detection results of FairMOT [31] and S2F2. The results marked with * are taken directly from the FairMOT paper. The MOT17 test results are taken from the evaluation server under the "private detection" protocol.

Method	Dataset	MOTA($\uparrow$)	MOTP($\uparrow$)	IDs($\downarrow$)	IDF1($\uparrow$)
*FairMOT**	MOT17 test	69.8	–	**3996**	**69.9**
Ours	MOT17 test	**70.0**	80.15	4590	**69.9**
*FairMOT**	MOT17 val	67.5	–	**408**	69.9
Ours	MOT17 val	**67.7**	80.3	513	**71.0**
FairMOT	StaticMOT	73.1	80.5	**2283**	76.4
Ours	StaticMOT	**73.6**	**80.5**	2307	**76.6**

left, (2) a person walks towards the viewpoint and is occluded by another person walking to the right, and (3) a person comes to a crosswalk and turns left instead of turning right to cross the street. In the first scenario, it is difficult for S2F2 to forecast sudden movements of the person. In the second scenario, it is possible for S2F2 to sample the wrong object center from our predicted flow when multiple people are overly close to each other. In the third scenario, our model incorrectly predicts the direction of that person because it is different from the majority of the people in the scene. More visualizations of our forecasting results and predicted future optical flow are shown in Fig. 8.

4.3   Multiple Object Tracking Results

In addition to forecasting, Table 4 further compares the tracking results of S2F2 and FairMOT [31], the framework that S2F2 is based on. From top to bottom, the three categories correspond to the models trained on the whole official MOT17 training dataset [14], the training split of MOT17 from [31], and our StaticMOT, respectively. For each category, S2F2 and FairMOT are trained with the same set of data samples, and do not use any additional fine-tuning. It is observed from the results that our performance is on par or even slightly better than that of FairMOT for certain metrics, implying that the addition of our forecasting module does not affect its tracking capability. Note that S2F2 performs slightly worse than FairMOT in terms of the ID switch (IDS) metric. This might be due to the fact that FairMOT is trained on independent images, while S2F2 is trained on image sequences, thus causing slight overfitting.

Fig. 4. Examples of the unsuccessful forecasting results made by S2F2. From the left to the right, a person (1) suddenly turns and runs to the left, (2) walks towards the viewpoint and is occluded by another person walking to the right, and (3) comes to a crosswalk and turns left instead of turning right to cross the street. The bounding boxes are highlighted in different colors to represent the ground truth (red), the past locations (white), and the predictions made by CV-CS (aqua) and those made by S2F2 (dark blue). The predictions are one second into the future. (Color figure online)

4.4   Ablation Studies

In this section, we dive into a set of ablation studies to discuss the rationales of our design decisions and validate them.

Inference Speed. In Fig. 5, we separately time the detection, tracking, and forecasting portions of S2F2 on videos from StaticMOT with different numbers of pedestrians to validate our claim of consistent computational burden. The inference time of the two stage tracker (i.e., STED) is also included. All models are run on a single NVIDIA Tesla V100 GPU. As shown in the figure, the forecasting portion of S2F2 takes approximately 0.01 s per frame regardless of the number of pedestrians in the scene. On the other hand, the two stage tracker's inference time grows with the number of pedestrians. This supports our claim.

GRU Encoder Optimization. In this section, we validate the effectiveness of the design of the GRU encoder adopted in S2F2 and compare it against two different variants. Figure 6 illustrates a comparison of the three architectures. The main objective of this ablation analysis is to validate whether incorporating features beneficial for predicting the optical flow from timestep $t - 1 \rightarrow t$ would help the prediction of the future optical flow maps $F = \{f_{t+1}, f_{t+2}, ..., f_{t+n}\}$. To achieve this objective, an additional "past flow decoder" with a design similar to the original future flow decoder block is incorporated into the variants shown in Fig. 6. It is trained using the unsupervised warping loss presented in Eq. (2) to predict the optical flow from $t-1 \rightarrow t$. The incorporation of the past flow decoder ensures that the relative motion between frames $t-1 \rightarrow t$ could be encoded in the feature embedding. For the two variants, $Ours + Past$ is the case where only the past flow decoder block is added. Notice that in $Ours + Past$, the gradients from both the past and future flow decoders are used for updating the GRU Encoder and the backbone network K. On the other hand, the variant $Ours + Past Detach$ further includes an additional "past GRU encoder" which is only updated by the gradients from the past flow decoder. The original GRU encoder is placed after the past GRU encoder, but is detached such that its gradients are not utilized

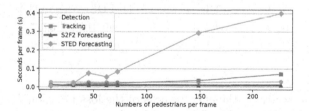

Fig. 5. A comparison of the inference time between a two-stage approach (STED) and our proposed one stage approach (S2F2).

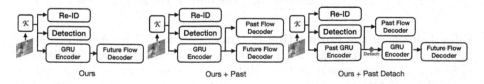

Fig. 6. An illustration of the three different model architectures discussed in Table 5.

for updating the past GRU encoder. This design aims to examine whether the features beneficial for predicting optical flows from $t-1 \rightarrow t$ could benefit the future flow prediciton.

Table 5 shows the results of the three different architectures on the MOT17 validation set, with MOTA representing the detection and tracking accuracy, and FDE representing the forecasting performance. It can be observed from Table 5 that both $Ours+Past$ and $Ours+PastDetach$ perform relatively unsatisfactory as compared to $Ours$. The detection results of $Ours+PastDetach$ are better than those of $Ours+Past$. However, the forecasting results demonstrate a different trend. The reasons are twofold. First, the features needed for predicting the optical flow from $t-1 \rightarrow t$ might not be suitable for predicting the future optical flow maps. This is supported by the evidence that $Ours+PastDetach$, which extracts features solely by the past GRU encoder, delivers the worst forecasting performance. Second, multi-task learning with tasks that need different representations might harm the performance of each individual tasks. As a result, $Ours+PastDetach$ shows better detection results as compared to $Ours+Past$.

Table 5. Ablation results for the GRU encoder optimization. All results are trained and validated on MOT17.

Ours + Past		Ours + PastDetach		Ours w/o L_{SSIM}		Ours	
MOTA(↑)	FDE(↓)	MOTA(↑)	FDE(↓)	MOTA(↑)	FDE(↓)	MOTA(↑)	FDE(↓)
66.0	43.097	66.2%	46.869	67.0	43.021	**67.7**	**39.891**

Table 6. Ablation results regarding changes to the tracking algorithm.

	Ours + BYTE		Ours w/o refinement		Ours	
Dataset	MOTA(↑)	FDE(↓)	MOTA(↑)	FDE(↓)	MOTA(↑)	FDE(↓)
MOT17	66.2	39.626	67.6	40.014	**67.7**	39.891
StaticMOT	73.4	16.146	73.3	16.249	**73.6**	16.228

An ablation study on the effectiveness of the loss function L_{SSIM} described in Sect. 3.4 is also presented in Table 5 under the column '$Ours$ w/o L_{SSIM}', corresponding to the case trained without L_{SSIM}. It can be observed that the performance declines if L_{SSIM} is not employed. Fig 7 further depicts that if L_{SSIM} helps S2F2 to concentrate on predicting the optical flows of the pedestrains.

Effectiveness of the Forecasting Refinement for Online Association. In this section, we validate the effectiveness of our forecasting refinement discussed in Sect. 3.5, and compare it with two different tracking variants. The results are presented in Table 6, in which $Ours+BYTE$ corresponds to the case where the tracking algorithm is replaced by ByteTrack [30] (denoted as BYTE). In this experiment, we use the implementation of BYTE that does not take Re-ID into consideration. On the other hand, *'Ours w/o refinement'* corresponds to the case where the original tracking algorithm from FairMOT [31] is utilized without the forecasting refinement. It can be observed from the results that our proposed forecasting refinement does benefit the detection and tracking performance, thus validating its effectiveness. In contrast, *Ours + BYTE* does not yield the most superior results, which might be due to the fact that ByteTrack [30] requires accurate detections. This can be inferred from the fact that *Ours + BYTE* performs better when the model is trained on StaticMOT (a larger dataset) than the case where the model is trained solely on MOT17 (a smaller dataset).

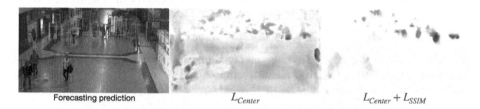

Forecasting prediction L_{Center} $L_{Center} + L_{SSIM}$

Fig. 7. Visualizations of the predicted flow maps from S2F2 trained with different loss terms.

Fig. 8. The tracking results and the predicted flow maps of S2F2 on the validation set of StaticMOT. Bounding boxes with different colors represent different identities.

5   Conclusion

In this paper, we presented the first single-stage framework, named S2F2, for predicting multiple human trajectories from raw video images. S2F2 performs detection, Re-ID, and forecasting of multiple pedestrians at the same time, with consistent computational burden even if the number of pedestrians grows. S2F2 is able to outperform two conventional trajectory forecasting algorithms, and a recent two-stage learning-based model [21], while maintaining its tracking performance on par with the contemporary MOT models. We hope this sheds light on single-stage pedestrian forecasting, and facilitates future works in this direction.

Acknowledgments. This work was supported by the Ministry of Science and Technology (MOST) in Taiwan under grant number MOST 111-2628-E-007-010. The authors acknowledge the financial support from MediaTek Inc., Taiwan and the donation of the GPUs from NVIDIA Corporation and NVIDIA AI Technology Center (NVAITC) used in this research work. The authors thank National Center for High-Performance Computing (NCHC) for providing computational and storage resources. Finally, the authors would also like to thank the time and effort of the anonymous reviewers for reviewing this paper.

References

1. Alahi, A., Goel, K., Ramanathan, V., Robicquet, A., Fei-Fei, L., Savarese, S.: Social lstm: human trajectory prediction in crowded spaces. In: Proceedings of the IEEE Conference on Computer Vision and Pattern Recognition, pp. 961–971 (2016)
2. Ansari, J.A., Bhowmick, B.: Simple means faster: Real-time human motion forecasting in monocular first person videos on cpu. In: 2020 IEEE/RSJ International Conference on Intelligent Robots and Systems (IROS), pp. 10319–10326. IEEE (2020)
3. Dendorfer, P., et al.: Mot20: a benchmark for multi object tracking in crowded scenes. [cs] arXiv:2003.09003 [cs] (2020)
4. Ess, A., Leibe, B., Schindler, K., van Gool, L.: A mobile vision system for robust multi-person tracking. In: IEEE Conference on Computer Vision and Pattern Recognition (CVPR 2008). IEEE Press (2008)
5. Gupta, A., Johnson, J., Fei-Fei, L., Savarese, S., Alahi, A.: Social gan: socially acceptable trajectories with generative adversarial networks. In: Proceedings of the IEEE Conference on Computer Vision and Pattern Recognition, pp. 2255–2264 (2018)
6. Ivanovic, B., Pavone, M.: The trajectron: probabilistic multi-agent trajectory modeling with dynamic spatiotemporal graphs. In: Proceedings of the IEEE/CVF International Conference on Computer Vision, pp. 2375–2384 (2019)
7. Jonschkowski, Rico, Stone, Austin, Barron, Jonathan T.., Gordon, Ariel, Konolige, Kurt, Angelova, Anelia: What matters in unsupervised optical flow. In: Vedaldi, Andrea, Bischof, Horst, Brox, Thomas, Frahm, Jan-Michael. (eds.) ECCV 2020. LNCS, vol. 12347, pp. 557–572. Springer, Cham (2020). https://doi.org/10.1007/978-3-030-58536-5_33
8. Kalman, R.E.: A new approach to linear filtering and prediction problems (1960)

9. Kendall, A., Gal, Y., Cipolla, R.: Multi-task learning using uncertainty to weigh losses for scene geometry and semantics. In: Proceedings of the IEEE Conference on Computer Vision and Pattern Recognition, pp. 7482–7491 (2018)

10. Lerner, A., Chrysanthou, Y., Lischinski, D.: Crowds by example. In: Computer Graphics Forum, vol. 26, pp. 655–664. Wiley Online Library (2007)

11. Liu, Yuan, Li, Ruoteng, Cheng, Yu., Tan, Robby T.., Sui, Xiubao: Object tracking using spatio-temporal networks for future prediction location. In: Vedaldi, Andrea, Bischof, Horst, Brox, Thomas, Frahm, Jan-Michael. (eds.) ECCV 2020. LNCS, vol. 12367, pp. 1–17. Springer, Cham (2020). https://doi.org/10.1007/978-3-030-58542-6_1

12. Luo, W., Yang, B., Urtasun, R.: Fast and furious: real time end-to-end 3D detection, tracking and motion forecasting with a single convolutional net. In: Proceedings of the IEEE Conference on Computer Vision and Pattern Recognition, pp. 3569–3577 (2018)

13. Makansi, O., Cicek, O., Buchicchio, K., Brox, T.: Multimodal future localization and emergence prediction for objects in egocentric view with a reachability prior. In: Proceedings of the IEEE/CVF Conference on Computer Vision and Pattern Recognition, pp. 4354–4363 (2020)

14. Milan, A., Leal-Taixé, L., Reid, I., Roth, S., Schindler, K.: MOT16: a benchmark for multi-object tracking. arXiv:1603.00831 [cs] (2016)

15. Neumann, L., Vedaldi, A.: Pedestrian and ego-vehicle trajectory prediction from monocular camera. In: Proceedings of the IEEE/CVF Conference on Computer Vision and Pattern Recognition, pp. 10204–10212 (2021)

16. Ranjan, A., et al.: Competitive collaboration: Joint unsupervised learning of depth, camera motion, optical flow and motion segmentation. In: Proceedings of the IEEE/CVF Conference on Computer Vision and Pattern Recognition, pp. 12240–12249 (2019)

17. Rasouli, A., Kotseruba, I., Tsotsos, J.K.: Are they going to cross? a benchmark dataset and baseline for pedestrian crosswalk behavior. In: Proceedings of the IEEE International Conference on Computer Vision Workshops, pp. 206–213 (2017)

18. Robicquet, Alexandre, Sadeghian, Amir, Alahi, Alexandre, Savarese, Silvio: Learning social etiquette: human trajectory understanding in crowded scenes. In: Leibe, Bastian, Matas, Jiri, Sebe, Nicu, Welling, Max (eds.) ECCV 2016. LNCS, vol. 9912, pp. 549–565. Springer, Cham (2016). https://doi.org/10.1007/978-3-319-46484-8_33

19. Shuai, B., Berneshawi, A.G., Modolo, D., Tighe, J.: Multi-object tracking with siamese track-rcnn. arXiv preprint arXiv:2004.07786 (2020)

20. Styles, O., Ross, A., Sanchez, V.: Forecasting pedestrian trajectory with machine-annotated training data. In: 2019 IEEE Intelligent Vehicles Symposium (IV), pp. 716–721. IEEE (2019)

21. Styles, O., Sanchez, V., Guha, T.: Multiple object forecasting: predicting future object locations in diverse environments. In: Proceedings of the IEEE/CVF Winter Conference on Applications of Computer Vision, pp. 690–699 (2020)

22. Tokmakov, P., Li, J., Burgard, W., Gaidon, A.: Learning to track with object permanence. arXiv preprint arXiv:2103.14258 (2021)

23. Wang, Y., Wang, P., Yang, Z., Luo, C., Yang, Y., Xu, W.: Unos: unified unsupervised optical-flow and stereo-depth estimation by watching videos. In: Proceedings of the IEEE/CVF Conference on Computer Vision and Pattern Recognition, pp. 8071–8081 (2019)

24. Wang, Zhongdao, Zheng, Liang, Liu, Yixuan, Li, Yali, Wang, Shengjin: Towards real-time multi-object tracking. In: Vedaldi, Andrea, Bischof, Horst, Brox, Thomas, Frahm, Jan-Michael. (eds.) ECCV 2020. LNCS, vol. 12356, pp. 107–122. Springer, Cham (2020). https://doi.org/10.1007/978-3-030-58621-8_7
25. Xingjian, S., Chen, Z., Wang, H., Yeung, D.Y., Wong, W.K., Woo, W.C.: Convolutional lstm network: a machine learning approach for precipitation nowcasting. Adv. Neural Inf. Process. Syst. **28**, 802–810 (2015)
26. Yagi, T., Mangalam, K., Yonetani, R., Sato, Y.: Future person localization in first-person videos. In: Proceedings of the IEEE Conference on Computer Vision and Pattern Recognition, pp. 7593–7602 (2018)
27. Yan, Y., et al.: Anchor-free person search. In: Proceedings of the IEEE/CVF Conference on Computer Vision and Pattern Recognition, pp. 7690–7699 (2021)
28. Yao, H.Y., Wan, W.G., Li, X.: End-to-end pedestrian trajectory forecasting with transformer network. ISPRS Int. J. Geo-Inf. **11**(1), 44 (2022)
29. Yin, Z., Shi, J.: Geonet: unsupervised learning of dense depth, optical flow and camera pose. In: Proceedings of the IEEE Conference on Computer Vision and Pattern Recognition, pp. 1983–1992 (2018)
30. t al Zhang, Y., e.: Bytetrack: multi-object tracking by associating every detection box. arXiv preprint arXiv:2110.06864 (2021)
31. Zhang, Y., Wang, C., Wang, X., Zeng, W., Liu, W.: Fairmot: on the fairness of detection and re-identification in multiple object tracking. Int. J. Comput. Vision **129**, 1–19 (2021)
32. Zhou, Xingyi, Koltun, Vladlen, Krähenbühl, Philipp: Tracking objects as points. In: Vedaldi, Andrea, Bischof, Horst, Brox, Thomas, Frahm, Jan-Michael. (eds.) ECCV 2020. LNCS, vol. 12349, pp. 474–490. Springer, Cham (2020). https://doi.org/10.1007/978-3-030-58548-8_28

Large-Displacement 3D Object Tracking with Hybrid Non-local Optimization

Xuhui Tian[1], Xinran Lin[1], Fan Zhong[1]([✉]), and Xueying Qin[2]

[1] School of Computer Science and Technology, Shandong University, Qingdao, China

zhongfan@sdu.edu.cn

[2] School of Software, Shandong University, Jinan, China

Abstract. Optimization-based 3D object tracking is known to be precise and fast, but sensitive to large inter-frame displacements. In this paper we propose a fast and effective non-local 3D tracking method. Based on the observation that erroneous local minimum are mostly due to the out-of-plane rotation, we propose a hybrid approach combining non-local and local optimizations for different parameters, resulting in efficient non-local search in the 6D pose space. In addition, a precomputed robust contour-based tracking method is proposed for the pose optimization. By using long search lines with multiple candidate correspondences, it can adapt to different frame displacements without the need of coarse-to-fine search. After the pre-computation, pose updates can be conducted very fast, enabling the non-local optimization to run in real time. Our method outperforms all previous methods for both small and large displacements. For large displacements, the accuracy is greatly improved (81.7% v.s. 19.4%). At the same time, real-time speed (>50 fps) can be achieved with only CPU. The source code is available at https://github.com/cvbubbles/nonlocal-3dtracking.

Keywords: 3D Tracking · Pose estimation

1 Introduction

3D object tracking aims to estimate the accurate 6-DoF pose of dynamic video objects provided with the CAD models. This is a fundamental technique for many vision applications, such as augmented reality [14], robot grasping [2], human-computer interaction [12], etc.

Previous methods can be categorized as optimization-based [4,16,18,21] and learning-based [3,13,25,26]. The optimization-based methods are more efficient

---

X. Tian and X. Lin—Equally contributed.

Supplementary Information The online version contains supplementary material available at https://doi.org/10.1007/978-3-031-20047-2_36.

and more precise, while the learning-based methods are more robust by leveraging the object-specific training process and the power of GPU. Our work will focus on the optimization-based approach, aiming at mobile applications that require fast high-precision 3D tracking (e.g. augmented reality).

In order to achieve real-time speed, previous optimization-based 3D tracking methods search for only the local minima of the non-convex cost function. Note that this is based on the assumption that frame displacement is small, which in practice is often violated due to fast object or camera movements. For large frame displacements, a good initialization is unavailable, then the local minima would deviate the true object pose. As shown in Fig. 1(a), when frame displacements become large, the accuracy of previous 3D tracking methods will decrease fast.

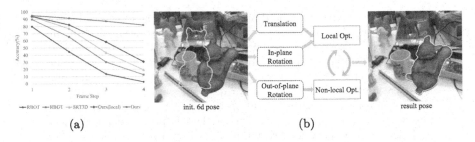

(a)   (b)

Fig. 1. (a) The accuracy of previous 3D tracking methods (RBOT [22], RBGT [18], SRT3D [19]) would decrease fast with the increase of displacements (frame step S). (b) The proposed hybrid non-local optimization method.

The coarse-to-fine search is commonly adopted in previous tracking methods for handling large displacements. For 3D tracking, it can be implemented by image pyramids [7,22] or by varying the length of search lines [18]. However, note that since the 3D rotation is independent of the object scale in image space, coarse-to-fine search in image space would take little effect on the rotation components. On the other hand, although non-local tracking methods such as particle filter [10] can overcome the local minimum, directly sampling in the 6D pose space would result in a large amount of computation, so previous methods [3,28] always require powerful GPU to achieve real-time speed.

In this paper, we propose the first non-local 3D tracking method that can run in real-time with only CPU. *Firstly*, by analyzing previous methods, we find that most tracking failures (e.g. near 90% for SRT3D [19])) are caused by the out-of-plane rotations. Based on this observation, we propose a hybrid approach for optimizing the 6D pose. As illustrated in Fig. 1(b), non-local search is applied for only out-of-plane rotation, which requires to do sampling only in a 2D space instead of the original 6D pose space. An efficient search method is introduced to reduce the invocations of local joint optimizations, by pre-termination and near-to-far search. *Secondly*, for better adaption to the non-local search, we propose a fast local pose optimization method that is more adaptive to frame displacements. Instead of using short search lines as in previous methods, we propose to use long search lines taking multiple candidate contour correspondences. The long search lines can be precomputed, and need not be recomputed when the pose is updated, which enables hundreds of pose update iterations to be conducted in real-time. A robust estimation method is introduced to deal with erroneous contour correspondences. As shown in Fig. 1(a), for the case of large displacements, our local method significantly outperforms previous methods, and the non-local method further improves the accuracy.

2 Related Work

Due to space limitation, here we only briefly introduce the methods that are closely related to our work. A more comprehensive review can be found in [19].

For textureless 3D object tracking, the optimization-based methods can be categorized as contour-based or region-based. The contour-based approaches have been studied for a long time [4,5,24]. However, early contour-based methods are known to be sensitive to background clutters that may cause wrong contour correspondences. To solve this problem, local color information is leveraged for improving the correspondences [8,17], which effectively improves accuracy.

Recent progress is mainly achieved by the region-based methods [7,18,19,29]. PWP3D [16] is the first real-time region-based method. Many methods are then proposed to improve the object segmentation. Hexner and Hagege [6] proposed a localized segmentation model to handle cluttered scenes. Tjaden et al. [23] extended the idea by using temporally consistent local color histograms. Zhong et al. [29] proposed to use polar coordinates for better handling occlusion. The recent works of Stobier et al. [18,19] proposed a sparse probabilistic model and Gaussian approximations for the derivatives in optimization, achieving state-of-the-art accuracy on the RBOT dataset [22] and can run at a fast speed. The above methods all do only local optimization, and thus are sensitive to large displacements.

The power of deep learning can be exploited for 3D tracking when GPU is available. The 6D pose refinement network of DeepIM [13] provides an effective way to estimate the pose difference between an input image and a rendered template. A similar network is adopted in SE(3)-TrackNet [26] for RGBD-based 3D tracking. A model-free 3D tracking method is proposed in BundleTrack [25], by leveraging an online optimization framework. In PoseRBPF [3], 6D pose tracking is formulated in a particle filter framework, with rotations searched globally in the 3D rotation space. This approach actually bridges 3D tracking with detection-based 6D pose estimation [11,15,27].

3 Adaptive Fast Local Tracking

To enable the non-local optimization in real-time, we first introduce a fast local optimization method that solves the local minima for arbitrary initial pose rapidly.

3.1   Robust Contour-Based Tracking

As in the previous method [22], the rigid transformation from the model space to the camera coordinate frame is represented as:

$$\mathbf{T} = \begin{bmatrix} \mathbf{R} \ \mathbf{t} \\ \mathbf{0} \ 1 \end{bmatrix} = \exp(\xi) \in \mathbb{SE}(3) \tag{1}$$

with $\xi \in \mathbb{R}^6$ the parameterization of $\mathbf{T}$.

Given a 3D model and an initial object pose, a set of 3D model points $\mathbf{X}_i$ ($i = 1, \cdots, N$) can be sampled on the projected object contour. Denoted by $\mathbf{x}_i^\xi$ the projection of $\mathbf{X}_i$ on image plane with respect to object pose ξ. As illustrated in Fig. 2(a), for each $\mathbf{x}_i^\xi$, a search line $l_i = \{\mathbf{o}_i, \mathbf{n}_i\}$ is assigned, with $\mathbf{o}_i$ the start point and $\mathbf{n}_i$ the normalized direction vector. l_i will be used to determine the image contour correspondence $\mathbf{c}_i$. The optimal object pose then is solved by minimizing the distance between the projected contour and the image contour:

$$E(\xi) = \sum_{i=1}^{N} \omega_i \parallel \mathbf{n}_i^\top (\mathbf{x}_i^\xi - \mathbf{o}_i) - d_i \parallel^\alpha \tag{2}$$

with d_i the distance from $\mathbf{c}_i$ to $\mathbf{o}_i$, i.e. $\mathbf{c}_i = \mathbf{o}_i + d_i \mathbf{n}_i$, so the cost function above actually measures the projected distance of $\mathbf{x}_i^\xi$ and $\mathbf{c}_i$ on the search line. ω_i is a weighting function for the i-th point. α is a constant parameter for robust estimation. $\mathbf{x}_i^\xi$ can be computed based on the pinhole camera projection function:

$$\mathbf{x}_i^\xi = \pi(\mathbf{K}(\mathbf{T}\widetilde{\mathbf{X}}_i)_{3 \times 1}), \quad \text{where } \mathbf{K} = \begin{bmatrix} f_x & 0 & c_x \\ 0 & f_y & c_y \\ 0 & 0 & 1 \end{bmatrix} \tag{3}$$

where $\widetilde{\mathbf{X}}_i$ is the homogeneous representation of $\mathbf{X}_i$, $\pi(\mathbf{X}) = [X/Z, Y/Z]^\top$ for 3D point $\mathbf{X} = [X, Y, Z]^\top$, $\mathbf{K}$ is the known 3×3 camera intrinsic matrix.

The above method extends previous contour-based methods [8,17] in the following aspects:

First, in previous methods, the search lines are generally centered at the projected point $\mathbf{x}_i^\xi$, and the image correspondences are searched in a fixed range on the two sides. This approach raises difficulty in determining the search range for the case of large displacements. In addition, since the search lines are dependent on the current object pose ξ, they should be recomputed once the pose is updated. The proposed search line method as shown in Fig. 2(a) can address the above problems by detaching the line configurations from ξ, which enables us to use long search lines that can be precomputed for all possible ξ in the range (see Sect. 3.2).

Second, our method takes robust estimation with $\alpha < 2$ to handle erroneous correspondences. In previous methods $\alpha = 2$, so the optimization process is sensitive to the correspondence errors, and complex filtering and weighting techniques thus are necessary [8,17]. We will show that, by setting α as a small value, erroneous correspondences can be well suppressed with a simple weighting function ω_i (see Sect. 3.3).

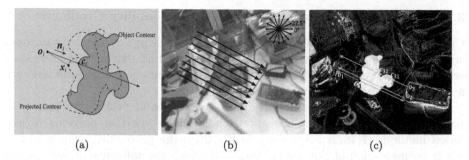

(a)   (b)   (c)

Fig. 2. (a) The adopted contour-based tracking model. (b) The search lines in one direction. The top right shows all of the directions for $D = 16$. (c) The foreground probability map and exemplar search lines. Note that the contour points of $\mathbf{o}_1$ and $\mathbf{o}_2$ are on the opposite sides of the object. $\mathbf{o}_3$ has two different contour points.

3.2 Precomputed Search Lines

Using long search lines would make it more difficult to determine the contour correspondences. On the one hand, there may be multiple contour points on the same search line, and the number is unknown. On the other hand, due to the background clutters, searching in a larger range would be more likely to result in an error. To overcome these difficulties, for each search line l_k we select multiple candidate contour points $\mathbf{c}_{km}$. Then during pose optimization, for $\mathbf{x}_i^\xi$ associated with l_k, $\mathbf{c}_{km}$ closest to $\mathbf{x}_i^\xi$ will be selected as the correspondence point $\mathbf{c}_i$. In this way, significant errors in $\mathbf{c}_{km}$ can be tolerated because $\mathbf{c}_{km}$ far from the projected contour would not be involved in the optimization.

For $\mathbf{x}_i^\xi$ with projected contour normal $\hat{\mathbf{n}}_i$, the associated search line can be determined as the one passing $\mathbf{x}_i^\xi$ and has direction vector $\mathbf{n}_i = \hat{\mathbf{n}}_i$. Therefore, a search line can be shared by all $\mathbf{x}_i^\xi$ on the line with the same projected normal, which enables the search lines to be precomputed. Figure 2(b) shows all search lines in one direction. Given the ROI region containing the object, each search line will be a ray going through the ROI region. The search lines in each direction are densely arranged, so every pixel in the ROI will be associated with exactly one search line in each direction.

In order to precompute all search lines, the range $[0°, 360°)$ are uniformly divided into D different directions ($D = 16$ in our experiments). The search lines in each of the D directions then can be precomputed. Note that a direction o and its opposite direction $o + 180°$ are taken as two different directions because the contour correspondences assigned to them are different (see Sect. 3.3). For arbitrary $\mathbf{x}_i^\xi$ in the ROI, there will be D search lines passing through it, one of which with the direction vector closest to $\hat{\mathbf{n}}_i$ is assigned to $\mathbf{x}_i^\xi$, and then the contour correspondence $\mathbf{c}_i$ can be found as the closest candidate point.

3.3   Contour Correspondences Based on Probability Gradients

Correspondences would take a great effect on the resulting accuracy, so have been studied much in previous methods. Surprisingly, we find that with the proposed search line and robust estimation methods, high accuracy can be achieved with a very simple method for correspondences.

For an input image, we first compute a foreground probability map $p(\mathbf{x})$ based on color histograms. The approach is widely used in previous region-based methods [7,18,22]. As shown in Fig. 2(c), the probability map is in fact a soft segmentation of the object, based on which the influence of background clutters and interior contours can be suspended effectively. Considering large object displacements, we estimate $p(\mathbf{x})$ based on the global color histograms. Note that although local color probabilities have been shown to handle complex and indistinctive color distributions better [7,22], the local window size is usually hard to be determined for the case of large displacement.

During tracking, foreground and background color histograms are maintained in the same way as [18], which produces probability densities $p^f(\mathbf{x})$ and $p^b(\mathbf{x})$ respectively for each pixel $\mathbf{x}$, then $p(\mathbf{x})$ is computed as:

$$p(\mathbf{x}) = \frac{p^f(\mathbf{x}) + \epsilon}{p^f(\mathbf{x}) + p^b(\mathbf{x}) + 2\epsilon} \tag{4}$$

where $\epsilon = 10^{-6}$ is a small constant, so $p(\mathbf{x})$ would be 0.5 if $p^f(\mathbf{x})$ and $p^b(\mathbf{x})$ are both zero (usually indicating a new color has not appeared before).

Given $p(\mathbf{x})$, for each search line l_k, the probability value $p_k(d)$ at the pixel location $\mathbf{x} = \mathbf{o}_k + d\mathbf{n}_k$ can be resampled with bilinear interpolation. Since $p(\mathbf{x})$ is a soft segmentation of the object, the probability gradients $\nabla_k = \frac{\partial p_k(d)}{\partial d}$ can be taken as the response of object contours along l_k. We thus can select the candidate contour correspondences $\mathbf{c}_{km}$ based on ∇_k. Specifically, standard 1D non-maximum suppression is first applied to ∇_k, then the M locations with the maximum gradient response are selected as $\mathbf{c}_{km}$. Finally, a soft weight is computed for $\mathbf{c}_{km}$ as:

$$\omega_{km} = (\frac{1}{W}\nabla_{km})^2 \tag{5}$$

where W is a normalizing factor computed as the maximum gradient response of all candidate correspondences, ∇_{km} is the gradient response of $\mathbf{c}_{km}$. ω_{km} will be used as the weight ω_i in Eq. (2) if $\mathbf{x}_i^\xi$ is matched with $\mathbf{c}_{km}$ (i.e. $\mathbf{c}_i = \mathbf{c}_{km}$).

The above method is pretty simple and elegant compared with previous methods. Note that unless there is not enough local maximum, each search line would take a fixed number of M candidates ($M = 3$ in our experiments). We did not even filter candidates with small responses as in usual cases. By taking a small α, the effect of erroneous correspondences can be well suppressed.

3.4 Pose Optimization

The cost function in Eq. (2) can be rewritten as

$$E(\xi) = \sum_{i=1}^{N} \omega_i \parallel F(\xi, i) \parallel^{\alpha}, \quad \text{where } F(\xi, i) = \mathbf{n}_i^{\top} (\mathbf{x}_i^{\xi} - \mathbf{o}_i) - d_i \qquad (6)$$

which can be solved with *iterative reweighted least square* (IRLS) by further rewriting as

$$E(\xi) = \sum_{i=1}^{N} \omega_i \psi_i F(\xi, i)^2, \quad \text{with } \psi_i = \frac{1}{\parallel F(\xi, i) \parallel^{2-\alpha}} \qquad (7)$$

with ψ_i fixed weights computed with the current ξ. ψ_i would penalize the correspondences with larger matching residuals, which are usually caused by erroneous correspondences. Using smaller α can better suppress erroneous correspondences, with some sacrifice in convergence speed.

Equation (7) is a nonlinear weighted least square problem that can be solved similarly as in previous methods [7,22]. Given the Jacobian $\mathbf{J}$ of $F(\xi, i)$, the pose update of each iteration can be computed as

$$\Delta \xi = -(\sum_{i=1}^{N} \omega_i \psi_i \mathbf{J} \mathbf{J}^{\top})^{-1} \sum_{i=1}^{N} \omega_i \psi_i \mathbf{J} F(\xi, i) \qquad (8)$$

Please refer the supplementary material for details. Note that for arbitrary $\mathbf{x}_i^{\xi}$, the corresponding $\mathbf{c}_i$ and d_i can be easily retrieved from the precomputed search lines, so the pose update iterations can be executed very fast.

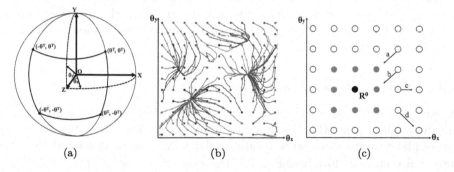

(a)   (b)   (c)

Fig. 3. (a) Parameterization of the out-of-plane rotation with θ_x and θ_y. (b) Convergence paths of the naive grid search in the 2D out-of-plane parameter space, with each path corresponds to the iterations of a local optimization. (c) The near-to-far search starting from $\mathbf{R}^0$. The iterations toward $\mathbf{R}^0$ (e.g. a, b) may be terminated soon by the *path pretermination*, while the iterations apart from $\mathbf{R}^0$ (e.g. c, d) may converge to other local minimum.

4   Hybrid Non-local Optimization

The $E(\xi)$ in Eq. (2) is obviously non-convex, so the method in Sect. 3.4 can obtain only the local minima. This is a common case in previous methods. Considering the complexity of the cost function and the real-time speed requirement, it is hard to be addressed with general non-convex optimization methods [9]. Here we propose an efficient non-local optimization method to address this problem.

4.1   The Hybrid Optimization

A rotation matrix $\mathbf{R}$ can be decomposed as in-plane rotation $\mathbf{R}^{in}$ and out-of-plane rotation $\mathbf{R}^{out}$, i.e., $\mathbf{R} = \mathbf{R}^{in}\mathbf{R}^{out}$. $\mathbf{R}^{out}$ will rotate a direction vector $\mathbf{v}$ to the view axis, and $\mathbf{R}^{in}$ is a rotation around the view axis. By fixing an up vector, $\mathbf{R}^{out}$ can be uniquely determined from $\mathbf{v}$, then $\mathbf{R}$ can be uniquely decomposed. Please see the supplementary material for the details.

By analyzing previous tracking methods, we find that most of the erroneous local minimums are due to out-of-plane rotations. The supplementary material contains loss distributions of RBOT [22] and SRT3D [19]. As can be found, about 70% of RBOT failures and 90% of SRT3D failures are due to out-of-plane rotation. Based on this observation, we propose a hybrid approach combining non-local search and continuous local optimization, with the non-local search performed only in the 2D out-of-plane rotation space, and then jointly optimized with other parameters using local optimization.

To facilitate the non-local sampling of $\mathbf{R}^{out}$, we parameterize it as a 2D vector. Since $\mathbf{R}^{out}$ can be determined with $\mathbf{v}$, it can be parameterized in the same way. As illustrated in Fig. 3(a), each $\mathbf{v}$ around the Z axis is parameterized as a 2D vector $\theta = [\theta_x, \theta_y]^\top$, with θ_x, $\theta_y \in (-\pi/2, \pi/2)$ the elevation angles of the projections of $\mathbf{v}$ on the XOZ and YOZ planes, respectively. Compared with the parameterization with elevation and azimuth angles, this method can facilitate determining the neighbors in each direction and is more uniform for sampling around the Z axis.

4.2   Efficient Non-local Search

A naive non-local search method now can be easily devised based on grid search. Given an initial pose $(\mathbf{R}^0, \mathbf{t}^0)$ and a maximum search range $\theta^T \in [0, \pi/2)$ for the out-of-plane rotation, a grid of rotation offsets Δ_{ij}^R can be generated from the direction vectors uniformly sampled in the range $\Omega = [-\theta^T, \theta^T] \times [-\theta^T, \theta^T]$. In our implementation a fixed interval $\pi/12$ is used for the sampling. For each grid point (i, j), the initial pose is reset as $(\Delta_{ij}^R\mathbf{R}^0, \mathbf{t}^0)$, then the local optimization method proposed in Sect. 3 is invoked to find the corresponding local minimum ξ_{ij}. The final pose is selected as ξ_{ij} that results in smallest contour matching error $E'(\xi) = \frac{1}{N'}E(\xi)$, where N' is the actual number of contour points involved in the computation of $E(\xi)$, excluding those occluded or out of image scope.

Algorithm 1 Non-local 3D Tracking

1: **Input**: initial pose $\{\mathbf{R}, \mathbf{t}\}$ and parameters e^T, θ^T
2: Precompute the search lines
3: $\{\mathbf{R}, \mathbf{t}\} \leftarrow localUpdates(\{\mathbf{R}, \mathbf{t}\})$ ▷ Please see text
4: $err \leftarrow E'(\{\mathbf{R}, \mathbf{t}\})$
5: **if** $err > e^T$ **then**
6:     $\mathbf{R}^0 = \mathbf{R}$
7:     Sampling Δ_{ij}^R from the range $[-\theta^T, \theta^T] \times [-\theta^T, \theta^T]$
8:     Visit grid points (i, j) in breadth-first search and **do**
9:         $\{\hat{\mathbf{R}}, \hat{\mathbf{t}}\} \leftarrow innerLocalUpdates(\{\Delta_{ij}^R \mathbf{R}^0, \mathbf{t}\})$ ▷ Please see text
10:         $\hat{err} \leftarrow E'(\{\hat{\mathbf{R}}, \hat{\mathbf{t}}\})$
11:         $err, \mathbf{R}, \mathbf{t} \leftarrow \hat{err}, \hat{\mathbf{R}}, \hat{\mathbf{t}}$ if $\hat{err} < err$
12:         Break if $err < e^T$
13: **end if**
14: $\{\mathbf{R}, \mathbf{t}\} \leftarrow localUpdates(\{\mathbf{R}, \mathbf{t}\})$

The above naive grid search is inefficient because the local optimizations are independent of each other, which incurs a large amount of redundant computation. We thus propose an improved version with the following improvements:

1) *grid pre-termination*. The grid search process is pre-terminated once it finds a pose ξ_{ij} that is accurate enough, i.e., the contour matching error $E'(\xi_{ij})$ is less than a threshold e^T. In this way, a large amount of computation can be saved if an accurate pose is found in the early stage. Since e^T is generally not easy to set manually, we adaptively estimate it as the median of the result matching errors of the previous 15 frames.

2) *path pre-termination*. As visualized in Fig. 3(b), the local optimizations contain a large number of overlaps in the space of Ω, which indicates that the same point in Ω may be searched multiple times. To avoid this, a new grid table that is 3 times finer than the searching grid is created for recording the visited locations in Ω, then the iterations of local optimization can be pre-terminated when it reaches a visited location. Note that this may harm the optimization of other parameters (in-plane rotation and translation), so we choose to disable the pretermination for iterations with a small step in Ω, which usually indicates that the current pose is close to a local minimum in Ω, so the optimization should continue for further optimizing in-plane rotation and translation.

3) *near-to-far search*. A near-to-far search is used instead of the sequential search in Ω. As illustrated in Fig. 3(c), starting from $\mathbf{R}^0$, the locations closer to $\mathbf{R}^0$ are visited first with a breadth-first search. As a result, for the case of small displacements, $\mathbf{R}^0$ is close to the true object pose, then the search process would terminate soon with the *grid pre-termination*. On the contrary, for the case of large displacements, a larger range will be searched automatically for smaller errors. This is a nice property making our method more adaptive to different displacements.

Algorithm 1 outlines the overall procedures of the proposed non-local search method. *localUpdates* is a procedure for local optimization, it accepts an initial pose and returns the optimized one. $\mathbf{R}^0, \mathbf{t}^0$ is computed as the result of a local tracking, if $\mathbf{R}^0, \mathbf{t}^0$ is already accurate enough, the non-local search process would completely be skipped. Note that this is a special case of the near-to-far search process mentioned above, with *grid pre-termination* activated for $\mathbf{R}^0, \mathbf{t}^0$. *innerLocalUpdates* is the version of *localUpdates* with the *path pretermination*. After the non-local search, *localUpdates* is called again to refine the pose.

5   Implementation Details

Similar to [18], the 3D model of each object is pre-rendered as 3000 template views to avoid online rendering. The view directions are sampled uniformly with the method introduced in [1]. For each template, $N = 200$ contour points $\mathbf{X}_i$ are sampled and stored together with their 3D surface normal. Given the pose parameter ξ, the image projection $\mathbf{x}_i^\xi$ as well as projected contour normals $\mathbf{n}_i$ can be computed fast with the camera projection function in Eq. (3).

The ROI region for the current frame is determined by dilating the object bounding box of the previous frame with 100 pixels on each side. For the efficient computation of the search lines in the direction o, the probability map $p(\mathbf{x})$ is first rotated around the center of the ROI to align the direction o with image rows. Each row of the rotated map $p^o(\mathbf{x})$ then is used for one search line. The probability gradient map ∇^o is computed from $p^o(\mathbf{x})$ using a horizontal Sobel operator with 7×7 kernel size. Compared with pixel difference, the smoothing process of the Sobel operator is helpful for suspending small response of contours and results in better accuracy. Note that for the opposite direction $o + 180°$, the probability gradient is negative to ∇^o at the same pixel location, and thus can be computed from ∇^o with little computation, saving nearly half of the computations for all directions.

The *localUpdates* in Algorithm 1 will execute the local pose optimization as in Eq. (8) up to 30 iterations, with the closest template view updated every 3 iterations. The iteration process will pre-terminate if the step $\| \Delta\xi \|$ is less than 10^{-4}. The robust estimation parameter α is fixed to 0.125. Note that this is a small value for better handling erroneous correspondences. For *innerLocalUpdates*, the above settings are the same except α, which is set as 0.75 for better convergence speed.

The non-local search range θ^T is adaptively estimated from the previous frames. When the frame t is successfully tracked, the displacement with the frame $t-1$ is computed the same as the rotation error in the RBOT dataset [22]. θ^T for the current frame then is computed as the median of the rotation displacements of the latest 5 frames.

6   Experiments

In experiments we evaluated our method with the RBOT dataset [22], which is the standard benchmark of recent optimization-based 3D tracking methods [7, 18,19,29]. The RBOT dataset consists of 18 different objects, and for each object,

4 sequences with different variants (i.e., *regular, dynamic light, noisy, occlusion*) are provided. The accuracy is computed the same as in previous works with the 5 cm–5° criteria [22]. A frame is considered as successfully tracked if the translation and rotation errors are less than 5 cm and 5°, respectively. Otherwise, it will be considered as a tracking failure and the pose will be reset with the ground truth. The accuracy is finally computed as the success rate of all frames.

6.1 Comparisons

Table 1 compares the accuracy of our method with previous methods, including RBOT [22], RBGT [18], SRT3D [19], etc. The cases of large displacements are tested with different frame step S. Each sequence of RBOT dataset contains 1001 frames, from which a sub-sequence $\{0, S, 2S, 3S, \cdots\}$ is extracted for given frame step S. The mean and maximum displacements for different S are included in Table 1. Note that the objects in RBOT actually move very fast, so $S = 4$ is

Table 1. Large-displacement tracking results on the *regular* variant of the RBOT dataset [22]. In [] is the mean and maximum displacements of rotation/translation corresponding to different frame step S. For $S > 1$, only the methods with published code are tested. *Ours⁻* is our method without the non-local optimization(lines 5–13 in Algorithm 1). Results of other variants can be found in the supplementary material.

Method	Ape	Soda	Vise	Soup	Camera	Can	Cat	Clown	Cube	Driller	Duck	Egg Box	Glue	Iron	Candy	Lamp	Phone	Squirrel	Avg.
$S = 1$ [Disp. Mean = 7.1°15.6 mm, Max = 14.8°30.1 mm]																			
[29]	88.8	41.3	94.0	85.9	86.9	89.0	98.5	93.7	83.1	87.3	86.2	78.5	58.6	86.3	57.9	91.7	85.0	96.2	82.7
[8]	91.9	44.8	99.7	89.1	89.3	90.6	97.4	95.9	83.9	97.6	91.8	84.4	59.0	92.5	74.3	97.4	86.4	99.7	86.9
[20]	93.0	55.2	99.3	85.4	96.1	93.9	98.0	95.6	79.5	**98.2**	89.7	89.1	66.5	91.3	60.6	98.6	95.6	99.6	88.1
[7]	94.6	49.4	99.5	91.0	93.7	96.0	97.8	96.6	90.2	**98.2**	93.4	90.3	64.4	94.0	79.0	**98.8**	92.9	99.8	89.9
[22]	85.0	39.0	98.9	82.4	79.7	87.6	95.9	93.3	78.1	93.0	86.8	74.6	38.9	81.0	46.8	97.5	80.7	99.4	79.9
[18]	96.4	53.2	98.8	93.9	93.0	92.7	99.7	97.1	92.5	92.5	93.7	88.5	70.0	92.1	78.8	95.5	92.5	99.6	90.0
[19]	98.8	65.1	99.6	96.0	**98.0**	96.5	100	98.4	94.1	96.9	98.0	95.3	79.3	96.0	90.3	97.4	**96.2**	99.8	94.2
Ours⁻	**99.8**	65.6	99.5	95.0	96.6	92.6	100	98.7	95.0	97.1	97.4	96.1	83.3	96.9	91.5	95.8	95.2	99.7	94.2
Ours	**99.8**	67.1	100	97.8	97.3	93.7	100	99.4	97.4	97.6	99.3	96.9	84.7	97.7	93.4	96.7	95.4	100	**95.2**
$S = 2$ [Disp. Mean = 14.0°30.7 mm, Max = 28.1°57.8 mm]																			
[22]	37.6	11.4	72.0	46.6	45.2	44.0	46.6	52.0	24.6	65.6	46.4	44.6	13.6	42.4	22.8	67.8	45.2	75.2	44.6
[18]	83.4	21.8	72.4	75.0	68.4	58.2	86.4	78.8	74.0	58.0	80.4	65.4	38.8	63.8	41.6	59.4	61.8	90.0	65.4
[19]	94.0	30.6	82.8	83.4	78.0	72.8	90.2	90.0	81.8	72.2	90.6	77.6	56.4	79.0	62.6	70.8	76.4	94.4	76.9
Ours⁻	97.2	38.4	94.6	85.8	87.2	78.2	91.4	92.6	84.6	82.8	93.6	82.2	61.6	87.4	66.8	77.4	78.8	98.2	82.2
Ours	100	49.0	99.4	96.8	94.4	90.2	99.6	99.4	95.2	93.2	98.8	92.6	72.0	95.4	88.0	93.4	89.8	100	**91.5**
$S = 3$ [Disp. Mean = 20.8°45.8 mm, Max = 39.5°81.0mm]																			
[22]	8.1	0.3	28.8	9.0	12.3	9.9	14.1	16.8	4.8	19.2	17.1	11.7	2.4	12.9	3.9	22.2	11.1	37.8	13.5
[18]	47.4	7.2	26.4	35.7	28.5	17.4	43.2	42.0	40.5	25.2	47.1	30.3	12.0	31.2	14.1	24.6	25.2	45.9	30.2
[19]	70.6	12.6	42.6	48.9	41.4	30.6	54.4	55.9	53.2	38.7	63.7	43.2	27.9	44.1	22.8	36.6	35.7	59.2	43.5
Ours⁻	81.7	15.9	69.1	68.2	55.3	44.7	65.5	74.8	68.5	53.8	81.4	51.7	34.5	68.8	35.1	41.7	50.8	88.3	58.3
Ours	99.4	37.8	99.4	94.9	91.6	83.5	99.4	98.5	93.1	84.7	99.7	87.4	62.2	91.6	79.3	85.3	80.2	100	**87.1**
$S = 4$ [Disp. Mean = 27.7°60.7 mm, Max = 54.6°97.6 mm]																			
[22]	0.8	0.0	5.6	2.0	3.2	2.4	3.6	1.6	0.4	5.2	2.4	2.8	0.4	3.2	0.4	2.8	1.2	7.6	2.5
[18]	22.0	2.0	10.0	14.8	12.4	4.8	18.4	17.2	16.4	10.8	22.0	14.0	4.8	12.8	5.2	8.4	10.4	19.6	12.6
[19]	36.4	3.2	15.2	22.4	17.2	10.0	26.0	26.0	28.0	16.8	37.6	18.0	10.4	19.2	6.8	12.8	16.4	27.2	19.4
Ours⁻	50.0	8.0	34.8	42.0	28.8	15.2	36.4	41.2	39.2	22.0	55.2	24.8	12.4	38.0	10.0	16.4	22.0	56.0	30.7
Ours	96.8	31.6	97.6	93.6	85.6	77.6	98.0	97.6	84.8	80.0	98.8	82.0	46.8	86.0	60.0	80.8	74.0	99.6	**81.7**

indeed very challenging. For the compared methods, the results of $S = 1$ are from the original paperw, and the results of $S > 1$ are computed with the authors' code with default parameters. Therefore, only the methods with published code are tested for $S > 1$. For our method, the same setting is used for all S.

As is shown, our method constantly outperforms previous methods for different frame steps. More importantly, the margin of accuracy becomes larger and larger with the increase of frame step, showing the effectiveness of our method in handling large displacements. When $S = 4$, the average frame displacement is $27.7°/60.7$ mm, which is hard for local tracking methods. In this case, the most competitive method SRT3D [19] can achieve only 19.4% accuracy, while our method still obtains 81.7% accuracy. Note that this accuracy is even higher than the accuracy of RBOT [22] for $S = 1$ (79.9%). We have also tested with stricter 2 cm–2° criteria and the tracking accuracy is 84.1%. As a comparison, in this case, SRT3D [19] achieves only 78.7% accuracy.

Table 1 also shows the results of the proposed local tracking method (*Ours⁻*). As can be found, our local method still significantly outperforms previous methods for large displacements. This is mainly attributed to the new search line model, which makes our method more adaptive to displacements. Note that our method does not even use coarse-to-fine search, while the compared methods all exploit coarse-to-fine search for handling large displacements.

(a) init.   (b) srt3d [19]   (c) ours prob.   (d) ours(local)   (e) ours

Fig. 4. Visual examples and comparisons for $S = 8$.

Figure 4 shows some challenging examples with $S = 8$. In the top row, the translation displacement is very large. Thanks to the use of long search lines, our local method can compensate for most translation errors and performs much better than SRT3D. In the bottom row, the rotation displacement is large and the probability map is very inaccurate, so both SRT3D and *Ours⁻* fail to converge properly. In both cases, our non-local method can result in the correct pose.

Due to the space limitation, results of other variants (*dynamic light, noisy, occlusion*) are put in the supplementary material. The trend is generally the same as the *regular* variant when compared with previous methods.

6.2   Time Analysis

Runtime is measured on a machine with Intel(R) Core(TM) i7-7700K CPU. The pre-computation needs to be done for each of the D directions ($D = 16$ in our experiments). We implement it in parallel with the OpenCV *parallel_for* procedure for acceleration, which requires about 4–7 ms for each frame, depending on the object size. As a comparison, a sequential implementation requires 11–20 ms. After the pre-computation, the pose update iterations in Eq. (8) can be executed very fast. For $N = 200$ as in our experiments, only about 0.03 ms is required for each pose update iteration.

Besides the pre-computation, no parallelism is used in other parts of our code. For $S = 1, 2, 3, 4$, the average runtime per frame is about 10.8 ms, 12.5 ms, 21.7 ms, 22.3 ms respectively, achieving average about 50–100 fps. The runtime varies a lot for different S because of the pre-termination and near-to-far strategies in the non-local search. This is a desirable feature making our system adapt better to different displacements. On the contrary, previous non-local methods such as particle filter usually require constant computation regardless of the displacements.

Table 2. Ablation studies to the non-local search (GP = *grid pretermination*, PP = *path pretermination*, N2F = *near-to-far search*). The results are computed with $S = 4$ for the *regular* variant. *UpdateItrs* is the average pose update iterations per frame.

	Naive	+GP	+PP	+GP&PP	+GP&PP&N2F	Local(*Ours⁻*)
UpdateItrs	1085	718	823	578	468	59
Time	47.7 ms	34.0 ms	37.9 ms	27.6 ms	22.3 ms	9.7 ms
Accuracy	85.1	83.5	84.6	82.7	81.7	30.7

6.3   Ablation Studies

Table 2 shows the ablation studies for the non-local search method. With the naive grid search, more than 1000 pose update iterations are required for each frame. Thanks to the proposed fast local optimization method, even the naive search can achieve near real-time speed. The three strategies all contribute significantly to higher efficiency. Using them all can reduce more than half of the time with only about 3% sacrifice in accuracy. Moreover, compared with the local method, it increases the absolute accuracy by more than 50% with only about 12 ms sacrifice in time.

Table 3 shows the ablation experiments for the parameters α and D. As can be seen, α would take a great effect on the accuracy. Using $\alpha > 1$ would significantly reduce the accuracy due to the erroneous contour correspondences. As shown in Fig. 4, the foreground probability map of some objects is very noisy.

Actually, for larger α, the reduction of accuracy are mainly due to the objects with indistinctive colors, as detailed in the supplementary material.

The number of directions D would also take significant effects. Surprisingly, even with only the horizontal and vertical directions (i.e., $D = 4$), our local method can still achieve 88.1% accuracy, which is competitive in comparison with previous methods other than SRT3D.

Table 4 shows the ablation experiments for the parameters M and N. Our method is very insensitive to the choice of M. We set $M = 3$ by default, but it is surprising that our method could benefit from using a larger M, which will increase the chance to find the correct correspondence, but at the same time introduce more noise. This further demonstrates the robustness of our method to erroneous contour correspondences.

The number of sampled contour points N also takes some effects on the accuracy. From Table 3 we can find that N is not difficult to set. For $N > 200$, the increase of N takes little effect on the accuracy. Note that the computation of our method is proportional to the number of sample points, so smaller N may be considered for applications that are more time-critical.

Table 3. Ablation studies to α, D with *Ours⁻* and the *regular* variant.

α	0.125	0.25	0.5	0.75	1.0	1.5	D	4	8	12	16	20
Acc.	94.2	94.2	93.6	92.1	88.8	72.3	Acc.	88.1	92.8	93.7	94.2	94.3

Table 4. Ablation studies to M and N with the *regular* variant.

M	1	3	5	7	9	15	N	50	100	200	300	400
Acc.	93.6	95.2	95.2	95.6	95.7	95.6	Acc.	93.9	94.6	95.2	95.3	95.2

6.4   Limitations

Our current method is still limited in some aspects that can be further improved. *Firstly*, the error function $E'(.)$ is very simple, and it may be failed to recognize the true object pose in complicated cases. For example, for the case of *noisy* variant and $S = 1$, the mean accuracy is reduced from 83.4% to 83.2% after adding the non-local optimization (see the supplementary material). Obviously, this case should not occur if the error function is reliable.

Secondly, the same as previous texture-less tracking methods, only the object shape is used for the pose estimation, so our method is not suitable for symmetrical objects (e.g., *soda* in the RBOT dataset). For symmetrical objects, additional cues such as interior textures should be considered for improvements.

Thirdly, since the correspondences are based on the probability map, the segmentation method would take a great effect on the accuracy of our method. Our current segmentation method is very simple considering the speed requirement, using better segmentation (e.g., those based on deep learning) would definitely improve the accuracy to a great extent.

7   Conclusions

In this paper we proposed a non-local 3D tracking method to deal with large displacements. To our knowledge, this is the first non-local 3D tracking method that can run in real-time on CPU. We achieve the goal with contributions in both local and non-local pose optimization. An improved contour-based local tracking method with long precomputed search lines is proposed, based on which an efficient hybrid non-local search method is introduced to overcome local minimums, with non-local sampling only in the 2D out-of-plane space. Our method is simple yet effective, and for the case of large displacements, large margin of improvements can be achieved. Future work may consider extending the idea to related problems, such as 6D pose estimation [27] and camera tracking [28].

Acknowledgements. This work is supported by NSFC project 62172260, and the Industrial Internet Innovation and Development Project in 2019 of China.

References

1. Arvo, J.: Fast random rotation matrices. In: Graphics gems III (IBM version), pp. 117–120. Elsevier (1992)
2. Choi, C., Christensen, H.I.: Real-time 3D model-based tracking using edge and keypoint features for robotic manipulation. In: IEEE International Conference on Robotics and Automation, pp. 4048–4055 (2010). https://doi.org/10.1109/ROBOT.2010.5509171
3. Deng, X., Mousavian, A., Xiang, Y., Xia, F., Bretl, T., Fox, D.: PoseRBPF: a Rao-Blackwellized particle filter for 6-D object pose tracking. IEEE Trans. Rob. **37**(5), 1328–1342 (2021). https://doi.org/10.1109/TRO.2021.3056043
4. Drummond, T., Cipolla, R.: Real-time visual tracking of complex structures. IEEE Trans. Patt. Anal. Mach. Intell. **24**(7), 932–946 (2002). https://doi.org/10.1109/TPAMI.2002.1017620
5. Harris, C., Stennett, C.: Rapid - a video rate object tracker. In: BMVC (1990)
6. Hexner, J., Hagege, R.R.: 2D–3D pose estimation of heterogeneous objects using a region based approach. Int. J. Comput. Vis. **118**(1), 95–112 (2016). https://doi.org/10.1007/s11263-015-0873-2
7. Huang, H., Zhong, F., Qin, X.: Pixel-wise weighted region-based 3D object tracking using contour constraints. IEEE Trans. Visual. Comput. Graph. 1 (2021). https://doi.org/10.1109/TVCG.2021.3085197
8. Huang, H., Zhong, F., Sun, Y., Qin, X.: An occlusion-aware edge-based method for monocular 3D object tracking using edge confidence. Comput. Graph. Forum **39**(7), 399–409 (2020). https://doi.org/10.1111/cgf.14154

9. Jain, P., Kar, P.: Non-convex optimization for machine learning. arXiv preprint arXiv:1712.07897 (2017)
10. Kwon, J., Lee, H.S., Park, F.C., Lee, K.M.: A geometric particle filter for template-based visual tracking. IEEE Trans. Pattern Anal. Mach. Intell. **36**(4), 625–643 (2013)
11. Labbé, Y., Carpentier, J., Aubry, M., Sivic, J.: CosyPose: consistent multi-view multi-object 6D pose estimation. In: Vedaldi, A., Bischof, H., Brox, T., Frahm, J.-M. (eds.) ECCV 2020. LNCS, vol. 12362, pp. 574–591. Springer, Cham (2020). https://doi.org/10.1007/978-3-030-58520-4_34
12. Lepetit, V., Fua, P.: Monocular model-based 3D tracking of rigid objects. Now Publishers Inc (2005)
13. Li, Y., Wang, G., Ji, X., Xiang, Y., Fox, D.: DeepIM: deep iterative matching for 6D pose estimation. In: Proceedings of the ECCV, pp. 683–698 (2018)
14. Marchand, E., Uchiyama, H., Spindler, F.: Pose estimation for augmented reality: a hands-on survey. IEEE Trans. Vis. Comput. Graph. **22**(12), 2633–2651 (2016). https://doi.org/10.1109/TVCG.2015.2513408
15. Peng, S., Liu, Y., Huang, Q., Zhou, X., Bao, H.: PVNet: pixel-wise voting network for 6DoF pose estimation. In: IEEE/CVF Conference on CVPR, pp. 4556–4565. IEEE, Long Beach, CA, USA, June 2019. https://doi.org/10.1109/CVPR.2019.00469
16. Prisacariu, V., Reid, I.: PWP3D: real-time segmentation and tracking of 3D objects. In: Proceedings of the 20th British Machine Vision Conference (September 2009). https://doi.org/10.1007/s11263-011-0514-3
17. Seo, B.K., Park, H., Park, J.I., Hinterstoisser, S., Ilic, S.: Optimal local searching for fast and robust textureless 3D object tracking in highly cluttered backgrounds. IEEE Trans. Vis. Comput. Graph. **20**(1), 99–110 (2014). https://doi.org/10.1109/TVCG.2013.94
18. Stoiber, M., Pfanne, M., Strobl, K.H., Triebel, R., Albu-Schaeffer, A.: A sparse gaussian approach to region-based 6DoF object tracking. In: Proceedings of the Asian Conference on Computer Vision (2020)
19. Stoiber, M., Pfanne, M., Strobl, K.H., Triebel, R., Albu-Schäffer, A.: SRT3D: a sparse region-based 3D object tracking approach for the real world. Int. J. Comput. Vis. **130**(4), 1008–1030 (2022). https://doi.org/10.1007/s11263-022-01579-8
20. Sun, X., Zhou, J., Zhang, W., Wang, Z., Yu, Q.: Robust monocular pose tracking of less-distinct objects based on contour-part model. IEEE Trans. Circuits Syst. Video Technol. **31**(11), 4409–4421 (2021). https://doi.org/10.1109/TCSVT.2021.3053696
21. Tjaden, H., Schwanecke, U., Schömer, E.: Real-time monocular segmentation and pose tracking of multiple objects. In: Leibe, B., Matas, J., Sebe, N., Welling, M. (eds.) ECCV 2016. LNCS, vol. 9908, pp. 423–438. Springer, Cham (2016). https://doi.org/10.1007/978-3-319-46493-0_26
22. Tjaden, H., Schwanecke, U., Schomer, E., Cremers, D.: A region-based gauss-newton approach to real-time monocular multiple object tracking. IEEE Trans. Pattern Anal. Mach. Intell. **41**(8), 1797–1812 (2019). https://doi.org/10.1109/TPAMI.2018.2884990
23. Tjaden, H., Schwanecke, U., Schömer, E.: Real-time monocular pose estimation of 3D objects using temporally consistent local color histograms. In: IEEE International Conference on Computer Vision (ICCV), pp. 124–132 (2017). https://doi.org/10.1109/ICCV.2017.23

24. Vacchetti, L., Lepetit, V., Fua, P.: Combining edge and texture information for real-time accurate 3D camera tracking. In: IEEE and ACM International Symposium on Mixed and Augmented Reality, pp. 48–56 (2004). https://doi.org/10.1109/ISMAR.2004.24

25. Wen, B., Bekris, K.: BundleTrack: 6D pose tracking for novel objects without instance or category-level 3D models. In: IEEE/RSJ International Conference on Intelligent Robots and Systems (IROS), pp. 8067–8074. IEEE (2021)

26. Wen, B., Mitash, C., Ren, B., Bekris, K.E.: se(3)-TrackNet: data-driven 6d pose tracking by calibrating image residuals in synthetic domains. In: IEEE/RSJ International Conference on Intelligent Robots and Systems (IROS), pp. 10367–10373. IEEE (2020)

27. Xiang, Y., Schmidt, T., Narayanan, V., Fox, D.: PoseCNN: a convolutional neural network for 6D object pose estimation in cluttered scenes. In: Robotics: Science and Systems XIV. Robotics: Science and Systems Foundation, June 2018. https://doi.org/10.15607/RSS.2018.XIV.019

28. Zhang, J., Zhu, C., Zheng, L., Xu, K.: ROSEFusion: random optimization for online dense reconstruction under fast camera motion. ACM Trans. Graph. (TOG) 40(4), 1–17 (2021)

29. Zhong, L., Zhao, X., Zhang, Y., Zhang, S., Zhang, L.: Occlusion-aware region-based 3D pose tracking of objects with temporally consistent polar-based local partitioning. IEEE Trans. Image Process. 29, 5065–5078 (2020). https://doi.org/10.1109/TIP.2020.2973512

FEAR: Fast, Efficient, Accurate and Robust Visual Tracker

Vasyl Borsuk[1,2]($\boxtimes$), Roman Vei[1,2], Orest Kupyn[1,2], Tetiana Martyniuk[1,2], Igor Krashenyi[1,2], and Jiři Matas[3]

[1] Ukrainian Catholic University, Lviv, Ukraine
{borsuk,vey,kupyn,t.martynyuk,igor.krashenyi}@ucu.edu.ua
[2] Piñata Farms, Los Angeles, USA
{vasyl,roman,orest,tetiana,igor}@pinatafarm.com
[3] Visual Recognition Group, Center for Machine Perception, FEE, CTU in Prague, Prague, Czech Republic
matas@cmp.felk.cvut.cz

Abstract. We present FEAR, a family of fast, efficient, accurate, and robust Siamese visual trackers. We present a novel and efficient way to benefit from dual-template representation for object model adaption, which incorporates temporal information with only a single learnable parameter. We further improve the tracker architecture with a pixel-wise fusion block. By plugging-in sophisticated backbones with the abovementioned modules, FEAR-M and FEAR-L trackers surpass most Siamese trackers on several academic benchmarks in both accuracy and efficiency. Employed with the lightweight backbone, the optimized version FEAR-XS offers more than 10 times faster tracking than current Siamese trackers while maintaining near state-of-the-art results. FEAR-XS tracker is **2.4x** smaller and **4.3x** faster than LightTrack with superior accuracy. In addition, we expand the definition of the model efficiency by introducing FEAR benchmark that assesses energy consumption and execution speed. We show that energy consumption is a limiting factor for trackers on mobile devices. Source code, pretrained models, and evaluation protocol are available at https://github.com/PinataFarms/FEARTracker.

Keyword: Object tracking

V. Borsuk and R. Vei—These authors contributed equally to this work.

Supplementary Information The online version contains supplementary material available at https://doi.org/10.1007/978-3-031-20047-2_37.

1 Introduction

Visual object tracking is a highly active research area of computer vision with many applications such as autonomous driving [15], surveillance [55], augmented reality [63], and robotics [44]. Building a general system for tracking an arbitrary object in the wild using only information about the location of the object in the first frame is non-trivial due to occlusions, deformations, lighting changes, background cluttering, reappearance, etc. [54]. Real-world scenarios often require models to be deployed on the edge devices with hardware and power limitations, adding further complexity (Fig. 1) . Thus, developing a robust tracking algorithm has remained a challenge.

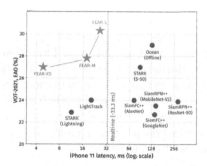

Fig. 1. The EAO-Latency trade-off plot. Compared to other state-of-the-art approaches (shown in blue), the FEAR-XS tracker (in red) achieves superior or comparable quality (EAO) while attaining outstanding speed on mobile devices; FEAR-L (in red) tracker runs in real-time on iPhone 11 and shows the best performance in EAO on VOT-2021.

The recent adoption of deep neural networks, specifically Siamese networks [28], has led to significant progress in visual object tracking [2,32,33,58,66,67, 69]. One of the main advantages of Siamese trackers is the possibility of end-to-end offline learning. In contrast, methods incorporating online learning [3,9, 39] increase computational complexity to an unacceptable extent for real-world scenarios [37].

Current state-of-the-art approaches for visual object tracking achieve high results on several benchmarks [29,30] at the cost of heavy computational load. Top-tier visual trackers like SiamRPNspsps [32] and Ocean [67] exploit complex feature extraction and cross-correlation modules, resulting in 54M parameters and 49 GFLOPs, and 26M parameters and 20 GFLOPs, respectively. Recently, STARK [59] introduced a transformer-based encoder-decoder architecture for visual tracking with 23.3M parameters and 10.5 GFLOPs. The large memory footprint cannot satisfy the strict performance requirements of real-world applications. Employing a mobile-friendly backbone into the Siamese tracker architecture does not lead to a significant boost in the inference time, as most memory and time-consuming operations are in the decoder or bounding box prediction modules (see Table 1). Therefore, designing a lightweight visual object tracking algorithm, efficient across a wide range of hardware, remains a challenging problem. Moreover, it is essential to incorporate temporal information into the algorithm to make a tracker robust to pose, lighting, and other object appearance changes. This usually assumes adding either dedicated branches to the model [59], or online learning modules [3]. Either approach results in extra FLOPs that negatively impact the run-time performance.

We introduce a novel lightweight tracking framework, *FEAR tracker*, that efficiently solves the above-mentioned problems. We develop a single-parameter *dual-template* module which allows to learn the change of the object appearance on the fly without any increase in model complexity, mitigating the memory bottleneck of recently proposed online learning modules [3, 4, 9, 11]. This module predicts the likelihood of the target object being close to the center of the search image, thus allowing to select candidates for the template image update. Furthermore, we interpolate the online selected dynamic template image feature map with the feature map of the original static template image in a learnable way. This allows the model to capture object appearance changes during inference. We optimize the neural network architecture to perform more than 10 times faster than most current Siamese trackers. Additionally, we design an extra lightweight FEAR-XS network that achieves real-time performance on mobile devices while still surpassing or achieving comparable accuracy to the state-of-the-art deep learning methods.

The main contributions of the paper are:

- A novel **dual-template representation** for object model adaptation. The first template, static, anchors the original visual appearance and thus prevents drift and, consequently, adaptation-induced failures. The other is dynamic; its state reflects the current acquisition conditions and object appearance. Unlike STARK [59], which incorporates additional temporal information by introducing *a separate score prediction head*, we introduce a *parameter-free* similarity module as a template update rule, optimized with the rest of the network. We show that a learned convex combination of the two templates is effective for tracking on multiple benchmarks.
- A lightweight tracker that combines a compact feature extraction network, the dual-template representation, and pixel-wise fusion blocks. The resulting **FEAR-XS tracker** runs at 205 FPS on iPhone 11, 4.2× faster than LightTrack [61] and 26.6× faster than Ocean [67], with high accuracy on multiple benchmarks - no state-of-the-art tracker is at the same time more accurate and faster than any of FEAR trackers. Besides, the algorithm is highly energy-efficient.
- We introduce **FEAR benchmark** - a new tracker efficiency benchmark and protocol. Efficiency is defined in terms of both energy consumption and execution speed. Such aspect of vision algorithms, important in real-world use, has not been benchmarked before. We show that current state-of-the-art trackers show high instantaneous speed when evaluated over a small test set, but slow down over time when processing large number of samples, as the device overheats when the tracker is not energy-efficient. In that sense, FEAR family fills the gap between speed and accuracy for real-time trackers.

2   Related Work

Visual Object Tracking. Conventional tracking benchmarks such as annual VOT challenges [30] and the Online Tracking Benchmark [54] have historically been dominated by hand-crafted features-based solutions [1,19,49]. With the rise of deep learning, they lost popularity constituting only 14% of VOT-ST2020 [29] participant models. Lately, short-term visual object tracking task [29] was mostly addressed using either discriminatory correlation filters [3,7,9,10,57,68] or Siamese neural networks [18,32,33,58,66,67,69], as well as both combined [36, 62,65]. Moreover, success of visual transformer networks for image classification [13] has resulted in new high-scoring models [6,50,59] for tracking.

Siamese Trackers. Trackers based on Siamese correlation networks perform tracking based on offline learning of a matching function. This function acts as a similarity metric between the features of the template image and the cropped region of the candidate search area. Siamese trackers initially became popular due to their impressive trade-off between accuracy and efficiency [2,33,47,51,69]; however, they could not keep up with the accuracy of online learning methods [3,9]. With recent modeling improvements, Siamese-based trackers [59,67] hold winning positions on the most popular benchmarks [14,22,30].

One of the state-of-the-art methods, Ocean [67], incorporates FCOS [48] anchor-free object detection paradigm for tracking, directly regressing the distance from the point in the classification map to the corners of the bounding box. Another state-of-the-art approach, STARK [59], introduces a transformer-based encoder-decoder in a Siamese fashion: flattened and concatenated search and template feature maps serve as an input to the transformer network.

Neither of the forenamed state-of-the-art architectures explicitly addresses the task of fast, high-quality visual object tracking across the wide variety of GPU architectures.

Recently, LightTrack [61] made a considerable step towards performant tracking on mobile, optimizing for FLOPs as well as model size via NAS [8,41]. Still, FLOP count does not always reflect actual inference time [52].

Efficient Neural Networks. Designing efficient and lightweight neural networks optimized for inference on mobile devices has attracted much attention in the past few years due to many practical applications. SqueezeNet [23] was one of the first works focusing on reducing the size of the neural network. They introduced an efficient downsampling strategy, extensive usage of 1×1 Convolutional blocks, and a few smaller modules to decrease the network size significantly. Furthermore, SqueezeNext [16] and ShiftNet [53] achieve extra size reduction without any significant drop of accuracy. Recent works focus not only on the size but also on the speed, optimizing FLOP count directly. MobileNets introduce new architecture components: MobileNet [21] uses depth-wise separable convolutions as a lightweight alternative to spatial convolutions, and MobileNet-v2 [45] adds memory-efficient inverted residual layers. ShuffleNet [64] utilizes group convolutions and shuffle operations to reduce the FLOP count further. More recently,

FBNet [52] also takes the hardware design into account, creating a family of mobile-optimized CNNs using neural architecture search.

For FEAR trackers, we followed best practices for designing efficient and flexible neural network architecture. For an extremely lightweight version, where possible, we used depth-wise separable convolutions instead of regular ones and designed the network layers such that the Conv-BN-ReLU blocks could be fused at the export step.

3   The Method

FEAR tracker is a single, unified model composed of a feature extraction network, a dual-template representation, pixel-wise fusion blocks, and task-specific subnetworks for bounding box regression and classification. Given a static template image, I_T, a search image crop, I_S, and a dynamic template image, I_d, the feature extraction network yields the feature maps over these inputs. The template feature representation is then computed as a linear interpolation between static and dynamic template image features. Next, it is fused with the search image features in the pixel-wise fusion blocks and passed to the classification and regression subnetworks. Every stage is described in detail further on, see the overview of the FEAR network architecture in Fig. 2.

3.1   FEAR Network Architecture

Feature Extraction Network. Efficient tracking pipeline requires a flexible, lightweight, and accurate feature extraction network. Moreover, the outputs of such backbone network should have high enough spatial resolution to have

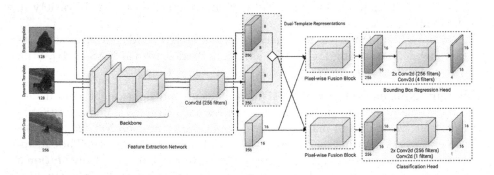

Fig. 2. The FEAR network architecture consists of 5 components: feature extraction network, dual-template representation, pixel-wise fusion blocks, and bounding box and classification heads. The CNN backbone extracts feature representations from the template and search images. The dual-template representation allows for a single-parameter dynamic template update (see Fig. 3). The pixel-wise fusion block effectively combines template and search image features (see Fig. 4). The bounding box and classification heads make the final predictions for the box location and its presence, respectively.

optimal feature capability of object localization [32] while not increasing the computations for the consecutive layers. Most of the current Siamese trackers [32,67] increase the spatial resolution of the last feature map, which significantly degrades the performance of successive layers. We observe that keeping the original spatial resolution significantly reduces the computational cost of both backbone and prediction heads, as shown in Table 1.

Table 1. GigaFLOPs, per frame, of the FEAR tracker and OceanNet [67] architectures; ↑ indicates the increased spatial resolutions of the backbone. We show in Sect. 4.4 that upscaling has a negligible effect on accuracy while increasing FLOPs significantly.

Model architecture	Backbone GigaFLOPs	Prediction heads GigaFLOPs
FEAR-XS tracker	0.318	0.160
FEAR-XS tracker ↑	0.840	0.746
OceanNet	4.106	1.178
OceanNet ↑ (original)	14.137	11.843

We use the first four stages of the neural network pretrained on the ImageNet [12] as a feature extraction module. The FEAR-M tracker adopts the vanilla ResNet-50 [17] as a backbone, and the FEAR-L tracker incorporates the RegNet [56] backbone to pursue the state-of-the-art tracking quality, yet remaining efficient.

The output of the backbone network is a feature map of stride *16* for the template and search images. To map the depth of the output feature map to a constant number of channels, we use a simple *AdjustLayer* which is a combination of Convolutional and Batch Normalization [24] layers.

To shift towards being more efficient during inference on mobile devices, for the mobile version of our tracker - FEAR-XS - we utilize the FBNet [52] family of models designed via NAS. Table 1 and Fig. 5 demonstrate that even a lightweight encoder does not improve the model efficiency of modern trackers due to the complex prediction heads. Thus, designing a lightweight and accurate decoder is still a challenge.

The dual-template representation with a dynamic template update allows the model to capture the appearance changes of objects during inference without the need to perform optimization on the fly. The general scheme of the Dynamic Template Update algorithm is shown in Fig. 3. In addition to the main static template I_T and search image I_S, we randomly sample a dynamic template image, I_d, from a video sequence during model training to capture the object under various appearances. We pass I_d through the feature extraction network, and the resulting feature map, F_d, is linearly interpolated with the main template feature map F_T via a learnable parameter w:

$$F'_T = (1 - w)F_T + wF_d \tag{1}$$

We further pass F'_T and F_S to the Similarity Module that computes cosine similarity between the dual-template and search image embeddings. The search image embedding e_S is obtained via the Weighted Average Pooling (WAP) [46] of F_S by the classification confidence scores; the dual-template embedding e_T is computed as an Average Pooling [31] of F'_T.

During inference, for every N frames we choose the search image with the highest cosine similarity with the dual-template representation, and update the dynamic template with the predicted bounding box at this frame. In addition, for every training pair we sample a negative crop I_N from a frame that does not contain the target object. We pass it through the feature extraction network, and extract the negative crop embedding e_N similarly to the search image, via WAP. We then compute Triplet Loss [20] with the embeddings e_T, e_S, e_N extracted from F'_T, F_S and F_N, respectively. This training scheme does provide a signal for the dynamic template scoring while also biasing the model to prefer more general representations.

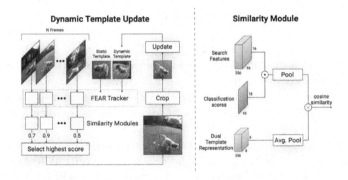

Fig. 3. Dynamic Template update. We compare the average-pooled dual-template representation with the search image embedding using cosine similarity, and dynamically update the template representation when object appearance changes dramatically.

Unlike STARK [59], which incorporates additional temporal information by introducing *a separate score prediction head* to determine whether to update the dynamic template, we present a *parameter-free* similarity module as a template update rule, optimized with the rest of the network. Moreover, STARK concatenates the dynamic and static template features, increasing the size of a tensor passed to the encoder-decoder transformer resulting in more computations. Our dual-template representation interpolates between the static and dynamic template features with *a single learnable parameter*, not increasing the template tensor size.

In Sect. 4, we demonstrate the efficiency of our method on a large variety of academic benchmarks and challenging cases. The dual-template representation module allows the model to efficiently encode the temporal information as well

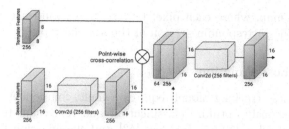

Fig. 4. The pixel-wise fusion block. The search and template features are combined using the point-wise cross-correlation module and enriched with search features via concatenation. The output is then forwarded to regression heads.

as the object appearance and scale change. The increase of model parameters and FLOPs is small and even negligible, making it almost a cost-free temporal module.

Pixel-Wise Fusion Block. The cross-correlation module creates a joint representation of the template and search image features. Most existing Siamese trackers use either simple cross-correlation operation [2,33,58] or more lightweight depth-wise cross-correlation [32]. Recently, Alpha-Refine [62] avoided correlation window blurring effect by adopting the pixel-wise correlation as it ensures that each correlation map encodes information of a local region of the target. Extending this idea, we introduce a pixel-wise fusion block which enhances the similarity information obtained via pixel-wise correlation with position and appearance information extracted from the search image (see Table 4).

We pass the search image feature map through a 3×3 Conv-BN-ReLU block, and calculate the point-wise cross-correlation between these features and template image features. Then, we concatenate the computed correlation feature map with the search image features, and pass the result through a 1×1 Conv-BN-ReLU block to aggregate them. With this approach, learned features are more discriminative and can efficiently encode object position and appearance: see Sect. 4.4 and Table 4 for the detailed ablation study. The overall architecture of a pixel-wise fusion block is visualized in Fig. 4.

Classification and Bounding Box Regression Heads. The core idea of a bounding box regression head is to estimate the distance from each pixel within the target object's bounding box to the ground truth bounding box sides [48,67]. Such bounding box regression takes into account all of the pixels in the ground truth box during training, so it can accurately predict the magnitude of target objects even when only a tiny portion of the scene is designated as foreground. The bounding box regression network is a stack of two simple 3×3 Conv-BN-ReLU blocks. We use just two such blocks instead of four proposed in Ocean [67] to reduce computational complexity. The classification head employs the same structure as a bounding box regression head. The only difference is that we use one filter instead of four in the last Convolutional block. This head predicts a 16×16 score map, where each pixel represents a confidence score of object appearance in the corresponding region of the search crop.

3.2   Overall Loss Function

Training a Siamese tracking model requires a multi-component objective function to simultaneously optimize classification and regression tasks. As shown in previous approaches [59,67], IoU loss [43] and classification loss are used to efficiently train the regression and classification networks jointly. In addition, to train FEAR trackers, we supplement those training objectives with **triplet loss**, which enables performing Dynamic Template Update. As seen in the ablation study, it improves the tracking quality by 0.6% EAO with only a single additional trainable parameter and marginal inference cost (see Table 4). To our knowledge, this is a novel approach in training object trackers.

The triplet loss term is computed from template (e_T), search (e_S), and negative crop (e_N) feature maps:

$$L_t = \max\left\{d(e_T, e_S) - d(e_T, e_N) + \text{margin}, 0)\right\}, \tag{2}$$

where $d(x_i, y_i) = \|x_i - y_i\|_2$. The regression loss term is computed as:

$$L_{reg} = 1 - \sum_i IoU(t_{reg}, p_{reg}), \tag{3}$$

where t_{reg} denotes the target bounding box, p_{reg} denotes the predicted bounding box, and i indexes the training samples. For classification loss term, we use Focal Loss [34]:

$$L_c = -(1 - p_t)^\gamma \log(p_t), \quad p_t = \begin{cases} p & \text{if } y = 1, \\ 1 - p & \text{otherwise.} \end{cases} \tag{4}$$

In the above, $y \in \{-1; 1\}$ is a GT class, and $0 \le p \le 1$ is the predicted probability for the class $y = 1$. The overall loss function is a linear combination of the three components with λ_1, λ_2, λ_3 being 0.5, 1.0, 1.0, respectively:

$$L = \lambda_1 * L_t + \lambda_2 * L_{reg} + \lambda_3 * L_c. \tag{5}$$

4   Experimental Evaluation

4.1   Implementation Details

Training. We implemented all of models using PyTorch [40]. The backbone network is initialized using the pretrained weights on ImageNet. All the models are trained using **4 RTX A6000** GPUs, with a total batch size of 512. We use ADAM [27] optimizer with a learning rate = $4 * 10^{-4}$ and a plateau learning rate reducer with a factor = 0.5 every 10 epochs monitoring the target metric (mean IoU). Each epoch contains 10^6 image pairs. The training takes 5 d to converge. For each epoch, we randomly sample 20,000 images from LaSOT [14], 120,000

from COCO [35], 400,000 from YoutubeBB [42], 320,000 from GOT10k [22] and
310,000 images from the ImageNet dataset [12], so, overall, 1,170,000 images are
used in each epoch.

From each video sequence in a dataset, we randomly sample a template
frame I_T and search frame I_S such that the distance between them is $d = 70$
frames. Starting from the $15th$ epoch, we increase d by 2 every epoch. It allows
the network to learn the correlation between objects on easier samples initially
and gradually increase complexity as the training proceeds. A dynamic template
image is sampled from the video sequence between the static template frame and
search image frame. For the negative crop, where possible, we sample it from
the same frame as the dynamic template but without overlap with this template
crop; otherwise, we sample the negative crop from another video sequence. The
value for d was found empirically. It is consistent with the note in TrackingNet
[38] that any tracker is reliable within 1 s. Our observations are that the appearance of objects does not change dramatically over 2 s (60 frames), and we set
$d = 70$ as a trade-off between the inference speed and the amount of additionally
incorporated temporal information.

Preprocessing. We extract template image crops with an additional offset of
20% around the bounding box. Then, we apply a light shift (up to 8px) and
random scale change (up to 5% on both sides) augmentations, pad image to the
square size with the mean RGB value of the crop, and resize it to the size of
128×128 pixels. We apply the same augmentations with a more severe shift (up
to 48px) and scale (between 65% and 135% from the original image size) for the
search and negative images. Next, the search image is resized to 256×256 pixels
with the same padding strategy as in the template image.

Finally, we apply random photometric augmentations for both search and
template images to increase model generalization and robustness under different
lighting and color conditions [5].

Testing: During inference, tracking follows the same protocols as in [2,33]. The
static template features of the target object are computed once at the first frame.
The dynamic template features are updated every 70 frames and interpolated
with the static template features. These features are combined with the search
image features in the correlation modules, regression, and classification heads to
produce the final output.

4.2   Tracker Efficiency Benchmark

Setup: Mobile devices have a limited amount of both computing power and
energy available to execute a program. Most current benchmarks measure only
runtime speed without taking into account the energy efficiency of the algorithm, which is equally important in a real-world scenario. Thus, we introduce
the **FEAR Benchmark** to estimate the effect of tracking algorithms on mobile
device battery and thermal state and its impact on the processing speed over

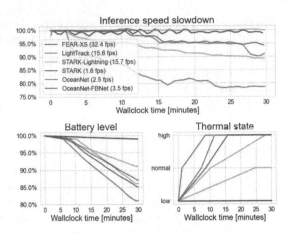

Fig. 5. Online Efficiency Benchmark on iPhone 8: battery consumption, device thermal state, and inference speed degradation over time. FEAR-XS tracker does not change the thermal state of the device and has a negligible impact on the battery level. Transformer-based trackers have a battery level drop comparable to the Siamese trackers, reaching a high thermal state in less than 10 min of online processing.

time. It measures the energy efficiency of trackers with online and offline evaluation protocols - the former to estimate the energy consumption for the real-time input stream processing and the latter to measure the processing speed of a constant amount of inputs.

The online evaluation collects energy consumption data by simulating a real-time (30 FPS) camera input to the neural network for 30 min. The tracker cannot process more frames than the specified FPS even if its inference speed is faster, and it skips inputs that cannot be processed on-time due to the slower processing speed. We collect battery level, device's thermal state, and inference speed throughout the whole experiment. The thermal state is defined by Apple in the official Thermal state iOS API [25]. The *high* thermal state refers to a critical thermal state when system's performance is significantly reduced to cool it down. The performance loss due to heat causes trackers to slow down, making it a critical performance metric when deployed to mobile devices. FEAR benchmark takes care of these issues providing fair comparison (see Fig. 5).

The offline protocol measures the inference speed of trackers by simulating a constant number of random inputs for the processing. All frames are processed one by one without any inference time restrictions. Additionally, we perform a model warmup before the experiment, as the first model executions are usually slower. We set the number of warmup iterations and inputs for the processing to 20 and 100, respectively.

In this work, we evaluate trackers on iPhone 7, iPhone 8 Plus, iPhone 11, and Pixel 4. All devices are fully charged before the experiment, no background tasks are running, and the display is set to the lowest brightness to reduce the energy consumption of hardware that is not involved in computations.

We observe that algorithms that reach the high system thermal state get a significant drop in the processing speed due to the smaller amount of processing units available. The results prove that the tracking speed is dependent on the energy efficiency, and both should be taken into account.

Online Efficiency Benchmark: Figure 5 summarizes the online benchmark results on iPhone 8. The upper part of the plot demonstrates the degradation of inference speed over time. We observe that FEAR-XS tracker and STARK-Lightning [60] backbone do not change inference speed over time, while Light-Track [61] and OceanNet [67] start to process inputs slower. Also, transformer network STARK-S50 degrades significantly and becomes 20% slower after 30 min of runtime. The lower part of the figure demonstrates energy efficiency of FEAR-XS tracker against competitors and its negligible impact on device thermal state. STARK-S50 and Ocean overheat device after 10 min of execution, LightTrack slightly elevates temperature after 24 min, STARK-Lightning overheats device after 27 min, while FEAR-XS tracker keeps device in a low temperature. Moreover, Ocean with a lightweight backbone FBNet [52] still consumes lots of energy and produces heat due to complex and inefficient decoder.

Additionally, we observe that STARK-Lightning reaches high thermal state without performance drop. Modern devices have a special hardware, called Neural Processing Unit (NPU), designed specifically for neural network inference. The Apple Neural Engine (ANE) is a type of NPU that accelerates neural network operations such as convolutions and matrix multiplies. STARK-Lightning is a transformer based on simple matrix multiplications that are efficiently computed by ANE and thus do not slow down over time.

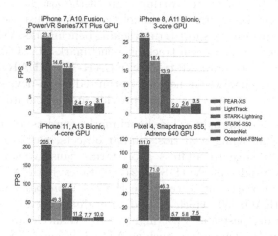

Fig. 6. Offline Efficiency Benchmark: mean FPS on a range of mobile GPU architectures. FEAR-XS tracker has superior processing speed on all devices while being an order of magnitude faster on a modern GPU – Apple A13 Bionic.

Offline Efficiency Benchmark: We summarize the results of offline benchmark in Fig. 6. We observe that FEAR-XS tracker achieves 1.6 times higher FPS than LightTrack [61] on iPhone 7 (A10 Fusion and PowerVR Series7XT GPU), iPhone 8 (A11 Bionic with 3-core GPU) and Google Pixel 4 (Snapdragon 855 and Adreno 640 GPU). Furthermore, FEAR-XS tracker is more than 4 times faster than LightTrack on iPhone 11 (A11 Bionic with 4-core GPU). FEAR-XS tracker achieves more than 10 times faster inference than OceanNet [67] and STARK [59] on all aforementioned mobile devices. Such low inference time makes FEAR-XS tracker a very cost-efficient candidate for use in resource-constrained applications.

Table 2. Extremely High FPS Tracking Matters. The metrics were computed from the same set of frames on 30 and 240 fps NFS benchmark [26]. FEAR-XS, tracking in over 200 fps, achieves superior performance than trackers limited to 30 fps by incorporating additional temporal information from intermediate frames.

FPS	Success score	Precision score	Success rate
30	0.618	0.753	0.780
240	**0.655**	**0.816**	**0.835**

4.3   Comparison with the State-of-the-Art

We compare FEAR trackers to existing state-of-the-art Siamese [32,58,61,67] and DCF [3,4,9] trackers in terms of model accuracy, robustness and speed. We evaluate performance on two short-term tracking benchmarks: VOT-ST2021 [30], GOT-10k [22] and two long-term tracking benchmarks: LaSOT [14], NFS [26]. We provide three version of FEAR tracker: **FEAR-XS**, **FEAR-M** and **FEAR-XL**. The first one is a lightweight network optimized for on-device inference while two latter networks are more heavy and provide more accurate results.

VOT-ST2021 Benchmark: This benchmark consists of 60 short video sequences with challenging scenarios: similar objects, partial occlusions, scale and appearance change to address short-term, causal, model-free trackers. Table 3a reports results on VOT-ST2021. It takes both Accuracy (A) and Robustness (R) into account to compute the *bounding box* Expected Average Overlap metric (EAO) [30] which is used to evaluate the overall performance. FEAR-L tracker demonstrates 1.3% higher EAO than Ocean [67] and outperforms trackers with online update, such as ATOM [9] and KYS [4], by 3% EAO. FEAR-XS tracker shows near state-of-the-art performance, outperforming Light-Track [61] and STARK-Lightning [60] by 3% and 4.4% EAO, respectively, while having higher FPS. Also, it is only 2% behind Ocean, yet having more than **18 times fewer parameters** than Ocean tracker and being **26 times faster** at model inference time (iPhone 11).

Table 3a additionally reports model weights memory consumption and peak memory consumption during the forward pass in megabytes. LightTrack and STARK-Lightning model sizes are 4.11MB and 6.28MB, respectively, while FEAR-XS consumes only 3MB. During the forward pass, the peak memory usage of FEAR-XS is 10.1MB, LightTrack consumes slightly less (9.21MB) by using fewer filters in bounding box regression convolutional layers, and STARK-Lightning has 30.69MB peak memory usage due to memory-consuming self-attention blocks.

GOT-10K Benchmark: GOT-10K [22] is a benchmark covering a wide range of different objects, their deformations, and occlusions. We evaluate our solution using the official GOT-10K submission page. FEAR-XS tracker achieves better results than LightTrack [61] and Ocean [67], while using 1.4 and 19 times fewer parameters, respectively. More details in the Table 3b.

LaSOT Benchmark: LaSOT [14] contains 280 video segments for long-range tracking evaluation. Each sequence is longer than 80 s in average making in the largest densely annotated long-term tracking benchmark. We report the *Success Score* as well as *Precision Score* and *Success Rate*. As presented in Table 3c, the *Precision Score* of FEAR-XS tracker is 3% and 2.8% superior than LightTrack

Table 3. Comparison of FEAR and the state-of-the-art trackers on common benchmarks: VOT-ST2021 [30], GOT-10K [22], LaSOT [14], and NFS [26]. FEAR trackers use much fewer parameters, achieves higher FPS; their accuracy and robustness is on par with the best. ①, ② and ③ indicate the top-3 trackers

	SiamFC++ (GoogleNet) [58]	SiamRPN++ (MobileNet-V2) [32]	SiamRPN++ (ResNet-50) [32]	ATOM [9]	KYS [4]	Ocean (offline) [67]	STARK (S50) [59]	STARK (lightning) [60]	LightTrack [61]	**FEAR-XS**	**FEAR-M**	**FEAR-L**
EAO	0.227	0.235	0.239	0.258	0.274	0.290③	0.270	0.226	0.240	0.270	0.278②	0.303①
Accuracy	0.418	0.432	0.438	0.457	0.453	0.479③	0.464	0.433	0.417	0.471	0.476②	0.501①
Robustness	0.667	0.656	0.668	0.691	0.736①	0.732②	0.719	0.627	0.684	0.708	0.728	0.755③
iPhone 11 FPS	7.11	6.86	3.49	-	-	7.72	11.2	87.41②	49.13	205.12①	56.20③	38.3
Parameters (M)	12.71	11.15	53.95	-	-	25.87	23.34	2.28③	1.97②	1.37①	9.67	33.65
Memory (MB)	24.77	21.63	103.74	-	-	102.81	109.63	6.28③	4.11②	3.00①	18.82	66.24
Peak memory (MB)	34.17	31.39	192.81	-	-	119.51	295.97	30.69	9.21①	10.10②	25.88③	85.97

(a) **VOT-ST2021** [30]

	SiamRPNspssps (ResNet-50) [32]	ATOM [9]	KYS [4]	Ocean (offline) [67]	STARK (S50) [59]	LightTrack [61]	**FEAR-XS**	**FEAR-M**	**FEAR-L**
Average Overlap	0.518	0.556	0.636③	0.592	0.672①	0.611	0.619	0.623	0.645②
Success Rate	0.618	0.634	0.751②	0.695	0.761①	0.710	0.722	0.730	0.746③

(b) **GOT-10K** [22]

	SiamRPNspssps (ResNet-50) [32]	ATOM [9]	KYS [4]	Ocean (offline) [67]	STARK (S50) [59]	STARK (lightning) [60]	LightTrack [61]	**FEAR-XS**	**FEAR-M**	**FEAR-L**
Success Score	0.503	0.491	0.541	0.505	0.586①	0.579	0.523	0.535	0.546	0.579③
Precision Score	0.496	0.483	0.539	0.517	0.701①	0.579③	0.515	0.545	0.556	0.609②
Success Rate	0.593	0.566	0.640	0.594	0.778①	0.690	0.596	0.641	0.638	0.686③

(c) **LaSOT** [14]

	SiamRPNspssps (ResNet-50) [32]	ATOM [9]	KYS [4]	Ocean (offline) [67]	STARK (S50) [59]	STARK (lightning) [60]	LightTrack [61]	**FEAR-XS**	**FEAR-M**	**FEAR-L**
Success Score	0.596	0.592	0.634③	0.573	0.681①	0.628	0.591	0.614	0.622	0.658②
Precision Score	0.720	0.711	0.766	0.706	0.825①	0.754	0.730	0.768③	0.745	0.814②
Success Rate	0.748	0.737	0.795	0.728	0.860①	0.796③	0.743	0.788	0.788	0.834②

(d) **NFS** [26]

[61] and Ocean [67], respectively. Besides, the larger FEAR-M and FEAR-L trackers further improve *Success Score* outperforming KYS [4] by 0.5% and 3.8%.

NFS Benchmark: NFS [26] dataset is a long-range benchmark, which has 100 videos (380K frames) captured with now commonly available higher frame rate (240 FPS) cameras from real world scenarios. Table 3d presents that FEAR-XS tracker achieves better *Success Score* (61.4%), being 2.3% and 4.1% higher than LightTrack [61] and Ocean [67], respectively. Besides, FEAR-L tracker outperforms KYS [4] by 2.4% *Success Score* and 4.8% *Precision Score*. Additionally, Table 2 reports the impact of extremely high FPS video processing on accuracy, implying the importance of developing a fast tracker capable to process videos in higher FPS.

4.4   Ablation Study

To verify the efficiency of the proposed method, we evaluate the effects of its different components on the VOT-ST2021 [30] benchmark, as presented in Table 4. The baseline model (#1) consists of the FBNet backbone with an increased spatial resolution of the final stage, followed by a plain pixel-wise cross-correlation operation and bounding box prediction network. The performance of the baseline is 0.236 EAO and 0.672 Robustness. In #2, we set the spatial resolution of the last stage to its original value and observe a negligible degradation of EAO while significantly increasing FPS on mobile. Adding our pixel-wise fusion blocks (#3) brings a 3% EAO improvement. This indicates that combining search image features and correlation feature maps enhances feature representability and improves tracking accuracy. Furthermore, the proposed dynamic template update module (#4) also brings an improvement of 0.6% in terms of EAO and 2.5% Robustness, showing the effectiveness of this module. The pixel-wise fusion block and dynamic template update brought a significant accuracy improvements while keeping almost the same inference speed. Note that the EAO metrics is calculated w.r.t. *bounding box* tracking.

Table 4. FEAR-XS tracker – Ablation study on VOT-ST2021 [30]

#	Component	EAO↑	Robustness↑	iPhone 11 FPS↑
1	*baseline*	0.236	0.672	122.19
2	+ lower spatial resolution	0.234	0.668	208.41
3	+ pixel-wise fusion block	0.264	0.683	207.72
4	+ dynamic template update	0.270	0.708	205.12

5   Conclusions

In this paper, we introduce the *FEAR tracker* family - an efficient and powerful new Siamese tracking framework that benefits from novel architectural blocks.

We validate FEAR trackers performance on several popular academic benchmarks and show that the models near or exceed existing solutions while reducing the computational cost of inference. We demonstrate that the FEAR-XS model attains real-time performance on embedded devices with high energy efficiency. Additionally, we introduce a novel tracker efficiency benchmark, where FEAR trackers demonstrate their energy efficiency and high inference speed, being more efficient and accurate than current state-of-the-art approaches at the same time.

Acknowledgements. We thank the Armed Forces of Ukraine for providing security to complete this work.

References

1. Bertinetto, L., Valmadre, J., Golodetz, S., Miksik, O., Torr, P.H.: Staple: complementary learners for real-time tracking. In: Proceedings of the IEEE Conference on Computer Vision and Pattern Recognition, pp. 1401–1409 (2016)
2. Bertinetto, L., Valmadre, J., Henriques, J.F., Vedaldi, A., Torr, P.H.S.: Fully-convolutional Siamese networks for object tracking. In: Hua, G., Jégou, H. (eds.) ECCV 2016. LNCS, vol. 9914, pp. 850–865. Springer, Cham (2016). https://doi.org/10.1007/978-3-319-48881-3_56
3. Bhat, G., Danelljan, M., Gool, L.V., Timofte, R.: Learning discriminative model prediction for tracking. In: Proceedings of the IEEE/CVF International Conference on Computer Vision, pp. 6182–6191 (2019)
4. Bhat, G., Danelljan, M., Van Gool, L., Timofte, R.: Know your surroundings: exploiting scene information for object tracking. In: Vedaldi, A., Bischof, H., Brox, T., Frahm, J.-M. (eds.) ECCV 2020. LNCS, vol. 12368, pp. 205–221. Springer, Cham (2020). https://doi.org/10.1007/978-3-030-58592-1_13
5. Buslaev, A., Iglovikov, V.I., Khvedchenya, E., Parinov, A., Druzhinin, M., Kalinin, A.A.: Albumentations: fast and flexible image augmentations. Information **11**(2), 125 (2020)
6. Chen, X., Yan, B., Zhu, J., Wang, D., Yang, X., Lu, H.: Transformer tracking. In: Proceedings of the IEEE/CVF Conference on Computer Vision and Pattern Recognition, pp. 8126–8135 (2021)
7. Chen, Y., Xu, J., Yu, J., Wang, Q., Yoo, B.I., Han, J.-J.: AFOD: adaptive focused discriminative segmentation tracker. In: Bartoli, A., Fusiello, A. (eds.) ECCV 2020. LNCS, vol. 12539, pp. 666–682. Springer, Cham (2020). https://doi.org/10.1007/978-3-030-68238-5_44
8. Chen, Y., Yang, T., Zhang, X., Meng, G., Xiao, X., Sun, J.: DetNAS: backbone search for object detection. Adv. Neural. Inf. Process. Syst. **32**, 6642–6652 (2019)
9. Danelljan, M., Bhat, G., Khan, F.S., Felsberg, M.: Atom: accurate tracking by overlap maximization. In: Proceedings of the IEEE/CVF Conference on Computer Vision and Pattern Recognition, pp. 4660–4669 (2019)
10. Danelljan, M., Bhat, G., Shahbaz Khan, F., Felsberg, M.: ECO: efficient convolution operators for tracking. In: Proceedings of the IEEE Conference on Computer Vision and Pattern Recognition, pp. 6638–6646 (2017)
11. Danelljan, M., Gool, L.V., Timofte, R.: Probabilistic regression for visual tracking. In: Proceedings of the IEEE/CVF Conference on Computer Vision and Pattern Recognition, pp. 7183–7192 (2020)

12. Deng, J., Dong, W., Socher, R., Li, L.J., Li, K., Fei-Fei, L.: Imagenet: a large-scale hierarchical image database. In: 2009 IEEE Conference on Computer Vision and Pattern Recognition, pp. 248–255. IEEE (2009)
13. Dosovitskiy, A., et al.: An image is worth 16 × 16 words: transformers for image recognition at scale. In: ICLR (2021)
14. Fan, H., et al.: LaSOT: a high-quality benchmark for large-scale single object tracking. In: Proceedings of the IEEE/CVF Conference on Computer Vision and Pattern Recognition (CVPR), June 2019
15. Gao, M., Jin, L., Jiang, Y., Guo, B.: Manifold Siamese network: a novel visual tracking convnet for autonomous vehicles. IEEE Trans. Intell. Transp. Syst. **21**(4), 1612–1623 (2020)
16. Gholami, A., et al.: SqueezeNext: hardware-aware neural network design. In: Proceedings of the IEEE Conference on Computer Vision and Pattern Recognition (CVPR) Workshops, June 2018
17. He, K., Zhang, X., Ren, S., Sun, J.: Deep residual learning for image recognition. In: Proceedings of the IEEE Conference on Computer Vision and Pattern Recognition, pp. 770–778 (2016)
18. Held, D., Thrun, S., Savarese, S.: Learning to track at 100 FPS with deep regression networks. In: Leibe, B., Matas, J., Sebe, N., Welling, M. (eds.) ECCV 2016. LNCS, vol. 9905, pp. 749–765. Springer, Cham (2016). https://doi.org/10.1007/978-3-319-46448-0_45
19. Henriques, J.F., Caseiro, R., Martins, P., Batista, J.: High-speed tracking with kernelized correlation filters. IEEE Trans. Pattern Anal. Mach. Intell. **37**(3), 583–596 (2014)
20. Hoffer, E., Ailon, N.: Deep metric learning using triplet network. In: Feragen, A., Pelillo, M., Loog, M. (eds.) SIMBAD 2015. LNCS, vol. 9370, pp. 84–92. Springer, Cham (2015). https://doi.org/10.1007/978-3-319-24261-3_7
21. Howard, A.G., et al.: MobileNets: efficient convolutional neural networks for mobile vision applications. arXiv preprint arXiv:1704.04861 (2017)
22. Huang, L., Zhao, X., Huang, K.: Got-10k: a large high-diversity benchmark for generic object tracking in the wild. IEEE Trans. Pattern Anal. Mach. Intell. **43**(5), 1562–1577 (2021)
23. Iandola, F.N., Han, S., Moskewicz, M.W., Ashraf, K., Dally, W.J., Keutzer, K.: SqueezeNet: alexnet-level accuracy with 50x fewer parameters and <0.5 mb model size. arXiv:1602.07360 (2016)
24. Ioffe, S., Szegedy, C.: Batch normalization: accelerating deep network training by reducing internal covariate shift. In: International Conference on Machine Learning, pp. 448–456. PMLR (2015)
25. iOS thermal state. https://developer.apple.com/documentation/foundation/processinfo/thermalstate
26. Kiani Galoogahi, H., Fagg, A., Huang, C., Ramanan, D., Lucey, S.: Need for speed: a benchmark for higher frame rate object tracking. In: Proceedings of the IEEE International Conference on Computer Vision, pp. 1125–1134 (2017)
27. Kingma, D.P., Ba, J.: Adam: a method for stochastic optimization. arXiv preprint arXiv:1412.6980 (2014)
28. Koch, G., et al.: Siamese neural networks for one-shot image recognition. In: ICML Deep Learning Workshop, vol. 2, Lille (2015)
29. Kristan, M., et al.: The eighth visual object tracking VOT2020 challenge results. In: Bartoli, A., Fusiello, A. (eds.) ECCV 2020. LNCS, vol. 12539, pp. 547–601. Springer, Cham (2020). https://doi.org/10.1007/978-3-030-68238-5_39

30. Kristan, M., et al.: A novel performance evaluation methodology for single-target trackers. IEEE Trans. Pattern Anal. Mach. Intell. **38**(11), 2137–2155 (2016). Nov
31. Lee, C.Y., Gallagher, P.W., Tu, Z.: Generalizing pooling functions in convolutional neural networks: mixed, gated, and tree. In: Proceedings of the 19th International Conference on Artificial Intelligence and Statistics, pp. 464–472 (2016)
32. Li, B., Wu, W., Wang, Q., Zhang, F., Xing, J., Yan, J.: SiamRPN++: evolution of Siamese visual tracking with very deep networks. In: Proceedings of the IEEE/CVF Conference on Computer Vision and Pattern Recognition, pp. 4282–4291 (2019)
33. Li, B., Yan, J., Wu, W., Zhu, Z., Hu, X.: High performance visual tracking with Siamese region proposal network. In: Proceedings of the IEEE Conference on Computer Vision and Pattern Recognition (CVPR), June 2018
34. Lin, T.Y., Goyal, P., Girshick, R.B., He, K., Dollár, P.: Focal loss for dense object detection. In: 2017 IEEE International Conference on Computer Vision (ICCV), pp. 2999–3007 (2017)
35. Lin, T.-Y., et al.: Microsoft COCO: common objects in context. In: Fleet, D., Pajdla, T., Schiele, B., Tuytelaars, T. (eds.) ECCV 2014. LNCS, vol. 8693, pp. 740–755. Springer, Cham (2014). https://doi.org/10.1007/978-3-319-10602-1_48
36. Ma, Z., Wang, L., Zhang, H., Lu, W., Yin, J.: RPT: learning point set representation for Siamese visual tracking. In: Bartoli, A., Fusiello, A. (eds.) ECCV 2020. LNCS, vol. 12539, pp. 653–665. Springer, Cham (2020). https://doi.org/10.1007/978-3-030-68238-5_43
37. Marvasti-Zadeh, S.M., Cheng, L., Ghanei-Yakhdan, H., Kasaei, S.: Deep learning for visual tracking: a comprehensive survey. IEEE Transactions on Intelligent Transportation Systems (2021)
38. Müller, M., Bibi, A., Giancola, S., Alsubaihi, S., Ghanem, B.: TrackingNet: a large-scale dataset and benchmark for object tracking in the wild. In: Ferrari, V., Hebert, M., Sminchisescu, C., Weiss, Y. (eds.) ECCV 2018. LNCS, vol. 11205, pp. 310–327. Springer, Cham (2018). https://doi.org/10.1007/978-3-030-01246-5_19
39. Nam, H., Han, B.: Learning multi-domain convolutional neural networks for visual tracking. In: Proceedings of the IEEE Conference on Computer Vision and Pattern Recognition, pp. 4293–4302 (2016)
40. Paszke, A., et al.: Pytorch: an imperative style, high-performance deep learning library. Adv. Neural Inf. Process. Syst. **32**, 1–12 (2019)
41. Pham, H., Guan, M., Zoph, B., Le, Q., Dean, J.: Efficient neural architecture search via parameters sharing. In: International Conference on Machine Learning, pp. 4095–4104. PMLR (2018)
42. Real, E., Shlens, J., Mazzocchi, S., Pan, X., Vanhoucke, V.: YouTube-boundingboxes: a large high-precision human-annotated data set for object detection in video. In: proceedings of the IEEE Conference on Computer Vision and Pattern Recognition, pp. 5296–5305 (2017)
43. Rezatofighi, H., Tsoi, N., Gwak, J., Sadeghian, A., Reid, I., Savarese, S.: Generalized intersection over union. In: The IEEE Conference on Computer Vision and Pattern Recognition (CVPR), June 2019
44. Robin, C., Lacroix, S.: Multi-robot target detection and tracking: taxonomy and survey. Auton. Robot. **40**(4), 729–760 (2016)
45. Sandler, M., Howard, A., Zhu, M., Zhmoginov, A., Chen, L.C.: Mobilenetv 2: inverted residuals and linear bottlenecks. In: Proceedings of the IEEE Conference on Computer Vision and Pattern Recognition, pp. 4510–4520 (2018)
46. Shin, H., Cho, H., Kim, D., Ko, D.K., Lim, S.C., Hwang, W.: Sequential image-based attention network for inferring force estimation without haptic sensor. IEEE Access **7**, 150237–150246 (2019)

47. Tao, R., Gavves, E., Smeulders, A.W.: Siamese instance search for tracking. In: Proceedings of the IEEE Conference on Computer Vision and Pattern Recognition, pp. 1420–1429 (2016)
48. Tian, Z., Shen, C., Chen, H., He, T.: FCOS: fully convolutional one-stage object detection. In: Proceedings of the IEEE/CVF International Conference on Computer Vision, pp. 9627–9636 (2019)
49. Vojír, T., Noskova, J., Matas, J.: Robust scale-adaptive mean-shift for tracking. In: SCIA (2013)
50. Wang, N., Zhou, W., Wang, J., Li, H.: Transformer meets tracker: Exploiting temporal context for robust visual tracking. In: Proceedings of the IEEE/CVF Conference on Computer Vision and Pattern Recognition, pp. 1571–1580 (2021)
51. Wang, Q., Teng, Z., Xing, J., Gao, J., Hu, W., Maybank, S.: Learning attentions: residual attentional Siamese network for high performance online visual tracking. In: Proceedings of the IEEE Conference on Computer Vision and Pattern Recognition, pp. 4854–4863 (2018)
52. Wu, B., et al.: FBNet: hardware-aware efficient convnet design via differentiable neural architecture search. The IEEE Conference on Computer Vision and Pattern Recognition (CVPR) (2019)
53. Wu, B., et al.: Shift: a zero flop, zero parameter alternative to spatial convolutions. In: Proceedings of the IEEE Conference on Computer Vision and Pattern Recognition, pp. 9127–9135 (2018)
54. Wu, Y., Lim, J., Yang, M.H.: Online object tracking: a benchmark. In: Proceedings of the IEEE Conference on Computer Vision and Pattern Recognition (CVPR), June 2013
55. Xing, J., Ai, H., Lao, S.: Multiple human tracking based on multi-view upper-body detection and discriminative learning. In: 2010 20th International Conference on Pattern Recognition, pp. 1698–1701. IEEE (2010)
56. Xu, J., Pan, Y., Pan, X., Hoi, S., Yi, Z., Xu, Z.: RegNet: self-regulated network for image classification. IEEE Transactions on Neural Networks and Learning Systems (2022)
57. Xu, T., Feng, Z.H., Wu, X.J., Kittler, J.: Learning adaptive discriminative correlation filters via temporal consistency preserving spatial feature selection for robust visual object tracking. IEEE Trans. Image Process. 28(11), 5596–5609 (2019)
58. Xu, Y., Wang, Z., Li, Z., Yuan, Y., Yu, G.: SiamFC++: towards robust and accurate visual tracking with target estimation guidelines. In: Proceedings of the AAAI Conference on Artificial Intelligence, vol. 34, pp. 12549–12556 (2020)
59. Yan, B., Peng, H., Fu, J., Wang, D., Lu, H.: Learning spatio-temporal transformer for visual tracking. arXiv preprint arXiv:2103.17154 (2021)
60. Yan, B., Peng, H., Fu, J., Wang, D., Lu, H.: Stark lightning (2021). https://github.com/researchmm/Stark
61. Yan, B., Peng, H., Wu, K., Wang, D., Fu, J., Lu, H.: Lighttrack: finding lightweight neural networks for object tracking via one-shot architecture search. In: CVPR 2021, June 2021
62. Yan, B., Zhang, X., Wang, D., Lu, H., Yang, X.: Alpha-refine: Boosting tracking performance by precise bounding box estimation. In: Proceedings of the IEEE/CVF Conference on Computer Vision and Pattern Recognition, pp. 5289–5298 (2021)
63. Zhang, G., Vela, P.A.: Good features to track for visual slam. In: Proceedings of the IEEE Conference on Computer Vision and Pattern Recognition, pp. 1373–1382 (2015)

64. Zhang, X., Zhou, X., Lin, M., Sun, J.: ShuffleNet: an extremely efficient convolutional neural network for mobile devices. In: Proceedings of the IEEE Conference on Computer Vision and Pattern Recognition, pp. 6848–6856 (2018)
65. Zhang, Z., Li, B., Hu, W., Peng, H.: Towards accurate pixel-wise object tracking by attention retrieval. arXiv preprint arXiv:2008.02745 (2020)
66. Zhang, Z., Peng, H.: Deeper and wider Siamese networks for real-time visual tracking. In: Proceedings of the IEEE/CVF Conference on Computer Vision and Pattern Recognition, pp. 4591–4600 (2019)
67. Zhang, Z., Peng, H., Fu, J., Li, B., Hu, W.: Ocean: object-aware anchor-free tracking. In: Vedaldi, A., Bischof, H., Brox, T., Frahm, J.-M. (eds.) ECCV 2020. LNCS, vol. 12366, pp. 771–787. Springer, Cham (2020). https://doi.org/10.1007/978-3-030-58589-1_46
68. Zheng, L., Tang, M., Chen, Y., Wang, J., Lu, H.: Learning feature embeddings for discriminant model based tracking. In: Vedaldi, A., Bischof, H., Brox, T., Frahm, J.-M. (eds.) ECCV 2020. LNCS, vol. 12360, pp. 759–775. Springer, Cham (2020). https://doi.org/10.1007/978-3-030-58555-6_45
69. Zhu, Z., Wang, Q., Li, B., Wu, W., Yan, J., Hu, W.: Distractor-aware Siamese networks for visual object tracking. In: Ferrari, V., Hebert, M., Sminchisescu, C., Weiss, Y. (eds.) ECCV 2018. LNCS, vol. 11213, pp. 103–119. Springer, Cham (2018). https://doi.org/10.1007/978-3-030-01240-3_7

PREF: Predictability Regularized Neural Motion Fields

Liangchen Song[1,2] , Xuan Gong[1,2] , Benjamin Planche[2(✉)] ,
Meng Zheng[2] , David Doermann[1] , Junsong Yuan[1] , Terrence Chen[2],
and Ziyan Wu[2]

[1] University at Buffalo, Buffalo, NY, USA
[2] United Imaging Intelligence, Cambridge, MA, USA
{liangchen.song,xuan.gong,benjamin.planche,
meng.zheng,ziyan.wu}@united-imaging.com

Abstract. Knowing the 3D motions in a dynamic scene is essential to many vision applications. Recent progress is mainly focused on estimating the activity of some specific elements like humans. In this paper, we leverage a neural motion field for estimating the motion of all points in a multiview setting. Modeling the motion from a dynamic scene with multiview data is challenging due to the ambiguities in points of similar color and points with time-varying color. We propose to regularize the estimated motion to be predictable. If the motion from previous frames is known, then the motion in the near future should be predictable. Therefore, we introduce a predictability regularization by first conditioning the estimated motion on latent embeddings, then by adopting a predictor network to enforce predictability on the embeddings. The proposed framework PREF (**P**redictability **RE**gularized **F**ields) achieves on par or better results than state-of-the-art neural motion field-based dynamic scene representation methods while requiring no prior knowledge of the scene.

Keywords: Neural fields · Motion estimation · Motion prediction

1 Introduction

Estimating motion in dynamic scenes is a fundamental and long-standing problem in computer vision [16]. Most of the existing 3D motion estimation works are concerned with specific objects like humans [42]. Still, knowing the 3D motion of all objects in a dynamic scene can be of great benefit to a number of vision applications like robot path planning [8]. Tracking all points in the space with only multiview data is obviously challenging, however, neural fields is a hot topic that has emerged recently [59], bringing hope to breakthroughs for this problem.

Supplementary Information The online version contains supplementary material available at https://doi.org/10.1007/978-3-031-20047-2_38.

(a) Topologically varying scene   (b) Physical motion for all points

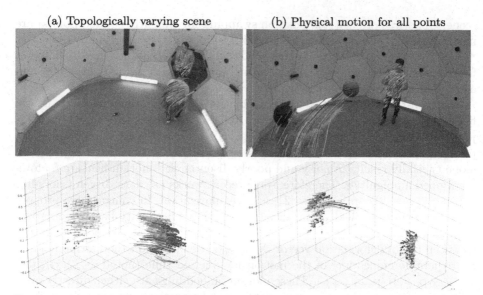

To see the animation, please view the document with compatible software, *e.g.*, *Adobe Acrobat* or *KDE Okular*; otherwise, the animation is also provided as a separate file in supplementary material.

Fig. 1. Our method can handle topologically varying scenes and estimate physical motion for all points in the space. *Topologically varying* means that the topology of the scene can change, such as a new person entering the scene in (a). All points in the space are tracked, such as the ball in (b). Only the sequence of images to be analyzed is used and no prior knowledge is required in our framework. (See supplementary material for an animated version of the figure.)

Neural fields, also known as coordinate-based neural networks, have demonstrated great potential in dynamic 3D scene reconstruction from multiview data [51,59]. Coordinate-based representations not only naturally support fine-grained modeling of the motion for points in space, but also require no prior knowledge about the geometry and track all points in space. In this paper, we address the problem of estimating 3D motion from multiview image sequences, for general scenes and for all points in the space (Fig. 1).

Despite recent progress on neural fields-based dynamic scene representation (*e.g.*, [9–11,20,21,25,36,37,41,52,56,57,63]), estimating 3D motion from multiview data remains challenging for the following reasons. First, motion ambiguity exists among points with the same color, so one cannot confidently track interchangeable points on non-rigid surfaces from visual observations alone (*c.f.* possibility of position swapping). Second, the color of any point may change over time. For example, spatially or temporally varying lighting conditions can blur the notion of a point's identity over time.

In this paper, we propose to *regularize the estimated motion to be predictable* to address the aforementioned ambiguity issues. The key insight behind motion predictability is that underlying motion patterns exist in a dynamic real-world scene. Chaotic motions (*e.g.*, position swapping for similarly-colored points) are not predictable and should be penalized. In our work, the motion in a scene is "*implicitly*" regularized by enforcing predictability, which is intrinsically different from explicitly designed regularizing terms, such as elastic regularization [36] and as-rigid-as-possible regularization [52].

State-of-the-art solutions use combinations of space-time radiance neural fields and neural motion fields to model dynamic scenes, optimizing these fields jointly over a set of visual observations in a self-supervised manner by comparing predicted images to actual observations. But vision-based supervision alone typically results in noisy and poorly disentangled motion fields, *c.f.* aforementioned ambiguities. Therefore, some recent works use data-driven priors like depth [57] and 2D optical flow [21] as a regularization. In contrast, we propose to improve motion field optimization through predictability-based regularization. Instead of learning a motion field M that maps each 3D position $\mathbf{p}$ and timestep t to a deformation vector $\Delta_{t \to t+\delta t}\mathbf{p}$, we condition the motion field on a predictable embedding of the motion for queried time (noted $\boldsymbol{\omega}_{t \to t+\delta t}$), *i.e.*, $\Delta_{t \to t+\delta t}\mathbf{p} = M(\mathbf{p}, \boldsymbol{\omega}_{t \to t+\delta t})$. These motion embeddings are either directly optimized jointly with the space-time field over observations, or are inferred by a predictor function P that takes a set of past embeddings and infers the next motion embedding. During scene optimization, we enforce each motion embedding regressed from the observations to be predictable by our model P. Therefore we promote the encoding of underlying motion patterns and penalize chaotic and unlikely-realistic deformations. In summary, our contributions are as follows:

- We propose to leverage predictability as a prior w.r.t.let@tokeneonedotthe motion in a dynamic scene. Predictability regularization implicitly penalizes chaotic motion estimation and can help solve the ambiguity of motion.
- We condition point motions on embedding vectors and design a predictor on the embedding space to enforce motion predictability.
- We demonstrate the benefits of the resulting additional supervision (predictability regularization) on motion learning through a variety of qualitative and quantitative evaluations.
- We provide insights into how the proposed framework can be leveraged for motion prediction as a by-product.

2   Related Work

Neural Fields. A neural field is a field that is parameterized fully or in part by a neural network [6,59]. Neural fields are widely used for implicitly encoding the geometry of a scene, such as occupancy [29] and distance function [7,35]. Our method is built on the milestone work NeRF [30], in which the radiance and density are encoded in neural fields. NeRF led to a series of breakthroughs in the fields of 3D scene understanding and rendering, such as relighting [2,3,46], human face and body capture [14,24,34,39,40,49], and city-scale reconstruction [43,50,53,58]. A recent method also named PREF [15] is developed for compact neural signal modeling.

Motion Estimation and 4D Reconstruction. Large-scale learning-based motion estimation from multiview data achieved impressive performance [22,42], but most methods are constrained to tracking some specific objects such as humans [42]. In this paper, we are concerned with estimating the motion of all points without access to any annotations, which is related to the 4D reconstruction problem where motion is usually estimated. Some methods have been developed with known geometry information such as depth or point cloud. Dynamic-Fusion [32], Schmidt *et al*let@tokeneonedot[44], Bozic *et al*let@tokeneonedot[5], and Yoon *et al*let@tokeneonedot[61] estimate motion from videos with depth. OFlow [33] and ShapeFlow [17] infer a deformation flow field with the knowledge of occupancy. More recently, motivated by the success of NeRF, a number of methods have been designed to reconstruct 4D scenes as well as motion directly from multiview data, which can be acquired from a multi-camera system or a single moving camera. D-NeRF [41], Nerfies [36] and NR-NeRF [52] set a canonical frame and align dynamic points to it. DCT-NeRF [56] proposes to track the trajectory of a point along all sequences. NSFF [21], VideoNeRF [57], and NeRFlow [9] propose to represent the dynamic scene with a 4D space-time field, thus able to handle topologically varying scenes. The 4D fields are under-determined, and precomputed data-driven priors are usually needed to achieve good performance. HyperNeRF [37] proposes to align frames towards a hyperspace for topologically varying scenes and achieves state-of-the-art performance without the need of data-driven priors. These methods are able to render visually appealing images for novel views and time, yet their performance on 3D motion estimation has room for improvements.

Scene Flow Estimation. 3D motion field is also known as dense scene flow [28,31,62]. Vedula *et al*let@tokeneonedot[54] introduced the concept and demonstrated a framework for acquiring dense, non-rigid scene flow from optical flow. Basha *et al*let@tokeneonedot[1] proposed a 3D point cloud parameterization of the 3D structure and scene flow with calibrated multi-view videos. Vogel *et al*let@tokeneonedot[55] suggested to represent the dynamic 3D scene by a collection of planar, rigidly moving, local segments. More recently, Yang *et al*let@tokeneonedot[60] proposed a framework adopting 3D rigid transformations for analyzing background segmentation and rigidly moving objects.

Predictability. The study of the predictability of time series data dates back to [4,38], in which predictability is interpreted as the ability to be decomposed into lower-dimensional components. The idea of extracting principal components as predictability is adopted for blind source separation in [48]. Differential entropy is used for measuring predictability in [12]. Our method shares a similar motivation as the above methods in terms of discovering low-rank structures, while predictability in our method is not explicitly defined but implicitly introduced through a predictor network.

3 Preliminaries

Our method is built upon the NeRF framework [30] and is inspired by recent progresses w.r.tlet@tokeneonedotdynamic scenes [21,57]. For each 3D point $\mathbf{p} = (x, y, z)$ in the considered space, we represent its volume density by $\boldsymbol{\sigma}(\mathbf{p})$, and its color from a viewing direction $\mathbf{d}$ by $\mathbf{c}(\mathbf{p}, \mathbf{d})$. In NeRF, these two attributes are defined as the output of a continuous function F modeled by a neural network, i.e., $(\mathbf{c}, \boldsymbol{\sigma}) = F(\mathbf{p}, \mathbf{d})$. This neural field can be queried to render images of the represented scene through volume rendering. For each camera ray $\mathbf{r}$ defined by its optical origin $\mathbf{o}$ and direction $\mathbf{d}$ intersecting a pixel, we compute the color $\mathbf{C}(\mathbf{r})$ of said pixel by sampling points along the ray, i.e., sampling $\mathbf{p}_i = \mathbf{o} + i\mathbf{d}$; then querying and accumulating their attributes according to F. Overall, the expected color $\mathbf{C}(\mathbf{r})$ of the ray $\mathbf{r}$ is:

$$\mathbf{C}(\mathbf{r}) = \int_{i_n}^{i_f} e^{-\int_{i_n}^{i} \sigma(\mathbf{p}_j) dj} \boldsymbol{\sigma}(\mathbf{p}_i) \mathbf{c}(\mathbf{p}_i, \mathbf{d}) di, \tag{1}$$

where i_n, i_f are near and far bounds. The integration in Eq. 1 is numerically approximated by summing up a set of points on the ray.

For dynamic scenes, existing solutions can be roughly categorized into two groups. Either methods model the motion and radiance with two distinct fields [36,41], or they are regularizing the motion from a space-time field [9,21,57]. In the former solutions, the color of a point $\mathbf{p}$ at time t is represented by $F_k(M(\mathbf{p}, t), \mathbf{d})$, where F_k represents the kth canonical time-invariant space and M is a learned neural motion field defining the motion $\Delta\mathbf{p}$ of any point $\mathbf{p}$ at time t w.r.tlet@tokeneonedotto their position in the canonical space. Our method falls into the latter category, in which each point in the dynamic scene is represented by a space-time field $F(\mathbf{p}, \mathbf{d}, t)$. Unlike canonical space-based methods, for the space-time field we need to specify the frame of F when joint training with a motion field M. We opt for space-time field rather than canonical-space one for two reasons. First, we presume that underlying patterns exist for the motion of a certain time range. So canonical-frame-based motion estimation frameworks are not suitable, since their motions are from the predefined canonical frame to another, whereas we need the motion between a certain range of frames. Second, space-time fields are more generic as they can handle non-existent geometry in the canonical frame (e.g., objects entering the scene mid-sequence). Note that for both categories, the scene fields are optimized jointly leveraging observation-based self-supervision, i.e., computing the image reconstruction loss for each time step t as:

$$\mathcal{L}_{\text{rec}} = \sum_{\mathbf{r}} \|\mathbf{C}_{\text{gt}}^t(\mathbf{r}) - \mathbf{C}^t(\mathbf{r})\|_2^2, \tag{2}$$

with $\mathbf{C}_{\text{gt}}^t$ is the observed pixel color and $\mathbf{C}^t$ is the color rendered from F and M.

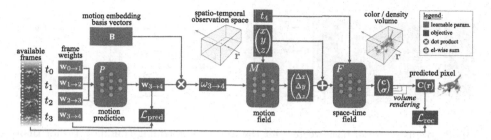

Fig. 2. Overview of the proposed framework. Three networks are trained jointly: the space-time field, the motion field and the predictor. The space-time field returns color and occupancy for each point at a specific time. The motion field predicts the motion of a point based on a motion embedding vector. The predictor generates the future motion embedding based on previously observed embeddings.

4 Method

4.1 Overview

Our framework consists of three components: a neural space-time field F, a motion field M and a motion predictor P. An overview of their interactions is presented in Fig. 2. In our framework and implementations, we do not model the viewing dependency effects with the space-time field, so the space-time field outputs the color and occupancy for each point (x, y, z, t), whereas the motion field provides the motion of any point between two time steps, according to the space-time field. Let the motion of point $\mathbf{p} = (x, y, z)$ from time t to $t + \delta t$ be $\Delta_{t \to t+\delta t}\mathbf{p}$, then for $\mathbf{p}$ at time t we have:

$$(\mathbf{c}_t, \boldsymbol{\sigma}_t) = F(\mathbf{p} + \Delta_{t \to t+\delta t}\mathbf{p}, t + \delta t). \tag{3}$$

The idea is that for a scene observed at time $t + \delta t$, we can obtain the attributes of $\mathbf{p}$ at time t by querying the space-time field with the point location at $t + \delta t$.

In our framework, the motion network is conditioned on an embedding vector $\boldsymbol{\omega}$ (instead of queried timestep) and the motion can be written as $\Delta_{t \to t+\delta t}\mathbf{p} = M(\mathbf{p}, \boldsymbol{\omega}_{t \to t+\delta t})$, where $\boldsymbol{\omega}_{t \to t+\delta t}$ depends on time t and interval δt. Replacing the temporal variable t with a vector $\boldsymbol{\omega}$ as input to M enables predictability via embedding, as further detailed in Sect. 4.2. All networks and the embedding vector w.r.tlet@tokeneonedottime t are optimized using the reconstruction loss $\mathcal{L}_{\text{rec}}$ (c.f. Eq. 2), with color C^t predicted from $F, M, \boldsymbol{\omega}_{t \to t+\delta t}$ according to Eqs. 1 and 3.

We define the predictor P as a function taking as input several motion embedding vectors of previous frames and inferring the motion embedding vectors for the future frames accordingly. Mathematically, we have $\boldsymbol{\omega}_{t \to t+\delta t} = P(\boldsymbol{\omega}_{\text{prev}})$ with $\boldsymbol{\omega}_{\text{prev}} = \{\boldsymbol{\omega}_{t-(i+1)\delta t \to t - i\delta t}\}_{i=1}^{\tau}$ set of τ previous frames' embeddings. For example, in Fig. 2, the embedding vector $\boldsymbol{\omega}_{3 \to 4}$ for motion from t_3 to t_4 is predicted from previous three embedding vectors, that is, $P(\{\boldsymbol{\omega}_{0 \to 1}, \boldsymbol{\omega}_{1 \to 2}, \boldsymbol{\omega}_{2 \to 3}\})$.

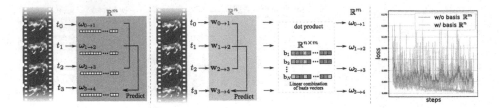

Fig. 3. We use a set of basis vectors for the motion embedding (middle), rather than associating each frame with a motion vector (left). The input and out space of the predictor switches to the linear combination weights by using these shared basis vectors. The comparison of training losses (right) indicates that the predictor converges faster on the space of linear combination weights.

4.2   Neural Motion Fields with Motion Embedding

The motion field is conditioned on an embedding vector, sampled from a latent space depicting motion patterns. Such embedding can be implemented in various ways. The simplest one is to associate each motion of interest with a trainable embedding vector. This technique has been widely used for conditioning neural fields w.r.tlet@tokeneonedotappearance [26] and deformation [36]. However, empirical studies show that associating each motion with motion embedding frequently and significantly slows down the convergence speed of the predictor, as demonstrated in Fig. 3. We presume that the phenomenon is caused by the large and unstructured solution space brought by frame-wise motion embedding. To validate the assumption and improve the convergence speed, we propose to reduce the dimension of the input and output space of the predictor.

Inspired by mixture-of-experts-based prediction networks [13,23,47], we design a set $\mathbf{B} \in \mathbb{R}^{n \times m}$ of n embedding basis vectors, $i.e.$, $\mathbf{B} = [\mathbf{b}_1, \cdots, \mathbf{b}_n]^T$ with $\mathbf{b}_i \in \mathbb{R}^m$ basis vector. $\mathbf{B}$ is shared across all frames. Then the motion embedding becomes $\boldsymbol{\omega}_{t \to t+\delta t} = \mathbf{w}_{t \to t+\delta t} \cdot \mathbf{B}$, with $\mathbf{w} \in \mathbb{R}^n$ optimizable linear combination weights. Accordingly, we redefine the model P to receive and predict these weight vectors instead of the embedding ones, thus reducing its input space and output space to $\mathbb{R}^n$, $i.e.$, with the dimensionality of basis vectors not affecting the predictor anymore. In our experiments, we set $n = 5$ and $m = 32$, so the dimension of the predictor's output space is reduced from 32 to 5. An illustration and comparison of the training losses between the two schemes are presented in Fig. 3.

4.3   Regularizing with Motion Prediction

Our proposed solution makes it possible to complement the usual self-supervision of space-time neural fields (through visual reconstruction only) by a regularization term over motion. However, while predicting motion embeddings is straightforward, $i.e.$, by simply forwarding the embedding vectors of previous frames into P, leveraging P for the regularization of M is not trivial.

In our framework, motion embeddings can be acquired either from reconstruction, *i.e.*, optimizing each embedding along with other components (*e.g.*, both the motion embedding $\omega_{3\rightarrow4} = \mathbf{w}_{3\rightarrow4} \cdot \mathbf{B}$ and the motion network $M(\mathbf{p}, \omega_{3\rightarrow4})$ can be optimized on observed images at $t = 3, 4$); or through the predictor (*e.g.*, $\omega_{3\rightarrow4} = P(\{\mathbf{w}_{t-1\rightarrow t}\}_{t=1}^{3}) \cdot \mathbf{B}$). We leverage this redundancy for regularization, *i.e.*, proposing a loss to minimize the difference between the self-supervised embeddings and their corresponding predicted versions:

$$\mathcal{L}_{\text{pred}} = \|P(\mathbf{w}_{\text{prev}}) - \arg\min_{\mathbf{w}_{t\rightarrow t+\delta t}} \mathcal{L}_{\text{rec}}\|_2^2, \text{ where } \mathbf{w}_{\text{prev}} = \{\mathbf{w}_{t-(i+1)\delta t\rightarrow t-i\delta t}\}_{i=1}^{\tau}. \quad (4)$$

In the above equation, the first term $P(\cdot)$ represents the motion embedding predicted according to previous τ frames, and the second term $\arg\min_{\mathbf{w}_{t\rightarrow t+\delta t}} \mathcal{L}_{\text{rec}}$ is the vector acquired from minimizing the reconstruction loss.

It is, however, impractical to compute this second term during training, since the reconstruction problem can take hours to solve via optimization. We propose instead to obtain $\mathbf{w}_{t\rightarrow t+\delta t}$ in an online manner, and to jointly optimize frame weights $\mathbf{w}$ over both $\mathcal{L}_{\text{rec}}$ and $\mathcal{L}_{\text{pred}}$ at each optimization step. That is, at each step, all current frame weights $\mathbf{w}$ are first used to compute $\mathcal{L}_{\text{pred}}$ and optimize downstream models accordingly, and are then themselves optimized w.r.t @tokeneonedot $\mathcal{L}_{\text{rec}}$. The details of implementing the two losses with batches of frames are introduced in the next section.

4.4 Optimization

During optimization, we sample a short sequence of frames from the training set. For simplifying the notations, we assume that the predictor takes $\tau = 3$ frames as input and predicts the motion of the next frame. An illustration is presented in Fig. 4. Four consecutive frames $(t_i, t_{i+1}, t_{i+2}, t_{i+3})$ are first sampled from the observed sequence and the corresponding embedding vectors ω are acquired as in Sect. 4.2. Note that training images can be sampled from different synchronized cameras if available.

We disentangle appearance- and motion-related information during optimization by applying $\mathcal{L}_{\text{rec}}$ to images reconstructed both with and without motion reparameterization. That is, we sample F for radiance/density values $(\mathbf{c}_t, \sigma_t)$ both as $F(\mathbf{p} + M(\mathbf{p}, \omega_{t\rightarrow t+\delta t}), t + \delta t)$ and as $F(\mathbf{p}, t)$ (*c.f.*, Fig. 4).

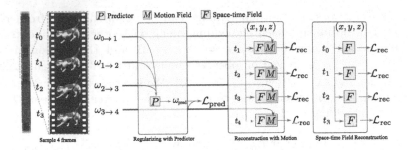

Fig. 4. System optimization, demonstrated on a batch of 4 frames. Predictor P infers a vector ω based on the preceding 3 frames; $\mathcal{L}_{\text{pred}}$ minimizes the difference between these predicted embeddings and their sampled equivalents; whereas reconstruction loss $\mathcal{L}_{\text{rec}}$ is applied to the predicted four frames, with and without motion reparameterization.

5   Experiments

We qualitatively and quantitatively evaluate our method in this section. *We urge the reader to check our video to better appraise the quality of motion.* The following three datasets are used for evaluation:

- **ZJU-MoCap** [40] is a multi-camera dataset, with videos of one person performing different actions. Since each video sequence records a single human, the scene is less topologically varying and we compare our method with canonical frame-based representations of dynamic scenes. We use videos from 11 cameras for evaluation.
- **Panoptic** [18] includes videos from multiple synchronized cameras under many different settings including multi-person activities and human-object interactions. We select 4 challenging and representative video clips from the 31 HD cameras and denote them as SPORTS, TOOLS, IAN, and CELLO. Each clip has 400 frames and all the clips involve human-object interaction.
- **Hypernerf** [37] is a single-camera dataset, *i.e.*, with one view available at each timestamp. Unlike the previous two datasets that use static cameras, in Hypernerf the multiview information is generated by moving the camera around. Hypernerf is challenging not only because of the single-camera setting, but also the topologically varying scenes.

Details about the clips (*e.g.*, starting and ending frame number) are included in the supplementary. All the sequences are split into short intervals consisting of 25 frames. On each interval, the networks are trained using an Adam optimizer [19] with a learning rate that decays from 5×10^{-4} to 5×10^{-6} every 50k iterations. During training, the two losses are added with a balancing parameter, *i.e.*, $\mathcal{L} = \mathcal{L}_{\text{rec}} + \gamma \mathcal{L}_{\text{pred}}$ with γ set to 0.01 in all experiments. A batch of 1,024 rays is randomly sampled from the selected frames for training the motion field and the space-time field. We observe that using viewing direction $\mathbf{d}$ in F leads to worse performance if the scene of interest mostly contains Lambertian surfaces. In our experiments, the viewing direction is not taken as the input for the space-time field, *i.e.*, a space-time irradiance field [57]. The network structures of the

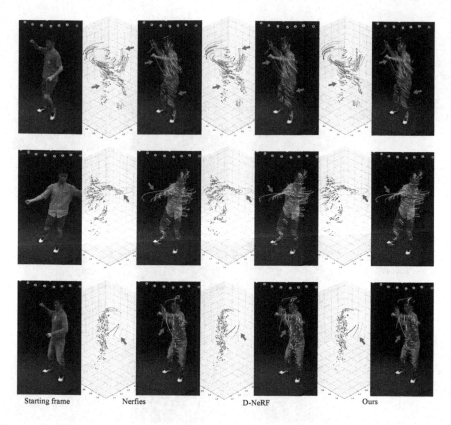

Starting frame   Nerfies   D-NeRF   Ours

Fig. 5. Comparison of the estimated motion on the ZJU-MoCap dataset. Only one person is captured for each sequence and we compare our method with canonical frame-based methods Nerfies [36] and D-NeRF [41]. Motion for 20 frames is demonstrated.

motion field and the space-time field are the same as in NeRF [30]. The predictor consists of 5 fully connected layers with a width of 128 and ReLU activations.

5.1 Qualitative Evaluation

We visually compare the estimated motion in this section. Since neural motion fields tracks all points in the space, we randomly sample points and then demonstrate their trajectory. Different sampling strategies are used for different datasets. For ZJU-MoCap, we first sample a dense grid of points and then remove the empty points with $\sigma < 20$, then we randomly sample points from the non-empty ones. For Panoptic, since background (walls and floors) is kept in the scenes, we sample meaningful points near the persons in the scene, leveraging provided people positions. For Hypernerf, since the scenes are all front-facing, we sample points on the surfaces according to the depth generated by the space-time field F from one view.

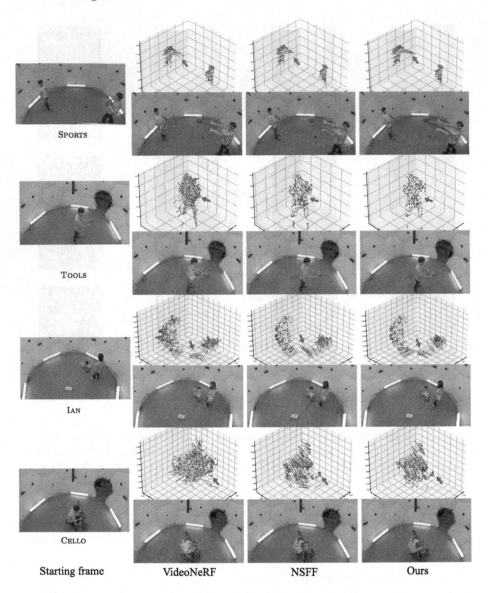

Fig. 6. Motion estimation comparison on the Panoptic dataset [18]. Motions estimated by VideoNeRF are more chaotic than NSFF, possibly due to the 2D optical flow supervision adopted in NSFF. Our method faithfully estimates the motions of people and objects, whereas NSFF fails to track some points, *e.g.*, the ball in SPORTS and IAN.

On Multi-Camera Dataset. We first present our results on ZJU-MoCap in Fig. 5. Since there is only one person in this dataset, the topology of the scene roughly remains unchanged and canonical space-based methods can be applied. Nerfies [36] and D-NeRF [41] are selected for comparison. As can be observed

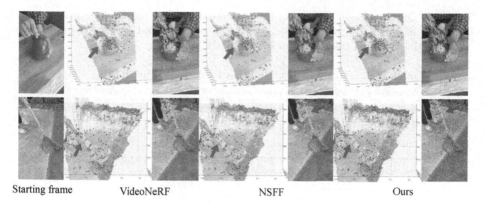

Fig. 7. Comparison of the estimated motion on the Hypernerf dataset [37]. We randomly sample points on the surfaces and then demonstrate their the motions.

from the images, our method can generate a smooth motion as opposed to the rugged and noisy motions from the other two methods.

Figure 6 demonstrate the performance of our method and competitors on the Panoptic dataset. The scenes contain complex geometries and objects may occur or disappear in the middle of a sequence. Two space-time field-based methods, VideoNeRF [57] and NSFF [21], are selected for comparison. Our method estimate the motion of both people and objects accurately, while VideoNeRF presents chaotic results and the motion from NSFF are occasionally inaccurate. The results on Figs. 5 and 6 validate our claim that our method can well track all points in the space without prior knowledge of the scene.

On Single-Camera Dataset. To further validate our method, we demonstrate motion estimation in single-camera settings, which are more commonly encountered by dynamic-scene novel-view rendering methods. We consider the challenging scenes captured by Hypernerf [37]. As shown in Fig. 7, we compare again to VideoNeRF [57] and NSFF [21]. We note that our results are more temporally consistent and accurate than competitors. These results highlight the practical value of our method, able to accurately handle single-camera image sequences captured in the wild.

5.2 Quantitative Evaluation

Quantitative evaluation is difficult for our task since manually labeling a dense set of points in the space is expensive, if not unfeasible. We thus use the sparser human body joints provided by the Panoptic dataset to quantify the accuracy of the estimated motion. MPJPE [45] and 3D-PCK [27] are two widely used metrics for evaluating 3D human pose tracking performance, but both of them do not suit our task since our tracking requires as input the position of points at the starting frame. We propose to calculate the tracking error across K frames

Table 1. Quantitatively evaluating the estimated motion on the Panoptic dataset. Locations of the body joints in the starting frame are used as the inputs and we calculate the averaged tracking error for the body joints.

	mMPJPE$_5$ (cm)			mMPJPE$_{10}$ (cm)			mMPJPE$_{15}$ (cm)		
	VideoNeRF	NSFF	Ours	VideoNeRF	NSFF	Ours	VideoNeRF	NSFF	Ours
SPORTS	5.942	5.171	**4.533**	8.346	7.933	**7.457**	11.569	11.254	**10.718**
TOOLS	3.378	2.341	**1.684**	4.105	2.879	**2.650**	4.931	3.984	**3.393**
IAN	3.448	**2.349**	2.402	5.059	**3.534**	3.792	6.767	5.282	**4.980**
CELLO	2.796	1.759	**1.612**	4.281	3.296	**2.572**	4.853	3.776	**3.457**

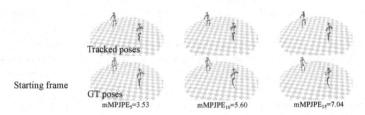

Fig. 8. Visualization of motion tracking results on the Panoptic dataset.

and use the averaged value as a metric. We denote the metric as mMPJPE$_K$ (mean MPJPE), computed as:

$$\text{mMPJPE}_K = \frac{1}{N_f}\frac{1}{K}\sum_{u=1}^{N_f}\sum_{v=u+1}^{u+K}\text{MPJPE}(P_{u\to v}, P_v^{\text{gt}}), \tag{5}$$

where K is the number of frames for evaluating the motion and N_f is the total number of frames in the sequence. $P_{i\to j}$ represents the estimated positions for the jth frame given positions for the ith one as inputs, and P_j^{gt} the ground-truth joint positions for the jth frame.

We report the mMPJPEK metric with $K = 5, 10, 15$ on the Panoptic dataset in Table 1. Our method achieves more accurate tracking performance than the other two methods except on IAN while tracking with 5 and 10 frames. NSFF requires both 2D optical flow and depth, while VideoNeRF requires depth information. As a comparison, we do not use any data-driven prior to guide the motion estimation module. Moreover, in Fig. 8 we visualize the tracked pose and the ground truth pose on one sequence and compute the corresponding mMPJPE metrics ($N_f = 1$ for one sequence).

Fig. 9. Accuracy evaluation of the motion predictor. Left: Plotting of the MPJPE of predicted future body joint locations. Horizontal lines are the mMPJPE$_{15}$ results on the corresponding scenes. Right: Visualization of predicted future motion of densely sampled points on the last observed frames and the 10th ground truth future frames.

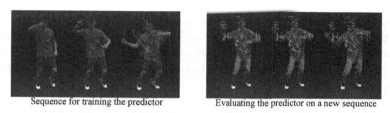

Fig. 10. Transferability of the motion predictor. We train the whole framework on the left-side sequence, then we freeze the predictor and fine tune other models on the right-side sequence. The next 10 frame motions are predicted from the last observed frame (the right-side first image) and visualized. The other two images are real movements in the future 5th frame and 10th frame.

5.3   Analysis of the Motion Predictor

We analyze the motion predictor P in two aspects: prediction accuracy and transferability. For the accuracy evaluation, we compare the predicted future locations of the body joints and the ground-truth future locations. The results are demonstrated in Fig. 9. The training sequences are separated into 20 intervals and we test the prediction results on each interval. The MPJPE of predicted body joint locations are averaged over all the intervals and plotted. We can observe in Table 1 that the model can predict the unseen motion of the next 5 time steps, with a low error close to the tracking error over actual observations.

We further demonstrate the transferability of the predictor in Fig. 10. Since the predictor generates motion codes in a latent space, the same model should work for motion sequences with similar patterns. We test the intuition on the ZJU-MoCap dataset, on two sequences in which the person does similar actions. We can observe from the right side of the figure that the predicted motions align with the real movements. The results demonstrate that the predictor is indeed transferable if the motions are similar.

6   Discussion

Limitations. Our method sometimes fail on non-rigid/monochromatic elements and the problem of motion estimation then gets underconstrained: Some points may converge into the same point for the non-rigid case and it may be hard to tell which part in the monochromatic area moved. We presume that a more advanced (possibly pre-trained) motion prediction model could be leveraged. Moreover, while our methods shows higher precision in estimating natural motion (*e.g.*, dense human motion tracking), it is among our future work to address some other challenging scenes (*e.g.*, scenes with chaotic particles).

Conclusion. We introduced a novel solution for the regularization and prediction of 3D dense motion in dynamic scenes. Leveraging advances in neural fields, we propose a combination of space-time and motion fields conditioned on motion embeddings. Through predictability-based regularization over these embeddings, we promote the encoding of scene-relevant motions and penalize ambiguous and noisy deformations. We acknowledge that this scheme may not benefit all types of scenes (*c.f.* above limitations), but it shows higher precision in natural settings.

References

1. Basha, T., Moses, Y., Kiryati, N.: Multi-view scene flow estimation: a view centered variational approach. Int. J. Comput. Vision **101**(1), 6–21 (2013)
2. Boss, M., Braun, R., Jampani, V., Barron, J.T., Liu, C., Lensch, H.: Nerd: neural reflectance decomposition from image collections. In: Proceedings of the IEEE/CVF International Conference on Computer Vision, pp. 12684–12694 (2021)
3. Boss, M., Jampani, V., Braun, R., Liu, C., Barron, J.T., Lensch, H.P.: Neural-pil: neural pre-integrated lighting for reflectance decomposition. Adv. Neural Inf. Process. Syst. **34**, 10691–10704 (2021)
4. Box, G.E., Tiao, G.C.: A canonical analysis of multiple time series. Biometrika **64**(2), 355–365 (1977)
5. Bozic, A., Palafox, P., Zollhöfer, M., Dai, A., Thies, J., Nießner, M.: Neural non-rigid tracking. Adv. Neural Inf. Process. Syst. **33**, 18727–18737 (2020)
6. Chen, A., Xu, Z., Geiger, A., Yu, J., Su, H.: Tensorf: tensorial radiance fields. In: Proceedings of the European Conference on Computer Vision (2022)
7. Chibane, J., Pons-Moll, G., et al.: Neural unsigned distance fields for implicit function learning. Adv. Neural Inf. Process. Syst. **33**, 21638–21652 (2020)
8. Chung, S.J., Paranjape, A.A., Dames, P., Shen, S., Kumar, V.: A survey on aerial swarm robotics. IEEE Trans. Rob. **34**(4), 837–855 (2018)
9. Du, Y., Zhang, Y., Yu, H.X., Tenenbaum, J.B., Wu, J.: Neural radiance flow for 4D view synthesis and video processing. In: Proceedings of the IEEE/CVF International Conference on Computer Vision (2021)
10. Fang, J., et al.: Fast dynamic radiance fields with time-aware neural voxels. arXiv preprint arXiv:2205.15285 (2022)
11. Gafni, G., Thies, J., Zollhofer, M., Nießner, M.: Dynamic neural radiance fields for monocular 4D facial avatar reconstruction. In: Proceedings of the IEEE/CVF Conference on Computer Vision and Pattern Recognition, pp. 8649–8658 (2021)

12. Goerg, G.: Forecastable component analysis. In: International Conference on Machine Learning, pp. 64–72. PMLR (2013)
13. Hassan, M., et al.: Stochastic scene-aware motion prediction. In: Proceedings of the IEEE/CVF International Conference on Computer Vision, pp. 11374–11384 (2021)
14. Hong, Y., Peng, B., Xiao, H., Liu, L., Zhang, J.: Headnerf: a real-time nerf-based parametric head model. In: Proceedings of the IEEE/CVF Conference on Computer Vision and Pattern Recognition, pp. 20374–20384 (2022)
15. Huang, B., Yan, X., Chen, A., Gao, S., Yu, J.: Pref: phasorial embedding fields for compact neural representations (2022)
16. Huang, T.S., Tsai, R.: Image sequence analysis: motion estimation. In: Huang, T.S. (ed.) Image Sequence Analysis, pp. 1–18. Springer, Heidelberg (1981). https://doi.org/10.1007/978-3-642-87037-8_1
17. Jiang, C., Huang, J., Tagliasacchi, A., Guibas, L.: Shapeflow: learnable deformations among 3D shapes. Adv. Neural Inf. Process. Syst. **33**, 9745–9757 (2020)
18. Joo, H., et al.: Panoptic studio: a massively multiview system for social motion capture. In: Proceedings of the IEEE International Conference on Computer Vision, pp. 3334–3342 (2015)
19. Kingma, D.P., Ba, J.: Adam: a method for stochastic optimization. In: Bengio, Y., LeCun, Y. (eds.) International Conference on Learning Representations (2015)
20. Li, T., et al.: Neural 3D video synthesis from multi-view video. In: Proceedings of the IEEE/CVF Conference on Computer Vision and Pattern Recognition, pp. 5521–5531 (2022)
21. Li, Z., Niklaus, S., Snavely, N., Wang, O.: Neural scene flow fields for space-time view synthesis of dynamic scenes. In: Proceedings of the IEEE/CVF Conference on Computer Vision and Pattern Recognition (2021)
22. Li, Z., Ji, Y., Yang, W., Ye, J., Yu, J.: Robust 3D human motion reconstruction via dynamic template construction. In: International Conference on 3D Vision, pp. 496–505. IEEE (2017)
23. Ling, H.Y., Zinno, F., Cheng, G., Van De Panne, M.: Character controllers using motion vaes. ACM Trans. Graph. (TOG) **39**(4), 40–1 (2020)
24. Liu, L., Habermann, M., Rudnev, V., Sarkar, K., Gu, J., Theobalt, C.: Neural actor: neural free-view synthesis of human actors with pose control. ACM Trans. Graph. (ACM SIGGRAPH Asia) **40**, 1–16 (2021)
25. Lombardi, S., Simon, T., Saragih, J., Schwartz, G., Lehrmann, A., Sheikh, Y.: Neural volumes: learning dynamic renderable volumes from images. ACM Trans. Graph. **38**(4), 1–14 (2019)
26. Martin-Brualla, R., Radwan, N., Sajjadi, M.S., Barron, J.T., Dosovitskiy, A., Duckworth, D.: Nerf in the wild: neural radiance fields for unconstrained photo collections. In: Proceedings of the IEEE/CVF Conference on Computer Vision and Pattern Recognition, pp. 7210–7219 (2021)
27. Mehta, D., et al.: Monocular 3D human pose estimation in the wild using improved cnn supervision. In: 2017 International Conference on 3D Vision (3DV), pp. 506–516. IEEE (2017)
28. Menze, M., Geiger, A.: Object scene flow for autonomous vehicles. In: Proceedings of the IEEE Conference on Computer Vision and Pattern Recognition, pp. 3061–3070 (2015)
29. Mescheder, L., Oechsle, M., Niemeyer, M., Nowozin, S., Geiger, A.: Occupancy networks: learning 3D reconstruction in function space. In: Proceedings of the IEEE/CVF Conference on Computer Vision and Pattern Recognition, pp. 4460–4470 (2019)

30. Mildenhall, B., Srinivasan, P.P., Tancik, M., Barron, J.T., Ramamoorthi, R., Ng, R.: NeRF: representing scenes as neural radiance fields for view synthesis. In: Vedaldi, A., Bischof, H., Brox, T., Frahm, J.-M. (eds.) ECCV 2020. LNCS, vol. 12346, pp. 405–421. Springer, Cham (2020). https://doi.org/10.1007/978-3-030-58452-8_24

31. Mittal, H., Okorn, B., Held, D.: Just go with the flow: self-supervised scene flow estimation. In: Proceedings of the IEEE/CVF Conference on Computer Vision and Pattern Recognition, pp. 11177–11185 (2020)

32. Newcombe, R.A., Fox, D., Seitz, S.M.: Dynamicfusion: reconstruction and tracking of non-rigid scenes in real-time. In: Proceedings of the IEEE Conference on Computer Vision and Pattern Recognition, pp. 343–352 (2015)

33. Niemeyer, M., Mescheder, L., Oechsle, M., Geiger, A.: Occupancy flow: 4D reconstruction by learning particle dynamics. In: Proceedings of the IEEE/CVF International Conference on Computer Vision, pp. 5379–5389 (2019)

34. Noguchi, A., Sun, X., Lin, S., Harada, T.: Neural articulated radiance field. In: Proceedings of the IEEE/CVF International Conference on Computer Vision, pp. 5762–5772 (2021)

35. Park, J.J., Florence, P., Straub, J., Newcombe, R., Lovegrove, S.: Deepsdf: learning continuous signed distance functions for shape representation. In: Proceedings of the IEEE/CVF Conference on Computer Vision and Pattern Recognition, pp. 165–174 (2019)

36. Park, K., et al.: Nerfies: deformable neural radiance fields. In: Proceedings of the IEEE/CVF International Conference on Computer Vision, pp. 5865–5874 (2021)

37. Park, K., et al.: Hypernerf: a higher-dimensional representation for topologically varying neural radiance fields. ACM Trans. Graph. **40**(6) (2021)

38. Pena, D., Box, G.E.: Identifying a simplifying structure in time series. J. Am. Stat. Assoc. **82**(399), 836–843 (1987)

39. Peng, S., et al.: Animatable neural radiance fields for modeling dynamic human bodies. In: Proceedings of the IEEE/CVF International Conference on Computer Vision, pp. 14314–14323 (2021)

40. Peng, S., et al.: Neural body: implicit neural representations with structured latent codes for novel view synthesis of dynamic humans. In: Proceedings of the IEEE/CVF Conference on Computer Vision and Pattern Recognition, pp. 9054–9063 (2021)

41. Pumarola, A., Corona, E., Pons-Moll, G., Moreno-Noguer, F.: D-nerf: neural radiance fields for dynamic scenes. In: Proceedings of the IEEE/CVF Conference on Computer Vision and Pattern Recognition, pp. 10318–10327 (2021)

42. Reddy, N.D., Guigues, L., Pishchulin, L., Eledath, J., Narasimhan, S.G.: Tessetrack: end-to-end learnable multi-person articulated 3D pose tracking. In: Proceedings of the IEEE/CVF Conference on Computer Vision and Pattern Recognition, pp. 15190–15200 (2021)

43. Rematas, K., et al.: Urban radiance fields. In: Proceedings of the IEEE/CVF Conference on Computer Vision and Pattern Recognition, pp. 12932–12942 (2022)

44. Schmidt, T., Newcombe, R., Fox, D.: Dart: dense articulated real-time tracking with consumer depth cameras. Auton. Robots **39**(3), 239–258 (2015)

45. Sigal, L., Balan, A.O., Black, M.J.: Humaneva: synchronized video and motion capture dataset and baseline algorithm for evaluation of articulated human motion. Int. J. Comput. Vision **87**(1), 4–27 (2010)

46. Srinivasan, P.P., Deng, B., Zhang, X., Tancik, M., Mildenhall, B., Barron, J.T.: Nerv: neural reflectance and visibility fields for relighting and view synthesis. In:

Proceedings of the IEEE/CVF Conference on Computer Vision and Pattern Recognition, pp. 7495–7504 (2021)

47. Starke, S., Zhang, H., Komura, T., Saito, J.: Neural state machine for character-scene interactions. ACM Trans. Graph. **38**(6), 209–1 (2019)

48. Stone, J.V.: Blind source separation using temporal predictability. Neural Comput. **13**(7), 1559–1574 (2001)

49. Su, S.Y., Yu, F., Zollhoefer, M., Rhodin, H.: A-nerf: articulated neural radiance fields for learning human shape, appearance, and pose. In: NeurIPS (2021)

50. Tancik, M., et al.: Block-nerf: scalable large scene neural view synthesis. In: Proceedings of the IEEE/CVF Conference on Computer Vision and Pattern Recognition, pp. 8248–8258 (2022)

51. Tewari, A., et al.: State of the art on neural rendering. Comput. Graph. Forum **39**(2), 701–727 (2020)

52. Tretschk, E., Tewari, A., Golyanik, V., Zollhöfer, M., Lassner, C., Theobalt, C.: Non-rigid neural radiance fields: reconstruction and novel view synthesis of a dynamic scene from monocular video. In: Proceedings of the IEEE/CVF International Conference on Computer Vision, pp. 12959–12970 (2021)

53. Turki, H., Ramanan, D., Satyanarayanan, M.: Mega-nerf: scalable construction of large-scale nerfs for virtual fly-throughs. In: Proceedings of the IEEE/CVF Conference on Computer Vision and Pattern Recognition, pp. 12922–12931 (2022)

54. Vedula, S., Baker, S., Rander, P., Collins, R., Kanade, T.: Three-dimensional scene flow. In: Proceedings of the Seventh IEEE International Conference on Computer Vision, vol. 2, pp. 722–729. IEEE (1999)

55. Vogel, C., Schindler, K., Roth, S.: Piecewise rigid scene flow. In: Proceedings of the IEEE International Conference on Computer Vision, pp. 1377–1384 (2013)

56. Wang, C., Eckart, B., Lucey, S., Gallo, O.: Neural trajectory fields for dynamic novel view synthesis. arXiv preprint arXiv:2105.05994 (2021)

57. Xian, W., Huang, J.B., Kopf, J., Kim, C.: Space-time neural irradiance fields for free-viewpoint video. In: Proceedings of the IEEE/CVF Conference on Computer Vision and Pattern Recognition, pp. 9421–9431 (2021)

58. Xiangli, Y., et al.: Citynerf: building nerf at city scale. arXiv preprint arXiv:2112.05504 (2021)

59. Xie, Y., et al.: Neural fields in visual computing and beyond. In: Computer Graphics Forum, vol. 41, pp. 641–676. Wiley Online Library (2022)

60. Yang, B., et al.: Learning object-compositional neural radiance field for editable scene rendering. In: Proceedings of the IEEE/CVF International Conference on Computer Vision, pp. 13779–13788 (2021)

61. Yoon, J.S., Kim, K., Gallo, O., Park, H.S., Kautz, J.: Novel view synthesis of dynamic scenes with globally coherent depths from a monocular camera. In: Proceedings of the IEEE/CVF Conference on Computer Vision and Pattern Recognition, pp. 5336–5345 (2020)

62. Zhai, M., Xiang, X., Lv, N., Kong, X.: Optical flow and scene flow estimation: a survey. Pattern Recogn. **114**, 107861 (2021)

63. Zhang, J., et al.: Editable free-viewpoint video using a layered neural representation. ACM Trans. Graph. **40**(4), 149:1–149:18 (2021)

View Vertically: A Hierarchical Network for Trajectory Prediction via Fourier Spectrums

Conghao Wong[1], Beihao Xia[1], Ziming Hong[1], Qinmu Peng[1], Wei Yuan[1], Qiong Cao[2], Yibo Yang[2], and Xinge You[1(✉)]

[1] Huazhong University of Science and Technology, Wuhan, China
conghao_wong@hust.edu.cn, xbh_hust@hust.edu.cn   , youxg@hust.edu.cn
[2] JD Explore Academy, Beijing, China

Abstract. Understanding and forecasting future trajectories of agents are critical for behavior analysis, robot navigation, autonomous cars, and other related applications. Previous methods mostly treat trajectory prediction as time sequence generation. Different from them, this work studies agents' trajectories in a "vertical" view, *i.e.*, modeling and forecasting trajectories from the spectral domain. Different frequency bands in the trajectory spectrums could hierarchically reflect agents' motion preferences at different scales. The low-frequency and high-frequency portions could represent their coarse motion trends and fine motion variations, respectively. Accordingly, we propose a hierarchical network V^2-Net, which contains two sub-networks, to hierarchically model and predict agents' trajectories with trajectory spectrums. The coarse-level keypoints estimation sub-network first predicts the "minimal" spectrums of agents' trajectories on several "key" frequency portions. Then the fine-level spectrum interpolation sub-network interpolates the spectrums to reconstruct the final predictions. Experimental results display the competitiveness and superiority of V^2-Net on both ETH-UCY benchmark and the Stanford Drone Dataset.

Keywords: Hierarchical trajectory prediction · Fourier spectrums

1 Introduction

Trajectory prediction aims at inferring agents' possible future trajectories considering potential influencing factors. It has been an essential but challenging task, which can be widely applied to behavior analysis [2,5,39], robot navigation [48], autonomous driving [8,9,19,22], tracking [38,43], detection [10,11,34], and many other computer vision tasks [36,53]. Researchers have widely studied interactive factors, including the agent-agent interaction [1,14] and the agent-scene interaction [21,42]. Another line of researchers have explored creative ways to model

---

C. Wong and B. Xia—Equal contribution.
Codes are available at https://github.com/cocoon2wong/Vertical.

© The Author(s), under exclusive license to Springer Nature Switzerland AG 2022
S. Avidan et al. (Eds.): ECCV 2022, LNCS 13682, pp. 682–700, 2022.
https://doi.org/10.1007/978-3-031-20047-2_39

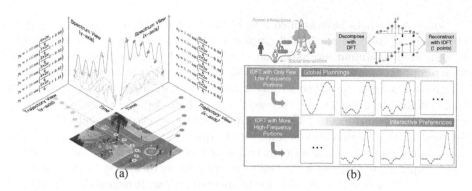

Fig. 1. V²-Net Motivation. (a) We show the trajectory in two views, the time sequences view and the Fourier spectrums view. The x-axis trajectory (green dots) and the y-axis trajectory (yellow dots) have similar "shapes", while they are quite different in the spectrum views (shown with amplitudes and phases), which motivates us to view trajectories "vertically" with spectrums rather than time sequences. (b) shows a trajectory with interactions. We utilize the first n/N low-frequency portions to reconstruct the trajectory, and the results show that different frequency portions have different contributions to their global plannings and interactive preferences. (Color figure online)

trajectories. Neural networks like Long-Short Term Memory Networks (LSTMs) [16,30,55], Graph Convolution Networks (GCNs) [24,46,56], and Transformers [13,57] are employed to encode agents' trajectories. Some researchers have also studied agents' multi-modal characteristics [5,17] and the distributions of their goals [7,12,40], thus forecasting multiple future choices.

However, most previous methods treat trajectory prediction as time sequence generation and predict trajectories recurrently, which could be challenging to reflect agents' motion preferences at different scales hierarchically. In other words, researchers usually tend to explore agents' behaviors and their changing trends dynamically but lack the overall analyses at different temporal scales. In fact, pedestrians always plan their activities at different levels simultaneously. For example, they may first determine their coarse motion trends and then make fine decisions to interactive variations. Although some methods [13,57,58] employ neural networks with attention mechanisms (like Transformers) as the backbone to model agents' status, they may still be difficult to directly represent agents' detailed motion differences at different temporal scales.

The Fourier transform (FT) and its variations have significantly succeeded in the signal processing community. Recently, researchers have also introduced FTs to some computer vision tasks, such as image de-noising [20], edge extraction [18], and image super-resolution [6]. FTs decompose sequential inputs into a series of sinusoids with different amplitudes and phases on different frequencies. Furthermore, these sinusoids could reflect the differentiated frequency response characteristics at different frequency scales, which could be difficult to obtain directly in the original signal. They provide a "vertical" view for processing and analyzing sequences, thus presenting elusive features in the original signals.

Some researchers have applied FTs in tasks similar to trajectory prediction. For example, Mao *et al.* [31,32] employ the discrete cosine transform (DCT) to help predict human motions. Cao *et al.* [3] use the graph Fourier transform to attempt to model interaction series in trajectory prediction. Unfortunately, FTs have not been employed to *model trajectories* in the trajectory prediction task directly. Inspired by the successful use of FTs, we try to employ the Discrete Fourier Transform (DFT) to obtain trajectory spectrums to capture agents' detailed motion preferences at different frequency scales. Figure 1(a) demonstrates an agent's two-dimensional trajectory in the time series and spectrum view, respectively. Although the two projection trajectories have similar shapes, they show considerable differences in the spectrum view. It means that the trajectory spectrums (including amplitudes and phases) obtained through FTs could reflect subtle differences that are difficult to discern within the time series.

Furthermore, some works have divided trajectory prediction into a two-stage pipeline, which we call the *hierarchical* prediction strategy. [29,47] divide this two-stage process into destination prediction and destination-controlled prediction. [28] introduces several "waypoints" to help predict agents' potential intentions rather than the only destination point. FTs decompose time series into the combination of different frequency portions. Inspired by these hierarchical approaches, a natural thought is to hierarchically predict agents' trajectories on different *frequency scales*, including: (a) *Global Plannings*, *i.e.*, agents' coarse motion trends. The low-frequency portions (slow-changing portions) in the trajectory spectrums could reflect their plannings globally. (b) *Interactive Preferences*, *i.e.*, agents' detailed interactions. The high-frequency portions (fast-changing portions) in the spectrums will directly show the rapidly changing movement rules, thus further describing their personalized interactive preferences.

Figure 1(b) demonstrates the trajectory reconstructed by different number of frequency portions. Agent's overall plannings could be reconstructed through a few low-frequency portions of the trajectory spectrum. By continually adding new high-frequency portions, the reconstructed trajectory would be able to reflect finer motion details and interactive preferences. Accordingly, we introduce a "coarse-fine" strategy to hierarchically model global plannings and interactive preferences by trajectory spectrums at different levels correspondingly.

In this paper, we propose the V^2-Net to hierarchically forecast trajectories in the spectrum view. It contains two sub-networks. The coarse-level keypoints estimation sub-network first predicts the "minimal" spectrums of agents' trajectories on several "key" frequency portions, and then the fine-level spectrum interpolation sub-network interpolates the spectrums to reconstruct the final predictions. Meanwhile, agents' social and scene interactions will also be concerned to make the network available to give predictions that conform to social rules and physical constraints. Our contributions are list as follows:

- We introduce the Fourier Transform to model and predict trajectories with spectrums to better capture agents' behaviors from a different perspective.

- A Transformer-based V²-Net containing coarse-level keypoints estimation and fine-level spectrum interpolation sub-networks is proposed to model and predict trajectories "coarse-to-fine" hierarchically.
- Experiments demonstrate that V²-Net achieves competitive performance on both ETH-UCY benchmark and the Stanford Drone Dataset.

2   Related Work

Trajectory Prediction. Recently, researchers have studied how interactive factors affect agents' trajectory plans, like social interaction [1,15,35,59] and scene interaction [30,55]. The modeling of agents' trajectories also matters how the trajectory prediction networks perform. Alahi *et al.* [1] treat this task as a sequence generation problem, and they employ LSTMs to model and predict pedestrians' positions in the next time step recurrently. A series of works have also introduced Graph Neural Networks (GNNs), *e.g.* Graph Attention Networks (GATs) [15,21,26] and GCNs [4,35], to handle interactive factors when forecasting. Moreover, the attention mechanism has been employed [50,54,59] to focus on the most valuable interactive targets to give reasonable predictions. With the success of Transformers [49] in sequence processing such as natural language processing, researchers [13,57] have employed Transformers to obtain better feature representations. Some researchers address agents' uncertainty and randomness by introducing generative models. Generative Adversarial Networks (GANs) are employed in [14,21,42] to generate multiple stochastic trajectories to suit agents' various future choices. Some works like [17,44] use the Conditional Variation AutoEncoder (CVAE) to achieve the similar goal.

Applications of Fourier Transforms. Many approaches achieve better performance in different computer vision tasks by introducing FTs. Cheng *et al.* [6] present a Fast Fourier Transform-based algorithm, which brings high computational efficiency and reliability for the multichannel interpolation in image super-resolution. Kaur *et al.* [18] propose a Fractional Fourier Transform based Riesz fractional derivative approach for edge detection and apply it to enhance images. Komatsu *et al.* [20] construct the 3-D mean-separation-type short-time DFT and apply it to denoise moving images. It is worth noting that FTs have been widely applied in handling time-series forecasting problems. Mao *et al.* [31,32] employ DCT to help predict human skeleton-graphs in motion forecasting. Cao *et al.* [3,4] propose spectral temporal graph to model interaction series (not trajectories) in trajectory forecasting. Forecasting trajectories could also be regarded as one of the time-series forecasting tasks [1]. The successful use of FTs motivates us to model *agents' trajectories* in the Fourier domain, therefore trying to obtain better representations. Unfortunately, there seems to be no method that directly uses FTs to describe agents' trajectories in the field of trajectory prediction. This paper attempts to model and forecast *agents' trajectories* in the spectrum view for the first time.

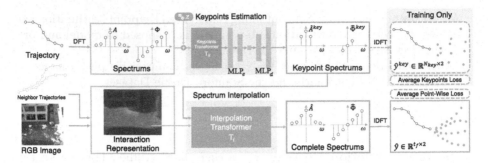

Fig. 2. V^2-Net Overview. The coarse-level keypoints estimation sub-network aims at forecasting the N_{key}-point keypoint spectrums $[A^{key}, \Phi^{key}]$ from the observed trajectory spectrums $[A, \Phi]$. The other fine-level spectrum interpolation sub-network aims at predicting the complete spectrums $[\hat{A}, \hat{\Phi}]$ on each future moment based on the keypoint spectrums and the interaction representations.

Hierarchical Trajectory Prediction. More and more researchers [7,12,40] have treated trajectory prediction as a "two-stage" problem and predict trajectories *hierarchically*. Some researchers divide this process into "destination prediction" and "destination-controlled prediction". Mangalam *et al.* [29] infer trajectory endpoints to assist in long-range multi-modal trajectory prediction. Tran *et al.* [47] attempt to obtain multi-modal goal proposals from the additional goal channel to generate multiple predictions. Wong *et al.* [51] use a set of generators to give destination proposals with different styles, and then interpolate to forecast multiple future predictions. Others like [28] also introduce several "waypoints" to help better predict agents' potential future intentions rather than the only destination points. These hierarchical approaches concern more on factor "destination" (or "waypoints") and "predictions". Considering the Fourier transforms could decompose time series into the combination of different frequency portions, a natural thought is to predict agents' future trajectories hierarchically on different *frequency scales*. Therefore, these two-stage factors may become the "low-frequency-portions" and "high-frequency-portions" for trajectory spectrums. It motivates us to forecast trajectories from coarse global plannings to fine interactive preferences with trajectory spectrums hierarchically.

3   Method

As shown in Fig. 2, V^2-Net has two main sub-networks, the coarse-level keypoints estimation sub-network and the fine-level spectrum interpolation sub-network.

Formulations. Let $p_t = (x_t, y_t) \in \mathbb{R}^2$ denote the two-dimensional coordinates of one agent at step t. Given a video clip $\{I\}$ that contains M agents' observed trajectories $\{X_i\}_{i=1}^M$ ($X_i = (p_1, p_2, ..., p_{t_h})^T$ represents i-th agent's observed trajectory) during the observation period, trajectory prediction aims to forecast

Table 1. Architecture details of the proposed V²-Net.

Layers	Network architecture
MLP_t	$(a_x, a_y, \phi_x, \phi_y) \rightarrow \text{fc}(64, \text{ReLU}) \rightarrow \text{fc}(64, \tanh) \rightarrow f_t$
MLP_c	$C \rightarrow \text{MaxPool}(5 \times 5) \rightarrow \text{Flatten} \rightarrow \text{fc}(64t_h, \tanh) \rightarrow \text{Reshape}(t_h, 64)$ $\rightarrow f_c$
T_k	$f_e \rightarrow \text{TransformerEncoder}\ (128) \rightarrow f_k';\ f_k', (a_x, a_y, \phi_x, \phi_y) \rightarrow \text{Trans-}$ formerDecoder $(128) \rightarrow f_k''$
MLP_e	$f_k'' \rightarrow \text{fc}(128, \tanh) \rightarrow \text{fc}(128) \rightarrow f$
MLP_d	$f \rightarrow \text{fc}(128, \text{ReLU}) \rightarrow \text{fc}(128, \text{ReLU}) \rightarrow \text{fc}(4N_{key}) \rightarrow \text{Reshape}\ (N_{key}, 4)$ $\rightarrow (a_x^{key}, a_y^{key}, \phi_x^{key}, \phi_y^{key})$
T_i	$[f_t^{key}, f_c] \quad \rightarrow \quad \text{TransformerEncoder} \quad (128) \quad \rightarrow \quad f_i';$ $f_i', (a_x^{key}, a_y^{key}, \phi_x^{key}, \phi_y^{key}) \rightarrow \text{TransformerDecoder}\ (4) \rightarrow (\hat{a}_x, \hat{a}_y, \hat{\phi}_x, \hat{\phi}_y)$

their possible future coordinates $\{\hat{Y}_i\}_{i=1}^M$ ($\hat{Y}_i = (\hat{p}_{t_h+1}, \hat{p}_{t_h+2}, ..., \hat{p}_{t_h+t_f})^T$ denotes one of the predictions) during the corresponding future t_f steps considering their observations and the interactive context.

Keypoints Estimation Sub-network. The coarse-level keypoints estimation sub-network aims to forecast agents' keypoint spectrums with *a lower spatio-temporal resolution*. An encoder-decoder structure is designed to generate multiple random predictions to adapt to agents' uncertainty and randomness.

We first use Discrete Fourier Transform (DFT) on agents' observed trajectories to obtain the t_h-point trajectory spectrums. We apply 1D-DFT on *each dimension* in the observed trajectory $X = \{(x_t, y_t)\}_{t=1}^{t_h}$ to obtain their spectrums, including the amplitudes $A = \{a_x, a_y\}$ and the phases $\Phi = \{\phi_x, \phi_y\}$:

$$\mathcal{X} = \text{DFT}[(x_1, x_2, ..., x_{t_h})] \in \mathbb{C}^{t_h}, \quad \mathcal{Y} = \text{DFT}[(y_1, y_2, ..., y_{t_h})] \in \mathbb{C}^{t_h},$$
$$A = \{a_x, a_y\} = \{\|\mathcal{X}\|, \|\mathcal{Y}\|\}, \quad \Phi = \{\phi_x, \phi_y\} = \{\arg \mathcal{X}, \arg \mathcal{Y}\}. \tag{1}$$

We employ an embedding MLP (the MLP_t in Table 1) to embed agents' observed trajectory spectrums $(a_x, a_y, \phi_x, \phi_y) \in \mathbb{R}^{t_h \times 4}$ into the high-dimensional f_t. Similar to previous works like S-GAN [14], we model agents' multimodality by sampling the random noise vector $z \sim \mathcal{N}(0, I)$ and then concatenating the corresponding random representations f_i to the f_t. The encoder for these noise vectors (we call the MLP_i) has the same structure like the MLP_t. We combine the above representations to obtain the embedded vector f_e. Formally,

$$f_t = \text{MLP}_t((a_x, a_y, \phi_x, \phi_y)) \in \mathbb{R}^{t_h \times 64},$$
$$f_i = \text{MLP}_i(z) \in \mathbb{R}^{t_h \times 64}, \tag{2}$$
$$f_e = [f_t, f_i] \in \mathbb{R}^{t_h \times 128}.$$

Here, $[a, b]$ represents the concatenation for vectors $\{a, b\}$ on the last dimension.

Then, we use a Transformer [49] named T_k to encode agents' behavior representations. The embedded vector f_e is passed to the Transformer encoder, and the spectrums $(a_x, a_y, \phi_x, \phi_y)$ are input to the Transformer decoder. The Transformer here is used as the feature extractor, and it does not contain the final output layer. We employ another MLP encoder (MLP_e) to aggregate features at different frequency nodes [51], thus inferring the behavior feature f:

$$f = \text{MLP}_e\left(T_k(f_e, (a_x, a_y, \phi_x, \phi_y))\right) \in \mathbb{R}^{t_h \times 128}. \tag{3}$$

The sub-network finally utilizes a decoder MLP (MLP_d) to predict agents' N_{key}-point ($N_{key} < t_f$) **keypoint spectrums** $[A^{key}, \Phi^{key}]$. Formally,

$$[A^{key}, \Phi^{key}] = (a_x^{key}, a_y^{key}, \phi_x^{key}, \phi_y^{key}) = \text{MLP}_d(f) \in \mathbb{R}^{N_{key} \times 4}. \tag{4}$$

We call N_{key} **the number of spectrum keypoints**.

When training the sub-network, agents' key spatial coordinates y^{key} (which are gathered from their entire ground-truth future trajectories) will be used as the supervision. Meanwhile, the Inverse DFT (IDFT) will be applied to obtain the predicted spatial keypoints $\hat{y}^{key}$. The network variables will be tuned by minimizing the average Euclidean distance between y^{key} and the predicted $\hat{y}^{key}$, therefore learning to predict the corresponding keypoint spectrums. We define the **Average Keypoints Loss** ($\mathcal{L}_{\text{AKL}}$) as:

$$\mathcal{L}_{\text{AKL}} = \|\hat{y}^{key} - y^{key}\|_2 = \frac{1}{N_{key}} \sum_{n=1}^{N_{key}} \|\hat{p}_{t_n^{key}} - p_{t_n^{key}}\|_2, \tag{5}$$

where

$$\hat{y}^{key} = \left(\text{IDFT}[a_x^{key} \exp(j\phi_x^{key})], \ \text{IDFT}[a_y^{key} \exp(j\phi_y^{key})]\right) \in \mathbb{R}^{N_{key} \times 2},$$
$$y^{key} = \left(p_{t_1^{key}}, p_{t_2^{key}}, ..., p_{t_{N_{key}}^{key}}\right)^T \in \mathbb{R}^{N_{key} \times 2}. \tag{6}$$

Spectrum Interpolation Sub-network. The fine-level spectrum interpolation sub-network reconstructs the complete trajectory spectrums from the keypoint spectrums with *a higher spatio-temporal resolution*. It aims to learn the spectrum biases between the complete spectrums and the keypoint spectrums.

The sub-network takes the N_{key}-point keypoint spectrums $[A^{key}, \Phi^{key}]$ as the input. Similar to Eq. 2, we have the representation f_t^{key}:

$$f_t^{key} = \text{MLP}_t((a_x^{key}, a_y^{key}, \phi_x^{key}, \phi_y^{key})) \in \mathbb{R}^{N_{key} \times 64}. \tag{7}$$

Note that MLP_t in Eq. 2 and Eq. 7 do not share weights.

Besides, agents' social and scene interactions will be concerned in this sub-network. In detail, we use a context embedding MLP (MLP_c) to encode the transferred images C [52] (which encodes both social interactions and scene constraints together in an energy map form by the scene visual image I and trajectories $\mathcal{T}$ via a CNN) into the context feature $f_c = \text{MLP}_c(C)$.

We employ a similar Transformer (called the Interpolation Transformer, T_i) to learn the spectrum biases. We pass the concatenated feature $f_e^{key} = [f_t^{key}, f_c]$ to the transformer encoder, and keypoint spectrums $[A^{key}, \Phi^{key}] = (a_x^{key}, a_y^{key}, \phi_x^{key}, \phi_y^{key})$ to the transformer decoder. The transformer here is used to forecast the **complete spectrums** $[\hat{A}, \hat{\Phi}] = (\hat{a}_x, \hat{a}_y, \hat{\phi}_x, \hat{\phi}_y)$. Then, we use the IDFT to obtain the reconstructed trajectory $\hat{y}_o$. Formally,

$$
\begin{aligned}
(\hat{a}_x, \hat{a}_y, \hat{\phi}_x, \hat{\phi}_y) &= T_i(f_e^{key}, (a_x^{key}, a_y^{key}, \phi_x^{key}, \phi_y^{key})) \in \mathbb{R}^{(t_h+t_f)\times 4}, \\
\hat{y}_o &= \left(\text{IDFT}[\hat{a}_x \exp(j\hat{\phi}_x)], \ \text{IDFT}[\hat{a}_y \exp(j\hat{\phi}_y)] \right) \in \mathbb{R}^{(t_h+t_f)\times 2}.
\end{aligned}
\tag{8}
$$

Finally, we have one of the V²-Net predictions:

$$
\hat{y} = \hat{y}_o[t_h :, :] \in \mathbb{R}^{t_f \times 2},
\tag{0}
$$

where the $[t_h :, :]$ indicates the slicing operation on tensors.

The spectrum interpolation sub-network learns to interpolate the "key" trajectory spectrums into the complete trajectory spectrums, thus reflecting agents' fine interactive details by predicting the remaining spectrum portions. Its variables will be tuned through the **Average Point-wise Loss** ($\mathcal{L}_{APL}$):

$$
\mathcal{L}_{APL} = \|\hat{y} - y\|_2 = \frac{1}{t_f} \sum_{t=t_h+1}^{t_h+t_f} \|\hat{p}_t - p_t\|_2.
\tag{10}
$$

Loss Functions. We use the joint loss function to tain V²-Net:

$$
\mathcal{L} = \mathcal{L}_{AKL} + \mathcal{L}_{APL}.
\tag{11}
$$

4 Experiments

Datasets. (a) **ETH-UCY Benchmark**: Many previous methods like [1,14,42] take several sub-datasets from ETH [38] and UCY [23] to train and evaluate their models with the "leave-one-out" strategy [1], which is called the ETH-UCY benchmark. It contains 1536 pedestrians with thousands of non-linear trajectories. The annotations are pedestrians' coordinates in meters. (b) **Stanford Drone Dataset**: The Stanford Drone Dataset [41] (SDD) has 60 bird-view videos captured by drones. More than 11,000 different agents are annotated with bounding boxes in pixels. It contains over 185,000 social interactions and 40,000 scene interactions, which is more complex and challenging.[1]

---

[1] Dataset splits used to train and validate on SDD are the same as [25].

Metrics. We employ two metrics to evaluate the prediction accuracy, including the Average Displacement Error (ADE) and the Final Displacement Error (FDE) [1,38]. ADE is the average point-wise Euclidean distance between groundtruth and predictions of all steps, and FDE is the Euclidean distance between the last point's prediction and groundtruth. Following [14], the reported metrics are the minimum value in 20 generations ("best-of-20"). For one prediction, we have:

$$\text{ADE} = \frac{1}{t_f} \sum_{t=t_h+1}^{t_h+t_f} \|p_t - \hat{p}_t\|_2, \quad \text{FDE} = \|p_{t_h+t_f} - \hat{p}_{t_h+t_f}\|_2. \tag{12}$$

Baselines. We choose several methods as our baselines, including S-GAN [14], SoPhie [42], Social-BiGAT [21], E-SR-LSTM [60], MANTRA [33], Multiverse [26], SimAug [25], PECNet [29], STAR [57], TPNMS [27], TF [13], Trajectron++ [44], Introvert [45], LB-EBM [37], Agentformer [58], Y-net [28], and SpecTGNN [3].

Implementation Details. We predict agents' trajectories in future $t_f = 12$ frames according to their $t_h = 8$ frames' observations. The frame rate is set to 2.5 frames per second when sampling trajectories. We train the entire V^2-Net with the Adam optimizer (learning rate lr = 0.0003) on one NVIDIA Tesla P4 graphic processor. V^2-Net is trained with the batch size bs = 2500 for 800 epochs on ETH-UCY and 150 epochs on SDD. Detailed layer connections, output units, and activations are listed in Table 1. We employ $L = 4$ layers of encoder-decoder structure with $H = 8$ attention heads in each Transformer-based sub-network. The output dimension of fully connected layers used in multi-head attention layers is set to 128. The default number of spectrum keypoints is set to $N_{key} = 3$. When training the network, we set $\{t_1^{key}, t_2^{key}, t_3^{key}\} = \{t_h + 4, t_h + 8, t_h + 12\}$.

4.1   Comparision to State-of-the-Art Methods

ETH-UCY. As shown in Table 2, V^2-Net achieves better performance on most ETH-UCY sub-datasets. It improves the metrics on eth by 23.3% and 28.8% compared with LB-EBM. Meanwhile, V^2-Net has better performance than Introvert on hotel by about 8.8% FDE. Compared with Introvert, its average ADE and FDE have been improved by 14.2% and 17.6%, respectively. Moreover, V^2-Net has achieved comparable average performance to the state-of-the-art Agentformer and Y-net. It shows V^2-Net's strong competitiveness on ETH-UCY. Especially, V^2-Net dramatically outperforms Agentformer and Y-net about 14.8% ADE on eth, which demonstrates its unique advantages.

SDD. As shown in Table 3, V^2-Net has better performance than the previous state-of-the-art methods on SDD. Compared to SpecTGNN, V^2-Net has significantly gained by 13.3% and 8.2% in ADE and FDE, respectively. V^2-Net also outperforms the state-of-the-art Y-net by 9.3% and 3.9%. In general, V^2-Net has a better prediction accuracy than other baselines on SDD. It is worth noting that SDD is more complex than ETH-UCY, which demonstrates V^2-Net's robustness and adaptability to larger and more challenging scenarios.

4.2   Quantitative Analysis

We design several model variations and run ablation studies to verify each design in the proposed V^2-Net. Quantitative results are shown in Table 4 and Table 5.

DFT on Trajectories. V^2-Net implements on the trajectory spectrums to focus on different frequency portions in different prediction stages. Variations a1 and a2 are trained with the same number of spectrum keypoints $N_{key} = 1$, while a1 does not use DFT/IDFT when predicting. It means that variation a2 obtains behavior features and interaction features from the spectrums, while a1 obtains them from the time series. Experiments show that a2 outperforms a1 by about 10% average ADE and FDE on ETH-UCY. In addition, we remove all other components from the model and design two minimal model variations min1 and min2 to demonstrate more directly the usefulness of introducing DFT for trajectory prediction. These two variations DO NOT take into account agents' interactions and multimodal properties, but only retain the Transformer backbone to achieve the "simple" trajectory prediction goal. We train both the two variations under the same conditions. Results in Table 5 favorably demonstrate the performance gains (12.9% on ADE and 11.1% on FDE) by using trajectory spectrums, independent of the rest of the designs in the proposed network. It proves the effectiveness of DFT in this task, and further demonstrates the considerable performance gain by implementing on the trajectory spectrums.

Table 2. Comparisons to baselines with the *best-of-20* on ETH-UCY. Metrics are shown in the format of "ADE/FDE" in meters.Lower means better.

Models	eth	hotel	univ	zara1	zara2	Average
Social-BiGAT [21]	0.69/1.29	0.49/1.01	0.55/1.32	0.30/0.62	0.36/0.75	0.48/1.00
E-SR-LSTM [60]	0.44/0.79	0.19/0.31	0.50/1.05	0.32/0.64	0.27/0.54	0.34/0.67
PECNet [29]	0.54/0.87	0.18/0.24	0.35/0.60	0.22/0.39	0.17/0.30	0.29/0.48
STAR [57]	0.56/1.11	0.26/0.50	0.52/1.13	0.40/0.89	0.52/1.13	0.41/0.87
TPNMS [27]	0.52/0.89	0.22/0.39	0.55/0.13	0.35/0.70	0.27/0.56	0.38/0.73
TF [13]	0.61/1.12	0.18/0.30	0.35/0.65	0.22/0.38	0.17/0.32	0.31/0.55
Trajectron++ [44]	0.43/0.86	0.12/0.19	**0.22**/0.43	0.17/0.32	**0.12**/0.25	**0.20**/0.39
Introvert [45]	0.42/0.70	0.11/0.17	**0.20/0.32**	**0.16**/0.27	0.16/0.25	0.21/0.34
LB-EBM [37]	0.30/0.52	0.13/0.20	0.27/0.52	0.20/0.37	0.15/0.29	0.21/0.38
Agentformer [58]	0.26/0.39	0.11/**0.14**	0.26/0.46	**0.15/0.23**	**0.14/0.23**	**0.18/0.29**
Y-net [28]	0.28/**0.33**	**0.10/0.14**	0.24/0.41	0.17/0.27	**0.13/0.22**	**0.18/0.27**
V^2-Net (Ours)	**0.23**/0.37	**0.11/0.16**	**0.21**/0.35	0.19/0.30	**0.14/0.24**	**0.18**/0.28

Table 3. Comparisons to baselines with the *best-of-20* on SDD. Lower means better.

Models	S-GAN [14]	SoPhie [42]	Multiverse [26]	SimAug [25]	PECNet
ADE/FDE	27.25/41.44	16.27/29.38	14.78/27.09	12.03/23.98	9.96/15.88

Models	MANTRA [33]	LB-EBM	SpecTGNN [3]	Y-net	V^2-Net (Ours)
ADE/FDE	8.96/17.76	8.87/15.61	8.21/12.41	7.85/11.85	**7.12/11.39**

Table 4. Ablation Studies. S1 and S2 represent the keypoints estimation stage and the spectrum interpolation stage, correspondingly. "D" indicates whether different variations model trajectories with spectrums. "N" indicates the number of spectrum keypoints. Results in "↑" are the percentage metric improvements compared to a1.

No.	S1	S2	D	N	eth	hotel	univ	zara1	zara2	↑ Gain (%)
a1	✓	✓	×	1	0.29/0.47	0.12/0.18	0.23/0.38	0.25/0.37	0.17/0.29	- (base)
a2	✓	✓	✓	1	0.23/0.39	0.12/0.17	0.23/0.37	0.22/0.32	0.16/0.26	7.9%/11.3%
b1	✓	✓	✓	3	0.23/0.37	0.11/0.16	0.21/0.35	0.19/0.30	0.14/0.24	16.2%/16.5%
b2	✓	✓	✓	4	0.24/0.38	0.12/0.17	0.22/0.36	0.21/0.32	0.16/0.26	9.5%/12.4%
b3	✓	✓	✓	6	0.29/0.49	0.13/0.17	0.23/0.38	0.26/0.37	0.21/0.31	-6.0%/-1.2%
c	✓	×	✓	3	0.24/0.37	0.12/0.16	0.23/0.35	0.21/0.30	0.15/0.25	9.6%/15.9%

Table 5. Validation of DFT. We design and run two minimal model variations to show the performance gain brought by DFT. Symbols are the same as Table 4.

No.	S1	S2	D	N	eth	hotel	univ	zara1	zara2	↑ Gain (%)
min1	✓	×	×	-	0.83/1.66	0.25/0.44	0.77/1.39	0.48/0.97	0.38/0.74	- (base)
min2	✓	×	✓	-	0.79/1.51	0.22/0.38	0.55/1.10	0.46/0.92	0.34/0.71	12.9%/11.1%

Number of Spectrum Keypoints N_key. The number of spectrum keypoints to be predicted matters how the keypoints estimation sub-network determines agents' overall motion trends. A smaller N_{key} might cause a looser planning division, making it challenging to reflect the differences between agents' similar future choices. On the contrary, a larger value may lead to a strict trends division, which could be difficult for the subsequent network to reflect agents' multiple uncertain future choices and motion preferences. Ablation experiments on variations a2, b1, b2, and b3 show the quantitative comparisons with different N_{key} configurations. The temporal keypoints are set to the equivalence point among the predicted period ($t_f = 12$). For example, when $N_{key} = 1$, we set $\{t_1^{key}\} = \{t_h + 12\}$, and when $N_{key} = 4$, we set $\{t_1^{key}, t_2^{key}, t_3^{key}, t_4^{key}\} = \{t_h + 3, t_h + 6, t_h + 9, t_h + 12\}$. It shows that variation b1 ($N_{key} = 3$) outperforms variation a2 ($N_{key} = 1$) with additional improvements by about 5% ADE and 6% FDE. However, The performance of variation b3 ($N_{key} = 6$) reduces by about 5% and 1% compared to variation a1. Please refer to visualized trajectories of different N_{key} variations in section "Qualitative Analysis" to see how they affect the prediction performance qualitatively.

Hierarchical Prediction. Similar to some *goal-driven methods*, V²-Net splits trajectory prediction into a two-stage "keypoints-interpolation" process. However, the most significant difference from these methods is that our model implements the entire process with trajectory spectrums rather than spatial coordinates. Correspondingly, the second stage "goal-conditioned prediction" has turned into the "spectrum interpolation". Although the first stage sub-network has already given a low-resolution prediction composed of a few keypoint spectrums, it is not easy to reflect agents' subtle interactions and activity differences. The spectrum interpolation sub-network aims to interpolate these "key" spectrums into the complete trajectory spectrums, thus reflecting agents' fine-level interactive preferences. Variation c only implements the S1 sub-network but utilizes linear interpolation to finish forecasting. Variations b1 and c could show the improvements brought by the interpolation sub-network. Results point out that b1 improves about 7% in ADE compared with variation c. It effectively reflects the superiority of the "coarse-to-fine" hierarchical prediction with spectrums.

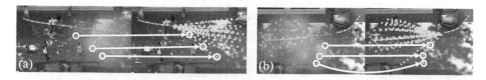

Fig. 3. Keypoints and Interpolation Illustration. We show the predicted spatial keypoints ($N_{key} = 3$) after IDFT and the corresponding predicted trajectories V²-Net finally outputs. Their corresponding time steps are distinguished with different color masks. Dots connected by white arrows belong to the same prediction steps.

(a) $N_{key} = 1$ (b) $N_{key} = 3$ (c) $N_{key} = 6$

Fig. 4. Number of Spectrum Keypoints and Prediction Styles. We show the visualized predictions with different N_{key} configurations. Each sample has 20 random predictions.

4.3   Qualitative Analysis

Coarse-Fine Prediction. V^2-Net predicts agents' multiple random keypoint spectrums at the first stage, and then uses a spectrum interpolation method to forecast the complete spectrums by considering interactions and fine activities. Figure 3 shows two visualized results at keypoints estimation and spectrum interpolation stages correspondingly. At the first stage, V^2-Net aims to predict keypoint spectrums with a low spatio-temporal resolution. We apply IDFT on these keypoint spectrums to show the corresponding spatial keypoints in Fig. 3. As shown in Fig. 3(a) and (b), these spatial keypoints could only represent the general trend of agents' future activities rather than the specific and precise coordinates. Then, the interpolation sub-network considers both physical constraints and social interactions to "fine-tune" these keypoints. For example, the marked keypoints in Fig. 3(b) indicate that the pedestrian could go toward the road. However, the corresponding final prediction shows that he might slow down and stay on the side of the road considering the scene's physical constraints.

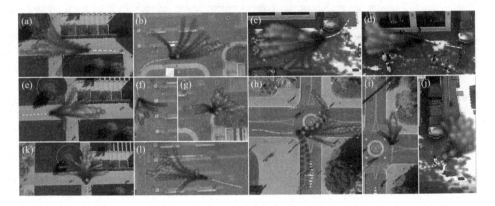

Fig. 5. Visualized Predictions. Each sample illustrates 20 random predictions.

Number of Spectrum Keypoints and Prediction Styles. The keypoint sub-network estimate agents' keypoint spectrums to determine their coarse future routes. Meanwhile, it contains a generative module to give agents multiple predictions by randomly sampling $z \sim N(0, I)$, therefore adapting to agents' uncertain future decisions. The number of spectrum keypoints N_{key} matters directly V^2-Net's stochastic performance, which can be seen in Fig. 4. It shows that Fig. 4(a) exhibits a looser restraint when generating trajectories. Obviously, it is caused by the insufficient trends constraints from the little N_{key}. Although (a) gives a large number of future predictions, most of them may be invalid or do not meet the scene constraints. Visualized results indicate that V^2-Net will give more rigorous predictions when N_{key} increases. It will forecast more acceptable predictions when increasing the N_{key} to 3 (Fig. 4(b)). However, its predictions will be limited to a small area when N_{key} is set to 6 (Fig. 4(c)). At this time, V²-Net could hardly reflect agents' multiple stochastic plannings under the constraints of such excessive keypoints. In short, with a low number of keypoints a wider spectrum of possibilities is covered (higher multimodality) and vice versa by increasing the number the trajectories become more plausible (collisions with static elements are avoided). It also explains the drop of quantitative performance when $N_{key} = 6$ in the above ablation studies. Furthermore, we can set different N_{key} in different prediction scenarios to achieve controllable predictions.

Visualization. As shown in Fig. 5, V²-Net could predict multiple trajectories considering both scene constraints and social interactions. For example, V²-Net gives a variety of different future options for bikers crossing the intersection (illustrated in Fig. 5(a)(c)(k)). In the prediction case (e) and (k), it considers the physical constraints of the environment and forecast to bypasses the grass. Additionally, it also shows strong adaptability in some unique prediction scenarios. For instance, it gives three kinds of predictions to the biker in case (h) to pass through the traffic circle: turning right, going ahead, and turning left. When turning left, the given predictions are not to turn left directly (just like turning right) but to go left after going around the traffic circle, which is consistent with the traffic rules around the circle. Case (i) presents similar results for the man passing the crossroads. It shows V²-Net could accurately describe the scene's physical constraints and agents' motion rules in various scenes.

Surprisingly, V²-Net could give "smoother" predictions due to the usage of DFT, like turning left in case (h). The spatio-temporal continuity between adjacent points in the predicted time series will be ensured with the superposition of a series of sinusoids. Therefore, the predictions could reflect the real physical characteristics of the target agent while keeping their interactive preferences.

Fig. 6. Failure prediction cases.

Limitations. As shown in Fig. 6, V²-Net has failed predictions for stationary agents and few interactive cases. Although not all predictions are regarded as failed predictions, some of them show not-so-reasonable movement trends for these standing still agents. Additionally, it may provide predictions not that suitable for the interactive context. We will fix this problem in the future.

5   Conclusion

In this work, we focus on giving predictions in two hierarchical steps by modeling their trajectories with spectrums from the global plannings and the interactive preferences. A Transformer-based V^2-Net, which consists of the coarse-level keypoints estimation sub-network and the fine-level spectrum interpolation sub network, is proposed to predict agents' trajectories hierarchically. Experimental results show that V^2-Net achieves the competitive performance on both ETH-UCY benchmark and the Stanford Drone Dataset. Although the proposed method shows higher prediction accuracy and provides better visualized results, there are still some failed predictions. We will address this problem and further explore feasible solutions to model and predict agents' possible trajectories.

Acknowledgements. This work was partially supported by the National Natural Science Foundation of China (Grant No. 62172177), and in part by the Fundamental Research Funds for the Central Universities (Grant No. 2021yjsCXCY040).

References

1. Alahi, A., Goel, K., Ramanathan, V., Robicquet, A., Fei-Fei, L., Savarese, S.: Social lstm: human trajectory prediction in crowded spaces. In: Proceedings of the IEEE Conference on Computer Vision and Pattern Recognition, pp. 961–971 (2016)
2. Alahi, A., et al.: Learning to predict human behavior in crowded scenes. In: Group and Crowd Behavior for Computer Vision, pp. 183–207. Elsevier (2017)
3. Cao, D., Li, J., Ma, H., Tomizuka, M.: Spectral temporal graph neural network for trajectory prediction. In: 2021 IEEE International Conference on Robotics and Automation (ICRA), pp. 1839–1845. IEEE (2021)
4. Cao, D., et al.: Spectral temporal graph neural network for multivariate time-series forecasting. Adv. Neural Inf. Process. Syst. **33**, 17766–17778 (2020)
5. Chai, Y., Sapp, B., Bansal, M., Anguelov, D.: Multipath: multiple probabilistic anchor trajectory hypotheses for behavior prediction. arXiv preprint arXiv:1910.05449 (2019)
6. Cheng, D., Kou, K.I.: Fft multichannel interpolation and application to image super-resolution. Signal Process. **162**, 21–34 (2019)
7. Choi, C., Malla, S., Patil, A., Choi, J.H.: Drogon: a trajectory prediction model based on intention-conditioned behavior reasoning. arXiv preprint arXiv:1908.00024 (2019)
8. Cui, H., et al.: Multimodal trajectory predictions for autonomous driving using deep convolutional networks. In: 2019 International Conference on Robotics and Automation (ICRA), pp. 2090–2096. IEEE (2019)
9. Deo, N., Trivedi, M.M.: Convolutional social pooling for vehicle trajectory prediction. In: Proceedings of the IEEE Conference on Computer Vision and Pattern Recognition Workshops, pp. 1468–1476 (2018)
10. Ergezer, H., Leblebicioğlu, K.: Anomaly detection and activity perception using covariance descriptor for trajectories. In: Hua, G., Jégou, H. (eds.) ECCV 2016. LNCS, vol. 9914, pp. 728–742. Springer, Cham (2016). https://doi.org/10.1007/978-3-319-48881-3_51

11. Fernando, T., Denman, S., Sridharan, S., Fookes, C.: Soft+ hardwired attention: an lstm framework for human trajectory prediction and abnormal event detection. Neural Netw. **108**, 466–478 (2018)
12. Girase, H., et al.: Loki: Long term and key intentions for trajectory prediction. In: Proceedings of the IEEE/CVF International Conference on Computer Vision, pp. 9803–9812 (2021)
13. Giuliari, F., Hasan, I., Cristani, M., Galasso, F.: Transformer networks for trajectory forecasting, pp. 10335–10342 (2021)
14. Gupta, A., Johnson, J., Fei-Fei, L., Savarese, S., Alahi, A.: Social gan: socially acceptable trajectories with generative adversarial networks. In: Proceedings of the IEEE Conference on Computer Vision and Pattern Recognition, pp. 2255–2264 (2018)
15. Huang, Y., Bi, H., Li, Z., Mao, T., Wang, Z.: Stgat: modeling spatial-temporal interactions for human trajectory prediction. In: Proceedings of the IEEE International Conference on Computer Vision, pp. 6272–6281 (2019)
16. Hug, R., Becker, S., Hübner, W., Arens, M.: Particle-based pedestrian path prediction using lstm-mdl models. In: 2018 21st International Conference on Intelligent Transportation Systems (ITSC), pp. 2684–2691. IEEE (2018)
17. Ivanovic, B., Pavone, M.: The trajectron: probabilistic multi-agent trajectory modeling with dynamic spatiotemporal graphs. In: Proceedings of the IEEE International Conference on Computer Vision, pp. 2375–2384 (2019)
18. Kaur, K., Jindal, N., Singh, K.: Fractional fourier transform based riesz fractional derivative approach for edge detection and its application in image enhancement. Signal Process. **180**, 107852 (2021)
19. Kim, B., Kang, C.M., Kim, J., Lee, S.H., Chung, C.C., Choi, J.W.: Probabilistic vehicle trajectory prediction over occupancy grid map via recurrent neural network. In: 2017 IEEE 20th International Conference on Intelligent Transportation Systems (ITSC), pp. 399–404. IEEE (2017)
20. Komatsu, T., Tyon, K., Saito, T.: 3-d mean-separation-type short-time dft with its application to moving-image denoising. In: 2017 IEEE International Conference on Image Processing (ICIP), pp. 2961–2965 (2017)
21. Kosaraju, V., Sadeghian, A., Martín-Martín, R., Reid, I., Rezatofighi, H., Savarese, S.: Social-bigat: multimodal trajectory forecasting using bicycle-gan and graph attention networks. Adv. Neural Inf. Process. Syst. **32**, 137–146 (2019)
22. Lee, N., Choi, W., Vernaza, P., Choy, C.B., Torr, P.H., Chandraker, M.: Desire: distant future prediction in dynamic scenes with interacting agents. In: Proceedings of the IEEE Conference on Computer Vision and Pattern Recognition, pp. 336–345 (2017)
23. Lerner, A., Chrysanthou, Y., Lischinski, D.: Crowds by example. Comput. Graph. Forum **26**(3), 655–664 (2007)
24. Li, S., Zhou, Y., Yi, J., Gall, J.: Spatial-temporal consistency network for low-latency trajectory forecasting. In: Proceedings of the IEEE/CVF International Conference on Computer Vision (ICCV), pp. 1940–1949 (2021)
25. Liang, J., Jiang, L., Hauptmann, A.: *SimAug*: learning robust representations from simulation for trajectory prediction. In: Vedaldi, A., Bischof, H., Brox, T., Frahm, J.-M. (eds.) ECCV 2020. LNCS, vol. 12358, pp. 275–292. Springer, Cham (2020). https://doi.org/10.1007/978-3-030-58601-0_17
26. Liang, J., Jiang, L., Murphy, K., Yu, T., Hauptmann, A.: The garden of forking paths: towards multi-future trajectory prediction. In: Proceedings of the IEEE/CVF Conference on Computer Vision and Pattern Recognition, pp. 10508–10518 (2020)

27. Liang, R., Li, Y., Li, X., Zhou, J., Zou, W., et al.: Temporal pyramid network for pedestrian trajectory prediction with multi-supervision. arXiv preprint arXiv:2012.01884 (2020)
28. Mangalam, K., An, Y., Girase, H., Malik, J.: From goals, waypoints & paths to long term human trajectory forecasting. arXiv preprint arXiv:2012.01526 (2020)
29. Mangalam, K., et al.: It is not the journey but the destination: endpoint conditioned trajectory prediction. In: Vedaldi, A., Bischof, H., Brox, T., Frahm, J.-M. (eds.) ECCV 2020. LNCS, vol. 12347, pp. 759–776. Springer, Cham (2020). https://doi.org/10.1007/978-3-030-58536-5_45
30. Manh, H., Alaghband, G.: Scene-lstm: a model for human trajectory prediction. arXiv preprint arXiv:1808.04018 (2018)
31. Mao, W., Liu, M., Salzmann, M.: History repeats itself: human motion prediction via motion attention. In: Vedaldi, A., Bischof, H., Brox, T., Frahm, J.-M. (eds.) ECCV 2020. LNCS, vol. 12359, pp. 474–489. Springer, Cham (2020). https://doi.org/10.1007/978-3-030-58568-6_28
32. Mao, W., Liu, M., Salzmann, M., Li, H.: Learning trajectory dependencies for human motion prediction. In: Proceedings of the IEEE/CVF International Conference on Computer Vision, pp. 9489–9497 (2019)
33. Marchetti, F., Becattini, F., Seidenari, L., Bimbo, A.D.: Mantra: memory augmented networks for multiple trajectory prediction. In: Proceedings of the IEEE/CVF Conference on Computer Vision and Pattern Recognition, pp. 7143–7152 (2020)
34. Mehran, R., Oyama, A., Shah, M.: Abnormal crowd behavior detection using social force model. In: 2009 IEEE Conference on Computer Vision and Pattern Recognition, pp. 935–942. IEEE (2009)
35. Mohamed, A., Qian, K., Elhoseiny, M., Claudel, C.: Social-stgcnn: a social spatiotemporal graph convolutional neural network for human trajectory prediction. In: Proceedings of the IEEE/CVF Conference on Computer Vision and Pattern Recognition, pp. 14424–14432 (2020)
36. Morris, B.T., Trivedi, M.M.: Trajectory learning for activity understanding: unsupervised, multilevel, and long-term adaptive approach. IEEE Trans. Pattern Anal. Mach. Intell. **33**(11), 2287–2301 (2011)
37. Pang, B., Zhao, T., Xie, X., Wu, Y.N.: Trajectory prediction with latent belief energy-based model. In: Proceedings of the IEEE/CVF Conference on Computer Vision and Pattern Recognition, pp. 11814–11824 (2021)
38. Pellegrini, S., Ess, A., Schindler, K., Van Gool, L.: You'll never walk alone: modeling social behavior for multi-target tracking. In: 2009 IEEE 12th International Conference on Computer Vision, pp. 261–268. IEEE (2009)
39. Phan-Minh, T., Grigore, E.C., Boulton, F.A., Beijbom, O., Wolff, E.M.: Covernet: multimodal behavior prediction using trajectory sets. In: Proceedings of the IEEE/CVF Conference on Computer Vision and Pattern Recognition, pp. 14074–14083 (2020)
40. Rhinehart, N., McAllister, R., Kitani, K., Levine, S.: Precog: prediction conditioned on goals in visual multi-agent settings. In: Proceedings of the IEEE International Conference on Computer Vision, pp. 2821–2830 (2019)
41. Robicquet, A., Sadeghian, A., Alahi, A., Savarese, S.: Learning social etiquette: human trajectory understanding in crowded scenes. In: Leibe, B., Matas, J., Sebe, N., Welling, M. (eds.) ECCV 2016. LNCS, vol. 9912, pp. 549–565. Springer, Cham (2016). https://doi.org/10.1007/978-3-319-46484-8_33

42. Sadeghian, A., Kosaraju, V., Sadeghian, A., Hirose, N., Rezatofighi, H., Savarese, S.: Sophie: an attentive gan for predicting paths compliant to social and physical constraints. In: Proceedings of the IEEE Conference on Computer Vision and Pattern Recognition, pp. 1349–1358 (2019)

43. Saleh, F., Aliakbarian, S., Salzmann, M., Gould, S.: Artist: autoregressive trajectory inpainting and scoring for tracking. arXiv preprint arXiv:2004.07482 (2020)

44. Salzmann, T., Ivanovic, B., Chakravarty, P., Pavone, M.: Trajectron++: dynamically-feasible trajectory forecasting with heterogeneous data. In: Vedaldi, A., Bischof, H., Brox, T., Frahm, J.-M. (eds.) ECCV 2020. LNCS, vol. 12363, pp. 683–700. Springer, Cham (2020). https://doi.org/10.1007/978-3-030-58523-5_40

45. Shafiee, N., Padir, T., Elhamifar, E.: Introvert: human trajectory prediction via conditional 3D attention. In: Proceedings of the IEEE/CVF Conference on Computer Vision and Pattern Recognition, pp. 16815–16825 (2021)

46. Sun, J., Jiang, Q., Lu, C.: Recursive social behavior graph for trajectory prediction. In: Proceedings of the IEEE/CVF Conference on Computer Vision and Pattern Recognition, pp. 660–669 (2020)

47. Tran, H., Le, V., Tran, T.: Goal-driven long-term trajectory prediction. In: Proceedings of the IEEE/CVF Winter Conference on Applications of Computer Vision, pp. 796–805 (2021)

48. Trautman, P., Krause, A.: Unfreezing the robot: navigation in dense, interacting crowds. In: 2010 IEEE/RSJ International Conference on Intelligent Robots and Systems, pp. 797–803. IEEE (2010)

49. Vaswani, A., et al.: Attention is all you need. Adv. Neural Inf. Process. Syst. **30**, 5998–6008 (2017)

50. Vemula, A., Muelling, K., Oh, J.: Social attention: modeling attention in human crowds. In: 2018 IEEE international Conference on Robotics and Automation (ICRA), pp. 1–7. IEEE (2018)

51. Wong, C., Xia, B., Peng, Q., You, X.: Msn: multi-style network for trajectory prediction. arXiv preprint arXiv:2107.00932 (2021)

52. Xia, B., Wong, C., Peng, Q., Yuan, W., You, X.: Cscnet: contextual semantic consistency network for trajectory prediction in crowded spaces. Pattern Recogn. **126**, 108552 (2022)

53. Xie, D., Shu, T., Todorovic, S., Zhu, S.C.: Learning and inferring "dark matter" and predicting human intents and trajectories in videos. IEEE Trans. Pattern Anal. Mach. Intell. **40**(7), 1639–1652 (2017)

54. Xu, Y., Piao, Z., Gao, S.: Encoding crowd interaction with deep neural network for pedestrian trajectory prediction. In: Proceedings of the IEEE Conference on Computer Vision and Pattern Recognition, pp. 5275–5284 (2018)

55. Xue, H., Huynh, D.Q., Reynolds, M.: SS-LSTM: a hierarchical lstm model for pedestrian trajectory prediction. In: 2018 IEEE Winter Conference on Applications of Computer Vision (WACV), pp. 1186–1194. IEEE (2018)

56. Xue, H., Huynh, D.Q., Reynolds, M.: Scene gated social graph: pedestrian trajectory prediction based on dynamic social graphs and scene constraints. arXiv preprint arXiv:2010.05507 (2020)

57. Yu, C., Ma, X., Ren, J., Zhao, H., Yi, S.: Spatio-temporal graph transformer networks for pedestrian trajectory prediction. In: Vedaldi, A., Bischof, H., Brox, T., Frahm, J.-M. (eds.) ECCV 2020. LNCS, vol. 12357, pp. 507–523. Springer, Cham (2020). https://doi.org/10.1007/978-3-030-58610-2_30

58. Yuan, Y., Weng, X., Ou, Y., Kitani, K.M.: Agentformer: agent-aware transformers for socio-temporal multi-agent forecasting. In: Proceedings of the IEEE/CVF International Conference on Computer Vision (ICCV), pp. 9813–9823 (2021)

59. Zhang, P., Ouyang, W., Zhang, P., Xue, J., Zheng, N.: SR-LSTM: state refinement for lstm towards pedestrian trajectory prediction. In: Proceedings of the IEEE Conference on Computer Vision and Pattern Recognition, pp. 12085–12094 (2019)
60. Zhang, P., Xue, J., Zhang, P., Zheng, N., Ouyang, W.: Social-aware pedestrian trajectory prediction via states refinement lstm. IEEE Trans. Pattern Anal. Mach. Intell. (2020)

HVC-Net: Unifying Homography, Visibility, and Confidence Learning for Planar Object Tracking

Haoxian Zhang[1] and Yonggen Ling[2]([⊠])

[1] Tencent AI Lab, Shenzhen, China
`leohxzhang@tencent.com`
[2] Tencent Robotics X, Shenzhen, China
`rolandling@tencent.com`

Abstract. Robust and accurate planar tracking over a whole video sequence is vitally important for many vision applications. The key to planar object tracking is to find object correspondences, modeled by homography, between the reference image and the tracked image. Existing methods tend to obtain wrong correspondences with changing appearance variations, camera-object relative motions and occlusions. To alleviate this problem, we present a unified convolutional neural network (CNN) model that jointly considers homography, visibility, and confidence. First, we introduce correlation blocks that explicitly account for the local appearance changes and camera-object relative motions as the base of our model. Second, we jointly learn the homography and visibility that links camera-object relative motions with occlusions. Third, we propose a confidence module that actively monitors the estimation quality from the pixel correlation distributions obtained in correlation blocks. All these modules are plugged into a Lucas-Kanade (LK) tracking pipeline to obtain both accurate and robust planar object tracking. Our approach outperforms the state-of-the-art methods on public POT and TMT datasets. Its superior performance is also verified on a real-world application, synthesizing high-quality in-video advertisements.

Keywords: Planar object tracking · Homography · Visibility · Confidence

1 Introduction

Planar object tracking is a classic computer vision task with a wide range of applications. Given the initial corners of a planar object in the reference frame, the primary goal of planar tracking is to estimate the movements of these corners, modeled by a

---

H. Zhang and Y. Ling—Equal Contribution listed alphabetically.

Supplementary Information The online version contains supplementary material available at https://doi.org/10.1007/978-3-031-20047-2_40.

geometric transformation called a homography, in consecutive frames. Though lots of advances have been made in past decades, obtaining accurate and robust results remains challenging. These difficulties are mainly caused by three factors: appearance variation, camera-object relative motion and occlusion.

Fig. 1. One of our synthetic frames in the lottery sequence of [23]. (a) A planar object to be tracked in the reference image, denoted by a green quadrilateral. (b) The estimated homography with very high tracking confidence in one video frame. (c) Corresponding visibility mask of the tracked object. (d) The synthetic frame after placing the CVF logo using results from (b) and (c). More results are shown in Fig. 7 and the supplemental.

The appearance variation is a camera-related issue. It is usually known as image blur, sensor noise, non-linear response of brightness. The camera-object relative motion leads to geometry transformations of an object on the image. Typical effects on the image plane are scale changes, rotations, translations, and perspective distortions. Occlusion is referred as the fact that the tracked object is occluded by another object. The situation becomes worse if the 'another object' looks very similar to the tracked object. These factors pose strong challenges for traditional keypoint-based methods that estimate the homography using hand-crafted features [6,12,35], since the extracted features are prone to be different under the influence of these factors. Learned features like D2-Net [14], LF-Net [45], and R2D2 [30] are proposed to decrease this influence. Direct methods [4,7], usually with the LK pipeline [4], estimate the homography iteratively. [4,7] assume the intensity consistency and compute the homography increment for each iteration. [9,24,27,46,47] extend direct methods with the learned 'feature consistency' assumption for increasing the robustness. We argue that efforts are still needed on better feature representation. Moreover, these methods have not discussed occlusions that are widely existed in real-world video sequences. The last to mention is the CNN-based method [11] that directly regresses the homography in one step with CNN. It is not robust to these three factors, neither.

In this work, we propose a novel CNN model for handling mentioned difficulties. The base of our model is correlation blocks (Sect. 3.3). It firstly extracts features in the intensity domain for handling appearance variations. Cost volumes, representing distributions of pixel correlations, are then constructed in the pixel displacement domain to account for the camera-object relative motion. We find that estimating the homography with these two cascaded steps is much better than methods with one step [9,11,24,27]. Moreover, in contrast to methods that learn homography alone [9,11,24,27], we learn it jointly with another task called visibility, which is defined as a binary mask that indicates which part of the reference image is visible on the tracked image (Fig. 2). A reference image pixel is regarded as visible if and only if it satisfies the homography constraint of the tracked planar object (geometry-induced) and it is not occluded by other objects on the tracked image (disocclusion-induced). Joint learning homography and visibility not only improves the correlation block representations, but also links camera-object relative motions with occlusions (Sect. 3.5). Lastly, as estimations with the LK pipeline are sensitive to initializations, we further improve the estimation robustness by monitoring the tracking quality and rebooting estimations. This is done by introducing a confidence module that evaluates the planar tracking quality from pixel correlation distributions obtained in correlation blocks (Sect. 3.7). By equipping all these presented modules with a LK pipeline, our model obtains both accurate and robust homography estimations. We achieve significantly higher homography precision than state-of-the-art homography estimation methods (Sect. 4). Besides, as a by-product, our model provides visibility masks that other works have not mentioned. With these masks, we are able to easily place planar advertisements in videos (Fig. 1).

Fig. 2. (from left to right) Reference image, current image, motion-induced visibility, disocclusion-induced visibility, combined visibility used in our model.

2   Related Work

2.1   Homography Estimation

Existing planar tracking methods for estimating the underlying homography can be roughly classified into three categories: keypoint-based methods [3,6,12,13,28,35], direct methods [4,5,7,10,26,31], and CNN-based methods [9,11,24,27]. Keypoint-based methods firstly detect and describe keypoints (using ORB [35], SIFT [12], SURF [6] and etc.) both in the reference planar region and subsequent consecutive frames. These keypoints are then matched by minimizing the distances in the descriptor space. Homography, the planar surface in the projection space is related, is then calculated with the obtained matches. To remove potential outlier matches, RANSAC [16] is usually performed. Different from keypoint-based methods, direct methods [4,7] assume that the planar template does not move fast in consecutive images. The homography is directly optimized by minimizing the photometric error between the planar template and its projection in the incoming video frames. Recently, CNN-based methods have been proposed. Homography is regressed from input images in one forward step [11,27,46,47]. [9,20,24,48] adopt the Lucas-Kanade framework [4] and compute homography with multiple iterations.

2.2 Object Segmentation

The visibility of planar object tracking is less discussed in the past. The closest work is segmentation. There are three main approaches for object segmentation according to the level of supervision required. Supervised methods require iterative human interactions for adding segmentation prior as well as refining segmentation outputs [2,15]. They obtain high-quality segmentations at the cost of extensive expert efforts. To relax this mass manual supervision, semi-supervised methods propagate sparse human labeling in the reference frame to the remaining frames, and then formulate the segmentation problem as an optimization problem with energy defined over graphs [1,29,42]. The last to mention is the unsupervised methods that do not require any manual annotation or utilize prior information on the segmented objects. Early unsupervised methods focus on over-segmentation [17] or motion segmentation [8]. They are extended to foreground-background separation in recent years [41,44].

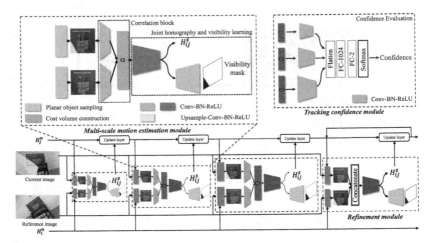

Fig. 3. The framework of our model. It follows the LK scheme. There are three modules: the multi-scale motion estimation module, the refinement module, and the tracking confidence module. The base of this model is correlation blocks that extract features in the intensity domain for handling appearance variations and construct cost volumes in the pixel displacement domain for handling motion-related issues in a cascaded way (Sect. 3.3). Pyramid blocks are build (Sect. 3.4), where homography and visibility are jointly learned (Sect. 3.5). The refinement module for further improvements is optional (Sect. 3.6). Tracking estimation confidence is also evaluated (Sect. 3.7).

2.3 Patch Similarity

The most related work to confidence prediction is to compute the similarity between two patches [18,36,37]. The confidence score is learned by training the network with reflective loss in [37]. The similarity is trained via a classification pipeline in [36]. Patched representation as well as robust feature comparison is jointly learned in [18].

3   Our Approach

3.1   The LK-based CNN Framework

Our model framework is shown in Fig. 3. We follows the LK scheme [4] to compute homography, denoted as $\mathbf{H}_{ij} \in \mathbb{R}^{3\times3}$. For each 3D object point o_k, its projection on image frame i and j is denoted as $\mathbf{p}_i^k$ and $\mathbf{p}_j^k$ respectively. According to the derivation from [19], we have $\mathbf{p}_i^k = \mathbf{H}_{ij}\mathbf{p}_j^k$. Supposing we have an initial homography $\mathbf{H}_{ij}$, the LK scheme consists of two iterated steps:
1) solving for homography increment $\delta\mathbf{H}_{ij}$,
2) updating homography $\mathbf{H}_{ij} \leftarrow \mathbf{H}_{ij} * \delta\mathbf{H}_{ij}$.
For the first step, the classic LK method [4] assume that intensities are consistent across images. We improve this step with three aspects. Firstly, as the intensity consistency assumption is prone to be broken in real-world cases with appearance variations and occlusions, we extend it with the 'feature consistency' assumption and improve the effectiveness of feature representation (Sect. 3.3). Secondly, homography increments are computed with difference scales (Sect. 3.4). Thirdly, based on the 'feature consistency' assumption, we compute homography increments with joint homography and visibility learning (Sect. 3.5). The improved first LK step is implemented as the multi-scale motion estimation module in our model. We also have an optional step without correlation block, i.e. the refinement module (Sect. 3.6). As computed homography increments are sensitive to homography initializations, we present a tracking confidence module to evaluate the estimation quality and re-initializes the homography computations (Sect. 3.7). We follow the same second step as the LK pipeline, where we update homography through update layers. Lastly, we notice that the concerned planar object tracking problem is to solve for homography between object projections on two images while existing LK-based methods consider homography between two images. We thus propose a sampling trick to turn the concerned problem into a classic LK-based homography problem that is more suitable for CNN models (Sect. 3.2).

3.2   Homography Surrogate and Sampling

The projection shape of a 3D plane on video images deforms as the camera moves relatively to the tracked object. Processing the full-resolution video images with CNNs will waste a lot of memory as well as computations on useless image regions outside the projection shape. What's worse, information on outside regions will distort the estimations and make CNN predictions more challenging. To this end, we propose a planar object sampling layer for CNNs for handling planar objects in arbitrarily deformed shapes or sizes. As shown in Fig. 4, the key idea is NOT to predict the original homography in the original image space. Instead, we predict a surrogate homography in the normalized space. We sample the planar

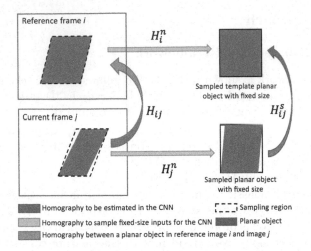

Fig. 4. The planar object sampling. We sample the planar object in the reference frame and in the current frame to fixed-size images with $\mathbf{H}_i^n$ and $\mathbf{H}_j^n$, and use our mode to predict the increment $\mathbf{H}_{ij}^s.\mathbf{H}_{ij}^s$ will be the identity matrix if and only if the sampled planar objects on both sampled images are aligned perfectly.$\mathbf{H}_j^n$ and $\mathbf{H}_{ij}^s$ are used as surrogates for $\mathbf{H}_{ij}$ and $\delta\mathbf{H}_{ij}$ respectively.

object in the reference image into a $W \times H$ template: $\mathbf{p}_i^n = \mathbf{H}_i^n\mathbf{p}_i$, where $\mathbf{H}_i^n$ can be easily computed using SVD [19] once the reference planar object with four-corner representation is given. We denote the homography used to sample the planar object in the current image into a $W \times H$ template as $\mathbf{H}_j^n$, and the homography between two normalized images i and j is $\mathbf{H}_{ij}^s$. We have:

$$\mathbf{H}_j^n = (\mathbf{H}_{ij}^s)^{-1}\mathbf{H}_i^n\mathbf{H}_{ij} = (\mathbf{H}_{ij}^s)^{-1}\mathbf{H}_{ij}^* \tag{1}$$

where $\mathbf{H}_{ij}^* = \mathbf{H}_i^n\mathbf{H}_{ij}$. We define $\mathbf{H}_j^n$ as a surrogate for $\mathbf{H}_{ij}$, and $\mathbf{H}_{ij}^s$ as a surrogate for $\delta\mathbf{H}_{ij}$. $\mathbf{H}_{ij}^s$ will be an identity matrix if and only if $\mathbf{H}_j^n$ is equal to ground truth $\mathbf{H}_{ij}^*$. If the final $\mathbf{H}_j^n$ is obtained, $\mathbf{H}_{ij}$ is computed as $\mathbf{H}_{ij} = (\mathbf{H}_i^n)^{-1}\mathbf{H}_j^n$. By using surrogates, we maintain a fixed-size input to CNNs.

3.3 Correlation Block

Different from previous works [11,24] that regress homography on images, we decompose the homography regression into two cascaded steps:

1) The first step is to extract features representing image local appearances. These features are designed to be robust for image blur, illumination variations, occlusions, scale changes, perspective distortions, etc., through data argumentation covering various image conditions. Since the template size is small, we use the U-Net structure [32] for simplicity. Other feature extraction structures, such as ResNet, EfficientNet and MultiResUNet, can also be used.

2) The second step is to construct cost volumes with extracted features, whose elements are pixel correlations between sampled images. These pixel correlations are designed to encode the relative geometry transformation between objects and cameras. Each element in this cost volume is computed as the correlation [40] between a pixel x_i in reference feature map $\mathbf{f}_r$ and a pixel x_j in the tracked feature map $\mathbf{f}_t$: $c(\mathbf{x}_i, \mathbf{x}_j) = \mathbf{f}_r(\mathbf{x}_i)^T \mathbf{f}_t(\mathbf{x}_j)$, where T is the transpose operator. Given a maximum displacement d_m, for each location $\mathbf{x}_i$ we compute correlations $c(\mathbf{x}_i, \mathbf{x}_j)$ for $\mathbf{x}_j$ s.t. $|\mathbf{x}_j - \mathbf{x}_i| <= d_m$. Correlations at each location $\mathbf{x}_i$ are reorganized in the channel dimension. Thus, the size of the 3D cost volume is $H \times W \times (2d_m + 1)^2$. d_m is set to be 4 at each pyramid here by balancing the complexity and movement range.

3.4   Pyramids

Inspired by the classic pyramid methods in image processing, we build correlation blocks in different scales. We sample objects with different template resolutions (1/16x, 1/4x, 1x). Homography increments are computed sequentially from the smallest resolution to the highest resolution.

3.5   Joint Learning of Homography and Visibility

Homography is obtained by information that is visible on both reference and tracked images. Hence, we learn homography jointly with visibility, in order to extract a more reliable feature representation. This leads to three loss functions during training: L_d, L_m, and L_v. For benefit of CNNs, we adopt representation in [11], where homography is represented by four corner displacements $\{d_1, d_2, d_3, d_4\}$. L_d is a homograph loss. It is defined as the $l1$ norm between the ground truth 4-point displacement d_k^* and the predicted 4-point displacement d_k at each scale level:

$$L_d = \frac{1}{4} \sum_{k=1}^{4} \|d_k^* - d_k\|_1 \tag{2}$$

L_m is a visibility loss. Pixel visibility prediction of the sampled tracked image is regarded as a 2-class classification problem. We denote the ground truth label and the predicted label for a pixel's visibility as m_k^* and m_k. Cross-entropy is adopted for the visibility loss L_m at each scale level:

$$L_m = -\frac{1}{N^k} \sum_{k=1}^{N^k} (m_k^* \log(m_k) + (1 - m_k^*) \log(1 - m_k)) \tag{3}$$

where N^k is the total number of pixels at each scale level. To further improve the feature representations used to construct cost volumes, we add a visible alignment loss L_v that minimizes the visible feature distance between extracted reference feature map $\mathbf{f}_r$ and tracked feature map $\mathbf{f}_t$. It is defined as followed,

$$L_v = \frac{1}{N^k} \sum_{\mathbf{x}_k} m_k^* \|\mathbf{f}_t'(\mathbf{x}_k) - \mathbf{f}_t(\mathbf{x}_k)\|_1 \tag{4}$$

where $\mathbf{x}_k$ is the pixel location on the sampled tracked image, $\mathbf{f}_t' = Warp(\mathbf{f}_r, \mathbf{H}_{tr})$ is a wrapped feature map from $\mathbf{f}_r$ to $\mathbf{f}_t$ using the homography $\mathbf{H}_{tr}$. The total loss is the combination of these three losses:

$$L_{all} = \lambda_d L_d + \lambda_m L_m + \lambda_v L_v \tag{5}$$

where λ_d, λ_m and λ_v are balancing parameters. In our experiments, they are all empirically set to be 1.0.

With the visibility loss, we explicitly connect homography with occlusion. This is in contrast to competing methods [9,24,27,46,47] that handle occlusions implicitly with the learned feature capability. Moreover, with the visible alignment loss, we ale able to connect homography, visibility and features in the correlation block.

Notice that, the supervised visibility mask varies in each scale level. It is generated at each training iteration.

3.6 Homography and Visibility Refinement

This module is similar to that of Sect. 3.5 expect that the correlation block is removed and the visible alignment loss is ignored. It is designed to capture tiny modifications to the homography and visibility. The VGG structure [39] is used for simplicity. Three iterations are usually conducted for convergence. Note that, this module is optional.

3.7 Estimation Confidence Evaluation

This section discusses the homography initialization in the LK pipeline (Sect. 3.1). The initial homography of the first scale level is equal to the homography obtained at the previous video frame $j - 1$. For the following scale levels, their initializations are equal to homography obtained at previous scale levels. For the refinement module, its first homography initial value is equal to the homography output from the multi-scale motion estimation module. In the following refinement step, its initial homography is equal to the homography in last iteration.

With this homography initialization mechanism, we see the significance of the homography obtained at the previous video frame $j - 1$, as it is the base of estimation in the current video frame j. However, though we have tried our best to improve the homography estimation robustness and accuracy, our trained model inevitably fails under extreme conditions, such as large appearance variations, rapid camera-object relative motions, and severe occlusions. That is, the homography obtained at the previous video frame $j - 1$ may be unreliable. To check this, we add a tracking confidence module to evaluate the estimation confidence. This confidence is regarded as a regression whose output ranges between 0 and 1. 0 indicates the estimation is unreliable while 1 indicates it is reliable. In contrast to previous works [18,36,37] that regress confidences from images, we regress them from cost volumes of correlation blocks. These multi-scale cost volumes, representing distributions of pixel correlations, encode the 'uncertainty' of the estimation. For an object pixel in the reference image, its corresponding pixel on the tracked image is ambiguous if the pixel correlation distribution is flat, or obvious if the pixel correlation distribution is concentrated on one specific location. We train this tracking confidence module after the multi-scale motion estimation module and the optional refinement module is trained using an independent dataset.

We consider the estimation as unreliable if the homography loss L_d between the ground truth and predicted homography is larger than 5 while reliable otherwise. We denote the ground truth label and the predicted label as p^* and p. Cross-entropy loss is used for confidence loss:

$$L_c = -(p^* \log(p) + (1 - p^*) \log(1 - p)) \tag{6}$$

In implementations, each cost volume of each pyramid layer is convoluted to a $\frac{H}{8} \times \frac{W}{8} \times 15$ feature map by several convolutional layers respectively. These feature maps are then followed by two fully connected (FC) layers, whose dropout ratio is set to 0.5, with 1024 and 2 channels. The final layer is a soft-max layer that output the confidence. 3×3 kernels are used in convolutional layers.

After the tracking confidence module is trained, we monitor the tracking confidence on the fly. If the homography obtained at the previous video frame $j-1$ is classified as unreliable, we use the homography estimated in more previous times (e.g. 2 to 60 frames before) for homography initialization and re-run our model pipeline. This process is repeated until this tracking is reliable.

4   Experiments

Similar to [9,11], we use the MS-COCO dataset [25] to generate the training data. All images are resized to 240×240. We randomly select an image, assign a 120×120 window to its center. We then randomly perturb the four corners of this window to generate a random homography. The corner displacement is uniformly distributed between $[-32, 32]$ in both horizontal and vertical directions. Pixels within the perturbed window are wrapped to a sample image whose size is $W \times H$. To increase the robustness of our network, we augment our samples with more conditions that we meet in real-world applications. We add variances of brightness, contrast, saturation and image blur to the sample images [38]. Moreover, we simulate real-world object occlusions by randomly placing arbitrary polygons, whose textures are cropped natural images from [25], into our training samples [38]. 280000 image pairs with ground truth homography are generated in total (Fig. 5). Among them, 200000 samples are used for training the motion estimation network and refinement network, 40000 samples are used for validation, and the rest 40000 samples are tested for ablation study (Sect. 4.2). GT visibility masks are generated at each training iteration.

4.1   Training and Quantitative Evaluation

In all experiments, we set $W = H = 120$. Adam [22] optimization with $\beta_1 = 0.9$, $\beta_2 = 0.999$ is used, and the batch size is set to 32. Batch normalization [21] is

Fig. 5. Samples of the generated dataset. First two rows are image pairs with variations of brightness, contrast, saturation, image blur, and occlusions. The last row shows ground truth visibility masks.

adopted for accelerating convergence. The learning rate is initialized to be 10^{-4}. It is then decreased by a factor of 10 every 5 epochs. After the model is trained, its processing rate is about 10hz on a commodity GPU card GeForce GTX 1080.

In this paper, two quantitative metrics, alignment error (AE) [34] and homography discrepancy (HD) [23], are used to evaluate the quality of predicted homography accuracy.

4.2   Ablation Study

In this section, we perform ablation studies to analyze the contribution of each component in our proposed model. All methods are trained on the training dataset as well as tested on the dataset from Sect. 4.1 introduction.

Homography Precision We firstly analyze component contributions to the homography precision. We train our model with increasing components proposed in this paper: the correlation block in Sect. 3.3 (D), pyramids in Sect. 3.4 (P), joint learning of homography and visibility in Sect. 3.5 (M), the refinement module in Sect. 3.6 (R): Ours-D, Ours-DP, Ours-DPR, Ours-DPM, Ours-DPMR. If our model is trained without any proposed components (Ours w/o DPMR), it is equivalent to DeepHomography [11]. Table 1 shows the results:

- From line 2 and line 7, we see that the model with correlation blocks (Ours-D) performs significantly better than that without them (Ours w/o DPMR).
- Pyramids (P) do help both approaches (Ours-D and Ours w/o DPMR). This improvement is more significant for the model Ours-D as the cost volume is constructed on limited displacements.
- The refinement module is able to capture tiny displacement between images. It further increases the accuracy for all models (Ours-DP vs Ours-DPR, Ours-DPM vs Ours-DPMR, Ours-P vs Ours-PR, Ours-PM vs Ours-PMR).

Table 1. Ablation study and comparison on our test set.

Method	AE [34]	HD [23]
Ours w/o DPMR	6.678	14.983
Ours-P	5.280	10.627
Ours-PR	2.970	5.104
Ours-PM	4.051	7.984
Ours-PMR	2.426	4.262
Ours-D	4.173	9.147
Ours-DP	1.145	2.216
Ours-DPR	**0.876**	1.739
Ours-DPM	1.097	2.107
Ours-DPMR	**0.876**	**1.695**

– By jointly training homography and visibility, our model generalizes better on each original task (Ours-DP vs Ours-DPM, Ours-P vs Ours-PM, and Ours-PR vs Ours-PMR).

Fig. 6. A challenging case with large and irregular occlusions.

Table 2. Visibility loss of models w/ or w/o the correlation block (D), w/ or w/o joint homography and visibility learning (M vs V).

Method	Ours-PVR	Ours-PMR	Ours-DPVR	Ours-DPMR
Visibility loss	0.347	0.346	0.335	**0.328**

Apart from the improvement to homography precision, we wonder whether learning of homography and visibility jointly (M) leads to higher visibility accuracy than learning these two tasks independently (V). We also test if the correlation block helps visibility accuracy. We train four models on the generated training dataset: Ours-PMR, Ours-DPMR, Ours-PVR and Ours-DPVR. We then compute the visibility loss (Sect. 3.5) on the test set. Results are shown in Table 2. We find that the correlation block and joint learning not only help the homography predictions but also improve the visibility estimations. We see strong connections between homography and visibility. Visibility, a by-product of our work, can be used for in-video advertising. We show one synthesized frame (Fig. 6) using our obtained visibility during experiments on the POT dataset [23]. We meet large and irregular occlusions that are challenging to our model. Fortunately, our model is able to overcome this difficulty.

Confidence Effectiveness. One way to evaluate the confidence effectiveness is to compute the classification statistics using the predicted confidence (0.5 is used as the threshold). We follow data generations in Sect. 4.1 introduction to generate an additional large dataset covering challenging conditions. This dataset, on which tracking is much harder than that of in Sect. 4.1 introduction, contains 50000 samples. The percents of training, validation and testing are 80%, 10% and 10% respectively. Our trained models (Ours-DPR and Ours-DPMR) are then run on this dataset. If the computed L_d is smaller than 5, the tracking result is labeled to be reliable. Otherwise, it is labeled to be unreliable. Obtained labels are adopted for training the confidence network and testing the confidence performance. PatchCon [36] that directly regresses this confidence from wrapped images is the baseline/competing method. Both OursCon and PatchCon are trained to evaluate pre-trained Ours-DPMR and Ours-DPR.

True-positive rate (TPR), false-positive rate (FPR), false-negative rate (FNR) and true-negative rate (TNR) are shown in Table 3. Comparing OursCon and PatchCon [36] that both evaluate Ours-DPMR, we see that tracking confidence predicted from correlation blocks is more accurate. Moreover, from OursCon +Ours-DPR and OursCon+Ours-DPMR, we see that joint learning of visibility mask and homography does improve the effectiveness of our correlation block and model generalization, leading to performance gains of confidence prediction.

Table 3. Classification statistics using the estimated confidence.

Method + Pre-trained Base	TPR	FPR	FNR	TNR
PatchCon [36]+Ours-DPMR	93.1%	14.5%	6.9%	85.5%
OursCon+Ours-DPMR	96.6%	**8.7%**	**3.4%**	91.3%
OursCon+Ours-DPR	96.5%	10.2%	3.5%	89.8%

Scale change	Rotation	Perspective distortion	Motion blur	Occlusion	Out of view

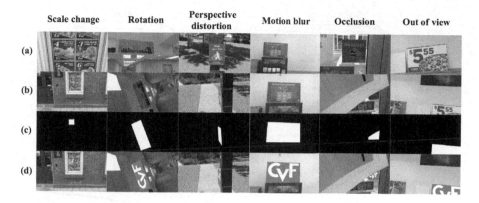

(a)

(b)

(c)

(d)

Fig. 7. Results obtained by our model in different conditions. (a) A planar object in the reference frame. (b) The tracked planar object in the current frame. (c) Predicted visibility mask corresponding to (b). (d) The synthetic frame after placing the CVF logo on (b). More results can be found in the supplementary material.

4.3   Comparisons on Other Datasets

Two public datasets, POT [23] and TMT [34], are used to evaluate the homography accuracy. State-of-the-art methods, including SIFT [12], SURF [6], L1 [5, 26], IVT [33], ESM [7], Gracker [43], DeepHomography [11], IC-STN [24], Ctx-Unsupervise [47], PFN [46], MHN [20] and DLKFM [48] are compared. Our models are all with our tracking confidence module (OursCon), except the one named Ours-DPMR w/o OursCon. The competing confidence prediction method, PatchCon [36], is also included for comparison (Ours-DPMR-PatchCon). The model with all our modules achieves the best performance.

POT is a planar object tracking benchmark containing 210 videos of 30 planar objects in natural environments. It contains scenes with various challenging conditions, including scale change, rotation, perspective distortion, motion blur, occlusion, out-of-view, and a combination of these factors. For better presentation, comparisons are shown with precision plots and success plots. Precision plot counts the percentage of frames whose AE is within the threshold t_p. Success plot counts the percentage of frames whose HD is within a threshold t_s. Results are shown in Fig. 8 and the supplementary material. Our proposed method shows superior performance in all scenes. Especially for scenes with motion blur, perspective distortion, scale change or combinations of these factors, our approach works much better because it is hard for non-learning algorithms to model the underlying variation or tuning related parameters manually.

TMT consists of sequences for manipulation tasks. There are 100 annotated and tagged sequences in total. Similar to POT, sequences in this dataset also have a large condition variation. We use the same evaluation metric as in [34]. That is, the success rate that counts the percentage of frames whose AE < 5.

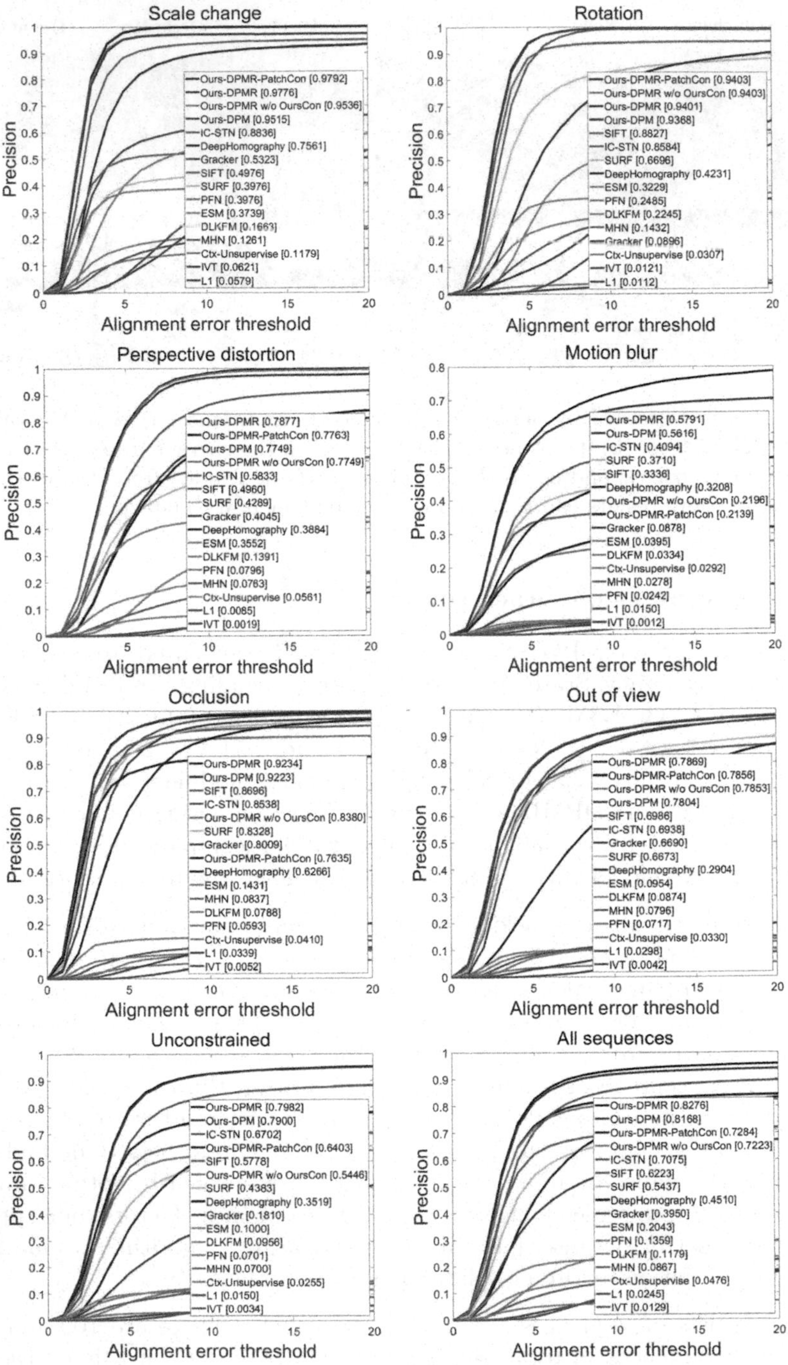

Fig. 8. The comparison of different approaches shown in precision plots on the POT dataset [23]. Curves with larger areas are better. The AE at threshold = 5 [34] is illustrated within brackets. Zoom-in is recommended. Video comparisons are in the supplementary material.

Comparison results are summarized in Table. 4. Overall, our model achieves a better or similar performance in all sequences compared to other methods.

Table 4. Success rate of different approaches on the TMT dataset with AE < 5 [34].Larger is better. Best and second best are colored. (*) Models of Ours-DPMR, Ours-DPMR-PatchCon and Ours-DPMR w/o OursCon perform the same. We omit rested notations for short.

Method	Cereal	Book1	Book2	Book3	Juice	Mug1	Mug2	Mug3	Bus	Highlight	Letter	Newspaper
SIFT [12]	0.92	0.74	1.00	0.84	0.89	0.91	0.43	0.55	0.19	0.97	0.18	0.16
SURF [6]	0.91	0.64	1.00	0.74	0.50	0.07	0.14	0.06	0.19	0.94	0.08	0.01
L1 [26]	0.24	0.10	0.79	0.42	0.16	0.10	0.30	0.54	0.57	0.67	0.19	0.61
IVT [33]	0.99	0.48	0.30	0.72	0.98	0.91	0.72	0.68	0.94	0.95	0.25	0.02
ESM [7]	1.00	1.00	1.00	0.34	1.00	1.00	0.89	1.00	1.00	0.76	1.00	1.00
Grackor [10]	0.91	1.00	1.00	0.88	1.00	1.00	0.83	0.75	0.97	1.00	0.78	1.00
DeepHomography	0.92	1.00	1.00	0.82	0.99	0.93	0.65	0.80	0.50	0.99	1.00	0.95
IC-STN [24]	0.92	1.00	1.00	0.82	1.00	1.00	0.77	0.79	0.99	0.98	1.00	0.95
PFN [46]	0.74	0.28	0.92	0.38	0.39	0.89	0.40	0.88	0.24	0.78	0.29	0.53
Ctx-Unsupervise	0.54	0.38	1.00	0.38	0.29	0.28	0.23	0.39	0.16	1.00	0.17	0.14
MHN [20]	0.62	0.18	0.92	0.40	0.63	0.99	0.50	0.41	0.50	0.76	0.22	0.14
DLKFM [48]	0.58	0.18	0.92	0.41	0.63	0.99	0.50	0.41	0.50	0.76	0.21	0.14
Ours-D	0.85	0.65	0.84	0.67	0.37	1.00	0.78	0.72	0.71	0.92	0.50	0.32
Ours-DP	0.93	1.00	1.00	0.86	1.00	1.00	0.84	0.81	0.97	1.00	1.00	0.93
Ours-DPR	0.93	1.00	1.00	0.88	1.00	1.00	0.83	0.80	0.95	1.00	1.00	0.98
Ours-DPM	0.93	1.00	1.00	0.88	1.00	1.00	0.72	0.83	0.99	1.00	1.00	0.93
Ours-DPMR (*)	0.93	1.00	1.00	0.88	1.00	1.00	0.89	0.85	0.99	1.00	1.00	1.00

We visualize some qualitative results obtained by our model during experiments and place a product (i.e. the CVF logo) on the tracked planar object in Fig. 1 and Fig. 7. More results can be found in the supplementary material.

5   Discussions and Limitations and Conclusions

The main limitation of our work is that the predicted visibility mask is not perfect. With the own constraints of LK-based methods, our approach is sometimes disturbed by the factor of similar occluded objects. In conclusion, we proposed a novel model for planar object tracking. Homography, visibility and confidence are jointly learned based on a correlation block. We achieved a superior planar tracking performance compared to state-of-the-art methods on the public dataset, provided visibility masks that other works had not discussed, calculated more reliable confidence than competing approaches. To better take multi-frame constraints and similar occlusions into consideration is our future work.

References

1. Badrinarayanan, V., Galasso, F., Cipolla, R.: Label propagation in video sequences. In: Proceedings of the IEEE International Conference on Computer Vision and Pattern Recognition (2010)
2. Bai, X., Wang, J., Simons, D., Sapiro, G.: Video snapCut: robust video object cutout using localized classifiers. ACM Trans. Graph. **28**(3), 1–11 (2009)
3. Baker, S., Matthews, I.: Equivalence and efficiency of image alignment algorithms. In: Proceedings of the IEEE International Conference on Computer Vision and Pattern Recognition (2001)
4. Baker, S., Matthews, I.: Lucas-Kanade 20 years on: a unifying framework. Int. J. Comput. Vis. **56**(3), 221–255 (2004). https://doi.org/10.1023/B:VISI.0000011205. 11775.fd
5. Bao, C., Wu, Y., Ling, H., Ji, H.: Real time robust l1 tracker using accelerated proximal gradient approach. In: Proceedings of the IEEE International Conference on Computer Vision and Pattern Recognition (2012)
6. Bay, H., Tuytelaars, T., Van Gool, L.: SURF: speeded up robust features. In: Leonardis, A., Bischof, H., Pinz, A. (eds.) ECCV 2006. LNCS, vol. 3951, pp. 404–417. Springer, Heidelberg (2006). https://doi.org/10.1007/11744023_32
7. Benhimane, S., Malis, E.: Real-time image-based tracking of planes using efficient second-order minimization. In: Proceedings of the IEEE/RSJ International Conference on Intelligent Robots and System (2004)
8. Brox, T., Malik, J.: Object segmentation by long term analysis of point trajectories. In: Daniilidis, K., Maragos, P., Paragios, N. (eds.) ECCV 2010. LNCS, vol. 6315, pp. 282–295. Springer, Heidelberg (2010). https://doi.org/10.1007/978-3-642-15555-0_21
9. Chang, C.H., Chou, C.N., Chang, E.Y.: CLKN: cascaded Lucas-Kanade networks for image alignment. In: Proceedings of the IEEE International Conference on Computer Vision and Pattern Recognition (2017)
10. Chen, L., Zhou, F., Shen, Y., Tian, X., Ling, H., Chen, Y.: Illumination insensitive efficient second-order minimization for planar object tracking. In: Proceedings of the IEEE International Conference on Robotics and Automation (2017)
11. DeTone, D., Malisiewicz, T., Rabinovich, A.: Deep image homography estimation. In: ArXiv preprint arXiv:1606.03798 (2016)
12. D.G. Lowe: object recognition from local scale-invariant features. In: Proceedings of the IEEE International Conference on Computer Vision (1999)
13. Dick, T., Quintero, C.P., Jägersand, M., Shademan, A.: Realtime registration-based tracking via approximate nearest neighbour search. In: Proceedings of Robotics: Science and Systems (2013)
14. Dusmanu, M., Rocco, I., Pajdla, T., Pollefeys, M., Sivic, J., Torii, A., Sattler, T.: D2-Net: a trainable CNN for joint detection and description of local features. In: Proceedings of the IEEE International Conference on Computer Vision and Pattern Recognition (2019)
15. Fan, Q., Zhong, F., Lischinski, D., Cohen-Or, D., Chen, B.: JumpCut: non-successive mask transfer and interpolation for video cutout. ACM Trans. Graph. **34**(6), 1–195 (2015)
16. Fischler, M.A., Bolles, R.C.: Random sample consensus: a paradigm for model fitting with applications to image analysis and automated cartography. Commun. ACM **24**(6), 381–395 (1981)

17. Grundmann, M., Kwatra, V., Han, M., Essa, I.: Efficient hierarchical graph-based video segmentation. In: Proceedings of the IEEE International Conference on Computer Vision and Pattern Recognition (2010)
18. Han, X., Leung, T., Jia, Y., Sukthankar, R., Berg, A.C.: Matchnet: Unifying feature and metric learning for patch-based matching. In: Proceedings of the IEEE International Conference on Computer Vision and Pattern Recognition (2015)
19. Hartley, R., Zisserman, A.: Multiple View Geometry in Computer Vision, 2nd edn. Cambridge University Press, Cambridge (2003)
20. Hoang Le, Feng Liu, S.Z.A.A.: Deep homography estimation for dynamic scenes. In: Proceedings of the IEEE International Conference on Computer Vision and Pattern Recognition (2020)
21. Ioffe, S., Szegedy, C.: Batch normalization: Accelerating deep network training by reducing internal covariate shift. arXiv preprint arXiv:1502.03167 (2015)
22. Kingma, D.P., Ba, J.: Adam: a method for stochastic optimization. arXiv preprint arXiv:1412.6980 (2014)
23. Liang, P., Wu, Y., Liu, H., Wang, L., Liao, C., Ling, H.: Planar object tracking in the wild: a benchmark. In: Proceedings of the IEEE International Conference on Robotics and Automation (2017)
24. Lin, C.H., Lucey, S.: Inverse compositional spatial transformer networks. In: Proceedings of the IEEE International Conference on Computer Vision and Pattern Recognition (2017)
25. Lin, T.-Y., et al.: Microsoft COCO: common objects in context. In: Fleet, D., Pajdla, T., Schiele, B., Tuytelaars, T. (eds.) ECCV 2014. LNCS, vol. 8693, pp. 740–755. Springer, Cham (2014). https://doi.org/10.1007/978-3-319-10602-1_48
26. Mei, X., Ling, H.: Robust visual tracking using l1 minimization. In: Proceedings of the IEEE International Conference on Computer Vision (2009)
27. Nguyen, T., Chen, S.W., Shivakumar, S.S., Taylor, C.J., Kumar, V.: Unsupervised deep homography: a fast and robust homography estimation model. IEEE Robot. Autom. Lett. 3(3), 2346–2353 (2018)
28. Ozuysal, M., Calonder, M., Lepetit, V., Fua, P.: Fast keypoint recognition using random ferns. IEEE Trans. Pattern Anal. Mach. Intell. 32(3), 448–461 (2009)
29. Ramakanth, S.A., Babu, R.V.: Seamseg: Video object segmentation using patch seams. In: Proceedings of the IEEE International Conference on Computer Vision and Pattern Recognition (2014)
30. Revaud, J., Weinzaepfel, P., de Souza, C.R., Humenberger, M.: R2D2: repeatable and reliable detector and descriptor. In: Neural Information Processing Systems (2019)
31. Richa, R., Sznitman, R., Taylor, R., Hager, G.: Visual tracking using the sum of conditional variance. In: Proceedings of the IEEE/RSJ International Conference on Intelligent Robots and System (2011)
32. Ronneberger, O., Fischer, P., Brox, T.: U-Net: convolutional networks for biomedical image segmentation. In: Navab, N., Hornegger, J., Wells, W.M., Frangi, A.F. (eds.) MICCAI 2015. LNCS, vol. 9351, pp. 234–241. Springer, Cham (2015). https://doi.org/10.1007/978-3-319-24574-4_28
33. Ross, D.A., Lim, J., Lin, R.S., Yang, M.H.: Incremental learning for robust visual tracking. Intl. J. Comput. Vis. 77(1–3), 125–141 (2008). https://doi.org/10.1007/s11263-007-0075-7
34. Roy, A., Zhang, X., Wolleb, N., Perez, Quenterio, C., Jagersand, M.: Tracking benchmark and evaluation for manipulation tasks. In: Proceedings of the IEEE International Conference on Robotics and Automation (2015)

35. Rublee, E., Rabaud, V., Konolige, K., Bradski, G.: ORB: an efficient alternative to SIFT or SURF. In: Proceedings of the IEEE International Conference on Computer Vision (2011)
36. Seki, A., Pollefeys, M.: Patch based confidence prediction for dense disparity map. In: Proceedings of the British Machine Vision Conference (2016)
37. Shaked, A., Wolf, L.: Improved stereo matching with constant highway networks and reflective loss. In: arXiv preprint arxiv:1701.00165 (2016)
38. Shorten, C., Khoshgoftaar, T.M.: A survey on image data augmentation for deep learning. J. Big Data **6**(1), 1–48 (2019)
39. Simonyan, K., Zisserman, A.: Very deep convolutional networks for large-scale image recognition. In: ArXiv preprint arXiv:1606.03798 (2014)
40. Sun, D., Yang, X., Liu, M.Y., Kautz, J.: PWC-Net: CNNs for optical flow using pyramid, warping, and cost volume. In: Proceedings of the IEEE International Conference on Computer Vision and Pattern Recognition (2018)
41. Taylor, B., Karasev, V., Soatto, S.: Causal video object segmentation from persistence of occlusions. In: Proceedings of the IEEE International Conference on Computer Vision and Pattern Recognition (2015)
42. Vijayanarasimhan, S., Grauman, K.: Active frame selection for label propagation in videos. In: Fitzgibbon, A., Lazebnik, S., Perona, P., Sato, Y., Schmid, C. (eds.) ECCV 2012. LNCS, vol. 7576, pp. 496–509. Springer, Heidelberg (2012). https://doi.org/10.1007/978-3-642-33715-4_36
43. Wang, T., Ling, H.: Gracker: a graph-based planar object tracker. IEEE Trans. Pattern Anal. Mach. Intell. **40**(6), 1494–1501 (2017)
44. Wang, W., Shen, J., Porikli, F.: Saliency-aware geodesic video object segmentation. In: Saliency-aware geodesic video object segmentation and Pattern Recognition (2015)
45. Yuki Ono, Eduard Trulls, P.F., Yi, K.M.: LF-Net: learning local features from images. In: Neural Information Processing Systems (2018)
46. Zeng, R., Denman, S., Sridharan, S., Fookes, C.: Rethinking planar homography estimation using perspective fields. In: Jawahar, C.V., Li, H., Mori, G., Schindler, K. (eds.) ACCV 2018. LNCS, vol. 11366, pp. 571–586. Springer, Cham (2019). https://doi.org/10.1007/978-3-030-20876-9_36
47. Zhang, J., et al.: Content-aware unsupervised deep homography estimation. In: Vedaldi, A., Bischof, H., Brox, T., Frahm, J.-M. (eds.) ECCV 2020. LNCS, vol. 12346, pp. 653–669. Springer, Cham (2020). https://doi.org/10.1007/978-3-030-58452-8_38
48. Zhao, Y., Huang, X., Zhang, Z.: Deep lucas-kanade homography for multimodal image alignment. In: Proceedings of the IEEE International Conference on Computer Vision and Pattern Recognition (2021)

RamGAN: Region Attentive Morphing GAN for Region-Level Makeup Transfer

Jianfeng Xiang[1,2,3,4], Junliang Chen[1,2,3,4], Wenshuang Liu[1,2,3,4],
Xianxu Hou[1,2,3,4], and Linlin Shen[1,2,3,4(✉)]

[1] Computer Vision Institute, School of Computer Science and Software Engineering,
Shenzhen University, Shenzhen, China
{xiangjianfeng2020,chenjunliang2016,liuwenshuang2018}@email.szu.edu.cn,
llshen@szu.edu.cn
[2] Shenzhen Institute of Artificial Intelligence and Robotics for Society,
Shenzhen, China
[3] Guangdong Key Laboratory of Intelligent Information Processing,
Shenzhen University, Shenzhen, China
[4] National Engineering Laboratory for Big Data System Computing Technology,
Shenzhen University, Shenzhen, China

Abstract. In this paper, we propose a region adaptive makeup transfer GAN, called RamGAN, for precise region-level makeup transfer. Compared to face-level transfer methods, our RamGAN uses spatial-aware Region Attentive Morphing Module (RAMM) to encode Region Attentive Matrices (RAMs) for local regions like lips, eye shadow and skin. After that, the Region Style Injection Module (RSIM) is applied to RAMs produced by RAMM to obtain two Region Makeup Tensors, γ and β, which are subsequently added to the feature map of source image to transfer the makeup. As attention and makeup styles are calculated for each region, RamGAN can achieve better disentangled makeup transfer for different facial regions. When there are significant pose and expression variations between source and reference, RamGAN can also achieve better transfer results, due to the integration of spatial information and region-level correspondence. Experimental results are conducted on public datasets like MT, M-Wild and Makeup datasets, both visual and quantitative results and user study suggest that our approach achieves better transfer results than state-of-the-art methods like BeautyGAN, BeautyGlow, DMT, CPM and PSGAN.

Keywords: Region makeup transfer · Region attention · GAN

1 Introduction

With the development of the times, human beings, especially women are paying more and more attention to their appearance and willing to spend a lot of time

Supplementary Information The online version contains supplementary material available at https://doi.org/10.1007/978-3-031-20047-2_41.

Fig. 1. Half face makeup (left) and step-by-step makeup (right).

and money on it. Among all facial beautification techniques, makeup is one of the most convenient and popular way, which usually applies some cosmetics like foundation, eye shadow, lipstick and so on, to generate good-looking appearance.

As facial makeup has become more and more popular, a large number of makeup transfer methods have been proposed in recent years. Makeup transfer is a computer vision task to render a non-makeup face image a makeup style without changing the face identity. Most of existing methods employ Generative Adversarial Networks (GANs) [4–6,8,18,26] to learn a mapping from non-makeup face image domain to the makeup one. CycleGAN [28] adopted cycle consistency loss to learn the mapping between two domains. BeautyGAN [14] adopted the dual input/output architecture, which can perform makeup transfer and removal simultaneously. It also introduced a pixel-level histogram matching loss to improve the appearance of the lips, eye shadow and skin regions. BeautyGlow [1] used the Glow [13] framework to perform makeup transfer. LADN [9] adopted multiple and overlapping local adversarial discriminators for heavy facial makeup. DMT [25] applied two encoders to decompose the input images into identity codes and makeup codes, and produced various outputs by combining the two codes. Recently, CPM [19] successfully achieved color/pattern makeup transfer with a color/pattern transfer branch. However, most of these methods have a shortcoming, i.e., they can only work well on frontal facial images since they lack a specific module to focus on the spatial information of the images. When these methods are directly applied to the unaligned images for makeup transfer, the generated results are always far from satisfactory.

The Attentive Makeup Morphing (AMM) module proposed by PSGAN [11] tried to model how a pixel in the source is morphed from the reference image, and integrated the spatial information by including the relative positions with landmarks and the facial regions of each pixel into the attention matrix. As an extension, PSGAN++ [15] equipped an Identity Distill Network (IDNet) with the AMM module to achieve makeup transfer and removal simultaneously. However, although PSGAN and PSGAN++ can achieve makeup transfer between faces with large variations, they can not achieve accurate region-level makeup transfer, i.e., they cannot well disentangle each region when implementing partial makeup transfer.

Therefore, we propose RamGAN, which consists of two core architectures, i.e., Region Attentive Morphing Module (RAMM) and Region Style Injection Module

(RSIM), for region-level makeup transfer. Figure 1 shows four examples of region-level makeup results transferred by our approach. In the first row of the left figure, the makeup of the reference is transferred to the left face of source and one can observe that RamGAN precisely preserves the right face of source. In the second row of the left figure, even when there is significant pose differences between source and reference, RamGAN still successfully transfers the makeup of reference to the lower part of source. In the right figure, we can observe that RamGAN can precisely transfer the makeup for local regions like skin, eye shadow and lip.

Figure 2 shows the main differences between our RamGAN and PSGAN. First of all, while PSGAN learns a relationship between the styles (γ and β) of reference and source, our RamGAN does not assume such a relationship and directly learns γ and β applied to source. To integrate spatial constrain, the attention matrix in AMM is calculated by measuring the similarity between pixels of source and reference by weighting both the relative position to 68 landmarks and the extracted visual features. However, when faces are occluded, some of the landmarks might not be accurately detected, which will significantly affect the accuracy of attention map. Instead, the attention maps of RamGAN, Region Attentive Matrices (RAMs), are calculated for each region, based on visual features only. The makeup transfer of our approach is thus more robust against large pose differences. Based on the RAMs, two Region Makeup Tensors (RMTs) are learned to transfer the style of source face.

In addition, in order to make sure that the regions are translated separately, that is, the translation of certain region does not affect other regions, we use Region Matching Loss (RML) and Background Loss to measure the similarity between the corresponding regions of no-makeup and local/global translated images.

Our contributions are mainly summarized as follows:

- We propose a makeup transfer framework based on spatial region attention, called RamGAN, to achieve robust makeup transfer between faces with large pose variations and accurate region transfer.
- The proposed Region Attentive Morphing Module (RAMM) adaptively and separately learns the makeup information through three Region Attentive Matrices (RAMs) and successfully achieves region-level makeup transfer.
- We propose Region Style Injection Module (RSIM) to accurately transfer makeup information of reference faces to the corresponding areas of non-makeup faces.
- Experimental results quantitatively and qualitatively demonstrate that our RamGAN framework achieves the start-of-the-art performance.

2　Methodology

2.1　Problem Formulation

Let $\mathcal{X} \subset \mathbb{R}^{3 \times H \times W}$ and $\mathcal{Y} \subset \mathbb{R}^{3 \times H \times W}$ be the source image domain and the reference image domain. Note that the pair of makeup and non-makeup images is not available, i.e., the identities of source and reference images are different.

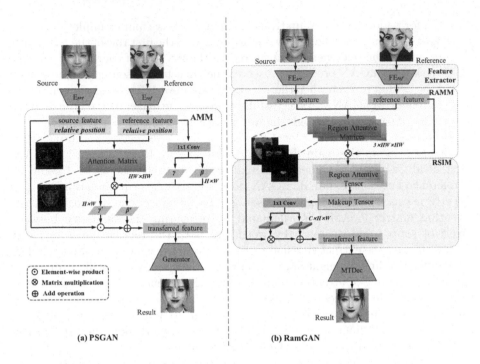

Fig. 2. An overview of PSGAN [11] **(a)** and our proposed RamGAN **(b)**.

Given a non-makeup sample $x \in \mathcal{X}$ and a makeup sample $y \in \mathcal{Y}$, the goal of the proposed RamGAN is to learn a mapping $G : x \rightarrow \tilde{y}_x$, where $\tilde{y}_x \in \mathcal{Y}$ possesses the makeup style of y and the identity of x.

2.2   Network Structure

As shown in Fig. 2(b), our proposed framework mainly consists of four modules, Feature Extractor, Region Attentive Morphing Module (RAMM), Region Style Injection Module (RSIM) and Makeup Transfer Decoder.

Feature Extractor. As shown in Fig. 2(b), the Feature Extractor consists of two encoder-bottleneck architectures, i.e. a source image encoder FE_x and a reference image encoder FE_y, which can extract the makeup-related features, e.g., the color of face, the size of eyes, etc. And these makeup-related features are fed to the RAMM subsequently. Note that the FE_x and FE_y share the same architecture, but do not share parameters. Mathematically, it is formulated as:

$$f_x = FE_x(x), \; f_y = FE_y(y), \tag{1}$$

where $f_x \in \mathbb{R}^{C \times H \times W}$ and $f_y \in \mathbb{R}^{C \times H \times W}$ are the source and reference feature map extracted by Feature Extractor. C, H and W are the number of channels, height and width of the feature map. FE_x and FE_y represent source image Feature Extractor and reference image Feature Extractor, respectively.

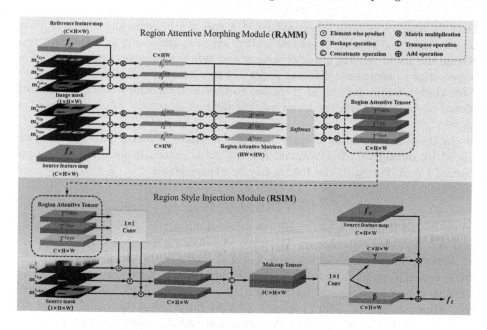

Fig. 3. Detailed architecture of the proposed RAMM and RSIM.

Region Attentive Morphing Module. Inspired by AMM module of PSGAN [11], we propose Region Attentive Morphing Module (RAMM) based on attention mechanism [2,3,22,24,27], which produces attention matrix for each of the facial regions like skin, lip and eye shadow. Figure 2 shows the main differences between AMM and our RAMM. The attention matrix of AMM models the relationship between each pixel in the source with all pixels in the reference. The relative positions with 68 landmarks and the facial regions of each pixel are also considered in AMM to integrate spatial information, such that the style of reference is transferred to that of closely related pixels in source, in terms of both spatial position and visual similarity. The attention matrix is then multiplied with the style features (γ and β) of reference and applied to the source face to transfer the makeup. Different with AMM, our RAMM extracts style features and learns attention matrix for each of the facial region, the style features of reference face regions are then multiplied with the corresponding attention matrix and input to the RSIM (Region Style Injection Module) to generate the style codes (γ and β) to transfer the makeup to source face.

As shown in the upper part of Fig. 3, our RAMM has 4 inputs, i.e., source feature map f_x, reference feature map f_y, source mask $m_x^{r_k}$ and reference mask $m_y^{r_k}$. The source feature map and reference feature map are element-wisely multiplied with corresponding facial parsing masks to get two regional feature maps.

$$f_x^{r_k} = \left(f_x \odot m_x^{r_k}\right), \; f_y^{r_k} = \left(f_y \odot m_y^{r_k}\right). \tag{2}$$

Here, $\odot$ denotes element-wise product, $f_x^{r_k}$ and $f_y^{r_k}$ indicate the source regional feature map and reference regional feature map, respectively, $m_x^{r_k}$ and $m_y^{r_k}$ represent the facial parsing mask of source and reference image, respectively. The superscript r_k represents different regions of face and $k \in \{\text{skin}, \text{lip}, \text{eye shadow}\}$. Note that different definitions of regions can be used. Specially, when we perform global makeup transfer, the facial mask is defined as $m_x^{global} = m_x^{r_{skin}} + m_x^{r_{lip}} + m_x^{r_{eye}}$.

In the following branch, three Region Attentive Matrices (RAMs) are produced by multiplying two regional feature maps, which is shown in the upper part of Fig. 3. Formally, the RAMs can be expressed as:

$$A^{r_k} = \mathbf{R}(f_x^{r_k})^T \otimes \mathbf{R}(f_y^{r_k}), \tag{3}$$

where $\otimes$ and $\mathbf{R}$ denote matrix multiplication and reshape operation, respectively, and A^{r_k} represents the Region Attentive Matrices for different regions.

Several differences exist between AMM of PSGAN and the proposed RAMM when calculating the attention matrix. First, both facial landmarks and facial parsing masks are required by AMM to integrate the spatial information into the attention matrix. The proposed RAMM only needs the facial masks. To integrate spatial constrain into the attention, AMM calculates the similarity between pixels of source and reference by weighting both the relative position to 68 landmarks and extracted visual features. They tested different weights and found 0.01 to be the best value, which actually emphasizes much more on the spatial positions. However, when there are significant pose variations between source and reference faces, some of the landmarks might be occluded and can't be detected. In this case, the position correspondence between source and reference might not be well established, which will significantly affect the accuracy of attention map. In contrast, our attention map is calculated for each region, based on visual features only. As faces are symmetric and the makeup styles of pixels are consistent within the same region, the makeup can still be successfully transferred to the corresponding regions when there are large pose differences between source and reference.

Figure 4 shows the attention maps generated by PSGAN and our RamGAN for two pairs of source and references. Due to the pose differences, PSGAN wrongly matches the pixels located on the upper lip and right eyes of source face to mouth and the centers of eyes in reference face, respectively. As a result, the eye shadow and lip color of the face generated by PSGAN are significantly different with that of reference. In contrast, our RamGAN can accurately attend the makeup style to that of the same region and successfully transfer the makeup style of each region.

| Source image (with a specific red point) | Reference image | Attention map (PSGAN) | Attention map (RamGAN) | Makeup result (PSGAN) | Makeup result (RamGAN) |

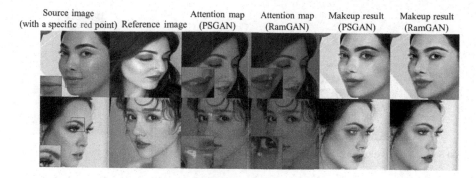

Fig. 4. The visualization of attention map on reference image. Given a specific red point in source image, we calculate the attentive values for pixels in the reference face and visualize the attention map. (Color figure online)

After obtaining the RAMs, a softmax layer is subsequently applied to RAMs, which enables the attentive values in RAMs become more gathered [11]. Finally, the RAMM applies RAMs to the regional reference feature with matrix multiplication to produce the Region Attentive Tensor (RAT), which is shown in the red dashed box in the Fig. 3. The RAT consists of three Attentive Tensors, each of which has C channels with spatial-aware attentive values for different regions. The process can be expressed as:

$$T^{r_k} = softmax(A^{r_k}) \otimes \mathbf{R}(f_y^{r_k}),\qquad(4)$$

where T^{r_k} represents Region Attentive Tensor for different regions, *softmax* represents softmax activation layer.

Region Style Injection Module. In order to accurately control the application of makeup to the target region, we introduce RSIM module. It first applies the RAT produced by RAMM to the source mask $m_x^{r_k}$ by element-wise multiplication and the output is concatenated along the channel dimension. The lower part of Fig. 3 shows the process of multiplication and concatenation. The output Makeup Tensor is fed into two 1×1 convolution layers separately to produce two Region Makeup Tensors (RMTs), $\gamma \in \mathbb{R}^{C \times H \times W}$ and $\beta \in \mathbb{R}^{C \times H \times W}$. The process can be defined as:

$$\begin{aligned} MT &= Cat\big(Conv(T^{r_k}) \odot m_x^{r_k}\big) \\ \gamma &= Conv_\gamma(MT), \beta = Conv_\beta(MT), \end{aligned}\qquad(5)$$

where $MT \in \mathbb{R}^{3C \times H \times W}$ denotes Makeup Tensor, *Cat* and *Conv* represent the concatenation and 1×1 convolution, respectively. Then γ and β are applied to the source feature map f_x to get the transferred feature map by matrix multiplication and addition. More specifically, the transferred feature map is computed by

$$f_t = \gamma f_x + \beta,\qquad(6)$$

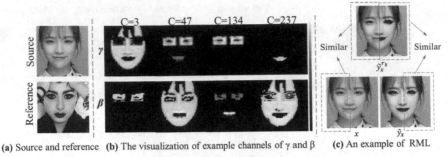

(a) Source and reference   (b) The visualization of example channels of γ and β   (c) An example of RML

Fig. 5. (a) Source and reference images. (b) Example channels of γ and β. (c) An example of Region Matching Loss.

where f_t represents the transferred feature map.

Note that the makeup matrices γ' and β' of PSGAN are duplicated and expanded along the channel dimension to produce the makeup tensors $\Gamma' \in \mathbb{R}^{C \times H \times W}$ and $B' \in \mathbb{R}^{C \times H \times W}$. It is unreasonable because all facial regions shared the same makeup features and thus the model has trouble in region-level makeup transfer. Different to PSGAN [11], our RMTs $\gamma \in \mathbb{R}^{C \times H \times W}$ and $\beta \in \mathbb{R}^{C \times H \times W}$ are tensors with spatial channel. We believe that makeup transfer is a region-to-region task and each channel of γ or β should focus on different facial regions. In Fig. 5(b), we visualize several channels of γ and β. From the figure, we can observe that different channels of γ or β response to different regions, i.e. our RMTs γ and β contain more spatial-aware information for region-level makeup transfer.

Makeup Transfer Decoder. MTDec utilizes a bottleneck-decoder architecture like StarGAN [6], which is a symmetric model of Feature Extractor. The transferred feature map f_t produced by RSIM is fed to the MTDec to generate the makeup result $\tilde{y}_x$, which can be expressed as:

$$\tilde{y}_x = MTDec(f_t). \tag{7}$$

2.3 Objective Function

Adversarial Loss. We employ adversarial loss to improve the quality of generated images. Given a source image domain $\mathcal{X}$ and a reference image domain $\mathcal{Y}$, we use two discriminators $D_\mathcal{X}$ and $D_\mathcal{Y}$ to distinguish generated images and real images and thus help the generator G synthesize realistic outputs. Therefore, the adversarial loss of discriminators and generator can be computed by

$$
\begin{aligned}
L_D^{adv} = {} & \mathbb{E}_{x \sim \mathcal{P}_\mathcal{X}} \left[\log D_\mathcal{X}(x) \right] + \mathbb{E}_{y \sim \mathcal{P}_\mathcal{Y}} \left[\log D_\mathcal{Y}(y) \right] \\
& + \mathbb{E}_{(x,y) \sim \mathcal{P}_{(\mathcal{X},\mathcal{Y})}} \left[\log \left(1 - D_\mathcal{X}(G(y,x)) \right) \right] \\
& + \mathbb{E}_{(x,y) \sim \mathcal{P}_{(\mathcal{X},\mathcal{Y})}} \left[\log \left(1 - D_\mathcal{Y}(G(x,y)) \right) \right]
\end{aligned}
\tag{8}
$$

$$L_G^{adv} = \mathbb{E}_{(x,y)\sim\mathcal{P}_{(\mathcal{X},\mathcal{Y})}}\left[\log\left(D_{\mathcal{X}}(G(y,x))\right)\right]$$
$$+ \mathbb{E}_{(x,y)\sim\mathcal{P}_{(\mathcal{X},\mathcal{Y})}}\left[\log\left(D_{\mathcal{Y}}(G(x,y))\right)\right]. \tag{9}$$

Makeup Loss. We use the makeup loss proposed in [14] to provide a coarse guidance for makeup transfer. Specifically, it employs a Histogram Matching (HM) function to adjust the color histogram distribution of the transferred image to match the reference one in each facial regions like eye shadows, lips, and facial skin. The makeup loss is a weighted sum of the regional losses

$$\mathcal{L}_G^{make} = \lambda_{lips}\mathcal{L}_{lips} + \lambda_{eyes}\mathcal{L}_{eyes} + \lambda_{skin}\mathcal{L}_{skin}, \tag{10}$$

where $\lambda_{skin}, \lambda_{eyes}$ and λ_{lips} are tunable hyper-parameters. Specifically, each loss item is a local histogram loss, which can be written as:

$$\mathcal{L}_k = \left\|\tilde{y}_x \odot m_x^{r_k} - \text{HM}\left(\tilde{y}_x \odot m_x^{r_k}, y \odot m_y^{r_k}\right)\right\|_2. \tag{11}$$

Region Matching Loss. As shown in Fig. 5(c), given a source image x, a global makeup image $\tilde{y}_x$ and a region makeup image $\tilde{y}_x^{r_k}$. We use Region Matching Loss (RML) [16,17] to measure the similarity between the kth regions of $\tilde{y}_x$ and $\tilde{y}_x^{r_k}$, and the similarity between other regions of x and $\tilde{y}_x^{r_k}$. Then, the RML is defined as follows:

$$\mathcal{L}_G^{rm} = \left\|\tilde{y}_x^{r_k} \odot m_x^{r_k}, \tilde{y}_x \odot m_x^{r_k}\right\|_1 + \left\|\tilde{y}_x^{r_k} \odot (1 - m_x^{r_k}), x \odot (1 - m_x^{r_k})\right\|_1, \tag{12}$$

where $1 - m_x^{r_k}$ inverts the mask to get the unrelated regions.

Background Loss. When performing region-level makeup transfer, we want to only change the target region, while keeping the other regions including hair, background, etc., unchanged. For this reason, we define the background loss as below

$$\mathcal{L}_G^{bg} = \left\|\tilde{y}_x \odot (1 - m_x^{r_k}), x \odot (1 - m_x^{r_k})\right\|_1. \tag{13}$$

Cycle Consistency Loss. Since we are performing image-to-image translation with unpaired images, we need an additional loss to ensure that the unrelated regions in source image are not modified. Here, we introduce the cycle consistency loss proposed in [28] and define the loss function as:

$$L_G^{cyc} = \left\|G(G(x,y),x) - x\right\|_1 + \left\|G(G(y,x),y) - y\right\|_1. \tag{14}$$

Perceptual Loss. Perceptual loss aims to preserve the identity between source and generated images. We use the VGG-16 model [21] pre-trained on ImageNet dataset [7] to compare the activation features of source image and generated image in the hidden layer. The perceptual loss can be expressed as:

$$L_G^{per} = \left\|\mathscr{F}_l(G(x,y)) - \mathscr{F}_l(x)\right\|_2 + \left\|\mathscr{F}_l(G(y,x)) - \mathscr{F}_l(y)\right\|_2, \tag{15}$$

where $\mathscr{F}_l(\cdot)$ denotes the output of the lth layer of the VGG-16 model.

728   J. Xiang et al.

Total Loss. The total loss for discriminator and generator of our method can be expressed as:

$$L_D = \lambda_{adv} L_D^{adv}$$
$$L_G = \lambda_{adv} L_G^{adv} + \lambda_{make} L_G^{make} + \lambda_{rm} L_G^{rm}$$
$$+ \lambda_{bg} L_G^{bg} + \lambda_{cyc} L_G^{cyc} + \lambda_{per} L_G^{per}. \tag{16}$$

3 Experiments

3.1 Dataset

Makeup Transfer Dataset. We train our RamGAN model on the Makeup Transfer (MT) dataset [14], which contains 1,115 non-makeup images and 2,719 makeup images. Most of these images consist of aligned faces with a resolution of 361 × 361 and provide face segmentation masks. We follow the strategy of [11] by randomly selecting 100 non-makeup and 250 makeup images as the test set and use the remaining images for training. For testing, we transfer the 100 non-makeup images with reference to each of the 250 makeup images and in total 25,000 makeup images can be generated for quality assessment.

Makeup Dataset. LADN [9] provides Makeup dataset, which contains 333 non-makeup images, 302 makeup images and 115 extreme makeup images with great variances on makeup color, style and region coverage. We randomly select 200 non-makeup images and 200 makeup images for experiments and in total 40,000 makeup images can be generated for quality assessment.

Makeup-Wild Dataset. Makeup-Wild [11] (M-Wild) dataset has 403 makeup images and 369 non-makeup images. Most of these images are faces with large pose variations. We randomly select 200 non-makeup images and 200 makeup images for experiments.

CPM-Real Dataset. CPM-Real [19] dataset has 3895 real face images. Most of these images have heavy and extreme makeup, including facial gems, face paintings, hennas, and festival makeups. We select 10 non-makeup images and 10 references with light makeup for user study.

3.2 Implementation Details

In all experiments, we resize the images to 256 × 256, and use the $relu\_4\_1$ feature layer of the pre-trained VGG16 for calculating the perceptual loss. The hyper-parameters of different loss functions are set as $\lambda_{adv} = 1$, $\lambda_{make} = 0.2$, $\lambda_{rm} = 5$, $\lambda_{bg} = 5$, $\lambda_{cyc} = 10$, $\lambda_{per} = 0.005$. We use Adam [12] as the optimizer, the maximum epochs for model training is 50, the learning rate is 0.0002, and the batch size is 4. We implement RamGAN with Pytorch [20] and conduct all the experiments on a NVIDIA Tesla V100 GPU.

3.3 Qualitative Results

We compare our proposed method with the general image-to-image translation method, CycleGAN [28] and several state-of-the-art makeup transfer methods like BeautyGAN [14], BeautyGlow[1] [1], PSGAN [11], DMT [25] and CPM [19].

Figure 6 compares the qualitative result of RamGAN with the above methods on frontal face makeup transfer. The results generated by CycleGAN have an unnatural color significantly different with the source image. Both BeautyGAN and CPM produce artifacts on the background or forehead of generated images. BeautyGlow seems to have a satisfactory result, but the color of faces, especially lips and skin, is not similar to the reference image. Comparatively, the results of PSGAN and DMT are more realistic than other methods. However, the eye shadows generated by PSGAN are all black, which are different with references. Only the results of DMT are comparable to our proposed RamGAN. However, DMT fails to achieve the makeup transfer when source and reference faces have a large difference in pose.

Fig. 6. Comparison of frontal face makeup transfer with several state-of-the-art methods.

We also conduct an evaluation on makeup transfer between faces with large pose variations in Fig. 7. Since these methods are not equipped with a specific module to learn the spatial information, the makeup is applied randomly to the face. For example, in the first row of Fig. 7, DMT transfers the lip region into an unnatural patch. And in the second row, the makeup image generated by DMT is irrelevant to reference. In the 5th column of Fig. 7, the faces generated by CPM are both deformed and blurry. Although the results generated by PSGAN are relatively satisfactory, the makeup styles are not accurately transferred to the appropriate regions, like eye shadow and lips, etc. As we analyzed above, the AMM module takes the relative position as the primary concern when calculating the attention matrix, which is not robust when the face is occluded.

---

[1] As the source code of BeautyGlow is not available, we directly used the makeup transfer results posted on https://github.com/BeautyGlow/BeautyGlow.github.io for the same source and reference images for comparison.

Fig. 7. Makeup transfer between faces with large pose differences.

To further illustrate that our method can not only perform global makeup transfer, but also has a strong regional controllability. We now compare step-by-step makeup transfer results with PSGAN [11]. In the first row of Fig. 8, when PSGAN performs step-by-step makeup transfer, especially changing skin color, the color of the area around eyes and lips changes simultaneously. This also proves that PSGAN cannot well disentangle each region. Though the AMM module enables pose and expression transfer, PSGAN can't perform well in region-level makeup transfer. In the second row of the figure, the proposed RamGAN succesfully achieves the step-by-step makeup transfer with a smoother and more natural transition for each region, even when there are large pose between source and reference faces.

Fig. 8. Step-by-step makeup results.

3.4   Quantitative Results

In this section, we demonstrate a qualitative comparison of the proposed Ram-GAN and other methods. We first compare Structural Similarity Index (SSIM) [23] score and Fréchet Inception Distance (FID) [10] with BeautyGAN, DMT, CPM and PSGAN on MT [14] test set, M-Wild dataset [11] and Makeup [9] dataset. Then, we conduct a user study on MT test set, M-Wild dataset, Makeup dataset and CPM-Real [19] dataset, respectively. The result images generated by all methods are aligned to the same resolution (256 × 256).

SSIM. Structural Similarity Index (SSIM) [23] is a metric to measure the structural similarity (illumination, reflectance etc.) of two images. We use the SSIM metric (bigger is better) to evaluate the quality of the makeup images by comparing them with source images. The average score for each method is reported in Table 1. The SSIM score of our method on MT test set, M-Wild dataset and Makeup dataset is **0.94**, **0.95** and **0.95**, respectively, which are higher than all other methods.

FID. Different from SSIM metric, Fréchet Inception Distance (FID) [10] is usually used to evaluate the quality and realness of the generated images. Therefore, we compute the FID score (smaller is better) between generated images and source images to measure our method. The result is shown in Table 1. We can see that our method achieves the lowest FID score among all methods.

Table 1. The SSIM/FID of different methods.

Dataset	BeautyGAN	DMT	CPM	PSGAN	Ours
MT	0.85/31.80	0.81/22.23	0.62/33.06	0.90/17.01	**0.94/13.20**
M-Wild	0.83/50.28	0.82/30.21	0.63/56.76	0.85/22.51	**0.95/16.70**
Makeup	0.86/38.21	0.90/21.16	0.66/43.68	0.90/14.83	**0.95/10.67**

User Study. To further measure the quality of images generated by our RamGAN, a user study is conducted among 65 volunteers (38 females and 27 males) aged from 20 years old to 30 years old. We randomly choose 10 non-makeup images and 10 makeup images from each of the MT test set, M-Wild dataset, Makeup dataset and CPM-Real dataset for experiments. For each of the 40 non-makeup images, the 40 makeup images are used as references and input to our RamGAN, BeautyGAN, DMT, CPM and PSGAN to generate in total 1,600 makeup transferred faces, for each model. We further divided the 1,600 makeup transfer tasks into three categories, i.e. frontal faces, faces with large pose variations and step-by-step transfer. Each volunteer was presented with the makeup faces generated by different approaches for each category of the tasks and asked to choose the best one, in terms of both image quality and identity preservation. For each category of task, four results (one from each dataset) transferred by each approach, $4 \times 5 = 20$ results, are randomly selected and shown to each of the volunteers. We in total collected 65 questionnaires and each questionnaire contain the best models chosen by volunteer for each category of the tasks.

Table 2. The ratio selected as best (%).

Makeup transfer tasks	BeautyGAN	DMT	CPM	PSGAN	Ours
Frontal faces	0.18	0.20	0.18	0.15	**0.29**
Faces with large pose variations	0.03	0.17	0.03	0.10	**0.67**
Step-by-step	—	—	0.08	0.15	**0.77**

Table 2 shows the ratio of each model chosen by volunteers and it shows that our RamGAN is the most frequently chosen model across all of the different tasks. Especially for makeup transfer across large pose variations and stey-by-step transfer, the ratio of our approach chosen by volunteers is significantly higher than other competing approaches. As the stey-by-step makeup transfer results of BeautyGAN and DMT are far from satisfactory, we don't include them into the questionnaire for the step-by-step task.

3.5   Ablation Studies

We now test the effectiveness of the proposed RAMM and Region Matching Loss (RML). As presented in previous sections, our RAMM mainly enables region-level transfer and RML further reduces the entanglement of different regions to the target region. Figure 9. shows the results of two examples for our RamGAN with and without the proposed RAMM and RML. As shown in the 4th column, the forehead of the lady's face in the first row and the mouth region in the second row are also changed when RamGAN without RML is trying to transfer the makeup of the mouth and eye regions, respectively. Instead, the target regions transferred by RamGAN with RML are much more precise and other regions are preserved much better. In the 5th column, there are obvious transition boundaries in the makeup faces transferred by RamGAN without RAM, which clearly justifies the usefulness of the proposed module.

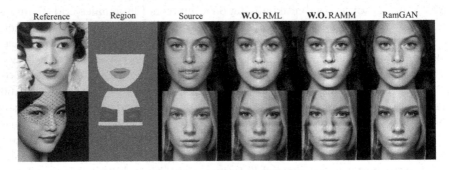

Fig. 9. The performance of RamGAN without RML (4th column) and without RAMM (5th column).

We now show the quantitative results of SSIM and FID for RamGAN without RAMM and RML in Table 3. One can observe from the table that RamGAN equipped with the two modules achieves much better results.

Table 3. The SSIM and FID of ablation study.

Metric	Dataset	**W.O.** RAMM	**W.O.** RML	RamGAN
SSIM	MT	0.72	0.61	**0.94**
	M-Wild	0.73	0.63	**0.95**
	Makeup	0.71	0.69	**0.95**
FID	MT	30.21	45.75	**13.20**
	M-Wild	35.73	50.83	**16.70**
	Makeup	32.36	16.19	**10.67**

3.6 More Visual Results

Based on our RAMM and RSIM, we can actually perform mixed style transfer by transferring different regions to the styles of different faces. Given three reference images, y_0, y_1, $y_2 \in \mathcal{Y}$, we can obtain the corresponding makeup-related features f_{y_0}, f_{y_1} and f_{y_2} extracted by Feature Extractor, respectively. Based on the facial region masks, $m_{y_0}^{r_{skin}}$, $m_{y_1}^{r_{lip}}$ and $m_{y_2}^{r_{eye}}$, we can obtain the corresponding regional feature maps $f_{y_0}^{r_{skin}}$, $f_{y_1}^{r_{lip}}$ and $f_{y_2}^{r_{eye}}$ with Eq. (2). Thereafter, different regions of a source face can be transferred to the styles of corresponding regions encoded in the three different feature maps. For example, in middle of the 2nd row of Fig. 10, the skin, lips and eye shadow of the source image are transferred to the styles of corresponding regions of the three references shown in the first row, respectively. The last facial image in the 2nd row shows the results of mixed transfer by integrating the styles of three regions of different reference faces, i.e. the skin, lips and eye shadow of the face are similar to the styles of the three reference faces shown in the first row, respectively. More results of interpolation between difference references can be found in the supplementary.

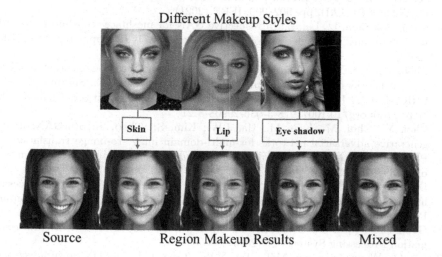

Fig. 10. The mixed trasfer of different makeup styles. First rows are different styles. Second rows are source image, region makeup transfer results (skin, lips and eye shadow), and mixed result.

4   Conclusions

In this paper, we discuss the makeup transfer task, which aims to render a non-makeup face image a makeup style without changing the face identity. We propose a region attentive morphing generative adversarial network (RamGAN) for facial makeup transfer. Our RamGAN can achieve state-of-the-art results, which performs region-level makeup transfer and makeup transfer between faces with large pose variations. Extensive experiments on various datasets further demonstrate that our method significantly outperforms the latest makeup transfer approaches e.g. BeautyGAN, BeautyGlow, DMT, CPM and PSGAN. Moreover, our method has a great advantage in precise region control. Therefore, we believe that our method can be applied to other regional image-to-image translation task.

Acknowledgements. This research was supported by National Natural Science Foundation of China under grant no. 91959108, and Guangdong Basic and Applied Basic Research Foundation under Grant no. 2020A1515111199 and 2022A1515011018.

References

1. Chen, H.J., Hui, K.M., Wang, S.Y., Tsao, L.W., Shuai, H.H., Cheng, W.H.: BeautyGlow: on-demand makeup transfer framework with reversible generative network. In: Proceedings of the IEEE/CVF Conference on Computer Vision and Pattern Recognition, pp. 10042–10050 (2019)
2. Chen, J., Lu, W., Shen, L.: Selective multi-scale learning for object detection. In: Farkaš, I., Masulli, P., Otte, S., Wermter, S. (eds.) ICANN 2021. LNCS, vol. 12892, pp. 3–14. Springer, Cham (2021). https://doi.org/10.1007/978-3-030-86340-1_1
3. Chen, J., Zhao, X., Shen, L.: Delving into the scale variance problem in object detection. In: 2021 IEEE 33rd International Conference on Tools with Artificial Intelligence (ICTAI), pp. 902–909. IEEE (2021)
4. Chen, W., Shen, L., Lai, Z.: Introspective GAN for meshface recognition. In: 2019 IEEE International Conference on Image Processing (ICIP), pp. 3472–3476. IEEE (2019)
5. Chen, W., Xie, X., Jia, X., Shen, L.: Texture deformation based generative adversarial networks for multi-domain face editing. In: Nayak, A.C., Sharma, A. (eds.) PRICAI 2019. LNCS (LNAI), vol. 11670, pp. 257–269. Springer, Cham (2019). https://doi.org/10.1007/978-3-030-29908-8_21
6. Choi, Y., Choi, M., Kim, M., Ha, J.W., Kim, S., Choo, J.: StarGAN: unified generative adversarial networks for multi-domain image-to-image translation. In: Proceedings of the IEEE Conference on Computer Vision and Pattern Recognition, pp. 8789–8797 (2018)
7. Deng, J., Dong, W., Socher, R., Li, L.J., Li, K., Fei-Fei, L.: ImageNet: a large-scale hierarchical image database. In: 2009 IEEE Conference on Computer Vision and Pattern Recognition, pp. 248–255. IEEE (2009)
8. Goodfellow, I., et al.: Generative adversarial nets. In: Advances in Neural Information Processing Systems 27 (2014)
9. Gu, Q., Wang, G., Chiu, M.T., Tai, Y.W., Tang, C.K.: LADN: local adversarial disentangling network for facial makeup and de-makeup. In: Proceedings of the IEEE/CVF International Conference on Computer Vision, pp. 10481–10490 (2019)

10. Heusel, M., Ramsauer, H., Unterthiner, T., Nessler, B., Hochreiter, S.: GANs trained by a two time-scale update rule converge to a local Nash equilibrium. In: Advances in Neural Information Processing Systems 30 (2017)

11. Jiang, W., et al.: PSGAN: pose and expression robust spatial-aware GAN for customizable makeup transfer. In: Proceedings of the IEEE/CVF Conference on Computer Vision and Pattern Recognition, pp. 5194–5202 (2020)

12. Kingma, D.P., Ba, J.: Adam: a method for stochastic optimization. arXiv preprint arXiv:1412.6980 (2014)

13. Kingma, D.P., Dhariwal, P.: Glow: generative flow with invertible 1x1 convolutions. arXiv preprint arXiv:1807.03039 (2018)

14. Li, T., et al.: BeautyGAN: instance-level facial makeup transfer with deep generative adversarial network. In: Proceedings of the 26th ACM International Conference on Multimedia, pp. 645–653 (2018)

15. Liu, S., et al.: PSGAN++: robust detail-preserving makeup transfer and removal. IEEE Trans. Pattern Anal. Mach. Intell. **44**, 8538–8551 (2021)

16. Liu, W., Chen, W., Shen, L.: Translate the facial regions you like using region-wise normalization. arXiv preprint arXiv:2007.14615 (2020)

17. Liu, W., Chen, W., Yang, Z., Shen, L.: Translate the facial regions you like using self-adaptive region translation. In: Proceedings of the AAAI Conference on Artificial Intelligence, vol. 35, pp. 2180–2188 (2021)

18. Liu, W., Chen, W., Zhu, Y., Shen, L.: SatGAN: augmenting age biased dataset for cross-age face recognition. In: 2020 25th International Conference on Pattern Recognition (ICPR), pp. 1368–1375. IEEE (2021)

19. Nguyen, T., Tran, A.T., Hoai, M.: Lipstick ain't enough: beyond color matching for in-the-wild makeup transfer. In: Proceedings of the IEEE/CVF Conference on Computer Vision and Pattern Recognition, pp. 13305–13314 (2021)

20. Paszke, A., et al.: PyTorch: an imperative style, high-performance deep learning library. Adv. Neural. Inf. Process. Syst. **32**, 8026–8037 (2019)

21. Simonyan, K., Zisserman, A.: Very deep convolutional networks for large-scale image recognition. arXiv preprint arXiv:1409.1556 (2014)

22. Vaswani, A., et al.: Attention is all you need. In: Advances in Neural Information Processing Systems, pp. 5998–6008 (2017)

23. Wang, Z., Bovik, A.C., Sheikh, H.R., Simoncelli, E.P.: Image quality assessment: from error visibility to structural similarity. IEEE Trans. Image Process. **13**(4), 600–612 (2004)

24. Xie, J., Luo, C., Zhu, X., Jin, Z., Lu, W., Shen, L.: Online refinement of low-level feature based activation map for weakly supervised object localization. In: Proceedings of the IEEE/CVF International Conference on Computer Vision, pp. 132–141 (2021)

25. Zhang, H., Chen, W., He, H., Jin, Y.: Disentangled makeup transfer with generative adversarial network. arXiv preprint arXiv:1907.01144 (2019)

26. Zhang, X., Zhu, Y., Chen, W., Liu, W., Shen, L.: Gated switchGAN for multi-domain facial image translation. IEEE Trans. Multimedia **24**, 1990–2003 (2021)

27. Zhao, X., Chen, J., Liu, M., Ye, K., Shen, L.: Multi-scale attention-based feature pyramid networks for object detection. In: Peng, Y., Hu, S.-M., Gabbouj, M., Zhou, K., Elad, M., Xu, K. (eds.) ICIG 2021. LNCS, vol. 12888, pp. 405–417. Springer, Cham (2021). https://doi.org/10.1007/978-3-030-87355-4_34

28. Zhu, J.Y., Park, T., Isola, P., Efros, A.A.: Unpaired image-to-image translation using cycle-consistent adversarial networks. In: Proceedings of the IEEE International Conference on Computer Vision, pp. 2223–2232 (2017)

SinNeRF: Training Neural Radiance Fields on Complex Scenes from a Single Image

Dejia Xu[1(✉)], Yifan Jiang[1], Peihao Wang[1], Zhiwen Fan[1], Humphrey Shi[2,3,4], and Zhangyang Wang[1]

[1] The University of Texas at Austin, Austin, USA
{dejia,atlaswang}@utexas.edu
[2] UIUC, Champaign, USA
[3] University of Oregon, Eugene, USA
[4] Picsart AI Research, New York, USA

Abstract. Despite the rapid development of Neural Radiance Field (NeRF), the necessity of dense covers largely prohibits its wider applications. While several recent works have attempted to address this issue, they either operate with sparse views (yet still, a few of them) or on simple objects/scenes. In this work, we consider a more ambitious task: training neural radiance field, over realistically complex visual scenes, by "looking only once", i.e., using only a **single** view. To attain this goal, we present a *Single View NeRF* (**SinNeRF**) framework consisting of thoughtfully designed semantic and geometry regularizations. Specifically, SinNeRF constructs a semi-supervised learning process, where we introduce and propagate geometry pseudo labels and semantic pseudo labels to guide the progressive training process. Extensive experiments are conducted on complex scene benchmarks, including NeRF synthetic dataset, Local Light Field Fusion dataset, and DTU dataset. We show that even whouzt pre-training on multi-view datasets, SinNeRF can yield photo-realistic novel-view synthesis results. Under the single image setting, SinNeRF significantly outperforms the current state-of-the-art NeRF baselines in all cases. Project page: https://vita-group.github.io/SinNeRF/.

1 Introduction

Synthesizing photo-realistic images has been one of the most essential goals in the area of computer vision. Recently, the field of novel view synthesis has gained tremendous popularity with the success of coordinate-based neural networks. Neural radiance field (NeRF) [31], as an effective scene representation, has prevailed among image-based rendering approaches.

D. Xu and Y. Jiang—Equal contribution.

Supplementary Information The online version contains supplementary material available at https://doi.org/10.1007/978-3-031-20047-2_42.

S. Avidan et al. (Eds.): ECCV 2022, LNCS 13682, pp. 736–753, 2022.
https://doi.org/10.1007/978-3-031-20047-2_42

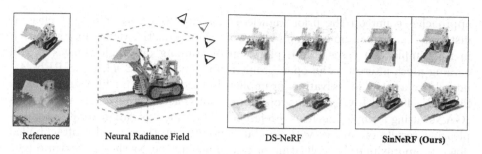

Reference   Neural Radiance Field   DS-NeRF   SinNeRF (Ours)

Fig. 1. Given only a single reference view as input, our novel semi-supervised framework effectively trains a neural radiance field. In contrast, previous method [9] shows inconsistent geometry when synthesizing novel views.

Despite its great success, NeRF is impeded by the stringent requirement of the dense views captured from different angles and the corresponding camera poses. As has been implied by recent literature [34], training a neural radiance field without sufficient views will end up with drastic performance degradation, including incorrect geometry and blurry appearance. Meanwhile, it could be challenging or even infeasible in real-world scenarios to collect a sufficiently dense coverage of views for specific applications such as AR/VR or autonomous driving. Motivated by this, many researchers attempt to address this fragility in the sparse view setting [6,9,21,24,34,62]. One line of research [6,62] aggregates available learning priors from adequate pre-training on large-scale datasets. Other approaches propose various regularizations on color and geometry of different views [9,21,24,34]. However, most aforementioned works still necessitate multiple view inputs, with a minimum requirement of three views [9,34] (Fig. 1).

In contrast to previous works, we push the setting of sparse views to the extreme by training a neural radiance field on only one single view. To our best knowledge, few efforts have been made to explore this circumstance before. PixelNeRF [62] takes the first attempt by pre-training a feature extractor on a large-scale dataset. Although they report impressive results on simple objects (e.g., ShapeNet dataset [5]), their performance on complex scenes [22] is less than satisfactory. Others [25,41] demonstrate good performance on novel-view synthesis. However, their platforms are based on other techniques (e.g., multiplane images). Different from those previous research, our work aims at training the neural radiance field from scratch, without bells and whistles, to generate photo-realistic novel views of complex scenes.

Nevertheless, training a neural radiance field with a single image is frustratingly challenging. First and foremost, reconstructing an accurate 3D shape from a single image meets several hurdles. Previous research has addressed reconstructing different types of objects from a single image [37,56]. Especially, Pixel2Mesh [56] proposes to reconstruct the 3D shape from a single image and expressed it in a triangular mesh. PIFu [37] adopts a 3D occupancy field to recover high-resolution surfaces of humans. NID [57] utilizes a pre-trained dictionary to acquire implicit fields from sparse measurements. However, all these approaches count on the prior knowledge specific to a certain object class or instance. Thus it can not work for complex scene reconstruction. Moreover, even in the simpler 2D cases, the exploration of training on single images is still gaining much interest as an open problem up to now [40,42,44,51]. SIREN [44] introduces a periodic activation for implicit functions to better fit a single image. SinGAN [40] and InGAN [42] propose to train generative adversarial networks (GANs) using a single image as a reference. Their models can generate visually-pleasing results of images with similar content, but their results often boiled down to approximately replicating or re-composing the patches or textural patterns from the given images, and hence cannot serve the purpose of modeling sophisticated 3D view transformations.

Our inspiration draws from generating pseudo labels according to the available single view, which enables us to design a semi-supervised training strategy to constrain the learned radiance field. Specifically, we design two categories of pseudo labels to capture complementary hidden information. The first one focuses on the geometry of the radiance field, where we reproject depth information between reference view and unseen views through image warping [19], thus ensuring multi-view geometry consistency of our trained radiance field. The second one focuses on the semantic fidelity of the unseen views. We utilize a discriminator and a pre-trained Vision Transformer (ViT [10]) to constrain the unseen views: the former helps improve each unseen view's local textures, while the latter focuses on the perceptual quality of their global structures.

Our main contributions can be summarized as follows:

- We propose SinNeRF, a novel semi-supervised framework to train a neural radiance field in complex scenes effectively, using a single reference view.
- We introduce and propagate geometry and semantic pseudo labels to jointly guide the progressive training process. The former is inspired by image warping to ensure multi-view geometry consistency, and the latter enforces the perceptual quality of local textures as well as global structures.
- We conduct extensive experiments on complex scene benchmarks and show that SinNeRF can yield photo-realistic novel-view synthesis results without bells and whistles. Under the single image setting, SinNeRF significantly outperforms state-of-the-art NeRF baselines in all cases.

2   Related Works

2.1   Neural Radiance Field

Neural Radiance Fields (NeRFs) [31] have demonstrated encouraging progress for view synthesis by learning an implicit neural scene representation. Since its origin, tremendous efforts have been made to improve its quality [2,3,7,17, 46,52], speed [15,32,36,47], artistic effects [13,20,53], and generalization ability [6,29,58,62]. Specifically, Barron et al. [2] propose to cast a conical frustum instead of a single ray for the purpose of anti-aliasing. Mip-NeRF 360 [3] further extends it to the unbounded scenes with efficient parameterization. KiloN-eRF [36] speeds up NeRF by adopting thousands of tiny MLPs. MVSNeRF [6] extracts a 3D cost volume [16,60] and renders high-quality images from novel viewpoints on unseen scenes. The most related works to SinNeRF target the sparse view setting [9,21,34,62] Especially, DS-NeRF [9] adopts additional depth supervision to improve the reconstruction quality. RegNeRF [34] proposes a normalizing flow and depth smoothness regularization. DietNeRF [21] utilizes the CLIP embeddings [35] to add semantic constraints for unseen views. However, the CLIP embeddings can only be obtained from low-resolution inputs due to memory issues. Thus it struggles to obtain texture details. Meanwhile, these methods can only perform well on at least two or three input views. Pixel-NeRF [62] utilizes a ConvNets encoder to extract context information by large-scale pre-training, and successfully renders novel views from a single input. However, it can only work on simple objects (e.g., ShapeNet [5]) while the results on complex scenes remain unknown. In our work, we focus on the challenging setting of using only one single view without any pre-training on multi-view datasets.

2.2 Single View 3D Reconstruction

Single view 3D reconstruction is a long-standing problem. Early methods use shape-from-shading [11] or adopt texture [26] and defocus [14] cues. These techniques rely on the existing regions of the images using a depth cue. More recent approaches hallucinate the invisible parts using learned priors. Johnston et al. [23] adopt an inverse discrete cosine transform decoder. Fan et al. [12] directly regresses the point clouds. Wu et al. [59] learns a mapping from input images to 2.5D sketches and maps the intermediate representations to the final 3D shapes. However, very few datasets are available for 3D annotation, and most of these methods use ShapeNet [5] which contains objects of simple shapes. There are also attempts to reconstruct the 3D shape of specific objects (e.g. humans). PiFU [37] utilizes a 3D occupancy field to recover the 3D geometry of clothed humans. DeepHuman [65] adopts an image-guided volume-to-volume translation framework. NormalGAN [55] conditions a generative adversarial network on the normal maps of the reference view.

Another line of research focuses on learning a 3D representation for view synthesis. Explicit representations involve volumetric representations [18,39,45], layer depth images (LDI) [41,49], and multiplane images (MPI) [30]. Implicit representations use coordinate-based networks to train a neural scene representation on one single view. PixelNeRF [62] takes the first attempt by utilizing a pre-trained feature extractor on large-scale dataset. Their results on complex scenes are less than satisfactory compared to their impressive results on simple objects from ShapeNet [5]. GRF [48] proposes a generative radiance field modeling 3D geometries by projecting the features of 2D images to 3D points. MINE [25] learns a continuous depth MPI and uses volumetric rendering to synthesize novel views. Our work is fundamentally different from existing works in these ways: 1) we train a neural scene representation from scratch without relying on pre-trained feature extractors or multi-plane images; 2) we conduct experiments on complex 3D environments and yield photo-realistic rendered results.

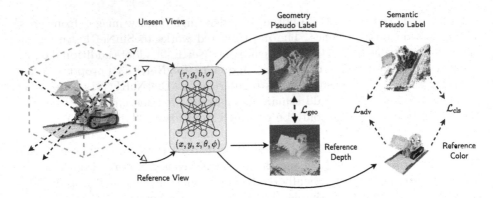

Fig. 2. An overview of our SinNeRF, where we synthesize patches from the reference view and unseen views. We train this semi-supervised framework via ground truth color and depth labels of the reference view and pseudo labels on unseen views. We use image warping to obtain geometry pseudo labels and utilize adversarial training as well as a pre-trained ViT for semantic pseudo labels.

2.3 Single Image Training

Single image training is a field of great interest in 2D computer vision. Sin-GAN [40] and InGAN [42] propose a generative adversarial network trained using a single image as reference. Their models can generate visually-pleasing results containing similar content of the image, but the diversity is limited, and their results often copy-paste different patches from the original image. Dmitry *et al.* [51] investigate the deep image prior of convolutional networks and show excellent results in image restoration. More recently, SIREN [44] proposes a periodic activation for implicit functions to fit a single image by supervising the gradients of networks. In this work, we make further attempts to adversarially train a radiance field using a single image (Fig. 2).

3 Method

3.1 Overview

The setting of only one single view available is challenging for NeRF, as training directly on the available view leads to overfitting on the reference view and results in a collapsed neural radiance field. To tackle this problem, we build our SinNeRF as a semi-supervised framework to provide necessary constraints on unseen views. We treat the reference view with RGB and available depth as the labeled set, while the unseen views are considered as the unlabeled set. To help the neural radiance field render reasonable results on the unseen views, we introduce two types of supervision signals from the perspective of geometry and semantic constraints. We will first introduce the preliminary of neural radiance field and semi-supervised learning framework, then the progressive training strategies.

3.2   Preliminary

Neural Radiance Fields (NeRFs) [31] synthesize images sampling 5D coordinates (location (x, y, z) and viewing direction (θ, ϕ)) along camera rays, map them to color (r, g, b) and volume density σ. Mildenhall *et al.* [31] first propose to use coordinate-based multi-layer perception networks (MLPs) to parameterize this function and then use volumetric rendering techniques to alpha composite the values at each location and obtain the final rendered images.

Given a pixel $r(t) = o + td$, where o is the camera origin and d is the ray direction, pixel's predicted color is defined as follows:

$$\hat{C}(r) = \int_{t_n}^{t_f} T(t)\sigma(r(t))c(r(t), d)dt, \tag{1}$$

where $T(t) = \exp\left(-\int_{t_n}^{t} \sigma(r(s))ds\right)$, $\sigma(\cdot)$ and $c(\cdot,)$ are densities and color predictions from the network. Due to the computational cost, the continuous integral is numerically estimated using quadrature [31]. NeRF [31] optimize the radiance field by minimizing the mean squared error between rendered color and the ground truth color,

$$\mathcal{L}_{\text{pix}} = \sum_{r \in R_i} ||(C(r) - \hat{C}(r))||^2, \tag{2}$$

where R_i is the set of input rays during training.

3.3   Geometry Pseudo Label

Directly overfitting on the reference images leads to a corrupted neural radiance field collapsing towards the provided views. The issue is much more severe when there is only one training image. Without multi-view supervision, NeRF is not able to learn the inherent geometry of the scene and thus fails to build a view-consistent representation. Similar to previous works [61] to reconstruct a 3D shape from a single image, we start by adopting the depth prior to reconstructing reasonable 3D geometry. As suggested by [9], adding another depth supervision can significantly improve the learned geometry. However, since only a single training view is available in our setting, simply adopting depth supervision can not produce a reasonable 3D shape, as shown in Fig. 3.

To best utilize the available information in the reference view, we propose to propagate it to other views through image warping [19]. For pixel $p_i(x_i, y_i)$ in reference view I_{ref}, the corresponding pixel $p_j(x_j, y_j)$ in the j-th unseen view I_{unseen} can be formulated as:

$$p_j = K_{\text{unseen}}T(K_{\text{ref}}^{-1}Z_i p_i), \tag{3}$$

where Z_i is the available depth of reference view, T refers to the relationship between camera extrinsic matrices from I_{ref} to I_{unseen}, and K_{ref} and K_{unseen} refer to the camera intrinsic matrices. We further adopt the Painter's Algorithm [33]when multiple points in the reference view are projected to the same point in the unseen view and select the point with the smallest depth as the warping result.

Through image warping, we then obtain the depth map of an unseen view, which further serves as the pseudo ground truth label. Nevertheless, there is still an unavoidable gap between this pseudo ground truth and its real correspondence, since small misalignment in the predicted depth map can cause large errors when projected to other views. Moreover, it is quite common that the projected results contain some uncertain regions due to the occlusion. To regularize the uncertain regions in the warped results, we utilize the self-supervised inverse depth smoothness loss [54], which uses the second-order gradients of the RGB pixel value to encourage the smoothness of the predicted depths:

$$\mathcal{L}_{\text{smooth}}\left(d_i\right) = e^{-\nabla^2 \mathcal{I}(\mathbf{x}_i)}\left(\left|\partial_{xx}d_i\right| + \left|\partial_{xy}d_i\right| + \left|\partial_{yy}d_i\right|\right), \tag{4}$$

where d_i is the depth map, $\nabla^2 \mathcal{I}(\mathbf{x}_i)$ refers to the Laplacian of pixel value at location x_i. Similar to [54], we calculate this loss on a downscaled resolution.

We also reproject the unseen views back to the reference view to enforce geometry consistency. In summary, the geometry pseudo label is utilized as follows,

$$\mathcal{L}_{\text{geo}} = \mathcal{L}_1(d_1, f(d_2)) + \mathcal{L}_1(f(d_1), d_2) + \lambda_4 \mathcal{L}_{\text{smooth}}, \tag{5}$$

where λ_4 is empirically set to be 0.1 in all our experiments, d_1 and d_2 refer to the depths of two views, and $f(\cdot)$ refers to the image warping result of the other view using the current view's depth information.

3.4   Semantic Pseudo Label

Since the rendered color and texture might still be inconstant across different views, image warping can only project depth information. We propose to adopt semantic pseudo labels to regularize the learned appearance representation. Unlike the geometry pseudo labels, where we enforce the consistency in 3D space, semantic pseudo labels are adopted to regularize the 2D image fidelity. Concretely speaking, we introduce a local texture guidance loss implemented by adversarial learning, and a global structure prior supported by a pre-trained ViT network. The two complementary guidances collaboratively help SinNeRF render visually-pleasing results in each view.

Local Texture Guidance. The local texture guidance is implemented via a patch discriminator. The outputs from NeRF are considered as fake samples, and the patches randomly cropped from the reference view are regarded as real samples. Since the available training data are too limited, the discriminator tends to memorize the entire training set. To overcome this issue, we adopt differentiable augmentation [64] for our discriminator to improve its data efficiency:

$$\begin{aligned}
\mathcal{L}_{\text{D}} &= \mathbb{E}_{\boldsymbol{x} \sim p_{\text{data}}(\boldsymbol{x})}\left[f_D(-D(T(\boldsymbol{x})))\right] + \mathbb{E}_{\boldsymbol{z} \sim p(\boldsymbol{z})}\left[f_D(D(T(G(\boldsymbol{z}))))\right], \\
\mathcal{L}_{\text{G}} &= \mathbb{E}_{\boldsymbol{z} \sim p(\boldsymbol{z})}\left[f_G(-D(T(G(\boldsymbol{z}))))\right], \\
\mathcal{L}_{\text{adv}} &= \mathcal{L}_{\text{D}} + \mathcal{L}_{\text{G}},
\end{aligned} \tag{6}$$

where T refers to the augmentation applied on both real and fake samples. We train the GAN framework using Hinge loss [27], so $f_D(x) = \max(0, 1 + x)$ and $f_G(x) = x$. The architecture of our discriminator is a cascade of convolutional layers. More details about the discriminator design is provided in the supplementary materials.

Global Structure Prior. Vision transformers (ViT) have been proven to be an expressive semantic prior, even between images with misalignment [1,50]. Similar to [21], we propose to adopt a pre-trained ViT for global structure guidance, which enforces semantic consistency between unseen views and the reference view. Although there exists pixel-wise misalignment between the views, we observe that the extracted representation of ViT is robust to this misalignment and provides supervision at the semantic level. Intuitively, this is because the content and style of the two views are similar, and a deep network is capable of learning invariant representation.

Here we adopt DINO-ViT [4], a self-supervised vision transformer trained on ImageNet [8] dataset. Unlike DietNeRF [21] which utilizes a CLIP-ViT [35] and adopts its projected images embeddings as features, we directly extract the [CLS] token from DINO-ViT's output. This approach is more straightforward since the [CLS] token serves as a representation of an entire image [10]. The intuition also aligns with the recent findings of [50], where ViT architecture can capture semantic appearance after self-supervised pre-training. We calculate L_2 distance between the extracted features,

$$\mathcal{L}_{\text{cls}} = ||f_{\text{vit}}(A) - f_{\text{vit}}(B)||^2 \tag{7}$$

where $f_{\text{vit}}(\cdot)$ refers to the extracted [CLS] tokens. A and B are patches from the reference view and an unseen view, respectively.

3.5 Progressive Training Strategy

To stabilize the training of the GAN framework, we apply a progressive sampling strategy to the training of a single view neural radiance field.

Progressive Strided Ray Sampling: We start from utilizing a stride sampling [38] of ray generation and progressively reduce the stride size during training. This design enables our SinNeRF to cover a much larger region with a limited amount of rays. Specifically, the $K \times K$ patch P of stride s containing point (u, v) is defined as a set of 2D image coordinates,

$$\mathcal{P}(u, v, s) = \{(u + sx, v + sy) \mid x, y \in \{0, \ldots, K\}\}. \tag{8}$$

Under this circumstance, the NeRF is able to generate a $K \times K$ patch representing a large aspect of the scene. During training, we randomly sample two patches in each iteration, with the first one from the reference view and the other one from a random unseen view. After that, the collaborative local texture guidance and global structure prior loss are applied on these patches to provide semantic guidance on the unseen views. Meanwhile, we obtain the geometry pseudo labels via image warping and add regularization on each patch's intersection with the corresponding patch's warped result. As the training goes into the latter stages, the stride s decreases so that the framework starts to focus on more local regions. Note that we randomly initialize the discriminator after reducing the stride size. This helps the discriminator focus on a fixed resolution, making the training more stable.

Progressive Gaussian Pose Sampling: After that, we propose to progressively enlarge the viewing angle during training. During training, we start at a local neighbor of the reference view and progressively rotate the camera pose more as the training proceeds. This helps the network to focus on dealing with the confident regions and stabilize training as the output image patches will have a good quality when the camera pose is only slightly different from the reference view. Specifically, we represent the distance between an unseen view and the reference view as Euler angles. Let (α, β, ϕ) denote the signed angles between the axis in the reference view's camera coordinate and the axis in the unseen views' camera coordinates. In each iteration, we sample α, β, ϕ each based on a Gaussian distribution $\mathcal{N}(0, \omega^2)$, where ω increases with more iterations.

We show the overall loss function as follows:

$$\mathcal{L}_{\text{total}} = \mathcal{L}_{\text{pix}} + \lambda_1 \mathcal{L}_{\text{geo}} + \lambda_2 \mathcal{L}_{\text{adv}} + \lambda_3 \mathcal{L}_{\text{cls}}, \tag{9}$$

where $\lambda_1, \lambda_2, \lambda_3$ are weighting factors. We anneal the loss weight during training. In the early stages where we use a large stride and the patch covers the major regions of the original image, the global structure prior is given a large weight λ_3 compared to the weight of local texture guidance λ_2. As the training proceeds, we reduce the stride to focus on reconstructing the high-frequency details. Consequently, we reduce the weight of global structure prior λ_3 and increase the weight of local texture guidance λ_2. In all our experiments, λ_1, λ_2, and λ_3 are initialized to be 8, 0.1, and 0, respectively. During the training process, we gradually decrease λ_2 to 0 and increase λ_3 to 0.1 with a linear function.

4   Experiment

4.1   Implementation Details

We use the same architecture as the original NeRF paper [31]. During training iterations, we randomly sample two patches of rays from both the reference view and a random sampled unseen view. The size of patches on NeRF synthetic (Blender) dataset, Local Light Field Fusion (LLFF) dataset, and DTU dataset are set as 64×64, 84×63, and 70×56, respectively. The rendered patches are then sent to the discriminator and DINO-ViT network, where we additionally resize its input patches to 224×224 resolution to fit the input resolution of DINO-ViT architecture. We train our framework using RAdam optimizer [28],

DS-NeRF [9]   PixelNeRF [62]   DietNeRF [21]   SinNeRF   Target Image

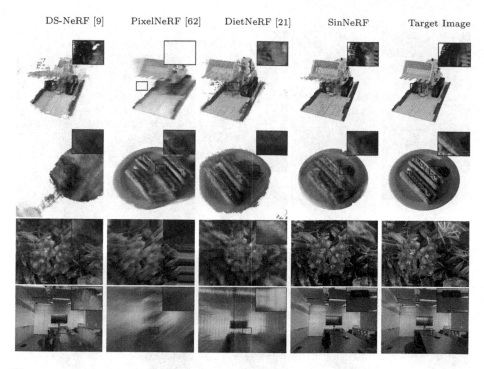

Fig. 3. Novel view synthesis results of different methods on NeRF synthetic and LLFF dataset.

with an initial learning rate of $1e - 3$. We decay the learning rate by half after every 10k iterations. The learning rate of the discriminator is kept to be 20% of the MLP's learning rate. The stride for sampling the patches starts at 6 and gradually reduces by 2 after every 10k iterations. All experiments of SinNeRF are conducted on an NVIDIA RTX A6000 GPU. The whole training process takes several hours for each scene. More implementation details and visual results are provided in the supplementary.

4.2   Evaluation Protocol

We perform experiments on NeRF synthetic dataset [31], Local Light Field Fusion (LLFF) dataset [30], and DTU dataset [22]. NeRF synthetic dataset contains complex objects with 360° view. LLFF provides complex forward-facing scenes. DTU consists of various objects placed on a table. We report metrics including PSNR, structural similarity index (SSIM), and LPIPS perceptual metric [63]. We compare our method with the state-of-the-art neural radiance field methods DietNeRF [21], PixelNeRF [62], and DS-NeRF [9]. We train DietNeRF and DS-NeRF for each scene since they are test-time optimization methods. As for PixelNeRF, we fine-tune the model on each scene before evaluation for a fair comparison.

DS-NeRF [9]   PixelNeRF [62]   DietNeRF [21]   SinNeRF   Target Image

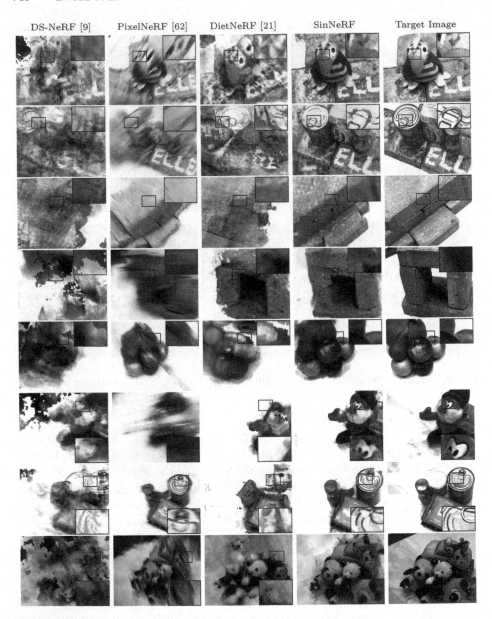

Fig. 4. Novel view synthesis results of different methods on DTU dataset.

4.3   View Synthesis on NeRF Synthetic Dataset

For NeRF synthetic dataset, each scene is rendered via Blender. Both ground truth rendered images of 100 camera poses and the original blender files are provided. We randomly select a single view as the reference view and refer to its surrounding views as unseen views. Then we use blender to render the ground

Table 1. Quantitative evaluation of our method against state-of-the-art methods on the NeRF synthetic dataset (Lego and Hotdog) and LLFF dataset (Flower and Room).

	PSNR↑				SSIM↑				LPIPS↓			
	Lego	Hotdog	Flower	Room	Lego	Hotdog	Flower	Room	Lego	Hotdog	Flower	Room
DS-NeRF	16.62	14.16	16.92	17.44	0.77	0.67	0.41	0.65	0.1682	0.2956	0.3900	0.3986
DietNeRF	15.07	16.28	13.35	15.77	0.72	0.69	0.20	0.49	0.2063	0.2633	0.7526	0.7512
PixelNeRF	14.25	16.67	13.20	12.88	0.72	0.71	0.19	0.41	0.2171	0.2381	0.6378	0.7633
SinNeRF	20.97	19.78	17.20	18.85	0.82	0.77	0.41	0.67	0.0932	0.1700	0.3724	0.3796

Table 2. Quantitative evaluation of our method against state-of-the-art methods on DTU dataset. We report average values across scenes.

	PSNR↑	SSIM↑	LPIPS↓
DS-NeRF	12.17	0.41	0.6493
DietNeRF	12.84	0.44	0.6409
PixelNeRF	12.06	0.42	0.6471
SinNeRF	16.52	0.56	0.5250

truth of the unseen views by rotating the world-to-camera matrix. Specifically, we generate 60 test set images by rotating the camera around the y-axis uniformly in $[-30°, 30°]$. The quantitative results are shown in Table 1. Our method achieves the best results both in pixel-wise error and perceptual quality.

We show the novel view synthesis results in the first two rows of Fig. 3. Each row corresponds to a fixed camera pose, and each column contains the results of a method. One can see that our method preserves the best geometry as well as perceptual quality. DS-NeRF's output contains a wrong geometry at the top of the lego. This is because DS-NeRF only utilizes supervision on the reference view and does not perform warping to other views. PixelNeRF's results contain "ghost" hotdogs since they do not explicitly regularize the geometry. Optimizing on unseen views, DietNeRF produces appealing results, but unfortunately with flaws in the novel view's geometry (e.g., the objects are no longer in the center). The results are also blurry since their CLIP embeddings are obtained at a low resolution.

4.4 View Synthesis on LLFF Dataset

For the local light field dataset, the images and the SfM results from colmap are provided. We randomly select a single view as the reference view and use its surrounding views as unseen views during training. For quantitative evaluation, we render the other views in the dataset whose ground truth images are available. We provide visual results in the last two rows of Fig. 3 and quantitative results in Table 1. Our method generates the most visually-pleasing results, while other methods tend to render obscure estimations on novel views. DS-NeRF shows realistic geometry, but the rendered images are blurry. PixelNeRF and DietNeRF

w/o $\mathcal{L}_{adv}$ w/o $\mathcal{L}_{cls}$ w/o $\mathcal{L}_{geo}$ Full Model   Target Image

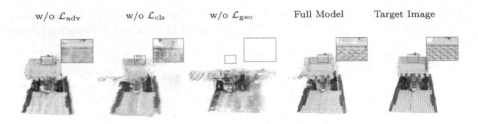

Fig. 5. Novel view synthesis from different variants of our proposed model.

Table 3. Ablation study on variants of pseudo labels. "w/o $\mathcal{L}_{adv}$" refers to the variant without the local texture guidance. "w/o $\mathcal{L}_{cls}$" refers to the variant without global structure prior. "w/o $\mathcal{L}_{geo}$" refers to removing the geometry pseudo labels and using depth supervision only on the reference view. Experiments are conducted on Lego scene.

Methods	PSNR↑	SSIM↑	LPIPS↓
w/o $\mathcal{L}_{geo}$	16.11 (-4.86)	0.74 (-0.08)	0.1919 $(+0.0987)$
w/o $\mathcal{L}_{cls}$	18.20 (-2.77)	0.76 (-0.06)	0.1348 $(+0.0146)$
w/o $\mathcal{L}_{adv}$	20.20 (-0.77)	0.79 (-0.03)	0.1306 $(+0.0294)$
Full model	**20.97**	**0.82**	**0.0932**

present good structures but wrong geometry due to their lack of local texture guidance and geometry pseudo label.

4.5 View Synthesis on DTU Dataset

For each scene in DTU dataset, 49 images and their fixed camera poses are provided. We use camera 2 as the reference view because its images contain most parts of the scene. We use 10 nearby cameras from the dataset as unseen views during training. Since the ground truth of these nearby views are provided, we render these views for quantitative evaluation. We provide visual results in Fig. 4 and quantitative results in Table 2. Our method demonstrates the most visually-pleasing results as well as the best quantitative performance. DS-NeRF generates realistic geometry, but the results contain severe artifacts. PixelNeRF and DietNeRF obtain a pleasing overall looking but suffer from wrong geometry.

4.6 Ablation Study

Variants of Pseudo Labels. In this section, we study the effectiveness of each component of our proposed method. We evaluate on the lego scene and provide the results in Fig. 5 and Table 3. Removing adversarial training leads to blurry artifacts. This is because the $\mathcal{L}_{cls}$ is only beneficial when the extracted patch has a receptive field large enough to cover the major structure of the image. The

Table 4. Ablation study on different choices of the global structure prior. Here "content loss" refers to calculating L_1 loss on the feature space of pretrained VGG-16 network [43]. "style loss" refers to minimizing gram matrix from the output of pre-trained VGG-16 network [43]. "self-similarity loss" [50] refers to calculating the self-similarity of the keys in ViT's self-attention layer. The $[CLS]$ denotes our proposed one, where we adopt the $[CLS]$ token from pretrained DINO-ViT approaches. $\mathcal{L}_{\text{cls}}$. Experiments are conducted on Lego scene.

	PSNR↑	SSIM↑	LPIPS↓
Style	15.49 (-5.48)	0.73 (-0.09)	0.2046 $(+0.1114)$
Self-similarity	18.67 (-2.30)	0.81 (-0.01)	0.1075 $(+0.0143)$
Content	19.20 (-1.76)	0.80 (-0.02)	0.1138 $(+0.0206)$
$[CLS]$(ours)	**20.97**	**0.82**	**0.0932**

variant without global structure prior contains wrong structure in novel views, which is due to the missing guidance on the overall semantic structure. Although there are still geometry pseudo labels available, the projected depth information only provides partial guidance and leaves the occluded regions unconstrained. Finally, the variant without geometry pseudo labels suffers from wrong geometry. There is only depth supervision of the reference view, and the unseen views are not properly regularized.

Different Choices of the Global Structure Prior. We study different model choices for our global structure prior in this section. The global structure prior is designed to focus on the overall semantic consistency between the unseen views and the reference view regardless of the pixel misalignment. Following this direction, we evaluate different architectures including both the ConvNets and ViTs. As shown in Table 4, we evaluate different kinds of the global structure prior by conducting experiments on the "lego" scene, including adopting the content, style, and self-similarity losses from a pre-trained VGG network between unseen views and reference view or minimizing the distance between the outputs of $[CLS]$ token from DINO-ViT [4] architecture. The quantitative results demonstrate that DINO-ViT shows a stronger global structure prior, suggesting that it is more robust to pixel misalignment.

5   Conclusions

We present SinNeRF, a framework to train a neural radiance field on a single view from a complex scene. SinNeRF is based on a semi-supervised framework, where geometry pseudo label and semantic pseudo label are synthesized to stabilize the training process. Comprehensive experiments are conducted on complex scene datasets, including NeRF synthetic dataset, Local Light Field Fusion (LLFF) dataset, and DTU dataset, where SinNeRF outperforms the current state-of-the-art NeRF frameworks. However, similar to most NeRF approaches, one limitation of SinNeRF is the training efficiency issue, which could be one of our future directions to explore further.

References

1. Amir, S., Gandelsman, Y., Bagon, S., Dekel, T.: Deep ViT features as dense visual descriptors. arXiv preprint arXiv:2112.05814 (2021)
2. Barron, J.T., Mildenhall, B., Tancik, M., Hedman, P., Martin-Brualla, R., Srinivasan, P.P.: Mip-NeRF: a multiscale representation for anti-aliasing neural radiance fields. In: Proceedings of the IEEE/CVF International Conference on Computer Vision, pp. 5855–5864 (2021)
3. Barron, J.T., Mildenhall, B., Verbin, D., Srinivasan, P.P., Hedman, P.: Mip-NeRF 360: unbounded anti-aliased neural radiance fields. arXiv preprint arXiv:2111.12077 (2021)
4. Caron, M., et al.: Emerging properties in self-supervised vision transformers. In: Proceedings of the IEEE/CVF International Conference on Computer Vision, pp. 9650–9660 (2021)
5. Chang, A.X., et al.: ShapeNet: an information-rich 3d model repository. arXiv preprint arXiv:1512.03012 (2015)
6. Chen, A., et al.: MVSNeRF: fast generalizable radiance field reconstruction from multi-view stereo. In: Proceedings of the IEEE/CVF International Conference on Computer Vision, pp. 14124–14133 (2021)
7. Chen, T., Wang, P., Fan, Z., Wang, Z.: Aug-NeRF: training stronger neural radiance fields with triple-level physically-grounded augmentations. In: Proceedings of the IEEE/CVF Conference on Computer Vision and Pattern Recognition, pp. 15191–15202 (2022)
8. Deng, J., Dong, W., Socher, R., Li, L.J., Li, K., Fei-Fei, L.: ImageNet: a large-scale hierarchical image database. In: 2009 IEEE Conference on Computer Vision and Pattern Recognition, pp. 248–255. IEEE (2009)
9. Deng, K., Liu, A., Zhu, J.Y., Ramanan, D.: Depth-supervised NeRF: fewer views and faster training for free. arXiv preprint arXiv:2107.02791 (2021)
10. Dosovitskiy, A., et al.: An image is worth 16x16 words: transformers for image recognition at scale. arXiv preprint arXiv:2010.11929 (2020)
11. Durou, J.D., Falcone, M., Sagona, M.: Numerical methods for shape-from-shading: a new survey with benchmarks. Comput. Vis. Image Underst. **109**(1), 22–43 (2008)
12. Fan, H., Su, H., Guibas, L.J.: A point set generation network for 3d object reconstruction from a single image. In: Proceedings of the IEEE Conference on Computer Vision and Pattern Recognition, pp. 605–613 (2017)
13. Fan, Z., Jiang, Y., Wang, P., Gong, X., Xu, D., Wang, Z.: Unified implicit neural stylization. arXiv preprint arXiv:2204.01943 (2022)
14. Favaro, P., Soatto, S.: A geometric approach to shape from defocus. IEEE Trans. Pattern Anal. Mach. Intell. **27**(3), 406–417 (2005)
15. Fridovich-Keil, S., Yu, A., Tancik, M., Chen, Q., Recht, B., Kanazawa, A.: Plenoxels: radiance fields without neural networks. In: Proceedings of the IEEE/CVF Conference on Computer Vision and Pattern Recognition, pp. 5501–5510 (2022)
16. Gu, X., Fan, Z., Zhu, S., Dai, Z., Tan, F., Tan, P.: Cascade cost volume for high-resolution multi-view stereo and stereo matching. In: Proceedings of the IEEE/CVF Conference on Computer Vision and Pattern Recognition, pp. 2495–2504 (2020)

17. Guo, Y.C., Kang, D., Bao, L., He, Y., Zhang, S.H.: NeRFReN: neural radiance fields with reflections. In: Proceedings of the IEEE/CVF Conference on Computer Vision and Pattern Recognition, pp. 18409–18418 (2022)
18. Henzler, P., Mitra, N.J., Ritschel, T.: Learning a neural 3d texture space from 2d exemplars. In: Proceedings of the IEEE/CVF Conference on Computer Vision and Pattern Recognition, pp. 8356–8364 (2020)
19. Huang, B., Yi, H., Huang, C., He, Y., Liu, J., Liu, X.: M3VSNet: unsupervised multi-metric multi-view stereo network. In: 2021 IEEE International Conference on Image Processing (ICIP), pp. 3163–3167. IEEE (2021)
20. Jain, A., Mildenhall, B., Barron, J.T., Abbeel, P., Poole, B.: Zero-shot text-guided object generation with dream fields. In: Proceedings of the IEEE/CVF Conference on Computer Vision and Pattern Recognition, pp. 867–876 (2022)
21. Jain, A., Tancik, M., Abbeel, P.: Putting NeRF on a diet: semantically consistent few-shot view synthesis. In: Proceedings of the IEEE/CVF International Conference on Computer Vision, pp. 5885–5894 (2021)
22. Jensen, R., Dahl, A., Vogiatzis, G., Tola, E., Aanæs, H.: Large scale multi-view stereopsis evaluation. In: Proceedings of the IEEE Conference on Computer Vision and Pattern Recognition, pp. 406–413 (2014)
23. Johnston, A., Garg, R., Carneiro, G., Reid, I., van den Hengel, A.: Scaling CNNs for high resolution volumetric reconstruction from a single image. In: Proceedings of the IEEE International Conference on Computer Vision Workshops, pp. 939–948 (2017)
24. Kim, M., Seo, S., Han, B.: InfoNeRF: ray entropy minimization for few-shot neural volume rendering. arXiv preprint arXiv:2112.15399 (2021)
25. Li, J., Feng, Z., She, Q., Ding, H., Wang, C., Lee, G.H.: MINE: towards continuous depth MPI with nerf for novel view synthesis. In: Proceedings of the IEEE/CVF International Conference on Computer Vision, pp. 12578–12588 (2021)
26. Li, Z., Snavely, N.: MegaDepth: learning single-view depth prediction from internet photos. In: Proceedings of the IEEE Conference on Computer Vision and Pattern Recognition, pp. 2041–2050 (2018)
27. Lim, J.H., Ye, J.C.: Geometric GAN. arXiv preprint arXiv:1705.02894 (2017)
28. Liu, L., et al.: On the variance of the adaptive learning rate and beyond. In: Proceedings of the Eighth International Conference on Learning Representations (ICLR 2020), April 2020
29. Liu, Y., et al.: Neural rays for occlusion-aware image-based rendering. In: Proceedings of the IEEE/CVF Conference on Computer Vision and Pattern Recognition, pp. 7824–7833 (2022)
30. Mildenhall, B., et al.: Local light field fusion: practical view synthesis with prescriptive sampling guidelines. ACM Trans. Graph. (TOG) **38**(4), 1–14 (2019)
31. Mildenhall, B., Srinivasan, P.P., Tancik, M., Barron, J.T., Ramamoorthi, R., Ng, R.: NeRF: representing scenes as neural radiance fields for view synthesis. In: Vedaldi, A., Bischof, H., Brox, T., Frahm, J.-M. (eds.) ECCV 2020. LNCS, vol. 12346, pp. 405–421. Springer, Cham (2020). https://doi.org/10.1007/978-3-030-58452-8_24
32. Müller, T., Evans, A., Schied, C., Keller, A.: Instant neural graphics primitives with a multiresolution hash encoding. arXiv preprint arXiv:2201.05989 (2022)
33. Newell, M.E., Newell, R., Sancha, T.L.: A solution to the hidden surface problem. In: Proceedings of the ACM Annual Conference, vol. 1, pp. 443–450 (1972)
34. Niemeyer, M., Barron, J.T., Mildenhall, B., Sajjadi, M.S., Geiger, A., Radwan, N.: RegNeRF: regularizing neural radiance fields for view synthesis from sparse inputs. arXiv preprint arXiv:2112.00724 (2021)

35. Radford, A., et al.: Learning transferable visual models from natural language supervision. In: International Conference on Machine Learning, pp. 8748–8763. PMLR (2021)
36. Reiser, C., Peng, S., Liao, Y., Geiger, A.: KiloNeRF: speeding up neural radiance fields with thousands of tiny MLPs. In: Proceedings of the IEEE/CVF International Conference on Computer Vision, pp. 14335–14345 (2021)
37. Saito, S., Huang, Z., Natsume, R., Morishima, S., Kanazawa, A., Li, H.: PIFu: pixel-aligned implicit function for high-resolution clothed human digitization. In: Proceedings of the IEEE/CVF International Conference on Computer Vision, pp. 2304–2314 (2019)
38. Schwarz, K., Liao, Y., Niemeyer, M., Geiger, A.: GRAF: generative radiance fields for 3d-aware image synthesis. Adv. Neural. Inf. Process. Syst. **33**, 20154–20166 (2020)
39. Seitz, S.M., Dyer, C.R.: Photorealistic scene reconstruction by voxel coloring. Int. J. Comput. Vision **35**(2), 151–173 (1999)
40. Shaham, T.R., Dekel, T., Michaeli, T.: SinGAN: learning a generative model from a single natural image. In: Proceedings of the IEEE/CVF International Conference on Computer Vision, pp. 4570–4580 (2019)
41. Shih, M.L., Su, S.Y., Kopf, J., Huang, J.B.: 3d photography using context-aware layered depth inpainting. In: Proceedings of the IEEE/CVF Conference on Computer Vision and Pattern Recognition, pp. 8028–8038 (2020)
42. Shocher, A., Bagon, S., Isola, P., Irani, M.: InGAN: capturing and remapping the "DNA" of a natural image. arXiv preprint arXiv:1812.00231 (2018)
43. Simonyan, K., Zisserman, A.: Very deep convolutional networks for large-scale image recognition. arXiv preprint arXiv:1409.1556 (2014)
44. Sitzmann, V., Martel, J., Bergman, A., Lindell, D., Wetzstein, G.: Implicit neural representations with periodic activation functions. Adv. Neural. Inf. Process. Syst. **33**, 7462–7473 (2020)
45. Sitzmann, V., Thies, J., Heide, F., Nießner, M., Wetzstein, G., Zollhofer, M.: DeepVoxels: learning persistent 3D feature embeddings. In: Proceedings of the IEEE/CVF Conference on Computer Vision and Pattern Recognition, pp. 2437–2446 (2019)
46. Suhail, M., Esteves, C., Sigal, L., Makadia, A.: Light field neural rendering. In: Proceedings of the IEEE/CVF Conference on Computer Vision and Pattern Recognition, pp. 8269–8279 (2022)
47. Sun, C., Sun, M., Chen, H.T.: Direct voxel grid optimization: super-fast convergence for radiance fields reconstruction. In: Proceedings of the IEEE/CVF Conference on Computer Vision and Pattern Recognition, pp. 5459–5469 (2022)
48. Trevithick, A., Yang, B.: GRF: learning a general radiance field for 3d representation and rendering. In: Proceedings of the IEEE/CVF International Conference on Computer Vision, pp. 15182–15192 (2021)
49. Tulsiani, S., Tucker, R., Snavely, N.: Layer-structured 3D scene inference via view synthesis. In: Ferrari, V., Hebert, M., Sminchisescu, C., Weiss, Y. (eds.) ECCV 2018. LNCS, vol. 11211, pp. 311–327. Springer, Cham (2018). https://doi.org/10.1007/978-3-030-01234-2_19
50. Tumanyan, N., Bar-Tal, O., Bagon, S., Dekel, T.: Splicing ViT features for semantic appearance transfer. arXiv preprint arXiv:2201.00424 (2022)
51. Ulyanov, D., Vedaldi, A., Lempitsky, V.: Deep image prior. In: Proceedings of the IEEE Conference on Computer Vision and Pattern Recognition, pp. 9446–9454 (2018)

52. Verbin, D., Hedman, P., Mildenhall, B., Zickler, T., Barron, J.T., Srinivasan, P.P.: Ref-NeRF: structured view-dependent appearance for neural radiance fields. arXiv preprint arXiv:2112.03907 (2021)

53. Wang, C., Chai, M., He, M., Chen, D., Liao, J.: CLIP-NeRF: text-and-image driven manipulation of neural radiance fields. In: Proceedings of the IEEE/CVF Conference on Computer Vision and Pattern Recognition, pp. 3835–3844 (2022)

54. Wang, C., Buenaposada, J.M., Zhu, R., Lucey, S.: Learning depth from monocular videos using direct methods. In: Proceedings of the IEEE Conference on Computer Vision and Pattern Recognition, pp. 2022–2030 (2018)

55. Wang, L., Zhao, X., Yu, T., Wang, S., Liu, Y.: NormalGAN: learning detailed 3D human from a single RGB-D image. In: Vedaldi, A., Bischof, H., Brox, T., Frahm, J.-M. (eds.) ECCV 2020. LNCS, vol. 12365, pp. 430–446. Springer, Cham (2020). https://doi.org/10.1007/978-3-030-58565-5_26

56. Wang, N., Zhang, Y., Li, Z., Fu, Y., Liu, W., Jiang, Y.-G.: Pixel2Mesh: generating 3D mesh models from single RGB images. In: Ferrari, V., Hebert, M., Sminchisescu, C., Weiss, Y. (eds.) ECCV 2018. LNCS, vol. 11215, pp. 55–71. Springer, Cham (2018). https://doi.org/10.1007/978-3-030-01252-6_4

57. Wang, P., Fan, Z., Chen, T., Wang, Z.: Neural implicit dictionary via mixture-of-expert training. In: International Conference on Machine Learning (2022)

58. Wang, Q., et al.: IBRNet: learning multi-view image-based rendering. In: Proceedings of the IEEE/CVF Conference on Computer Vision and Pattern Recognition, pp. 4690–4699 (2021)

59. Wu, J., Wang, Y., Xue, T., Sun, X., Freeman, B., Tenenbaum, J.: MarrNet: 3D shape reconstruction via 2.5 D sketches. In: Advances in Neural Information Processing Systems 30 (2017)

60. Yao, Y., Luo, Z., Li, S., Fang, T., Quan, L.: MVSNet: depth inference for unstructured multi-view stereo. In: Ferrari, V., Hebert, M., Sminchisescu, C., Weiss, Y. (eds.) ECCV 2018. LNCS, vol. 11212, pp. 785–801. Springer, Cham (2018). https://doi.org/10.1007/978-3-030-01237-3_47

61. Yin, W., et al.: Learning to recover 3d scene shape from a single image. In: Proceedings of the IEEE/CVF Conference on Computer Vision and Pattern Recognition, pp. 204–213 (2021)

62. Yu, A., Ye, V., Tancik, M., Kanazawa, A.: pixelNeRF: neural radiance fields from one or few images. In: Proceedings of the IEEE/CVF Conference on Computer Vision and Pattern Recognition, pp. 4578–4587 (2021)

63. Zhang, R., Isola, P., Efros, A.A., Shechtman, E., Wang, O.: The unreasonable effectiveness of deep features as a perceptual metric. In: CVPR (2018)

64. Zhao, S., Liu, Z., Lin, J., Zhu, J.Y., Han, S.: Differentiable augmentation for data-efficient GAN training. In: Conference on Neural Information Processing Systems (NeurIPS) (2020)

65. Zheng, Z., Yu, T., Wei, Y., Dai, Q., Liu, Y.: DeepHuman: 3d human reconstruction from a single image. In: Proceedings of the IEEE/CVF International Conference on Computer Vision, pp. 7739–7749 (2019)

Entropy-Driven Sampling and Training Scheme for Conditional Diffusion Generation

Guangcong Zheng[1], Shengming Li[1], Hui Wang[1], Taiping Yao[2], Yang Chen[2], Shouhong Ding[2], and Xi Li[1,3,4(✉)]

[1] College of Computer Science and Technology, Zhejiang University, Hangzhou, China
{guangcongzheng,shengming22,wanghui_17,xilizju}@zju.edu.cn
[2] Youtu Lab, Tencent, Shanghai, China
{taipingyao,wizyangchen,ericshding}@tencent.com
[3] Shanghai Institute for Advanced Study, Zhejiang University, Hangzhou, China
[4] Shanghai AI Laboratory, Shanghai, China

Abstract. Denoising Diffusion Probabilistic Model (DDPM) is able to make flexible conditional image generation from prior noise to real data, by introducing an independent noise-aware classifier to provide conditional gradient guidance at each time step of denoising process. However, due to the ability of the classifier to easily discriminate an incompletely generated image only with high-level structure, the gradient, which is a kind of class information guidance, tends to vanish early, leading to the collapse from conditional generation process into the unconditional process. To address this problem, we propose two simple but effective approaches from two perspectives. For sampling procedure, we introduce the entropy of predicted distribution as the measure of guidance vanishing level and propose an entropy-aware scaling method to adaptively recover the conditional semantic guidance. For the training stage, we propose the entropy-aware optimization objectives to alleviate the overconfident prediction for noisy data. On ImageNet1000 256×256, with our proposed sampling scheme and trained classifier, the pretrained conditional and unconditional DDPM model can achieve 10.89% (4.59 to 4.09) and 43.5% (12 to 6.78) FID improvement, respectively. Code is available at https://github.com/ZGCTroy/ED-DPM.

Keywords: Denoising diffusion probabilistic model · Conditional generation · Distribution entropy · Gradient vanishing

1 Introduction

Conditional image generation, usually class conditional, aims to generate the specific class of high-quality images. There are many generative models that are able

---

G. Zheng and S. Li—The first two authors contributed equally to this paper.

Supplementary Information The online version contains supplementary material available at https://doi.org/10.1007/978-3-031-20047-2_43.

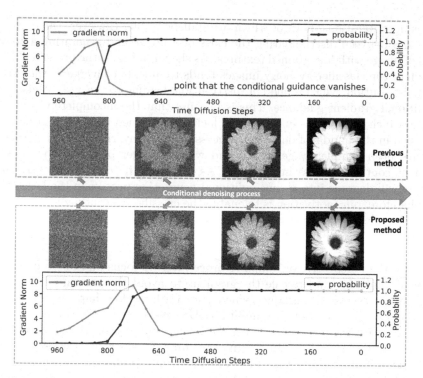

Fig. 1. The visualization of denoising sampling process. The classifier gradient, a kind of class information in conditional generation, quickly converge to 0 in the previous method. It will lead to the collapse from conditional generation to unconditional generation, while our method recovers the gradient guidance and succeed to generate fine-grained features in the subsequent iterations.

to make high-quality conditional generation based on the joint training scheme, such as Generative Adversial Networks (GAN) [2, 7] or Variational Autoencoder (VAE) [27, 38]. However, when the condition requirement is changed, the generative models will be retrained, which is very inconvenient.

Denoising Diffusion Probabilistic Model (DDPM) [10, 23, 33] is a class of iterative generation models, which has achieved remarkable performance in unconditional image generation recently. The flexibility of DDPM [6, 32] is that it can be easily extended to conditional variants by introducing an independent noise-aware classifier. Recent researches modeled the prior denoising distribution by training an unconditional DDPM, following the training scheme of Denoising Score Matching [39], and computed likelihood score by backwarding the classifier gradient. Dhariwal *et al.* [6] further proposed fixed scaling factor to improve the predicted probability of generated samples for DDPM, achieving superior performance than GAN on several image generation benchmarks. In conditional generation process of DDPM, by backwarding the gradient of classification probability to image, the classifier provides high-level semantic information in the early stage of iterations, and gradually strengthens fine-grained features in the subsequent iterations, both of which are indispensable. However, there exists a huge gap between discriminating the class of a image and generating a specific class of image with fine-grained textures. As shown in Fig. 1, the predicted distribution of the classifier for noisy images tends to quickly converge to the desired class distribution, which is one-hot distribution, leading to the early vanishing of conditional gradient guidance. This is because that the incompletely generated image, which is still a noisy image and lacks fine-grained features, can be easily classified in the middle of denoising process. In this way, the image is considered to have been completely generated and will no longer be guided by classifier gradient containing class information. As a result, the conditional generation process will degrade into an unconditional generation process in the later stage.

Therefore, our motivation is to enable the classifier to continuously give conditional guidance throughout the entire denoising process. We propose two simple but effective schemes from the procedure of sampling and the design of classifier training.

From the perspective of sampling procedure, we focus on how to detect the gradient vanishing and rescale the gradient to avoid the existence of gradient vanishing or recover the gradient when the vanishing does happen. We propose **E**ntropy-**D**riven conditional **S**ampling (EDS) method, which is able to adaptively measure the level of gradient vanishing and rescale the gradient guidance to a appropriate level. In design of training classifier, we propose **E**ntropy-**C**onstraint **T**raining (ECT), which will penalize the classifier when it gives a overconfident classification probability to a generated noisy image, thus constraining the classifier to provide more gentle guidance.

Our contributions can be summarized as follows:

- We are the first to discover the problem of vanishing gradient guidance for DDPM-based conditional generation methods, and point out that category information guidance should be continuously provided throughout the entire generation process.
- We propose EDS to alleviate the vanishing guidance by dynamically measuring and rescaling gradient guidance. At the classifier training stage, to alleviate the vanishing gradient caused by one-hot label supervision, we utilize discrete uniform distribution to build an entropy-aware optimization term, which is **E**ntropy-**C**onstraint **T**raining scheme (ECT).
- We conduct experiments on ImageNet1000 and achieve state-of-the-art FID (Fréchet Inception Distance) results at various resolutions. On ImageNet1000 256×256, with our proposed sampling scheme and trained classifier, the pre-trained conditional and unconditional DDPM model can achieve 10.89% (4.59 to 4.09) and 43.5% (12 to 6.78) FID (Fréchet Inception Distance) improvement, respectively.

2   Related Work

2.1   Denoising Diffusion Probabilistic Model

Denoising diffusion probabilistic models (DDPM) is the latest generation model which achieve superior generation performance than traditional generative models like Generative Adversial Networks (GAN) [2,7,8], Variational Autoencoders (VAE) [25,27,38] on several benchmarks about unconditional generation. Its key idea is to model the diffusion process based on total T time steps, which adds noise gradually to the clean data, and its reverse process, which denoises the white noise into the clean sample. Accordingly, its diffusion process is modeled as a fixed Markov Chain and its transition kernel is formulated as:

$$q(\mathbf{x}_t|\mathbf{x}_{t-1}) := \mathcal{N}(\mathbf{x}_t; \sqrt{1 - \beta_t}\mathbf{x}_{t-1}, \beta_t\mathbf{I}), \tag{1}$$

where $\beta_1, ..., \beta_T$ are the fixed variance parameters, which are not learnable. According to the transition kernel above, when the clean data $\mathbf{x}_0$ is given, the noisy data $\mathbf{x}_t$ can be sampled with a closed-form distribution:

$$q(\mathbf{x}_t|\mathbf{x}_0) = \mathcal{N}(\mathbf{x}_t; \sqrt{\bar{\alpha}_t}\mathbf{x}_0, (1 - \bar{\alpha}_t)\mathbf{I}), \tag{2}$$

where $\alpha_t = 1 - \beta_t$ and $\bar{\alpha}_t = \prod_{s=1}^{t} \alpha_s$. When t is close to T, x_T can be approximated as a Gaussian distribution.

Given a prior diffusion process, DDPM aims to model its reverse process to sample from the data distribution. The optimization objective of the reverse transition can be derived from a variational bound [13]. Thus, DDPM introduced the variational solution [13] and assumed that its reverse transition kernel also subjects to Gaussian distribution, which is the same as the diffusion process. In this way, the generation process parameterized the mean of the Gaussian transition distribution and fixed its variance as follows:

$$p_\theta(\mathbf{x}_{t-1}|\mathbf{x}_t) = \mathcal{N}(\mathbf{x}_{t-1}; \mu_\theta(\mathbf{x}_t), \sigma_t^2\mathbf{I})$$
$$\mu_\theta(\mathbf{x}_t) = \frac{1}{\sqrt{\alpha_t}}(\mathbf{x}_t - \frac{1 - \alpha_t}{\sqrt{1 - \bar{\alpha}_t}}\epsilon_\theta(\mathbf{x}_t)), \tag{3}$$

where $\epsilon_\theta(\mathbf{x}_t)$ is a noise estimator modeled by a neural network. The variance is designed as the hyperparameters for training diffusion models.

Recently, there were some researches [6,34,36,37] which indicated that the noise estimator can be regarded as an approximation of score function so that the sampling process is equivalent to solving a stochastic differential equation. Based on above, Song et al. [34] proposed an effective sampling process that shares the same training objectives as DDPM and its corresponding denoising process, which is also the iteration solution to solve the stochastic differential equation, is designed as follows:

$$\mathbf{x}_{t-1} = \sqrt{\alpha_{t-1}}f_\theta(\mathbf{x}_t, t) + \sqrt{1 - \alpha_{t-1} - \sigma_t^2}\epsilon_\theta(\mathbf{x}_t) + \sigma_t^2\mathbf{z}, \tag{4}$$

where $f_\theta(\mathbf{x}_t, t)$ is the prediction of clean data x_0 when noisy data $\mathbf{x}_t$ is observed and noise prediction $\epsilon_\theta(\mathbf{x}_t)$ is given. The $f_\theta(\mathbf{x}_t, t)$ can be expressed as:

$$f_\theta(\mathbf{x}_t, t) = \frac{\mathbf{x}_t - \sqrt{1 - \alpha_t}\epsilon_\theta(\mathbf{x}_t)}{\sqrt{\alpha_t}}, \tag{5}$$

When the variance σ_t is set to 0, the sampling process becomes deterministic. At the same time, the non-Markovian diffusion process [34] allows the generation quality to remain unchanged within fewer denoising steps, which is called the DDIM sampling process.

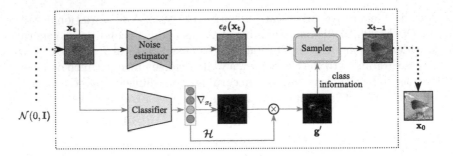

Fig. 2. Pipeline for Entropy-driven Sampling process. Sampler represents a class of iteration method (DDPM or DDIM), which is non-parametric. All models are pretrained without gradient updating in the sampling process.

2.2   Conditional Image Generation

Conditional image generation aims to generate samples with desired condition information. The condition can be extended to multi-modal information, such as class [20,25,27], text [26,40,41], and low-resolution image [3]. Most previous work modeled this by the joint training scheme with both condition and random noise, utilizing generative models like GAN or VAE.

Considering that Denoising Diffusion Probabilistic Model (DDPM) has made remarkable progress in recent years [5,11,12,17,21,24,34,35], there raised many researches [4,6,14,16,18,30,31] which applied DDPM to conditional generation. Due to the ideal theoretical properties of DDPM, it can be extended flexibly to conditional variants using the Bayes theorem without retraining, which is similar to score-based generative models [19,36,37]. In this paper, we focus on the class-conditional generation task, in which the condition is represented by a class discrete distribution, and design a more effective sampling and training scheme to improve the generation quality for DDPM, further exploring its potential in image generation aspects.

3   Proposed Methods

We start by introducing the conditional generation process for diffusion models with classifier guidance (Sect. 3.1). For ease of description, we will firstly introduce our dynamic scaling technology to recover gradient guidance adaptively in the sampling process and its motivation (Sect. 3.2). Then, we describe the entropy-aware optimization loss for alleviating vanishing conditional guidance from training perspective (Sect. 3.3), utilizing the uniform distribution, which is a more dense distribution.

3.1   Conditional Diffusion Generation

The goal of conditional image generation is to model probability density $p(\mathbf{x}|\mathbf{y})$. To be specific, in class-conditional image generation, $\mathbf{y}$ represents the desired

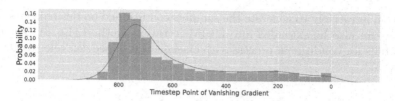

Fig. 3. The various gradient vanishing points for different samples. We randomly generate 5000 samples and define the time point, whose gradient norm that is smaller than 0.15 as the gradient vanishing point. Premature vanishing of gradients occurs in almost every sample.

class label, which tends to be one-hot distribution, and **x** represents the image sample. For diffusion models, it can be implemented by introducing an independent classifier, as shown in Fig. 2. Specifically, the goal is converted into modeling the conditional transition distribution $p(\mathbf{x}_{t-1}|\mathbf{x}_t, \mathbf{y})$, derived from Markov chain sampling scheme:

$$p_\varphi(\mathbf{x}_0|\mathbf{y}) = \int p_\varphi(\mathbf{x}_{0:T}|\mathbf{y})d\mathbf{x}_{1:T},$$

$$p_\varphi(\mathbf{x}_{0:T}|\mathbf{y}) = p(\mathbf{x}_T)\prod_{t=1}^{T} p_\varphi(\mathbf{x}_{t-1}|\mathbf{x}_t, \mathbf{y}), \tag{6}$$

where φ represents the model and T is the total length of Markov chain, which tends to be large. Then, we decompose the conditional transition distribution into two independent terms:

$$p_\varphi(\mathbf{x}_{t-1}|\mathbf{x}_t, \mathbf{y}) = Z p_\theta(\mathbf{x}_{t-1}|\mathbf{x}_t) p_\phi(\mathbf{y}|\mathbf{x}_t), \tag{7}$$

where Z is a normalizing constant independent from $\mathbf{x}_{t-1}$ and φ can be seen as the combination of models θ and ϕ, which is proven theoretically [6,32]. Furthermore, the log density of Eq. (7) can be approximated as a Gaussian distribution [6]:

$$\log(p_\varphi(\mathbf{x}_{t-1}|\mathbf{x}_t, \mathbf{y})) \approx \log p(\mathbf{z}) + \log Z$$

$$\mathbf{z} \sim \mathcal{N}(\frac{1}{\sqrt{\alpha_t}}(\mathbf{x}_t - \frac{1-\alpha_t}{\sqrt{1-\bar{\alpha}_t}}\epsilon_\theta(\mathbf{x}_t)) + \sigma_t^2\mathbf{g}, \sigma_t^2\mathbf{I}), \tag{8}$$

where $\mathbf{g} = s\nabla_{\mathbf{x}_t}\log p_\phi(\mathbf{y}|\mathbf{x}_t)$ and s is the gradient scale. $\mathbf{g}$ can be derived by backwarding the gradient of a pretrained classifier on noisy data $\mathbf{x}_t$. Usually, s is set to a constant [6] to improve the predicted probability. $\epsilon_\theta(\mathbf{x}_t)$ is the pretrained noise estimator for diffusion models and σ_t^2 is the hyperparameters for unconditional DDPM to control the variance.

In this way, unconditional diffusion models with parameterized noise estimator ϵ_θ can be extended to conditional generative models by introducing the condition-aware guidance $\nabla_{\mathbf{x}_t}\log p_\phi(\mathbf{y}|\mathbf{x}_t)$, as shown in Fig. 2. Specifically, we start with the prior noise $\mathbf{x}_T \sim \mathcal{N}(0, \mathbf{I})$, and utilize DDPM-based (Eq. 8) sampler to make transition iteratively to generate the samples conditioned on desired class **y**. The sampler can also be extended into DDIM iteration method (Eq. 3). The extension details for conditional process with classifier guidance can refer to Dhariwal *et al.* [6,37].

3.2   Entropy-Driven Conditional Sampling

During the conditional generation process, we observe that the guidance provided from noise-aware classifier tends to vanish prematurely, which could be attributed to the discrepancy between generative pattern and discriminative pattern. For example, the noisy samples with high-level semantic information, such as contour or the color, may be guided iteratively by the classifier with nearly one-hot distribution, in which situation the gradient guidance tends to be weak or vanish, while the samples still lack the condition-aware semantic details. In this way, the condition-aware textures of generated samples are guided by unconditional denoising process (Eq. 3).

An intuitive solution is to manually select a time step during the sampling process, after which the semantic details tend to vanish in most instances, and rescale the conditional gradient by an empirical constant after the selected time step. However, since the stochasticity in the generation process of diffusion models [4], the denoising trajectories for generated samples would differ from each other. It will lead to the various initial vanishing points, as shown in Fig. 3. At the same time, considering the learning bias of classifier for different conditional classes, the level of recovery factor for each class may also differ. In summary, the effective scaling factor can be related to the current time step, the class condition, and the stochasticity of generation process. The experiment design and results about more intuitive approaches can be seen in Sect. 4.3.

Algorithm 1. Entropy-driven sampling scheme (DDPM/DDIM)

Require: a pretrained diffusion model $\epsilon_\theta(\mathbf{x}_t)$, classifier $p_\phi(\hat{\mathbf{y}}|\mathbf{x}_t)$, and desired class condition **y**

1: $\mathbf{x}_T \sim \mathcal{N}(\mathbf{0}, \mathbf{I})$
2: **for** $t = T, \ldots, 1$ **do**
3:     $s \leftarrow \gamma * \frac{\mathcal{H}(\mathcal{U}(\hat{\mathbf{y}}))}{\mathcal{H}(p_\phi(\hat{\mathbf{y}}|\mathbf{x}_t))}$ if EDS, else $s \leftarrow \gamma$
4:     **if** use DDPM **then**
5:         $\mathbf{z} \sim \mathcal{N}(\mathbf{0}, \mathbf{I})$ if $t > 1$, else $\mathbf{z} \leftarrow \mathbf{0}$
6:         $\mathbf{g} \leftarrow s \cdot \nabla_{\mathbf{x}_t} \log p_\phi(\mathbf{y}|\mathbf{x}_t)$,
7:         $\mathbf{x}_{t-1} \leftarrow \frac{1}{\sqrt{\alpha_t}}\left(\mathbf{x}_t - \frac{1-\alpha_t}{\sqrt{1-\bar{\alpha}_t}}\epsilon_\theta(\mathbf{x}_t)\right) + \sigma_t^2\mathbf{g} + \sigma_t\mathbf{z}$
8:     **else if** use DDIM **then**
9:         $\hat{\epsilon} \leftarrow \epsilon_\theta(\mathbf{x}_t) - s \cdot \nabla_{\mathbf{x}_t} \log p_\phi(\mathbf{y}|\mathbf{x}_t)$,
10:        $\mathbf{x}_{t-1} \leftarrow \sqrt{\bar{\alpha}_{t-1}}(\frac{\mathbf{x}_t - \sqrt{1-\bar{\alpha}_t}\hat{\epsilon}}{\sqrt{\bar{\alpha}_t}}) + \sqrt{1-\bar{\alpha}_{t-1}}\hat{\epsilon}$
11:    **end if**
12: **end for**
13: **return** $\mathbf{x}_0$

Motivated from above, we propose an dynamic scaling technology for the conditional diffusion generation to recover the semantic details adaptively for each sample. We noticed that, when time step is close to T, the predicted distribution tends to be dense, which can be nearly approximated as uniform distribution. The reason is that the noisy data derived from Eq. 1 can be approximated as random noise, $\mathcal{N}(0, \mathbf{I})$, in which state the gradient guidance is obvious. As time step declines to 0 inversely, the noise hidden in sample will be removed gradually and the predicted distribution tends to be close to one-hot, in which case the classifier gradient is invalid to provide semantic details for generation. Statistically, entropy can represent the sparsity of the predicted distribution, inspiring us to take it into consideration:

$$
\begin{aligned}
\mathcal{H}(p_\phi(\tilde{\mathbf{y}}|\mathbf{x}_t)) &= -\mathbb{E}_{\tilde{\mathbf{y}}|\mathbf{x}_t} \log p_\phi(\tilde{\mathbf{y}}|x_t) \\
&= -\sum_{i=1}^{|Y|} p_\phi(\tilde{\mathbf{y}}_i|\mathbf{x}_t) \log p_\phi(\tilde{\mathbf{y}}_i|\mathbf{x}_t),
\end{aligned}
\tag{9}
$$

where $p_\phi(\tilde{\mathbf{y}}|\mathbf{x}_t)$ represents the predicted distribution from classifier and Y represents the set of all class conditions.

In this paper, we utilize $\mathcal{H}(p_\phi(\tilde{\mathbf{y}}|\mathbf{x}_t))$ to adaptively fit various gradient vanishing time step. Furthermore, the entropy $\mathcal{H}(p_\phi(\tilde{\mathbf{y}}|\mathbf{x}_t))$ can also capture bias caused by different conditions, due to its sample-aware rescaling effect. Thus, when we sample from a pretrained noise estimator ϵ_θ in Eq. 8 conditionally, we reformulate the gradient term $\mathbf{g}$ as following, which is shown in Fig. 2:

$$
\begin{aligned}
\mathbf{g}' &= s(x_t, \phi) * \nabla_{\mathbf{x}_t} \log p_\phi(\mathbf{y}|\mathbf{x}_t), \\
s(x_t, \phi) &= \gamma * \frac{\mathcal{H}(\mathcal{U}(\tilde{\mathbf{y}}))}{\mathcal{H}(p_\phi(\tilde{\mathbf{y}}|\mathbf{x}_t))}
\end{aligned}
\tag{10}
$$

where γ is a hyper-parameter to balance the guiding gradient and entropy-aware scaling factor $s(\mathbf{x}_t, \phi)$. In order to maintain the numerical range, we renormalize the entropy by its theoretical upper bound $\mathcal{H}(\mathcal{U}(\tilde{\mathbf{y}}))$, where $\mathcal{U}(\tilde{\mathbf{y}})$ represents the uniform distribution of class variable, so that the gradients are almost not rescaled when t is close to T.

3.3   Training Noise-Aware Classifier with Entropy Constraint

From the training perspective, the vanishing gradient can be partly attributed to the label supervision pattern for noise-aware classifier. Since one-hot distribution is very sparse and is utilized to supervise the noisy data, the predicted distributions are inclined to converge to one-hot under noisy samples in the sampling process, so that the gradient guidances are too weak to generate condition-aware semantic details at sampling stage.

Specifically, given the dataset $(\mathbf{x}_0, \mathbf{y}) \sim \mathbb{D}$ and a prior diffusion process (Eq. 1), the classifier will be trained under noisy data $\mathbf{x}_t$ to build the gradient field in Eq. 8 of each time step. To alleviate the weak guidance caused by the

---

Algorithm 2. Entropy-constraint training scheme.

Require: training set $\mathbb{D}$, a neural classifier ϕ, training set $\mathbb{D}$, total time steps T
1: **repeat**
2:     $(\mathbf{x}_0, \mathbf{y}) \leftarrow$ sample from $\mathbb{D}$
3:     $t \sim \mathcal{U}(\{1, \ldots, T\})$
4:     $\mathbf{x}_t \sim q(\mathbf{x}_t | \mathbf{x}_0)$ (Eq. 2)
5:     $L_{CE} \leftarrow \mathbf{y} \log p_\phi(\tilde{\mathbf{y}} | \mathbf{x}_t)$
6:     **if** use ECT **then**
7:         $L_{ECT} \leftarrow -\mathcal{H}(p_\phi(\tilde{\mathbf{y}} | \mathbf{x}_t))$
8:         Take gradient descent step on $\nabla_\phi(L_{CE} + \eta L_{ECT})$
9:     **else**
10:         Take gradient descent step on $\nabla_\phi L_{CE}$
11:     **end if**
12: **until** converged

---

sparsity, we utilize discrete uniform distribution, which is a dense distribution and has maximum entropy, as a perturbing distribution and introduce the optimization term at the training stage of the classifier to constrain the predicted distribution from the classifier as followed:

$$
\begin{aligned}
\mathcal{L}_{ECT}(\mathbf{x}_t, \mathbf{y}) &= D_{KL}(p_\phi(\tilde{\mathbf{y}} | \mathbf{x}_t) \| \mathcal{U}(\tilde{\mathbf{y}})) \\
&= \mathbb{E}_{\tilde{\mathbf{y}} | \mathbf{x}_t} \log p_\phi(\tilde{\mathbf{y}} | \mathbf{x}_t) - \mathbb{E}_{\tilde{\mathbf{y}} | \mathbf{x}_t} \log \mathcal{U}(\tilde{\mathbf{y}}) \\
&= -\mathcal{H}(p_\phi(\tilde{\mathbf{y}} | \mathbf{x}_t)) + \mathbf{C},
\end{aligned}
\tag{11}
$$

where $\mathbf{C}$ is a constant term independent from the parameter ϕ. This loss term is equivalent to maximizing entropy of the predicted distribution $p(\tilde{\mathbf{y}} | \mathbf{x}_t)$. The whole training loss of guiding classifier is composed of the normal cross-entropy loss and entropy constraint training loss (ECT), which is formally given by:

$$
\mathcal{L}_{tot}(\mathbf{x}_t, \mathbf{y}) = \mathcal{L}_{CE}(\mathbf{x}_t, \mathbf{y}) + \eta \mathcal{L}_{ECT}(\mathbf{x}_t, \mathbf{y}),
\tag{12}
$$

where η is a hyper-parameter to adjust the divergence about predicted label distribution and the uniform distribution.

Different from Entropy-driven Sampling, the proposed training scheme tries to alleviate the vanishing guidance by adjusting the gradient direction in sampling process, instead of the gradient scale. Thus, entropy-constrain training scheme can be complementary with entropy-driven sampling.

4 Experiments

In this section, we present experiments to verify the effectiveness and motivation of our proposed schemes. More visualization of generated samples and ablation experiments about hyperparameters can be found in supplementary materials.

4.1 Experiment Setup

Dataset. We perform our experiments mainly on ImageNet dataset [28] at 256×256 resolutions. ImageNet contains 14,197,122 images with 1000 classes in total, which is a very challenging benchmark for conditional image generation.

Implementation Details. For verifying the effect of proposed schemes, we apply the neural network architecture, ablated diffusion model (ADM), proposed by Dhariwal et al. [6]. ADM is mainly based on the UNet, with increased depth versus width, the number of attention heads, and rescaling residual connections with $\frac{1}{\sqrt{2}}$. It is also possible to train a conditional diffusion models. We call the conditional diffusion architecture [6] as CADM for short. Correspondingly, UADM means unconditional diffusion architecture. UADM-G and CADM-G additionally use noise-aware classifier guidance to perform conditional generation, separately.

Our training hyperparameters of noise-aware classifier, including batch size, total number of iterations, and decay rate, are kept the same as those of Dhariwal *et al.* [6] for fair comparison. We adopt the fixed linear variance schedule $\beta_1, ..., \beta_T$ [10,23] for prior noising process Eq. 1 and choose T as 1000. In this paper, we set η to 0.2 to keep a slight disturbance during training stage of classifier in all experiments. The selection details of γ can be seen in supplementary materials. All the experiments are conducted on 16 NVIDIA 3090s.

Evaluation Metrics. We select FID (Fréchet Inception Distance) [9] as our default evaluation metric, which is the most widely used metric for generation evaluation. FID [9] measures the KL divergence of two Gaussian distributions, which is computed by the real reference samples and the generated samples, in the feature space of Inception-V3. To capture more spatial relationships, sFID are proposed as a variant of FID, which is more sensitive to the consistent image distribution with high-level structures.

In addition, we apply several other metrics for more comprehensive evaluations. Inception Score (IS) was proposed [1], to measure the mutual information between input sample and the predicted class. Improved Precision and Recall metrics are proposed [15] for further evaluation of generative models. Precision is computed by estimating the proportion of generated samples that fall into real data manifold, measuring the sample fidelity. By contraries, recall is computed by estimating the proportion of real samples which fall into generated data manifold, measuring the sample diversity. Following Dhariwal et al. [6], we randomly generated **50k** images to compute all the above metrics based on **10k** real images when compared with previous methods. For consistent comparisons, we use the evaluation metrics for all methods based on the same codebase as Dhariwal *et al.* [6].

4.2 Comparison with State-of-the-Art Methods

In this section, we show the comparison results of our proposed schemes with other SOTA methods. Based on UADM and CADM architectures [6]. All results

Table 1. Comparison results with state-of-the-art generative models on ImageNet1000 256 × 256. Annotation '(25)' means the DDIM [34] sampling method with 25 steps. Otherwise, it means DDPM sampling method with 250 steps.

Method	FID ↓	sFID ↓	IS ↑	Prec ↑	Rec ↑	Prec+Rec ↑
DCTransformer [22]	36.51	8.24	–	0.36	**0.67**	1.03
VQ-VAE-2 [27]	31.11	17.38	–	0.36	0.57	0.93
IDDPM [23]	12.26	5.42	–	0.70	0.62	1.32
SR3 [29]	11.30	–	–	–	–	–
BigGAN-deep [2]	6.95	7.36	–	**0.87**	0.28	1.15
UADM-G(25 steps) [6]	14.21	8.53	83	0.7	0.46	1.16
UADM-G(25 steps)+**EDS+ECT**	8.28	6.37	163.17	0.76	0.44	1.20
CADM-G(25 steps) [6]	5.44	5.32	194.48	0.81	0.49	1.30
CADM-G(25 steps)+**EDS+ECT**	4.67	5.12	**235.24**	0.82	0.47	1.29
UADM-G [6]	12	10.4	95.41	0.76	0.44	1.20
UADM-G+**EDS+ECT**	6.78	6.56	168.78	0.81	0.45	1.26
CADM [6]	10.94	6.02	100.98	0.69	0.63	1.32
CADM-G [6]	4.59	5.25	186.70	0.82	0.52	**1.34**
CADM-G+**EDS+ECT**	**4.09**	**5.07**	221.57	0.83	0.50	1.33

of other previous methods are cited from Dhariwal *et al.* [6]. As shown in Table 1, we achieve the best results in terms of FID metric. Compared to UADM-G in ImageNet 256 × 256, our methods achieve relatively about 40% improvement on FID metric (from 14.21 to 8.28, from 12.0 to 6.78) based on both DDPM and DDIM sampling iteration methods, with comparable or even better precision and recall. For the CADM architecture, our proposed schemes still maintain a significant improvement margin on FID metric (from 5.44 to 4.67, from 4.59 to 4.09), and comparable precision and recall.

It is worth mentioning that our method based on the UADM architecture outperformed BigGAN-deep in terms of FID by 0.17 margin (6.78 vs 6.95), with no dependency on conditional architecture CADM, which has not been achieved in previous work [6,10,23].

4.3 Ablation Study

Effect of Proposed Schemes. To further verify the contribution of each component of proposed schemes, we conduct ablation experiments on both UADM and CADM architectures, as shown in Table 2. It can be concluded that EDS and ECT both improve the generation quality. Combining with two schemes, the generation results can be further improved, with more semantic details achieved from the improved direction (ECT) and scale (EDS) aspects of the guidance gradient.

Table 2. Ablation study of our proposed methods EDS and ECT on ADM-G under DDIM 25 steps and DDPM 250 steps on ImageNet1000 256×256.

Method	+ECT	+EDS	FID ↓	sFID ↓	IS ↑	Precision ↑	Recall ↑
UADM-G (25 steps)	✗	✗	14.21	8.53	83	0.7	**0.46**
	✗	✓	10.09	6.86	133.71	0.73	0.45
	✓	✗	12.21	8.14	100.95	0.74	0.44
	✓	✓	**8.28**	**6.37**	**163.17**	**0.76**	0.44
CADM-G (25 steps)	✗	✗	5.46	5.32	194.48	0.81	0.48
	✗	✓	4.82	**5.04**	218.97	0.80	**0.50**
	✓	✗	5.34	5.3	196.8	0.81	0.49
	✓	✓	**4.67**	5.12	**235.24**	**0.82**	0.48
UADM-G	✗	✗	12.0	10.4	95.41	0.76	0.44
	✗	✓	7.98	10.61	**178.73**	**0.82**	0.40
	✓	✗	10.79	10.49	117.56	0.79	0.41
	✓	✓	**6.78**	**6.56**	168.78	0.81	**0.45**
CADM-G	✗	✗	4.59	5.25	186.7	0.82	0.52
	✗	✓	**4.01**	5.15	217.25	0.82	0.52
	✓	✗	4.62	5.16	182.48	0.81	**0.53**
	✓	✓	4.09	**5.07**	**221.57**	**0.83**	0.50

Effect of Entropy-Driven Sampling. In this part, we design various intuitive scaling methods and compare them under optimal hyperparameters with EDS. We select the scaling method with constant recovery factor for all time range [6] as our baseline. Intuitively, we can manually select vanishing time point through observing Fig. 3 and Fig. 1 i.e., 700, and finetune the constant rescaling factor to adjust the weak gradient for all generated samples, which we called Constant (range 0–700). The constant scale can be further adjusted to time-aware form, such like $T - t$. We call this method as Timestep-aware, which can dynamically adjust the scaling factor according to time step in sampling process. In this way, the sample-aware vanishing characteristic is ignored and the scale cannot fit the various vanishing level.

To verify that entropy-aware scaling could better fit the initial time steps of vanishing guidance, we design another approach which is based on norm of gradient map. Specifically, we empirically select a norm bound M for gradient. When the norm of gradient map is smaller than the threshold vanishing norm bound M, we regard that the gradient guidance is weak and need to be rescaled. Thus, s in Eq. 10 is rewritten as followed:

$$s = \begin{cases} 1, & \|\nabla_{\mathbf{x}_t} \log p_\phi(\mathbf{y}|\mathbf{x}_t)\|_2 < M \\ C, & \text{Otherwise} \end{cases} \qquad (13)$$

The rescaling factor C is a large constant. Compared to the methods above, it can be experimentally verified that EDS not only fits the sample-aware initial

Table 3. Sample quality comparison with several intuitive sampling schemes. Generate 5,000 samples for more efficient comparisons.

Method	FID	IS	Precision	Recall
Baseline	20.17	84.53	0.71	0.59
Constant (range 0–700)	19.84	88.42	0.70	0.61
Timestep-aware	19.42	87.42	0.70	0.63
Gradient Norm	19.08	93.14	0.71	0.63
Entropy-driven	**16.56**	**133.26**	**0.73**	**0.66**

time steps of weak guidance, but also provides a reasonable rescaling factor for recovery, as shown in Table 3.

4.4 Qualitative Results

Gradient Map Visualization. We collected several gradient maps **g** derived from the classifier in the previous sampling process and our EDS process, with an equal time interval. From Fig. 4, it can be observed that the classifier provides high-level semantic guidance at the beginning. Gradually, the classifier will provide condition-aware texture guidance. Compared with EDS, which can maintain guidance of semantic details throughout the denoising process for refined generation results, sampling scheme based on the fixed scaling factor lost a lot of condition-aware details (first line) or introduce unnatural details (third line) at the later sampling stage.

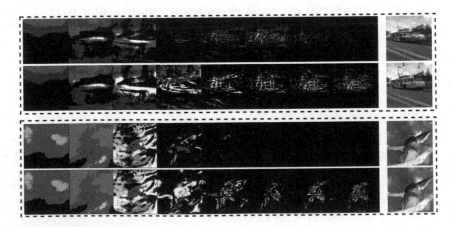

Fig. 4. Gradient map comparison between UADM-G [6] (the first line of each image box) and our UADM-G + EDS (the second line of each image box) on ImageNet1000 256 × 256, DDIM 25 steps.

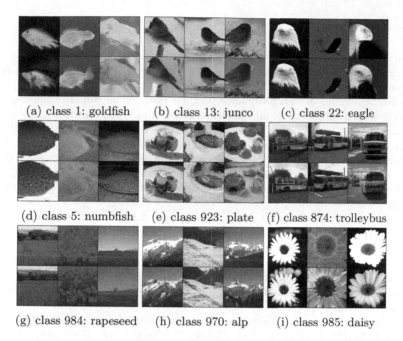

(a) class 1: goldfish   (b) class 13: junco   (c) class 22: eagle

(d) class 5: numbfish   (e) class 923: plate   (f) class 874: trolleybus

(g) class 984: rapeseed   (h) class 970: alp   (i) class 985: daisy

Fig. 5. Sample quality comparison between UADM-G [6] (the first line of each box) and our UADM-G+ECT+EDS (the second line of each box) on ImageNet1000 256 × 256, DDIM 25 steps.

Generation Results Visualization. We visualized various generated images conditioned on different classes and compared our final generated results with that of previous SOTA method [6] on UADM architecture. DDIM is adopted as the deterministic generation process to generate samples with the same initial noise. From Fig. 5, previous SOTA method cannot generate condition-aware semantic details such like beaks of birds Fig. 5b or petal texture Fig. 5i, while our method can generate more refined textures, with similar high-level structure.

5   Conclusion

In this paper, we proposed an entropy-aware scaling technology for the guiding classifier in sampling and constrain the predicted distribution in training. Experiments demonstrate that our methods can recover textures in generated samples, achieving state-of-the-art generation results.

Acknowledgements. This work is supported in part by National Key Research and Development Program of China under Grant 2020AAA0107400, Zhejiang Provincial Natural Science Foundation of China under Grant LR19F020004, National Natural Science Foundation of China under Grant U20A20222.

References

1. Barratt, S., Sharma, R.: A note on the inception score. arXiv:1801.01973 (2018)
2. Brock, A., Donahue, J., Simonyan, K.: Large scale GAN training for high fidelity natural image synthesis. arXiv:1809.11096 (2018)
3. Bulat, A., Yang, J., Tzimiropoulos, G.: To learn image super-resolution, use a GAN to learn how to do image degradation first. In: Ferrari, V., Hebert, M., Sminchisescu, C., Weiss, Y. (eds.) ECCV 2018. LNCS, vol. 11210, pp. 187–202. Springer, Cham (2018). https://doi.org/10.1007/978-3-030 01231-1_12
4. Choi, J., Kim, S., Jeong, Y., Gwon, Y., Yoon, S.: ILVR: conditioning method for denoising diffusion probabilistic models. In: Proceedings of the IEEE/CVF International Conference on Computer Vision (ICCV), pp. 14367–14376, October 2021
5. De Bortoli, V., Thornton, J., Heng, J., Doucet, A.: Diffusion Schrödinger bridge with applications to score-based generative modeling. In: Advances in Neural Information Processing Systems 34 (2021)
6. Dhariwal, P., Nichol, A.: Diffusion models beat GANs on image synthesis. In: Advances in Neural Information Processing Systems 34 (2021)
7. Donahue, J., Simonyan, K.: Large scale adversarial representation learning. arXiv:1907.02544 (2019)
8. Goodfellow, I.J., et al.: Generative adversarial networks. arXiv:1406.2661 (2014)
9. Heusel, M., Ramsauer, H., Unterthiner, T., Nessler, B., Hochreiter, S.: GANs trained by a two time-scale update rule converge to a local Nash equilibrium. In: Advances in Neural Information Processing Systems 30 (NIPS 2017) (2017)
10. Ho, J., Jain, A., Abbeel, P.: Denoising diffusion probabilistic models. In: NeurIPS (2020)
11. Huang, C.W., Lim, J.H., Courville, A.C.: A variational perspective on diffusion-based generative models and score matching. In: Advances in Neural Information Processing Systems 34 (2021)
12. Kingma, D.P., Salimans, T., Poole, B., Ho, J.: Variational diffusion models. arXiv preprint arXiv:2107.00630 (2021)
13. Kingma, D.P., Welling, M.: Auto-encoding variational Bayes. Stat **1050**, 1 (2014)
14. Kong, Z., Ping, W., Huang, J., Zhao, K., Catanzaro, B.: DiffWave: a versatile diffusion model for audio synthesis. arXiv:2009.09761 (2020)
15. Kynkäänniemi, T., Karras, T., Laine, S., Lehtinen, J., Aila, T.: Improved precision and recall metric for assessing generative models. In: Advances in Neural Information Processing Systems 32 (2019)
16. Liu, J., Li, C., Ren, Y., Chen, F., Liu, P., Zhao, Z.: DiffSinger: singing voice synthesis via shallow diffusion mechanism. arXiv preprint arXiv:2105.02446 (2021)
17. Luhman, E., Luhman, T.: Knowledge distillation in iterative generative models for improved sampling speed. arXiv:2101.02388 (2021)
18. Lyu, Z., Kong, Z., Xu, X., Pan, L., Lin, D.: A conditional point diffusion-refinement paradigm for 3d point cloud completion. arXiv preprint arXiv:2112.03530 (2021)
19. Meng, C., Song, Y., Song, J., Wu, J., Zhu, J.Y., Ermon, S.: SDEdit: image synthesis and editing with stochastic differential equations. arXiv preprint arXiv:2108.01073 (2021)
20. Mirza, M., Osindero, S.: Conditional generative adversarial nets. arXiv:1411.1784 (2014)
21. Nachmani, E., Roman, R.S., Wolf, L.: Non gaussian denoising diffusion models. arXiv preprint arXiv:2106.07582 (2021)

22. Nash, C., Menick, J., Dieleman, S., Battaglia, P.W.: Generating images with sparse representations. arXiv:2103.03841 (2021)
23. Nichol, A., Dhariwal, P.: Improved denoising diffusion probabilistic models. arXiv preprint arXiv:2102.09672 (2021)
24. Nie, W., Vahdat, A., Anandkumar, A.: Controllable and compositional generation with latent-space energy-based models. In: Advances in Neural Information Processing Systems 34 (2021)
25. van den Oord, A., Vinyals, O., Kavukcuoglu, K.: Neural discrete representation learning. arXiv:1711.00937 (2017)
26. Ramesh, A., et al.: Zero-shot text-to-image generation. arXiv preprint arXiv:2102.12092 (2021)
27. Razavi, A., van den Oord, A., Vinyals, O.: Generating diverse high-fidelity images with VQ-VAE-2. arXiv:1906.00446 (2019)
28. Russakovsky, O., et al.: ImageNet large scale visual recognition challenge. arXiv:1409.0575 (2014)
29. Saharia, C., Ho, J., Chan, W., Salimans, T., Fleet, D.J., Norouzi, M.: Image super-resolution via iterative refinement. arXiv:arXiv:2104.07636 (2021)
30. Sasaki, H., Willcocks, C.G., Breckon, T.P.: UNIT-DDPM: unpaired image translation with denoising diffusion probabilistic models. arXiv preprint arXiv:2104.05358 (2021)
31. Sinha, A., Song, J., Meng, C., Ermon, S.: D2C: diffusion-decoding models for few-shot conditional generation. In: Advances in Neural Information Processing Systems 34 (2021)
32. Sohl-Dickstein, J., Weiss, E.A., Maheswaranathan, N., Ganguli, S.: Deep unsupervised learning using nonequilibrium thermodynamics. arXiv:1503.03585 (2015)
33. Song, J., Meng, C., Ermon, S.: Denoising diffusion implicit models. In: International Conference on Learning Representations (2020)
34. Song, J., Meng, C., Ermon, S.: Denoising diffusion implicit models. arXiv:2010.02502 (2020)
35. Song, Y., Durkan, C., Murray, I., Ermon, S.: Maximum likelihood training of score-based diffusion models. In: Advances in Neural Information Processing Systems 34 (2021)
36. Song, Y., Ermon, S.: Generative modeling by estimating gradients of the data distribution. arXiv:1907.05600 (2020)
37. Song, Y., Sohl-Dickstein, J., Kingma, D.P., Kumar, A., Ermon, S., Poole, B.: Score-based generative modeling through stochastic differential equations. arXiv:2011.13456 (2020)
38. Vahdat, A., Kautz, J.: NVAE: a deep hierarchical variational autoencoder. arXiv:2007.03898 (2020)
39. Vincent, P.: A connection between score matching and denoising autoencoders. Neural Comput. 23(7), 1661–1674 (2011)
40. Wang, H., Lin, G., Hoi, S.C.H., Miao, C.: Cycle-consistent inverse GAN for text-to-image synthesis (2021)
41. Xia, W., Yang, Y., Xue, J.H., Wu, B.: TediGAN: text-guided diverse face image generation and manipulation. In: Proceedings of the IEEE/CVF Conference on Computer Vision and Pattern Recognition, pp. 2256–2265 (2021)

Author Index